Mastering AutoCAD 2000

PRAISE FROM OUR READERS FOR THE PREVIOUS EDITION OF *MASTERING AUTOCAD*

SYBEX
www.sybex.com

Mastering™ AutoCAD® 2000

George Omura

SYBEX®

San Francisco • Paris • Düsseldorf • Soest • London

Associate Publisher: Amy Romanoff
Contracts and Licensing Manager: Kristine O'Callaghan
Acquisitions & Developmental Editor: Melanie Spiller
Project Editor: Rebecca Rider
Editor: Sarah Lemaire
Technical Editor: Sam Sol Matzkin
Book Designers: Patrick Dintino, Catalin Dulfu
Graphic Illustrators: Tony Jonick, Jerry Williams
Electronic Publishing Specialist: Franz Baumhackl
Production Coordinator: Shannon Murphy
Proofreader: Andrea Fox
Indexer: Ted Laux
Companion CD: Ginger Warner
Cover Designer: Design Site
Cover Illustrator/Photographer: Sergie Loobkoff

SYBEX is a registered trademark of SYBEX Inc.

Mastering is a trademark of SYBEX Inc.

Screen reproductions produced with Collage Complete. Collage Complete is a trademark of Inner Media Inc.

Netscape Communications, the Netscape Communications logo, Netscape, and Netscape Navigator are trademarks of Netscape Communications Corporation.

Netscape Communications Corporation has not authorized, sponsored, endorsed, or approved this publication and is not responsible for its content. Netscape and the Netscape Communications Corporate Logos are trademarks and trade names of Netscape Communications Corporation. All other product names and/or logos are trademarks of their respective owners.

The CD Interface music is from GIRA Sound AURIA Music Library © GIRA Sound 1996.

The New San Francisco Library was designed by Pei Cobb Freed & Partners and Simon Martin-Vegue Winkelstein Moris Associated Architects. Floor plans prepared by SMWM and Technical Publications. Exterior elevations prepared by PCF & P.

TRADEMARKS: SYBEX has attempted throughout this book to distinguish proprietary trademarks from descriptive terms by following the capitalization style used by the manufacturer.

The author and publisher have made their best efforts to prepare this book, and the content is based upon final release software whenever possible. Portions of the manuscript may be based upon pre-release versions supplied by software manufacturer(s). The author and the publisher make no representation or warranties of any kind with regard to the completeness or accuracy of the contents herein and accept no liability of any kind including but not

Library of Congress Card Number: 99-61306
ISBN: 0-7821-2501-8

Manufactured in the United States of America

10 9 8 7 6 5 4 3 2

To my family and my teachers

ACKNOWLEDGMENTS

There are many hard-working people giving their best effort to produce *Mastering AutoCAD 2000*. I'd like to offer my sincerest gratitude to those people who helped bring this book to you.

Heartfelt thanks go to the editorial and production teams at Sybex for their efforts in getting this book to press on an incredible schedule. Developmental Editor Melanie Spiller got things going and offered many great suggestions. Project Editor Rebecca Rider did a great job managing the project. Sam Sol Matzkin, technical editor, provided helpful suggestions and made sure I was on the right track. Sarah Lemaire edited this edition with precision and care. Franz Baumhackl, electronic publishing specialist, created the pages you see before you, and Shannon Murphy, production coordinator, steadfastly proofread every one of those pages. Finally, Ginger Warner and Heather O'Connor compiled the CD and made it easy and fun to use.

Thanks also go to the people at Autodesk for their support. Cynde Hargrave helped coordinate our efforts with Autodesk. Kathy Fanning was always very helpful in answering my many questions, and Denis Cadu provided the materials I needed and was also always quick to respond to my questions. I'd also like to thank Jeff Allen and Dan Morrison on the AutoCAD 2000 Beta Team for providing software on a timely basis.

I also wish to thank the many contributors to this book. First, a big thanks to Mike Gunderloy for his great work on ActiveX Automation. Many thanks to my friend and colleague R. Bob Callori for his work on the *AutoCAD Instant Reference* on the CD-ROM. David Fry and Bill Hill helped sort out the features of this new version of AutoCAD 2000.

The handiwork of Paul Richardson and Christine Merredith of Technical Publications can be seen in the sidebars that discuss the San Francisco Main Library. Thanks for the use of your wonderful drawings. And while we are on the subject, thanks also go to the architectural firms of Pei Cobb Freed & Partners and Simon Martin-Vegue Winkelstein Moris Associated Architects for generously granting permission to reproduce drawings from their design of the San Francisco Main Library.

And finally, a great big thanks to my wife and sons who are always behind my work 100 percent.

CONTENTS AT A GLANCE

TABLE OF CONTENTS

PART II   Building on the Basics

5   Editing for Productivity   **229**

PART III   **Becoming an Expert**

10   Storing and Linking Data with Graphics   539

PART IV   Modeling and Imaging in 3D

15   Introducing 3D   813

INTRODUCTION

Welcome to *Mastering AutoCAD 2000*. As many readers have already discovered, *Mastering AutoCAD* offers a unique blend of tutorial and reference book that offers everything you need to get started and stay ahead with AutoCAD.

How to Use This Book

Rather than just showing you how each command works, *Mastering AutoCAD 2000* shows you AutoCAD 2000 in the context of a meaningful activity. You will learn how to use commands while working on an actual project and progressing toward a goal. It also provides a foundation on which you can build your own methods for using AutoCAD and become an AutoCAD expert yourself. For this reason, I haven't covered every single command or every permutation of a command response. The *AutoCAD 2000 Instant Reference*, which is included on the companion CD-ROM, will fill that purpose nicely. This online resource will help you quickly locate the commands you need. You should think of *Mastering AutoCAD 2000* as a way to get a detailed look at AutoCAD as it is used on a real project. As you follow the exercises, I encourage you to also explore AutoCAD on your own, applying the techniques you learn to your own work.

Both experienced and beginning AutoCAD users will find this book useful. If you are not an experienced user, the way to get the most out of this book is to approach it as a tutorial—chapter by chapter. You'll find that each chapter builds on the skills and information you learned in the previous one. To help you navigate, the exercises are shown in numbered steps. To address the needs of all readers worldwide, the exercises are given in both English feet and inch measurements and metric measurements.

This book can also be used as a ready reference for your day-to-day problems and questions about commands. Optional exercises at the end of each chapter will help you review what you have learned and look at different ways to apply the information you've learned. Experienced users will also find this book to be a handy reference tool.

Finally, if you run into problems using AutoCAD, check out the *Troubleshooting* section in Appendix A. You'll find a listing of the more common issues readers face when first learning AutoCAD.

Getting Information Fast

I've included plenty of *Notes*, *Tips*, and *Warnings*. Notes supplement the main text, Tips are designed to make practice easier, and Warnings steer you away from pitfalls. Also, in each chapter you will find more extensive tips and discussions in the form of specially screened *sidebars*. To encourage you along the way, some of the sidebars show you how topics in each chapter were applied to a real-world project, the San Francisco Main Library. Together the Notes, Tips, Warnings, and sidebars provide a wealth of information I have gathered over years of using AutoCAD on a variety of projects in different office environments. You may want to browse through the book, just reading the margin notes and sidebars, to get an idea of how they might be useful to you.

Another quick reference you'll find yourself turning to often is Appendix D. This appendix contains tables of all the system variables and dimension variables with comments on their use. If you experience any problems, you can consult the *Troubleshooting* section in Appendix A.

What to Expect

Mastering AutoCAD 2000 is divided into six parts, each representing a milestone in your progress toward becoming an expert AutoCAD user. Here is a description of those parts and what they will show you.

Part I: The Basics

As with any major endeavor, you must begin by tackling small, manageable tasks. In this first part, you will get familiar with the way AutoCAD looks and feels. Chapter 1, *This Is AutoCAD*, shows you how to get around in AutoCAD. In Chapter 2, *Creating Your First Drawing*, you will learn how to start and exit the program and how to respond to AutoCAD commands. Chapter 3, *Learning the Tools of the Trade*, tells you how to set up a work area, edit objects, and lay out a drawing. In Chapter 4, *Organizing Your Work*, you will explore some tools unique to CAD: symbols, blocks, and layers. As you are introduced to AutoCAD, you will also get a chance to make some drawings that you can use later in the book and perhaps even in future projects of your own.

Part II: Building on the Basics

Once you have the basics down, you will begin to explore some of AutoCAD's more subtle qualities. Chapter 5, *Editing for Productivity*, tells you how to reuse drawing setup information and parts of an existing drawing. In Chapter 6, *Enhancing Your Drawing Skills*, you will learn how to assemble and edit a large drawing file. Chapter 7, *Printing and Plotting*, shows you how to get your drawing onto hard copy. Chapter 8, *Adding Text to Drawings*, tells you how to annotate your drawing and edit your notes. Chapter 9, *Using Dimensions*, gives you practice in using automatic dimensioning, another unique CAD capability. Along the way, I will be giving you tips on editing and problems you may encounter as you begin to use AutoCAD for more complex tasks.

Part III: Becoming an Expert

At this point, you will be on the verge of becoming a real AutoCAD expert. Part III is designed to help you polish your existing skills and give you a few new ones. Chapter 10, *Storing and Linking Data with Graphics*, tells you how to attach information to drawing objects and how to link your drawing to database files. In Chapter 11, *Working with Pre-existing Drawings and Raster Images*, you will learn techniques for transferring paper drawings to AutoCAD. In Chapter 12, *Advanced Editing Methods*, you will complete the apartment building tutorial. During this process you will learn how to integrate what you've learned so far and gain some tips on working in groups. Chapter 13, *Drawing Curves and Solid Fills*, gives you an in-depth look at some special drawing objects, such as spline and fitted curves. In Chapter 14, *Getting and Exchanging Data from Drawings*, you will practice getting information about a drawing and learn how AutoCAD can interact with other applications, such as spreadsheets and desktop-publishing programs. You'll also learn how to copy and paste data.

Part IV: Modeling and Imaging in 3D

While 2D drafting is AutoCAD's workhorse application, AutoCAD's 3D capabilities give you a chance to expand your ideas and look at them in a new light. Chapter 15, *Introducing 3D*, covers AutoCAD's basic features for creating three-dimensional drawings. Chapter 16, *Using Advanced 3D Features*, introduces you to some of the program's more powerful 3D capabilities. Chapter 17, *3D Rendering in AutoCAD*, shows how you can use AutoCAD to produce lifelike views of your 3D drawings. Chapter 18, *Mastering 3D Solids*, is a guided tour of AutoCAD Release 14's solid-modeling feature.

Part V: Taking AutoCAD to the Limit

In the last part of the book, you will learn how you can take full control of AutoCAD. Chapter 19, *Introduction to Customization*, gives you a gentle introduction to the world of AutoCAD customization. You'll learn how to load and use existing utilities that come with AutoCAD and find out how you can publish high-resolution drawings on the Web. Chapter 20, *Integrating AutoCAD into Your Projects*, shows you how you can adapt AutoCAD to your own work style. Customizing menus, line types, and screens are only three of the many topics. Chapter 21, *Introduction to VBA in AutoCAD*, shows you how you can tap the power of VBA. Chapter 22, *Integrating AutoCAD into Your Work Environment*, explores the methods and tools offered by AutoCAD to help you manage your design projects. Two additional chapters about VBA and ActiveX are on the CD that accompanies this book.

Part VI: Appendices

Finally, this book has four appendices. Appendix A, *Hardware and Software Tips*, offers information on hardware related to AutoCAD. It also provides tips on improving AutoCAD's performance and troubleshooting. Appendix B, *Installing and Setting Up AutoCAD*, contains an installation and configuration tutorial. If AutoCAD is not already installed on your system, you should follow this tutorial before starting Chapter 1. Appendix C, *What's on the Companion CD-ROM*, describes the utilities available on the companion CD-ROM. Appendix D, *System and Dimension Variables*, will illuminate the references to the system variables scattered throughout the book. Appendix D also discusses the many dimension settings and system features AutoCAD has to offer.

The Minimum System Requirements

This book assumes you have an IBM-compatible Pentium computer that will run AutoCAD and support a mouse. Your computer should have at least one CD-ROM drive and a hard disk with 100MB or more free space after AutoCAD is installed (about 70MB for AutoCAD to work with and another 50MB available for drawing files). In addition to these requirements, you should also have enough free disk space to allow for a Windows virtual memory page file of at least 60MB. Consult your Windows manual or Appendix A of this book for more on virtual memory.

AutoCAD 2000 runs best on systems with at least 64MB or more of RAM, though you can get by with 32MB. Your computer should also have a high-resolution monitor and a color display card. The current standard is the Super Video Graphics Array (SVGA) display with a resolution of 1024×768 or greater. This is quite adequate for most AutoCAD work. The computer should also have at least one serial port. If you have only one, you may want to consider having another installed. I also assume you are using a mouse and have the use of a printer or a plotter. Most computers come equipped with a sound card. You'll need a sound card to take advantage of some of the multimedia tutorials that come with AutoCAD. A CD-ROM or DVD-ROM is needed to install AutoCAD and the software from this book. Finally, you'll want to have an Internet connection to take full advantage of the support offerings from Autodesk.

If you want a more detailed explanation of hardware options with AutoCAD, see Appendix A. You will find a general description of the available hardware options and their significance to AutoCAD.

Doing Things in Style

Much care has been taken to see that the stylistic conventions in this book—the use of uppercase or lowercase letters, italic or boldface type, and so on—will be the ones most likely to help you learn AutoCAD. On the whole, their effect should be subliminal. However, you may find it useful to be conscious of the following rules that we have followed:

1. Pull-down selections are shown by a series of menu options separated by the ➤ symbol (e.g., Choose File ➤ New).

2. Keyboard entries are shown in boldface (e.g., enter **Rotate**).

3. Command-line prompts are also shown in a different font (e.g., `Select objects:`).

For most functions, this book describes how to select options from toolbars and the menu bar. In addition, where applicable, I include related keyboard shortcuts and command names in parentheses. By providing command names, I have provided continuity for those readers already familiar with earlier releases of AutoCAD.

What's on the CD-ROM

Finally, a CD-ROM is included with this book that contains a wealth of utilities, symbols libraries, and sample programs that can greatly enhance your use of Auto-CAD. Two chapters that cover ActiveX and additional information on VBA are also included. Two online books—the *AutoCAD 2000 Instant Reference* and the *ABCs of AutoLISP*—function as easy-to-use, online references that compliment *Mastering AutoCAD 2000* and will prove invaluable for quick command searches and customization tips. Appendix C gives you detailed information about the CD-ROM, but here's a brief rundown of what's available. Check it out!

Software

An AEC add-on to AutoCAD offers the typical symbols and wall and door utilities needed to construct architectural drawings. It is a simple, straightforward add-on to AutoCAD that won't take you months to master. Two versions of the AEC add-on are included: one for US users and another for metric users.

Eye2eye is a utility that makes perspective viewing of your 3D work a simple matter of moving camera and target objects. This utility lets you easily fine-tune your perspective views so you can in turn use them to create rendered images using Auto-CAD 2000's enhanced rendering tools.

I've also included trial versions of Tutohelp, an interactive software program to help you learn and review AutoCAD; Visual Stitcher, a powerful but easy-to-use image stitching application; Whip! 4, the Netscape Communicator plug-in that allows you to view AutoCAD drawings over the Internet; PaintShop Pro, a tool that will round out your graphic editing needs; and QuickView, a utility that helps you manage your files.

Electronic Resources

If you just need to find information about a command quickly, the electronic version of the *AutoCAD 2000 Instant Reference* is here to help you. It is a comprehensive guidebook that walks you through every feature and command of AutoCAD 2000. *Mastering AutoCAD* and the *AutoCAD Instant Reference* have always been a great combination.

And if you want in-depth coverage of AutoLISP, AutoCAD's macro programming language, you can delve into the *ABCs of AutoLISP*. This book is an AutoLISP electronic reference and tutorial. AutoCAD users and developers alike have found the original *ABCs of AutoLISP* book an indispensable resource in their customization efforts. Now in its new HTML format, it's even easier to use.

Drawing Files for the Exercises

I have also included drawing files from all the exercises throughout this book. These are provided so that you can pick up an exercise anywhere in the book, without having to work through the book from front to back. You can also use these sample files to repeat exercises or to just explore how files are organized and put together.

New Features of AutoCAD 2000

AutoCAD 2000 offers a higher level of speed, accuracy, and ease of use. It has always provided drawing accuracy to 16 decimal places. With this kind of accuracy, you can create a computer model of the earth and include details down to submicron levels. It also means that no matter how often you edit an AutoCAD drawing, its dimensions will remain true. The interface is more consistent than in prior releases, so learning and using AutoCAD is easier than ever.

Other new features include:

- The Multiple Document Environment (MDE) allows you to open multiple files at once.

- WYSIWYG plotting lets you see your drawing as it will look when you plot.

- Objects now have line-width control.

- Polar Tracking and Object Snap Tracking allow you to align points in space.

- The AutoCAD DesignCenter gives you control over your library of drawings.

- The 3DOrbit and Camera tools greatly improve your ability to view 3D models.

- IntelliMouse support makes viewing a drawing effortless.

- Context-sensitive popup menus make AutoCAD easier to use.

- Viewports can now be of any shape, including closed spline curves.

- Multiple Layout tabs allow you to create multiple Paper Space layouts.

- Express tools that let you create custom hatch patterns and custom shape files.

- Expanded Internet support makes it easier to share data with others.

- Partial opening of files lets you conserve memory for large drawings.

Finally, AutoCAD offers one of the most easily customizable versions yet, with customization options through VBA and AutoLISP, as well as with easily customizable menus and toolbars.

The AutoCAD Package

This book assumes you are using AutoCAD 2000. If you are using an earlier version of AutoCAD, you will want to refer to *Mastering AutoCAD 14* or *Mastering AutoCAD 14 Premium Edition*.

When you purchase AutoCAD 2000, you will receive the following manuals:

- *The AutoCAD Command Reference*

- *The AutoCAD User's Guide*

- *The Installation Guide*

- *The Customization Guide*

- *The AutoCAD Migration Assistance*

NOTE *The AutoCAD User's Guide* and *The Installation Guide* are included in both hard copy and electronic formats. All the other manuals are in electronic format only. Hard copy versions of *The AutoCAD Command Reference* and *The Customization Guide* are available for purchase from Autodesk. You can also purchase hard copy editions of the *ActiveX/VBA Developer's Guide*, *Visual LISP Tutorial*, and *The Visual LISP Developer's Guide* from Autodesk.

In addition, the AutoCAD package contains the AutoCAD Learning Assistant. This is a CD-ROM–based multimedia training and reference tool designed for those users who are upgrading from earlier versions of AutoCAD. It offers animated video clips, tips, and tutorials on a variety of topics. You'll need a sound card to take full advantage of the Learning Assistant.

You'll probably want to read the installation guide for Windows first and then browse through *The AutoCAD Command Reference* and *The AutoCAD User's Guide* to get a feel for the kind of information available there. You may want to save *The Customization Guide* for when you've become more familiar with AutoCAD. If you're upgrading, *The Migration Assistance* offers a full range of tools to help you upgrade your work environment to AutoCAD 2000 including a few tools that can help you with your day-to-day work.

AutoCAD comes on a CD-ROM and offers several levels of installation. This book assumes that you will install the Full installation, which includes the Internet and Express Tools. You'll also want to install the ActiveX Automation software, also included on the AutoCAD CD-ROM, if you plan to explore this new feature.

The Digitizer Template

If you intend to use a digitizer tablet in place of a mouse, Autodesk also provides you with a digitizer template. Commands can be selected directly from the template by pointing at the command on the template and pressing the pick button. Each command is shown clearly by name and a simple icon. Commands are grouped on the template by the type of operation the command performs. Before you can use the digitizer template, you must configure the digitizer. See Appendix A, *Hardware and Software Tips*, for a more detailed description of digitizing tablets; and see Appendix B for instructions on configuring the digitizer.

NOTE This book doesn't specifically discuss the use of the digitizer for selecting commands because the process is straightforward. If you are using a digitizer, you can use its puck like a mouse for the all of exercises in this book.

I hope that *Mastering AutoCAD 2000* will be of benefit to you and that, once you have completed the tutorials, you will continue to use the book as a reference. If you have comments, criticisms, or ideas about how the book can be improved, you can write to me or send e-mail to me at the address below. And thanks for choosing *Mastering AutoCAD 2000*.

George Omura
P.O. Box 6357
Albany, CA 94706-0357
gomura@sirius.com

PART I

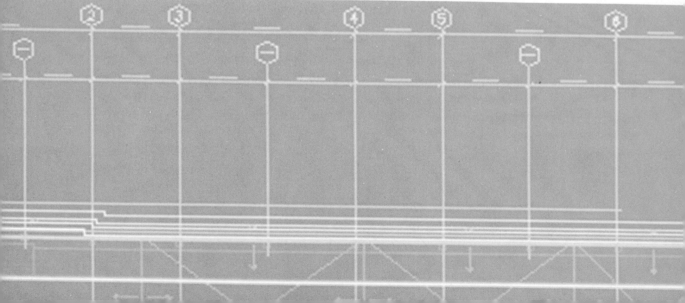

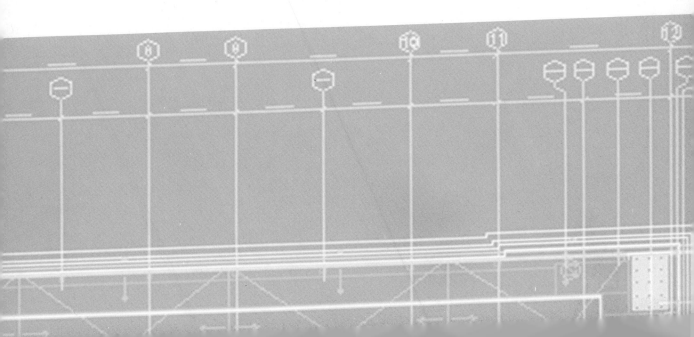

The Basics

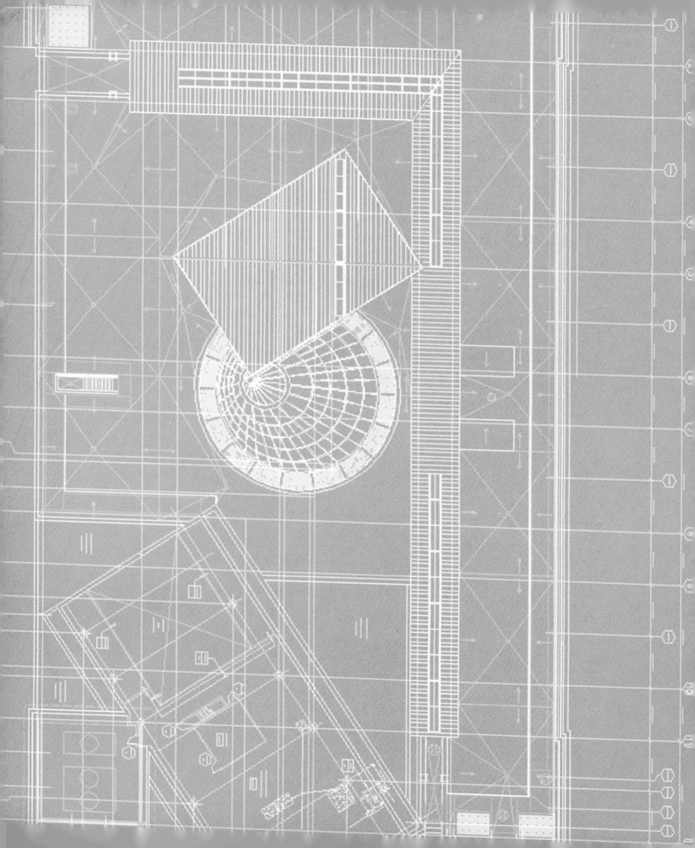

This Is AutoCAD

- Taking a Guided Tour

- Working with AutoCAD

- If You Want to Experiment...

Over the years, AutoCAD has evolved from a DOS-based, command-line-driven program to a full-fledged Windows application. AutoCAD 2000 continues this trend with a new look and a wealth of new features that allow you to work more efficiently and with less effort. Like Release 14, AutoCAD 2000 is strictly a Windows 95/98/NT program; there are no UNIX or DOS versions.

By concentrating on a single operating system, Autodesk is able to create a more efficient, faster AutoCAD. AutoCAD 2000 offers the speed you demand with the convenience of a Windows multitasking environment. You'll also find that Auto-CAD makes great use of the Windows environment. For example, you can use Windows's OLE features to paste documents directly into AutoCAD from Microsoft Excel, Windows Paint, or any other programs that support OLE as a server application. And, as in Releases 13 and 14, you can export AutoCAD drawings directly to other OLE clients. This means no more messy conversions and reworking to get spreadsheet, database, text, or other data into AutoCAD. It also means that if you want to include a photograph in your AutoCAD drawing, all you have to do is cut and paste. Text-based data can also be cut and pasted, saving you time in transferring data, such as layer or block names.

NOTE   OLE stands for *Object Linking and Embedding*—a Windows feature that lets different applications share documents. See Chapter 14 for a more detailed discussion of OLE.

With Windows, you have the freedom to arrange AutoCAD's screen by clicking and dragging its components. AutoCAD 2000 now sports a look that is more in line with the Microsoft Office suite of applications, with Excel-like sheet tabs and borderless toolbar buttons. The changes in AutoCAD 2000 are not only skin deep either. Among the many new features of AutoCAD 2000, you can now open multiple documents during a single session of AutoCAD. This means an easier exchange of data between different files, and the ability to compare files more easily. AutoCAD 2000 also introduces a wealth of new tools to help you manage your drawing projects. If you are new to AutoCAD, this is the version you may have been waiting for. Even with its many new features, the programmers at Autodesk have managed to make AutoCAD easier to use than previous releases. AutoCAD's interface has been trimmed down and is more consistent than prior versions. They have even improved the messages you receive from AutoCAD to make them more understandable.

But in one sense, AutoCAD 2000 represents a return to an old feature of Auto-CAD: Autodesk has begun to listen to the user community again and has clearly incorporated many of the wish-list features users have been asking for over the years. So whether you're an old hand at AutoCAD or whether you are just starting out, AutoCAD 2000 offers a powerful drawing and design tool that is easier to use than ever.

So let's get started! This first chapter looks at many of AutoCAD's basic operations, such as opening and closing files, getting a close-up look at part of a drawing, and making changes to a drawing.

Taking a Guided Tour

First, you will get a chance to familiarize yourself with the AutoCAD screen and how you communicate with AutoCAD. As you do these exercises, you will also get a feel for how to work with this book. Don't worry about understanding or remembering everything that you see in this chapter. You will get plenty of opportunities to probe the finer details of the program as you work through the later chapters. If you are already familiar with earlier versions of AutoCAD, you may want to read through this chapter anyway, to get acquainted with new features and the graphical interface. To help you remember the material, you will find a brief exercise at the end of each chapter. For now, just enjoy your first excursion into AutoCAD.

> **TIP** Consider purchasing either *Mastering Windows 95* by Robert Cowart or *The ABCs of Windows 95* by Sharon Crawford, both published by Sybex. For Windows 98, try *Windows 98: No Experience Required,* also by Sharon Crawford. For Windows NT, *Windows NT Server Complete,* edited by Mark Minasi, is a good bet.

If you already installed AutoCAD, and you are ready to jump in and take a look, then proceed with the following steps to launch the program:

1. Click the Start button in the lower-left corner of the Windows 95/98 or Windows NT 4 screen. Then choose Program ➤ AutoCAD 2000 ➤ Auto-CAD 2000. You can also double-click the AutoCAD 2000 icon on your Windows Desktop.

2. The opening greeting, called a *splash screen,* tells you which version of Auto-CAD you are using, to whom the program is registered, and the AutoCAD dealer's name and phone number, should you need help.

3. Next, the Create New Drawing dialog box appears. This dialog box is a convenient tool for setting up new drawings. You'll learn more about this tool in later chapters. For now, click Cancel in the Create New Drawing dialog box.

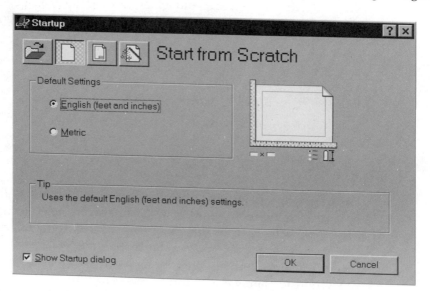

Message to Veteran AutoCAD Users

Autodesk is committed to the Windows operating environment. The result is a graphical user interface (GUI) that is easier on the AutoCAD neophyte, but perhaps a bit foreign to a veteran AutoCAD user.

If you've been using AutoCAD for a while, and you prefer the older interface, you can still enter AutoCAD commands through the keyboard, and you can still mold AutoCAD's interface into one that is more familiar to you.

You can, for example, restore the side menu that appears in the DOS version of AutoCAD. Here's how it's done:

1. Select Tools ➤ Options.

2. In the Options dialog box, click the Display tab.

3. Click the check box labeled Display AutoCAD Screen Menu in Drawing Window.

4. Finally, click OK. The side menu appears.

Continued on next page

A word of caution: If you are accustomed to pressing Ctrl+C to cancel an operation, you must now retrain yourself to press the Esc (Escape) key. Ctrl+C now conforms to the Windows standard, making this key combination a shortcut for saving marked items to the Clipboard. Similarly, instead of using F1 to view the full text window, you must use F2. F1 is most commonly reserved for the Help function in Windows applications.

If you prefer entering commands from the keyboard, you'll also want to know about some changes to specific commands in AutoCAD 2000. Several commands that usually invoke dialog boxes can be used through the Command window prompt. Here is a list of those commands:

Bhatch	Boundary	Group	Hatchedit	Image
Layer	Linetype	Mtext	Pan	Block
XBind	Style	Osnap	Xref	Wblock

When you enter these commands from the keyboard, you normally see a dialog box. In the case of the Pan command, you will see the real-time Pan hand graphic. To utilize these commands from the command prompt, add a minus sign (-) to the beginning of the command name. For example, to use the old Layer command in the command-line method, enter **–layer** at the command prompt. To use the old Pan command, enter **–pan** at the command prompt.

Even if you don't care to enter commands from the keyboard, knowing about the use of the minus sign can help you create custom macros. See Chapter 20 for more on AutoCAD customization.

The AutoCAD Window

The AutoCAD program window is divided into five parts:

- Pull-down menu bar
- Docked and floating toolbars
- Drawing area
- Command window
- Status bar

NOTE   A sixth hidden component, the Aerial View window, displays your entire drawing and lets you select close-up views of parts of your drawing. After you've gotten more familiar with AutoCAD, consult Chapter 6 for more on this feature.

Figure 1.1 shows a typical layout of the AutoCAD program window. Along the top is the *menu bar*, and at the bottom are the *Command window* and the *status bar*. Just below the menu bar and to the left of the window are the *toolbars*. The *drawing area* occupies the rest of the screen.

Many of the elements in the AutoCAD window can be easily moved and reshaped. Figure 1.2 demonstrates how different AutoCAD can look after some simple rearranging of window components. Toolbars can be moved from their default locations to any location on the screen. When they are in their default location, they are in their *docked* position. When they are moved to a location where they are free-floating, they are *floating*.

FIGURE 1.1:

A typical arrangement of the elements in the Auto-CAD window

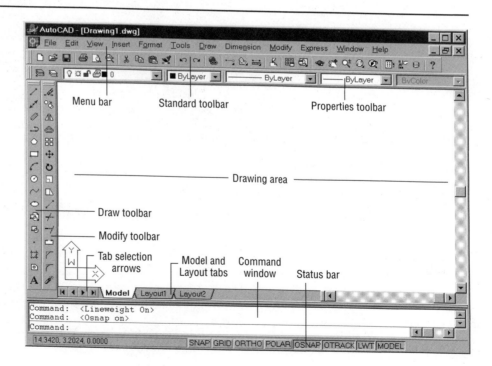

FIGURE 1.2:

An alternative arrangement of the elements in the AutoCAD window

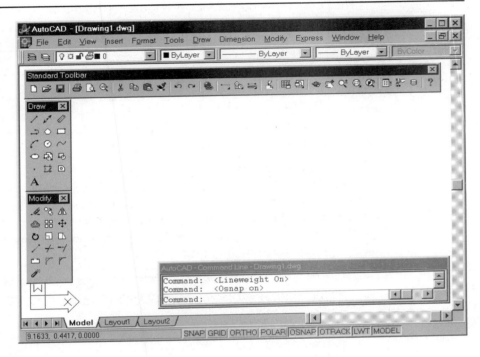

The menu bar at the top of the drawing area (as shown in Figure 1.3) offers pull-down menus from which you select commands in a typical Windows fashion. The toolbars offer a variety of commands through tool buttons and drop-down lists. For example, the *layer* name or number that you are presently working on is displayed in a drop-down list in the Object Properties toolbar. The layer name is preceded by tools that inform you of the status of the layer. The tools and lists on the toolbar are plentiful, and you'll learn more about all of them later in this chapter and as you work through this book.

NOTE   A *layer* is like an overlay that allows you to separate different types of information. AutoCAD allows an unlimited number of layers. On new drawings, the default layer is 0. You'll get a detailed look at layers and the meaning of the Layer tools in Chapter 4.

The Draw and Modify toolbars (Figure 1.4) offer commands that create new objects and edit existing ones. These are just two of many toolbars available to you.

FIGURE 1.3:

The components of the menu bar and the Standard toolbar

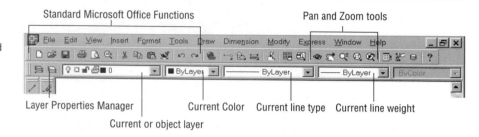

The drawing area—your workspace—occupies most of the screen. Everything you draw appears in this area. As you move your mouse around, you see crosshairs appear to move within the drawing area. This is your drawing cursor that lets you point to locations in the drawing area. At the bottom of the drawing area, the status bar (see Figure 1.5) gives you information at a glance about the drawing. For example, the coordinate readout toward the far left of the status line tells you the location of your cursor. By the way, your screen may show the drawing area in black. You can set the drawing area background color using the Options dialog box. Appendix B describes how this can be done. The figures in this book show the drawing area background in white for clarity.

FIGURE 1.4:

Here are the Draw and Modify toolbars as they appear when they are floating.

A set of tabs gives you access to the Layout views of your drawing. These are views that let you layout your drawing like a desktop publishing program. You'll learn about the Layout tabs in Chapter 7. The arrows to the left of the tabs let you navigate the tabs when there are more tabs than can fit in the window. The Command window can be moved and resized in a manner similar to toolbars. By default, the Command window is in its docked position, shown here. Let's practice using the coordinate readout and drawing cursor.

Some AutoCAD users prefer to turn off the scrollbars to the right and at the bottom of the drawing area. This allows you to maximize the size of the drawing area. Settings that control the scroll bars and other screen-related functions can be found in the Options dialog box. See Appendix B for more information on the Options dialog box.

FIGURE 1.5:

The status bar and Command window

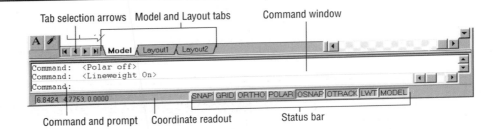

Picking Points

1. Move the cursor around in the drawing area. As you move, note how the coordinate readout changes to tell you the cursor's location. It shows the coordinates in an *X,Y* format.

2. Now place the cursor in the middle of the drawing area and press and immediately release the left mouse button. You have just picked a point. Move the cursor, and a rectangle follows. This is a *selection window*; you'll learn more about this window in Chapter 2.

3. Move the cursor a bit in any direction; then press and let go of the left mouse button again. Notice that the rectangle disappears.

4. Try picking several more points in the drawing area.

If you accidentally press the right mouse button, a popup menu appears. This will be a surprise to both new and experienced AutoCAD users. In AutoCAD 2000, a right mouse click frequently brings up a popup menu with options that are context sensitive. This means that the contents of the popup menu depend on where you right-click as well as the command that is active at the time of your right-click. If options are not appropriate at the time of the right-click, AutoCAD treats the right-click as a ⏎. You'll learn more about these options as you progress through the book. For now, if you happen to open this menu by accident, press the Esc key to dismiss it.

The ↲ symbol is used in this book to denote the Enter key. Whenever you see it, press the Enter key, also known as the Return key.

Terminology to Remember: The operation you performed in steps 1 and 2—placing the cursor on a specific point and pressing the left mouse button—is referred to as *clicking* or *clicking a point*.

UCS Icon

In the lower-left corner of the drawing area, you see a thick, L-shaped arrow outline. This is the *User Coordinate System (UCS)* icon, which tells you your orientation in the drawing. This icon becomes helpful as you start to work with complex 2D drawings and 3D models. The *X* and *Y* inside the icon indicate the x- and y-axes of your drawing. The *W* tells you that you are in what is called the *World Coordinate System*. Chapter 16 discusses this icon in detail. For now, you can use it as a reference to tell you the direction of the axes.

If you can't find the UCS icon... The UCS icon can be turned on and off, so if you are on someone else's system and you don't see the icon, don't panic. It also changes shape depending on whether you are in Paper Space mode in the Layout tab or in Model Space mode! If you don't see the icon or it doesn't look like it does in this chapter, see *Switching to Paper Space* in Chapter 12 for more information on Paper Space and Model Space. Chapter 16 can give you more information on the UCS icon.

The Command Window

At the bottom of the screen, just above the status bar, is a small horizontal window called the *Command window*. Here AutoCAD displays responses to your input. It shows three lines of text. The bottom line shows the current messages and the top two lines show messages that have scrolled by, or in some cases, components of the current message that do not fit in a single line. Right now, the bottom line displays the message Command (see Figure 1.5). This tells you that AutoCAD is waiting for your instructions. As you click a point in the drawing area, you'll see the message Other corner. At the same time, the cursor starts to draw a selection window that disappears when you click another point.

As a new user, it is important to pay special attention to messages displayed in the Command window because this is how AutoCAD communicates with you. Besides giving you messages, the Command window records your activity in AutoCAD. You can use the scroll bar to the right of the Command window to review previous messages. You can also enlarge the window for a better view. (Chapter 2 discusses these components in more detail.)

NOTE   As you become more familiar with AutoCAD, you may find you don't need to rely on the Command window as much. For new users, however, the Command window can be quite helpful in understanding what steps to take as you work.

Now let's look at AutoCAD's window components in detail.

The Pull-Down Menus

Like most Windows programs, the pull-down menus available on the menu bar offer an easy-to-understand way to access the general controls and settings for AutoCAD. Within these menus you'll find the commands and functions that are the heart of AutoCAD. By clicking menu items, you can cut and paste items to and from AutoCAD, change the settings that make AutoCAD work the way you want it to, set up the measurement system you want to use, access the help system, and much more.

TIP   To close a pull-down menu without selecting anything, press the Esc key. You can also click any other part of the AutoCAD window or click another pull-down menu.

The pull-down menu options perform four basic functions:

- Display additional menu choices
- Display a dialog box that contains settings you can change
- Issue a command that requires keyboard or drawing input
- Offer an expanded set of the same tools found in the Draw and Modify toolbars

As you point to commands and options in the menus or toolbars, AutoCAD provides additional help for you in the form of brief descriptions of each menu option, which appear in the status bar.

Here's an exercise to let you practice with the pull-down menus and get acquainted with AutoCAD's interface:

1. Click View in the menu bar. The list of items that appears includes the commands and settings that let you control the way AutoCAD displays your drawings. Don't worry if you don't understand them; you'll get to know them in later chapters.

2. Move the highlight cursor slowly down the list of menu items. As you highlight each item, notice that a description of it appears in the status line at the bottom of the AutoCAD window. These descriptions help you choose the menu option you need.

3. Some of the menu items have triangular pointers to their right. This means the command has additional choices. For instance, highlight the Zoom item, and you'll see another set of options appear to the right of the menu.

NOTE   If you look carefully at the command descriptions in the status bar, you'll see an odd word at the end. This is the keyboard command equivalent to the highlighted option in the menu or toolbar. You can actually type in these keyboard commands to start the tool or menu item that you are pointing to. You don't have to memorize these command names, but knowing them will be helpful to you later if you want to customize AutoCAD.

This second set of options is called a *cascading menu*. Whenever you see a pull-down menu item with the triangular pointer, you know that this item opens a cascading menu offering a more detailed set of options.

You might have noticed that other pull-down menu options are followed by an ellipsis (…). This indicates that the option brings up a dialog box, as the following exercise demonstrates:

1.   Move the highlight cursor to the Tools option in the menu bar.

NOTE   If you prefer, you can click and drag the highlight cursor over the pull-down menu to select an option.

2.   Click the Options item. The Options dialog box appears.

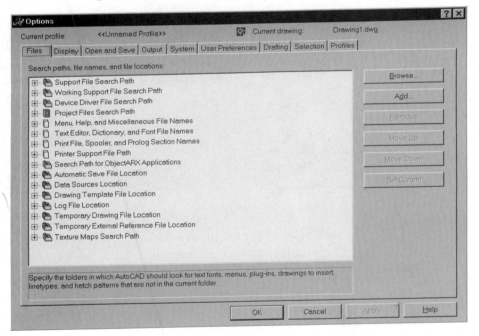

NOTE   If you're familiar with the Windows 95/98 Explorer, you should feel at home with the Files tab of the Options dialog box. Clicking the plus sign to the left of the items in the list expands the option to display more detail.

This dialog box contains several "pages," indicated by the tabs across the top, that contain settings for controlling what AutoCAD shows you on its screens, where you want it to look for special files, and other "housekeeping" settings. You needn't worry about what these options mean at this point. Appendix B describes the Options dialog box in more detail.

3. In the Options dialog box, click the tab labeled Open and Save. The options change to reveal new options.

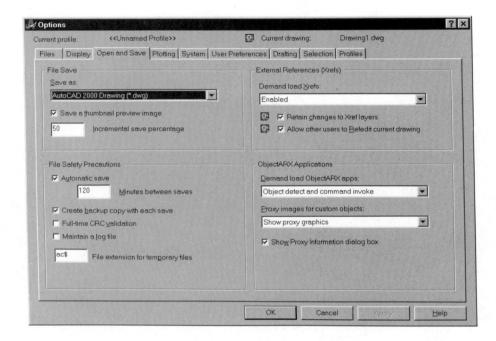

In the middle-left side of the dialog box, you'll see a check box labeled Automatic Save, with the Minutes Between Saves input box set to 120 minutes. This setting controls how frequently AutoCAD performs an automatic save.

4. Change the 120 to 20, and then click OK. You have just changed AutoCAD's Automatic Save feature to automatically save files every 20 minutes instead of every two hours. (Let this be a reminder to give your eyes a rest!)

5. Finally, click the OK button at the bottom of the dialog box to save your changes and dismiss the dialog box.

The third type of item you'll find on pull-down menus is a command that directly executes an AutoCAD operation. Let's try an exercise to explore these commands.

1. Click the Draw option from the menu bar, and then click the Rectangle command. Notice that the Command window now shows the following prompt:

```
Specify first corner point or [Chamfer/Elevation/Fillet/
Thickness/Width]:
```

AutoCAD is asking you to select the first corner for the rectangle, and in brackets, it is offering a few options that you can take advantage of at this point in the command. Don't worry about those options right now. You'll have an opportunity to learn about command options in Chapter 2.

2. Click a point roughly in the lower-left corner of the drawing area, as shown in Figure 1.6. Now as you move your mouse, you'll see a rectangle follow the cursor with one corner fixed at the position you just selected. You'll also see the following prompt in the Command window:

    Specify other corner point:

3. Click another point anywhere in the upper-right region of the drawing area. A rectangle appears (see Figure 1.7). You'll learn more about the different cursor shapes and what they mean in Chapter 2.

At this point you've seen how most of AutoCAD's commands work. You'll find that dialog boxes are offered when you want to change settings, while many drawing and editing functions present messages in the Command window. Also, be aware that many of the pull-down menu items are duplicated in the toolbars that you will explore next.

FIGURE 1.6:

Selecting the first point of a rectangle

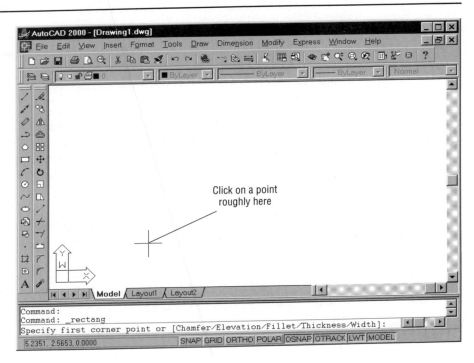

FIGURE 1.7:

Once you've selected your first point of the rectangle, the cursor disappears and you see a rectangle follow the motion of your mouse.

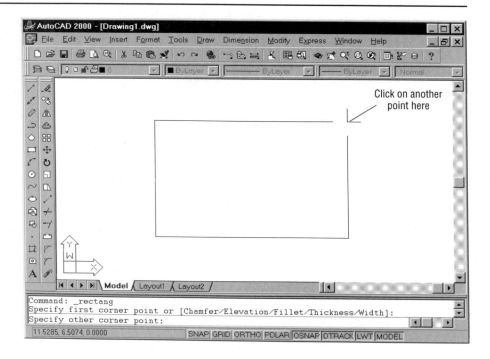

Click on another point here

Communicating with AutoCAD

AutoCAD is the perfect servant: It does everything you tell it to, and no more. You communicate with AutoCAD using the pull-down menus and the toolbars. These devices invoke AutoCAD commands. A command is a single-word instruction you give to AutoCAD telling it to do something, such as draw a line (the Line tool in the Draw toolbar) or erase an object (the Erase tool in the Modify toolbar). Whenever you invoke a command, by either typing it in or selecting a menu or toolbar item, AutoCAD responds by presenting messages to you in the Command window or by displaying a dialog box.

The messages in the Command window often tell you what to do next, or they offer a list of options. A single command often presents several messages, which you answer to complete the command. These messages serve as an aid to new users who need a little help. If you ever get lost while using a command, or forget what you are supposed to do, look at the Command window for clues. As you become more comfortable with AutoCAD, you will find that you won't need to refer to these messages as frequently.

Continued on next page

As an additional aid, you can right-click to display a context-sensitive menu. If you are in the middle of a command and are not selecting points, this menu offers a list of options specifically related to that command. For example, if you had right-clicked your mouse before picking the first point for the rectangle command in the previous exercise, a popup menu would have appeared, offering the same options that were listed in the command prompt, plus some additional options.

A dialog box is like a form you fill out on the computer screen. It lets you adjust settings or make selections from a set of options pertaining to a command. You'll get a chance to work with commands and dialog boxes later in this chapter.

The Toolbars

While the pull-down menus offer a full range of easy-to-understand options, they require some effort to navigate. The toolbars, on the other hand, offer quick, single-click access to the most commonly used AutoCAD features. In the default AutoCAD window arrangement, you see the most commonly used toolbars. Other toolbars are available but they are hidden from view until you open them.

The tools in the toolbars perform three types of actions, just like the pull-down menu commands: They display further options, open dialog boxes, and issue commands that require keyboard or cursor input.

The Toolbar Tool Tips

AutoCAD's toolbars contain tools that represent commands. To help you understand each tool, a *tool tip* appears just below the arrow cursor when you rest the cursor on a tool. Each tool tip helps you identify the tool with its function. A tool tip appears when you follow these steps:

1. Move the arrow cursor onto one of the toolbar tools and leave it there for a second or two. Notice that the command's name appears nearby—this is the tool tip. In the status bar, a brief description of the button's purpose appears (see Figure 1.8).

2. Move the cursor across the toolbar. As you do, notice that the tool tips and status bar descriptions change to describe each tool. The keyboard command equivalent of the tool is also shown in the status bar at the end of the description.

FIGURE 1.8:

Tool tips show you the function of each tool in the toolbar. AutoCAD also displays a description of the tool in the status bar.

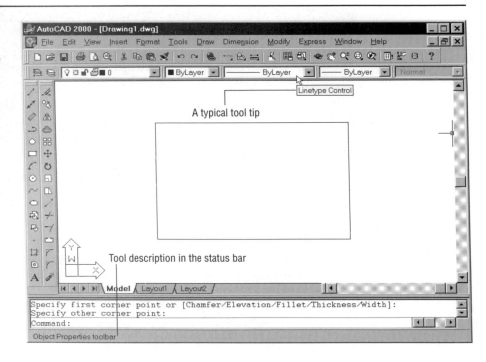

Flyouts

Most toolbar tools start a command as soon as you click them, but other tools display a set of additional tools (similar to the menus in the menu bar) that are related to the tool you have selected. This set of additional tools is called a toolbar *flyout*. If you've used other Windows graphics programs, chances are you've seen flyouts. Look closely at the tools just below the Express or Dimension pull-down menu options on your screen or in Figure 1.8. You'll be able to identify which toolbar tools have flyouts; they'll have a small right-pointing arrow in the lower-right corner of the tool.

TIP   Remember: When an instruction says, "click," you should lightly press the left mouse button until you hear a click; then immediately let it go. Don't hold it down.

The following steps show you how a flyout works:

1. Move the cursor to the Zoom Window tool in the Standard toolbar. Click and hold the left mouse button to display the flyout. Don't release the mouse button.

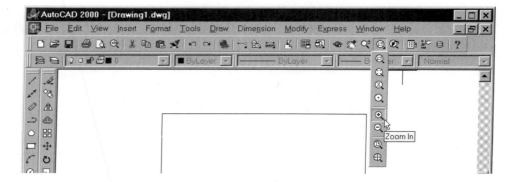

2. Still holding down the left mouse button, move the cursor over the flyout; notice that the tool tips appear here as well. Also, notice the description in the status bar.

3. Move the cursor to the Zoom Window tool at the top of the flyout and release the mouse button.

4. You won't need to use this tool yet, so press the Esc key to cancel this tool.

As you can see from this exercise, you get a lot of feedback from AutoCAD!

Moving the Toolbars

One unique characteristic of AutoCAD's toolbars is their mobility. They can be either floating anywhere on the AutoCAD window or in a *docked* position. Docked means the toolbar is placed against the top and side borders of the AutoCAD window, so that the toolbar occupies a minimal amount of space. If you want to, you can move the toolbar to any location on your desktop, thus turning it into a floating toolbar.

Later in this section you'll find descriptions of all of AutoCAD's toolbars, but first try the following exercise to move the Object Properties toolbar away from its current position in the AutoCAD window.

1. Move the arrow cursor so that it points to the vertical bars, called *grab bars*, to the far left of the Object Properties toolbar, as shown here:

2. Press and hold down the left mouse button. Notice that a gray rectangle appears by the cursor.

3. Still holding down the mouse button, move the mouse downward. The gray box follows the cursor.

4. When the gray box is over the drawing area, release the mouse button and the Object Properties toolbar—now a floating toolbar—moves to its new location.

NOTE   **Terminology to Remember:** The action you perform in steps 2 and 3 of this exercise—holding down the mouse/pick button while simultaneously moving the mouse—is called *click and drag*. (If you have used other Windows applications, you already know this.) From now on, this book will use the term "click and drag" to describe this type of action.

You can now move the Object Properties toolbar to any location on the screen that suits you. You can also change the shape of the toolbar. Try the following steps:

1. Place the cursor on the bottom-edge border of the Object Properties toolbar. The cursor becomes a double-headed arrow, as shown here:

2. Click and drag the border downward. The gray rectangle jumps to a new, taller rectangle as you move the cursor.

3. When the gray rectangle changes to the shape you want, release the mouse button to reshape the toolbar.

4. To move the toolbar back into its docked position, place the arrow cursor on the toolbar's title bar and slowly click and drag the toolbar so that the

cursor is in position in the upper-left corner of the AutoCAD window. Notice how the gray outline of the toolbar changes as it approaches its docked position.

5. When the outline of the Object Properties toolbar is near its docked position, release the mouse button. The toolbar moves back into its previous position in the AutoCAD window.

TIP

You can also move a toolbar from a docked position to a floating one by double-clicking the toolbar's grab bar. Double-click the title bar of a floating toolbar to move the toolbar to its docked position.

You can move and reshape any of AutoCAD's toolbars to place them out of the way, yet still have them at the ready to give you quick access to commands. You can also put them away altogether when you don't need them and bring them back at will, as shown in the following steps:

1. Click and drag the Draw toolbar from its position at the left of the AutoCAD window to a point near the center of the drawing area. Remember to click and drag the grab bars at the top of the toolbar.

2. Click the Close button in the upper-left corner of the Draw floating toolbar. This is the small square button with the *x* in it. The toolbar disappears.

NOTE

Terminology to Remember: When this book asks you to select an option from the pull-down menu, you will see the notation *Menu* ➤ *Option*. For cascading menus, the notation will be *Menu* ➤ *Option* ➤ *Option;* the second ➤ *Option* is in a cascading menu. In either case, the selected menu option issues a command that performs the function being discussed. As mentioned earlier, the actual command name appears in the status bar when you point to a menu option or toolbar tool.

---

3. To recover the Draw toolbar, right-click any toolbar—the Properties toolbar, for example. A popup list of toolbars appears.

4. Locate and select Draw in the popup list of toolbars. The Draw toolbar reappears.

5. Click and drag the Draw toolbar back to its docked position in the far-left side of the AutoCAD window.

AutoCAD remembers your toolbar arrangement between sessions. When you exit and then reopen AutoCAD later, the AutoCAD window appears just as you left it.

You may have noticed several other toolbars listed in the popup list of toolbars that don't appear in the AutoCAD window. To keep the screen from becoming cluttered, many of the toolbars are not placed on the screen. The toolbars you'll be using most often are displayed first; others that are less frequently used are kept out of sight until they are needed. Here are brief descriptions of all the toolbars available on the popup list:

3D Orbit   Tools to control 3D views.

Dimension   Commands that help you dimension your drawings. Many of these commands are duplicated in the Dimension pull-down menu. See Chapter 9.

Draw   Commands for creating common objects, including lines, arcs, circles, curves, ellipses, and text. This toolbar appears in the AutoCAD window by default. Many of these commands are duplicated in the Draw pull-down menu.

Inquiry   Commands for finding distances, point coordinates, object properties, mass properties, and areas.

Insert   Commands for importing other drawings, raster images, and OLE objects.

Layouts   Tools that let you set up drawing layouts for viewing, printing, and plotting.

Modify   Commands for editing existing objects. You can Move, Copy, Rotate, Erase, Trim, Extend, and so on. Many of these commands are duplicated in the Modify pull-down menu.

Modify II   Commands for editing special complex objects such as polylines, multilines, 3D solids, and hatches.

Object Properties   Commands for manipulating the properties of objects. This toolbar is normally docked below the pull-down menu bar.

Object Snap   Tools to help you select specific points on objects, such as endpoints and midpoints. See Chapter 3.

Refedit   Tools that allow you to make changes to symbols or background drawings that are imported as external reference drawings. See Chapter 12.

Reference   Commands that control cross-referencing of drawings. See Chapters 6 and 12.

Render   Commands to operate AutoCAD's rendering feature. See Chapter 17.

Shade   Offers tools to control the way 3D models are displayed. See Chapter 15 for more on Shade.

Solids   Commands for creating 3D solids. See Chapter 18.

Solids Editing   Command for editing 3D solids. See Chapter 18.

Standard Toolbar   The most frequently used commands for view control, file management, and editing. This toolbar is normally docked below the pull-down menu bar.

Surfaces   Commands for creating 3D surfaces. See Chapters 15 and 16.

UCS   Tools for setting up a plane on which to work. UCS stands for User Coordinate System. This is most useful for 3D modeling, but it can be helpful in 2D drafting, as well. See Chapter 16.

UCS II   Tools for selecting from a set of predefined user coordinate systems.

View   Offers tools to control the way you view 3D models. See Chapter 15 for more on 3D views.

Viewports   Tools that let you create and edit multiple views to your drawing. See Chapter 12 for more in viewports.

Web   Tools for accessing the World Wide Web.

Zoom   Commands that allow you to navigate your drawing.

You'll get a chance to work with all of the toolbars as you work through this book. Or, if you plan to use the book as a reference rather than working through it as a chapter-by-chapter tutorial, any exercise you try explains which toolbar to use for performing a specific operation.

Menus versus the Keyboard

Throughout this book, you will be told to select commands and command options from the pull-down menus and toolbars. For new and experienced users alike, menus and toolbars offer an easy-to-remember method for accessing commands. If you are an experienced AutoCAD user who is used to the earlier versions of AutoCAD, you still have the option of entering commands directly from the keyboard. Most of the commands you know and love still work as they did from the keyboard.

Another method for accessing commands is to use *accelerator keys,* which are special keystrokes that open and activate pull-down menu options. You might have noticed that the commands in the menu bar and the items in the pull-down menus all have an underlined character. By pressing the Alt key followed by the key corresponding to the underlined character, you activate that command or option, without having to engage the mouse. For example, to issue File ➤ Open, press Alt, then F, then finally O (Alt+F+O).

Many tools and commands have keyboard *shortcuts;* shortcuts are one-, two-, or three-letter abbreviations of a command name. As you become more proficient with AutoCAD, you may find these shortcuts helpful. As you work through this book, the shortcuts will be identified for your reference.

Finally, if you are feeling adventurous, you can create your own accelerator keys and keyboard shortcuts for executing commands by adding them to the AutoCAD support files. Chapters 19 and 20 discuss customization of the menus, toolbars, and keyboard shortcuts.

Working with AutoCAD

Now that you've been introduced to the AutoCAD window, let's try using a few of AutoCAD's commands. First, you'll open a sample file and make a few simple modifications to it. In the process, you'll become familiar with some common methods of operation in AutoCAD.

Opening an Existing File

In this exercise, you will get a chance to see and use a typical Select File dialog box. To start with, you will open an existing file.

1. From the menu bar, choose File ➤ Close. A message appears asking you if you want to save the changes you've made to the current drawing. Click No.

2. Choose File ➤ Open. The Select File dialog box appears. This is a typical Windows file dialog box, with an added twist. The large Preview box on the right allows you to preview a drawing before you open it, thereby saving time while searching for files.

3. In the Select File dialog box, go to the Directories list and locate the directory named Figures (you may need to scroll down the list to find it). Point to it and double-click (press the mouse/pick button twice in rapid succession). (If you're having trouble opening files with a double-click, here's another way to do it until you are more proficient with the mouse: Click the file once to highlight it, and then click the OK button.) The file list on the left changes to show the contents of the Figures directory.

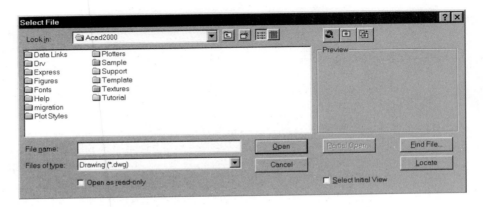

4. Move the arrow to the file named Nozzle3d and click it. Notice that the Nozzle3d.dwg filename now appears in the File Name input box above the file list. Also, the Preview box now shows a thumbnail image of the file.

NOTE

The Nozzle3D drawing is included on the companion CD-ROM. If you cannot find this file, be sure you have installed the sample drawings from the companion CD-ROM. See Appendix C for installation instructions.

5. Click the OK button at the bottom of the Select File dialog box. AutoCAD opens the Nozzle3d file, as shown in Figure 1.9.

FIGURE 1.9:

In the early days, this nozzle drawing became the unofficial symbol of Auto-CAD, frequently appearing in ads for AutoCAD third-party products.

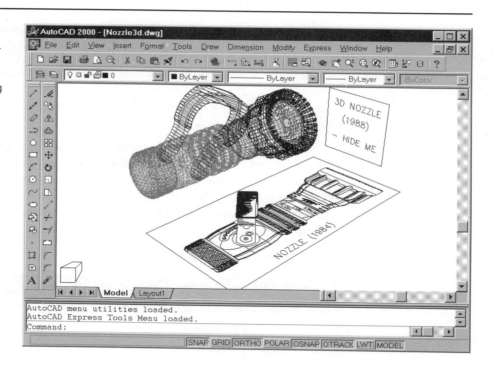

The Nozzle3d file opens to display the entire drawing. Also, the AutoCAD window's title bar displays the name of the drawing. This offers easy identification of the file. This particular file contains both a 2D and 3D model of a fire hose nozzle. The opening view is actually a 3D view.

Getting a Closer Look

One of the most frequently used commands is the Zoom command. Zoom lets you get a closer look at a part of your drawing. It offers a variety of ways to control your view. Now you'll enlarge a portion of the Nozzle drawing to get a more detailed look. To tell AutoCAD what area you wish to enlarge, you use what is called a *window*.

1. Choose View ➢ 3D Views ➢ Plan View ➢ World UCS. Your view changes to display a two-dimensional view looking down on the drawing.

2. Click the Zoom Window button on the Standard toolbar.

You can also Choose View ➢ Zoom ➢ Window from the pull-down menu or type the command: **Z⏎ W⏎**.

3. The Command window displays the `First corner:` prompt. Look at the top image of Figure 1.10. Move the crosshair cursor to a location similar to the one shown in the figure, then left-click the mouse. Move the cursor and the rectangle appears, with one corner fixed on the point you just picked, while the other corner follows the cursor.

4. The Command window now displays the `Specify first corner:` and `Specify opposite corner:` prompts. Position the other corner of the window so it encloses the handle of the nozzle, as shown in the top image of Figure 1.10, and left-click the mouse again. The handle enlarges to fill the screen (see the bottom image of Figure 1.10).

NOTE   If you decide that you don't like the position of the first point you pick while defining the zoom window, you can right-click the mouse, then re-select the first point. This only works when you enter Z (⏎) W (⏎) to issue the Zoom Window command or when you select Zoom Window from the Standard toolbar.

FIGURE 1.10:

Placing the Zoom window around the nozzle handle. After clicking the Zoom Window button in the Standard toolbar, select the two points shown in this figure.

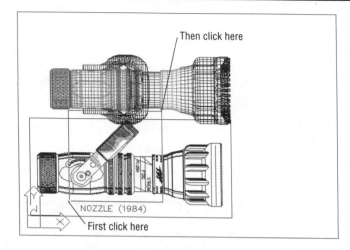

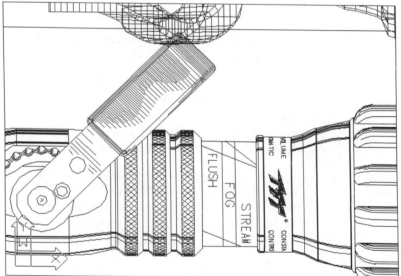

In this exercise, you used the Window option of the Zoom command to define an area to enlarge for your close-up view. You saw how AutoCAD prompts you to indicate first one corner of the window and then the other. These messages are helpful for first-time users of AutoCAD. You will be using the Window option frequently—not just to define views, but also to select objects for editing.

Getting a close-up view of your drawing is crucial to working accurately with a drawing, but you'll often want to return to a previous view to get the overall picture. To do so, click the Zoom Previous button on the Standard toolbar.

Do this now, and the previous view—one showing the entire nozzle—returns to the screen. You can also get there by choosing View ≻ Zoom ≻ Previous.

You can quickly enlarge or reduce your view using the Zoom Realtime button on the Standard toolbar.

NOTE   You can also zoom in and out using the Zoom In and Zoom Out buttons in the Zoom Window flyout of the Standard toolbar. The Zoom In button shows a magnifying glass with a plus sign; the Zoom Out button shows a minus sign. If you have a mouse equipped with a scroll wheel, you can zoom in and out just by turning the wheel. The location of the cursor at the time you move the wheel will determine the center of the zoom. A click-and-drag of the scroll wheel will let you pan your view.

1. Click the Zoom Realtime button on the Standard Toolbar.

The cursor changes into a magnifying glass.

2. Place the Zoom Realtime cursor slightly above the center of the drawing area, and then click and drag downward. Your view zooms out to show more of the drawing.

3. While still holding the left mouse button, move the cursor upward. Your view zooms in to enlarge your view. When you have a view similar to the

one shown in Figure 1.11, release the mouse button. (Don't worry if you don't get the *exact* same view as the figure. This is just for practice.)

4. You are still in Zoom Realtime mode. Click and drag the mouse again to see how you can further adjust your view. To exit, select another command besides a Zoom or Pan command, press the Esc key, or right-click your mouse.

5. Go ahead and right-click now. A popup menu appears.

This menu lets you select other display-related options.

6. Click Exit from the popup menu to exit the Zoom Realtime command.

As you can see from this exercise, you have a wide range of options for viewing your drawings, just by using a few buttons. In fact, these three buttons, along with the scroll bars at the right side and bottom of the AutoCAD window are all you need to control the display of your 2D drawings.

FIGURE 1.11:

The final view you want to achieve in step 3 of the exercise

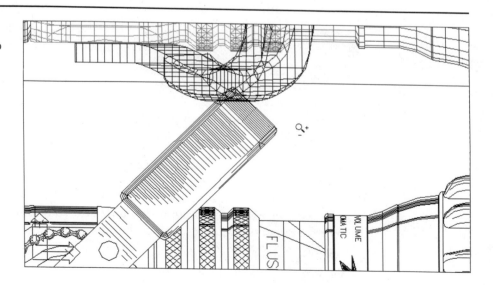

The Aerial View Window

The *Aerial View* window is an optional AutoCAD display tool. It gives you an overall view of your drawing, regardless of the magnification you are using for the drawing editor. Aerial View also makes it easier to get around in a large-scale drawing. You'll find that this feature is best suited to complex drawings that cover great areas, such as site plans, topographical maps, or city planning documents.

The Aerial View is not discussed much in this chapter, because it can be a bit confusing for the first-time AutoCAD user. However, as you become more comfortable with AutoCAD, you may want to try it out. You'll find a detailed description of the Aerial View window in Chapter 6.

Saving a File As You Work

It is a good idea to periodically save your file as you work on it. You can save it under its original name (with File ➢ Save) or under a different name (with File ➢ Save As), thereby creating a new file.

By default, AutoCAD automatically saves your work at 120-minute intervals under the name AUTO.SV$; this is known as the *Automatic Save* feature. Using settings in the Options dialog box or system variables, you can change the name of the autosaved file and control the time between autosaves. See the *Using Auto-CAD's Automatic Save Feature* sidebar in Chapter 3 for details.

Let's first try the Save command. This quickly saves the drawing in its current state without exiting the program.

Choose File ➢ Save. You will notice some disk activity while AutoCAD saves the file to the hard disk. As an alternative to choosing File ➢ Save from the menu, you can type **Alt+F S**. This is the accelerator key, also called *hotkey*, for the File ➢ Save command.

Now try the Save As command. This command brings up a dialog box that allows you to save the current file under a new name.

1. Choose File ➢ Save As, or type **Saveas**↵ at the command prompt. The Select File dialog box appears. Note that the current filename, Nozzle3d.dwg, is highlighted in the File Name input box at the bottom of the dialog box.

2. Type **Myfirst**. As you type, the name Nozzle3d disappears from the input box and is replaced by Myfirst. You don't need to enter the .dwg filename extension. AutoCAD adds it to the filename automatically when it saves the file.

3. Click the Save button. The dialog box disappears, and you will notice some disk activity.

You now have a copy of the nozzle file under the name Myfirst.dwg. The name of the file displayed in the AutoCAD window's title bar has changed to Myfirst. From now on, when you use the File ➤ Save option, your drawing will be saved under its new name. Saving files under a different name can be useful when you are creating alternatives or when you just want to save one of several ideas you have been trying out.

If you are working with a monitor that is on the small side, you may want to consider closing the Draw and Modify toolbars. The Draw and Modify pull-down menus offer the same commands, so you won't lose any functionality by closing these toolbars. If you really want to maximize your drawing area, you can also turn off the scroll bars and reduce the Command window to a single line. See *Setting Options* in Appendix B for details on how to do this.

Making Changes

You will be making frequent changes to your drawings. In fact, one of Auto-CAD's chief advantages is the ease with which you can make changes. The following exercise shows you a typical sequence of operations involved in making a change to a drawing:

1. From the Modify toolbar, click the Erase tool (the one with a pencil eraser touching paper). This activates the Erase command. You can also choose Modify ➤ Erase from the pull-down menu.

Notice that the cursor has turned into a small square; this square is called the *pickbox*. You also see `Select object:` in the command prompt area. This message helps remind new users what to do.

2. Place the pickbox on the diagonal pattern of the nozzle handle (see Figure 1.12) and click it. The 2D image of the nozzle becomes highlighted. The pickbox and the `Select object:` prompt remain, telling you that you can continue to select objects.

3. Now press ↵. The nozzle and the rectangle disappear. You have just erased a part of the drawing.

FIGURE 1.12:

Erasing a portion of the nozzle handle

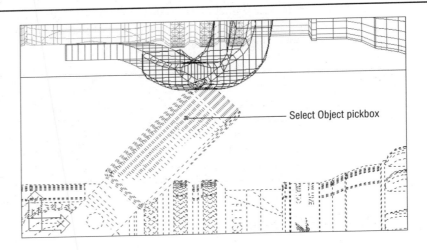

Select Object pickbox

In this exercise, you first issued the Erase command, and then selected an object by clicking it using a pickbox. The pickbox tells you that you must select items on the screen. Once you've done that, press ↵ to move on to the next step. This sequence of steps is common to many of the commands you will work with in AutoCAD.

Opening Multiple Files

With AutoCAD 2000, you can now have multiple documents open at the same time. This can be especially helpful if you want to exchange parts of drawings between files or if you just want to have another file open for reference. Try the following exercise to see how multiple documents work in AutoCAD:

1. Choose File ➤ New.

2. In the Create New Drawing dialog box, click the Start from Scratch button at the top of the dialog box.

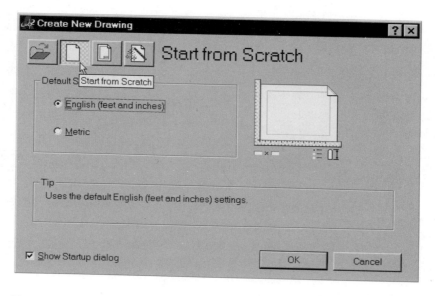

3. Click the English radio button, then click OK. You'll get a blank drawing file.

4. Choose Window ➤ Tile Vertically to get a view of both drawing files. The options in the Window pull-down menu act just like their counterparts in other Windows programs that allow multiple document editing.

5. Click in the window with the Nozzle3d drawing to make it active.

6. Choose View ➤ Zoom ➤ All to get an overall view of the drawing.

7. Click the words Nozzle 1984 near the bottom of the drawing.

8. Click and drag on the words Nozzle 1984. You'll see a small rectangle appear next to the cursor.

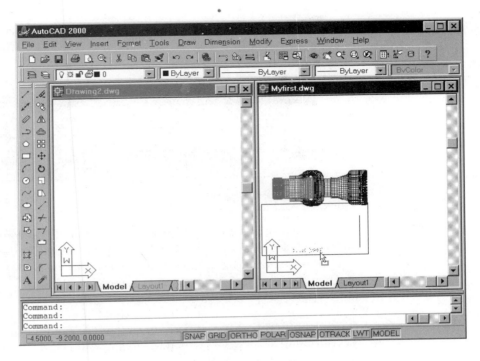

9. While still holding the left mouse button, drag the cursor to the new file window. When you see the words Nozzle 1984 appear in the new drawing window, release the mouse button. You've just copied a text object from one file to another.

Now you have two files open at once. You can have as many files open as you want, as long as you have adequate memory to accommodate them. You can control the individual document windows as you would any window using the Window pull-down menu or the window control buttons in the upper-right corner of the document window.

Closing AutoCAD

When you are done with your work on one drawing, you can open another drawing, temporarily leave AutoCAD, or close AutoCAD entirely. To close all the open files at once and exit AutoCAD, use the Exit option on the File menu.

1. Choose File ➤ Exit, the last item in the File menu. A dialog box appears, asking you if you want to "Save Changes to Myfirst.dwg?" and offering three buttons labeled Yes, No, and Cancel.

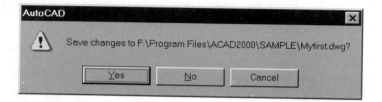

2. Click the No button.

3. AutoCAD displays another message asking you if you want to save Drawing2.dwg, which is the new drawing you opened in the last exercise. Click the No button again. AutoCAD closes both the nozzle drawing and the new drawing and exits without saving your changes.

Whenever you attempt to exit a drawing that has been changed, you get this same inquiry box. This request for confirmation is a safety feature that lets you change your mind and save your changes before you exit AutoCAD. In the previous exercise, you discarded the changes you made, so the nozzle drawing reverts back to its state before you erased the handle. The new drawing is completely discarded and no file is saved.

If you only want to exit AutoCAD temporarily, you can minimize it so it appears as a button on the Windows 95/98 or Windows NT 4 toolbar. You do this by clicking the Minimize button in the upper-right corner of the AutoCAD window; the Minimize button is the title bar button that looks like an underscore (_). Alternatively, you can use the Alt+Tab key combination to switch to another program.

If You Want to Experiment...

Try opening and closing some of the sample drawing files.

1. Start AutoCAD by choosing Start ➤ Programs ➤ AutoCAD 2000 ➤ Auto-CAD 2000.

2. Click File ➤ Open.

3. Use the dialog box to open the Myfirst file again. Notice that the drawing appears on the screen with the handle enlarged. This is the view you had on screen when you used the Save command in the earlier exercise.

4. Erase the handle, as you did in the earlier exercise.

5. Click File ➤ Open again. This time, open the Dhouse file from the companion CD-ROM. Notice that you now see the Save Changes inquiry box that you saw when you used the Exit option earlier. File ➤ Open acts just like Exit, but instead of exiting AutoCAD altogether, it closes the current file and then opens a different one.

6. Click the No button. The 3D Dhouse drawing opens.

7. Click File ➤ Exit. Notice that you exit AutoCAD without getting the Save Changes dialog box. This is because you didn't make any changes to the Dhouse file.

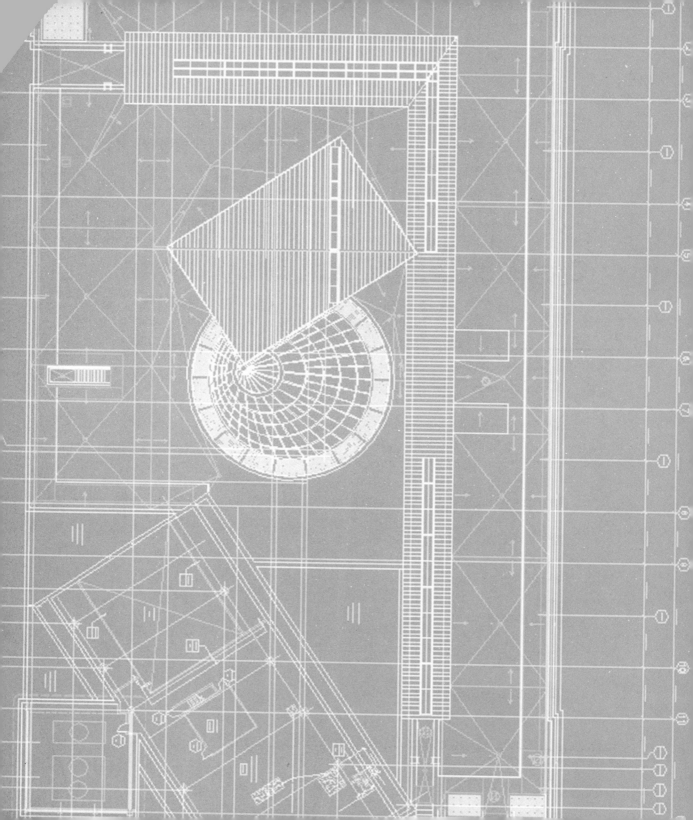

CHAPTER
TWO

Creating Your First Drawing

- Getting to Know the Draw Toolbar

- Starting Your First Drawing

- Specifying Distance with Coordinates

- Interpreting the Cursor Modes and Understanding Prompts

- Selecting Objects

- Editing with Grips

- Getting Help

- Displaying Data in a Text Window

- If You Want to Experiment...

2

This chapter examines some of AutoCAD's basic functions. You will get the chance to practice with the drawing editor by building a simple drawing to use in later exercises. You'll learn how to give input to AutoCAD, interpret prompts, and get help when you need it. This chapter also covers the use of coordinate systems to give AutoCAD exact measurements for objects. You'll see how to select objects you've drawn, and how to specify base points for moving and copying.

If you're not a beginning AutoCAD user, you might want to move on to the more complex material in Chapter 3. You can use the files supplied on the companion CD-ROM of this book to continue the tutorials at that point.

Getting to Know the Draw Toolbar

Your first task in learning how to draw in AutoCAD is to try and draw a line. But before you begin drawing, take a moment to familiarize yourself with the toolbar you'll be using more than any other to create objects with AutoCAD: the Draw toolbar.

1. Start AutoCAD just as you did in the first chapter, by clicking Start ➤ Programs ➤ AutoCAD 2000 ➤ AutoCAD 2000.

2. When the Startup Drawing wizard appears, click the Cancel button. You'll learn about setting up a drawing later in this chapter and in Chapter 3.

3. In the AutoCAD window, move the arrow cursor to the top icon in the Draw toolbar, and rest it there so that the tool tip appears.

4. Slowly move the arrow cursor downward over the other tools in the Draw toolbar, and read each tool tip.

NOTE   Moving the arrow cursor onto an element on the screen is also referred to as *pointing to* that element.

In most cases, you'll be able to guess what each tool does by looking at its icon. The icon with an arc, for instance, indicates that the tool draws arcs; the one with the ellipse shows that the tool draws ellipses; and so on. For further clarification, the tool tip gives you the name of the tool. In addition, the status bar at the bottom of the AutoCAD Window gives you information about a tool. For example, if you point to the Arc icon just below the Rectangle icon, the status bar reads `Creates an Arc`. It also shows you the actual AutoCAD command name: `Arc`. This command is what you type in the Command window to invoke the Arc tool. You also use this word if you are writing a macro or creating your own custom tools.

Figure 2.1 and Table 2.1 will aid you in navigating the two main toolbars, Draw and Modify. You'll get experience with many of AutoCAD's tools as you work through this book.

FIGURE 2.1:

The tools available on these Draw and Modify toolbars are listed by number in Table 2.1.

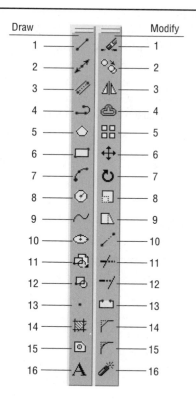

TABLE 2.1: The Options That Appear on the Draw and Modify Toolbars and Flyouts

Draw Toolbar		Draw Toolbar	
1	Line	9	Spline
2	Construction Line (Xline)	10	Ellipse
3	Multiline (Mline)	11	Insert Block
4	Polyline (Pline)	12	Make Block
5	Polygon	13	Point
6	Rectangle	14	Hatch
7	Arc	15	Region
8	Circle	16	Multiline Text

Continued on next page

TABLE 2.1 CONTINUED: The Options That Appear on the Draw and Modify Toolbars and Flyouts

Modify Toolbar		Modify Toolbar	
1	Erase	9	Stretch
2	Copy Object	10	Lengthen
3	Mirror	11	Trim
4	Offset	12	Extend
5	Array	13	Break
6	Move	14	Chamfer
7	Rotate	15	Fillet
8	Scale	16	Explode

As you saw in Chapter 1, clicking a tool issues a command. Some tools allow *clicking and dragging*, which opens a *flyout*. A flyout offers further options for that tool. You can identify flyout tools by a small triangle located in the lower-right corner of the tool.

1. Click and drag the Distance tool on the Standard toolbar. A flyout appears with a set of tools. As you can see, there are a number of additional tools for gathering information about your drawing.

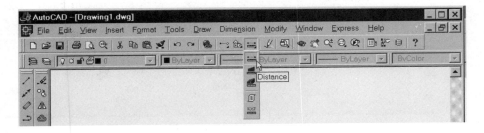

2. Move the cursor down the flyout to the second-to-last tool, until the tool tip reads "List"; then let go of the mouse button. Notice that the icon representing the Distance tool now changes and becomes the icon from the flyout that

represents List. By releasing the mouse, you've also issued the List command. This command lists the properties of an object.

3.   Press the Esc key twice to exit the List command.

TIP

If you find you are working a lot with one particular flyout, you can easily turn that flyout into a floating toolbar, so that all the flyout options are readily available with a single click.

By making the most recently selected option on a flyout the default option for the toolbar tool, AutoCAD gives you quick access to frequently used commands. A word of caution, however: This feature can confuse the first-time AutoCAD user. Also, the grouping of options on the flyout menus is not always self-explanatory—even to a veteran AutoCAD user.

Working with Toolbars

As you work through the exercises, this book will show you graphics of the tools to choose, along with the toolbar or flyout that contains the tool. Don't be alarmed, however, if the toolbars you see in the examples don't look exactly like those on your screen. To save page space, I have oriented the toolbars and flyouts horizontally for the illustrations; the ones on your screen may be oriented vertically, like the Draw and Modify toolbars to the left of the AutoCAD window. Although the shape of your toolbars and flyouts may differ from the ones you see in this book, the contents are the same. So when you see a graphic showing a tool, focus on the tool icon itself with its tool tip name, along with the name of the toolbar in which it is shown.

Starting Your First Drawing

In Chapter 1, you looked at a pre-existing sample drawing. This time you will begin to draw on your own drawing, by creating a door that will be used in later exercises. First, though, you must learn how to tell AutoCAD what you want and, even more important, to understand what AutoCAD wants from you.

NOTE   In this chapter, you'll start to see instructions for both English measurement and metric users. In general, you will see the instructions for English measurement given first, followed by the metric instructions. You won't be dealing with inches or centimeters yet, however. You're just getting to know the AutoCAD system.

1. Choose File ➤ Close to close the current file. Notice that the toolbars disappear and the AutoCAD drawing window appears blank when no drawings are open.

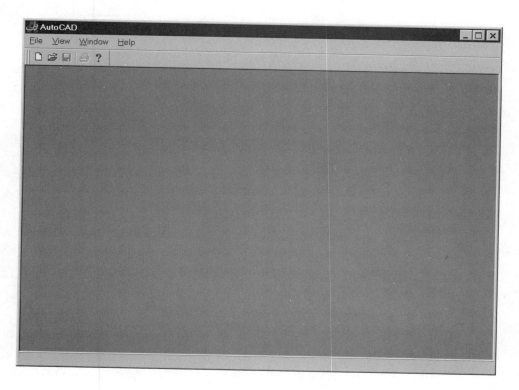

2. Choose File ➤ New. The Create New Drawing dialog box appears.

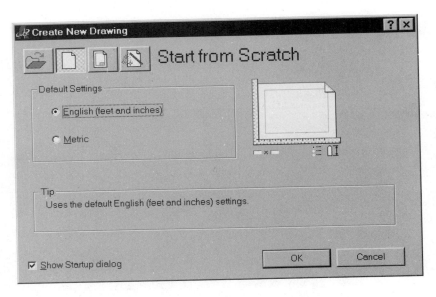

3. Click the Use a Wizard button at the top of the dialog box.

4. Select Quick Setup from the list box.

5. Click OK. The Units dialog appears.

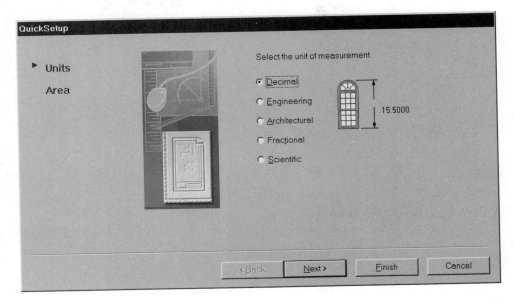

6. For now, you'll use the default decimal units as indicated by the radio buttons. You'll learn more about these options in the next chapter. Go ahead and click Next again in the Units dialog. The Area dialog appears.

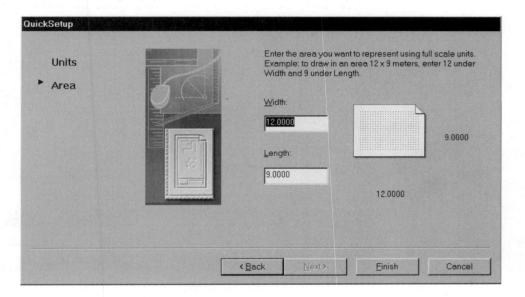

7. Double-click the Width input box and enter **12**. Metric users should enter **40**.

8. Press the Tab key to move to the next input box and enter **9**. Metric users should enter **30**.

9. Click Finish. A new drawing file appears in the AutoCAD window.

10. Choose View ➤ Zoom ➤ All from the menu bar. This ensures that your display covers the entire area you specified in steps 7 and 8.

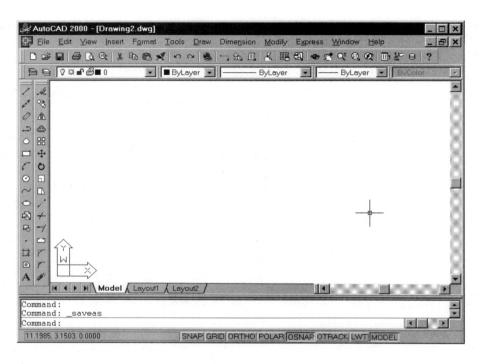

11. To give your new file a unique name, choose File ➤ Save As.

12. At the Save Drawing As dialog box, type **Door**. As you type, the name appears in the File Name input box.

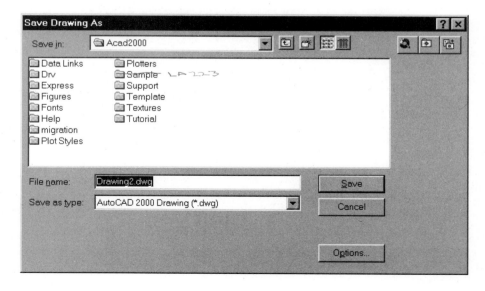

13.   Double-click the `Sample` folder shown in the main file list of the dialog box. By doing this, you open the `Sample` subdirectory.

14.   Click Save. You now have a file called `Door.dwg`, located in the `Sample` subdirectory of your `AutoCAD2000` directory. Of course, your drawing doesn't contain anything yet. You'll take care of that next.

The new file shows a drawing area roughly 14 inches wide by 9 inches high. Metric users will have a file that shows an area roughly 40 mm wide by 30 mm high. This area is your workspace, though you're not limited to it in any way. There are no visual clues to indicate the size of the area. To check the area size for yourself, move the crosshair cursor to the upper-right corner of the screen, and observe the value shown in the coordinate readout. This is the standard AutoCAD default drawing area for new drawings.

To begin a drawing, follow these steps:

1.   Click the Line tool on the Draw toolbar, or type **L↵**. You've just issued the Line command. AutoCAD responds in two ways. First, you see the message

   `Specify first point:`

   in the command prompt, asking you to select a point to begin your line. Also, the cursor has changed its appearance; it no longer has a square in the crosshairs. This is a clue telling you to pick a point to start a line.

NOTE   You can also type **Line↵** in the Command window to start the Line command.

---

2.   Using the left mouse button, select a point on the screen near the center. As you select the point, AutoCAD changes the prompt to

   `Specify next point or [Undo]:`

   Now as you move the mouse around, notice a line with one end fixed on the point you just selected, and the other end following the cursor (see the top image of Figure 2.2). This action is called *rubber-banding*.

FIGURE 2.2:

Two rubber-banding lines

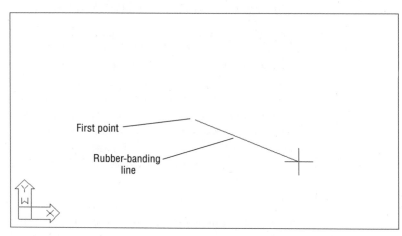

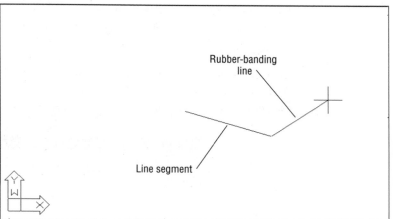

If you move the cursor to a location directly to the left or right of the point you clicked on, you'll see a dotted horizontal line appear, along with a tool tip–like message that appears at the cursor. This action also occurs when pointing directly up or down. In fact, your cursor will seem to jump to a horizontal or vertical position.

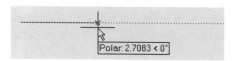

This is a feature called *Polar Tracking*. It helps to restrict your line to an exact horizontal or vertical direction like a T-square and triangle. It can be turned on or off by clicking the Polar button in the status bar. If you don't see it, chances are it's just been turned off. You'll learn more about Polar Tracking in Chapter 3.

Now continue with the Line command:

3. Move the cursor to a point below and to the right of the first point you selected, and press the left mouse button again. The first rubber-banding line is now fixed between the two points you selected, and a second rubber-banding line appears (see the bottom image of Figure 2.2).

4. If the line you drew isn't the exact length you want, you can back up during the Line command and change it. To do this, click Undo in the Standard toolbar, or type **U**↵ from the keyboard. Now the line you drew previously will rubber-band as if you hadn't selected the second point to fix its length.

You've just drawn, and then undrawn, a line of an arbitrary length. The Line command is still active. There are two things that tell you that you are in the middle of a command, as mentioned above. If you don't see the word Command in the bottom of the Command window, you know a command is still active. Also, the cursor will be the plain crosshair without the little box at its intersection.

Getting Out of Trouble

Beginners and experts alike are bound to make a few mistakes. Before you get too far into the tutorial, here are some powerful yet easy-to-use tools to help you recover from accidents.

Backspace (←)   If you make a typing error, you can use the Backspace key to back up to your error, and then retype your command or response. Backspace is located in the upper-right corner of the main keyboard area.

Escape (Esc)   This is perhaps the single most important key on your keyboard. When you need to quickly exit a command or dialog box without making changes, just press the Esc key in the upper-left corner of your keyboard. Press it twice if you want to cancel a selection set of objects or to make absolutely sure you've canceled a command.

Tip: Use the Esc key before editing with grips or issuing commands through the keyboard. You can also press Esc twice to clear grip selections.

U.⏎   If you accidentally change something in the drawing and want to reverse that change, click the Undo tool in the Standard toolbar (the left-pointing curved arrow). You can also type **U.⏎** at the **command** prompt. Each time you do this, AutoCAD will undo one operation at a time, in reverse order, so the last command performed will be undone first, then the next-to-last command, and so on. The prompt displays the name of the command being undone, and the drawing reverts to its state prior to that command. If you need to, you can undo everything back to the beginning of an editing session.

Redo.⏎   If you accidentally Undo one too many commands, you can redo the last undone command by clicking the Redo tool (the right-pointing curved arrow) in the Standard toolbar. Or type **Redo.⏎**. Unfortunately, Redo only restores one command and it can only be invoked immediately after an Undo.

Specifying Distances with Coordinates

Next, you will continue with the Line command to draw a *plan view* (an overhead view) of a door, to no particular scale. Later, you will resize the drawing to use in future exercises. The door will be 3.0 units long and 0.15 units thick. For metric users, the door will be 9 units long and 0.5 units thick. To specify these exact distances in AutoCAD, you can use either *relative polar coordinates* or *Cartesian coordinates*.

The English and metric distances are not equivalent in the exercises of this chapter. For example, 3 units in the English-based drawing are not equal to 9 metric units. These distances are arbitrary and based on how they will appear in the figures of this chapter.

Specifying Polar Coordinates

To enter the exact distance of 3 (or 9 metric) units to the right of the last point you selected, do the following:

1. Type **@3<0**. Metric users should type **@9<0**. As you type, the letters appear in the command prompt.

2. Press ⏎. A line appears, starting from the first point you picked and ending 3 units to the right of it (see Figure 2.3). You have just entered a relative polar coordinate.

FIGURE 2.3:

Notice that the rubber-banding line now starts from the last point selected. This tells you that you can continue to add more line segments.

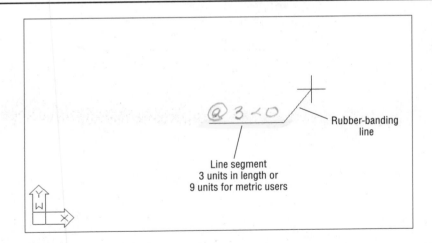

The "at" sign (@) you entered tells AutoCAD that the distance you are specifying is from the last point you selected. The 3 (or 9 metric) is the distance, and the less-than symbol (<) tells AutoCAD that you are designating the angle at which the line is to be drawn. The last part is the value for the angle, which in this case is 0. This is how to use polar coordinates to communicate distances and direction to AutoCAD.

NOTE   If you are accustomed to a different method for describing directions, you can set AutoCAD to use a vertical direction or downward direction as 0°. See Chapter 3 for details.

Angles are given based on the system shown in Figure 2.4, where 0° is a horizontal direction from left to right, 90° is straight up, 180° is horizontal from right to left, and so on. You can specify degrees, minutes, and seconds of arc if you want to be that exact. We'll discuss angle formats in more detail in Chapter 3.

FIGURE 2.4:

AutoCAD's default system for specifying angles

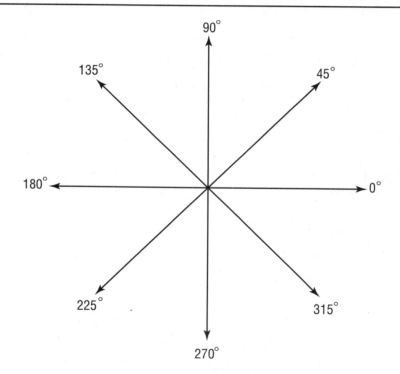

Specifying Relative Cartesian Coordinates

For the next line segment, let's try another method of specifying exact distances.

1. Enter **@1,0.15**↵. Metric users should enter **@0,0.5**↵. A short line appears above the endpoint of the last line.

TIP   This section indicates the metric users should enter **@0,0.5**↵ for the distance. You can also enter **0,.5** (zero comma point five). The leading zero is included for clarity. Metric users should be aware that the comma is used as a separator between the *x* and *y* components of the coordinate. Commas are not used for decimal points. In AutoCAD you must use a period to denote a decimal point.

Once again, the @ tells AutoCAD that the distance you specify is from the last point picked. But in this example, you give the distance in *x* and *y* values. The *x* distance, 0, is given first, followed by a comma, and then the *y* distance, 0.15. This is how to specify distances in relative Cartesian coordinates.

2.   Enter **@-3,0**↵. Metric users should enter **@-9,0**↵. The result is a drawing that looks like Figure 2.5.

The distance you entered in step 2 was also in *x,y* values, but here you used a negative value to specify the *x* distance. Positive values in the Cartesian coordinate system are from left to right and from bottom to top (see Figure 2.6). (You may remember this from your high school geometry class!) If you want to draw a line from right to left, you must designate a negative value.

FIGURE 2.5:

These three sides of the door were drawn using the Line tool. Points are specified using either relative Cartesian or polar coordinates.

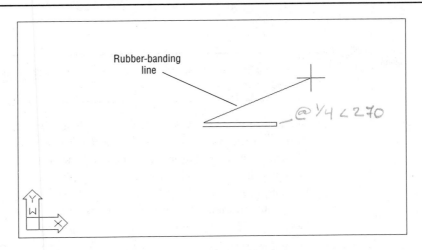

Rubber-banding line

FIGURE 2.6:

Positive and negative Cartesian coordinate directions.

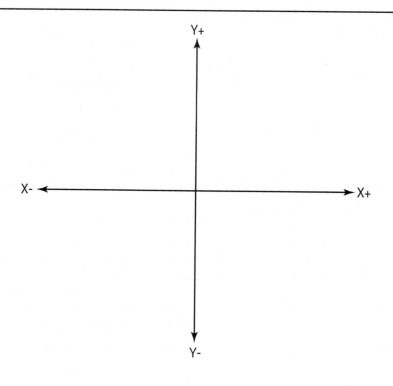

To finish drawing a series of lines without closing them, you can press Esc, ↵, or the spacebar.

3. Now type **C↵**. This C stands for the Close command. It closes a sequence of line segments. A line connecting the first and last points of a sequence of lines is drawn (see Figure 2.7), and the Line command terminates. The rubber-banding line also disappears, telling you that AutoCAD has finished drawing line segments. You can also use the rubber-banding line to indicate direction while simultaneously entering the distance through the keyboard. See the *A Fast Way to Enter Distances* sidebar in this chapter.

FIGURE 2.7:

Distance and direction input for the door. Distances for metric users are shown in brackets.

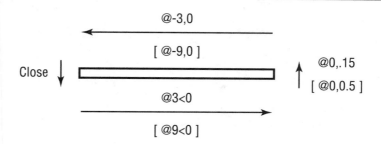

A Fast Way to Enter Distances

A third method for entering distances is to simply point in a direction with a rubber-banding line, and then enter the distance through the keyboard. For example, to draw a line 3 units long from left to right, click the Line tool from the Draw toolbar, click a start point, and then move the cursor so the rubber-banding line points to the right at some arbitrary distance. While holding the cursor in the direction you want, type **3⏎**. The rubber-banding line becomes a fixed line 3 units long.

Using this method, called the *Direct Distance* method, along with the Ortho mode or Polar Snap described in Chapter 3, can be a fast way to draw objects of specific lengths. Use the standard Cartesian or polar coordinate methods when you need to enter exact distances at angles other than those that are exactly horizontal or vertical.

Cleaning Up the Screen

On some systems, the AutoCAD Blipmode setting may be turned on. This causes tiny cross-shaped markers, called *blips*, to appear where you've selected points. These blips can be helpful to keep track of the points you've selected on the screen. You can also enter **R⏎**.

Blips aren't actually part of your drawing and do not print. Still, they can be annoying. To clear the screen of blips, click the Redraw tool in the toolbar (it's the one that looks like a pencil point drawing an arc), or type **R⏎**. The screen quickly redraws the objects, clearing the screen of the blips. You can also choose View ➤ Redraw View to accomplish the same thing. As you will see later in this book, Redraw can also clear up other display problems.

Continued on next page

Another command, Regen, does the same thing as Redraw, but also updates the drawing display database—which means it takes a bit longer to restore the drawing. Regen is used to update certain types of changes that occur in a drawing. You will learn about Regen in Chapter 7.

To turn Blipmode on and off, type **blipmode**↵ at the command prompt, and then enter **on**↵ or **off**↵.

Interpreting the Cursor Modes and Understanding Prompts

The key to working with AutoCAD successfully is understanding the way it interacts with you. This section will help you become familiar with some of the ways AutoCAD prompts you for input. Understanding the format of the messages in the Command window and recognizing other events on the screen will help you learn the program more easily.

As the Command window aids you with messages, the cursor also gives you clues about what to do. Figure 2.8 illustrates the various modes of the cursor and gives a brief description of the role of each mode. Take a moment to study this figure.

The Standard cursor tells you that AutoCAD is waiting for instructions. You can also edit objects using grips when you see this cursor. The Point Selection cursor appears whenever AutoCAD expects point input. It can also appear in conjunction with a rubber-banding line. You can either click a point or enter a coordinate through the keyboard. The Object Selection cursor tells you that you must select objects— either by clicking them or by using any of the object selection options available. The Osnap marker appears along with the Point Selection cursor when you invoke an Osnap. Osnaps let you accurately select specific points on an object, such as endpoints or midpoints. The tracking vector appears when you use the Polar Tracking or Object Snap Tracking feature. Polar Tracking aids you in drawing orthogonal lines while Object Snap Tracking helps you align point in space relative to the geometry of existing objects. Object Snap Tracking works in conjunction with Osnap. You'll learn more about the tracking vector in Chapters 3 and 4.

FIGURE 2.8:

The drawing cursor's modes

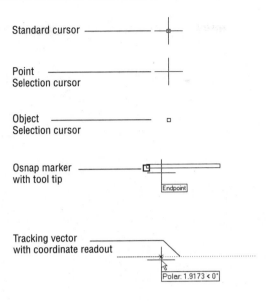

Standard cursor

Point
Selection cursor

Object
Selection cursor

Osnap marker
with tool tip

Endpoint

Tracking vector
with coordinate readout

Polar: 1.9173 < 0°

TIP If you are an experienced AutoCAD user and prefer to use the older style crosshair cursor that crosses the entire screen, use the Pointer tab of the Preferences dialog box (Tools ➤ Preferences) to set the cursor size. Set the Percent of Screen Size option near the bottom of the dialog box to 100. The cursor then appears as it did in prior versions of AutoCAD. As the option implies, you can set the cursor size to any percentage of the screen you want. The default is 6%.

Choosing Command Options

Many commands in AutoCAD offer several options, which are often presented to you in the Command window in the form of a prompt. This section uses the Arc command to illustrate the format of AutoCAD's prompts.

Usually, in a floor-plan drawing in the U.S., an arc is drawn to indicate the direction of a door swing. Figure 2.9 shows some of the other standard symbols used in architectural style drawings. This is a small sampling of the symbols available on the CD-ROM included with this book. See Appendix C for more information.

FIGURE 2.9:

Samples of standard symbols used in architectural drawings

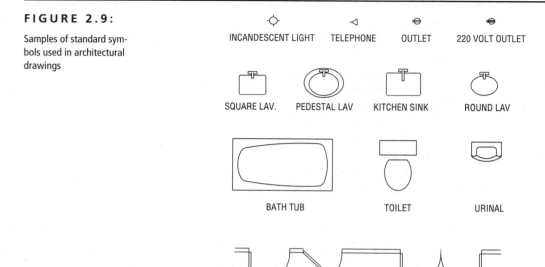

Next, you'll draw the arc for the door you started in the previous exercise.

1. Click the Arc tool in the Draw toolbar. The prompt `Specify start point of arc or [CEnter]:` appears, and the cursor changes to point selection mode.

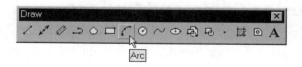

Let's examine this `Specify start point of arc or [CEnter]:` prompt. The start point contains two options. The *default* option is the one stated in the main part of the prompt. In this case, the default option is to specify the start point of the arc. If other options are available, they will appear within brackets.

In the Arc command, you see the word CEnter within brackets telling you that if you prefer, you can also start your arc by selecting a center point instead of a start point. If multiple options are available, they appear within the brackets and are separated by slashes (/). The default is the option AutoCAD assumes you intend to use unless you tell it otherwise.

2. Type CE↵ to select the Center option. The prompt Specify center point of arc: appears. Notice that you only had to type in the **CE** and not the entire word **Center**.

NOTE   When you see a set of options in the Command window, note their capitalization. If you choose to respond to prompts using the keyboard, these capitalized letters are all you need to enter to select that option. In some cases, the first two letters are capitalized to differentiate two options that begin with the same letter, such as LAyer and LType.

---

3. Now pick a point representing the center of the arc near the upper-left corner of the door (see the first image of Figure 2.10). The prompt Specify start point of arc: appears.

4. Type @3<0. Metric users should type @9<0. The prompt Specify end point of arc or [Angle/chord Length]: appears.

5. Move the mouse and a temporary arc appears, originating from a point 3 units to the right of the center point you selected and rotating about that center, as in the top continued image of Figure 2.10. (Metric users will see the temporary arc originating 9 units to the right of the center point.)

   As the prompt indicates, you now have three options. You can enter an angle, a chord length, or the endpoint of the arc. The prompt default, to specify the endpoint of the arc, picks the arc's endpoint. Again, the cursor is in a point selection mode, telling you it is waiting for point input. To select this default option, you only need to pick a point on the screen indicating where you want the endpoint.

6. Move the cursor so that it points in a vertical direction from the center of the arc. You'll see the Polar Tracking vector snap to a vertical position.

7. Click any location with the Polar Tracking vector in the vertical position. The arc is now fixed in place, as in the bottom continued image of Figure 2.10.

FIGURE 2.10:

Using the Arc command

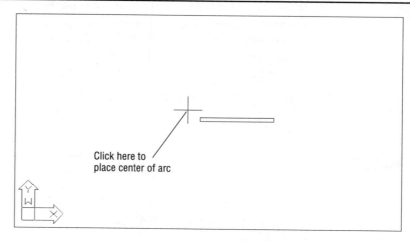

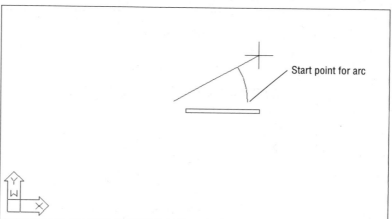

This exercise has given you some practice working with AutoCAD's Command window prompts and entering keyboard commands—skills you will need when you start to use some of the more advanced AutoCAD functions.

As you can see, AutoCAD has a distinct structure in its prompt messages. You first issue a command, which in turn offers options in the form of a prompt. Depending on the option you select, you get another set of options or you are prompted to take some action, such as picking a point, selecting objects, or entering a value.

As shown in Figure 2.11, the sequence is something like a tree. As you work through the exercises, you will become intimately familiar with this routine. Once you understand the workings of the toolbars, the Command window prompts, and the dialog boxes, you can almost teach yourself the rest of the program!

FIGURE 2.10 CONTINUED:

Using the Arc command

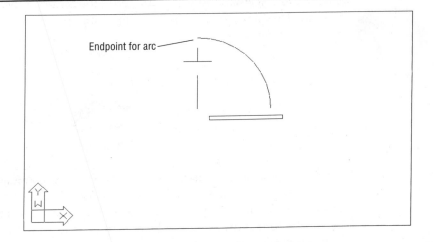

FIGURE 2.11:

A typical command structure, using the Arc command as an example. You will see different messages depending on the options you choose as you progress through the command. This figure shows the various pathways to creating an arc.

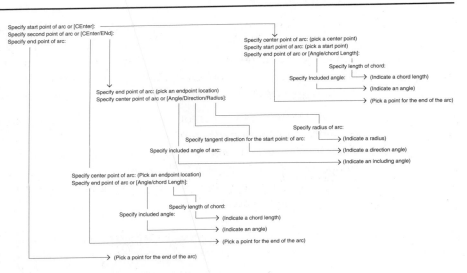

Selecting Options from a Popup Menu

Now you know that you can select command options by typing them in. You can also right-click at any time during a command to open a popup menu containing those same options. For example, in step 2 in the previous exercise, you typed **C↵** to tell AutoCAD that you wanted to select the center of the arc. Instead of typing, you can also right-click the mouse to open a popup menu of options applicable to the Arc command at that time.

Notice that in addition to the options shown in the command prompt, the popup menu also shows you a few more options, namely Enter, Cancel, Pan, and Zoom. The Enter option is the same as pressing ↵. Cancel cancels the current command. Pan and Zoom allow you to make adjustments to your view as you are working through the current command.

As you work with AutoCAD, you'll find that you can right-click at any time to get a list of options. This list is context sensitive, so you'll only see options that pertain to the command or activity that is currently in progress. Also, when AutoCAD is expecting a point, an object selection, or a numeric value, you do not get a popup menu with a right-click. Instead, AutoCAD will treat a right-click as a ↵.

Be aware that the location of your cursor when you right-click determines the contents of the popup list. You've already seen that you can right-click a toolbar to get a list of other toolbars. A right-click in the Command window displays a list of operations you can apply to the command line, such as repeating one of the last five commands you've used, or copying the most recent history of command activity to the clip board.

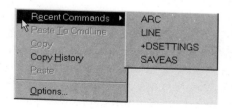

A right-click in the drawing area when no command is active gives you a set of basic options for editing your file, like Cut, Paste, Undo, Repeat the last command, Pan, and Zoom, to name a few.

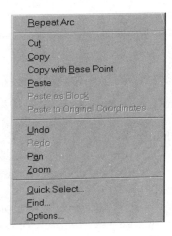

If you're ever in doubt over what to do in AutoCAD, you can right-click any time to see a list of options. You'll learn more about these options later in this book. For now, let's move on to the topic of selecting objects.

TIP   If you're a veteran AutoCAD user, and you prefer to have the right-click issue a ⏎ at all times, as in previous versions, instead of opening the popup menu, you can configure AutoCAD to do just that. See *Configuring AutoCAD* in Appendix B for details on how to set up the mouse's right-click action. Be aware, however, that the tutorials in this book assume that AutoCAD is configured for the new right-click popup menu.

Selecting Objects

AutoCAD provides many options for selecting objects. This section has two parts: The first part deals with object selection methods unique to AutoCAD, and the second part deals with the more common selection method used in most popular graphic programs, the *Noun/Verb* method. Because these two methods play a major role in working with AutoCAD, it's a good idea to familiarize yourself with them early on.

TIP
In case you need to select objects by their characteristics rather than by their location, Chapter 12 describes the Object Selection Filters tool. This feature lets you easily select a set of objects based on their properties, including object type, color, layer assignment, and so on.

Selecting Objects in AutoCAD

Many AutoCAD commands prompt you to `Select objects:`. Along with this prompt, the cursor changes from crosshairs to a small square (look back at Figure 2.8). Whenever you see the `Select objects:` prompt and the square cursor, you have several options while making your selection. Often, as you select objects on the screen, you will change your mind about a selection or accidentally pick an object you do not want. Let's take a look at most of the selection options available in AutoCAD, and learn what to do when you make the wrong selection.

Before you continue, you'll turn off two features that, while extremely useful, can be confusing to new users. These features are called Running Osnaps and Osnap Tracking. You'll get a chance to explore these features in depth later in this book.

1. First, check to see if either Running Osnaps or Osnap Tracking is turned on. To do this, look at the buttons labeled OSNAP and OTRACK in the status bar at the bottom of the AutoCAD window. If they are turned on, they look like they are depressed.

If they look like this graphic, proceed.

2. To turn off Running Osnap or Osnap Tracking, click the button labeled OSNAP or OTRACK in the status bar at the bottom of the AutoCAD window. When turned off, they will look like they are *not* depressed.

Now let's go ahead and see how to select an object in AutoCAD.

1. Choose Move from the Modify toolbar.

2. At the `Select objects:` prompt, click the two horizontal lines that comprise the door. As you saw in the last chapter, whenever AutoCAD wants you to select objects, the cursor turns into the small square pickbox. This tells you that you are in *Object Selection mode*. As you pick an object, it is *highlighted*, as shown in Figure 2.12.

NOTE   *Highlighting* means an object changes from a solid image to one composed of dots. When you see an object highlighted on the screen, you know that you have chosen that object to be acted upon by whatever command you are currently using.

FIGURE 2.12:

Selecting the lines of the door and seeing them highlighted

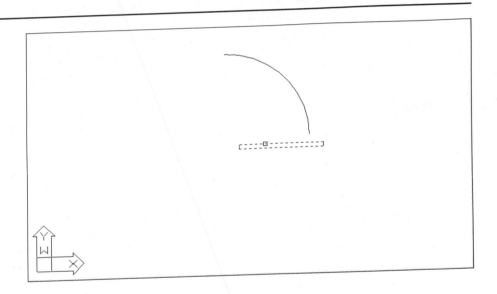

3. After making your selections, you may decide to deselect some items. Click Undo in the Standard toolbar, or enter **U**↵ from the keyboard.

Notice that one line is no longer highlighted. The Undo option deselects objects, one at a time, in reverse order of selection.

4. There is another way to deselect objects: Hold down the Shift key and click the remaining highlighted line. It reverts to a solid line, showing you that it is no longer selected for editing.

By now you have deselected both lines. Let's try using another method for selecting groups of objects.

5. Another option for selecting objects is to *window* them. Type **W**↵. The cursor changes to a Point Selection cursor, and the prompt changes to

   First corner:

6. Click a point below and to the left of the rectangle representing the door. As you move your cursor across the screen, the window appears and stretches across the drawing area.

7. Once the window completely encloses the door but not the arc, click this location and the entire door is highlighted. This window selects only objects that are completely enclosed by the window, as shown in Figure 2.13.

NOTE

You might remember that you used a window with the Zoom command in Chapter 1. That window option under the Zoom command does not select objects. Rather, it defines an area of the drawing you want to enlarge. Remember that the window option works differently under the Zoom command than it does for other editing commands.

WARNING

If you are using a mouse you're not familiar with, it's quite easy to accidentally click the right mouse button when you really wanted to click the left mouse button, and vice versa. If you click the wrong button, you'll get the wrong results. On a two-button mouse, the right button will either act like the ↵ key or open a context-sensitive popup menu, depending on your current operation. A ↵ will be issued if you are selecting objects, but otherwise, the popup menu appears.

---

8. Now that you have selected the entire door but not the arc, press ↵. *It is important to remember to press ↵ as soon as you have finished selecting the objects you want to edit.* Pressing ↵ tells AutoCAD when you have finished selecting objects. A new prompt, Specify base point or displacement:, appears. The cursor changes to its Point Selection mode.

Now you have seen how the selection process works in AutoCAD—but you're in the middle of the Move command. The next section discusses the prompt that's now on your screen and describes how to enter base points and displacement distances.

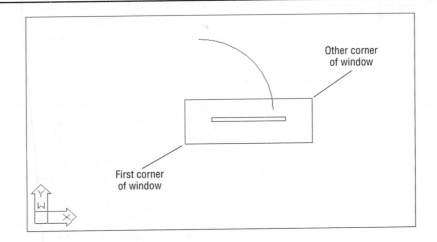

FIGURE 2.13:

Selecting the door within a window

Other corner
of window

First corner
of window

Providing Base Points

When you move or copy objects, AutoCAD prompts you for a *base point*, which is a difficult concept to grasp. AutoCAD must be told specifically *from* where and *to* where the move occurs. The base point is the exact location from which you determine the distance and direction of the move. Once the base point is determined, you can tell AutoCAD where to move the object in relation to that point.

1. To select a base point, hold down the Shift key and press the right mouse button. A menu pops up on the screen. This is the *Object Snap (Osnap)* menu.

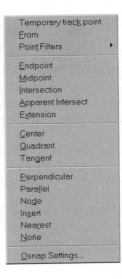

2. Choose Intersection from the Osnap menu. The Osnap menu disappears.

3. Move the cursor to the lower-right corner of the door. Notice that as you approach the corner, a small x-shaped graphic appears on the corner. This is called an *Osnap marker*.

4. After the x-shaped marker appears, hold the mouse motionless for a second or two. A tool tip appears telling you the current Osnap point AutoCAD has selected.

5. Now press the left mouse button to select the intersection indicated by the Osnap marker. Whenever you see the Osnap marker at the point you wish to select, you don't have to point exactly at the location with your cursor. Just left-click the mouse and the exact Osnap point is selected (see Figure 2.14). In this case, you selected the exact intersection of two lines.

6. At the `Specify second point of displacement or <use first point as displacement>:` prompt, hold down the Shift key and press the right mouse button again. You'll use the Endpoint Osnap this time, but instead of clicking the option with the mouse, type **E**.

7. Now pick the lower-right end of the arc you drew earlier. (Remember that you only need to move your cursor close to the endpoint until the Osnap marker appears.) The door moves so that the corner of the door connects exactly with the endpoint of the arc (see Figure 2.15).

As you can see, the Osnap options allow you to select specific points on an object. You used Endpoint and Intersect in this exercise, but other options are available. Chapter 3 discusses some of the other Osnap options. You may have also noticed that the Osnap marker is different for each of the options you used. You'll learn more about Osnaps in Chapter 3. Now let's continue with our look at point selection.

NOTE You might have noticed the statement `Use first point as displacement` in the prompt in step 6. This means that if you press ↵ instead of clicking a point, the object will move a distance based on the coordinates of the point you selected as a base point. If, for example, the point you click for the base point is at coordinate 2,4, the object will move 2 units in the x-axis and 4 in the y-axis.

CASEY KIGHT

FIGURE 2.14:

Using the Osnap cursor

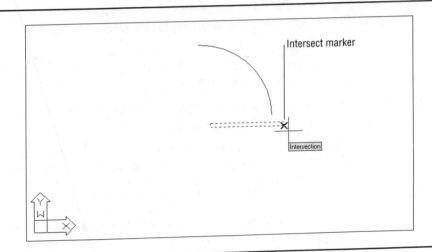

Intersect marker

Intersection

FIGURE 2.15:

The rectangle in its new
position after using the
Endpoint Osnap

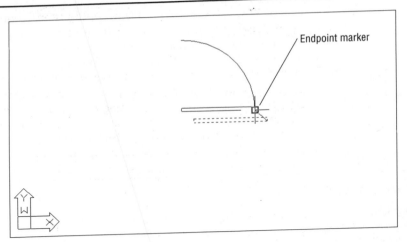

Endpoint marker

If you want to specify an exact distance and direction by typing in a value, select
any point on the screen as a base point. Or you can just type @ followed by ↵ at the
base point prompt; then enter the second point's location in relative coordinates.
Remember that @ means the last point selected. In this next exercise, you'll try moving the entire door an exact distance of 1 unit in a 45° angle. Metric users will move
the door 3 units in a 45° angle.

1.   Click the Move tool from the Modify toolbar.

2. Type **P**↵. The set of objects you selected in the previous command is highlighted. **P** is a selection option that selects the previously selected set of objects.

3. You're still in the Object Selection mode, so click the arc to include it in the set of selected objects. Now the entire door, including the arc, is highlighted, as shown in Figure 2.16.

4. Now press ↵ to tell AutoCAD that you have finished your selection. The cursor changes to Point Selection mode.

5. At the `Base point or displacement:` prompt, choose a point on the screen between the door and the left side of the screen (see Figure 2.16).

6. Move the cursor around slowly and notice that the door moves as if the base point you selected were attached to the door. The door moves with the cursor, at a fixed distance from it. This demonstrates how the base point relates to the objects you select.

7. Now type **@1<45**↵. Metric users should type **@3<45**↵. The door moves to a new location on the screen at a distance of 1 unit (or 3 for metric users) from its previous location and at an angle of 45°.

> **TIP**
>
> If AutoCAD is waiting for a command, you can repeat the last command used by pressing the spacebar or by pressing the ↵ key. You can also right-click in the drawing area and select the option at the top of the list. If you right-click the Command window, a popup list offers the most recent commands.

FIGURE 2.16:

The highlighted door and the base point just to the left of the door. Note that the base point does not need to be on the object that you are moving.

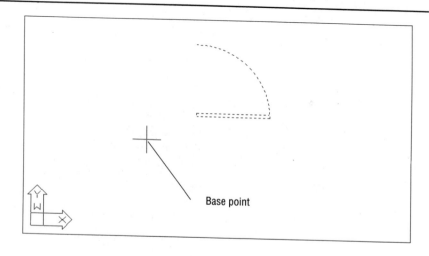

Base point

This exercise illustrates that the base point does not have to be on the object you are manipulating. The base point can be virtually anywhere on your drawing. You also saw how to reselect a group of objects that were selected previously, without having to duplicate the selection process.

Other Selection Options

There are several other selection options you haven't tried yet. This sidebar describes these other options. You'll see how these options work in exercises later in this book. Or if you are adventurous, try them out now on your own. To use these options, type their keyboard abbreviations (shown in brackets in the following list) at any `Select object:` prompt.

All [all↵]   Selects all the objects in a drawing except those in frozen or locked layers (see Chapter 4 for more on layers).

Crossing [c↵]   Is similar to the Select Window option but selects anything that crosses through the window you define.

Crossing Polygon [cp↵]   Acts exactly like WPolygon (see below) but, like the Select Crossing option, selects anything that crosses through a polygon boundary.

Fence [f↵]   Selects objects that are crossed over by a temporary line called a *fence*. This operation is like crossing out the objects you want to select with a line. When you invoke this option, you can then pick points, as when you are drawing a series of line segments. When you are done drawing the fence, press ↵, then go on to select other objects, or press ↵ again to finish your selection.

Last [l↵]   Selects the last object you entered.

Multiple [m↵]   Lets you select several objects first, before AutoCAD highlights them. In a very large file, picking objects individually can cause AutoCAD to pause after each pick, while it locates and highlights each object. The Multiple option can speed things up by letting you first pick all the objects quickly, and then highlight them all by pressing ↵. This has no menu equivalent.

Previous [p↵]   Selects the last object or set of objects that was edited or changed.

Window [w↵]   Forces a standard selection window. This option is useful when your drawing area is too crowded to use the Autoselect feature to place a window around a set of objects (see the Auto entry in this sidebar). It prevents you from accidentally selecting an object with a single pick when you are placing your window.

Continued on next page

Window Polygon [wp↵] Lets you select objects by enclosing them in an irregularly shaped polygon boundary. When you use this option, you see the prompt `First polygon point:`. You then pick points to define the polygon boundary. As you pick points, the prompt `Undo/<Endpoint of line>:` appears. Select as many points as you need to define the boundary. You can undo boundary line segments as you go by clicking the Undo tool on the Standard toolbar, or by pressing the U key. With the boundary defined, press ↵. The bounded objects are highlighted and the `Select object` prompt returns, allowing you to use more selection options.

The following two selection options are also available, but seldom used. They are intended for use in creating custom menu options or custom toolbar tools.

Auto [au↵] Forces the standard automatic window or crossing window when a point is picked and no object is found (see *Using Autoselect* later in this chapter). A standard window is produced when the two window corners are picked from left to right. A crossing window is produced when the two corners are picked from right to left. Once this option is selected, it remains active for the duration of the current command. Auto is intended for use on systems where the Automatic Selection feature has been turned off.

Single [si↵] Forces the current command to select only a single object. If you use this option, you can pick a single object; then the current command acts on that object as if you had pressed ↵ immediately after selecting the object. This has no menu equivalent.

Selecting Objects before the Command: Noun/Verb

Nearly all graphics programs today have tacitly acknowledged the *Noun/Verb* method for selecting objects. This method requires you to select objects *before* you issue a command to edit them. The next set of exercises shows you how to use the Noun/Verb method in AutoCAD.

You have seen that when AutoCAD is waiting for a command, it displays the crosshair cursor with the small square. This square is actually a pickbox superimposed on the cursor. It tells you that you can select objects, even while the command prompt appears at the bottom of the screen and no command is currently active. The square momentarily disappears when you are in a command that asks you to select points. From now on, this crosshair cursor with the small box will be referred to as the *Standard cursor*.

This chapter presents the standard AutoCAD method for object selection. Auto-CAD also offers selection methods with which you may be more familiar. Refer to the section on the Object Selection Settings dialog box in Appendix B to learn how you can control object selection methods. This appendix also describes how you can change the size of the pickbox cursor.

Now try moving objects by first selecting them and then using the Move command.

1. First, press the Esc key twice to make sure AutoCAD isn't in the middle of a command you may have accidentally issued. Then click the arc. The arc is highlighted, and you may also see squares appear at its endpoints and its mid-point. These squares are called *grips*. You may know them as *workpoints* from other graphics programs. You'll get a chance to work with them a bit later.

2. Choose Move from the Modify toolbar. The cursor changes to Point Selection mode. Notice that the grips on the arc disappear, but the arc is still selected.

3. At the Base point: prompt, pick any point on the screen. The prompt To point: appears.

4. Type @1<0.⏎. Metric users should type @3<0.⏎. The arc moves to a new location 1 unit (3 units for metric users) to the right.

If you find that this exercise does not work as described here, chances are the Noun/Verb setting has been turned off on your copy of AutoCAD. Refer to Appendix B to find out how to activate this setting.

In this exercise, you picked the arc *before* issuing the Move command. Then, when you clicked the Move tool, you didn't see the Select object: prompt. Instead, AutoCAD assumed you wanted to move the arc that you had selected and went directly to the Base point: prompt.

Using Autoselect

Next you will move the rest of the door in the same direction using the Autoselect feature.

1. Pick a point just above and to the left of the rectangle representing the door. Be sure not to pick the door itself. Now a window appears that you can drag

across the screen as you move the cursor. If you move the cursor to the left of the last point selected, the window appears dotted (see the top image of Figure 2.17). If you move the cursor to the right of that point, it appears solid (see the bottom image of Figure 2.17).

2. Now pick a point below and to the right of the door, so that the door is completely enclosed by the window, as shown in the bottom image of Figure 2.17. The door is highlighted (and again, you may see small squares appear at the line's endpoints and midpoints).

3. Click the Move tool again. Just as in the last exercise, the `Base point:` prompt appears.

4. Pick any point on the screen; then enter @1<0↵. Metric users should enter @3<0↵. The door joins with the arc.

The two different windows you have just seen—the solid one and the dotted one—represent a *standard window* and a *crossing window*. If you use a standard window, anything that is completely contained within the window is selected. If you use a crossing window, anything that crosses through the window is selected. These two types of windows start automatically when you click any blank portion of the drawing area with a Standard cursor or Point Selection cursor; hence the name Autoselect.

Next, you will select objects with an automatic crossing window.

1. Pick a point below and to the right of the door. As you move the cursor to the left, the crossing (dotted) window appears.

2. Select the next point so that the window encloses the door and part of the arc (see Figure 2.18). The entire door, including the arc, is highlighted.

3. Click the Move tool.

4. Pick any point on the screen; then enter @1<180↵. Metric users should type @3<180↵. The door moves back to its original location.

You'll find that in most cases, the Autoselect standard and crossing windows are all you need when selecting objects. They really save you time, so you'll want to get familiar with these features.

Before continuing, you need to use File ➤ Save to save the Door file. You won't want to save the changes you make in the next section, so saving now stores the current condition of the file on your hard disk for safekeeping.

FIGURE 2.17:

The dotted window (top image) indicates a crossing selection; the solid window (bottom image) indicates a standard selection window.

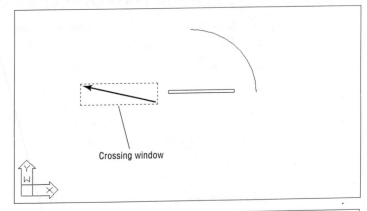

Crossing window

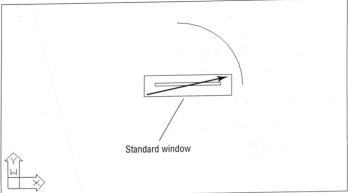

Standard window

FIGURE 2.18:

The door enclosed by a crossing window

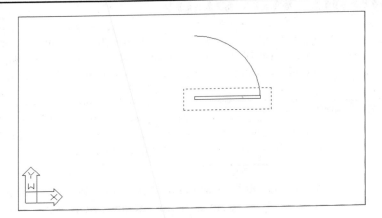

Restrictions on Noun/Verb Object Selection

If you prefer to work with the Noun/Verb selection feature, you should know that its use is limited to the following subset of AutoCAD commands, listed here in no particular order:

Array	Mirror	Wblock	Block
Dview	Move	Erase	Explode
Change	Rotate	Chprop	Hatch
Scale	Copy	List	Stretch

For all other modifying or construction-oriented commands, the Noun/Verb selection method is inappropriate because for those commands you must select more than one set of objects. But you do not need to remember this list. You'll know if a command accepts the Noun/Verb selection method right away. Commands that don't accept the Noun/Verb selection method clear the selection and then display a `Select object:` prompt.

NOTE   If you want to take a break, now is a good time to do it. If you wish, exit AutoCAD and return to this point in the tutorial later. When you return, start AutoCAD and open the Door file.

Editing with Grips

Earlier, when you selected the door, little squares appeared at the endpoints and midpoints of the lines and arcs. These squares are called *grips*. Grips can be used to make direct changes to the shape of objects, or to quickly move and copy them.

WARNING   If you did not see small squares appear on the door in the previous exercise, your version of AutoCAD may have the Grips feature turned off. Before continuing with this section, refer to the information on grips in Appendix B.

So far, you have seen how operations in AutoCAD have a discrete beginning and ending. For example, to draw an arc, you first issue the Arc command and then go through a series of operations, including answering prompts and picking points. When you are done, you have an arc and AutoCAD is ready for the next command.

The Grips feature, on the other hand, plays by a different set of rules. Grips offer a small yet powerful set of editing functions that don't conform to the lockstep command/prompt/input routine you have seen so far. As you work through the following exercises, it is helpful to think of the grips feature as a "subset" to the standard method of operation within AutoCAD.

To practice using the Grips feature, you'll make some temporary modifications to the door drawing.

Stretching Lines Using Grips

In this exercise, you'll stretch one corner of the door by grabbing the grip points of two lines.

1. Press the Esc key to make sure AutoCAD has your attention and you're not in the middle of a command. Click a point below and to the left of the door to start a selection window.

2. Click above and to the right of the rectangular part of the door to select it.

3. Place the cursor on the lower-left corner grip of the rectangle, *but don't press the pick button yet.* Notice that cursor jumps to the grip point.

4. Move the cursor to another grip point. Notice again how the cursor jumps to it. When the cursor is placed on a grip, the cursor moves to the exact center of the grip point. This means, for example, that if the cursor is placed on an endpoint grip, it is on the exact endpoint of the object.

5. Move the cursor to the upper-left corner grip of the rectangle and click it. The grip becomes a solid color, and is now a *hot grip.* The prompt displays the following message:

   ```
   **STRETCH**

   Specify stretch point or [Base point/Copy/Undo/eXit]:
   ```

   This prompt tells you that the Stretch mode is active. Notice the options shown in the prompt. As you move the cursor, the corner follows and the lines of the rectangle stretch (see Figure 2.19).

NOTE When you select a grip by clicking it, it turns a solid color and is known as a *hot grip.* You can control the size and color of grips using the Grips dialog box; see Appendix B for the details.

6. Move the cursor upward toward the top end of the arc and click that point. The rectangle deforms, with the corner placed at your pick point (see Figure 2.19).

FIGURE 2.19:

Stretching lines using hot grips. The top image shows the rectangle's corner being stretched upward. The bottom image shows the new location of the corner at the top of the arc.

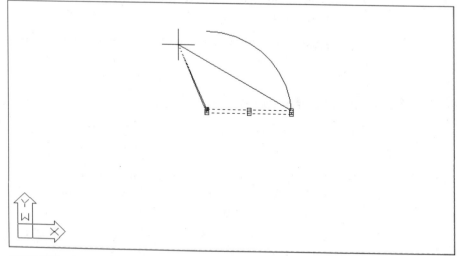

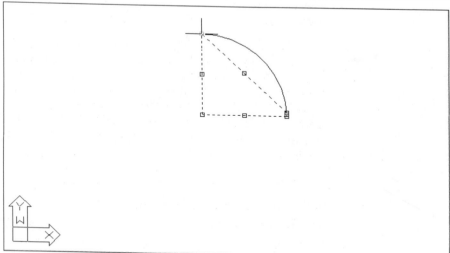

NOTE   When you click the corner grip point, AutoCAD selects the overlapping grips of two lines. When you stretch the corner away from its original location, the end-points of both lines follow.

Here you saw that a command called **STRETCH** is issued simply by clicking a grip point. As you will see, a handful of other hot grip commands are also available.

1. Notice that the grips are still active. Click the grip point that you moved before to make it a hot grip again.

2. Right-click the mouse. A popup list of grip edit options appears.

3. Select Base Point from the list, and then click a point to the right of the hot grip. Now as you move the cursor, the hot grip moves relative to the cursor.

4. Right-click again, and then select the Copy option from the popup list and enter @1<-30.↵. Metric users should enter @3<-30.↵. Instead of moving the hot grip and changing the lines, copies of the two lines are made, with their endpoints 1 unit (or 3 units for metric users) below and to the right of the first set of endpoints.

5. Pick another point just below the last. More copies are made.

6. Press ↵ or enter X↵ to exit the Stretch mode. You can also right-click again and select Exit from the popup list.

In this exercise, you saw that you can select a base point other than the hot grip. You also saw how you can specify relative coordinates to move or copy a hot grip. Finally, with grips selected on an object, a right-click of the mouse opens a popup list showing grip edit options.

Moving and Rotating with Grips

As you've just seen, the Grips feature offers an alternative method of editing your drawings. You've already seen how you can stretch endpoints, but there is much more you can do with grips. The next exercise demonstrates some other options. You will start by undoing the modifications you made in the last exercise.

1. Click the Undo tool in the Standard toolbar, or type **U**↵. The copies of the stretched lines disappear.

2. Press ↵ again. The deformed door snaps back to its original form.

TIP   Pressing ↵ at the command prompt causes AutoCAD to repeat the last command entered—in this case, **U**.

---

3. Select the entire door by first clicking a blank area below and to the right of the door.

4. Move the cursor to a location above and to the left of the rectangular portion of the door, and click. Since you went from right to left, you created a crossing window. Recall that the crossing window selects anything enclosed and crossing through the window.

5. Click the lower-left grip of the rectangle to turn it into a hot grip. Just as before, as you move your cursor, the corner stretches.

6. Right-click the mouse. Then in the grip edit popup list, select Move. The Command window displays the following:

    ```
    **MOVE**
    <Move to point>/Base point/Copy/Undo/eXit:
    ```

    Now as you move the cursor, the entire door moves with it.

7. Position the door near the center of the screen and click there. The door moves to the center of the screen. Notice that the command prompt returns, yet the door remains highlighted, telling you that it is still selected for the next operation.

8. Click the lower-left grip again, and right-click the mouse. This time, select Rotate from the popup list. The Command window displays the following:

    ```
    **ROTATE** <Rotation angle>/Base point/copy/Undo/Reference/eXit:
    ```

    As you move the cursor, the door rotates about the grip point.

9. Position the cursor so that the door rotates approximately 180° (see Figure 2.20). Then, while holding down the Shift key, press the mouse/pick button. A copy of the door appears in the new rotated position, leaving the original door in place.

10. Press ↵ to exit the Grip Edit mode.

NOTE

You've seen how the Move command is duplicated in a modified way as a hot grip command. Other hot grip commands (Stretch, Rotate, Scale, and Mirror) also have similar counterparts in the standard set of AutoCAD commands. You'll see how those work later in this book in Chapters 9 and 12.

After you've completed any operation using grips, the objects are still highlighted with their grips still active. To clear the grip selection, press the Esc key twice.

FIGURE 2.20:

Rotating and copying the door using a hot grip. Notice that more than one object is being affected by the grip edit, even though only one grip is "hot."

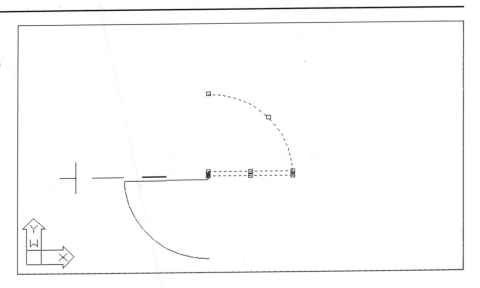

In this exercise, you saw how hot grip options appear in a popup list. Several other options are available in that list, including Exit, Base Point, Copy, and Undo. You can also make adjustments to an object's properties using the Properties option.

Many of these grip edit options are also available by pressing the spacebar or ↵ while a grip is selected. With each press, the next option becomes active. The

do not save changes

options then repeat if you continue to press ↵. The Shift key acts as a shortcut to the Copy option. You only have to use it once; then each time you click a point thereafter, a copy is made.

A Quick Summary of the Grips Feature

The exercises in this chapter using hot grips include only a few of the grips options. You'll get a chance to use other hot grip options in later chapters. Meanwhile, here is a summary of the grips feature:

- Clicking endpoint grips causes those endpoints to stretch.

- Clicking midpoint grips of lines causes the entire line to move.

- If two objects meet end to end and you click their overlapping grips, both grips are selected simultaneously.

- You can select multiple grips by holding down the Shift key and clicking the desired grips.

- When a hot grip is selected, the Stretch, Move, Rotate, Scale, and Mirror options are available to you by right-clicking the mouse.

- *Or* you can cycle through the Stretch, Move, Rotate, Scale, and Mirror options by pressing ↵ while a hot grip is selected.

- All the hot grip options allow you to make copies of the selected objects by either using the Copy option or by holding down the Shift key while selecting points.

- All the hot grip options allow you to select a base point other than the originally selected hot grip.

Getting Help

Eventually, you will find yourself somewhere without documentation and you will have a question about an AutoCAD feature. AutoCAD provides an online help facility that gives you information on nearly any topic related to AutoCAD. Here's how to find help:

1. Click Help in the menu bar and choose AutoCAD Help Topics. A Help window appears.

2. If it isn't already selected, click the Contents tab. This window shows a table of contents. There are two more tabs labeled Index and Find, and each offers assistance in finding specific topics.

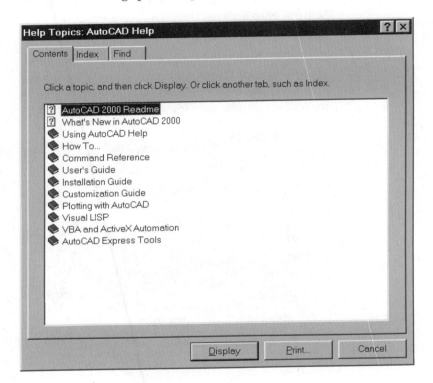

NOTE   You can also press F1 to open the AutoCAD Help window.

3. Scan down the screen until you see the topic named Command References, and double-click it. The list expands to show more topics.

4. Double-click the item labeled Commands. The Help window expands to show a list of command names.

5. At the top of the list is a set of alphabet buttons. In the main window, you see a list of commands beginning with "3D." You can click the alphabetical button to go to a listing of commands that start with a specific letter. For now, scroll down the list and click the word "Copy" shown in green. A detailed description of the Copy command appears.

6. Click the Help Topics button at the top of the window. The Help Topics dialog box appears.

7. Click the Find tab. If this is the first time you've selected the Find tab, the Find Setup wizard appears. This dialog box offers options for the search database that Find uses to locate specific words.

8. Accept the default option by clicking the Next button at the bottom of the dialog box. The Find options appear with a list of topics in alphabetical order. You can enter a word to search for in the drop-down list at the top of the dialog, or you can choose a topic in the list box.

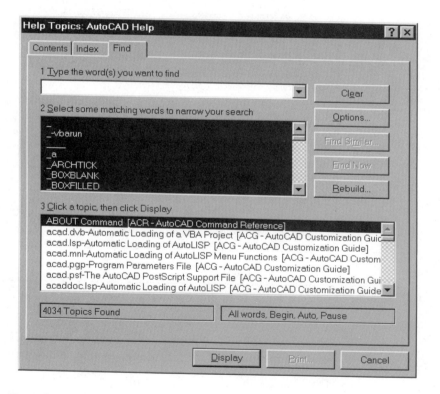

9. Type the word **Change**. The list box immediately goes to the word "Change" in the list.

10. Click the word "CHANGE" in all capital letters. Notice that the list box at the bottom of the dialog box changes to show some options.

11. Double-click Change Command [ACR] in the list. A description of the Change command appears.

AutoCAD also provides *context-sensitive help* to give you information related to the command you are currently using. To see how this works, try the following:

1. Close or minimize the Help window and return to the AutoCAD window.

2. Click the Move tool in the Modify toolbar to start the Move command.

3. Press the F1 function key, or choose Help ➤ AutoCAD Help Topics. The Help window appears, with a description of the Move command.

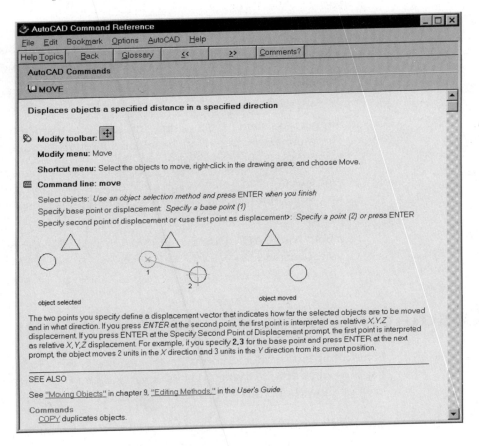

4. Click the Close button or press the Esc key.

5. Press the Esc key to exit the Move command.

If you are already familiar with the basics of AutoCAD, you may want to install the AutoCAD Learning Assistant. This tool offers quick tips and brief tutorials on a wide variety of topics, including working in collaborative groups, and making the most of the Windows environment. The Learning Assistant is on its own CD-ROM as part of the AutoCAD 2000 package.

Additional Sources for Help

The Help Topics tool is the main online source for reference material, but you can also find answers to your questions through the other options found in the Help menu. Here is a brief description of the other Help menu options:

What's New   Gives you an overview of the new features found in AutoCAD 2000. If you're an experienced AutoCAD user and just want to know about the new features in AutoCAD 2000, this is a good place to start.

Learning Assistant   Offers new users some quick tutorials that show you how to use AutoCAD commands together to accomplish a task.

Support Assistant   Offers a series of answers to frequently asked questions. This unique support tool can be updated through the Autodesk Web site.

Autodesk on the Web   Offers a listing of popular pages on the Autodesk Web site. You can find news about updates, locate downloadable tools and upgrades, and find the latest AutoCAD plug-ins for specific jobs you're trying to tackle.

About AutoCAD   Displays information about the version of AutoCAD you are using.

Displaying Data in a Text Window

Some commands produce information that requires a Text window. This frequently happens when you are trying to get information about your drawing. The following exercise shows how you can get an enlarged view of messages in a Text window.

1. Click the List tool in the Standard toolbar. (It's the icon that looks like a piece of paper with writing on it. Remember that it is in the Distance flyout tool.) This tool offers information about objects in your drawing.

2. At the Select objects: prompt, click one of the arcs and press ↵. Information about the arc is displayed in the AutoCAD Text window (see Figure 2.21). Toward the bottom is the list of the arc's properties. Don't worry if

you don't understand this listing. As you work through this book, you'll learn what the different properties of an object mean.

3. Press F2. The AutoCAD Text window closes.

TIP   The F2 function key offers a quick way to switch between the drawing editor and the Text window.

The Text window not only shows you information about objects, it also displays a history of the command activity for your AutoCAD session. This can be helpful for remembering data you may have entered earlier in a session, or for recalling an object's property that you have listed earlier. The scroll bar to the right of the Text window lets you scroll to earlier events. You can even set the number of lines AutoCAD retains in the Text window using the Preferences dialog box, or you can have AutoCAD record the Text window information in a text file.

4. Now you are done with the door drawing, so choose File ➤ Close.

5. At the Save Changes dialog box, click the No button. (You've already saved this file in the condition you want it in, so you do not need to save it again.)

FIGURE 2.21:

The AutoCAD text screen showing the data displayed by the List tool

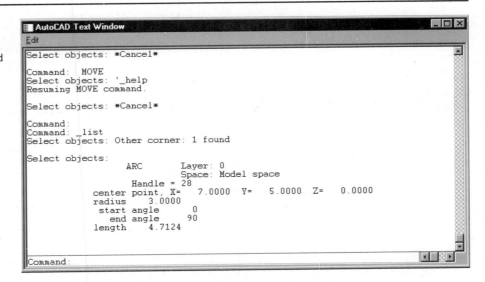

When you have more than one document open, the Text window will display a listing for the drawing that is currently active.

If You Want to Experiment...

Try drawing the latch shown in Figure 2.22.

1. Start AutoCAD, open a new file, and name it Latch.

2. When you get to the drawing editor, use the Line command to draw the straight portions of the latch. Start a line as indicated in the figure; then enter relative coordinates from the keyboard. For example, for the first line segment, enter @4<180↵ to draw a line segment 4 units long from right to left.

3. Draw an arc for the curved part. To do this, click the Arc tool from the Draw toolbar.

4. Use the Endpoint Osnap to pick the endpoint indicated in the figure to start your arc.

5. Type E↵ to issue the End option of the Arc command.

6. Using the Endpoint Osnap again, click the endpoint above where you started your line. A rubber-banding line and a temporary arc appear.

7. Type D↵ to issue the Direction option for the Arc command.

8. Position your cursor so the ghosted arc looks like the one in the figure, and then press the mouse/pick button to draw in the arc.

FIGURE 2.22:

Try drawing this latch. Dimensions are provided for your reference.

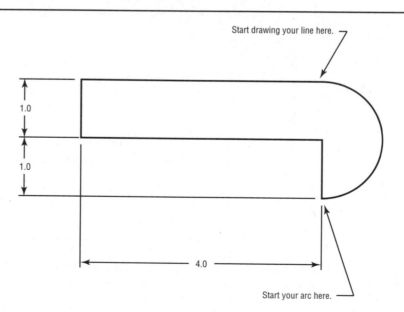

HUNG

LIKE
A
HORSE

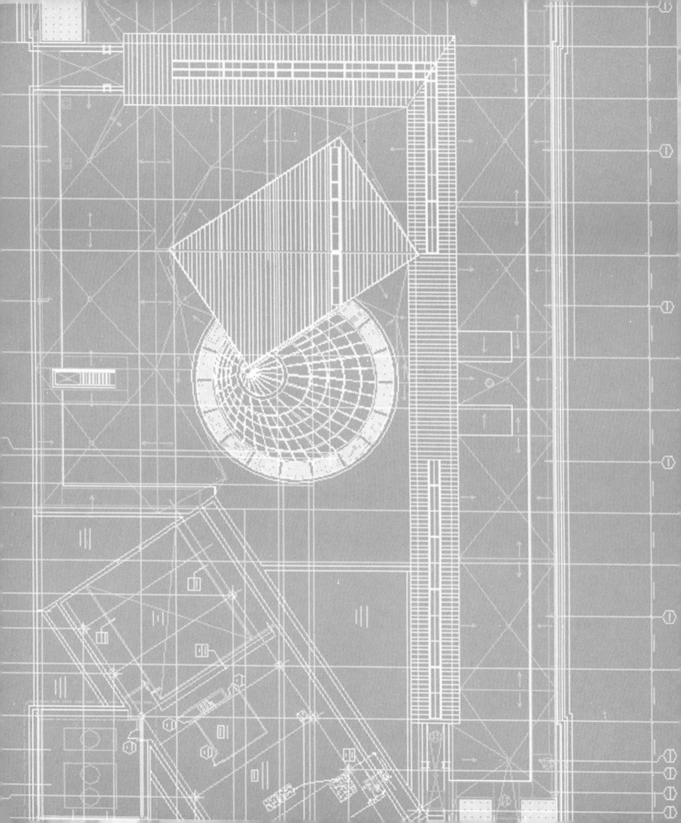

Learning the Tools of the Trade

- Setting Up a Work Area

- Using the AutoCAD Modes as Drafting Tools

- Exploring the Drawing Process

- Planning and Laying Out a Drawing

- If You Want to Experiment...

Chapters 1 and 2 covered the most basic information you need to understand the workings of AutoCAD. Now you will put this knowledge to work. In this architectural tutorial, which begins here and continues through Chapter 12, you will draw an apartment building composed of studios. The tutorial illustrates how to use AutoCAD commands and gives you a solid understanding of the basic AutoCAD package. With these fundamentals, you can use AutoCAD to its fullest potential, regardless of the kinds of drawings you intend to create or the enhancement products you may use in the future.

In this chapter you will start drawing an apartment's bathroom fixtures. In the process, you will learn how to use AutoCAD's basic tools.

Setting Up a Work Area

Before beginning most drawings, you should set up your work area. To do this, determine the *measurement system,* the *drawing sheet size,* and the *scale* you want to use. The default work area is roughly 9"×16" at full scale, given a decimal measurement system where 1 unit equals 1 inch. Metric users will find that the default area is roughly 550mm by 300mm, where 1 unit equals 1mm. If these are appropriate settings for your drawing, then you don't have to do any setting up. It is more likely, however, you will be making drawings of various sizes and scales. For example, you may want to create a drawing in a measurement system where you can specify feet, inches, and fractions of inches at 1"=1' scale, and print the drawing on an 8 1/2" × 11" sheet of paper.

In Chapter 2, you used the Create New Drawing wizard to set up a drawing file. The Create New Drawing wizard is a great tool, but it hides many of the drawing setup tools you'll need to know to work with AutoCAD. In this section, you will learn how to set up a drawing exactly the way you want.

Using the English and Metric Examples

Many of the exercises in this chapter are shown in both the metric and English measurement system. Please be sure that if you start with the English system, you continue with it throughout this book. Also note that the metric settings described in this book are only approximations of their English equivalents, and they may not be the exact translation between the two measurements. For example, the drawing scale for the metric example is

Continued on next page

1:10 which is close to the 1"=1'-0" scale used in the English example. In the grid example, you are asked to use a 30-unit grid, which is close to the 1-foot grid of the English example. Dimension of objects will be similar, but not exact. For example, the English version of the tub will measure 2'8" by 5'0", while the Metric version of the tub will be 81cm by 152cm. The actual metric equivalent of 2'8" by 5'0" is 81.28cm by 152.4cm. In the tub example, we've rounded to the nearest centimeter.

Metric users should also be aware that AutoCAD uses a period as a decimal point instead of a comma. Commas are used in AutoCAD to separate the *x*, *y*, and *z* components of a coordinate.

Specifying Units

Start by creating a new file called Bath.

1. If you haven't already done so, start up AutoCAD. If AutoCAD is already running, choose File ➤ New.

2. In the Create New Drawing dialog box, click the Start from Scratch button and select English from the Select Default Setting list. Metric users can select Metric.

3. Click OK to open the new file.

4. Choose File ➤ Save As.

5. In the Save Drawing As dialog box, enter **Bath** for the filename.

6. Check to make sure you are saving the drawing in the Samples subdirectory, or the directory you have chosen to store your exercise files, and then click Save.

The first thing you want to tell AutoCAD is the *unit style* you intend to use. So far, you've been using the default, which is decimal inches. In this unit style, whole units represent inches, and decimal units are decimal inches. If you want to be able to enter distances in feet, then you must change the unit style to a style that accepts feet as input. This is done through the Drawing Units dialog box.

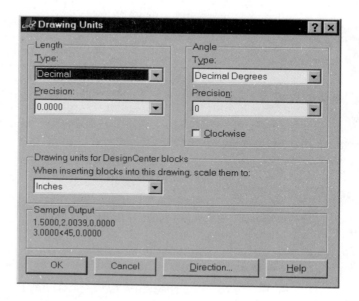

If you are a civil engineer, you should know that the Engineering unit style allows you to enter feet and decimal feet for distances. For example, the equivalent of 12'-6" would be 12.5'. Earlier versions of AutoCAD did not have this feature, so engineers had to resort to using the Decimal unit style and feet as the base unit instead of inches. This caused problems when architectural drawings were combined with civil drawings. The scales of each type of drawing did not match. Even though this feature has existed since Release 12 of AutoCAD, old habits die hard. If you use the Engineering unit style, you will ensure that your drawings will conform to the scale of drawings created by your architectural colleagues. And you will have the ability to enter decimal feet.

1. Choose Formats ➤ Units, or type **Un**↵. The Drawing Units dialog box appears. Let's look at a few of the options available.

2. Click the Type drop-down list in the Length button group. Notice the unit styles shown in the list.

3. Click Architectural in the list. Once you've selected Architectural, the Sample Output section of the dialog box shows you what the architectural style looks like in AutoCAD. Metric users should keep this setting as Decimal.

TIP   The Drawing Units settings can also be controlled using several system variables. To set the unit style, you can type **'lunits.⏎** at the command prompt. (The apostrophe lets you enter this command while in the middle of other commands.) At the `New value for Lunits <2>:` prompt, enter **4** for Architectural. See Appendix D for other settings.

4. Click the Precision drop-down list just below the Type list. Notice the options available. You can set the smallest unit AutoCAD will display in this drawing. For now, leave this setting at its default value of 1/16". Metric users will keep the setting to 0.0000.

5. Close the drop-down list by pressing the Esc key and then click the Direction button at the bottom of the dialog box. The Direction Control dialog box appears. This dialog box lets you set the direction for the 0° angle and the direction for positive degrees. For now, don't change these settings—you'll read more about them in a moment.

6. Click the Cancel button.

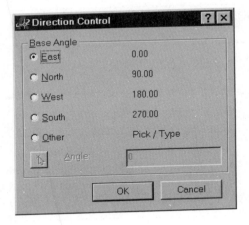

7. Now click the drop-down list in the Drawing Units for DesignCenter Blocks group. The list shows various units of measure.

8. Click Inches, or if you are a metric user, choose Centimeters. This option allows you to control how AutoCAD translates drawing scales when you import drawings from outside the current drawing. You'll learn more about this feature in Chapter 22.

9. Click OK in the Drawing Units dialog box to return to the drawing.

NOTE   Remember that the status bar displays a description of the tool or pull-down menu option, including the command name. If you prefer entering commands from the keyboard, look at the tool description in the status bar during the exercises. The command name is listed last. You can type in the command name to issue the command instead of clicking the tool during any of these exercises. Command names are also useful when you want to create your own custom macros. You'll get a chance to create some macros in Chapter 19. Be aware that many commands have shortcut names. For example, the Units command has the shortcut Un, which you saw in step 1 of the previous exercise.

If you use the English system of measurement, you selected Architectural measurement units for this tutorial, but your own work may require a different unit style. You saw the unit styles available in the Drawing Units dialog box. Table 3.1 shows examples of how the distance 15.5 is entered in each of these styles.

TABLE 3.1:   Measurement Systems Available in AutoCAD

Measurement System	AutoCAD's Display of Measurement
Scientific	1.55E+01 (inches or metric)
Decimal	15.5000 (inches or metric)
Engineering	1'-3.5" (input as 1'3.5")
Architectural	1'-3 1/2" (input as 1'3-1/2")
Fractional	15 1/2" (input as 15-1/2")

In the previous exercise, you needed to change only two settings. Let's take a look at the other Drawing Units settings in more detail. As you read, you may want to refer to the illustration of the Drawing Units dialog box.

Fine-Tuning the Measurement System

Most of the time, you will be concerned only with the units and angles settings of the Drawing Units dialog box. But as you saw from the last exercise, you can control many other settings related to the input and display of units.

TIP   To find the distance between two points, choose Distance from the Standard toolbar, or type **Di↵**, and then click the two points (**Di** is the shortcut for entering **Dist↵**). But if you find that this command doesn't give you an accurate distance measurement, examine the Precision option in the Drawing Units dialog box. If it is set too high, the value returned by the Dist command may be rounded to a value greater than your tolerances allow, even though the distance is drawn accurately.

The Precision drop-down list in the Length group lets you specify the smallest unit value that you want AutoCAD to display in the status line and in the prompts. If you choose a measurement system that uses fractions, the Precision list includes fractional units. This setting can also be controlled with Luprec system variables.

The Angle group lets you set the style for displaying angles. You have a choice of five angle styles: decimal degrees, degrees/minutes/seconds, grads, radians, and surveyor's units. In the Angle group's Precision drop-down list, you can determine the degree of accuracy you want AutoCAD to display for angles. These settings can also be controlled with the Aunits and Auprec system variables.

NOTE   You can find out more about system variables in Appendix D.

The Direction Control dialog box lets you set the direction of the 0° base angle. The default base angle (and the one used throughout this book) is a direction from left to right. However, there may be times when you will want to designate another direction as the 0° base angle. You can also tell AutoCAD which direction is positive, either clockwise or counterclockwise. This book uses the default, which is counterclockwise. These settings can also be controlled with the Angbase and Angdir system variables.

The Drawing Units for DesignCenter Blocks setting in the Drawing Units dialog box lets you control how external files are scaled as they are imported into your current drawing. For example, in older versions of AutoCAD, engineers often used one foot as their unit of measure so that they could enter values in decimal feet. In prior versions of AutoCAD, importing such a file into your architectural drawing would show an engineering drawing that is 1/12 the size that it should be. To fix this, you would have to scale the inserted engineering drawing by a factor of 12 to get it to match your architectural drawing.

The Drawing Units for DesignCenter Blocks setting lets you compensate for drawings of different scale by offering an automatic scale translation when files are imported. If you know that you will be importing engineering drawings that use decimal feet as the unit of measure, you can set the Drawing Units for DesignCenter Blocks value to feet, then the imported engineering drawing will be imported at a scale that matches your architectural drawing. The Insunits system variable also controls the Drawing Units for DesignCenter Blocks setting.

TIP   If you're new to AutoCAD, don't worry about the Drawing Units for DesignCenter Blocks setting right now. Make a mental note of it. It may come in handy in your work in the future.

Things to Watch Out for When Entering Distances

When you are using Architectural units, there are two points you should be aware of:

- Hyphens are used only to distinguish fractions from whole inches.

- You cannot use spaces while specifying a dimension. For example, you can specify eight feet, four and one-half inches as 8'4-1/2" or 8'4.5, but not as 8'-4 1/2".

These idiosyncrasies are a source of confusion to many architects and engineers new to AutoCAD because the program often displays architectural dimensions in the standard architectural format but does not allow you to enter dimensions that way.

When entering distances and angles in unusual situations, here are some tips:

- When entering distances in inches and feet, you can omit the inch (") sign. If you are using the Engineering unit style, you can enter decimal feet and forego the inch sign entirely.

- You can enter fractional distances and angles in any format you like, regardless of the current unit style. For example, you can enter a distance as **@1/2<1.5708r** even if your current unit system is set for decimal units and decimal degrees (**1.5708r** is the radian equivalent of 90°).

- If you have your angle units set to degrees, grads, or radians, you do not need to specify g, r, or d after the angle. You do have to specify g, r, or d, however, if you want to use these units when they are not the current default angle system.

- If your current angle system is set to something other than degrees, but you want to enter angles in degrees, you can use a double less-than symbol (<<) in place of the single less-than symbol (<) to override the current angle system of measure. The << also assumes the base angle of 0° to be a direction from left to right and the positive direction to be counterclockwise.

Continued on next page

- If your current angle system uses a different base angle and direction (other than left to right for 0° and a counterclockwise direction for positive angles), and you want to specify an angle in the standard base direction, you can use a triple less-than symbol (<<<) to indicate angle.

- You can specify a denominator of any size when specifying fractions. However, be aware that the value you have set for the maximum number of digits to the right of decimal points (under the Precision setting in the Length button group of the Drawing Units dialog box) will restrict the actual fractional value AutoCAD uses. For example, if your units are set for a maximum of 2 digits of decimals and you give a fractional value of 5/32, AutoCAD rounds it out to 3/16 or 0.16.

- You are allowed to enter decimal feet for distances in the Architectural unit style. For example, 6'-6" can be entered as **6.5'**.

Setting Up the Drawing Limits

One of the big advantages in using AutoCAD is that you can draw at full scale; you aren't limited to the edges of a piece of paper the way you are in manual drawing. But you still have to consider what will happen when you want a printout of your drawing. If you're not careful, you may create a drawing that won't fit on the paper size you want at the scale you want. When you start a new drawing, it helps to limit your drawing area to one that can be scaled down to fit on a standard sheet size. While this is not absolutely necessary with AutoCAD, the limits give you a frame of reference between your work in AutoCAD and the final printed output.

In order to set up the drawing work area, you need to understand how standard sheet sizes translate into full-scale drawing sizes. Table 3.2 lists widths and heights of drawing areas in inches, according to scales and final printout sizes. The scales are listed in the far-left column; the output sheet sizes are listed across the top.

Let's take an example: To find the area needed in AutoCAD for your bathroom drawing, look across from the scale 1"=1' to the column that reads 8 1/2" × 11" at the top. You'll find the value 102×132. This means the drawing area needs to fit within an area 102" × 132" (8.5 feet by 11 feet) in AutoCAD in order to fit a printout of a 1"=1'-0" scale drawing on an 8 1/2" × 11" sheet of paper. You may want the drawing area to be oriented horizontally, so that the 11 feet will be in the x-axis and the 8.5 feet will be in the y-axis.

If you're a metric user, you'll be drawing the bathroom at a scale of 1 to 10. This is a scale that is close to the 1" = 1'-0" scale used for the English measurements in the exercises. So for an A4 sheet, your work area should be 297cm × 210cm. This is the equivalent of an A4 sheet (210mm × 297mm) enlarged by a factor of 10.

TABLE 3.2: Work Area in Drawing Units (Inches) by Scale and Plotted Sheet Size

Scale	8 1/2"×11"	11"×17"	17"×22"	18"×24"	22"×34"	24"×36"	30"×42"	36"×48"
3"=1'	34×44	44×68	68×88	72×96	88×136	96×144	120×168	144×192
1 1/2"=1'	68×88	88×136	136×176	144×192	176×272	192×288	240×336	288×384
1"=1'	102×132	132×204	204×264	216×288	264×408	288×432	360×504	432×576
3/4"=1'	136×176	176×272	272×352	288×384	352×544	384×576	480×672	576×768
1/2"=1'	204×264	264×408	408×528	432×576	528×816	576×864	720×1008	864×1152
1/4"=1'	408×528	528×816	816×1056	864×1152	1056×1632	1152×1728	1440×2016	1728×2304
1/8"=1'	816×1056	1056×1632	1632×2112	1728×2304	2112×3264	2304×3456	2880×4032	3456×4608
1/16"=1'	1632×2112	2112×3264	3264×4224	3456×4608	4224×6528	4608×6912	5760×8064	6912×9216
1/32"=1'	3264×4224	4224×6528	6528×8448	6912×9216	8448×13056	9216×13824	11520×16128	13824×18432
1"=10'	1020×1320	1320×2040	2040×2640	2160×2880	2640×4080	2880×4320	3600×5040	4320×5760
1"=20'	2040×2640	2640×4080	4080×5280	4320×5760	5280×8160	5760×8640	7200×10080	8640×11520
1"=30'	3060×3960	3960×6120	6120×7920	6480×8640	7920×12240	8640×12960	10800×15120	12960×17280
1"=40'	4080×5280	5280×8160	8160×10560	8640×11520	10560×16320	11520×17280	14400×20160	17280×23040
1"=50'	5100×6600	6600×10200	10200×13200	10800×14400	13200×20400	14400×21600	18000×25200	21600×28800
1"=60'	6120×7920	7920×12240	12240×15840	12960×17280	15840×24480	17280×25920	21600×30240	25920×34560

Now that you know the area you need, you can use the Limits command to set up the area.

1. Choose Format ➤ Drawing Limits.

2. At the `Specify lower left corner or [ON/OFF] <0'-0",0'-0">:` prompt, specify the lower-left corner of your work area. Press ↵ to accept the default.

3. At the `Specify upper right corner <1'0",0'9">:` prompt, specify the upper-right corner of your work area. (The default is shown in brackets.) Enter **132,102**. Or if you prefer, you can enter **11',8'6**, since you've set up your drawing for architectural units. Metric users should enter **297,210**.

4. Next, choose View ➤ Zoom ➤ All. You can also select the Zoom All tool from the Zoom Window flyout on the Standard toolbar, or type **Z↵ A↵**. Although it appears that nothing has changed, your drawing area is now set to a size that will allow you to draw your bathroom at full scale.

TIP   You can toggle through the different Coordinate Readout modes by pressing F6, or by clicking the coordinate readout of the status bar. For more on the Coordinate Readout modes, see Chapter 1 and the *Using the Coordinate Readout as Your Scale* section later in this chapter.

---

5. Move the cursor to the upper-right corner of the drawing area and watch the coordinate readout. Notice that now the upper-right corner has a y-coordinate of approximately 8'-6" or 300 for metric users. The x-coordinate will vary depending on the proportion of your AutoCAD window. The coordinate readout also displays distances in feet and inches.

In step 5 above, the coordinate readout shows you that your drawing area is larger than before, but there are no visual clues to tell you where you are or what distances you are dealing with. To help you get your bearings, you can use the Grid mode, which you will learn about shortly. But first, let's take a closer look at scale factors and how they work.

NOTE   The steps you've just take to set up your drawing are duplicated in the Advanced Setup option of the Create New Drawing wizard. This section showed you the detailed method of setting up your drawing so you'll understand exactly what is going on, but if you prefer, you can use the Create New Drawing wizard to set up future drawings. You can then use the Drawing Units dialog box to fine-tune your drawing or make adjustments later.

Understanding Scale Factors

When you draft manually, you work on the final drawing directly with pen and ink or pencil. With a CAD program, you are a few steps removed from the actual finished product. Because of this, you need to have a deeper understanding of your drawing scale and how it is derived. In particular, you need to understand scale factors.

For example, one of the more common uses of scale factors is in translating text size in your CAD drawing to the final plotted text size. When you draw manually, you simply draw your notes at the size you want. In a CAD drawing, you need to translate the desired final text size to the drawing scale.

When you start adding text to your drawing (Chapter 8), you have to specify a text height. The scale factor helps you determine the appropriate text height for a particular drawing scale. For example, you may want your text to appear 1/8" high in your final plot. But if you drew your text to 1/8" in your drawing, it would appear as a dot when plotted. The text has to be scaled up to a size that, when scaled back down at plot time, appears 1/8" high. So, for a 1/4" scale drawing you multiply the 1/8" text height by a scale factor of 48 to get 6". Your text should be 6" high in the CAD drawing in order to appear 1/8" high in the final plot.

All the drawing sizes in Table 3.2 were derived by using scale factors. Table 3.3 shows scale factors as they relate to standard drawing scales. These scale factors are the values by which you multiply the desired final printout size to get the equivalent full-scale size. For example, if you have a sheet size of 11" × 17", and you want to know the equivalent full-scale size for a 1/4"-scale drawing, you multiply the sheet measurements by 48. In this way, 11" becomes 528" (48" × 11") and 17" becomes 816" (48" × 17"). Your work area must be 528" × 816" if you intend to have a final output of 11" × 17" at 1/4"=1'. You can divide these inch measurements by 12" to get 44' × 68'.

TIP   If you get the message ****Outside limits**, it means you have selected a point outside the area defined by the limits of your drawing *and* the Limits command's limits-checking feature is on. (Some third-party programs may use the limits-checking feature.) If you must select a point outside the limits, issue the Limits command and then enter **off** at the ON/OFF <Lower left corner>: prompt to turn off the limits-checking feature.

The scale factor for fractional inch scales is derived by multiplying the denominator of the scale by 12, and then dividing by the numerator. For example, the scale factor for 1/4"=1'-0" is (4×12)/1, or 48/1. For 3/16"=1'-0" scale, the operation is (16 × 12)/3 or 64. For whole-foot scales like 1"=10', multiply the feet side of the equation by 12. Metric scales require simple decimal conversions.

TABLE 3.3: Scale Conversion Factors

Scale Factors for Engineering Drawing Scales

1"= n	10'	20'	30'	40'	50'	60'	100'	200'
Scale factor	120	240	360	480	600	720	1200	2400

Scale Factors for Architectural Drawing Scales

n = 1'-0"	1/16"	1/8"	1/4"	1/2"	3/4"	1"	1 1/2"	3"
Scale factor	192	96	48	24	16	12	8	4

If you are using the metric system, the drawing scale can be used directly as the scale factor. For example, a drawing scale of 1:10 has a scale factor of 10; a drawing scale of 1:50 has a scale factor of 50; and so on. Table 3.4 shows drawing areas based on scale and sheet size. The sheet sizes are shown across the top while the scales are shown in the column to the far left.

Metric users need to take special care regarding the base unit. The examples in this book will use centimeters as a base unit, which means that if you enter a distance as 1, you can assume the distance to be 1cm. If you want to use millimeters as the base unit, multiply the sheet-size values in Table 3.4 by 10.

Metric users should note that the scale factor will vary depending on whether you are using millimeters, centimeters, or meters as the basis for the final plot size. For example, a drawing that uses millimeters as its base unit of drawing measure (1 drawing unit = 1 millimeter) would use a scale factor of 1 to 500 if the final output is to be at a scale of 1:50 centimeters.

TABLE 3.4: Work Area in Metric Units (Centimeters) by Scale and Plotted Sheet Size. Multiply Work Area Sizes by 10 for Millimeter Equivalents.

Scale	A0 or F 841mm× 1189mm (33.11"× 46.81")	A or D 594mm× 841mm (23.39"× 33.11")	A2 or C 420mm× 594mm (16.54"× 23.39")	A3 or B 297mm× 420mm (11.70"× 16.54")	A4 or A 210mm× 297mm (8.27"× 11.70")
1:5	420cm× 594cm	297cm× 420cm	210cm× 297cm	148cm× 210cm	105cm× 148cm
1:10	841cm× 1189cm	594cm× 841cm	420cm× 594cm	297cm× 420cm	210cm× 297cm
1:20	1682cm× 2378cm	1188cm× 1682cm	840cm× 1188cm	594cm× 840cm	420cm× 594cm
1:25	2102.5cm× 2972.5cm	1485cm× 2102.5cm	1050cm× 1485cm	742.5cm× 1050cm	5250cm× 742.5cm
1:33 1/3	2803cm× 3962cm	1980cm× 2803cm	1399cm× 1980cm	990cm× 1399cm	700cm× 990cm
1:40	3360cm× 4756cm	2376cm× 3360cm	1680cm× 2376cm	1188cm× 1680cm	840cm× 1188cm
1:50	4200cm× 5940cm	2970cm× 4200cm	2100cm× 2970cm	1480cm× 2100cm	1050cm× 1480cm
1:75	6307cm× 8917cm	4455cm× 6307cm	3150cm× 4455cm	2227cm× 3150cm	1575cm× 2227cm
1:10	8410cm× 11890cm	5940cm× 8410cm	4200cm× 5940cm	2970cm× 4200cm	2100cm× 2970cm
1:125	10512cm× 14862cm	7425cm× 10512cm	5250cm× 7425cm	3712cm× 5250cm	2625cm× 3712cm

You will be using scale factors to specify text height and dimension settings, so getting to understand them now will pay off later.

Using the AutoCAD Modes as Drafting Tools

After you have set up your work area, you can begin the plan of a typical bathroom in your studio. You will use this example to learn about some of AutoCAD's drawing aids. These tools might be compared to a background grid (*Grid mode*), scale (*Coordinate Readout mode*), and a T-square and triangle (*Object Snap Tracking mode* and *Polar Tracking mode*). These drawing modes can be indispensable tools when used properly. The Drafting Settings dialog box helps you visualize the modes in an organized manner and simplifies their management.

Using the Grid Mode as a Background Grid

Using the *Grid mode* is like having a grid under your drawing to help you with layout. In AutoCAD, the Grid mode also lets you see the limits of your drawing and helps you visually determine the distances you are working with in any given view. In this section, you will learn how to control the grid's appearance. The F7 key toggles the Grid mode on and off; you can also click the GRID button in the status bar. Start by setting the grid spacing.

1. Choose Tools ➣ Drafting Settings, or type **Rm**↲ to display the Drafting Settings dialog box, showing all the mode settings.

2. Click the Snap and Grid tab at the top of the dialog box. You see four button groups: Snap, Grid, Polar Spacing, and Snap Type & Style.

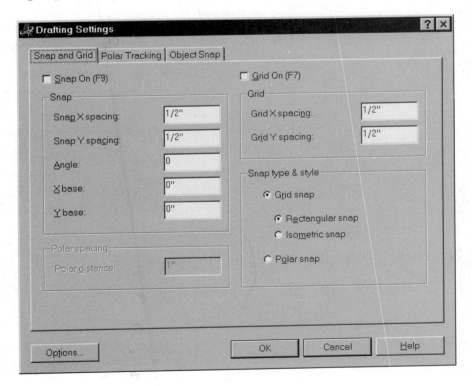

3. Let's start with the Grid group. Notice that the Grid X Spacing input box contains a value of 1/2". Metric users see a value of 10.

4. Double-click the Grid X Spacing input box. The 1/2" (or 10 for metric users) highlights. You can now type in a new value for this setting.

TIP

You can use the Gridunit system variable to set the grid spacing. Enter **'Gridunit.⏎**, and at the New value for GRIDUNIT <0'0",0'0">: prompt, enter **12,12** or (**30,30** for metric users). Note that the Gridunit value must be entered as an *x,y* coordinate.

---

5. Type **12** for 12", then press the Tab key to move to the Grid Y Spacing input box. Metric users should type **30**, then press Tab. Notice that the Grid Y Spacing input box automatically changes to the same value as the X spacing value you just entered. In the case of the English measurement, the value also changes from 12 to 1'. AutoCAD assumes you want the X and Y grid spacing to be the same, unless you specifically ask for a different Y setting.

TIP

If you want to change an entry in an input box, you can double-click the input box to highlight the whole entry, and then replace the entry by simply typing in a new one. If you just want to change a part of the entry, click the input box and then use the cursor keys to move the vertical bar cursor to the exact character you want to change. You can use the Backspace key to delete characters.

---

6. Click the Grid On check box. This setting makes the grid visible. Also notice the F7 in parentheses. This tells you that the F7 function key also controls the Grid On/Off function.

7. Click OK. The grid now appears as an array of dots with a 12" spacing in your drawing area (30cm if you are following the metric version of this tutorial). The grid dots will not print or plot with your drawing.

With the grid at a 12-unit spacing (30cm for metric users), you can see your work area more clearly. It also gives you a visual reference for your drawing. You can see what a 1-foot (or 30-cm) distance looks like in your drawing. Since the grid appears only within the drawing limits, you are better able to see your work area. In the next section, you'll see how the Snap mode works.

8. Press F7, or click the word GRID in the status bar (you can also hold down the Ctrl key and press **G**). The grid disappears.

9. Press F7 again to turn the grid back on again.

TIP   If your view is such that the grid spacing appears quite small, AutoCAD will not display the grid in order to preserve the readability of the drawing. If this situation occurs, you will see the message `Grid too dense to display` in the Command window.

TIP   In this exercise, you set the grid spacing to be equal to the scale factor of your drawing. This makes the grid spacing equivalent to 1" intervals of the final plotted drawing. For example, if your drawing is 1/4" = 1'-0" scale, you could set your grid spacing to 48. The grid spacing would then reflect the 1-inch spacing for a 1/4" scale drawing. If you're a metric user, you can keep the grid spacing to 10 to display the equivalent distance of 10cm. 30 was used in this exercise for the metric grid spacing to closely match the display of the English version in order to keep the figures consistent.

Using the Snap Modes

The *Snap mode* has no equivalent in hand drafting. This mode forces the cursor to step a specific distance. Snap mode is useful if you want to maintain accuracy while entering distances with the cursor.

There are actually two snap modes available in AutoCAD: *Grid Snap* and *Polar Snap*. Experienced users will know how to use the Grid Snap, but the Polar Snap is new in AutoCAD 2000. You'll start by looking at the Grid Snap mode.

The F9 key toggles the Grid Snap mode on and off. Or, just like the Grid mode, there is a SNAP button in the status bar that you can click. Follow these steps to access the Grid Snap mode:

1. Choose Tools ➤ Drafting Settings, or type **Rm↵**. The Drafting Settings dialog box appears again.

2. In the Snap group of the dialog box, double-click the Snap X Spacing input box and type **4**. Then press the Tab key to move to the next option. Metric users should enter **10**. As with the grid setting, AutoCAD assumes you want

the X and Y snap spacing to be the same, unless you specifically ask for a different Y setting.

3. Click the Snap On check box so that a checkmark appears.

4. Click OK and start moving the cursor around. Notice how the cursor seems to move in "steps" rather than in a smooth motion. Also notice that the SNAP button in the status bar appears to be depressed, indicating that the Snap mode is on.

5. Press F9 or click the word SNAP in the status bar (you can also hold down the Ctrl key and press **B**); then move the cursor slowly around the drawing area. The Snap mode is now off.

6. Press F9 again to turn the Snap mode back on.

TIP   You can use the Snapunit system variable to set the snap spacing. Enter **'Snap-unit**⏎. Then at the `New value for SNAPUNIT <0'0",0'0">:` prompt, enter **4,4** (**10,10** for metric users). Note that the Snapunit value must be entered as an *x,y* coordinate.

Take a moment to look at the Drafting Settings dialog box. The other options in the Snap group allow you to set the snap origin point (X Base and Y Base), rotate the cursor to an angle other than its current 0–90° (Angle), and set the horizontal snap spacing to a value different from the vertical spacing (Snap X Spacing and Snap Y Spacing).

In the Snap Type & Style group, you can change the snap and grid configuration to aid in drawing isometric drawings by choosing the Isometric Snap radio button. The Polar Snap option allows you to set a snap distance for the Polar Snap feature. When you click the Polar Snap radio button, the Polar Distance option at the lower left of the dialog box changes from gray to black and white to allow you to enter a Polar Snap distance. The next exercise discusses these features, as do Chapters 6 and 15.

NOTE   The Snaptype system variable can be used to set the snap to either the Grid Snap or Polar Snap while the Snapstyl system variable turns the isometric Grid Snap on and off. The Polardist system variable controls the snap distance for the Polar Snap feature.

Using Grid and Snap Together

You can set the grid spacing to be the same as the snap setting, allowing you to see every snap point. Let's take a look at how Grid and Snap modes work together.

TIP   You can take a shortcut to the Drafting Settings dialog box by right-clicking the SNAP, GRID, POLAR, or OTRACK button in the status bar, then selecting Settings from the popup menu.

---

1. Open the Drafting Settings dialog box.

2. Make sure the Snap and Grid tab is selected, then double-click the Grid X Spacing input box in the Grid group, and type **0**.

3. Click OK. Now the grid spacing has changed to reflect the 4" (or 10cm) snap spacing. Move the cursor, and watch it snap to the grid points.

4. Open the Drafting Settings dialog box again.

5. Double-click the Snap X Spacing input box in the Snap group, and type **1** (or **3** for metric users).

6. Click OK. The grid automatically changes to conform to the new snap setting. When the grid spacing is set to 0, the grid then aligns with the snap points. At this density, the grid is overwhelming.

7. Open the Drafting Settings dialog box again.

8. Double-click the Grid X Spacing input box in the Grid group, and type **12** (**30** for metric users).

9. Click OK. The grid spacing is now at 12 (or 30) again, which is a more reasonable spacing for the current drawing scale.

With the snap spacing set to 1 (3 for metric users), it is difficult to tell if the Snap mode is turned on based on the behavior of the cursor, but the coordinate readout in the status bar gives you a clue. As you move your cursor, the coordinates appear as whole numbers with no fractional distances. Metric users will notice the coordinate readout displaying values that are multiples of 3.

As you move the cursor over the drawing area, the coordinate readout in the lower-left corner of the AutoCAD window dynamically displays the cursor's position in absolute Cartesian coordinates. This allows you to find a position on your drawing by locating it in reference to the drawing origin—0,0—that is in the lower-left corner of the drawing. You can also set the coordinate readout to display relative coordinates by clicking the readout itself or by pressing the F6 key. Throughout these exercises, coordinates will be provided to enable you to select points using the dynamic coordinate readout. (If you want to review the discussion of AutoCAD's coordinates display, see Chapter 1.)

Next, you'll learn how to use the snap tools as your virtual drawing scale, T-square, and triangle.

Using Polar Tracking and Snap as Your Scale, T-Square, and Triangle

Now you will draw the first item in the bathroom: the toilet. It is composed of a rectangle representing the tank, and a truncated ellipse representing the seat. To construct the toilet, you'll use the Polar Tracking and Polar Snap tools. Polar Tracking helps you align your cursor to exact horizontal and vertical angles, much like a T-square and triangle. Polar Snap is similar to Grid Snap in that it forces the cursor to move in exact increments. The main difference is that Polar Snap only works in conjunction with Polar Tracking.

Start by setting up Polar Snap.

1. Open the Drafting Settings dialog box again.

2. Make sure the Snap and Grid tab is selected, then click the Polar Snap radio button in the Snap Type & Style button group.

3. Double-click the Polar Distance setting, and type **.5** for a 1/2-inch Snap setting. Metric users should type **1** for a 1-cm Polar Snap setting.

4. Click OK to dismiss the Drafting Settings dialog box.

You've just set the Polar Snap setting to .5 or one-half (1cm for metric users). As you move the cursor over the drawing area, notice that the Snap mode seems to be off. When Polar Snap is active, you'll only have the snap in effect when you are actually drawing an object. You can, however, switch between Grid Snap and Polar Snap on the fly. In the next exercise, you'll see how this is done.

1. Click the Line tool on the Draw toolbar, or type **L↵**. You could also select Draw ➤ Line from the pull-down menu.

Click polar button

2. Right-click the SNAP button in the status bar.

3. Select Grid Snap On from the popup menu. This places you in the Grid Snap mode.

4. Press F6 until you see the *x,y* coordinates dynamically update as you move the cursor. You can also click directly on the coordinate readout to cycle through the static, dynamic, and polar readout. Notice that as you move your cursor, the coordinate readout shows the cursor moving in increments that you set for the Grid Snap.

5. Using your coordinate readout for guidance, start your line at the coordinate 5'-7", 6'-3". Metric users should use 171,189 as the starting coordinate.

6. Right-click the SNAP button again, then select Polar Snap in the popup menu.

7. Move the cursor directly to the right. The Polar Tracking cursor appears, along with the Polar Tracking readout. Notice that the readout shows distances in 1/2" increments (or 1-unit increments for metric users). It also shows you the angle in the standard AutoCAD distance and angle format. Even though the Grid Snap is set to 1 (or 3 for metric users), when Polar Tracking is active and Polar Snap is on, the snap distance changes to the value you set for Polar Snap.

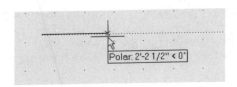

8. Move the cursor until the Polar Snap readout lists 1'-10"< 0, and pick this point. Metric users should use a Polar Tracking readout of 56.0000<0. As in Chapter 2, when you move the cursor around, the rubber-banding line follows it at any angle.

9. Move the cursor downward until the coordinate readout lists 0'-9"< 270 and click this point. Metric users should use a readout of 23.0000<270.

10. Continue drawing the other two sides of the rectangle by using the Polar Tracking readout. You should have a drawing that looks like Figure 3.1.

FIGURE 3.1:

A Plan view of the toilet tank

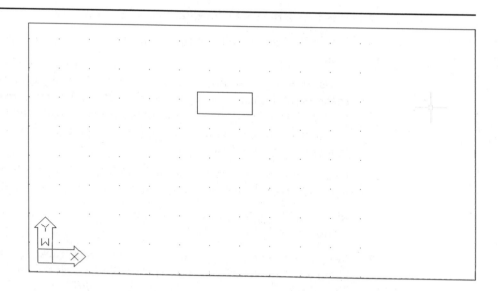

As you can see from the exercise, you can use Polar Tracking to restrain your cursor to horizontal and vertical positions, just like a T-square and triangle. Later, you'll learn how you can set up Polar Tracking to set the angle to any value you wish in a way similar to an adjustable triangle.

In some situations, you may find that you do not want Polar Tracking on. You can turn it off by clicking the POLAR button in the status bar. In fact, this is exactly what you did in Chapter 2. You can also use the F10 function key to turn Polar Tracking on or off.

NOTE

In step 4, the coordinate readout displayed some extra values. The third coordinate that you see at the end of the coordinate readout listing indicates the z value of the coordinate. This extra coordinate is significant only when you are doing 3D modeling, so for the time being, you can ignore it. If you'd like to know more about the additional z-coordinate listing in the coordinate readout, see Chapter 16.

While this exercise tells you to use the Line tool to draw the tank, you can also use the Rectangle tool. The Rectangle tool creates what is known as a *polyline,* which is a set of line or arc segments that acts like a single object. You'll learn more about polylines in Chapter 13.

The Ortho Mode

In addition to the Polar Tracking mode, you can further restrain the cursor to a vertical or horizontal direction by using the Ortho mode. To use the Ortho mode, press F8, or click the word Ortho in the status bar (you can also hold down the Ctrl key and press **O** to toggle on the Ortho mode). When you move the cursor around while drawing objects, the rubber-banding line only moves vertically or horizontally. With the Ortho mode turned on, Polar Tracking is automatically turned off.

In previous versions of AutoCAD, the Ortho mode was the only option available for restraining your line work to a vertical or horizontal direction. Polar Tracking is a much more flexible tool for this purpose.

By using the Snap modes in conjunction with the coordinate readout and Polar Tracking, you can locate coordinates and measure distances as you draw lines. This is similar to the way you would draw using a scale. Be aware that the smallest distance the coordinate readout and Polar Tracking readout register depends on the area you have displayed in your drawing area. For example, if you are displaying an area the size of a football field, the smallest distance you can indicate with your cursor may be 6" or 15cm. On the other hand, if your view shows an area of only one square inch or centimeter, you can indicate distances as small as 1/1000 of an inch or centimeter using your cursor.

Setting the Polar Tracking Angle

You've seen how Polar Tracking lets you draw exact vertical and horizontal lines. You can also set Polar Tracking to draw lines at other angles, such as 30 or 45 degrees. To change the angle Polar Tracking uses, you use the Polar Tracking tab of the Drafting Settings dialog box.

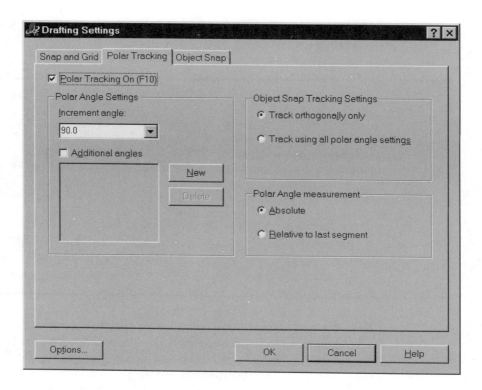

Open this dialog box by right-clicking the POLAR button in the status bar and then selecting Settings from the popup menu. Or you can select Tools ➤ Drafting Settings from the menu bar and then click the Polar Tracking tab.

To change the Polar Tracking angle, enter an angle in the Increment Angle input box, or select a predefined angle from the drop-down list. This can be done while drawing a series of line segments, for example, so that you can set angles "on the fly."

There are numerous other settings available in the Polar Tracking tab. Here is a listing of their functions for your reference:

Additional Angles   This check box and list box let you enter a specific angle for Polar Tracking. For example, if you want Polar Tracking to snap to 12 degrees and only 12 degrees, click the New button next to the Additional Angles list box and enter **12**. The value you enter appears in the list box, and when the Additional Angles check box is checked, Polar Tracking snaps to 12 degrees. To delete a value from the list box, highlight it and click the Delete button.

The Additional Angles option differs from the Increment Angle setting in that the Increment Angle setting causes Polar Tracking to snap to every increment of its setting while Additional Angles only snaps to the angle specified. You can enter as many angles as you wish in the Additional Angles list box.

Object Snap Tracking Settings   These settings let you control whether Object Snap Tracking uses strictly orthogonal directions (0, 90, 180, and 270 degrees) or the angles set in the Polar Angle button group of this dialog box. See *Aligning Objects Using Object Snap Tracking* later in this chapter.

Polar Angle Measurement   These radio buttons let you determine the zero angle on which Polar Tracking bases its incremental angles. The Absolute option uses the current AutoCAD setting for the 0° angle. The Relative to Last Segment option uses the last drawn object as the 0° angle. For example, if you draw a line at a 10° angle, and have the Relative to Last Segment option selected with the Increment Angle set to 90, Polar Tracking snaps to 10, 100, 190, and 280 degrees, relative to the actual 0° direction.

Exploring the Drawing Process

This section explores some of the more common AutoCAD commands and shows you how to use them to complete a simple drawing. As you draw, watch the prompts and notice how your responses affect them. Also note how you use existing drawing elements as reference points.

While drawing with AutoCAD, you create gross geometric forms to determine the basic shapes of objects, and then modify the shapes to fill in detail. This is where the differences between drawing with AutoCAD and manual drafting become more apparent. In essence, you alternately create and edit objects to build your drawing.

AutoCAD offers 14 basic drawing types. These are lines, arcs, circles, text, traces, polylines, points, 3D Faces, ellipses, elliptical arcs, spline curves, solids, regions, and multiline text. All drawings are built on these objects. In addition, there are five different 3D meshes, which are three-dimensional surfaces composed of 3D Faces. You are familiar with lines and arcs; these, along with circles, are the most commonly used objects. As you progress through the book, you will learn about the other objects and how they are used.

Locating an Object in Reference to Others

To define the toilet seat, you will use an ellipse.

1. Click the Ellipse tool in the Draw toolbar, or type **El**↵. You can also choose Draw ➢ Ellipse ➢ Axis, End.

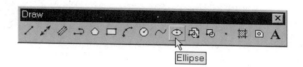

2. At the Specify axis endpoint of ellipse or [Arc/Center]: prompt, pick the midpoint of the bottom horizontal line of the rectangle. Do this by bringing up the Osnap popup menu and selecting Midpoint; then move the cursor toward the bottom line. (Remember, to bring up the Osnap menu, Shift+click the right mouse button.) When you see the Midpoint Osnap marker appear on the line, press the left mouse button.

3. At the Specify other endpoint of axis: prompt, move the cursor down until the Polar Tracking readout lists 1'-10"< 270. Metric users should use a readout of 55.0000<270.

4. Pick this as the second axis endpoint.

5. At the Specify distance to other axis or [Rotation]: prompt, move the cursor horizontally from the center of the ellipse until the Polar Tracking readout lists 0'-8"< 180. Metric users should use a readout of 20.0000<180.

6. Pick this as the axis distance defining the width of the ellipse. Your drawing should look like Figure 3.2.

NOTE   As you work with AutoCAD, you will eventually run into NURBS. NURBS stands for Non-Uniform Rational B-Splines—a fancy term meaning that curved objects are based on accurate mathematical models. When you trim the ellipse in a later exercise, it becomes a NURBS curve, not a segmented polyline as in earlier versions of AutoCAD. You'll learn more about both polylines and NURBS curves in Chapter 13.

FIGURE 3.2:

The ellipse added to the tank

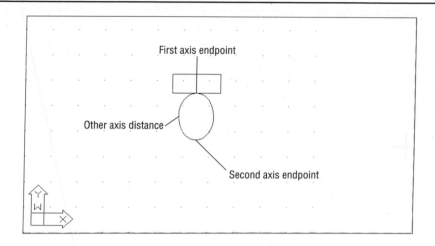

First axis endpoint

Other axis distance

Second axis endpoint

Getting a Closer Look

During the drawing process, you will want to enlarge areas of a drawing to more easily edit its objects. In Chapter 1, you already saw how the Zoom capability is used for this purpose.

1. Click the Zoom Window tool on the Standard toolbar, or type **Z**↵ **W**↵. You can also Choose View ➤ Zoom ➤ Window.

2. At the `First corner:` prompt, pick a point below and to the left of your drawing at or near coordinate 5'-0", 3'-6". Metric users should use the coordinate of 150.0000,102.0000.

3. At the `Other corner:` prompt, pick a point above and to the right of the drawing, at or near coordinate 8'-3", 6'-8" (246.0000,195.0000 for metric users), so that the toilet is completely enclosed by the View window. To obtain this view, use the Zoom Window tool. You can also use the Zoom Realtime tool in conjunction with the Pan Realtime tool. The toilet enlarges to fill more of the screen (see Figure 3.3).

TIP

To issue the Zoom Realtime tool from the keyboard, type **Z⏎⏎**. If you have a mouse with a scroll wheel, you can place the cursor on the toilet and turn the wheel to zoom into the image.

FIGURE 3.3:

A close-up of the toilet drawing

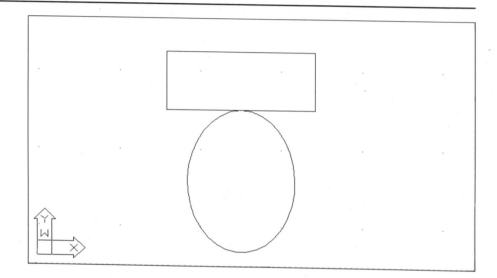

Modifying an Object

Now let's see how editing commands are used to construct an object. To define the back edge of the seat, let's put a copy of the line defining the front of the toilet tank 3" (7cm for metric users) toward the center of the ellipse.

1. Click the Copy Object tool in the Modify toolbar, or type **co⏎**. You can also select Modify ➢ Copy from the pull-down menu.

TIP

You can also use the Grip Edit tools to make the copy. See Chapter 2 for more on grip editing.

2. At the Select objects: prompt, pick the horizontal line that touches the top of the ellipse. The line is highlighted. Press ↵ to confirm your selection.

3. At the <Base point or displacement>/Multiple: prompt, pick a base point near the line. Then move the cursor down until the Polar Tracking readout lists 0'-3"< 270 or 7.0000<270 for metric users.

4. Pick this point. Your drawing should look like Figure 3.4.

FIGURE 3.4:

The line copied down

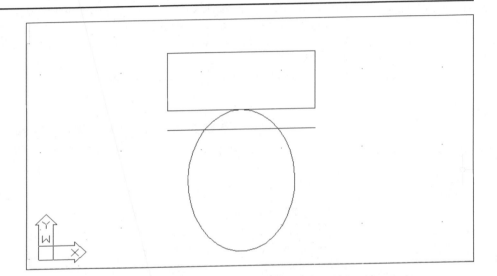

Architects and Their Symbols

You may be asking yourself if there is a set of standard architectural measurements for common items, such as the aforementioned toilet tank. Some items, such as doors and kitchen appliances, do have "standard" sizes that architects would learn in the course of their professional training. In this particular example, the 3-inch offset is really arbitrary because the toilet symbol is just that, a *symbol* representing a toilet and not necessarily an exact representation of one. When you see a toilet symbol in an architectural drawing, it's saying "put the toilet here." The actual brand of toilet is specified in the *specs*, which are written documents that go with the drawings.

Notice that the Copy command acts exactly like the Move command you used in Chapter 2, except that Copy does not alter the position of the objects you select.

Trimming an Object

Now you must delete the part of the ellipse that is not needed. You will use the Trim command to trim off part of the ellipse.

1. First, turn the Snap mode off by pressing F9 or clicking the word SNAP in the status bar. Snap mode may be a hindrance at this point in your editing session because it may keep you from picking the points you want. Snap mode forces the cursor to move to points at a given interval, so you will have difficulty selecting a point that doesn't fall exactly at one of those intervals.

2. Click the Trim tool in the Modify toolbar.

You will see this prompt:

```
Current settings: Projection=UCS Edge=None
Select cutting edges ...
```

3. Click the line you just created—the one that crosses through the ellipse—and press ↵ to finish your selection.

4. At the `Select object to trim or [Project/Edge/Undo]:` prompt, pick the topmost portion of the ellipse above the line. This trims the ellipse back to the line.

5. Press ↵ to exit the Trim command.

Selecting Close or Overlapping Objects

At times, you will want to select an object that is in close proximity to or lying underneath another object, and AutoCAD won't obey your mouse click. It's frustrating when you click the object you want to select but AutoCAD selects the one next to it instead. To help you make your selections in these situations, AutoCAD provides Object Selection Cycling. To use it, hold down the Ctrl key while simultaneously clicking the object you want to select. If the wrong object is highlighted, press the left mouse button again (you do not need to

Continued on next page

hold down the Ctrl key for the second time), and the next object in close proximity is high-lighted. If several objects are overlapping or close together, just continue to press the left mouse button until the correct object is highlighted. When the object you want is finally highlighted, press ↵ and continue with further selections.

In step 2 of the previous exercise, the Trim command produces two messages in the prompt. The first prompt, `Select cutting edges:`, tells you that you must first select objects to define *the edge to which you wish to trim an object*. In step 4, you are again prompted to select objects, this time to select the *objects to trim*. Trim is one of a handful of AutoCAD commands that asks you to select two sets of objects: The first set defines a boundary, and the second is the set of objects you want to edit. The two sets of objects are not mutually exclusive. You can, for example, select the cutting edge objects as objects to trim. The next exercise shows how this works.

First you will undo the trim you just did; then you will use the Trim command again in a slightly different way to finish off the toilet.

1. Click the Undo button in the Standard toolbar, or enter **U**↵ at the command prompt. The top of the ellipse reappears.

2. Start the Trim tool again by clicking it in the Modify toolbar.

3. At the `Select cutting edges:` prompt, click the ellipse and the line cross-ing the ellipse (see the top image of Figure 3.5).

4. Press ↵ to finish your selection and move to the next step.

NOTE   These Trim options—Project, Edge, and Undo—are described in *The Trim Options* section later in this chapter.

---

5. At the `Select object to trim or [Project/Edge/Undo]:` prompt, click the top portion of the ellipse, as you did in the previous exercise. The ellipse trims back.

6. Click a point near the left end of the trim line, past the ellipse. The line trims back to the ellipse.

7. Click the other end of the line. The right side of the line trims back to meet the ellipse. Your drawing should look like the bottom image of Figure 3.5.

8. Press ↵ to exit the Trim command.

9. Choose File ➤ Save to save the file in its current state. You might want to get in the habit of doing this every 20 minutes.

FIGURE 3.5:

Trimming the ellipse and the line

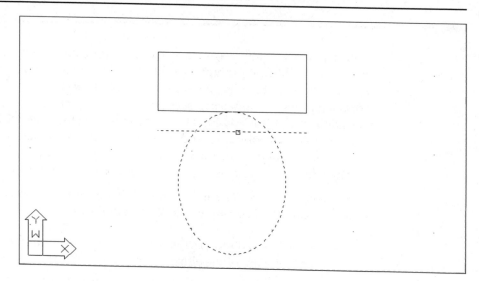

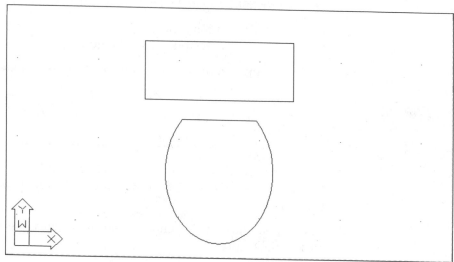

Here you saw how the ellipse and the line are both used as trim objects, as well as the objects to be trimmed.

The Trim Options

AutoCAD offers three options for the Trim command: Edge, Project, and Undo. As described in the following paragraphs, these options give you a higher degree of control over how objects are trimmed.

Edge [E]   Allows you to trim an object to an apparent intersection, even if the cutting-edge object does not intersect the object to be trimmed (see the top of Figure 3.6). Edge offers two options: Extend and No Extend. These can also be set using the Edgemode system variable.

Project [P]   Is useful when working on 3D drawings. It controls how AutoCAD trims objects that are not coplanar. Project offers three options: None, UCS, and View. None causes Trim to ignore objects that are on different planes, so that only coplanar objects will be trimmed. If you choose UCS, the Trim command trims objects based on a Plan view of the current UCS and then disregards whether the objects are coplanar or not (see the middle of Figure 3.6). View is similar to UCS but uses the current view's "line of sight" to determine how non-coplanar objects are trimmed (see the bottom of Figure 3.6).

Undo [U]   Causes the last trimmed object to revert to its original length.

You've just seen one way to construct the toilet. However, there are many ways to construct objects. For example, you could have just trimmed the top of the ellipse, as you did in the first Trim exercise, and then used the Grips feature to move the endpoints of the line to meet the endpoints of the ellipse. As you become familiar with AutoCAD, you will start to develop your own ways of working, using the tools best suited to your style.

NOTE   If you'd like to take a break, now would be a good time. You can exit AutoCAD, then come back to the Bath drawing file when you are ready to proceed.

FIGURE 3.6:

The Trim tool's options

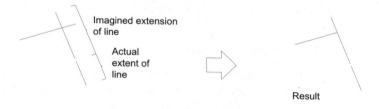

Imagined extension of line

Actual extent of line

Result

With the Extend option, objects will trim even if the trim object doesn't actually intersect with the object to be trimmed.

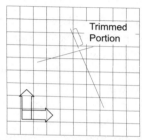

Trimmed Portion

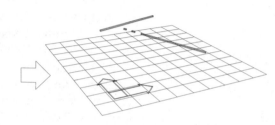

With the UCS option, objects in 3D space will trim on a plane perpendicular to the current UCS...

but when viewed in 3D or in another UCS, may appear to be trimmed incorrectly.

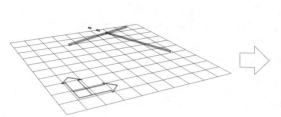

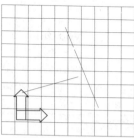

With the View option, objects in 3D space will trim according to your point of view...

but when they are viewed in plan, they may appear to be trimmed incorrectly.

Planning and Laying Out a Drawing

For the next object, the bathtub, you will use some new commands to lay out parts of the drawing. This will help you get a feel for the kind of planning you must do to use AutoCAD effectively. You'll also get a chance to use some of the keyboard shortcuts built into AutoCAD. First, though, go back to the previous view of your drawing, and arrange some more room to work.

1. Return to your previous view, the one shown in Figure 3.7. A quick way to do this is to click the Zoom Previous tool on the Standard toolbar, or Choose View ➤ Zoom ➤ Previous. Your view returns to the one you had before the last Zoom command (Figure 3.7).

FIGURE 3.7:

The view of the finished toilet after using the Zoom Previous tool. You can also obtain this view using the Zoom All tool from the Zoom Window flyout.

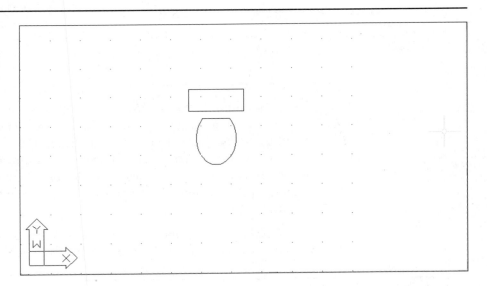

You'll begin the bathtub by using the Line command to draw a rectangle 2'-8"×5'-0" (81cm × 152cm for metric users) on the left side of the drawing area. For a change this time, you'll use a couple of shortcut methods: the Line command's keyboard shortcut and the Direct Distance method for specifying distance and direction.

2. Turn the Grid Snap mode on by right-clicking the SNAP button on the status bar and selecting Grid Snap from the popup menu.

3. Type **L↵** and pick the coordinate location 0'-9", 0'-10" at the Specify first point: prompt. Metric users use the coordinate 24.0000,27.0000. You can

either use the cursor in conjunction with the coordinate readout or enter the coordinate from the keyboard. Metric users can leave off the zero decimal values while entering coordinates through the keyboard.

4. Place your cursor so that the rubber-banding line is pointing directly to the left and type **2'8"**; then press ↵ for the first side of the tub. Metric users should enter **81**↵. Notice that the rubber-banding line is now fixed at the length you typed.

5. Now point the rubber-banding line upward toward the top of the screen and type **5'**; then press ↵ for the next side. Metric users should enter **152**↵.

6. Point the rubber-banding line directly to the right of the last point and type **2'8"** (**81** for metric users); then press ↵ for the next side.

7. Type **C**↵ to close the rectangle.

NOTE   Instead of pressing ↵ during the Direct Distance method, you can press the space-bar key or right-click and select Enter from the popup menu.

Now you have the outline of the tub. Notice that when you enter feet and inches from the keyboard, you must avoid hyphens or spaces. Thus, 2 feet 8 inches is typed as **2'8"**. Also notice that you didn't have to enter the at sign (@) or angle specification. Instead, you used the *Direct Distance method* for specifying direction and distance. You can use this method for drawing lines or moving and copying objects at right angles. The Direct Distance method is less effective if you want to specify exact angles other than right angles.

Besides the Direct Distance method, you used a keyboard shortcut to start the Line command, instead of using the Line tool on the Draw toolbar.

TIP   Some of the keyboard shortcuts for tools or commands you've used in this chapter are CO (Copy), E (Erase), EL (Ellipse), F (Fillet), M (Move), O (Offset), and TR (Trim). Remember that keyboard shortcuts, like keyboard commands, can only be entered when the command prompt is visible in the Command window.

Making a Preliminary Sketch

The following exercise will show you how planning ahead will make your use of AutoCAD more efficient. When drawing a complex object, you will often have to do some layout before you do the actual drawing. This is similar to drawing an accurate pencil sketch using construction lines that you later trace over to produce a finished drawing. The advantage of doing this in AutoCAD is that your drawing doesn't lose any accuracy between the sketch and the final product. Also, Auto-CAD allows you to use the geometry of your sketch to aid you in drawing. While planning your drawing, think about what it is you want to draw, and then decide what drawing elements will help you create that object.

You will use the Offset command to establish reference lines to help you draw the inside of the tub. This is where the Osnap overrides are quite useful. See *The Osnap Options* sidebar, later in this chapter.

Setting Up a Layout

The Offset tool of the Modify toolbar allows you to make parallel copies of a set of objects, such as the lines forming the outside of your tub. Offset is different from the Copy command; Offset allows only one object to be copied at a time, but it can remember the distance you specify. The Offset option does not work with all types of objects. Only lines, arcs, circles, and 2D polylines can be offset.

In this exercise, you will use standard lines to lay out your drawing. Standard lines are best suited for the layout of the bathtub in this situation. In Chapter 5 you will learn about two other objects, construction lines (Xlines) and Rays, which are specifically designed to help you lay out a drawing.

1. Click the Offset tool in the Modify toolbar, or type **o⏎**. You can also select Modify ➤ Offset from the pull-down menu.

2. At the Specify offset distance or [Through] <Through>: prompt, enter **3⏎**. This specifies the distance of 3" as the offset distance. Metric users should enter **7** for 7cm, which is roughly equivalent to 3 inches.

3. At the Select object to offset or <exit>: prompt, click the bottom line of the rectangle you just drew.

4. At the Specify point on side to offset: prompt, pick a point inside the rectangle. A copy of the line appears. You don't have to be exact about

where you pick the side to offset; AutoCAD only wants to know on which side of the line you want to make the offset copy.

5. The prompt Select object to offset or <exit>: appears again. Click another side to offset; then click again on a point inside the rectangle.

6. Continue to offset the other two sides; then offset these four new lines inside the rectangle toward the center. You will have a drawing that looks like Figure 3.8.

7. When you are done, exit the Offset command by pressing ↵.

FIGURE 3.8:

The completed layout

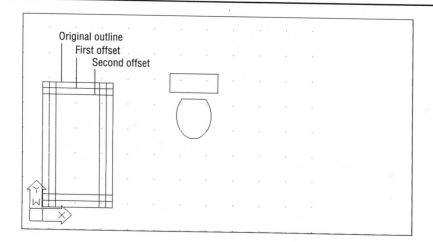

Using the Layout

Now you will begin to draw the inside of the tub, starting with the narrow end. You will use your offset lines as references to construct the arcs that make up the tub. Also in this exercise, you'll set up some of the Osnap tools to be available automatically whenever AutoCAD expects a point selection.

1. Choose Tools ➤ Drafting Settings, then select the Object Snap tab. You can also type **os**↵. You can also right-click the OSNAP button on the status bar, then select Settings from the popup menu.

2. Press the Clear All button at the right side of the dialog box. This turns off any options that might be selected in this dialog box.

3. Click the check boxes labeled Endpoint, Midpoint, and Intersection so that an X appears in the boxes and make sure the Object Snap On option is checked; then click OK.

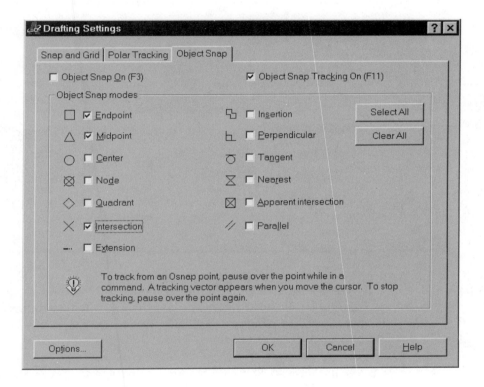

NOTE	Take a look at the graphic symbols next to each of the Osnap options in the Object Snap tab. These are the Osnap markers that appear in your drawing as you select Osnap points. Each Osnap option has its own marker symbol. As you work with the Osnaps, you'll become more familiar with how they work.

Making Adjustments to the AutoSnap Feature

When you click the Options button in the Object Snap tab of the Drafting Settings dialog box, you'll see the Drafting Settings tab of the Options dialog box. This tab offers a set of options pertaining to the AutoSnap feature. AutoSnap looks at the location of your cursor during Osnap selections and locates the Osnap point nearest your cursor. AutoSnap then displays a graphic called a *marker* showing you the Osnap point it has found. If it is the one you want, you simply left-click your mouse to select it.

The AutoSnap settings allow you to control its various features. The following is a listing of each of the settings and their purpose.

Marker   Turns the graphic marker on or off.

Magnet   Causes the Osnap cursor to "jump to" inferred Osnap points.

Display AutoSnap Tooltip   Turns the Osnap tool tip on or off.

Display AutoSnap Aperture Box   Turns the old style Osnap cursor box on or off.

AutoSnap Marker Size   Controls the size of the graphic marker.

AutoSnap Marker Color   Controls the color of the graphic marker.

You've just set up the Endpoint, Midpoint, and Intersection Osnaps to be on by default. This is called a *Running Osnap* where AutoCAD automatically selects the nearest Osnap point without your intervention. Now let's see how Running Osnaps works.

1. In the Draw toolbar, click the Arc tool, or type **a↵**. (See Figure 3.9 for other Arc options available from the pull-down menu. This figure shows each pull-down menu option name with a graphic above it depicting the arc and numbers indicating the sequence of points to select. For example, if you want to know how the Draw ➢ Arc ➢ Start, Center, End option works, you can look to the graphic at the bottom-right corner of the figure. It shows the point selection sequence for drawing an arc using that option; 1 for the start point, 2 for the center point, and then 3 for the end of the arc.)

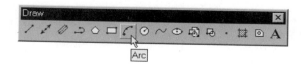

FIGURE 3.9:

If you look at the Draw ➤ Arc cascading menu, you'll see some additional options for drawing arcs. These options provide "canned" responses to the Arc command so that you only have to select the appropriate points as indicated in the pull-down menu option name.

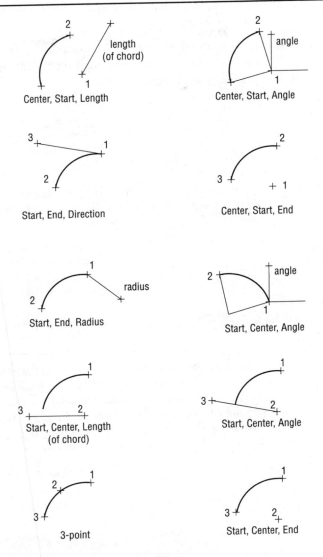

Center, Start, Length

Center, Start, Angle

Start, End, Direction

Center, Start, End

Start, End, Radius

Start, Center, Angle

Start, Center, Length (of chord)

Start, Center, Angle

3-point

Start, Center, End

2. For the first point of the arc, move the cursor toward the intersection of the two lines as indicated in the first image of Figure 3.10. Notice that the Intersection Osnap marker appears on the intersection.

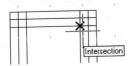

3. With the Intersection Osnap marker on the desired intersection, click the left mouse button.

4. Now move the cursor to the midpoint of the second horizontal line near the top. When the Midpoint Osnap marker appears at the midpoint of the line, press the left mouse button.

5. Finally, use the Intersection Osnap marker to locate and select the intersection of the two lines at the upper-left side of the bathtub.

The top image of Figure 3.10 shows the sequence we've just described.

Next, you will draw an arc for the left side of the tub.

1. In the Draw toolbar, click the Arc tool again.

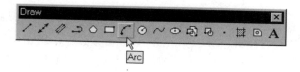

2. Type @↵. This selects the last point you picked as the start of the next arc.

FIGURE 3.10:

The top, left side, and bottom of the tub

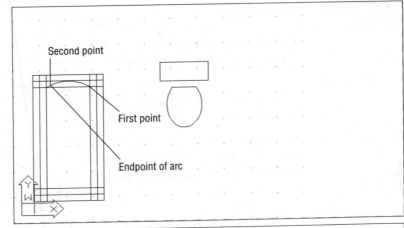

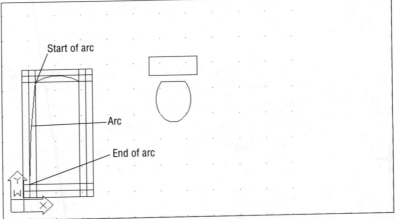

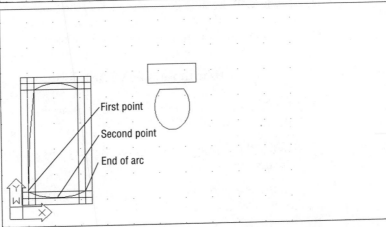

If you accidentally select additional points after the last exercise and prior to step 1, you may not get the results described here. If this happens, issue the Arc command again and then use the Endpoint Osnap and select the endpoint of the last arc.

3. Type **E↵** to tell AutoCAD that you want to specify the other end of the arc, instead of the next point. Alternately, you can right-click and select End from the popup menu.

4. At the End point prompt, use the Intersection Osnap to pick the intersection of the two lines in the lower-left corner of the tub. See the middle image of Figure 3.10 for the location of this point.

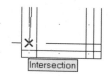

5. Type **D↵** to select the Direction option. You can also right-click and then select Direction from the popup menu. The arc drags as you move the cursor, along with a rubber-banding line from the starting point of the arc.

6. Move the cursor to the left of the dragging arc until it touches the middle line on the left side of the tub. Then pick that as shown in the middle image of Figure 3.10.

In step 3, the rubber-banding line indicates the direction of the arc. Be sure Ortho mode is off, because Ortho mode forces the rubber-banding line and the arc in a direction you don't want. Check the status bar; if the ORTHO button looks like it's depressed, press F8 or click the ORTHO button to turn Ortho mode off.

Now you will draw the bottom of the tub.

1. Click the Arc tool in the Draw toolbar again. You can also press ↵ to replay the last command.

2. Using the Endpoint Osnap marker, pick the endpoint of the bottom of the arc just drawn.

3. Using the Midpoint Osnap marker, pick the middle horizontal line at the bottom of the tub.

4. Finally, pick the intersection of the two lines in the lower-right corner of the tub (see the bottom image of Figure 3.10).

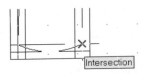

Now create the right side of the tub by mirroring the left side.

5. Click the Mirror tool on the Modify toolbar.

6. At the `Select objects:` prompt, pick the long arc on the left side of the tub. The arc is highlighted. Press ↵ to indicate that you've finished your selection.

7. At the `Specify first point of mirror line:` prompt, pick the midpoint of the top horizontal line. By now, you should know how to use the automatic Osnap modes you set up earlier.

8. At the `Specify second point of mirror line:` prompt, use the Polar Tracking mode to pick a point directly below the last point selected.

9. At the `Delete source objects? [Yes/No] <N>:` prompt, press ↵ to accept the default, No. A mirror image of the arc you picked appears on the right side of the tub. Your drawing should look like Figure 3.11.

In this exercise, you were able to use the Osnaps in a Running Osnap mode. You'll find that you will use the Osnaps nearly all the time as you create your drawings. For this reason, you may choose to have Running Osnaps on all the time. Even so, there will be times when Running Osnaps may get in the way. For example, they may be a nuisance in a crowded drawing when you want to use a Zoom window. The Osnaps can cause you to select an inappropriate window area by automatically selecting Osnap points.

Fortunately, you can turn Running Osnaps on and off quite easily by clicking the OSNAP button in the status bar. This toggles the Running Osnaps on or off. If you don't have any Running Osnaps set, then click the Object Snap tab of the Options dialog box.

FIGURE 3.11:

The inside of the tub completed with the layout lines still in place

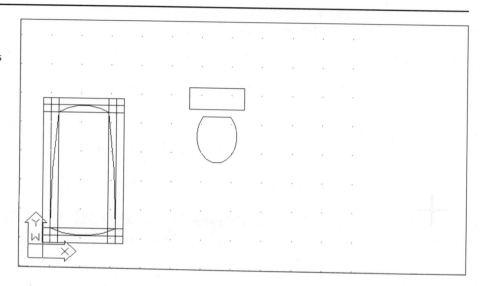

Erasing the Layout Lines

For the next step, you will erase the layout lines you created using the Offset command. But this time, try selecting the lines *before* issuing the Erase command.

> **TIP**
>
> If the following exercise doesn't work as described, be sure you have the Noun/Verb selection setting turned on. See Appendix B for details.

1. Click each internal layout line individually.

    If you have problems selecting just the lines, try using a window to select single lines. (Remember, a window selects only objects that are completely within the window.) You might also try the Object Selection Cycling option, as explained earlier in this chapter in the *Selecting Close or Overlapping Objects* sidebar.

2. Once all the layout lines are highlighted, enter **E↵** to use the keyboard shortcut for the Erase command, or right-click and select Erase from the popup menu. Your drawing will look like Figure 3.12.

    If you right-click to use the popup menu in step 2, you'll notice that you have several other options besides Erase. You can move, copy, scale, rotate, and mirror the objects you have selected. These options act just like the standard Modify toolbar options. Be aware that these commands act somewhat differently from the hot-grip options described in Chapter 2.

TIP

If you find you need more control over the selection of objects, you will find the Add/Remove selection mode setting useful. This setting lets you deselect a set of objects within a set of objects you've already selected. While in Object Selection mode, enter **R**↵; then proceed to use a window or other selection tool to remove objects from the selection set. Enter **A**↵ to continue to add more options to the selection set. Or if you only need to deselect a single object, Shift+click it.

FIGURE 3.12:

The drawing after erasing the layout lines

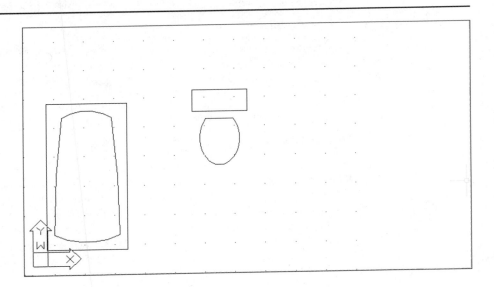

The Osnap Options

In the previous exercise, you made several of the Osnap settings automatic so that they were available without having to select them from the Osnap popup menu. Another way to invoke the Osnap options is by typing in their keyboard equivalents while selecting points or by right-clicking while selecting points to open the Osnap popup menu.

Continued on next page

Here is a summary of all the available Osnap options, including their keyboard shortcuts. You've already used many of these options in this chapter and in the previous chapter. Pay special attention to those options you haven't yet used in the exercises but may find useful to your style of work. The full name of each option is followed by its keyboard shortcut name in brackets. To use these options, you can enter either the full name or abbreviation at any point prompt. You can also pick these options from the popup menu obtained by Shift+clicking the right mouse button.

Tip: Sometimes you'll want to have one or more of these Osnap options available as the default selection. You can set Osnaps to be on at all times (called a *Running Osnap*). Choose Tools ➤ Drafting Settings from the menu bar, then click the Object Snap tab. You can also right-click the OSNAP button in the status bar, then select Settings from the popup menu.

Available Osnap options:

Apparent Intersection [apint]   Selects the apparent intersection of two objects. This is useful when you want to select the intersection of two objects that do not actually intersect. You will be prompted to select the two objects.

Center [cen]   Selects the center of an arc or circle. You must click the arc or circle itself, not its apparent center.

Endpoint [endp]   Selects all the endpoints of lines, polylines, arcs, curves, and 3D Face vertices.

Extension [ext]   Selects a point that is aligned with an imagined extension of a line. For example, you can pick a point in space that is aligned with an existing line, but is not actually on that line. To use that point, type **ext↵** during point selection or select Extension from the Osnap popup menu, then move the cursor to the line whose extension you want to use and hold it there until you see a small, cross-shaped marker on the line. The cursor also displays a tool tip with the word "extension" letting you know that the Extension OSNAP is active.

From [fro]   Selects a point relative to a picked point. For example, you can select a point that is 2 units to the left and 4 units to the right of a circle's center. This option is usually used in conjunction with another Osnap option, such as From Endpoint or From Midpoint.

Insert [ins]   Selects the insertion point of text, blocks, Xrefs, and overlays.

Intersection [int]   Selects the intersection of objects.

Midpoint [mid]   Selects the midpoint of a line or arc. In the case of a polyline, it selects the midpoint of the polyline segment.

Continued on next page

Nearest [nea]   Selects a point on an object nearest the pick point.

Node [nod]   Selects a point object.

None [non]   Temporarily turns off Running Osnaps.

Parallel [par]   Lets you draw a line segment that is parallel to another existing line segment. To use this option, type **par.↵** during point selection or select Parallel from the Osnap popup menu, then move the cursor to the line you want to be parallel to and hold it there until you see a small, cross-shaped marker on the line. The cursor also displays a tool tip with the word "parallel" letting you know that the Parallel OSNAP is active.

Perpendicular [per]   Selects a position on an object that is perpendicular to the last point selected. Normally, this option is not valid for the first point selected in a string of points.

Quadpoint [qua]   Selects the nearest cardinal (north, south, east, or west) point on an arc or circle.

Quick [qui]   Improves the speed at which AutoCAD selects geometry by sacrificing accuracy. You use Quick in conjunction with one of the other Osnap options. For example, to speed up the selection of an intersection, you enter **QUICK,INT↵** at a point prompt, and then select the intersection of two objects.

Tangent [tan]   Selects a point on an arc or circle that represents the tangent from the last point selected. Like the Perpendicular option, Tangent is not valid for the first point in a string of points.

TIP   When preparing to erase an object that is close to other objects, you may want to select the object first, using the Noun/Verb selection method. This way you can carefully select objects you want to erase before you actually invoke the Erase command.

Putting On the Finishing Touches

The inside of the tub still has some sharp corners. To round out these corners, you can use the versatile Fillet command on the Modify toolbar. Fillet allows you to join lines and arcs end to end, and it can add a radius where they join, so there is a smooth transition from arc to arc or line to line. Fillet can join two lines that do not intersect, and it can trim two crossing lines back to their point of intersection.

1. Click the Fillet tool on the Modify toolbar, or type **f**↵. You can also choose Modify ➤ Fillet from the pull-down menu.

2. At the prompt

   ```
   Current settings: Mode = TRIM, Radius = 0'-0 1/2"
   Select first object or [Polyline/Radius/Trim]:
   ```

   enter **R**↵ or right-click and select Radius from the popup menu.

3. At the `Specify fillet radius <0'-0 1/2">:` prompt, enter **4**↵. This tells AutoCAD that you want a 4" radius for your fillet. Metric users will see a value of `<10.0000>` for the default radius. Go ahead and keep this value, but keep in mind that you can alter the radius value at this prompt.

4. Press ↵ to invoke the Fillet command again; this time, pick two adjacent arcs. The fillet arc joins the two larger arcs.

5. Press ↵ again and fillet another corner. Repeat until all four corners are filleted. Your drawing should look like Figure 3.13.

6. Save and close the Bath file.

FIGURE 3.13:

A view of the finished toilet and tub with the tub corners filleted

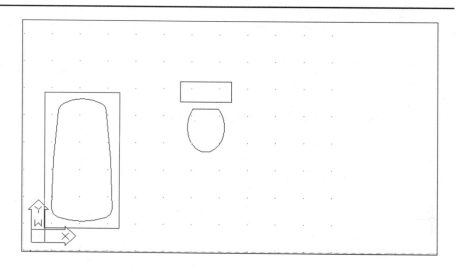

Using AutoCAD's Automatic Save Feature

As you work with AutoCAD, you may notice that AutoCAD periodically saves your work for you. Your file is saved not as its current filename, but as a file called `Auto.sv$`. The default time interval between automatic saves is 120 minutes. You can change this interval by doing the following:

1. Enter **Savetime.↵** at the command prompt.

2. At the `Enter new value for SAVETIME < 120 >:` prompt, enter the desired interval in minutes. Or, to disable the automatic save feature entirely, enter **0** at the prompt.

Aligning Objects Using Object Snap Tracking

You saw how to use lines to construct an object like the bathtub. In many situations, using these *construction lines* is the most efficient way to draw, but they can also be a bit cumbersome. AutoCAD 2000 offers another tool that helps you align locations in your drawing to existing objects without having to draw intermediate construction lines. The tool is called *Object Snap Tracking* or *Osnap Tracking*.

Osnap Tracking is like an extension of Object Snaps that allows you to *align* a point to the geometry of an object instead of just selecting a point on an object. For example, with Osnap Tracking, you can select a point that is exactly at the center of a rectangle.

In the following set of exercises, you will draw a plan view of a bathroom sink as an introduction to the Osnap Tracking feature. This drawing will be used as a symbol in later chapters.

TIP If you're a veteran AutoCAD user, think of Object Snap Tracking as an improved version of the XY filter tool. XY filters allow you to selectively filter out the *x, y,* or *z* coordinate of any point location. Object Snap Tracking allows you to do that and more, in a way that is visually easier to comprehend.

Doing a Quick Setup

First, as a review, you'll open a new file using the Create New Drawing wizard. Since this drawing will be used as a symbol for insertion into other CAD drawings, don't worry about setting it up to conform to a sheet size. Chances are, you won't be printing out individual symbols.

1. Select File ➤ New to create a new drawing for your bathroom sink.

2. In the Create New Drawing wizard, click the Use a Wizard button at the top to the far right of the window.

3. Select Quick Setup from the list box, then click OK.

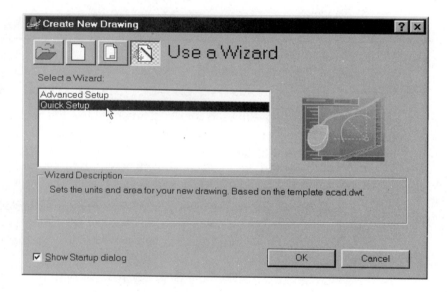

4. In the Units dialog box, choose Architectural, then click Next. This option performs the same operation as the Drawing Units dialog box you saw earlier in this chapter.

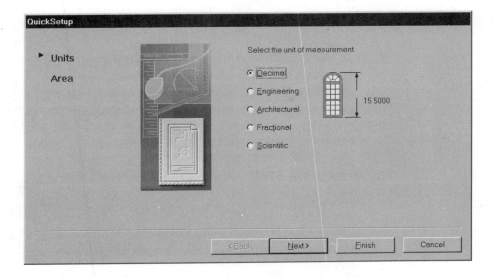

5.   In the Area dialog box, enter **48** for the width and **36** for the length. Metric users should enter **122** for the width and **92** for the length. Click Finish when you've entered the width and length values. This option performs the same operation as the Format ➤ Drawing Limits command on the menu bar.

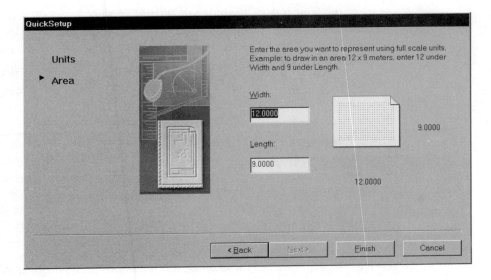

6. Click the GRID button in the status bar, then choose View ➣ Zoom ➣ All from the menu bar. This allows you to see your entire work area.

7. Use File ➣ SaveAs to save the file under the name of Sink.

As you saw in steps 4 and 5, the Create New Drawing wizard simplifies the drawing setup process by limiting the options you need to work with. Still, it helps to know what the wizard is really doing behind the scenes. Also, the wizard does not translate your work area into a plotted sheet size.

Drawing the Sink

Now you're ready to draw the sink. Start with the outline of the sink countertop.

1. Click the GRID button in the status bar to turn off the grid. It was helpful to let you see the work area but you don't need it now.

2. Click the Rectangle tool in the Draw toolbar or type **rec**↵.

3. At the prompt

```
Specify first corner point or [Chamfer/Elevation/Fillet/
Thickness/Width]:
```

enter **0,0**↵. This places one corner of the rectangle in the origin of the drawing.

4. At the `Specify other corner point:` prompt, enter **@2'4,1'6**↵. Metric users should enter **@71,46**↵. This makes the rectangle 2'-4" wide by 1'-6" deep or 71cm by 46cm for metric users. Your drawing will look like Figure 3.14.

5. Use View ➣ Zoom ➣ Extents to enlarge the view of the sink outline. Then use the Zoom Realtime tool in the Standard toolbar to adjust your view so it looks similar to the one shown in Figure 3.15.

Rectangle Options

You may have noticed that the Rectangle tool offers a number of options, namely, Chamfer, Elevation, Fillet, Thickness, and Width. Two of these options, Chamfer and Fillet, are equivalent to the Chamfer and Fillet tools on the Modify toolbar. They are offered as options in the Rectangle tool as a convenience. The options Elevation and Thickness are standard properties that all objects possess. You'll learn more about these properties in the chapters that describe how to create 3D drawings. The last option, Width, is a special property of polyline objects. You'll learn about polyline widths in Chapter 13.

FIGURE 3.14:

The outline of the sink

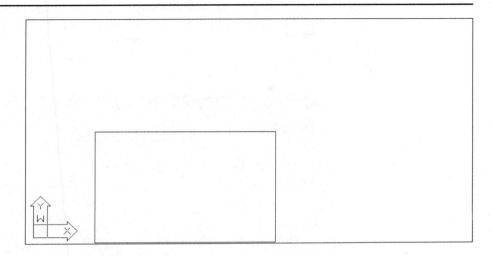

FIGURE 3.15:

The view of the sink after making some adjustments

Next you'll draw the bowl of the sink. The bowl will be represented by an ellipse. You'll want to place the center of the ellipse at the center of the rectangle you've just drawn. To do this, you will use the midpoint of two adjoining sides of the rectangle as alignment locations. This is where the Osnap Tracking tool will be useful.

First, make sure Running Osnaps are turned on and that they are set to the Midpoint option. Then make sure Osnap Tracking is turned on.

1. Right-click the OTRACK button in the status bar. The Object Snap tab of the Drafting Settings dialog box appears.

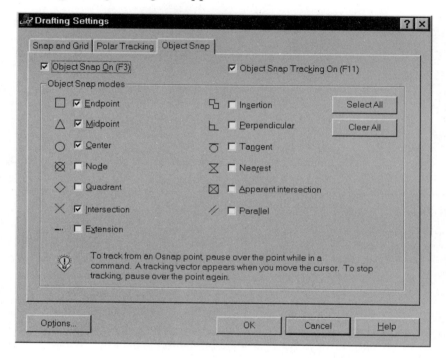

2. Make sure that the Midpoint option in the Object Snap Modes button group is checked.

3. Make sure also that Object Snap On and Object Snap Tracking On are both checked. Click OK.

Finally, you are ready to draw the ellipse.

1. Click the Ellipse tool in the Draw toolbar.

2. At the `Specify axis endpoint of ellipse or [Arc/Center]:` prompt, type **C** or right-click and select Center from the popup menu.

3. Move your cursor to the top, horizontal edge of the rectangle, until you see the midpoint tool tip.

4. Now move the cursor directly over the Midpoint Osnap marker. Without clicking the mouse, hold the cursor there for a second until you see a small cross appear. Look carefully because the cross is quite small. This is the Osnap Tracking marker.

NOTE   You can alternately insert and remove the Osnap Tracking marker by passing the cursor over the Osnap marker.

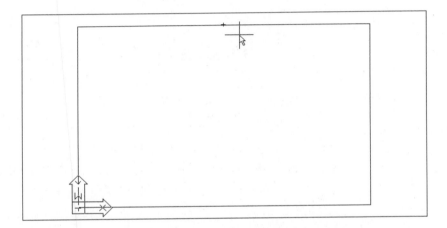

5. Now as you move the cursor downward, a dotted line appears, emanating from the midpoint of the horizontal line.

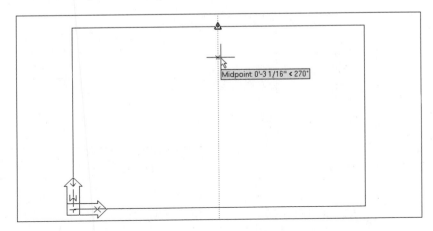

The cursor also shows a small X following the dotted line as you move it.

6. Now move the cursor to the midpoint of the left-hand vertical side of the rectangle. Don't click, but hold it there for a second until you see the small cross. Now as you move the cursor away, a horizontal dotted line appears with an X following the cursor.

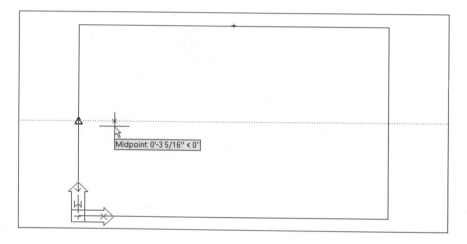

7. Now move the cursor to the center of rectangle. The two dotted lines appear simultaneously and a small X appears at their intersection.

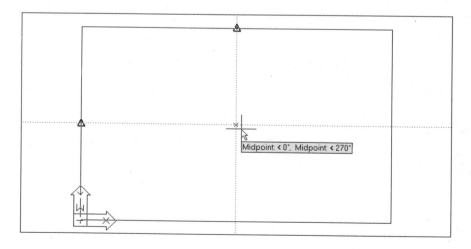

8. With the two dotted lines crossing and the X at their intersection, click the left mouse button. You have selected the exact center of the rectangle.

9. Point the cursor to the right and enter **8.⏎** to make the width of the bowl 16". Metric users should enter **20.⏎** for a 20cm wide bowl.

10. Point the cursor downward and enter **6.⏎** to make the length of the bowl 12". Metric users should enter **15.⏎** for a bowl with a length of 15cm. The basic symbol for the sink is complete (see Figure 3.16).

11. Choose File ➤ Save. You can exit AutoCAD now and take a break.

In this exercise, you saw how Osnap Tracking allowed you to align two locations to select a point in space. While you only used the Midpoint Osnap setting in this exercise, you are not limited to only one Osnap setting. You can use as many as you need to in order to select the appropriate geometry. You can also use as many alignment points as you need, although in this exercise, you only used two. If you like, erase the ellipse and repeat this exercise until you get the hang of using the Osnap Tracking feature.

NOTE   As with all the other buttons in the status bar, you can turn Osnap Tracking on or off by clicking the OTRACK button.

FIGURE 3.16:

The completed bathroom sink

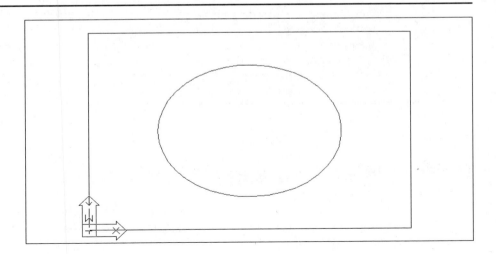

Using Osnap Tracking and Polar Tracking Together

In addition to selecting as many tracking points as you need, you can also use different angles besides the basic orthogonal angles of 0, 90, 180, and 270 degrees. For example, you can have AutoCAD locate a point that is aligned vertically to the top edge of the sink and at a 45° angle from a corner.

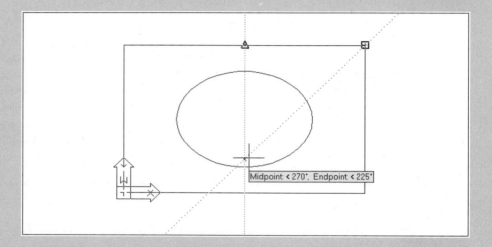

This can be accomplished by using the settings in the Polar Tracking tab of the Drafting Settings dialog box (see *Setting the Polar Tracking Angle* earlier in this chapter). If you set the Increment angle to 45° and turn on the Track Using All Polar Angle Settings option, you will be able to use 45° in addition to the orthogonal directions. You'll see firsthand how this works in Chapter 5.

If You Want to Experiment...

As you draw, you will notice that you are alternately creating objects, and then copying and editing them. This is where the difference between hand drafting and CAD really begins to show.

Try drawing the wide flange beam shown in Figure 3.17. The figure shows you what to do, step by step. Notice how you are applying the concepts of layout and editing to this drawing.

FIGURE 3.16:

The completed
bathroom sink

1. Draw a box 7 units wide by 8 units high using the Line command.

2. Draw a vertical line through the center of the box.

3. Offset the top and bottom lines of the box a distance of 0.7 units. Offset the center at 0.35 units.

4. Break the sides of the box between the two offset lines.

5. Trim the top and bottom offset lines between the center three vertical lines.

6. Set the fillet radius to 0.4; then fillet the vertical offset lines with the horizontal offset lines.

7. Erase the center vertical line. You have finished the wide flange beam.

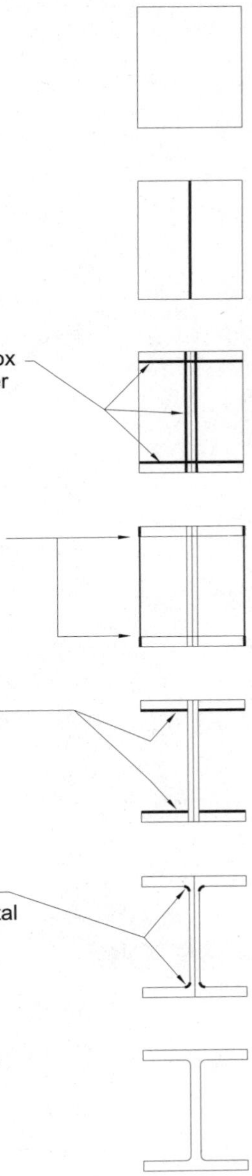

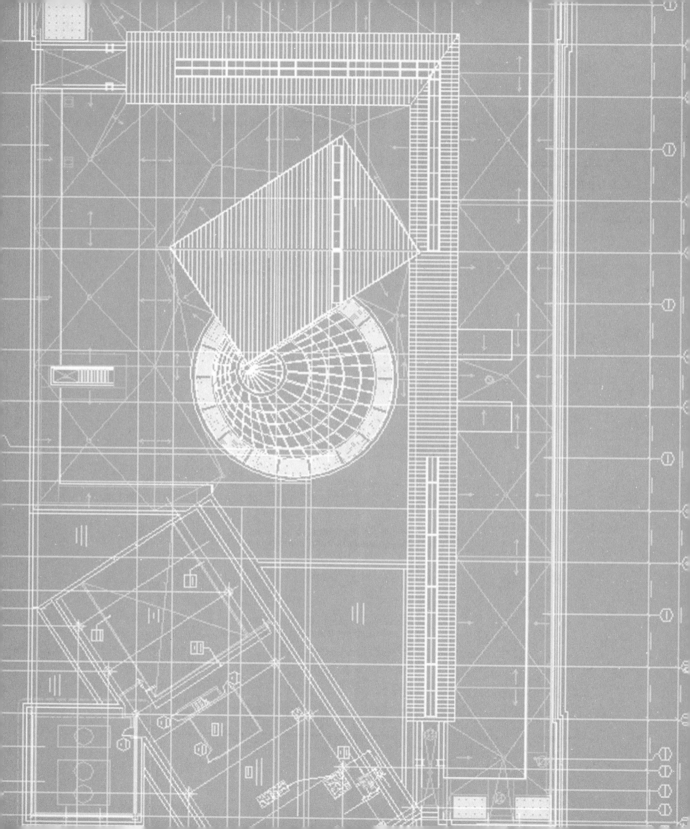

CHAPTER
FOUR

Organizing Your Work

- Creating a Symbol

- Inserting a Symbol

- Modifying a Block

- Organizing Information with Layers

- Keeping Track of Blocks and Layers

- Finding Files on Your Hard Disk

- Inserting Symbols with Drag and Drop

- If You Want to Experiment...

4

Drawing the tub and toilet in Chapter 3 may have taken what seemed to you an inordinate amount of time. As you continue to use AutoCAD, however, you will learn to draw objects more quickly. You will also need to draw fewer of them because you can save drawings as symbols to be used like rubber stamps, duplicating drawings instantaneously wherever they are needed. This saves you a lot of time when you're composing drawings.

To make effective use of AutoCAD, you should begin a *symbols library* of drawings you use frequently. A mechanical designer might have a library of symbols for fasteners, cams, valves, or any type of parts for his or her application. An electrical engineer might have a symbols library of capacitors, resistors, switches, and the like. A circuit designer will have yet another unique set of frequently used symbols. This book's companion CD-ROM contains a variety of ready-to-use symbols libraries. Check them out—you're likely to find some you can use.

In Chapter 3, you drew two objects—a bathtub and a toilet—that architects often use. In this chapter, you will see how to create symbols from those drawings. You will also learn about layers and how you can use them to organize information.

Symbols for Projects Large and Small

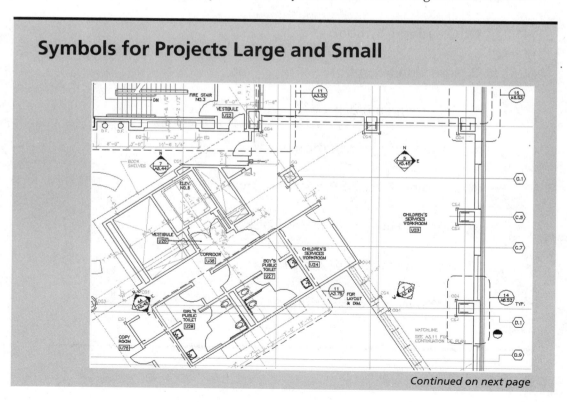

Continued on next page

A symbols library was a crucial part of the production of the San Francisco Main Library construction documents. Shown here is a portion of an AutoCAD floor plan of the library where some typical symbols were used.

Notice the familiar door symbols, like the door you created in Chapter 2. And yes, there are even toilets in the lower half of the plan in the public restrooms. The method for drawing the wide flange demonstrated at the end of Chapter 3 is similar to the one that was used to create the I-beam column symbols shown here.

Symbol use isn't restricted to the building components. Room number labels, diamond-shaped interior elevation reference symbols, and the hexagonal column grid symbols are all common to an architectural drawing, regardless of the project's size. As you work through this chapter, keep in mind that all of the symbols used in the library drawings were created using the tools presented here.

Creating a Symbol

To save a drawing as a symbol, you use the Block tool. In word processors, the term *block* refers to a group of words or sentences selected for moving, saving, or deletion. A block of text can be copied elsewhere within the same file, to other files, or to a separate file on disk for future use. AutoCAD uses blocks in a similar fashion. Within a file, you can turn parts of your drawing into blocks that can be saved and recalled at any time. You can also use entire existing files as blocks.

1. Start AutoCAD and open the existing Bath file. Use the one you created in Chapter 3 or open 04-BATH.dwg on the companion CD-ROM. The drawing appears just as you left it in the last session.

2. In the Draw toolbar, click the Make Block tool or type **B↵**, the keyboard shortcut for the Make Block tool.

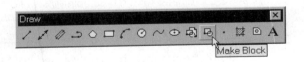

CMK

The Block Definition dialog box appears.

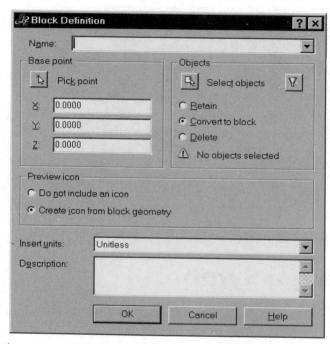

3. Type **Toilet**↵ into the Name input box.

   cmk

4. In the Base Point button group of the dialog box, click the Pick Point button. This option enables you to select a base point for the block using your cursor. (The insertion base point of a block is similar to the base point you used as a handle on an object in Chapter 2.) When you've selected this option, the Block Definition dialog box temporarily disappears.

5. Using the Midpoint Osnap, pick the midpoint of the back of the toilet as the base point. Remember that you learned how to set up some Running Osnaps in Chapter 3; all you need to do is point to the midpoint of a line to display the Midpoint Osnap marker, and then left-click your mouse. Once you've selected a point, the Block Definition dialog box reappears. Notice that the *x,*

y, and z values in the Base Point button group now display the coordinates of the point you picked.

6. Next, you need to select the actual objects that you want as part of the block. Click the Select Objects button in the Objects button group. Once again, the dialog box momentarily disappears. You now see the familiar object selection prompt in the Command window and the cursor becomes an object selection cursor. Click a point below and to the left of the toilet. Then window the entire toilet. The toilet is now highlighted.

WARNING Make sure you use the Select Objects option in the Block Definition dialog box to select the objects you want to turn into a block. AutoCAD lets you create a block that contains no objects. This can cause some confusion and frustration, even for an experienced user.

---

7. Press ↵ to confirm your selection. The Block Definition dialog box appears again.

8. Select Inches from the Insert Units drop-down list. Metric users should select Centimeters.

9. Click the Description list box and enter **Standard Toilet**.

10. Make sure the Retain radio button in the Objects button group is checked, and then click OK. The toilet drawing is now a block with the name Toilet.

11. Repeat the blocking process for the tub, but this time use the upper-left corner of the tub as the insertion base point and give the block the name Tub. Enter **Standard Tub** for the description.

NOTE You can press ↵ or right-click the mouse and select Repeat Make Block from the popup menu to start the Make Block tool again.

When you turn an object into a block, it is stored within the drawing file, ready to be recalled at any time. The block remains part of the drawing file even when you end the editing session. When you open the file again, the block will be available for your use. In addition, you can access blocks from other drawings using a feature called the AutoCAD DesignCenter. You'll learn more about the DesignCenter later in Chapter 22.

A block acts like a single object, even though it is really made up of several objects. One unique characteristic of a block is that when you modify a block, all instances of that block are updated to reflect the modifications. For example, you can insert several copies of the toilet into a drawing, then later, if you decide the toilet needs to be of a different shape, you can edit the Toilet block and all of the other copies of the toilet are updated automatically.

In earlier versions of AutoCAD, you had to redraw a block and then redefine the block using the steps in the previous exercise. AutoCAD 2000 offers a new, easier way to make changes to blocks called In-Place Xref and Block Edit. You'll learn more about this feature later in this chapter.

Restoring Objects That Have Been Removed by the Make Block Tool or the Block Command

In prior versions of AutoCAD, the Block command was the only command available to create blocks. This is a command-line version of the Make Block tool and is still available to those users who are more comfortable entering commands via the keyboard. To use it, you must enter the word **Block** preceded by a minus sign at the command prompt, as in **–Block**. When you use the Block command, the objects you turn into a block automatically disappear. AutoCAD's Block tool (Bmake) gives you the option of removing or maintaining the block's source objects by way of the Retain option, shown in step 10 of the previous exercise.

If you use the Block command, or if for some reason you leave the Retain option unchecked in the Block Definition dialog box, the source objects you select for the block disappear. You can restore the source using the Oops command. Oops can also be used in any situation where you want to restore an object you accidentally erased. To use it, simply type **OOPS↵** in the Command window. The source objects reappears in their former condition and location, not as a block.

Understanding the Block Definition Dialog Box

The Block Definition dialog box offers several options that can help make the use of blocks easier. If you're interested in these options, take a moment to review the Block Definition dialog box in step 2 of the previous exercise as you read the descriptions of the dialog box options. Or if you prefer, you can continue with the tutorial and come back to this section later.

You've already seen how the Name option of the Block Definition dialog box lets you enter a name for your block. AutoCAD does not let you complete the block creation until you enter a name.

You've also seen how to select a base point for your block. The base point is like the handle of the block. It is the reference point you use when you insert the block back into the drawing. In the exercise, you used the Pick Point option to indicate a base point, but you also have the option to enter x, y, and z-coordinates just below the Pick Point option. In most cases, however, you will want to use the Pick Point option to indicate a base point that is on or near the set of objects you are converting to a block.

The Objects button group of the Block Definition dialog box lets you select the objects that make up the block. You use the Select Objects button to visually select the objects you want to include in the block you are creating. The Quick Select button to the right of the Select Objects button lets you filter out objects based on their properties. You'll learn more about this tool later in Chapter 12.

Other options in the Objects button group allow you to determine what to do with the objects you are selecting for your block. Here is a listing of the options and what they mean:

Retain   Keeps the objects you select for your block as they are, unchanged.

Convert to block   Converts the objects you select into the block you are defining. It then acts like a single object once you've completed the Block command.

Delete   Deletes the objects you selected for your block. This is what AutoCAD did in earlier versions. You might also notice that a warning message appears at the bottom of the Objects button group. This warning tells you if you've selected objects for the block. Once you've selected objects, this warning changes to tell you how many objects you've selected.

The Preview Icon options let you control whether a preview image is stored with the block or not. This option is new in AutoCAD 2000 and it lets you easily locate and identify blocks in a drawing. You can, for example, peek into another drawing file without actually opening the file, and browse through the blocks that are contained in that file.

The Insert Units option lets you determine how the object is to be scaled when it is inserted into the drawing. By default, this value will be the same as the current drawing's insert value.

The Description input box lets you include a brief verbal description or keyword for the block. This option is helpful when you need to find a specific block in a set of drawings. You'll learn more about searching for blocks later in this chapter and in Chapter 22.

Inserting a Symbol

The Tub and Toilet blocks can be recalled at any time, as many times as you want. In the following exercise, you'll first draw the interior walls of the bathroom and then insert the tub and toilet.

1. First, delete the original tub and toilet drawings. Click the Erase tool in the Modify toolbar, then enter **All**.↵↵. This erases the entire visible contents of the drawing. (It has no effect on the blocks you created previously.)

2. Draw a rectangle 5' × 7'-6". Metric users should draw a 152cm × 228cm rectangle. Orient the rectangle so the long sides go from left to right and the lower-left corner is at coordinate 1'-10",1'-10" (or coordinate 56.0000,56.0000 for metric users). If you draw the rectangle using the Rectangle tool, make sure you explode it using the Explode tool. This is important for later exercises. Your drawing should now look like Figure 4.1.

FIGURE 4.1:

The interior walls of the bathroom

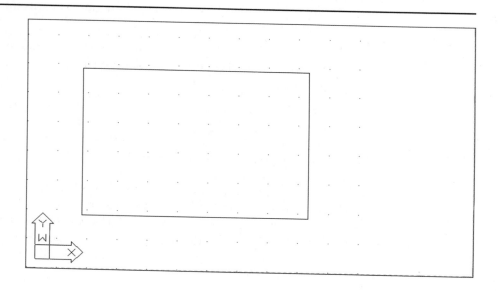

> **NOTE** The Insert Block tool can also be found in the Insert toolbar. The Insert toolbar can be opened using the Toolbars dialog box. To open the Toolbars dialog box, right-click any open toolbar, or choose Insert.

3.   In the Draw toolbar, click the Insert Block tool or type **I⤶**.

The Insert dialog box appears.

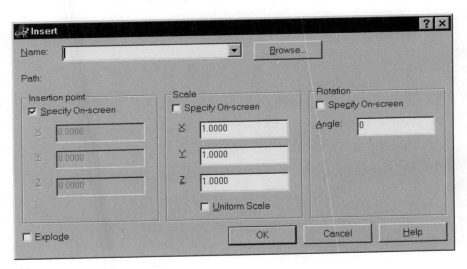

4.   Click the Name drop-down list at the top of the dialog box. A list of the available blocks in the current drawing appears.

5.   Click the block name TUB.

6.   In the Rotation button group on the right side of the dialog box, click the Specify On-Screen check box. This option allows you to graphically specify the rotation angle of the block as you insert it.

7.   Click OK and you see a preview image of the tub attached to the cursor. The upper-left corner you picked for the tub's base point is now on the cursor intersection.

8. At the Specify insertion point: prompt, pick the upper-left intersection of the room as your insertion point. Once you've picked the insertion point, notice that as you move your cursor, the preview image of the tub appears distorted.

9. At the Specify rotation angle <0>: prompt, notice that you can rotate the block. This lets you visually specify a rotation angle for the block. You won't actually use this feature at this time so press ↵ to accept the default of 0. You should have a drawing that looks like the top image of Figure 4.2.

FIGURE 4.2:

The bathroom, first with the tub and then with the toilet inserted

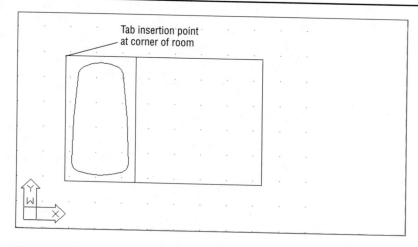

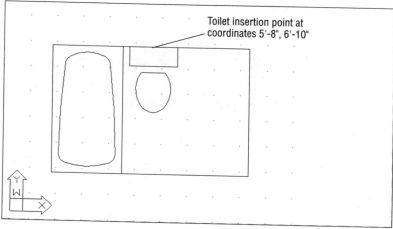

CASEY RIGHT

10. Open the Insert dialog box again but this time, select TOILET in the Name drop-down list.

11. Remove the check next to the Specify On-Screen option in the Rotation button group of the dialog box.

5'7 not 5'8

12. Place the toilet at the midpoint of the line along the top of the rectangle representing the bathroom wall as shown in the bottom image of Figure 4.2. Notice that once you select the insertion point, the toilet appears in the drawing; you are not prompted for a rotation angle for the block.

Scaling and Rotating Blocks

In step 8, you can see the tub rotate as you move the cursor. You can pick a point to fix the block in place, or you can enter a rotation value. This was the result of selecting the Specify On-Screen option in the Insert dialog box. You may find that you want the Rotation's Specify On-Screen option turned on most of the time to allow you to adjust the rotation angle of the block while you are placing it in the drawing.

You aren't limited to scaling or rotating a block when it is being inserted into a drawing. You can always use the Scale or Rotate tools, or modify an inserted block's properties to stretch it in one direction or another. You'll learn about modifying a block's properties later in this chapter.

The other options in the Insert dialog box that you did not use are the Scale button group options. These options let you scale the block to a different size. You can scale the block uniformly, or you can distort the block by individually changing its X, Y, or Z scale factor. With the Specify On-Screen option unchecked, you can enter specific values in the X, Y, and Z input boxes to stretch the block in any direction. If you turn on the Specify On-Screen option, you'll be able to visually adjust the X, Y, and Z scale factors in real time. While these options are not used often, they can be useful in special situations, where a block needs to be stretched one way or another to fit in a drawing

Using an Existing Drawing as a Symbol

Now you need a door into the bathroom. Since you have already drawn a door and saved it as a file, you can bring the door into this drawing file and use it as a block.

1. In the Draw toolbar, click the Insert Block tool or type **I↵**.

2. In the Insert dialog box, click the Browse button at the top of the dialog box. The Select Drawing File dialog box appears.

3. Locate the Door file and double-click it. You may need to go to a different drive and folder from the default folder shown in the Select Drawing File dialog box.

4. When you return to the Insert dialog box, make sure the Specify On-Screen options for the Scale and Rotation button groups are checked, then click OK. As you move the cursor around, notice that the door appears above and to the right of the cursor intersection, as in Figure 4.3.

5. At this point, the door looks too small for this bathroom. This is because you drew it 3 units long, which translates to 3". Metric users drew the door 9cm long. Pick a point near coordinates 7'-2",2'-4", so that the door is placed in the lower-right corner of the room. Metric users should use the coordinate 210,70.

6. If you take the default setting for the X scale of the inserted block, the door will remain 3" long or 9cm long for metric users. However, as mentioned earlier, you can specify a smaller or larger size for an inserted object. In this case, you want a 3' door. Metric users want a 90cm door To get that from a 3" door, you need an X scale factor of 12 or 10 for metric users. (You may want to look again at Table 3.3 in Chapter 3 to see how this is determined.) Enter 12.↵ now, at the X scale factor prompt. Metric users should enter 10.↵.

7. Press ↵ twice to accept the default y = x and the rotation angle of 0°.

FIGURE 4.3:

The door drawing being inserted in the Bath file

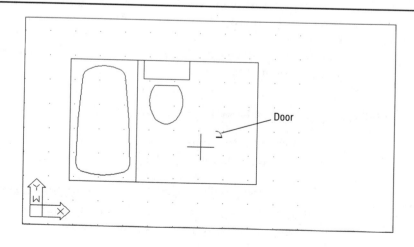

Now the command prompt appears, but nothing seems to happen to the drawing. This is because when you enlarged the door, you also enlarged the distance between the base point and the object. This brings up another issue to be aware of when you're considering using drawings as symbols: All drawings have base points. The default base point is the absolute coordinate 0,0, otherwise known as the *origin*, which is located in the lower-left corner of any new drawing. When you drew the door in Chapter 2, you didn't specify the base point. So when you try to bring the door into this drawing, AutoCAD uses the origin of the door drawing as its base point (see Figure 4.4).

FIGURE 4.4:

By default, a drawing's origin is also its insertion point. You can change a drawing's insertion point using the Base command.

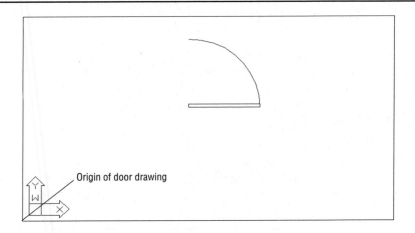

Origin of door drawing

Because the door appears outside the bathroom, you must first use the Zoom ➢ All option to show more of the drawing, and then the Move command on the Modify toolbar to move the door to the right-side wall of the bathroom. Let's do this now.

1. Click View ➢ Zoom ➢ All from the menu bar pull-down menu. Zoom All displays the area set by the limits of your drawing (Format ➢ Drawing Limits), plus any other objects that may be outside those limits. The view of the room shrinks away and the door is revealed. Notice that it is now the proper size for your drawing (see Figure 4.5).

2. Choose Move from the Modify toolbar, or type **M↵**.

3. To pick the door you just inserted, at the `Select objects:` prompt, click a point anywhere on the door and press ↵. Notice that now the entire door is highlighted. This is because a block is treated like a single object, even though it may be made up of several lines, arcs, and so on.

4. At the Specify base point: prompt, turn the Running Osnaps back on and pick the lower-left corner of the door. Remember that pressing the F3 function key or double-clicking the word OSNAP in the status bar toggles the Running Osnaps on or off.

5. At the Second point: prompt, use the Nearest Osnap override, and position the door so your drawing looks like Figure 4.6.

FIGURE 4.5:

The enlarged door

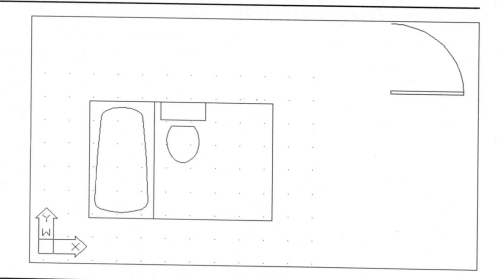

FIGURE 4.6:

The door on the right side wall of the bathroom

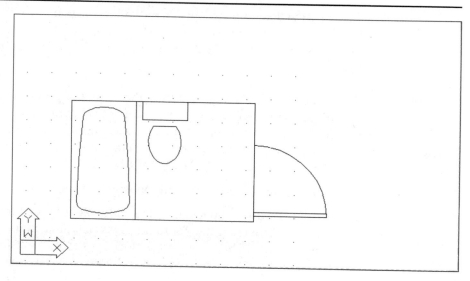

Because the door is an object you will use often, it should be a common size so you don't have to specify an odd value every time you insert it. It would also be helpful if the door's insertion base point were in a more convenient location, that is, a location that would allow you to place the door accurately within a wall opening. Next, you will modify the Door block to better suit your needs.

Modifying a Block

There are actually two ways in which you can modify a block. One way is to completely redefine the block. Before AutoCAD 2000, this was the only way to make changes to a block. A second method for modifying blocks is to use the Reference Edit tool, which is new in AutoCAD 2000. The Reference Edit tool lets you quickly modify a block in its existing location. Reference Edit offers more flexibility when editing blocks and another type of object called an *Xref*, but it also has a few limitations. In this chapter, you'll learn how to redefine a block by making changes to the door symbol. Later, in Chapter 6, you'll see how the Reference Edit tool allows you to quickly modify a block that will then affect other copies of the block throughout a drawing.

Unblocking and Redefining a Block

To modify a block, you break it down into its components, edit them, and then turn them back into a block. This is called *redefining* a block. If you redefine a block that has been inserted in a drawing, each occurrence of that block within the current file changes to reflect the new block definition. You can use this block redefinition feature to make rapid changes to a design.

TIP   If the Regenauto setting is turned off, you have to issue a Regen command to see changes made to redefined blocks. See Chapter 6 for more on Regenauto.

To separate a block into its components, use the Explode command.

1. Choose Explode from the Modify toolbar. You can also type **X**↵ to start the Explode command.

2. Click the door and press ⏎ to confirm your selection.

TIP You can simultaneously insert and explode a block by clicking the Explode check box in the lower-left corner of the Insert dialog box.

Now you can edit the individual objects that make up the door, if you so desire. In this case, you only want to change the door's insertion point because you have already made it a more convenient size. So now you'll turn the door back into a block, this time using the door's lower-left corner for its insertion base point.

3. In the Draw toolbar, select Make Block or type **B**⏎.

4. In the Block Definition dialog box, select the name Door from the Name drop-down list.

5. Click the Pick Point button and pick the lower-left corner of the door.

6. Click the Select Objects button and select the components of the door. Press ⏎ when you've finished making your selection.

7. Select the Convert to Block option in the Objects button group. This automatically converts the selected objects into a block.

8. Select Inches from the Insert Units drop-down list, then enter **Standard door** in the Description list box.

9. Now click OK. You see a warning message that reads DOOR is already defined. Do you want to re-define it? You don't want to accidentally redefine an existing block. In this case, you know you want to redefine the door, so click the Yes button to proceed.

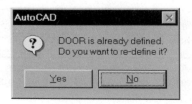

10. Choose Erase from the Modify toolbar, then click the door. Notice that the entire door is one object instead of individual lines and an arc. Had you not selected the Convert to Block option in step 7, the components of the block would have remained as individual objects.

11. Now insert the door block again using the Block button in the Insert dialog box. This time, however, use the Nearest Osnap override and pick a point on the right-side wall of the bathroom, near coordinate 9'-4",2'-1". *Presisely*

12. Use the Grips feature to mirror the door, using the wall as the mirror axis so that the door is inside the room. Your drawing will look like Figure 4.7.

TIP   To mirror an object using grips, first be sure that the Grips feature is on. Select the objects to mirror, click a grip, and then press the right mouse button. Select Mirror from the popup list that appears; then indicate a mirror axis with the cursor.

FIGURE 4.7:

The bathroom floor plan thus far

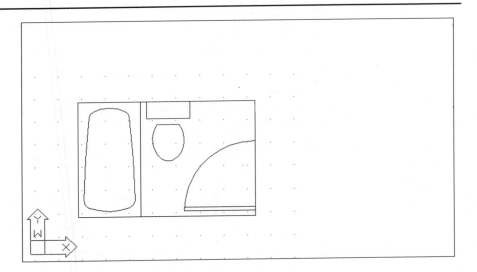

In step 9, you received a warning message telling you that you were about to redefine the existing door block. But you inserted the door as a file, not as a block. Whenever you insert a drawing file using the Insert Block tool, the drawing automatically becomes a block in the current drawing. When you redefine a block, however, you do not affect the drawing file you imported. AutoCAD only changes the block within the current file. Next, you'll see how you can update an external file with a redefined block.

TIP   The Select Object and Select Point buttons appear in other dialog boxes. Make note of their appearance and remember that when you select them, the dialog box temporarily disappears to allow you to select points or objects, and otherwise perform operations that require a clear view of the drawing area.

Saving a Block as a Drawing File

You've seen that, with very little effort, you can create a symbol that can be placed anywhere in a file. Suppose you want to use this symbol in other files. When you create a block using the Block command, the block exists within the current file only until you specifically instruct AutoCAD to save it as a drawing file on disk. For an existing drawing that has been brought in and modified, such as the door, the drawing file on disk associated with that door is not automatically updated. To update the Door file, you must take an extra step and use the Export option on the File menu. Let's see how this works.

TIP AutoCAD 2000 allows you to extract blocks that are embedded in other drawings by using a new feature called the DesignCenter. See *Exchanging Data Between Open Files* in Chapter 22.

Start by turning the Tub and Toilet blocks into individual files on disk.

1. Click File ➤ Export. The Export Data dialog box opens. This dialog box is a simple file dialog box.

2. Open the List Files of Type drop-down list and select Block (*.dwg).

TIP If you prefer, you can skip step 2, and instead, in step 3, enter the full filename, including the .dwg extension, as in Tub.dwg.

---

3. Double-click the File Name input box and enter **Tub**.

4. Click the Save button. The dialog box closes.

5. At the [= (block=output file)/* (whole drawing)] <define new drawing>: prompt, enter the name of the block you wish to save to disk as the tub file—in this case, also **Tub**. The Tub block is now saved as a file.

6. Repeat steps 1 through 3 for the Toilet block. Give the file the same name as the block.

NOTE AutoCAD gives you the option to save a block's file under the same name as the original block or with a different name. Usually you will want to use the same name, which you can do by entering an equal sign (=) after the prompt.

NOTE   Normally, AutoCAD saves a preview image with a file. This allows you to preview a drawing file prior to opening it. Preview images are not included with files that are exported with the File ➢ Export option or the Wblock command, which is discussed in the next section.

Replacing Existing Files with Blocks

The Wblock command does the same thing as File ➢ Export, but output is limited to AutoCAD *.dwg files. (Veteran AutoCAD users should note that Wblock is now incorporated into the File ➢ Export option.) Let's try using the Wblock command this time to save the Door block you modified.

1. Issue the Wblock command by typing **Wblock**↵, or use the keyboard shortcut by typing **w**↵. The Write Block dialog box appears.

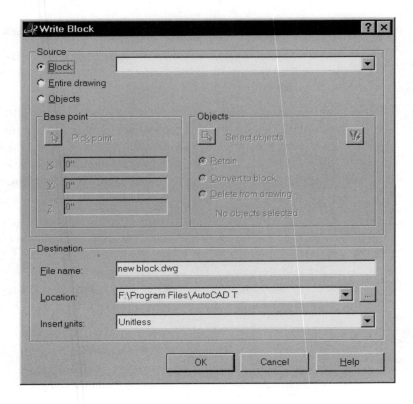

2. In the Source button group, click the Block radio button.

3. Next, select Door from the drop-down list. Notice that the options under the Destination button group change to reflect the location of the old `Door.dwg` file from which the Door block was originally inserted. You can keep the old name or enter a different name if you prefer.

4. In this case, you want to update the door you drew in Chapter 2, so click OK.

5. You'll see a warning message telling you that the `Door.dwg` file already exists. Go ahead and click Yes to confirm that you want to overwrite the old door drawing with the new door definition.

In this exercise, you typed the Wblock command at the command prompt instead of using File ➤ Export. The results are the same, regardless of which method you use. If you are in a hurry, the File ➤ Export command is a quick way to save part of your drawing as a file. The Wblock option may be easier for new users to use since it offers options in a dialog box.

Understanding the Write Block Dialog Box Options

The Write Block dialog box offers a way to save parts of your current drawing as a file. As you can see from the dialog box shown in step 1 of the previous exercise, you have several options to work with.

In the previous exercise, you used the Block option of the Source button group to select an existing block as the source object to be exported. You can also export a set of objects by choosing the Objects option. If you choose this option, the Base Point and Objects button groups become available. These options work the same way as their counterparts in the Block Definition dialog box that you saw earlier when you created the Tub and Toilet blocks.

The third option in the Source button group, Entire Drawing, lets you export the whole drawing to its own file. This may seem to duplicate the File ➤ Save As option in the menu bar, but saving the entire drawing from the Write Block dialog box actually performs some additional operations, such as stripping out unused blocks or other unused components. This has the effect of reducing file size. You'll learn more about this feature later in this chapter.

Other Uses for Blocks

So far, you have used the Make Block tool to create symbols, and the Export and Wblock commands to save those symbols to disk. As you can see, symbols can be created and saved at any time while you are drawing. You have made the tub and toilet symbols into drawing files that you can see when you check the contents of your current directory.

However, creating symbols is not the only use for the Insert Block, Block, Export, and Wblock commands. You can use them in any situation that requires grouping objects (though you may prefer to use the more flexible Object Group command discussed in the next section). You can also use blocks to stretch a set of objects along one axis. Export and Wblock also allow you to save a part of a drawing to disk. You will see instances of these other uses of the Block, Export, and Wblock commands throughout Chapters 5–8 and in Chapter 12.

Make Block, Export, and Wblock are extremely versatile commands and, if used judiciously, can boost your productivity and simplify your work. If you are not careful, however, you can also get carried away and create more blocks than you can keep track of. Planning your drawings helps you determine which elements will work best as blocks, and to recognize situations where other methods of organization will be more suitable.

An Alternative to Blocks

Another way to create symbols is by creating shapes. Shapes are special objects made up of lines, arcs, and circles. They can regenerate faster than blocks and they take up less file space. Unfortunately, shapes are considerably more difficult to create and less flexible to use than blocks.

You create shapes by using a coding system developed by Autodesk. The codes define the sizes and orientations of lines, arcs, and circles. You first sketch your shape, convert it into the code, and then copy that code into a DOS text file. You can also use the Make Shape Express tool described in Chapter 19 to create a shape from an AutoCAD drawing. This book doesn't go into detail on this subject, so if you want to know more about shapes, see your *AutoCAD Customization Manual*.

Another way of using symbols is to use AutoCAD's external reference capabilities. External referenced files, known as Xrefs, are files inserted into a drawing in a way similar to blocks. The difference is that Xrefs do not actually become part of the drawing's database. Instead, they are loaded along with the current file at startup time. It is as if AutoCAD opens several drawings at once: the main file you specify when you start AutoCAD, and the Xrefs associated with the main file.

By keeping the Xrefs independent from the current file, you make sure that any changes made to the Xrefs automatically appear in the current file. You don't have to update the Xrefs, as you must for blocks. For example, if you use the External Reference option on the Reference toolbar (discussed in Chapter 12) to insert the Tub drawing, and later you make changes to the tub, the next time you open the Bath file, you will see the new version of the tub.

Xrefs are especially useful in workgroup environments, where several people are working on the same project. One person might be updating several files that have been inserted into a variety of other files. Before Xrefs were available, everyone in the workgroup had to be notified of the changes and had to update all the affected blocks in all the drawings that contained them. With Xrefs, the updating is automatic. There are many other features unique to these files, discussed in more detail in Chapters 6 and 12.

Grouping Objects

Blocks are an extremely useful tool, but for some situations, they are too restricting. At times, you will want to group objects together so they are connected, yet can still be edited individually. For example, consider a space planner who has to place workstations in a floor plan. Though each workstation is basically the same, there may be some slight variations in each station that would make the use of blocks unwieldy. For instance, one workstation may need a different configuration to accommodate special equipment while another workstation may need to be slightly larger than the standard size. A better way is to draw a prototype workstation and then turn it into a group. The group can be copied into position, then edited for each individual situation, without the group losing its identity as a group. The following exercises demonstrate how this works.

1. Open the drawing named `office1.dwg` from the companion CD-ROM.

2. Use the Zoom command to enlarge just the view of the workstation, as shown in the top image of Figure 4.8.

3. Type G (↵) or Group (↵) to start the Group command. The Object Grouping dialog box appears.

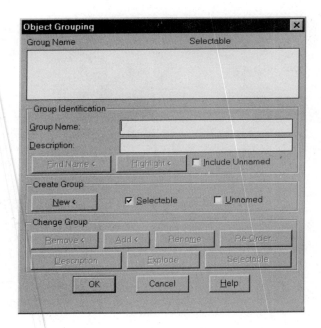

4. Type **Station1**. As you type, your entry appears in the Group Name input box.

5. Click New in the Create Group button group, about midway in the dialog box. The dialog box temporarily disappears to allow you to select objects for your new group.

6. At the `Select objects:` prompt, window the entire workstation and press ↵. The Object Grouping dialog box returns. Notice that the name `Station1` appears in the Group Name list box at the top of the dialog box.

7. Click OK. You have just created a group.

Now, whenever you want to select the workstation, you can click any part of it and the entire group is selected. At the same time, you can still modify individual parts of the group—the desk, partition, and so on—without losing the grouping of objects.

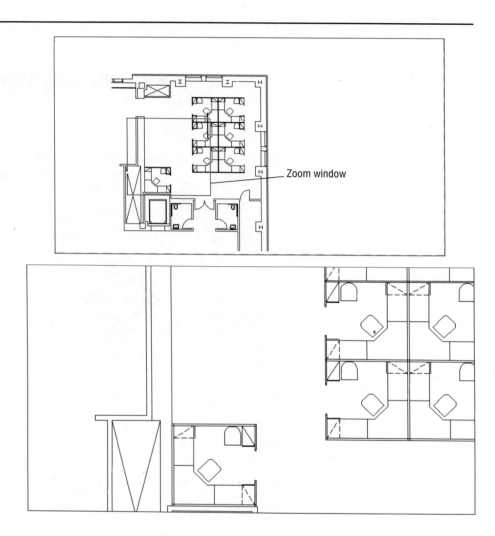

Zoom window

Modifying Members of a Group

Next, you will make copies of the original group and modify the copies. Figure 4.9 is a sketch of the proposed layout that uses the new workstations. Look carefully and you'll see that some of the workstations in the sketch are missing a few of the standard components that exist in the Station1 group. One pair of stations has a partition removed; another station has no desk.

FIGURE 4.9:

A sketch of the new office layout

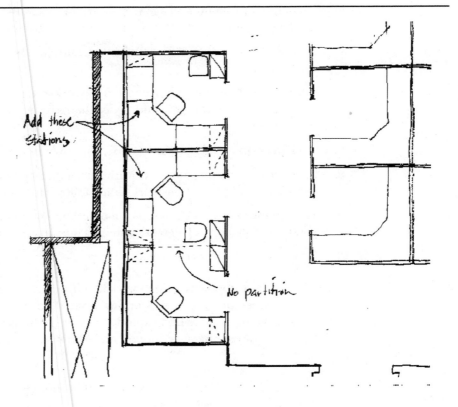

This next exercise shows you how to complete your drawing to reflect the design requirements of the sketch.

1. Click Copy on the Modify toolbar or type **Co**↵, and click the Station1 group you just created. Notice that you can click any part of the station to select the entire station. If only a single object is selected, press Ctrl-A and try clicking another part of the group.

2. Press ↵ to finish your selection.

3. At the `Base point:` prompt, enter **@**↵. Then enter **@8'2"<90** to copy the workstation 8 feet, 2 inches vertically. Metric users should enter **@249<90**.

| TIP | In step 3, you can also use the Direct Distance method by typing **@**↵, then pointing the rubber-banding line 90 degrees and typing **8'2"**↵. |

4. Issue the Copy command again, but this time click the copy of the workstation you just created. Notice that it, too, is a group.

5. Copy this workstation 8'2" (249cm) vertically, just as you did the original workstation.

6. Next, you'll use grips to mirror the first workstation copy. Click the middle workstation to highlight it, and notice that grips appear for all the entities in the group.

7. Click the grip in the middle-left side, as shown in Figure 4.10.

8. Right-click the mouse and select Mirror from the popup list. Notice that a temporary mirror image of the workstation follows the movement of your cursor.

9. Turn on the Ortho mode and pick a point directly to the right of the hot grip you picked in step 7. The workstation is mirrored to a new orientation.

10. Press the Esc key twice to clear the grip selection.

Now that you've got the workstations laid out, you need to remove some of the partitions between the new workstations. If you had used blocks for the workstations, you would have to first explode the workstations whose partitions you wish to edit. Groups, however, let you make changes without undoing their grouping.

1. Press Ctrl+A. This temporarily turns off groupings. You'll see the message <Group off> in the Command window.

2. Using a window, erase the short partition that divides the two copies of the workstations, as shown in Figure 4.11.

3. Press Ctrl+A again to turn groupings back on. You'll see the message <Group on> in the Command window.

4. To check your workstations, click one of them to see if all of its components are highlighted together.

TIP   You can also use the Pickstyle system variable to control groupings. See Appendix D for more information on Pickstyle.

FIGURE 4.10:

Mirroring the new group using grips

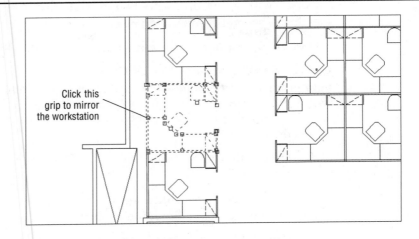

Click this grip to mirror the workstation

FIGURE 4.11:

Remove the partitions between the two workstations.

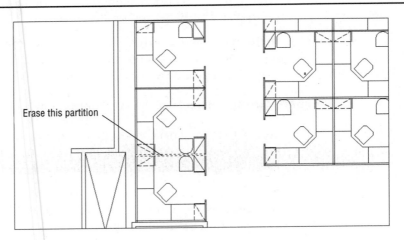

Erase this partition

Working with the Object Grouping Dialog Box

Each group has a unique name, and you can also attach a brief description of the group in the Object Grouping dialog box. When you copy a group, AutoCAD assigns an arbitrary name to the newly created group. Copies of groups are considered unnamed, but can still be listed in the Object Grouping dialog box by clicking the Unnamed check box. You can use the Rename button in the Object Grouping dialog box to rename unnamed groups appropriately.

Objects within a group are not bound solely to that group. One object can be a member of several groups, and you can have nested groups.

Here are descriptions of the options available in the Object Grouping dialog box:

Group Identification   Use the Group Identification button group to identify your groups, using unique elements that let you remember what each group is for.

> **Group Name**   This input box lets you create a new group by naming it first.
>
> **Description**   This input box lets you include a brief description of the group.
>
> **Find Name**   This button lets you find the name of a group by temporarily closing the Object Grouping dialog box so you can click a group.
>
> **Highlight**   This button highlights a group that has been selected from the group list. This helps you locate a group in a crowded drawing.
>
> **Include Unnamed**   This check box determines whether unnamed groups are included in the Group Name list. Check this box to display the names of copies of groups for processing by this dialog box.

Create Group   Here's where you control how a group is created.

> **New**   Lets you create a new group. It temporarily closes the dialog box so you can select objects for grouping. To use this button, you must have either entered a group name or checked the Unnamed check box.
>
> **Selectable**   This check box lets you control whether the group you create is selectable or not. See the description of the Selectable button in the Change Group button group just below.
>
> **Unnamed**   This check box lets you create a new group without naming it.

Change Group   These buttons are available only when a group name is highlighted in the Group Name list at the top of the dialog box.

> **Remove**   Lets you remove objects from a group.
>
> **Add**   Lets you add objects to a group. While using this option, grouping is temporarily turned off to allow you to select objects from other groups.
>
> **Rename**   Lets you rename a group.
>
> **Reorder**   Lets you change the order of objects in a group.

Description   Lets you modify the description of a group.

Explode   Separates a group into its individual components.

Selectable   Turns individual groupings on and off. When a group is selectable, it is selectable as a group. When a group is not selectable, the individual objects in a group can be selected, but not the group.

Organizing Information with Layers

Another tool for organization is the *layer*. Layers are like overlays on which you keep various types of information (see Figure 4.12). In a floor plan of a building, for example, you want to keep the walls, ceiling, plumbing fixtures, wiring, and furniture separate, so you can display or plot them individually or combine them in different ways. It's also a good idea to keep notes and reference symbols about each element of the drawing, as well as the drawing's dimensions, on their own layers. As your drawing becomes more complex, the various layers can be turned on and off to allow easier display and modification.

For example, one of your consultants may need a plot of just the dimensions and walls, without all the other information; another consultant may need only a furniture layout. Using manual drafting, you would have to redraw your plan for each consultant. With AutoCAD, you can turn off the layers you don't need and plot a drawing containing only the required information. A carefully planned layering scheme helps you produce a document that combines the different types of information needed in each case.

Using layers also enables you to modify your drawings more easily. For example, suppose you have an architectural drawing with separate layers for the walls, the ceiling plan, and the floor plan. If any change occurs in the wall locations, you can turn on the ceiling plan layer to see where the new wall locations will affect the ceiling, and then make the proper adjustments.

AutoCAD allows an unlimited number of layers, and you can name each layer anything you want.

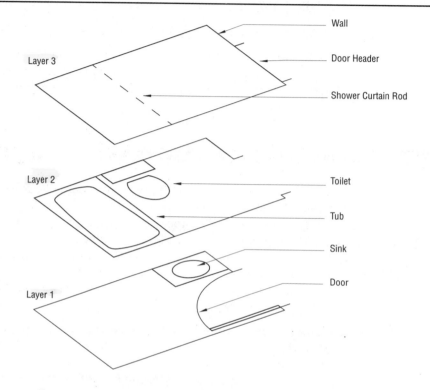

FIGURE 4.12:

A comparison of layers and overlays

Wall

Door Header

Shower Curtain Rod

Toilet

Tub

Sink

Door

Layer 3

Layer 2

Layer 1

Creating and Assigning Layers

To continue with your bathroom, you will create some new layers.

1. Open the Bath file you created earlier in this chapter. If you didn't create one, use the file 04b-bath.dwg from the companion CD-ROM.

2. To display the Layer Properties Manager dialog box, click the Layers tool in the Properties toolbar, or choose Format ➤ Layers from the pull-down menu. You can also type **LA↵** to use the keyboard shortcut.

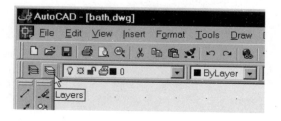

Getting Multiple Uses from a Drawing Using Layers

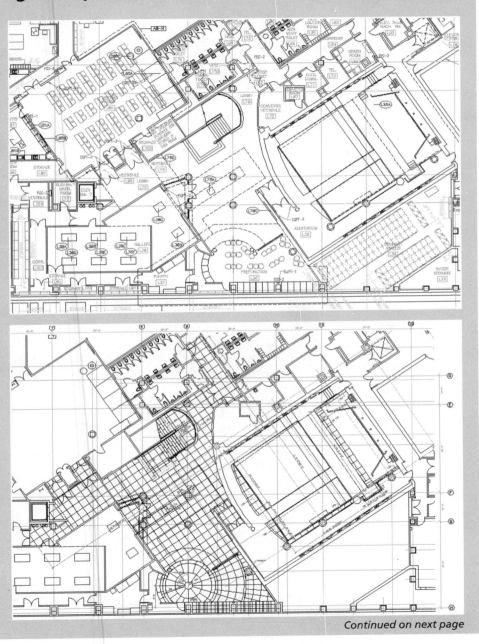

Continued on next page

Layering allows you to use a single AutoCAD drawing for multiple purposes. A single drawing may serve to show both the general layout of the plan and more detailed information such as equipment layout or floor paving layout.

These two reproductions of the San Francisco Main Library's lower level show how one floor plan file was used for two different purposes. The top view shows the layout of furnishings and the bottom view shows a paving layout. In each case, the same floor plan file was used, but in the upper panel, the paving information is on a layer that is turned off. Layers also facilitate the use of differing scales in the same drawing. Frequently, a small-scale drawing of an overall plan will contain the same data for an enlarged view of other portions of the plan, such as a stairwell or elevator core. The detailed information, such as notes and dimensions, may be on a layer that is turned off for the overall plan.

NOTE
The Layer Properties Manager dialog box shows you at a glance the status of your layers. Right now, you only have one layer, but as your work expands, so will the number of layers. You will then find this dialog box indispensable.

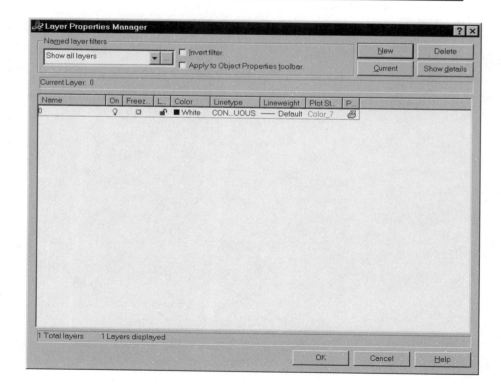

3. Click the New button in the upper-right corner of the dialog box. A new layer named Layer 1 appears in the list box. Notice that the name is highlighted. This tells you that by typing, you can change the default name to something better suited to your needs.

4. Type **Wall**. As you type, your entry replaces the Layer 1 name in the list box.

5. Click the Show Details button, also located in the upper-right corner of the dialog box. Additional layer options appear.

6. With the Wall layer name highlighted, click the downward-pointing arrow to the right of the Color drop-down list. You see a listing of colors that you can assign to the Wall layer.

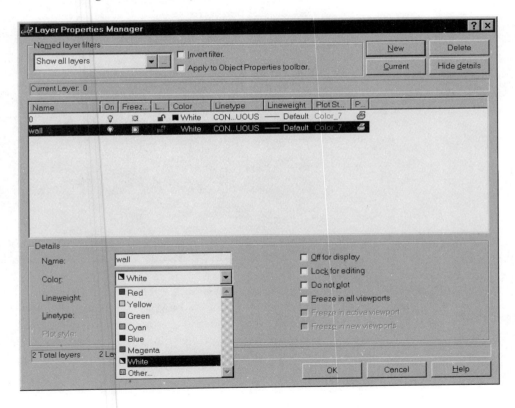

At first glance, this list may seem a bit limited, but you actually have a choice from 256 colors.

NOTE   Though it isn't readily apparent, all the colors in the Color drop-down list, except for the first seven, are designated by numbers. So when you select a color after the seventh color, the color's number rather than its name appears in the Color input box at the bottom of the dialog box.

7. Click Other from the list, or click the white color swatch (black if your background color is white) in the Wall layer listing, next to the word CONTINUOUS.

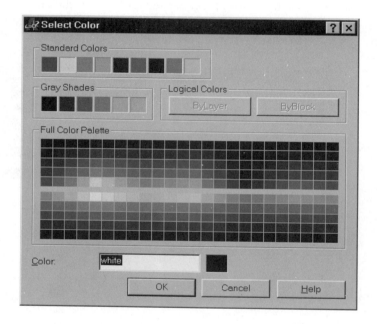

8. In the top row of Standard Colors, click the green square and then click OK. Notice that the color swatch in the Wall layer listing is now green. You could have just chosen green from the Colors drop-down list, but I wanted you to select green from the Select Color dialog box so you would be aware that many other colors are available.

9. When the Layer Properties Manager dialog box returns, click OK to close it.

The New Layer Properties Manager Dialog Box

NEW!

The Layer dialog box conforms to the Windows interface standard. Notice that the bar at the top of the Layer Name list box offers several buttons for the various layer properties. Just as you can adjust the Windows Explorer, you can adjust the width of each column in the list of layers by clicking and dragging either side of the column head buttons. You can also sort the layer list based on a property simply by clicking on the property name at the top of the list. And, just as with other Windows list boxes, you can Shift+click names to select a block of layer names, or Ctrl+click individual names to select multiples that do not appear together. These features will become helpful as your list of layers enlarges.

Controlling Layers through the Layer Command

You have seen how the Layer Properties Manager dialog box makes it easy to view and edit layer information, and how layer colors can be easily selected from an on-screen toolbar. But layers can also be controlled through the command prompt.

1. First, press the Esc key to make sure any current command is canceled.

2. At the command prompt, enter **–Layer**↵. Make sure you include the minus sign in front of the word **Layer**. The following prompt appears:

   ```
   [?/Make/Set/New/ON/OFF/Color/Ltype/LWeight/Plot/Freeze/Thaw/
   LOck/Unlock]:
   ```

   You'll learn about many of the options in this prompt as you work through this chapter.

3. Enter **N**↵ to select the New option.

4. At the `New layer name(s):` prompt, enter **Wall2**↵. The `?/Make/Set/New/ ON/ OFF/Color/Ltype/LWeight/Plot/Freeze/Thaw/LOck/Unlock]:` prompt appears again.

5. Enter **C**↵.

6. At the `Enter color name or number (1-255):` prompt, enter **Yellow**↵. Or you can enter **2**↵, the numeric equivalent to the color yellow in AutoCAD.

7. At the `Enter name list of layer(s) for color 2 (yellow) <0>:` prompt, enter **Wall2**↵. The `?/Make/Set/New/ON/OFF/Color/Ltype/LWeight/ Plot/Freeze/Thaw/LOck/Unlock]:` prompt appears again.

8. Press ↵ to exit the Layer command.

Each method of controlling layers has its own advantages. The Layer Properties Manager dialog box offers more information about your layers at a glance. On the other hand, the Layer command offers a quick way to control and create layers if you're in a hurry. Also, if you intend to write custom macros, you will want to know how to use the Layer command as opposed to the Layer Properties Manager dialog box, because dialog boxes cannot be controlled through custom toolbar buttons or scripts.

TIP

Another advantage to using the keyboard commands is that you can recall previously entered keystrokes by using the Up and Down arrow keys. For example, to recall the layer named Wall2 you entered in step 4 earlier, press the Up arrow key until Wall2 appears in the prompt. This saves time when you are performing repetitive operations such as creating multiple layers. This feature does not work with tools selected from the toolbars.

Assigning Layers to Objects

When you create an object, that object is assigned to the current layer. Until now, only one layer has existed—Layer 0—which contains all the objects you've drawn so far. Now that you've created some new layers, you can reassign objects to them using the Properties tool on the Object Properties toolbar.

NEW!

1. Select the four lines that represent the bathroom walls. If you have problems singling out the wall to the left, use a window to select the wall line.

2. With the cursor in the drawing area, right-click the mouse, then select Properties at the bottom of the popup menu. The Properties dialog box appears.

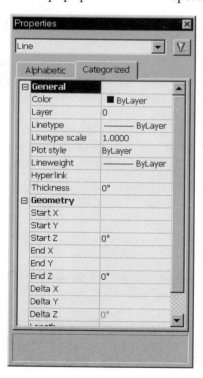

This dialog box lets you modify the properties of an object or set of objects (see *Understanding Object Properties* for more on the properties of objects).

3. Click the Categorized tab at the top of the dialog box. The list changes to show the properties according to property categories.

4. Click the Layer option from the listing in the Properties dialog box. Notice that an arrow appears in the layer name to the right of the Layer option.

5. Click the downward-pointing arrow to the far right of the Layer option. A list of all the available layers appears.

6. Select the Wall layer from the list. Notice that the wall lines you selected change to a green color. This tells you that that the objects have been assigned to the Wall layer. Remember that you assigned a green color to the Wall layer.

7. Dismiss the Properties dialog box by clicking the X button in the upper-left corner of the dialog box.

The bathroom walls are now on the new layer, Wall, and the walls are changed to green. Layers are more easily distinguished from one another when colors are used to set them apart.

Understanding Object Properties

It helps to think of the components of AutoCAD as having properties. For example, a line has geometric properties, such as the length, and coordinates that define its endpoints. An arc has a radius, a center, and beginning and ending coordinates. And even though a layer is not an object you can grasp and manipulate, it can have properties such as color, line types, and line weight.

By default, objects take on the color, line type, and weight of the layer to which they are assigned, but you can also assign these properties directly to individual objects. These general properties can be manipulated through both the Properties dialog box and the Properties toolbar.

While many of the options in the Properties dialog box may seem cryptic to you, don't worry about them at this point. As you work with AutoCAD, these properties will become more familiar to you. You'll find that you really won't be too concerned with the geometric properties, since you'll be manipulating those through the standard editing tools in the Modify toolbar. The other properties will be explained in the rest of this chapter and in other chapters.

Next, you will practice the commands you learned in this section and try out some new ones by creating some new layers and changing the layer assignments of the rest of the objects in your bathroom.

1. Bring up the Layer Properties Manager dialog box (use Format ➤ Layers or click the Layers button in the Properties toolbar). Create a new layer called Fixture and give it the color blue.

TIP You can change the name of a layer by clicking it in the Layer Properties Manager dialog box. Once it is highlighted, click it again so a box surrounds the name. You can then rename the layer. This works in the same way as renaming a file or folder in Windows 95.

2. Click the Tub and Toilet blocks, then right-click your mouse and select Properties from the popup menu.

3. Click Layer in the list of properties, then select Fixture from the drop-down layer list to the right of the Layer listing.

4. Click the X in the upper-right corner of the Properties dialog box to dismiss it, then press the Esc key to clear your selection.

5. Now create a new layer for the door, name the layer Door, and make it red.

NOTE Within a block, you can change the color assignment and line type of only those objects that are on Layer 0. See the sidebar *Controlling Colors and Line Types of Blocked Objects* in this chapter.

6. Just as you have done with the walls and fixtures, use the Properties dialog box to change the door to the Door layer.

7. Use the Layer Properties Manager dialog box to create three more layers for the ceiling, door jambs, and floor, as shown in Table 4.1. Remember that you can open the Select Color dialog box by clicking the color swatch of the layer listing.

In step 3 above, you used the Properties dialog box that offered several options for modifying the block. The Properties dialog box displays different options depending on the objects you have selected. With only one object selected, AutoCAD presents options that apply specifically to that object. With several objects selected, you'll see a more limited set of options because AutoCAD can change only those properties that are common to all the objects selected.

TABLE 4.1: Create These Layers and Set Their Colors as Indicated

Layer Name	Layer Color (Number)
Ceiling	Magenta (6)
Jamb	Green (3)
Floor	Cyan (4)

Controlling Colors and Line Types of Blocked Objects

Layer 0 has special importance to blocks. When objects assigned to Layer 0 are used as parts of a block, those objects take on the characteristics of the layer on which the block is inserted. On the other hand, if those objects are on a layer other than Layer 0, they maintain their original layer characteristics even if you insert or change that block to another layer. For example, suppose the tub is drawn on the Door layer, instead of on Layer 0. If you turn the tub into a block and insert it on the Fixture layer, the objects the tub is composed of will maintain their assignment to the Door layer, although the Tub block is assigned to the Fixture layer.

It might help to think of the block function as a clear plastic bag that holds together the objects that make up the tub. The objects inside the bag maintain their assignment to the Door layer even while the bag itself is assigned to the Fixture layer.

AutoCAD also allows you to have more than one color or line type on a layer. For example, you can use the Color and Linetype buttons in the Change Properties dialog box (the Object Properties button on the Standard toolbar) to alter the color or line type of an object on layer 0. That object then maintains its assigned color and line type—no matter what its layer assignment. Likewise, objects specifically assigned a color or line type are not affected by their inclusion into blocks.

Working on Layers

So far you have created layers and then assigned objects to those layers. However, the current layer is still Layer 0, and every new object you draw will be on Layer 0. Here's how to change the current layer.

1. Click the arrow button next to the layer name on the Object Properties toolbar. A drop-down list opens, showing you all the layers available in the drawing.

Notice the icons that appear next to the layer names; these control the status of the layer. You'll learn how to work with these icons later in this chapter. Also notice the box directly to the left of each layer name. This shows you the color of the layer.

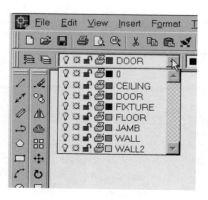

2. Click the Jamb layer name. The drop-down list closes, and the name Jamb appears in the toolbar's layer name box. Jamb is now the current layer.

NOTE   You can also use the Layer command to reset the current layer. To do this here, enter **−Layer** (be sure to include the minus sign) at the command prompt, and at the ?/Make/Set/New/ON/OFF/Color/Ltype/LWeight/Plot/Freeze/Thaw/LOck/Unlock]: prompt, enter **S** for Set. At the New current layer: prompt, enter **Jamb** and then press ⏎ twice to exit the Layer command.

---

3. Zoom in on the door and draw a 5" line; start at the lower-right corner of the door and draw toward the right. Metric users should draw a 13-cm line.

4. Draw a similar line from the top-right end of the arc. Your drawing should look like Figure 4.13.

Because you assigned the color green to the Jamb layer, the two lines you just drew to represent the door jambs are green. This gives you immediate feedback about what layer you are on as you draw.

Now you will use the part of the wall between the jambs as a line representing the door header (the part of the wall above the door). To do this, you will have to cut the line into three line segments, and then change the layer assignment of the segment between the jambs.

1. In the Modify toolbar, click the Break tool or type **br↵**.

2. At the Select objects: prompt, click the wall between the two jambs.

3. At the Enter second point (or F for first point): type **F**. This issues the first point option.

4. At the First point: prompt, use the Endpoint Osnap override to pick the endpoint of the door's arc that is touching the wall, as shown in Figure 4.13.

5. At the Enter second point: prompt, type **@↵** to signify that you want the second point of the break to be at the same location as the first point.

6. Click Break on the Modify toolbar, and then repeat steps 2 through 5, this time using the jamb near the door hinge location to locate the break point (see Figure 4.13).

FIGURE 4.13:

Door at wall with door jamb added

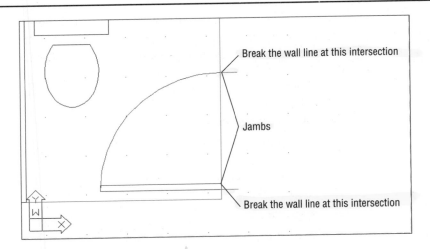

Though it may not be obvious, you've just broken the right-side wall line into three line segments; one at the door opening and two more on either side of the jambs. You can also use the Break command to produce a gap in a line segment.

Next, you'll change the Layer property of the line between the two jambs to the Ceiling layer. But instead of using the Properties tool, as you've done in earlier exercises, you'll use a shortcut method.

1. Click the line between the door jambs to highlight it. Notice that the layer listing in the Properties toolbar changes to Wall. Whenever you select an object to expose its grips, the Layer, Color, Linetype, and Line Width listings in the Properties toolbar change to reflect those properties of the selected object.

2. Click the layer name in the Properties toolbar. The Layer drop-down list appears.

3. Click the Ceiling layer. The list closes and the line you selected changes to the magenta color showing you that it is now on the Ceiling layer. Also notice that the color list in the Properties toolbar also changes to reflect the new color for the line.

4. Press the Esc key twice to clear the grip selection. Notice that the layer returns to Jamb, the current layer.

5. Click the Zoom Previous tool in the Standard toolbar, or choose View ➤ Zoom ➤ Previous to return to the previous view.

In this exercise, you saw that by selecting an object with no command active, the object's properties are immediately displayed in the Properties toolbar under the Layer, Color, and Linetype boxes. Using this method, you can also change an object's color, line type, and line width independent of its layer. Just as with the Properties tool, you can select multiple objects and change their layers through the Layer drop-down list. These options in the Properties toolbar offer a quick way to edit some of the properties of objects.

Now you'll finish the bathroom by adding a sink to a layer named Casework.

1. Open the Layer Properties Manager dialog box and create a new layer called Casework.

2. When the Casework layer name appears in the Layer drop-down list, click the button labeled Current at the top of the dialog box.

3. Click the color swatch for the Casework layer, and then select Blue from the Select Color dialog box. Click OK to exit the dialog box.

4. Click OK on the Layer Properties Manager dialog box. Notice that the layer listing in the Properties toolbar indicates that the current layer is Casework.

Now you'll add the sink. As you draw, the objects will appear in blue, the color of the Casework layer.

5. Click View ➤ Zoom ➤ All.

6. Click the Insert Block tool on the Draw toolbar, then click the Browse button in the Insert dialog box.

7. Locate the Sink file and double-click it.

8. In the Insert dialog box, make sure that the Specify On-Screen options in both the Scale and Rotation button groups are not checked, then click OK.

9. Place the sink roughly in the upper-right corner of the bathroom plan, then use the Move command to place it accurately in the corner, as shown in Figure 4.14.

FIGURE 4.14:

Bathroom with sink and countertop added

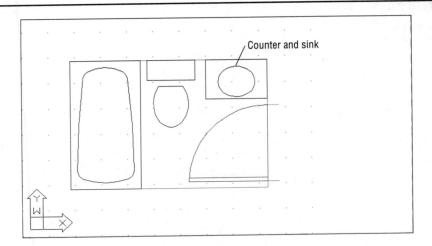

Counter and sink

Controlling Layer Visibility

I mentioned earlier that at times you'll want to be selective about what layers you are working with on a drawing. In this bathroom, there is a door header that would normally appear only in a reflected ceiling plan. To turn off a layer so that it becomes invisible, use the Off button in the Layer Properties Manager dialog box.

1. Open the Layer Properties Manager dialog box by clicking the Layers tool in the Properties toolbar.

2. Click the Ceiling layer in the Layer drop-down list.

3. Click the lightbulb icon in the Layer drop-down list next to the Ceiling layer name. You can also highlight the Ceiling layer in the Layer Properties Manager dialog box, then click the check box labeled On in the Details group so that no check appears there. In either case, the lightbulb icon changes from yellow to gray to indicate that the layer is off.

TIP   By momentarily placing the cursor on an icon in the Layer drop-down list, you get a tool tip giving you a brief description of the icon's purpose.

---

4. Click the OK button to exit the Layer Properties Manager dialog box. When you return to the drawing, the header disappears because you have made it invisible by turning off its layer (see Figure 4.15).

FIGURE 4.15:

Bathroom with Ceiling layer turned off

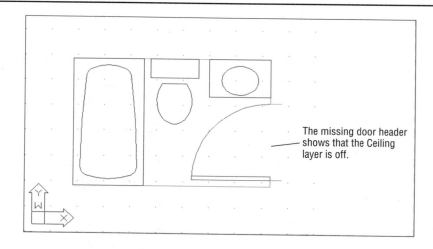

The missing door header shows that the Ceiling layer is off.

You can also control layer visibility using the Layer drop-down list on the Object Properties toolbar.

1. On the Object Properties toolbar, click the Layer drop-down list.

2. Find the Ceiling layer and notice that its lightbulb icon is gray. This tells you that the layer is off and not visible.

3. Click the lightbulb icon to make it yellow.

4. Now click the drawing area to close the Layer drop-down list, and the door header reappears.

Figure 4.16 explains the role of the other icons in the Layer drop-down list.

FIGURE 4.16:

The Layer drop-down list icons

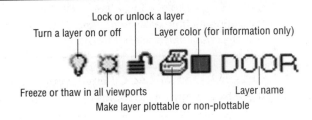

Lock or unlock a layer

Turn a layer on or off   Layer color (for information only)

Freeze or thaw in all viewports   Layer name

Make layer plottable or non-plottable

Finding the Layers You Want

With only a handful of layers, it's fairly easy to find the layer you want to turn off. It becomes much more difficult, however, when the number of layers exceeds 20 or 30. The Layer Properties Manager dialog box offers some useful tools to help you find the layers you want fast.

Now suppose you have several layers whose names begin with C, such as C-lights, C-header, and C-pattern, and you want find those layers quickly. You can click the Name button at the top of the layer list to sort the layer names in alphabetical order. Click the Name button again to reverse the order. To select those layers for processing, click the first layer name that starts with C; then scroll down the list until you find the last layer of the group and Shift+click it. All the layers between those layers will be selected. If you want to deselect some of those layers, hold down the Ctrl key while clicking the layer names you don't want to include in your selection. Or Ctrl+click other layer names you do want selected.

The Color and Linetype buttons at the top of the list let you control what layers appear in the list by virtue of their color or line-type assignments. Other buttons sort the list by virtue of the status: On/Off, Freeze/Thaw, Lock/Unlock, and so forth. See the *Other Layer Options* sidebar later in this chapter.

Now try changing the layer settings again, turning off all the layers except Wall and Ceiling and leaving just a simple rectangle. In the exercise, you'll get a chance to experiment with the On/Off options of the Layer Properties Manager dialog box.

1. Click the Layers button in the Object Properties toolbar, or on Format ➤ Layers in the pull-down menus.

2. Click the topmost layer name in the List box; then Shift+click the bottom-most layer name. All the layer names are highlighted.

TIP   Another way to select all the layers at once in the Layer Properties Manager dialog box is to right-click the Layer drop-down list; then click the Select All option from the popup menu that appears. And if you want to clear your selections, right-click the layer list and select Clear All.

3. Ctrl+click the Wall and Ceiling layers to deselect them and thus exempt them from your next action.

4. Click the lightbulb icon of any of the highlighted layer names or click the On check box in the Details section of the dialog box to clear the checkmark.

5. A message appears warning you that the current layer will be turned off. Click OK in the message box. The lightbulb icons turn gray to show that the selected layers have been turned off.

6. Click OK. The drawing now appears with only the Wall and Ceiling layers displayed (see Figure 4.17).

7. Open the Layer Properties Manager dialog box again and select all the layers as you did in steps 2 and 3, and then click the On button, or any of the gray lightbulbs, to turn on all the layers at once.

8. Click OK to return to the drawing.

FIGURE 4.17:

Bathroom with all layers except Wall and Ceiling turned off

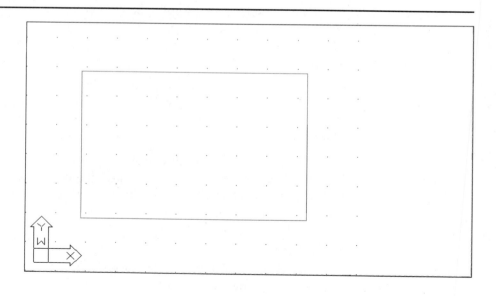

In this exercise, you turned off a set of layers with a single click on a lightbulb icon. You can freeze/thaw, lock/unlock, or change the color of a group of layers in a similar manner by clicking the appropriate layer property. For example, if you click a color swatch of one of the selected layers, the Select Color dialog box appears, allowing you to set the color for all the selected layers.

Other Layer Options

You may have noticed the *Freeze* and *Thaw* buttons in the Layer Properties Manager dialog box. These options are similar to the On and Off buttons—however, Freeze not only makes layers invisible, it also tells AutoCAD to ignore the contents of those layers when you use the All response to the `Select objects:` prompt. Freezing layers can save time when you issue a command that regenerates a complex drawing. This is because AutoCAD ignores objects on frozen layers during Regen. You will get firsthand experience with Freeze and Thaw in Chapter 6.

Another pair of Layer Properties Manager options, Lock and Unlock, offer a function similar to Freeze and Thaw. If you lock a layer, you can view and snap to objects on that layer, but you can't edit those objects. This feature is useful when you are working on a crowded drawing and you don't want to accidentally edit portions of it. You can lock all the layers except those you intend to edit, and then proceed to work without fear of making accidental changes.

Three more options, Lineweight and Plot Style and Plot are new in AutoCAD 2000. Lineweight lets you control the width of lines in a layer. In prior versions of AutoCAD, you could only control line widths through the plotter. Plot Style lets you assign plotter configurations to specific layers. (You'll learn more about plot styles in Chapter 7.) Plot lets you determine whether a layer gets printed in hard-copy output. This can be useful for setting up layers you might use for layout purposes only.

Taming an Unwieldy List of Layers

Chances are, you will eventually end up with a fairly long list of layers. Managing such a list can become a nightmare, but AutoCAD provides the Layer Filter dialog box to help you locate and isolate only those layers you need to work with.

To use layer filters, click the Show drop-down list near the top of the Layer Properties Manager dialog box. This drop-down list contains a list of options described here in Table 4.2. See *Using External References* in Chapter 6 for information on Xref-dependent layers.

TABLE 4.2: The Filter Options

Filter Options	What It Filters
Show all layers	All layers regardless of their status
Show all used layers	All layers that have objects assigned to them
Show all Xref-dependent layers	All layers that contain Xref objects

You can also create your own filter criteria and add it to this drop-down list by clicking on the Ellipsis button with the three dots on it.

When you click this button, the Named Layer Filters dialog box appears. Here you can create a filter list based on the layer's characteristics.

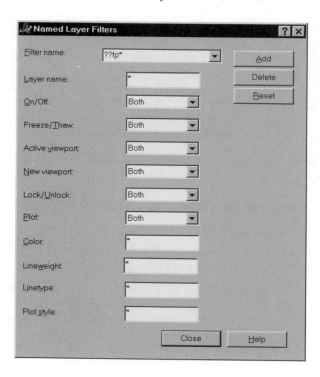

Now suppose you have a drawing whose layer names are set up to help you easily identify floor plan data versus ceiling plan data as in the following list.

A-FP-WALL-JAMB

A-RP-WIND-JAMB

A-FP-WIND-SILL

A-CP-WIND-HEAD

A-CP-DOOR-HEAD

L-FP-CURB

C-FP-ELEV

NOTE   These layer examples are loosely based on a layer-naming convention devised by the American Institute of Architects. As you can see from this example, careful naming of layers can help you manage them.

The first character in the layer name designates the discipline related to that layer: A for architectural, L for landscape, C for civil, and so on. In this example, layers whose names contain the two characters FP signify floor plan layers. CP designates ceiling information.

If you want to isolate only those layers that have to do with floor plans, regardless of their discipline, enter **??FP*** in the Layer Name input box. You can then give this filter criteria the name Floor Plan by entering **Floor Plan** in the Filter Name input box. Then click OK to dismiss the Named Layer Filters dialog box. You can then pick Floor Plan from the Named Layer Filters drop-down list and only those layers whose names contain the letters FP as their third and fourth characters will appear in the list of layers. You can then easily turn all these layers off, change their color assignment, or change other settings quickly, without having to wade through other layers you don't want to touch. You can further create other named layer filters to isolate other groups of layers. AutoCAD keeps these filter lists for future use until you delete them using the Delete option in the Named Layer Filters dialog box.

NOTE   In the ??FP* example, the question marks (??) tell AutoCAD that the first two characters in the layer name can be anything. The "FP" tells AutoCAD that the layer name must contain F and P in these two places of the name. The asterisk (*) at the end tells AutoCAD that the remaining characters can be anything. The question marks and asterisk are known as *wildcard characters*. They are commonly used filtering tools for the UNIX operating system and in Windows.

The other four input boxes near the bottom, Color, Lineweight, Linetype, and Plot Style, let you control what layers appear in the list by virtue of their settings as they relate to these four options. The six popup lists let you filter layers by virtue of the status: On/Off, Freeze/Thaw, Lock/Unlock, and so forth. See the *Other Layer Options* sidebar earlier in this chapter.

As the number of layers in a drawing grows, you will find layer filters to be an indispensable tool. But bear in mind that the successful use of the layer filters depends on a careful layer-naming convention. If you are producing architectural plans, you may want to consider the American Institute of Architects (AIA) layering guidelines.

Assigning Line Types to Layers

You will often want to use different line types to show hidden lines, center lines, fence lines, or other noncontinuous lines. You can set a layer to have not only a color assignment but also a line-type assignment. AutoCAD comes with several line types, as shown in Figure 4.18. From the top of one image to the bottom of the continued image of Figure 4.18, we can see Standard line types, then ISO and Complex line types, and then a series of lines that can be used to illustrate gas and water lines in civil work, or batt insulation in a wall cavity. ISO line types are designed to be used with specific plotted line widths and line-type scales. For example, if you are using a pen width of .5mm, the line-type scale of the drawing should be set to .5 as well. (See Chapter 12 for more information on plotting and line-type scale.) The complex line types at the bottom of the figure offer industry-specific lines such as gas and water lines for civil work, and a line type that can be used to symbolize batt insulation in a wall cavity. You can also create your own line types (see Chapter 19).

WARNING   Be aware that line types that contain text, such as the gas sample, use the current text height and font to determine the size and appearance of the text displayed in the line. A text height of 0 (zero) displays the text properly in most cases. See Chapter 8 for more on text styles.

AutoCAD stores line-type descriptions in an external file named Acad.lin. You can edit this file in a word processor to create new line types or to modify existing ones. You will see how this is done in Chapter 19.

Adding a Line Type to a Drawing

To see how line types work, add a dash-dot line in the bathroom plan to indicate a shower curtain rod.

1. Open the Layers Properties Manager dialog box.

2. Click New and then type **Pole** to create a new layer called Pole.

TIP　If you are in a hurry, you can simultaneously load a line type and assign it to a layer using the Layer command. In this exercise, you would enter **–Layer.⏎** at the command prompt. Then enter **L⏎**, **dashdot⏎**, **pole⏎**, and then ⏎ to exit the Layer command.

---

3. Click the word CONTINUOUS at the far right of the Pole layer listing (under the Linetype column). The Select Linetype dialog box appears.

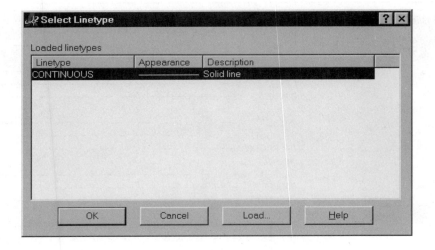

The Select Linetype dialog box offers a list of line types to choose from. In a new file such as the Bath file, only one line type is available by default. You must load any additional line type you may want to use.

4. Click the Load button at the bottom of the dialog box. The Load or Reload Linetypes dialog box appears.

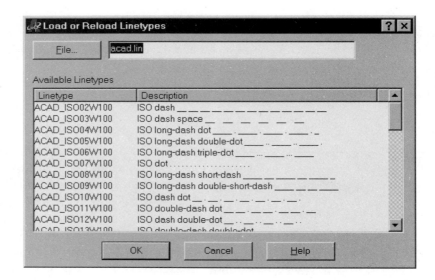

FIGURE 4.18:

Standard AutoCAD
line types

BORDER	
BORDER2	
BORDERX2	
CENTER	
CENTER2	
CENTERX2	
DASHDOT	
DASHDOT2	
DASHDOTX2	
DASHED	
DASHED2	
DASHEDX2	
DIVIDE	
DIVIDE2	
DIVIDEX2	
DOT	
DOT2	
DOTX2	
HIDDEN	
HIDDEN2	
HIDDENX2	
PHANTOM	
PHANTOM2	

**FIGURE 4.18
CONTINUED:**

Standard AutoCAD
line types

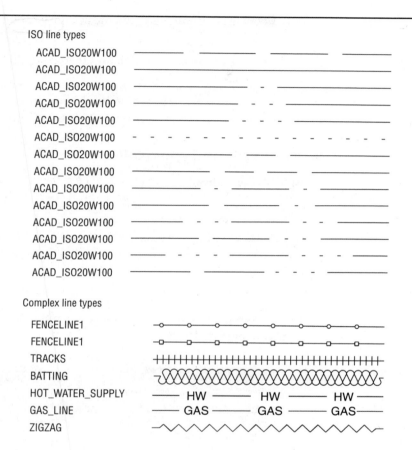

ISO line types

ACAD_ISO20W100
ACAD_ISO20W100
ACAD_ISO20W100
ACAD_ISO20W100
ACAD_ISO20W100
ACAD_ISO20W100
ACAD_ISO20W100
ACAD_ISO20W100
ACAD_ISO20W100
ACAD_ISO20W100
ACAD_ISO20W100
ACAD_ISO20W100
ACAD_ISO20W100
ACAD_ISO20W100

Complex line types

FENCELINE1
FENCELINE1
TRACKS
BATTING
HOT_WATER_SUPPLY
GAS_LINE
ZIGZAG

Notice that the list of line-type names is similar to the Layer drop-down list. You can sort the names alphabetically or by description by clicking the Linetype or Description buttons at the top of the list.

5. In the Available Linetypes list, scroll down to locate the Dashdot line type, click it, and then click OK.

6. Notice that the Dashdot line type is now added to the line types available in the Select Linetype dialog box.

7. Click Dashdot to highlight it; then click OK. Now Dashdot appears in the Pole layer listing under Linetype.

8. With the Pole layer still highlighted, click the Current button to make the Pole layer current.

9. Click OK to exit the Load or Reload Linetype dialog box.

10. Turn off the Running Osnap mode; then draw a line across the opening of the tub area, from coordinate 4'-4",1'-10" to coordinate 4'-4",6'-10". Metric users should draw a line from coordinate 133,56 to 133,208.

Controlling Line-Type Scale

Although you have designated this line to be a Dashdot line, it appears to be solid. Zoom in to a small part of the line, and you'll see that the line is indeed as you specified.

Since you are working at a scale of 1"=1', you must adjust the scale of your line types accordingly. This, too, is accomplished in the Layer Properties Manager dialog box.

1. Select Format ➤ Linetype from the pull-down menus. You can also select Other from the Linetype drop-down list in the Properties toolbar. The Linetype Manager dialog box appears.

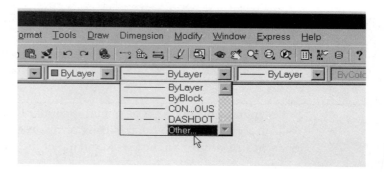

2. Click the Show Details button in the upper-right corner of the dialog box. You'll see some additional options appear at the bottom.

NOTE   You may notice that the Linetype tab of the Layer Properties Manager dialog box also contains the Load and Delete button options that you saw in step 4 of the previous exercise. These offer a way to directly load or delete a line type without having to go through a particular layer's line-type setting.

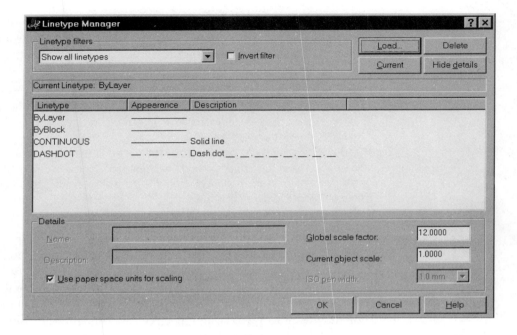

3. Double-click the Global Scale Factor input box, and then type **12** (Metric users type **30**). This is the scale conversion factor for a 1"=1' scale (see Table 3.3).

4. Click OK. The drawing regenerates, and the shower curtain rod is displayed in the line type and at the scale you designated.

5. Click the Zoom Previous tool so your drawing looks like Figure 4.19.

FIGURE 4.19:

The completed bathroom

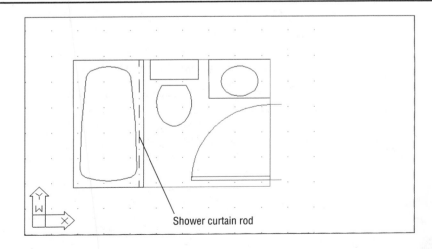

Shower curtain rod

TIP
You can also use the Ltscale system variable to set the line-type scale. Type **Ltscale⏎**, and at the LTSCALE New scale factor <1.0000>: prompt, enter **12⏎**.

TIP
If you change the line type of a layer or object but the object remains a continuous line, check the Ltscale system variable. It should be set to your drawing scale factor. If this doesn't work, set the Viewres system variable to a higher value (see Chapter 6). (Viewres can also be set by the Arc and Circle Smoothness option in the Display tab of the Options dialog box.) Line-type scales act differently depending on whether you are in Model Space or in a drawing layout. See Chapter 12 for more on Model Space and layouts.

Remember that if you assign a line type to a layer, everything that you draw on that layer will be of that line type. This includes arcs, polylines, circles, and traces. As explained in the *Setting Individual Colors, Line Types, and Line-Type Scales* sidebar, you can also assign different colors and line types to individual objects, rather than relying on their layer assignment to define color and line type. However, you may want to avoid assigning colors and line types directly to objects until you have some experience with AutoCAD and a good grasp of your drawing's organization.

In the last exercise, you changed the global line-type scale setting. This affects all noncontinuous line types within the current drawing. You can also change the line-type scale of individual objects using the Properties button on the Object Properties toolbar. Or you can set the default line-type scale for all new objects, with the Current Object Scale option in the Linetype Manager dialog box.

When individual objects are assigned a line-type scale, they are still affected by the global line-type scale set by the Ltscale system variable. For example, say you assign a line-type scale of 2 to the curtain rod in the previous example. This scale is then multiplied by the global line-type scale of 12, for a final line-type scale of 12.

TIP
The default Linetype Scale setting for individual objects can also be set using the Celtscale system variable. Once set, only newly created objects are affected. You must use the Properties tool to change the line-type scale of individual existing objects.

If the objects you draw appear in a different line type from that of the layer they are on, check the default line type using the Linetype Control drop-down list on the Object Properties toolbar. You can also click Format ➤ Linetype. Then, in the Line-type Manager dialog box, highlight ByLayer in the Linetype list, and then click the Current button. In addition, check the line-type scale of the object itself, using the Properties dialog box. A different line-type scale can make a line appear to have an assigned line type that may not be what you expect. See the next sidebar, *Setting Individual Colors, Line Types, and Line-Type Scales.*

WARNING   The display of line types also depends on whether you are in Paper Space or draw-ing layout. If your efforts to control line-type scale have no effect on your line type's visibility, you may be in a drawing layout. See Chapter 12 for more informa-tion on how to control line-type scale while in a layout view.

If you are working through the tutorial, your last task here is to set up an inser-tion point for the current drawing, to facilitate its insertion into other drawings in the future.

1. Type **Base**⤶.

2. At the Base point: prompt, pick the upper-left corner of the bathroom. The bathroom drawing is now complete.

3. Choose File ➤ Save to record your work up to now.

Setting Individual Colors, Line Types, and Line-Type Scales

If you prefer, you can set up AutoCAD to assign specific colors and line types to objects, instead of having objects take on the color and line-type settings of the layer on which they reside. Normally, objects are given a default color and line type called *ByLayer,* which means each object takes on the color or line type of its assigned layer. (You've probably noticed the word ByLayer in the Object Properties toolbar and in various dialog boxes.)

Use the Properties tool on the Object Properties toolbar to change the color or line type of existing objects. This tool opens a dialog box that lets you set the properties of individual objects. For new objects, use the Color tool on the Object Properties toolbar to set the

Continued on next page

current default color to red (for example), instead of ByLayer. The Color tool opens the Select Color dialog box, where you select your color from a toolbar. Then everything you draw will be red, regardless of the current layer color.

For line types, you can use the Linetype drop-down list in the Object Properties toolbar to select a default line type for all new objects. The list only shows line types that have already been loaded into the drawing, so you must have first loaded a line type before you can select it.

Another possible color and line-type assignment is *ByBlock,* which is also set with the Properties button. ByBlock makes everything you draw white, until you turn your drawing into a block and then insert the block on a layer with an assigned color. The objects then take on the color of that layer. This behavior is similar to that of objects drawn on Layer 0. The ByBlock line type works similarly to the ByBlock color.

Finally, if you want to set the line-type scale for each individual object, instead of relying on the global line-type scale (the Ltscale system variable), you can use the Properties button to modify the line-type scale of individual objects. Or you can use the Object Creation Modes dialog box (via the Object Creation button in the Object Properties toolbar) to set the line-type scale to be applied to new objects. In place of using the Properties button, you can set the Celtscale system variable to the line-type scale you want for new objects.

As mentioned earlier, you should stay away from assigning colors and line types to individual objects until you are comfortable with AutoCAD; and even then, use color and line-type assignments carefully. Other users who work on your drawing may have difficulty understanding your drawing's organization if you assign color and line-type properties indiscriminately.

Controlling Line Weights

You may have noticed an option in the Layer Properties Manager dialog box called *Lineweight*. With AutoCAD 2000, you can control the thickness of your lines by adjusting the Lineweight setting, either through layer assignments or through direct object property assignment. This means that now you have true WYSIWYG drawing in AutoCAD.

In previous versions of AutoCAD, you had to assign final plotted line weights to objects based on their color. This method made it difficult to control how your plots would look because you didn't really see the thickness of lines on the computer screen. You had to do some mental gymnastics to translate the colors on your screen to the final plotted line weights.

With the introduction of the Lineweight option, you have greater control over the look of your drawings. This can save time since you don't have to print your drawing out just to check for line weights. You'll be able to see how thick or thin your lines are as you edit your drawing.

This feature isn't discussed in detail in this chapter, but be aware that it is available. You'll get a chance to delve into line weights in Chapter 7.

Keeping Track of Blocks and Layers

The Insert and the Layer Properties Manager dialog boxes let you view the blocks and layers available in your drawing, by listing them in a window. The Layer Properties Manager dialog box also includes information on the status of layers. However, you may forget the layer on which an object resides. You've seen how the Properties option on the popup menu shows you the properties of an object. The List button on the Object Properties toolbar also allows you to get information about individual objects.

1. Click and hold the Distance tool so that a flyout appears.

2. Drag the pointer down to the List tool and select it.

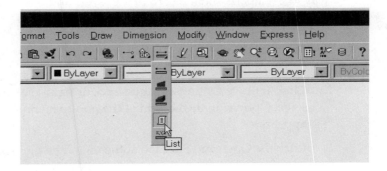

TIP   If you just want to quickly check which layer an object is on, click it. Its layer will appear in the Layer list of the Properties toolbar.

3. At the `Select object:` prompt, click the Tub block and then press ↵. The AutoCAD Text window appears.

4. In the Text window, a listing appears that shows not only the layer that the tub is on, but its space, insertion point, name, color, line type, rotation angle, and scale.

The information you see in the Text window is duplicated in the Properties dialog box that you see when you right-click your mouse and choose Properties. But having the data in the Text window gives you the flexibility to record the data in a text file, in case you need to store data about parts of your drawing. You can also use the Text window to access and store other types of data regarding your drawings.

NOTE   The Space property you see listed for the Tub block designates whether the object resides in Model Space or Layout Space. You'll learn more about these spaces in Chapters 6 and 12.

Using the Log File Feature

Eventually, you will want a permanent record of block and layer listings. This is especially true if you work on drawing files that are being used by others. Here's a way to get a permanent record of the layers and blocks within a drawing using the Log File option under the Environment Preferences.

1. Minimize the Text window (click the Minimize button in the upper-right corner of the Text window).

2. Click Tools ➤ Options, or type **op**↵, or right-click the drawing area. Then select Options in the bottom of the popup menu. The Options dialog box appears.

3. Click the Open and Save tab at the top of the dialog box.

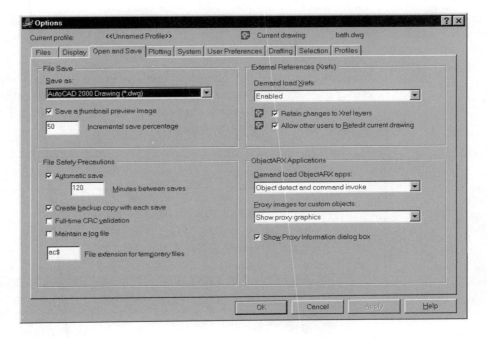

4. Click the Maintain a Log File check box in the bottom-left side of the dialog box. A checkmark appears in the check box.

5. Click OK, then type **–LAYER.⏎** (don't forget the minus sign) at the command prompt, and then type **?.⏎⏎**. The AutoCAD Text window appears and a listing of all the layers scrolls into view.

6. Press F2 to return to the AutoCAD drawing screen. Then open the Options dialog box again.

7. Make sure you have the Open and Save tab selected, then click the Maintain a Log File check box again, and then click OK.

8. Use Windows Notepad to open the AutoCAD log file, Acad.log, located in the \AutoCAD2000\ directory. Notice that the layer listing is recorded there.

With the Log File feature, you can record virtually anything that appears in the command prompt. You can even record an entire AutoCAD session. The log file can also be helpful in constructing script files to automate tasks (see *Automating a Slide Presentation* in Chapter 15 for more information on scripts). To have hard copy of the log file, just print it from an application such as Windows Notepad or your favorite word processor.

If you wish, you can arrange to keep the Acad.log file in a directory other than the default AutoCAD subdirectory. This setting is also in the Options dialog box under the Files tab. Locate Log File Location in the Search Path, File Names, and File Locations list box. Click the plus sign next to this listing. The listing expands to show the location for the log file.

NOTE   See Appendix B for more on the AutoCAD Options dialog box settings.

You can double-click the file location listing to open a Select a File dialog box and specify a different location and filename for your log file. This dialog box is a typical Windows file dialog box.

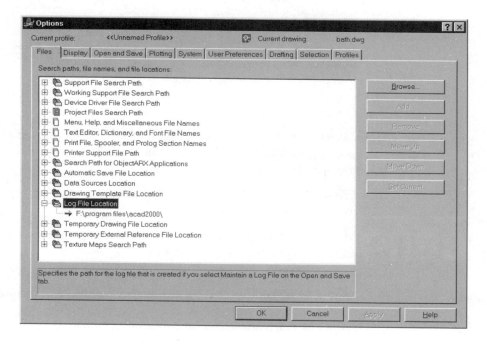

Once you've settled on a location on disk for the log file, use the File Manager to associate the log file with the Windows Notepad or Write application. Then click and drag the file to the AutoCAD program group. This gives you quick access to your log file by simply double-clicking its icon in the AutoCAD program group.

Finding Files on Your Hard Disk

As your library of symbols and files grows, you may begin to have difficulty keeping track of them. Fortunately, AutoCAD offers a utility that lets you quickly locate a file anywhere in your computer. The Find File utility searches your hard disk for specific files. You can have it search one drive or several, or you can limit the search to one directory. You can limit the search to specific filenames or use DOS wildcards to search for files with similar names.

The following exercise steps you through a sample Find File task:

1. Click File ➤ Open. In the Select File dialog box, click Find File to display the Browse/Search dialog box.

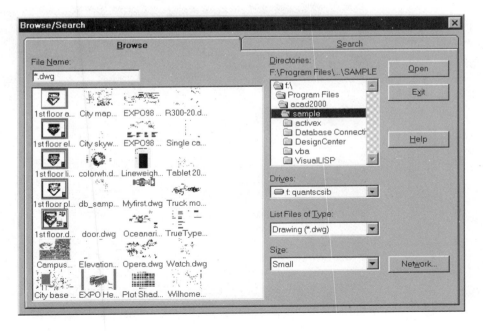

TIP

The Find File utility can also be accessed using the Find File button in any AutoCAD file dialog box, including the File option of the Insert Block tool. Find File can help you access and maintain your symbols library.

The Browse/Search dialog box has two tabs: Browse and Search. The Browse tab contains all the drawings in the current directory, displayed as thumbnail views so you can easily identify them. You can open a file by double-clicking its thumbnail view, or by entering its name in the File Name input box at the top.

The Size drop-down list in the Browse tab of the Browse/Search dialog box lets you choose the size of the thumbnail views shown in the list box—small, medium, and large. You can scroll through the views using the scroll bars at the bottom of the list box.

2. Click the Search tab to open the page of Search functions. Use the Search Pattern input box to enter the name of the file for which you wish to search. The default is *.dwg, which causes the Find File utility to search for all AutoCAD drawing files. Several other input boxes help you set a variety of other search criteria, such as the date stamp of the drawing, the type of drawing, and the drive and path to be searched. For now, leave these settings as is.

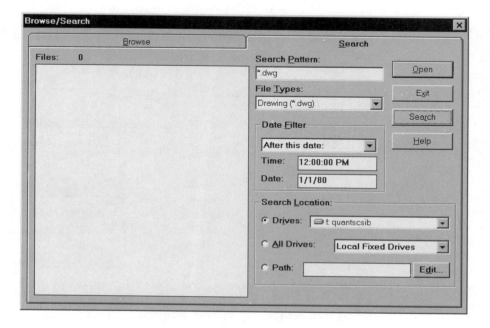

3. Click the Search button. In a few seconds, a listing of files that meet the criteria specified in the input boxes appears in the Files list on the left, along with thumbnail views of each file. You can click a filename in the list, and then click the Open button to open the file in the drawing editor.

4. When you're ready, click Exit to exit the Browse/Search dialog box, and then click Cancel to exit the Open File dialog box.

NOTE   In the Browse/Search dialog box, a drawing from a pre-Release 13 version of AutoCAD is represented as a box with an X through it.

In this exercise, you performed a search using the default settings. These settings caused AutoCAD to search for files with the .dwg filename extension, created after 12:00 midnight on January 1, 1980, in the \ACADWIN\ directory.

Here are the functions of the items in the Browse/Search dialog box:

Search Pattern   Lets you give specific filename search criteria using DOS wildcard characters.

File Types   Lets you select from a set of standard file types.

Date Filter   Lets you specify a cutoff time and date. Files created before the specified time and date are ignored.

Drives   Lets you specify the drives to search.

All Drives   Lets you search all the drives on your computer.

Path   Lets you specify a path to search.

Search   This button begins the search process.

Open   This button opens the file highlighted in the file list, after a search is performed.

Help   This button provides information on the use of Browse/Search.

Edit   This button, next to the Path input box, opens another dialog box, displaying a directory tree from which you can select a search path.

Using the AutoCAD DesignCenter to Manage Drawings and Blocks

If you need a more powerful tool to manage your drawings, then you'll want to get to know the AutoCAD DesignCenter. The DesignCenter is new in AutoCAD 2000. It lets you locate and manage AutoCAD drawing files and blocks that reside within drawings. It also allows you to search for and import settings from other drawings, such as layers, line types, text, and dimension styles (you'll learn about text and dimension styles in Chapters 8 and 9) and Xrefs. If your work involves raster images, you can use the DesignCenter to view and import Targa, TIFF, BMP, JPEG, and other image files. You'll get a chance to learn more about the DesignCenter in Chapter 22, which discusses project management issues.

Inserting Symbols with Drag and Drop

If you prefer to manage your symbols library using Windows Explorer, or to use another third-party file manager for locating and managing your symbols, you'll appreciate AutoCAD's support for Drag and Drop. With this feature, you can click and drag a file from the Windows Explorer into the AutoCAD window. You can also drag and drop from the Windows Find File or Folder utility. AutoCAD automatically starts the Insert command to insert the file. Drag and Drop also works with a variety of other AutoCAD support files.

AutoCAD supports Drag and Drop for other types of data from applications that support Microsoft's ActiveX technology. Table 4.3 shows a list of files with which you can use Drag and Drop, and the functions associated with them.

TABLE 4.3: AutoCAD Support for Drag and Drop

File Type	Command Issued	Function Performed When File Is Dropped
.dxf	Dxfin	Imports .dxf files
.dwg	Insert	Imports or plots drawing files
.txt	Dtext	Imports texts via Dtext

Continued on next page

TABLE 4.3 CONTINUED: AutoCAD Support for Drag and Drop

File Type	Command Issued	Function Performed When File Is Dropped
.lin	Linetype	Loads line types
.mnu, .mns, .mnc	Menu	Loads menus
.ps	Psin	Imports PostScript files
.psb, .shp, .shx	Style	Loads fonts or shapes
.scr	Script	Runs script
.lsp	(Load..)	Loads AutoLISP routine
.exe, .exp	(Xload..)	Loads ADS application

> **TIP**
>
> You can also drag and drop from folder shortcuts placed on your desktop or even from a Web site.

If You Want to Experiment...

If your application is not architecture, you may want to experiment with creating other types of symbols. You might also start thinking about a layering system that suits your particular needs.

Open a new file called Mytemp. In it, create layers numbered 1 through 8 and assign each layer the color that corresponds to its number. For example, give Layer 1 the color 1 (red), Layer 2 the color 2 (yellow), and so on. Draw each part shown in Figure 4.20, and turn each part into a file on disk using the Export (File ➤ Export) or the Wblock command. When specifying a filename, use the name indicated for each part in the figure. For the insertion point, also use the points indicated in the figure. Use the Osnap modes (Chapter 2) to select the insertion points.

When you are done creating the parts, exit the file using File ➤ Exit, and then open a new file. Set up the drawing as an engineering drawing with a scale of 1/4"=1" on an 11" × 17" sheet. Create the drawing in Figure 4.21 using the Insert Block command to place your newly created parts.

FIGURE 4.20:

A typical set of symbols

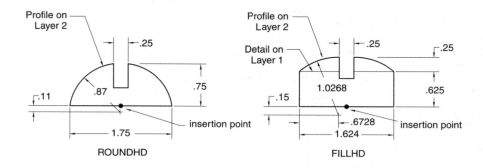

ROUNDHD

FILLHD

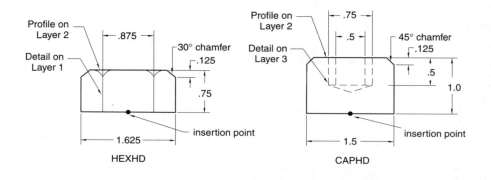

HEXHD

CAPHD

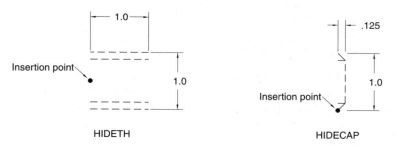

HIDETH

HIDECAP

Note:
Give Layer 3 the HIDDEN line type.
Put all of HIDETH and HIDECAP on Layer 3.
Don't draw dimensions; just use them for reference.

FIGURE 4.21:

Draw this part using the symbols you create.

1. Set the snap mode to .125 and be sure it is on. Set Ltscale to .25. Draw the figure at right using the dimensions shown as a guide.

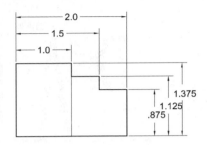

2. Insert the HEXHD drawing at the location shown in the figure at right. Enter .25 for a scale value and when you are asked for a rotation angle, visually orient it as shown.

3. Insert the HIDETH file at the same point and scale as the HEXHD file then explode it.

4. Insert the HIDECAP file as shown to the right. Enter .25 for the scale and rotate it so it looks like the this figure.

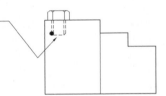

5. Do the same sequence of steps to add the screw shown at the right. This time, use a scale factor of .125 when you insert the ROUNDHD file. When you insert the HIDETH file, enter a value of 1 for the X scale factor and .125 for the Y scale factor.

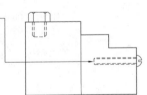

PART II

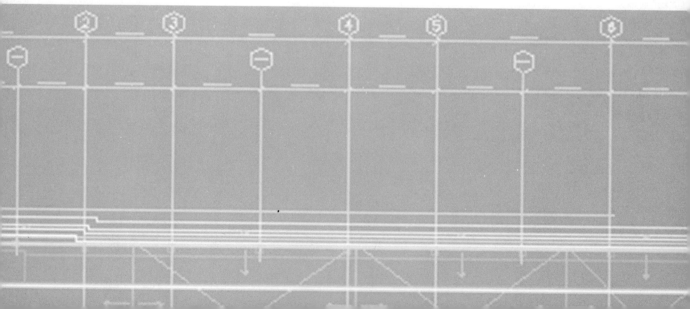

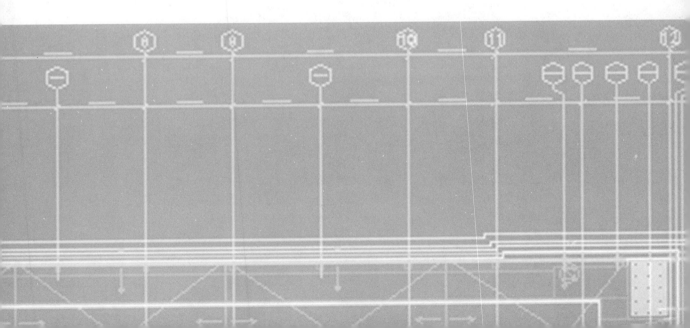

Building on the Basics

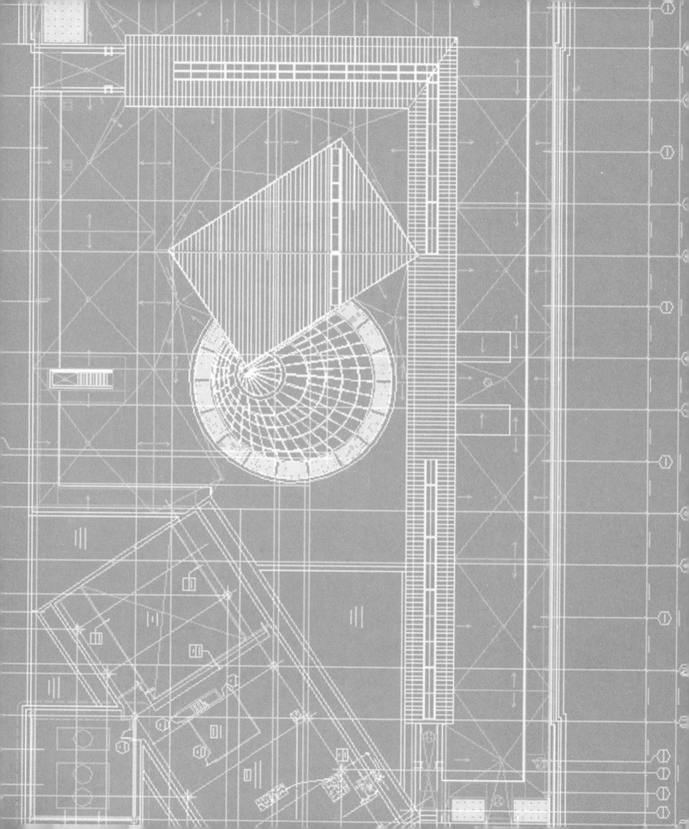

Editing for Productivity

- Creating and Using Templates

- Copying an Object Multiple Times

- Developing Your Drawing

- Drawing Parallel Lines

- Eliminating Layers, Line Types, Shapes, and Styles

- If You Want to Experiment…

There are at least five commands devoted to duplicating objects, ten if you include the Grips options. Why so many? If you're an experienced drafter, you know that technical drawing is often tedious. So AutoCAD offers a variety of ways to reuse existing geometry, thereby automating much of the repetitious work usually associated with manual drafting.

In this chapter, as you finish drawing the studio apartment unit, you will explore some of the ways to exploit existing files and objects while constructing your drawing. For example, you will use existing files as prototypes for new files, eliminating the need to set up layers, scales, and sheet sizes for similar drawings. With AutoCAD you can also duplicate objects in multiple arrays. You have already seen how to use the Osnap overrides on objects to locate points for drawing complex forms. This chapter describes other ways of using lines to aid your drawing.

And, because you will begin to use the Zoom command more in the exercises of this chapter, you will review this command as you go along. You'll also discover the Pan command—another tool to help you get around in your drawing.

You're already familiar with many of the commands you will use to draw the apartment unit. So, rather than going through every step of the drawing process, the exercises will sometimes ask you to copy the drawing from a figure, using notes and dimensions as guides and putting objects on the indicated layers. If you have trouble remembering a command you've already learned, just go back and review the appropriate section of the book.

Creating and Using Templates

If you are familiar with the Microsoft Office suite, you are probably familiar with templates. A template is a blank file that is already set up for a specific application. For example, you might want to have letters set up in a way that is different from a report or invoice. You can have a template for each type of document, each set up for the needs of that document. That way, you don't have to spend time reformatting each new document you create.

Similarly, AutoCAD offers templates, which are drawing files that contain custom settings designed for a particular function. Out of the box, AutoCAD offers templates for ISO, ANSI, DIN, and JIS standard drawing formats. But you aren't limited to these "canned" templates. You can create your own templates set up for your particular style and method of drawing.

If you find that you use a particular drawing setup frequently, you can turn one or more of your typical drawings into a template. For example, you may want to create a set of drawings with the same scale and sheet size as an existing drawing. By turning a typical drawing into a template, you can save a lot of setup time for subsequent drawings.

Creating a Template

The following exercise guides you through creating and using a template drawing for your studio's kitchenette. Because the kitchenette will use the same layers, settings, scale, and sheet size as the bathroom drawing, you can use the Bath file as a prototype.

1. Start AutoCAD in the usual way.

2. Click File ➤ Open.

3. In the Select File dialog box, locate the Bath file you created in the last chapter. You can also use the file 04c-bath.dwg from the companion CD-ROM.

4. Click the Erase button on the Modify toolbar; then type **all**↵↵. This erases all the objects that make up the bathroom.

5. Choose File ➤ Save As. Then in the Save Drawing As dialog box, open the Save as Type drop-down list and select Drawing Template File (*.dwt). The file list window changes to display the current template files in the \Template\ folder.

NOTE   When you choose the Drawing Template File option in the Save Drawing As dialog box, AutoCAD automatically opens the folder containing the template files. The standard AutoCAD installation creates the folder named Template to contain the template files. If you wish to place your templates in a different folder, you can change the default template location using the Options dialog box. (Tools ➤ Options). Use the Files tab and then double-click the Template Drawing File Location in the list. Double-click the folder name that appears just below Template Drawing File Location; then select a new location from the Browse for Folder dialog box that appears.

---

6. Double-click the File Name input box and enter the name **8x11h**. If you're a metric user, save the drawing as **A4plan**.

7.   Click Save. The Template Description dialog box appears.

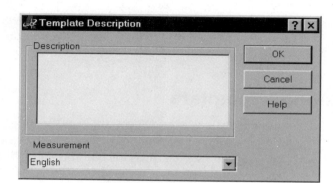

8.   Enter the following description: **Architectural One inch scale drawing on 8 1/2 by 11 inch media**. Metric users should enter the description: **Architectural 1:10 scale drawing on A4 media**.

9.   Select English or Metric from the Measurement drop-down list, depending on the unit system you're using.

10.   Click OK. You have just created a template.

11.   Close the current file without saving it. You don't want to save this file with the objects deleted.

Notice that the current drawing is now the template file you just saved. As with other Windows programs, the File ➤ Save As option makes the saved file current. This also shows that you can edit template files just as you would regular drawing files.

Using a Template

Now let's see how a template is used. You'll use the template you just created as the basis for a new drawing you will work on in this chapter.

1.   Choose File ➤ New.

2.   In the Create New Drawing dialog box, click the Use a Template button. A list box entitled Select a Template appears, along with a Preview window.

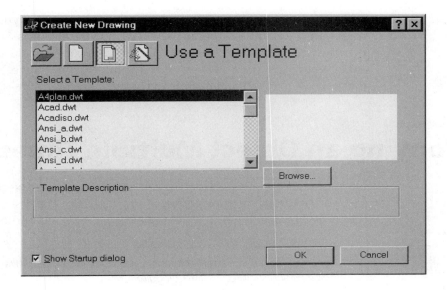

3. Click the filename `8x11h.dwt` from the Select a Template list box. Metric users should click the filename `A4plan.dwt`. The file is displayed in the Preview window. Since it is a blank file, you won't see anything in the Preview window. Notice that the description you entered earlier in the Template Description dialog box appears in the Template Description area below the list.

TIP The More Files option at the top of the Use a Template window lets you browse your hard drive to locate other files for use as a template.

4. Click OK. It may not be obvious, but your new file is set up with the same architectural units and drawing limits as the bathroom drawing. It also contains the Door, Toilet, and Tub blocks.

5. Now you need to give your new file a name. Choose File ➢ Save As. Then in the Save Drawing As dialog box, enter **Kitchen** for the filename and select the appropriate folder in which to save your new kitchen file.

6. Click Save to create the Kitchen file and close the dialog box.

You've created and used your own template file. Later, when you have established a comfortable working relationship with AutoCAD, you can create a set of templates that are custom made to your particular needs.

However, you don't need to create a template every time you want to reuse settings from another file. You can use an existing file as the basis or prototype for a new file without creating a template. Open the prototype file and then use File ➤ Save As to create a new version of the file under a new name. You can then edit the new version without affecting the original prototype file.

Copying an Object Multiple Times

Now let's explore the tools that let you quickly duplicate objects. In the next exercise, you will begin to draw parts to a small kitchen. The first exercise introduces the Array command, which enables you to draw the gas burners of a range top.

> **NOTE** An array can be in either a circular pattern, called a *polar array,* or a matrix of columns and rows, called a *rectangular array.*

Making Circular Copies

To start the range top, you have to first set the layer on which you want to draw, and then draw a circle representing the edge of one burner.

1. Set the current layer to Fixture, and turn the Grid Snap mode on by right-clicking the SNAP button in the status bar, then selecting Grid Snap On.

> **NOTE** Since you used the Bath file as a template, the Running Osnaps for Endpoint, Midpoint, and Intersection are already turned on and available in this new file.

2. Click the Circle tool on the Draw toolbar, or type **C↵**.

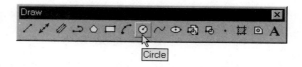

3. At the Specify Center point for circle or [3p/2p/Ttr (Tan tan tan radius)]: prompt, pick a point at coordinate 4',4'. Metric users should pick a point at coordinate 120,120.

4. At the Specify radius of circle or [Diameter]: prompt, enter **3**↵. Metric users should enter **7.6**↵. The circle appears.

Now you're ready to use the Array command to draw the burner grill. You will first draw one line representing part of the grill, and then use the Array command to create the copies.

1. Turn off both the Polar Snap and Grid Snap modes by clicking the SNAP button in the status bar and draw a 4"-long line starting from the coordinate 4'-1", 4'-0" and ending to the right of that point. Metric users should draw a line 9cm long starting at coordinate 122,120 and ending to the right of that point.

2. Zoom into the circle and line to get a better view. Your drawing should look like Figure 5.1.

FIGURE 5.1:

A close-up of the circle and line

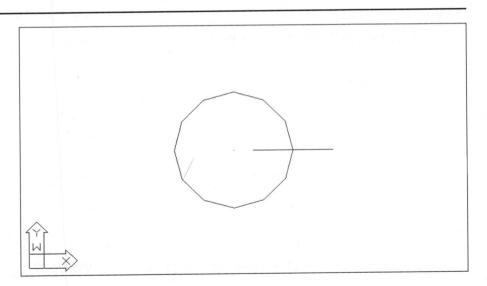

3. Click Array on the Modify toolbar, or type **AR**↵.

4. At the `Select objects:` prompt, enter **L↵**. This highlights the line you just drew.

5. Press ↵ to confirm your selection.

6. At the `Enter type of array [Rectangular/Polar] <R>:` prompt, type **P↵** to use the Polar array option. You can also right-click and select Polar from the popup menu.

7. At the `Specify Center point of array:` prompt, pick the center of the circle. To do this, Shift+right-click, then select Center from the popup menu.

TIP

Remember, to access Osnaps other than those set up as Running Osnaps, Shift+right-click the mouse, then select the Osnap from the popup menu.

WARNING

If you use the Center Osnap, you must place the cursor on the circle's circumference, not on the circle's center point.

---

8. At the `Enter the number of items in the array:` prompt, enter **8↵**. This tells AutoCAD you want seven copies plus the original.

9. At the `Specify the angle to fill (+=ccw,-=cw) <360>:` prompt, press ↵ ↵ to accept the default. The default value of 360 tells AutoCAD to copy the objects so that they are spaced evenly over a 360° arc. (If you had instead entered 180°, the lines would be evenly spaced over a 180° arc, filling only half the circle.)

NOTE

If you want to copy in a clockwise (CW) direction, you must enter a minus sign (–) before the number of degrees.

---

10. At the `Rotate objects ? <Y>:` prompt, press ↵ again to accept the default. The line copies around the center of the circle, rotating as it copies. Your drawing will look like Figure 5.2.

NOTE

In step 10, you could have the line maintain its horizontal orientation as it is copied around by entering **N↵**. But since you want it to rotate about the array center, accept the default, **Y**.

FIGURE 5.2:

The completed gas burner

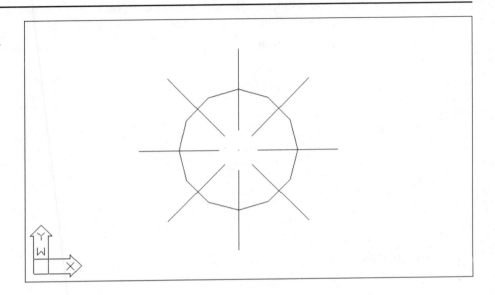

Making Row and Column Copies

Now you will draw the other three burners of the gas range by creating a rectangular array from the burner you just drew. You will first zoom back a bit to get a view of a larger area. Then you will proceed with the Array command.

1. Choose View ➤ Zoom ➤ Scale, or type **Z↵ S↵**.

2. Enter **.5x↵**. Your drawing will look like Figure 5.3.

TIP If you're not too fussy about the amount you want to zoom out, you can choose View ➤ Zoom ➤ Out to quickly reduce your view, or use the Zoom Realtime tool on the Standard toolbar. If you have a scroll mouse, you can use the scroll wheel to zoom out.

Entering **.5x** for the Zoom Scale value tells AutoCAD you want a view that reduces the width of the current view to fill half the display area, allowing you to see more of the work area. If you specify a scale value greater than 1 (5, for example), you will magnify your current view. If you leave off the **x**, your new view will be in relation to the drawing limits rather than the current view.

Now you will finish the range top. Here you will get a chance to use the Rectangular Array option to create three additional burners.

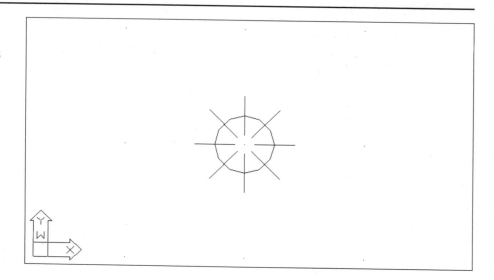

3. Click the Array tool on the Modify toolbar again, or type **AR↵**.

4. At the `Select objects:` prompt, use a window to select the entire burner. Then press ↵ to confirm your selection.

5. Enter **R↵** at the `Enter the type of array [Rectangular/Polar] <R>:` prompt to select the Rectangular option.

6. As mentioned earlier, a rectangular array is a matrix of columns and rows. At the `Enter number of rows (––) <1>:` prompt, enter **2↵**. This tells AutoCAD the number of copies you want vertically.

7. At the `Enter number of columns ( ||| ) <1>:` prompt, enter **2↵** again. This tells AutoCAD the number of copies you want horizontally.

8. At the Enter distance between rows or specify unit cell(—):
    prompt, enter **14**↵. Metric users should enter **35.5**↵. This tells AutoCAD that the
    vertical distance between the rows of burners is 14", 35.5cm for metric users.

9. At the Specify the distance between columns (|||): prompt, enter **16**↵
    to tell AutoCAD you want the horizontal distance between the columns of
    burners to be 16". Metric users should enter **40.6**↵. Your screen will look like
    Figure 5.4.

> **NOTE**
>
> The Array command "remembers" whether you last used the Polar or Rectangular
> array option and offers that option as the default.

FIGURE 5.4:

The burners arrayed

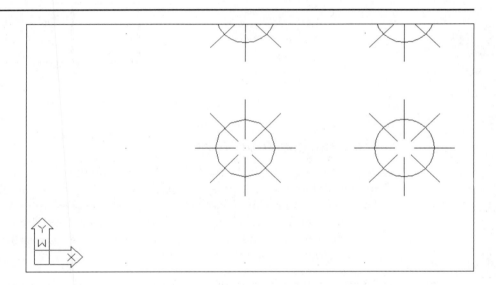

AutoCAD usually draws a rectangular array from bottom to top, and from left
to right. You can reverse the direction of the array by giving negative values for
the distance between columns and rows.

> **TIP**
>
> At times, you may want to do a rectangular array at an angle. To accomplish this,
> first set the Snap Angle setting in the Snap and Grid tab of the Drafting Settings
> dialog box (Tools ➤ Drafting Settings) to the desired angle. Then proceed with
> the Array command. Another method is to set the UCS to the desired angle.
> See *Defining a UCS* in Chapter 11. A quick way to set the Snap angle is to type
> **'Snapang**↵ at the command prompt, then enter the desired angle.

You can also use the cursor to graphically indicate an *array cell* (see Figure 5.5). An array cell is a rectangle defining the distance between rows and columns. You may want to use this option when an object is available to use as a reference from which to determine column and row distances. For example, you may have drawn a crosshatch pattern, as on a calendar, within which you want to array an object. You use the intersections of the hatch lines as references to define the array cell, which is one square in the hatch pattern.

FIGURE 5.5:

An array cell

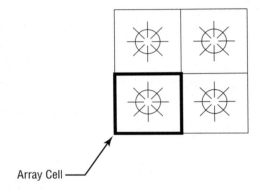

Array Cell ——

Fine-Tuning Your View

Notice that most of the burners do not appear on the display shown back in Figure 5.4. To move the view over so you can see all the burners, use the Pan command. Pan is similar to Zoom in that it changes your view of the drawing. However, Pan does not alter the magnification of the view the way Zoom does. Rather, Pan maintains the current magnification while moving your view across the drawing, just as you would pan a camera across a landscape.

NOTE   If you have a scroll mouse, you can click and drag the scroll wheel to perform the same action as the Pan Realtime tool.

To activate the Pan command, follow these steps.

1.   Click the Pan Realtime tool on the Standard toolbar, or type **P↵**.

A small hand-shaped cursor appears in place of the AutoCAD cursor.

2. Place the hand cursor in the center of the drawing area and then click and drag it downward and to the left. The view follows the motion of your mouse.

3. Continue to drag the view until it looks similar to Figure 5.6; then let go of the mouse.

To finish the kitchen, you will want a view that shows more of the drawing area. Continue with the following steps.

4. Now right-click the mouse. A popup menu appears.

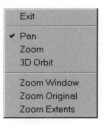

5. Select Zoom from the list. The cursor changes to the Zoom Realtime cursor.

6. Now place the cursor close to the top of the screen and click and drag the cursor downward to zoom out until your view looks like the top panel of Figure 5.7. You may need to click and drag the zoom cursor a second time to achieve this view.

7. Right-click the mouse again, and then choose Exit from the popup menu. You're now ready to add more information to the kitchen drawing.

8. Now complete the kitchenette as indicated in the bottom panel of Figure 5.7.

FIGURE 5.6:

The panned view of the top range. Metric dimensions are shown in brackets.

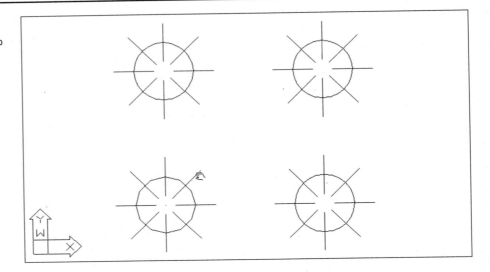

This exercise showed you how you can fine-tune your view by easily switching between Pan Realtime and Zoom Realtime. Once you get the hang of these two tools working together, you'll be able to quickly access the best view for your needs. The other options in the popup list—Zoom Window, Zoom Previous, and Zoom Extents—perform the same functions as the tools of the same name on the Standard toolbar and View pull-down menu.

NOTE   The Zoom Window option in the Zoom popup menu functions in a slightly different way from the standard Zoom Window. Instead of picking two points, you click and drag a window across your view.

While we're on the subject of display tools, don't forget the scroll bars to the right and bottom of the AutoCAD drawing area. They work like any other Windows scroll bar, offering a simple way to move up, down, left, or right of your current view.

TIP   If for some reason the scroll bars do not appear in AutoCAD, or if you prefer to turn them off, do the following. Go to the Display tab of the Options dialog box (Tools ➤ Options) and make sure that Display Scroll Bars in the Drawing Window option is either checked to turn them on or unchecked to turn them off.

FIGURE 5.7:

The final view of the range top burners (top image) and the finished kitchen (bottom image)

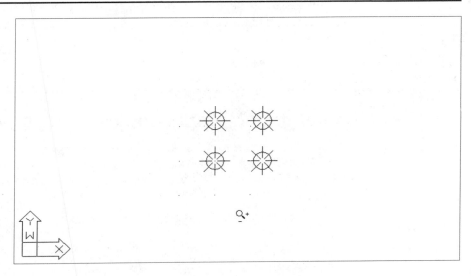

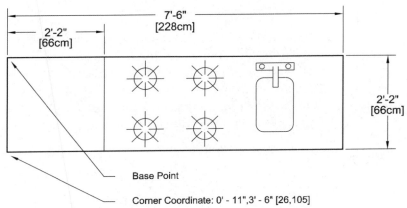

Base Point

Corner Coordinate: 0' - 11",3' - 6" [26,105]

Put Entire Kitchen on Fixture Layer

Before you save and close the kitchen file, there is one more thing you need to do. You will be using this drawing as a symbol and inserting it into the overall plan of the studio apartment unit. To facilitate accurate placement of the kitchen, you will want to change the location of the base point of this drawing to the upper-left corner of the kitchen. This will then be the "handle" of the drawing.

1. Choose Draw ➢ Block ➢ Base from the pull-down menu.

2. At the Enter base point: prompt, pick the upper-left corner of the kitchen, as indicated in the bottom image of Figure 5.7. The kitchen drawing is complete.

3. Click File ➢ Save.

Making Random Multiple Copies

The Draw ➢ Array command is useful when you want to make multiple copies in a regular pattern. But what if you need to make copies in a random pattern? You have two alternatives for accomplishing this: the Copy command's Multiple option and the Grips Move option.

To use the Copy command to make random multiple copies:

1. Click Copy Objects on the Modify toolbar, or type **CO↵**.

2. At the Select objects: prompt, select the objects you want to copy and press ↵ to confirm your selections.

3. At the Specify base point or displacement or [Multiple]: prompt, enter **M↵** to select the Multiple option.

4. At the Base point: prompt, select a base point as usual.

5. At the Specify second point or displacement or <use first point as displacement>: prompt, select a point for the copy. You will be prompted again for a second point, allowing you to make yet another copy of your object.

6. Continue to select points for more copies as desired.

7. Press ↵ to exit the Copy command when you are done.

When you use the Grips feature to make multiple random copies, you get an added level of functionality because you can also rotate, mirror, and stretch copies by using the popup menu (right-click while a grip is selected). Of course, you must have the Grips feature turned on; it is usually on by default but you may find yourself on a system that has it turned off for some reason.

1. Press the Esc key twice to make sure you are not in the middle of a command; then select the objects you want to copy.

2. Click a grip point as your base point.

3. Right-click your mouse and select Move.

4. Right-click again and select Copy.

Continued on next page

> **5.** Click the location for the copy. Notice that the rubber-banding line persists and you still see the selected objects follow the cursor.
>
> **6.** If desired, click other locations for more copies.
>
> Finally, you can make square-arrayed copies using grips by doing steps 1 through 3 above, but instead of step 4, Shift+click a copy location. Continue to hold down the Shift key and select points. The copies snap to the angle and distance you indicate with the first Shift+select point. Release the Shift key and you can make multiple random copies.

Developing Your Drawing

As mentioned briefly in Chapter 3, when using AutoCAD, you first create the most basic forms of your drawing; then you refine them. In this section you will create two drawings—the studio apartment unit and the lobby—that demonstrate this process in more detail.

First, you will construct a typical studio apartment unit using the drawings you have created thus far. In the process, you will explore the use of lines as reference objects.

You will also further examine how to use existing files as blocks. In Chapter 4, you inserted a file into another file. There is no limit to the size or number of files you can insert. As you may already have guessed, you can also *nest* files and blocks, that is, insert blocks or files within other blocks or files. Nesting can help reduce your drawing time by allowing you to build one block out of smaller blocks. For example, you can insert your door drawing into the bathroom plan. The bathroom plan can in turn be inserted into the studio unit plan, which also contains doors. Finally, the unit plan can be inserted into the overall floor plan for the studio apartment building.

Importing Settings

In this exercise, you will use the Bath file as a prototype for the studio unit plan. However, you must make a few changes to it first. Once the changes are made, you will import the bathroom and thereby import the layers and blocks contained in the bathroom file.

As you go through this exercise, observe how the drawings begin to evolve from simple forms to complex, assembled forms.

1. First, open the Bath file. If you skipped drawing the Bath file in Chapter 4, use the file named `04c-bath.dwg` from the companion CD-ROM.

2. Use the Base command and select the upper-left corner of the bathroom as the new base point for this drawing, so you can position the Bath file more accurately.

3. Save the Bath file. If you use the file from the CD-ROM, use File ➤ Save As and save it as **Bath**.

4. Choose File ➤ Close to close the Bath drawing.

Next, you will create a new file. But this time, instead of using the Start from Scratch or Use a Template option in the Create New Drawing dialog box, you'll try out the Use a Wizard option.

1. Choose File ➤ New.

2. In the Create New Drawing dialog box, choose Use a Wizard. You'll see two options in the Select a Wizard list box. Choose Quick Setup and then click OK. The Quick Setup dialog box appears.

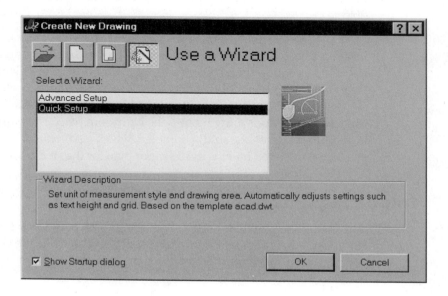

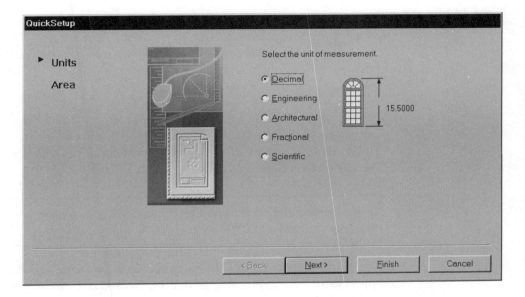

3. Click the Architectural radio button. Metric users should use the default Decimal units.

4. Click Next.

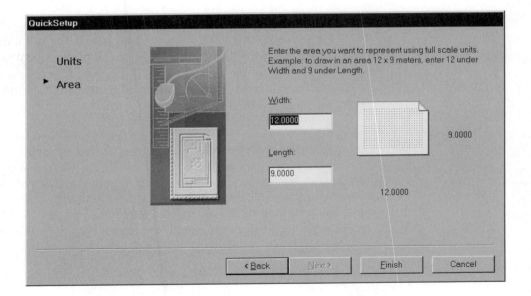

5. Enter **528** in the Width input box and **408** in the Length input box. These are the appropriate dimensions for an 8 1/2" x 11" drawing at 1/4"=1'-0" scale. Metric users should enter **1485** for the width and **1050** for the length. This is the work area for a 1:50 scale drawing on an A4 sheet.

6. Click Finish.

7. Use Tools ➤ Drafting Settings to set the snap spacing to 1" and the grid spacing to 48". This sets the grid spacing to display the equivalent of 1-inch intervals for a 1/4"=1' -0" scale drawing. Metric users should set the snap spacing to 1 and the grid spacing to 120.

NOTE If you need to find out the equivalent drawing area for a given sheet size and scale, see *Setting Up a Work Area* in Chapter 3.

Your drawing is now set up. However, this time, you used the Quick Setup Wizard option to set it up. In fact, the Quick Setup Wizard does nothing more than combine the Format ➤ Units and Format ➤ Drawing Limits options into one dialog box.

Now let's continue by laying out a typical studio unit. You'll also discover how importing a file also imports a variety of drawing items such as layers and line types.

1. Begin the unit by drawing two rectangles, one 14' wide by 24' long, and the other 14' wide by 4' long. Metric users should make the rectangles 426cm wide by 731cm long and 427cm wide by 122cm long. Place them as shown in Figure 5.8. The large rectangle represents the interior of the apartment unit, and the small rectangle represents the balcony. The size and location of the rectangles are indicated in the figure.

NOTE If you used the Rectangle tool to draw the interior and balcony of the apartment unit, then make sure you use the Explode tool on the Modify toolbar to explode the rectangles. The Rectangle tool draws a polyline rectangle instead of simple line segments, so you need to explode the rectangle to reduce it to its component lines. You'll learn more about polylines in Chapter 13.

2. Click the Insert Block tool on the Draw toolbar.

3. In the Insert Dialog box, click the Browse button and locate and select the bathroom drawing using the Select Drawing File dialog box. Then click Open.

FIGURE 5.8:

The apartment unit interior and balcony. Metric locations and dimensions are shown in brackets.

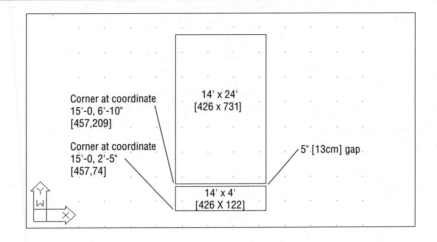

Corner at coordinate
15'-0, 6'-10"
[457,209]

Corner at coordinate
15'-0, 2'-5"
[457,74]

14' x 24'
[426 x 731]

5" [13cm] gap

14' x 4'
[426 X 122]

TIP

If you are using the **04c-bath.dwg** file from the CD-ROM, do the following: After performing step 3, change the name that appears in the Block input box to **Bath** instead of **04c-bath** before you click OK. This gives the inserted file a block name of Bath, even though its originating filename is **04c-bath**.

---

4. Click OK in the Insert dialog box, and then click the upper-left corner of the unit's interior as the insertion point (see Figure 5.9). You can use the Endpoint Osnap to accurately place the bathroom. Use a scale factor of 1.0 and a rotation angle of 0°.

NOTE

Because the Running Osnaps have not been set up in this file, you need to use the Osnap popup menu (Shift+right-click) to access the Endpoint Osnap. You can set up the Running Osnaps to take advantage of Tahoe's Auto Snap functions by right-clicking the Osnap box in the status bar. Set the Running Osnaps as described in the *Using the Layout* section of Chapter 3.

---

5. Change the two rectangles that you drew earlier to the Wall layer. To do this, select the two rectangles so they are highlighted, then open the Layer drop-down list in the Properties toolbar and select Wall. Press the Esc key twice to clear the selection.

TIP   You can also use the Match Properties tool on the Standard toolbar to change layer settings of an object to those of another object in the drawing. See *How to Quickly Match a Hatch Pattern and Other Properties* in Chapter 6.

FIGURE 5.9:

The unit after the bathroom is inserted

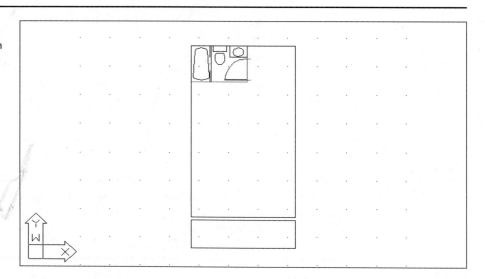

By inserting the bathroom, you imported the layers and blocks contained in the Bath file. You were then able to move previously drawn objects to the imported layers. If you are in a hurry, this can be a quick way to duplicate layers that you know exist in another drawing. This method is similar to using an existing drawing as a template, but it allows you to start work on a drawing before deciding which template to use.

WARNING   If two drawings contain the same layers and blocks, and one of these drawings is imported into the other, the layer settings and block definitions of the *current* file will take priority over those of the *imported* file. This is important to remember in cases where the layer settings and block definitions are different in the two files.

Importing Settings from External Reference Files

As explained in the Chapter 4 sidebar, *An Alternative to Blocks*, you can use the External Reference (Xref) Attach option to use another file as a background or Xref file. Xref files are similar to blocks except that they do not actually become part of the current drawing's database; nor do the settings from the cross-referenced file automatically become part of the current drawing.

If you want to import layers, line types, text styles, and so forth from an Xref file, you must use the Xbind command, which you will learn more about as you work through this book. Xbind allows you to attach dimension style settings (discussed in Chapter 9 and in Appendix D), layers, line types, or text styles (discussed in Chapter 8) from a cross-referenced file to the current file.

You can also use Xbind to turn a cross-referenced file into an ordinary block, thereby importing all the new settings contained in that file.

See Chapter 12 for a more detailed description of how to use the External References (Xref) and Xbind commands.

Another tool for importing settings is the AutoCAD DesignCenter. You'll learn about the DesignCenter in Chapter 22.

Using Osnap Tracking to Place Objects

You will draw lines in the majority of your work, so it is important to know how to manipulate lines to your best advantage. In this section, you will look at some of the more common ways to use and edit these fundamental drawing objects. The following exercises show you the process of drawing lines, rather than just how individual commands work. While you're building walls and adding doors, you'll get a chance to become more familiar with Polar Tracking and Osnap Tracking.

Roughing In the Line Work

The bathroom you inserted in the last section has only one side of its interior walls drawn (walls are usually shown by double lines). In this next exercise, you will draw the other side. Rather than trying to draw the wall perfectly the first time, you will "sketch" in the line work and then perform a clean-up process, in a way similar to manual drafting.

1. Zoom into the bathroom so that the entire bathroom and part of the area around it are displayed, as in Figure 5.10.

NOTE You may notice that some of the arcs in your bathroom drawing are not smooth. Don't be alarmed; this is how AutoCAD displays arcs and circles in enlarged views. The arcs will be smooth when they are plotted. If you want to see them now as they actually are stored in the file, you can regenerate the drawing by typing **Regen.⌐** at the command prompt. Chapter 6 discusses regeneration in more detail.

FIGURE 5.10:

The enlarged view of the bathroom

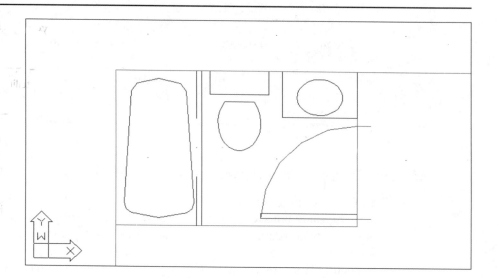

2. Select Wall from the Layer drop-down list in the Properties toolbar to make Wall the current layer.

3. Make sure that the OTRACK button on the status bar is depressed indicating that Osnap Tracking is turned on.

SNAP GRID ORTHO POLAR OSNAP OTRACK LWT MODEL

4. Choose Line from the Draw menu, or type **L**⏎.

5. At the `Specify first point:` prompt, open the Osnap menu and select the Endpoint Osnap.

6. Move your cursor over the lower-right corner of the bathroom so that the Endpoint Osnap marker appears, but don't click it. As you move the cursor downward, the tracking vector appears.

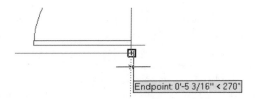

If the tracking vector doesn't appear at first, move your cursor over the corner again until the tracking vector does appear.

TIP   Remember that a little cross appears at the Osnap location telling you that the Osnap Tracking has "locked on" to that location.

---

7. With the tracking vector visible, point the cursor directly downward from the corner, then type **5**⏎. Metric users should type **13**⏎ while pointing the cursor downward. Now a line starts 5" (or 13cm) below the lower-right corner of the bathroom.

8. Continue the line horizontally to the left to slightly cross the left wall of the apartment unit, as illustrated in the top image of Figure 5.11. Press ⏎.

In the foregoing exercise, Osnap Tracking mode allowed you to specify a starting point of a line at an exact distance from the corner of the bathroom. In step 6, you used the Direct Distance method for specifying distance and direction.

NOTE   If you prefer, you can also select From from the Osnap popup menu, then open the Osnap popup menu again and select Endpoint. Select the corner, then enter a polar coordinate such as **@5<-90** to accomplish the same task as this exercise.

FIGURE 5.11:

The first wall line and the wall line by the door

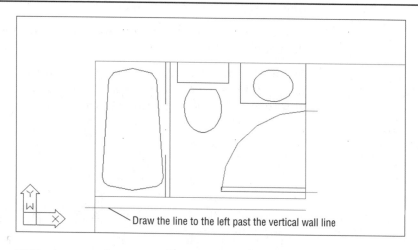

Draw the line to the left past the vertical wall line

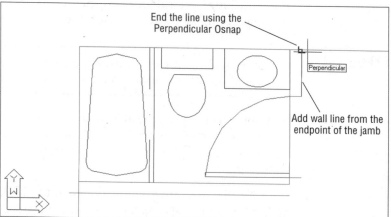

End the line using the Perpendicular Osnap

Perpendicular

Add wall line from the endpoint of the jamb

Understanding the Osnap Tracking Vector

The Osnap Tracking vector only comes into play after you've placed an Osnap marker on a location, in this case, the corner of the bathroom. It won't appear at any other time. If you have both Running Osnaps and Osnap Tracking turned on, you'll get the tracking vector every time the cursor lands on an Osnap location. This can be a bit confusing to novice users, so you may want to use Osnap Tracking sparingly until you become more comfortable with it.

Continued on next page

Also, since Polar Tracking uses a tracking vector, you may get the two confused. Remember that Polar Tracking lets you point the cursor in a specific direction while selecting points. If you're an experienced AutoCAD user, you can think of it as a more intelligent Ortho mode. On the other hand, Osnap Tracking lets you align points to Osnap locations. Experienced AutoCAD users can think of Osnap Tracking as a more intelligent XYZ filter option.

Now let's continue with the line work.

1. Draw another line upward from the endpoint of the top door jamb to meet the top wall of the unit (see the bottom image of Figure 5.11). Use the Polar Tracking mode and the Perpendicular Osnap to pick the top wall of the unit. This causes the line to end precisely on the wall line in perpendicular position, as in the bottom image of Figure 5.11.

TIP   The Perpendicular Osnap override can also be used to draw a line perpendicular to a nonorthogonal line—one at a 45° angle, for instance.

2. Draw a line connecting the two door jambs. Then change that line to the Ceiling layer (see first panel of Figure 5.12).

3. Draw a line 6" downward from the endpoint of the door jamb nearest the corner as shown in the second panel of Figure 5.12.

FIGURE 5.12:

The corner of the bathroom wall and the filleted wall around the bathroom

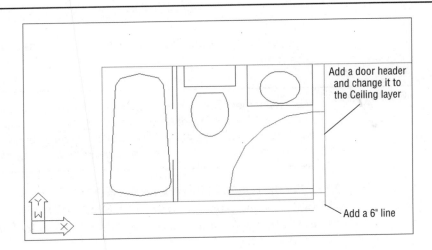

Add a door header and change it to the Ceiling layer

Add a 6" line

FIGURE 5.12 CONTINUED:

The corner of the bathroom wall and the filleted wall around the bathroom

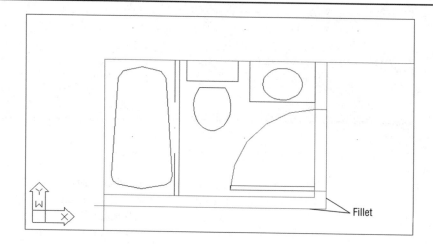

Cleaning Up the Line Work

You've drawn some of the wall lines, approximating their endpoint locations. Next you will use the Fillet command to join lines exactly end to end.

1. Click the Fillet tool on the Modify toolbar.

2. Type **R↵ 0↵** to set the fillet radius to 0; then press ↵ to repeat the Fillet command.

> **NOTE**
>
> There is another command, the Chamfer command, that performs a similar function to the Fillet command. Unlike Fillet, the Chamfer command allows you to join two lines with an intermediate beveled line rather than an arc. Chamfer can be set to join two lines at a corner in exactly the same manner as Fillet.

3. Fillet the two lines by picking the vertical and horizontal lines, as indicated in the second panel of Figure 5.12. Notice that these points lie on the portion of the line you want to keep. Your drawing will look like the second panel of Figure 5.12.

If you are a veteran AutoCAD user, you should note that the default value for the Fillet command is now .5 instead of 0.

4. Fillet the bottom wall of the bathroom with the left wall of the unit, as shown in Figure 5.13. Make sure the points you pick on the wall lines are on the side of the line you want to keep, not the side you want trimmed.

5. Fillet the top wall of the unit with the right-side wall of the bathroom as shown in Figure 5.13.

FIGURE 5.13:

The cleaned-up wall intersections

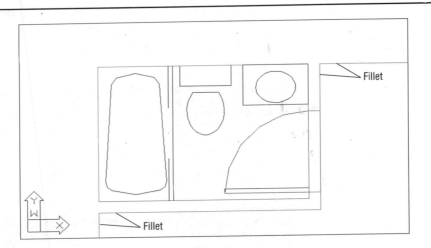

You can select two lines at once for the fillet operation by using a Crossing window by typing **C⏎** at the `Select first object:` prompt. The two endpoints closest to the fillet location are trimmed.

Where you select the lines affects how the lines are joined. As you select objects for Fillet, the side of the line where you click is the side that remains when the lines are joined. Figure 5.14 illustrates how the Fillet command works and shows what the Fillet options do.

If you select two parallel lines during the Fillet command, the two lines are joined with an arc.

FIGURE 5.14:

The place where you click the object to select it determines what part of an object gets filleted.

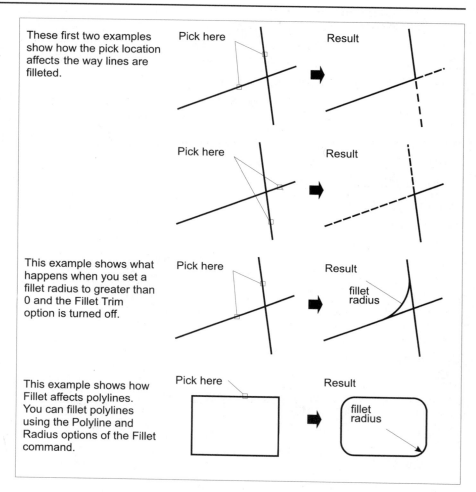

These first two examples show how the pick location affects the way lines are filleted.

Pick here   Result

Pick here   Result

This example shows what happens when you set a fillet radius to greater than 0 and the Fillet Trim option is turned off.

Pick here   Result

fillet radius

This example shows how Fillet affects polylines. You can fillet polylines using the Polyline and Radius options of the Fillet command.

Pick here   Result

fillet radius

Now import the Kitchen plan you drew earlier in this chapter.

1. Click Insert Block on the Draw toolbar, then click Browse and locate the kitchen drawing you created earlier in this chapter. Make sure you leave the Specify On-Screen option unchecked under the Scale and Rotation button groups of the Insert dialog box.

2. Place the kitchen drawing at the wall intersection below the bathtub (see the top image of Figure 5.15).

TIP   If you didn't complete the kitchen earlier in this chapter, you can insert the `04a-kitchen.dwg` file from the companion CD-ROM.

3. Adjust your view with Pan and Zoom so that the upper portion of the apartment unit is centered in drawing area, as illustrated in the top image of Figure 5.15.

FIGURE 5.15:

The view after using Pan, with the door inserted and the jamb and header added

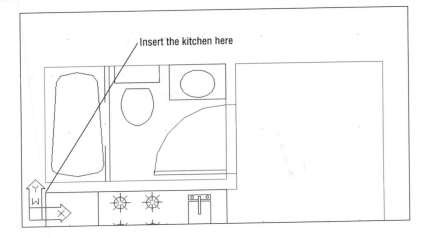

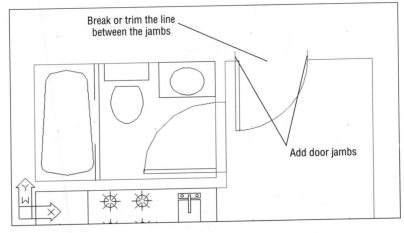

In this exercise, you'll use a number of new tools together to streamline the drawing process. You'll practice using the Osnap Tracking feature and the From

Osnap option to place the entry door at an exact distance from the upper corner of the floor plan.

1. Open the Insert dialog box again by right-clicking the Command window. Select Recent Commands ➤ Insert from the popup menu.

2. Select Door from the Name drop-down list.

3. Make sure the Specify On-Screen option is checked for the Rotation button group and Specify On-Screen is not checked in the Scale button group, then click OK. You'll see the Door follow the cursor in the drawing window.

4. Shift+right-click the mouse to open the Osnap popup menu, then select From.

5. Make sure the OSNAP and OTRACK buttons on the status bar are on, then use the Endpoint Running Osnap to pick the corner where the upper horizontal wall line meets the bathroom wall.

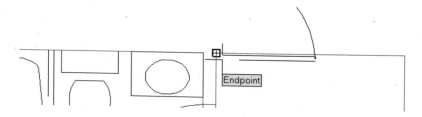

6. Move the cursor over the Osnap marker so that the Osnap Tracking vector appears from the corner. Now as you move the cursor away to the right, you'll see the Osnap Tracking vector extend from the corner.

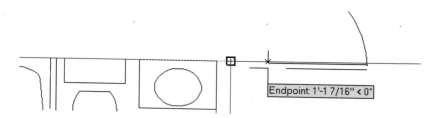

7. Now, move the cursor to the right so that the tracking vector readout shows roughly 6 inches, or 15cm for metric users.

8. With the cursor in this position, enter **5**↵. Metric users should enter **13**↵. The door is placed exactly 5 (or 13) units to the right of the corner.

9. At the `Rotation angle:` prompt, enter **270**⏎. Or if you prefer, turn on Polar Tracking to orient the door so that it is swinging *into* the studio. You've now accurately placed the entry door in the studio apartment.

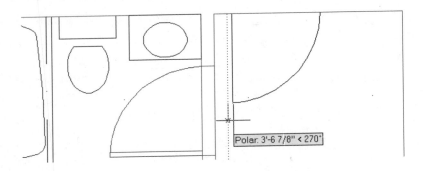

10. Make sure the door is on the Door layer.

TIP   For a shortcut to setting an object's layer, you can select the object or objects, and then select a layer from the Layer drop-down list in the Properties toolbar.

Now add the finishing touches to the entry door.

1. Add 5" (13cm for metric users) door jambs and change their layer property to the Jamb layer, as shown in the bottom image of Figure 5.15.

2. Choose the Break tool in the Modify toolbar, and then select the header over the entry door (see the bottom image of Figure 5.15).

NOTE   If you need some help with the Break command, see *Modifying an Object* in Chapter 3, and the *Different Methods for Using the Break Command* sidebar, here in Chapter 5.

---

3. Type **F**⏎ to use the first point option; then select the endpoint of one of the door jambs.

4. At the `Specify second break point:` prompt, select the endpoint of the other jamb as shown in the bottom image of Figure 5.15.

5. Draw the door header on the Ceiling layer, as shown in Figure 5.16.

6. Click Offset on the Modify toolbar and offset the top wall lines of the unit and the door header up 5" (13cm for metric users), so they connect with the top end of the door jamb, as shown in Figure 5.16. Don't forget to include the short wall line from the door to the bathroom wall.

7. Use File ➤ Save As to save your file under the name Unit.

FIGURE 5.16:

The other side of the wall

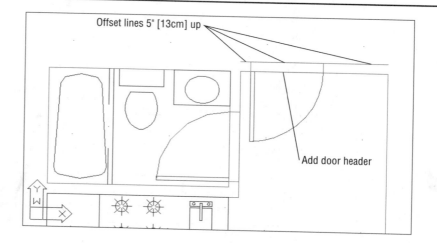

Different Methods for Using the Break Command

In the exercise for finishing the Unit plan, you used the Break command to accurately place a gap in a line over the entry door. In Chapter 3, you broke a line at a single point to create multiple, contiguous line segments. In both cases you used the F option. You can also break a line without the F option with a little less accuracy. By not using the F option, the point at which you select the object is used as the first break point. If you're in a hurry, you can dispense with the F option and simply place a gap in an approximate location. You can then later use other tools to adjust the gap.

In addition, you can use locations on other objects to select the first and second points of a break. For example, you may want to align an opening with another opening some distance away. Once you've selected the line to break, you can then use the F option and select two points on the existing opening to define the first and second break points. The break points will align in an orthogonal direction to the selected points.

Using Polar and Osnap Tracking as a Construction Line Tool

Now you need to extend the upper wall line 5" (13cm for metric users) beyond the right-side interior wall of the unit. To accomplish this, you will use Polar Tracking to locate the endpoint of the line. Start by changing the Polar Tracking setting to include a 45° angle.

1. Right-click the Polar button in the status bar, then select Settings. The Polar Tracking tab of the Drafting Settings dialog box appears.

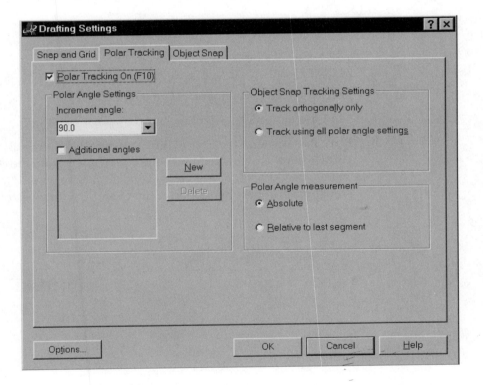

2. Select 45 from the Increment Angle drop-down list in the upper-left corner of the dialog box.

3. In the Object Snap Tracking Settings button group, make sure that the Track Using All Polar Angle Settings option is selected, then click OK.

You're ready to extend the wall line. For this operation, you'll use grip editing.

1. Click the wall line at the top of the plan to the right of the door to select it and expose its grips.

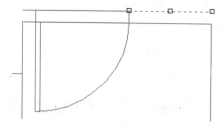

2. Click the ORTHO mode button to turn on Ortho mode in the status bar. This keeps the wall line straight as you edit it.

3. Click the right-most grip of the line to make it "hot."

4. Place the cursor on the upper-right corner of the plan until you see the End-point Osnap marker, then move the cursor away from the corner at a 45° angle. The Osnap Tracking vector appears at a 45° angle. Notice the small X that appears at the intersection of the Osnap Tracking vector and the line.

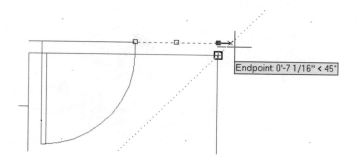

With the Osnap Tracking vector and the line intersecting, click the mouse button. The line changes to extend exactly 5 units beyond the vertical interior wall of the plan.

5. Press the Esc key twice to clear your selection, then repeat the process for the horizontal wall line to the left of the door to extend that line to the left corner.

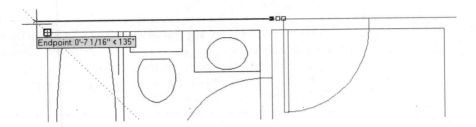

6. Click View ➤ Zoom ➤ All to view the entire drawing. It will look like Figure 5.17.

TIP   With Polar Tracking set to 45 and Osnap Tracking turned on, you may find that you are selecting points that you don't really want to select in a crowded drawing. Just remember that if a drawing becomes too crowded, you can turn these options off temporarily by clicking the OTRACKor POLAR buttons in the status bar.

FIGURE 5.17:

The studio unit thus far

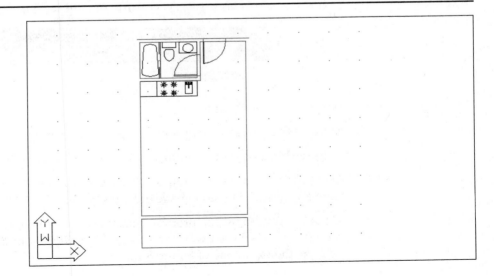

In this exercise, you used Polar Tracking and the Ortho mode to accurately position the two lines used for the exterior walls of the studio unit. This shows you how you can take advantage of existing geometry with a combination of tools in the status bar.

NOTE If you prefer to use an actual line as a construction tool, you can use the *ray*. A ray is a line that starts from a point you select and continues off to some infinite distance. You specify the start point and angle of the ray. You can place a ray at the corner at a 45° angle, then fillet the ray to the horizontal wall line to shorten or lengthen the line to the appropriate length.

Now you will finish the balcony by adding a sliding glass door and a rail. This time, you will use lines for construction as well as for parts of the drawing. First, you'll add the door jamb by drawing an Xline. An Xline is a line that has an infinite length, but unlike the ray, it extends in both directions. After drawing the Xline, you'll use it to quickly position the door jambs.

1. Zoom into the balcony area.

2. Click the Construction Line tool on the Draw toolbar, or type **XL↵**. You'll see this prompt:

    ```
    Specify a point or [Hor/Ver/Ang/Bisect/Offset]:
    ```

3. Type **O↵** to select the Offset.

4. At the `Offset distance:` prompt, type **4'↵**. Metric users should type **122↵**.

5. At the `Select objects:` prompt, click the wall line at the right of the unit.

6. At the `Side to offset:` prompt, click a point to the left of the wall. The Xline appears (see the top image of Figure 5.18).

7. At the `Select objects:` prompt, click the left wall line, and then click to the right of the selected wall to create another Xline. Your drawing should look like the top image of Figure 5.18.

Next, you'll edit the Xlines to form the jambs.

8. Click Trim from the Modify toolbar.

9. Select the Xlines and the two horizontal lines representing the wall between the unit and the balcony, and press ↵. You can use either a crossing window or select each line individually. You have just selected the objects to trim to.

FIGURE 5.18:

Drawing the door opening

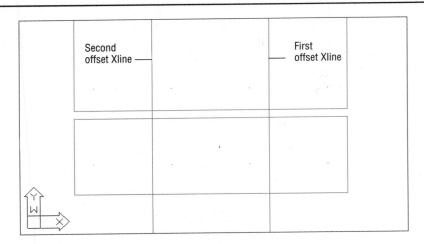

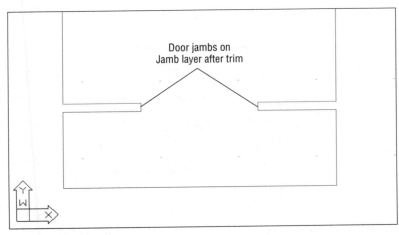

You can also use the Fence selection option to select the lines to be trimmed. See *Other Selection Options* in Chapter 2 or *Building on Previously Drawn Objects* in Chapter 12.

10. Click the horizontal lines at any point between the two Xlines. Then click the Xlines above and below the horizontal lines to trim them. Your drawing will look like the bottom image of Figure 5.18.

11. Add lines on the Ceiling layer to represent the door header.

12. Now draw lines between the two jambs (on the Door layer) to indicate a sliding glass door (see Figure 5.19).

FIGURE 5.19:

Finishing the sliding glass door

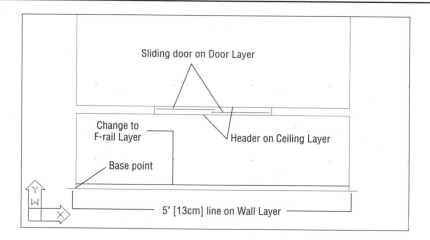

The Xline Options

There is more to the Xline command than you have seen in the exercises of this chapter. Here is a list of the Xline options and their use:

Hor   Draws horizontal Xlines as you click points.

Ver   Draws vertical Xlines as you click points.

Angle   Draws Xlines at a specified angle as you pick points.

Bisect   Draws Xlines bisecting an angle or a location between two points.

Offset   Draws Xlines offset at a specified distance.

The wall facing the balcony is now complete. To finish off the unit, you need to show a handrail and the corners of the balcony wall.

1. Offset the bottom line of the balcony 3" toward the top of the drawing. Metric users should offset the line 7.6 units.

2. Create a new layer called **F-rail**, and assign this offset line to it.

3. Add a 5" (13cm for metric users) horizontal line to the lower corners of the balcony, as shown in Figure 5.19.

4. Now choose Draw ➤ Block ➤ Base from the pull-down menu to set the base point at the lower-left corner of the balcony at the location shown in Figure 5.19.

5. Change the lines indicating walls to the Wall layer, and put the sliding glass door on the Door layer (see Figure 5.19).

6. Zoom back to the previous view. Your drawing should now look like Figure 5.20.

7. Click File ➤ Save to save the drawing.

FIGURE 5.20:

The completed studio apartment unit

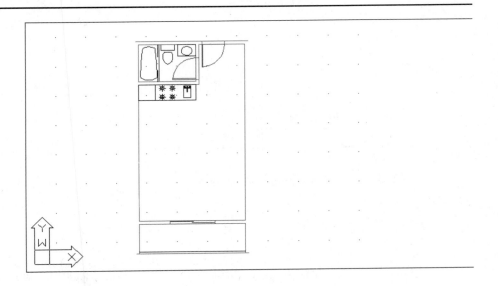

Your studio apartment unit plan is now complete. The exercises you've just completed show you a typical set of operations you'll perform while building your drawings. In fact, nearly 80 percent of what you will do in AutoCAD is represented here.

Now, to review the drawing process, and to create a drawing you'll use later, you're going to draw the apartment building's lobby. As you follow the steps, refer to Figure 5.21.

As is usual in floor plans, the elevator is indicated by the box with the large X through it, and the stair shaft is indicated by the box with the row of vertical lines through it. If you are in a hurry, there is a finished version of this file on the companion CD-ROM.

FIGURE 5.21:

Drawing the lobby plan. Metric dimensions are shown in brackets.

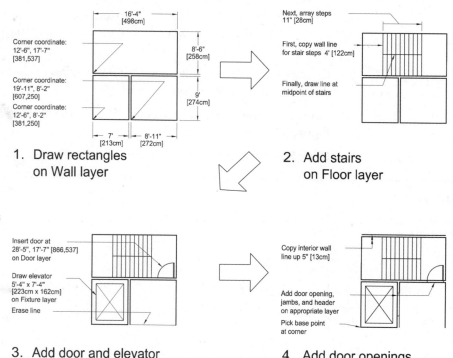

1. Draw rectangles on Wall layer

2. Add stairs on Floor layer

3. Add door and elevator

4. Add door openings

Take the following steps to draw the apartment building lobby:

1. Create a new file called Lobby, using the Unit file as a prototype. (Open the Unit file, choose File ➢ Save As, and enter **Lobby** for the new filename).

2. Erase the entire unit (Erase ➢ All).

3. Begin by drawing the three main rectangles that represent the outlines of the stair shaft, the elevator shaft, and the lobby.

4. To draw the stairs, offset the stair shaft's left wall to the right a distance of 4' (122cm). This creates the first line representing the steps.

5. Array this line in one row of ten columns, using 11" (28cm) column spacing.

6. Draw the center line dividing the two flights of stairs.

7. Draw the elevator and insert the door. Practice using Xlines here.

8. Draw the door jambs. Edit the door openings to add the door headers. Your plan should resemble the one in Figure 5.21, step 4.

9. Once you are finished, save the Lobby file.

How to Quickly Set the Current Layer to That of an Existing Object

As your list of layers grows, you may find it difficult to quickly locate the exact layer you want. You may know that you want to draw objects on the same layer as an existing object in a drawing, but you are not sure what that layer is.

In previous versions of AutoCAD, you would have to take the following steps:

1. Determine the layer of the object whose layer you want to match.

2. Open the layer list.

3. Scroll down the list until you find the layer name.

4. Select the layer.

If the list of layers is quite long, you may forget the name of the layer before you find it in the list!

AutoCAD offers the *Make Object's Layer Current* tool to help you easily set the current layer. This tool can be found on the Object Properties toolbar next to the Layers tool.

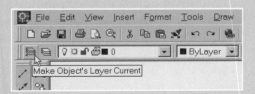

Continued on next page

The Make Object's Layer Current tool is a simple yet powerful tool that lets you set the current layer by selecting an object in the drawing instead of selecting its name from a list. To use it, click the Make Object's Layer Current tool and then click the object whose layer you want to make current. This reduces the three-step or four-step process of earlier AutoCAD versions to one click.

Remember this tool the next time you are faced with a drawing that has a very large list of layers.

Finding Distances Along Arcs

You've seen how you can use lines to help locate objects and geometry in your drawing. But if you need to find distances along a curved object such as an arc, lines don't always help. This section describes two ways to find exact distances on arcs. Try these exercises when you're not working through the main tutorial.

Finding a Point at a Particular Distance from Another Point

At times you'll need to find the location of a point on an arc that lies at a known distance from another point on the arc. The distance can be described as a cord of the arc, but how do you find the exact cord location? To find a cord along an arc, follow these steps.

1. Click the Circle tool on the Draw toolbar or type **C**↵.

2. Use the Endpoint Osnap to click the endpoint of an arc.

3. At the `Specify radius of circle or [Diameter]:` prompt, enter the length of the cord distance you wish to locate along the arc.

The point where the circle intersects the arc is the endpoint of the cord distance from the endpoint of the arc (see Figure 5.22). You can then use the Intersect Osnap override to select the circle and arc intersection.

FIGURE 5.22:

Finding a cord distance
along an arc using a circle

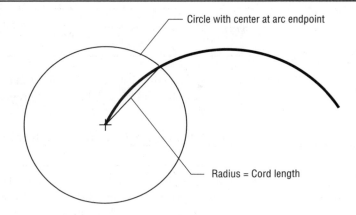

Circle with center at arc endpoint

Radius = Cord length

Finding an Exact Distance Along an Arc

To find an exact distance along an arc or curve (nonlinear), or to mark off specific distance increments along an arc or curve, do the following:

1. Choose Format ➤ Point Style from the pull-down menu to open the Point Style dialog box.

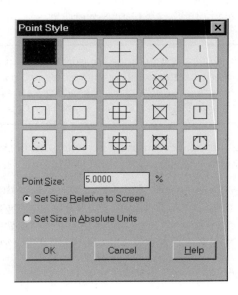

> **TIP**   You can also set the point style by setting the Pdmode system variable to 3. See Appendix D for more on Pdmode.

2. In the Point Style dialog box, click the icon that looks like an X, in the top row. Also be sure the Set Size Relative to Screen radio button is selected. Then click OK.

3. Choose Draw ➤ Point ➤ Measure from the pull-down menu or type **me**.↵.

> **TIP**   Another command called Divide (Draw ➤ Point ➤ Divide) marks off a line, arc, or curve into equal divisions, as opposed to divisions of a length you specify. You might use Divide to divide an object into twelve equal segments, for example. Aside from this difference in function, Divide works in exactly the same way as Measure.

4. At the `Select object to measure:` prompt, click the arc near the end from which you wish to find the distance.

5. At the `Specify length of segment or [Block]:` prompt, enter the distance you are interested in. A series of Xs appears on the arc, marking off the specified distance along the arc. You can select the exact location of the Xs using the Node Osnap override (see Figure 5.23).

> **TIP**   The Block option of the Measure command allows you to specify a block to be inserted at the specified segment length, in place of the Xs on the arc. You have the option to align the block with the arc as it is inserted. (This is similar to the polar array's Rotate Objects As They Are Copied option.)

The Measure command also works on Bezier curves. You'll get a more detailed look at the Measure command in Chapter 13.

As you work with AutoCAD, you'll find that constructing temporary geometry such as the circle and points in the two foregoing examples will help you solve problems in new ways. Don't hesitate to experiment! Remember, you've always got the Save and Undo commands to help you recover from mistakes.

FIGURE 5.23:

Finding an exact distance along an arc using points and the Measure command

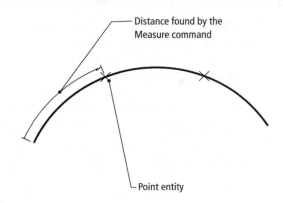

Distance found by the Measure command

Point entity

Changing the Length of Objects

Suppose, after finding the length of an arc, you realize you need to lengthen the arc by a specific amount. The Modify ➤ Lengthen command lets you lengthen or shorten arcs, lines, splines, and elliptical arcs. Here's how to lengthen an arc.

1. Click the Lengthen tool on the Modify toolbar or type **len**↵.

2. At the Select an object or [DElta/Percent/Total/DYnamic]: prompt, type **T**↵.

3. At the Specify total length or [Angle] <1.0000)>: prompt, enter the length you want for the arc.

4. At the Select an object to change or [Undo]: prompt, click the arc you wish to change. Be sure to click at a point nearest the end you want to lengthen. The arc increases in length to the size you specified.

The Lengthen command also shortens an object if it is currently longer than the value you enter.

In this short example, you have learned how to change an object to a specific length. You can use other criteria to change an object's length, using these options available in the Lengthen command:

DElta   Lets you lengthen or shorten an object by a specific length. To specify an angle rather than a length, use the Angle suboption.

Percent   Lets you increase or decrease the length of an object by a percentage of its current length.

Total   Lets you specify the total length or angle of an object.

DYnamic   Lets you graphically change the length of an object using your cursor.

Creating a New Drawing Using Parts from Another Drawing

This section will explain how to use the Wblock command (which you learned about in Chapter 4), to create a separate stair drawing using the stair you've already drawn for the lobby. Although you haven't turned the existing stair into a block, you can still use Wblock to turn parts of a drawing into a file.

1.   If you closed the Lobby file, open it now. If you didn't create the Lobby drawing, open the Lobby.dwg file from the companion CD-ROM.

2.   Click File ➤ Export or type **export**↵.

3.   When the Export Data File dialog box appears, enter **stair.dwg** in the File Name input box and click Save. By including the .dwg filename extension, AutoCAD knows that you want to export to a drawing file and not some other format, such as a .dxf or .wmf file format.

4.   At the Enter name of existing block or [= (block=output file)/* (whole drawing)] <define new drawing>: prompt, press ↵. When you export to a .dwg format, AutoCAD assumes you want to export a block. Bypassing this prompt by pressing ↵ tells AutoCAD that you want to create a file from part of the drawing, rather than from a block.

5.   At the Insertion base point: prompt, pick the lower-right corner of the stair shaft. This tells AutoCAD the base point for the new drawing.

6. At the Select objects: prompt, use a window to select the stair shaft, as shown in Figure 5.24.

7. When the stair shaft, including the door, is highlighted, press ↵ to confirm your selection. The stair disappears.

8. Since you want the stair to remain in the lobby drawing, click the Undo button to bring it back. Undo does not affect any files you may export with File ➤ Export, Wblock, or the Make Block tool.

FIGURE 5.24:

A selection window enclosing the stair shaft

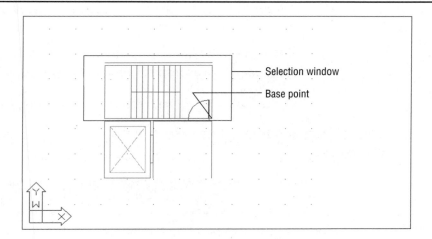

Drawing Parallel Lines

Frequently, when working on an architectural project, you will first do your schematic layout using simple lines for walls. Then, as the design requirements begin to take shape, you can start to add more detailed information about the walls, for example, indicating wall materials or locations for insulation. AutoCAD provides *multilines* (the multiline command) for this purpose. Multilines are double lines that can be used to represent walls. Multilines can also be customized to display solid fills, center lines, and additional line types shown in Figure 5.25. You can save your custom multilines as Multiline styles, which are in turn saved in special files for easy access from other drawings.

TIP   Multilines are especially useful for metric users who need to represent cavity walls.

FIGURE 5.25:

Samples of multiline styles

Dots indicate
pick points.

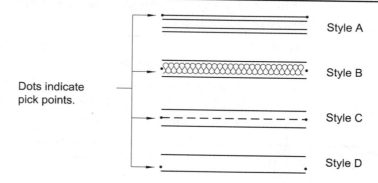

Style A

Style B

Style C

Style D

The following exercise shows you how you might continue to build information into your drawings by using multilines to indicate wall types.

1. Click the Multiline tool on the Draw toolbar, or type **ML**↵. You'll see two lines in the prompt area:

    ```
    Current settings: Justification = Top, Scale = 1.00, Style = STANDARD
    Specify start point or [Justification/Scale/STyle]:
    ```

NOTE   The first line in the prompt area gives you the current settings for Multiline.

---

2. Type **S**↵ (for Scale).

3. At the `Enter mline scale <1.00>:` prompt, type **5**↵.

4. Pick a point to start the double line.

5. Continue to select points to draw more double line segments, or type **C**↵ to close the series of lines.

Let's take a look at the meaning of the multiline settings included in the prompt you saw in steps 1 and 2 above.

> **Justification**   Controls how far off center the double lines are drawn. The default sets the double lines equidistant from the points you pick. By changing the justification value to be greater than or less than 0, you can have AutoCAD draw double lines off center from the pick points.

Scale   Lets you set the width of the double line.

Close   Closes a sequence of double lines, much as the Line command's Close option does.

Style   Lets you select a style for multilines. You can control the number of lines in the multiline, as well as the line types used for each line in the multiline style, by using the Mledit command.

Customizing Multilines

In Chapter 4 you learned how to make a line appear dashed or dotted using line types. In a similar way, you can control the appearance of multilines using the Multiline Style dialog box. This dialog box allows you to

- Set the number of lines that appear in the multiline.
- Control the color of each multiline.
- Control the line type of each multiline.
- Apply a fill between the outermost lines of a multiline.
- Control if and how ends of multilines are closed.

To access the Multiline Styles dialog box, choose Format ➢ Multiline Style from the pull-down menu, or type **Mlstyle**⏎ at the command prompt.

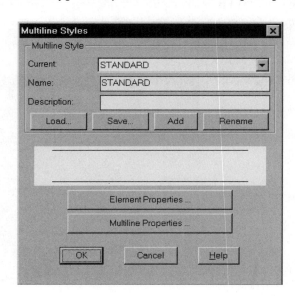

WARNING   Once you have drawn a multiline in a particular style, you cannot modify the style settings for that style in the Element Properties and Multiline Properties dialog boxes described later in this section. The Multiline Styles dialog box only allows you to set up styles before they are used in a drawing.

At the top of the Multiline Styles dialog box, a group of buttons and input boxes allow you to select the multiline style you want to work with. The Current popup list offers you a selection of existing styles. In the Name input box you can name a new style you are creating, or rename an existing style. The Description input box lets you attach a description to a multiline style for easy identification. You use the Add and Save buttons to create and save multiline styles as files so they can be accessed by any AutoCAD drawing. With the Load button, you can retrieve a saved style for use in the current drawing. Rename lets you change the name of a multiline style (the default style in a new drawing is called Standard).

In the lower half of the Multiline Styles dialog box are two buttons—Element Properties and Multiline Properties—that allow you to make adjustments to the multiline style currently indicated at the top of the dialog box. This multiline is also previewed in the middle of the dialog box.

Element Properties

In the Element Properties dialog box, you control the properties of the individual elements of a newly created style, including the number of lines that appear in the multiline, their color, and the distance they appear from your pick points.

The Element Properties settings are not available for existing multiline styles.

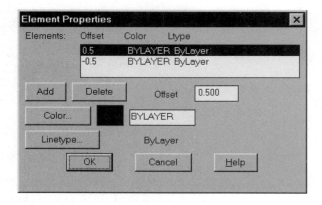

For example, click the Add button, and another line is added to your multiline. The offset distance of the new line appears in the list box. The default value for new lines is 0.0, which places the line at the center of the standard multiline. To delete a line, highlight its offset value in the list box and click the Delete button. To change the amount of offset, highlight it and enter a new value in the Offset input box.

To change the color and line type of individual lines, use the Color and Line-type buttons, which open the Color and Select Linetype dialog boxes, both of which you have already worked with. Figure 5.26 contains some examples of multilines and their corresponding Element Properties settings.

TIP

You can easily indicate an insulated wall in an architectural drawing by adding a third center line (offset of 0.0), and giving that center line a *batting* line. This line type draws an S-shaped pattern typically used to represent fiberglass batt insulation in a floor plan. To see how other wall patterns can be created, see the sections on line-type customization in Chapter 20.

Multiline Properties

The Multiline Properties button lets you control how the multiline is capped at its ends, as well as whether joints are displayed.

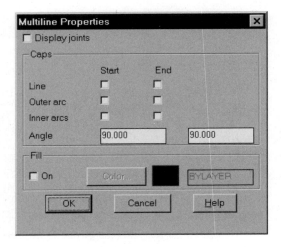

To turn a cap on, click the check box next to the type of cap you want. If you prefer, you can give your multiline style a solid fill, using the Fill check box.

FIGURE 5.26:

Samples of multiline styles
you can create

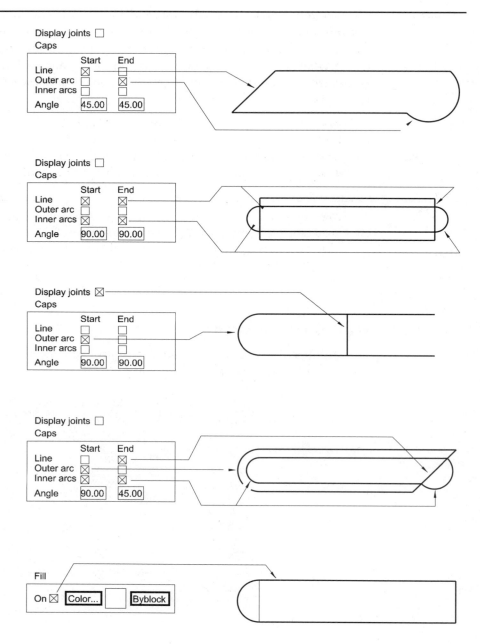

TIP

A solid-filled multiline can be used where you need to fill in a wall with a solid shade (or *pouche,* to use the drafting term). You can quickly add a pouche by setting one multiline offset to be 0.0 and the other to be the width of the wall. Then trace either the inside or outside of the wall to be pouched, using the multiline style with the Fill option turned on.

Joining and Editing Multilines

Multilines are unique in their ability to combine several line types and colors into one entity. For this reason, you need special tools to edit them. On the Modify menu, the Edit multiline option (and the Mledit command) have the sole purpose of allowing you to join multilines in a variety of ways, as demonstrated in Figure 5.27.

FIGURE 5.27:

The Mledit options and their meanings

CLOSED CROSS Trims one of two intersecting multilines so that they appear overlapping.	
OPEN CROSS Trims the outer lines of two intersecting multilines.	
MERGED CROSS Joins two multilines into one multiline.	
CLOSED TEE Trims the leg of a tee intersection to the first line.	
OPEN TEE Joins the outer lines of a multiline tee intersection.	
MERGED TEE Joins all the lines in a multiline tee intersection.	
CORNER JOINT Joins two multilines into a corner joint.	
ADD VERTEX Adds a vertex to a multiline. The vertex can later be moved.	
DELETE VERTEX Deletes a vertex to straighten a multiline.	
CUT SINGLE Creates an opening in a single line of a multiline.	
CUT ALL Creates a break across all lines in a multiline.	
WELD Closes a break in a multiline.	

Here's how to use the Mledit command.

1. Type **Mledit.↵** at the command prompt. The Multiline Edit Tools dialog box appears (see Figure 5.28), offering a variety of ways to edit your multilines.

FIGURE 5.28:

Multiline Edit Tools dialog box

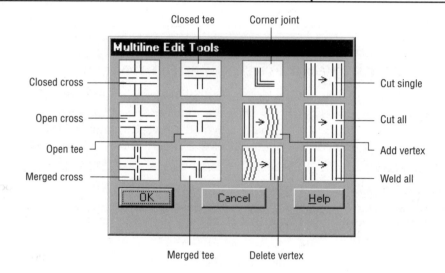

2. Click the graphic that best matches the edit you want to perform.

3. Select the multilines you want to join or edit.

Another option is to explode multilines and edit them using the editing tools you've used in this and previous chapters. When a multiline is exploded, it is reduced to its component lines. Line-type assignments and layers are maintained for each component.

If you are doing a lot of work with multilines, you can open the Modify II toolbar. It contains the Edit Multiline button that opens the Multiline Edit Tools dialog box. To open the Modify II toolbar, right-click any toolbar and then click the Modify II check box in the Toolbars dialog box.

Eliminating Blocks, Layers, Line Types, Shapes, and Styles

A template may contain blocks and layers you don't need in your new file. For example, the lobby you just completed contains the bathroom block because you used the Unit file as a prototype. Even though you erased this block, it remains in the drawing file's database. It is considered "unused" because it doesn't appear as part of the drawing. Such extra blocks can slow you down by increasing the amount of time needed to open the file. They will also increase the size of your file unnecessarily. There are two tools for eliminating unused elements from a drawing: Purge and the File ➤ Export option.

Selectively Removing Unused Elements

The Purge command is used to remove unused individual blocks, layers, line types, shapes, and text styles from a drawing file. To help keep the file size down and to make layer maintenance easier, you will want to purge your drawing of unused elements.

As you will see in the File ➤ Drawing Utilities ➤ Purge cascading menu and the Purge command prompt, you can purge other unused drawing elements, such as line types and layers, as well. Bear in mind, however, that the Purge command does not delete certain primary drawing elements—namely, layer 0, the Continuous line type, and the standard text style.

1. Click File ➤ Open and open the Lobby file.

2. Click File ➤ Drawing Utilities ➤ Purge ➤ Blocks.

3. At the Enter names to purge <*>: prompt, enter the name of a specific block, or press ↵ to purge all the blocks.

4. Go ahead and press ↵. You should now see the Verify each name to be purged? [Yes/No] <Y>: prompt. This lets you selectively purge blocks by displaying each block name in succession.

5. Press ↵ again.

6.   At the `Purge block BATH? <N>:` prompt, enter **Y**↵. This prompt repeats for each unused block in the file. Continue to enter **Y**↵ to all the prompts until the Purge command is completed.

The Lobby file is now purged of most, but not all, of the unused blocks. Now let's take a look at how to delete all the unused elements at once.

Opening a File as Read-Only

When you open an existing file, you might have noticed the Read Only Mode check box in the Open Drawing dialog box. If you open a file with this option checked, AutoCAD does not let you save the file under its original name. You can still edit the drawing any way you please, but if you attempt to use File ➤ Save, you will get the message `Drawing file is write-protected.` You can, however, save your changed file under another name.

The read-only mode provides a way to protect important files from accidental corruption. It also offers another method for reusing settings and objects from existing files by letting you open a file as a prototype, and then saving the file under another name.

Removing All Unused Elements

The Purge command does not remove nested blocks on its first pass. For example, although you purged the Bath block from the Lobby file, it still contains the Tub and Toilet blocks that were nested in the Bath block. To remove them using the Purge command, you must start the command again and remove the nested blocks. For this reason, Purge can be a time-consuming way to delete large numbers of elements.

NOTE Cross-referenced files do not have to be purged because they never actually become part of the drawing's database.

In contrast, the File ➤ Export option enables you to remove *all* unused elements—including blocks, nested blocks, layers, line types, shapes, and styles—all at once. You cannot select specific elements or types of elements to remove.

Be careful: In a given file, there may be a block that is unused but that you want to keep, so you may want to keep a copy of the unpurged file.

1. Choose File ➢ Close and at the Save Changes to Drawing warning, click No.

2. Choose File ➢ Open.

3. In the Select File dialog box, select the Lobby file again. Because you didn't save changes to it from the last exercise, this has the effect of reverting back to the condition before you used the Purge command.

4. Click File ➢ Export.

5. In the Export Data File dialog box, enter **Lobby1.dwg**. This tells AutoCAD to create a new file called Lobby1, which will be the Lobby file with the unused elements removed.

NOTE   If you specify an existing file, a warning message appears telling you that a file with that name already exists, and a request to confirm if you want to replace it. Click Yes to replace the file or No to enter a new name.

---

6. At the Enter name of existing block or [= (block=output file)/* (whole drawing)] <define new drawing>: prompt, enter *↵. This tells AutoCAD that you want to create a new file containing all the drawing elements of the current file, including settings. AutoCAD saves the current file to disk, omitting all the unused blocks, layers, and so forth.

7. Now open the Lobby1 file and click Insert Block on the Draw toolbar.

8. Click the Block button to get a view of blocks contained in this file. Note that the list shows only the Door block. All the unused blocks have been purged.

Remember: Although File ➢ Export offers a quick way of clearing out the deadwood in a file, the command indiscriminately strips a file of all unused elements. So exercise care when you use this method of purging files.

If You Want to Experiment...

Try using the techniques you learned in this chapter to create new files. Use the files you created in Chapter 4 as prototypes to create the symbols shown in Figure 5.29.

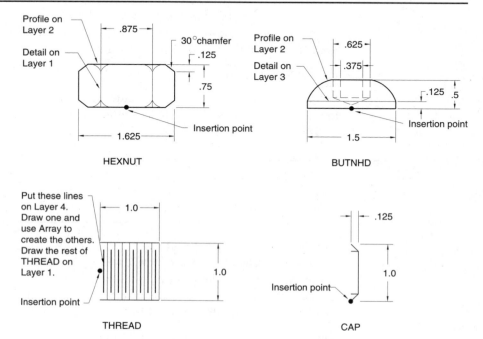

Note:
Create four layers named 1, 2, 3, and 4, if they do not already exist.
Give each layer the same color as their number.
Give Layer 3 the HIDDEN line type.
Don't draw dimensions, just use them for reference.

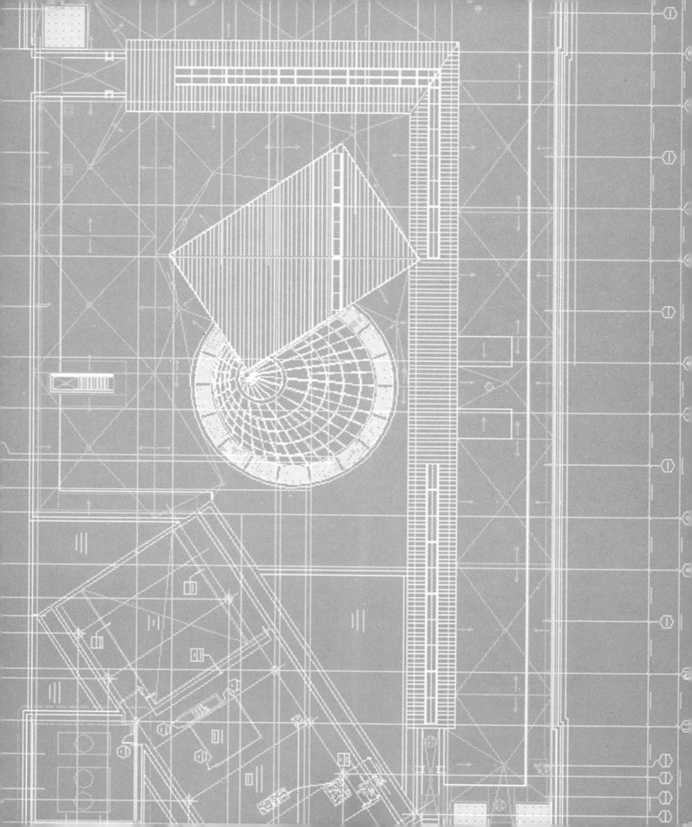

CHAPTER

SIX

6

Enhancing Your
Drawing Skills

- Assembling the Parts

- Taking Control of the AutoCAD Display

- Using Hatch Patterns in Your Drawings

- Updating Blocks

- Using External References

- If You Want to Experiment...

Now that you have created drawings of a typical apartment unit, and the apartment building's lobby and stairs, you can assemble them to complete the first floor of the apartment building. In this chapter, you will take full advantage of AutoCAD's features to enhance your drawing skills, as well as to reduce the time it takes for you to create accurate drawings.

As your drawing becomes larger, you will find that you need to use the Zoom and Pan commands more often. Larger drawings also require some special editing techniques. You will learn how to assemble and view drawings in ways that will save you time and effort as your design progresses. Along the way, you'll see how you can enhance the appearance of your drawings by adding hatch patterns.

Assembling the Parts

Start by creating a new file for the first floor.

1. Create a new file named Plan to contain the drawing of the apartment building's first floor. This is the file that you will use to assemble the unit plans into an apartment building.

TIP If you're just opening AutoCAD, you can click the Open a Drawing button in the Start Up wizard, and then double-click the Browse Files button from the Select a File list.

---

2. Set the Units style to Architectural (Format ➢ Units).

3. Set up the drawing for a 1/8"=1'-0" scale on a 24" × 18" drawing area (Format ➢ Drawing Limits). If you look at Table 3.2 in Chapter 3 you'll see that such a drawing requires an area 2304 units wide by 1728 units deep. Metric users should set up a drawing at 1:100 scale on an A2 sheet size. If you look at Table 3.3, you'll see that your drawing area should be 5940cm by 4200cm.

4. Create a layer called Plan1 and make it the current layer.

5. Use the Drawing Aids dialog box to set the Snap mode to 1, and set the grid to 8', which is the distance required to display 1-inch divisions in a 1/8"=1'-0" scale drawing. Metric users can set the Grid mode to 250.

6. Turn on the grid.

7. Choose View ≻ Zoom ≻ All, or type **Z**↵ **A**↵, to get an overall view of the drawing area.

If you prefer, you can specify the insertion point in the Insert dialog box by removing the checkmark from the Specify on Screen check box. The Input options in the dialog box then become available to receive your input.

Now you're ready to start building a floor plan of the first floor from the Unit plan.

1. Make sure Running Osnaps are turned off, then insert the `Unit.dwg` drawing at coordinate 31'–5",43'–8" (957,1330 for metric users). Accept the default.

2. Zoom in to the apartment unit plan.

3. Click Mirror on the Modify toolbar. Then select the Unit plan and press ↵.

4. At the `Specify first point of the mirror line:` prompt, Shift+right-click the mouse and select From.

5. Shift+right-click again and select Endpoint.

6. Select the endpoint of the upper-right corner of the apartment unit, as shown in Figure 6.1.

FIGURE 6.1:

The Unit plan mirrored

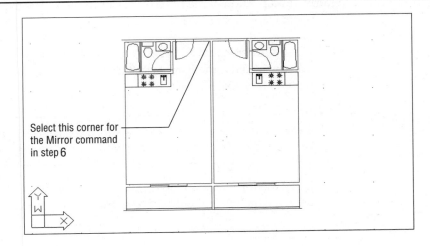

Select this corner for the Mirror command in step 6

7. Enter **@2.5<0**↵. Metric users should enter **@6.5<0**↵. A rubber-banding line appears indicating the mirror axis.

8. Turn on the Ortho mode and select any point to make the mirror axis point in a vertical orientation.

9. At the `Delete Source Objects? [Yes/No] <N>:` prompt, press ↵. You will get a 5" wall thickness between two studio units. Your drawing should be similar to Figure 6.1.

10. Press ↵ to reissue the Mirror command and select both units.

11. Use the From Osnap again and, using the Endpoint Osnap, select the same corner you selected in step 6.

12. Enter **@24<90** to start a mirror axis 24 inches directly above the selected point. Metric users should enter **@61<90**.

13. With the Ortho mode on, select a point so that the mirror axis is exactly horizontal.

14. Press ↵ to keep the original units and complete the mirror operation.

NOTE The Extents option forces the entire drawing to fill the screen at the leftmost side of the display area.

With the tools you've learned about so far, you've quickly and accurately set up a fairly good portion of the floor plan. Continue with the next few steps to "rough-in" the main components of the floor.

1. Click View ➤ Zoom ➤ Extents, or type **Z**↵ **E**↵, to get a view of the four plans. You can also use the Extents tool on the Zoom Window tool flyout. Your drawing will look like Figure 6.2.

TIP If you happen to insert a block in the wrong coordinate location, you can use the Properties dialog box to change the insertion point for the block.

---

2. Copy the four units to the right at a distance of 28'-10" (878cm for metric users), which is the width of two units from centerline to centerline of walls.

3. Insert the lobby at coordinate 89'-1",76'-1" (2713,2318 for metric users).

4. Copy all the unit plans to the right 74'-5" (2267cm for metric users), the width of four units plus the width of the lobby.

FIGURE 6.2:

The Unit plan, duplicated four times

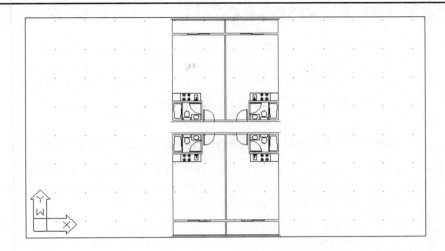

NOTE

From this point on, this book will use the nickname "Zoom All" to refer to the View ➤ Zoom ➤ All command.

5.   Click View ➤ Zoom ➤ All, or type **Z**↵ **A**↵, to view the entire drawing, which look like Figure 6.3. You can also use the Zoom All tool on the Zoom Window flyout.

6.   Now use the File ➤ Save option to save this file to disk.

FIGURE 6.3:

The Plan drawing

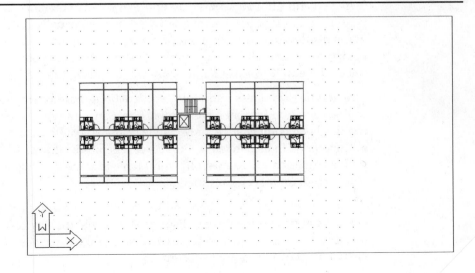

Taking Control of the AutoCAD Display

By now you should be familiar with the Pan and Zoom functions in AutoCAD. There are many other tools at your disposal that can help you get around in your drawing. In this section, you'll get a closer look at the different ways you can view your drawing.

Understanding Regeneration and Redraw

AutoCAD uses two methods for refreshing your drawing display: the drawing regeneration or *regen* and the *redraw*. Each method serves a particular purpose, though they may not be clear to a new user.

AutoCAD stores drawing data in two ways; one is like a database of highly accurate coordinate information and object properties. This is the core information you supply as you draw and edit your drawing. The other way is a less accurate, simplified database of just the display information. AutoCAD uses this second database to allow quick manipulation of the display of your drawing. For the purposes of this discussion, I'll call this simplified database the "virtual display" because it is like a computer model of the overall display of your drawing. This virtual display is in turn used as the basis for what is shown in the drawing area. When you issue a redraw, you are telling AutoCAD to reread this virtual display data and display that information in the drawing area. A regen, on the other hand, causes AutoCAD to rebuild the virtual display based on information from the core drawing database.

As you edit drawings, you may find that some of the lines in the display disappear or otherwise appear corrupted. Redraw will usually restore such distortions in the display. In earlier versions of AutoCAD, the Blipmode system variable was turned on by default, causing markers called *blips* to appear wherever points were selected. Redraw was, and still is, useful in clearing the screen of these blips.

Regens are used less frequently, and are brought to bear when changes occur to settings and options that have a global effect on a drawing, such as a line-type scale change, layer color change, or text style changes (you'll learn more about text styles in Chapter 8). In fact, in many situations, regens are performed automatically when such changes occur. You usually don't have to issue the Regen command on your own, except under certain situations.

Regens can also occur when you select a view of a drawing that is not currently included as part of the virtual display. The virtual display contains display data for a limited area of a drawing. If you zoom or pan to a view that is outside that virtual display area, a regen occurs.

NOTE You may notice that the Pan Realtime and Zoom Realtime commands do not work beyond a certain area in the display. When you've reached a point where these commands seem to stop working, you've come to the limits of the virtual display data. To go beyond these limits, AutoCAD must rebuild the virtual display data from the core data; in other words, do a drawing regeneration.

In past versions of AutoCAD, regens were to be avoided at all cost, especially in large files. A regen on a very large file could take several minutes to complete. Today, with faster processors, large amounts of RAM, and a retooled AutoCAD, regens are not the problem they once were. Still, they can be annoying in multi-megabyte files, and if you are using an older Pentium-based computer, regens can still be a major headache. For these reasons, it pays to understand the finer points of controlling regens.

In this section, you will discover how to manage regens, thus reducing their impact on complex drawing. You can control how regens impact your work in three ways:

- By taking advantage of AutoCAD's many display-related tools
- By setting up AutoCAD so that regens do not occur automatically
- By freezing layers that do not need to be viewed or edited

This chapter will explore these methods in the upcoming sections.

Exploring Other Ways to Control AutoCAD's Display

Perhaps one of the easiest ways to avoid regens is by making sure you don't cross into an area of your drawing that falls outside of the virtual display's area. If you use Pan Realtime and Zoom Realtime, you are automatically kept safely within the bounds of the display list. In this section, you'll be introduced to other tools that will help keep you within those boundaries.

Controlling Display Smoothness

The virtual display can be turned on or off using the Viewres command. The Viewres setting is on by default, and for the most part, should remain on. You can turn it off by typing **Viewres**↵ **No**↵ at the command prompt. However, I don't recommend this. With Viewres off, a regen occurs every time you change your view using Pan or Zoom.

The Viewres command also controls the smoothness of line types, arcs, and circles when they appear in an enlarged view. With the display list active, line types sometimes appear as continuous, even when they are supposed to be dotted or dashed. You may have noticed in previous chapters that on-screen arcs appear to be segmented lines, although they are always plotted as smooth curves. You can adjust the Viewres value to control the number of segments an arc appears to have: the lower the value, the fewer the segments and the faster the redraw and regeneration. However, a low Viewres value causes noncontinuous line types, such as dashes or center lines, to appear as continuous.

> **TIP**
>
> The Arc and Circle Smoothness setting in the Display tab of the Options dialog box has the same effect as the Viewres setting.

Another way to accelerate screen redraw is to keep your drawing limits to a minimum area. If the limits are set unnecessarily high, AutoCAD may slow down noticeably. Also, make sure the drawing origin falls within the drawing limits.

> **TIP**
>
> A good value for the Viewres setting is 500. At this setting, line types display properly, and arcs and circles have a reasonably smooth appearance. At the same time, redraw speed is not noticeably degraded. However, you may want to keep Viewres lower still if you have a limited amount of RAM. High Viewres settings can adversely affect AutoCAD's overall use of memory.

Using the Aerial View

Let's take a tour of a tool that lets you navigate drawings that represent very large areas. It's called the Aerial view.

1. Click View ➤ Aerial View on the menu bar. The Aerial View window appears, as shown in Figure 6.4.

2. Click the Aerial View window. As you move your mouse, notice what happens in the AutoCAD window. Your view pans, following your motion in the Aerial View window. A bold rectangle in the Aerial View window representing your AutoCAD view moves with your cursor.

3. Click the Aerial View window again. Now as you move your cursor from left to right, the view in the AutoCAD window zooms in and out. This is the Zoom mode of the Aerial view. The rectangle in the Aerial View window now shrinks and expands as you move the cursor from left to right indicating the size of the area being displayed in the AutoCAD window.

FIGURE 6.4:

The Aerial View window and its components

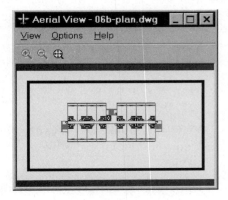

4. Move the cursor to the left so that the rectangle representing your AutoCAD view is about half the size of the overall view of the plan, then right-click. Your AutoCAD view becomes fixed. Also notice that the magnification icon in the Aerial View toolbar becomes available.

As you can see from this exercise, you can cycle through the Pan and Zoom feature of the Aerial view by clicking the mouse. If you simply want to pan the view, you can right-click in step 2 of the last exercise to fix your view in place. Or you can rapidly alternate between the Pan and Zoom modes by clicking the mouse until you've reached the location and view size you want.

The bold rectangle shows you exactly where you are in the overall drawing at any given time. This feature is especially useful in drawings of large areas that may take several pans to cross.

TIP   The View ➤ Zoom ➤ Dynamic option performs a similar function to the Aerial View window, but instead of opening a separate window, the Dynamic option temporarily displays the overall view in the drawing area.

The Aerial View window is a great tool when you are working on a drawing that requires a lot of magnification in your zoomed-in views. It is also helpful when you need to maintain an overall view of a drawing as you work on closer detail. You may not find it very helpful on drawings that don't require lots of magnification, like the bathroom drawing you worked on in Chapters 3 and 4.

You were able to use the major features of the Aerial view in this exercise. Here are a few more features you can try on your own:

View ➤ Zoom In   Zooms in on the view defined by the bold rectangle in the Aerial view.

View ➤ Zoom Out   Zooms out of magnified view on the view in the Aerial view.

View ➤ Global   Displays an overall view of your drawing in the Aerial View window. Global is like a View ➤ Zoom ➤ Extents option for the Aerial view.

Options ➤ Auto Viewport   Controls whether a selected viewport is automatically displayed in the Aerial View window. When checked, this option will cause the Aerial View window to automatically display the contents of a viewport when it becomes active. (See Chapters 12 and 16 for more on viewports.)

Options ➤ Dynamic Update   Controls how AutoCAD updates the Aerial View window. When this setting is on, AutoCAD updates the Aerial view in real time as changes in the drawing occur. When it is off, changes in the drawing will not appear in the Aerial view until you click the Aerial View window.

Options ➤ Realtime Zoom   Controls whether the AutoCAD display is updated in real time as you zoom and pan in the Aerial View window.

Saving Views

Another way of controlling your views is by saving them. You might think of saving views as a way of creating a bookmark or placeholder in your drawing. You'll see how to save views in the following set of exercises.

A few walls in the Plan drawing are not complete. You'll need to zoom in to the areas that need work to add the lines, but these areas are spread out over the drawing. You could use the Aerial View window to view each area. There is, however, another way to edit widely separated areas: First, save views of the areas you want to work on, and then jump from saved view to saved view. This technique is especially helpful when you know you will often want to return to a specific area of your drawing.

1. First, close the Aerial View window by clicking the Close button in the upper-left corner of the window.

2. Click View ➤ Zoom ➤ All, or type **Z**↲ **A**↲, to get an overall view of the plan.

3. Click View ➤ Named Views or type **V**↲. The View dialog box appears.

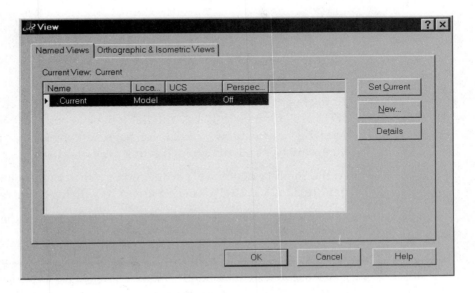

In the View dialog box, you can call up an existing view (Set Current), create a new view (New), or get detailed information about a view (Details). You can also select the Orthographic & Isometric Views tab to select from a set of predefined views. You'll learn more about these options in Chapter 15.

4. Make sure the Named Views tab is selected, then click the New button. The New View dialog box appears.

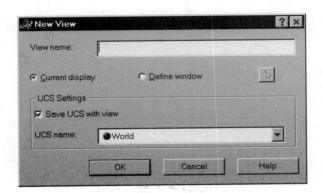

You'll notice some options that deal with the User Coordinate System (UCS). You'll get a chance to look at the UCS in Chapter 15. For now, you'll concentrate on creating a new view.

5. Click the Define Window radio button. Notice that the grayed button to the right, the Define View Window button, becomes available.

6. Click the Define View Window button. The dialog boxes momentarily disappear.

7. At the Specify first corner: prompt, click near the coordinate 26',40' (1715,1150 for metric users). You don't have to be exact because you are selecting view windows. Also, if you have Running Osnaps turned on, you may want to turn it off while selecting view windows.

8. At the Specify opposite corner prompt, click a location near the coordinate 91',82' (2600,2500 for metric users). The dialog boxes reappear.

9. Click the View Name input box and type **First** for the name of the view you just defined.

10. Click the OK button. The New View dialog box closes, and you see First listed in the Name list.

11. Repeat steps 3 through 9 to define five more views, named Second, Third, etc. Use Figure 6.5 as a guide for where to define the windows. Click OK when you are done.

Now let's see how to recall these views that you've saved.

1. With the View dialog box open, click First in the list of views.

2. Click the Set Current button and then click OK. Your screen displays the first view you selected.

FIGURE 6.5:

Save view windows in these locations for the Plan drawing.

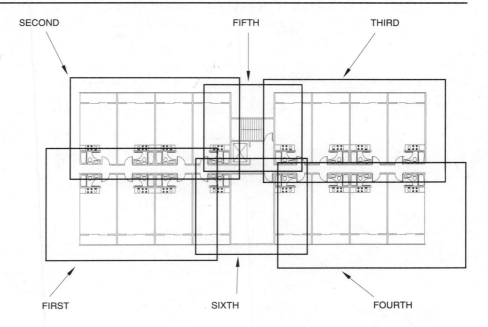

SECOND   FIFTH   THIRD

FIRST   SIXTH   FOURTH

TIP   To set the current view, you can also right-click the view name in the View dialog box. You can then choose Set Current, Delete, Details, or Rename from a popup list.

---

3. Set the current layer to Wall, and proceed to add the stairs and exterior walls of the building, as shown in Figure 6.6. (Remember that you exported the stairs from the Lobby drawing in the last chapter. You can also use the Stair.dwg file from the companion CD-ROM.)

4. Use the View dialog box again to restore the view named Second. Then add the walls, as shown in Figure 6.7.

TIP   Remember that, when AutoCAD is idle, you can right-click the Command window, then select Recent Commands to repeat a recently issued command. You can also right-click the drawing area when AutoCAD is idle and repeat the last command.

---

5. Continue to the other views and add the rest of the exterior walls, as you have done with First and Second. Use the four panels of Figure 6.8 as a guide to completing the views.

FIGURE 6.6:

The stairs added to the restored First view

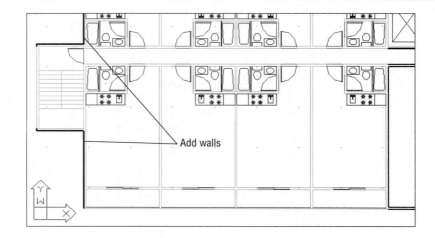

FIGURE 6.7:

Walls added to the restored Second view

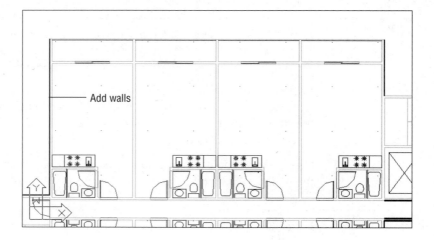

FIGURE 6.8:

Walls, stairs, and doors added to the other views

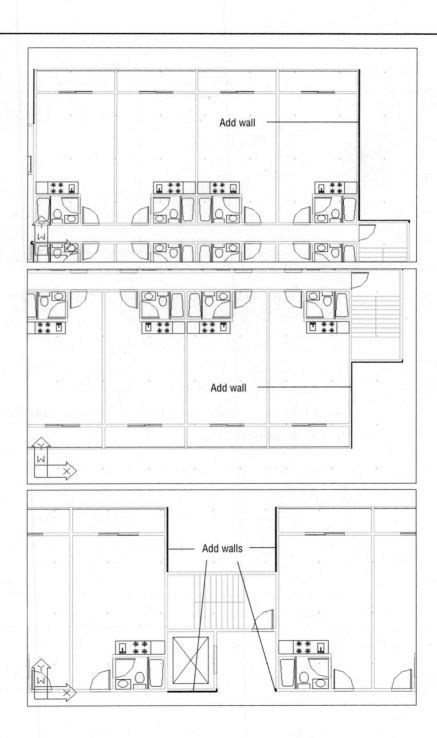

FIGURE 6.8 CONTINUED:

Walls, stairs, and doors added to the other views

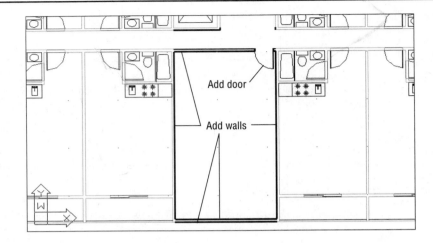

If you prefer, you can use the keyboard to invoke the View command and thus avoid all the dialog boxes.

1. Click View ➤ Zoom ➤ Extents, or type **Z**↵ **E**↵.

2. Enter **–View**↵ **s**↵ at the command prompt or use the **–V**↵ **s**↵ shortcut. (Don't forget the minus sign in front of **View** or **V**.)

3. At the `Enter view name to save:` prompt, enter **Overall**↵.

4. Now save the Plan file to disk.

As you can see, this is a quick way to save a view. With the name Overall assigned to this view, you can easily recall the Overall view at any time. (The View ➤ Zoom ➤ All option gives you an overall view, too, but it may zoom out too far for some purposes, or it may not show what you might consider to be an overall view.)

TIP   Another useful tool for getting around in your drawing is the Zoom toolbar. It contains tools for Zoom Window, Dynamic, Scale, Center, In, Out, All, and Extent. To open the Zoom toolbar, right-click any toolbar, then click Zoom in the popup list.

Opening a File to a Particular View

The Select File dialog box contains a Select Initial View check box. If you open an existing drawing with this option checked, you are greeted with a Select Initial View dialog box just before the opened file appears on the screen. This dialog box lists any views saved in the file. You can then go directly to a view by double-clicking the view name. If you have saved views and you know the name of the view you want, using Select Initial View saves time when you're opening very large files.

Understanding the Frozen Layer Option

As mentioned earlier, you may wish to turn certain layers off altogether to plot a drawing containing only selected layers. But even when layers are turned off, AutoCAD still takes the time to redraw and regenerate them. The Layer Properties Manager dialog box offers the Freeze option that acts like the Off option, except that Freeze causes AutoCAD to ignore frozen layers when redrawing and regenerating a drawing. By freezing layers that are not needed for reference or editing, you can reduce the time AutoCAD takes to perform regens. This can be helpful in very large, multi-megabyte files.

You should be aware, however, that the Freeze option affects blocks in an unusual way. Try the following exercise to see firsthand how the Freeze option makes entire blocks invisible.

1. Use the Layer Properties Manager dialog box to set the current layer to 0.

TIP   You can freeze and thaw individual layers by clicking the Sun icon in the Layers popup list in the Object Properties toolbar.

2. Click the yellow lightbulb icon in the Plan1 layer listing to turn off that layer, and then click OK. Nothing happens to your drawing. Turning off the Plan1 layer, the layer on which the unit blocks were inserted, has no effect.

3. Now use the Layer Properties Manager dialog box to turn off all of the layers.

4. Choose View ➤ Regen, or type re↵.

5. Open the Layer Properties Manager dialog box again and turn all of the layers back on.

6. Now click the Plan1 layer's Freeze/Thaw icon, which is the one that looks like a sun. (Note that you cannot freeze the current layer.) The yellow sun icon changes to a gray snowflake indicating that the layer is now frozen.

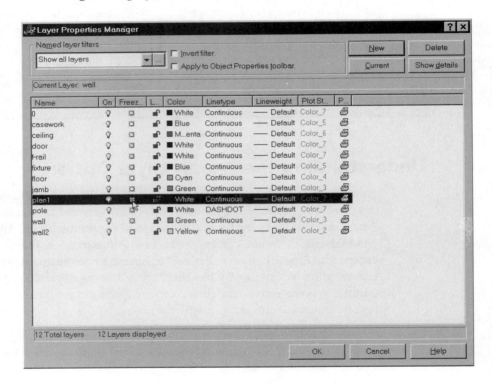

7. Click OK. Now the unit blocks disappear. Even though none of the objects within the unit blocks were drawn on the Plan1 layer, when Plan1 is frozen, so are the entire contents of the blocks assigned to the Plan1 layer.

TIP Remember that you can right-click a blank area of the Layer Properties Manager dialog box, then choose Select All from the popup menu to select all the layers at once.

8. Issue the Regen command again and pay attention to the time it takes. The regen is faster this time.

9. Now, thaw layer Plan1 by opening the Layer Properties Manager dialog box and clicking the Snowflake icon in the Plan1 layer listing.

10. Turn off the Ceiling layer. Exit the dialog box.

In this relatively small file, the differences between the regen times of the Off state versus the Freeze state are small. But in larger files, the difference can be significant. As your drawings become larger, try this exercise again to see how Off versus Freeze affects your regen speed.

Making Good Use of Freeze and Off

The previous exercise showed the effect that freezing a layer has on blocks. When the layer of a block is frozen, the entire block is made invisible, regardless of the layer assignments of the objects contained in the block.

Keep in mind that when blocks are on layers that are not frozen, the individual objects that are a part of a block are still affected by the status of the layer to which they are assigned.

You can take advantage of this feature by using layers to store parts of a drawing that you may want to plot separately. For example, three floors in your apartment building plan may contain the same information, with some specific variation on each floor. In this case, you can have one layer contain blocks of the objects common to all the floors. Another layer contains the blocks and objects specific to the first floor, and additional layers contain information specific to the second and third floors. When you want to view or plot one floor, you can freeze the layers associated with the others. With respect to Freeze/Thaw visibility, external referenced files inserted using the external reference (Xref) command also act like blocks. For example, you can Xref several drawings on different layers. Then, when you want to view a particular Xref drawing, you can freeze all the layers except the one containing that drawing.

In larger projects, you may not want to combine all of your floors into one file, but instead combine different types of data such as electrical, mechanical, interior, site, and lease data. When you want to plot an interior plan, for example, you turn off or freeze layers associated with other disciplines. In fact, this is how the San Francisco Main Library project was organized. However, you may still use common data such as structural grids, columns, elevator core, and stair drawings as part of all your floor plan files.

Using layers and blocks in these ways requires careful planning and record keeping. If used successfully, however, this technique can save substantial time when you're working with drawings that use repetitive objects or that require similar information that can be overlaid.

Taking Control of Regens

If you work with extremely large files and regen times become a problem, you can control regeneration by setting the Regenmode system variable to 0 (zero). You can also use the Regenauto command to accomplish the same thing, by typing **Regenauto↵ Off↵**.

If you then issue a command that normally triggers a regen, AutoCAD will give the message Regen queued. For example, when you globally edit attributes, redefine blocks, thaw frozen layers, change the Ltscale setting, or, in some cases, change a text style, you will get the Regen queued message. You can "queue up" regens then at a time you choose. You can issue a regen to update all the changes at once by choosing View ➤ Regen, or by typing **Re↵**. This way, only one regen occurs instead of several.

By taking control of when regens occur, you can reduce the overall time you spend editing large files.

Using Hatch Patterns in Your Drawings

To help communicate your ideas to others, you will want to add graphic elements that represent types of materials, special regions, or textures. AutoCAD provides *hatch patterns* for quickly placing a texture over an area of your drawing. In this section, you will add a hatch pattern to the floor of the studio apartment unit, thereby instantly enhancing the appearance of one drawing. In the process, you'll learn how to quickly update all the units in the overall floor plan to reflect the changes in the unit.

Creating Multiple Views

So far, you've looked at ways to help you get around in your drawing while using a single view window. You also have the capability to set up multiple views of your drawing, called *viewports*. With viewports, you can display more than one view of your drawing at one time in the AutoCAD drawing area. For example, you can have one viewport to show a close-up of the bathroom, another viewport to display the overall plan view, and yet another to display the unit plan.

Continued on next page

When viewports are combined with AutoCAD's Paper Space feature, you can plot multiple views of your drawing. Paper Space is a display mode that allows you to "paste-up" multiple views of a drawing, much like a page layout program. To find out more about viewports and Paper Space, see Chapter 12.

Placing a Hatch Pattern in a Specific Area

It's always a good idea to provide a separate layer for hatch patterns. By doing so, you can turn them off if you need to. For example, in Chapter 3, you saw how the San Francisco Main Library floor plan displayed the floor paving pattern in one drawing while in another drawing, it was turned off so it wouldn't distract from other information.

In the following exercise, you will add a hatch pattern representing floor tile. This will give you the opportunity to learn the different methods of creating and controlling hatch patterns.

1. Open the Unit file. Keep in mind that you still have the Plan file open as well.

2. Zoom into the bathroom and kitchen area.

3. Create a new layer called Flr-pat.

4. Make Flr-pat the current layer.

Once you've set up the layer for the hatch pattern, you can place the pattern in the drawing.

1. Click the Hatch tool on the Draw toolbar or type **H.↵**. Hatch is also located in the Draw pull-down menu.

The Boundary Hatch dialog box appears.

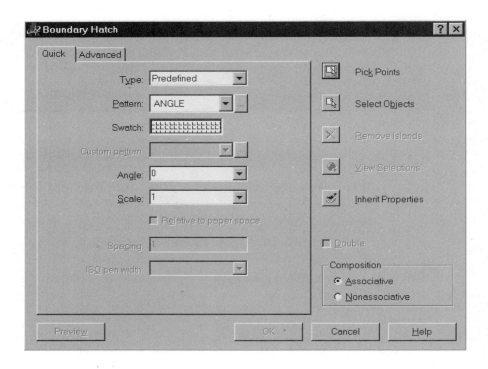

TIP

Say you want to add a hatch pattern that you have previously inserted in another part of the drawing. You may think that you have to guess at its scale and rotation angle. But with the Inherit Properties option in the Boundary Hatch dialog box, you can select a previously inserted hatch pattern as a prototype for the current hatch pattern. However, this feature does not work with exploded hatch patterns.

---

2. Under Type, open the popup list and select User-Defined. The User-Defined option lets you define a simple crosshatch pattern by specifying the line spacing of the hatch and whether it is a single- or double-hatch pattern. The Angle and Spacing input boxes become available, so you can enter values.

3. Double-click the Spacing input box near the bottom and enter **6** (metric users should enter **15**). This tells AutoCAD you want the hatch's line spacing to be 6" or 15cm. Leave the Angle value at 0 because you want the pattern to be aligned with the bathroom.

4. Click the check box labeled Double (just to the right of the Spacing input box). This tells AutoCAD you want the hatch pattern to run both vertically and horizontally. Also notice that the Swatch button offers a sample view of your hatch pattern.

5. Click the Pick Points button.

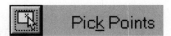

The dialog box momentarily disappears, allowing you to pick a point inside the area you want hatched.

6. Click a point anywhere inside the bathroom floor area, below the toilet. Notice that a highlighted outline appears in the bathroom. This is the boundary AutoCAD has selected to enclose the hatch pattern. It outlines everything including the door swing arc.

TIP   If you have text in the hatch boundary, AutoCAD will avoid hatching over it, unless the Ignore option is selected in the Boundary Style options of the Advanced Hatch settings. See *Using Advanced Hatch Settings* in this chapter for more on the Ignore setting.

7. Press ↵ to return to the Boundary Hatch dialog box.

8. Click the Preview button in the lower-left corner of the dialog box. The hatch pattern appears everywhere on the floor except where the door swing occurs.

9. Right-click to return to the dialog box.

10. Click the Pick Points button again, pick a point inside the door swing, and press ↵.

11. Click Preview again. The hatch pattern now covers the entire floor area.

12. Right-click to return to the dialog box.

13. Click the OK button to place the hatch pattern in the drawing.

The Boundary Hatch dialog box lets you first define the boundary within which you want to place a hatch pattern. You do this by simply clicking a location inside the boundary area, as in step 6. AutoCAD finds the actual boundary for you. There are many options that give you control over how a hatch boundary is selected. If you want to find out more, look at *Understanding the Boundary Hatch Options* later in this chapter.

Positioning Hatch Patterns Accurately

In the last exercise, the hatch pattern was placed in the bathroom without regard for the location of the lines that make up the pattern. In most cases, however, you will want to have accurate control over where the lines of the pattern are placed.

> **TIP**
>
> You can also click the Swatch button to browse through a graphical representation of the predefined hatch patterns.

Hatch patterns use the same origin as the snap origin (see Chapter 3 for more information about the snap origin). By default, this origin is the same as the drawing origin, 0,0. You can change the snap origin (and thus the hatch pattern origin) by using the Snapbase system variable. The following exercise guides you through the process of placing a hatch pattern accurately, using the example of adding floor tile to the kitchenette.

1. Pan your view so that you can see the area below the kitchenette, and using the Rectangle tool in the Draw toolbar, draw the 3'0" × 8'0" outline of the floor tile area, as shown in Figure 6.9. Metric users should create a rectangle that is 91cm by 228cm. You may also use a closed polyline.

> **TIP**
>
> If you know the coordinates of the new snap origin, you can enter them in the Drawing Aids dialog box under the X Base and Y Base input boxes instead of using the Snapbase system variable.

2. At the command prompt, type **Snapbase**⏎.

3. At the Enter new value for Snapbase <0'-0",0'-0">: prompt, use the Endpoint Osnap and click the lower-left corner of the area you just defined (see Figure 6.9).

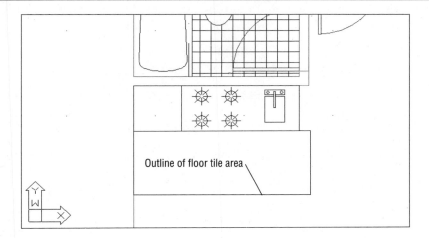

Outline of floor tile area

4. Click the Hatch tool in the Draw toolbar.

5. In the Boundary Hatch dialog box, make sure that Predefined is selected in the Type pull-down list.

6. Click the button labeled with the ellipses (…) just to the right of the Pattern drop-down list.

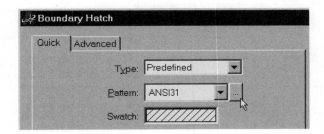

The Hatch Pattern Palette dialog box appears.

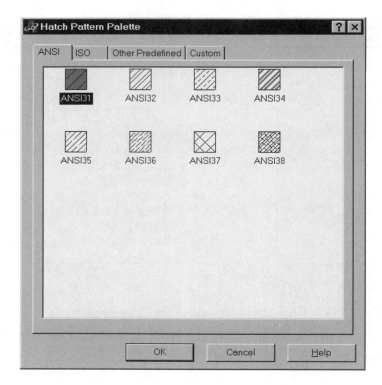

NOTE   If you know the name of the pattern you want, you can also select it from the Pattern drop-down list in the Boundary Hatch dialog box.

7. This dialog box lets you select a predefined pattern either from a list to the left, or from a graphic that shows what the pattern looks like.

8. Select the Other Predefined tab, then locate and click AR-PARQ1.

9. Click OK to exit the dialog box.

10. Click the Pick Points button.

11. Click the interior of the area to be tiled, and press ↵. Metric users should double-click the Scale input box and enter **2.54** to scale this pattern appropriately to match the proportions of the English measurement example.

12. Click OK. A parquet-style tile pattern appears in the defined area.

13. Now save the Unit file, but keep it open.

TIP   You can use the Solid predefined hatch pattern at the top of the list to create solid fills. This is a vast improvement over the Solid command that was used in earlier versions of AutoCAD for solid fills.

Notice that each tile is shown whole; none of the tiles is cut off as in the bathroom example. This is because you first used the Snapbase system variable to set the origin for the hatch pattern. You can now move the Snapbase setting back to the 0,0 setting and not affect the hatch pattern.

In the foregoing exercise, you got a chance to use a predefined hatch pattern. Figure 6.10 shows you all the patterns available. You can also create your own custom patterns, as described in Chapters 19 and 20.

FIGURE 6.10:

Predefined hatch patterns available in AutoCAD

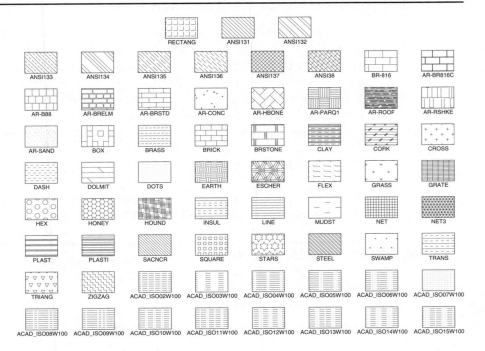

In the next exercise, you'll use this updated Unit file to update all the units in the Plan file.

NOTE
The predefined patterns with the AR prefix are architectural patterns that are drawn to full scale. In general, you will want to leave their scale settings at 1. You can adjust the scale after you have placed the hatch pattern using the Properties tool, as described later in this chapter.

NOTE
If you are a veteran AutoCAD user, you may hesitate to use many hatch patterns in an already crowded drawing. In the past, hatch patterns were memory hogs. You'll be happy to know that AutoCAD 2000 has made hatch patterns much more memory efficient. Also, AutoCAD 2000 has a solid hatch for solid fills also.

Updating Blocks in the Plan File

As you progress through a design project, you make countless revisions. With traditional drafting methods, revising a drawing like the studio apartment floor plan takes a good deal of time. If the bathroom layout is changed, for example, you have to erase every occurrence of the bathroom and redraw it 16 times. With AutoCAD, on the other hand, revising this drawing can be a very quick operation. The studio unit you just modified can be updated throughout the overall plan drawing by replacing the current Unit block with the updated Unit file. AutoCAD can update all occurrences of the Unit block. The following exercise will show you how this is accomplished.

1. Make sure you've saved the Unit file with the changes, then return to the Plan file that is still open. Choose Window ➤ Plan.dwg.

WARNING
This method does not update exploded blocks. If you plan to use this method to update parts of a drawing, do not explode the blocks you plan to update. See Chapter 4.

---

2. Click the Insert Block tool on the Draw toolbar.

3. Click the Browse button, and from the Select Drawing File dialog box, double-click the Unit filename.

4. Click OK. A warning message tells you that a block already exists with the same name as the file. You have the option to cancel the operation or redefine the block in the current drawing.

5. Click Yes. The drawing regenerates (unless you have Regenauto turned off.)

6. At the `Insertion point:` prompt, press the Esc key. You do this because you really don't want to insert a Unit plan into your drawing, but rather are just using the Insert feature to update an existing block. The Insert Dialog box returns.

7. Click Cancel to return to the drawing.

8. If Regenauto is turned off, type **Regen**↵ to view the results of the Insert dialog box.

NOTE   If Regenauto is turned off, you must use the Regen command to force a regeneration of the drawing before the updated Unit block appears on the display, even though the drawing database has been updated.

---

9. Now zoom in to one of the units. You will see that the floor tile appears in all the units as you drew it in the Unit file (see Figure 6.11).

Nested blocks must be updated independently of the parent block. For example, if you had modified the Toilet block while editing the Unit file, and then updated the Unit drawing in the Plan file, the old Toilet block would not have been updated. Even though the toilet is part of the Unit file, it is still a unique, independent block in the Plan file, and AutoCAD will not modify it unless specifically instructed to do so. In this situation, you must edit the original Toilet block, and then update it in both the Plan and Unit files.

TIP   If you want to substitute one block for another within the current file, type **–Insert**↵. (Don't forget the minus sign in front of the word **Insert**). At the `Block name` prompt, enter the block name followed by an equal sign (=), then the name of the new block or the filename. Do not include spaces between the names and the equal sign.

FIGURE 6.11:

The Plan drawing with the tile pattern

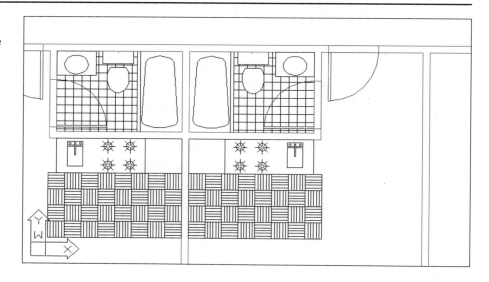

Also, block references and layer settings of the current file take priority over those of the imported file. For example, if a file to be imported has layers of the same name as the current file, but those layers have color and line-type assignments that are different from the current file's, the current file's layer color and line-type assignments will determine those of the imported file. This does not mean, however, that the actual imported file on disk is changed; only the inserted drawing is affected.

Substituting Blocks

In the example under the section *Updating Changes in the Plan File,* you updated a block in your Plan file using the Browse option in the Insert dialog box. In that exercise, the block name and the filename were the same. You can also replace a block with another block or file of a different name. Here's how to do this.

1. Open the Insert dialog box.

2. Click the Browse button, locate and select the file you want to use as a substitute, and then click Open. The Insert dialog box reappears.

3. Change the name in the Block input box to the name of the block you want replaced.

Continued on next page

> **4.** Click OK. A warning message appears telling you that a block with this name already exists. Click OK again to proceed with the block substitution.
>
> You can use this method of replacing blocks if you would like to see how changing one element of your project can change your design. You might, for example, draw three different apartment unit plans, and give each plan a unique name. You could then generate and plot three apartment building designs in a fraction of the time it would take you to do it by hand.
>
> Block substitution can also reduce a drawing's complexity and accelerate regenerations. To do this, you temporarily replace large, complex blocks with schematic versions of those blocks. For example, you might replace the Unit block in the Plan drawing with another drawing that contains just a single-line representation of the walls and bathroom fixtures. You would still have the wall lines for reference when inserting other symbols or adding mechanical or electrical information, but the drawing would regenerate much faster. When doing the final plot, you would reinsert the original Unit block showing every detail.

Changing the Hatch Area

You may have noticed the Associative option in the Boundary Hatch dialog box. When this option is checked, AutoCAD creates an associative hatch pattern. Associative hatches will adjust their shapes to any changes in their associated boundary, hence the name. The following exercise demonstrates how this works.

Suppose you want to enlarge the tiled area of the kitchen by one tile. Here's how it's done.

1. Return to the Unit file (Window ➤ Unit.dwg) then click the outline border of the hatch pattern you created earlier. Notice the grips that appear around the hatch pattern area.

NOTE   You may need to zoom in closer to the pattern area or use the object selection cycling feature to select the hatch boundary. For more on selection cycling, see *Singling Out Proximate Objects* in Chapter 12.

---

2. Shift+click the grip in the lower-left corner of the hatch area.

TIP If the boundary of the hatch pattern consists of line segments, you can use a crossing window or polygon-crossing window to select the corner grips of the hatch pattern.

3. With the lower-left grip highlighted, Shift+click the lower-right grip.

4. Now click the lower-right grip again, but don't Shift+click this time.

5. Enter @12<–90 (@30<–90 for metric users) to widen the hatch pattern by 1 foot. The hatch pattern adjusts to the new size of the hatch boundary.

6. Press the Esc key twice to clear any grip selections.

7. Save the Unit file to disk and exit the file.

8. Return to the Plan file (Window ➢ Plan.dwg) and repeat the steps in the *Updating Changes in the Plan File* exercise prior to this one to update the units again.

The Associative feature of hatch patterns can save time when you need to make modifications to your drawing. But you should be aware of its limitations. There are several ways a hatch pattern can lose its associativity. They are:

- Erasing or exploding a hatch boundary

- Erasing or exploding a block that forms part of the boundary

- Moving a hatch pattern away from its boundary

- Moving a hatch boundary away from the hatch pattern

These situations frequently arise when you edit an unfamiliar drawing. Often, boundary objects are placed on a layer that is off or frozen, so the boundary objects are not visible. Or the hatch pattern may be on a layer that is turned off and you proceed to edit the file, not knowing that a hatch pattern exists. When you encounter such a file, take a moment to check for hatch boundaries so you can deal with them properly.

Modifying a Hatch Pattern

Like everything else, you or someone involved in your project will eventually want to change a hatch pattern in some way. The Properties tool in the Object

Properties toolbar offers most of the settings you'll need to make changes to your hatch patterns.

1. Return to the Unit drawing by choosing Window ➤ Unit.dwg.

2. Press the Esc key twice to clear any grip selections that may be active from earlier exercises.

3. Click the hatch pattern, then right-click and select Properties from the popup menu. The Properties dialog box appears, displaying the options available for the hatch pattern. Make sure the Categorized tab is selected.

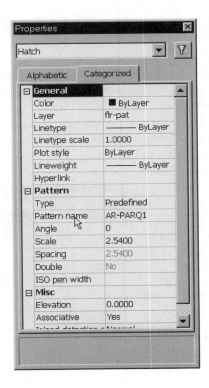

4. Click Pattern Name under the Pattern category. A button with ellipses appears to the far right of the Pattern Name listing next to the hatch pattern name.

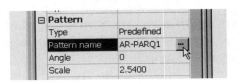

5. Click this button with the ellipses. The Hatch Pattern Palette appears.

6. Locate and click the pattern named AR-BRSTD. It's the pattern that looks like brick.

7. Click OK to change the hatch pattern area to the new pattern.

8. Press the Esc key to clear the selection of the hatch pattern, then click the X in the upper-right corner of the Properties dialog box to close it. Or, you can continue to try out different hatch patterns by repeating steps 5, 6, and 7. Just press the Esc key when you are done.

9. You want to keep the old pattern in our drawing, so at this point, exit the Unit file without saving it.

In this exercise, you were able to change the hatch pattern by editing the Properties of the pattern. While you only changed the pattern type, other options are available to you. You can, for example, change the pattern from a predefined one to a user-defined one by clicking on the Type listing. You'll see the Ellipses button appear to the far right of the listing, in a way similar to the Pattern Name listing in step 4 of the previous exercise. When you click this Ellipses button, you'll see the Hatch Pattern Type dialog box appear.

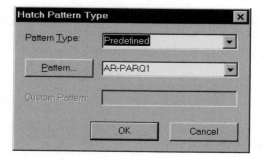

You can then select User-Defined from the Pattern Type drop-down list.

The other items listed in the Hatch Pattern Type dialog box duplicate some of the options in the Boundary Hatch dialog box. They let you modify the individual properties of the selected hatch pattern. The next section, *Understanding the Boundary Hatch Options*, describes these other properties in detail.

If you find that you are creating and editing hatch patterns frequently, you will find the Modify II toolbar useful. It contains an Edit Hatch tool that gives you ready access to the Hatchedit dialog box. To open the Modify II toolbar, right-click any toolbar, and then click the Modify II check box in the Toolbars dialog box that appears.

TIP   If you're working through the tutorial in this chapter, this would be a good place to take a break or stop. You can pick up the next exercise at another time.

Understanding the Boundary Hatch Options

The Boundary Hatch dialog box offers many other options that you didn't explore in these exercises. For example, instead of selecting the area to be hatched by clicking a point, you can select the actual objects that bound the area you wish to hatch using the Select Objects button. The Swatch button opens the Hatch Pattern Palette dialog box that lets you select a predefined hatch pattern from a graphic window.

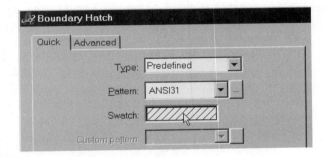

The Hatch Pattern Palette dialog box offers several tabs that further divide the types of hatch patterns into four different categories: ANSI, ISO, Other Predefined, and Custom. The Custom tab is empty until you create your own set of custom hatch patterns. See Chapter 20 for details on how to create custom hatch patterns.

TIP   If you're working on the tutorial, you may want to skip this section and proceed to the *Positioning Hatch Patterns Accurately* section. Come back to this section later to get a better understanding of the Boundary Hatch options.

Other options in the right-hand column of the Boundary Hatch dialog box include Remove Islands, View Selections, and Inherit Properties.

Remove Islands   Lets you remove an area within a hatch pattern boundary that has been removed from the hatch pattern. An example of this is the toilet seat in the bathroom. This option is only available when you select a hatch area using the Pick Points option and an island has been detected.

View Selections   Temporarily closes the dialog box and then highlights the objects that have been selected as the hatch boundary by AutoCAD.

Inherit Properties   Lets you select a hatch pattern from an existing one in the drawing. This is helpful when you want to add a hatch pattern that already exists, but you do not know its name or its scale, rotation, or other properties.

At the very bottom of the column of options is the Composition button group. This option lets you determine whether the hatch pattern being inserted is associative or nonassociative. An associative hatch pattern automatically changes to fill its boundary whenever that boundary is stretched or edited.

Using the Advanced Hatch Options

AutoCAD's Boundary Hatch command has a fair amount of intelligence. As you saw in the last exercise, it was able to detect not only the outline of the floor area, but also the outline of the toilet seat that represents an island within the pattern area. If you prefer, you can control how AutoCAD treats these island conditions and other situations by selecting options available when you click the Advanced tab in the Boundary Hatch dialog box.

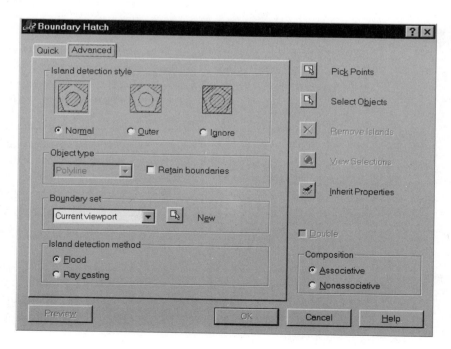

In addition to controlling the Island Detection feature of hatch patterns, the Advanced tab lets you fine-tune other aspects of hatch pattern creation.

Island Detection Style

The Island Detection Style button group at the top of the dialog box controls how nested boundaries affect the hatch pattern. The graphics in this button group show examples of the effect of the selected option. The Island Detection Style options include the following:

Normal   Causes the hatch pattern to alternate between nested boundaries. The outer boundary is hatched; if there is a closed object within the boundary, it is not hatched. If another closed object *is* inside the first closed object, *that* object is hatched. This is the default setting.

Outer   Applies the hatch pattern to an area defined by the outermost boundary and by any boundaries nested within the outermost boundary. Any boundaries nested within the nested boundaries are ignored.

Ignore   Supplies the hatch pattern to the entire area within the outermost boundary, ignoring any nested boundaries.

NOTE   Hatch patterns are like blocks in that they act like single objects. You can explode a hatch pattern to edit its individual lines.

Object Type

The Boundary Hatch command can also create an outline of the hatch area using one of two objects: 2D regions, which are like 2D planes, or polyline outlines. Boundary Hatch actually creates such a polyline boundary temporarily, to establish the hatch area. These boundaries are automatically removed after the hatch pattern is inserted. If you want to retain the boundaries in the drawing, make sure the Retain Boundaries check box is checked. Retaining the boundary can be useful in situations where you know you will be hatching the area more than once, or if you are hatching a fairly complex area.

TIP   Retaining a hatch boundary is useful if you want to know the hatched area's dimensions in square inches or feet, because you can find the area of a closed polyline using the List command. The Boundary command creates a polyline outline or region within a selected area. It works much like the Boundary Hatch command but does not add a hatch pattern.

Island Detection Method

You may have noticed that the Boundary Hatch command did not place a hatch pattern on the toilet seat. This is because the Island Detection feature was turned on. The toilet seat is like an island within the hatch area. The Island Detection Method radio buttons let you control whether islands such as the toilet seat are detected or not. The Flood option detects islands and hatches around them. The Ray Casting option determines the boundary outline by first looking for the nearest object to your pick point, then tracing along that object in a counterclockwise direction.

Boundary Set Options

The Boundary Hatch feature is view dependent; that is, it locates boundaries based on what is visible in the current view. If the current view contains lots of graphic data, AutoCAD can have difficulty finding a boundary, or it may be very slow in finding a boundary. If you run into this problem, or if you want to single out a specific object for a point selection boundary, you can further limit the area that AutoCAD uses to locate hatch boundaries by using the Boundary Set options.

New   Lets you select the objects from which you want AutoCAD to determine the hatch boundary, instead of searching the entire view. The screen clears and lets you select objects. This option discards previous boundary sets. It is useful for hatching areas in a drawing that may contain many objects that you do not want to include in the hatch boundary.

Current viewport   Tells you that AutoCAD will use all of the current view to determine the hatch boundary. Once you select a set of objects using the New button, you also see Existing Set as an option in this drop-down list. You can then use this drop-down list to choose the entire view or the objects you select for the hatch boundary.

The Boundary Set options are designed to give you more control over the way a point selection boundary is created. These options have no effect when you use the Select Objects button to select specific objects for the hatch boundary.

Tips for Using the Boundary Hatch

Here are a few tips on using the Boundary Hatch feature:

- Watch out for boundary areas that are part of a very large block. AutoCAD examines the entire block when defining boundaries. This can take time if the block is quite large. Use the Boundary Set option to "focus in" on the set of objects you want AutoCAD to use for your hatch boundary.

- The Boundary Hatch feature is view dependent; that is, it locates boundaries based on what is visible in the current view. To ensure that AutoCAD finds every detail, zoom in to the area to be hatched.

- If the area to be hatched will cover a very large area yet will require fine detail, first outline the hatch area using a polyline (see Chapter 13 for more on polylines). Then use the Select Objects option in the Boundary Hatch dialog box to select the polyline boundary manually, instead of depending on Boundary Hatch to find the boundary for you.

- Consider turning off layers that might interfere with AutoCAD's ability to find a boundary. For example, in the previous exercise, you could have turned off the Door layer, and then used Pick Points to locate the boundary of the hatch pattern.

- Boundary Hatch works on nested blocks as long as the nested block entities are parallel to the current UCS and are uniformly scaled in the x- and y-axes.

How to Quickly Match a Hatch Pattern and Other Properties

Another tool to help you edit hatch patterns is the Match Properties tool, which is similar to the Format Painter in the Microsoft Office suite. This tool lets you change an existing hatch pattern to match another existing hatch pattern. Here's how to use it.

1. Click the Match Properties tool in the Standard toolbar.

Continued on next page

2. Click the hatch pattern you want to copy.

3. Click the hatch pattern you want to change.

The selected pattern changes to match the pattern selected in step 2.

The Match Properties tool transfers other properties as well, such as layer, color, and linetype settings. You can select the properties that are transferred by opening the Property Settings dialog box.

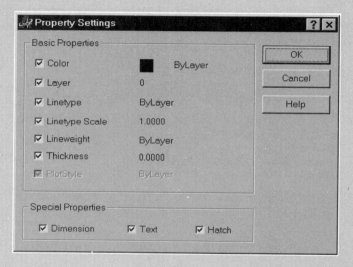

To open this dialog box, type **S⏎** after selecting the object in step 2, or right-click and select Settings from the popup menu. You can then select the properties you wish to transfer from the options shown. All the properties are selected by default. Note that text and dimension style settings can also be transferred. You'll learn more about text and dimension styles in Chapters 8 and 9.

Space Planning and Hatch Patterns

Suppose you are working on a plan within which you are constantly repositioning equipment and furniture, or you are in the process of designing the floor covering. You may be a little hesitant to place a hatch pattern on the floor because you don't want to have to rehatch the area each time you move a piece of equipment or change the flooring. You have two options in this situation: You can use the Boundary Hatch's associative capabilities to include the furnishings in the boundary set, or you can put AutoCAD's 3D features to work.

Using Associative Hatch

Associative Hatch is the most straightforward method. Make sure the Associative option is checked in the Boundary Hatch dialog box and include your equipment or furniture in the boundary set. You can do this by using the Select Objects option in the dialog box.

Once the pattern is in place, you can move the furnishings in your drawing and the hatch pattern automatically adjusts to their new location. One drawback, however, is that AutoCAD attempts to hatch the interior of your furnishings if they cross over the outer boundary of the hatch pattern. Also, if any boundary objects are erased or exploded, the hatch pattern no longer follows the location of your furnishings. To avoid these problems, you can use the method described in the next section.

Using 3D Features to Trick AutoCAD

The second method for masking hatch patterns requires the use of some 3D features of AutoCAD.

1. First, draw the equipment at an elevation above the floor level by setting up AutoCAD to draw objects with a z-coordinate other than 0.

2. Use the 3DFace command to generate a 3D surface that matches the outline of the equipment. Or, if your equipment outline is a fairly complex shape, use a region (regions are discussed in Chapter 18).

3. Make sure the 3DFaces are drawn at an elevation that places them between the floor and the equipment.

4. Turn each individual piece of equipment, complete with 3DFace, into blocks or groups so that you can easily move them around.

5. Hatch the entire floor, making sure the hatch pattern is at an elevation below the 3DFace elevation (see Figure 6.12).

NOTE   See Chapter 15 for more on drawing objects in 3D.

TIP   You can change the z-coordinate of virtually any object by using the Properties dialog box. To do this, select the object you want to change, then click the Properties tool in the Standard toolbar. Edit the Position Z value in the dialog box.

FIGURE 6.12:

Using 3D functions for space planning

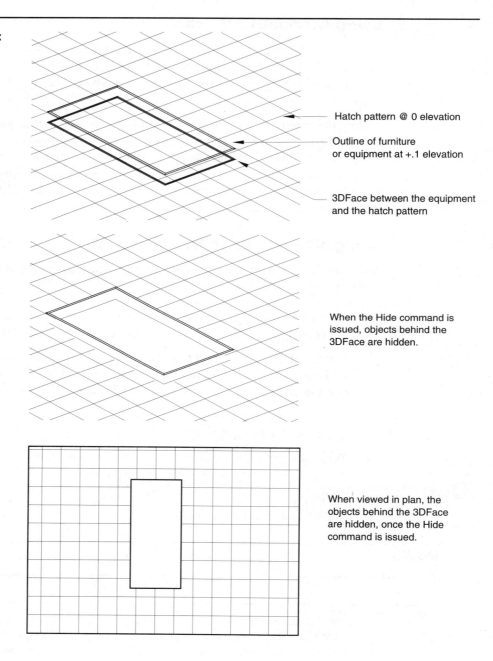

Hatch pattern @ 0 elevation

Outline of furniture or equipment at +.1 elevation

3DFace between the equipment and the hatch pattern

When the Hide command is issued, objects behind the 3DFace are hidden.

When viewed in plan, the objects behind the 3DFace are hidden, once the Hide command is issued.

WARNING   One drawback to the 3D method is that the Hide command turns solids and wide polylines into outlines.

As you work with the drawing, the floor pattern shows through the equipment. Don't worry—when it's time to plot your drawing, you can use the Plot command's Hide option, discussed in Chapter 15, or the Mview command's Hideplot option, discussed in Chapter 18. This causes anything behind the 3DFace to be hidden in the plotter output, which means that any hatch pattern underneath your equipment does not appear. You can also use the Hide command from time to time to see what your design will look like without having to wait for hard copy—like using paper cutouts over a plan.

Using AutoCAD 3D features this way can save you time and give you more flexibility in your work. And although the Hide command takes a minute or two to do its work, it is still faster than rehatching an area each time you make a change to its configuration. For more on the 3D functions mentioned here, see Part IV of this book.

NOTE   A third method for masking hatch patterns is to use two Express tools called Wipeout and Text Mask. Text Mask masks the area behind text to make text more readable when situated over a hatch pattern. Wipeout is a more generalized masking tool that can be used to mask areas behind odd shapes. See Chapter 19 for details on both these tools.

Using External References

This chapter's discussion about freezing layers mentioned that you can insert drawing files as external references, in a way similar to inserting blocks. To accomplish this, you use the Insert ➤ External Reference (Xref) command. The difference between Xref files and blocks is that Xref files do not actually become part of the drawing's database. Instead, they are "loaded" along with the current file at startup time. It is as if AutoCAD were opening several drawings at once: the currently active file you specify when you start AutoCAD, and any file inserted as an Xref.

If you keep Xref files independent from the current file, any changes you make to the Xref automatically appear in the current file. You don't have to manually update the Xref file as you do blocks. For example, if you used Xref to insert the Unit file into the Plan file, and you later made changes to the Unit file, the next time you opened the Plan file, you would see the new version of the Unit file in place of the old.

TIP You cannot Xref a file if the file has the same name as a block in the current drawing. If this situation occurs, but you still need to use the file as an Xref, you can rename the block of the same name using the Rename command. See Chapter 8.

Another advantage of Xref files is that since they do not actually become part of a drawing's database, drawing size is kept to a minimum. This translates to more efficient use of your hard disk space.

NOTE Xref files, like blocks, cannot be edited. You can, however, use Osnaps to snap to location in an Xref file, or freeze or turn off the Xref file's insertion layer to make it invisible.

Attaching a Drawing as an External Reference

The next exercise shows how to use an Xref in place of an inserted block to construct the studio apartment building. You'll start with creating a new Unit file by copying the old one. Then you bring a new toolbar, the External Reference toolbar, to the screen.

1. Return to the Unit file; use File ➢ Save As to save it under the name Unitxref.dwg. You can also use the Unitxref.dwg file from the companion CD-ROM.

2. Return to the Plan file, and choose Save As and save the file under the name Planxref. The current file is now Planxref.

3. Erase all of the objects (**E**↵ **All**↵) and purge the Unit, Stair, and Lobby blocks. (By doing steps 2 and 3, you save yourself from having to set up a new file.)

4. Choose File ➢ Drawing Utilities ➢ Purge ➢ All to purge the drawing.

5. Click Insert ➤ Xref Manager, or type **XR**↵, to open the Xref Manager dialog box.

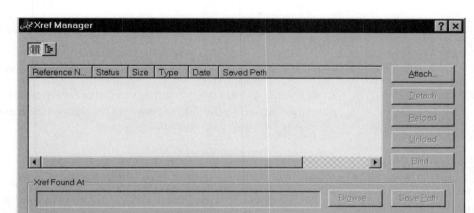

6. Click the Attach button in the Xref Manager dialog box. The Select Reference File dialog box appears. This is a typical AutoCAD File dialog box complete with a preview window.

7. Locate and select the Unitxref.dwg file, and then click Open. The External Reference dialog box appears.

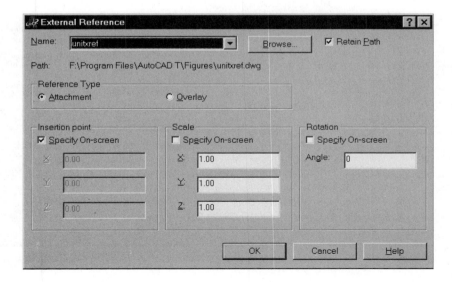

Notice that this dialog box looks similar to the Insert dialog box. It offers the same options for insertion point, scale, and rotation.

8. You'll get a description of the options presented in this dialog box. For now, click OK.

9. Enter **31'–5",43'–8"** (metric users enter **957,1330**) for the insertion point.

10. After the Unitxref.dwg file is inserted, recreate the same layout of the floor plan you created in the first section of this chapter by copying and mirroring the Unitxref.dwg external reference.

11. Save and exit the Unitxref file.

You now have a drawing that looks like the Plan.dwg file, you created earlier in this chapter, but instead of using blocks that are detached from their source file, you have a drawing composed of Xrefs. These Xrefs are the actual Unitxref.dwg files and they are loaded into AutoCAD at the same time that you open the Planxref.dwg file.

Next, you'll modify the Unitxref.dwg file, then see the results in the Planxref.dwg file.

1. Return to the Unitxref.dwg drawing.

2. Erase the hatch pattern and kitchen outline for the floors, and save the file.

3. Open Planxref.dwg again, and notice that the Unitxref Xrefs have been updated automatically to reflect the erasure of the hatch pattern. This automatic updating does not occur with block insertions.

Importing Blocks, Layers, and Other Named Elements from External Files

You can use the Xbind command to import blocks and other drawing components from another file. First, use External Reference Attach to cross-reference a file; type **Xbind** at the command prompt. In the Xbind dialog box, click the plus sign next to the Xref file-name, and then select Block. Locate the name of the block you want to import, click the Add button, and click OK. Finally, use Detach from the Reference dialog box to remove the Xref file. The imported block remains as part of the current file. (See Chapter 12 for details on importing drawing components.) For general import of drawing components, you can also use the AutoCAD DesignCenter described in Chapter 22.

Here you saw how an Xref file doesn't have to be updated the way blocks do. Since Xrefs are loaded along with the drawing file that contains them, the containing file, which in this case was the Plan file, automatically displays any changes made to the Xref. Also, you avoid the task of having to update nested blocks, because Auto-CAD updates nested Xrefs, as well as non-nested Xrefs.

Editing Xrefs and the Files That Contain Them at the Same Time

In the exercise in the section *Attaching a Drawing as an External Reference*, you closed the `Planxref.dwg` file, edited the `Unitxref.dwg` file, then reopened the `Planxref.dwg` file. This demonstrates that the Xref is automatically updated when you open the `Planxref.dwg` file. You could have also kept the `Planxref.dwg` file open while editing the `Unitxref.dwg` file, then refreshed the `Unitxref.dwg` Xref from the Xref Manager dialog box.

To refresh an Xref, open the Xref Manager dialog box while in the `Planxref.dwg` file. Highlight the Unitxref name in the Xref Manager dialog box list box, then click the Reload button, then click OK. Since both the Xref file and the containing file are opened, you'll get the message `File is open for editing. Unable to Demand load, Perform a full read instead?` You can click OK at this message, then the Xref will be updated. By the way, this warning message is the same message you'd get if someone else is working on the Unitxref file over a network while you're attempting to update the Xref in the `Planxref.dwg` file.

TIP   If you find that you use the Xrefs frequently, you may want to place the Insert tool-bar permanently in your AutoCAD window. It contains tools for inserting both blocks and Xrefs. To open the Insert toolbar, right-click any toolbar, and then click the Insert check box in the Toolbar dialog box.

Other Differences between External References and Blocks

Here are a few other differences between external references (Xrefs) and inserted blocks that you will want to keep in mind:

- Any new layers, text styles, or line types brought in with cross-referenced files do not become part of the current file. If you want to import any of these items, you can use the Xbind command (described in Chapter 12).

- If you make changes to the layers of a cross-referenced file, those changes are not retained when the file is saved, unless you have checked the Retain Changes to Xref Layers option in the Open and Save tab of the Options dialog box. This option can be found in the External References (Xrefs) button group. This option instructs AutoCAD to remember any layer color or visibility settings from one editing session to the next. In the standard AutoCAD settings, this option is on by default.

TIP   Another way to ensure that layer settings for Xrefs are retained is to enter **Visretain.┘** at the command prompt. At the `New value for VISRETAIN <0>:` prompt, enter **1**.

- To segregate layers in Xref files from the ones in the current drawing, the Xref file's layers are prefixed with their file's name. A vertical bar separates the filename prefix and the layer name, as in Unitxref│wall.

- Xrefs cannot be exploded. You can, however, convert an Xref into a block, and then explode it. To do this, you must use the Bind button in the External Reference dialog box. This opens another dialog box that offers two ways of converting an Xref into a block. See the *Options in the External Reference Dialog Box* section for more information on this dialog box.

- If an Xref is renamed or moved to another location on your hard disk, AutoCAD won't be able to find that file when it opens other files to which the Xref is attached. If this happens, you must use the Browse option in the External Reference dialog box to tell AutoCAD where to find the cross-reference file.

WARNING   Take care when relocating an Xref file with the Browse button. The Browse button can assign a file of a different name to an existing Xref as a substitution.

Xref files are especially useful in workgroup environments where several people are working on the same project. For example, one person might be updating several files that are inserted into a variety of other files. Using blocks, everyone in the workgroup would have to be notified of the changes and would have to update all the affected blocks in all the drawings that contained them. With cross-referenced files, however, the updating is automatic, so you avoid confusion about which files need to have their blocks updated.

External References in the San Francisco Main Library Project

While these exercises demonstrate how Xrefs work, you aren't limited to using them in the way shown here. Perhaps one of the more common ways of using Xrefs is to combine a single floor plan with different title block drawings, each with its own layer settings and title block information. In this way, single-drawing files can be reused in several drawing sheets of a final construction document set. This helps keep data consistent across drawings and reduces the number of overall drawings needed.

This is exactly how Xrefs were used in the San Francisco Main Library drawings. One floor plan file contained most of the main information for that floor. The floor plan was then used as an Xref in another file that contained the title block, as well as additional information such as furnishings or floor finish reference symbols. Layer visibility was controlled in each title block drawing so only the data related to that drawing appeared.

Multiple Xref files were also used by segregating the structural column grid layout drawings from the floor plan files. In other cases, portions of plans from different floors were combined into a single drawing using Xrefs, as shown in Figure 6.13.

FIGURE 6.13:

A sample sheet from the San Francisco Main Library construction documents showing enlarged paving plans from various floors. Each floor is an Xref from a complete floor plan drawing file.

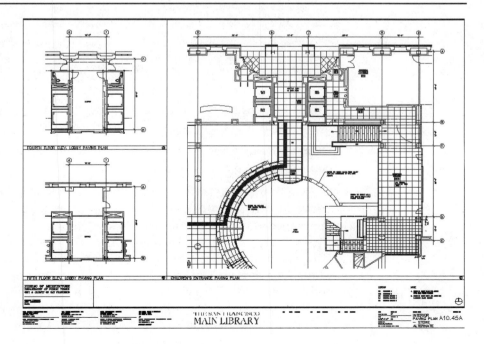

Other External Reference Options

There are many other features unique to cross-referenced files. Let's briefly look at some of the other options in the Xref Manager dialog box.

Options in the Xref Manager Dialog Box

The following options are found in the main External Reference dialog box. All but the Attach option are available only when an Xref is present in the current drawing and its name is selected from the list of Xrefs shown in the main part of the dialog box.

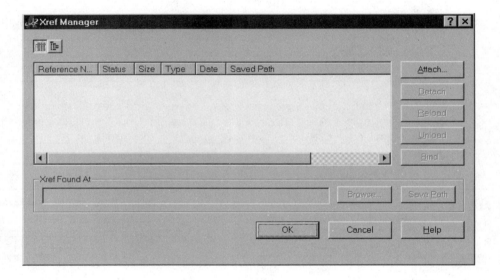

Attach   Opens the Select Reference dialog box, allowing you to select a file to attach and set the parameters for the attachment.

Detach   Detaches an Xref from the current file. The file is then completely disassociated from the current file.

Unload   Similar to Detach but maintains a link to the Xref file so that it can be quickly reattached. This has an effect similar to freezing a layer and can reduce redraw, regen, and file-loading times.

Reload   Restores an unloaded Xref.

Bind   Converts an Xref into a block. Bind offers two options: Bind (again) and Insert. Bind's Bind option maintains the Xref's named elements (layers, line types, and text and dimension styles) by creating new layers in the current file with the Xref's filename prefix (see Chapter 12). The Insert option does not attempt to maintain the Xref's named elements but merges them with named elements of the same name in the current file. For example, if both the Xref and the current file have layers of the same name, the objects in the Xref are placed in the layers of the same name in the current file.

Browse   Opens the Select New Path dialog box from which you can select a new file or location for a selected Xref.

Save Path   Saves the file path displayed in the Xref Found At input box. See the Include Path option in the following section.

List View/Tree View   These two buttons are in the upper-left corner of the Xref Manager dialog box. They let you switch between a List view of your Xrefs and a hierarchical Tree view. The Tree view can be helpful in determining how the Xrefs are nested.

NOTE   The Xref list works like other Windows lists, offering the ability to sort by name, status, size, type, date, or path. To sort by name, for example, click the Reference Name button at the top of the list.

The External Reference Dialog Box

The External Reference dialog box shown in the previous exercise offers these options:

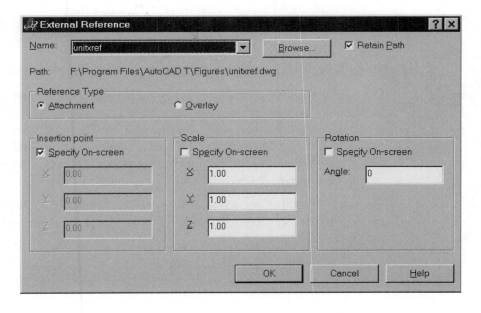

Browse   Opens the Select Reference File dialog box to allow you to change the file you are importing as an Xref.

Attachment   Causes AutoCAD to include other Xref attachments that are nested in the selected file.

Overlay   Causes AutoCAD to ignore other Xref attachments that are nested in the selected file. This avoids multiple attachments of other files and eliminates the possibility of circular references (referencing the current file into itself through another file).

Retain Path   Lets you determine whether AutoCAD stores the path information to the Xref in the current drawing's database, or discards it. If you choose not to use this option, AutoCAD uses the default file search path to locate the Xref the next time the current file is open. If you plan to send your files to someone else, you may want to turn this option off; otherwise the person you send the file has to duplicate the exact file path structure of your computer before the Xrefs will load properly.

Specify On-Screen   Appears in three places. It gives you the option to enter insertion point, scale factors, and rotation angles within the dialog box or in the Command window, in a way similar to inserting blocks. If you check this option for any of the corresponding parameters, the parameters change to allow input. If they are checked, you are prompted for those parameters after you click OK to close the dialog box. With all three Specify On-Screen check boxes unchecked, the Xref will be inserted in the drawing using the settings indicated in the dialog box.

Clipping Xref Views and Improving Performance

Xrefs are frequently used to import large drawings for reference or backgrounds. Multiple Xrefs, such as a floor plan, column grid layout, and site plan drawing, might be combined into one file. One drawback to multiple Xrefs in earlier versions of AutoCAD is that the entire Xref is loaded into memory, even if only a small portion of the Xref is used for the final plotted output. For computers with limited resources, multiple Xrefs could slow the system to a crawl.

AutoCAD 2000 offers two tools that help make display and memory use more efficient when using Xrefs: The Xclip command and the Demand Load option in the Options dialog box.

Clipping Views

Xclip is the name of a command accessed by choosing Modify ➤ Clip ➤ Xref. This command allows you to clip the display of an Xref or block to any shape you desire as shown in Figure 6.14. For example, you may want to display only an L-shaped portion of a floor plan to be part of your current drawing. Xclip lets you define such a view.

FIGURE 6.14:

The top panel shows a polyline outline of the area to be isolated with Xclip. The middle panel shows how the Xref appears after Xclip is applied. The last panel shows a view of the plan with the polyline's layer turned off.

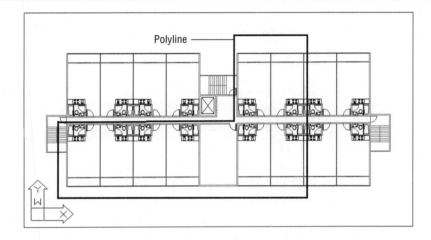

Polyline

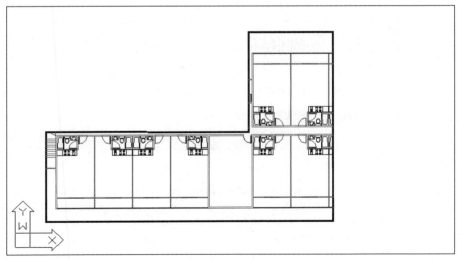

FIGURE 6.14: CONTINUED

The top panel shows a polyline outline of the area to be isolated with Xclip. The middle panel shows how the Xref appears after Xclip is applied. The last panel shows a view of the plan with the polyline's layer turned off.

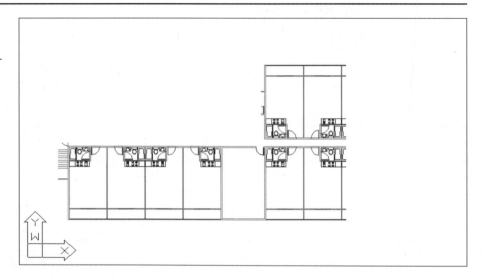

Blocks and multiple Xrefs can be clipped as well. And you can specify a front and back clipping distance so that visibility of objects in 3D space can be controlled (see *Using 3D Features to Trick AutoCAD* in this chapter). You can define a clip area using polylines or spline curves, although curve-fitted polylines will revert to decurved polylines. (See Chapter 13 for more on polylines and spline curves.)

NOTE To see a detailed tutorial on clipping Xrefs, see Chapter 12.

Controlling Xref Settings in the Options Dialog Box

The External Reference button group in the Open and Save tab of the Options dialog box offers some tools to help you manage memory use and other features related to Xrefs. If you're working on large projects with others in a workgroup, you'll want to be aware of these settings and what they do.

The Demand Load Xref drop-down list offers three settings: Disabled, Enabled, and Enabled with Copy. Demand Load is enabled by default in the standard AutoCAD drawing setup. Besides reducing the amount of memory an Xref consumes, Demand Load also prevents other users from editing the Xref while it is being viewed as part of your current drawing. This is done to help aid drawing version control and drawing management. The third Demand Load option, Enabled with Copy, creates a copy of the source Xref file, and then uses the copy, thereby allowing other AutoCAD users to edit the source Xref file.

Demand loading improves performance by loading only the parts of the referenced drawing that are needed to regenerate the current drawing. You can set the location for the Xref copy in the Files tab of the Options dialog box under Temporary External Reference File Location.

Two other options are also available in the Options dialog box.

Retain Changes to Xref-Layers   Instructs AutoCAD to remember any layer color or visibility settings of Xrefs from one editing session to the next. In the standard AutoCAD settings, this option is on by default.

Allow Other Users to Refedit Current Drawing   Lets others edit the current drawing using the Modify ➢ In-Place Xref and Block Edit ➢ Edit Reference command (Refedit). You'll learn about this command in the next section.

Special Save As Options That Affect Demand Loading

AutoCAD offers a few additional settings that boost the performance of the Demand load feature mentioned in the previous section. When you choose File ➢ Save As to save a file in the standard .dwg format, you see a button labeled Options. If you click the Options button, the Export Options dialog box appears. This dialog box offers the Index Type dropdown list. The index referred to can help improve the speed of demand loading. The index options are:

None   No index is created.

Layer   AutoCAD loads only layers that are both turned on and thawed.

Spacial   AutoCAD loads only portions of an Xref or raster image within a clipped boundary.

Layer & Spacial   This option turns on both the Layer and Spacial options.

Editing Xrefs In Place

You've seen different methods for editing blocks and Xrefs as external files. AutoCAD 2000 offers a way to edit a block or Xref directly within a file, without having to edit an external file. To do this, you use the In-Place Xref and Block Edit option in the Modify pull-down menu. This option issues the Refedit command. The following exercise demonstrates how Refedit works.

1. If it isn't already open, open the Planxref.dwg file.

2. Zoom into the Unit plan in the lower-left corner of the drawing so you see a view similar to Figure 6.15.

3. Choose Modify ➤ In-Place Xref and Block Edit ➤ Edit Reference from the menu bar.

4. At the Select reference: prompt, click the kitchenette in the corner unit. The Reference Edit dialog box appears.

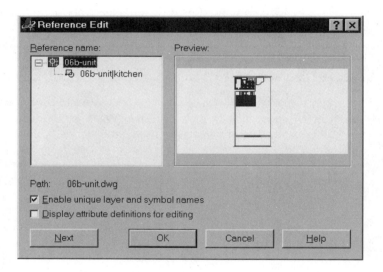

5. The Reference Edit dialog box contains two windows. The right-hand window shows the entire Xref that you are editing. The window to the left shows a listing of the specific item you selected in the Xref. Notice that the listing shows the hierarchical relationship of the kitchenette block in relation to the Unitxref Xref.

6. In the left-hand window, click the Kitchen listing, then click OK. The Reference Edit dialog box disappears.

7. Use a selection window to select the entire lower-left corner unit. Notice that only the kitchenette is highlighted while all other objects become gray.

8. Press ↲. The Refedit toolbar appears. You can now edit the kitchenette.

> You can open the Refedit toolbar so that it stays on the screen by right-clicking any toolbar, then selecting Refedit from the popup menu.

The Refedit command isolates the objects you select in step 7 for editing. You cannot edit anything else until you choose Modify ➢ In-Place Xref and Block Edit ➢ Save Reference Edit or Modify ➢ In-Place Xref and Block Edit ➢ Discard Reference Edit from the menu bar.

Note that at this point, you are actually able to edit a block within an Xref. Now let's continue editing the kitchenette.

1. Zoom in on the kitchenette, then move the four burners to the right 8 inches (20cm for metric users).

2. Erase the sink.

3. Click the Save Back Changes to Reference button on the Refedit toolbar.

You may also select Modify ➢ In-Place Xref and Block Edit ➢ Save Reference Edit from the menu bar.

4. A warning message appears telling you that the changes you've made to the Xref will be saved to disk. Click OK.

5. Zoom back to your previous view. Notice that the other units now reflect the changes you made to the Unitxref Xref (see Figure 6.16).

6. Open the Unitxref.dwg file. Notice that the kitchen now reflects the changes you made to the Xref of the unit in the Planxref file. This shows you that by choosing to save the reference edit in step 3, you actually save the changes back to the Xref's source file.

FIGURE 6.15:

The enlarged view of the
Unit Xref in the Planxref file

FIGURE 6.15:

The enlarged view of the
Unit Xref in the Planxref file

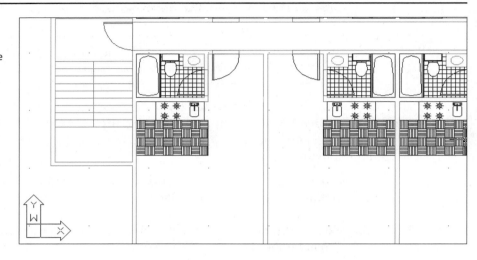

FIGURE 6.16:

The Xrefs after being edited

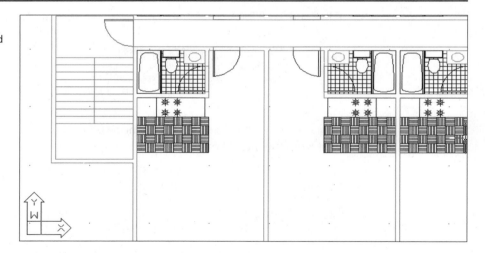

As you saw from these two exercises, you can actually edit a specific block within an Xref, but you must click that block when you are prompted to select objects at the beginning of the Refedit command.

The Reference Edit dialog box offers you the option to isolate the block itself, or select the next object up in the block/Xref hierarchy. You can also cycle through the hierarchy using the Next button just below the hierarchy listing.

In these exercises, you edited a block contained within an Xref, but you could have just as easily edited a single block or a block nested inside another block. Changes in blocks will not affect other files, however. The changes remain within the current file until you explicitly export the changed block to a file, as you saw in earlier exercises.

Adding and Removing Objects from Blocks and Xrefs

In the previous exercises, you removed objects from the Kitchen block simply by using the Erase command. You can also move objects from a block or Xref into the current drawing without actually erasing it. To do this, select Modify ➤ In-Place Xref and Block Edit ➤ Remove From Working Set. This removes the object from the block or Xref without erasing it. Likewise, you can add new objects to the block or Xref using select Modify ➤ In-Place Xref and Block Edit ➤ Add to Working Set. Both of these options are the Refset command with different options applied. To see how Refset works, try the following exercise.

1. Close the Unitxref file.

2. In the Planxref file, zoom into the kitchenette to get a view similar to Figure 6.17.

3. Choose Modify ➤ In-Place Xref and Block Edit ➤ Edit Reference.

4. Click the kitchenette.

5. Click the Kitchen listing in the Reference Edit dialog box, then click OK.

6. Select the entire kitchenette again.

7. Use the Move tool to move the two right-hand burners just to the right of the kitchenette, as shown in Figure 6.17.

8. Click the Transfer (Remove) Objects from the Refedit Working Set button in the Refedit toolbar, or select Modify ➤ In-Place Xref and Block Edit ➤ Remove From Working Set.

9. Select the two burners you just moved, then press ↵.

Notice that the burners become grayer to show that they are now removed from the working set. They remain as part of the Planxref drawing, but they are no longer part of the Kitchen block.

Now add a rectangle to the Kitchen block in place of the burners.

1. Draw a 7" by 16" (18cm by 40cm) rectangle in place of the moved burners, as shown in Figure 6.17.

2. Select the rectangle you drew in place of the moved burners, then press ↵.

3. Click Save Back Changes to Reference Tool on the Refedit toolbar or select Modify ➤ In-Place Xref and Block Edit ➤ Save Reference Edits.

4. Zoom out enough to see the other units in the drawing (see Figure 6.18).

FIGURE 6.17:

Moving the burners out of the Kitchen block and the rectangle in

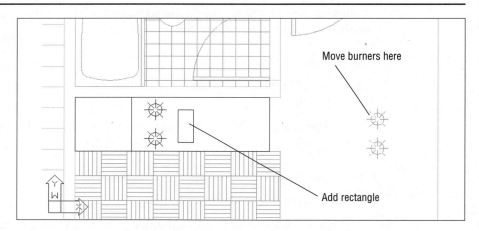

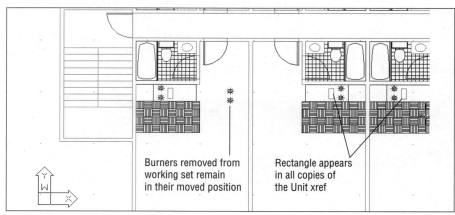

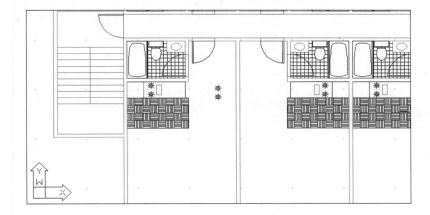

FIGURE 6.18:

The Planxref drawing with the changes made to the Unitxref Xref

Notice that now you see that the burners have been replaced by the rectangle in all the other Xref units. The burners you moved are still there in the lower-right corner unit, but they have been removed from all of the Xrefs. It is as if you had extracted them from the block and placed them in the Plan drawing.

Once you start the Refedit command, any new objects that you create are added to the working set automatically, until you save your reference edits. When you drew the rectangle in step 1, for example, it was automatically included in the working set, which is the set of objects included in the block or Xref you are currently working on. You didn't have to specifically add it to the working set. If you want to include existing objects in the working set, use the Modify ➤ In-Place Xref and Block Edit ➤ Add to Working Set option, or select it from the Refedit toolbar

You've completed the exercises in this chapter so you can exit AutoCAD without saving these changes.

If You Want to Experiment...

If you'd like to see firsthand how block substitution works, try doing the exercise in Figure 6.19. It shows how quickly you can change the configuration of a drawing by careful use of block substitution. As you work through the exercise, keep in mind that some planning is required to use blocks in this way. If you know that you will have to try various configurations in a drawing, plan to set up files to accommodate them.

FIGURE 6.19:

An exercise in block substitution

1. Open a file called PART1 and draw the object shown at right.

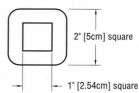

2" [5cm] square

1" [2.54cm] square

2. Next to that object, draw the object shown at right. Use the Wblock command and turn it into a file called TAB1.
(Note the insertion point location.)

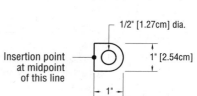

1/2" [1.27cm] dia.

Insertion point at midpoint of this line

1" [2.54cm]

1" [2.54cm]

3. Draw the object shown at right and turn it into a file called TAB2.

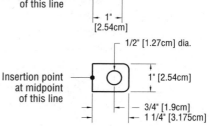

1/2" [1.27cm] dia.

Insertion point at midpoint of this line

1" [2.54cm]

3/4" [1.9cm]

1 1/4" [3.175cm]

4. Insert TAB1 into the drawing in four places as shown in here. You can insert one then use the Polar option under the Array command for the other three tabs.

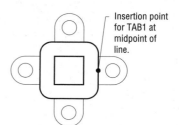

Insertion point for TAB1 at midpoint of line.

5. Start the Insert command again but at the prompt

Block name (or ?):

enter TAB1=TAB2. The drawing regenerates and an alternate version of the part appears with TAB2 replacing TAB1. Cancel the Insert command.

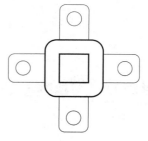

You might also want to try the exercise using Xrefs instead of inserting files as blocks. Once you've attached the Xref, try substituting the Tab1 Xref with the Tab2 Xref by using the Browse button in the External Reference dialog box. Highlight Tab1 in the list of Xrefs, and then click Browse and select Tab2. The current file still calls the Xref Tab1 by its original name, but instead loads Tab2 in its place.

TIP   You can substitute Xrefs in a way similar to blocks as shown in this example.

By now, you may be anxious to see how your drawings look on paper. In the next chapter, you will explore the use of AutoCAD's printing and plotting commands.

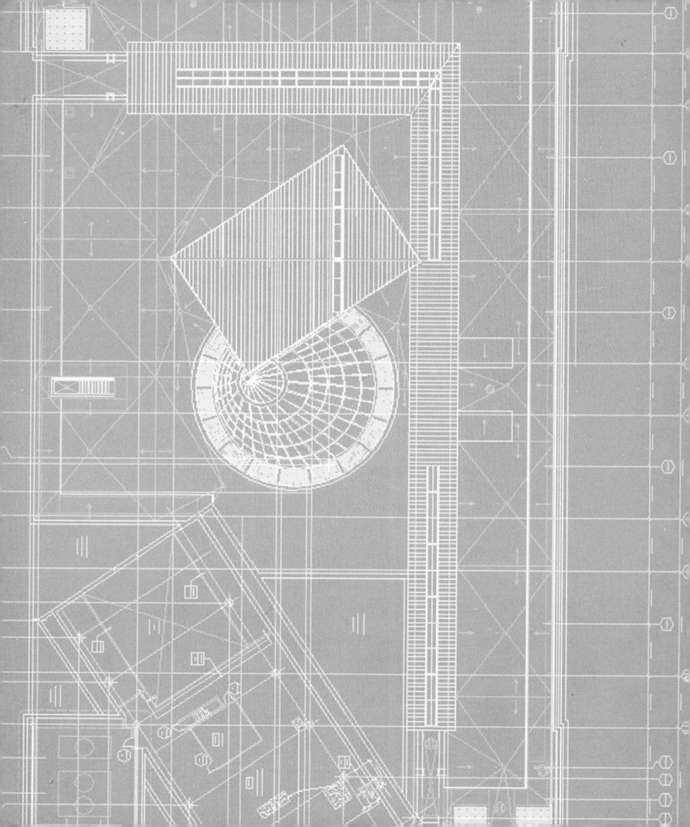

CHAPTER
SEVEN

7

Printing and Plotting

Getting hard copy output from AutoCAD is something of an art. You'll need to be intimately familiar with both your output device and the settings available in AutoCAD. You will probably spend a good deal of time experimenting with AutoCAD's plotter settings and with your printer or plotter to get your equipment set up just the way you want.

With the huge array of output options available, this chapter can only provide a general discussion of plotting. It's up to you to work out the details and fine-tune the way you and AutoCAD together work with your plotter. This chapter describes the features available in AutoCAD and discusses some general rules and guidelines to follow when setting up your plots.

You'll start out by getting an overview of the plotting features in AutoCAD. Then you'll delve into the finer details of setting up your drawing and controlling your plotter.

NOTE If you've used an earlier version of AutoCAD, be sure you read through this chapter. Virtually every aspect of printing and plotting has changed in AutoCAD 2000.

Plotting the Plan

To see firsthand how the Plot command works, you'll plot the Plan file using the default settings on your system. Start by getting a preview of your plot, before you commit to actually printing your drawing.

1. First, be sure your printer or plotter is connected to your computer and is turned on.

2. Start AutoCAD and open the Plan file.

3. Choose View ➢ Zoom ➢ All to display the entire drawing.

4. Choose File ➢ Plot. The Plot dialog box appears. You may also see the *Fast Track to Plotting Help* message asking you if you would like to see the provided Plotting Help documents and animation files. At some point in the future you may want to review these documents. For now, click No.

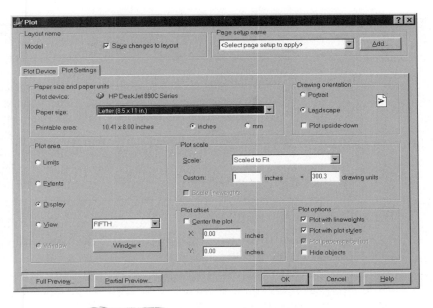

5. Make sure the Plot Settings tab is selected, then click the Display radio button in the Plot Area button group. This tells AutoCAD to plot the drawing as it looks in the drawing window.

6. Make sure the Scaled to Fit option is selected in the Plot Scale button group.

7. Click the Full Preview button in the lower-left corner of the dialog box. AutoCAD works for a moment, then displays a sample view showing you how your drawing will appear on your printer output.

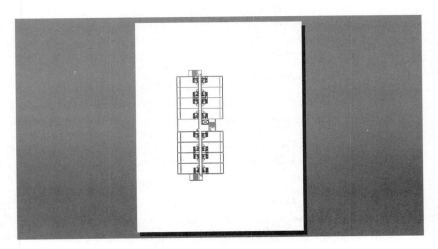

NOTE   The print preview depends on the type of output device you chose when you installed AutoCAD or when you last selected a Plotter Device option (described in *Selecting an Output Device* in this chapter). The print preview is also affected by other settings in the Plot dialog box, such as those in the Drawing Orientation, Plot Offset, and Plot Area group. The previous example shows a typical preview view using the Windows default system printer in portrait mode.

The preview image displays the paper in its orientation as it leaves the printer. This may be a bit confusing if you are printing in landscape mode. The image appears sideways, which is the proper orientation for the landscape image in relation to the paper, even though the paper appears in a portrait orientation.

Notice that the view also shows the Zoom Realtime cursor. You can use the Zoom/Pan Realtime tool to get a close-up look at your print preview. Now go ahead and plot the file.

8. Right-click, then select Plot from the popup menu. AutoCAD sends the drawing to your printer.

9. Your plotter or printer prints out the plan to no particular scale.

You've just done your first plot just to see how the drawing looks on paper. You used the minimal settings to ensure that the complete drawing appears on the paper. Next, try plotting your drawing to an exact scale.

WARNING   It is important to make sure you use the appropriate unit settings in this chapter. If you've been using the metric measurements for previous exercises, make sure you use the metric settings in the exercises of this chapter, otherwise your results will not coincide with the exercises in this chapter.

1. Choose File ➤ Plot again.

2. If your last printout was not oriented on the paper correctly, then select the Landscape option in the Drawing Orientation button group.

3. Open the Scale drop-down list and select 1/16" = 1'-0". Metric users should select 1:20. As you can see, you have quite a few choices for the scale of your output.

4. In the Paper Size and Paper Units button group, select the Inches radio button then select Letter (8.5 × 11 in.). Metric users should click the mm radio button, and select A4 (210 × 297mm). The options available in this drop-down list will

depend on your Windows system printer or the output device you have configured for AutoCAD.

5. In the Plot Area button group, click the Limits option. This tells AutoCAD to use the limits of your drawing to determine which part of your drawing to plot.

6. Click Full Preview again to get a preview of your plot.

7. Right-click and select Plot. This time, your printout is to scale.

Here, you were asked to make a few more settings in the Plot dialog box. A number of settings work together to produce a drawing that is to scale and that fits properly on your paper. This is where it pays to understand the relationship between your drawing scale and your paper's size, as it was discussed in Chapter 3.

> **NOTE**   The next section is lengthy, but doesn't contain any exercises. If you prefer to continue with the exercises in this chapter, skip to *WYSIWYG Plotting Using Layout Tabs*. Make sure to come back and read the following section while the previous exercises are still fresh in your mind.

Understanding the Plotter Settings

In this section, you'll explore all of the settings that are available in the Plot Settings tab of the Plot dialog box. These settings give you control over the size and orientation of your image on the paper. They also let you control what part of your drawing gets printed. All of these settings work together to give you control over how your drawing will fit on your printed output.

> **WARNING**   If you're a veteran AutoCAD user, be aware that AutoCAD 2000 now relies mainly on the Windows system printer configuration instead of its own plotter drivers. This give you more flexibility and control over your output, but it also may create some confusion if you're used to the previous method that AutoCAD used to set up plots. Just be aware that you'll need to understand the Windows system printer settings, in addition to those offered by AutoCAD.

Paper Size and Paper Units

The options in this group allow you to select the paper size and the measurement system you are using. You can select a paper size from the Paper Size drop-down list.

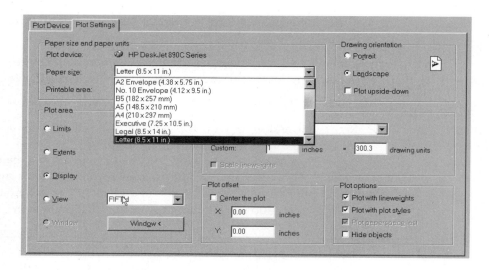

These sizes are derived from the sizes available from your currently selected system printer. You'll find out how to select a different printer later in this chapter.

The Printable Area radio buttons offer Inches and mm. When you select one of these options, the Printable Area listing changes to show you the area in the units you selected. Options in the Plot Scale button group also change to reflect the measurement system choice.

Drawing Orientation

When you used the Full Preview option in the first exercise of this chapter, you saw your drawing as it would be placed on the paper. A landscape orientation places the image on the paper so that the width of the paper is greater than the height of the paper. In the figure shown in our example, it was placed in what is called a landscape orientation. You can rotate the image on the paper 90 degrees into what is called a Portrait orientation by selecting the Portrait Radio button (see Figure 7.1) in the Drawing Orientation button group. A third option, Plot Upside-Down, lets you change the orientation further by turning the landscape or portrait orientation upside down. These three settings let you orient the image in any one of four orientations on the sheet.

Note that in AutoCAD, the preview displays the paper in the orientation that it leaves the printer. So for most small-format printers, if you're printing in the portrait orientation, the image appears in the same orientation as you see it when you are editing the drawing. If you're using the landscape orientation, the preview image is turned sideways. For large-format plotters, the preview may be oriented in the opposite direction.

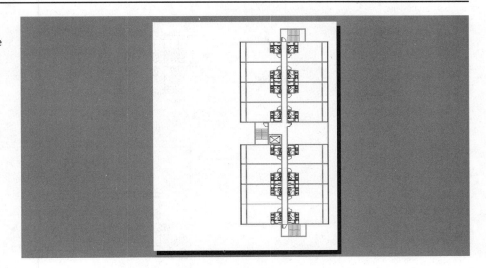

Plot Area

The Radio buttons on the lower-left side of the Plot dialog box let you specify which part of your drawing you wish to plot. You might notice some similarities between these settings and the Zoom command options.

Limits

The Limits printing option uses the limits of the drawing to determine what to print (see Figure 7.2). If you let AutoCAD fit the drawing onto the sheet (by selecting Scaled to Fit from the Scale drop-down list), the plot displays exactly the same thing that you would see on the screen had you selected View ➤ Zoom ➤ All.

Extents

The Extents option draws the entire drawing, eliminating any space that may border the drawing (see Figure 7.3). If you let AutoCAD fit the drawing onto the sheet (that is, you select Scaled to Fit from the Scale drop-down list), the plot displays exactly the same thing that you would see on the screen if you had selected View ➤ Zoom ➤ Extents.

FIGURE 7.2:

The screen display and the printed output when Limits is chosen

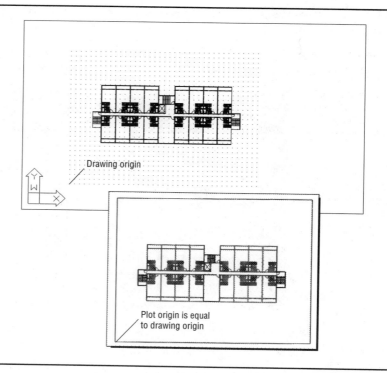

Drawing origin

Plot origin is equal to drawing origin

FIGURE 7.3:

The printed output when Extents is chosen

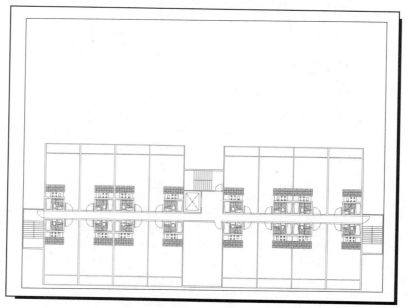

Display

Display is the default option; it tells AutoCAD to plot what is currently displayed on the screen (see panel 1 of Figure 7.4). If you let AutoCAD fit the drawing onto the sheet (that is, you select the Scaled to Fit option from the Scale drop-down list), the plot is exactly the same as what you see on your screen (panel 2 of Figure 7.4).

FIGURE 7.4:

The screen display and the printed output when Display is chosen and no Scale is used (the drawing is scaled to fit the sheet)

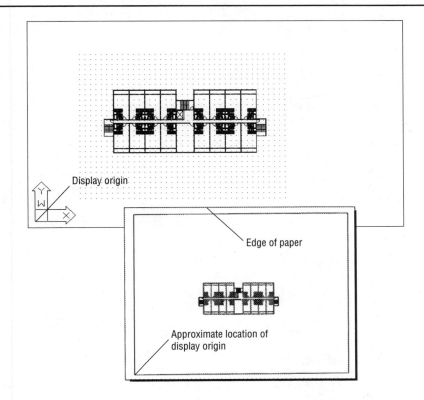

Display origin

Edge of paper

Approximate location of display origin

View

The View printing option uses a previously saved view to determine what to print (see Figure 7.5). To use this option, you must first create a view. Then click the View Radio button. You can then select a view from the drop-down list, just to the right of the View Radio button.

If you let AutoCAD fit the drawing onto the sheet (by selecting Scaled to Fit from the Scale drop-down list), the plot displays exactly the same thing that you would see on the screen if you had recalled the view you are plotting.

FIGURE 7.5:

A comparison of the saved view and the printed output

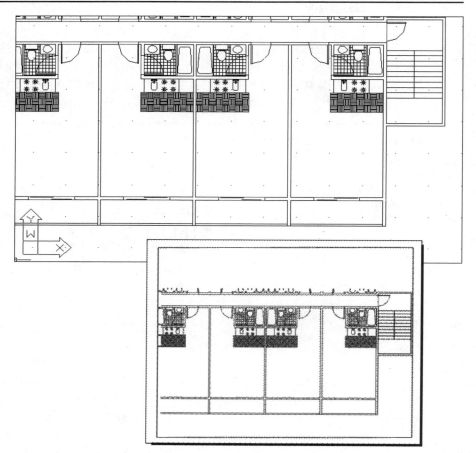

FIGURE 7.5:

A comparison of the saved view and the printed output

Window

The Window option allows you to use a window to indicate the area you wish to plot (see Figure 7.6). Nothing outside the window prints.

To use this option, click the Window button, then indicate a window in the drawing editor. The dialog box temporarily closes to allow you to select points. When you're done, click OK.

If you let AutoCAD fit the drawing onto the sheet using the Scaled to Fit option in the Scale drop-down list, the plot displays exactly the same thing that you enclose within the window.

FIGURE 7.6:

A selected window and the resulting printout

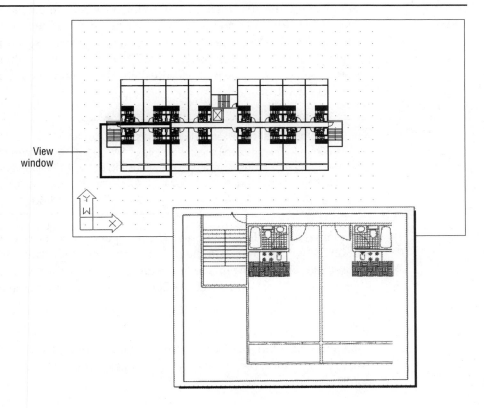

View window

TIP

Do you get a blank print, even though you selected Extents or Display? Chances are the Scaled to Fit option is not selected, or the Plotted Inches = Drawing Units setting is inappropriate for the sheet size and scale of your drawing. If you don't care about the scale of the drawing, then make sure the Scaled to Fit option is selected. Otherwise, make sure the Plot Scale settings are set correctly. The next section describes how to set the scale for your plots.

Plot Scale

In the previous section, the descriptions of several Plot Area options indicate that the Scaled to Fit option must be selected. Bear in mind that when you apply a scale factor to your plot, it changes the results of the Plot Area settings, and some problems can arise. This is usually where most new users have difficulty.

For example, the apartment plan drawing fits nicely on the paper when you use Scaled to Fit. But if you tried to plot the drawing at a scale of 1"=1', you would probably get a blank piece of paper because, at that scale, hardly any of the drawing would fit on your paper. AutoCAD would tell you that it was plotting and then tell you that the plot was finished. You wouldn't have a clue as to why your sheet was blank.

NOTE　Remember that the `Plan1.dwg` file was set up for an 18" × 24" (A2 or 594mm × 420mm for metric users) sheet at a scale of 1/8" = 1'-0" (1:10 for metric users). If you select these settings from the Plot Settings tab of the Plot dialog box (provided your printer or plotter supports 18" × 24" or A2 paper) and you also select Limits for your plot area, your drawing will fit on the paper and will be at the appropriate scale.

If an image is too large to fit on a sheet of paper because of improper scaling, the plot image will be placed on the paper differently, depending on whether the plotter uses the center of the image or the lower-left corner for its origin (see Figure 7.1). Keep this in mind as you specify Scale factors in this area of the dialog box.

Scale

You can select a drawing scale from a set of predefined scales. These are offered through the Scale drop-down list. These options cover the most common scales you'll need to use.

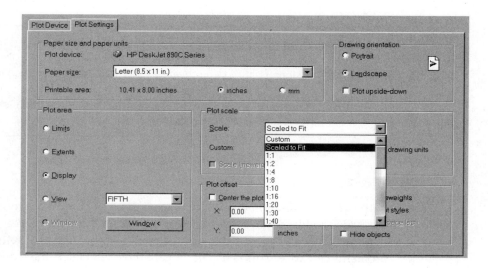

You've already seen how one option from this drop-down list, Scaled to Fit, allows you to avoid giving a scale altogether and forces the drawing to fit on the sheet. This works fine if you are doing illustrations that are not to scale. If you select another option like 1/8" = 1'-0", you'll see the Custom input boxes change to reflect this scale. The Inches input box changes to 1 and the Drawing Units input box changes to 96, the scale factor for a 1/8" scale drawing.

Custom

If you can't find the scale you want from the Scale drop-down list, you can use the two Custom input boxes that are provided in the Plot Scale button group: Inches (or mm if you select mm in the Paper Size and Paper Units button group) and Drawing Units.

Through these input boxes, you can indicate how the drawing units within your drawing relate to the final plotted distance in inches or millimeters. For example, if your drawing is of a scale factor of 96, follow these steps.

1. Double-click the Inches input box, enter **1**, and press the Tab key.

2. Double-click the Drawing Units input box, enter **96**, and press the Tab key.

Metric users who want to plot to a scale of 1:10 should enter **1** in the mm input box and **10** in the Drawing Units input box.

If you are more used to the Architectural unit style in the English measurement system, you can enter a scale as a fraction. For example, for a 1/8" scale drawing:

1. Double-click the Inches input box and enter **1/8** and press the Tab key.

2. Double-click the Drawing Units input box and enter **12** and press the Tab key

You can specify a different scale from the one you chose while setting up your drawing, and AutoCAD will plot your drawing to that scale. You are not restricted in any way as to scale, but entering the correct scale is important: If it is too large, AutoCAD will think your drawing is too large to fit on the sheet, although it will attempt to plot your drawing anyway.

NOTE   See Chapter 3 for a discussion on unit styles and scale factors.

TIP
If you plot to a scale that is different from the scale you originally intended, objects and text will appear smaller or larger than would be appropriate for your plot. You'll need to edit your text size to match the new scale. This can be done using the Properties dialog box. Select the text whose height you want to change, click the Properties tool on the Standard toolbar, and then change the Height setting in the Properties dialog box.

Scale Lineweights

AutoCAD 2000 offers the option to assign line weights to objects either by their layer assignments or by directly assigning a line weight to individual objects. The line weight option, however, doesn't have any meaning until you specify a scale for your drawing. Once you do specify a scale, the Scale Lineweights option is available. Check this box if you want the line weight assigned to layers and objects to appear correctly in your plots. You'll get a closer look at line weights and plotting later in this chapter.

Plot Offset

Frequently, your first plot of a drawing shows the drawing positioned incorrectly on the paper. You can fine-tune the location of the drawing on the paper using the Plot Offset settings.

To adjust the position of your drawing on the paper, you enter the location of the view origin in relation to the plotter origin in x- and y-coordinates (see Figure 7.7).

For example, suppose you plot a drawing, then realize that it needs to be moved 1" to the right and 3" up on the sheet. You can replot the drawing by making the following changes.

1. Double-click the X input box, type **1**, and press the Tab key.
2. Double-click the Y input box, type **3**, and press the Tab key.

Now proceed with the rest of the plot configuration. With the above settings, when the plot is done, the image is shifted on the paper exactly 1" to the right and 3" up.

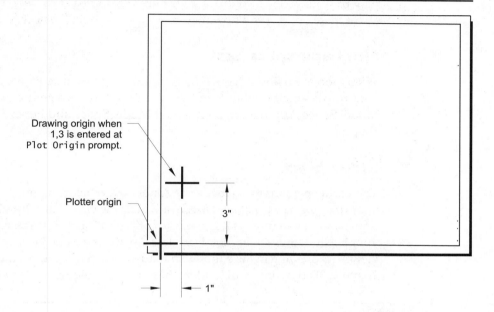

Adjusting the image location on a sheet

Drawing origin when
1,3 is entered at
Plot Origin prompt.

Plotter origin

3"

1"

Plot Options

The options in the Plot Options button group, with the exception of Hide Objects, are new in AutoCAD 2000. These new features offer a greater amount of control over your output and require some detailed instruction. Here is a brief description of these options. You'll learn more about them in the next section.

Plot with Lineweights

As mentioned earlier, AutoCAD 2000 lets you assign line weights to objects either through their layer assignment or by directly assigning a line weight to the object itself. If you use this feature in your drawing, this option lets you turn line weights on or off in your output.

Plot with Plot Styles

Plot styles are new in AutoCAD 2000 and they give you a high degree of control over your drawing output. You can control whether your output is in color or black and white, and you can control whether filled areas are drawn in a solid color or a pattern. You can even control the way lines are joined at corners. You'll learn more about these options and how they affect your work in the next section.

Plot Paperspace Last

When you are using Layout Space, otherwise known as Paper Space, this option determines whether objects in Paper Space are drawn before or after objects in Model Space. You'll learn more about Model Space and Paper Space later in this chapter.

Hide Objects

This option pertains to 3D models in AutoCAD. When you draw in 3D, you will see your drawing as a *wireframe view*. In a wireframe view, your drawing looks like it's transparent even though it is made up of "solid" surfaces. You can view and plot your 3D drawings so that solid surfaces are opaque using hidden line removal. To view a 3D drawing in the editor with hidden lines removed, use the Hide command. To plot a 3D drawing with hidden lines removed, use the Hide Objects option.

WARNING   Hide Objects does not work for views in the Layout tab viewport described in the next section. Instead, you need to set the viewport's Hideplot property to On. (Click the viewport, right-click, then select Hideplot ➤ On). For more on Hideplot, see Chapter 18.

WYSIWYG Plotting Using Layout Tabs

You've probably noticed the tabs at the bottom of the drawing area labeled Model, Layout 1, and Layout 2. So far, you've done all of your work in the Model tab, also known as *Model Space*. The other two Layout tabs open views to your drawing that are specifically geared toward printing and plotting. The Layout views allow you to control drawing scale, add title blocks, and even set up different layer settings from those in the Model tab. You can think of the Layout tabs as page layout spaces that act like a desktop-publishing program.

You can have as many Layout tabs as you like, each set up for a different type of output. You can, for example, have two or three different Layout tabs each set up for a different scale drawing or with different layer configurations for reflected ceiling plans, floor plans, or equipment plans. You can even set up multiple views of your drawing at different scales within a single Layout tab.

NOTE When you create a new file, you see two Layout tabs. If you open a pre-AutoCAD 2000 file, you only see one Layout tab.

To get familiar with the Layout tabs, try the following exercise.

1. With the Plan file open, click the tab labeled Layout 1. You see the Page Setup dialog box.

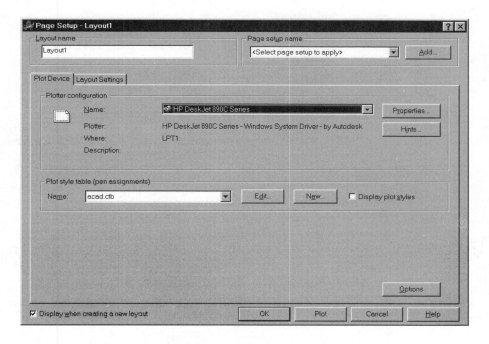

Make sure the Layout Settings tab is selected, then select Letter (8.5 × 11in.) from the Paper Size drop-down list. Metric users should choose A4 (210 × 297mm). Notice that the Page Setup dialog box is identical to the Plot dialog box.

2. Click OK. A view of your drawing appears on a gray background as shown in Figure 7.8. This is a view of your drawing as it will appear when plotted on

your current default printer or plotter. The white area represents the printer or plotter paper.

3. Try zooming in and out using the Realtime Zoom tool. Notice that the entire image zooms in and out, including the area representing the paper.

FIGURE 7.8:

A view of the Layout 1 tab

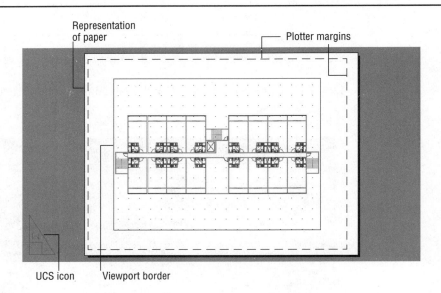

Representation of paper

Plotter margins

UCS icon · Viewport border

Let's take a moment to look at the different elements of the Layout 1 tab. As mentioned previously, the white background represents the paper on which your drawing will be printed. The dashed line immediately inside the edge of the white area represents the limits of your printer's margins. Finally, the solid rectangle that surrounds your drawing is the outline of the Layout viewport. A viewport is an AutoCAD object that works like a window into your drawing from the Layout tab. You may also notice the triangular symbol in the lower-left corner of the view.

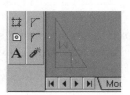

This is the UCS icon for the Layout tab. It tells you that you are currently in the Layout tab space. The significance of this icon will be clearer in the following exercise.

1. Try selecting part of your drawing by clicking in the lobby area. Nothing is selected.

2. Now click the solid rectangle surrounding the drawing as shown in Figure 7.9. This is the viewport into the Model tab. Notice that you can select it.

3. Right-click and select Properties from the popup menu. You can see from the Properties dialog box that the viewport is just like any other AutoCAD object with layer, line-type, and color assignments. You can even hide the viewport outline by turning off its layer.

4. Close the Properties dialog box.

5. With the viewport still selected, click the Erase tool in the Modify toolbar. The view of your drawing disappears with the erasure of the viewport. Remember that the viewport is like a window into the drawing you created in the Model tab. Once the viewport is erased, the drawing view goes with it.

6. Type **U**↵ or click the Undo button in the Standard toolbar to restore the viewport.

7. Double-click anywhere within the viewport's boundary. Notice that the UCS icon you're used to seeing appears in the lower-left corner of the viewport. The Layout UCS icon disappears.

8. Now try clicking the lobby of your drawing. You can now select parts of your drawing.

9. Try zooming and panning your view. Changes in your view only take place within the boundary of the viewport.

10. Choose View ➢ Zoom ➢ All or type **Z**↵ **A**↵ to display the entire drawing in the viewport.

11. To return to Paper Space, double-click an area outside the viewport.

TIP   You can also type **PS**↵ to return to Paper Space and **MS**↵ to access the space within the viewport.

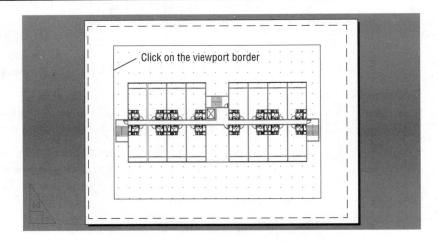

This exercise shows you the unique characteristics of the Layout tab. The objects within the viewport are inaccessible until you double-click the interior of the viewport. You can then move about and edit your drawing within the viewport, just as you would while in the Model tab.

The Layout tabs can contain as many viewports as you like, and each viewport can hold a different view of your drawing. Each viewport can be sized and arranged in any way you like or you can even create multiple viewports, giving you the freedom to lay out your drawing as you would a page in a desktop-publishing program. You can also draw in the Layout tab, or import Xrefs and blocks for title blocks and borders.

Plot Scale in the Layout Tab Viewports

In the first part of this chapter, you plotted your drawing from the Model tab. You learned that to get the plot to fit onto your paper, you either had to use the Scaled to Fit option in the Plot Settings tab of the Plot dialog box, or you had to indicate a specific drawing scale, plot area, and drawing orientation.

The Layout tab works in a different way: It is designed to allow you to plot your drawing at a 1-to-1 scale. Instead of specifying the drawing scale in the Plot dialog box, as you did when you plotted from the Model tab, your drawing scale is determined by the size of your view in the Layout tab viewport. You can set the viewport view to an exact scale by making changes to the properties of the viewport.

To set the scale of a viewport in a Layout tab, try the following exercise.

1. Press the Esc key twice to clear any selections. Then click the viewport border to select it.

2. Right-click, then select Properties from the popup menu. The Properties dialog box for the viewport appears.

3. Make sure the Categorized tab is selected, then locate the Standard Scale option under the Misc category. Go ahead and click the Standard Scale option. The item to the right of the Standard Scale option turns into a list box.

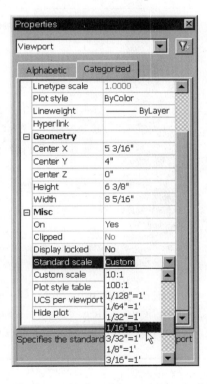

4. Open the list box and select 1/16" = 1' (metric users should select 1:20). The view in the drawing window changes to reflect the new scale for the viewport. Now most of the drawing fits into the viewport and it is now to scale.

NOTE   The scale of 1/16" = 1' is very similar to the metric 1:200 scale, but since you used centimeters instead of millimeters as the base unit for the metric version of the Plan file, you drop the second 0 in 200, so the metric scale becomes 1:20.

---

5. Close the Properties dialog box.

6. Use the viewport grips to enlarge the viewport enough to display all of the drawing as shown in Figure 7.10: You only need to move a single corner grip. As you move a corner grip, notice that the viewport maintains a rectangular shape.

7. Choose File ➤ Plot, then in the Plot dialog box, make sure the Scale option in the Plot Settings tab is set to 1:1 then click OK. Your drawing is plotted as it appears in the Layout tab and it is plotted to scale.

8. After reviewing your plot, close the drawing without saving it.

FIGURE 7.10:

The enlarged viewport

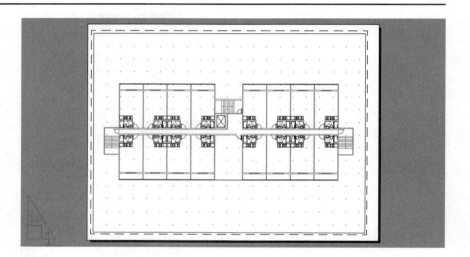

In step 4, you saw that you can select a scale for a viewport by selecting it from the Properties dialog box. If you look just below the Standard Scale option, you'll see the Custom Scale option. Both of these options work like their counterpart, the Plot scale group, in the Plot Settings tab of the Plot dialog box.

TIP   Veteran AutoCAD users can still use the View ➤ Zoom ➤ Scale option to control the scale of the viewport view.

Layout tabs and viewports work in conjunction with your plotter settings to give you a better idea of how your plots will look. In fact, there are numerous plotter settings that can dramatically change the appearance of your Layout tab view and your plots. In the next section, you'll learn how some of the plotter settings can enhance the appearance of your drawings. You'll also learn how Layout tabs can display those settings so you can see on your computer screen exactly what will appear on your paper output.

Controlling the Appearance of the Layout Tabs

The Options dialog box offers a set of controls dedicated to the Layout tabs. If you don't like some of the graphics in the Layout tab, you can turn them off. Open the Options dialog box and select the Display tab. You'll see a set of options in the Layout Elements group.

```
┌ Layout elements ─────────────────────────────┐
│   ☑ Display Layout and Model tabs             │
│   ☑ Display margins                           │
│   ☑ Display paper background                  │
│      ☑ Display paper shadow                   │
│   ☑ Show Page Setup dialog for new layouts    │
│   ☑ Create viewport in new layouts            │
└───────────────────────────────────────────────┘
```

As you can see in the Layout Elements group, you can control the display of the tabs themselves, the margins, the paper background, and the paper shadow. In addition, you can set whether or not AutoCAD automatically creates a viewport or opens the Page Setup dialog box when you open a Layout tab for the first time.

Setting Color, Line Corner Styles, and Shading Patterns with Plot Styles

AutoCAD 2000 introduces a new feature called *plot style tables*. Plot style tables are settings that give you control over how objects in your drawing are translated into hard copy plots. You can control how colors are translated into line weight and how area fills are converted into shades of gray or screened colors, as well as many other output options. You can also control how the plotter treats each individual object in a drawing.

If you don't use plot style tables, your plotter will produce output as close as possible to what you see in the drawing editor, including colors. You can, however, force your plotter to plot all colors in black, for example. You can also assign a fill pattern or screen to a color. This can be useful for charts and maps that require area fills of different gradations.

The following set of exercises will show you firsthand how plot style tables can be used to enhance your plotter output. You'll look at how you can adjust the line weight of the walls in the Plan file and make color changes to your plotter output.

Choosing between Color and Named Plot Style Tables

AutoCAD offers two types of plot style tables: color and named. Color plot style tables allow you to assign plotting properties to the AutoCAD colors. For example, you can assign a 0.50mm pen width to the color red so that anything that is red in your drawing is plotted with a line width of 0.50mm. You can, in addition, set the pen color to black so that everything that is red in your drawing is plotted in black.

Named plot style tables let you assign plotting properties directly to objects in your drawing, instead of relying on their color property. They also allow you to assign plotter properties directly to layers. For example, with named plot styles, you can assign a black pen color and a 0.50mm pen width to a single circle in a drawing, regardless of its color.

Named plot styles are more flexible than color plot styles, but if you already have a library of AutoCAD drawings set up for a specific set of plotter settings, the color plot styles would be a better choice when opening those older files in AutoCAD 2000. This is because color plot styles are more similar to the older method of assigning AutoCAD colors to plotter pens. You may also want to use color plot style tables with files that you intend to share with an individual or office that is still using earlier versions of AutoCAD.

The type of plot style table assigned to a drawing depends on the settings in the Plotting tab of the Options dialog box at the time the file is created. In the case of drawings created in earlier versions of AutoCAD, the type of plot style table used depends on the settings of the Output tab of the Options dialog box the first time the file is opened in AutoCAD 2000. Once a choice is made between color or named plot styles, your drawing cannot change to the other type of plot style. So choose wisely.

Here's how to set up the plot style type for new and pre-AutoCAD 2000 files.

1. Open the Options dialog box and select the Output tab.

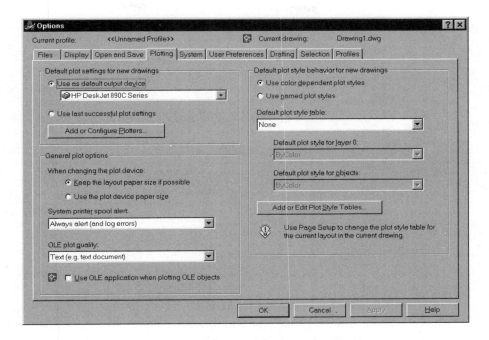

2. In the Default Plot Style Behavior button group, click Use Color Dependant Plot Styles. In a later exercise, you'll use the Use Named Plot Styles option.

3. Click OK to return to the drawing.

Once you've set up AutoCAD for color plot style tables, any new drawings you create are only allowed to use color plot style tables. You can change this setting at any time for new files, but once a file is saved, the type of plot style that is current when the file is first created is the only type of plot style available to that file. If you find that you need to change a color plot style to a named plot style drawing, the AutoCAD Migration Assistance utilities offer a tool for just this purpose. See Appendix B for more information on Migration Assistance.

Next, you'll set up a custom color plot style table. Plot style tables are stored as files with the .CTB or .STB filename extension. The tables that end with .CTB are color plot style tables. The table files that end with .STB are named plot style tables.

TIP   Veteran AutoCAD users who use Hewlett-Packard InkJet plotters may be familiar with many of the settings available in the plot style table options. These are similar to the settings offered by the Hpconfig command from prior versions of AutoCAD.

Creating a Color Plot Style Table

You can have several plot style table files on hand to quickly apply plot styles to any given plot or Layout tab. Each plot style table can be set up to create a different look to your drawing. These files are stored in the Plot Styles directory off of the main AutoCAD directory. Take the following steps to create a new plot style table. You'll use an existing file that was created in Release 14 as an example to demonstrate the plot style features.

NOTE

If you change your mind about a selection you make while using a wizard, you can move forward or backward by using the Next and Back buttons.

---

1. Open the sample file from the companion CD called `Plan-color.dwg`, then click the Layout 1 tab.

2. In the Page Setup dialog box, click the Plot Device tab. Notice that the Page Setup dialog box is similar to the Plot dialog box. The main difference is that the Page Setup dialog box has an extra button at the bottom labeled Plot.

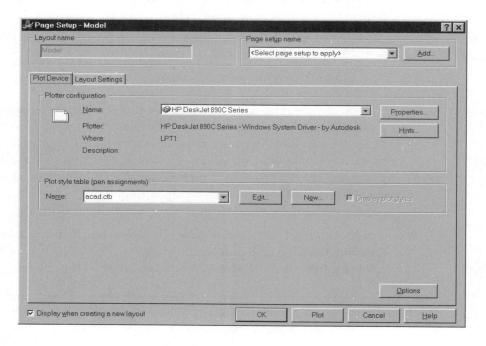

3. In the Plot Style Table button group, click the New button to the right. This opens the Add Color-Dependent Plot Style Table wizard.

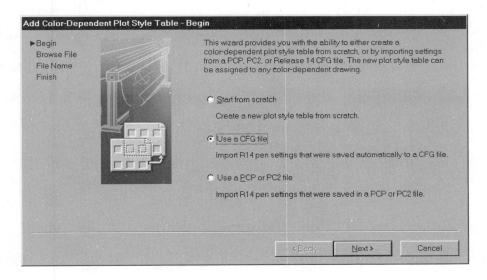

4. Select the Start From Scratch radio button, then click Next. The next page of the wizard asks for a filename. You can also specify whether this new plot style table you are creating will be the default for all drawings from now on, or whether you want to apply this plot style table just to the current drawing.

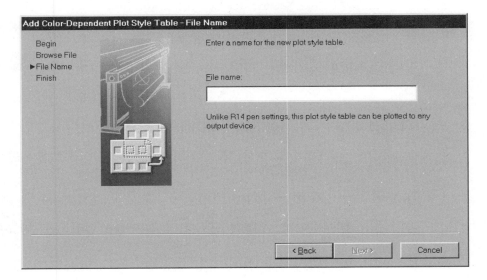

5. Enter **Mystyle** for the filename, then click Next. The next page of the wizard lets you edit your plot style and assign the plot style to your current, new, or old drawings. You'll learn about editing plot styles a bit later.

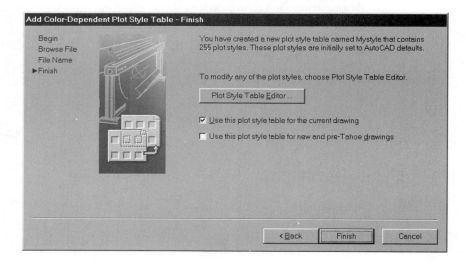

6. Go ahead and click Finish. You return to the Page Setup dialog box.

With the Add Color-Dependant Plot Style Table wizard, you can create a new plot style table from scratch, or you can create one based on an AutoCAD R14 CFG, PCP or PC2 file. You can also access the Add Color-Dependent Plot Style Table wizard by choosing File ➤ Plot Style Manager, then double-clicking the Add Color-Dependent Plot Style Table Wizard icon.

The steps shown here are the same whether your drawing is set up for color plot styles or named plot styles.

Editing and Using Plot Style Tables

You now have your own plot style table. In the next exercise, you'll get to edit the plot style and see firsthand how plot styles affect your drawing.

1. While in the Page Setup dialog box, make sure the Plot Device tab is selected.

2. The filename Mystyle.ctb should appear in the Name drop-down list of the Plot Style Table group. If it isn't, open the Name drop-down list, then locate and select Mystyle.ctb.

3. Click the Edit button to the right of the drop-down list. The Plot Style Table Editor appears. Make sure the Form View tab is selected.

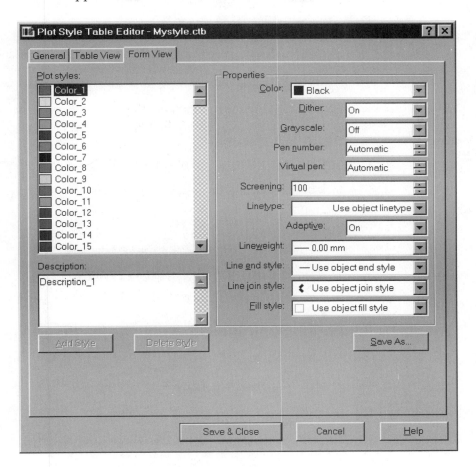

TIP

You can also open and edit existing plot style tables by choosing File ➤ Plot Style Manager. The Plot Styles dialog box appears. You can then double-click the plot style you want to edit. A third option is to double-click the Plot Style Table file in the Plot Style subdirectory of the \AutoCAD2000\ main directory.

The Plot Style Table Editor dialog box offers three tabs that give you control over how each color in AutoCAD is plotted. The Form View tab lets you select a color from a list box, then set the properties of that color using the options on the right side of the tab.

The Table View tab displays each color as a column of properties. Each column is called a *plot style*. The property names are listed in a column to the far left. While the layout is different, both the Table View and the Form View offer the same functions.

Next, you'll continue by changing the line width property of the color 3 (green) plot style. Remember that green is the color assigned to the Wall layer of your Plan drawing.

4. Click the Color_3 listing in the Plot Styles list box

5. Click the Lineweight drop-down list and select 0.50 mm.

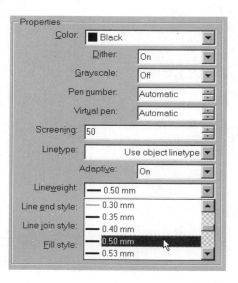

6. Click Save & Close. You return to the Page Setup dialog box.

7. Click the Display Plot Styles check box in the Plot Style Table group, then click OK.

8. Zoom into the plan to enlarge the view of a unit bathroom and entrance as shown here.

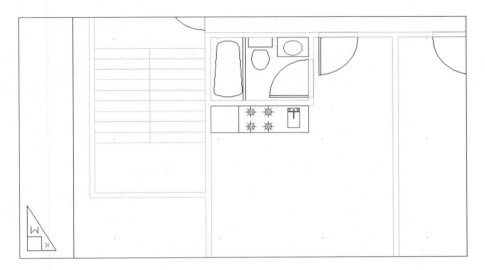

Making Your Plot Styles Visible

You won't see any changes in your drawing yet. You'll need to make one more change to your drawing options.

1. Choose Format ➤ Lineweight. The Lineweight Settings dialog box appears.

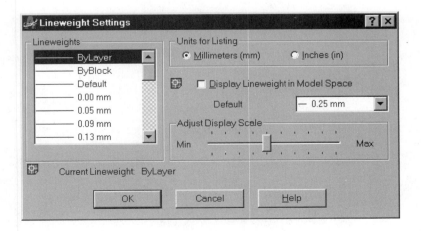

TIP You can also open the User Preferences tab of the Options dialog box, then click the Lineweight Settings button to open the Lineweight Settings dialog box.

The Lineweight Settings dialog box lets you control the appearances of line weights in the drawing editor. If line weights are not showing up, this is the place to look to make them viewable. You can find out more about the Lineweight Settings dialog box in Chapter 12.

2. Click the check box labeled Display Lineweight in Model Space to turn on this option.

3. Click OK, then click OK in the Options dialog box.

4. Choose View ➤ Regen All. Notice that now the green lines have a width or line weight.

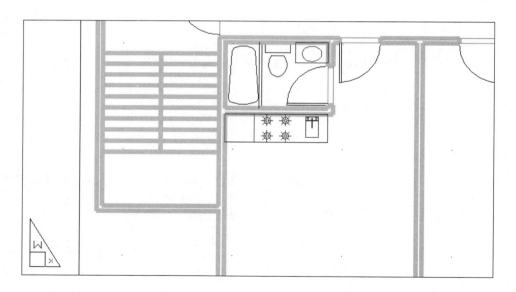

Lineweights Past and Present

In *Editing and Using Plot Style Tables*, you learned how you can assign a line weight to an AutoCAD color. In fact, this is the method used in earlier versions of AutoCAD for controlling line weight. But prior to AutoCAD 2000, there was no way to view the effects of line weight settings until you produced a printout, nor was there a tool like the Plot Style Manager to help you take control over how AutoCAD colors were plotted. The plot style table not only gives you a higher degree of control over the translation of AutoCAD colors to final plot but it adds some additional features. And the Layout tabs let you "proof" your color settings before you commit your drawing to paper.

With AutoCAD 2000, you can also assign line weights through the Layer Properties Manager. You may recall in Chapter 3 that layers have a line-weight property that can be set inside the Layer Properties Manager dialog box. You can also assign line weights directly to objects through the Properties dialog box. If you assign line weights through layers or object properties, then you can use the Use Object Lineweight option in the Plot Style Table Editor to display and plot the line weights as you intend them.

Remember that if you want to view any line-weight setting, make sure that you turn on the Display Lineweight in Model Space option as described in *Making Your Plot Styles Visible*.

Making Changes to Multiple Plot Styles

Chances are, you'll want to plot your drawing in black and white for most of your work. You can edit your color plot style table to plot one or all of your AutoCAD colors as black instead of the AutoCAD colors.

You saw how you can open the Plot Style Table Editor from the Page Setup dialog box to edit your color plot style table. In this exercise, you'll try a different route.

1. Choose File ➤ Plot Style Manager. The Plot Styles window appears. This is a view to the Plot Style directory under the \AutoCAD2000\ directory.

2. Locate the file Mystyle.ctb and double-click it. The Plot Style Table Editor appears.

3. In the Plot Style Table Editor dialog box, make sure the Form View tab is selected.

4. Click Color_3 in the Plot Styles list box.

5. Click the Color drop-down list and select Black.

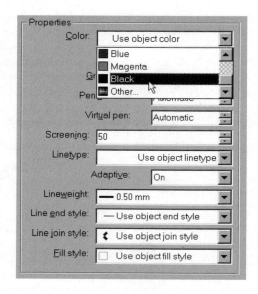

6. Click Save & Close, then close the Plot Styles window.

7. Choose View ➤ Regen All to view your drawing. Now the green objects appear black in the Layout tab.

8. Click the Model tab to view your drawing in Model Space. Notice that the objects are still in their original colors. This shows you that you haven't actually changed the colors of your objects or layers. You've only changed the color of the plotted output.

Next try changing all of the output colors to black.

1. Follow steps 1 and 2 of the previous exercise to open the Mystyle.ctb file again.

2. Make sure the Form View tab is selected, then click Color_1 in the Plot Styles list box.

3. Shift-click Color_9 in the Plot Styles list box. All of the plot styles from Color_1 to Color_9 are selected.

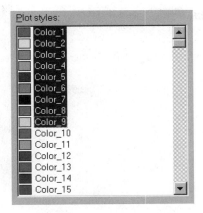

4. Click the Color drop-down list and select Black.

5. Click Save & Close, then click OK to close the Page Setup dialog box.

6. Choose View ➤ Regen All. Now all of the colors have changed to black.

Now when you plot your drawing, you will get a plot that is composed entirely of black lines.

Setting Up Line Corner Styles

You may notice that the corners of the wall lines appear to be notched instead of having a crisp, sharp corner.

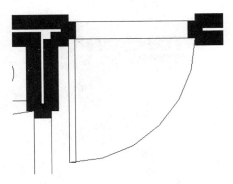

You can adjust the way AutoCAD draws these corners at plot time through the Plot Style Table Editor.

1. Once again, open the Mystyle.ctb plot style table, as you did in the previous exercise.

2. Make sure the Form View tab is selected, then click Color_3 in the Plot Styles list box.

3. Click the Line End Style drop-down list and select Square.

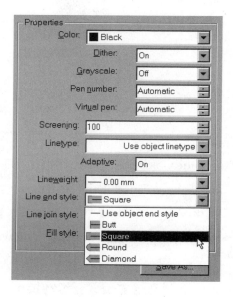

4. Click Save & Close, then click OK to close the Page Setup dialog box.

5. Choose View ➤ Regen All to view your changes. Notice that now the corners meet in a sharp angle.

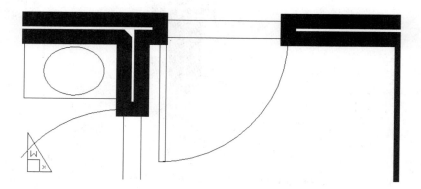

The Square option in the Line End Style drop-down list extends the endpoints of contiguous lines so that their corners meet in a clean corner instead of a notch. The Line Join Style drop-down list offers a similar set of settings for polylines. For example, you can round the corner of polyline corners using the Round option in the Line Join Style drop-down list.

Setting Up Screen Values for Solid Areas

The last option you'll look at is how to change a color into a screened area. Frequently, you'll want to add a gray or colored background to an area of your drawing to emphasize that area graphically, as in a focus area in a map or to designate functions in a floor plan. The setting you're about to use will allow you to create shaded backgrounds.

1. Go to the Page Setup dialog box again and open the Plot Style Table Editor. By now you should be able to do this easily on your own.

2. Select Color_3 from the Plot Styles list box.

3. Go to the Screening list box and double-click the number 100. The number becomes highlighted.

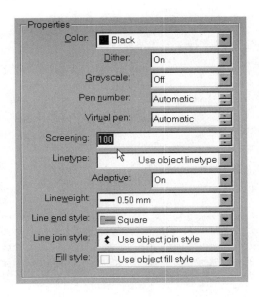

4. Type **50**⏎.

5. Click Save & Close, then click OK in the Page Setup dialog box.

6. Choose View ➤ Regen All. Notice that now the walls are a shade of gray instead of solid black.

As you can see from these exercises, you turned a wide black line into a gray one. In this example, the Screening option lets you "tone down" the chosen color from a solid color to a color that has 50 percent of its full intensity.

You can use the Screening option in combination with color to obtain a variety of tones. If you need to cover large areas with color, you can use the Solid hatch pattern to fill those areas, then use the Screening option in the Plot Style Table Editor to make fine adjustments to the area's color.

TIP   You'll want to know about the Draworder command in conjunction with solid filled areas. This command lets you control how overlapping areas are displayed. See *Controlling Object Visibility and Overlap with Raster Images* in Chapter 11 for more information.

Colors and Line Weights in the San Francisco Main Library

Technical drawings can have a beauty of their own, but they can also be deadly boring. What really sets a good technical drawing apart from a poor one is the control of line weights. Knowing how to vary and control line weights in both manual and CAD drawings can make a huge difference in the readability of the drawing.

In the San Francisco Main Library project, the designers at SMWM Associates were especially concerned with line weights in the reflected ceiling plan. Figure 7.11 shows a portion of the reflected ceiling plan from the library drawings. As you can see, it contained a good deal of graphical information, which, without careful line weight control, could become confusing. (While you can't see it in the black-and-white print, a multitude of colors were used to vary line weight.) When the electronic drawings were plotted, colors were converted into lines of varying thickness. Bolder lines were used to create emphasis in components such as walls and ceiling openings, while fine lines were used to indicate ceiling tile patterns.

Continued on next page

By emphasizing certain lines over others, visual monotony is avoided and the various components of the drawing can be seen more easily.

FIGURE 7.11:

A sample portion of the reflected ceiling plan of the San Francisco Main Library. These plans were carefully color coded to control the line weights of the plotter drawing.

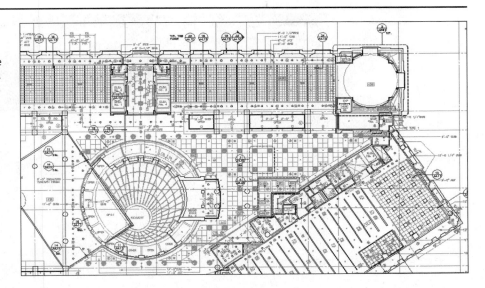

Other Options in the Plot Style Table Editor

You've seen a lot of the plot style options so far, but there are many others that you may want to use in the future. This section describes those options that were not covered in the previous exercises.

NOTE   The options in the Plot Style Table Editor are the same regardless of whether you are editing a color plot style table or a named plot style table.

The General Tab

You didn't really look at the General tab of the Plot Style Table Editor in the exercise presented earlier. Here is a view of the General tab and a description of the options offered there.

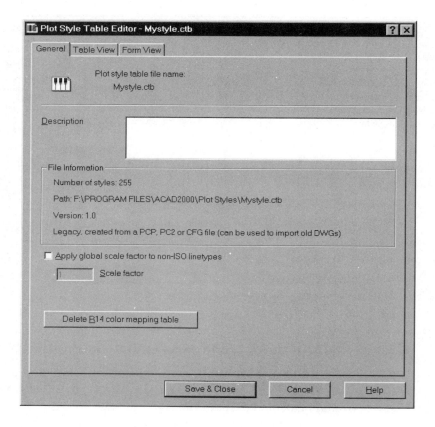

The General tab offers information regarding the plot style you are currently editing. You can enter a description of the style in the large input box that dominates the tab. This can be useful if you plan to include the plot style with a drawing you are sending to someone else for plotting.

The File Information group gives you the basic information on the file location and name, as well as the number of color styles included in the plot style table.

The Apply Global Scale Factor to Non-ISO Linetypes check box lets you determine whether ISO line-type scale factors are applied to all line types. When this item is checked, the Scale Factor input box becomes active, allowing you to enter a scale factor.

ISO Pen Widths

You may have noticed a setting called ISO Pen Width in the Linetype Manager dialog box discussed in Chapter 4 (Format ➤ Linetype). This setting is in the form of a pull-down list. When you select a pen width from that list, the line-type scale is updated to conform to the ISO standard for that width. However, this setting has no effect on the actual plotter output. If you are using ISO standard widths, it is up to you to match the color of the lines to their corresponding widths in the Plot Style Table Editor.

The Form View Tab

The Form View tab contains the same settings as the Table View tab but in a different format. Instead of displaying each color as a column of properties, the properties are listed as options along the right side, while the colors are listed in a list box.

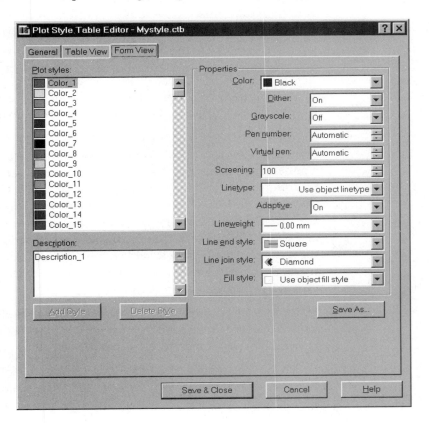

To modify the properties of a color, you select the color from the list, then edit the values in the Properties button group in the right side of the dialog box. So to change the screen value of the Color_3 style, highlight Color_3 in the Plot Styles list, then double-click the Screening input box and enter a new value.

You've already seen what the Screening, Color, Lineweight, and Line Join Style options do. Here's a description of the other style properties.

NOTE The names of the properties in the Table View tab are slightly different from those in the Form View tab. The Table View property names are shown enclosed in brackets in this listing.

Description Allows you to enter a description for each individual color.

Dither [Enable Dithering] Dithering is a method that enables your plotter to simulate colors beyond the basic 256 colors available in AutoCAD. While this option is desirable when you want to create a wider range of colors in your plots, it can also create some distortions in your plots, including broken, fine lines and false colors. For this reason, dithering is usually turned off. This option is not available in all plotters.

[Convert to] Grayscale Converts colors to grayscale.

[Use Assigned] Pen Number Lets you determine what pen number is assigned to each color in your drawing. This option only applies to pen plotters.

Virtual Pen [Number] Many inkjet and laser plotters offer "virtual pens" to simulate the processes of the old-style pen plotters. Frequently, such plotters offer as many as 255 virtual pens. Plotters with virtual pens often let you assign AutoCAD colors to a virtual pen number. This is significant if the virtual pens of your plotter can be assigned screening width, end style, and joint styles. You can then use the virtual pen settings instead of using the settings in the Plot Style Table Editor. This option is most beneficial for users who already have a library of drawings that are set up for plotters with virtual pen settings.

You can set up your inkjet printer for virtual pens under the Vector Graphics listing of the Device and Documents Setting tab of the Plotter Configuration Editor. See Appendix A for more on setting up your printer or plotter configuration.

Linetype If you prefer, you can use this setting to control line types in AutoCAD based on the color of the object. By default, this option is set to Use Object Linetype. This book recommends that you leave this option at its default.

Adaptive [Adjustment] Controls how non-continuous line types begin and end. This option is on by default, which forces line types to begin and end in a line segment. With the option turned off, the same line type is drawn without regard for its ending. In some cases, this may produce a line that appears incomplete. For more on adaptive adjustment, see *The Line-Type Code* in Chapter 20.

Line End Style Lets you determine the shape of the end of simple lines that have a line weight greater than zero.

Line Join Style Lets you determine the shape of the corners of polylines.

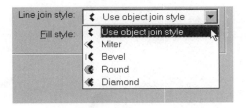

Fill Style Lets you set up a color to be drawn as a pattern when used in a solid filled area. The patterns appear as follows:

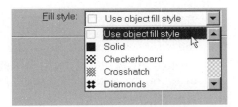

Add Style Allows you to add more plot styles or colors.

Delete Style Deletes the selected style.

Save As Lets you save the current plot style table.

The Table View Tab

The Table View tab offers the same settings as the Form View tab, only in a different format. Each plot style is shown as a column with the properties of each plot style listed along the left side of the tab. To change a property, click the property in the column.

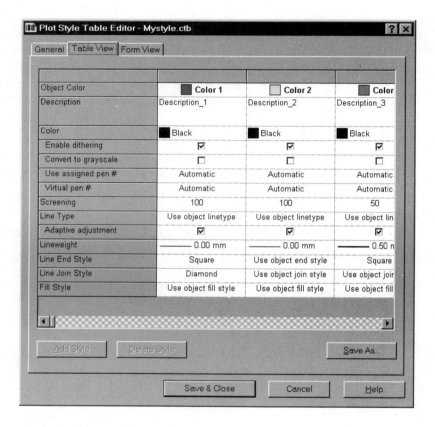

To apply the same setting to all plot styles at once, right-click a setting you want to use from a single plot style, then select Copy from the popup menu. Right-click again on the setting, then select Paste to All Styles.

Assigning Plot Styles Directly to Layers and Objects

So far, you've learned that you can control how AutoCAD translates drawing colors into plotter output. You also have the option to assign plot styles directly to objects or layers. In order to do this, you need make a few changes to the settings in AutoCAD and you also need to have a named plot style table. So far, you've

only been working with a color plot style table. In this sec͡
set up AutoCAD with a named plot style table to assign plot s͡ɩ͡͡
you'll create a new plot style table.

Using Named Plot Style Tables

Before you can start to assign plot styles to objects and layers, you need to make
some changes to the AutoCAD Options dialog box. You'll also want to create your
own named plot style table.

1. Choose Tools ➢ Options, then select the Output tab.

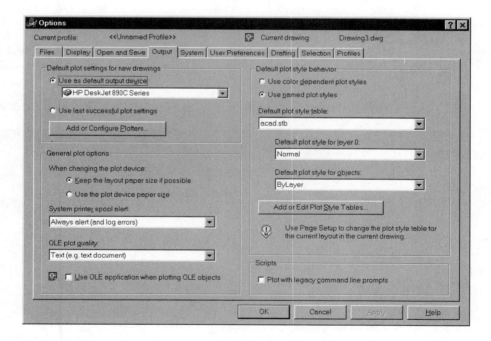

This tab offers a variety of settings geared toward your plotter or printer.

2. In the upper-right corner of the dialog box, click the Use Named Plot Styles
   radio button.

3. Click OK to close the Options dialog box.

To create and try out a new named plot style, you'll open an existing file from an
earlier version of AutoCAD. In the next few exercises, you'll use the Plan-named.dwg
file from the companion CD-ROM. This is a Release 14 file that will be assigned the

type of plot style table that is currently the default as determined by the Use Named Plot Styles option you just set in the previous exercise.

1. Open the Plan-name.dwg file from the companion CD-ROM.

2. Choose File ➤ Plot Style Manager. This opens a window to the Plot Styles directory.

3. Double-click the Add-A-Plot Style Table Wizard icon. The Plot Style Table wizard appears.

4. Click Next, then choose Start From Scratch on the Begin page, then click Next. The Pick Plot Style Table page appears.

5. Click the radio button labeled Named Plot Style Table, then click next. The File Name page appears.

6. Enter **Mynamedstyle1** in the File Name input box, then click Next. The Finish page appears. Here you can exit or you can proceed to edit the new plot style table. This time you'll go ahead and edit the table from the wizard.

7. Click the Plot Style Table Editor button. The Plot Style Table Editor appears.

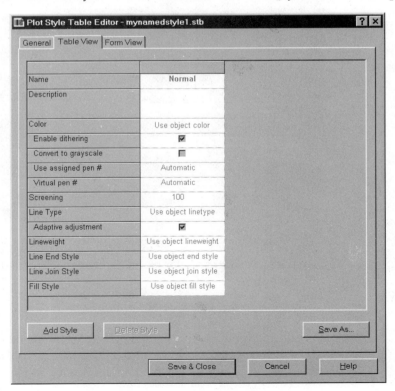

Notice that you only have one style named. Unlike the color plot style tables, you aren't assigning a style to each AutoCAD color, so you don't need a style for each of the 255 colors. Instead, you can create a limited set of styles, giving each style the characteristics you would like to apply to objects. Continue by adding some additional plot styles.

1. Click the Add Style button. A new column appears labeled Style 1.

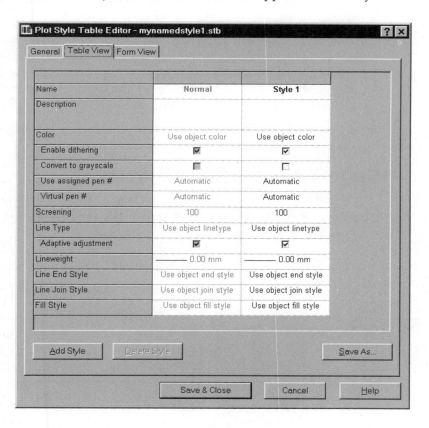

The name is highlighted so that if you choose, you can give the style a different name at this point, simply by typing it in.

2. Select the Form View tab, then select Style_1 from the Plot Styles list.

3. Click the Lineweight drop-down list and select 0.50mm.

4. Click the Add Style button, then in the Add Plot Style dialog box, click OK.

5. Select Style_2 from the Plot Styles list, then click the Lineweight drop-down list and select 0.70mm.

6. Click Save & Close. You return to the Add Plot Style Table wizard.

7. Click Finish to exit the wizard, then close the Plot Styles window.

8. Return to the Options dialog box, click the Default Plot Style Table drop-down list and select the plot style you just created, `Mynamedstyle1.stb`.

9. Click OK to exit the Options dialog box.

You may have noticed that the Add a Plot Style Table wizard works in a slightly different way when you start it from the Plot Styles window. It adds an extra option (in step 5 of the exercise before the last one) that lets you choose between a color plot style table and a named plot style table.

Now you're ready to start assigning plot styles to the objects in your drawing.

Assigning Plot Styles to Objects

Once you've set up AutoCAD to use named plot styles, you can begin to assign plot styles to objects through the Properties dialog box. Here are the steps to take to assign plot styles to objects.

1. Back in the `Plan-named.dwg` file, click the Layout1 tab.

2. If the Page Setup dialog box does not appear, choose File ➤ Page Setup.

NOTE If you remove the check from the Display When Creating a New Layout check box in the lower-left corner of the Page Setup dialog box, AutoCAD does not display the Page Setup dialog box the first time you select a Layout tab.

3. In the Page Setup dialog box, select the Plot Device tab, then select `Mynamedstyle1.stb` from the Name drop-down list in the Plot Style Table group.

4. Make sure the Display Plot Styles check box is checked.

5. Click OK to close the dialog box.

6. Choose Format ➤ Lineweight, and make sure there is a check in the Display Lineweight in Model Space check box, then click OK.

7. Set up your view of the unit so you see a close-up of the lower-left corner unit.

8. Select the line representing the outer wall of the unit at the bottom-left side of the plan, then right-click and select Properties.

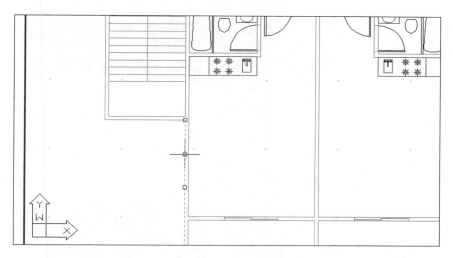

9. In the Properties dialog box, click the Plot Style option. A downward-pointing arrow appears in the Plot Style value listing.

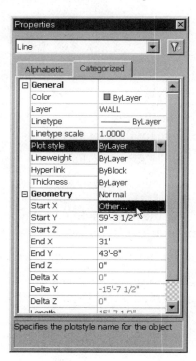

10. Click the downward-pointing arrow, then select Other from the list. The Select Plot Style dialog box appears.

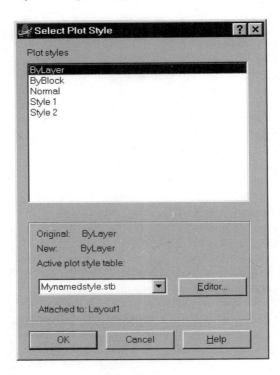

11. Select Style 1, then click OK.

12. Click the Plot Styles list box again and make sure that Style 1 shows up as the value for the Plot Style in the Properties dialog box.

13. Close the Properties dialog box.

14. Choose View ➤ Regen All.

If you have the line-weight visibility turned on, you'll see the results in the drawing editor.

Another way to assign plot styles to individual objects is through the Plot Style Control drop-down list.

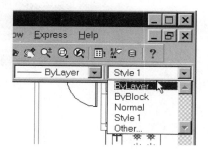

This allows you to select a plot style in a manner similar to the Layer & Linetype drop-down list. You can assign plot styles to individual objects by selecting the objects and then selecting a plot style from the Plot Style Control drop-down list. If you are using a color plot style table like the one you created in earlier exercises, the Plot Style Control drop-down list is unavailable.

Assigning Plot Style Tables to Layers

You can also assign named plot style tables to layers. This has a similar effect to using the color plot style tables. The main difference is that with named plot style tables, you assign the plot style tables directly to the layer instead of assigning a plot style to the color of a layer. Here's how to assign a plot style table to a layer.

1. Click the Layer tool in the Properties toolbar.

2. In the Layer Properties Manager dialog box, select the Wall layer.

3. Click the Plot Style column of Wall layer listing.

The Select Plot Style dialog box appears.

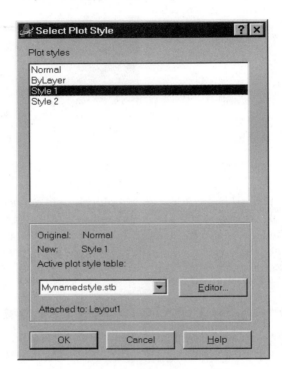

4. Select Style 1 from the Plot Styles list.

5. Click OK. The Layer Properties Manager appears again, this time showing the Plot Style property for the Wall layer listed as Style 1.

6. Close the Layer Properties Manager dialog box, then choose View ➣ Regen All. Your view of the plan changes to reflect the new plot style assignment to the Wall layer.

Plotting Multiple Layout Tabs

When you first open a Layout tab, you see the Page Setup dialog box. Since Layout tabs show you the layout of your drawing as it will appear when it is plotted, layouts need to be linked to a sheet size. You can also link each Layout tab to a different plot style table. This means that you can produce two completely different looking plots from the same drawing file. This chapter already explained that you can set up several layouts, each with their own layer settings and title block information. With the ability to attach different plot style tables to each Layout tab, you can also plot presentation-style drawings alongside construction documents.

Once you've got your Layout tabs set up, the Plot dialog box offers a set of options that will allow you to plot multiple tabs at once. The What to Plot button group in the Plot Device tab of the Plot dialog box offers four options: Current Tab, Selected Tabs, All Layout Tabs and Number of Copies.

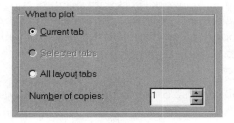

The functions of these options are pretty clear, although one option needs a bit of explaining. If you want to selectively plot certain tabs in your drawing, you can Shift+click the tabs just before you plot. You can then choose the Selected Tabs radio button in the Plot Device tab of the Plot dialog box to plot the selected Layout tabs.

The Plot to File button group lets you save your plots to a file on your hard drive. This can be helpful if you have multiple plotters and printers. You can save your plot files and send them to the different printers or plotters at a later time. This can be helpful if you are on a network and want to send plots to a network plotter. Or you can send your plot file over the Internet for plotting at a remote location.

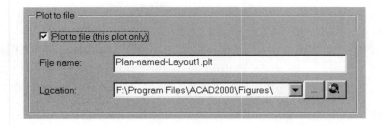

Adding an Output Device

This chapter mentioned that you can have AutoCAD set up for more than one output device. You can do this even if you only have one printer or plotter connected to your computer. There are many reasons why you might want to have multiple printer configurations in AutoCAD. You may want to have your system set up so that you can print to a remote location over a network or the Internet. There are also other printer configurations that are strictly file oriented, such as the AutoCAD DWF format for Internet Web pages, or raster file output. (See Chapter 19 for more on DWF files).

AutoCAD works best with printers and plotters configured as Windows system devices. While you can add devices through the AutoCAD Plot Manager, Autodesk recommends that you set up your plotters and printers as Windows devices, then use the System Printer option in AutoCAD to select your output device.

You can also configure additional printers through the AutoCAD Plot Manager. Here's how it's done.

1.   Choose File ➤ Plotter Manager. The Plotters window appears.

You can also get to this window by clicking the Add or Configure Plotter button in the Output tab of the Options dialog box. It's just an Explorer window showing you the contents of the Plotters directory under the main AutoCAD directory.

2. Double-click the Add-A-Plotter Wizard icon. The Add Plotter wizard appears.

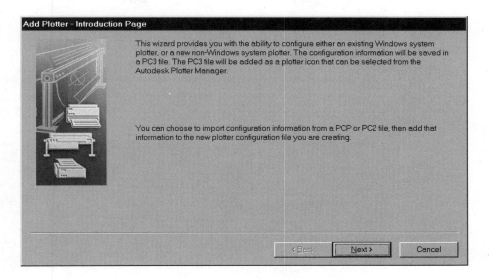

3. Click Next. The next page of the wizard lets you select the type of setup you want.

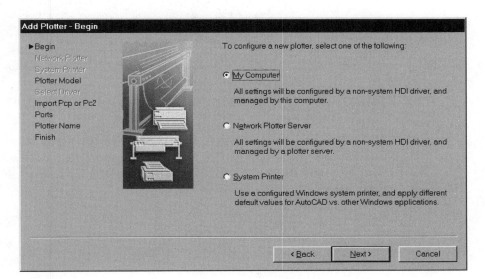

Here you are offered three options: My Computer, Network Plotter Server, and System Printer. The My Computer and the Network Plotter Server options offer plotter options based on AutoCAD-specific drivers. The main difference between these two options is that the Network Plotter option asks you for a network server name. Otherwise, they both offer the same set of options.

4. If you click the My Computer option, then click Next, you see a listing of plotter models that are supported by AutoCAD directly through AutoCAD's own drivers.

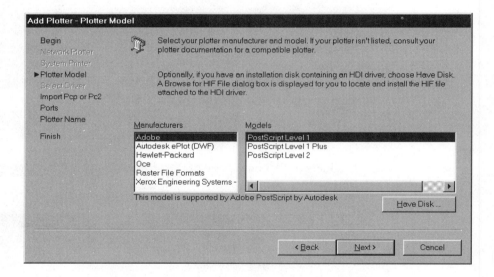

If you use a PostScript device, or if you want to convert drawings to raster formats, this is the place to select those options.

5. Once you've made a selection, click Next. You are then asked if you want to use an existing PCP or PC2 configuration file for the selected plotter. PCP and PC2 configurations files are plotter configuration files from earlier releases of AutoCAD.

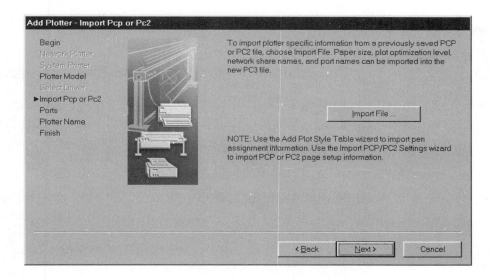

6. Click Next on the Import PCP or PC2 page and if you selected My Computer in step 4, the Ports page appears.

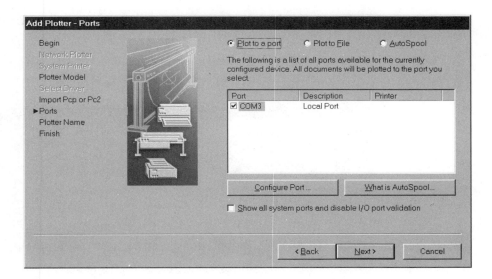

If you selected a different option in step 4, you should skip this option and the Plotter Name page appears.

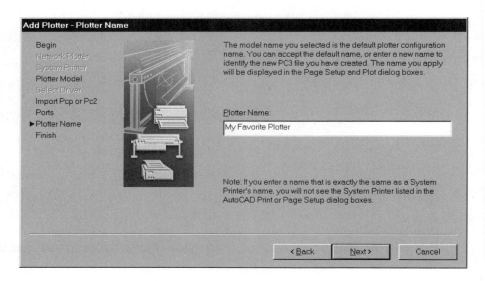

7. Enter a name for this configuration in the space provided, then click Next.

8. The Finish page of the Add Plotter wizard gives you the option to make adjustments to the configuration you've just created. Click Finish to exit the Add Plotter wizard. Your new configuration appears in the Plotters window.

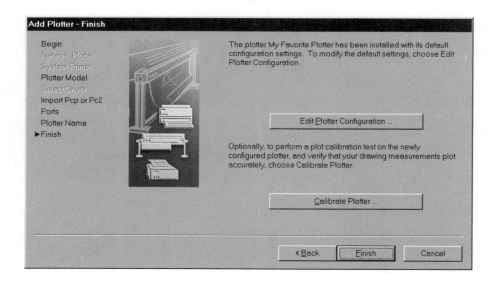

In step 7, you can further adjust the plotter settings by clicking the Edit Plotter Configuration button. If you click this button, the Plotter Configuration Editor dialog box appears.

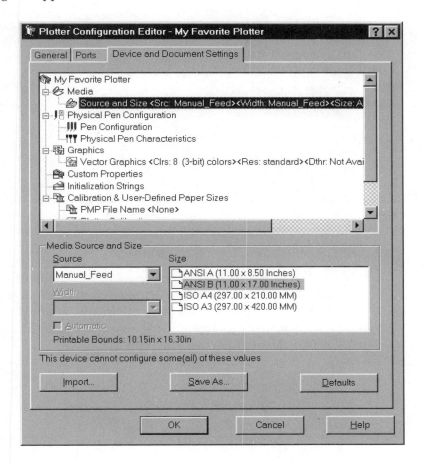

This editor lets you fine-tune your plotter settings. For example, you can calibrate your plotter for more accurate scaling of your plots, or if you're creating a raster file output configuration, you can create a custom page setting for extremely high-resolution raster images.

Once you've set up a plotter, the plotter information is stored as a file with the .PC3 filename extension. This file is stored in the `Plotters` subdirectory of the main AutoCAD directory.

Plotting Image Files

If your work involves the production of manuals, reports, or similar documents, you may want to add the Raster File Export option to your list of plotter configurations. The Raster File Export option lets you plot your drawings as PCX, Targa, Tiff, or BMP files that you can later import into documents that accept bitmap images. Images can be up to 8000 × 8000 pixels and can contain as many colors as the file format allows. If you need several different raster formats, you can use multiple instances of this or any plotter configuration.

If you would like to convert your 3D wireframe models into 2D line drawings, add the PostScript file output format. Like the DXB option, you can plot a 3D image to a file, and then import the resultant EPS file using File ➤ Import. For best results, make sure that when you configure the PostScript printer, you use the highest resolution available, and that you use the largest media size possible when you're plotting.

Editing a Plotter Configuration

In step 7 of the previous exercise, you exited the Add Plotter wizard without editing the newly created plotter configuration. You can always go back and edit the configuration by opening the Plotters window (File ➤ Plotter Manager) and double-clicking the configuration you want to edit. You can also double-click the .PC3 file of the configuration you want to edit.

Many users will use their Windows system printer or plotter for other applications besides AutoCAD and frequently, the AutoCAD settings for that printer will be different from the settings used for other applications. You can set up AutoCAD to automatically use its own settings so you don't have to reconfigure your Windows system printer every time you switch applications. To do this, take the following steps.

1. Choose File ➤ Page Setup.

2. Select the Plot Device tab in the Page Setup dialog box.

3. Select the printer that you want to configure in the Name drop-down list of the Plotter Configuration group.

4. Click the Properties button to the right of the drop-down list. The Plotter Configuration Editor appears.

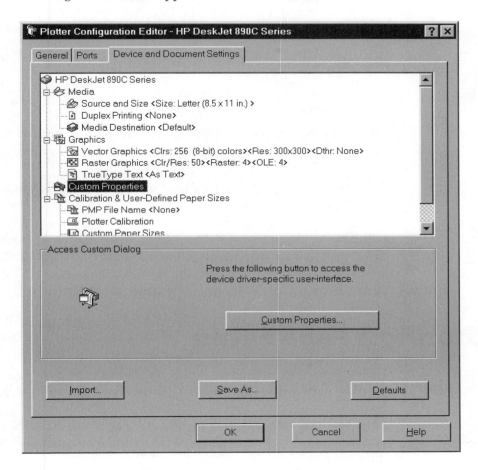

A list box appears, showing all of the properties of the printer or plotter. Not all of these properties are editable, however. Each time you click a property in the list box, the options in the lower half of the dialog box change to offer the options associated with that property.

5. Click the Custom Properties item in the list box. The options in the lower half of the dialog box change to display the Custom Properties button.

6. Click the Custom Properties button. You'll see the Windows system printer options appear. These are the same options you see when you edit the properties of your printer from the Start ➤ Settings ➤ Printers option on the Windows Desktop.

7. Adjust these settings the way you want them when you plot from AutoCAD, then click OK.

8. Back in the Plotter Configuration Editor dialog box, click the Save As button. A standard file dialog box appears.

9. Enter the name of the plot configuration you've set up, or accept the default name, which is usually the name of the Windows printer or plotter, then click OK.

10. Click OK in the Plotter Configuration Editor dialog box, then click OK in the Page Setup dialog box.

The Plotter Configuration Editor offers a wide variety of options that are fairly technical in nature. If you want to know more about the Plotter Configuration Editor, you'll find a detailed description in Appendix A.

Storing a Page Setup

Unlike most other programs, AutoCAD offers hundreds of page setup options. It can be quite a chore keeping track of and maintaining all of these options. But as you settle into using AutoCAD, you'll probably find that you will set up a few plotter configurations and stick to them. AutoCAD 2000 lets you save a page setup under a name to help you store and manage those settings you use the most.

The Page Setup Name option in the upper-right corner of the Plot or Page Setup dialog box lets you store the settings from these dialog boxes under a name. When you click the Add button, the User Defined Page Setups dialog box appears.

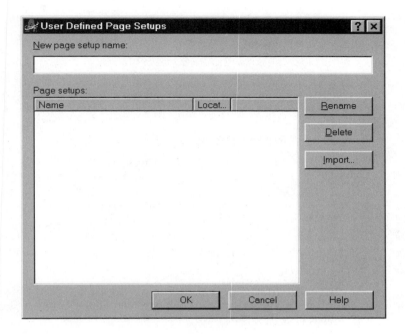

To save the current page setup, enter a name in the New Page Setup Name input box, then click OK. The name you enter appears in the Page Setup Name drop-down list of the Plot or Page Setup dialog box. You can also import other user-defined page setups by using the Import button. Since page setups are stored in the drawing, the Import button opens a standard file dialog box that displays drawing files.

Understanding the Plotting Tab in the Options Dialog Box

You've worked with the Output tab in the Options dialog box on a few occasions in this chapter. This tab contains several options related to plotting. Here's a summary of those options and their purpose.

Default Plot Settings for New Drawings

The settings in this group let you control the default plot settings for new drawings and for drawings from earlier versions of AutoCAD that are opened for the first time in Auto-CAD 2000. The Use As Default Output Device radio button and drop-down list let you

Continued on next page

select the default plotter or printer to be used with new drawings. When selected, the Use Last Successful Plot Settings radio button uses the last successful plotter settings for subsequent plots. This is how earlier versions of AutoCAD worked. The Add or Configure Plotters option opens the Plotters window. This is the same as selecting Files ➢ Plot Manager from the AutoCAD menu bar. From the Plotters window, you can launch the Add Plotter wizard to add new plotter configurations. You can also edit existing plotter configurations.

General Plot Options

These options control some of the general plotter parameters. The Keep the Layout Paper Size If Possible radio button causes AutoCAD to attempt to plot to the paper size specified in the Plot Settings tab of the Plot dialog box, regardless of the actual paper size in the plotter. If the specified size is larger than the capacity of the plotter, a warning message is displayed. The Use the Plot Device Paper Size option causes AutoCAD to use the paper size specified by the system printer or the PC3 plot configuration file currently in use. Both of these settings are also controlled by the Paperupdate system variable.

The System Printer Spool Alert drop-down list offers control over printer spooling alert messages. The OLE Plot Quality drop-down list offers control over the quality of OLE objects embedded or linked to a drawing. This setting can also be controlled through the Olequality system variable.

When the Use OLE Application When Plotting OLE Objects check box is checked, AutoCAD will launch any application that is associated with an OLE object embedded or linked to the AutoCAD drawing that is currently being plotted. This helps improve the plot quality of OLE objects. This option can also be set through the Olestartup system variable.

Default Plot Style Behavior

You've used two of these options in exercises in this chapter. These options control the type of plot styles used in AutoCAD. In the case of named plot styles, you can also select a default plot style for Layer 0 and a default plot style for objects. Note that the Use Color Dependant Plot Styles and Use Named Plot Styles radio buttons do not have an effect on the current drawing; they only affect new drawings and pre-AutoCAD 2000 drawings being opened for the first time. The Default Plot Style Table drop-down list lets you select a default plot style table for new and pre-AutoCAD 2000 drawings. These settings are also controlled by the Pstylepolicy system variable.

The Add or Edit Plot Style Tables button opens the Plot Styles dialog box. From there, you can double-click an existing plot style table file or start the Add a Plot Style Table wizard to create a new plot style.

Continued on next page

Scripts

The Plot with Legacy Command Line Prompts check box lets you run plot scripts that were created for earlier versions of AutoCAD. It enables the command-line version of the Plot command.

Plotter and Printer Hardware Considerations

Positioning an AutoCAD drawing on the printer output is something of an art. Before you are faced with a deadline with hundreds of plots to produce, you may want to create some test plots and carefully refine your plotter settings so that you'll have AutoCAD set up properly for those rush jobs.

Part of the setup process will be to understand how your particular printer or plotter works. Each device has its own special characteristics, so a detailed description of printer hardware setup is beyond the scope of this section. However, you will learn about a few guidelines that will make the process easier.

Understanding Your Plotter's Limits

If you're familiar with a word-processing or desktop-publishing program, you know that you can set the margins of a page, thereby telling the program exactly how far from each edge of the paper you want the text to appear. With AutoCAD, you don't have that luxury. To accurately place a plot on your paper, you must know the plotter's *hard clip limits*. The hard clip limits are like built-in margins, beyond which the plotter will not plot. These limits vary from plotter to plotter (see Figure 7.12).

It's crucial that you know your printer or plotter's hard clip limits in order to place your drawings accurately on the sheet. Take some time to study your plotter manual and find out exactly what these limits are. Then make a record of them and store it somewhere, in case you or someone else needs to format a sheet in a special way.

Hard clip limits for printers often depend on the software that drives them. You may need to consult your printer manual, or use the trial-and-error method of plotting several samples to see how they come out.

Once you've established the limits of your plotter or printer, you'll be better equipped to fit your drawing within those limits. You can then establish some standard drawing limits based on your plotter's limits. You'll also need to know the dimensions of those hard clip limits to define custom sheet sizes. While AutoCAD offers standard sheet sizes in the Paper Size and Orientation button group of the Plot Configuration dialog box, these sizes do not take into account the hard clip limits.

FIGURE 7.12:

The hard clip limits of a plotter

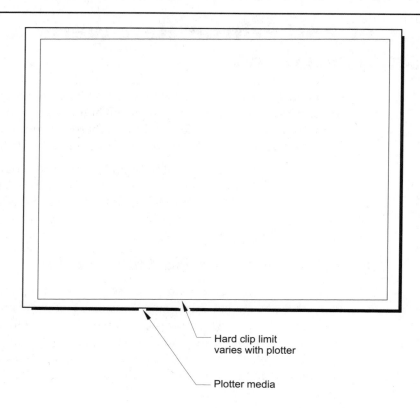

Hard clip limit
varies with plotter

Plotter media

Knowing Your Plotter's Origins

Another important consideration is the location of your plotter's origin. For example, on some plotters, the lower-left corner of the plot area is used as the origin. Other plotters use the center of the plot area as the origin. When you plot a drawing that is too large to fit the sheet on a plotter that uses a corner for the origin, the image is pushed toward the top and to the right of the sheet (see Figure 7.13). When you plot a drawing that is too large to fit on a plotter that uses the center of the paper as the origin, the image is pushed outward in all directions from the center of the sheet.

FIGURE 7.13:

Plotting an oversized image on a plotter that uses the lower-left corner for its origin

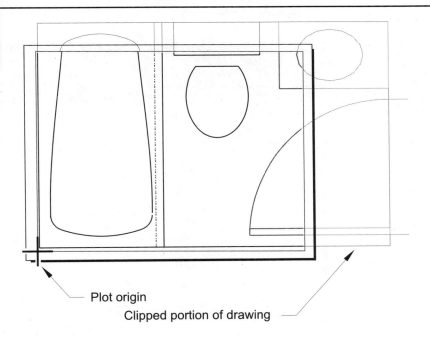

Plot origin

Clipped portion of drawing

In each situation, the origin determines a point of reference from which you can relate your drawing in the computer to the physical output. Once you understand this, you're better equipped to accurately place your electronic drawing on the physical media.

Batch Plotting

AutoCAD 2000 includes a tool that enables you to plot several unattended draw-ings at once. This can be helpful when you've finished a set of drawings and would like to plot them during a break or overnight. Here's how to use the Batch Plot utility.

1. From the Windows Desktop, choose Start ➤ Programs ➤ AutoCAD 2000➤ Batch Plot Utility. The Batch Plot Utility window appears, along with an AutoCAD session.

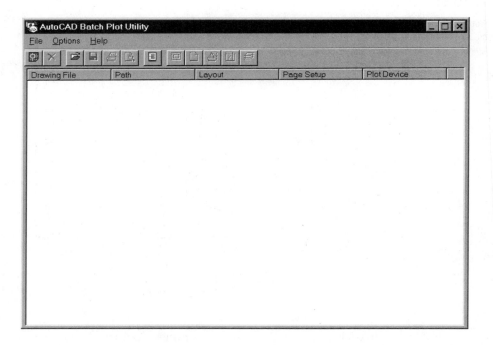

2. Click the Add Drawing button. The Add Drawing dialog box appears. This is a typical Windows file dialog box.

3. Locate and select a file you wish to plot. The name of the file you select appears in the list box of the Batch Plot Utility window.

4. Repeat steps 2 and 3 until you've included all the drawings you wish to plot in your list.

5. Choose File ➤ Plot to plot the list of files.

Once you've compiled a list of files for plotting, you can save the list by selecting File ➤ Save List. A saved list can be later opened using the File ➤ Open List option. The filename will have the .BP3 file extension

If you have special requirements for each file, such as a special plotter or layout you want to use, you can make those settings and save them along with the list. These options can be found by clicking a drawing name then selecting the option from the Options pull-down menu, or by right-clicking a listed file. Here is a description of those options.

Layouts Opens a dialog box that lets you select the Layout tabs for a file for plotting.

Page Setups Opens a dialog box that allows you import the Page Setup settings from an existing drawing

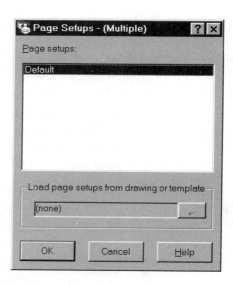

Plot Devices   Opens a dialog box that lets you select a plot configuration file for the listed file.

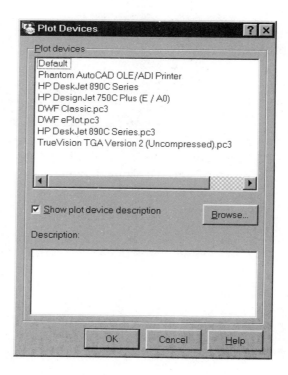

Plot Settings   Opens a dialog box that lets you select the plot area, the scale, and whether or not you want to plot to a file.

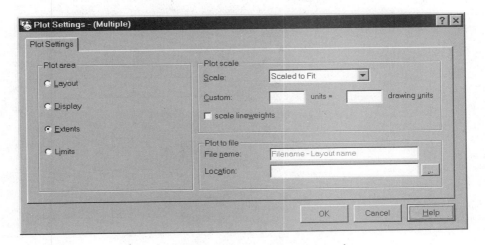

Layers   Opens the Plot Settings dialog box with the Layers tab selected. The Layers tab lets you control which layers get plotted for a particular file.

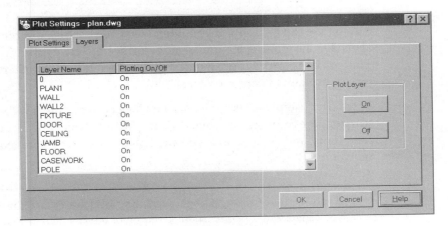

If you wish to maintain a log of the plots you create with the Batch Plot Utility, you can do so by choosing File ➤ Logging. The Logging dialog box appears, offering options for the log file location and a description for the log.

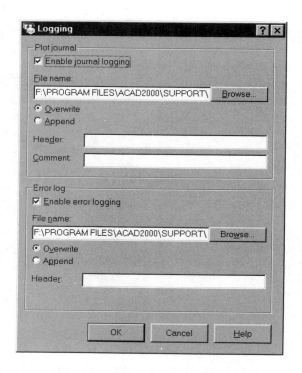

A log file can be useful if you intend to send plot files to a remote site. You can also have the logging feature create an error log where error messages are stored. This can be helpful for unattended plots when you might otherwise miss error messages that may occur during a plot.

Another useful tool is the File ≻ Plot Test option. The Plot Test checks to make sure that the resources for each drawing are available. The resources include Xref files, fonts, and custom line-type and hatch patterns that are required to open or plot a file.

TIP   If you have already set up a system using scripts for accessing the Plot command, you can restore the command-line version of the Plot command by changing the Plotlegacy system variable to 1. This system variable can also be turned on by placing a check in the Plot with Legacy Command Line Prompts option in the Output tab of the Options dialog box. Bear in mind that, due to minor changes in the way that command-line plotting works, you may need to make changes to your plot script. See Chapter 15 for more information about scripts.

Sending Your Drawings to a Service Bureau

Using a plotting service can be a good alternative to purchasing your own plotter. Or you might consider using a low-cost plotter for check plots and then sending the files to a service bureau for your final product. Most reprographic services, such as blueprinters, offer plotting in conjunction with their other services. Quite often these services include a high-speed modem that allows you to send files over phone lines, eliminating the need for using courier services or regular mail.

If you foresee the need for service bureaus, consider establishing a relationship with one or two service bureaus fairly early. Send them some sample plot files to make sure that they will produce the results you want. One of the greatest difficulties you may face while using a service bureau is miscommunication between what you want and what they provide in the way of plotter output.

You may be able to make use of the PC3 and other plotter setting files as part of your relationship with a service bureau. Plot configuration files and plot style table files can help communicate exactly what you're expecting from your plots.

If You Want to Experiment...

At this point, since you aren't rushing to meet a deadline, you may want to experiment with some of the plotter and printer variables and see firsthand what each one does. Try plotting the `Plan-color.dwg` and `Plan-named.dwg` files using the plot style tables you created earlier in this chapter. Also, try changing other plot style table options to see the results on paper.

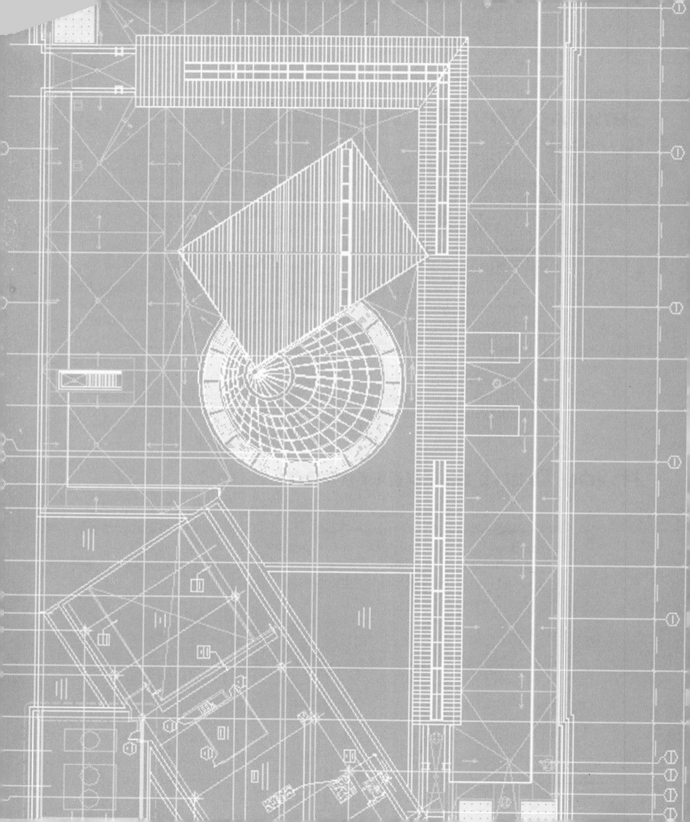

CHAPTER

EIGHT

8

Adding Text to Drawings

- Adding Text to a Drawing

- Understanding Text Formatting in AutoCAD

- Organizing Text by Styles

- What Do the Fonts Look Like?

- Adding Special Characters

- Adding Simple Text Objects

- Checking Spelling

- Substituting Fonts

- Accelerating Zooms and Regens with Qtext

- Express Tools Text-Editing Utilities

- If You Want to Experiment...

One of the more tedious drafting tasks is applying notes to your drawing. Anyone who has had to draft a large drawing containing a lot of notes knows the true meaning of writer's cramp. AutoCAD not only makes this job go faster by allowing you to type your notes right into the same document as the corresponding drawing, it also helps you to create more professional-looking notes by using a variety of fonts, type sizes, and type styles.

In this chapter, you will add notes to your apartment building plan. In the process, you will explore some of AutoCAD's text creation and editing features. You will learn how to control the size, slant, type style, and orientation of text, and how to import text files.

Adding Text to a Drawing

In this first section, you will add some simple labels to your Unit drawing to identify the general design elements: the bathroom, kitchen, and living room.

1. Start AutoCAD and open the Unit file. If you haven't created the Unit file, you can use the file called `08a-unit.dwg` from the companion CD-ROM. Once open, use File ➤ Save As to save the Unit drawing to a file called `Unit.dwg`.

2. Create a layer called Notes and make it the current layer. Notes is the layer on which you will keep all your text information.

3. Turn off the Flr-pat layer. Otherwise, the floor pattern you added previously will obscure the text you enter during the exercises in this chapter.

TIP   It's a good idea to keep your notes on a separate layer, so you can plot drawings containing only the graphics information, or freeze the Notes layer to save redraw/ regeneration time.

---

4. Set up your view so it looks similar to the top image in Figure 8.1.

5. Choose the Multiline Text tool from the Draw toolbar, or type **MT**.⏎.

FIGURE 8.1:

The top image shows the points to pick to place the text boundary window. The bottom image shows the completed text.

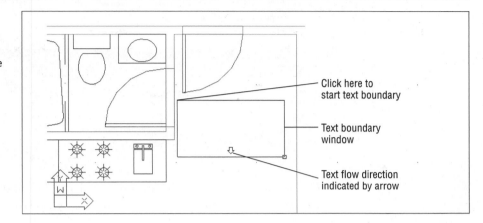

Click here to start text boundary

Text boundary window

Text flow direction indicated by arrow

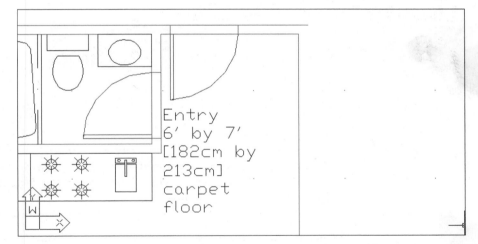

Entry
6' by 7'
[182cm by
213cm]
carpet
floor

6. Click the first point indicated in the top image of Figure 8.1 to start the text boundary window. This boundary window indicates the area in which to place the text. Notice the arrow near the bottom of the window. It indicates the direction of the text flow.

NOTE   You don't have to be too precise about where you select the points for the boundary because you can make adjustments to the location and size later.

7. Click the second point indicated in the top image of Figure 8.1. The Multi-line Text Editor appears.

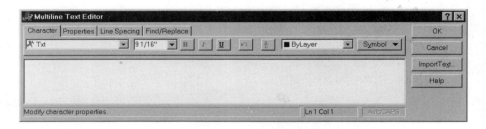

8. You could start typing the text for the room label, but first you need to select a size. Point to the Font Height drop-down list and click it. The default font size highlights.

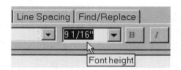

9. Enter **6** to make the default height 6 inches. Metric users should enter **15** for a text height of 15cm.

> **NOTE** Why make the text so high? Remember that you are drawing at full scale, and anything you draw will be reduced in the plotted drawing. Text height is discussed in more detail later in this chapter.

10. Click the main text window and type the word **Entry**. As you type, the word appears in the text window, just as it will appear in your drawing. As you will see later, the text also appears in the same font as the final text.

> **NOTE** The default font is a native AutoCAD font called `Txt.shx`. As you will see later, you can also use TrueType fonts and PostScript fonts.

11. Press ↵ to advance one line; then enter **6' by 7'**.

12. Press ↵ to advance another line and enter **[182cm by 213cm]**.

13. Press ↵ again to advance another line and enter **carpet floor**.

14. Click OK. The text appears in the drawing (see the bottom image of Figure 8.1).

The Text window works like any text editor, so if you make a typing error, you can highlight the error and then retype the letter or word. You can also perform other word processing functions such as search and replace, import text, or make font changes.

The following sections discuss some of the many options you have available for formatting text.

TIP   If text is included in an area where a hatch pattern is to be placed, AutoCAD automatically avoids hatching over the text. If you add text over a hatched area, you must rehatch the area to include the text in the hatch boundary.

Understanding Text Formatting in AutoCAD

AutoCAD offers a wide range of text-formatting options. You can control fonts, text height, justification, line spacing, and width. You can even include special characters such as degree symbols or stacked fractions. In a departure from the somewhat clumsy text implementation of earlier AutoCAD versions, you now have a much wider range of controls over your text.

Adjusting the Text Height and Font

Let's continue our look at AutoCAD text by adding a label for the living room of the studio apartment. You'll use the Multiline Text tool again, but this time you'll get to try out some of its other features. In this first exercise, you'll see how you can adjust the size of text in the editor.

1. Pan your view so that the kitchen is just at the top of the drawing, as shown in the top image of Figure 8.2.

2. Click the Multiline Text tool again; then select a text boundary window, as shown in the top image of Figure 8.2.

3. In the Multiline Text dialog box, start typing the following text:

   Living Room
   14'-0" by 16'-5"
   [427cm by 500cm]

As you type, notice that the words "Living" and "Room" become two separate lines even though you did not press ↵ between them. AutoCAD uses word wrap to fit the text inside the text boundary area.

4. Highlight the text 14'-0" by 16'-5" (427cm by 500cm) as you would in any word processor. For example, you can click the end of the line to place the cursor there; then Shift+click the beginning of the line to highlight the whole line.

5. Click the Font Height drop-down list and enter **6**↵. The highlighted text changes to a smaller size.

6. Highlight the words "Living Room."

7. Click the Font drop-down list. A list of font options appears.

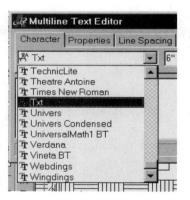

8. Scroll up the list until you find Arial. This is a standard TrueType font available in all installations of Windows NT or Windows 95/98. Notice that the text changes to reflect the new font.

9. With the words "Living Room" still highlighted, click the Underline tool.

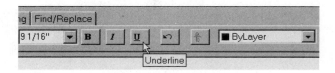

10. Click OK. The label appears in the area you indicated in step 2 (see the bottom image of Figure 8.2).

FIGURE 8.2:

Placing the text boundary window for the living room label and the final label

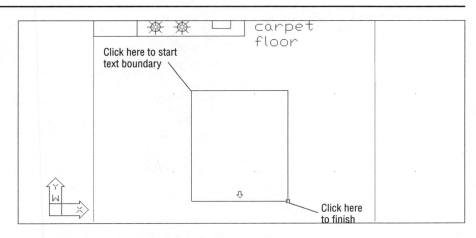

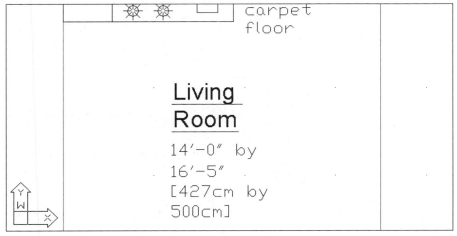

Using PostScript Fonts

If you have PostScript fonts that you would like to use in AutoCAD, you need to compile them into AutoCAD's native font format. The following steps show you how it's done.

1. Type **Compile**↵. The Compile Shape or Font File dialog box appears.

2. Select PostScript Font (*.pfb) from the File of Type drop-down list.

3. Double-click the PostScript font you want to convert into the AutoCAD format. AutoCAD will work for a moment; then you'll see this message:

   ```
   "Compiling shape/font description file"

   Compilation successful. Output file Program Files\AutoCAD2000\
   FONTS\fontname.shx contains 59578 bytes.
   ```

When AutoCAD is done, you have a file with the same name as the PostScript font file, but with the .shx filename extension. If you place your newly compiled font in AutoCAD's Fonts folder, it will be available in the Style dialog box.

When you work with AutoCAD's .shx font files, it is important to remember that

- License restrictions still apply to the AutoCAD-compiled version of the PostScript font.

- Like other fonts, compiled PostScript fonts can use up substantial disk space, so compile only the fonts you need.

While using the Multiline Text tool, you may have noticed the [Height/Justify/ Line spacing/Rotation/Style/Width] prompt immediately after you picked the first point of the text boundary. You can use any of these options to make on-the-fly modifications to the height, justification, line spacing, rotation style, or width of the multiline text.

For example, right after clicking the first point for the text boundary, you can type **R**↵ and then specify a rotation angle for the text windows, either graphically with a rubber-banding line or by entering an angle value. Once you've entered a rotation angle, you can resume selecting the text boundary.

Adding Color, Stacked Fractions, and Special Symbols

In the previous exercise, you were able to adjust the text height and font, just as you would in any word processor. You saw how you can easily underline portions of your text using the tool buttons in the editor. Other tools allow you to set the color for individual characters or words in the text, create stacked fractions, or insert special characters. Here's a brief description of how these tools work:

- To change the color of text, highlight it and then select the color from the Text Color drop-down list.

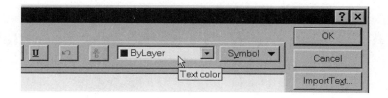

- To turn a fraction into a stacked fraction, highlight the fraction and then click the Stack/Unstack tool.

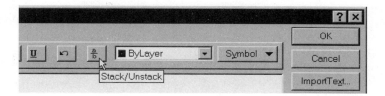

- To add a special character, place the cursor at the location of the character and then click the Symbol tool. A drop-down list appears offering options for special characters.

The Symbol tool offers three standard options that are typical for most technical drawings: the Degree, Plus/Minus, and Diameter signs. When you select these options, AutoCAD inserts the proper AutoCAD text code in the text that corresponds to these symbols. They don't appear in the editor as symbols. Instead, they appear as a special code. However, once you return to the drawing, you'll see the text with the proper symbol. You'll get a more detailed look at special symbols later in this chapter.

Adjusting the Width of the Text Boundary Window

While your text font and height is formatted correctly, it appears stacked in a way that is too tall and narrow. The following steps will show you how to change the boundary to fit the text.

1. Click any part of the text you just entered to highlight it.

2. Click the upper-right grip.

3. Drag the grip to the right to the location shown in Figure 8.3; then click that point.

4. Click any grip and then right-click the mouse and select Move.

5. Move the text to a location that is more centered in the room.

FIGURE 8.3:

Adjusting the text boundary window

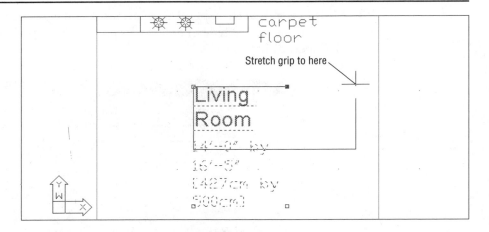

AutoCAD's word-wrap feature automatically adjusts the text formatting to fit the text boundary window. This feature is especially useful to AutoCAD users because other drawing objects often impact the placement of text. As your drawing changes, you will need to make adjustments to the location and boundary of your notes and labels.

Adjusting the Text Alignment

The text is currently aligned on the left side of the text boundary. For a label such as the one in the living room, it is more appropriate to center the text. Here's how you can make changes to the text alignment:

1. If the text is not yet selected, click it.

2. Right-click, then select Properties. The Properties dialog box for the selected text appears.

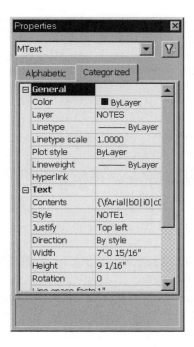

3. Make sure the Categorized tab is selected, then scroll down the Properties listing until you can see all of the Text options.

4. Notice that the text appears in the Contents input box. Also included is some special code that helps format the text. If you only wanted to make changes to the text, this is one place you could do it.

WARNING   The code you see mixed in with the text in the Contents input box is normally hidden from you in the Multiline Text Editor, and you don't really need to concern yourself with it. If you edit the text in the Contents input box, make sure you don't change the coding unless you know what you are doing.

5. Click the Contents label in the left-hand column. This exposes the Ellipses button to the far right.

6. Click the Ellipses button. The Multiline Text Editor appears with the text.

TIP   You can go directly to the Multiline Text Editor by right-clicking after selecting text and selecting Mtext Edit.

7. Click the Properties tab in the Multiline Text Editor. The editor changes to display a different set of options.

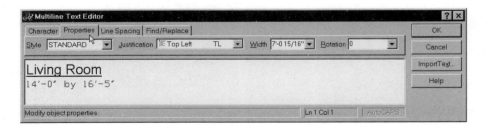

8. Click the Justification drop-down list. The alignment options appear.

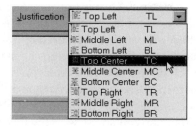

9. Click Top Center. The living room label moves to a centered position above the second line.

10. Click OK and then close the Properties dialog box. The text changes to align through the center of the text, as shown in Figure 8.4.

FIGURE 8.4:

The text aligned using the Top Center alignment option

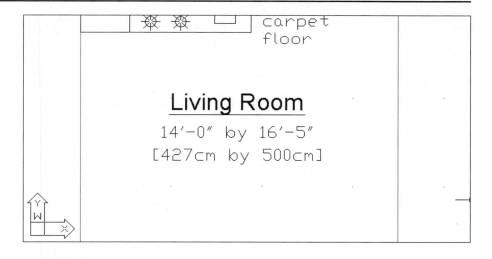

You can also change the justification of text in the Multiline Text Editor dialog box. Select the multiline text you want to edit, then right-click and select Properties. Click the setting just to the right of the Justify option. It becomes a drop-down list. Open the list and select the justification style you want. The text changes as you select the justification style.

Text Alignment and Osnaps

While it's clear that the text is now aligned through the center of the text, one important change occurred that is not so obvious. You may have noticed that the object alignment list offered three centered options: Top Center, Middle Center, and Bottom Center. All three of these options have the same effect on the text's appearance, but they each have a different effect on how Osnaps act upon the text. Figure 8.5 shows where the Osnap point occurs on a text boundary, depending on which alignment option is selected. A multiline text object only has one insertion point on its boundary that you can access with the Insert Osnap.

The Osnap point also appears as an extra grip point on the text boundary when you click the text. If you click the text you just entered, you will see that a grip point now appears at the top center of the text boundary.

FIGURE 8.5:

The location of the Insert Osnap points on a text boundary based on its alignment setting

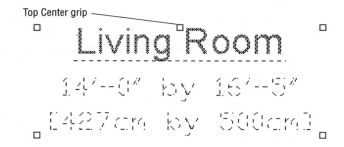

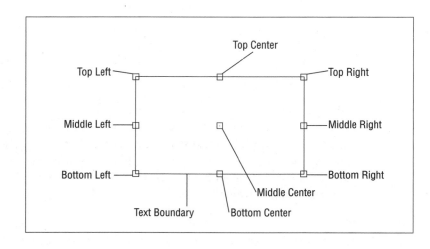

Knowing where the Osnap points occur can be helpful when you want to align the text with other objects in your drawing. In most cases, you can use the grips to align your text boundary, but the Top Center and Middle Center alignment options allow you to use the center and middle portions of your text to align the text with other objects.

Adjusting Line Spacing

Another text-editing feature that is related to text alignment is the Line Spacing option. You can adjust line spacing between the range of 0.5 and 4 times the height of the text. Here's how it works.

1. Type **Ed↵** or choose Modify ➣ Text. This issues the Ddedit command.

2. Click the words "Living Room." The Multiline Text Editor dialog box appears.

3. Select the Line Spacing tab. You see the options for line spacing.

You can select from a set of predefined line spacing values by selecting from the Line Spacing drop-down list to the far right. You can also enter a custom line spacing value by entering it into the drop-down list.

4. Click the current value shown in the drop-down list to the far right.

5. Enter **4x↵**. Once you press ↵, the value changes to reflect the spacing of the text at 4 times the height of the text.

6. Click OK. The Multiline Text Editor closes and the text in the drawing changes to the new line spacing.

7. Type **U↵** or click the Undo button in the Standard toolbar. You don't need to save this change to the text.

In step 5 you had to enter an **x** after the **4** to indicate that you want a line spacing value that is 4 times the text height. You can also enter an exact text height value, but be aware that the height value must be between 0.5 and 4 times the current text height.

While you changed the line-spacing value of an existing text object in this exercise, you can use the same option in the Line Spacing tab to set the line spacing for new text.

Editing Existing Text

It is helpful to think of text in AutoCAD as a collection of text documents. Each text boundary window you place is like a separate document. To create and edit these documents, you use the Multiline Text Editor.

You've already seen how you can access existing text using the Properties tool on the Object Properties toolbar when you modified the formatting of the living room label. Of course, you can use the same tool to change the content of the text. In the following example, you'll use a shortcut to the Multiline Text Editor dialog box to add more text to the living room label.

1. Type **Ed**↵ or choose Modify ➤ Text. This issues the Ddedit command.

NOTE   The Ddedit command does not allow Noun/Verb selection.

2. Click the words "Living Room." The Multiline Text Editor dialog box appears.

3. Place and click the text cursor on the end of the line that reads "Living Room"; then type ↵**230 square feet**.

4. Click OK. The text appears in the drawing with the addition line.

5. The Ddedit command is still active, so press ↵ to exit Ddedit.

In step 5, the Ddedit command remains active so you can continue to edit other text objects. In addition to pressing ↵ to exit the command, you can select another text object.

As with the prior exercise, you can change the formatting of the existing or new text while in the Multiline Text Editor dialog box. Notice that the formatting of the new text is the same as the text that preceded it. Just as in Microsoft Word, the formatting of text is dependent on the paragraph or word to which it is added. If you had added the text after the last line, it would appear in the AutoCAD Txt font and in the same 6-inch height.

Converting Text to Lowercase or Uppercase

If you find you need to change the case of existing text, you can do so with the Multiline Text Editor. Here are the steps. You don't need to apply these steps to your drawing exercises.

1. Choose Modify ➤ Text or enter **MT**↵ to start the editor.

2. Highlight the text you want to change.

3. Right-click, then select Change Case ➤ UPPERCASE or Change Case ➤ lowercase, depending on which option you want.

4. Click OK to exit the Multiline Text Editor.

If you want new text to be all uppercase, double-click the AutoCAPS button in the lower-right corner of the Multiline Text Editor.

Modify character properties.   Ln 1 Col 1   AutoCAPS

This turns on the Caps Lock on your keyboard. You can do this before importing text to convert an external file to all caps while it is being imported.

Understanding Text and Scale

In the first few exercises of this chapter, you were asked to make the text height 6 inches. This is necessary to give the text the proper scale for the drawing. But where did we come up with the number 6? Why not 4 or 10? The 6-inch height was derived by carefully considering the desired final height of the text in relation to the designated scale of the drawing. Just as in Chapter 3 where you applied a scale factor to a drawing's final sheet size to accommodate a full-scale drawing, you need to make a scale conversion for your text size to make the text conform to the drawing's intended scale.

Text scale conversion is a concept many people have difficulty grasping. As you discovered in previous chapters, AutoCAD allows you to draw at full scale, that is, to represent distances as values equivalent to the actual size of the object. When you later plot the drawing, you tell AutoCAD at what scale you wish to plot and the program reduces the drawing accordingly. This allows you the freedom to enter measurements at full scale and not worry about converting them to various scales every time you enter a distance. Unfortunately, this feature can also create problems when you enter text and dimensions. Just as you had to convert the plotted sheet size to an enlarged size equivalent at full scale in the drawing editor, you must convert your text size to its equivalent at full scale.

To illustrate this point, imagine you are drawing the Unit plan at full size on a very large sheet of paper. When you are done with this drawing, it will be reduced to a scale that allows it to fit on an 81/2" × 11" sheet of paper. So you have to make your text quite large to keep it legible once it is reduced. This means that if you want text to appear 1/8" high when the drawing is plotted, you must convert it to a considerably larger size when you draw it. To do this, you multiply the desired height of the final plotted text by a scale conversion factor.

If your drawing is at 1/8"=1' scale, you multiply the desired text height, 1/8", by the scale conversion factor of 96 (Table 3.3 shows scale factors as they relate to standard drawing scales) to get a height of 12". This is the height you must make your text to get 1/8"-high text in the final plot. Table 8.1 shows you some other examples of text height to scale.

TABLE 8.1: 1/8"-High Text Converted to Size for Various Drawing Scales

Drawing Scale	Scale Factor	AutoCAD Drawing Height for 1/8"-High Text
1/16" = 1'-0"	192	24.0"
1/8" = 1'-0"	96	12.0"
1/4" = 1'-0"	48	6.0"
1/2" = 1'-0"	24	3.0"
3/4" = 1'-0"	16	2.0"
1" = 1'-0"	12	1.5"
1 1/2" = 1'-0"	8	1.0"
3" = 1'-0"	4	0.5"

Organizing Text by Styles

If you understand the Multiline Text Editor and text scale, you know all you need to know to start labeling your drawings. As you expand your drawing skills and your drawings become larger, you will want to start organizing your text into *styles*. You can think of text styles as a way to store your most common text formatting. Styles will store text height and font information, so you don't have to reset these options every time you enter text. But styles also include some settings not available in the Multiline Text Editor.

Creating a Style

In the prior examples, you entered text using the AutoCAD default settings for text. Whether you knew it or not, you were also using a text style: AutoCAD's default style called Standard. The Standard style uses the AutoCAD Txt font and numerous other settings that you will learn about in this section. These other settings include width factor, obliquing, and default height.

TIP If you don't like the way the AutoCAD default style is set up, open the `Acad.dwt` file and change the Standard text style settings to your liking. You can also add other styles that you use frequently.

The previous exercises in this chapter demonstrate that you can modify the formatting of a style as you enter the text. But for the most part, once you've set up a few styles, you won't need to adjust settings like fonts and text height each time you enter text. You'll be able to select from a list of styles you've previously created, and just start typing.

To create a style, choose Format ➤ Text Style and then select from the available fonts. This next exercise will show you how to create a style.

1. Click Format ➤ Text Style, or type **St**↵. The Text Style dialog box appears.

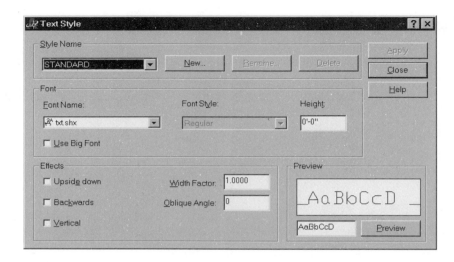

2. Click the New button in the Style Name group. The New Text Style dialog box appears.

3. Enter **Note1** for the name of your new style; then click OK.

4. Now select a font for your style. Click the Font Name drop-down list in the Font group.

5. Locate the Courier New TrueType font and select it.

6. In the Height input box, enter **6**.

7. Click Apply and then click Close.

Dressing Up Your Drawings with Display Fonts

Display fonts are fonts used in situations where appearances are important. In a typical architectural project, for example, display fonts are frequently used for presentation drawings of floor plans and building elevations. Traditionally, architects have used a device called a Kroy label machine to generate text for presentations. The Kroy machine is slow and somewhat time-consuming to use because you have to apply the lettering by hand to your artwork. With TrueType support, you can add display fonts directly to your CAD drawings, thereby saving time and gaining a higher degree of control over your presentation artwork.

Using a Type Style

Now let's see how your new text style looks by adding more text to the Unit.dwg drawing.

1. Pan your view so the balcony is centered in the AutoCAD drawing area, as shown in Figure 8.6.

2. Click the Multiline Text tool on the Draw toolbar.

3. Place the text boundary as shown in the top image of Figure 8.6. Notice that the font and height settings reflect the Note1 style you created earlier.

4. Enter the following text:

   Balcony ⏎
   14'-0" by 4'-0"⏎
   [427cm by 122cm]

5. Highlight the word "Balcony," and then click the Underline button.

6. With Balcony still highlighted, click the Font Height drop-down list and enter **9**⏎.

7. Click the Properties tab.

8. Highlight all of the text and then select Top Center from the Justification drop-down list.

9. Click OK. The text appears over the balcony in the style you selected.

A newly created style becomes the default style, and you didn't have to explicitly select your new Note1 style in order to use it.

You can also change an existing piece of text to a different style. The following steps show you how.

1. Return to your previous view of the "Living Room" text.

2. Type **Ed**⏎ and select the text.

3. Click the Properties tab in the Multiline Text Editor.

4. Highlight one line of the text.

5. Click the Style drop-down list and select Note1. Notice that all the text is converted to the new style.

WARNING   When you change the style of a text object, it loses any custom formatting it may have, such as font or height changes that are different from those of the text's default style settings.

---

6. Click OK. The living room label is now in your Note1 style (see Figure 8.7).

FIGURE 8.6:

Adding the balcony label using the Note1 text style

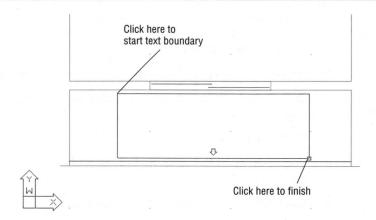

Click here to start text boundary

Click here to finish

Balcony
14'-0" by 4'-0"
[427cm by 122cm]

FIGURE 8.7:

The living room label converted to the Note1 style

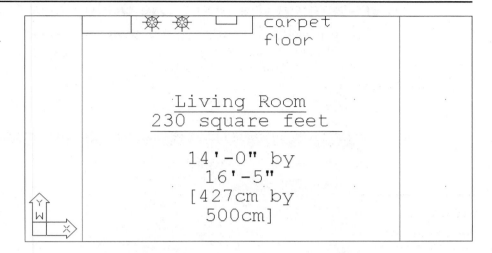

carpet
floor

Living Room
230 square feet

14'-0" by
16'-5"
[427cm by
500cm]

WARNING   The Style input box in the Modify Mtext dialog box (found via the Properties tool) allows you to select a new style for a text object. This option does not affect the style of text if the text has other custom format changes, such as a font and size change from its default settings.

Setting the Current Default Style

The last exercise showed you how you can change the style of existing text. But suppose you want all the new text you create to be of a different style than the current default style. You can change the current style by using the Text Style dialog box. Here's how it's done.

1. Click Format ➤ Text Style, or type **St↵**. The Text Style dialog box appears.

2. Select a style name from the Style Name drop-down list. For this exercise, choose Standard to return to the Standard style.

3. Click Close.

Once you've done this, the selected style will be the default until you select a different style. AutoCAD records the current default style with the drawing data when you issue a File ➤ Save command, so that the next time you work on the file you will still have the same default style.

Understanding the Text Style Dialog Box Options

Now you know how to create a new style. As mentioned before, there are other settings in the Text Style dialog box that you didn't apply in an exercise. Here is a listing of those settings and their purposes. Some of them, like the Width Factor, can be quite useful. Others like the Backwards and Vertical options are rarely used.

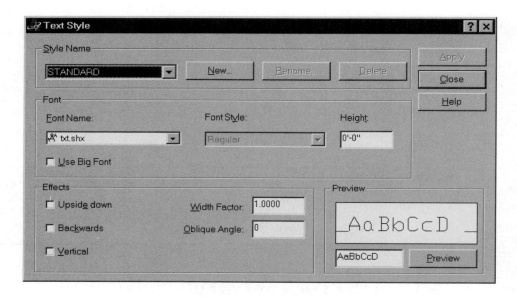

Style Name

New   Lets you create a new text style.

Rename   Lets you rename an existing style. This option is not available for the Standard style.

Delete   Deletes a style. This option is not available for the Standard style.

Font

Font Name   Lets you select a font from a list of available fonts. The list is derived from the font resources available to Windows NT or Windows 95/98, plus the standard AutoCAD fonts.

Font Style   Offers variations of a font such as italic or bold, when they are available.

Height   Lets you enter a font size. A 0 height has special meaning when entering text using the Dtext command, described later in this chapter.

Effects

Upside down   Prints the text upside down.

Backwards   Prints the text backwards.

Width Factor   Adjusts the width and spacing of the characters in the text. A value of 1 keeps the text at the its normal width. Values greater than 1 expands the text while values less than 1 compress the text.

This is the Simplex font expanded by 1.4

This is the simplex font using a width factor of 1

This is the simplex font compressed by .6

Oblique Angle   Skews the text at an angle. When this option is set to a value greater than 0, the text appears to be italicized. A value of less than 0 (-12, for example) causes the text to "lean" to the left.

This is the simplex font
using a 12—degree oblique angle

Renaming a Text Style

You can use the Rename option in the Text Style dialog box to rename a style. An alternate method is to use the Ddrename command. This is a command that allows you to rename a variety of AutoCAD settings. Here's how to use it.

NOTE This exercise is not part of the main tutorial. If you are working through the tutorial, make note of it and then try it out later.

1. Click Format ➤ Rename, or enter **Ren.**⌐ at the command prompt. The Rename dialog box appears.

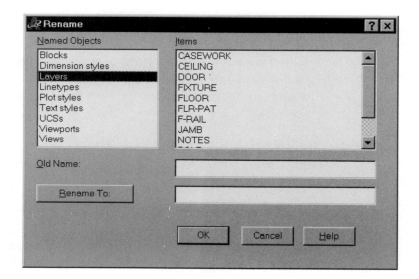

NOTE The Ddrename command allows you to rename blocks, dimension styles, layers, line types, user coordinate systems, viewports, and views, as well as text styles.

2. In the Named Objects list box, click Style.

3. Click the name of the style you wish to change from the list to the right; the name appears in the Old Name input box below the list.

4. In the input box next to the Rename To button, enter the new name, click the Rename To button, and then click OK.

NOTE If you are an experienced AutoCAD user and accustomed to entering the Rename command at the command prompt, you still can. Then answer the prompts that appear.

TIP	If you need to change the style of one text object to match that of another, you can use the Match Properties tool. See the *How to Quickly Match a Hatch Pattern and Other Properties* sidebar in Chapter 6 for details on how to use this tool.

What Do the Fonts Look Like?

You've already seen a few of the fonts available in AutoCAD. Chances are, you are familiar with the TrueType fonts available in Windows. You have some additional AutoCAD fonts from which to choose. In fact, you may want to stick with the AutoCAD fonts for all but your presentation drawings, as other fonts can consume more memory.

Figure 8.8 shows the basic AutoCAD text fonts. The Roman font is perhaps the most widely used because it offers a reasonable appearance while not consuming much memory. Figure 8.9 lists the Symbols and Greek fonts.

FIGURE 8.8:

The standard AutoCAD text fonts

This is Txt
This is Monotxt
This is Simplex   (Old version of Roman Simplex)
This is Complex   (Old version of Roman Complex)
This is Italic   (Old version of Italic Complex)
This is Romans   (Roman Simplex)
This is Romand   (Roman double stroke)
This is Romanc   (Roman Complex)
This is Romant   (Roman triple stroke)
This is Scripts   (Script Simplex)
This is Scriptc   (Script Complex)
This is Italicc   (Italic Complex)
This is Italict   (Italic triple stroke)
Τηισ ισ Γρεεκσ   (This is Greeks - Greek Simplex)
Τηισ ισ Γρεεκχ   (This is Greekc - Greek Complex)
This is Gothice   (Gothic English)
This is Gothicg   (Gothic German)
This is Gothici   (Gothic Italian)

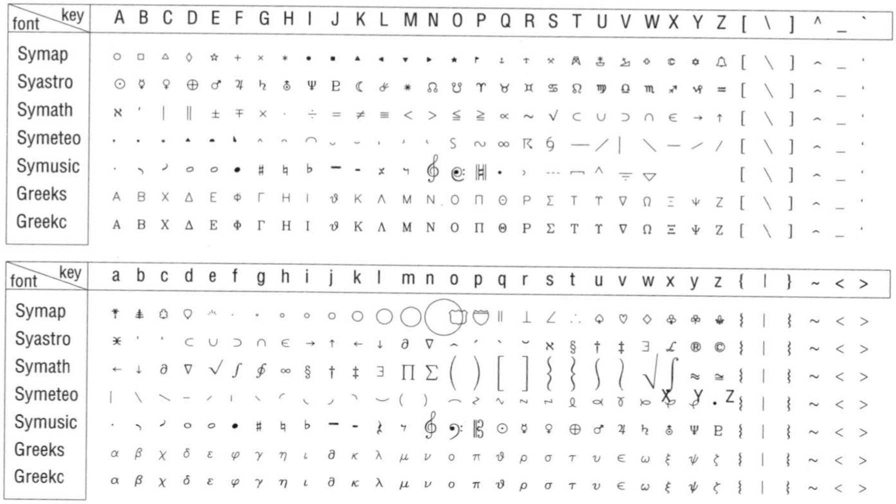

FIGURE 8.9:

The AutoCAD symbols and Greek fonts

The Textfill System Variable

Unlike the standard stick-like AutoCAD fonts, TrueType and PostScript fonts have filled areas. These filled areas take more time to generate, so if you have a lot of text in these fonts, your redraw and regen times will increase. To help reduce redraw and regen times, you can set AutoCAD to display and plot these fonts as outline fonts, even though they are filled in their true appearance.

To change its setting, type **Textfill⏎** and then type **0⏎**. This turns off text fill for PostScript and TrueType fonts. For plots, you can remove the checkmark on the option labeled Text Fill (this is the same as setting the Textfill system variable to 0).

This section showed you samples of the AutoCAD fonts. You can see samples of all the fonts, including TrueType fonts, in the Preview window of the Text Style dialog box. If you use a word processor, you're probably familiar with at least some of the TrueType fonts available in Windows and AutoCAD.

Adding Special Characters

Earlier in this chapter, you saw that you can add special characters using the Symbol button in the Multiline Text Editor. For example, you use the Degrees symbol to designate angles and the Plus/Minus symbol for showing tolerance information. The Diameter characters are already available as special characters. AutoCAD also offers a nonbreaking space. You can use the nonbreaking space when you have a space between two words but you do not want the two words to be separated by a line break.

WARNING   The Character Map dialog box is a Windows accessory. If it does not appear when you select Other from the Symbol drop-down list, you may need to install the Character Map from your Windows installation CD.

By clicking the Other option in the Symbol drop-down list, you can also add other special characters from the Windows Character Map dialog box.

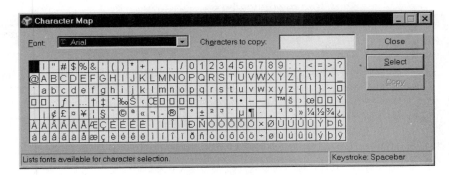

Characters such as the trademark (™) and copyright (©) symbols are often available. The contents of the Symbol drop-down list will vary depending on the font you have currently selected. You can click and drag or just click your mouse over the Character Map to see an enlarged view of the character you are pointing to.

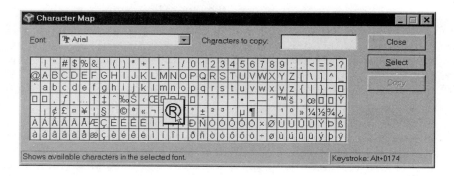

To use the characters from this dialog box, proceed with the following steps.

1. Choose Other from the Symbol drop-down list in the Multiline Text Editor.

NOTE

This is not part of the regular tutorial in this chapter but you can experiment with these steps on your own.

---

2. Highlight the character you want.

3. Either double-click the character or click the Select button. The character appears in the box at the upper-right corner of the dialog box.

4. Click Copy to copy the character to the Clipboard.

5. Close the dialog box.

6. In the Multiline Text Editor, place the cursor where you want the special character to appear.

7. Press Ctrl+V to paste the character into your text. You can also right-click the mouse and choose Paste from the pop-up list.

Importing Text Files

With multiline text objects, AutoCAD allows you to import ASCII text or Rich Text Format (RTF) files. Here's how you go about importing text files.

1. In the Multiline Text Editor dialog box, click Import Text.

2. In the Open dialog box, locate a valid text file. It must be either a file in a raw text (ASCII) format, such as a Notepad (.txt) file, or a Rich Text Format (.rtf) file. RTF files are capable of storing formatting information, such as boldface and varying point sizes.

3. Once you've highlighted the file you want, double-click it or click Open. The text appears in the Edit Mtext window.

4. You can then click OK and the text will appear in your drawing.

In addition, you can use the Windows Clipboard and Cut and Paste feature to add text to a drawing. To do this, take the following steps:

1. Use the Cut or Copy option in any other Windows program to place text into the Windows Clipboard.

2. Go to AutoCAD and then choose Edit ➤ Paste. The OLE Properties dialog box appears, allowing you to adjust the height, width, and other properties of the pasted object.

3. Click OK and the pasted text appears in your drawing. It is not, however, editable within AutoCAD.

Because AutoCAD is an OLE client, you can also attach other types of documents to an AutoCAD drawing file. See Chapter 14 for more on AutoCAD's OLE support.

Adding Simple Text Objects

You may find that you are entering a lot of single words or simple labels that don't require all the bells and whistles of the Multiline Text Editor. AutoCAD offers the *single-line text object* that is simpler to use and can speed text entry if you are only adding small pieces of text.

Continue the tutorial on the Unit.dwg file by trying the following exercise.

1. Adjust your view so it looks like Figure 8.10.

2. Enter **Dt⏎**, or choose Draw ➤ Text ➤ Single Line Text. This issues the Dtext command.

3. At the DTEXT Justify/Style/<Start point>: prompt, pick the starting point for the text you are about to enter, just below the kitchen at coordinate 16'-2",21'-8" (490,664 for metric users). By picking a point, you are accepting <Start point>, which is the default.

4. At the Height prompt, enter **6"** (**15** for metric users) to indicate the text height.

5. At the Insertion angle <0>: prompt, press ⏎ to accept the default, 0°. You can specify any angle other than horizontal (for example, if you want your text to be aligned with a rotated object). You'll see a text I-beam cursor at the point you picked in step 3.

6. At the Text prompt, enter the word **Kitchenette**. As you type, the word appears in the drawing as well as in the Command window.

NOTE   If you make a typing error, use the Right and Left arrow keys to move the text cursor in the Command window to the error; then use the Backspace key to correct the error. You can also paste text from the Clipboard into the cursor location using the Ctrl+V keyboard shortcut or by right-clicking in the Command window to access the popup menu.

---

7. Press ⏎ to move the cursor down to start a new line.

8. This time you want to label the bathroom. Pick a point to the right of the door swing at coordinate 19'-11",26'-5" (610,805 for metric users). The text cursor moves to that point.

9. Type **Bathroom⏎**. Figure 8.10 shows how your drawing should look now.

10. Press ⏎ again to exit the Dtext command.

Adding simple labels to the
kitchen and bath using the
Dtext command

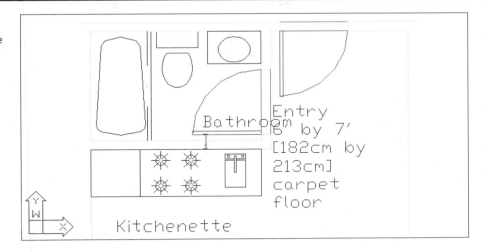

TIP

If for some reason you need to stop entering single-line text objects to do something else in AutoCAD, you can continue text where you left off by pressing ↵ at the **Start point:** prompt of the Dtext command. The text continues immediately below the last line of text entered.

Here you were able to add two single lines of text in different parts of your drawing fairly quickly. Dtext uses the current default text style settings (remember that earlier you set the text style to Standard), so the kitchen and bath labels use the Standard style.

Editing Single-Line Text Objects

Editing single-line text objects uses the same tools as those for multiline text, though the dialog boxes that result are different. In this exercise, you'll change the labels in both the kitchen and bath using the Ddedit command.

1. Type **ED**↵ or choose Modify ➢ Object ➢ Text.

2. Click the Kitchenette label. A small Edit Text dialog box appears.

3. Using the cursor, highlight the "ette" in kitchenette and delete it.

4. Click OK. (Notice that Ddedit is still active.)

5. Click the Bathroom label.

6. In the Edit Text dialog box that appears, change **Bathroom** to **Bath**.

7. Click OK and then press ↵ to exit the Ddedit command.

As you can see, even the editing is simplified. You are limited to editing the text only. This can be an advantage, however, when you need to edit several pieces of text. You don't have other options to get in the way of your editing.

You can change other properties of single-line text using the Properties dialog box. For example, suppose you want to change the Bath label to a height of 9 inches.

1. Click the Bath text, then right-click and select Properties. The Properties dialog box appears.

2. Select the Height value in the Properties dialog box and change it to **9"**.

3. Press ↵ and the text in the drawing increases in size to 9 inches high.

4. Click the Undo tool on the menu bar to undo the change in text height.

5. Click File ➤ Save to save the changes you've made thus far.

6. Close the Properties dialog box.

The Properties dialog box lets you change the Height, Rotation, Width Factor, Obliquing, Justification, and Style of a single-line text object. You can also modify the text content.

TIP   Unlike prior versions of AutoCAD, the `Height:` prompt appears in the Dtext command even if the current style has a non-zero height.

Justifying Single-Line Text Objects

Justifying single-line text objects works in a slightly different way from multiline text. For example, if you change the justification setting to Center, the text moves so the center of the text is placed at the text insertion point. In other words, the insertion point stays in place while the text location adjusts to the new justification setting. Figure 8.11 shows the relationship between single-line text and the insertion point based on different justification settings.

FIGURE 8.11:

Text inserted using the various justification options

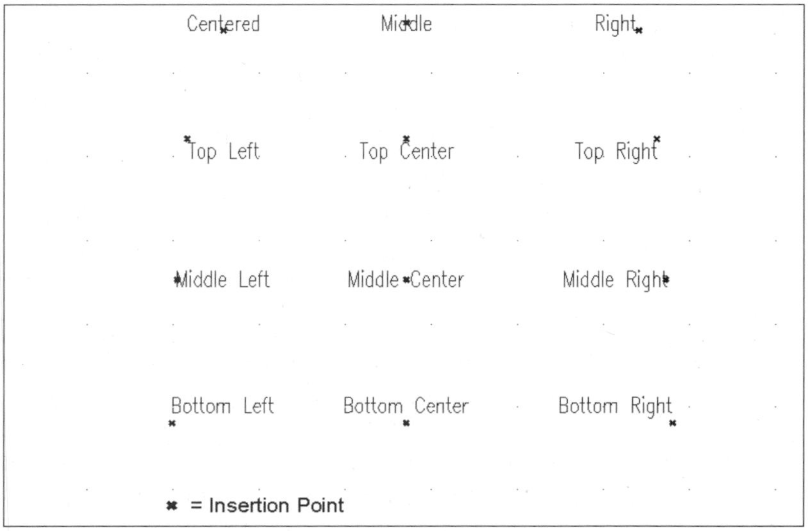

```
      Centered          Middle            Right

      Top Left        Top Center        Top Right

      Middle Left    Middle Center     Middle Right

      Bottom Left    Bottom Center     Bottom Right


      * = Insertion Point
```

To set the justification of text as you enter it, you must enter **J**↵ at the `Justify/Style/<Start point>:` prompt after issuing the Dtext command.

Once you've issued the Dtext's Justify option, you get the prompt:

`Align/Fit/Center/Middle/Right/TL/TC/TR/ML/MC/MR/BL/BC/BR:`

Here are descriptions of each of these options (I've left Fit and Align until last, because these options require a bit more explanation):

Center   Center causes the text to be centered on the start point, with the baseline on the start point.

Middle   Middle causes the text to be centered on the start point, with the baseline slightly below the start point.

Right   Right causes the text to be justified to the right of the start point, with the baseline on the start point.

TL, TC, and TR   TL, TC, and TR stand for top left, top center, and top right. Text using these justification styles appears entirely below the start point, justified left, center, or right, depending on which option you choose.

ML, MC, and MR   ML, MC, and MR stand for middle left, middle center, and middle right. These styles are similar to TL, TC, and TR, except that the start point determines a location midway between the baseline and the top of the lowercase letters of the text.

BL, BC, and BR   BL, BC, and BR stand for bottom left, bottom center, and bottom right. These styles, too, are similar to TL, TC, and TR, but here the start point determines the bottom-most location of the letters of the text (the bottom of letters that have descenders, such as p, q, and g).

Align and Fit Options   With the Align and Fit justification options, you must specify a dimension within which the text is to fit. For example, suppose you want the word "Refrigerator" to fit within the 26"-wide box representing the refrigerator. You can use either the Fit or the Align option to accomplish this. With Fit, AutoCAD prompts you to select start and end points, and then stretches or compresses the letters to fit within the two points you specify. You use this option when the text must be a consistent height throughout the drawing and you don't care about distorting the font.

Align works like Fit, but instead of maintaining the current text style height, the Align option adjusts the text height to keep it proportional to the text width, without distorting the font. Use this option when it is important to maintain the font's shape and proportion. Figure 8.12 demonstrates how Fit and Align work.

FIGURE 8.12:

The word "Refrigerator" as it appears normally and with the Fit and Align options selected

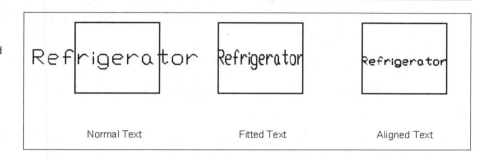

Normal Text   Fitted Text   Aligned Text

Using Special Characters with Single-Line Text Objects

Just as with multiline text, you can add a limited set of special characters to single-line text objects. For example, you can place the degree symbol (°) after a number, or you can *underscore* (underline) text. To accomplish this, you use double percent (%%) signs in conjunction with a special code. For example, to underscore text, you enclose that text with the %% signs and follow it with the underscore code. So, to get this text: "This is underscored text." you enter this at the prompt:

This is %%uunderscored%%u text.

Overscoring (putting a line above the text) operates in the same manner. To insert codes for symbols, you just place the codes in the correct positions for the symbols that they represent. For example, to enter 100.5°, you type **100.5%%d**.

Here is a list of the codes you can use:

Code	Special Characters
%%o	Toggles overscore on and off.
%%u	Toggles underscore on and off.
%%d	Places a degree sign (°) where the code occurs.
%%p	Places a plus-minus sign where the code occurs.
%%%	Forces a single percent sign; useful when you want a double percent sign to appear, or when you want a percent sign in conjunction with another code.

Code	Special Characters
%%*nnn*	Allows the use of extended Unicode characters when these characters are used in a text-definition file; *nnn* is the three-digit value representing the character.

Using the Character Map Dialog Box to Add Special Characters

You can add special characters to a single line of text in the same way you would with multiline text. You may recall that to access special characters, you use the Character Map dialog box. This dialog box can be opened directly from the Windows Explorer.

Using Windows Explorer, locate the file `Charmap.exe` in the `Windows` folder. Double-click it and the Character Map dialog box appears. You can then use the procedure discussed in the *Adding Special Characters* section earlier in this chapter to cut and paste a character from the Character Map dialog box. If you find you use the Character Map dialog box often, create a shortcut for it and place the shortcut in your AutoCAD Program group.

Keeping Text from Mirroring

At times you will want to mirror a group of objects that contain some text. This operation causes the mirrored text to appear backward. You can change a setting in AutoCAD to make the text read normally, even when it is mirrored.

1. Enter **Mirrtext⏎**.

2. At the `New value for MIRRTEXT <1>:` prompt, enter **0⏎**.

Now, any mirrored text that is not in a block will read normally. The text's *position,* however, will still be mirrored, as shown in the graphic below. Mirrtext is set to 0 by default.

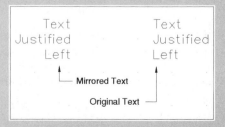

Checking Spelling

Although AutoCAD is primarily a drawing program, you will find that some of your drawings contain more text than graphics. Autodesk has recognized this and included a spelling checker starting in AutoCAD Release 14. If you've ever used the spelling checker in a typical word processor, such as Microsoft Word, the AutoCAD spelling checker's operation will be familiar to you. These steps show you how it works.

1. Choose Tools ➤ Spelling from the pull-down menu, or type **Sp**↵.

2. At the `Select objects:` prompt, select any text object you want to check. You can select a mixture of multiline and single-line text. When the spelling checker finds a word it does not recognize, the Check Spelling dialog box appears.

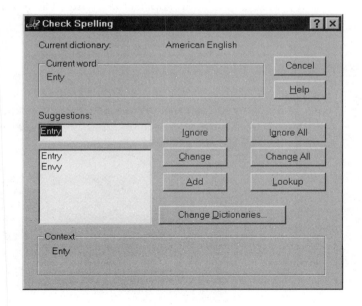

In the Check Spelling dialog box, you'll see the word in question, along with the spelling checker's suggested alternate word in the Suggestions input box. If the spelling checker finds more than one suggestion, a list of suggested alternate words appears below the input box. You can then highlight the desired replacement and click the Change button to change the misspelled word, or click Change All to change all occurrences of the word in the selected text. If the suggested word is inappropriate, choose another word from the replacement list (if any), or enter your own spelling in the Suggestions input box. Then choose Change or Change All.

Here is a list of the options available in the Check Spelling dialog box:

Ignore   Skips the word.

Ignore All   Skips all the occurrences of the word in the selected text.

Change   Changes the word in question to the word you have selected (or entered) from the Suggestions input box.

Change All   Changes all occurrences of the current word, when there are multiple instances of the misspelling.

Add   Adds the word in question to the current dictionary.

Lookup   Checks the spelling of the word in question. This option is for the times when you want to find another word that doesn't appear in the Suggestions input box.

Change Dictionaries   Lets you use a different dictionary to check spelling. This option opens the Change Dictionaries dialog box, described in the upcoming section.

Choosing a Dictionary

The Change Dictionaries option opens the Change Dictionaries dialog box, where you can select a particular main dictionary for foreign languages, or create or choose a custom dictionary. Main dictionary files have the .dct extension. The Main dictionary for the U.S. version of AutoCAD is Enu.dct.

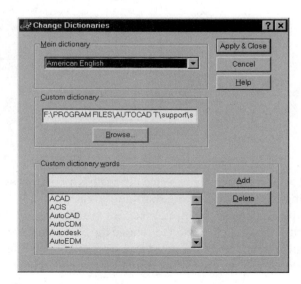

In the Change Dictionaries dialog box, you can also add or delete words from a custom dictionary. Custom dictionary files are ASCII files with the .cus extension. Because they are ASCII files, they can be edited outside of AutoCAD. The Browse button lets you view a list of existing custom dictionaries.

If you prefer, you can also select a main or custom dictionary using the Dctust and Dctmain system variables. See Appendix D for more on these system variables.

A third place where you can select a dictionary is in the Files tab of the Options dialog box (Tools ➤ Options). You can find the Dictionary listing under Text Editor, Dictionary, and Font File Names. Click the plus sign next to this listing and then click the plus sign next to the Main Dictionary listing to expose the dictionary options.

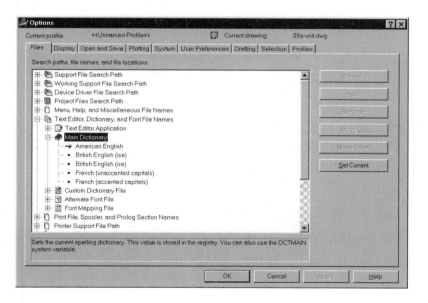

From here, you can double-click the dictionary you prefer. The pointing hand icon moves to the selected dictionary.

Substituting Fonts

There will be times when you want to change all the fonts in a drawing quickly. For instance, you may want to convert PostScript fonts into a simple Txt.shx font to help shorten redraw times while you are editing. Or you may need to convert the font of a drawing received from another office to a font that conforms to your own office standards. In AutoCAD 2000, the Fontmap system variable works in conjunction with a font-mapping table, allowing you to easily substitute fonts in a drawing.

The font-mapping table is an ASCII file called `Acad.fmp`. You can also use a file you create yourself. You can give this file any name you choose, as long as it has the .fmp extension.

This font-mapping table contains one line for each font substitution you want AutoCAD to make. A typical line in this file would read as follows:

```
romant; C:\ProgramFiles\Acad2000\Font\Txt.shx
```

In this example, AutoCAD is directed to use the `Txt.shx` font in place of the Romant.shx font. To execute this substitution, you type:

Fontmap ↵ *Fontmap_filename*

where *Fontmap_filename* is the font-mapping table you've created. This tells AutoCAD where to look for the font-mapping information. Then you issue the Regen command to view the font changes. To disable the font-mapping table, you type:

Fontmap ↵ .↵

You can also specify a font-mapping file in the Files tab of the Options dialog box. Look for the Text Editor, Dictionary, and Font File Names listing. Click the plus sign next to this listing and then click the plus sign next to the Font Mapping File listing to expose the current default font-mapping filename.

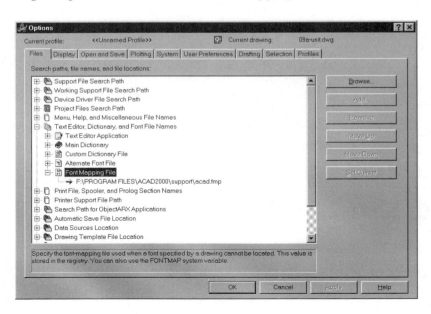

You can double-click this filename to open a Select a File dialog box. From there, you can select a different font-mapping file.

See Appendix D for more on the Fontmap system variable and other system variables.

Making Substitutions for Missing Fonts

When text styles are created, the associated fonts do not become part of the drawing file. Instead, AutoCAD loads the needed font file at the same time that the drawing is loaded. So if a text style in a drawing requires a particular font, AutoCAD looks for the font in the AutoCAD search path; if the font is there, it is loaded. Usually this isn't a problem if the drawing file uses the standard fonts that come with AutoCAD or Windows. But occasionally you will encounter a file that uses a custom font.

In earlier versions of AutoCAD, when you attempted to open such a file, you saw an error message. This missing-font message would often send the new AutoCAD user into a panic.

Fortunately, AutoCAD automatically substitutes an existing font for the missing font in a drawing. By default, AutoCAD substitutes the Txt.shx font, but you can specify another font using the Fontalt system variable. Type **Fontalt.** at the command prompt and then enter the name of the font you want to use as the substitute.

You can also select an alternate font through the Files tab of the Options dialog box. Locate the Text Editor, Dictionary, and Font File Names listing and then click the plus sign at the left. Locate the Alternate Font File listing that appears and click the plus sign at the left. The current alternate is listed. You can double-click the font name to select a different font through a Standard File dialog box.

Be aware that the text in your drawing will change in appearance, sometimes radically, when you use a substitute font. If the text in the drawing must retain its appearance, you should substitute a font that is as similar in appearance to the original font as possible.

Accelerating Zooms and Regens with Qtext

If you need to edit a drawing that contains a lot of text, but you don't need to edit the text, you can use the Qtext command to help accelerate redraws and regenerations when you are working on the drawing. Qtext turns lines of text into rectangular boxes, saving AutoCAD from having to form every letter. This allows you to see the note locations so you don't accidentally draw over them.

TIP Selecting a large set of text objects for editing can be annoyingly slow. To improve the speed of text selection (and object selection in general), turn off the Highlight and Dragmode system variables. This disables certain convenience features but may improve overall performance, especially on large drawings. See Appendix D for more information on these system variables.

The following steps tell you how to turn on Qtext.

1. Enter **Qtext↵** at the command prompt.

2. At the ON/OFF <OFF>: prompt, enter **ON↵**.

3. To display the results of Qtext, issue the Regen command from the prompt.

NOTE You may also open the Options dialog box (Tools ➤ Options), select the Display tab, then click on the *Show text boundary frame only* option to display text as rectangular regions.

When Qtext is off, text is generated normally. When Qtext is on, rectangles show the approximate size and length of text, as shown in Figure 8.13.

FIGURE 8.13:

View of the Unit file labels with the Qtext system variable turned on

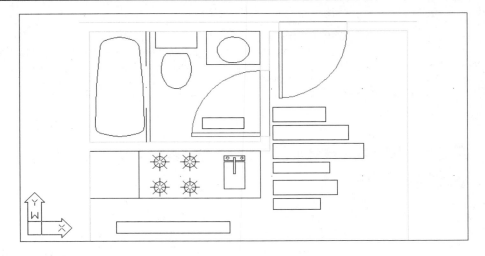

Manipulating Text beyond Labels

This chapter concentrates on methods for adding labels to your drawing, but you also use text in other ways with AutoCAD. Many of the inquiry tools in AutoCAD, such as Dist and List, produce text data. You can use the Windows Clipboard to manipulate such data to your benefit.

For example, you can duplicate the exact length of a line by first using the List command to get a listing of its properties. Once you have the property list in the AutoCAD Text window, you can highlight its length listing and then press Ctrl+C to copy it to the Windows Clipboard. Next, you can start the line command and then pick the start point for the new line. Click the Command window and press Ctrl+V to paste the line length data into the Command window; then add the angle data or use the Direct Distance method to draw the line.

Any text data from dialog box input boxes or the AutoCAD Text window can be copied to the Clipboard using the Ctrl+C keyboard shortcut. That data can likewise be imported into any part of AutoCAD that accepts text.

Consider using the Clipboard the next time you need to transfer data within AutoCAD, or even when you need to import text from some other application.

Express Tools Text-Editing Utilities

Finally, before ending this chapter, you will want to know about a set of bonus utilities that give you the following capabilities:

- Draw text along an arc. If the arc changes, the text follows.
- Adjust the width of a single-line text object to fit within a specified area.
- Explode text into lines.
- Mask areas behind text so that the text is readable when placed over hatch or solid fill patterns.
- Search and replace text for a set of single-line text objects.
- Import external text files.
- Convert single-line text to multiline text.

These functions can save hours of your time when editing a complex drawing that is full of text. You can find out how to access these tools in Chapter 19.

Some additional text-editing tools are included on the companion CD-ROM to this book. These tools let you edit single-line text objects in a word-processing environment (Edsp.lsp), change the oblique angle of a set of text (Oblique.lsp), and change a set of single-line text objects into sequential numbers (Ets.lsp). See Appendix C for details.

If You Want to Experiment...

At this point, you may want to try adding some notes to drawings you have created in other *If You Want to Experiment...* sections of this book. Also, try the exercise shown in Figure 8.14. In addition, you might try importing a finish or door schedule from a word processor in the Monotxt font, to see how that works. If your application is mechanical, you might try importing a parts list.

FIGURE 8.14:

The sample mechanical drawing with notes added

1. Open the file called PART1 that you created in the last chapter. Using the Style command, create a style called Notes. Use the Romans font and give the style a height of .12 units and a width factor of .8.

2. Add the notes shown in this figure using the Dtext command. Place the notes approximately as shown.

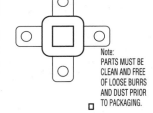

3. When you've finished typing the note, but before you exit Dtext, pick the point shown in this figure. Notice that the Dtext cursor moves to the point you pick.

Pick this point

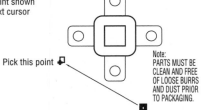

4. Continue to add this second note to your drawing. Press return twice at the end of the last line to exit the Dtext command.

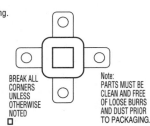

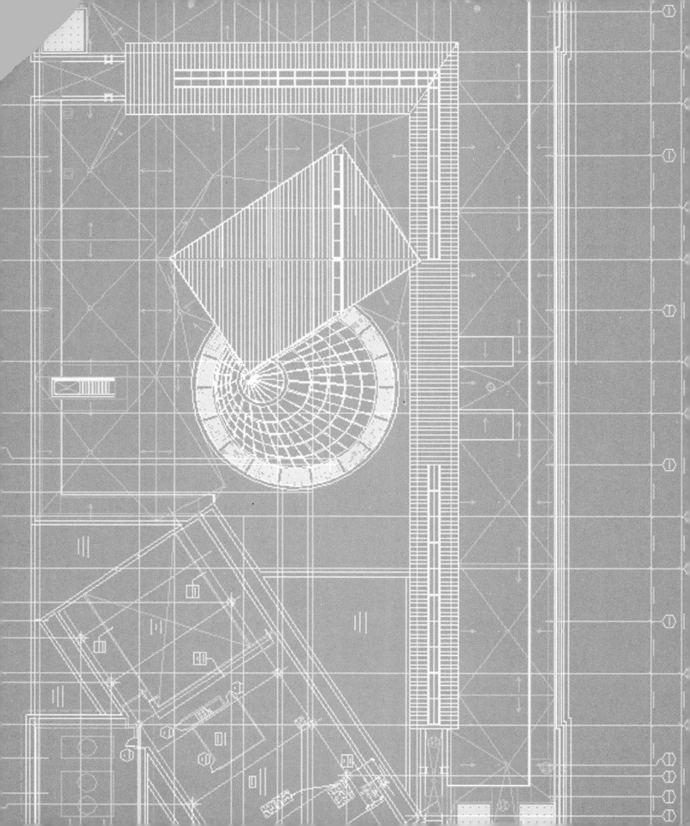

CHAPTER
NINE

Using Dimensions

Before you determine the dimensions of a project, your design is in flux and many questions may be unanswered. Once you begin dimensioning, you will begin to see if things fit or work together. Dimensioning can be crucial to how well a design works and how quickly it develops. The dimensions answer questions about code conformance if you are an architect; they answer questions about tolerances, fit, and interference if you are involved in mechanical applications. Once you and your design team have reached a design on a schematic level, communicating even tentative dimensions to others on the team can accelerate design development. Dimensions represent a point from which you can further develop your ideas.

With AutoCAD, you can easily add tentative or final dimensions to any drawing. AutoCAD gives you an accurate dimension without your having to take measurements. You simply pick the two points to be dimensioned and the dimension line location, and AutoCAD does the rest. AutoCAD's *associative dimensioning* capability automatically updates dimensions whenever the size or shape of the dimensioned object is changed. These dimensioning features can save you valuable time and reduce the number of dimensional errors in your drawings.

AutoCAD's dimensioning feature has many settings. Though they give you an enormous amount of flexibility in formatting your dimensions, all these settings can be somewhat intimidating to the new user. This chapter will ease you into dimensioning by first showing you how to create a *dimension style*.

Understanding the Components of a Dimension

Before you get started with the exercises in this chapter, it will help you to know the names of the different parts of a dimension. Figure 9.1 shows a sample of a dimension with the different parts labeled. The *dimension line* is the line that represents the distance being dimensioned. It is the line with the arrows on either end. The *extension lines* are the lines that originate from the object being dimensioned. They show you the exact location from which the dimension is taken. The *dimension text* is the actual dimension value, usually shown inside or above the dimension line.

Other components of a dimension line include the *dimension line extension*. This is the part of the dimension line that extends beyond the extension line. Dimension line extensions are usually only used on architectural dimensions. The extension lines usually extend beyond the dimension lines in all types of dimensions. The extension line offset from origin is the distance from the beginning of the extension line to the object being dimensioned.

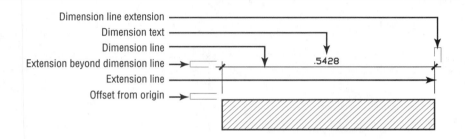

You can control each of these components by creating or editing dimension styles. Dimension styles are the settings that determine the look of your dimensions. You can store multiple styles within a single drawing. Your first exercise in this chapter will show you how to create a dimension style.

Creating a Dimension Style

Dimension styles are similar to text styles. They determine the look of your dimensions as well as the size of dimensioning features, such as the dimension text and arrows. You might set up a dimension style to have special types of arrows, for instance, or to position the dimension text above or in line with the dimension line. Dimension styles also make your work easier by allowing you to store and duplicate your most common dimension settings.

AutoCAD gives you one of two default dimension styles called *ISO-25*, or *Standard*, depending on whether you use the metric or English measurement system. You will probably add many other styles to suit the style of drawings you are creating. You can also create variations of a general style for those situations that call for only minor changes in the dimension's appearance.

In this first section you'll learn how to set up your own dimension style based on the Standard dimension style (see Figure 9.2). For metric users, the settings will be different but the overall methods will be the same.

FIGURE 9.2:

AutoCAD's Standard dimension style compared with an architectural-style dimension

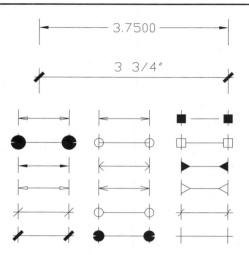

1. Open the Unit file you edited in the last chapter. If you didn't create one, use the 09a-unit.dwg file on the companion CD-ROM and rename it Unit.dwg.

2. Issue Zoom All to display the entire floor plan.

3. Click Format ➤ Dimension Style, or type **D**↵ at the command prompt. The Dimension Style Manager dialog box appears.

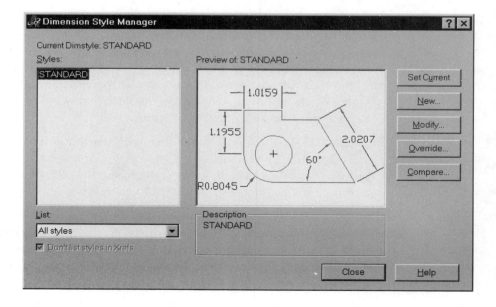

4. Select Standard from the Styles list box. Metric users should select ISO-25.

5. Click New. The New Dimension Style dialog box appears.

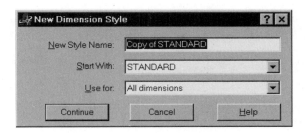

6. With the Copy of Standard or ISO-25 name highlighted in the New Style Name input box, enter **My Architectural**.

7. Click Continue. The detailed New Dimension Style dialog box appears.

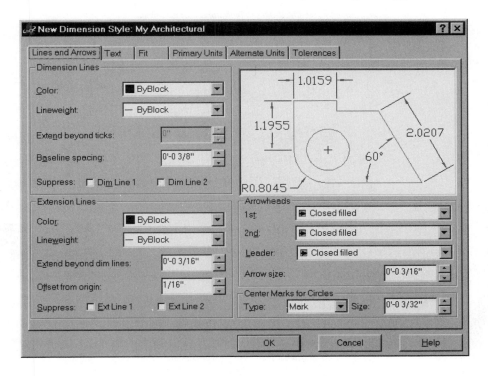

You've just created a dimension style called My Architectural, but at this point, it is identical to the Standard style on which it is based. Nothing has happened to the Standard style; it is still available if you need to use it.

Setting Up the Primary Unit Style

Now you need to set up your new dimension style so that it conforms to the U.S. architectural style of dimensioning. Let's start by changing the unit style for the dimension text. Just as you changed the overall unit style of AutoCAD to a feet-and-inches style for your toilet and tub drawing in Chapter 3, you must do the same for your dimension styles. Setting the overall unit style does not automatically set the dimension unit style.

1. In the New Dimension Style dialog box, click the Primary Units tab. The options for the Primary Units style appear.

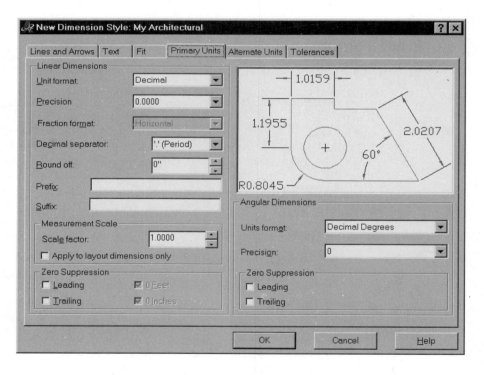

2. In the Linear Dimensions button group, open the Unit Format drop-down list and choose Architectural. Notice that this drop-down list contains the same unit styles as the main Units dialog box (Format ➤ Units). Metric users can skip this option.

NOTE   You might notice the Decimal Separator option a few settings below the Unit Format option. The Decimal Separator option lets you choose between a period or a comma for decimal points. Metric users will often use the comma for a decimal point while U.S. users will use a period. This option doesn't have any meaning for feet-and-inch measurements, so it is dimmed when the Architectural unit format is selected.

---

3. Select 0'-0 1/4" from the Precision option, just below the Unit Format list. Metric users should select 0.00. The Precision option allows you to set the level of precision that is displayed in the dimension text. It doesn't limit the precision of AutoCAD's drawing database. This value is only used to limit the display of dimension text values.

NOTE   Every dimension style setting has an equivalent system variable. See Appendix D for more on system variables that are directly associated with dimensions.

---

4. Just below the Precision option, open the Fraction Format drop-down list and select Diagonal. Notice what happens to the graphic in the right-hand corner of the dialog box. The fractional dimensions change to show you how your dimension text will look. Metric users can skip this step, since it isn't available when the Decimal unit format is selected.

5. In the Zero Suppression button group in the lower-left corner, click 0 Inches to turn off this check box. If you leave it turned on, indications of 0 inches will be omitted from the dimension text. (In architectural drawings, 0 inches are shown as in this dimension: 12'-0".) Metric users can ignore this option.

If you use the English measurement system, you have set up My Architectural's dimension unit style to show dimensions in feet and inches, the standard method for U.S. construction documents. Metric users have just changed the precision value and kept the Decimal unit system.

Setting the Height for Dimension Text

Along with the unit style, you will want to adjust the size of the dimension text. The Text tab of the New Dimension Style dialog box lets you set a variety of text options, including text location relative to the dimension line, style, and height.

1.   Click the Text tab to display the text options.

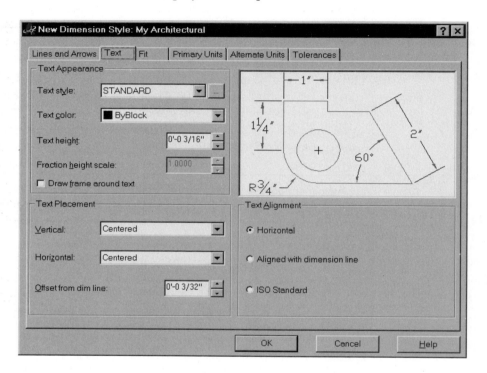

2.   Highlight the contents of the Text Height input box.

3.   Type **1/8**↵ to make the text height 1/8" high. Metric users should enter **0.3**↵ for the text height.

Unlike the text you created in Chapter 8, you specify the text height by its final plot size. You then specify an overall dimension scale factor that affects the sizing of all of the dimensioning settings such as text and arrows.

If you want to use a specific text style for your dimensions, select a text style in the Text Style drop-down list in the Text tab. If the style you select happens to have a height specification greater than 0, then that height will override any text height settings you may enter here in the Text tab.

Setting the Location and Orientation of Dimension Text

AutoCAD's default setting for the placement of dimension text puts the text in line with the dimension line, as shown in the example at the top of Figure 9.2. However, you want the new Architectural style to put the text above the dimension line, as is done at the bottom of Figure 9.2. To do that, you will use the Text Placement and Text Alignment options in the Text tab of the New Dimension Style dialog box.

1. In the Text Alignment group in the lower-right corner of the dialog box, click the Aligned with Dimension Line radio button.

2. In the Text Placement group, open the drop-down list labeled Vertical and select Above. Notice how the appearance of the sample image changes to show you how your new settings will look.

3. Again in the Text Placement group, change the Offset from Dim Line to 1/16. This setting controls the size of the gap between the dimension line and the dimension text.

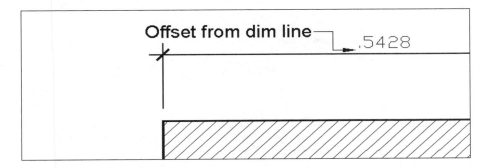

Each time you change a setting, you get immediate feedback on how your changes will affect your dimension style by watching the graphic.

NOTE   Metric users may not need to change these settings, depending on your preference for dimension styles.

Choosing an Arrow Style and Setting the Dimension Scale

Next, you want to specify a different type of arrow for your new dimension style. For linear dimension in architectural drawings, a diagonal line or "tick" mark is typically used, rather than an arrow.

In addition, you want to set the scale for the graphical components of the dimension, such as the arrows and text. Recall from Chapter 8 that text must be scaled up in size in order to appear at the proper size in the final output of the drawing. Dimensions, too, must be scaled so they look correct when the drawing is plotted. The arrows are controlled by settings in the Lines and Arrows tab and the overall scale of the dimension style is set in the Fit tab.

1. Click the Lines and Arrows tab. You see the options for controlling the arrow style and dimension line extensions.

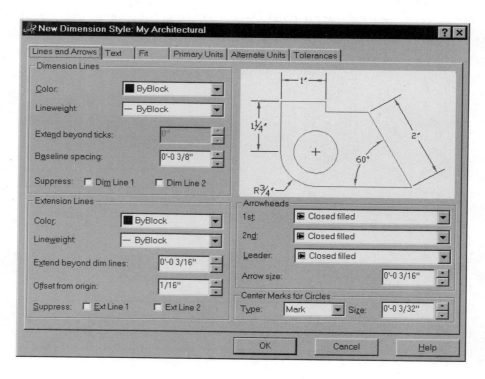

2. In the Arrowheads group, open the drop-down list labeled 1st and choose Architectural Tick. The graphic next to the arrowhead name shows you what the arrowhead looks like.

See Appendix D for details on how you can create your own arrowheads. Also, AutoCAD 2000 lets you setup a separate arrow style for leaders.

3. In the Arrowheads group, change the Arrow Size setting to **1/8**. Metric users should enter **.3**.

4. In the Dimension Lines group, highlight the value in the Extend Beyond Ticks input box, then enter **1/16**. (Metric users should enter **0.15**.) This causes the dimension lines to extend past the tick arrows. This is a standard graphic practice used for dimensioning linear dimensions in architectural plans.

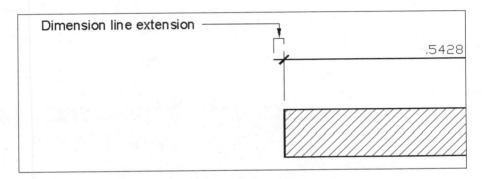

5. In the Extension Lines group, change the Extend Beyond Dim Lines setting to **1/8**. Metric users should change this to **.3**. This setting determines the distance that the extension line extends past the dimension line.

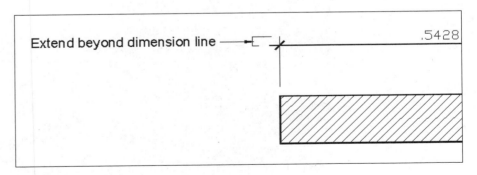

6. Again in the Extension Lines group, change the Offset From Origin setting to **1/8**. Metric users should change this to **.3**. This sets the distance from the point being dimensioned to the beginning of the dimension extension line.

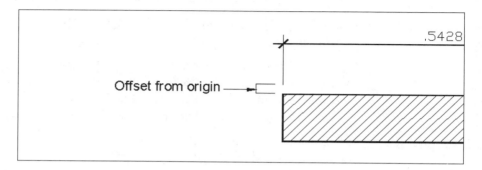

7. Click the Fit tab of the New Dimension Style dialog box to display the options for overall dimension scale and miscellaneous settings.

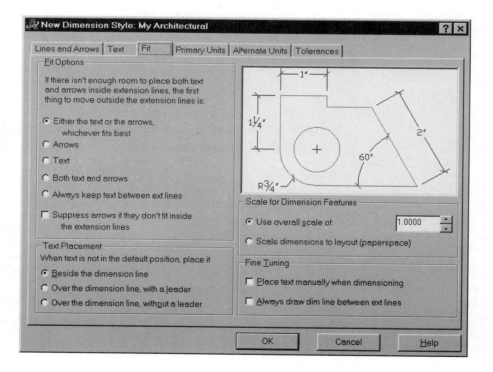

8. In the Scale For Dimension Features group, select the Use Overall Scale of radio button.

9. Double-click the list box just to the right of the Use Overall Scale of radio button, then enter **48**. This is the scale factor for a 1/4" scale drawing. Metric users should enter **50**.

   All of the values that you enter for the various options in the New Dimension Style dialog box will be multiplied by this value to obtain the final size of the dimension components. For example, the text height you entered earlier, 1/8", will be multiplied by 48 for a dimension text height of 6". For metric users, the text height of 0.3 will be multiplied by 50 for a text height of 15cm.

TIP   If you use the Scale Dimensions to Layout (Paperspace) option in the Scale for Dimension Features group of the Fit tab, AutoCAD uses the layout viewport scale to size the dimension components. See Chapter 7 for more information on viewport scale settings. This can be useful if you have a drawing that you want to print at multiple scales.

Fitting Text and Arrows in Tight Places

Every now and then, you'll need to dimension a small gap or a small width of an object that won't allow a dimension text to fit within the dimension. The Fit tab offers a few other settings that control how dimensions act when the extension lines are too close. The Text Placement group offers three options to place the text in tight situations.

Beside the Dimension Line   Places text next to the extension line but close to the dimension line. You'll see how this affects your dimension later.

Over the Dimension Line, with a Leader   Places the dimension text farther away from the dimension line and includes an arrow or leader from the dimension line to the text.

Over the Dimension Line without a Leader   Does the same as the previous setting, but does not include the leader.

The options in the Fit Options group let you control how text and arrows are placed when there isn't enough room for both of them between the extension lines.

Setting Up Alternate Units

You can use the Alternate Units tab of the New Dimension Style dialog box to set up AutoCAD to display a second dimension in centimeters or millimeters. Likewise, if you are a metric user, you can set up a second dimension to display feet and inches. In most situations, you won't need to use these alternate units, but for our exercise you'll use them for the benefit of AutoCAD users in all parts of the world.

Now take the following steps to add alternate units to your dimension style.

TIP   If you decide later that you do not want the alternate units to be displayed, you can turn them off by returning to this dialog box and removing the check in the Display Alternate Units check box.

1. In the New Dimension Style dialog box, select the Alternate Units tab.

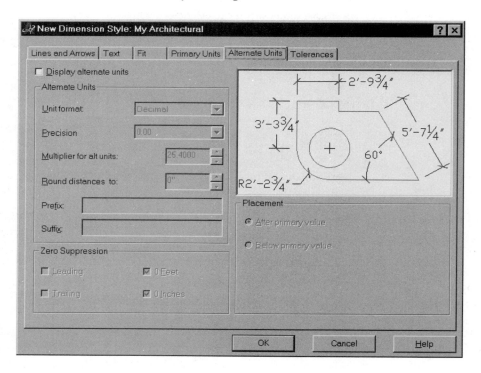

2. Click the Display Alternate Units check box. The options in the tab become available for your input.

3. Select the appropriate option from the Unit Format drop-down list. U.S. users should select Decimal to show metric alternate units. Metric users should select Architectural.

4. Select 0.00 from the Precision drop-down list. Metric users should select 1/4".

5. Enter a scale factor for your alternate dimension in the Multiplier for Alt Units input box. For U.S. users, the default value is 25.4. This value converts feet-and-inch dimensions to millimeters. In our metric examples, you've been using centimeters so change this setting to **2.54**. Metric users should enter **0.3937** to convert centimeters to feet and inches.

6. In the Placement group, select the Below Primary Value option.

7. Click OK to exit the New Dimension Style dialog box. The Dimension Style Manager dialog box reappears.

Setting the Current Dimension Style

Before you can begin to use your new dimension style, you must make it the current default.

1. Click My Architectural in the Styles list box in the Dimension Style Manager dialog box.

2. Click the Set Current button in the far-right side of the dialog box.

3. Click Close to exit the Dimension Style Manager dialog box.

You're now ready to use your new dimension style.

In the next set of exercises, you will be using the My Architectural style you just created. To switch to another style, open the Dimension Style Manager dialog box again, select the style you want from the Styles list, and click Set Current, just as you did in the previous exercise.

Modifying a Dimension Style

To modify an existing dimension style, open the Dimension Style Manager dialog box, highlight the style you want to edit, then click Modify. The Modify Dimension Style dialog box appears, which is virtually identical to the New Dimension Style dialog box you've been working with. You can then make changes to the different components of the selected dimension style. When you've finished making changes and closed both dialog boxes, all of the dimensions associated with the edited style will update automatically in your drawing. For example, if you decide you need to change the dimension scale of a style, you can open the Modify Dimension Style dialog box and change the Scale value in the Fit tab. In prior versions of AutoCAD, you had to use the Update option and manually select each dimension that required the new setting.

This section introduced you to the various settings that let you set the appearance of a dimension style. This section didn't discuss every option, so if you want to learn more about the other dimension style options, consult Appendix D. There you'll find descriptions of all the items in the Dimension Style dialog box, plus reference material covering the system variables associated with each option.

Using Grids in Architectural Dimensions

Common, if not essential, elements in architectural drawings are the building grids. These are the center lines of the main structural components, which are usually the columns and structural walls of the building. Grids are labeled similarly to map grids, with numeric labels going horizontally and alphabetical labels going vertically. A circle or hexagon is used at the end of the grid to label it. The grids are the first items dimensioned and all other building components are dimensioned from the grid lines. The San Francisco Main Library made ample use of grids, incorporating both major and minor grid systems. There, a hexagon was used to label the grids.

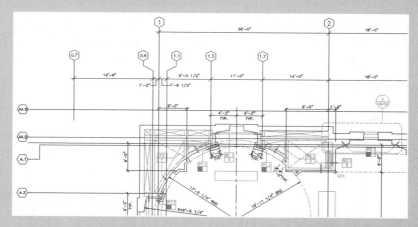

Continued on next page

Since the structural components of a building are usually the first parts that are put in place, they play a crucial role in locating other components of the building during the construction process. When producing floor plans, the grid is usually the first thing an architect draws, mimicking to some degree the construction process. All other elements of the plan are then drawn in relation to that grid.

While working in AutoCAD, you can use a grid to start to build your drawing. Once the grid is in place, you can use the Offset tool to locate walls or other building components. Using AutoCAD's tracking feature, you can easily align drawing elements to grid lines.

Drawing Linear Dimensions

The most common type of dimension you'll be using is the *linear dimension*. The linear dimension is an orthogonal dimension measuring the width and length of an object. AutoCAD offers three dimensioning tools for this purpose: Linear (Dimlinear), Continue (Dimcont), and Baseline (Dimbase). These options are readily accessible from the Dimension toolbar or the Dimension pull-down menu.

WARNING In the following exercise, you'll see figures displaying dimensions with feet and inches as the primary unit style above the dimension line. Metric dimensions will be shown below the primary units. If you have been following the exercises using the metric system, your display will have the two dimensions switched with metric dimensions above the dimension line and the feet and inches below.

Finding the Dimension Toolbar

Before you apply any dimension, you'll want to open the Dimension toolbar. This toolbar contains nearly all the commands necessary to draw and edit your dimensions.

Right-click any toolbar. At the popup menu, click Dimension from the list of toolbars. The Dimension toolbar appears.

The Dimension commands are also available from the Dimension pull-down menu.

Now you're ready to begin dimensioning.

Placing Horizontal and Vertical Dimensions

Let's start by looking at the basic dimensioning tool, Linear Dimension. The Linear Dimension button (the Dimlinear command) on the Dimension toolbar accommodates both the horizontal and vertical dimensions.

In this exercise, you'll add a vertical dimension to the right side of the Unit plan.

1. To start either a vertical or horizontal dimension, click Linear Dimension on the Dimension toolbar, or enter **Dli.⏎** at the command prompt. You can also choose Dimension ➤ Linear from the pull-down menu.

2. The Specify first extension line origin or <select object>: prompt is asking you for the first point of the distance to be dimensioned. An extension line is the line that connects the object being dimensioned to the dimension line. Use the Endpoint Osnap override and pick the upper-right corner of the entry, as shown in Figure 9.3.

3. At the Specify second extension line origin: prompt, pick the lower-right corner of the living room, as shown in Figure 9.3.

4. In the next prompt,

    ```
    Specify dimension line location or
    [Mtext/Text/Angle/Horizontal/Vertical/Rotated]:
    ```

    the dimension line is the line indicating the direction of the dimension and containing the arrows or tick marks. Move your cursor from left to right, and a temporary dimension appears. This allows you to visually select a dimension line location.

NOTE In step 4, you have the option to append information to the dimension's text or change the dimension text altogether. You'll see how later in this chapter.

5. Enter **@4'<0**↵ to tell AutoCAD you want the dimension line to be 4' to the right of the last point you selected. Metric users should enter **@122<0**↵. (You could pick a point using your cursor, but this doesn't let you place the dimension line as accurately.) After you've done this, the dimension is placed in the drawing, as shown in Figure 9.3.

FIGURE 9.3:

The dimension line added to the Unit drawing

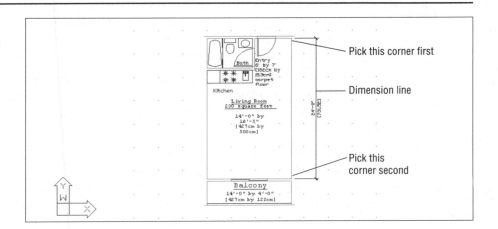

Continuing a Dimension

You will often want to enter a group of dimensions strung together in a line. For example, you may want to continue dimensioning the balcony and have the continued dimension aligned with the dimension you just entered. To do this, use the

Continue option found in both the Dimension toolbar and the Dimension pull-down menu.

1. Click the Continue Dimension option on the Dimension toolbar, or enter **Dco**↵. You can also choose Dimension ➤ Continue from the pull-down menu.

2. At the `Specify a second extension line origin or [Undo/Select] <Select>:` prompt, pick the upper-right corner of the balcony (see the top image of Figure 9.4).

3. Pick the right end of the rail on the balcony. See the bottom image of Figure 9.4 for the results.

4. Press ↵ twice to exit the command.

TIP   If you find you've selected the wrong location for a continued dimension, you can click the Undo tool or press **U**↵ to back up your dimension.

The Continue Dimension option adds a dimension from where you left off. The last drawn extension line is used as the first extension line for the continued dimension. AutoCAD keeps adding dimensions as you continue to pick points, until you press ↵.

You probably noticed that the last two dimensions you just added overlap each other. This is the result of the 5" dimensions not having enough space to fit between the dimension extension lines. You'll learn about dimension style settings that can remedy this problem. For now, let's continue with adding dimensions to the plan.

Continuing a Dimension from a Previous Dimension

If you need to continue a string of dimensions from an older linear dimension, instead of the most recently added one, press ↵ at the `Specify a second extension line origin or (<select>/Undo):` prompt you saw in step 2 of the previous exercise. Then, at the `Select continued dimension:` prompt, click the extension line from which you wish to continue.

The dimension string
continued and completed

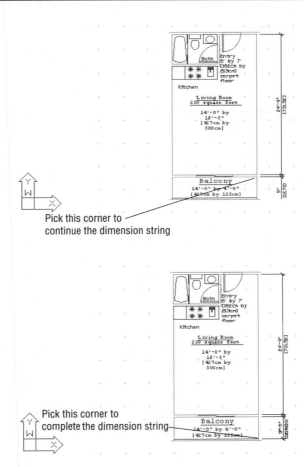

Pick this corner to
continue the dimension string

Pick this corner to
complete the dimension string

Drawing Dimensions from a Common Base Extension Line

Another method for dimensioning objects is to have several dimensions originate from the same extension line. To accommodate this, AutoCAD provides the Baseline option on the Dimension toolbar or Dimension pull-down menu. To see how this works, you will start another dimension—this time a horizontal one—across the top of the plan.

1. Click Linear Dimension on the Dimension toolbar. Or, just as you did for the vertical dimension, you can type **Dli↵** to start the horizontal dimension. This option is also on the Dimension pull-down menu.

2. At the `Specify first extension line origin or <select object>:` prompt, use the endpoint Osnap to pick the upper-left corner of the bathroom, as shown in Figure 9.5.

3. At the `Specify second extension line origin:` prompt, pick the upper-right corner of the bathroom, as shown in Figure 9.5.

4. At the prompt;

```
Specify dimension line location or
   [Mtext/Text/Angle/Horizontal/Vertical/Rotated]:
```

pick a point above the unit plan, as shown in Figure 9.5. If you need to, pan your view downward to fit the dimension in.

TIP   Since you usually pick exact locations on your drawing as you dimension, you may want to turn on the Running Osnaps to avoid the extra step of selecting Osnaps from the Osnap popup menu.

FIGURE 9.5:

The bathroom with horizontal dimensions

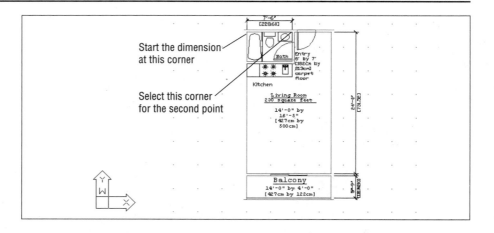

Now you're all set to draw another dimension continuing from the first extension line of the dimension you just drew.

5. Click the Baseline Dimension option on the Dimension toolbar. Or you can type **Dba**⏎ at the command prompt to start a baseline dimension.

6. At the `Specify second extension line origin or [Undo/Select] <Select>:` prompt, click the upper-right corner of the entry, as shown in Figure 9.6.

7. Press ⏎ twice to exit the Baseline Dimension command.

8. Pan your view down so it looks similar to Figure 9.6.

FIGURE 9.6:

The overall width dimension

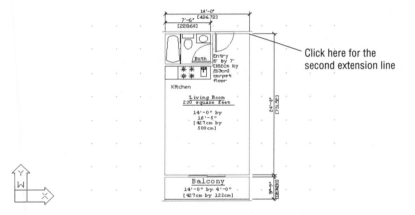

In this example, you see that the Baseline Dimension option is similar to the Continue Dimension option, except that the Baseline Dimension option allows you to use the first extension line of the previous dimension as the base for a second dimension.

Continuing from an Older Dimension

You may have noticed in step 7 that you had to press ⏎ twice to exit the command. As with Continue Dimension, you can draw the baseline dimension from an older dimension by pressing ⏎ at the `Specify a second extension line origin [Undo/Select] <select>:` prompt. You then get the `Select base dimension:` prompt, at which you can either select another dimension or press ⏎ again to exit the command.

Editing Dimensions

As you begin to add more dimensions to your drawings, you will find that Auto-CAD will occasionally place a dimension text or line in an inappropriate location, or you may need to make a modification to the dimension text. In this section, you'll take an in-depth look at how dimensions can be modified to suit those special circumstances that always crop up.

Appending Data to Dimension Text

So far in this chapter, you've been accepting the default dimension text. You can append information to the default dimension value, or change it entirely if you need to. At the point when you see the temporary dimension dragging with your cursor, enter **T**↵. Then, by using the less than (<) and greater than (>) symbols, you can add text either before or after the default dimension or replace the symbols entirely to replace the default text. The Properties button on the Object Properties toolbar lets you modify the existing dimension text in a similar way. Let's see how this works by changing an existing dimension's text in your drawing.

1. Choose Modify ➤ Text or type **ED**↵.

2. Next, click the last horizontal dimension you added to the drawing at the top of the screen.

3. Press ↵. The Multiline Text Editor dialog box appears.

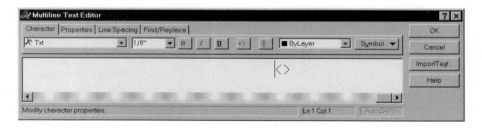

4. Click the Contents input box, move the cursor behind the <> sign, and then type **to face of stud**.

5. Click OK. The dimension changes to read "14'-0' to face of stud." The text you entered is appended below the dimension text.

6. Because you don't really need the new appended text for the tutorial, click the Undo button in the Standard toolbar to remove the appended text.

TIP Place your appended text in front of the <> symbols if you want to add text to the beginning of the dimension text. You can also replace the dimension text entirely by replacing the <> sign in the Contents input box with new text. If you want to restore a dimension that has been modified, delete everything in the Contents input box, including space. Or, include a space to leave the dimension text blank.

NOTE In this exercise, you were only able to edit a single dimension. To append text to several dimensions at once, you need to use the Dimension Edit tool. See the *Making Changes to Multiple Dimensions* sidebar in this chapter for more on this command.

You can also have AutoCAD automatically add a dimension suffix or prefix to all dimensions, instead of just a chosen few, by using the Suffix or Prefix option in the Primary Units tab of the Dimension Style dialog box. See Appendix D for more on this feature.

Making Changes to Multiple Dimensions

The Dimension Edit tool offers a quick way to edit existing dimensions. It gives you the ability to edit more than one dimension's text at one time. One common use for the Dimension Edit tool might be to change a string of dimensions to read "Equal", instead of showing the actual dimensioned distance. The following example shows an alternative to the Properties tool for appending text to a dimension.

1. Click the Dimension Edit tool in the Dimension toolbar, or type **Ded⏎**.

2. At this prompt:

   ```
   Enter type of dimension Edit [Home/New/Rotate/Oblique]<Home>:
   ```

   type **N⏎** to use the New option. The Multiline Text Editor appears showing the <> brackets in the text box.

3. Click the space behind or in front of the <> brackets, and then enter the text you want to append to the dimension. Or you can replace the brackets entirely to replace the dimension with your text.

Continued on next page

4. Click OK.

5. At the `Select objects:` prompt, pick the dimensions you wish to edit. The `Select objects:` prompt remains, allowing you to select several dimensions.

6. Press ↵ to finish your selection. The dimension changes to include your new text or to replace the existing dimension text.

The Dimension Edit tool is useful in editing dimension text, but you can also use this command to make graphical changes to the text. Here is a listing of the other Dimension Edit tool options:

Home   Moves the dimension text to its standard default position and angle.

Rotate   Allows you to rotate the dimension text to a new angle.

Oblique   Skews the dimension extension lines to a new angle. See the *Skewing Dimension Lines* section later in this chapter.

Locating the Definition Points

AutoCAD provides the associative dimensioning capability to automatically update dimension text when a drawing is edited. Objects called *definition points* are used to determine how edited dimensions are updated.

The definition points are located at the same points you pick when you determine the dimension location. For example, the definition points for linear dimensions are the extension line origin and the intersection of the extension line/dimension line. The definition points for a circle diameter are the points used to pick the circle and the opposite side of the circle. The definition points for a radius are the points used to pick the circle, plus the center of the circle.

Definition points are actually point objects. They are very difficult to see because they are usually covered by the feature that they define. You can, however, see them indirectly using grips. The definition points of a dimension are the same as the dimension's grip points. You can see them simply by clicking a dimension. Try the following:

1. Make sure the Grips feature is turned on (see Chapter 2 to refresh your memory on the Grips feature).

2. Click the longest of the three vertical dimensions you drew in the earlier exercise. You will see the grips of the dimension, as shown in Figure 9.7.

FIGURE 9.7:

The grip points are the same as the definition points on a dimension.

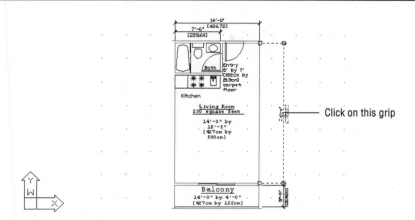

Click on this grip

Making Minor Adjustments to Dimensions Using Grips

The definition points, whose location you can see through their grips, are located on their own unique layer called Defpoints. Definition points are displayed regardless of whether the Defpoints layer is on or off. To give you an idea of how these definition points work, try the following exercises, which show you how to directly manipulate the definition points.

1. With the grips visible, click the grip near the dimension text.

TIP

Since the Defpoints layer has the unique feature of being visible even when turned off, you can use it as a layer for laying out your drawing. While Defpoints is turned off, you can still see objects assigned to it, but the objects won't plot.

2. Move the cursor around. Notice that when you move the cursor vertically, the text moves along the dimension line. When you move the cursor horizontally, the dimension line and text move together, keeping their parallel orientation to the dimensioned floor plan.

Here the entire dimension line, including the text, moves. In a later exercise, you'll see how you can move the dimension text independently of the dimension line.

3. Enter **@9'<0↵**. Metric users should enter **@275<0↵**. The dimension line, text, and the dimension extensions move to the new location to the right of the text (see Figure 9.8).

FIGURE 9.8:

Moving the dimension line using its grip

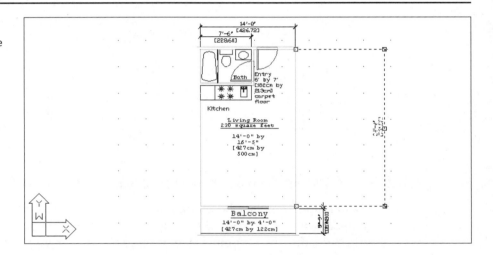

If you need to move several dimension lines at once, select them all at the command prompt; then Shift+click one set of dimension-line grips from each dimension. Once you've selected the grips, click one of the hot grips again. You can then move all the dimension lines at once.

In step 3 of the last exercise you saw that you can specify an exact distance for the dimension line's new location by entering a relative polar coordinate. Cartesian coordinates work just as well. You can even use object snaps to relocate dimension lines. Next, try moving the dimension line back using the Perpendicular Osnap.

1. Click the grip at the bottom of the dimension line you just edited.

2. Shift+click the right mouse button and choose Perpendicular from the Osnap popup menu.

3. Place the cursor on the vertical dimension line that dimensions the balcony and click it.

4. The selected dimension line moves to align with the other vertical dimension, back to its original location.

Changing Style Settings of Individual Dimensions

In some cases, you will have to make changes to an individual dimension's style setting in order to edit that dimension. For example, if you try to move the text of a typical linear dimension, you'll find that the text and dimension lines are inseparable. You need to make a change to the dimension style setting that controls how AutoCAD locates dimension text in relation to the dimension line. This section describes how you can make changes to the style settings of individual dimensions to facilitate changes in the dimension.

TIP If you need to change the dimension style of a dimension to match that of another, you can use the Match Properties tool. See the *How to Quickly Match a Hatch Pattern and Other Properties* sidebar in Chapter 6 for details on how to use this tool.

Moving a Fixed Dimension Text

You may remember that in an earlier exercise where you added a continued dimension, two dimensions' text ended up overlapping each other. In situations like that, you will want to manually move an overlapping dimension text away from the dimension line, but as you saw in an earlier exercise, this cannot be done with the current settings.

In the next exercise, you will make a change to a single dimension's style settings. Then you'll use grips to move the dimension text away from the dimension line.

1. Press the Esc key twice to cancel the grip selection from the previous exercise.

2. Zoom into lower-right side of the balcony area so you have a view similar to Figure 9.9.

3. Click the 5" dimension to expose its grips. This may be a bit tricky since it closely overlaps the 3'-9" dimension. If you need to, use the Selection Cycling feature to isolate the 5" dimension. (See *Singling Out Proximate Objects* in Chapter 12.)

4. Click the Properties tool in the Standard toolbar.

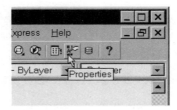

5. Scroll down the list of properties until you see an option called Fit, then click the plus sign to the left of the Fit option. A new set of options appears below the Fit option.

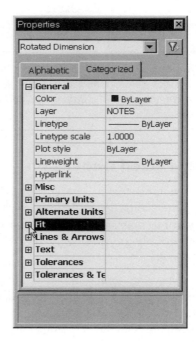

6. Scroll down the list further until you see the Keep Dim Line with Text option, then click this option.

7. Click the arrow that appears next to it to open the drop-down list, then select the Move Text, Add Leader option.

The dimension moves away from its original location to a new one away from the 3'-9" balcony dimension.

8. Close the Properties dialog box.

9. AutoCAD uses the grip on the 5" dimension to move it to a new location next to dimension extension lines as shown in Figure 9.9.

10. Zoom back to your previous view.

11. Now choose File ➤ Save to save this file in its current state.

In the Properties dialog box, the Move Text, Add Leader option in the Fit options lets you move the dimension text independently of the dimension line. It also causes a leader to be drawn from the dimension line to the text.

As you can see from this exercise, the Properties dialog box gives you access to many of the settings that you saw for setting up dimension styles. The main difference here is that the Properties dialog box only affects the dimensions that you have selected.

FIGURE 9.9:

Selecting then moving
the 5" dimension

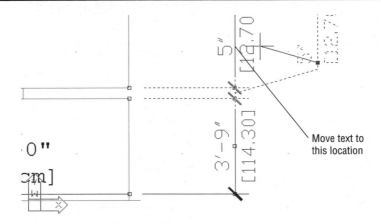

In the previous exercise, you changed the format setting of a single dimension *after* it was placed. These settings can be made a standard part of your Architectural dimension style by using the Modify button in the Dimension Style Manager dialog box.

> **TIP**   If you have multiple dimension styles and you want to change an existing dimension to the current dimension style, use the Dimension Update tool. Click the Dimension Update tool on the Dimension toolbar, or choose Dimension Update from the pull-down menu. Then select the dimensions you want to change. Press ↵ when you are done selecting dimensions. The selected dimensions will be converted to the current style.

Rotating a Dimension Text

Once in a while, a dimension text works better if it is kept in a horizontal orientation, even if the dimension itself is not horizontal. If you find you need to rotate dimension text, here's the way to do it.

1. First, click the Undo button twice in the toolbar or type **U↵↵** to return the 5" dimension to its original location.

2. Click the Dimension Edit tool in the Dimension toolbar.

3. At the `Enter type of dimension editing [Home/New/Rotate/Oblique]` `<Home>`: prompt, enter **R**↵.

4. At the `Enter text angle:` prompt, type **45**↵ to rotate the text to a 45° angle.

5. At the `Select objects:` prompt, click the 5" dimension text again. Press ↵.

6. Click the Undo button to undo the text rotation. You won't want to save this change to your drawing.

TIP   You can also choose Dimension ➤ Align Text ➤ Angle, select the dimension text, and then enter an angle. A 0-degree angle will cause the dimension text to return to its default angle.

The Dimension Text Edit tool (Dimtedit command) also allows you to align the dimension text to either the left or right side of the dimension line. This is similar to the Alignment option in the Multiline Text Editor that controls text justification.

As you have seen in this section, the Grips feature is especially well suited to editing dimensions. With grips, you can stretch, move, copy, rotate, mirror, and scale dimensions.

Modifying the Dimension Style Settings Using Override

In the *Moving a Fixed Dimension Text* section, you used the Properties button on the toolbar to facilitate the moving of the dimension text. You can also use the Dimension ➤ Override option (Dimoverride command) to accomplish the same thing. The Override option allows you to make changes to an individual dimension's style settings. Here's an example showing how the Override option can be used in place of the Properties button in the first exercise of the *Moving a Fixed Dimension Text* section.

1. Press the Esc key twice to make sure you are not in the middle of a command. Then choose Dimension ➤ Override from the pull-down menu.

2. At the next prompt:

`Enter dimension variable name to override or [Clear overrides]:` type **Dimfit** ↵.

Continued on next page

3. At the `Current value <3>:` prompt, enter **4**↵. This has the same effect as selecting Move Text, Add Leader from the Fit option of the Properties dialog box.

4. The `Enter dimension variable to override…` prompt appears again, allowing you to enter another dimension variable. Press ↵ to move to the next step.

5. At the `Select objects:` prompt, select the dimension you want to change. You can select a group of dimensions if you want to change several dimensions at once. Press ↵ when you are done with your selection. The dimension settings will change for the selected dimensions.

As you can see from this example, the Dimoverride command requires that you know exactly which dimension variable to edit in order to make the desired modification. In this case, setting the Dimfit variable to 4 lets you move the dimension text independently of the dimension line. If you find the Dimoverride command useful, consult Appendix D to find which system variable corresponds to the Dimension Style dialog box settings.

Understanding the Dimension Text Edit Tool

One dimension text-editing tool you haven't used yet is the Dimension Text Edit tool.

While it may sound as though this tool allows you to edit dimension text, its purpose is to allow you to quickly position dimension text to either the left, right, or center of the dimension line. To use it, choose Dimension Text Edit from the toolbar, then click the dimension text you want to move. You'll see the prompt

```
Click on a dimension and the Select dimension: Specify new location for
dimension text or [Left/Right/Center/Home/Angle]:
```

You can then enter the letter of the option you want. For example, if you enter **L**↵, the dimension text moves to the left side of the dimension line.

Editing Dimensions and Other Objects Together

Certainly it's helpful to be able to edit a dimension directly using its grips. But the key feature of AutoCAD's dimensions is their ability to *automatically* adjust themselves to changes in the drawing. As long as you include the dimension's definition points when you select objects to edit, the dimensions themselves will automatically update to reflect the change in your drawing.

To see how this works, try moving the living room closer to the bathroom wall. You can move a group of lines and vertices using the Stretch command and the Crossing option.

1. Click the Stretch tool in the Modify palette, or type **S**↵ and then **C**↵. You will see the following prompt:

    ```
    At the Select objects to stretch by crossing-window or -polygon...
    Select objects: C
    Specify first corner:
    ```

2. Pick a crossing window, as illustrated in Figure 9.10. Then press ↵ to confirm your selection.

FIGURE 9.10:

The Stretch crossing window

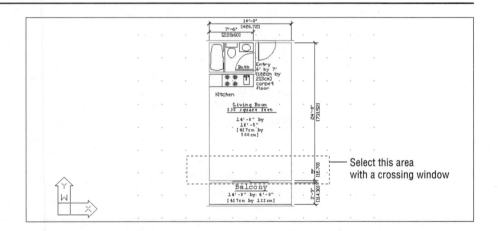

3. At the Specify base point or displacement: prompt, pick any point on the screen.

4. At the Specify second point of displacement: prompt, enter **@2'<90** to move the wall 2' in a 90° direction. The wall moves, and the dimension text changes to reflect the new dimension, as shown in Figure 9.11.

TIP

In some situations, you may find that a crossing window selects objects other than those you want to stretch. This frequently occurs when many objects are close together at the location of a vertex you want to stretch. To be more selective about the vertices you move and their corresponding objects, use a standard window instead of a crossing window to select the vertices. Then pick the individual objects whose vertices you wish to move.

FIGURE 9.11:

The moved wall, with the updated dimensions

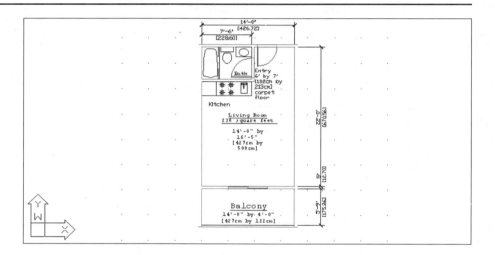

When you selected the crossing window corners, you included the definition points of both vertical dimensions. This allowed you to move the dimension extension lines along with the wall, thereby updating the dimensions automatically.

Understanding the Stretch Command

The tool you used for moving the wall and the dimension line extensions is the Stretch command. This is one of the most useful, yet least understood commands offered by AutoCAD. Think of the Stretch command as a vertex mover: Its sole purpose is to move the vertices (or endpoints) of objects.

Continued on next page

The Stretch command actually requires you to do two things: select the objects you want to edit, and then select the vertices you wish to move. The crossing window and the Cpolygon window are convenient ways of killing two birds with one stone because they select objects and vertices in one operation. But when you want to be more selective, you can click objects and window vertices instead. For example, consider the exercise in this chapter where you moved a wall with the Stretch command. To move the walls but not the dimension-line extensions, take the following steps:

1. Click the Stretch tool on the Modify toolbar or click Stretch on the Modify pull-down menu. You may also type **S**↵.

2. At the `Select objects:` prompt, enter **W**↵ (Window) or **WP**↵ (Window Polygon).

3. Window the vertices you wish to move. Since the Window and Window Polygon selection options select objects completely enclosed within the window, most of the items you want to stretch will already be selected.

4. Click the vertical walls to include them in the set of objects to be edited.

5. Press ↵ to finish your selection.

6. Indicate the base point and second point for the stretch.

You could also use the Remove Selection option and click the dimensions to deselect them in the previous exercise. Then, when you enter the base and second points, the walls move but the dimensions stay in place.

Stretch will stretch only the vertices included in the last window, crossing window, crossing polygon, or window polygon (see Chapter 2 for more on these selection options). Thus, if you had attempted to window another part of your drawing in the wall-moving exercise, nothing would have moved. Before Stretch will do anything, objects need to be highlighted (selected) and their endpoints windowed.

The Stretch command is especially well suited to editing dimensioned objects, and when you use it with the Crossing Polygon (CP) or Window Polygon (WP) selection options, you have substantial control over what gets edited.

You can also use the Mirror, Rotate, and Stretch commands with dimensions. The polar arrays also work, and Extend and Trim can be used with linear dimensions.

When editing dimensioned objects, be sure to select the dimension associated with the object being edited. As you select objects, using the Crossing (C) or Crossing Polygon (CP) selection option helps you include the dimensions. For more on these selection options, see the *Other Selection Options* sidebar in Chapter 2.

TIP   If you have some dimension text that overlaps a hatch pattern, and the hatch pattern obscures the text, you can use the Wipeout tool on the Express toolbar to mask out portions of the hatch. If a hatch pattern or solid fill completely covers a dimension, you can use the Draworder command to have AutoCAD draw the dimension over the hatch or solid fill. See Chapter 19 for more on the Bonus Tools and Chapter 13 for more on the Draworder command.

Adding a String of Dimensions with a Single Operation

AutoCAD 2000 offers a method for creating a string of dimensions using a single operation. The Qdim command lets you select a set of objects instead of having to select points. The following exercise demonstrates how the Qdim command works.

1. Zoom out so you have an overall view of the Unit floor plan.

2. Choose Dimension ➢ Qdim or click Quick Dimension on the Dimension toolbar.

3. At the `Select geometry to dimension:` prompt, place a selection window around the entire left-side wall of the unit.

4. Press ↵ to finish your selection. The following prompt appears:

   ```
   Specify dimension line position, or
   [Continuous/Staggered/Baseline/Ordinate/Radius/Diameter/datumPoint/
   Edit] <Continuous>:
   ```

5. Click a point to the left of the wall to place the dimension. A string of dimensions appears, displaying all the dimensions for the wall.

6. When you are done reviewing the results of this exercise, exit the file without saving it.

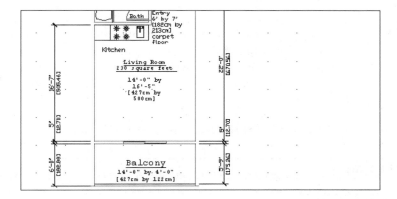

The prompt in step 4 indicates several types of dimensions you can choose from. For example, if you want the dimensions to originate from a single baseline, you can enter **B** ↵ in step 5 to select the Baseline option.

The Qdim command can be a time-saver when you want to dimension a wall quickly. It may not work in all situations, but if the object you're dimensioning is fairly simple, it may be all you need.

TIP   In this exercise, you used a simple window to select the wall. For more complex shapes, try using a crossing polygon selection window. See *Other Selection Options* in Chapter 2 for more on crossing polygons.

Removing the Alternate Dimensions

In the beginning of this chapter, you set up the My Architectural dimension style to include an alternate dimension. You can remove those alternate dimensions by turning off the alternate dimension features. Here's how it's done.

1. Choose Dimension ➤ Style or enter **D** ↵.

2. In the Dimension Style Manager dialog box, select the style that uses the Alternate Units. In the Styles list box, click Modify.

3. Select the Alternate Units tab.

4. Click the Display Alternate Units check box to remove the checkmark.

5. Click OK, then click Close in the Dimension Style Manager dialog box.

The dimensions that use the style you just edited change to remove the alternate dimensions. You can also perform the reverse operation and add alternate dimensions to an existing set of dimensions. Follow the steps shown here, but instead of removing the checkmark in step 4, add the checkmark and make the appropriate setting changes to the rest of the Alternate Units tab.

Using Osnap While Dimensioning

WARNING There is a drawback to setting a Running Osnap mode: When your drawing gets crowded, you may end up picking the wrong point by accident. However, you can easily toggle the Running Osnap mode off by clicking the OSNAP label in the status bar.

You may find that when you pick intersections and endpoints frequently, as during dimensioning, it is a bit inconvenient to use the Osnap popup menu. In situations where you know you will be using certain Osnaps frequently, you can use Running Osnaps. You can do so in the following two ways:

- Click Tools ➤ Drafting Settings. In the Object Snap tab of the Drafting Settings dialog box, make sure the Object Snap On check box is checked and then select the desired default Osnap mode. You can pick more than one mode, for example, Intersection, Endpoint, and Midpoint, so that whichever geometry you happen to be nearest will be the point selected.

- Another way to accomplish this is to type **–osnap**↵ at the command prompt, and then enter the name of the Osnap modes you want to use. If you want to use more than one mode, enter their names separated by commas; for example:

```
endpoint,midpoint,intersect
```

Once you've designated your Running Osnaps, the next time you are prompted to select a point, the selected Osnap modes are automatically activated. You can still override the default settings using the Osnap popup menu (Shift+click the right mouse button). You can toggle the Running Osnaps on or off by clicking the OSNAP label in the status bar, or by pressing F3. The toggle feature is especially helpful in crowded drawings where you may accidentally select an Osnap location while panning or zooming or selecting points for other operations.

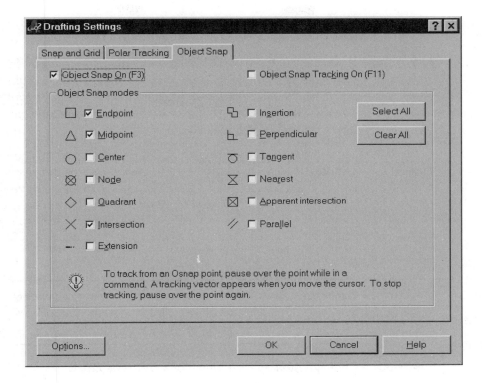

Dimensioning Nonorthogonal Objects

So far, you've been reading about how to work with linear dimensions. You can also dimension nonorthogonal objects, such as circles, arcs, triangles, and trapezoids. In this section, you will practice dimensioning nonorthogonal objects by drawing an elevation of a window in the set of plans for your studio apartment building. You'll start by setting up the drawing, then drawing the window itself.

1.   Create a new file called Window.

2.   In the Create New Drawing wizard, click the Start From Scratch icon at the top, then click the English radio button if you are using feet and inches or click the Metric radio button. This is important because depending on which option you select, AutoCAD will set up the drawing with different dimension style defaults. AutoCAD will create a style called ISO-25 as the default style for metric users.

3. Set the file up as an architectural drawing at a scale of 3"=1'-0" on an 8 1/2" × 11" sheet. Metric users set up an A4 sheet at a scale of 1:4.

4. If you are using the English measurement system, start by setting the dimension scale to 4. Normally, you would use the Dimension Style Manager dialog box to set the dimension scale. A shortcut to do this is by typing **Dimscale**↵ 4↵. This changes the scale factor of the current dimension style to 4. Metric users can use the default setting.

5. There are two more settings that English system users should set. Enter **Dimtih**↵ 0↵. This turns off the setting that forces the dimension text to be horizontal. Next type **Dimtad**↵ 1↵. This turns on the text-above-dimension feature. You'll want these two settings on to match the appearance of text in the metric ISO-25 style. Again, metric users do not have to change these settings.

Now you are ready to start drawing the window.

WARNING   In the figures shown for the following exercises, you'll see both English and metric dimensions for the benefit of users of both systems. Your view will only contain the measurement in the system you've chosen in the previous exercise.

---

1. Click Polygon on the Draw toolbar, or type **Pol**↵.

2. At the Enter number of sides: prompt, enter 6↵.

3. At the Specify center of polygon or [Edge]: prompt, pick the center of the polygon at coordinate 22,18. Metric users use 59,42 for the center coordinate.

TIP   You can turn on the Snap mode to help you locate points for this exercise.

---

4. Enter C↵ at the Enter an option [Inscribe in circle/circumscribe-about circle] <I>: prompt to select the Circumscribe option. This tells AutoCAD to place the polygon outside the temporary circle used to define the polygon.

5. At the Specify radius of circle: prompt, you will see the hexagon drag along with the cursor. You can pick a point with your mouse to determine its size.

6. Enter 8↵ to get an exact size for the hexagon. Metric users enter **20.32**↵.

7. Draw a circle with a radius of 7" using 22,18 as its center. Metric users draw a circle with a radius of 17.78 using 59.42 for the center location. Your drawing will look like Figure 9.12.

FIGURE 9.12:

The window frame

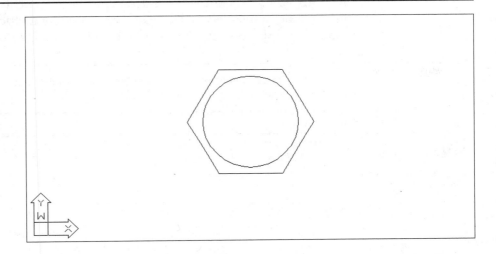

Dimensioning Nonorthogonal Linear Distances

Now you will dimension the window. The unusual shape of the window prevents you from using the horizontal or vertical dimensions you've used already. However, the Dimension ➤ Aligned option will allow you to dimension at an angle.

1. Click the Aligned Dimension tool on the Dimension toolbar. You can also enter **Dal**↵ to start the aligned dimension or select Dimension ➤ Aligned.

2. At the Specify first extension line origin or <select object>: prompt, press ↵. You could have picked extension line origins as you did in earlier examples, but using the ↵ shows you firsthand how the Select option works.

3. At the `Select object to dimension:` prompt, pick the upper-right face of the hexagon near coordinate 2'-5",1'-10" (75,55 for metric users). As the prompt indicates, you can also pick an arc or circle for this type of dimension.

4. At the `Specify dimension line location or [Mtext/Text/Angle]:` prompt, pick a point near coordinate 34,26 (90,60 for metric users). The dimension appears in the drawing as shown in Figure 9.13.

TIP   Just as with linear dimensions, you can enter **T**↵ at step 4 to enter alternate text for the dimension.

FIGURE 9.13:

The aligned dimension of a nonorthogonal line

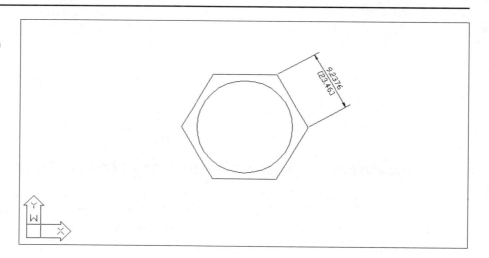

Next, you will dimension a face of the hexagon. Instead of its actual length, however, you will dimension a distance at a specified angle—the distance from the center of the face.

1. Click the Linear Dimension tool on the Dimension toolbar.

2. At the `Specify first extension line origin or <select> object:` prompt, press ↵.

3. At the `Select object to dimension:` prompt, pick the lower-right face of the hexagon near coordinate 30,16 (77,33 for metric users).

4. At the `Specify dimension line location or`
    `[Mtext/Text/Angle/Horizontal/Vertical/Rotated]:`prompt, type **R**↵ to select the rotated option.

5. At the `Dimension line angle <0>:` prompt, enter **30**↵.

6. At the `Dimension line location:` prompt, pick a point near coordinate 35,8 (88,12 for metric users). Your drawing will look like Figure 9.14.

FIGURE 9.14:

A linear dimension using the Rotated option

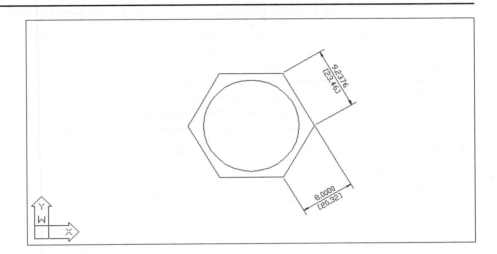

Dimensioning Radii, Diameters, and Arcs

To dimension circular objects, you use another set of options from the Draw ➤ Dimensioning menu.

1. Click Angular Dimension on the Dimension toolbar. Or you can enter **Dan**↵ or choose Dimension ➤ Angular from the pull-down menu to start the angular dimension.

2. At the `Select arc, circle, line, or <Specify vertex>:` prompt, pick the upper-left face of the hexagon near coordinate 15,22 (44,57 for metric users).

3. At the Select second line: prompt, pick the top face at coordinate 21,26 (54,62 for metric users).

4. At the Specify dimension arc line location or [Mtext/Text/Angle]: prompt, notice that as you move the cursor around the upper-left corner of the hexagon, the dimension changes, as shown in the top images of Figure 9.15.

5. Pick a point near coordinate 21,23 (49,50 for metric users). The dimension is fixed in the drawing (see the bottom image of Figure 9.15).

TIP   If you need to make subtle adjustments to the dimension line or text location, you can do so using grips, after you have placed the angular dimension.

FIGURE 9.15:

The angular dimension added to the window frame

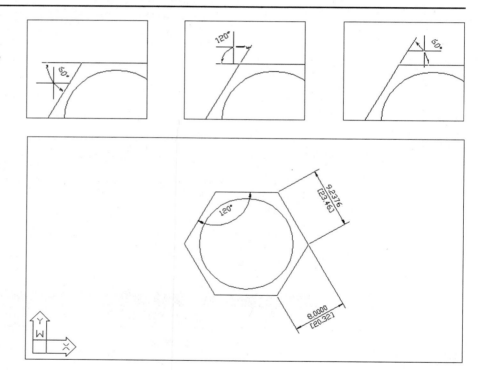

Now try the Diameter option, which shows the diameter of a circle.

1. Click the Diameter Dimension tool on the Dimension toolbar. Or you can
    enter **Ddi**↵ at the command prompt.

2. At the Select arc or circle: prompt, pick the circle.

3. At the Specify dimension line location or [Mtext/Text/Angle]:
    prompt, you will see the diameter dimension drag along the circle as you
    move the cursor. If you move the cursor outside the circle, the dimension
    will change to display the dimension on the outside (see the top image of
    Figure 9.16).

NOTE   If the dimension text can't fit within the circle, AutoCAD gives you the option to
place the dimension text outside the circle as you drag the temporary dimension
to a horizontal position.

---

4. Place the cursor inside the circle so that the dimension arrow points in a
    horizontal direction, as shown in the bottom image of Figure 9.16.

5. With the text centered, click the mouse.

The Radius Dimension tool on the Dimension toolbar gives you a radius dimension just as the diameter dimension provides a circle's diameter.

Figure 9.17 shows a radius dimension on the outside of the circle, but you can
place it inside in a manner similar to the diameter dimension. The Center Mark
tool on the Dimension toolbar just places a cross mark in the center of the selected
arc or circle.

FIGURE 9.16:

Dimension showing the diameter of a circle

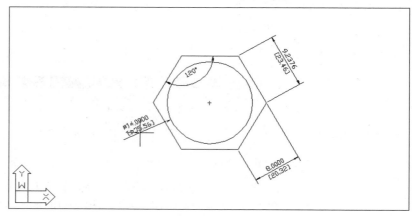

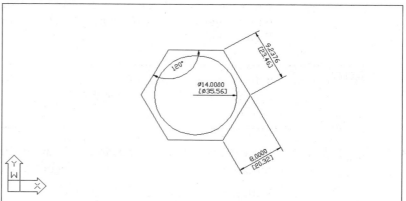

FIGURE 9.17:

A radius dimension shown on the outside of the circle

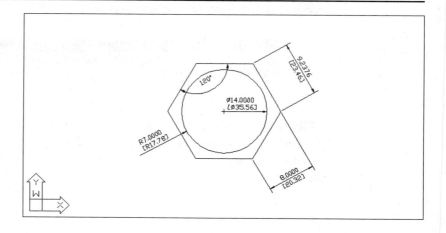

TIP You can alter the format of diameter dimensions by changing the Dimtix and Dimtofl dimension variable settings. For example, to have two arrows appear across the diameter of the circle, turn both Dimtix and Dimtofl on. See Appendix D for more details.

Adding a Note with an Arrow

Finally, there is the Dimension ➤ Leader option, which allows you to add a note with an arrow pointing to the object the note describes.

1. Click the Leader tool on the Dimension toolbar, or enter **Le.⏎**, or select Dimension ➤ Leader from the pull-down menu.

2. At the `Specify first leader point, or [Settings]<Settings>:` prompt, pick a point near the top-left edge of the hexagon at coordinate 16,24 (45,59 for metric users).

3. At the `Specify next point:` prompt, enter **@6<110⏎**. Metric users should enter **@15<110** ⏎.

4. At the `Specify next point:` prompt, you can continue to pick points just as you would draw lines. For this exercise, however, press ⏎ to finish drawing leader lines.

TIP You can also add multiline text at the leader. See the next section, *Exploring the Leader Options*.

5. At the `Enter first line of annotation text <Mtext>:` prompt, type **Window frame.⏎⏎** as the label for this leader. Your drawing will look like Figure 9.18.

Exploring the Leader Options

The Leader tool is a deceptively simple tool with numerous options. In step 2 of the previous exercise, you can enter **S⏎** to open the Leader Settings dialog box.

From here, you can have the Leader tool perform any number of functions, depending on the type of leader you want. The following subsection lists the options and their functions.

FIGURE 9.18:

The leader with a note
added

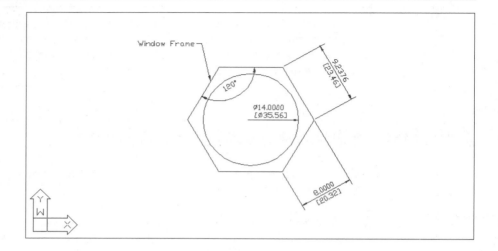

Annotation Tab

The options in the Annotation tab let you control the type of annotation that is
attached to the leader. AutoCAD uses the Mtext option by default, which places a
multiline text object at the end of the leader. Here are the other options organized
by button groups.

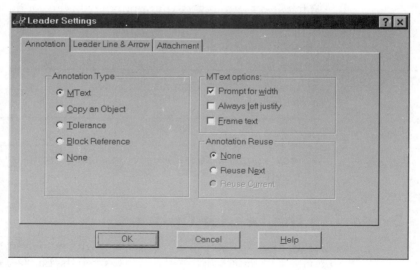

Annotation Type Button Group

Copy an Object   Prompts you to select text, tolerance, or blocks to be copied to the endpoint of the leader.

Tolerance   Opens the Tolerance dialog box when you've finished drawing the leader lines. See *Adding Tolerance Notation* later in this chapter.

Block Reference   Lets you insert a block at the end of the leader.

None   Ends the leader without adding a note.

Mtext Options Button Group

Prompt for Width   Asks you to select a width for multiline text.

Always Left Justify   Left justifies multiline text.

Frame Text   Draws a frame around the text.

Annotation Reuse Button Group

None   Always prompts you for annotation.

Reuse Next   Reuses the annotation you enter for the next leader.

Reuse Current   Reuses the current annotation text.

Leader Line & Arrow Tab

The options in the Leader Line & Arrow tab give you control over the leader line and arrow. You can select an arrow that is different from the default, or you can constrain the lines to follow a specific angle.

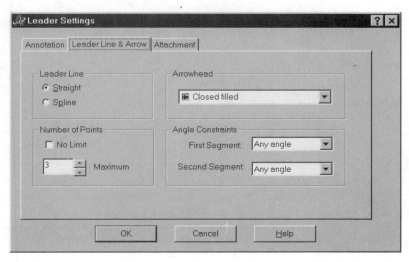

Leader Line   Lets you select from either a straight line or spline for your lines. (see Figure 9.19).

Number of Points   Lets you constrain the number of points you select before the command prompts you for the annotation.

Arrowhead   Lets you select an arrowhead from a list similar to the one in the Dimension Style dialog box.

Angle Constraints   Lets you constrain the angle at which the leader line extends from the arrow and the second point.

Attachment Tab

The options in the Attachment tab let you control how the leader connects to Mtext annotation, depending on which side of the leader the annotation appears. The location of the leader endpoint in relation to the note is frequently a focus of drafting standards. These options let you customize your leader to produce results that conform to the standards you work with.

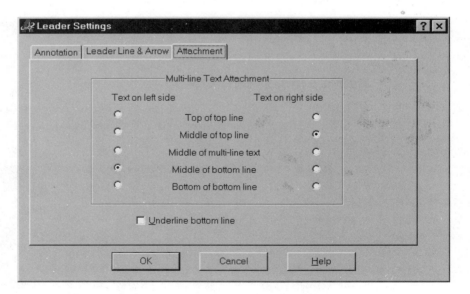

TIP

Just as with other dimensions, and objects in general, you can modify some of the properties of a leader using the Properties dialog box. You can, for example, change a straight leader to a spline leader.

The leader with a note added

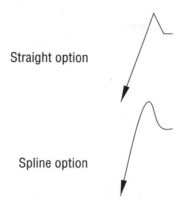

Straight option

Spline option

Skewing Dimension Lines

At times, you may find it necessary to force the extension lines to take on an angle other than 90° to the dimension line. This is a common requirement of isometric drawings, where most lines are at 30° or 60° angles instead of 90°. To facilitate non-orthogonal dimensions like these, AutoCAD offers the Oblique option.

1. Choose Dimension ➤ Oblique, or type **Ded↵ O↵**. You can also select Dimension Edit tool from the Dimension toolbar, and then type **O↵**.

2. At the `Select object` prompt, pick the aligned dimension at the upper-right of the drawing and press ↵ to confirm your selection.

3. At the `Enter obliquing angle (Press enter for none):` prompt, enter **60** for 60 degrees. The dimension will skew so that the extension lines are at 60°, as shown in Figure 9.20.

4. Exit AutoCAD. You are done with the tutorials in this chapter.

FIGURE 9.20:

A dimension using the Oblique option

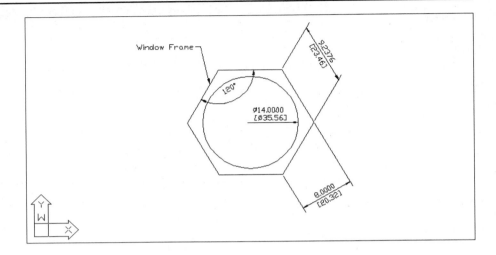

Applying Ordinate Dimensions

In mechanical drafting, *ordinate dimensions* are used to maintain the accuracy of machined parts by establishing an origin on the part. All major dimensions are described as x-coordinates or y-coordinates of that origin. The origin is usually an easily locatable feature of the part, such as a machined bore or two machined surfaces. Figure 9.21 shows a typical application of ordinate dimensions. In the lower-left corner, note the two dimensions whose leaders are jogged. Also note the origin location in the upper-right corner.

To use AutoCAD's Ordinate Dimension command, perform the following steps.

1. Click Tools ➤ UCS ➤ Origin, or type **UCS↵ Or↵**.

2. At the Specify new origin point <0,0,0>: prompt, click the exact location of the origin of your part.

3. Toggle the Ortho mode on.

4. Click the Ordinate Dimension tool on the Dimension toolbar. You can also enter **Dor↵** to start the ordinate dimension.

5. At the Select feature location: prompt, click the item you want to dimension.

NOTE

The direction of the leader determines whether the dimension will be of the Xdatum or the Ydatum.

---

6. At the Specify leader endpoint or [Xdatum/Ydatum/Mtext/Text/ Angle]: prompt, indicate the length and direction of the leader. Do this by positioning the rubber-banding leader perpendicular to the coordinate direction you want to dimension, and then clicking that point.

FIGURE 9.21:

A drawing using ordinate dimensions

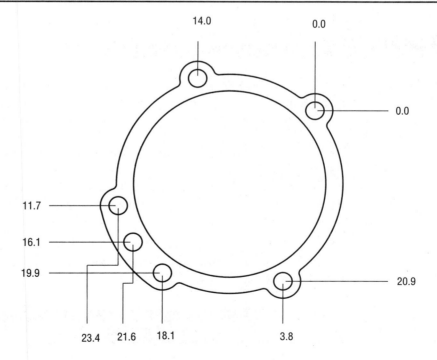

In steps 1 and 2, you used the UCS feature to establish a second origin in the drawing. The Ordinate Dimension tool then uses that origin to determine the ordinate dimensions. You will get a chance to work with the UCS feature in Chapter 16.

You may have noticed options in the Command window for the Ordinate Dimension tool. The Xdatum and Ydatum options force the dimension to be of the x- or y-coordinate no matter what direction the leader takes. The Mtext option opens the Multiline Text Editor, allowing you to append or replace the ordinate dimension text. The Text option lets you enter a replacement text directly through the Command window.

> **TIP** As with all other dimensions, you can use grips to make adjustments to the location of ordinate dimensions.

If you turn Ortho mode off, the dimension leader will be drawn with a jog to maintain orthogonal (look back at Figure 9.20).

Adding Tolerance Notation

In mechanical drafting, tolerances are a key part of a drawing's notation. They specify the allowable variation in size and shape that a mechanical part can have. To help facilitate tolerance notation, AutoCAD provides the Tolerance command, which offers common ISO tolerance symbols together with a quick way to build a standard *feature control* symbol. Feature control symbols are industry-standard symbols used to specify tolerances. If you are a mechanical engineer or drafter, AutoCAD's tolerance notation options will be a valuable tool. However, a full discussion of tolerances requires a basic understanding of mechanical design and drafting and is beyond the scope of this book.

To use the Tolerance command, choose Tolerance from the Dimension toolbar, or type **Tol**⏎ at the command prompt, or select Dimension ➤ Tolerance from the drop-down menu.

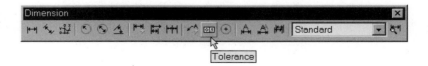

The Geometric Tolerance dialog box appears.

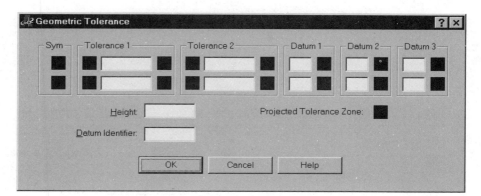

This is where you enter tolerance and datum values for the feature control symbol. You can enter two tolerance values and three datum values. In addition, you can stack values in a two-tiered fashion.

If you click a box in the Sym group, the Tolerance Symbol dialog box appears.

The top image of Figure 9.22 shows what each symbol in the Tolerance Symbol dialog box represents. The bottom image shows a sample drawing with a feature symbol used on a cylindrical object.

In the Geometric Tolerance dialog box, if you click a box in any of the Datum groups, or a box in the right side of the Tolerance groups, the Material Condition dialog box appears.

FIGURE 9.22:

The tolerance symbols

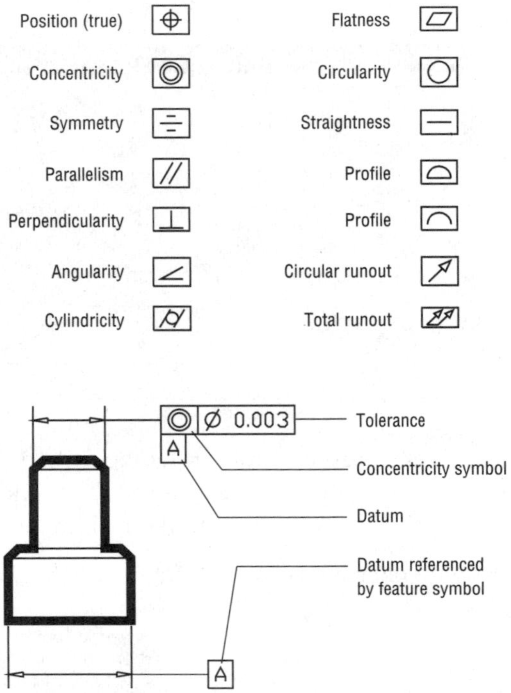

Position (true)	⊕	Flatness	▱
Concentricity	◎	Circularity	○
Symmetry	⌯	Straightness	—
Parallelism	∥	Profile	⌓
Perpendicularity	⊥	Profile	⌒
Angularity	∠	Circular runout	↗
Cylindricity	⌭	Total runout	⌰

◎ Ø 0.003 ——— Tolerance
A
—— Concentricity symbol
—— Datum
—— Datum referenced by feature symbol
A

Understanding the Power of the Properties Dialog Box

In both this and the previous chapter, you made frequent use of the Properties dialog box. By now, you may have recognized that the Properties dialog box is like a gateway to editing virtually any object. It allows you to edit the general properties of layer, color, and line type assignments. When used with individual objects, it allows you to edit properties that are unique to the selected object. For example, through this tool, you are able to change a spline leader with an arrow into one with straight-line segments and no arrow.

If the Properties dialog box does not offer specific options to edit the object, then it offers a button to open a dialog box that will. If you edit a multiline text object with the Properties dialog box, for example, you have the option to open the Multiline Text Editor. The same is true for dimension text.

Continued on next page

With AutoCAD 2000, Autodesk has made a clear effort to make AutoCAD's interface more consistent. The text-editing tools now edit text of all types, single-line, multiline, and dimension text, so you don't have to remember which command or tool you need for a particular object. Likewise, the Properties dialog box offers a powerful means to editing all types of objects in your drawing.

As you continue with the rest of this tutorial, you may want to experiment with the Properties dialog box with new objects you learn about. In addition to allowing you to edit properties, the Properties dialog box can show you the status of an object, much like the List tool.

If You Want to Experiment...

At this point, you might want to experiment with the settings described in this chapter to identify the ones that are most useful for your work. You can then establish these settings as defaults in a prototype file or the Acad.dwt file.

It's a good idea to experiment even with the settings you don't think you will need often—chances are you will have to alter them from time to time.

As an added exercise, try the steps shown in Figure 9.23. This exercise will give you a chance to see how you can update dimensions on a drawing that has been scaled down.

FIGURE 9.23:

A sample mechanical drawing with dimensions

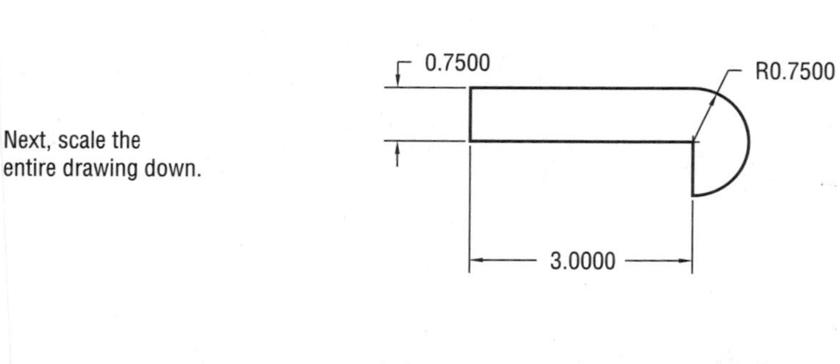

PART III

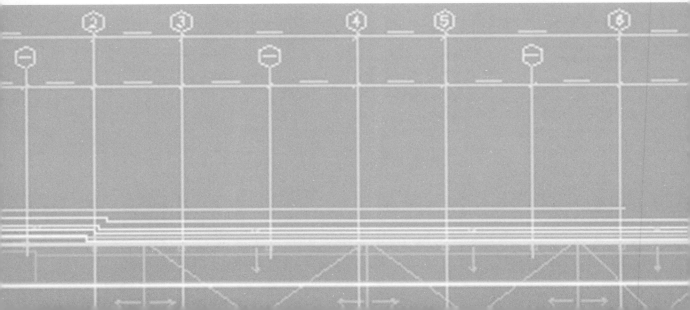

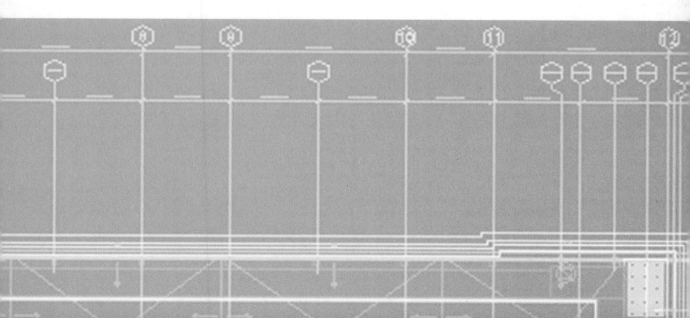

Becoming an Expert

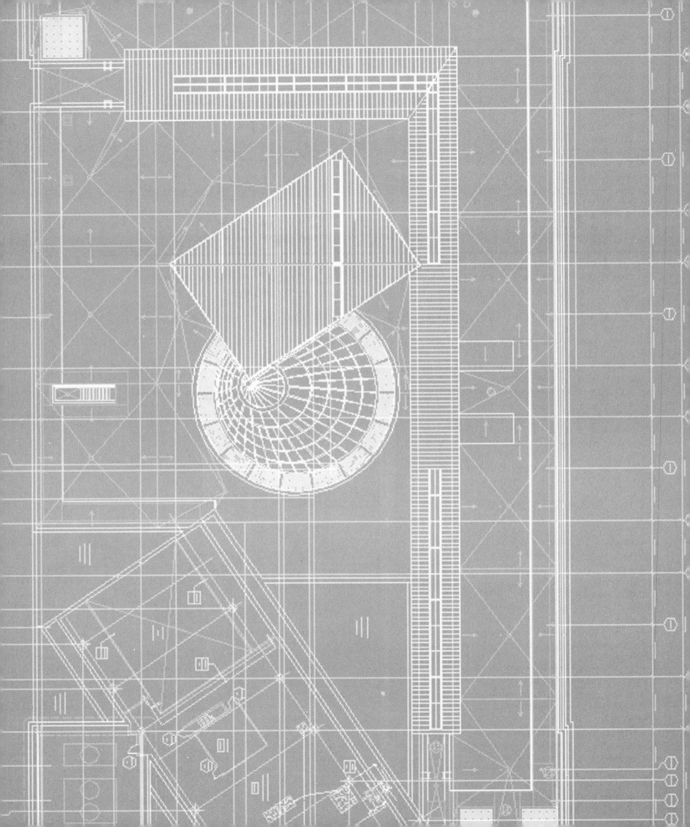

10

Storing and Linking Data with Graphics

- Creating Attributes

- Editing Attributes

- Extracting and Exporting Attribute Information

- Accessing External Databases

- Linking Objects to a Database

- If You Want to Experiment…

Attributes are unique to computer-aided design and drafting; nothing quite like them exists in traditional drafting. Because of this, they are often poorly understood. Attributes enable you to store information as text that you can later extract to use in database managers, spreadsheet programs, and word processors. By using attributes, you can keep track of virtually any object in a drawing, or maintain textural information within the drawing that can be queried.

Keeping track of objects is just one way of using attributes. You can also use them in place of text objects in situations where you must enter the same text, with minor modifications, in many places in your drawing. For example, if you are drawing a schedule that contains several columns of information, you can use attributes to help simplify your data entry.

Attributes can also be used where you anticipate global editing of text. For example, suppose a note that refers to a part number occurs in several places. If you think you will want to change that part number in every note, you can make the part a block with an attribute. Later, when you know the new part number, you can use the global editing capability of the Attribute feature to change the old part number for all occurrences in one step.

TIP You can even set up a default value for the attribute, such as *hollow core*, or *hc*. With this value in place, you only have to enter a value when it deviates from the default.

In this chapter you will use attributes for one of their more common functions: maintaining lists of parts. In this case, the parts are doors. This chapter will also describe how to import these attributes into a database management program. As you go through these exercises, think about the ways attributes can help you in your particular application.

Creating Attributes

Attributes depend on blocks. You might think of an attribute as a tag attached to a block, where the tag contains information about the block. For example, you could have included an attribute definition with the door drawing you created in Chapter 2. If you had, then every time you subsequently inserted the door you would have been prompted for a value associated with that door. The value could be a number, a height or width value, a name, or any type of text information you want.

When you insert the block, you are prompted for an attribute value. Once you enter a value, it is stored as part of the block within the drawing database. This value can be displayed as text attached to the door, or it can be made invisible. The value can be changed at any time. You can even specify what the prompts say in asking you for the attribute value.

However, suppose you don't have the attribute information when you design the door. As an alternative, you can add the attribute to a *symbol* that is later placed by the door when you know enough about the design to specify what type of door goes where. The standard door type symbol suits this purpose nicely because it is an object that can be set up and used as a block independent of the actual door block.

NOTE   A *door type symbol* is a graphic code used to indicate special characteristics of the associated door. The code refers to a note on another drawing or in a set of written specifications.

In the following exercises, you will create a door type symbol with attributes for the different values normally assigned to doors, namely size, thickness, fire rating, material, and construction.

Adding Attributes to Blocks

In this exercise, you will create a door type symbol, which is commonly used to describe the size, thickness, and other characteristics of any given door in an architectural drawing. The symbol is usually a circle, hexagon, or diamond, with a number in it. The number is usually cross-referenced to a schedule that lists all the door types and their characteristics.

While in this exercise you will be creating a new file containing attribute definitions, you can also include such definitions in blocks you create using the Make Block tool (the Block command) or in files you create using the Wblock command. Just create the attribute definitions, then include them with the Block or Wblock selections.

1. Create a new file and call it S-door (for symbol-door). Since the symbol will fit in the default limits of the drawing, you don't have to change the limits setting.

TIP

Since this is a new drawing, the circle is automatically placed on Layer 0. Remember that objects in a block that are on Layer 0 take on the color and line-type assignment of the layer on which the block is inserted.

2. Draw a circle with a radius of 0.125 (0.3 for metric users) and with its center at coordinate 7,5.

3. Next, zoom in to the circle so it is about the same size as shown in Figure 10.1.

4. If the circle looks like an octagon, Choose View ➢ Regen, or type **Re**↵ to regenerate your drawing.

5. Choose Draw ➢ Block ➢ Define Attributes, or type **At**↵. The Attribute Definition dialog box appears.

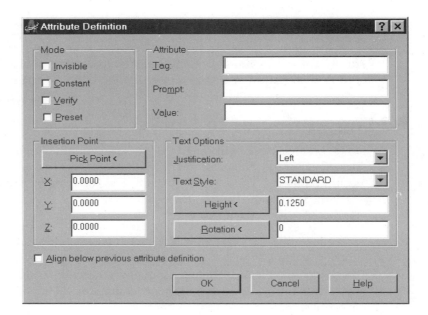

6. Click the input box labeled Tag in the Attribute group. Enter **d-type**.

NOTE

The Attribute Tag is equivalent to the field name in a database; it can be up to 31 characters long but it cannot contain spaces. If you plan to use the attribute data in a database program, check that program's manuals for other restrictions on field names.

7. Press the Tab key or click the input box labeled Prompt, and enter **Door type**. Here, you enter the text for the prompt that will appear when you insert the block containing this attribute. Often the prompt is the same as the tag, but it can be anything you like. Unlike the tag, the prompt can include spaces.

TIP   Use a prompt that gives explicit instructions so the user will know exactly what is expected. Consider including an example within the prompt. (Enclose the example in brackets to imitate the way AutoCAD prompts often display defaults.)

---

8. Click the input box labeled Value. This is where you enter a default value for the door type prompt. Enter a hyphen.

TIP   If an attribute is to contain a number that will later be used for making sorts in a database, use a default value such as 000 to indicate the number of digits required. The zeros may also serve to remind the user that values less than 100 must be preceded by a leading zero, as in 099.

---

9. Click the Justification pull-down list, and then highlight Middle. This allows you to center the attribute on the circle's center. You might notice several other options in the Text Options group. Since attributes appear as text, you can apply the same settings to them as you would to single-line text.

10. Double-click the input box next to the button labeled Height <, and then enter **0.125**. (Metric users should enter **0.3**.) This makes the attribute text 0.125 inches (0.3cm) high.

11. Check the box labeled Verify in the Mode group. This option instructs Auto-CAD to verify any answers you give to the attribute prompts at insertion time. (You'll see later in this chapter how Verify works.)

12. Click the button labeled Pick Point < in the Insertion Point group. The dialog box closes momentarily to let you pick a location for the attribute.

13. Using the Center Osnap, pick the center of the circle. You need to place the cursor on the circle's circumference, not in the circle's center, to obtain the center using the Osnap. The Attribute Definition dialog box reappears.

14. Click OK. The attribute definition appears at the center of the circle (see Figure 10.1).

You have just created your first attribute definition. The attribute definition displays its tag in all uppercase letters to help you identify it. When you later insert this file into another drawing, the tag turns into the value you assign to it when it is inserted. If you only want one attribute, you can stop here and save the file. The next section shows you how you can quickly add several more attributes to your drawing.

FIGURE 10.1:

The attribute inserted in the circle and the second attribute added

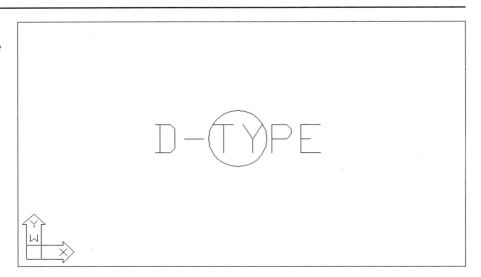

Changing Attribute Specifications

Next, you will add a few more attribute definitions, but instead of using the Attribute Definition dialog box, you will make an arrayed copy of the first attribute, and then edit the attribute definition copies. This method can save you time when you want to create several attribute definitions that have similar characteristics. By making copies and editing them, you'll also get a chance to see firsthand how to make changes to an attribute definition.

1. Click Array on the Modify toolbar, or type **Ar↵**.

2. At the `Select objects:` prompt, click the attribute definition you just created, and then press ↵.

3. At the Enter the type of array [Rectangular/Polar] <R>: prompt, type **R**↵.

4. At the Enter number of rows: prompt, enter **7**↵.

5. At the Enter number of columns: prompt, press ↵.

6. At the Enter distance between Rows: prompt, enter **–.18**↵ (**-0.432**↵ for metric users). This is about 1.5 times the height of the attribute definition. Be sure to include the minus sign. The minus sign causes the array to be drawn downward.

7. Issue a Zoom Extents or use the Zoom Realtime tool to view all the attributes.

Now you are ready to modify the copies of the attribute definitions.

1. Press the Esc key twice to clear any selections or commands, then click the attribute definition just below the original to select it.

2. Right-click, then select Properties from the popup menu. You can also select Properties from the Standard toolbar.

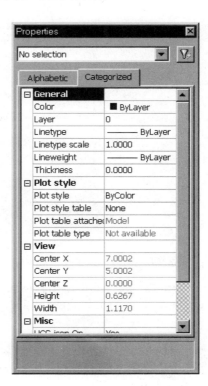

TIP

The Text Edit tool (**Ed↵** or Modify ➤ Object ➤ Text) lets you edit the tag, prompt, and default value of an attribute definition. However, it doesn't let you change an attribute definition's *mode*.

3. Make sure the Categorized tab is selected, then scroll down the list of properties until you see the Invisible option.

4. Double-click the No setting to the right of the Invisible option. The setting changes to Yes.

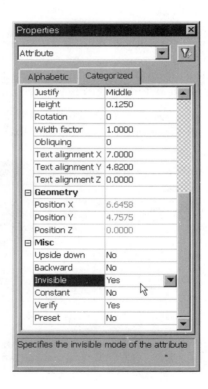

5. Scroll back up the list of properties and locate the Tag option.

6. Highlight the Tag value to the right, then type **D-SIZE** ↵. The attribute changes to reflect the change in the tag value.

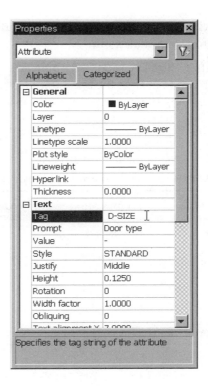

7. Highlight the Prompt value and type **Door size**↵.

8. In the Value field, type **3'-0"**↵. Metric users should type **90**↵.

Make sure you press ↵ after entering a new value for the properties in the Properties dialog box. The ↵ confirms your new entry.

---

9. Press the Esc key to clear the selection of the attribute you've been editing, then click the next attribute down so you can display its properties in the Properties dialog box.

10. Continue to edit this and the rest of the attribute definition properties using the attributes settings listed in Table 10.1. To do this, repeat steps 4 through 9 for each attribute definition, replacing the Tag, Prompt, and Default Value with those shown in Table 10.1. Also, make sure all but the original attributes have the Invisible option turned on.

11. When you've finished editing the attribute definition properties, close the Properties dialog box.

12. After you have modified all the attributes, use the Draw ➤ Block ➤ Base option to change the base point of this drawing to the center of the circle. Use the Center Osnap to get the exact center.

13. Now you have finished creating your door type symbol with attributes. Save the S-door file.

TABLE 10.1: Attributes for the Door Type Symbol (Make Sure the Invisible Option Is Checked.)

Tag	Prompt	Default Value
D-number	Door number	-
D-thick	Door thickness	-
D-rate	Fire rating	-
D-matrl	Door material	-
D-const	Door construction	-

When you later insert a file or block containing attributes, the attribute prompts will appear in the order that their associated definitions were created. If the order of the prompts at insertion time is important, you can control it by editing the attribute definitions so their creation order corresponds to the desired prompt order.

Understanding Attribute Definition Modes

In the Attribute Definition dialog box, you saw several check boxes in the Mode group. This section briefly described what two of these modes do, but below is a list describing all of the modes together in one place for your reference. You won't be asked to use any of the other modes in this tutorial, so the following set of descriptions is provided in case they might be useful for your work.

Invisible   Controls whether the attribute is shown as part of the drawing.

Continued on next page

Constant   Creates an attribute that does not prompt you to enter a value. Instead, the attribute simply has a constant, or fixed, value you give it during creation. The Constant mode is used in situations where you know you will assign a fixed value to an object. Once they are set in a block, constant values cannot be changed using the standard set of attribute editing commands.

Verify   Causes AutoCAD to review the attribute values you enter at insertion time and asks you if they are correct.

Preset   Causes AutoCAD to automatically assign the default value to an attribute when its block is inserted. This saves time because a preset attribute will not prompt you for a value. Unlike the Constant mode, you can edit an attribute that has the Preset option turned on.

You can have all four modes on, all four off, or any combination of modes. With the exception of the Invisible mode, none of these modes can be altered once the attribute becomes part of a block. Later, this chapter will discuss how to make an invisible attribute visible.

Inserting Blocks Containing Attributes

In the last section, you created a door type symbol at the desired size for the actual plotted symbol. This means that whenever you insert that symbol, you have to specify an x and y scale factor appropriate to the scale of your drawing. This allows you to use the same symbol in any drawing, regardless of its scale. (You could have several door type symbols, one for each scale you anticipate using, but this would be inefficient.)

1. Open the Plan file you created in earlier exercises. Or you can use the f10a-plan.dwg file from the companion CD-ROM. Metric users can use the file named 06b-plan-metric.dwg.

2. Choose View ➤ Named View to restore the view named First.

3. Be sure the Ceiling and Flr-Pat layers are off. Normally in a floor plan, the door headers are not visible, and they will interfere with the placement of the door reference symbol.

4. Click the Insert Block tool or type I⏎ to open the Insert dialog box.

5. In the Insert dialog box, click the Browse button.

6. Locate the S-door file in the file list and double-click it.

7. In the Scale button group, make sure the Uniform Scale check box is selected, then enter **96** in the X input box. Metric users should enter **100** in the X input box. You created the S-door file at the actual plotted size so you'll need to scale it up by the drawing scale factor to make it the appropriate size for this drawing.

8. Click OK.

9. Insert the symbol in the doorway of the lower-left unit, near coordinate 41'-3",72'-4". Metric users should use coordinate 1256,2202. When you've clicked the location, the Edit Attributes dialog box appears.

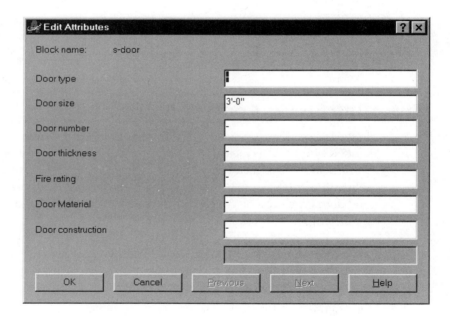

10. In the Door Type input box, enter **A**↵. Note that this prompt is the prompt you created. Note also that the default value is the hyphen you specified.

NOTE Attribute data is case sensitive, so any text you enter in all capital letters will be stored in all capital letters.

11. In the Door Number input box, change the hyphen to **116**. Continue to change the values for each input box, as shown in Table 10.2.

12. Now you've finished and the symbol appears. The only attribute you can see is the one you selected to be visible: the door type.

TIP If the symbol does not appear, go back to the **s-door.dwg** file and make sure you have set the base point to the center of the circle.

---

13. Add the rest of the door type symbols for the apartment entry doors by copying or arraying the door symbol you just inserted. You can use the previously saved views to help you get around the drawing quickly. Don't worry that the attribute values won't be appropriate for each unit. This chapter will show you how to edit the attributes in a later section.

TABLE 10.2: Attribute Values for the Typical Studio Entry Door

Prompt	Value
Door type	A
Door number	Same as room number
Door thickness	1 3/4"
Fire rating	20 min.
Door material	Wood
Door construction	Solid core

As a review exercise, you'll now create another file for the apartment number symbol (shown in Figure 10.2). This will be a rectangular box with the room number that you will place in each studio apartment.

1. Save the Plan file and then open a new file called S-apart (for the apartment number symbol).

2. Give the apartment number symbol attribute the tag name **R-number**, the prompt **Room number**, a default value of **000**, and a text height of **0.125** inches.

3. Make the base point of this drawing the lower-left corner of the rectangle.

4. Save and close S-apart.

5. Open the Plan file again and insert the apartment number symbol (using an x-scale factor of 96) into the lower-left unit. Give this attribute the value of 116.

6. Copy or array the room number symbol so that there is one symbol in each of the units. You'll learn how to modify the attributes to reflect their proper values in the following section, *Editing Attributes*. Figure 10.3 shows what the view should look like once you've entered the door symbols and apartment numbers.

FIGURE 10.2:

The apartment number symbol

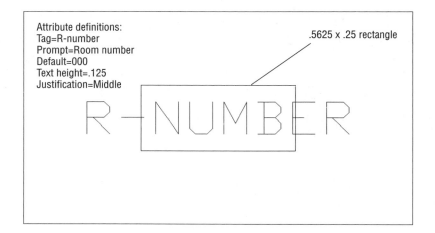

FIGURE 10.3:

An overall view of the plan with door symbols and apartment numbers added

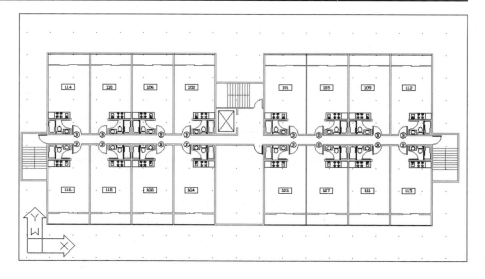

Editing Attributes

Because drawings are usually in flux even after actual construction or manufacturing begins, you will eventually have to edit previously entered attributes. In the example of the apartment building, many things can change before the final set of drawings is completed.

Attributes can be edited individually (one at a time) or they can be edited globally (meaning you can edit several occurrences of a particular attribute tag all at one time). In this section you will make changes to the attributes you have entered so far, using both individual and global editing techniques, and you will practice editing invisible attributes.

Editing Attributes One at a Time

AutoCAD offers an easy way to edit attributes one at a time through a dialog box. The following exercise demonstrates this feature.

1. Use the View ➤ Named View option to restore the First view.

2. Choose Modify ➤ Attribute ➤ Single, or enter **Ate.⤶** at the command prompt.

3. At the Select Block: prompt, click the apartment number attribute in the unit just to the right of the first unit in the lower-left corner. A dialog box appears, showing you the value for the attribute in an input box. Note that the value is already highlighted and ready to be edited.

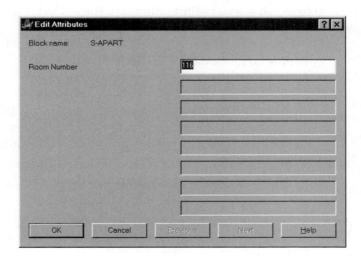

4. Type **112** and then click OK to make the change.

5. Do this for each room number, using Figure 10.4 to assign room numbers.

TIP The Edit Attributes option is useful for reviewing attributes as well as editing them because both visible and invisible attributes are displayed in the dialog box.

FIGURE 10.4:

Apartment numbers for one floor of the studio apart-ment building

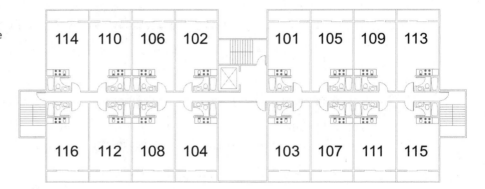

Editing Several Attributes in Succession

You can take advantage of the Tab key and the spacebar to quickly edit a series of attributes. In a dialog box, the Tab key moves you to the next option. In AutoCAD, the spacebar reissues the previous command. By combining these two tools, you can make quick work of editing attributes. The following steps describe the process.

1. Choose Modify ➢ Attribute ➢ Single, or enter **Ate⏎** at the command prompt to start the attribute-editing process.

2. Select the first attribute you want to edit.

3. In the Edit Attributes dialog box, enter the new value for the attribute. The old attribute value should already be highlighted. For blocks with multiple attributes, you may need to press the Tab key until you get to the value you want to edit.

4. After entering the new attribute value, press the Tab key to advance to the OK button.

5. Press the spacebar twice—once to accept the OK button, and again to reissue the Edit Attributes command.

6. Click the next attribute you want to edit and repeat the process.

If you are comfortable with the keyboard, you can get into a rhythm of selecting and editing attributes using these steps, especially if the block contains only one attribute.

Making Minor Changes to an Attribute's Appearance

Eventually, there will be situations where you will want to make a change to an attribute that doesn't involve its value, such as moving the attribute's location relative to the block it is associated with, or changing its color, its angle, or even its text style. To make these types of changes, you must use the Attedit command. Here's how to do it.

1. Choose Modify ➤ Attribute ➤ Global, or type **Attedit**↵ at the command prompt.

2. At the `Edit Attributes One at a Time? [Yes/No] <Y>`: prompt, press ↵ to accept the default, Y.

TIP

If you just want to change the location of individual attributes in a block, you can move attributes using grips. Click the block to expose the grips and then click the grip connected to the attribute. Or if you've selected several blocks, Shift+click the attribute grips; then move the attributes to their new location. They will still be attached to their associated blocks.

---

3. At the `Enter block Name Specification <*>`: prompt, press ↵. Optionally, you can enter a block name to narrow the selection to specific blocks.

4. At the `Enter attribute Tag Specification <*>`: prompt, press ↵. Optionally, you can enter an attribute tag name to narrow your selection to specific tags.

5. At the `Enter attribute Value Specification <*>`: prompt, press ↵. Optionally, you can narrow your selection to attributes containing specific values.

6. At the `Select Attributes`: prompt, you can pick the set of blocks that contain the attributes you wish to edit. Once you press ↵ to confirm your

selection, one of the selected attributes becomes highlighted, and an "x" appears at its base point (see Figure 10.5).

FIGURE 10.5:

Close-up of attribute with "x"

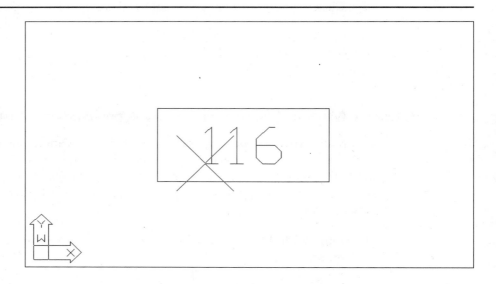

7. At the prompt

    ```
    Enter an option [Value/Position/Height/Angle/Style/Layer/Color/
    Next] <N>:
    ```

    enter the option that best describes the attribute characteristic you wish to change. After you make the change, the prompt returns, allowing you to make another change to the attribute. If you press ↵ to accept the default, N, another attribute highlights with an x at its base.

8. The prompt

    ```
    Enter an option [Value/Position/Height/Angle/Style/Layer/Color/
    Next] <N>:
    ```

    appears again, allowing you to make changes to the next attribute.

9. This process repeats until all the attributes have been edited or until you press the Esc key.

TIP   At some point you may find that an attribute would function better as a single-line text object. An Express tool called Explode Attribute to Text is available in the Express Text Tools toolbar. See Chapter 19 for more information on this tool.

Making Global Changes to Attributes

There will be times when you'll want to change the value of several attributes in a file to be the same value. You can use the Edit Attribute Globally option to make any global changes to attribute values.

Suppose you decide you want to change all the entry doors to a type designated as B, rather than A. Perhaps door type A was an input error, or type B happens to be better suited for an entry door. The following exercise demonstrates how this is done.

1. Use the View Control dialog box (View ➤ Named View) to restore the view named Fourth. Pan your view down so you can see the door reference symbol for all the rooms in this view of the drawing.

2. Choose Modify ➤ Attribute ➤ Global, or type **Attedit**↵ at the command prompt.

3. At the `Edit Attributes One at a Time? [Yes/No]<Y>:` prompt, enter **N**↵ for No. You will see the message `Global edit of attribute values`. This tells you that you are in the Global Edit mode.

4. At the `Edit Only Attributes Visible On Screen? [Yes/No] <Y>:` prompt, press ↵. As you can see from this prompt, you have the option to edit all attributes, including those out of the view area. You'll get a chance to work with this option later in the chapter.

5. At the `Enter block Name Specification <*>:` prompt, press ↵. Optionally, you can enter a block name to narrow the selection to specific blocks.

6. At the `Enter attribute Tag Specification <*>:` prompt, press ↵. Optionally, you can enter an attribute tag name to narrow your selection to specific tags.

7. At the `Enter attribute Value Specification <*>:` prompt, press ↵. Optionally, you can narrow your selection to attributes containing specific values.

8. At the `Select Attributes:` prompt, select the door type symbols for units 103 to 115.

WARNING   When you are editing attributes, make sure you click the attribute itself and not other graphic components of the block containing the attribute.

---

9. At the Enter string to Change: prompt, enter **A↵**.

10. At the Enter new String: prompt, enter **B↵**. The door type symbols all change to the new value.

In step 8 above, you are asked to select the attributes to be edited. AutoCAD limits the changes to those attributes you select. If you know you need to change every single attribute in your drawing, you can do so by answering the series of prompts in a slightly different way, as in the following exercise.

1. Try the same procedure again, but this time enter **N** at the Edit Only Attributes Visible On Screen: prompt (step 4 in the previous exercise). The message Drawing must be regenerated afterwards appears. The display flips to Text mode.

2. Once again, you are prompted for the block name, the tag, and the value (steps 5, 6, and 7 in the previous exercise). Respond to these prompts as you did before. Once you have done that, you get the message 16 attributes selected. This tells you the number of attributes that fit the specifications you just entered.

3. At the Enter String to Change: prompt, enter **A↵** to indicate you want to change the rest of the A attribute values.

4. At the Enter new String: prompt, enter **B↵**. A series of Bs appear, indicating the number of strings that were replaced.

WARNING   If the Regenauto command is off, you must regenerate the drawing to see the change.

TIP   If you find that this method for globally editing attributes is too complex, Auto-CAD offers the Global Attribute Edit Express tool in the Express Text Tool toolbar. See Chapter 19 for details.

You may have noticed in the last exercise that the Select Attribute: prompt is skipped and you go directly to the String to Change: prompt. AutoCAD assumes that you want it to edit every attribute in the drawing, so it doesn't bother asking you to select specific attributes.

Using Spaces in Attribute Values

At times, you may want the default value to begin with a blank space. This enables you to specify text strings more easily when you edit the attribute. For example, you may have an attribute value that reads 3334333. If you want to change the first 3 in this string of numbers, you have to specify **3334** when prompted for the string to change. If you start with a space, as in **_3334333** (I'm only using an underline here to represent the space; it doesn't mean you type an underline character), you can isolate the first 3 from the rest by specifying **_3** as the string to change (again, type a space instead of the underline).

You must enter a backslash character (\) before the space in the default value to tell Auto-CAD to interpret the space literally, rather than as a press of the spacebar (which is equivalent to pressing ↵).

Making Invisible Attributes Visible

Invisible attributes, such as those in the door reference symbol, can be edited globally using the tools just described. You may, however, want to be a bit more selective about which invisible attribute you want to modify. Or you may simply want to make them temporarily visible for other editing purposes. This section describes how you can make invisible attributes visible.

1. Enter **Attdisp**↵.

TIP

You may also use the View menu to change the display characteristics of attributes. Choose View ➤ Display ➤ Attribute Display, and then click the desired option on the cascading menu.

2. At the Enter attribute visibility setting [Normal/ON/OFF] <ON>: prompt, enter **ON**↵. Your drawing will look like Figure 10.6. If Regenauto is turned off, you may have to issue the Regen command. At this point, you could edit the invisible attributes individually, as in the first attribute-editing exercise. For now, set the attribute display back to normal.

3. Enter **Attdisp**↵ again; then at the Enter attribute visibility setting [Normal/ON/OFF] <ON>: prompt, enter **N**↵ for normal.

You get a chance to see the results of the On and Normal options. The Off option makes all attributes invisible, regardless of the mode used when they were created.

FIGURE 10.6:

The drawing with all the attributes visible (door type symbols are so close together that they overlap)

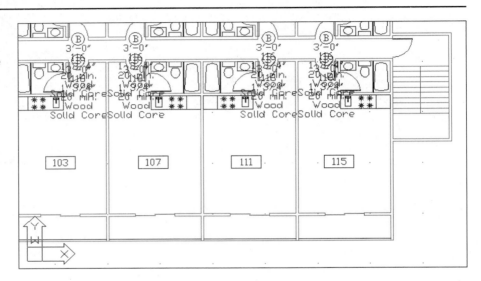

Because the attributes were not intended to be visible, they appear to overlap each other and cover other parts of the drawing when they are made visible. Just remember to turn them back off when you are done reviewing them.

Redefining Blocks Containing Attributes

Finally, you should be aware that attributes act differently from other objects when included in redefined blocks. Normally, blocks that have been redefined change their configuration to reflect the new block definition. But if a redefined block contains attributes, the attributes will maintain their old properties. This means that the old attribute position, style, and so on, do not change even though you may have changed them in the new definition.

Fortunately, AutoCAD offers a tool specifically designed to let you update blocks with attributes. The following steps describe how you would go about updating attribute blocks.

1. Before you use the command to redefine an attribute block, you must first create the objects and attribute definitions that are going to make up the

new replacement attribute block. The simplest way to do this is to explode a copy of the attribute block you wish to update. This ensures that you have the same attribute definitions in the updated block.

2. Make your changes to the exploded attribute block.

WARNING Before you explode the attribute block copy, be sure that it is at a 1-to-1 scale. This is important, because if you don't use the original size of the block, you could end up with all of your new attribute blocks at the wrong size. Also be sure you use some marker device, such as a line, to locate the insertion point of the attribute block *before* you explode it.

---

3. Type **Attredef**⏎.

4. At the Enter name of Block you wish to Redefine: prompt, enter the appropriate name.

5. At the Select Objects for New Block: prompt, select all the objects, including the attribute definitions, you want to include in the revised attribute block.

6. At the Insertion Base Point of New Block: prompt, pick the same location as used for the original block.

Once you pick the insertion point, AutoCAD takes a few seconds to update the blocks. The amount of time will vary depending on the complexity of the block and the number of times the block occurs in the drawing. If you include a new attribute definition with your new block, it too will be added to all the updated blocks, with its default value. Attribute definitions that are deleted from your new definition will be removed from all the updated blocks.

Common Uses for Attributes

Attributes are an easy way to combine editable text with graphic symbols without resorting to groups or separate text and graphic elements. One of the more common uses of attributes is in column grid symbols. Attributes are well suited for this purpose because they maintain their location in relation to the circle or hexagon shape usually used for grid symbols, and they can be easily edited.

Continued on next page

The illustration in this sidebar shows a portion of the San Francisco Main Library with a typical set of grid symbols. Each symbol contains an attribute similar to the one you created earlier for the room numbers. Other symbols in the figure are also blocks with attributes for text.

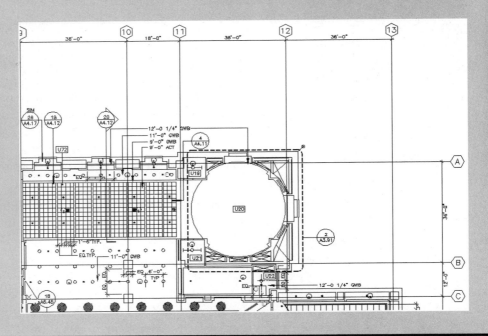

Extracting and Exporting Attribute Information

Once you have entered the attributes into your drawing, you can extract the information contained in the attributes and use that information in other programs. You may, for example, want to keep track of the door information in a database manager. This is especially useful if you have a project such as a large hotel that contains thousands of doors.

TIP

If you simply want to get a count of blocks in your drawing, check out the Count Blocks utility that is included on the companion CD-ROM for just that purpose. See Appendix C for details.

The first step in extracting attribute information is to create a template file using Windows Notepad. Do not use Windows WordPad because WordPad will introduce special codes to the file that can cause the extraction to fail. The template file used with attributes is an ASCII text file containing a list of the attributes you wish to extract and their characteristics. You can also extract information about the block an attribute is associated with. The block's name, x-coordinate and y-coordinate, layer, orientation, and scale are all available for extraction.

NOTE

Don't confuse this attribute template file with the drawing template file you use to set up various default settings.

Determining What to Extract

In the template file, for every attribute you want to extract, you must specify the attribute's tag name followed by a code that determines whether the attribute value is numeric or text, and how many spaces to allow for the value. If it is a numeric value, you must indicate how many decimal places to give the number. If you are familiar with database management programs, you'll know that these are typical variables you determine when you set up a database.

WARNING

You cannot have a blank line anywhere in the template file because AutoCAD will reject it. Also, the last line in the file must end with a ⏎, or your data will not be extracted.

For example, to get a list of rooms containing the B door type, you would create a text file with the following contents:

D-ROOM N005000
D-TYPE C001000

The first item on each line (D-ROOM and D-TYPE in this example) is the tag of the attribute you want to list. This is followed by at least one space, and then by a code that describes the attribute. This code may look a little cryptic at first glance. The following list describes how the code is broken down from left to right:

- The first character of the code is always a C or an N to denote a character (C) or numeric (N) value.

- The next three digits are where you enter the number of spaces the value will take up. You can enter any number from 001 to 999, but you must enter zeros for null values. The D-ROOM example shows the value of 005 for five spaces. The two leading zeros are needed because AutoCAD expects to see three digits in this part of the code.

- The last three digits are for the number of decimal places to allow if the value is numeric. For character values, these must always be zeros. Once again, AutoCAD expects to see three digits in this part of the code, so even if there are no decimal digits for the value, you must include 000.

Now you will use the Windows Notepad application to create a template file. If you like, you can use any Windows word processor that is capable of saving files in the ASCII format.

1. In Windows 95 and Windows NT, locate and start up the Notepad application from the Accessories program group.

2. Enter the following text as it is shown. Press ⏎ at the end of *each* line, including the last.

    D-NUMBER C005000
    D-THICK C007000
    D-RATE C010000
    D-MATRL C015000

3. When you have finished entering these lines of text, choose File ➤ Save, and then enter **Door.txt** for the filename. For ease of access, you should save this file to your current default directory, or the \AutoCAD2000\ directory.

4. Close Notepad and return to AutoCAD.

You've just completed the setup for attribute extraction. Now that you have a template file, you can extract the attribute data.

Text Editor Line Endings

It is very important that the last line of your file end with a single ↵. AutoCAD will return an error message if you either leave the ↵ off or have an extra ↵ at the end of the file. Take care to end the line with a ↵ and don't add an extra one. If the extraction doesn't work, check to see if there isn't an extra ↵ at the end of the file.

Extracting Block Information Using Attributes

This chapter mentioned that you can extract information regarding blocks, as well as attributes. To do this, you must use the following format:

```
BL:LEVEL        N002000
BL:NAME         C031000
BL:X            N009004
BL:Y            N009004
BL:Z            N009004
BL:NUMBER       N009000
BL:HANDLE       C009000
BL:LAYER        C031000
BL:ORIENT       N009004
BL:XSCALE       N009004
BL:YSCALE       N009004
BL:ZSCALE       N009004
BL:XEXTRUDE     N009004
BL:YEXTRUDE     N009004
BL:ZEXTRUDE     N009004
```

WARNING   A template file containing these codes must also contain at least one attribute tag, because AutoCAD must know which attribute it is extracting before it can identify which block the attribute is associated with. The code information for blocks works the same as for attributes.

This example includes some typical values for the attribute codes. The following list describes what each line in the above example is used for.

LEVEL   Returns the nesting level.

NAME   Returns the block name.

X   Returns the x-coordinate of the insertion point.

Y   Returns the y-coordinate of the insertion point.

Z   Returns the z-coordinate of the insertion point.

NUMBER   Returns the order number of the block.

HANDLE   Returns the block's handle. If no handle exists, a 0 is returned.

LAYER   Returns the layer the block is inserted on.

ORIENT   Returns the insertion angle.

XSCALE   Returns the X scale.

YSCALE   Returns the Y scale.

ZSCALE   Returns the Z scale.

XEXTRUDE   Returns the block's X extrusion direction.

YEXTRUDE   Returns the block's Y extrusion direction.

ZEXTRUDE   Returns the block's Z extrusion direction.

Performing the Extraction

AutoCAD allows you to extract attribute information from your drawing as a list in one of three different formats:

- CDF (comma-delimited format)
- SDF (space-delimited format)
- DXF (data exchange format)

Using the CDF Format

The CDF format can be read by many popular database management programs, as well as programs written in the programming language BASIC. This is the format you will use in this exercise.

1. Type **Ddattext**↵. The Attribute Extraction dialog box appears.

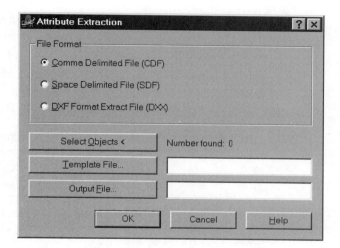

2. If it isn't already selected, click the radio button labeled Comma Delimited File (CDF).

3. Click the Template File button. Then, using the Template File dialog box, locate and select the Door.txt file you created earlier.

TIP You can select filenames of existing template and output files by clicking the Template File or Output File buttons in the Attribute Extraction dialog box. The File dialog box appears, allowing you to select files from a list.

4. Click the Output File button. Then, using the File dialog box, enter the name **Plan.txt** for your output file and place it in the \Program Files\AutoCAD2000 directory.

5. Click OK in the Attribute Extraction dialog box. The message 16 records in extract file appears.

NOTE You may have noticed the Select Objects< button in the Attribute Extraction dialog box. When you click this button, the dialog box temporarily closes to let you single out attributes to extract by picking their associated blocks from the display.

AutoCAD has created a file called Plan.txt that contains the extracted list. Let's take a look at its contents.

1. Open the Notepad application (Start ➤ Programs ➤ Accessories ➤ Notepad).

2. Choose File ➤ Open to open `Plan.txt` from the current directory. (In this exercise, the template file is located in the `\Program Files\AutoCAD2000` directory.) The following list appears:

```
'116','1 3/4"','20 MIN','WOOD','SOLID CORE'
'114','1 3/4"','20 MIN','WOOD','SOLID CORE'
'112','1 3/4"','20 MIN','WOOD','SOLID CORE'
'110','1 3/4"','20 MIN','WOOD','SOLID CORE'
'108','1 3/4"','20 MIN','WOOD','SOLID CORE'
'106','1 3/4"','20 MIN','WOOD','SOLID CORE'
'102','1 3/4"','20 MIN','WOOD','SOLID CORE'
'104','1 3/4"','20 MIN','WOOD','SOLID CORE'
'107','1 3/4"','20 MIN','WOOD','SOLID CORE'
'105','1 3/4"','20 MIN','WOOD','SOLID CORE'
'101','1 3/4"','20 MIN','WOOD','SOLID CORE'
'103','1 3/4"','20 MIN','WOOD','SOLID CORE'
'111','1 3/4"','20 MIN','WOOD','SOLID CORE'
'109','1 3/4"','20 MIN','WOOD','SOLID CORE'
'113','1 3/4"','20 MIN','WOOD','SOLID CORE'
'115','1 3/4"','20 MIN','WOOD','SOLID CORE'
```

Since you picked the comma-delimited format (CDF), AutoCAD placed commas between each extracted attribute value (or *field*, in database terminology).

NOTE Notice that the individual values are enclosed in single quotes. These quotes delimit character values. If you had specified numeric values, the quotes would not have appeared. Also note that the fields are in the order they appear in the template file.

The commas are used by some database management programs to indicate the separation of fields in ASCII files. This example shows everything in uppercase letters because that's the way they were entered when the attribute blocks were inserted in the working example. The extracted file maintains the case of whatever you enter for the attribute values.

Using Other Delimiters with CDF   Some database managers require the use of other symbols, such as double quotes and slashes, to indicate character values and field separation. AutoCAD allows you to use a different symbol in place of the single quote or comma. For example, if the database manager you use requires double-quote delimiters for text in the file to be imported, you can add the statement

```
c:quote "
```

to the template file to replace the single quote with a double quote. A line from an extract file using `c:quote  "` in the template file would look like this:

```
"115","1 3/4" ","20 MIN","WOOD","SOLID CORE"
```

Notice that the single quote (') is replaced by a double quote ("). You can also add the statement

```
c:delim /
```

to replace the comma delimiter with the slash symbol. A line from an extract file using both `c:quote  "` and `c:delim  /` in the template file would look like this:

```
"115"/"1 3/4" "/"20 MIN"/"WOOD"/"SOLID CORE"
```

Here, the comma is replaced by a forward slash. You can add either of these statements to the beginning or end of your template file.

Using the SDF Format

Like the CDF format, the space-delimited format (SDF) can be read by most database management programs. This format is the best one to use if you intend to enter information into a word-processed document because it leaves out the commas and quotes. You can even import it into an AutoCAD drawing using the method described in Chapter 8. In this exercise, you will use the SDF option to extract the same list you extracted a moment ago using CDF.

1. Type **Ddattext⏎** at the command prompt.

2. In the Attribute Extraction dialog box, use the same template filename, but for the attribute extract filename, use `Plan-SDF.txt` to distinguish this file from the last one you created.

3. Click the SDF radio button, and then click OK. You will see a message that reads `16 records in extract file`.

4. After AutoCAD has extracted the list, use Windows WordPad to view the contents of the file. You will see a list similar to this one:

```
116 1 3/4" 20 MIN WOOD SOLID CORE
114 1 3/4" 20 MIN WOOD SOLID CORE
112 1 3/4" 20 MIN WOOD SOLID CORE
110 1 3/4" 20 MIN WOOD SOLID CORE
108 1 3/4" 20 MIN WOOD SOLID CORE
106 1 3/4" 20 MIN WOOD SOLID CORE
102 1 3/4" 20 MIN WOOD SOLID CORE
104 1 3/4" 20 MIN WOOD SOLID CORE
```

```
107 1 3/4" 20 MIN WOOD SOLID CORE
105 1 3/4" 20 MIN WOOD SOLID CORE
101 1 3/4" 20 MIN WOOD SOLID CORE
103 1 3/4" 20 MIN WOOD SOLID CORE
111 1 3/4" 20 MIN WOOD SOLID CORE
109 1 3/4" 20 MIN WOOD SOLID CORE
113 1 3/4" 20 MIN WOOD SOLID CORE
115 1 3/4" 20 MIN WOOD SOLID CORE
```

This format shows text without any special delimiting characters.

5. Now save the Plan.dwg file for future chapters.

Using the DXF Format

The third file format is the data exchange format (DXF). There are actually two methods for DXF extraction. The Attribute Extraction dialog box you saw earlier offers the DXF option. This option extracts only the data from blocks containing attributes. Choose the File ➤ Export option; then select .DXF from the List Files of Type drop-down list to convert an entire drawing file into a special format for data exchange between AutoCAD and other programs (for example, other PC CAD programs). Chapter 14 discusses the DXF format in more detail.

NOTE As an alternate, you can choose File ➤ Export, then in the Export Data dialog box, choose DXX Extract (*.DXX) from the List Files of Type drop-down list. Enter a name for the extracted data file in the File Name input box, and then click OK. Finally, in the drawing editor, select the attributes you want to extract. The DXX format is a subset of the DXF format.

Using Extracted Attribute Data with Other Programs

You can import any of these lists into any word-processing program that accepts ASCII files. They will appear as shown in our examples.

As mentioned earlier, the extracted file can also be made to conform to other data formats.

Microsoft Excel

Excel has no specific requirements for the formatting of AutoCAD extracted data. Choose File ➤ Open from the Excel pull-down menu, and then select the Text File option from the Files of Type drop-down list in the File dialog box. Next, select the text file you want to import, then click Open. Excel then opens an easy-to-use import tool that steps you through the import process. You can choose the delimiting method, regardless of whether the field contains text, date, or another type of data, and other formatting options.

If you are a database user familiar with Microsoft Visual Basic, you will want to look at the sample Visual Basic utility supplied with AutoCAD. It shows how you can use VBA to export attribute data directly from AutoCAD to Excel without having to create a template file or perform an export using the Ddattext command. You can find the sample program in the \sample\activeX\ExtAttr directory. See Chapter 20 for more on this and other useful VBA-related utilities.

Microsoft Access

Like Excel, you can open the exported attribute data directly in Access. First, create a new database table. Then use the File ➤ Get External Data ➤ Import option in the Access pull-down menu, and then choose Text Files from the Files of Type drop-down list. After selecting the attribute-extracted file, Access offers an easy-to-use import tool that steps you through the process of importing the file. You can specify field and record names, as well as the delimiting method.

If you plan to update the attribute data file on a regular basis, you can have the file linked, instead of imported (File ➤ Get External Data ➤ Link Tables). A linked file is best suited for situations where you want to read the data without changing it. You can generate reports, link the attribute data to other databases, perform searches, or sort the attribute data.

As with Excel, if you are a Visual Basic user, you can add controls to enhance your attribute data link to Access.

Accessing External Databases

AutoCAD offers a way to access an external database from within AutoCAD through the dbConnect Manager. With the dbConnect Manager, you can read and manipulate data from external database files. You can also use dbConnect Manager to *link* parts of your drawing to an external database.

There are numerous reasons for doing this. The most obvious is to keep inventory on parts of your drawing. If you are an interior designer doing office planning, you can link inventory data from a database to your drawing, with a resulting decrease in the size of your drawing file. If you are a facilities manager, you can track the movement of people and facilities using AutoCAD linked to a database file.

This section will avoid the more complex programming issues of database management systems, and it does not discuss the SQL language, which can be used to query and edit your database files through dbConnect. Still, you should be able to make good use of the dbConnect Manager with the information provided here. You'll also be departing from the studio apartment example to make use of an office plan example that has already been created by Autodesk.

AutoCAD and Your Database

These exercises do assume that you are somewhat familiar with databases. For example, these exercises will refer frequently to something called a *table*. A table is an SQL term referring to the row-and-column data structure of a typical database file. Other terms I'll use are *rows*, which are the records in a database, and *columns*, which refer to the database fields. Finally, it is *very* important that you follow the instructions in these beginning exercises carefully. If anything is missed in the beginning, later exercises will not work properly. AutoCAD uses Windows Open Database Connectivity (ODBC) to help link drawings to databases. ODBC is an interface that lets diverse programs connect to a variety of different types of databases. It serves as a translator between the program, which in this case is AutoCAD, and the database file you want your program to "talk to." Before ODBC can do its translating, you need to install a driver that allows ODBC to communicate with the particular database type you want to work with. The following drivers are already included with Windows ODBC:

- Microsoft Access
- Microsoft dBase
- Microsoft Excel
- Microsoft Fox Pro
- Microsoft Oracle
- Microsoft Paradox
- Microsoft SQL Server
- Microsoft Text files
- Microsoft Visual Fox Pro

If your database type is not listed here, you'll need to obtain an ODBC driver for it. Also, you may need to configure the ODBC driver before you can connect your database to AutoCAD. You can do this through the ODBC Data Source Administrator in the Windows Control Panel. See Appendix B for information on how to do this.

Setting Up Your System for Database Access

The dbConnect Manager doesn't create new database files. You must use existing files or create them yourself before you use this tool. In addition, you will need to set up a Data Link file that will direct AutoCAD to the database file you want to work with. You can create a Data Link file through the Microsoft Data Link dialog box. The Data Link dialog box lets you create and manage Data Link files. Once you've created and set up a Data Link file, you can begin to access and link databases to AutoCAD drawings.

In the first set of exercises below, you'll learn how to create a new Data Link file that tells AutoCAD where to look for database information, Then for the rest of the tutorial, you will use a Microsoft Access file provided to you from the CD-ROM included with this book. The file is called db-Mastersample.mdb and it is installed when you install the sample figures from the CD-ROM. Look for it among those sample figures.

The db-mastersample.mdb file contains three tables: Computer, Employee, and Inventory. These are based on the sample dBase files offered with earlier versions of AutoCAD. The contents of Employee table are shown in Figure 10.7.

FIGURE 10.7:

The contents of the Employee table from the db-mastersample.mdb file

EMP_ID	LAST_NAME	FIRST_NAME	DEPT	TITLE	ROOM	EXT
1000	Meredith	Dave	Sales	V.P.	101	8600
1001	Williams	Janice	Sales	Western Region Mgr.	102	8601
1003	Smith	Jill	Sales	Central Region Mgr.	104	8603
1004	Nelson	Kirk	Sales	Canadian Sales Mgr.	109	8640
1005	Clark	Karl	Sales	Educational Sales Mgr.	106	8605
1006	Wilson	Cindy	Accounting	Accountant	109	8606
1007	Ortega	Emilio	Accounting	Accountant	109	8607
1008	Benson	Adam	Accounting	Accountant	109	8608
1009	Rogers	Kevin	Accounting	Accountant	109	8609
1011	Thompson	Frank	Engineering	Mechanical Engineer	123	8611
1012	Simpson	Paul	Engineering	Mechanical Engineer	124	8612
1013	Debrine	Todd	Engineering	Design Engineer	125	8613
1014	Frazier	Heather	Engineering	Application Engineer	126	8614
1016	Taylor	Patrick	Engineering	Software Engineer	128	8616
1017	Chang	Yuan	Engineering	Software Engineer	129	8617
1018	Dempsy	Phil	Engineering	Application Engineer	112	8618
1019	Kahn	Jenny	Engineering	Programmer	113	8619
1020	Moore	George	Engineering	Programmer	114	8620
1021	Price	Mark	Engineering	Software Engineer	115	8621
1022	Quinn	Scott	Engineering	Software Engineer	116	8622
1023	Sanchez	Maria	Engineering	Mechanical Engineer	117	8623
1024	Ross	Ted	Engineering	Application Engineer	118	8624
1025	Saunders	Terry	Engineering	Software Engineer	119	8625
1026	Fong	Albert	Engineering	Programmer	120	8626

Creating a Data Link File

A Data Link file is like a switchboard that connects applications to database files. The application can be anything that requires Data Link files for database connections, not just AutoCAD. You can have as many Data Link files as you need for your application, and as you'll see, you'll be able to access all of them from the AutoCAD dbConnect Manager.

1. Using Windows Explorer, locate the Data Link folder under the main Auto-CAD folder. Typically, this would be `C:\Program Files\AutoCAD2000 \Data Link`.

2. Right-click a blank area in the folder listing, then in the popup menu, choose New ➢ Microsoft Data Link. A new file appears called `New Microsoft Data Link.UDL`.

3. Rename this file `My Acad Data Link.UDL`.

You've just created a Data Link file. You may have noticed two other UDL files in the Data Link folder. These are sample files provided by Autodesk that allow you to explore AutoCAD's dbConnect feature on your own.

Configuring Data Links

Next, you'll configure your new Data Link file to locate the sample database files.

1. With the Data Link folder open, double-click `My Acad Data Link.UDL`. The Data Link Properties dialog box appears.

   You have two basic options in this dialog box. You can connect to a database through the Data Source Name (DSN) setting that is controlled through the ODBC Data Source Administrator in the Windows Control Panel, or you can create a link to a database directly from this dialog box. In this exercise, you'll use the Build option to create a database directly through this dialog box.

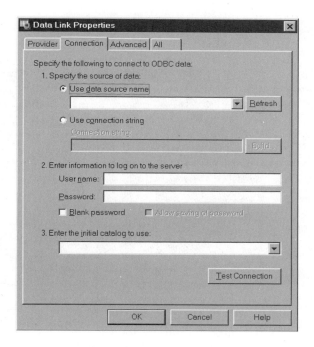

2. Click the Use Connection String radio button.

3. Click the Build button next to the Connection String input box. The Select Data Source dialog box appears.

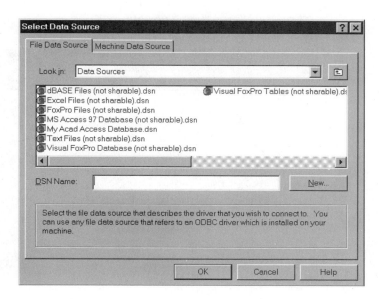

4. Click New next to the DSN Name input box. The Create New Data Source wizard appears.

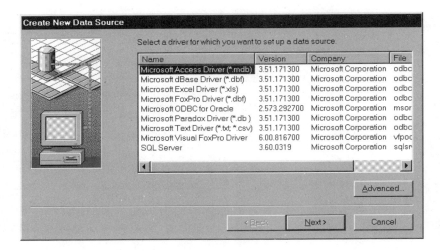

5. Select Microsoft Access Driver (*.mdb), then click Next.

6. On the next page, click the Browse button.

7. In the Save As dialog box, enter **My Acad Access Database**, then click Save. The previous dialog box reappears.

8. Click Next, then in the last dialog box, click Finish. The ODBC Microsoft Access 97 Setup dialog box appears.

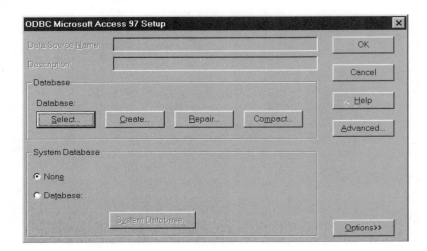

You've just created a file DSN that will direct AutoCAD to the database of your choice. But once a file DSN is created, it needs to be configured. This is where you indicate the exact location of the database file you want to use with this setup.

1. Click the Select button in the Database group. The Select Database dialog box appears. This is a standard file dialog box.

2. Locate `db-Mastersample.mdb` and select it. If you followed the installation instructions in Appendix C for installing the figures, `db-Mastersample.mdb` will be located in the `\Program Files\AutoCAD2000\Figures` folder.

3. Click OK in the ODBC Microsoft Access 97 Setup dialog box. The Select Data Source dialog box reappears.

4. Select `My Acad Access Database.dns` from the list, then click OK.

5. Click OK in the ODBC Microsoft Access 97 Setup dialog box.

6. Click OK in the Data Link Properties dialog box.

NOTE
You can also create a new Data Link file or edit an existing one by choosing dbConnect ➤ Data Sources ➤ Configure after you have clicked the dbConnect tool. The Configure a Data Source dialog box appears and asks for a data source name. Enter a new name or select the name of an existing Data Link file from the Data Link list box. Enter a name and then click OK. The Data Link Properties dialog box appears and you can set up the Data Link file.

Most of the steps you took in this exercise are the same steps you would take to create a file DSN through the ODBC Data Source Administrator in the Windows Control Panel. The Build button is a convenient way to access the ODBC Data Source Administrator through the Data Link Properties dialog box. See Appendix B for more on how to use the ODBC Data Source Administrator.

NOTE
AutoCAD is set up to look in the `AutoCAD 2000\Data Link` folder for Data Link files. You can direct AutoCAD to look in a different folder by changing settings in the Files tab of the Options dialog box. Look for the Data Source Location listing and edit its value. See Appendix B for more on editing values in the Options dialog box.

Opening a Database from AutoCAD

Now you're ready to access your database files directly from AutoCAD. In the following exercise, you'll take the first step by making a connection between a database table and AutoCAD.

1. Open the dbSample.dwg file from \Program Files\AutoCAD2000\Figures directory. This is the directory where the sample files from the Mastering AutoCAD CD are stored.

WARNING   If dbConnect does not find the My Acad Data Link file, be sure that the \Program Files\AutoCAD2000\Data Link directory is included in the Data Source Location listing in the Files tab of the Options dialog box. This option can be found by clicking Tools ➤ Options. Then in the Options dialog box, click the tab labeled Files. The Data Link subdirectory should be listed in the Data Source Location listing. Be sure to close and restart AutoCAD after making the environment change.

---

2. Choose Tools ➤ dbConnect or click the dbConnect tool on the Standard toolbar. You can also type **dbc**↵.

The dbConnect dialog box appears.

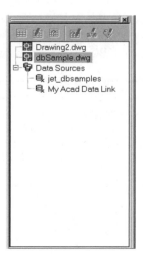

3. Right-click My Acad Data Link. Then in the popup menu, select Connect. The directory listing of the tables in the Access database file appears below My Acad Data Link.

4. Click the Edit Table tool in the dbConnect dialog box, or right-click the Employee listing, then select Edit Table from the popup menu.

The Data View dialog box appears. Your view of the Data View dialog box may be wider that the one shown here.

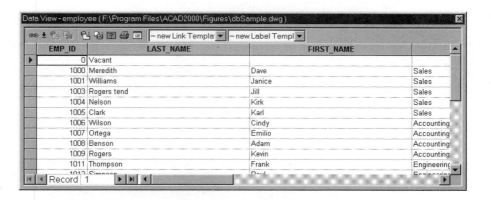

TIP

If you right-click the label at the top of each field in the Data View dialog box, you will see a popup menu that lets you sort the table by values in the field, control alignment of the field values, and perform simple find or replace functions. You can also resize the column widths by clicking and dragging the borders between the column headings.

You are now connected to the Employee table of the db-Mastersample.mdb database.

Take a moment to look at the dbConnect dialog box. You may need to move the Data View dialog box out of the way for the moment. There is a set of buttons along the top. These buttons duplicate the options you saw in step 4 in the popup menu. Also notice that you now have two more options in the menu bar: dbConnect and Data View. Most of the options in these two pull-down menus are duplicated in other parts of the dbConnect and Data View dialog boxes.

You've already seen that dbConnect's Edit Table tool opens the Data View dialog box to allow you to edit a database table. The View tool opens a view of the database, without allowing you to edit anything. You'll learn about the functions of the New Link and New Label template options later in this tutorial

Finding a Record in the Database

Now that you are connected to the database, suppose you want to find the record for a specific individual. You might already know that the individual you're looking for is in the Accounting department.

1. Click the Query icon in the Data View toolbar.

The New Query dialog box appears.

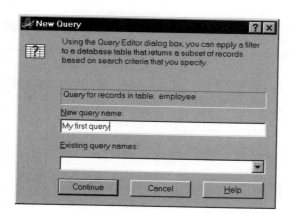

2. Type **My first query** in the New Query Name input box. You can save queries under different names in case you need to repeat a query later.

3. Click Continue. The Query Editor dialog box appears.

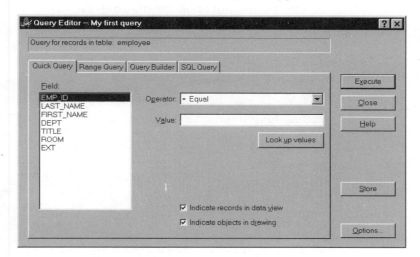

The Query Editor dialog box lets you set the criteria for your query. As you can see from the numerous tabs, you can use several methods to query the database. Try using the Quick Query method, which is the tab already selected.

4. Highlight DEPT in the Field list box.

5. Click the Look Up Values button just below the Value input box. A listing of the DEPT categories appears.

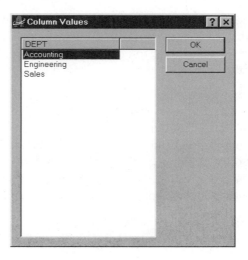

6. Select Accounting from the list, then click OK.

7. Click Store. This saves the current query under the name that you entered in the New Query dialog box. The name "My first query" appears in the dbConnect dialog box, just under the drawing name.

8. Click Execute. The Data View dialog box changes to show only the Accounting department records.

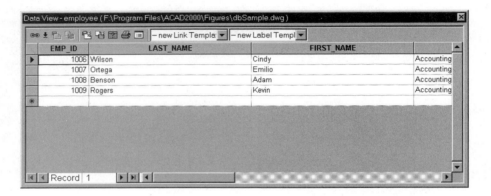

9. After reviewing the results of this exercise, right-click the Employee listing in the dbConnect dialog box, then select Edit Table to restore the view of the entire table.

You've just seen how you can locate and view a set of records in a database. If you want to edit any of those records, you only need to highlight the field of a record you want to change, then enter a new value. If you open the Data View window using the View option in the dbConnect dialog box, you are locked out of making changes to your database. In some cases, the View option is the only option available to access a database. You may be limited to the View option if the database is locked or if the ODBC driver for a database does not allow editing.

You used the Store option to store your query. By storing a query, you can quickly re-execute the query from the dbConnect dialog box. To do this, right-click the query name "My first query" in the dbConnect dialog box, then select Execute. You can also make modifications to a stored query. Right-click the query name in the dbConnect dialog box, then select Edit Query from the popup menu. The Query Editor dialog box appears, allowing you to make changes and re-execute your query. Other options in the popup menu allow you to rename the query or delete it altogether.

TIP
You can launch a new query from the dbConnect dialog box. Right-click the database filename, then select New Query. You see the New Query dialog box from step 1 of the previous exercise. You can then proceed with your query, just as you did in this exercise.

The ability to access databases in this way can help you connect AutoCAD graphic data with database information. For example, you may want to keep track of tenant information in your studio apartment building. As you will see later, you can actually link graphics to database records so you can quickly access data regarding a particular tenant. Another application might be generating a bill of materials for a mechanical project, where records in the database relate to parts in a mechanical assembly.

Adding a Row to a Database Table

Now let's get back to our office example. Suppose you have a new employee who needs to be set up in an office. The first thing you need to do is add his or her name to the database. Here's how it's done.

1. In the Data View dialog box, right-click any button to the far left of the table, then select New Record from the popup menu. A blank row appears and the cursor appears in the first field of the row for entering data.

2. Enter the following data in the blank row. To add an item, click the appropriate field, and then enter the new data. After you type in the new data, press the Tab key to move to the next field.

   ```
   EMP_ID   2000
   LAST_NAME   Ryan
   FIRST_NAME   Roma
   DEPT   Creative Resources
   TITLE   Producer/Lyricist
   ROOM   122
   EXT   8888
   ```

3. Press ⏎ after entering the last entry. You've just added a new record to the database.

Keeping Your Windows Organized

If you plan to work with a database for an extended period of time, you will find it easier to work with the dbConnect and Data View dialog boxes by docking them in your Auto-CAD windows.

First, maximize the AutoCAD window to fill your entire screen. Next, right-click the title bar of either dialog box and make sure that Allow Docking is checked in the popup menu. Move both dialog boxes into the AutoCAD window. You can place the dbConnect dialog box at either side of the window and the Data View dialog box at the bottom. While this will reduce the size of your AutoCAD drawing window, it will help you keep the dbConnect and Data View windows out of your way and in a place that is easy to get to.

Linking Objects to a Database

So far, you've looked at ways you can access and edit an external database file. You can also *link* specific drawing objects to elements in a database. But before you can link your drawing to data, you must create a *link template*. Link templates let you set up different sets of links to a database. For example, you can set up a link template that associates all of the phones in your AutoCAD drawing to records in your database file. Another link template can link the room numbers in your drawing to the LAST_NAME records in your database file.

This section will show you how to create a link to the database by linking your new employee to one of the vacant rooms.

Creating a Link

In the following set of exercises, you will link an AutoCAD object to the record you just added to the Employee database table. The first step is to set up a link template.

1. Close the Data View dialog box.

2. Highlight the Employee table listing in the dbConnect dialog box, then click the New Link Template tool in the dbConnect toolbar. You can also right-click the Employee listing and select New Link Template from the popup menu.

The New Link Template dialog box appears.

3. Notice that it has a similar format to the New Query dialog box. You can enter a name for your link template in the New Link Template Name input box.

4. Enter **Room Number** for the name, then click Continue. The Link Template dialog box appears.

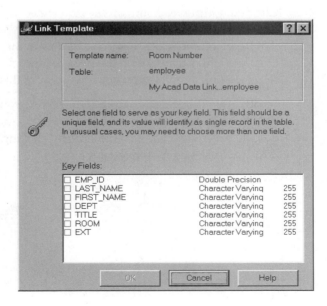

The Link Template dialog box lets you select a field to act as your key field. You can select more than one field for your key field.

A key field is any field whose values uniquely identify that table. For example, the set of values of the Employee ID is unique to this table. You further improve uniqueness by including another field, like the room numbers. The choice of fields is somewhat arbitrary but you will want to select fields that will not change frequently.

5. Click LAST_NAME and ROOM, then click OK. Now the Room Number template appears in the dbConnect dialog box.

You've just created a link template. You'll see your link template listed in the dbConnect dialog box under the drawing name. If you need to edit this link template, you can do so by right-clicking its name in the dbConnect dialog box, then selecting Redefine. Right now, you'll continue to add a link between your drawing and the database.

You are ready to add a link to room 122. The first step is to set up your AutoCAD drawing so you can easily access the rooms you will be linking to. Then you will locate the record that is associated with room 122 in the Data View dialog box.

1. Zoom into the set of rooms in the lower-right corner of the plan so your view looks like Figure 10.8.

2. Click the Employee listing in the dbConnect dialog box, then click the Edit Table tool in the dbConnect toolbar. The Data View dialog box appears. Notice that Room Number appears in the list box in the toolbar. This tells you which link template you are using. If you have more than one link template, you can select the link template you want to use from this list box.

3. Scroll down the records to locate the record you added in the previous exercise. You can also use the New Query option to isolate the record, or you can quickly get to the end of the records by clicking the end-of-table navigation arrow at the bottom of the dialog box.

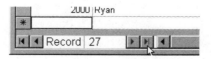

4.   Once you've found the record, click any field of the record.

5.   Click the Link and Label Settings tool in the toolbar and make sure that the Create Link option is selected. This option determines what type of link AutoCAD will create.

6.   Click the Link! tool in the toolbar. The Data View dialog box disappears and you see the selection cursor in the AutoCAD window.

7.   Click the room number 122 and the phone in the upper-left corner of the room, then press ↵ to finish your selection. The Data View dialog box returns. Now you see that the record is highlighted in yellow, indicating that it is linked to an object in the current drawing.

8.   In the Data View dialog box, link the records for room 116 and 114 to the same room numbers in the drawing. Remember to first select the record you want to link and click the Link! tool, then select the room number you want to link to. Room 116 is assigned to employee number 1022 and room number 114 is assigned to employee 1020.

Now you have a link established between the records for rooms 122, 116, and 114 in the database and their room numbers in your drawing. Next you'll learn how you can use those links to locate objects in the drawing or records in your database.

FIGURE 10.8:

The view of the drawing showing the rooms to the right of 122

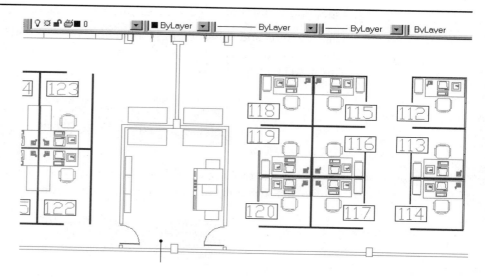

Locating Database Records through Drawing Objects

Now that you've got database links established, you can begin to make use of them. In the following exercise, you'll see how you can locate a database record by selecting an object in your drawing.

1. Go to the top of the table by clicking the first record button at the bottom of the Data View dialog box.

2. Click the View Linked Record in Table button in the Data View toolbar. The dialog box disappears.

3. Click the telephone in the upper-left corner of room 122, then click room numbers 114 and 116.

4. Press ↵ when you've completed your selections. The Data View dialog box appears again with the records for employees 1020, 1022, and 2000 highlighted.

As you can see from step 3, you can select several objects. AutoCAD isolates all of the records that are linked to the selected objects. You can go a step further and have AutoCAD display only the records associated with the linked objects.

1. Right-click the Room Number link template in the dbConnect dialog box, then select Link Select. The Link Select dialog box appears

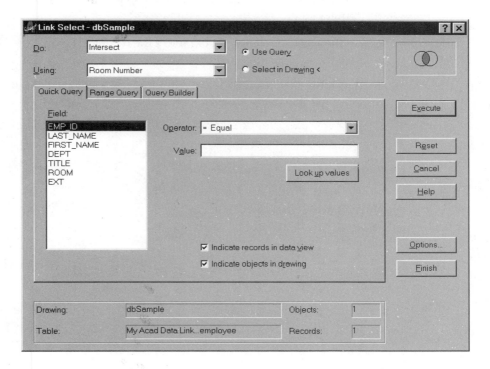

2. Click the Select in Drawing < radio button near the top of the dialog box.

3. Click the Select button. The dialog box disappears to allow you to select objects in the drawing.

4. Select room number 116, then press ↵. The Link Select dialog box reappears.

5. Click Finish. The Data View dialog box now displays only the record linked to the room number you selected.

The Link Select dialog box offers many more features that allow you to locate data either within your drawing or in your database.

Finding and Selecting Graphics through the Database

You've just seen how you can use links to locate records in a database. Links can also help you find and select objects in a drawing that are linked to a database. The next exercise shows, in a simplified way, how this works.

1. Click the Employee listing in the dbConnect dialog box, then click the Edit Table tool to open the entire table.

2. In the Data View dialog box, select the record for employee 2000. You can use the Last Record button to take you there.

3. Click the View Linked Objects in Drawing tool in the toolbar. The display shifts to center the linked object in the AutoCAD window.

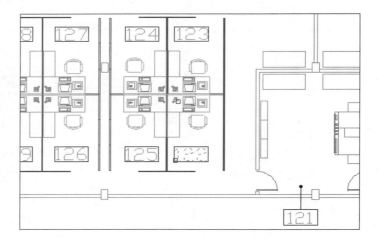

4. Move the Data View dialog box out of the way temporarily so you can view your drawing. Notice that the room number 122 and the telephone are highlighted and their grips are exposed.

Once these steps have been taken, you can use the Previous Object Selection option to select those objects that were highlighted in step 3.

In this example, you only selected objects in one office. However, you can create a record called Vacant, and then link all the vacant offices to this one record. When a new employee is hired, you can then quickly locate all the vacant rooms in the floor plan to place the new employee. If you continue to link each database record with rooms in the drawing, you can then later locate a person's room through the same process.

Adding Labels with Links

Database links can help you add labels to a drawing by using the data from a database table for the label text. The following exercise will show you how you can add the employee name and telephone extension number to the sample drawing.

1. In the Data View dialog box, click the Link and Label Settings tool in the toolbar and make sure that the Create Freestanding Labels option is selected. When you do this, the tool to the left changes to the Create Freestanding Label tool.

2. Click the button to the right of employee number 2000 to select that record.

3. Click the Create Freestanding Label tool in the toolbar. The New Label Template dialog box appears.

4. Enter the name **Employee Names**, then click Continue. The Label Template dialog box appears.

Notice that it looks quite similar to the Multiline Text Editor.

5. Click the Character tab and highlight the text in the text box.

6. Click the Text Height drop-down list and enter **6.**↵.

7. Click the Label Fields tab.

8. Select Last Name from the Field drop-down list, then click Add. The LAST_NAME entry appears in the text box.

9. Select Title from the Field drop-down list, then click Add again. The TITLE entry appears in the text box.

10. Click OK. The dialog box disappears and the point selection cursor appears in the AutoCAD window.

11. Click a clear location in room 122. The last name and title of employee 2000 appear as text in the drawing. Notice that these are the actual field values from the record you selected in step 2 and that they are the values from the fields you selected in steps 5 and 6.

Notice that now you have a listing in the dbConnect dialog box called Employee Names. This is the Label template you created in steps 4 through 10.

Next, you'll add a few more employee name labels to the floor plan. First you'll turn on the AutoView Linked Objects in Drawing tool so you can pan to the selected room number automatically. Then you'll proceed to add the new labels.

1. In the Data View dialog box, click the AutoView Linked Objects in Drawing tool.

2. In the Data View dialog box, click the button to the far left of the record for employee number 1020. Your view of the drawing pans to the link in room 114 that is already established in the drawing.

3. Click the Create Freestanding Label tool.

4. In the drawing, click a clear space in room 114 to place the label.

5. In the Data View dialog box, select the record for employee number 1022, then click the Create Freestanding Label tool.

6. In the drawing, click a free space in room 116 to place a label there.

Each label you add is linked to its corresponding record in the database. Notice that the label template appears just below the link template in the dbConnect dialog box. This tells you that the label template is dependent on the link template.

If you want to create labels based on different field data, you can create other label templates that include different sets of field values.

Adding Linked Labels

Now suppose you want to automatically label all of the links in the drawing. For example, suppose you want to show the telephone extension number for each link. In the next exercise, you'll create a new label template for the telephone extension field of the database table.

1. In the dbConnect dialog box, highlight the Employee listing, then click the New Label Template tool or right-click and select New Label Template from the popup menu.

2. In the New Label Template dialog box, enter **Extension** in the input box, then click Continue.

3. In the Label Template dialog box, select the Character tab.

4. Highlight the value in the Font Height drop-down list and enter **8**↵.

5. Select the Label Fields tab and select Ext from the Field drop-down list.

6. Click Add, then click OK to exit the dialog box.

You now have a label template for the telephone extension numbers. This label template is also dependent on the link template you created earlier in this set of exercises. You can use this template to automatically add phone extension labels to the drawing.

1. In the Data View dialog box, make sure the Extension label template shows in the Label Template drop-down list.

2. Click the Link and Label Settings tool and select Create Attached Labels.

3. Select the record for employee number 1020, then click the Create Attached Label tool. Extension number labels appear on each item that is linked to the record. The labels are placed on top of the object they are linked to.

4. Click the extension label that is on top of the employee name, then use its grip to move it away from the name. This shows you that the labels can be adjusted to a new position once they are placed.

5. Repeat steps 3 and 4 for employee numbers 1022 and 2000.

Each label you add with the Create Attached Label tool is linked to its associated record in the database.

Hiding Labels

You can edit the label in your drawing as you would any other multiline text object. Another characteristic of database labels is that you can control their visibility.

1. Right-click the Extension label template listed in the dbConnect dialog box, then select Hide Labels. The labels associated with the extension label template disappear.

2. Right-click the link template again and click Show Labels. The label reappears.

If you want to delete all of the labels associated with a label template, right-click the label template's name in the dbConnect dialog box, then select Delete Labels from the popup menu. Once you've done this, you can delete the label template as well by right-clicking the label template name and selecting Delete from the popup menu.

Editing Links

People and databases are always changing, so you need a way to update the links between your database and objects in your drawing. AutoCAD offers the Link Manager for this purpose.

Suppose you want to delete the link between the room number 116 in your drawing and the record for employee 1022.

1. Choose dbConnect ➤ Links ➤ Link Manager.

2. Click the room number 116 in your drawing. The Link Manager dialog box appears.

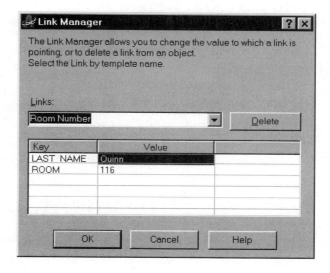

3. Click the Delete button.

4. Click OK. The link is removed and the linked label disappears.

You can also delete all the links associated with a link table by choosing dbConnect ➤ Links ➤ Delete Links. A dialog box appears, displaying a list of link tables.

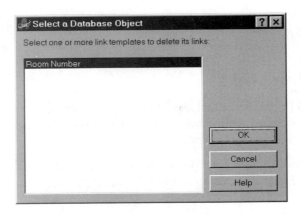

Select the link table whose links you want to delete, then click OK.

Where to Go from Here

You've seen how you can access and link your drawing to a database. This brief tutorial can help you find the information you will need to develop your own database needs.

If you understand SQL, you can take advantage of it to perform more sophisticated searches. You can also expand the functionality of the dbConnect Manager. These topics are, unfortunately, beyond the scope of this book. For more detailed ence manual.

If You Want to Experiment...

Attributes can be used to help automate data entry into drawings. To demonstrate this, try the following exercise.

Create a drawing file called Record with the attribute definitions shown in Figure 10.9. Note the size and placement of the attribute definitions as well as the new base point for the drawing. Save and exit the file, and then create a new drawing called Schedule containing the schedule shown in Figure 10.10. Use the Insert command and insert the Record file into the schedule at the point indicated. Note that you are prompted for each entry of the record. Enter any value you like for each prompt. When you are done, the information for one record is entered into the schedule.

FIGURE 10.9:

The Record file with attribute definitions

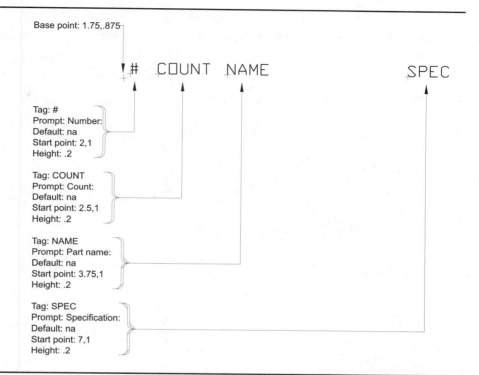

Base point: 1.75,.875

COUNT NAME   SPEC

Tag: #
Prompt: Number:
Default: na
Start point: 2,1
Height: .2

Tag: COUNT
Prompt: Count:
Default: na
Start point: 2.5,1
Height: .2

Tag: NAME
Prompt: Part name:
Default: na
Start point: 3.75,1
Height: .2

Tag: SPEC
Prompt: Specification:
Default: na
Start point: 7,1
Height: .2

FIGURE 10.10:

The Schedule drawing with Record inserted

Insert RECORD here.

NO	COUNT	PART NAME	SPECIFICATION
1	4	screw	5/16-18UNC-C.R.S.

5 1/2"
\(1/2" spacing
between lines\)

5/8" — 1 1/4" — 3 1/4" — 4 5/8"

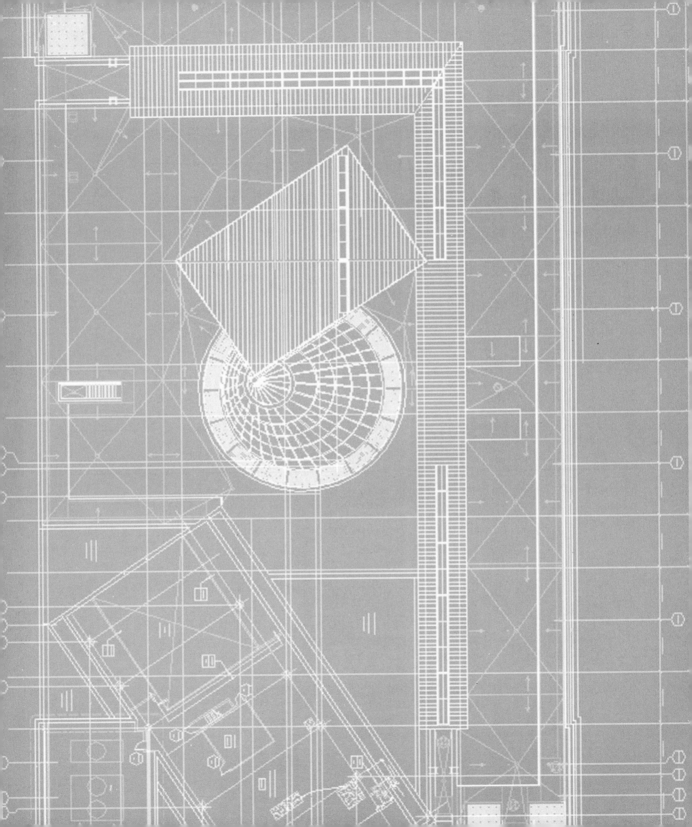

Working with Pre-existing Drawings and Raster Images

- Tracing, Scaling, and Scanning Drawings

- Importing and Tracing Raster Images

- Importing PostScript Images

- If You Want to Experiment...

11

At times you will want to turn a hand-drafted drawing into an AutoCAD drawing file. It may be that you are modifying a design you created before you started using AutoCAD, or that you are converting your entire library of drawings for future AutoCAD use. Or perhaps you want to convert a sketch into a formal drawing. This chapter discusses three ways to enter a hand-drafted drawing: tracing, scaling, and scanning. Each of these methods of drawing input has its advantages and disadvantages.

Tracing, Scaling, and Scanning Drawings

Tracing with a digitizing tablet is the easiest method to enter a hand-drafted drawing into AutoCAD, but a traced drawing usually requires some cleaning up and reorganization. If dimensional accuracy is not too important, tracing is the best method for entering existing drawings into AutoCAD. It is especially useful for drawings that contain irregular curves, such as the contour lines of a topographical map.

TIP   Even if you don't plan to trace drawings into AutoCAD, you still should read this section on tracing because some of the information presented here will help your everyday editing tasks.

Scaling a drawing is the most flexible method because you don't need a tablet to do it and generally, you are faced with less clean-up afterward. Scaling also affords the most accurate input of orthogonal lines because you can read dimensions directly from the drawing and enter those same dimensions into AutoCAD. The main drawback with scaling is that if the drawing does not contain complete dimensional information, you must constantly look at the hand-drafted drawing and measure distances with a scale. Also, irregular curves are difficult to scale accurately.

Scanning offers some unique opportunities with AutoCAD 2000, especially if you have a lot of RAM and a fast hard drive. Potentially, you can scan a drawing and save it on your computer as an image file, and then import the image into AutoCAD and trace over it. You still need to perform some clean-up work on the traced drawing, but because you can see your tracing directly on your screen, you have better control and you won't have quite as much cleaning up to do as you do when tracing from a digitizer.

There are also vectorizing programs that will automatically convert an image file into a vector file of lines and arcs. These programs may offer some help, but will require the most cleaning up of the options presented here. Like tracing, scanning is best used for drawings that are difficult to scale, such as complex topographical maps containing more contours than are practical to trace on a digitizer, or non-technical line art, such as letterhead and logos.

Tracing a Drawing

The most common method for entering a hand-drafted drawing into AutoCAD is tracing with a digitizer. If you are working with a large drawing and you have a small tablet, you may have to cut the drawing into pieces that your tablet can manage, trace each piece, and then assemble the completed pieces into the large drawing. However, the best solution is to have a large tablet.

The following exercises are designed for a 4" × 5" (10cm × 12.7cm) or larger tablet. The sample drawings are small enough to fit completely on this size of tablet. You can use either a stylus or a puck to trace them, but the stylus offers the most natural feel because it is shaped like a pen. A puck has crosshairs that you have to center on the line you want to trace, and this requires a bit more dexterity.

NOTE If you don't have a digitizing tablet, you can use scaling to enter the utility room drawing used in this section's tracing exercise. (You will insert the utility room into your apartment building plan in Chapter 12.)

Reconfiguring the Tablet for Tracing

When you first installed AutoCAD, you configured the tablet to use most of its active drawing area for AutoCAD's menu template. Because you will need the tablet's entire drawing area to trace this drawing, you now need to reconfigure the tablet to eliminate the menu. Otherwise, you won't be able to pick points on the drawing outside the 4" × 3" (10cm × 7.6cm) screen pointing area AutoCAD normally uses (see Figure 11.1).

TIP You can save several different AutoCAD configurations that can be easily set using the Options dialog box (see Appendix B).

FIGURE 11.1:

The tablet's active drawing area

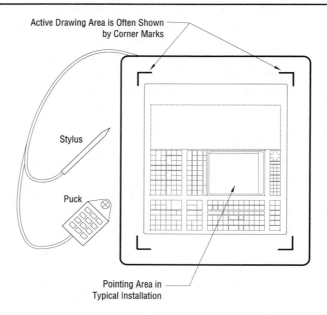

Active Drawing Area is Often Shown by Corner Marks

Stylus

Puck

Pointing Area in Typical Installation

TIP

Remember that in AutoCAD, the *x* and *y* components of a coordinate are separated by a comma. The comma between two numbers does not denote a decimal separation.

Here are the steps to follow:

1. Start AutoCAD and create a new file called Utility.

2. Set up the file as a 1/4"=1'-scale architectural drawing on an 8 1/2" × 11" sheet (limits set to 0,0 for the lower-left corner and 528,408 for the upper-right corner). Metric users should set up their drawing as a 1:50 scale drawing on an A4 size sheet. (Limits for metric users should be 0,0 for the lower-left corner and 1480,1050 for the upper-right corner).

3. Choose Tools ➤ Tablet ➤ Configure, or type **Ta↵ CFG↵**.

4. At the Enter number of tablet menus desired (0-4): prompt, enter **0↵**.

NOTE

When selecting points on the tablet, take care not to accidentally press the pick button twice, as this will give you erroneous results. Many tablets have sensitive pick buttons that can cause problems when you are selecting points.

5. At the Do you want to respecify the Fixed Screen Pointing Area?: prompt, enter **Y**↵.

6. At the Digitize lower left corner of screen pointing area: prompt, pick the lower-left corner of the tablet's active drawing area.

NOTE   On some tablets, a light appears to show you the active area; other tablets use a permanent mark, such as a corner mark. AutoCAD won't do anything until you have picked a point, so you don't have to worry about picking a point outside this area.

---

7. At the Digitize upper right corner of screen pointing area: prompt, pick the upper-right corner.

8. At the Do you want to specify the Floating Screen pointing area <N>: prompt, press ↵.

Now as you move your stylus or puck, you'll notice a difference in the relationship between your hand movement and the screen cursor. The cursor moves more slowly and it is active over more of the tablet surface.

Calibrating the Tablet for Your Drawing

Now make a photocopy of Figure 11.2, which represents a hand-drafted drawing of a utility room for your apartment building. Place the photocopied drawing on your tablet so that it is aligned with the tablet and completely within the tablet's active drawing area (see Figure 11.3).

Before you can trace anything into your computer, you must calibrate your tablet. This means you must give some points of reference so AutoCAD can know how distances on the tablet relate to distances in the drawing editor. For example, you may want to trace a drawing that was drawn at a scale of 1/8"=1'-0". You will have to show AutoCAD two specific points on this drawing, as well as where those two points should appear in the drawing editor. This is accomplished by using the Tablet command's Cal option.

NOTE   When you calibrate a tablet, you are setting ratios for AutoCAD; for example, 2 inches on your tablet equals 16 feet in the drawing editor.

FIGURE 11.2:

The utility room drawing

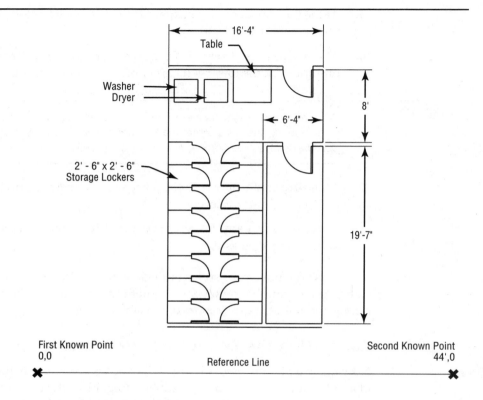

In Figure 11.2, we have already determined the coordinates for two points on a reference line.

1. Choose Tools ➤ Tablet ➤ Calibrate, or enter **Tablet⏎ Cal⏎** at the command prompt.

2. The prompt `Digitize point #1:` appears, asking you to pick the first point for which you know the absolute coordinates. Pick the X on the left end of the reference line.

3. At the `Enter coordinates for point #1:` prompt, enter **0,0⏎**. This tells AutoCAD that the point you just picked is equivalent to the coordinate 0,0 in your drawing editor.

4. Next, the `Digitize point #2:` prompt asks you to pick another point for which you know the coordinates. Pick the X on the right end of the reference line.

5. At the Enter coordinates for point #2: prompt, enter **44',0**↵. Metric users should enter **1340,0**↵.

6. At the Digitize point #3 (or RETURN to end): prompt, press ↵. The tablet is now calibrated.

FIGURE 11.3:

The drawing placed on the tablet

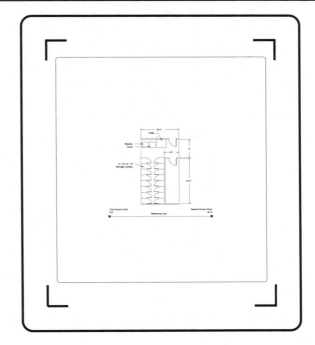

The word TABLET appears on the status bar to tell you that you are in Tablet mode. While in Tablet mode, you can trace the drawing but you cannot access the menus in Windows with some digitizers. (Check your digitizer manual for further information.) If you want to pick a menu item, you must toggle the Tablet mode off by using the F4 function key. Or you can enter commands through the keyboard. (If you need some reminders of the keyboard commands, type **Help**↵, and click Commands in the Help dialog box to get a list.)

Calibrating More Than Two Points

In step 6 of the previous exercise, you bypassed the prompt that offered you the chance to calibrate a third point. In fact, you can calibrate as many as 31 points.

Why would anyone want to calibrate so many points? Often the drawing or photograph you are trying to trace will be distorted in one direction or another. For example, blueline prints are usually stretched in one direction because of the way prints are rolled through a print machine.

NOTE   This section is not crucial to the tutorial and can be skipped for now. You may want to just skim through it and read it more carefully later on.

You can compensate for distortions by specifying several known points during your calibration. For example, we could have included a vertical distance on the utility room drawing to indicate a distance in the y-axis. You could have then picked that distance and calibrated its point. AutoCAD would then have a point of reference for the y distance as well as the x distance. If you calibrate only two points, as you did in the previous exercise, AutoCAD will scale x and y distances equally. Calibrating three points causes AutoCAD to scale x and y distances separately, making adjustments for each axis based on their respective calibration points.

Now suppose you want to trace a perspective view of a building, but you want to "flatten" the perspective so that all the lines are parallel. You can calibrate the four corners of the buildings facade to stretch out the narrow end of the perspective view to be parallel with the wide end. This is a limited form of what cartographers call *rubber-sheeting*, where various areas of the tablet are stretched by specific scale factors.

When you select more than two points for calibration, you will get a message similar to that shown in Figure 11.4. Let's take a look at the parts of this message.

In the text window, you see the labels "Orthogonal," "Affine," and "Projective." These are the three major types of calibrations or transformation types. The orthogonal transformation scales the x-axis and y-axis using the same values. Affine transformation scales the x-axis and y-axis separately and requires at least three points. The projective transformation stretches the tablet coordinates differently, depending on where you are on the tablet. It requires at least four calibration points.

Just below each of these labels you will see either "Success," "Exact," or "Impossible." This tells you whether any of these transformation types are available to you. Because this example shows what you see when you pick three points, you get Impossible for the projective transformation.

The far-left column tells you what is shown in each of the other three columns.

FIGURE 11.4:

AutoCAD's assessment of
the calibration

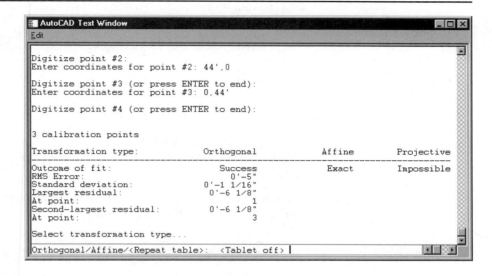

Finally, the prompt at the bottom of the screen lets you select which transformation type to use. If you calibrate four or more points, the projective transformation is added to the prompt. The Repeat Table option simply refreshes the table.

Take care when you calibrate points on your tablet. Here are a few things to watch out for when calibrating your tablet:

- Use only known calibration points.

- Try to locate calibration points that cover a large area of your image.

- Don't get carried away. Try to limit calibration points to only those necessary to get the job done.

Tracing Lines from a Drawing

Now you are ready to trace the utility room. If you don't have a digitizer, you can skip this exercise. A traced file is included on the companion CD-ROM that you can use for later exercises.

1. Make sure the ORTHO and POLAR buttons are off in the status bar.

| SNAP | GRID | ORTHO | POLAR | OSNAP | OTRACK | LWT |

2. Click the Line tool on the Draw toolbar, or type **L**↵.

3. Trace the outline of all the walls except the storage lockers.

4. Add the doors by inserting the Door file at the appropriate points and then mirroring them. The doors may not fit exactly, but you'll get a chance to make adjustments later.

5. Trace the washer and, because the washer and dryer are the same size, copy the washer over to the position of the dryer.

> **TIP** Once a tablet has been calibrated, you can trace your drawing from the tablet, even if the area you are tracing is not displayed in the drawing editor.

At this point, your drawing should look something like the top image of Figure 11.5—a close facsimile of the original drawing, but not as exact as you might like. Zoom in to one of the doors. Now you can see the inaccuracies of tracing. Some of the lines are crooked, and others don't meet at the right points. These inaccuracies are caused by the limited resolution of your tablet, coupled with the lack of steadiness in the human hand. The best digitizing tablets have an accuracy of 0.001 inch, which is actually not very good when you are dealing with tablet distances of 1/8" and smaller. In the following section, you will clean up your drawing.

> **NOTE** The raggedness of the door arc is the result of the way AutoCAD displays arcs when you use the Zoom command. See Chapter 6 for further explanation.

Cleaning Up a Traced Drawing

In this section, you'll reposition a door jamb, straighten some lines, adjust a dimension, and add the storage lockers to the utility room. If you didn't have a chance to digitize your own Utility file, use the file `11a-util.dwg` from the companion CD-ROM to do the following exercises.

FIGURE 11.5:

The traced drawing, and a close-up of the door

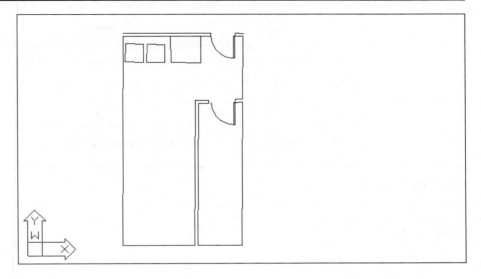

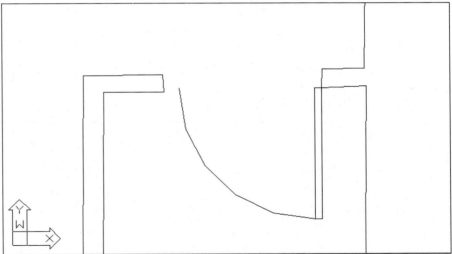

Moving the End of a Wall   In Figure 11.5, one of the door jambs is not in the right position (the bottom image gives you the best look). In this next exercise, you will fix this by repositioning a group of objects while keeping their vertices intact, using the Grips feature.

1.   Enlarge your view so it looks similar to the bottom image of Figure 11.5.

2. Pick a crossing window enclosing the door jamb to be moved (see the top image of Figure 11.6).

3. Click one of the grips at the end of the wall, and then Shift+click the other grip. You should have two hot grips at the door jamb.

4. Click the lower of the two hot grips, and drag the corner away to see what happens (see the bottom image of Figure 11.6).

5. Use the Endpoint Osnap to pick the endpoint of the arc. The jamb repositions itself, and all the lines follow (see Figure 11.7).

FIGURE 11.6:

A window crossing the door jamb, and the door jamb being stretched

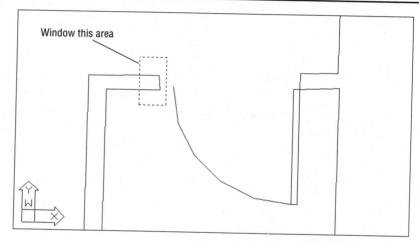

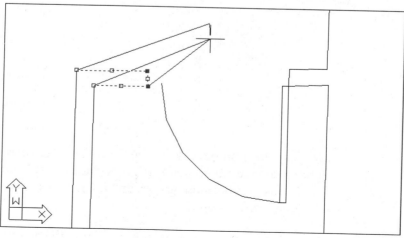

FIGURE 11.7:

The repositioned door jamb

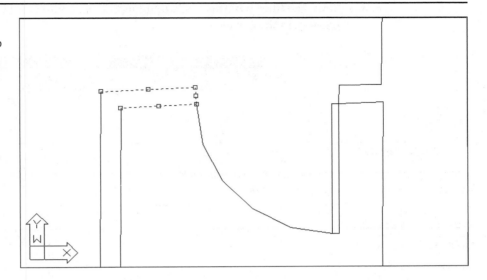

If AutoCAD doesn't respond in the way described in this section, make sure the Noun/Verb selection setting and the Grips feature are both turned on.

Straightening Lines   Another problem in this drawing is that some of the lines are not orthogonal. To straighten them, you use the Change command, together with the Ortho mode. In the following exercise, you'll use the Change command keyboard shortcut.

1. Press the Esc key to clear any grip selections that may be active.

2. Toggle the Ortho mode on.

3. Type **–Ch.⏎** at the command prompt to start this operation. Make sure you include the minus sign.

4. At the Object selection: prompt, pick the four lines representing the walls just left of the door, and press ⏎ to confirm your selection.

5. At the Specify change point or [Properties]: prompt, click the corner where the two walls meet. The four lines straighten out, as shown in Figure 11.8.

6. Once the lines have been straightened, use the Fillet tool in the Modify toolbar to join the corners.

The Change command's Change Point option changes the location of the endpoint closest to the new point location. This can cause erroneous results when you are trying to modify groups of lines.

FIGURE 11.8:

The lines after using the Change Point option of the Change command

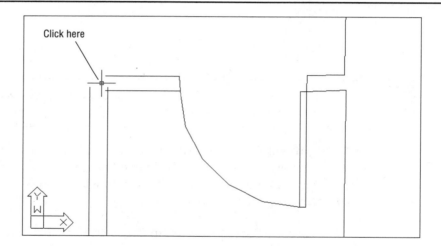

As you have just seen, you can use the Change command to quickly straighten a set of lines. When used carefully, this command can be a real time-saver.

Be aware that the Change command moves the nearest endpoints of selected lines to the new location. This can cause unpredictable results in some situations (see Figure 11.10). Note that the Change command does not affect polyline line segments.

In addition to straightening lines, you can use the Change command to align a set of lines to another line. For example, when used with the Perpendicular Osnap, several lines can be made to align at a perpendicular angle to another line. However, this only works with the Ortho mode on.

You also can extend several lines to be perpendicular to a nonorthogonal line. To do so, you have to rotate the cursor to that line's angle (see the top image in Figure 11.9), using the Snapang system variable. (You can also use the Snap Angle input box in the Tools ➤ Drawing Aids dialog box to rotate the cursor.) Then use the process just described to extend or shorten the other lines (see the bottom image of Figure 11.9).

When changing several lines to be perpendicular to another line, you must carefully choose the new endpoint location. Figure 11.10 shows what happens to the same line shown in the top image of Figure 11.9 when perpendicular reference is placed in the middle of the set of lines. Some lines are straightened to a perpendicular orientation, while others have the wrong endpoints aligned with the reference line.

Before moving on to the next section, use the Change command to straighten the other lines in your drawing. Start by straightening the corner to the right of the door in Figure 11.8.

1. Issue the Change command again.

2. Select the four lines that represent the walls to the right of the door, and then press ↵.

3. Click a point near the corner.

4. Chances are, the two vertical lines are not aligned. Move the top line so that it aligns with the lower one. You can use the Perpendicular Osnap to help with the alignment.

5. Use the Change command on each of the other corners until all the walls have been straightened. You can also use Change in a similar way to straighten the door jambs.

6. Once you've straightened the lines, use the Fillet tool on the Modify toolbar to join the corners end to end.

FIGURE 11.9:

You can use the Change command to quickly straighten a set of non-parallel lines and to align their endpoints to another reference line.

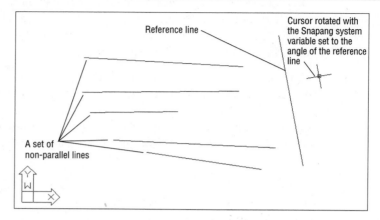

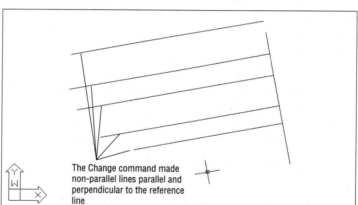

FIGURE 11.10:

The results of the Change command can be unpredictable if the endpoint location is too close to the lines being changed.

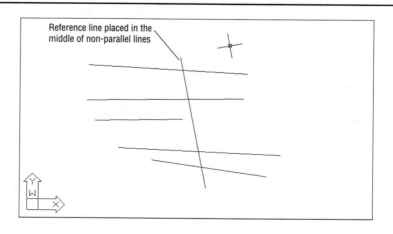

FIGURE 11.10 CONTINUED:

The results of the Change command can be unpredictable if the endpoint location is too close to the lines being changed.

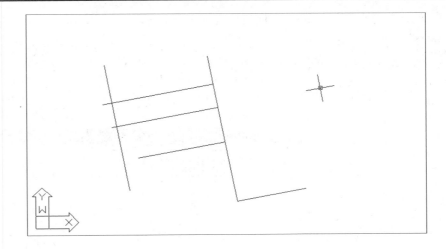

TIP
When using the Fillet tool to join lines, you can issue the Fillet command, and then type **C**↵ and enclose the two lines you wish to fillet with a crossing window.

Adjusting the Room Size   The overall interior dimension of the original utility room drawing is 16'-4"×28'-0". Chances are that the dimensions of the drawing you traced will vary somewhat from these. You will need to adjust your drawing to fit these dimensions.

1. Draw a horizontal line 16'-4" long (498cm for metric users) from the left wall; then draw a vertical line 28' long (856.6cm for metric users) from the bottom wall line, as shown in Figure 11.11.

2. Use the two lines you drew in step 1 to adjust the walls to their proper positions (see Figure 11.11). You can either use the Grips feature or click Stretch on the Modify toolbar.

3. Choose Draw ➤ Block ➤ Base, or type **Base**. Then make the upper-left corner of the utility room the base point.

4. To add the storage lockers, begin by drawing one 30" × 30" (76cm × 76cm for metric users) locker accurately.

5. Use the Mirror and Array commands to create the other lockers. Both of these commands are available on the Modify toolbar. (For entering objects repeatedly, this is actually a faster and more accurate method than tracing. If you traced each locker, you would also have to clean up each one.)

Finally, you may want to add the dimensions and labels shown earlier in Figure 11.2.

1. Create a layer called Notes to contain the dimensions and labels.

2. Set the Dimscale dimension setting to **48** (**50** for metric users) before you start dimensioning. To do this, choose Dimension Style from the Dimension toolbar. Make sure the Standard dimension style is selected, then click Modify. In the Modify Dimension Style dialog box, select the Fit tab and click the Use Overall Scale Of radio button. Next, enter **48** (**50** for metric users) in the input box to the right of the Use Overall Scale Of radio button. (See Chapter 9 for details on this process.)

NOTE   You can also set the Dimscale dimension setting by typing **Dimscale⏎**, and then entering the desired scale of **48**.

---

3. Select the Text tab and set the text height to 1/8" (0.3 for metric users).

4. When you are done, click OK, then click Close and save the file and exit AutoCAD.

TIP   Make sure that the text style that you are using with your dimension style is set to a height of 0 if you want the dimension style text height to take effect.

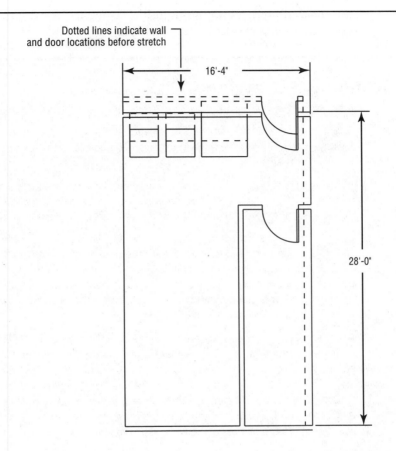

FIGURE 11.11:

The walls stretched to the proper dimensions

Working Smarter with Digitizers

In the first exercise of this chapter, you traced an entire drawing. However, you could have just traced the major lines with the Ortho mode on, and then used the Offset command to draw the wall thickness. The Fillet and Trim commands (see Chapter 5) could then be used to clean up the drawing where lines cross or where they don't meet.

If you are a civil engineer, you would take a different approach. In laying out a road, for instance, you might first trace the center lines, and then use the Offset option on the Modify toolbar to place the curb and gutter. You could trace curved features using arcs (just to see what the radius of the curve is), and then redraw the arc accurately, joining straight-line segments. The digitizer can be a great tool if it is used with care and a touch of creativity.

Scanning a Drawing

No discussion of drawing input can be complete without mentioning scanners. Imagine how easy it would be to convert an existing library of drawings into AutoCAD drawing files by simply running them through a scanning device. Unfortunately, scanning drawings is not quite that simple.

In scanning, the drawing size can be a problem. Desktop scanners are generally limited to an 8 1/2 " × 14" or 26cm × 37cm sheet size. Some low-cost handheld scanners will scan a 22 "×14" or 56cm × 37cm area. Larger format scanners are available but more expensive.

Once the drawing is scanned and saved as a file, you have two paths to importing it into AutoCAD. One path is to convert the scanned image into AutoCAD objects such as lines, arcs, and circles. This requires special software and is usually a fairly time-consuming process. Finally, the drawing usually requires some clean-up, which can take even longer than cleaning up a traced drawing. The poorer the condition of the original drawing, the more clean-up you'll have to do.

Another path is to import a scanned image directly into AutoCAD and then use some or all of the scanned image in combination with AutoCAD objects. You can trace over the scanned image using the standard AutoCAD tools and then discard the image when you are done, or you can use the scanned image as part of your AutoCAD file. With Auto-CAD's ability to import raster images, you can, for example, import a scanned image of an existing paper drawing, and then mask off the area you wish to edit. You can then draw over the masked portions to make the required changes.

Whether a scanner can help you depends on your application. If you have drawings that would be very difficult to trace—large, complex topographical maps, for example—a scanner may well be worth a look. You don't necessarily have to buy one; some scanning services offer excellent value. And if you can accept the quality of a scanned drawing before it is cleaned up, you can save a lot of time. On the other hand, a drawing composed mostly of orthogonal lines and notes may be more easily traced by hand with a large tablet or entered directly by using the drawing's dimensions.

Scanning can be an excellent document management tool for your existing paper drawings. You might consider scanning your existing paper drawings for archiving purposes.

You can then use portions or all of your scanned drawings later, without committing to a full-scale, paper-to-AutoCAD scan conversion.

Importing and Tracing Raster Images

If you have a scanner and you would like to use it to import drawings and other images into AutoCAD, you can use AutoCAD's raster image import capabilities. There are many reasons for wanting to import a scanned image. In architectural plans, a vicinity map is frequently used to show the location of a project. With the permission of its creator, you can scan a map into AutoCAD and incorporate it into a cover sheet. That cover sheet may also contain other images, such as photographs of the site, computer renderings and elevations of the project, and company logos.

Another use for importing scanned images is to use the image as a reference to trace over. You can trace a drawing with greater accuracy using a scanned image as opposed to digitizing tablet. With the price of scanners falling to below $100, a scanner is a cost-effective tool for tracing a wide variety of graphic material. In this section, you'll learn firsthand how you can import an image as a background for tracing.

The Insert ➢ Image Manager option in the pull-down menu opens the Image Manager dialog box, which in turn allows you to import a full range of raster image files.

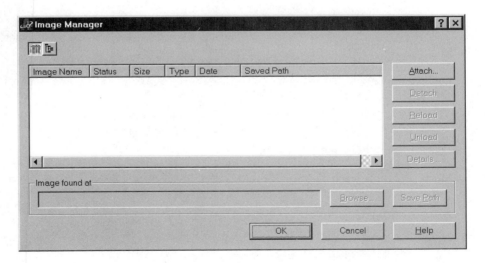

If you read Chapter 6, then this dialog box should look familiar. It looks and works just like the External Reference dialog box. The similarities are more than just cosmetic. Just like external references (Xrefs), raster images are loaded when the current file is open but they are not stored as part of the current file when the file is saved. This helps keep file sizes down, but it also means that you need to keep track of inserted raster files. You will need to make sure that they are kept together with the AutoCAD files in which they are inserted.

Tips for Importing Raster Images

When you scan a document into your computer, you get a raster image file. Unlike Auto-CAD files, raster image files are made up of a matrix of colors that form a picture. Vector files, like those produced by AutoCAD, are made up of lines, arcs, curves, and circles. The two formats, raster and vector, are so different that it is difficult to accurately convert one format to the other. It is easier to trace a raster file in AutoCAD than it is to try to have some computer program make the conversion for you.

But even tracing a raster image file can be difficult if the image is of poor quality. Here are a few points you should consider if you plan to use raster import for tracing drawings:

- Scan in your drawing using a grayscale or color scanner, or convert your black-and-white scanned image to grayscale using your scanner software.

- Use a paint program or your scanner software to clean up unwanted gray or spotted areas in the file before importing it into AutoCAD.

- If your scanner software or paint program has a de-speckle or de-spot routine, use it. It can help clean up your image and ultimately reduce the raster image file size.

- Scan at a reasonable resolution. Remember that the human hand is usually not more accurate than a few thousandths of an inch, so scanning at 150 to 200 dpi may be more than adequate.

- If you plan to make heavy use of raster import, upgrade your computer to the fastest processor you can afford and don't spare the memory.

The raster import commands can incorporate paper maps or plans into 3D AutoCAD drawings for presentations. I know of one architectural firm that produces some very impressive presentations with very little effort, by combining 2D scanned images with 3D massing models for urban design studies. (A *massing model* is a model that shows only the rough outline of buildings without giving too much detail. Massing models show the general scale of a project without being too fussy.) Raster images do not, however, appear in perspective views.

TIP   AutoCAD offers a "suitcase" utility called Pack 'n Go that will collect AutoCAD files and their related support files, such as raster images, external references, and fonts, into any folder or drive that you specify. See Chapter 19 for details.

Another similarity between Xrefs and imported raster images is that you can clip a raster image so that only a portion of the image is displayed in your drawing. Portions of a raster file that are clipped are not stored in memory, so your system won't get bogged down, even if the raster file is huge.

The following exercise gives you step-by-step instructions on importing a raster file. It also gives you a chance to see how scanned resolution translates into an image in AutoCAD. This is important for those readers interested in scanning drawings for the purpose of tracing over them.

1. Create a new file called Rastertrace.

2. Set up the file as a 1/4"=1'-scale architectural drawing on an 8 1/2" × 11" sheet (limits set to 0,0 for the lower-left corner and 528,408 for the upper-right corner). Metric users should set up their drawing as a 1:50 scale drawing on an A4 size sheet. (Limits for metric users should be 0,0 for the lower-left corner and 1480,1050 for the upper-right corner).

3. Choose View ➢ Zoom ➢ All to make sure the entire drawing limits are displayed on the screen.

4. Draw a line across the screen from coordinates 0,20' to 60',20'. Metric users should draw the line from 0,600 to 1820,600. You will use this line in a later exercise.

5. Click Insert ➢ Image Manager, or type **Im**↵ to open the Image Manager dialog box.

6. Click the Attach button in the upper-right corner of the dialog box. The Select File to Attach dialog box appears. This is a typical AutoCAD File dialog box complete with a preview window.

7. Locate and select the `Raster1.jpg` file from the companion CD-ROM. Notice that you can see a preview of the file in the right side of the dialog box.

8. Click Open. The Image dialog box appears. Click OK.

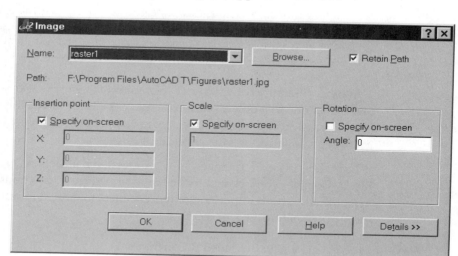

9. Press ↵ at the Insertion Point: prompt to accept the 0,0 coordinates.

10. At the Scale Factor: prompt, use the cursor to scale the image so it fills about half the screen, as shown in Figure 11.12.

TIP

You can bypass the Image dialog box and go directly to the Attach Image dialog box by entering **Iat**↵ at the command prompt.

The Image Dialog Box Options

The Attach Image dialog box you saw in step 7 of the previous exercise helps you manage your imported image files. It is especially helpful when you have a large number of images in your drawing. Like the External Reference dialog box, you can temporarily unload images (to help speed up the editing of AutoCAD objects), reload, detach, and relocate raster image files. Refer to *Other External Reference Options* in Chapter 6 for a detailed description of these options.

FIGURE 11.12:

Manually scaling the raster image

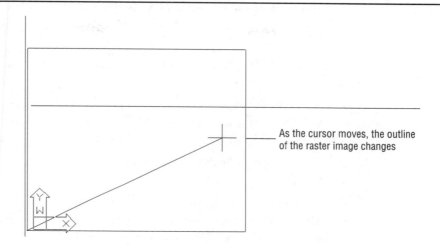

As the cursor moves, the outline of the raster image changes

Scaling a Raster Image

The `Raster1.jpg` file from the companion CD-ROM is a scanned image of Figure 11.2. It was scanned as a grayscale image at 100 dpi. This shows that you can get a reasonable amount of detail at a fairly low scan resolution.

Now suppose you want to trace over this image to start an AutoCAD drawing. The first thing you'll want to do is to scale the image to the appropriate size. You can scale an image file to full size. Try the following steps to see how you might begin the process.

1. Choose View ➢ Zoom ➢ Extents.

2. Click Scale on the Modify toolbar.

    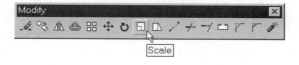

3. Click the edge of the raster image to select it. A crosshatch appears across the image to tell you that it is selected.

4. Press ↵ to finish your selection.

5. At the `Base Point:` prompt, click the X in the lower-left corner of the image—the one you used in the first exercise to calibrate your digitizing tablet.

6. At the `Scale factor>/Reference:` prompt, enter **R**↵ to use the Reference option.

7. At the `Reference Length:` prompt, type **@**↵. This tells AutoCAD that you want to use the last point selected as one end of the reference length. Once you enter the @ symbol, you'll see a rubber-banding line emanating from the X.

8. At the `Second Point:` prompt, click the X at the lower-right corner of the image.

9. At the `New Length:` prompt, enter **44'**↵. Metric users should enter **1341**↵. The image enlarges. Remember that this reference line is 44 feet or 1341cm in length relative to the utility room plan.

The image is now scaled properly for the plan it portrays. You can proceed to trace over the image. You can also place the image on its own layer and turn it off from time to time to check your trace work. Even if you don't trace the scanned floor plan line for line, you can read the dimensions of the plan from your computer monitor, instead of having to go back and forth between measuring the paper drawing and drawing the plan on the computer.

Controlling Object Visibility and Overlap with Raster Images

With the introduction of raster image support, AutoCAD inherits a problem fairly common to programs that use them. Raster images will obscure other objects that were placed before the raster image. The image you imported in the last exercise, for example, obscures the line you drew when you first opened the file. In most cases, this overlap may not be a problem, but there will be situations where you will want AutoCAD vector objects to overlap an imported raster image. An example of this would be a civil engineering drawing showing an AutoCAD drawing of a new road superimposed over an aerial view of the location for the road.

Paint and page-layout programs usually offer a "to front" and "to back" tool to control the overlap of objects and images. AutoCAD offers the Draworder command. Here's how it works.

1. Choose View ➤ Zoom ➤ Extents to get an overall view of the image.

2. Choose Tools ➤ Display Order ➤ Bring Above Object.

3. At the `Select objects:` prompt, select the horizontal line you drew when you first opened the file.

4. You could go on to select other objects. Press ↵ to finish your selection.

5. At the `Select Reference Objects:` prompt, click the edge of the raster image of the Utility room.

The drawing regenerates and the entire line appears, no longer obscured by the raster image.

The Draworder command you just used actually offers four options. On the pull-down menu, these options are:

Tools ➣ Display Order ➣ Bring to Front   Places an object or set of objects at the top of the draw order for the entire drawing. The effect is that the objects are completely visible.

Tools ➣ Display Order ➣ Send to Back   Places an object or set of objects at the bottom of the draw order for the entire drawing. The effect is that the objects may be obscured by other objects in the drawing.

Tools ➣ Display Order ➣ Bring Above Object   Places an object or set of objects above another object in the draw order. This has the effect of making the first set of objects appear above the second selected object.

Tools ➣ Display Order ➣ Bring Under Object   Places an object or set of objects below another object in the draw order. This has the effect of making the first set of objects appear underneath the second selected object.

You can also use the **Dr** keyboard shortcut to issue the Draworder command. If you do this, you see this prompt:

```
Above object/Under object/Front/<Back>:
```

You must then select the option by entering through the keyboard the capitalized letter of the option.

Although this section discussed the display order tools in relation to raster images, they can also be invaluable in controlling visibility of line work in conjunction with hatch patterns and solid fills. See Chapter 13 for a detailed discussion of the display order tools and solid fills.

TIP   Under certain conditions, the draw order of external reference files may not appear properly. If you encounter this problem, open the Xref file and make sure the draw order is correct. Then use the Wblock command to export all its objects to a new file. Use the new file for the external reference instead of the original external reference.

Clipping a Raster Image

In Chapter 6, you saw how you can clip an external reference object so that only a portion of it appears in the drawing. You can also clip imported raster images in the same way. Just as with Xrefs, you can create a closed outline of the area you want to clip, or you can specify a simple rectangular area. In the following exercise, you'll try out the Imageclip command to control the display of the raster image.

1. Choose Modify ➢ Clip ➢ Image, or type **Icl**↵.

2. At the Select Image to Clip: prompt, click the edge of the raster image.

3. At the ON/OFF/Delete/<New boundary>: prompt, press ↵ to create a new boundary.

4. At the Polygonal/<Rectangular>: prompt, enter **P**↵ to draw a polygonal boundary.

5. Select the points shown in the top image of Figure 11.13 and then press ↵ when you are done. The raster image is clipped to the boundary you created, as shown in the continued image of Figure 11.13.

As the prompt in step 3 indicates, you can turn the clipping off or on, or delete an existing clipping boundary through the Clip Image option.

Once you have clipped a raster image, you can adjust the clipping boundary using its grips.

1. Click the boundary edge of the raster image to expose its grips.

2. Click a grip in the upper-right corner, as shown in the continued image of Figure 11.13.

3. Drag the grip up and to the right, and then click a point. The image adjusts to the new boundary.

FIGURE 11.13:

Adjusting the boundary of a clipped image

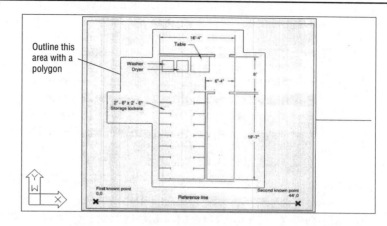

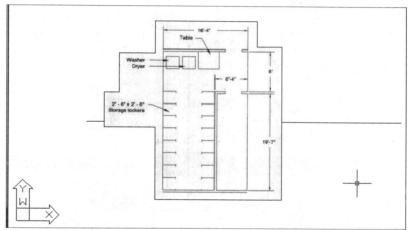

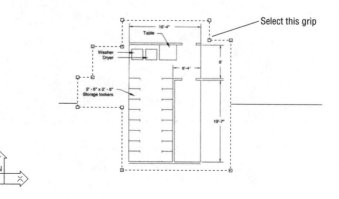

In addition to hiding portions of a raster image that may be unimportant to you, clipping an image file reduces the amount of RAM the raster image uses during your editing session. AutoCAD only loads the visible portion of the image into RAM. The rest is ignored.

TIP   The Wipeout tool in the Bonus Standard toolbar can also mask out a portion of a raster image. This is useful if you want to hide portions of a raster image that may make it difficult to view overlapping AutoCAD objects such as text or dimensions. Wipeout can also be useful as a general masking tool for AutoCAD objects. See Chapter 19 for details on how this tool works.

Adjusting Brightness, Contrast, and Strength

AutoCAD offers a tool that allows you to adjust the brightness, contrast, and strength of a raster image. Try making some adjustments to the raster image of the utility room in the following exercise.

1. Choose Modify ➤ Object ➤ Image ➤ Adjust, or type **Iad**↵.

2. At the Select Image to Adjust: prompt, click the edge of the raster image, then press ↵. The Image Adjust dialog box appears.

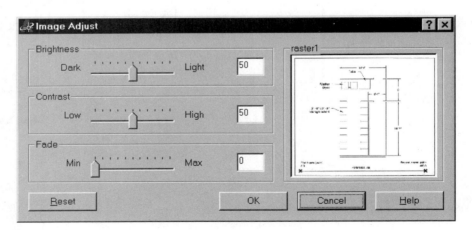

3. Click and drag the Fade slider to the right so that it is near the middle of the slider scale. Or enter **50** in the Fade input box that is just to the right of the slider. Notice how the sample image fades to the AutoCAD background color as you move the slider.

4. Click OK. The raster image appears faded.

You can adjust the brightness and contrast using the other two sliders in the Image Adjust dialog box. The Reset button resets all the settings to their default value.

By using the Image Adjust option in conjunction with image clipping, you can create special effects. Figure 11.14 shows an aerial view of downtown San Francisco. This view consists of two copies of the same raster image. One copy serves as a background, which was lightened using the same method demonstrated in the previous exercise. The second copy is the darker area of the image with a triangular clip boundary applied. You might use this technique to bring focus to a particular area of a drawing you are preparing for a presentation.

Figure 11.14 also contains AutoCAD text and line objects drawn over the image. The text labels make use of the Wipeout bonus tool to hide their background, making them easier to read. The Draworder command is also instrumental in creating this type of image by allowing you to control which object appears on top of others.

TIP	If the draw order of objects appears incorrectly after opening a file or performing a Pan or Zoom, issue a Regen to recover the correct draw order view.

FIGURE 11.14:

Two copies of the same image can be combined to create emphasis on a portion of the drawing.

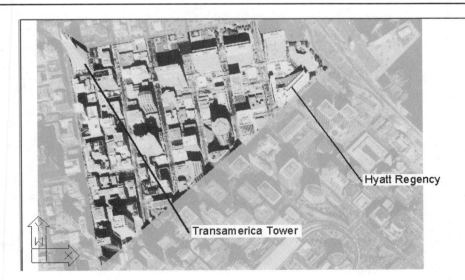

Turning Off the Frame, Adjusting Overall Quality, and Controlling Transparency

Three other adjustments can be made to your raster image: frame visibility, image quality, and image transparency.

By default, a raster image displays an outline or frame. In many instances, this frame may detract from your drawing. You can globally turn off image frames by choosing Modify ➢ Object ➢ Image ➢ Frame, then entering **On** or **Off**, depending on whether you want the frame visible or invisible (see Figure 11.15). You can also type **Imageframe↵ Of↵**.

FIGURE 11.15:

A raster image with the frame on (top) and off (bottom)

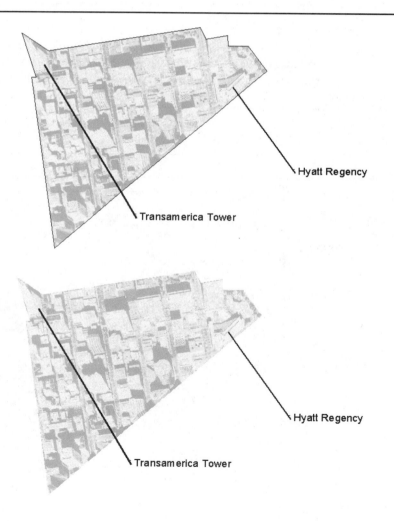

Hyatt Regency

Transamerica Tower

Hyatt Regency

Transamerica Tower

WARNING If you turn off the frame of raster images, you will not be able to select them for editing. You can use this to your advantage if you don't want a raster image to be moved or otherwise edited. To make a raster image selectable, turn on the image frame setting.

If your drawing doesn't require the highest quality image, you can set the image quality to Draft mode. You might use Draft mode when you are tracing an image, or when the image is already of a high quality. To set the image quality, choose Modify ➤ Object ➤ Image ➤ Quality, and then enter **H** for high quality or **D** for Draft mode. In Draft mode, your drawing will regenerate faster.

The High mode softens the pixels of the raster image, giving the image a smoother appearance. The Draft mode displays the image in a "raw," pixelated state. If you look carefully at the regions between the building and its shadow in the second image of Figure 11.16, you will see that it appears a bit jagged. The first image of Figure 11.16 uses the High setting to soften the edges of the building. You may need to look closely to see the difference.

FIGURE 11.16:

A close-up of a raster image with quality set to High

FIGURE 11.16 CONTINUED:

A close-up of a raster image with quality set to Draft

Finally, you can control the transparency of raster image files that allow transparent pixels. Some file formats, such as the CompuServe GIF 89a format, allow you to set a color in the image to be transparent (usually the background color). Most image-editing programs support this format because it is a popular one used on Web pages.

By turning on the Transparency setting, objects normally obscured by the background of a raster image may show through. Choose Modify ➤ Object ➤ Image ➤ Transparency, and then select the raster image that you wish to make transparent. Enter **On** or **Off**, depending on whether you want the image to be transparent or not. Unlike the Frame and Quality options, Transparency works on individual objects rather than globally.

TIP

If you want quick access to the Transparency setting, along with other raster image settings, the Properties tool in the Object Properties toolbar offers many of the same adjustments described in this section. You can access the Image Adjust dialog box, hide or display clipped areas, or hide the entire raster image.

Importing PostScript Images

In addition to raster import, you can use the built-in PostScript import feature to import PostScript files. This feature can be accessed by choosing Insert ➤ Encapsulated PostScript or by typing **Import**↵↵. The Import File dialog box lets you easily locate the file to be imported. Select Encapsulated PostScript (.eps) from the List Files of Type pull-down list, and then browse to find the file you want. Once you select a file, the rest of the program works just like the raster import commands. You are asked for an insertion point, a scale, and a rotation angle. Once you've answered all the prompts, the image appears in the drawing.

TIP   AutoCAD supports Drag and Drop for many raster file formats, including PostScript .eps files.

You can make adjustments to the quality of imported PostScript files by using the Psquality system variable (enter **Psquality**↵). This setting takes an integer value in the range -75 to 75, with 75 being the default. The absolute value of this setting is taken as the ratio of pixels to drawing units. If, for example, Psquality is set to 50 or -50, then Psin converts 50 pixels of the incoming PostScript file into one drawing unit. You use negative values to indicate that you want outlines of filled areas rather than the full painted image. Using outlines can save drawing space and improve readability on monochrome systems or systems with limited color capability.

Finally, if Psquality is set to 0, only the bounding box of the imported image is displayed in the drawing. Though you may only see a box, the image data is still incorporated into the drawing and will be maintained as the image is exported (using Psout).

Another system variable you should know about is Psdrag, which controls how the imported PostScript image appears at the insertion point prompt. Normally, Psdrag is set to 0, so Psin displays just the outline (bounding box) of the imported file as you move it into position. To display the full image of the imported PostScript file as you locate an insertion point, you can set Psdrag to 1.

TIP   If you need PostScript fonts in your .eps output files, you can use AutoCAD fonts as substitutes. AutoCAD converts fonts with specific code names to PostScript fonts during the .eps export process. See Appendix B for details.

If You Want to Experiment...

If you want to see firsthand how the PostScript import and export commands work, you can try the following exercise.

1. Open the Plan file.

This sequence of steps is a quick way to convert a 3D model into a 2D line drawing. You may want to make note of this as you work through the later chapters on 3D.

2. Choose File ➤ Export to open the Export Data dialog box. Select Encapsulated PostScript (.eps) in the List Files of Type pull-down list. You can also type **Psout**⏎ at the command prompt. The Create PostScript File dialog box appears and allows you to select or enter a filename.

3. Click the Options button. The PostScript Out Options dialog box appears.

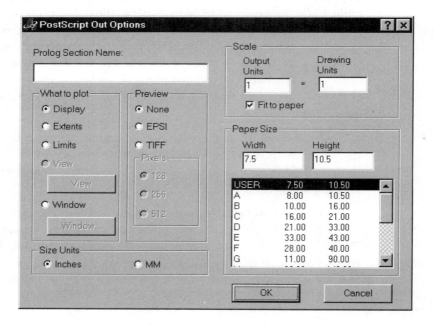

This dialog box offers options similar to the Plot Configuration dialog box.

4. Select the desired area to plot, sheet size, scale, and units from the dialog box; then click OK.

5. In the File dialog box, click Save to accept the suggested PostScript filename of Plan.eps.

6. Click Save in the Export Data dialog box.

TIP

You may notice that arcs, circles, and curves are not very smooth when you use this method to export, and then import, PostScript files. To improve the appearance of arcs and curves, specify a large sheet size at the Enter the Size or Width,Height (in Inches) <USER>: prompt.

---

7. Choose Insert ➤ Encapsulated PostScript to open the Select PostScript File dialog box.

8. Locate and select the Plan.eps file. You will be prompted for the insertion point and scale factor. Position and size the image as required. The file then appears in your drawing.

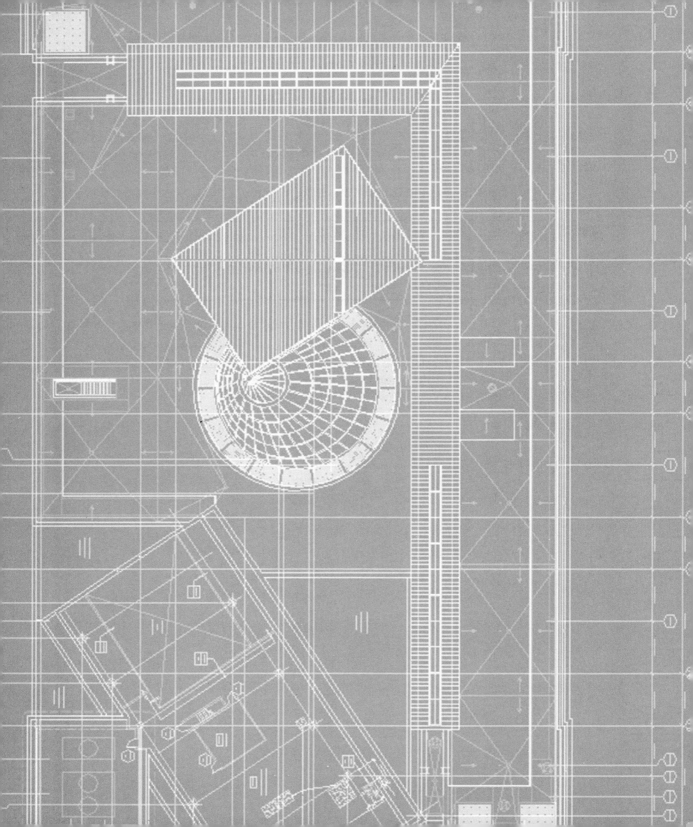

CHAPTER
TWELVE

12

Advanced Editing Methods

- Editing More Efficiently

- Using Grips to Simplify Editing

- Using External References (Xrefs)

- Using the Layout Tabs and Paper Space

- Working with Paper Space Viewports

- Understanding Line Weights, Line Types, and Dimensions in Paper Space

- Advanced Tools: Quick Select, Selection Filters, and the Calculator

- If You Want to Experiment...

Because you may not know all of a project's requirements when it begins, you usually base the first draft of a design on projected needs. As the plan goes forward, you make adjustments for new requirements as they arise. As more people enter the project, additional design restrictions come into play and the design is further modified. This process continues throughout the project, from the first draft to the end product.

In this chapter, you will review much of what you've already learned. Throughout the process, you will look at some techniques for setting up drawings to help manage the continual changes a project undergoes. You will also be introduced to new tools and techniques you can use to minimize duplication of work. AutoCAD can be a powerful timesaving tool if used properly. This chapter examines methods of harnessing that power.

Editing More Efficiently

The apartment building plan you've been working on is currently incomplete. For example, you need to add the utility room you created in Chapter 11. In the real world, this building plan would also undergo innumerable changes as the project developed. Wall and door locations would change, and more notes and dimensions would be added. However, in the space of this book's tutorials, this book can't develop these drawings to full completion. But, it can give you a sample of what is in store while using AutoCAD on such a project.

In this section, you will add a closet to the Unit plan (you will update the Plan file later in this chapter). In the editing you've already done, you've probably found that you use the following commands frequently: Move, Offset, Fillet, Trim, Grips, and the Osnap overrides. Now you will learn some ways to shorten your editing time by using them more efficiently.

Quick Access to Your Favorite Commands

As you continue to work with AutoCAD, you'll find that you use a handful of commands 90 percent of the time. You can collect your favorite commands into a single toolbar using AutoCAD's toolbar customization feature. This way, you can have ready access to your most frequently used commands. Chapter 20 gives you all the information you need to create your own custom toolbars.

Editing an Existing Drawing

First, let's look at how you can add a closet to the Unit plan. You'll begin by copying existing objects to provide the basis for the closet.

1. Open the Unit file.

2. Make Wall the current layer by trying the following: Click the Make Object's Layer Current tool on the Object Properties toolbar, and then click a wall line.

3. Make sure the Notes and Flr-pat layers are frozen. This will keep your drawing clear of objects you won't be editing.

TIP   If you didn't create a Unit plan, you can use **12a-unit.dwg** from the companion CD-ROM.

---

4. If they are not already on, turn on Noun/Verb Selection and the Grips feature. Also turn off Running Osnaps and Polar Tracking for now. They may get in the way of point selection in these exercises.

5. Click the right-side wall, and then click its midpoint grip.

6. Enter **C**↵ to start the Copy mode; then enter **@2'<180**↵. Metric users should enter **@60<180**↵ (see Figure 12.1).

7. Press the Esc key to exit the Grip mode.

8. Zoom in to the entry area shown in Figure 12.2.

9. Click Offset on the Modify toolbar, or type **O**↵.

10. At the `Offset distance or through:` prompt, use the Nearest Osnap and pick the outside wall of the bathroom near the door, as shown in Figure 12.2.

11. At the `Second point:` prompt, use the Perpendicular Osnap override and pick the other side of that wall (see Figure 12.2).

12. Click the copy of the wall line you just created, and then click a point to the left of it.

13. Press ↵ to exit the Offset command.

FIGURE 12.1:

Copying the wall to start the closet

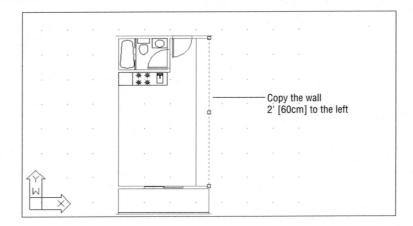

Copy the wall
2' [60cm] to the left

FIGURE 12.2:

Using an existing wall as a distance reference for copying

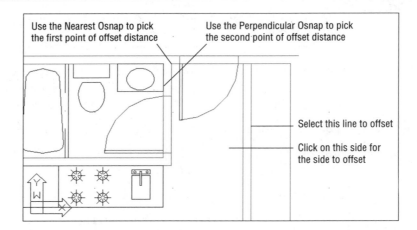

Use the Nearest Osnap to pick the first point of offset distance

Use the Perpendicular Osnap to pick the second point of offset distance

Select this line to offset

Click on this side for the side to offset

In steps 9 and 10 of the previous exercise, you determined the offset distance by selecting existing geometry. If you know you want to duplicate a distance, but don't know what that distance is, you can often use existing objects as references.

Next, use the same idea to copy a few more lines for the other side of the closet.

1. Click to highlight the two horizontal lines that make up the wall at the top of your view.

2. Shift+click the midpoint grips of these lines (see Figure 12.3).

3. Click again one of the midpoint grips, and then enter **C**↵ to select the Copy option.

4. Enter **B**↵ to select a base point option.

5. Use the upper-right corner of the bathroom for the base point, and the lower-right corner of the kitchen as the second point.

6. Press the Esc key twice to clear the grip selection.

FIGURE 12.3:

Adding the second closet wall

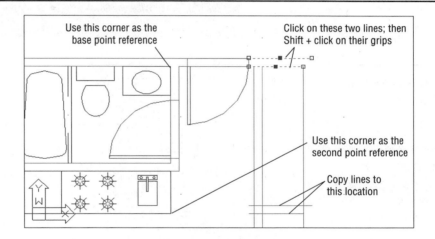

NOTE   In these exercises, you are asked to enter the grip options through the keyboard. This can be a quicker method to access the Copy and Base grip options. You can also right-click your mouse and select the Copy and Base options from the popup menu.

Now you've got the general layout of the closet. The next step is to clean up the corners. First, you'll have to do a bit of prep work and break the wall lines near the wall intersections, as shown in Figure 12.4.

1. Click Break on the Modify toolbar. This tool creates a gap in a line, arc, or circle.

2. Click the vertical wall to the far right at a point near the location of the new wall (see Figure 12.4).

3. Click the vertical line again near the point you selected in step 2 to create a small gap, as shown in Figure 12.4.

4. Use the Break tool again to create a gap in the horizontal line at the top of the unit, near the door, as shown in Figure 12.4.

5. Click Fillet on the Modify toolbar, or type **F↵** and join the corners of the wall, as shown in Figure 12.5.

FIGURE 12.4:

Breaking the wall lines

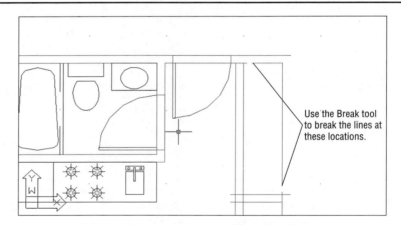

FIGURE 12.5:

Filleting the corners

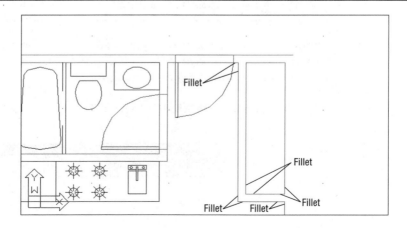

TIP   If Fillet is not trimming lines, type **Trimmode.⏎ 1.⏎**. This sets the Trimmode system variable to 1 which causes the Fillet and Chamfer tools to "trim" objects back to their intersection points.

In steps 2 and 3 above, you didn't have to be too exact about where to pick the break points because Construct ➤ Fillet takes care of joining the wall lines exactly. Now you are ready to add the finishing touches.

1. At the closet door location, draw a line from the midpoint of the interior closet wall to the exterior (see the top image of Figure 12.6). Make sure this line is on the Jamb layer.

2. Offset the new line 3' in both directions (90cm for metric users). These new lines are the closet door jambs.

3. Erase the first line you drew at the midpoint of the closet wall.

4. Click Trim on the Modify toolbar, or type **Tr.⏎**.

5. Click the two jambs, and then press ⏎.

6. Type **F.⏎** to invoke the Fence selection option; then click a point to the left of the wall, as shown in the bottom image of Figure 12.6.

7. As you move the cursor, you see a rubber-banding line from the last point you picked. Click a point to the right of the closet wall so the rubber-banding line crosses over the two wall lines, as shown in the top image of Figure 12.6.

8. Press ⏎ to finish your fence selection. The wall lines trim back to the jambs.

9. Press ⏎ again to exit the Trim command.

10. As shown in Figure 12.7, add the door headers and the sliding doors and assign these objects to their appropriate layers.

11. Use File ➤ Save to save the file. If you used the file from the companion CD-ROM, use File ➤ Save As and save the file under the name Unit.

FIGURE 12.6:

Constructing the closet door jambs

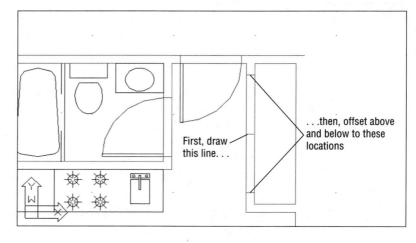

First, draw this line. . .

. . .then, offset above and below to these locations

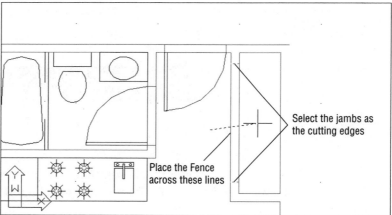

Place the Fence across these lines

Select the jambs as the cutting edges

TIP You can use the Match Properties tool to make a set of objects match the layer of another object. Click Match Properties on the Standard toolbar, select the objects whose layer you want to match, and then select the objects you want to assign to the objects layer. See Chapter 6 for more on the Match Properties tool.

FIGURE 12.7:

The finished closet

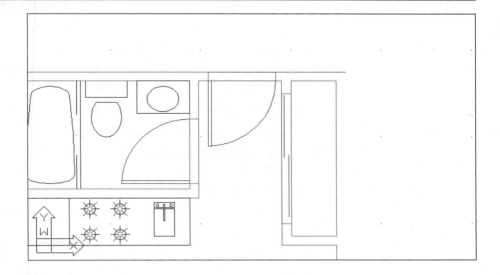

In this exercise, you used the Fence selection option to select the objects you wanted to trim. You could have selected each line individually by clicking them, but the Fence selection option offered you a quick way to select a set of objects without having to be too precise about where they are selected. You'll get a closer look at the Fence selection option a bit later in this chapter.

This exercise also showed that it's easier to trim lines back and then draw them back in than to try to break them precisely at each jamb location. At first this may seem counterproductive, but trimming the lines and then drawing in headers actually takes fewer steps and is a less tedious operation than some other routes. And the end result is a door that is exactly centered on the closet space.

Building on Previously Drawn Objects

Suppose your client decides your apartment building design needs a few one-bedroom units. In this exercise, you will use the studio unit drawing as a basis for the one-bedroom unit. To do so, you will double the studio's size, add a bedroom, move the kitchenette, rearrange and add closets, and move the entry doors. In the process of editing this new drawing, you will see how you can build on previously drawn objects.

Start by setting up the new file. As you work through this exercise, you'll be using commands that you've seen in previous exercises, so I won't bother describing every detail. But do pay attention to the process taking place, as shown in Figures 12.8 through 12.12.

1. You've already saved the current Unit file. Now use File ➤ Save As to save this file under the name of Unit2.dwg. This way, you can use the current file as the basis for the new one-bedroom unit.

2. Turn on the Notes layer and type **Z**↵ **A**↵ to get an overall view of the drawing.

3. Move the dimension string at the right of the unit, 14'-5" (439cm) further to the right, and copy the unit the same distance to the right. Your drawing should look like Figure 12.8.

FIGURE 12.8:

The copied unit

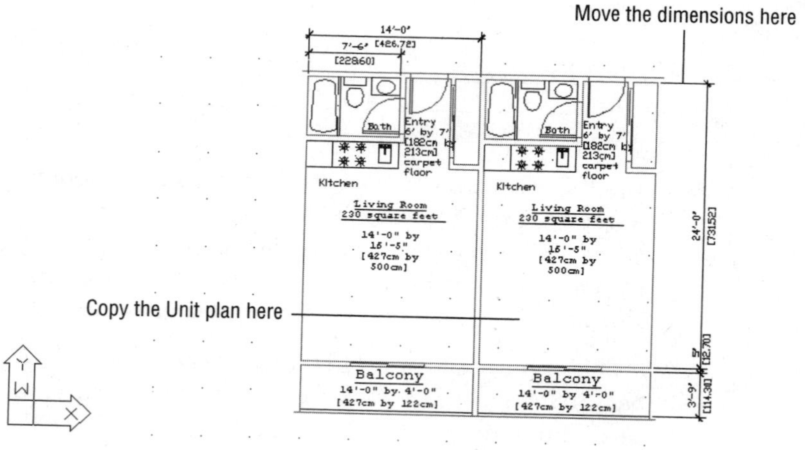

4. Now erase the bathroom, kitchen, door, closet, room labels, and wall lines, as shown in Figure 12.9.

NOTE   Although you could be more selective in step 4 about the objects you erase, and then add line segments where there are gaps in walls, this is considered bad form. When editing files, it's wise to keep lines continuous rather than fragmented. Adding line segments increases the size of the drawing database and slows down editing operations.

FIGURE 12.9:

Objects to be erased

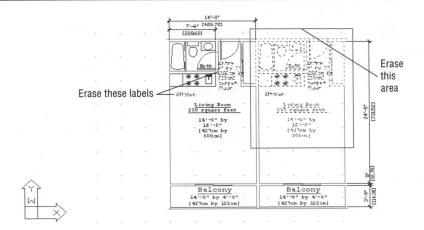

Using the Temporary Tracking Point Feature

The living room of this one-bedroom unit will be on the right side. You will want to move the Living Room label from the left half to the right half. Normally, you would probably just move the label without worrying about accuracy, but we'll use this opportunity to show how the Temporary Tracking Point feature works. In the next exercise, you will place the Living Room label in the center of the living room area.

1. Make sure the OSNAP and POLAR buttons are off in the status bar then click the Living Room label in the unit to the left.

2. Click the top-center grip in the label, as shown in the first image of Figure 12.10.

FIGURE 12.10:

Using the Tracking feature to move the Living Room label to the center of the new living room

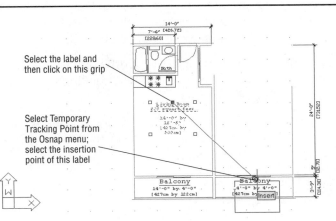

FIGURE 12.10 CONTINUED:

Using the Tracking feature to move the Living Room label to the center of the new living room

Select Temporary Tracking Point from the Osnap menu; select the midpoint of this line

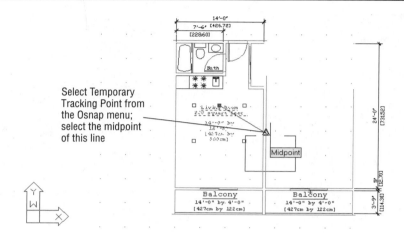

3. Shift+right-click the mouse to open the Osnap menu.

4. Select Temporary Tracking Point.

5. Shift+right-click again, and then select Insert from the Osnap menu.

6. Click the insertion point of the Balcony label of the unit to the right, as shown in the first image of Figure 12.10. Notice a tracking vector emanating from the selected insertion point, as shown in the second image of Figure 12.10.

7. Shift+right-click and select Temporary Tracking Point.

8. Shift+right-click again and select Midpoint.

9. This time, click the midpoint of the vertical wall between the two units as shown in the second image of Figure 12.10. Notice that a tracking vector now emanates from a point that represents the intersection of the text insertion point and the midpoint of the wall.

10. Move the text to the middle of the room to the right, as shown in Figure 12.11. Notice that two tracking vectors appear and converge in the middle of the room.

11. With the tracking vectors crossing and the text in the approximate location shown in Figure 12.11, click the mouse. The text moves to the middle of the unit to the right.

FIGURE 12.11:

The tracking vectors intersect in the middle of the room.

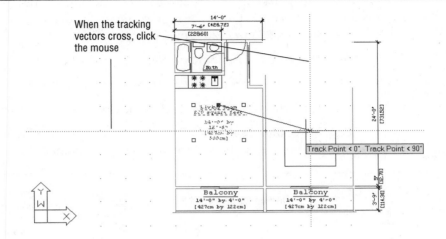

In earlier chapters, you saw how to use the Object Snap Tracking feature with Running Osnaps. Here, you used Object Snap Tracking in a slightly different way through the Temporary Tracking Point feature. The Temporary Tracking Point feature works by allowing you to select points that are aligned orthogonally, like the insertion point of the balcony text and the midpoint of the wall in the previous exercise. But unlike Object Snap Tracking with Running Osnaps, the Temporary Tracking Point feature lets you focus on specific object snap points.

The following example shows how you can use Temporary Tracking Point in conjunction with the Polar Tracking tool to move the endpoint of a line to align with the endpoint of another line.

1. Click the line at the top-right side of the unit to expose its grips, as shown in the top image of Figure 12.12.

2. Click the grip at the right end of the line.

3. As in the previous exercise, select Temporary Tracking Point from the Osnap menu.

4. Open the Osnap menu again and select Endpoint.

5. Click the POLAR button in the status bar to turn it on.

6. Select the rightmost endpoint of the short line at the bottom-right corner of the unit, as shown in the top image of Figure 12.12.

7. Move the cursor so that the Polar Tracking vector crosses the Osnap Tracking vector in the upper-right corner of the drawing, as shown in the bottom image of Figure 12.12, then click that point.

8. Press the Esc key twice to clear the grip selection.

9. Move the kitchen to the opposite corner of the unit, as shown in Figure 12.13.

10. Click the Move tool and select the closet area, as shown in Figure 12.13.

11. Move the closet down 5'-5" (165cm), as shown in Figure 12.14. You can use the corners of the bathroom as reference points.

FIGURE 12.12:

Stretching a line using the Tracking function

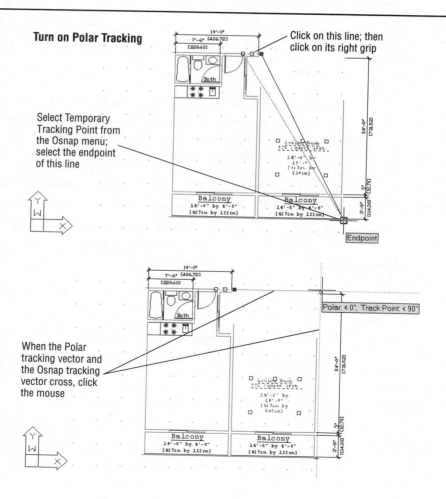

FIGURE 12.13:

Moving the closet and kitchen

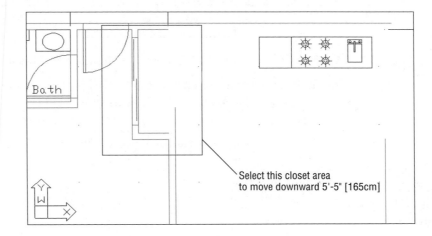

Select this closet area
to move downward 5'-5" [165cm]

When a drawing gets crowded, you may find that Running Osnaps get in the way of your work. The Temporary Tracking Point feature lets you access the Osnap Tracking vector without having to turn on Running Osnaps.

The Temporary Tracking Point feature and the other tools that use tracking vectors take a little practice to use, but once you understand how they work, they are an indispensable aid in your drawing.

Working with the Fence Selection Option

Next, you'll work on finishing the new bedroom door and entry. Once again, you will get a chance to work with the Fence selection option. Fence is a great tool for selecting locations on objects that would otherwise be difficult to select. With Fence, you can select objects by crossing over them with a rubber-banding line. It's like selecting objects by crossing them out. In addition, the point at which the rubber-banding line crosses the object is equivalent to a pick point. This is important when using commands that respond differently depending on where objects are selected. The following exercise shows how the Fence selection option can be helpful in selecting objects in tight spaces.

1. Copy the existing entry door downward, including header and jambs (see Figure 12.14). Use the Endpoint override to locate the door accurately.

2. Clean up the walls by adding new lines and filleting others, as shown in Figure 12.15.

Use the midpoint of the door header as the first axis endpoint.

3. Mirror the door you just copied so it swings in the opposite direction.

4. Use Stretch (click Stretch on the Modify toolbar) to move the entry door a distance of 8' (244cm) to the right, as shown in Figure 12.16. Remember to use a crossing window to select the objects and endpoints you want to stretch.

5. Once you've moved the entry door, mirror it in the same way you mirrored the other door.

FIGURE 12.14:

Using an existing door to create a door opening

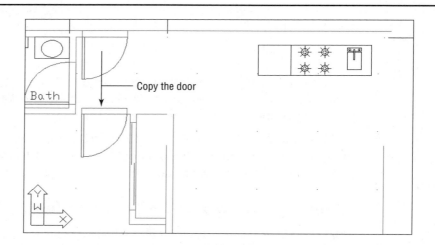

FIGURE 12.15:

Cleaning up the wall

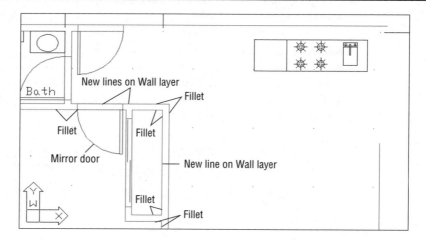

FIGURE 12.16:

Moving the door

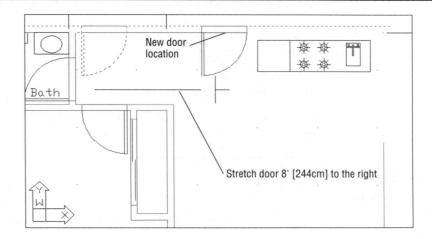

In the foregoing exercise, you once again used parts of a previous drawing instead of creating new parts. In only a few instances are you adding new objects.

1. Now set the view of your drawing so it looks similar to Figure 12.17 and turn off Polar Tracking and Running Osnaps, if they are on.

2. Click Extend on the Modify toolbar, or type **Ex↵** at the command prompt.

3. At the `Select boundary edge(s)… Select objects:` prompt, pick the wall at the bottom of the screen, as shown in Figure 12.17, and press ↵. Just as with Trim, the Extend command requires that you first select a set of objects to define the boundary of the extension, and then select the objects you wish to extend.

4. At the `Select object to extend:` prompt, you need to pick the two lines just below the closet door. To do this, first enter **F↵** to use the Fence selection option.

5. At the `First Fence point:` prompt, pick a point just to the left of the lines you want to extend.

6. Make sure the Ortho mode is off. Then at the `Undo/<Endpoint of line>:` prompt, pick a point to the right of the two lines so that the fence crosses over them (see the top image of Figure 12.17).

7. Press ↵. The two lines extend to the wall.

8. Press ↵ again to exit the Extend command.

9. Click Trim, and then select the two lines you just extended.

10. Press ↵ to finish your selection.

11. Type **F↵**, and then pick two points to place a fence between the endpoints of the two selected lines (see the bottom image of Figure 12.17).

12. Use a combination of Trim and Fillet to clean up the other walls.

13. Add another closet door on the right side of the new closet space you just created. Your drawing should look like Figure 12.18.

FIGURE 12.17:

Adding walls for a second closet

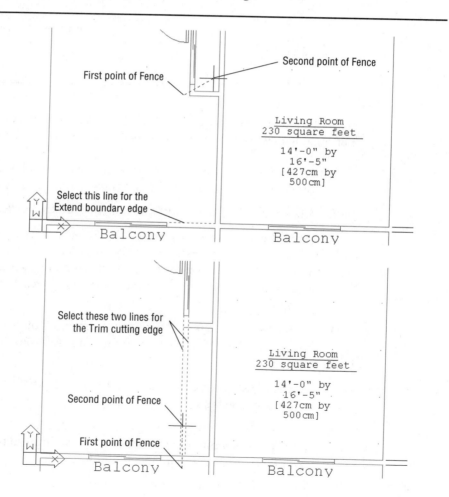

FIGURE 12.18:

The second closet

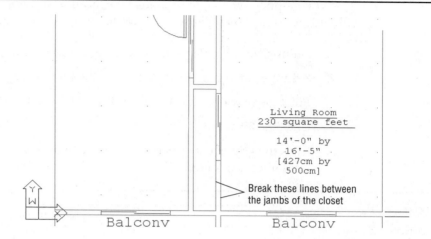

The Extend tool works just like the Trim tool: First you select the boundary objects, and then you select the objects you want to modify. Here again, you used the Fence selection option to select the object to extend. In this situation, the Fence option is crucial because it may be more difficult to select the lines individually.

> **TIP** The Trim and Extend tools do not allow you to trim or extend objects in a block. Fortunately, AutoCAD 2000 includes two bonus utilities on the Express Standard toolbar that will let you select trim and extend boundary objects from within a block. See Chapter 19 for details.

Using Grips to Simplify Editing

Throughout this book, I've shown you ways of using the Grips feature to edit drawings. When and how you use them will really depend on your preference, but there are situations where grip editing makes more sense. Here you'll explore some very basic situations where grips can be useful.

Now, suppose you want to change the location and orientation of the kitchen. In this exercise, you will use the Grips feature to do just that.

1. Set up a view similar to the one in Figure 12.19 and turn Polar Tracking on.

2. Add the horizontal line at the top of the kitchen, as shown in Figure 12.19.

3. Fillet the new line with the vertical wall line to the right of the unit.

4. Click the kitchen.

5. Click the grip in the upper-left corner to make it a hot grip. The grip changes from hollow to solid.

FIGURE 12.19:

Finishing the kitchen wall and selecting the kitchen rotation base point

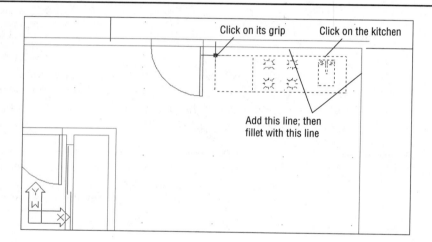

6. Right-click the mouse and then choose Rotate from the popup menu. (You can also press ⏎ two times until you see the *** ROTATE *** message at the prompt.)

TIP

Remember that the spacebar acts the same as the ⏎ key for most commands, including the Grips modes.

7. Enter **–90** or rotate the kitchen by pointing the cursor downward until the tracking vector appears, then click the mouse.

8. Click the kitchen grip again; then, using the Endpoint Osnap, click the upper-right corner of the room.

9. Press the Esc key twice to clear the grip selection. Your drawing should look like Figure 12.20.

FIGURE 12.20:

The revised kitchen

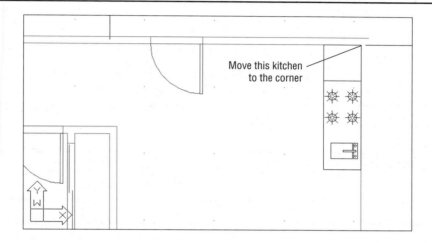

Because the kitchenette is a block, its grip point is the same as its insertion point. This makes the kitchenette block—as are all blocks—a great candidate for grip editing. Remember that the door, too, is a block.

Displaying Grips of Objects within a Block

You can set up AutoCAD to display the grips on all the entities within a block. This allows you to use those grips as handles for any of the grip operations such as Move, Rotate, or Scale. However, you cannot edit individual objects within the block.

To display all the grips within a block, type **Gripblock⏎ 1⏎**. You can also turn on the Enable Grips within a Block option in the Grips dialog box (Tools ➤ Grips).

Now suppose you want to widen the entrance door from 36" to 42" (90cm to 105cm for metric users). Try the following exercise involving a door and its surrounding wall.

1. Use a crossing window to select the door jamb to the left of the entry door, as shown in Figure 12.21.

2. Shift+click both of the door jamb's corner grips.

3. Click the bottom corner grip again. It is now a hot grip.

4. At the ** Stretch ** prompt, enter @6<180 (metric users should enter @15<180). The door should now look like Figure 12.21. You can also use the Direct Distance method: With Polar Tracking on, point the cursor to the left, then type 6↵.

NOTE   The Stretch hot grip command will ignore a block as long as you do not include its insertion point in the stretch window.

FIGURE 12.21:

The widened door opening

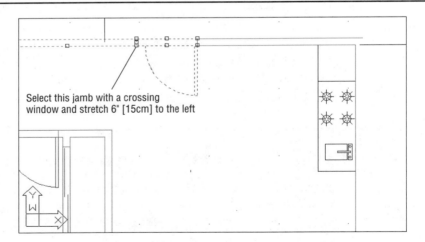

Select this jamb with a crossing window and stretch 6" [15cm] to the left

Notice that in step 4 you didn't have to specify a base point to stretch the grips. AutoCAD assumes the base to be the original location of the selected hot grip (the grip selected in step 3).

Now you can enlarge the door using the Grips command's Scale option. Scale allows you to change the size of an object or a group of objects. You can change the size visually, by entering a scale value, or by using an object for reference. In this exercise, you will use the current door width as a reference.

1. Press the Esc key twice to clear your selection set.

2. Click the door, and then click the door's grip point at the hinge side.

3. Right-click the mouse and select Scale.

4. At the `<Scale factor>/Base point/Copy/Undo/Reference/eXit:` prompt, enter **R↵** to select the Reference option.

5. At the `Reference length:` prompt, type **@↵** to indicate that you want to use the door insertion point as the first point of the reference length.

6. At the `Second point:` prompt, click the grip at the endpoint of the door's arc at the wall line (see the top image in Figure 12.22). Now as you move the cursor, the door changes in size relative to the distance between the grip and the end of the arc.

7. At the `<New length>/Base point/Copy/Undo/Reference/eXit:` prompt, use the Endpoint Osnap again and click the door jamb directly to the left of the arc endpoint. The door enlarges to fit the new door opening (see the bottom image in Figure 12.22).

8. To finish this floor plan, zoom out to get the overall view of the unit, turn on the Flr-pat layer, and then erase the floor pattern in the bedroom area just below the bathroom.

9. Save the file.

You could have used the Modify ➤ Scale option to accomplish the operation performed in the above exercise with the Scale hot grip command. The advantage to using grips is that you don't need to use the Osnap to select exact grip locations, thereby reducing the number of steps you must take to accomplish this task.

In the next section, you will update the Plan file to include the revised studio apartment and the one-bedroom unit you have just created (see Figure 12.23). You will be making changes such as these throughout the later stages of your design project. As you have seen, AutoCAD's ability to make changes easily and quickly can ease your work and help you test your design ideas more accurately.

FIGURE 12.22:

The enlarged door

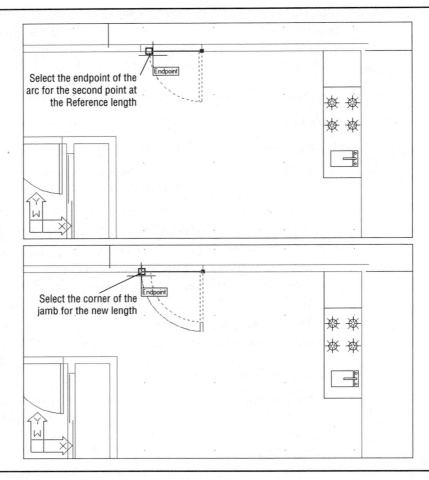

Select the endpoint of the arc for the second point at the Reference length

Endpoint

Select the corner of the jamb for the new length

Endpoint

FIGURE 12.23:

The finished one-bedroom unit

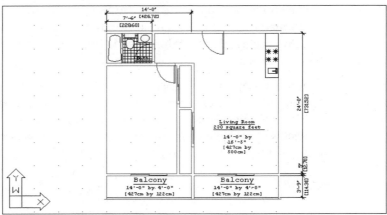

Singling Out Proximate Objects

Chapter 3 mentioned that you will encounter situations where you need to select an object that is overlapping or very close to another object. Often in this situation, you end up selecting the wrong object. To help you select the exact object you want, Auto-CAD offers the Selection Cycling tool and the Object Selection Settings dialog box.

Selection Cycling

Selection Cycling lets you cycle through objects that overlap until you select the one you want. To use this feature, hold down the Ctrl key and click the object you want to select. If the first object highlighted is not the one you want, click again, but this time, don't hold down the Ctrl key. When several objects are overlapping, just keep clicking until the right object is highlighted and selected. When the object you want is highlighted, press ↵, and then go on to select other objects or press ↵ to finish the selection process. You may want to practice using selection cycling a few times to get the hang of it. It can be a bit confusing at first, but once you've gotten accustomed to how it works, the Selection Cycling tool can be invaluable.

Object Sorting

If you are a veteran AutoCAD user, you may have grown accustomed to selecting the most recently created object of two overlapping objects by simply clicking it. In later versions of AutoCAD, you don't always get to the most recently drawn object when you click overlapping objects. But AutoCAD offers user-definable controls that set the method of selecting overlapping objects. These controls change the way AutoCAD selects overlapping objects.

If you prefer, you can set up AutoCAD to offer the most recently drawn object. You can use the User Preferences tab of the Options dialog box to set up the selection method. To get there, click Tools ➤ Options, then click the User Preferences tab.

The Object Sorting Methods button group of this tab lets you set the sort method for a variety of operations. If you enable any of the operations listed, AutoCAD sorts objects based on the order that they were added to the drawing. You will probably not want to change the sort method for Object Snaps or Regens. But by checking Object Selection, you can control which of two overlapping lines are selected when you click them. For plotting and for PostScript output, you can control the overlay of screened or hatched areas.

These settings can also be controlled through system variables. See Appendix D for details.

> **NOTE**
>
> When you use the Draworder command (the Tools ➤ Display Order options), all the options in the Object Sorting Methods button group of the User Preferences tab of the Options dialog box are turned on.

Using External References (Xrefs)

Chapter 6 mentioned that careful use of blocks, external references (Xrefs), and layers can help you improve your productivity. In this section you will see firsthand how to use these features to help reduce design errors and speed up delivery of an accurate set of drawings. You do this by controlling layers in conjunction with blocks and external referenced files to create a common drawing database for several drawings.

Preparing Existing Drawings for Cross-Referencing

Chapter 6 discussed how you can use Xrefs to assemble one floor of the apartment. In this section you will explore the creation and use of Xrefs to build multiple floors, each containing slightly different sets of drawing information. By doing so, you will learn how Xrefs allow you to use a single file in multiple drawings to save time and reduce redundancy. You'll see that by sharing common data in multiple files, you can reduce your work and keep the drawing information consistent.

You'll start by creating the files that you will use later as Xrefs.

1. Open the Plan file. If you didn't create the Plan file, you can use the 12a-plan.dwg file from the companion CD-ROM (see Figure 12.24).

FIGURE 12.24:

The overall plan

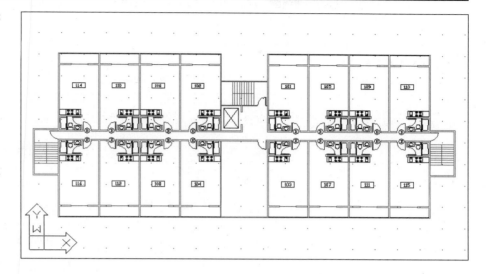

2. Turn off the Notes layer to get a clear, uncluttered view of the individual unit plans.

3. Use the Wblock command (enter **W**↵ at the command prompt) and write the eight units in the corners of your plan to a file called **Floor1.dwg** (see Figure 12.25). When you select objects for the Wblock, be sure to include the door symbols for those units. Use 0,0 for the Wblock insertion base point.

FIGURE 12.25:

Units to be exported to the Floor1 file

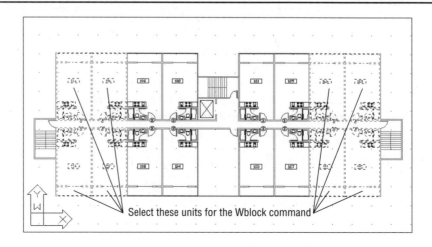

Select these units for the Wblock command

4. Using Figure 12.26 as a guide, insert Unit2 into the corners where the other eight units were previously.

FIGURE 12.26:

Insertion information for Unit2. Metric coordinates are shown in brackets.

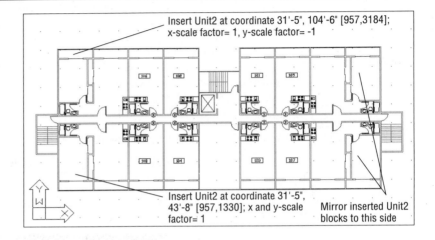

Insert Unit2 at coordinate 31'-5", 104'-6" [957,3184]; x-scale factor= 1, y-scale factor= -1

Insert Unit2 at coordinate 31'-5", 43'-8" [957,1330]; x and y-scale factor= 1

Mirror inserted Unit2 blocks to this side

NOTE If you didn't create the Unit2 file earlier in this chapter, use the Unit2.dwg file from the companion CD-ROM.

5. Once you've accurately placed the corner units, use the Wblock command to write these corner units to a file called Floor2.dwg. Again, use the 0,0 coordinate as the insertion base point for the Wblock.

6. Now use File ➤ Save As to turn the remaining set of unit plans into a file called Common.dwg.

You've just created three files: Floor1, Floor2, and Common. Each of these files contains unique information about the building. Next, you'll use the Xref command to recombine these files for the different floor plans in your building.

Assembling External References to Build a Drawing

Next, you will create composite files for each floor, using external references of only the files needed for the individual floors. You will use the Attach option of the Xref command to insert all the files you exported from the Plan file.

1. Close the Common.dwg file, open a new file, and call it Xref-1.

2. Set up this file as an architectural drawing 8 1/2" × 11" with a scale of 1/16"=1'. The upper-right corner limits for such a drawing are 2112, 1632. Metric users should set up a drawing at 1:200 scale on an A4 sheet size. If you look at Table 3.4, you'll see that your drawing area should be 4200cm by 5940cm.

NOTE   You are asked to use a small paper size since it is the most common size available to readers. Normally, you would specify a larger size and scale for architectural drawings.

---

3. Set the Ltscale value to **192**. Metric users should set it to **200**.

4. Open the Reference toolbar by right-clicking a toolbar, and then selecting Reference from the popup menu.

5. Click External Reference Attach on the Reference toolbar, or type **Xa↵**.

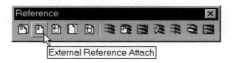

The Select Reference File dialog box appears.

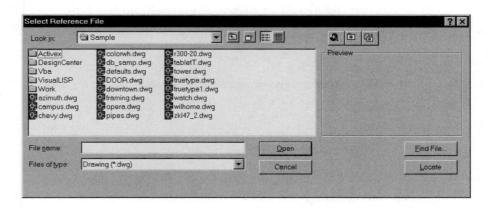

6. Locate and select the Common.dwg file.

7. In the External Reference dialog box, make sure the Specify On-Screen check box in the Insertion Point group is not checked. Then make sure the X, Y, and Z values in the Insertion Point group are all 0.

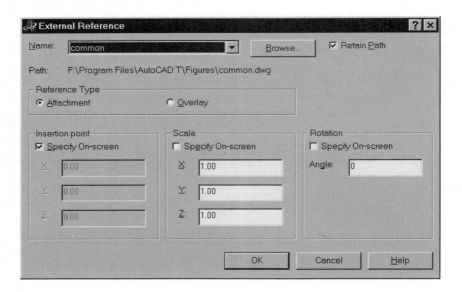

NOTE   Because the insertion points of all the files are the same, namely 0,0, they will fit together perfectly when they are inserted into the new files.

8. Click OK. The Common.dwg file appears in the drawing.

9. Click the External Reference Attach tool on the Reference toolbar again, and then click the Browse button to insert the Floor1 file.

10. Repeat step 10 to insert the Col-grid.dwg file as an Xref. The Col-grid.dwg file can be found on the companion CD-ROM. You now have the plan for the first floor.

11. Save this file.

Now use the current file to create another file representing a different floor.

1. Use File ➤ Save As to save this file as Xref-2.dwg.

2.   Click the External Reference tool in the Reference toolbar or type **Xr**⏎.

3.   In the Xref Manager dialog box, highlight Floor1 in the list of Xrefs, and then click Detach.

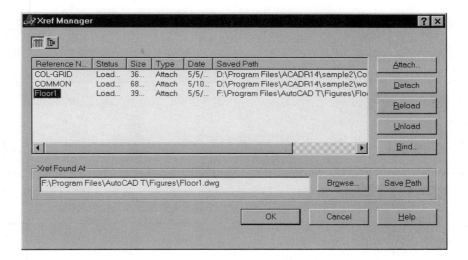

4.   Click Attach. In the External Reference dialog box, click Browse.

5.   ˙Locate and select Floor2.dwg.

6.   In the External Reference dialog box, make sure that the X, Y, and Z values in the Insertion Point group are all set to 0.

7.   Click OK. The Floor2 drawing appears in place of Floor1.

WARNING   If you move an external reference file after you have inserted it into a drawing, AutoCAD may not be able to find it later when you attempt to open the drawing. If this happens, you can use the Browse option in the External Reference dialog box to tell AutoCAD the new location of the external referenced file.

Now when you need to make changes to Xref-1 or Xref-2, you can edit the individual external referenced files that they comprise. Then, the next time you open either Xref-1 or Xref-2, the updated Xrefs will automatically appear in their most recent forms.

External references do not need to be permanent. As you saw in the previous exercise, you can attach and detach them easily at any time. This means, if you need to get information from another file—to see how well an elevator core aligns, for example—you can temporarily attach as an external reference the other file to quickly check alignments, and then detach it when you are done.

Think of these composite files as final plot files that are only used for plotting and reviewing. Editing can then be performed on the smaller, more manageable external referenced files. Figure 12.27 illustrates the relationship of these files.

FIGURE 12.27:

Diagram of external referenced file relationships

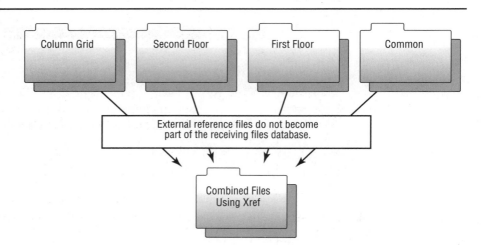

The combinations of external references are limited only by your imagination, but avoid multiple external references of the same file.

TIP

Because Xref files do not become part of the file they are referenced into, you must take care to keep Xref files in a location where AutoCAD can find them when the referencing file is opened. This can be a minor annoyance when you need to send files to others outside your office. To help you keep track of external references, AutoCAD offers the Pack 'n Go tool in the Express Standard toolbar. See Chapter 19 for details.

Updating Blocks in External References

There are several advantages to using external reference files. Because the Xrefs don't become part of the drawing file's database, the referencing files remain quite small. Also, because Xref files are easily updated, work can be split up among several people in a workgroup environment or on a network. For example, in our hypothetical apartment building, one person can be editing the Common file while another works on Floor1, and so on. The next time the composite Xref-1.dwg or Xref-2.dwg file is opened, it will automatically reflect any new changes made in the external referenced files. Now let's see how to set this up.

1. Open the Common.dwg file.

2. Next, you will update the Unit plan you edited earlier in this chapter. Click Insert Block on the Draw toolbar.

3. In the Insert dialog box, click the File button, and then locate and select Unit.dwg. Then click Open here, and again in the Insert dialog box.

4. At the warning message, click OK.

5. At the Insertion point: prompt, press the Esc key.

6. Enter **RE↵** to regenerate the drawing. You will see the new Unit plan in place of the old one (see Figure 12.28). You may also see all the dimensions and notes for each unit.

7. If the Notes layer is on, use the Layer & Linetype Properties dialog box or the Layer drop-down list to turn it off.

8. Using the Insert Block tool on the Draw toolbar again, replace the empty room across the hall from the lobby with the utility room you created in Chapter 11 (see Figure 12.29). If you didn't create the utility room drawing, use the Utility.dwg file from the companion CD-ROM.

FIGURE 12.28:

The Common file with the revised Unit plan

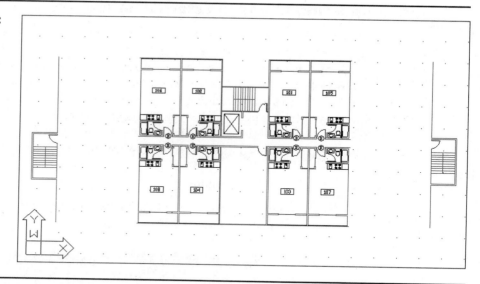

FIGURE 12.29:

The utility room installed

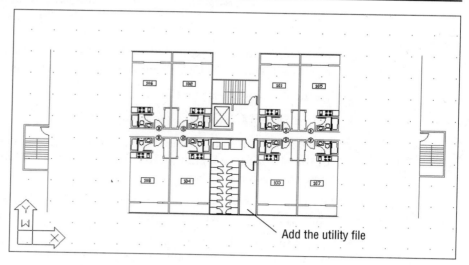

Add the utility file

9. Save the Common file.

10. Now open the Xref-1 file. You will see the utility room and the typical units in their new form. Your drawing should look like the top image of Figure 12.30.

11. Open Xref-2. You see that the utility room and typical units are updated in this file as well (see the bottom image of Figure 12.30).

FIGURE 12.30:

The Xref-1 file with the units updated

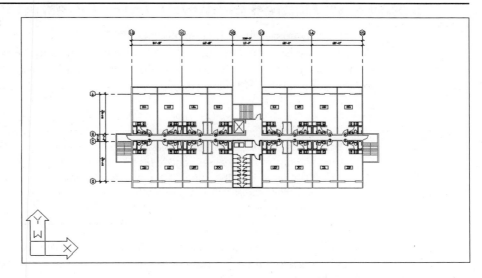

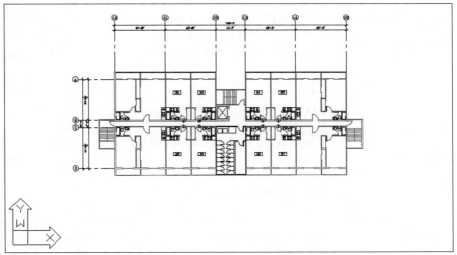

If this were a typical manually drafted project, someone would have had to make changes to both plans shown in Figure 12.30, duplicating a great deal of work.

Importing Named Elements from External References

Chapter 5 discussed how layers, blocks, line types, and text styles—called *named elements*—are imported along with a file that is inserted into another. External reference files, on the other hand, do not import named elements. You can, however, review their names and use a special command to import the ones you want to use in the current file.

You can set the Visretain system variable to 1 to force AutoCAD to remember layer settings of external referenced files. Or turn on the Retain Changes to Xref Layers option in the Open and Save tab of the Options dialog box. You can also use the Layer Manager Express utility to save layer settings for later recall. The Layer Manager is described in detail in Chapter 19.

AutoCAD renames named elements from Xref files by giving them the prefix of the filename from which they come. For example, the Wall layer in the `Floor1` file will be called Floor1 | WALL in the `Xref-1` file; the Toilet block will be called Floor1 | TOILET. You cannot draw on the layer Floor | WALL, nor can you insert Floor1 | TOILET; but you can view external referenced layers in the Layer Control dialog box, and you can view external referenced blocks using the Insert dialog box.

Next, you'll look at how AutoCAD identifies layers and blocks in external referenced files, and you'll get a chance to import a layer from an Xref.

1. While in the `Xref-1` file, open the Layer Properties Manager dialog box. Notice that the names of the layers from the external referenced files are all prefixed with the filename and the vertical bar (|) character. Exit the Layer Manager Properties dialog box.

NOTE

You can also open the Layer Control popup list to view the layer names.

2. Click the External Reference Bind tool on the Reference toolbar, or enter **Xb⏎**.

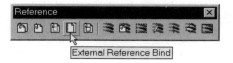

The Xbind dialog box appears.

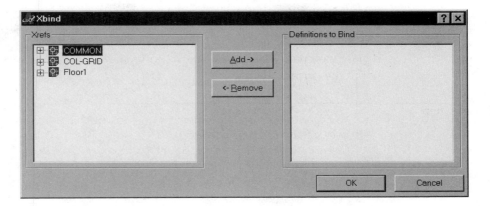

You see a listing of the current Xrefs. Each listing shows a plus sign to the left. This list box follows the Microsoft Windows 95 format for expandable lists, much like the directory listing in the Windows Explorer.

3. Click the plus sign next to the Floor1 Xref listing. The list expands to show the types of elements available to bind.

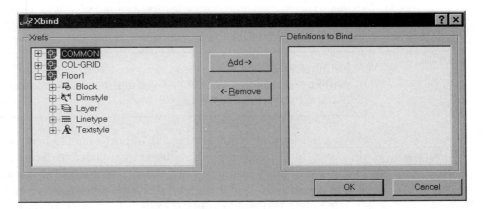

4. Now click the plus sign next to the Layer listing. The list expands further to show the layers available for binding.

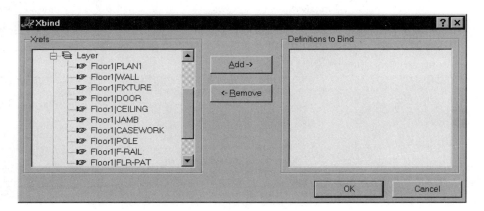

5. Locate Floor1 | WALL in the listing, click it, and then click the Add button. Floor1 | WALL is added to the list to the right: Definitions to Bind.

6. Click OK to bind the Floor1 | WALL layer.

7. Now open the Layer & Linetype Properties dialog box.

8. Scroll down the list and look for the Floor1 | WALL layer. You will not find it. In its place is a layer called Floor1$0$wall.

TIP The AutoCAD DesignCenter lets you import settings and other drawing components from any drawing, not just Xref drawings. You'll learn more about the AutoCAD DesignCenter in Chapter 22.

As you can see, when you use Xbind to import a named item, such as the Floor1 | WALL layer, the vertical bar (|) is replaced by two dollar signs surrounding a number, which is usually zero. (If for some reason the imported layer name Floor1$0$wall already exists, then the zero in that name is changed to 1, as in Floor1$1$wall.) Other named items are also renamed in the same way, using the 0 replacement for the vertical bar.

While you used the Xbind dialog box to bind a single layer, you can also use it to bind multiple layers, as well as other items from Xrefs attached to the current drawing.

TIP You can bind an entire Xref to a drawing, converting it into a simple block. By doing so, you have the opportunity to maintain unique layer names of the Xref being bound, or merge the Xref's similarly named layers with those of the current file. See Chapter 6 for details.

Nesting External References and Using Overlays

External references can be nested. For example, if the `Common.dwg` file created in this chapter used the `Unit.dwg` file as an external reference rather than an inserted block, you would still get the same result in the `Xref-1.dwg` file. That is, you would see the entire floor plan, including the unit plans, when you open `Xref-1.dwg`. In this situation, `Unit.dwg` is nested in the `Common.dwg` file, which is in turn external referenced in the `Xref-1.dwg` file.

Though nested Xrefs can be helpful, take care in using external references in this way. For example, you might create an external reference using the `Common.dwg` file in the `Floor1.dwg` file as a means of referencing walls and other features of the `Common.dwg` file. You might also reference the `Common.dwg` file into the `Floor2.dwg` file for the same reason. Once you do this, however, you will have three versions of the Common plan in the `Xref-1.dwg` file, because each Xref now has `Common.dwg` attached to it. And because AutoCAD would dutifully load `Common.dwg` three times, `Xref-1.dwg` would occupy substantial computer memory, slowing your computer down when you edit the `Xref-1.dwg` file.

To avoid this problem, use the Overlay option of the External Reference dialog box. An overlayed external reference cannot be nested. For example, if you use the Overlay option when inserting the `Common.dwg` file into the `Floor1.dwg` and `Floor2.dwg` files, the nested `Common.dwg` files are ignored when you open the `Xref-1.dwg` file, thereby eliminating the redundant occurrence of `Common.dwg`. In another example, if you use the Overlay option to import the `Unit.dwg` file into the `Common.dwg` file and then attach the `Common.dwg` into `Xref-1.dwg` as an Xref, you do not see the Unit plan in `Xref-1.dwg`. The nested `Unit.dwg` drawing is ignored.

Using the Layout Tabs and Paper Space

Your set of drawings for this studio apartment building would probably include a larger scale, more detailed drawing of the typical Unit plan. You already have the beginnings of this drawing in the form of the Unit file.

As you have seen, the notes and dimensions you entered into the Unit file can be turned off or frozen in the Plan file so they don't interfere with the graphics of the drawing. The Unit file can be part of another drawing file that contains more detailed information on the typical unit plan at a larger scale. To this new drawing you can add other notes, symbols, and dimensions. Whenever the Unit file is altered, you update its occurrence in the large-scale drawing of the typical unit as well as in the Plan file (see Figure 12.31). The units are thus quickly updated, and good correspondence is ensured among all the drawings for your project.

FIGURE 12.31:

Relationship of drawing files in a project

Unit Plan File

External referenced files do not become part of the receiving files database.

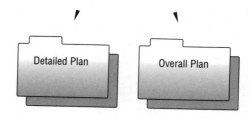

Detailed Plan

Overall Plan

Now suppose that you want to combine drawings having different scales in the same drawing file—for example, the overall plan of one floor plus an enlarged view of one typical unit. This can be accomplished by using the Layout tabs and a feature called Paper Space.

Understanding Model Space and Paper Space

So far, you've looked at ways to help you get around in your drawing while using a single view. This single view representation of your AutoCAD drawing is called the *Model Space* display mode. You also have the capability to set up multiple views of your drawing, called *floating viewports*. Floating viewports can be created by using the Layout tabs to work in *Paper Space* display mode.

To get a clear understanding of the Model Space and Paper Space modes, imagine that your drawing is actually a full-size replica or model of the object you are drawing. Your computer screen is your window into a "room" where this model is being constructed, and the keyboard and mouse are your means of access to this room. You can control your window's position in relation to the object through the use of Pan, Zoom, View, and other display-related commands. You can also construct or modify the model by using drawing and editing commands. Think of this room as your Model Space.

So far, you have been working on your drawings by looking through a single "window" into Model Space. Now suppose you have the ability to step back and add windows with different views looking into your Model Space. The effect is as if you have several video cameras in your Model Space "room," each connected to a different monitor. You can view all your windows at once on your computer screen, or enlarge a single window to fill the entire screen. Further, you can control the shape of your windows and easily switch from one window to another. This is what Paper Space is like.

Paper Space lets you create and display multiple views of Model Space. Each view window, called a *viewport*, acts like an individual virtual screen. One viewport can have an overall view of your drawing, while another can be a close-up. Layer visibility can also be controlled individually for each viewport, allowing you to display different versions of the same area of your drawing. You can move, copy, and stretch viewports, and even overlap them.

NOTE   Another type of viewport called the *Tiled* viewport can be set up in Model Space. Chapter 16 discusses this type of viewport.

Perhaps one of the more powerful features of Paper Space is that you can plot several views of the same drawing on one sheet of paper. You can also include graphic objects such as borders and notes that appear only in Paper Space. In this function, Paper Space acts very much like a page-layout program such as Quark or Adobe PageMaker. You can "paste up" different views of your drawing and then add borders, title blocks, general notes, and other types of graphic and textural data. Figure 12.32 shows the Plan drawing set up in Paper Space mode to display several views.

FIGURE 12.32:

Different views of the same drawing in Paper Space

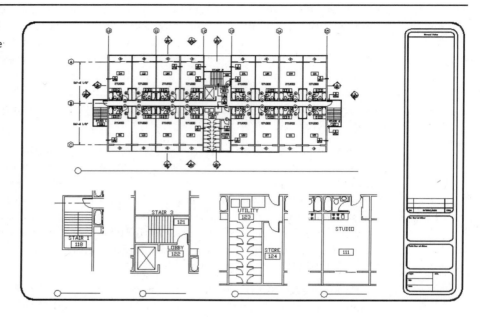

Creating a Paper Space Layout

Your gateway to Paper Space is the Layout tab at the bottom of the AutoCAD Window. When the Model tab is selected, you are in Model Space. When you select the Layout tab, you are in Paper Space.

> **TIP**
>
> You can also use a system variable to switch between tabs. When Tilemode is set to 1 (On), the default setting, you are in Model Space. When it is set to 0 (Off), you are in Paper Space.

Let's start with the basics of entering Paper Space.

1. If it isn't already open, open the Xref-1 file, making sure your display shows all of the drawing.

2. Click the Layout1 tab or click MODEL on the status bar. The Page Setup dialog box appears, allowing you to set up your plotter or printer for this Layout tab.

3. Make sure that the Layout Setting tab is selected, then select the Letter (8.5" × 11") paper size option from the Paper Size drop-down list. Metric users

should select A4 (210mm × 297mm). The paper size you select here determines the shape and margin of the Paper Space layout area.

4. Click OK when you've selected a paper size. The drawing appears in your Paper Space view. Note that the word "PAPER" replaces the word "MODEL" in the status bar; this tells you at a glance that you are in Paper Space.

In step 3, AutoCAD stops to ask you what paper size you want. AutoCAD bases the Paper Space work area on the paper size that you specify. Once you've opened a Layout tab for the first time, and specified a sheet size, the area shown in Paper Space reflects the area of the paper size you select in step 3. From then on, you won't see the Page Setup dialog box again. If for some reason you need to change the paper size, you can do so by opening the Layout tab you want to change, then choosing File ➤ Page Setup to open the Page Setup dialog box.

Creating New Paper Space Viewports

As you saw in Chapter 7, the different look of the Layout tab tells you that you are in Paper Space. You also learned that a viewport is automatically created when you first open a Layout tab Paper Space view. The viewport displays an overall view of your drawing to no particular scale.

In this section, you will work with multiple viewports in Paper Space, instead of just the default single viewport you get when you open the Layout tab. This first exercise shows you how to create three new viewports at once.

1. Right-click the Draw or Modify toolbar, and select Viewports to open the Viewports toolbar. You'll use this toolbar a bit later in this exercise.

2. Click the viewport border to select it. The viewport border is the solid rectangle surrounding your drawing, just inside the dashed rectangle.

3. Click the Erase tool to erase the viewport. Your drawing disappears. Don't panic; remember that the viewport is like a window to Model Space. The objects in Model Space are still there.

4. Click Display Viewports Dialog in the Viewports toolbar. You can also choose View ➤ Viewports ➤ New Viewports. The Viewports dialog box appears. This dialog box contains a set of predefined viewport layouts.

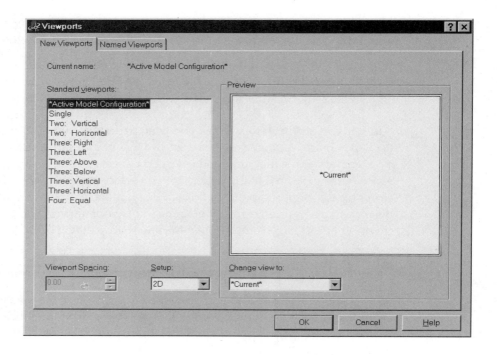

You'll learn more about the Viewports dialog box and its options in Chapter 16.

5. Click the Three Above option in the Standard Viewports list box. The box to the right shows a sample view of the Three Above layout you selected.

6. Click OK. The `Specify first corner or [Fit] <Fit>:` prompt appears.

7. Press ⏎ to accept the default Fit option. The Fit option fits the viewport layout to the maximum area allowed in your Paper Space view. Three rectangles appear in the formation, shown in Figure 12.33. Each of these is a viewport to your Model Space. The viewport at the top fills the whole width of the drawing area; the bottom half of the screen is divided into two viewports.

8. Press ⏎.

When you create new viewports, AutoCAD automatically fills the viewport with the extents of your Model Space drawing. You can specify an exact scale for each viewport, as you'll see later.

FIGURE 12.33:

The newly created viewports

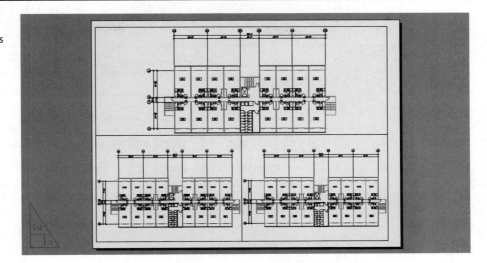

Notice that the dashed line representing your paper margin has disappeared. That's because the viewports are pushed to the margin limits, thereby covering the dashed line.

You could have kept the original viewport that appeared when you first opened the Layout1 tab, then added two new viewports. Completely replacing the single viewport is a bit simpler since it fits the viewports in the allowed space for you.

Reaching Inside Viewports

Now suppose you need to have access to the objects within the viewports in order to adjust their display and edit your drawing.

1. Click PAPER on the status bar. This gives you control over Model Space even though you are in Paper Space. (You can also enter **MS**↵ as a keyboard short-cut to entering Model Space mode.)

    The first thing you notice is that the UCS icon changes back to its L-shaped arrow form. It also appears in each viewport, as if you had three AutoCAD windows instead of just one.

2. Move your cursor over each viewport. Notice that in one of the viewports the cursor appears as the AutoCAD crosshair cursor, while in the other viewports it appears as an arrow pointer. The viewport that shows the AutoCAD

cursor is the active one; you can pan and zoom, as well as edit objects in the active viewport.

TIP

If your drawing disappears from a viewport, you can usually retrieve it by using View ➤ Zoom ➤ Extents (**Zoom**↵ **E**↵).

---

3. Click the lower-left viewport to activate it.

4. Click View ➤ Zoom ➤ Window and window the elevator area.

5. Click the lower-right viewport and use View ➤ Zoom ➤ Window to enlarge your view of a typical unit. You can also use the Pan Realtime and Zoom Real-time tools.

TIP

If you don't see the UCS Icon, it has been turned off. Type **UCSicon**↵ **On**↵ to turn it on. See Chapter 16 for more on the UCS Icon.

When you click the PAPER button on the status bar, the UCS icon again changes shape—instead of one triangular-shaped icon, you have three arrow-shaped ones, one for each viewport on the screen. Also, as you move your cursor into the currently active viewport, the cursor changes from an arrow into the usual crosshair. Another way to tell which viewport is the active one is by its double border.

TIP

You can also switch between Model Space and Paper Space by double-clicking an area in either region. For example, to go to Model Space from Paper Space, double-click inside a viewport. To get back to Paper Space, double-click the area outside the viewport. If you have an enlarged view of a viewport and no portion of the Paper Space area is available to click, use the PAPER button on the status bar.

You can move from viewport to viewport even while you are in the middle of most commands. For example, you can issue the Line command, then pick the start point in one viewport, then go to a different viewport to pick the next point, and so on. To activate a different viewport, you simply click it (see Figure 12.34).

TIP

You may find it difficult to access the contents of overlapping viewports, especially if the viewports are the same size or if one is enclosed by another. In this situation, you can move between viewports by entering Ctrl-R repeatedly until you get to the viewport you want.

FIGURE 12.34:

The three viewports, each with a different view of the plan

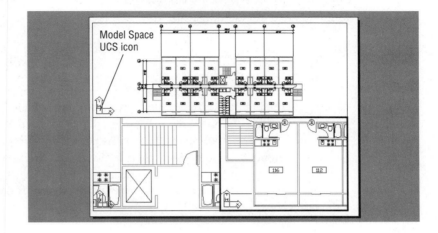

Model Space
UCS icon

You've seen how you can zoom into a viewport view, but what happens when you use the Zoom command while in Paper Space? Try the following exercise to find out.

1. Click the MODEL button on the status bar or double-click an area outside the viewports to return to Paper Space.

2. Click the Realtime Zoom tool in the Standard toolbar, then zoom into the Paper Space view. The entire view enlarges, including the views in the viewports.

3. Choose View ➢ Zoom ➢ All or enter Z↵ A↵ to return to the overall view of Paper Space.

This brief exercise shows that you can use the Zoom tool in Paper Space just as you would in Model Space. All the display-related commands are available, including the Pan Realtime command.

Getting Back to Full-Screen Model Space

Once you've created viewports, you can then re-enter Model Space through the viewport using the MODEL/PAPER button on the status bar. This button performs two functions: It shows you which space you are in and it allows you to switch between the two spaces. But what if you want to quickly get back into the old familiar full-screen Model Space you were in before you entered Paper Space? The following exercise demonstrates how this is done.

1. Click the Model tab at the bottom of the drawing area, or enter **Tm↵ 1↵**. Your drawing returns to the original full-screen Model Space view—everything is back to normal.

2. Click the Layout1 tab, or enter **Tm↵ 0↵**. You are back in Paper Space. Notice that all the viewports are still there when you return to Paper Space. Once you've set up Paper Space, it remains part of the drawing until you delete all the viewports. Also notice that you didn't see the Page Setup dialog box this time. Once you've chosen a sheet size, AutoCAD assumes that you will continue to use that sheet size and other page setup information until you tell it otherwise.

You may prefer doing most of your drawing in Model Space, using Paper Space for setting up views for plotting. Since viewport layouts are retained, you won't lose anything when you go back to Model Space to edit your drawing.

Working with Paper Space Viewports

Paper Space is intended as a page-layout or composition tool. You can manipulate viewports' sizes, scale their view independently of one another, and even set layering and line-type scales independently. Let's try manipulating the shape and location of viewports using the Modify toolbar options.

1. Turn off Running Osnaps if it is on.

2. Click the bottom edge of the lower-left viewport to expose its grips (see the top image of Figure 12.35).

3. Click the upper-right grip, and then drag it to the location shown in the top image of Figure 12.35.

4. Press the Esc key and then erase the lower-right viewport by clicking Erase in the Modify toolbar. Then click the bottom edge of the viewport.

5. Move the lower-left viewport so it is centered in the bottom half of the window, as shown in the bottom image of Figure 12.35.

FIGURE 12.35:

Stretching, erasing, and moving viewports

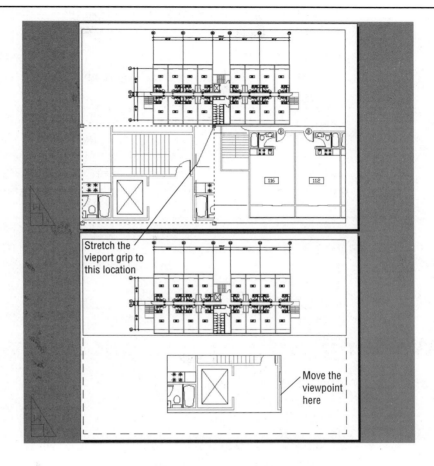

In this exercise, you clicked the viewport edge to select it for editing. If, while in Paper Space, you attempt to click the image within the viewport, you will not select anything. Later you will see, however, that you can use the Osnap modes to snap to parts of the drawing image within a viewport.

Viewports are recognized as AutoCAD objects so they can be manipulated by all the editing commands, just like any other object. In the foregoing exercise you moved, stretched, and erased viewports. Next, you'll see how layers affect viewports.

1. Create a new layer called Vport.

2. Use the Properties dialog box to change the viewport borders to the Vport layer.

3. Finally, turn off the Vport layer. The viewport borders disappear.

4. After reviewing the results of step 3, turn the Vport layer back on.

A viewport's border can be assigned a layer, color, line type, and even a line weight. If you put the viewport's border on a layer that has been turned off or frozen, that border becomes invisible, just like any other object on such a layer. Making the borders invisible is helpful when you want to compose a final sheet for plotting. Even when turned off, the active viewport has a heavy border around it when you switch to floating model, and all the viewports still display their views.

Disappearing Viewports

As you add more viewports to a drawing, you may discover that some of them blank out, even though you know you haven't turned them off. Don't panic. AutoCAD limits the number of viewports that display their contents at any given time to 48. (A viewport that displays its contents is said to be active.) This limit is provided because too many active viewports can bog down a system.

If you are using a slow computer with limited resources, you can lower this limit to 2 or 3 viewports to gain some performance. Then only 2 or 3 viewports will display their contents. (All viewports that are turned on will still plot, regardless of whether their contents are visible or not.) Zooming into a blank viewport restores its visibility, thereby allowing you to continue to work with enlarged Paper Space views containing only a few viewports.

The Maxactvp system variable controls this value. Type **Maxactvp** and then enter the number of viewports you want to have active at any given time.

Scaling Views in Paper Space

Paper Space has its own unit of measure. You have already seen how you are required to specify a paper size when opening a Layout tab to a Paper Space view. When you first enter Paper Space, regardless of the area your drawing occupies in Model Space, you are given limits that are set by the paper size you specify in the Page Setup dialog box. If you keep in mind that Paper Space is like a paste-up area that is dependant on the printer you have configured for AutoCAD, then this difference of scale becomes easier to comprehend. Just as you might paste up photographs and maps representing several square miles onto an 11" × 17" board, so can you use Paper Space to paste up views of scale drawings representing city blocks or houses on an 8 1/2" × 11" sheet of paper. But in AutoCAD, you have the freedom to change the scale and size of the objects you are pasting up.

NOTE   While in Paper Space, you can edit objects in a Model Space viewport, but to do so, you must use Floating Model Space. You can then click a viewport, and then edit within that viewport. While in this mode, objects that were created in Paper Space cannot be edited. View ➤ Paper Space brings you back to the Paper Space environment.

If you want to be able to print your drawing at a specific scale, then you must carefully consider scale factors when composing your Paper Space paste-up. Let's see how to put together a sheet in Paper Space and still maintain accuracy of scale.

1. Make sure you're in Paper Space. Check to see if the word PAPER appears on the status bar. If MODEL appears there, click that button to change it to PAPER.

2. Click the topmost viewport's border to select it.

3. Right-click, then select Properties at the bottom of the - menu. The Properties dialog box appears.

4. Scroll down the list of properties until you see the Standard Scale listing.

5. Click the Custom setting next to the Standard Scale listing, then click the downward-pointing arrow that appears next to Custom to open the list.

6. Select 1/32" = 1' from the drop-down list. Notice how the view in the top viewport changes.

7. Press the Esc key twice to clear the selection of the viewport.

8. Click the lower viewport border. The information in the Properties dialog box changes to reflect the properties of the newly selected viewport.

9. Click the Standard Scale Custom listing and open the drop-down list as you did in step 5.

10. Select 3/16" = 1' from the list. Notice that the view in the viewport changes to reflect the new scale (see Figure 12.36).

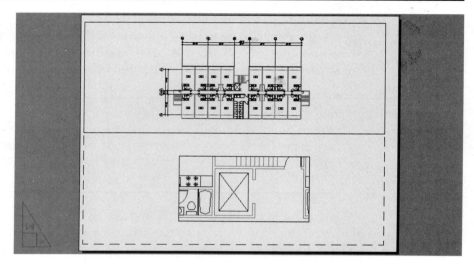

It's easy to adjust the width, height, and location of the viewports so that they display only the parts of the unit you want to see. While in Paper Space, use the Stretch, Move, or Scale command to edit any viewport border or just use the viewport's grips to edit its size. The view within the viewport itself remains at the same scale and location, while the viewport changes in size. You can move and stretch viewports with no effect on the size and location of the objects within the view.

If you have a situation where you need to overlay one drawing on top of another, you can overlap viewports. Use the Osnap overrides to select geometry within each viewport, even while in Paper Space. This allows you to align one viewport on top of another at exact locations.

You can also add a title block in Paper Space at a 1:1 scale to frame your viewports and then plot this drawing from Paper Space at a scale of 1:1. Your plot appears just as it does in Paper Space, at the appropriate scale. Paper Space provides a dashed line to show you where the nonprintable areas occur near the edge of the paper.

While working in Paper Space, pay close attention to whether you are in Paper Space or Floating Model Space mode. It is easy to accidentally perform a pan or zoom within a Floating Model Space viewport when you intend to pan or zoom your Paper Space view. This can cause you to lose your viewport scaling or alignment with other parts of the drawing. It's a good idea to save viewport views using View ➤ Named Views in case you happen to accidentally change a viewport view.

Another way to prevent your viewport view from being accidentally altered is to turn on View Lock. To do this, while in Paper Space, click a viewport border. Right-click to open the popup menu, then select View Lock ➢ On. Once locked, you cannot pan or zoom a viewport view. You also cannot change the size of the viewport. This setting is also available in the viewport's Properties dialog box.

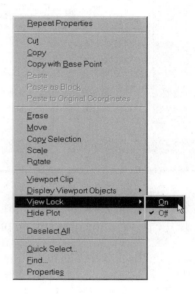

Setting Layers in Individual Viewports

Another unique feature of Paper Space viewports is their ability to freeze layers independently. You could, for example, display the usual plan information in the overall view of a floor but show only the walls in the enlarged view of one unit.

You control viewport layer visibility through the Layer Properties Manager dialog box. You may have noticed that there are three sun icons for each layer listing.

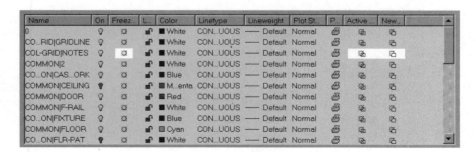

You're already familiar with the sun icon farthest to the left. This is the Freeze/Thaw icon that controls the freezing and thawing of layers globally. Just to the right of that icon is a sun icon with a transparent rectangle. This icon controls the freezing and thawing of layers in individual viewports. The next exercise shows you firsthand how it works.

1. Click the PAPER button on the status bar to go to Floating Model Space.

2. Activate the lower viewport.

3. Open the Layer Properties Manager dialog box.

4. Locate the COMMON | WALL layer, then click its name to help you isolate this layer.

WARNING The Cur VP and New VP options in the Layer Control dialog box cannot be used while you are in tiled Model Space.

5. Click the column labeled Active VP Freeze for the selected layer. The Active VP Freeze column is the second column from the right side of the dialog box. The icon looks like a transparent rectangle over a sun. Once you've clicked the icon, the sun changes into a snowflake telling you that the layer is now frozen for the current viewport.

6. Click OK. The active viewport regenerates, with the Wall layer of the Common Xref made invisible in the current viewport. However, the walls remain visible in the other viewport (see Figure 12.37).

7. After reviewing the effects of the Active VP Freeze setting, go back to the Layer Properties Manager and thaw the COMMON | WALL layer by clicking its Active VP Freeze icon again so it turns back into a sun.

8. Click OK to exit the dialog box.

FIGURE 12.37:

The drawing editor with the Wall layer turned off in the active viewport

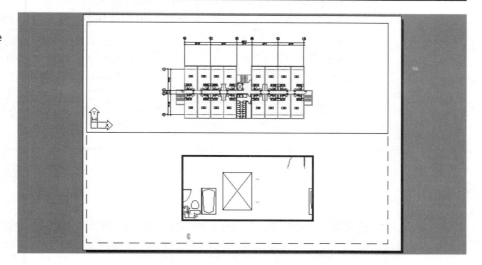

You might have noticed another, similar sun icon next to the one you used in the previous exercise. This icon shows an opaque rectangle over the sun. This icon controls layer visibility in any new viewports you might create next, rather than controlling existing viewports.

If you prefer, you can also use the Layer Control popup list in the toolbar to freeze layers in individual viewports. Select the layer from the list, and then click the same sun icon with the small rectangle below it. Now save and exit the Xref-1 file.

Masking Out Parts of a Drawing

Chapter 6 described a method for using 3D Faces to hide floor patterns under equipment or furniture in a floor layout. You can use a similar method to hide irregularly-shaped areas in a Paper Space viewport. This would be desirable for plotting site plans, civil plans, or floor plans that require portions of the drawing to be masked out. Or you may want to mask part of a plan that is overlapped by another to expose dimension or text data.

This section concludes the apartment building tutorial. Although you haven't drawn the complete building, you've already learned all the commands and techniques you need to do so. Figure 12.38 shows you a completed plan of the first floor; to complete your floor plans and get some practice using AutoCAD, you may want to add the symbols shown in this figure to your Plan file.

Since buildings like this one often have the same plans for several floors, the plan for the second floor can also represent the third floor. Combined with the first floor, this gives you a three-level apartment building. This project might also have a ground-level garage, which would be a separate file. The Col-grid.dwg file can be used in the garage file as a reference for dimensions. The other symbols can be blocks stored as files that can be retrieved in other files.

FIGURE 12.38:

A completed floor of the apartment building

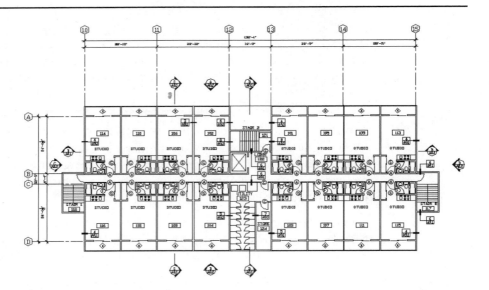

Paper Space and the San Francisco Main Library Project

The San Francisco Main Library project made extensive use of Paper Space. As you've seen in earlier chapters, the library project used multiple instances of the same file to show different types of information. Paper Space was instrumental in enabling the CAD specialists to manage large amounts of drawing data. One floor plan drawing served as the basis for several sheets including floor plans, reflected ceiling plans, equipment plans, exit plans, and others.

Continued on next page

The first image of the two graphics in this sidebar shows a Paper Space view of a drawing from the San Francisco Main Library construction document set. This particular sheet shows the floor pattern layout of some of the main circulation areas.

The title block is inserted in Paper Space as a block, rather than as an Xref. This was done because each drawing has unique drawing title information that is kept as attribute data in the title block. The attributes can be easily updated from a dialog box.

The plan drawings are Xrefs inserted into Model Space, with Paper Space viewports displaying selected areas. The viewport borders are turned on in this view to show how they are arranged. These borders are turned off when the drawing is plotted.

Notice that the grid reference symbols are in their own viewport adjacent to the main enlarged floor plan. These adjacent grid viewports display portions of the drawing that are actually some distance away from the floor plan shown in the main viewport. The second image in this sidebar shows the overall floor plan with the viewport areas outlined. Here you can see that the column grid symbols are actually at the edge of the drawing.

This example shows how viewports helped the creator of this drawing reuse existing data. If a change is made to the overall plan including the column grids, the enlarged plan of the entry is automatically updated.

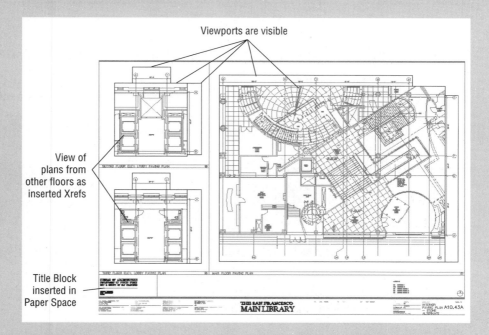

Viewports are visible

View of plans from other floors as inserted Xrefs

Title Block inserted in Paper Space

Continued on next page

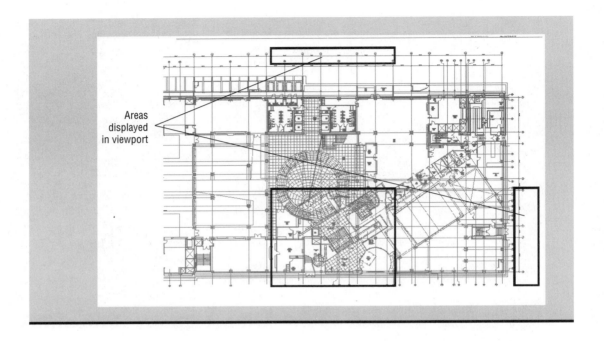

Areas displayed in viewport

Creating and Using Multiple Paper Space Layouts

You're not limited to just one Paper Space layout. You can have as many Paper Space layouts as you want, with each layout set up for a different sheet size containing different views of your drawing. You can use this feature to set up multiple drawing sheets based on a single AutoCAD drawing file. Imagine that you have a client that requires full sets of plans in both 1/8" = 1' scale and 1/16" = 1' scale. You can set up two Layout tabs, each with a different sheet size and viewport scale.

You can also set up different Paper Space layouts for the different types of drawings. In the San Francisco Main Library project, a single drawing contained the data for mechanical layout, equipment and furnishing, floor plans, and reflected ceiling plans. While that project used multiple files to set the layers for each plan, a single file with multiple Layout tabs can serve the same purpose in AutoCAD 2000.

To create new Layout tabs, do the following.

1. Right-click any tab.

2. Select New Layout from the popup menu. A new tab is added to those that already exist.

3. Click the new tab. The Page Setup dialog box appears.

4. Click OK. The new tab appears with its single default viewport.

When you click a new tab, the Page Setup dialog box appears just as it did in the first exercise of this section. The Layout tab popup menu also offers the From Template option. The From Template option lets you create a Paper Space layout based on an AutoCAD template file. AutoCAD offers several standard layouts that include title blocks based on common sheet sizes.

The Layout tab popup menu also offers options that allow you to delete, rename, move, copy, or select all the tabs. If you find that there are more tabs than can fit in the space provided, you can navigate the tabs using the arrows just to the left of the tabs.

Creating Odd-Shaped Viewports

There are many situations when a rectangular viewport will not provide a view appropriate for what you want to accomplish. For example, you may want to isolate part of a floor plan that is L-shaped or even circular. You can create viewports from virtually shape you need, as the following exercise demonstrates.

Now suppose you want to set up this Layout tab to show only the lower apartment units and the elevators and stairs.

1. Click the Clip Existing Viewport tool in the Viewports toolbar. You can also choose Modify ➢ Clip ➢ Viewport.

2. At the Select viewport to clip: prompt, click the viewport border.

3. At the Select clipping object or [Polygonal] <Polygonal>: prompt, press ↵.

4. Turn off Running Osnaps and draw the outline shown in Figure 12.39.

5. When you have finished selecting points, press ↵. The viewport changes to conform to the new shape.

6. Click the viewport border to expose its grips.

7. Click a grip and move it to a new location. Notice that the viewport view conforms to the new shape as shown in the bottom view of Figure 12.39.

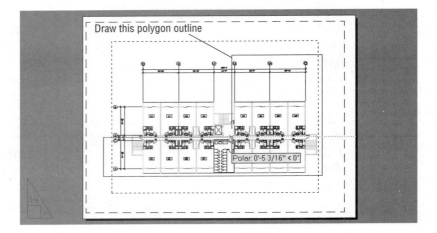

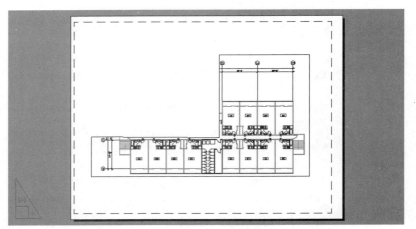

The new viewport shape gives you more flexibility in isolating portions of a drawing. This can be especially useful if you have a large project that is divided into smaller sheets. You can set up several Layout tabs, each displaying a different portion of the plan.

What if you want a viewport that is not rectilinear? The next exercise shows you how to create a circular viewport.

1. Erase the viewport you just modified.

2. Draw a circle that roughly fills the Paper Space area.

3. Click the Convert Object to Viewport option on the Viewports toolbar or select View ➤ Viewports ➤Object.

4. Click the circle. The plan appears inside the circle, as shown in Figure 12.40.

To simplify this exercise, you were asked to draw a circle to use as the basis for a new viewport. You are not limited to circles; you can use any closed polyline or spline of any shape (see Chapter 13 for a detailed discussion on polylines and splines). You can also use the Polygon tool in the Draw toolbar to create a shape, then turn it into a viewport.

FIGURE 12.40:

A circular viewport

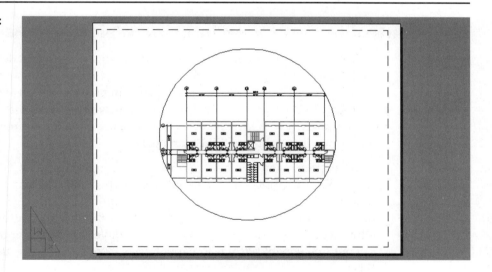

If you look carefully at the series of prompts for the last exercise, you'll notice that the Convert Object to Viewports option invokes a command-line version of the Vports command (**–vports**). The command-line version of Vports offers some options that the standard Vports command does not. The following options are available with the command-line version of Vports:

```
[ON/OFF/Fit/Hideplot/Lock/Object/Polygonal/Restore/2/3/4] <Fit>:
```

You used two of the options in these last two exercises, the Polygon option and the Object option. If you're an experienced AutoCAD user, you may notice that this command-line version of Vports is the same as the Mview command of earlier releases. You can still use the Mview command if you prefer.

Understanding Line Weights, Line Types, and Dimensions in Paper Space

There are a number of features in AutoCAD that act differently depending on whether you are in Paper Space or Model Space. The most visible of these features are line weights, line types, and dimensions. In this section, you'll take a closer look at these features and you'll see how to use them in conjunction with Paper Space.

Controlling and Viewing Line Weights in Paper Space

Line weights can greatly improve the readability of technical drawings. You can make important features stand out with bold line weights while keeping the "noise" of smaller details from overpowering a drawing. In architectural floor plans, walls are traditionally drawn with heavier lines, so the outline of a plan can be easily read. Other features exist in a drawing for reference only, so they are drawn in a lighter weight than normal.

In Chapter 7, you saw how to control line weights in AutoCAD using plot style tables. You can apply either a named plot style table or a color plot style table to a drawing. If you already have a library of AutoCAD drawings, you might want to use color plot style tables for backward compatibility. AutoCAD 2000 also allows you to assign line weights directly to layers or objects and view the results of your line weight settings in Paper Space. Here's an exercise that demonstrates this feature.

1. Click the Layout1 tab, then open the Layer Properties Manager dialog box.

2. Right-click the Layer list, then choose Select All.

3. Click the Lineweight column. The Lineweight dialog box appears.

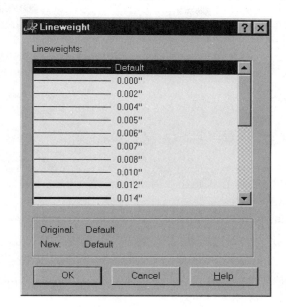

4. Select 0.005" (0.13mm) from the list then click OK. You've just assigned the 0.005" (0.13mm) line weight to all layers.

5. Right-click again and select Clear All.

6. Ctrl+click the layers COMMON | WALL and Floor1 | WALL to select them.

7. Click the Lineweight column for either of the two selected layers. The Lineweight dialog box opens again.

8. Select 0.016" (0.4mm) from the dialog box, then click OK. You've just assigned the 0.016" (0.4mm) line weight to the two selected layers.

9. Click OK in the Layer Properties Manager dialog box.

While you set the line weights for the layers in the drawing, you need to make a few more changes to the file settings before they are visible in Paper Space.

1. Choose Format ➤ Lineweights. The Lineweight Settings dialog box appears.

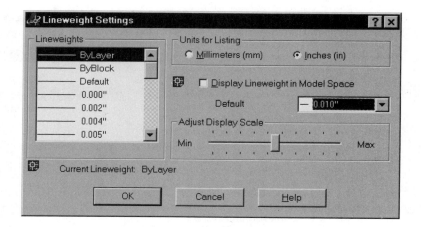

2. Click the Display Lineweight in Model Space check box, then click OK.

3. Make sure you are in Paper Space, then zoom into the drawing so you have a view similar to the one shown in Figure 12.41.

4. Choose View ➤ Regen All. You'll see the lines representing the walls appear with thickness.

FIGURE 12.41:

An enlarged view of the plan with line weights displayed

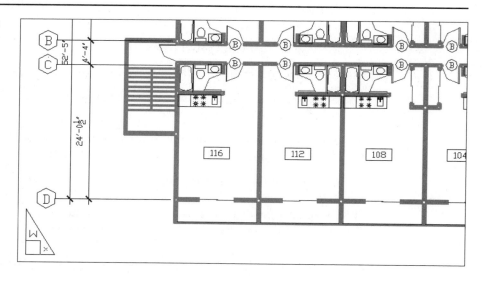

With the ability to display line weights in Paper Space, you have better control over your output. Instead of using a trial-and-error method to print your drawing, then checking your printout to see if the line weights are correct, AutoCAD 2000 lets you see the line weights right on your screen.

This exercise showed you how to set line weights so that they appear in Paper Space as they will when you plot your drawing. If you normally plot your drawings in black, you can go one step further and set all of your layer colors to black to really see how your plots will look. But you'll need to save your layer settings so you can restore the layers back to their original colors. The Layer Manager tool in the Express pull-down menu can save layer settings for you, including color settings. See Chapter 19 for more on the Express tools. Another way to view your drawing in black and white without affecting your layer settings is to use the color plot style table described in Chapter 7.

TIP   When line weight display is turned on, you'll see line weights in Model Space as well as in Paper Space. Line weights can be distracting while you work on your drawing in Model Space but you can quickly turn them off by typing **Lwdisplay↵ 0↵** at the command prompt. Typing **Lwdisplay↵ 1↵** turns the line weight display back on.

The Lineweight Settings Dialog Box

There were a number of other settings in the Lineweight Settings dialog box that you didn't use in the exercise. Here is a description of those settings for your reference.

Units for Listing   You can choose between millimeters and inches for the unit of measure for line weights. The default is millimeters.

Adjust Display Scale   This setting lets you control just how thick line weights appear in the drawing. Move the slider to the right for thicker lines and to the left for thinner lines. This setting only affects the display on your monitor. As you move the slider, you can see a sample of the results in the Lineweights list box to the left of the dialog box.

Default Drop-Down list   This drop-down list lets you select the default line weight that you see in the Layer Properties Manager dialog box. It is set to 0.01 inch (0.25mm) by default. You may want to lower the default line weight to .005 inch (.13mm) just as a matter of course, since most printers these days can print lines to that size and even smaller.

Line-Type Scales and Paper Space

As you have seen from previous exercises, drawing scales have to be carefully controlled when creating viewports. Fortunately, this is easily done through the Properties dialog box. While Paper Space offers the flexibility of combining different scale images in one display, it also adds to the complexity of your task in controlling that display. Your drawing's line-type scale, in particular, needs careful attention.

In Chapter 4, you saw that you had to set the line-type scale to the scale factor of the drawing in order to make the line type visible. If you intend to plot that same drawing from Paper Space, you will have to set the line-type scale back to 1 to get the line types to appear correctly. This is because AutoCAD faithfully scales line types to the current unit system. Remember that Paper Space units differ from Model Space units. So when you scale a Model Space image down to fit within the smaller Paper Space area, the line types remain scaled to the increased line-type scale settings. In the case of that Chapter 4 example, line types are scaled up by a factor of 48. This causes noncontinuous lines to appear as continuous in Paper Space because you only see a small portion of a greatly enlarged noncontinuous line type.

The Psltscale system variable allows you to determine how line-type scales are applied to Paper Space views. You can set Psltscale so that the line types will appear the same, regardless of whether you view them directly in tiled Model Space, or through a viewport in Paper Space. By default, this system variable is set to 1. This causes AutoCAD to scale all the line types uniformly across all the viewports in Paper Space. You can set Psltscale to 0 to force the viewports to display line types exactly as they appear in Model Space.

This setting can also be controlled in the Linetype Manager dialog box, accessed by choosing Format ➢ Linetype. When you click the Show Details button, you see a setting called Use Paper Space Units for Scaling in the lower-right corner. When this is checked, Psltscale is set to 1. When it is unchecked, Psltscale is set to 0.

Dimensioning in Paper Space

At times, you may find it more convenient to add dimensions to your drawing in Paper Space rather than directly on your objects in Model Space. There are several dimension settings you will want to know about that will enable you to do this.

To have your dimensions produce the appropriate values in Paper Space, you need to have AutoCAD adjust the dimension text to the scale of the viewport from which you are dimensioning. You can have AutoCAD scale dimension values so they correspond to a viewport zoom-scale factor. The following steps show you how this setting is made.

1. Open the Dimension Style Manager dialog box.

2. Select the dimension style you want to edit and click Modify.

3. Click the Primary Units tab.

4. In the Measurement Scale button group, enter the scale factor of the viewport you intend to dimension in the Scale Factor input box. For example, if the viewport is scaled to a 1/2"=1'-0" scale, enter **24**.

5. Click the Apply to Layout Dimensions Only check box so that a check appears there.

6. Click OK, and then click Close in the Dimension Style Manager dialog box. You are ready to dimension in Paper Space.

Remember that you can snap to objects in a floating viewport so you can add dimensions as you normally would in Model Space.

WARNING   While AutoCAD offers the capability of adding dimensions in Paper Space, you may want to refrain from doing so until you have truly mastered AutoCAD. Because Paper Space dimensions aren't visible in Model Space, it is easy to forget to update your dimensions when your drawing changes. Dimensioning in Paper Space can also create confusion for others editing your drawing at a later date.

Other Uses for Paper Space

The exercises presented in this section should give you a sense of how you work in Paper Space. We've given examples that reflect the more common uses of Paper Space. Remember that Paper Space is like a page-layout portion of AutoCAD—separate yet connected to Model Space through viewports.

You needn't limit your applications to floor plans. Interior and exterior elevation, 3D models, and detail sheets can all take advantage of Paper Space. When used in conjunction with AutoCAD raster import capabilities, Paper Space can be a powerful tool for creating large-format presentations.

Advanced Tools: Quick Select, Selection Filters, and the Calculator

Before ending this chapter, you will want to know about two other tools that are extremely useful in your day-to-day work with AutoCAD: selection filters and the Calculator. The discussion of these tools is saved until the end of this chapter because you don't really need them until you've become accustomed to the way AutoCAD works. Chances are you've already experimented with some of the Auto-CAD menu options not yet discussed in the tutorial. Many of the pull-down menu options and their functions are self-explanatory. Selection Filters and the Calculator, however, do not appear in any of the menus and require some further explanation.

Let's start with selection filters. There are actually two selection-filtering tools in AutoCAD. The Quick Select tool offers a quick way to locate objects based on their properties. The Filter tool lets you select objects based on a more complex set of criteria.

Filtering Selections

Suppose you need to take just the walls of your drawing and isolate them in a separate file. One way to do this is to turn off all the layers except the Wall layer. Then you can use the Wblock command and select the remaining walls, using a window to write the wall information to a file. Filters can simplify this operation by allowing you to select groups of objects based on their properties.

1. Open the Unit file.

2. Type **w⏎** to start the Wblock command. Then in the Write Block dialog box, enter **Unitwall** in the File Name input box.

3. Make sure the Object radio button is selected in the top of the dialog box, then click the Select Objects button in the Objects group. The dialog box disappears to allow you to select objects.

4. At the `Object Selection:` prompt, type **'Filter⏎**. The Object Selection Filters dialog box appears.

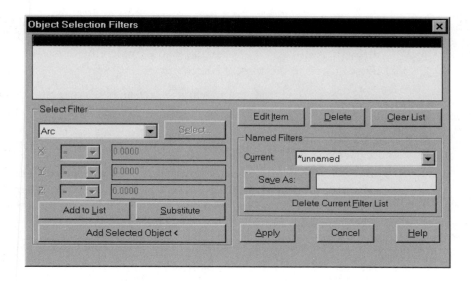

5. Open the drop-down list in the Select Filter button group.

6. Scroll down the list and find and highlight the Layer option.

7. Click the Select button next to the drop-down list to get a list of layers, highlight Wall, and then click OK.

8. In the Object Selection Filters dialog box, click the Add to List button toward the bottom of the Select Filter button group. Layer = Wall is added to the list box.

9. Click Apply. The Object Selection Filters dialog box closes.

10. Type **all**↵ to select everything in the drawing. Only the objects assigned to the Wall layer are selected. You'll see a message in the Command window indicating how many objects were found and how many were filtered out.

11. Press ↵ and you'll see the message `Exiting Filtered selection. 14 found.`

12. Press ↵ again to complete the Wblock command. All the walls are written out to a file called `Unitwall`.

13. After reviewing the results of the exercise, type **U**↵ or click the Undo button in the Standard toolbar to undo the Wblock command.

In this exercise, you filtered out a layer using the Wblock command. Once a filter is designated, you then select the group of objects you want AutoCAD to filter through. AutoCAD finds the objects that match the filter requirements and passes those objects to the current command.

As you've seen from the previous exercise, there are many options to choose from in this utility. Let's take a closer look.

Working with the Object Selection Filters Dialog Box

To use the Object Selection Filters dialog box, first select the criteria for filtering from the pull-down list. If the criteria you select is a named item (layers, line types, colors, or blocks), you can then click the Select button to choose specific items from a list. If there is only one choice, the Select button is dimmed.

Once you've determined what to filter, you must add it to the list by clicking the Add to List button. The filter criteria then appears in the list box at the top of the Object Selection Filters dialog box. Once you have something in the list box, you can then apply it to your current command or to a later command. AutoCAD remembers your filter settings, so if you need to reselect a filtered selection set, you don't have to redefine your filter criteria.

Saving Filter Criteria

If you prefer, you can preselect filter criteria. Then, at any `Select objects:` prompt, you can click Selection Filters on the toolbar (or type **'Filter.↵**), highlight the appropriate filter criteria in the list box, and click Apply. The specifications in the Object Selection Filters dialog box remain in place for the duration of the current editing session.

You can also save a set of criteria by entering a name in the input box next to the Save As button and then clicking the button. The criteria list data is saved in a file called `Filter.nfl`. You can then access the criteria list at any time by opening the Current drop-down list and choosing the name of the saved criteria list.

Filtering Objects by Location

Notice the X, Y, and Z pull-down lists just below the main Select Filter drop-down list in the Object Selection Filters dialog box. These lists become accessible when you select a criteria that describes a geometry or a coordinate (such as an arc's radius or center point). You can use these lists to define filter selections even more specifically, using greater than (>), less than (<), equal to (=), or not equal to (!=) comparisons (called *relational operators*).

For example, suppose you want to grab all the circles whose radii are greater than 4.0 units. To do this, choose Circle Radius from the Select Filter drop-up list. Then in the X list, select the >. Enter **4.0** in the input box to the right of the X list, and click Add to List. You see the item

```
Circle Radius > 4.0000
```

added to the list box at the top of the dialog box. You used the > to indicate a circle radius greater than 4.0 units.

Creating Complex Selection Sets

There will be times when you want to create a very specific filter list. For instance, say you need to filter out all the door blocks on the layer Floor2 *and* all arcs with a radius equal to 1. To do this, you use the *grouping operators* found at the bottom of the Select Filter drop-down list. You'll need to build a list as follows:

```
** Begin OR
** Begin AND
Entity = Block
Layer = Floor2
** End AND
** Begin AND
Entity = Arc
Arc Radius = 1.0000
** End AND
** End OR
```

Notice that the Begin and End operators are balanced; that is, for every Begin OR or Begin AND, there is an End OR or an End AND.

This list may look rather simple, but it can get confusing—mostly because of the way you normally think of the terms AND and OR. If criteria are bounded by the AND grouping operators, then the objects must fulfill *both* criteria before they are selected. If criteria are bounded by the OR grouping operators, then the objects fulfilling *either* criteria will be selected.

Here are the steps to build the list shown just above.

1. In the Select Filter drop-down list, choose ****Begin OR**, and click Add to List. Then do the same for ****Begin AND**.

2. Click Block in the Select Filter drop-down list, and then click Add to List.

3. For the layer, click Layer from the Select Filter drop-down list. Then click Select, choose the layer name, and click Add to List.

4. In the Select Filter drop-down list, choose `**End AND` and click Add to List. Then do the same for `**Begin AND`.

5. Select Arc from the Select Filter drop-down list and click Add to List.

6. Select Arc Radius from the Select Filter list, and enter **1.0** in the input box next to the X drop-down list. Be sure the equal sign (=) shows in the X drop-down list, and then click Add to List.

7. Choose `**End AND` and click Add to List. Then do the same for `**End OR`.

If you make an error in any of the above steps, just highlight the item, select an item to replace it, and click the Substitute button instead of the Add to List button. If you only need to change a value, click Edit Item near the center of the dialog box.

Quick Select

The Filter command offers a lot of power in isolating specific types of objects, but in many situations, you may not need such an elaborate tool. The Qselect command can filter your selection based on the object properties, which are more common filter criteria. To access the Qselect command, choose Tools ➤ Quick Select or right-click the drawing area when no command is active and choose Quick Select from the popup menu. The Quick Select dialog box appears.

Quick Select is also offered as an option on a few dialog boxes. Try using the Wblock command again, this time using the Quick Select option offered in its dialog box.

1. With the Unit file open, type **W**↵ to start the Wblock command, then at the Write Block dialog box, enter **Unitwall2** in the File Name input box.

2. Make sure the Object radio button is selected in the top of the dialog box. Then click the Quick Select button to the right of the Select Objects button in the Objects group. The Quick Select dialog box appears.

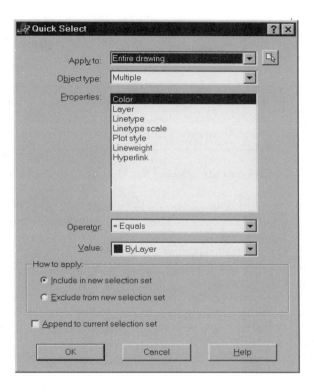

3. Select Layer from the Properties list.

4. Select Wall from the Value drop-down list near the bottom of the dialog box.

5. Click the Select Objects button in the upper-right corner of the dialog box. The dialog box disappears to allow you to select objects.

6. Select the entire drawing using a window, then press ↵ to finish your selection. The Quick Select dialog box returns.

7. Click OK, then click OK in the Write Block dialog box. The walls disappear indicating that they have been written to a file.

The Qselect command selects objects based on the object's properties, as shown in the Properties list box. You can apply the selection criteria based on the entire drawing, or you can use the Select Objects button in the upper-right corner of the dialog box to isolate a set of objects to which you want to apply the selection criteria.

In this last exercise, you used Quick Select from within another dialog box. As mentioned earlier, you can also use Quick Select by choosing Tools ➢ Quick Select or by right-clicking the drawing area when no command is active and choosing

Quick Select from the popup menu. Quick Select then makes use of the Noun/ Verb selection method so you select objects using Quick Select first, then you apply editing commands to the selected objects.

If you want to use Quick Select with a command that does not allow the Noun/ Verb selection method, you can first select objects using Quick Select, then start the command you want to use and use the Previous Selection option.

Here is a description of the Quick Select dialog box options.

Apply to   Lets you determine the set of objects you want to apply the Quick Select filters to. The default is the entire drawing, but you can use the Select Objects button to select a set of objects to apply the filters to. If a set of objects has been selected before issuing the Quick Select command, you also see the Current Selection option in the Apply To drop-down list.

Object Type   Lets you limit the filter to specific types of objects such as lines, arcs, circles, etc. The Multiple option lets you filter your selection from all the objects in the drawing regardless of its type.

Properties   Once you select an object type, you can then select the property of the object type you want to filter. The Properties list changes to reflect the properties that are available to be filtered.

Operator   Offers a set of criteria to apply to the property you select in the Properties list to make your selection. You can select objects that are *equal to* or *not equal to* the criteria you select in the Object Type and Properties lists. Depending on the property you select, you also may have the option to select objects that are greater than or less than a given property value. For example, you can select all lines whose x-coordinate is less than 5 by choosing Line from the Object Type drop-down list and Start X from the Properties list. You then select < Less Than from the Operator drop-down list and enter **5** in the Value input box.

Value   Displays the different values of the property you select in the Properties list. For example, If you select Layer from the Properties list, the Value option lists all the layers available.

How to Apply   Lets you determine whether to include or exclude the filtered objects in a new selection set.

Append to Current Selection Set   Lets you append the filtered objects to an existing selection set or create an entirely new selection set.

Finding Geometry with the Calculator

Another useful AutoCAD tool is the Geometry Calculator. Like most calculators, it adds, subtracts, divides, and multiplies. If you enter an arithmetic expression such as 1 + 2, the calculator returns 3. This is useful for doing math on the fly, but the Calculator does much more than arithmetic, as you will see in the next examples.

Finding the Midpoint between Two Points

One of the most common questions heard from AutoCAD users is, "How can I locate a point midway between two objects?" You can draw a construction line between the two objects, and then use the Midpoint override to select the midpoint of the construction line. The Calculator offers another method that doesn't require drawing additional objects.

In the following exercise, you start a line midway between the center of an arc and the endpoint of a line. Draw a line and an arc and try this out.

1. Start the Line command, and at the From point prompt, type 'Cal⏎.

2. At the >> Expression: prompt, enter **(end + cen)/2**⏎.

3. At the >> Select entity for END snap: prompt, the cursor turns into a square. Place the square on the endpoint of a line and click it.

4. At the >> Select entity for CEN snap: prompt, click an arc. The line starts midway between the arc's center and the endpoint of the line.

TIP Typing the Calculator expressions may seem a bit too cumbersome to use on a regular basis, but if you find you could use some of its features, you can create a toolbar macro to simplify the Calculator's use. See Chapter 20 for more on customizing toolbars.

Using Osnap Modes in Calculator Expressions

In the foregoing exercise, you used Osnap modes as part of arithmetic expressions. The Calculator treats them as temporary placeholders for point coordinates until you actually pick the points (at the prompts shown in steps 3 and 4 above).

The expression:

```
(end + cen)/2
```

finds the average of two values. In this case, the values are coordinates, so the average is the midpoint between the two coordinates. You can take this one step further and find the centroid of a triangle using this expression:

```
(end + end + end)/3
```

Note than only the first three letters of the Osnap mode are entered in Calculator expressions. Table 12.1 shows what to enter in an expression for Osnap modes.

TABLE 12.1:   The Geometry Calculator's Osnap Modes

Calculator Osnap	Meaning
End	Endpoint
Ins	Insert
Int	Intersection
Mid	Midpoint
Cen	Center
Nea	Nearest
Nod	Node
Qua	Quadrant
Per	Perpendicular
Tan	Tangent
Rad	Radius of object
Cur	Cursor pick

Two items are included in Table 12.1 that are not really Osnap modes, though they work similarly when they are used in an expression. The first is Rad. When you include Rad in an expression, you get the following prompt:

```
Select circle, arc or polyline segment for RAD function:
```

You can then select an arc, polyline arc segment, or circle, and its radius is used in place of Rad in the expression.

The other item, Cur, prompts you for a point. Instead of looking for specific geometry on an object, it just locates a point. You could have used Cur in the previous exercise in place of the End and Cen modes, to create a more general-purpose mid-point locator as in the following form:

```
(cur + cur)/2
```

Since AutoCAD does not provide a specific tool to select a point midway between two other points, the form shown here would be useful as a custom toolbar macro. You'll learn how to create macros in Chapter 19.

Finding a Point Relative to Another Point

Another common task in AutoCAD is starting a line at a relative distance from another line. The following steps describe how to use the Calculator to start a line from a point that is 2.5" in the x-axis and 5.0" in the y-axis from the endpoint of another line.

1. Start the Line command. At the First point prompt, enter 'Cal↵.

2. At the >> Expression: prompt, enter **end + [2.5,5.0]**↵.

3. At the >> Select entity for END snap: prompt, pick the endpoint. The line starts from the desired location.

In this example, you used the Endpoint Osnap mode to indicate a point of reference. This is added to Cartesian coordinates in square brackets, describing the distance and direction from the reference point. You could have entered any coordinate value within the square brackets. You could also have entered a polar coordinate in place of the Cartesian coordinate, as in the following: **end + [5.59<63]**.

You don't have to include an @, because the Calculator assumes you want to add the coordinate to the one indicated by the Endpoint Osnap mode. Also, it's not necessary to include every coordinate in the square brackets. For example, to indicate a displacement in only one axis, you can leave out a value for the other two coordinates, as in the following examples:

```
[4,5] = [4,5,0] [,1] = [0,1,0]
[,,2] = [0,0,2]
```

Adding Feet and Inch Distances on the Fly

If you use feet and inches, one of the more frustrating situations you may have run across is having to stop in the middle of a command to find the sum of two or more distances. Say you start the Move command, select your objects, and pick a base point. Then you realize you don't know the distance for the move, but you do know that the distance is the sum of two values—unfortunately, one value is in feet and the other is in inches. Usually in this situation you would have to reach for pen and paper (or, if you've got one, a feet-and-inches calculator), then figure out the distance, and then return to your computer to finish the task. AutoCAD's Geometry Calculator puts an end to this runaround.

The following shows you what to do if you want to move a set of objects a distance that is the sum of 12' 6-5/8" and 115-3/4".

1. Issue the Move command, select objects, and pick a base point.

2. At the Second point: prompt, start the Calculator.

3. At the >> Expression: prompt, enter [@12'6" + 115-3/4" < 45]. Then press ↵, and the objects move into place at the proper distance.

WARNING   You must always enter an inch symbol (") when indicating inches in the Calculator.

In this example, you are mixing inches and feet, which under normal circumstances is a time-consuming calculation. Notice that the feet-and-inches format follows the standard AutoCAD syntax (no space between the feet and inch values). The coordinate value in square brackets can have any number of operators and values, as in the following:

    [@4 * (22 + 15) - (23.3 / 12) + 1 < 13 + 17]

This expression demonstrates that you can also apply operators to angle values.

Guidelines for Working with the Calculator

You may be noticing some patterns in the way expressions are formatted for the Calculator. Here are some guidelines to remember:

- Coordinates are enclosed in square brackets.

- Nested or grouped expressions are enclosed in parentheses.

- Operators are placed between values, as in simple math equations.

- Object snaps can be used in place of coordinate values.

Table 12.2 lists all the operators and functions available in the Calculator. You may want to experiment with these other functions on your own.

TABLE 12.2: The Geometry Calculator's Functions

Operator/Function	What It Does	Example
+ or -	Add or subtract numbers or vectors	2 - 1 = 1 [a,b,c] + [x,y,z] = [a+x, b+y, c+z]
* or /	Multiply or divide numbers or vectors	2 * 4.2 = 8.4 a*[x,y,z] = [a*x, a*y, a*z]
^	Exponentiation of a number	3^2 = 9
sin	Sine of angle	sin (45) = 0.707107
cos	Cosine of angle	cos (30) = 0.866025
tang	Tangent of angle	tang (30) = 0.57735
asin	Arcsine of a real number	asin (0.707107) = 45.0
acos	Arccosine of a real number	acos (0.866025) = 30.0
atan	Arctangent of a real number	atan (0.57735) = 30.0
ln	Natural log	ln (2) = 0.693147
log	Base-10 log	log (2) = 0.30103
exp	Natural exponent	exp (2) = 7.38906
exp10	Base-10 exponent	exp10 (2) = 100
sqr	Square of number	sqr (9) = 81.0
abs	Absolute value	abs (−3.4) = 3.4
round	Rounds to nearest integer	round (3.6) = 4
trunc	Drops decimal portion of real number	trunc (3.6) = 3
r2d	Converts radians to degrees	r2d (1.5708) = 90.0002
d2r	Converts degrees to radians	d2r (90) = 1.5708
pi	The constant pi	3.14159

The Geometry Calculator is capable of much more than the typical uses you've seen here. A description of its full capabilities extends beyond the scope of this text. Still, the processes described in this section will be helpful as you use AutoCAD. If you want to know more about the Calculator, consult the *AutoCAD Command Reference* and the *User's Guide* that comes with AutoCAD 2000.

If You Want to Experiment...

You may want to experiment further with Paper Space to become more familiar with it. Try the following exercise. In it you will add two more viewports using the View ➤ Viewports (Floating) options (Mview and Copy commands). In the process, you'll find that editing Paper Space views requires frequent shifts from Model Space to Paper Space and back.

1. Open the Xref1 file you used for the earlier Paper Space exercise.

2. If you aren't already in Paper Space, click the Layout1 tab and make sure PAPER appears in the status bar.

3. Stretch the lower viewport so that it occupies the lower-right third of the screen (see the top image of Figure 12.42).

4. Switch to Floating Model Space and click the lower viewport.

5. Pan the view so the entire stair is displayed.

6. Return to Paper Space to create a new viewport.

7. Choose View ➤ Viewports ➤ New Viewport, or type **vports**⏎.

8. In the Viewports dialog box, make sure the New Viewports tab is selected and select Single from the list.

9. Click OK, then click the lower-left corner of the screen.

10. At the Other corner prompt, size the viewport so that it is similar to the viewport on the right, as shown in the bottom image of Figure 12.42.

11. Click the PAPER button in the status bar to go to Floating Model Space, then click the lower-left viewport.

12. Type **Regen**⏎. Notice that only the current viewport regenerates.

13. Use the Zoom and Pan commands to display the stairway at the far left of the floor plan.

14. Return to Paper Space and copy the new viewport to the right.

15. Return to Floating Model Space and use the Realtime Pan tool to pan the view in the new viewport to display the stairway to the far right of the floor plan. Notice that when you use the Realtime Pan tool, you can pan across the entire AutoCAD window; you're not limited to panning just inside the viewport area. You can also use the scroll bar to pan the active viewport.

16. Return to Paper Space to resize the viewports to display only the stairs, as in Figure 12.43.

FIGURE 12.42:

Creating new viewports in Paper Space

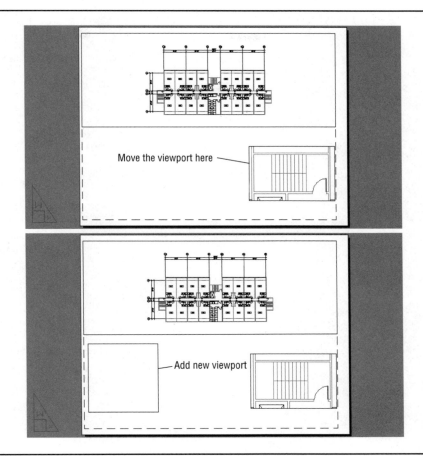

FIGURE 12.43:

Creating new viewports in Paper Space

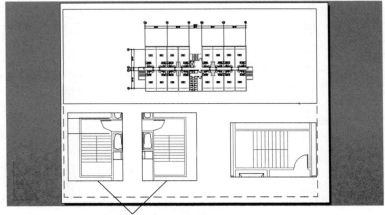

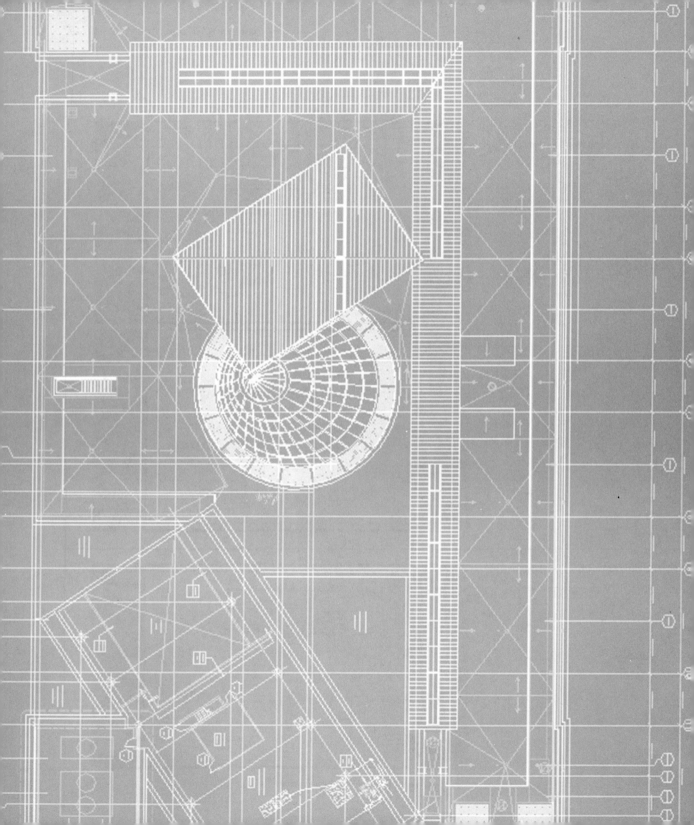

Drawing Curves and Solid Fills

- ■ Introducing Polylines

- ■ Editing Polylines

- ■ Creating a Polyline Spline Curve

- ■ Using True Spline Curves

- ■ Marking Divisions on Curves

- ■ Sketching with AutoCAD

- ■ Filling In Solid Areas

- ■ If You Want to Experiment…

So far in this book, you've been using basic lines, arcs, and circles to create your drawings. Now it's time to add polylines and spline curves to your repertoire. Polylines offer many options for creating forms, including solid fills. Spline curves are perfect for drawing smooth, nonlinear objects. The splines are true *NURBS* curves. NURBS stands for Non-Uniform Rational B-Splines.

Introducing Polylines

Polylines are like composite line segments and arcs. A polyline may look like a series of line segments, but it acts like a single object. This characteristic makes polylines useful for a variety of applications, as you'll see in the upcoming exercises.

Drawing a Polyline

First, to introduce you to the polyline, you will begin a drawing of the top view of the joint in Figure 13.1.

FIGURE 13.1:

A sketch of a metal joint

1. Open a new file and save it as Joint2d. Don't bother to make special setting changes, because you will do this drawing with the default settings.

2. Set the limits to **0,0** for the lower-left corner and **12,9** for the upper-right corner, then choose View ➤ Zoom ➤ All or type **Z↵ A↵**.

3. Click the Polyline tool on the Draw toolbar, or type **Pl↵**.

4. At the `Specify start point:` prompt, enter a point at coordinate 3,3 to start your polyline.

5. At the `Specify next point or [Arc/Close/Halfwidth/Length/Undo/Width]:` prompt, enter **@3<0**↵ to draw a horizontal line of the joint.

NOTE   You can draw polylines just as you do with the Line command. Or you can use the other Pline options to enter a polyline arc, specify the polyline thickness, or add a polyline segment in the same direction as the previously drawn line.

6. At the prompt

   `Specify next point or [Arc/Close/Halfwidth/Length/Undo/Width]:`

   enter **A**↵ to continue your polyline with an arc.

NOTE   The Arc option allows you to draw an arc that starts from the last point you selected. Once selected, the Arc option offers additional options. The default Save option is the endpoint of the arc. As you move your cursor, an arc follows it in a tangential direction from the first line segment you drew.

7. At the prompt

   `Specify endpoint of arc or`

   `[Angle/CEnter/CLose/Direction/Halfwidth/Line/Radius/Second pt/Undo/Width]:`

   enter **@4<90**↵ to draw a 180° arc from the last point you entered. Your drawing should now look like Figure 13.2.

8. Continue the polyline with another line segment. To do this, enter **L**↵.

9. At the prompt

   `Specify next point or [Arc/Close/Halfwidth/Length/Undo/Width]:`

   enter **@3<180**↵. Another line segment continues from the end of the arc.

10. Press ↵ to exit Pline.

You now have a sideways, U-shaped polyline that you will use in the next exercise to complete the top view of your joint.

FIGURE 13.2:

A polyline line and arc

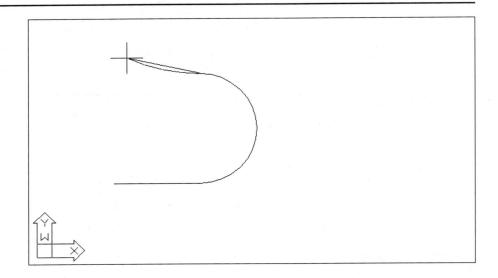

Polyline Options

Let's pause from the tutorial to look at some of the Polyline options you didn't use.

Close Draws a line segment from the last endpoint of a sequence of lines to the first point picked in that sequence. This works exactly like the Close option for the Line command.

Length Enables you to specify the length of a line that will be drawn at the same angle as the last line entered.

Halfwidth Creates a tapered line segment or arc by specifying half its beginning and ending widths (see Figure 13.3).

Width Creates a tapered line segment or arc by specifying the full width of the segment's beginning and ending points.

Undo Deletes the last line segment drawn.

If you want to break down a polyline into simple lines and arcs, you can use the Explode option on the Modify toolbar, just as you would with blocks. Once a polyline is exploded, it becomes a set of individual line segments or arcs.

FIGURE 13.3:

Tapered line segment and
arc created with Halfwidth

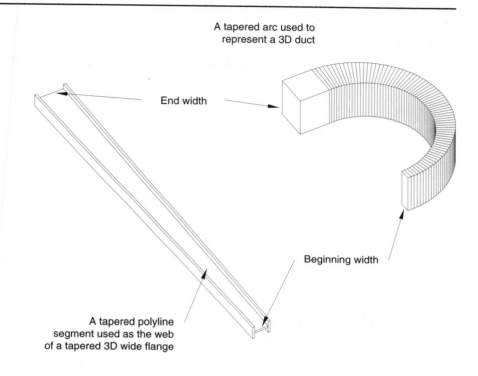

A tapered arc used to
represent a 3D duct

End width

Beginning width

A tapered polyline
segment used as the web
of a tapered 3D wide flange

To turn off the filling of solid polylines, open the Options dialog box and select
the Display tab. Remove the check from the Apply Solid Fill option in the Display
Performance group. (The options in the Display Performance group are explained
in detail later in this chapter in the section on solid fills.)

NOTE   The Fillet tool on the Modify toolbar can be used to fillet all the vertices of a polyline composed of straight-line segments. To do this, click Fillet, and then set your
fillet radius. Click Fillet again, type **P**↲ to select the Polyline option, and then pick
the polyline you want to fillet.

Editing Polylines

You can edit polylines with many of the standard editing commands. To change
the properties of a polyline, click the Properties tool on the Standard toolbar. The
Stretch command on the Modify toolbar can be used to displace vertices of a

polyline, and the Trim, Extend, and Break commands on the Modify toolbar also work with polylines.

In addition, there are many editing capabilities offered only for polylines. For instance, later in this chapter you will see how to smooth out a polyline using the Curve Fit option in the Pedit command and the Modify Polyline dialog box. In the next exercise, you'll use the Offset command on the Modify toolbar to add the inside portion of the joint.

1. Click the Offset tool in the Modify toolbar, or type **O⏎**.

2. At the `Specify offset distance or [Through] <1.0000>:` prompt, enter **1**.

3. At the `Select object to offset or <exit>:` prompt, pick the U-shaped polyline you just drew.

4. At the `Specify point on side to offset:` prompt, pick a point toward the inside of the U. A concentric copy of the polyline appears (see Figure 13.4).

5. Press ⏎ to exit the Offset command.

The concentric copy of a polyline made with Modify ➢ Offset can be very useful when you need to draw complex parallel curves like the ones in Figure 13.5.

Next, complete the top view of the joint.

1. Connect the ends of the polylines with two short line segments (see Figure 13.6).

WARNING   The objects to be joined must touch the existing polyline exactly endpoint to endpoint, or else they will not join. To ensure that you place the endpoints of the lines exactly on the endpoints of the polylines, use the Endpoint Osnap override to select each polyline endpoint.

FIGURE 13.4:

The offset polyline

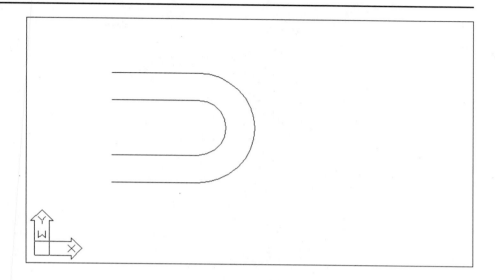

FIGURE 13.5:

Sample complex curves drawn by using offset polylines

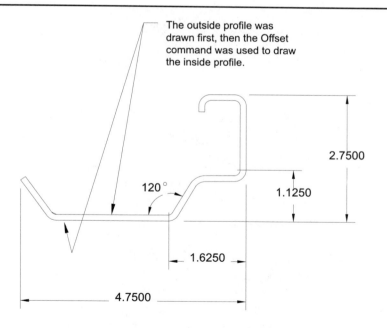

The outside profile was drawn first, then the Offset command was used to draw the inside profile.

120°

2.7500

1.1250

1.6250

4.7500

FIGURE 13.6:

The joined polyline

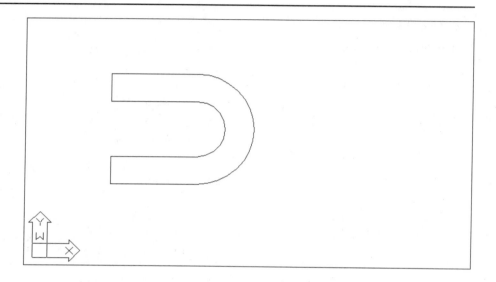

2. Choose Modify Polyline, or type **Pe**↵. You can also choose Edit Polyline from the Modify II toolbar.

3. At the Select polyline: prompt, pick the outermost polyline.

4. At the prompt

       Enter option [Close/Join/Width/Edit vertex/Fit/Spline/
       Decurve/Ltype gen/Undo]:

    enter **J**↵ for the Join option.

5. At the Select objects prompt, select all the objects you have drawn so far.

6. Once all the objects are selected, press ↵ to join them all into one polyline. It appears that nothing has happened, though you will see the message 4 segments added to polyline in the Command window. The 4 segments in the message are the 4 objects in your drawing.

7. Press ↵ again to exit the Pedit command.

8. Click the drawing to expose its grips. The entire object is hightlighted, telling you that all the lines have been joined into a single polyline.

   By using the Width option under Edit Polyline, you can change the thickness of a polyline. Let's change the width of your polyline, to give some thickness to the outline of the joint.

1. Click the Edit Polyline tool on Modify II toolbar again.

2. Click the polyline.

3. At the prompt

   ```
   [Close/Join/Width/Edit vertex/Fit/Spline/Decurve/Ltype gen/Undo]:
   ```

   enter **W**↵ for the Width option.

4. At the `Enter new width for all segments:` prompt, enter **.03**↵ for the new width of the polyline. The line changes to the new width (see Figure 13.7), and you now have a top view of your joint.

5. Press ↵ to exit the Pedit command.

6. Save this file.

FIGURE 13.7:

The polyline with a new thickness

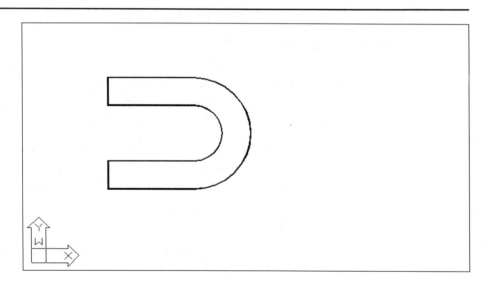

Now here's a brief look at a few of the Pedit options you didn't try firsthand:

Close   Connects the two endpoints of a polyline with a line segment. If the polyline you selected to be edited is already closed, this option changes to Open.

Open   Removes the last segment added to a closed polyline.

Spline/Decurve   Smooths a polyline into a spline curve (discussed in detail later in this chapter).

Edit Vertex   Lets you edit each vertex of a polyline individually (discussed in detail in the next section).

Fit   Turns polyline segments into a series of arcs.

Ltype Gen   Controls the way non-continuous line types pass through the vertices of a polyline. If you have a fitted or spline curve with a non-continuous line type, you should turn this option on.

TIP   You can change the thickness of regular lines and arcs by using Pedit to change them into polylines, and then using the Width option to change their width.

Smoothing Polylines

There are many ways to create a curve in AutoCAD. If you don't need the representation of a curve to be exactly accurate, you can use a polyline curve. In the following exercise, you will draw a polyline curve to represent a contour on a topographical map.

1. Open the Topo.dwg drawing that is included on the CD-ROM that comes with this book. The top image of Figure 13.8 contains the drawing of survey data. Some of the contours have already been drawn in between the data points.

2. Zoom in to the upper-right corner of the drawing, so your screen looks like the bottom image of Figure 13.8.

3. Click the Polyline tool in the Draw toolbar. Using the Center Osnap, draw a polyline that connects the points labeled "254.00." Your drawing should look like the continued image of Figure 13.8.

4. When you have drawn the polyline, press ↵.

FIGURE 13.8:

The Topo.dwg drawing shows survey data portrayed in an AutoCAD drawing. Notice the dots indicating where elevations were taken. The actual elevation value is shown with a diagonal line from the point.

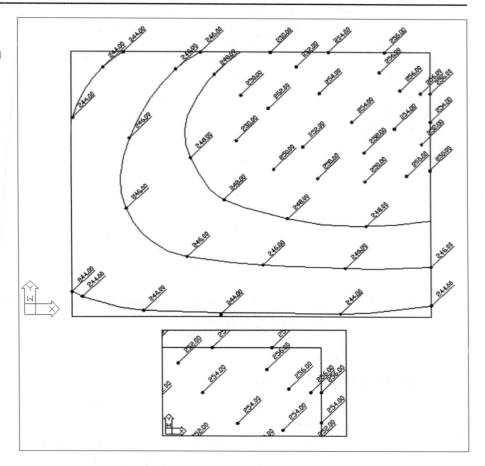

TIP

If Running Osnaps are not set, you can select Tools ➤ Drafting Settings or type **Os**↵ to open the Osnap Settings dialog box. From there, you can select Center to turn on the Center Running Osnaps dialog box. See Chapter 3 for more on this dialog box.

FIGURE 13.8 CONTINUED:

The Topo.dwg drawing shows survey data portrayed in an AutoCAD drawing. Notice the dots indicating where elevations were taken. The actual elevation value is shown with a diagonal line from the point.

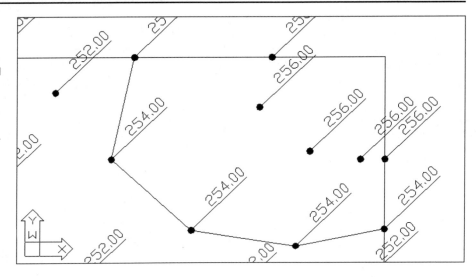

Next you will convert the polyline you just drew into a smooth contour line.

1. Choose Modify ➤ Polyline, or type **Pe**↵.

2. At the `PEDIT Select objects:` prompt, pick the contour line you just drew.

3. At the prompt

   ```
   Enter an option [close/Join/Width/Edit vertex/Fit/Spline/
   Decurve/Ltype gen/Undo]:
   ```

   press **F**↵ to select the Fit option. This causes the polyline to smooth out into a series of connected arcs that pass through the data points.

4. Press ↵ to end the Pedit command.

Your contour is now complete. The Fit curve option under the Pedit command causes AutoCAD to convert the straight-line segments of the polyline into arcs. The endpoints of the arcs pass through the endpoints of the line segments, and the curve of each arc depends on the direction of the adjacent arc. This gives the effect of a smooth curve. Next, you'll use this polyline curve to experiment with some of the editing options unique to the Pedit command.

Turning Objects into Polylines and Polylines into Splines

There may be times when you will want to convert regular lines, arcs, or even circles into polylines. You may want to change the width of lines, or join lines together to form a single object such as a boundary. Here are the steps to take to convert lines, arcs, and circles into polylines.

1. Choose Modify ➤ Polyline. You can also type **Pe**↵ at the command prompt.

2. At the `Select polyline:` prompt, pick the object you wish to convert. If you want to convert a circle to a polyline, you must first break the circle (using the Break option on the Modify toolbar) so that it becomes an arc of approximately 359°.

3. At the prompt

   ```
   Object selected is not a polyline. Do you want to turn it
   into one? <Y>:
   ```

   press ↵ twice. The object is converted into a polyline.

If you have a polyline you would like to turn into a true spline curve, do the following:

1. Choose Modify ➤ Polyline, or type **Pe**↵. Select the polyline you want to convert.

2. Type **S**↵ to turn it into a polyline spline; then press ↵ to exit the Pedit command.

3. Click the Spline tool in the Draw Toolbar or type **Spl**↵. You can also select Draw ➤ Spline from the pull-down menu.

4. At the `Specify first point or [Object]:` prompt, type **O**↵ for the Object option.

5. At the `Select objects:` prompt, click the polyline spline. Though it may not be apparent at first, the polyline is converted into a true spline.

You can also use the Spline Edit tool (Modify ➤ Spline or **Spe**↵) on a polyline spline. If you do, the polyline spline is automatically converted into a true spline.

Editing Vertices

One of the Pedit options that hasn't yet been discussed, Edit Vertex, is almost like a command within a command. Edit Vertex has numerous suboptions that allow you to fine-tune your polyline by giving you control over its individual vertices. This section discusses the Edit Vertex option in depth.

To access the Edit Vertex options, follow these steps.

1. First, turn off the Data and Border layers to hide the data points and border.

2. Issue the Pedit command again. Then select the polyline you just drew.

3. Type E⏎ to enter the Edit Vertex mode. An X appears at the beginning of the polyline, indicating the vertex that will be affected by the Edit Vertex options.

> **WARNING** When using Edit Vertex, you must be careful about selecting the vertex to be edited. Edit Vertex has six options, and you often have to exit the Edit Vertex operation and use Pedit's Fit option to see the effect of Edit Vertex's options on a curved polyline.

Edit Vertex Suboptions

Once you've entered the Edit Vertex mode of the Pedit command, you have the option to perform the following functions:

- Break the polyline between two vertices
- Insert a new vertex
- Move an existing vertex
- Straighten a polyline between two vertices
- Change the tangential direction of a vertex
- Change the width of the polyline at a vertex

These functions are presented in the form of the following prompt:

```
[Next/Previous/Break/Insert/Move/Regen/Straighten/Tangent/Width/eXit]
<N>:
```

This section examines each of the options presented in this prompt, starting with the Next and Previous options.

Next and Previous   The Next and Previous options enable you to select a vertex for editing. When you started the Edit Vertex option, an X appeared on the selected polyline to designate its beginning. As you select Next or Previous, the X moves from vertex to vertex to show which one is being edited. Let's try this out.

1. Press ↵ a couple of times to move the X along the polyline. (Because Next is the default option, you only need to press ↵ to move the X.)

2. Type **P**↵ for Previous. The X moves in the opposite direction. Notice that now the default option becomes P.

TIP

To determine the direction of a polyline, note the direction the X moves in when you use the Next option. Knowing the direction of a polyline is important for some of the other Edit Vertex options discussed below.

Break   The Break option breaks the polyline between two vertices.

1. Position the X on one end of the segment you want to break.

2. Enter **B**↵ at the command prompt.

3. At the `Enter an option [Next/Previous/Go/eXit] <N>:` prompt, use Next or Previous to move the X to the other end of the segment to be broken.

4. When the X is in the proper position, pick Go from the Edit Vertex menu or enter **G**↵, and the polyline will be broken (see Figure 13.9).

NOTE

You can also use the Break and Trim options on the Modify toolbar to break a polyline anywhere, as you did when you drew the toilet seat in Chapter 3.

Insert   Next, try the Insert option, which inserts a new vertex.

1. Type **X**↵ to temporarily exit the Edit Vertex option. Then type **U**↵ to undo the break.

2. Type **E**↵ to return to the Edit Vertex option, and position the X before the new vertex.

3. Press ↵ to advance the X marker to the next point.

4. Enter **I**↵ to select the Insert option.

5. When the prompt `Specify location for new vertex:` appears, along with a rubber-banding line originating from the current X position (see Figure 13.10), pick a point indicating the new vertex location. The polyline is redrawn with the new vertex.

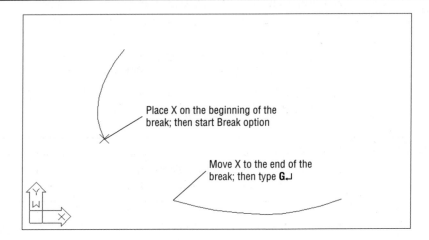

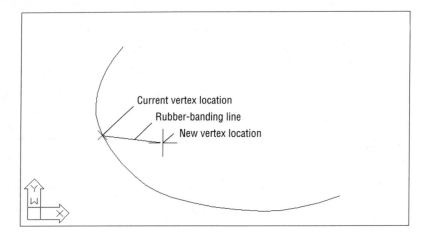

Notice that the inserted vertex appears between the currently marked vertex and the *next* vertex, so the Insert option is sensitive to the direction of the polyline. If the polyline is curved, the new vertex will not immediately be shown as curved (see the top image of Figure 13.11). You must smooth it out by exiting the Edit Vertex option and then using the Fit option, as you did to edit the site plan (see the bottom image of Figure 13.11). You can also use the Stretch command (on the Modify toolbar) to move a polyline vertex.

FIGURE 13.11:

The polyline before and after the curve is fitted

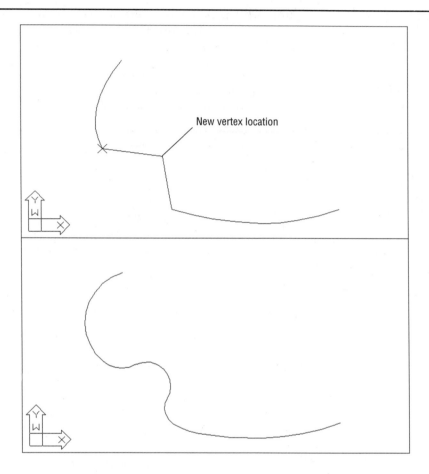

New vertex location

Move   In this brief exercise, you'll use the Move option to move a vertex.

1. Undo the inserted vertex by exiting the Edit Vertex option (**X.**⏎) and typing **U.**⏎.

2. Restart the Edit Vertex option, and use the Next or Previous option to place the X on the vertex you wish to move.

3. Enter **M.**⏎ for the Move option.

4. When the Specify new location for marked vertex: prompt appears, along with a rubber-banding line originating from the X (see the top image of

Figure 13.12), pick the new vertex. The polyline is redrawn (see the bottom image of Figure 13.12). Again, if the line is curved, the new vertex appears as a sharp angle until you use the Fit option (see the continued image of 13.12).

You can also move a polyline vertex using its grip.

FIGURE 13.12:

Picking a new location for a vertex, with the polyline before and after the curve is fitted

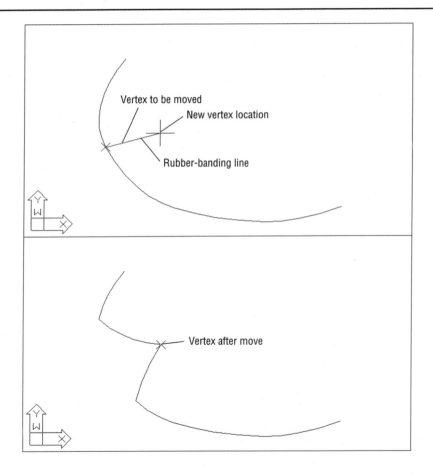

FIGURE 13.12
CONTINUED:

Picking a new location for a vertex, with the polyline before and after the curve is fitted

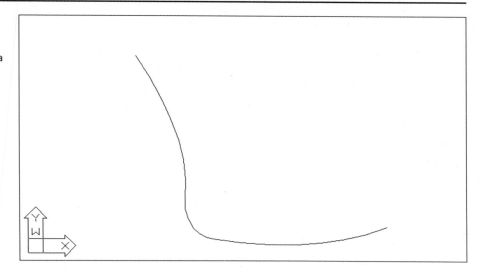

Straighten   The Straighten option straightens all the vertices between two selected vertices, as shown here in the following exercise.

1.   Undo the moved vertex (from the previous exercise).

2.   Start the Edit Vertex option again, and select the starting vertex for the straight line.

3.   Enter **S↵** for the Straighten option.

4.   At the `Enter option [Next/Previous/Go/eXit] <N>:` prompt, move the X to the location for the other end of the straight-line segment.

5.   Once the X is in the proper position, enter **G↵** for the Go option. The polyline straightens between the two selected vertices (see Figure 13.13).

TIP   The Straighten option offers a quick way to delete vertices from a polyline.

FIGURE 13.13:

A polyline after straightening

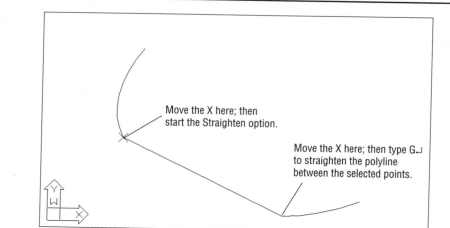

Move the X here; then start the Straighten option.

Move the X here; then type G↵ to straighten the polyline between the selected points.

Tangent   The Tangent option alters the direction of a curve on a curve-fitted polyline.

1. Undo the straightened segment from the previous exercise.

2. Restart the Edit Vertex option, and position the X on the vertex you wish to alter.

3. Enter **T↵** for the Tangent option. A rubber-banding line appears (see the top image of Figure 13.14).

4. Point the rubber-banding line in the direction for the new tangent, and click the mouse. An arrow appears, indicating the new tangent direction (see the bottom image of Figure 13.14).

Don't worry if the polyline shape does not change. You must use Fit to see the effect of Tangent (see the continued image of Figure 13.14).

FIGURE 13.14:

Picking a new tangent
direction

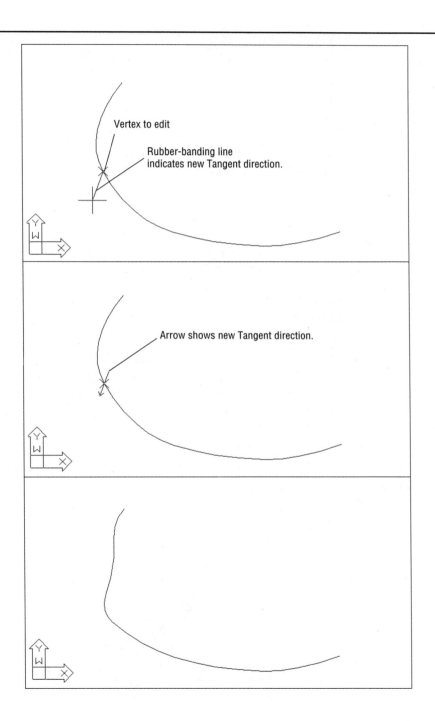

Width   Finally, try out the Width option. Unlike the Pedit command's Width option, the Edit Vertex/Width option enables you to alter the width of the polyline at any vertex. Thus, you can taper or otherwise vary polyline thickness.

1. Undo the tangent arc from the previous exercise.

2. Return to the Edit Vertex option, and place the X at the beginning vertex of a polyline segment you want to change.

3. Type **W↵** to issue the Width option.

4. At the `Specify starting width for next segment <0.0000>:` prompt, enter a value, **12** for example, indicating the polyline width desired at this vertex.

5. At the `Specify ending width for next segment <12.0000>:` prompt, enter the width, **24** for example, for the next vertex.

Again (as with Tangent), don't be alarmed if nothing happens after you enter this Width value. To see the result, you must exit the Edit Vertex command (see Figure 13.15).

NOTE   The Width option is useful when you want to create an irregular or curved area in your drawing that is to be filled in solid. This is another option that is sensitive to the polyline direction.

FIGURE 13.15:

A polyline with the width of one segment increased

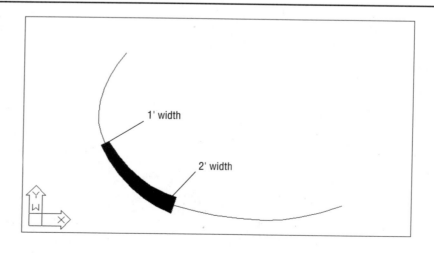

As you have seen throughout these exercises, you can use the Undo option to reverse the last Edit Vertex option used. And you can use the Edit option to leave Edit Vertex at any time. Just enter **X**↵, and this brings you back to the Pedit prompt:

```
Enter an option [Close/Join/Width/Edit vertex/Fit/Spline/Decurve/Ltype
gen/Undo]:
```

Creating a Polyline Spline Curve

The Pedit command's Spline option (named after the spline tool used in manual drafting) offers you a way to draw smoother and more controllable curves than those produced by the Fit option. A polyline spline does not pass through the vertex points as a fitted curve does. Instead, the vertex points act as weights pulling the curve in their direction. The polyline spline only touches its beginning and end vertices. Figure 13.16 illustrates this concept.

NOTE   A polyline spline curve does not represent a mathematically true curve. See *Using True Spline Curves* later in this chapter to learn how to draw a more accurate spline curve.

FIGURE 13.16:

The polyline spline curve pulled toward its vertices

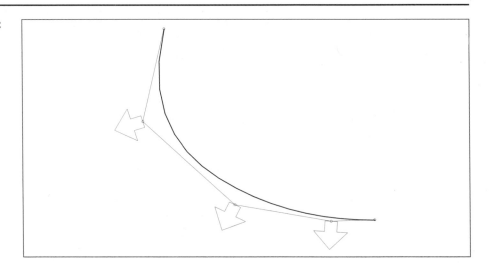

Let's see how using a polyline spline curve might influence the way you edit a curve.

1. Undo the width changes you made in the previous exercise.

2. To change the contour into a polyline spline curve, choose Modify ➤ Polyline.

3. Then pick the polyline to be curved.

4. At the prompt

   ```
   Enter an option [Close/Join/Width/Edit vertex/Fit/Spline/
   Decurve/Ltype gen/Undo]:
   ```

   enter **S.⏎**. Your curve changes to look like Figure 13.17.

5. Press ⏎ to exit Edit Polyline.

The curve takes on a smoother, more graceful appearance. It no longer passes through the points you used to define it. To see where the points went and to find out how spline curves act, do the following:

1. Make sure the Noun/Verb Selection mode and the Grips feature are turned on.

2. Click the curve. You'll see the original vertices appear as grips (see the top image of Figure 13.18).

FIGURE 13.17:

A spline curve

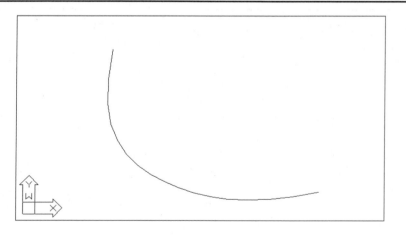

FIGURE 13.18:

The fitted curve changed
to a spline curve, with the
location of the second
vertex and the new curve

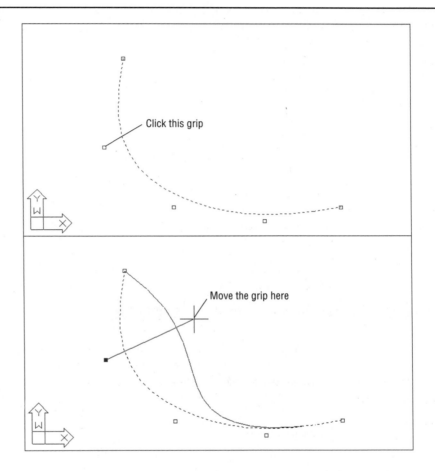

3. Click the grip that is second from the top of the curve, as shown in the bottom image of Figure 13.18, and move the grip around. Notice how the curve follows, giving you immediate feedback on how the curve will look.

4. Pick a point as shown in the continued image of Figure 13.18. The curve is fixed in its new position.

**FIGURE 13.18
CONTINUED:**

The fitted curve changed to a spline curve, with the location of the second vertex and the new curve

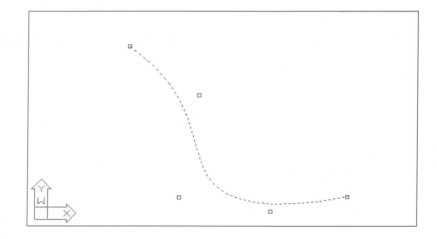

Using True Spline Curves

So far, you've been working with polylines to generate spline curves. The advantage to using polylines for curves is that they can be enhanced in other ways. You can modify their width, for instance, or join several curves together. But at times you will need a more exact representation of a curve. The Spline object, created with Draw ➤ Spline, offers a more accurate model of spline curves, as well as more control over its shape.

Drawing a Spline

The next exercise demonstrates the creation of a spline curve.

1. Undo the changes made in the last two exercises.

2. Turn the Data layer on so you can view the data points.

3. Adjust your view so you can see all the data points with the elevation of 250.00 (see Figure 13.19).

4. Click the Spline tool on the Draw toolbar, or type **Spl**↵.

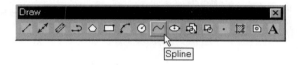

5. At the `Specify first point or [Object]:` prompt, use the Center Osnap to start the curve on the first data point in the lower-right corner (see Figure 13.19). The prompt changes to `Specify next point or [Close/Fit tolerance] <start tangent>:`.

6. Continue to select the 250.00 data points until you reach the last one. Notice that as you pick points, a curve appears, and bends and flows as you move your cursor.

7. Once you've selected the last point, press ↵. Notice that the prompt changes to `Specify start tangent:`. Also, a rubber-banding line appears from the first point of the curve to the cursor. As you move the cursor, the curve adjusts to the direction of the rubber-banding line. Here, you can set the tangency of the first point of the curve (see the top image of Figure 13.20).

FIGURE 13.19:

Starting the Spline curve at the first data point

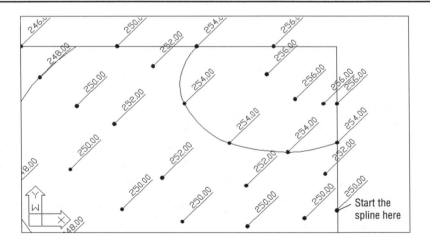

FIGURE 13.20:

The last two prompts of the Spline command let you determine the tangent direction of the spline.

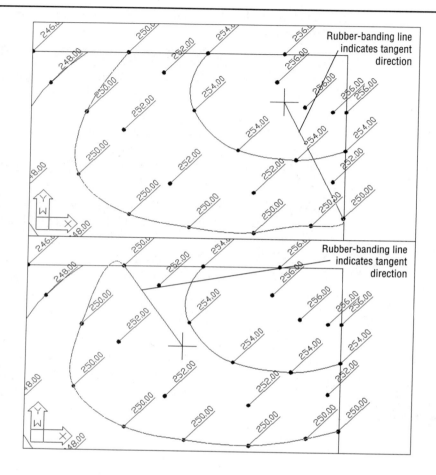

8.   Press ↵. This causes AutoCAD to determine the first point's tangency based on the current shape of the curve. A rubber-banding line appears from the last point of the curve. As with the first point, you can indicate a tangent direction for the last point of the curve (see bottom image of Figure 13.20).

9.   Press ↵ to exit the Spline command without changing the endpoint tangent direction.

You now have a smooth curve that passes through the points you selected. These points are called the *control points*. If you click the curve, you'll see the grips appear at the location of these control points, and you can adjust the curve simply by clicking the grip points and moving them. (You may need to turn off the Data layer to see the grips clearly.)

TIP   See Chapter 2 for more detailed information on grip editing.

You may have noticed two other options—Fit Tolerance and Close—as you were selecting points for the spline in the last exercise. Here is a description of these options.

Fit Tolerance   Lets you change the curve so that it doesn't actually pass through the points you pick. When you select this option, you get the prompt Enter Fit Tolerance <0.0000>:. Any value greater than 0 causes the curve to pass close to, but not through the points. A value of 0 causes the curve to pass through the points. (You'll see how this works in a later exercise.)

Close   Lets you close the curve into a loop. If you choose this option, you are prompted to indicate a tangent direction for the closing point.

Fine-Tuning Spline Curves

Spline curves are different from other types of objects, and many of the standard editing commands won't work on splines. AutoCAD offers the Modify ➤ Object ➤ Spline option (Splinedit command) for making changes to splines. The following exercise will give you some practice with this command. You'll start by focusing on Splinedit's Fit Data option, which lets you fine-tune the spline curve.

Controlling the Fit Data of a Spline

The following exercise will demonstrate how the Fit Data option lets you control some of the general characteristics of the curve.

1. Choose Modify ➤ Spline, or type **Spe**↵ at the command prompt.

2. At the Select Spline: prompt, select the spline you drew in the previous exercise.

3. At the prompt

    Enter an option [Fit data/Close/Move vertex/Refine/rEverse/Undo]:

    type **F**↵ to select the Fit Data option.

NOTE   The Fit Data option is similar to the Edit Vertex option of the Pedit command in that Fit Data offers a subset of options that let you edit certain properties of the spline.

Controlling Tangency at the Beginning Points and Endpoints

4.   At the prompt

    `[Add/Close/Delete/Move/Purge/Tangents/toLerance/eXit] <eXit>:`

    type **T↵** to select the Tangents option. Move the cursor, and notice that the curve changes tangency through the first point, just as it did when you first created the spline (Figure 13.20).

5.   Press ↵. You can now edit the other endpoint tangency.

6.   Press ↵ again. You return to the prompt

    `[Add/Close/Delete/Move/Purge/Tangents/toLerance/eXit] <eXit>:`

Adding New Control Points   Now add another control point to the spline curve.

7.   At the prompt

    `[Add/Close/Delete/Move/Purge/Tangents/toLerance/eXit] <eXit>:`

    type **A↵** to access the Add option.

8.   At the `Specify control point <exit>:` prompt, click the third grip point from the bottom end of the spline (see the top image of Figure 13.21). A rubber-banding line appears from the point you selected. That point and the next point are highlighted. The two highlighted points tell you that the next point you select will fall between these two points. You also see the `Specify new point <exit>:` prompt.

9.   Click a new point. The curve changes to include that point. In addition, the new point becomes the highlighted point, indicating that you can continue to add more points between it and the other highlighted point (see the bottom image of Figure 13.21).

10.   Press ↵. The `Specify control point <exit>:` prompt appears, allowing you to select another point if you so desire.

11. Press ↵ again to return to the prompt

    `[Add/Close/Delete/Move/Purge/Tangents/toLerance/eXit] <eXit>:`

    Press X to exit.

FIGURE 13.21:

Adding a new control point to a spline

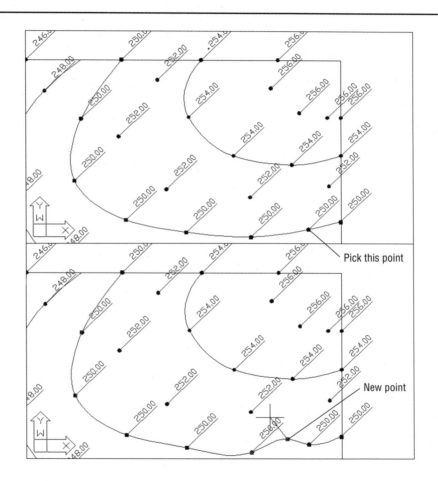

Adjusting the Spline Tolerance Setting   Before ending the description of the Fit Data options, let's look at how Tolerance works.

1. At the prompt

    `[Add/Close/Delete/Move/Purge/Tangents/toLerance/eXit] <eXit>:`

type **L**↵ to select the Tolerance option. This option sets the tolerance between the control point and the curve.

2. At the `Enter fit tolerance <0.0000>:` prompt, type **30**↵. Notice how the curve no longer passes through the control points, except for the beginning and endpoints (see Figure 13.22). The fit tolerance value you enter determines the maximum distance away from any control point the spline can be.

3. Type **X**↵ to exit the Fit Data option.

FIGURE 13.22:

The spline after setting the control point tolerance to 30

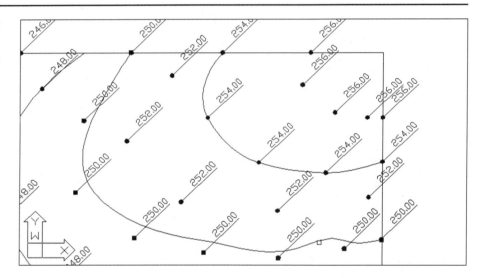

You've seen how you can control many of the shape properties of a spline through the Fit Data option. Here are descriptions of the other Fit Data options you didn't try in these exercises:

Delete   Removes a control point in the spline.

Close   Lets you close the spline into a loop.

Move   Lets you move a control point.

Purge   Deletes the fit data of the spline, thereby eliminating the Fit Data option for the purged spline. (See *When* Can't *You Use Fit Data?* just below.)

When *Can't* You Use Fit Data?   The Fit Data option of the Splinedit command offers many ways to edit a spline; however, this option is not available to all spline curves. When you invoke certain of the other Splinedit options, a spline curve will lose its fit data, thereby disabling the Fit Data option. These operations are as follows:

- Fitting a spline to a tolerance (Spline/Fit Tolerance) and moving its control vertices.

- Fitting a spline to a tolerance (Spline/Fit Tolerance) and opening or closing it.

- Refining the spline.

- Purging the spline of its fit data using the Purge option (Modify ≻ Fit Data ≻ Purge) or type **Splinedit**.┘.

Also, note that the Fit Data option is not available when you edit spline curves that have been created from polyline splines. See the *Turning Objects into Polylines and Polylines into Splines* sidebar earlier in this chapter.

Adjusting the Control Points with the Refine Option

While you are still in the Splinedit command, let's look at another of its options, Refine, with which you can fine-tune the curve:

1. Type **U**┘ to undo the changes you made in the previous exercise.

2. At the prompt

   ```
   [Fit data/Close/Move vertex/Refine/rEverse/Undo]:
   ```

   type **R**┘. The Refine option lets you control the "pull" exerted on a spline by an individual control point. This isn't quite the same effect as the Fit Tolerance option you used in the previous exercise.

3. At the prompt

   ```
   Enter a refine option [Add control point/Elevate order/
   Weight/eXit] <eXit>:
   ```

   type **W**┘. The first control point is highlighted.

4. At the next prompt

   ```
   Enter new weight (current = 1.000) or [Next/Previous/Select Point/
   eXit] <N>:
   ```

   press ┘ three times to move the highlight to the fourth control point.

5. Type **25**┘. The curve not only moves closer to the control point, it also bends around the control point in a tighter arc (see Figure 13.23).

FIGURE 13.23:

The spline after increasing the Weight value of a control point

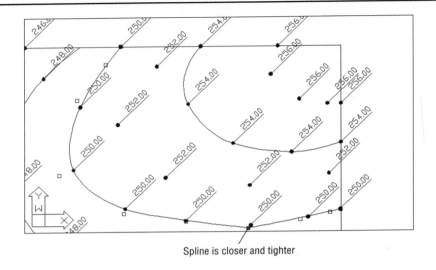

Spline is closer and tighter

You can use the Weight value of Splinedit's Refine option to pull the spine in tighter. Think of it as a way to increase the "gravity" of the control point, causing the curve to be pulled closer and tighter to the control point.

Continue your look at the Splinedit command by adding more control points—without actually changing the shape of the curve. You do this using Refine's Add Control Point and Elevate Order options.

1. Type **1**↵ to return the spline to its former shape.

2. Type **X**↵ to exit the Weight option; then type **A**↵ to select the Add Control Point option.

3. At the Specify a point on the spline <exit>: prompt, click the second-to-last control point toward the top end of the spline (see the top image of Figure 13.24). The point you select disappears and is replaced by two control points roughly equidistant from the one you selected (see the bottom image of Figure 13.24). The curve remains unchanged. Two new control points now replace the one control point you selected.

4. Press ↵ to exit the Add Control Point option.

5. Now type **E**↵ to select the Elevate Order option.

6. At the Enter new order <4>: prompt, type **6↵**. The number of control points increases, leaving the curve itself untouched.

7. Type **X↵** twice to exit the Refine option and then the Splinedit command.

FIGURE 13.24:

Adding a single control point using the Refine option

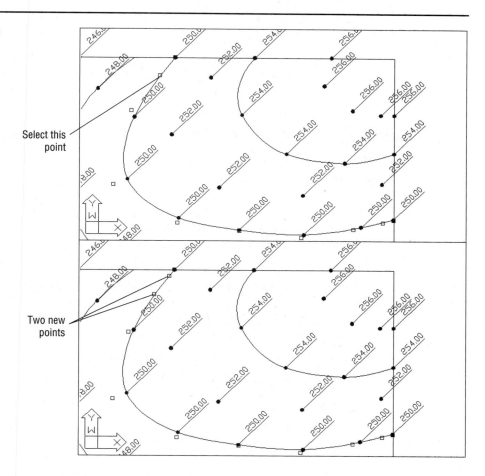

Select this point

Two new points

You would probably never edit contour lines of a topographical map in quite the way these exercises have shown. But by following this tutorial, you have explored all the potential of AutoCAD's spline object. Aside from its usefulness for drawing contours, it can be a great tool for drawing free-form illustrations. It is also an excellent tool for mechanical applications, where precise, non-uniform curves are required, such as drawings of cams or sheet metal work.

Marking Divisions on Curves

Perhaps one of the most difficult things to do in manual drafting is to mark regular intervals on a curve. AutoCAD offers the Divide and Measure commands to help you perform this task with speed and accuracy.

The Divide and Measure commands are discussed here in conjunction with polylines, but you can use these commands on any object except blocks and text.

Dividing Objects into Segments of Equal Length

The Divide command is used to divide an object into a specific number of equal segments. For example, suppose you needed to mark off the contour you've been working on in this chapter into nine equal segments. One way to do this is to first find the length of the contour by using the List command, and then sit down with a pencil and paper to figure out the exact distances between the marks. But there is another, easier way.

The Divide command places a set of point objects on a line, arc, circle, or polyline, marking off exact divisions. This next exercise shows how it works.

1. Open the file called 13a-divd.dwg from the companion CD-ROM. This is a file similar to the one you have been working with in the prior exercises.

2. Choose Draw ➤ Point ➤ Divide, or type **Div**↵.

3. At the Select object to divide: prompt, pick the spline contour line.

4. The Enter number of segments or [Block]: prompt that appears next is asking for the number of divisions you want on the selected object. Enter **9**↵.

The command prompt now returns, and it appears that nothing has happened. But AutoCAD has placed several points on the contour indicating the locations of the nine divisions you have requested. To see these points more clearly, follow these steps:

5. Click Format ➤ Point Style. The Point Style dialog box appears.

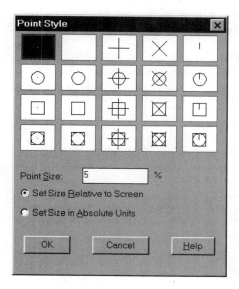

6. Click the X point style in the upper-right side of the dialog box, click the Set Size Relative to Screen radio button, and then click OK.

7. If the Xs don't appear, choose View ➤ Regen or enter **Re**↵. A set of Xs appear, showing the nine divisions (see Figure 13.25).

TIP

You can also change the point style by changing the Pdmode system variable. When Pdmode is set to 3, the point appears as an X. See Appendix D for more information on Pdmode.

The Divide command uses *point* objects to indicate the division points. Point objects are created by using the Point command; they usually appear as dots. Unfortunately, such points are nearly invisible when placed on top of other objects. But, as you have seen, you can alter their shape using the Point Style dialog box. You can use these X points to place objects or references to break the object being divided. (The Divide command does not actually cut the object into smaller divisions.)

TIP

If you are in a hurry, and you don't want to bother changing the shape of the point objects, you can do the following: Set the Running Osnaps to Node. Then, when you are in Point Selection mode, move the cursor over the divided curve. When the cursor gets close to a point object, the Node Osnap marker appears.

FIGURE 13.25:

Using the Divide and
Measure commands on
a polyline

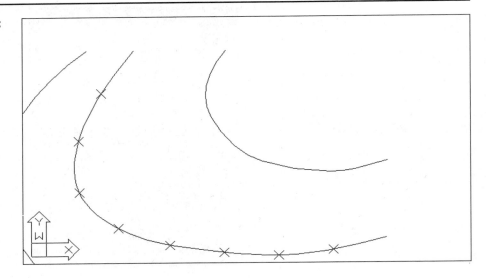

Dividing Objects into Specified Lengths

The Measure command acts just like Divide; however, instead of dividing an object into segments of equal length, the Measure command marks intervals of a specified distance along an object. For example, suppose you need to mark some segments exactly 5' apart along the contour. Try the following exercise to see how the Measure command is used to accomplish this task.

1. Erase the X-shaped point objects.

2. Choose Draw ➤ Point ➤ Measure, or type **Me**↵.

3. At the Select object to measure: prompt, pick the contour at a point closest to its lower endpoint. I'll explain shortly why this is important.

4. At the Specify lengthof segment or [Block]: prompt, enter **60**↵. The X points appear at the specified distance.

5. Now exit this file.

NOTE   The Measure command is AutoCAD's equivalent of the divider tool in manual drafting. A *divider* is a V-shaped instrument, similar to a compass, used to mark off regular intervals along a curve or line.

Bear in mind that the point you pick on the object to be measured determines where the Measure command begins measuring. In the last exercise, for example, you picked the contour near its bottom endpoint. If you had picked the top of the contour, the results would have been different because the measurement would have started at the top, not the bottom.

Marking Off Intervals Using Blocks Instead of Points

You can also use the Block option under the Divide and Measure commands to place blocks at regular intervals along a line, polyline, or arc. Here's how to use blocks as markers:

1. First, be sure the block you want to use is part of the current drawing file.

2. Start either the Divide or Measure command.

3. At the `Specify length of segment or [Block]:` prompt, enter **B**↵.

4. At the `Enter name of block to insert:` prompt, enter the name of a block.

5. At the `Align Block with Object? [Yes/No]:` prompt, press ↵ if you wish the blocks to follow the alignment of the selected object. (Entering **N**↵ causes each block to be inserted at a 0-degree angle.)

6. At the `Enter the number of Segments:` prompt, enter the number of segments. The blocks appear at regular intervals on the selected object.

One example of using Divide's or Measure's Block option is to place a row of sinks equally spaced along a wall. Or you might use this technique to make multiple copies of an object along an irregular path defined by a polyline. In civil projects, a fence line can be indicated using Divide or Measure to place Xs along a polyline.

Sketching with AutoCAD

No discussion of polylines would be complete without mentioning the Sketch command. Though AutoCAD isn't a sketch program, you *can* draw "freehand" using the Sketch command. With Sketch, you can rough in ideas in a free-form way, and later overlay a more formal drawing using the usual lines, arcs, and circles. You can use Sketch with a mouse, but it makes more sense to use this command with a digitizing tablet that has a stylus. The stylus affords a more natural way of sketching.

Freehand Sketching with AutoCAD

Here's a step-by-step description of how to use Sketch.

1. Make sure the Ortho and Snap modes are turned off. Then type **Skpoly**↵ **1** ↵. This sets the Sketch command to draw using polylines.

2. Type **Sketch**↵ at the command prompt.

3. At the `Record increment <0.1000>:` prompt, enter a value that represents the smallest line segment you will want Sketch to draw. This command approximates a sketch line by drawing a series of short line segments. So the value you enter here determines the length of those line segments.

4. At the `Sketch. Pen eXit Quit Record Erase Connect .` prompt, press the pick button and then start your sketch line. Notice that the message <Pen down> appears, telling you that AutoCAD is recording your cursor's motion.

NOTE   You can also start and stop the sketch line by pressing the P key.

---

5. Press the pick button to stop drawing. The message <Pen up> tells you Auto-CAD has stopped recording your cursor motion. As you draw, notice that the line is green. This indicates that you have drawn a temporary sketch line and have not committed the line to the drawing.

6. A line drawn with Sketch is temporary until you use Record to save it, so turn the sketch line into a polyline now by typing **R**.

7. Type **X**↵ to exit the Sketch command.

Here are some of the other Sketch options:

Connect   Allows you to continue a line from the end of the last temporary line drawn. Type **C** and then move the cursor to the endpoint of the temporary line. AutoCAD automatically starts the line, and you just continue to draw. This only works in the <Pen up> mode.

Period (.)   Allows you to draw a single straight-line segment by moving the cursor to the desired position and then pressing the period key. This only works in the <Pen up> mode.

Record, **Erase**, **Quit**, and **Exit**   Control the recording of lines and exiting from the Sketch command. Record is used to save a temporary sketched line; once a line has been recorded, you must edit it as you would any other line. With Erase, you can erase temporary lines before you record them. Quit ends the Sketch command without saving unrecorded lines. On the other hand, the Exit option on the Sketch menu automatically saves all lines you have drawn, and then exits the Sketch command.

Filling In Solid Areas   → use the same in the topo drawing

You have learned how to create a solid area by increasing the width of a polyline segment. But suppose you want to create a simple solid shape or a very thick line. AutoCAD provides the Solid, Trace, and Donut commands to help you draw simple filled areas. The Trace command acts just like the Line command (with the added feature of drawing wide line segments), so only the Solid and Donut commands are discussed here.

> **TIP**
>
> You can create free-form, solid-filled areas using the new Solid hatch pattern. Create an enclosed area using any set of objects, and then use the Hatch tool to apply a solid hatch pattern to the area. See Chapter 6 for details on using the Hatch tool.

Drawing Solid Filled Areas

If you've ever played with a paint program, you know how to do a solid fill. It's usually accomplished with a paint bucket tool. This is a tool that always looks like a paint bucket and it seems to be a universal tool among paint programs. In Auto-CAD, doing solid fills is not quite so obvious. It's actually one of many hatch patterns offered with the Boundary Hatch tool. Here is a short exercise to demonstrate how to use the Boundary Hatch tool to do a solid fill.

1.   Open the file `13a-htch.dwg` from the companion CD-ROM.

2.   Click the Hatch tool on the Draw toolbar.

3.   In the Boundary Hatch dialog box, click the Pick Points button.

4. Click the area bounded by the border and contour line in the upper-right corner of the drawing, as shown in the top image of Figure 13.26. Then press ↵. You have the option here to click more areas if you so desire.

5. Back in the Boundary Hatch dialog box, click the Pattern button.

6. In the Hatch Pattern Palette dialog box, click the Ellipses button and select the solid box under the Other Predefined tab.

7. Click OK, and then click Apply. A solid fill is applied to the selected area, as shown in the bottom image of Figure 13.26.

FIGURE 13.26:

Locating the area to fill, and the final result of the solid hatch

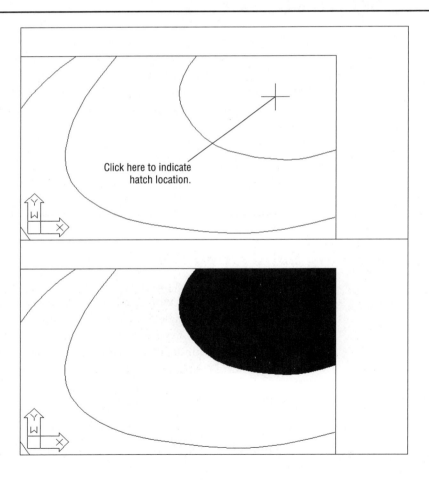

Overlapping Solid Lines and Shaded Fills

If you use an inkjet plotter, raster plotter, or laser printer that can convert solid areas into screened or gray-shaded areas, you may encounter the problem of shading areas overlapping lines and hiding them. This problem may not be apparent until you actually plot the drawing; it frequently occurs when a gray-shaded area is bounded by lines (see Figure 13.27).

The left side of Figure 13.27 shows how shading or solid fills can cover line work. The outline of the walls is obscured by the shading. The right side of Figure 13.27 shows how the drawing was intended to be displayed and printed.

FIGURE 13.27:

Problems that occur with overlapping lines and gray areas

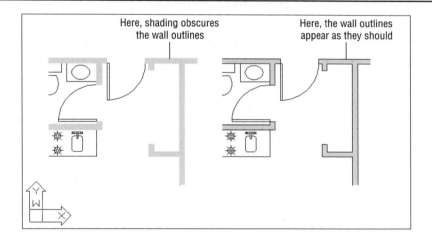

Most other graphics programs have specific tools to handle this overlapping difficulty. These tools are commonly named Move to Front or Move to Back, indicating that you move an object in front of or behind another object. AutoCAD offers the Draworder command to perform the same function as the Move to Back and Move to Front tools of other programs.

To force an object to appear above another, choose Tools ➤ Display Order ➤ Bring to Front, and then select the object that you want to overlap all the others. Or use Tools ➤ Display Order ➤ Send to Back to place an object behind other objects. You can also select specific objects to overlay or underlay using the Tools ➤ Display Order ➤ Bring Above Object and Send Under Object options. For more detailed instructions on how to use Draworder, see *Controlling Object Visibility and Overlap with Raster Images* in Chapter 11.

Drawing Filled Circles

If you need to draw a thick circle, like an inner tube, or a solid filled circle, perform the following steps.

1. Choose Draw ➤ Donut, or type **Do**⏎ at the command prompt.

2. At the `Specify inside diameter of donut <0'-0">:` prompt, enter the desired diameter of the donut "hole." This value determines the opening at the center of your circle.

3. At the `Specify outside diameter of donut <1.0000>:` prompt, enter the overall diameter of the circle.

4. At the `Specify center of doughnut or <exit>:` prompt, click the desired location for the filled circle. You can continue to select points to place multiple donuts (see Figure 13.28).

5. Press ⏎ to exit this process.

FIGURE 13.28:

Drawing wide circles using the Donut command

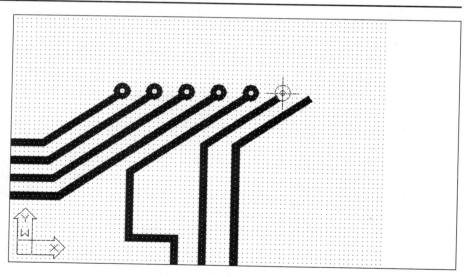

If you need to fill only a part of a circle, such as a pie slice, you can use the Donut command to draw a full, filled circle. Then use the Trim or Break option on the Modify toolbar to cut out the portion of the donut you don't need.

Toggling Solid Fills On and Off

Once you have drawn a solid area with the Pline, Solid, Trace, or Donut commands, you can control whether the solid area is actually displayed as filled in. Open the Options dialog box (Tools ➤ Options), then select the Display tab. Locate the Display Performance group in the lower-right corner of the dialog box. The Apply Solid Fill option controls whether or not solid areas are displayed. If the Solid Fill check box does not show a checkmark, thick polylines, solids, traces, and donuts appear as outlines of the solid areas (see Figure 13.29).

NOTE You can shorten regeneration and plotting time if solids are not filled in.

FIGURE 13.29:

Two polylines with the Fill option turned on (top) and turned off (bottom)

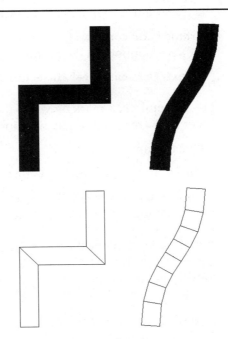

WARNING If Regenauto is turned off, you have to issue the Regen command to display the effects of the Fill command.

The Drawing Aids Solid Fill option is an easy-to-remember way to control the display of solid fills. Or you can enter **Fill⏎** at the command prompt; then, at the ON/OFF <ON>: prompt, enter your choice of **on** or **off**.

If You Want to Experiment...

There are many valuable uses for polylines beyond those covered in this chapter. I encourage you to become familiar with this unique object so you can take full advantage of AutoCAD.

To further explore the use of polylines, try the following exercise, illustrated in Figure 13.30. It will give you an opportunity to try out some of the options discussed in this chapter that weren't included in exercises.

1. Open a new file called PART13. Set the Snap mode to .25 and be sure that Snap mode is on. Use the Pline command to draw the object shown at step 1 of Figure 13.30. Draw it in the direction indicated by the arrows and start at the upper-left corner. Use the Close option to add the last line segment.

2. Start the Pedit command, select the polyline, and then type E↵ to issue the Edit Vertex option. At the prompt

    ```
    [Next/Previous/Break/Insert/Move/Regen/Straighten/Tangent/Width/
    eXit] <N>:
    ```

    press ↵ until the X mark moves to the first corner, shown in Figure 13.30. Enter an S↵ for the Straighten option.

3. At the prompt

    ```
    Enter an option [Next/Previous/Go/eXit] <N>:
    ```

    press ↵ twice to move the X to the other corner shown in Figure 13.30. Press G↵ for Go to straighten the polyline between the two selected corners.

4. Press ↵ twice to move the X to the upper-right corner, and then enter I ↵ for Insert. Pick a point as shown in Figure 13.30. The polyline changes to reflect the new vertex. Enter an X↵ to exit the Edit Vertex option, and then press ↵ to exit the Pedit command.

5. Start the Fillet command and use the Radius option to set the fillet radius to .30. Press ↵ to start the Fillet command again, but this time use the Polyline option and pick the polyline you just edited. All the corners fillet to the .30 radius. Add the .15 radius circles as shown in Figure 13.30 and exit the file with the End command.

FIGURE 13.30:

Drawing a simple plate
with curved edges

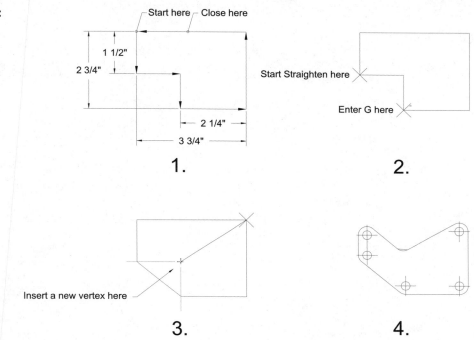

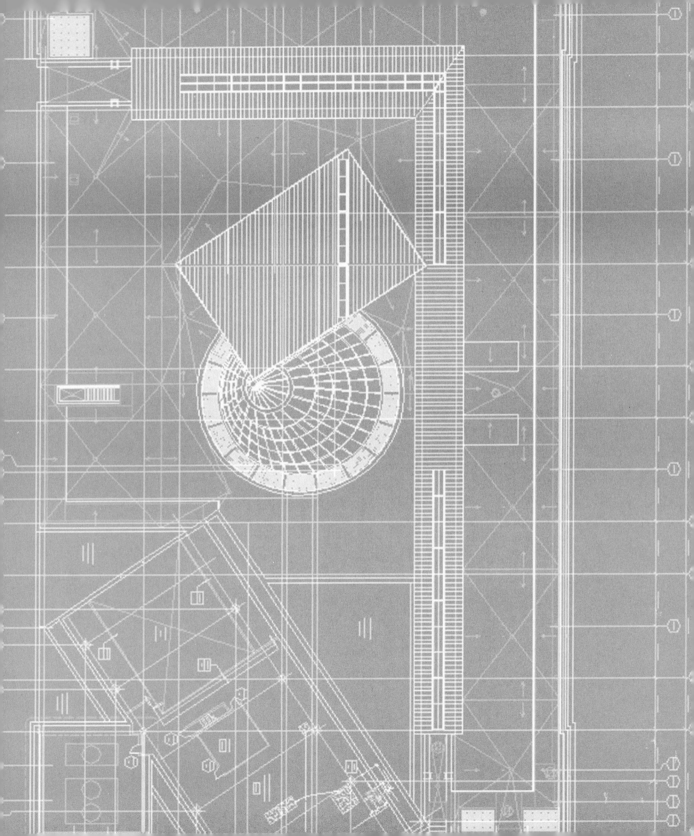

Getting and Exchanging Data from Drawings

- Finding the Area of Closed Boundaries

- Getting General Information

- Exchanging CAD Data with Other Programs

- Using AutoCAD Drawings in Desktop Publishing

- Combining Data from Different Sources

- If You Want to Experiment…

AutoCAD drawings contain a wealth of data. In them, you can find graphic information such as distances and angles between objects, as well as precise areas and the properties of objects. But as you become more involved with AutoCAD, you will find that you also need data of a different nature. For example, as you begin to work in groups, the various settings in a drawing become important. Statistics on the amount of time you spend on a drawing are needed when you are billing computer time. As your projects become more complex, file maintenance requires a greater degree of attention. To take full advantage of AutoCAD, you will want to exchange much of this data with other people and other programs.

In this chapter, you will explore the ways in which all types of data can be extracted from AutoCAD and made available to you, your coworkers, and other programs. First, you will discover how to get specific data on your drawings. Then you will look at ways to exchange data with other programs—such as word processors, desktop-publishing software, and even other CAD programs.

Finding the Area of Closed Boundaries

One of the most frequently sought pieces of data you can extract from an AutoCAD drawing is the area of a closed boundary. In architecture, you want to find the area of a room or the footprint of a building. In civil engineering, you want to determine the area covered by the boundary of a property line, or the area of cut for a roadway. In this section, you'll learn how you can use AutoCAD to obtain exact area information from your drawings.

TIP   To find absolute coordinates in a drawing, use the ID command. Choose Tools ➤ Inquiry ➤ ID Point, or type **ID**↵. At the **ID Point:** prompt, use the Osnap overrides to pick a point, and its x-, y-, and z-coordinates are displayed on the prompt line.

Finding the Area or Location of an Object

Architects, engineers, and facilities planners often need to know the square footage of a room or a section of a building. A structural engineer might want to find the cross-sectional area of a beam. In this section, you will practice determining the areas of both regular and irregular objects.

First you will find out the square-foot area of the living room and entry of your studio unit plan.

1. Start AutoCAD and open the Unit file you created earlier, or use the **14a-unit.dwg** file from the companion CD-ROM.

2. Enter **Blipmode⤶ on⤶**. This turns on a marking feature that displays a tiny cross called *blips* whenever you click in the drawing area. The blips do not print and can be cleared from the screen with a redraw. You'll use it to help keep track of your point selections in this exercise.

3. Zoom into the living room and entry area so you have a view similar to Figure 14.1.

4. Choose Tools ➢ Inquiry ➢ Area, or type **Area⤶** at the command prompt. You can also click and drag List on the Standard toolbar, and then select Area.

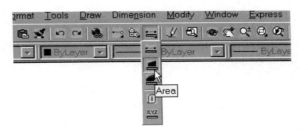

5. Using the Endpoint Osnap, start with the lower-left corner of the living room and select the points indicated in Figure 14.1. You are indicating the boundary of the entry and living room area.

6. When you have come full circle to the eighth point shown in Figure 14.1, press ⤶. You get the message

    ```
    Area = 39570.00 sq in (274.7917 sq ft), Perimeter = 76'-0"
    ```

7. Now turn off Blipmode by typing **Blipmode⤶ off⤶**. Then choose View ➢ Redraw to clear the blips from the screen.

There is no limit to the number of points you can pick to define an area, so you can obtain the areas of very complex shapes. Use the Blipmode feature to keep track of the points you select so you don't lose track of the beginning of the point selections.

FIGURE 14.1:

Selecting the points to determine the area of the living room and entry

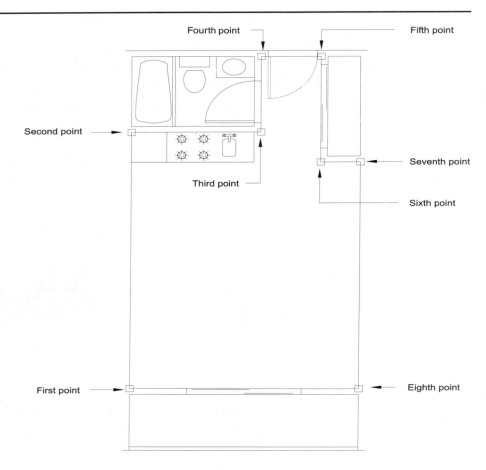

Using Boundary

Using the Object option of the Area command, you can also select circles and polylines for area calculations. Using this option in conjunction with another AutoCAD utility called Boundary, you can quickly get the area of a bounded space. Recall from the discussion on hatch patterns in Chapter 6 that a region polyline is drawn when you use the Hatch function; Boundary works similarly. Where Hatch generates a hatch pattern that conforms to the outline of a boundary, Boundary generates a polyline outline without adding the hatch. The following steps show you how to use it.

1.   Set the current layer to Floor.

2. Turn off the Door and Fixture layers. Also make sure the Ceiling layer is turned on. You want the boundary to follow the interior wall outline, so you need to turn off any objects that will affect the outline, such as the door and kitchen.

3. Choose Draw ➤ Boundary, or type **bo**↵. The Boundary Creation dialog box appears. Notice that it is actually the Boundary Hatch dialog box with several of the options dimmed.

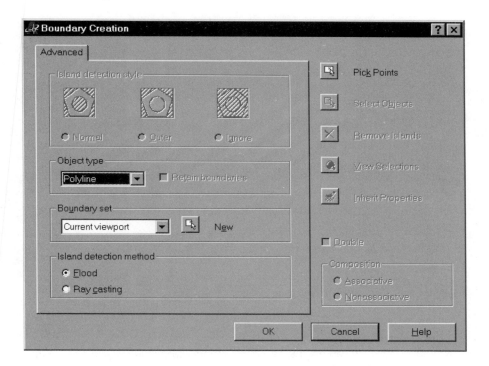

WARNING   There is one caveat to using Boundary: You must be sure the area you are trying to define has a continuous border. If there are any gaps at all, no matter how small, Boundary will give you an error message.

---

4. Click the Pick Points button. The Boundary Creation dialog box closes.

5. At the Select internal point: prompt, click in the interior of the unit plan. The outline of the interior is highlighted (see Figure 14.2).

FIGURE 14.2:

Once you select a point on the interior of the plan using Boundary, an outline of the area is highlighted and surrounded by a dotted line.

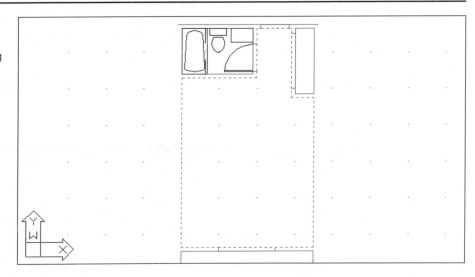

6.   Press ↵. Boundary draws an outline of the floor area using a polyline. Since the current layer is Floor, the boundary is drawn on the Floor layer and given the default cyan color of the layer.

7.   Choose Tools ➢ Inquiry ➢ Area again, or type **Area**↵ at the command prompt. Then enter **O**↵ for the Object option.

8.   Click the boundary; when it is highlighted, press ↵. Again you get the following message:

```
Area = 39570.00 sq in (274.7917 sq ft), Perimeter = 76'-0"
```

TIP   If you need to recall the last area calculation value you received, enter **'Setvar**↵ **Area**↵. The area is displayed in the prompt. Enter **'Perimeter**↵ to get the last perimeter calculated.

The Boundary command creates a polyline that conforms to the boundary of an area. This feature, combined with the ability of the Area command to find the area of a polyline, makes short work of area calculations. As you saw in step 3, Boundary uses the same dialog box as Boundary Hatch. See Chapter 6 for the options available in the Boundary Hatch dialog box.

Finding the Area of Complex Shapes

The Boundary command works fine as long as the area does not contain *islands* that you do not want included in the area calculation. An island is a closed area within a larger area within which you are attempting to hatch or create a boundary. In the case of the Flange part, the islands are the two circles at the lower end of the part.

For areas that do contain islands, you must enlist the aid of the other Area command options: Object, Add, and Subtract. Using Add and Subtract, you can maintain a running total of several separate areas being calculated. This gives you flexibility in finding areas of complex shapes.

The exercise in this section guides you through the use of these options. First, you'll look at how you can keep a running tally of areas. For this exercise, you will use a flange shape that contains circles. This shape is composed of simple arcs, lines, and circles.

1. Exit the Unit file and open the file named `Flange.dwg` from the companion CD-ROM (see Figure 14.3). Don't bother to save changes in the Unit file.

2. Choose Draw ➢ Boundary.

3. In the Boundary Dialog box, click Pick Points.

4. Click in the interior of the flange shape. Notice that the entire shape is highlighted, including the circle islands.

5. Press ↵.

FIGURE 14.3:

A flange to a mechanical device

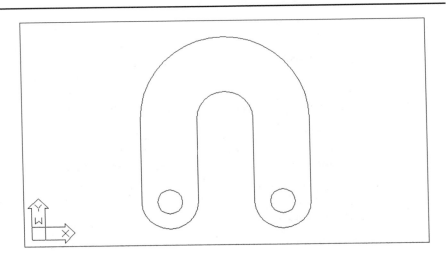

You now have a polyline outline of the shape. As you saw in the previous exercise, the polyline aids you in quickly obtaining the area. Now let's continue by using the Area command's Add and Subtract options.

1. Choose Tools ➤ Inquiry ➤ Area.

2. Type **A**↵ to enter the Add mode, and then type **O**↵ to select an object.

3. Click the outline of the flange. You see the following message:

   ```
   Area = 33.8496, Perimeter = 30.8496
   Total area = 33.8496
   ```

4. Press ↵ to exit the Add mode.

5. Type **S**↵ to enter the Subtract mode, and then type **O**↵ to select an object.

6. Click one of the circles. You see the following message:

   ```
   Area = 0.6070, Perimeter = 2.7618
   Total area = 33.2426
   ```

   This shows you the area and perimeter of the selected object and shows a running count of the total area of the flange outline minus the circle.

7. Click the other circle. You see the following message:

   ```
   Area = 0.6070, Perimeter = 2.7618
   Total area = 32.6356
   ```

   Again, you see a listing of the area and perimeter of the selected object along with a running count of the total area, which now shows a value of 32.6456. This last value is the true area of the flange.

8. Press ↵ twice to exit the Area command.

In the exercise, you first selected the main object outline and then subtracted the island objects. You don't have to follow this order; you can start by subtracting areas to get negative area values, and then add other areas to come up with a total. You can also alternate between Add and Subtract modes, in case you forget to add or subtract areas.

You may have noticed that the Area command prompt offered Specify first corner point or [Object/Add/Subtract]: as the default option for both the Add and Subtract modes. Instead of using the Object option to pick the circles, you could have started selecting points to indicate a rectangular area, as you did in the first exercise of this chapter.

It is important to remember that whenever you press ↵ while selecting points for an area calculation, AutoCAD automatically connects the first and last points and returns the calculated area. If you are in the Add or Subtract mode, you can then continue to select points, but the additional areas are calculated from the *next* point you pick.

As you can see from these exercises, it is simpler to first outline an area with a polyline, wherever possible, and then use the Object option to add and subtract area values of polylines.

In this example, you obtained the area of a mechanical object. However, the same process works for any type of area you want to calculate. It can be the area of a piece of property on a topographical map, or the area of a floor plan. For example, you can use the Object option to find an irregular area like the one shown in Figure 14.4, as long as it is a polyline.

FIGURE 14.4:

The site plan with an area to be calculated

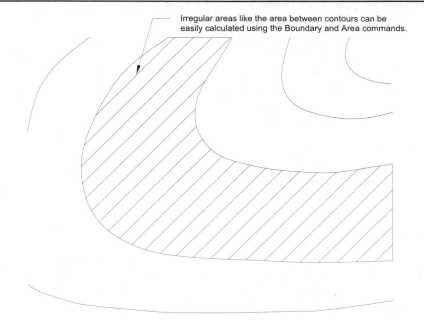

Irregular areas like the area between contours can be easily calculated using the Boundary and Area commands.

Recording Area Data in a Drawing File

Once you find the area of an object, you'll often need to record it somewhere. You can write it down in a project logbook, but this is easy to overlook. A more dependable way to store area information is to use *attributes*.

Consider the following example: In a building project, you can create a block that contains attributes for the room number, room area, and the date when the room area was last taken. You might make the area and date attributes invisible, so only the room number appears. This block can then be inserted into every room. Once you find the area, you can easily add it to your block attribute with the Ddatte command. In fact, such a block could be used with any drawing in which you wished to store area data. See Chapter 10 for more on attributes.

TIP Appendix C describes an AutoLISP program on your companion CD-ROM that lets you easily record area data in a drawing file.

Getting General Information

So far in this book, you've seen how to get data about the geometry of your drawings. There is also a set of tools available to access the general state of your drawings. You can gather information about the time at which a drawing was created and last edited, or the status of current settings in a file. In this section, you will practice extracting this type of information from your drawing, using the tools found in the Tools ➢ Inquiry option's cascading menu.

Determining the Drawing's Status

When you work with a group of people on a large project, keeping track of a drawing's setup becomes crucial. The Status command enables you to obtain some general information about the drawing you are working on, such as the base point, current mode settings, and workspace or computer memory use. The Status command is especially helpful when you are editing a drawing someone else has worked on, because you may want to identify and change settings for your own style of working. When you select Tools ➢ Inquiry ➢ Status, you get a list like the one shown in Figure 14.5.

NOTE If you have problems editing a file created by someone else, the difficulty can often be attributed to a new or different setting you are not used to working with. If you find that AutoCAD is acting in an unusual way, use the Status command to get a quick glimpse of the file settings before you start calling for help.

FIGURE 14.5:

The Status screen of the AutoCAD Text Window

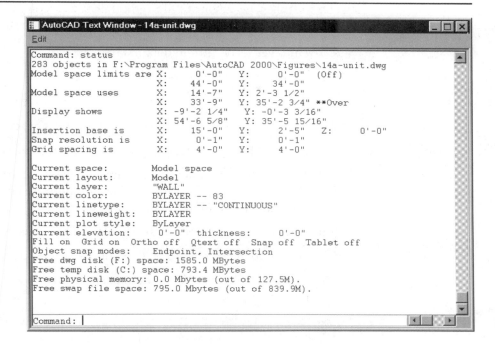

```
AutoCAD Text Window - 14a-unit.dwg                              _ □ ×
Edit

Command: status
283 objects in F:\Program Files\AutoCAD 2000\Figures\14a-unit.dwg
Model space limits are X:       0'-0"    Y:      0'-0"   (Off)
                        X:      44'-0"    Y:     34'-0"
Model space uses        X:      14'-7"    Y: 2'-3 1/2"
                        X:      33'-9"    Y: 35'-2 3/4" **Over
Display shows           X: -9'-2 1/4"     Y:  -0'-3 3/16"
                        X: 54'-6 5/8"     Y: 35'-5 15/16"
Insertion base is       X:      15'-0"    Y:      2'-5"   Z:      0'-0"
Snap resolution is      X:       0'-1"    Y:      0'-1"
Grid spacing is         X:       4'-0"    Y:      4'-0"

Current space:          Model space
Current layout:         Model
Current layer:          "WALL"
Current color:          BYLAYER -- 83
Current linetype:       BYLAYER -- "CONTINUOUS"
Current lineweight:     BYLAYER
Current plot style:     ByLayer
Current elevation:      0'-0"  thickness:     0'-0"
Fill on  Grid on  Ortho off  Qtext off  Snap off  Tablet off
Object snap modes:      Endpoint, Intersection
Free dwg disk (F:) space: 1585.0 MBytes
Free temp disk (C:) space: 793.4 MBytes
Free physical memory: 0.0 Mbytes (out of 127.5M).
Free swap file space: 795.0 Mbytes (out of 839.9M).

Command: |
```

Here is a brief description of each item on the Status screen. Note that some of the items you see listed on the screen will vary somewhat from what we've shown here, but the information applies to virtually all situations except where noted.

(number) **objects in** *D:\Directory\Subdirectory*   The number of entities or objects in the drawing.

Model space limits are   The coordinates of the Model Space limits (see Chapter 3 for more details on limits).

Model space uses   The area the drawing occupies; equivalent to the extents of the drawing.

**Over: If present, this item means that part of the drawing is outside the limit boundary.

Display shows   The area covered by the current view.

Insertion base is, Snap resolution is, and Grid spacing is   The current default values for these mode settings.

Current space   Model Space or Paper Space.

Current layout   The current tab.

Current layer   The current default layer.

Current color   The color assigned to new objects.

Current linetype   The line type assigned to new objects.

Current lineweight   The current default lineweight setting.

Current plot style   The current plot style table used for the drawing.

Current elevation/thickness   The current default z-coordinate for new objects, plus the default thickness of objects; these are both 3D-related settings (see Chapter 15 for details).

Fill, Grid, Ortho, Qtext, Snap, and Tablet   The status of these options.

Object snap modes   The current default Osnap setting.

Free dwg disk (*drive:*)   The amount of space available to store drawing-specific temporary files.

Free temp disk (*drive:*)   The amount of space you have left on your hard drive for AutoCAD's resource temporary files.

Free physical memory   The amount of free RAM available.

Free swap file space   The amount of Windows swap file space available.

NOTE   When you are in Paper Space, the Status command displays information regarding the Paper Space limits. See Chapter 12 for more on Model Space and Paper Space.

In addition to being useful in understanding a drawing file, the Status command is an invaluable tool for troubleshooting. Frequently, problems can be isolated by a technical support person using the information provided by the Status command.

NOTE   For more information on memory use, see Appendix A.

Keeping Track of Time

The Time command allows you to keep track of the time spent on a drawing, for billing or analysis purposes. You can also use the Time command to check the current time and find out when the drawing was created and most recently edited. Because the AutoCAD timer uses your computer's time, be sure the time is set correctly in DOS.

To access the Time command, enter **Time**↵ at the command prompt, or select Tools ➤ Inquiry ➤ Time. You get a message like the one in Figure 14.6.

FIGURE 14.6:

The Time screen in the AutoCAD Text Window

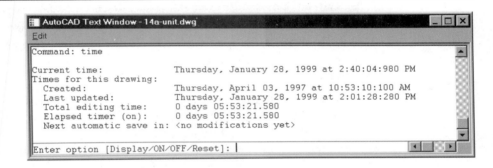

The first three lines of this message tell you the current date and time, the date and time the drawing was created, and the last time the drawing was saved or ended.

The fourth line shows the total time spent on the drawing from the point at which the file was opened. This elapsed timer lets you time a particular activity, such as changing the width of all the walls in a floor plan or redesigning a piece of machinery. You can turn the elapsed timer on or off, or reset it, by entering **ON, OFF,** or **Reset** at the prompt shown as the last line of the message. The last line tells you when the next automatic save will be.

Getting Information from System Variables

If you've been working through this book's ongoing studio apartment building tutorial, you'll have noticed occasional mentions of a *system variable* in conjunction with a command. You can check the status or change the setting of any system variable while you are in the middle of another command. To do this, you simply type an apostrophe ('), followed by the name of the system variable, at the command prompt.

For example, if you have started to draw a line and you suddenly decide you need to rotate your cursor 45°, you can do the following steps.

1. At the Specify next point or [Undo]: prompt, enter **'snapang**.

2. At the Enter new value for SNAPANG <0>: prompt, enter a new cursor angle. Once you have entered an angle value, you are returned to the Line command with the cursor in its new orientation.

You can also recall information such as the last area or distance calculated by AutoCAD. Because the Area system variable duplicates the name of the Area command, you need to choose Tools ➤ Inquiry ➤ Set Variables, and then type **Area.⏎** to read the last area calculation. You can also type **'Setvar⏎ Area.⏎**. The Tools ➤ Inquiry ➤ Set Variables option also lets you list all the system variables and their status, as well as access each system variable individually by entering a question mark (**?**).

Many of the system variables give you direct access to detailed information about your drawing. They also let you fine-tune your drawing and editing activities. In Appendix D you'll find all the information you need to familiarize yourself with the system variables available. Don't feel that you have to memorize them all at once; just be aware that they are available.

NOTE   Many of the dialog box options you have been using throughout this book, such as the options found in the Options dialog box, are actually system variable settings.

Keeping a Log of Your Activity

At times you may find it helpful to keep a log of your activity in an AutoCAD session. A log is a text file containing a record of your activities in AutoCAD. It may also contain notes to yourself or others about how a drawing is set up. Such a log can help you determine how frequently you use a particular command, or it can help you construct a macro for a commonly used sequence of commands.

The following exercise demonstrates how you can save and view a detailed record of an AutoCAD session using the Log feature.

1. Click Tools ➤ Options. In the Options dialog box, click the Open and Save tab at the top of the dialog box. A new set of options appears.

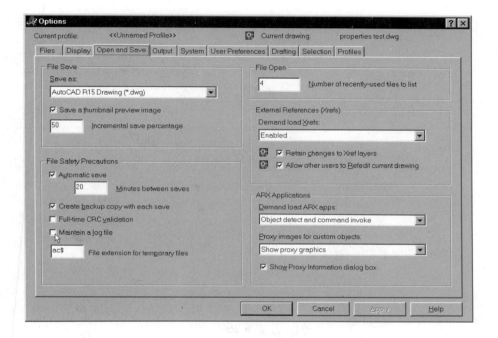

TIP

As a shortcut, you can quickly turn the Maintain a Log File feature on and off by typing **Logfileon**↵ and **Logfileoff**↵ at the command prompt in AutoCAD.

2. Click the check box labeled Maintain a Log File in the File Safety Precautions group, and then click OK.

3. Choose Tools ➤ Inquiry ➤ Status.

4. Return to the Open and Save tab of the Options dialog box, and then click the Maintain a Log File check box again to remove the X.

5. Click OK to exit the dialog box.

6. Switch over to Windows and start the Notepad application, or any text editor.

7. With the text editor, open the file called Acad.log in the \Program Files \AutoCAD2000\ directory. This is the file that stores the text data from the command prompt whenever the Log File option is turned on. You must turn off the Log File option before you can actually view this file in AutoCAD.

Since Acad.log is a standard text file, you can easily send it to other members of your workgroup, or print it out for a permanent record.

TIP   If you cannot find `Acad.log`, open the Options dialog box and select the Files tab. Click the plus sign to the left of the Log File Location option in the list box. A listing appears showing you where the `Acad.log` file is stored. If you like, you can modify this setting to indicate a new location for the `Acad.log` file.

Easy Access to the `Acad.log` File

If you want to have easy access to the `Acad.log` file, place a shortcut to it in your Auto-CAD 2000 program group. Here's how it's done:

1. Open Windows Explorer and locate and highlight the `Acad.log` file.

2. Right-click the `Acad.log` file.

3. In the popup menu, select Create Shortcut. A new file named Shortcut to Acad.log is created.

4. Shift+click and drag this Shortcut file to the Desktop. (A Shift+click on a file moves the file instead of making a copy.)

5. Right-click the Start button.

6. Click the Open option in the popup menu. The Start Menu window appears.

7. Double-click the Programs icon in the Start Menu window. The Programs Window appears.

8. Adjust your view of the Programs window so you can see the AutoCAD 2000 program group icon.

9. Click and drag the Shortcut to Acad.log file into the AutoCAD 2000 program group icon.

Once this is done, you can open the `Acad.log` file by choosing Start ➤ Programs ➤ Auto-CAD 2000 ➤ Shortcut to Acad.log from the Windows 95/98 or Windows NT 4 Start menu. Note that you cannot access this file while AutoCAD is open and the Log file feature is turned on.

Capturing and Saving Text Data from the AutoCAD Text Window

If you are working in groups, it is often quite helpful to have a record of the status, editing time, and system variables for particular files readily available to other group members. It is also convenient to keep records of block and layer information, so you can see if a specific block is included in a drawing or what layers are normally on or off.

You can use the Windows Clipboard to capture and save such data from the AutoCAD text window. The following steps show you how it's done.

1. Move the arrow cursor to the command prompt at the bottom of the AutoCAD window.

2. Right-click the mouse. A popup menu appears.

3. Click Copy History. The content of the text window is copied to the Clipboard.

By default, the text window stores 400 lines of text. You can change this number by changing the options in the Text Window group in the Display tab of the Options dialog box.

If you only want to copy a portion of the text window to the Clipboard, perform the following steps:

1. Press the F2 function key to open the text window.

2. Using the I-beam text cursor, highlight the text you wish to copy to the Clipboard.

3. Right-click your mouse, and then choose Copy from the popup menu. You can also choose Edit ➤ Copy from the text window's menu bar. The highlighted text is copied to the Clipboard.

4. Open Notepad or another word-processing application and paste the information.

You may notice four other options on the popup menu: Recent Commands, Copy History, Paste, and Options. Recent Commands offers a list of the most recent commands to choose from. You'll find that for most activities, you use a handful of command repeatedly. The Recent Commands option can save you time by giving you a shortcut to those commands you use the most. The Paste option pastes the first line of the contents of the Clipboard into the command line or input box of a dialog box. This can be useful for entering repetitive text or for storing and retrieving a frequently used command. The Options option opens the Options dialog box.

TIP   Items copied to the Clipboard from the AutoCAD text window can be pasted into dialog box input boxes. This can be a quick way to transfer layers, line types, or other named items from the text window into dialog boxes.

Storing Searchable Information in AutoCAD Files

As you start to build a library of AutoCAD files, you'll have to start thinking about how to manage those files. Keeping track of AutoCAD files can be a daunting task. Most AutoCAD users start to name files by their job number to keep things organized. But even the best organization schemes don't help if you need to find that one special among thousands of files in your library. In this section, you'll learn how to include information in an AutoCAD file that can be later used to locate the file using the Windows Find utility.

NOTE   AutoCAD 2000 offers the DesignCenter, a tool that can help you locate a file more easily based on a keyword or description. Chapter 22 contains a complete discussion of the DesignCenter.

To add general information about your drawing file that is searchable, use the Drawing Properties dialog box. To do this, choose File ➤ Drawing Properties. The Properties dialog box appears. There are four tabs in this dialog box. Here's a description of those tabs.

General

The General tab of the Properties dialog box gives you general information about the file. This information is similar to what you would see if you use the Properties options in the Windows Explorer to view the properties of a file.

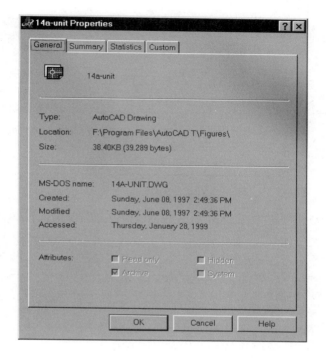

Summary

In the Summary tab, enter any text in the Title, Subject, Author, and Keywords fields that is appropriate to the drawing. The information you enter here is stored with the drawing and can be used to locate the file through the AutoCAD DesignCenter or the Windows Find Files or Folders utility (Start ➤ Find ➤ Files or Folders).

In addition, you can enter a base location for hyperlink links that are applied to objects in your drawing. This base location can be a directory in your computer or network, or an Internet Web address. See Chapter 24 for more information on hyperlinks.

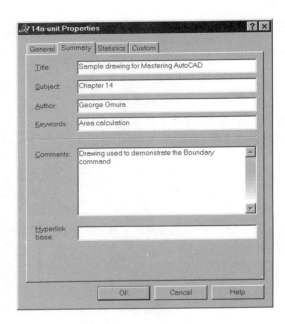

Statistics

The Statistics tab contains the name of the person who last edited the drawing, as well as the time spent on the file.

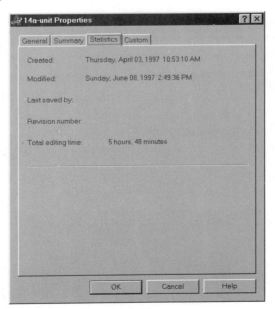

Custom

The Custom tab contains two columns of input boxes. This tab lets you store additional custom data with the drawing that is also searchable. For example, you might enter **Job Number** in the Name column, then enter **9901** in the Value column. You might also include information such as project manager names, consultants, or revision numbers. You can then locate the file using the AutoCAD DesignCenter or the Windows Find utility by doing a search for those two keywords.

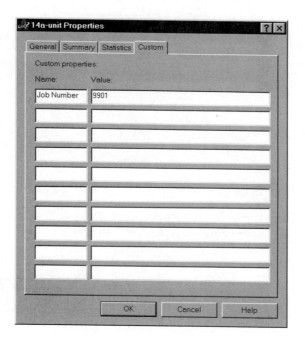

Searching for AutoCAD Files

Once you've included information in the Properties dialog box of a file, you can use the AutoCAD DesignCenter or Windows Find functions to locate your file.

The following exercise will show you how to use the Windows Find utility to locate a file.

1.   Choose Start ➤ Find ➤ Files or Folders from the Windows Desktop. The Find All Files dialog box appears.

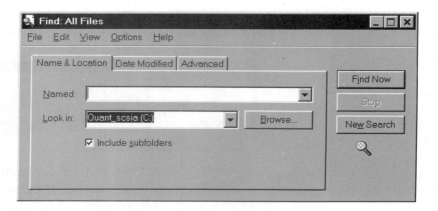

2.   In the Name & Location tab, select the drive location you want to search.

3.   Click the Advanced tab, then select AutoCAD Drawing from the Of Type drop-down list. You can also choose All Files and Folders, although this choice will slow down the search process.

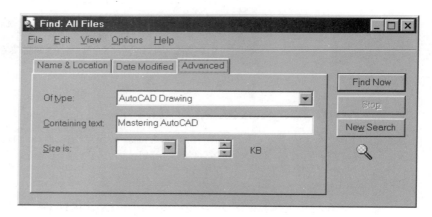

4.   Enter a word in the Containing Text input box that you know is included in the file's Properties dialog box.

5.   Click Find Now to start the search.

After a few moments, the file containing the word you entered in step 4 appears in the file list at the bottom of the dialog box. Double-click the filename in the list box to open it, or just note the location.

Recovering Corrupted Files

No system is perfect. Eventually, you will encounter a file that is corrupted in some way. AutoCAD offers two tools that can frequently salvage a corrupted file: Audit and Recover. Audit allows you to check a file that you are able to open, but you suspect has some problem. Recover allows you to open a file that is so badly corrupted that Auto-CAD is unable to open it in a normal way. You can access these tools from the File ➢ Drawing Utilities cascading menu. The functions of these options are as follows:

Audit   Checks the current file for any errors and displays the results in the text window.

Recover   Attempts to recover damaged or corrupted AutoCAD files. The current file is closed in the process as Recover attempts to open the file to be recovered.

More often than not, these tools will do the job, although they aren't a panacea for all file corruption problems. In the event that you cannot recover a file even with these tools, make sure your computer is running smoothly and that other systems are not faulty.

Exchanging CAD Data with Other Programs

AutoCAD offers many ways to share data with other programs. Perhaps the most common type of data exchange is simply to share drawing data with other CAD programs. In this section, you'll look at how you can export and import CAD drawings using the .dxf file format. You'll also look at how you can use bitmap graphics, both to and from AutoCAD, through the Windows Clipboard.

Other types of data exchange involve text, spreadsheets, and databases. Chapter 10 covers database links, but this section will describe how you can include text, spreadsheet, and database files in a drawing or include AutoCAD drawings in other program files using a Windows feature called Object Linking and Embedding (OLE).

Using the .dxf File Format

A .dxf file is a DOS text file containing all the information needed to reconstruct a drawing. It is often used to exchange drawings created with other programs. Many micro-CAD programs, including some 3D perspective programs, can generate or read files in .dxf format. You may want to use a 3D program to view your drawing in a Perspective view, or you may have a consultant who uses a different CAD program that accepts .dxf files. There are many 3D rendering programs that read .dxf files, on both Windows and Macintosh computers. Most 2D drafting programs also read and write .dxf files.

Be aware that not all programs that read .dxf files will accept all the data stored therein. Many programs that claim to read .dxf files will "throw away" much of the .dxf file's information. Attributes are perhaps the most commonly ignored objects, followed by many of the 3D objects, such as meshes and 3D Faces. But .dxf files, though not the most perfect medium for translating data, have become something of a standard.

> **NOTE**   AutoCAD no longer supports the IGES (Initial Graphics Exchange Specification) standard for CAD data translation.

Exporting .dxf Files

To export your current drawing as a .dxf file, try the following exercise:

1. Choose File ➤ Save As. The Save Drawing As dialog box appears.

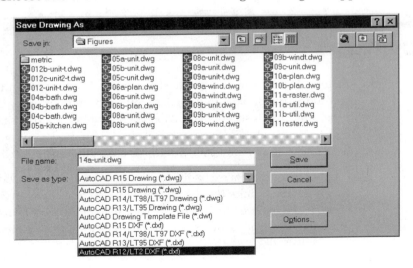

2. Click the Save as Type drop-down list. You have the option to export your drawing under a number of formats, including four different .dxf formats.

3. Select the appropriate .dxf format, and then enter a name for your file. You do not have to include the .dxf filename extension.

4. Select a folder for the file, and then click Save.

In step 2, you can select from the following .dxf file formats:

- AutoCAD 2000 DXF
- AutoCAD R14 DXF
- AutoCAD R13/LT95 DXF
- AutoCAD R12/LT2 DXF

Choose the format appropriate to the program you are exporting to. In most cases, the safest choice is AutoCAD R12/LT2 DXF if you are exporting to another CAD program, though AutoCAD will not maintain the complete functionality of AutoCAD 2000 for such files.

Once you've selected a .dxf format from the Save as Type drop-down list, you can set more detailed specifications by clicking the Options button in the Save Drawing As dialog box. Doing so opens the Saveas Options dialog box. For DXF files, select the DXF Options tab. This is what it looks like.

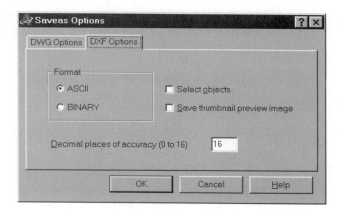

The DXF Options tab contains the following options:

Format Lets you choose between ASCII (plain text) or binary file formats. Most other programs accept ASCII, so it is the safest choice. Some programs accept binary .dxf files, which have the advantage of being more compact than the ASCII format.

Select Objects   Lets you select specific objects within the drawing for export. You have the option to select objects after you have closed the Export Options dialog box and selected Save from the Export Data dialog box.

Save Thumbnail Preview Image   Lets you save an image with the file so that when you use the AutoCAD File ➤ Open option, you can see a preview image of the DXF file.

Decimal Places of Accuracy   Allows you to determine the accuracy of the exported file. Keeping this value low helps reduce the size of the export file, particularly if it is to be in the ASCII format. Some CAD programs do not support the high accuracy of AutoCAD, so using a high value here may have no significance.

TIP   You can also type **Dxfout.⏎** at the command prompt to open the Create DXF File dialog box. This is a standard Windows file dialog box that includes the Options button described here. This dialog box displays only .dxf file formats in the Save As Type drop-down list.

Opening or Importing .dxf Files

Some offices have standardized their CAD drawings on the .dxf file format. This is most commonly seen in offices that use a variety of CAD software besides Auto-CAD. AutoCAD 2000 can be set up to read and write DXF files by default, instead of the standard DWG file format. Here's how it's done.

1.   Choose Tools ➤ Options to open the Options dialog box.

2.   Select the Open and Save tab.

3.   Select from any of the DXF formats from the Save As drop-down list

4.   Click OK.

Once you do this, all of your drawings are automatically saved in the DXF format of your choice. AutoCAD also displays DXF files in the File dialog box when you choose File ➤ Open.

You can also set the default AutoCAD file type by clicking the Options button in the Save Drawing As dialog box. As you saw in an earlier section, the Saveas

Options dialog box offers DWG Options. You can select a default file type from the Save All Drawings As drop-down list.

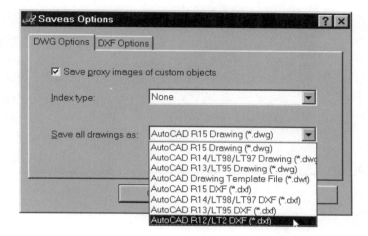

If you just need to open a DXF file once in a while, you can do so by selecting DXF from the File of Type drop-down list in the Select File dialog box. This is the dialog box you see when you choose File ➤ Open. You can also import .dxf files into the current open file, provided that the .dxf file does not contain blocks or other named elements that do not exist in the current file.

1. Type **Dxfin**↵ at the command prompt. The Select .DXF File dialog box appears. This is a typical Windows file dialog box.

2. Locate and select the .dxf file you wish to import.

3. Double-click the filename to begin importing it.

If the import drawing is large, AutoCAD may take several minutes to import it.

Exchanging Files with Earlier Releases

One persistent dilemma that has plagued AutoCAD users is how to exchange files between earlier versions of the program. In the past, if you upgraded your AutoCAD, you were locked out from exchanging your drawings with people using earlier versions. Release 12 alleviated this difficulty by making Release 12 files compatible with Release 11 files.

Continued on next page

With Release 13, the file structure was radically different from earlier versions of AutoCAD. Then AutoCAD 14 made it possible to freely exchange files between Release 13 and 14.

AutoCAD 2000 has some new features, like multiple layouts and searchable properties, that do not translate to earlier versions. If compatibility with earlier versions is more important than the new features of AutoCAD 2000, then you can set up AutoCAD 2000 to read and write to any release of AutoCAD back to Release 13. Or if you're willing to work with DXF files, you can set up AutoCAD 2000 to automatically read and write Auto-CAD 12 DXF files.

To set up AutoCAD to automatically read and write earlier versions, use the Options dialog box to set the default file type as described in *Opening or Importing .dxf Files*, but instead of selecting a DXF file type, select the DWG file type you want to use

Using AutoCAD Drawings in Desktop Publishing

As you probably know, AutoCAD is a natural for creating line art, and because of its popularity, most desktop-publishing programs are designed to import AutoCAD drawings in one form or another. Those of you who employ desktop-publishing software to generate user manuals or other technical documents will probably want to use AutoCAD drawings in your work. This section will examine ways to output AutoCAD drawings to formats that most desktop-publishing programs can accept.

There are two methods for exporting AutoCAD files to desktop-publishing formats: raster export and vector file export.

Exporting Raster Files

In some cases, you may only need a rough image of your AutoCAD drawing. You can export your drawing as a raster file that can be read in virtually any desktop-publishing and word-processing program. To do this, you must create a new plotter configuration that plots to an image file instead of an output device. The section called *Adding an Output Device* in Chapter 7 describes how to use the Add-a-Plotter wizard to add a plotter configuration to AutoCAD. Here is some additional information on how to use that wizard to set up AutoCAD for raster file output.

1. On the Begin page of the Add-a-Plotter wizard, choose My Computer.

2. On the Plotter Model page of the Add-a-Plotter wizard, select Raster file formats from the Manufacturers list, then select the type of raster file you want to use from the Models list. For example, you can choose Truevision TGA Version 2 from the list. This is one of the more universal file types.

3. Skip over the Import PCP or PC2 page and the Ports page.

4. Enter a name for your raster output settings on the Plotter Name page.

5. On the Finish page, click the Enter Plotter Configuration button. The Plotter Configuration Editor dialog box appears.

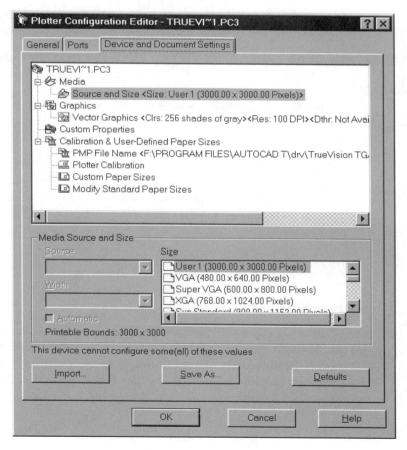

6. Click the Source and Size listing that appears in the large list box in the top of the dialog box. A list of options appears in the Size list box in the lower-right corner of the dialog box. Select an image size from the list or create a custom size by doing the following steps.

7. Click Custom Paper Sizes from the large list box at the top of the dialog box. The options change in the lower half of the dialog box.

8. Click the Add button. The Custom Paper Size wizard appears.

9. Select the Start from Scratch radio button, then click Next. The Media Bounds page appears.

10. Enter a height and width in pixels for your image file, then click Next. The Paper Size Name page appears. Enter a name that best describes the size of the image file, then click Next. The File Name page appears.

11. Enter a name for the Plotter Model Parameters file. This is a file that stores specific setting information about the plotter. Click Next when you are done.

12. On the Finish page, click Finish. The Plotter Configuration Editor dialog box reappears. Click OK, then click Finish in the Add-a-Plotter wizard.

Once you've finished creating a plotter configuration, it appears as a file in the Plotter subdirectory of the AutoCAD2000 directory. You can access this file through Windows Explorer, or from AutoCAD by clicking Files ➤ Plotter Manager.

To create a raster file version of your drawing, choose File ➤ Plot, then in the Plot dialog box, choose the Plot Device tab and select your Raster File plotter configuration from the Name drop-down list of the Plotter Configuration group. You can then proceed to plot your drawing, but instead of paper output, you'll get a raster file.

If you need to make changes to your Raster File configuration, choose File ➤ Plotter Manager, then in the Plotter window, double-click your Raster File configuration file. You will see the same Plotter Configuration Editor you used to set up the raster plotter configuration.

You can set up a different plotter configuration for each type of raster file you use. You can also set up plotter configurations for different resolutions, if you choose. To learn more about plotting in general, consult Chapter 7. Appendix A offers detailed information on the Plotter Configuration Editor.

Exporting Vector Files

If you need to preserve the accuracy of your drawing, or if you wish to take advantage of TrueType or PostScript fonts, you can use either the .dxf, .wmf, or PostScript vector formats.

For vector format files, .dxf is the easiest to work with, and with TrueType support, .dxf can preserve font information between AutoCAD and desktop-publishing programs that support the .dxf format. The .wmf, Windows Meta-File, format, is also a commonly accepted file format for vector information, and it preserves TrueType fonts and line weights that may be used in your drawings.

PostScript is a raster/vector hybrid file format that AutoCAD supports; unfortunately, AutoCAD has dropped direct PostScript font support since Release 14. However, you can still use substitute fonts to stand in for PostScript fonts. These substitute fonts are converted to true PostScript fonts when AutoCAD exports the drawing. You won't actually see the true results of your PostScript output until you actually print your drawing out on a PostScript printer.

The .dxf file export was covered in the *Using the .dxf File Format* section of this chapter, so this section will concentrate on the .wmf and PostScript file formats.

TIP

If you are a circuit board designer or drafter, you may want to use the PostScript Out option to send your layout to PostScript typesetting devices. This saves time and file size since the PostScript Out option converts AutoCAD entities into true PostScript descriptions.

WMF Output

The Windows MetaFile (WMF) file type is one of the more popular vector file formats in Windows. It can be opened and edited by most illustration programs, including CorelDraw and Adobe Illustrator. Most word-processing, database, and spreadsheet programs can also import WMF files. It's a great option for Auto-CAD file export because it preserves TrueType fonts and now that AutoCAD offers line-weight settings, you can export WMF files that preserve line weights as well.

To export WMF files, do the following.

1.   Choose File ➤ Export. The Export Data dialog box appears.

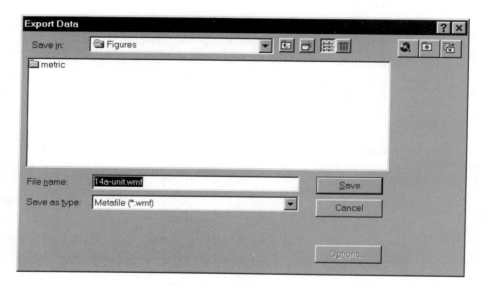

2.   The default file type in this dialog box happens to be WMF, so all you need to
      do is enter a name and location for your WMF file, then click OK. The dialog
      box closes and a prompt appears asking you to select objects.

3.   Select the objects you want to export to the WMF file and press ↵ when you
      are finished. The objects are saved to your WMF file.

PostScript Output

AutoCAD is capable of exporting to the Encapsulated PostScript file format (.eps).
You actually have two ways of obtaining PostScript output. You can use the File ➤
Export option on the menu bar, or you can install a PostScript printer driver and
plot your drawing to an .eps file. In Chapter 11, the *If You Want to Experiment...*
section described the steps for using File ➤ Export to export .eps files. To set up
AutoCAD to plot your drawing to an .eps file, follow the same steps described
in the previous *Exporting Raster Files* section, but in step 2, select the option that
reads Adobe from the Manufacturers list and then select the appropriate PostScript
level from the Models list.

WARNING   AutoCAD does not preserve font information when creating .eps files from the printer option. It also produces larger files, especially if your drawing contains a lot of area fills and filled fonts.

PostScript Font Substitution

This chapter mentioned earlier that AutoCAD substitutes its own fonts with PostScript fonts when a file is exported to an .eps file using the Export Data dialog box. If your work involves PostScript output, you will want to know these font names in order to make the appropriate substitution. Table 14.1 shows a listing of AutoCAD font names and their equivalent PostScript names.

To take advantage of AutoCAD's ability to translate fonts, you need to create AutoCAD fonts that have the names listed in the first column of Table 14.1. You then need to use those fonts when creating text styles in AutoCAD. Then Auto-CAD will convert the AutoCAD fonts into the corresponding PostScript fonts.

Creating the AutoCAD fonts can be simply a matter of copying and renaming existing fonts to those listed in Table 14.1. For example, you could make a copy of the Romans.shx font and name it Agd.shx. Better yet, if you have the PostScript .pfb file of the font, you can compile it into an AutoCAD font file and rename the compiled file appropriately. By compiling the .pfb file, you get a close approximation of its appearance in AutoCAD. See the *Using PostScript Fonts* sidebar in Chapter 8 for a description on how to compile PostScript fonts.

TABLE 14.1:   A Partial Listing of AutoCAD Font Filenames and Their Corresponding PostScript Fonts

AutoCAD Font Name	PostScript Font Name	AutoCAD Font Name	PostScript Font Name
agd	AvantGarde-Demi	agdo	AvantGarde-DemiOblique
agw	AvantGarde-Book	agwo	AvantGarde-BookOblique
bdps	Bodoni-Poster	bkd	Bookman-Demi
bkdi	Bookman-DemiItalic	bkl	Bookman-Light
bkli	Bookman-LightItalic	c	Cottonwood
cibt	CityBlueprint	cob	Courier-Bold

Continued on next page

TABLE 14.1 CONTINUED: A Partial Listing of AutoCAD Font Filenames and Their Corresponding PostScript Fonts

AutoCAD Font Name	PostScript Font Name	AutoCAD Font Name	PostScript Font Name
cobo	Courier-BoldOblique	cobt	CountryBlueprint
com	Courier	coo	Courier-Oblique
eur	EuroRoman	euro	EuroRoman-Oblique
fs	FreestyleScript	ho	Hobo
hv	Helvetica	hvb	Helvetica-Bold
hvbo	Helvetica-BoldOblique	hvn	Helvetica-Narrow
hvnb	Helvetica-Narrow-Bold	hvnbo	Helvetica-Narrow-BoldOblique
hvno	Helvetica-Narrow-Oblique	hvo	Helvetica-Oblique
lx	Linotext	ncb	NewCenturySchlbk-Bold
ncbi	NewCenturySchlbk-BoldItalic	nci	NewCenturySchlbk-Italic
ncr	NewCenturySchlbk-Roman	par	PanRoman
pob	Palatino-Bold	pobi	Palatino-BoldItalic
poi	Palatino-Italic	por	Palatino-Roman
rom	Romantic	romb	Romantic-Bold
romi	Romantic-Italic	sas	SansSerif
sasb	SansSerif-Bold	sasbo	SansSerif-BoldOblique
saso	SansSerif-Oblique	suf	SuperFrench
sy	Symbol	te	Technic
teb	Technic-Bold	tel	Technic-Light
tib	Times-Bold	tibi	Times-BoldItalic
tii	Times-Italic	tir	Times-Roman
tjrg	Trajan-Regular	vrb	VAGRounded-Bold
zcmi	ZapfChancery-MediumItalic	zd	ZapfDingbats

If you are using PostScript fonts not listed in Table 14.1, you can add your own AutoCAD-to-PostScript substitution by editing the `Acad.psf` file. This is a plain text file that contains the font substitution information as well as other PostScript translation data.

TIP

The HPGL plot file format is another vector format you can use to export your AutoCAD drawings. Use the method described earlier in *Exporting Raster Files* to add the HPGL plotter driver to your printer/plotter configuration.

Combining Data from Different Sources

Imagine being able to import and display spreadsheet data in an AutoCAD drawing. Further imagine that you can easily update that spreadsheet data, either from directly within the drawing or remotely by editing the source spreadsheet document. With a little help from a Windows feature called *Object Linking and Embedding (OLE)*, such a scenario is within your grasp. The data is not limited to spreadsheets; it can be a word-processed document, a database report, or even a sound or video clip.

To import data from other applications, you use the Cut and Paste features found in virtually all Windows programs. You cut the data from the source document, then paste it into AutoCAD.

When you paste data into your AutoCAD file, you have the option to have it *linked* to the source file or to *embed* it. If you link it to the source file, then the pasted data is updated whenever the source file is modified. This is similar to an Auto-CAD cross-referenced file. (See Chapter 12 for more on cross-referenced files.)

You can also paste data into AutoCAD without linking it; then it is considered an embedded object. You can still open the application associated with the data by double-clicking it, but the data is no longer associated with the source file. This is similar to a drawing inserted as a block where changes in the source drawing file have no effect on the inserted block.

Let's see firsthand how OLE works. The following exercise shows how to link an Excel spreadsheet to AutoCAD. You will need a copy of Microsoft Excel for

Windows 95/98 or Windows NT, but if you have another application that supports OLE, you can follow along.

1. Open the file called `14a-plan-xls.dwg` from the companion CD-ROM. This is a copy of the plan you may have created in earlier exercises.

2. Open the Excel spreadsheet called `14a-plan.xls`, also from the companion CD-ROM.

3. In Excel, highlight the door data, as shown in Figure 14.7, by clicking cell A1 and dragging to cell G17.

4. Choose Edit ➤ Copy. This places a copy of the selected data into the Windows Clipboard.

5. Switch to AutoCAD, either by clicking a visible portion of the AutoCAD window, or by clicking the AutoCAD button in the Taskbar at the bottom of the Windows Desktop.

6. Choose Edit ➤ Paste Special. The Paste Special dialog box appears.

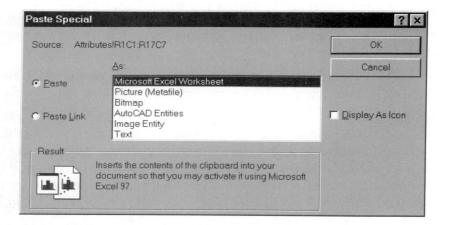

7. Click the Paste Link radio button to tell AutoCAD you want this paste to be a link. Notice that the list of source types changes to show only one option: Microsoft Excel Worksheet.

8. Click OK. The spreadsheet data appears in the drawing (see Figure 14.8).

FIGURE 14.7:

The Excel spreadsheet

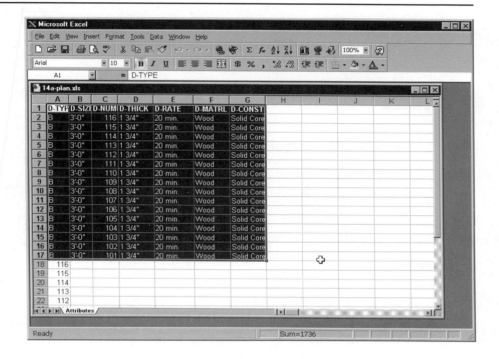

FIGURE 14.8:

The AutoCAD drawing with the spreadsheet pasted

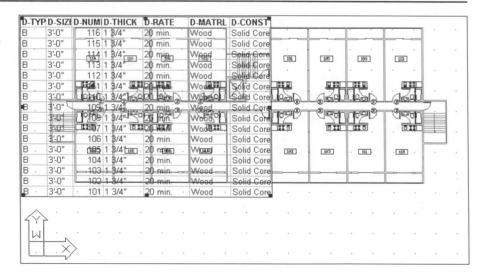

9. Place the cursor on the upper-left corner of the spreadsheet so that a double-headed diagonal arrow appears, and then click and drag the corner downward and to the right to make the size shown in Figure 14.9.

FIGURE 14.9:

Resizing the spreadsheet within AutoCAD

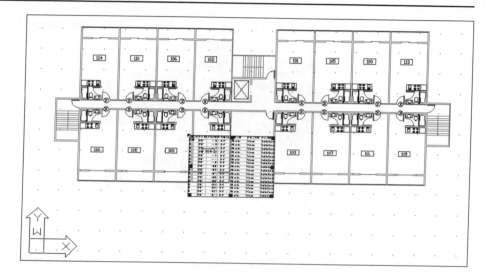

10. Place the cursor over the spreadsheet data so it looks like a cross, and then click and drag the spreadsheet to the lower-right corner of the drawing.

11. Zoom into the spreadsheet so you can read its contents clearly.

As you saw in steps 8 and 9, you can resize a pasted object using the corner or side grips. The corner grips maintain the original proportion of the inserted object.

You now have a linked object inserted into the AutoCAD drawing. You can save this file and send it off to someone else, along with the pasted document, 14a-plan.xls. The other person will be able to open the AutoCAD file and view the drawing with the spreadsheet.

WARNING Objects that are pasted into AutoCAD are maintained within AutoCAD until you use the Erase command to delete them. They act like other AutoCAD objects where layers are concerned. One limitation to pasted objects is that they do not appear in prints or plots unless you use the Windows system printer or plotter.

Now let's see how the link feature works by making some changes to the spreadsheet data.

1. Go back to Excel by clicking the Excel button in the Windows toolbar.

2. Click the cell just below the column heading D-RATE.

3. Change the cell's contents by typing **No Rating**.↵.

4. Go back to AutoCAD and notice that the corresponding cell in the inserted spreadsheet has changed to reflect the change you made to the original document. Since you inserted the spreadsheet as a linked document, OLE updates the pasted copy whenever the original source document changes.

5. Now close both the Excel spreadsheet and the AutoCAD drawing.

Editing Links

Once you've pasted an object with links, you can control the link by selecting Edit ➤ OLE Links (Olelinks). If there are no linked objects in the drawing, this option does nothing; otherwise it opens the Links dialog box.

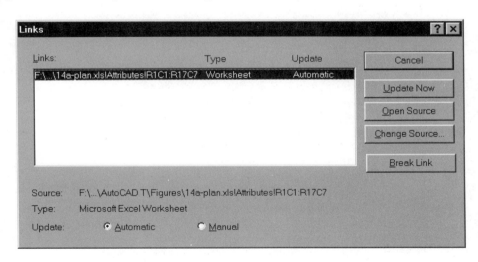

The following list describes the options available in the Links dialog box:

Cancel   Does just that. It cancels the link between a pasted object and its source file. Once this option is used, changes in the source file have no effect on the pasted object. This is similar to using the Bind option in the Xref command.

Update Now   Updates an object's link when the Manual option is selected.

Open Source   Opens the application associated with the object and lets you edit it.

Change Source   Lets you change the object's link to a different file. When you select this option, AutoCAD opens the Change Link dialog box, which lets you select another file of the same type. For example, if you are editing the link to a sound file, the Change Link dialog box will display files with the .wav file extension.

Automatic and **Manual**   Radio buttons control whether linked objects are updated automatically or manually.

Break Link   Disconnects the link between the inserted data and the source document. The inserted data then becomes embedded, rather than linked.

Adding Sound, Motion, and Photos to Your Drawings

You've already seen how you can include scanned images in AutoCAD drawings through the Raster Image tools. Through Object Linking and Embedding, you can also include sound files, video clips, and animation. Imagine how you might be able to enhance your AutoCAD files with these types of data. You can include voice annotation or, if the file is to go to a client, an animated walk-through of your building or mechanical design. The potential for this feature is enormous.

Options for Embedding Data

If you don't need to link the imported data to its source, the Paste Special dialog box lets you convert the imported data to a number of other formats. Here is a brief description of each format that is available:

Picture (Metafile)   Imports the data as vector or bitmap graphics, whichever is appropriate. If applicable, text is also maintained as text, though not editable within AutoCAD.

Bitmap   Imports the data as a bitmap image, closely reflecting the appearance of the data as it appears on your computer screen in the source application.

AutoCAD Entities   Converts the data into AutoCAD objects such as lines, arcs, and circles. Text is converted into AutoCAD single-line text objects.

Image Entity   Converts the data into an AutoCAD raster image. You can then edit it using the raster image-related tools found in the Modify ➤ Object ➤ Image cascading menu of the menu bar. See Chapter 11 for more on how to use raster images.

Text   Converts the data into AutoCAD multiline text objects.

The options you see in the Paste Special dialog box will depend on the type of data being imported. You saw how the Microsoft Excel Worksheet option maintains the imported data as an Excel worksheet. If the contents of the Clipboard come from another program, you are offered that program as a choice in place of Excel.

NOTE   The Edit ➤ Paste option embeds OLE data objects into AutoCAD, as does the Paste From Clipboard tool in the Standard toolbar.

Using the Clipboard to Export AutoCAD Drawings

Just as you can cut and paste data into AutoCAD from applications that support OLE, you can also cut and paste AutoCAD images to other applications. This can be useful as a way of including AutoCAD images into word-processed documents, spreadsheets, or desktop-publishing documents. It can also be useful in creating background images for visualization programs such as 3D Studio, or paint programs such as Fractal Painter.

NOTE   If you cut and paste an AutoCAD drawing to another file using OLE, then send the file to someone using another computer, they must also have AutoCAD installed before they can edit the pasted AutoCAD drawing.

The receiving application does not need to support OLE, but if it does, then the exported drawing can be edited with AutoCAD and will maintain its accuracy as a CAD drawing. Otherwise, the AutoCAD image will be converted to a bitmap graphic.

To use the Clipboard to export an object or set of objects from an AutoCAD drawing, use the Edit ➤ Copy option. You are then prompted to select the objects you want to export. If you want to simultaneously export and erase objects from AutoCAD, choose Edit ➤ Cut.

If you want the AutoCAD image to be linked to AutoCAD, use Edit ➤ Copy Link. You won't be prompted to select objects. The current visible portion of your drawing will be exported. If you want the entire drawing to be exported, use View ➤ Zoom ➤ Extents before using the Copy Link option. Otherwise, set up AutoCAD to display the portion of your drawing you want exported, before using Copy Link.

In the receiving application, choose Edit ➤ Paste Special. You'll see a dialog box similar to AutoCAD's Paste Special dialog box. Select the method for pasting your AutoCAD image, and then click OK. If the receiving application does not have a Paste Special option, choose Edit ➤ Paste. The receiving application converts the image into a format it can accept.

TIP   You can copy multiple viewport views from Paper Space into the Clipboard using the Edit ➤ Copy Link option.

If You Want to Experiment...

With a little help from a Visual Basic macro and OLE, you can have Excel extract attribute data from a drawing, and then display that data in a spreadsheet imported into AutoCAD. The following exercise uses a Visual Basic macro embedded in the 14a-plan.xls file you used in an earlier exercise.

1. Open the 14a-plan-xls.dwg file in AutoCAD again.

2. Open the 14a-plan.xls file in Excel.

3. Repeat the exercise in the *Combining Data from Different Sources* section of this chapter, but stop before exiting the two files.

4. In AutoCAD, choose Modify ➤ Attribute ➤ Single, and then click the door symbol in room 115.

5. Change the Fire Rating Attribute value to 1 hour, and then click OK.

6. Go to Excel, and then choose Tools ➤ Macro ➤ Macros.

7. In the Macros dialog box, highlight the Extract macro, and then click Run. Excel takes a moment to extract the attribute data from the open file; then it displays the data in the spreadsheet.

8. Return to AutoCAD and check the Fire Rating Value for room 115 in the imported spreadsheet. It reflects the change you made in the attribute in step 4.

9. Close both the files.

The macro you used in the Excel file is a small sample of what can be done using AutoCAD's implementation of Visual Basic Automation. You'll learn more about VBA in Chapter 21.

In this chapter, you have seen how AutoCAD allows you to access information ranging from the areas of objects to information from other programs. You may never use some of these features, but knowing they are there may, at some point, help you to solve a production problem.

You've just completed Part III of our tutorial. If you've followed the tutorial from the beginning, this is where you get a diploma. You have reached Expert status in 2D drawing and have the tools to tackle any drawing project thrown at you. You only need to log in some time on a few real projects to round out your experience.

From now on, you won't need to follow the book's chapters in order. If you're interested in 3D, go ahead and continue to Part IV, where you'll get thorough instructions on 3D drawing and imaging with AutoCAD. Otherwise, you can skip to Part V to become a full-fledged AutoCAD power user.

Also, don't miss the appendices and the CD-ROM—they are packed with information that will answer many of your specific questions or problems. Of course, the entire book is a ready reference to answer questions as they arise or to refresh your memory about specific commands.

Good luck!

PART IV

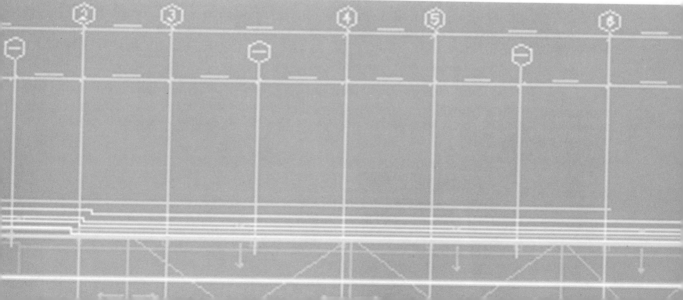

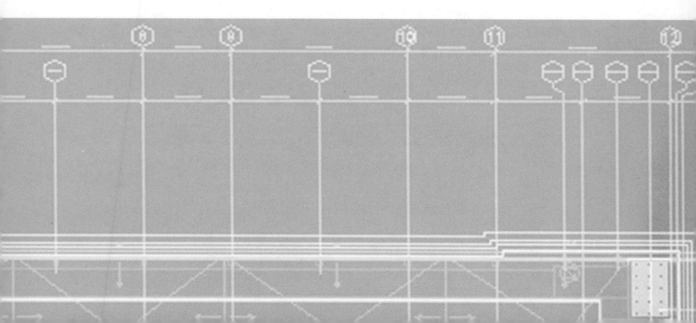

Modeling and Imaging in 3D

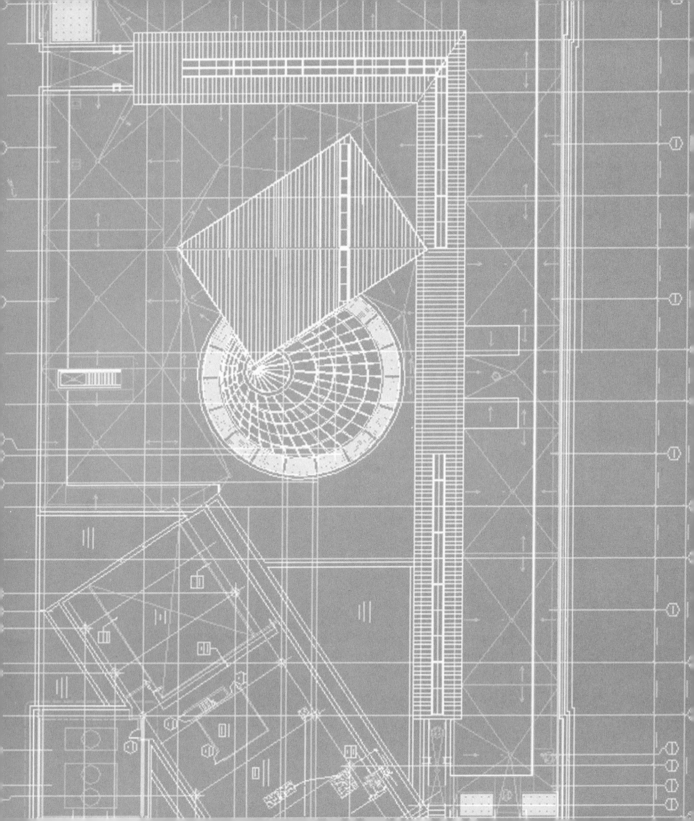

CHAPTER
FIFTEEN

15

Introducing 3D

- Creating a 3D Drawing

- Viewing a 3D Drawing

- Visualizing Your Model

- Getting the 3D Results You Want

- Drawing 3D Surfaces

- Creating and Using Slides

- If You Want to Experiment…

Viewing an object in three dimensions lets you have a sense of its true shape and form. It also helps you conceptualize the design, which results in better design decisions. Finally, using three-dimensional objects helps you communicate your ideas to those who may not be familiar with the plans, sections, and side views of your design.

A further advantage to drawing in three dimensions is that you can derive 2D drawings from your 3D model, which might otherwise take considerably more time with standard 2D drawing methods. For example, you could model a mechanical part in 3D and then quickly derive its top, front, and right-side views using the techniques discussed in this chapter.

AutoCAD offers two methods for creating 3D models: *surface modeling* and *solid modeling*. This chapter will introduce you to surface modeling. You'll get a chance to explore solid modeling in Chapter 18.

With surface modeling, you use two types of objects. One is called a *3D Face*, which you will learn about later in this chapter. The other is the standard AutoCAD set of objects you've been using all along, but with a slight twist. By changing the thickness property of objects, you can create 3D surfaces. These surfaces, along with some 3D editing tools, let you create virtually any 3D form you may need.

In this chapter, you will use AutoCAD's 3D capabilities to see what your studio apartment looks like from various angles.

Creating a 3D Drawing

By now, you are aware that AutoCAD objects have properties that can be manipulated to set color, line type, line weight, and layer assignments. Another property called *thickness* lets you turn two-dimensional objects into 3D forms. For example, to draw a cube, you first draw a square, and then change the thickness property of the square to some value greater than 0 (see Figure 15.1). This thickness property is a value given as a z-coordinate. Imagine that your screen's drawing area is the drawing surface. A z-coordinate of 0 is on that surface. A z-coordinate greater than 0 is a position closer to you and above that surface. Figure 15.2 illustrates this concept.

FIGURE 15.1:

Creating a cube by changing its thickness

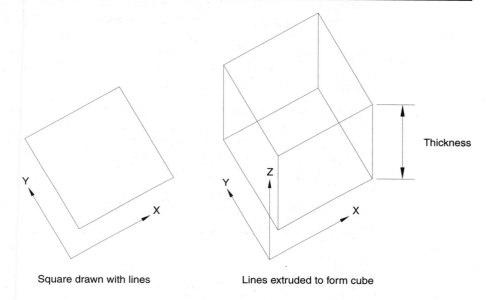

Square drawn with lines   Lines extruded to form cube

FIGURE 15.2:

The z-coordinate in relation to the x-coordinate and y-coordinate

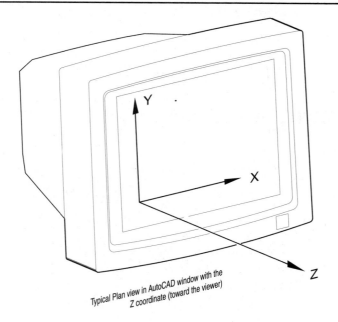

Typical Plan view in AutoCAD window with the Z coordinate (toward the viewer)

When you draw an object with thickness, you don't see the thickness until you view the drawing from a different angle. This is because normally your view is perpendicular to the imagined drawing surface. At that angle, you cannot see the thickness of an object because it projects toward you—just as a sheet of paper looks like a line when viewed from one end. Thus, to view an object's thickness, you must change the angle at which you view your drawing.

Another object property related to 3D is *elevation*. You can set AutoCAD so that everything you draw has an *elevation*. By default, objects have a zero elevation. This means that objects are drawn on the imagined 2D plane of Model Space, but you can set the z-coordinate for your objects so that whatever you draw is above or below that surface. An object with an elevation value other than 0 rests not *on* the imagined drawing surface but *above* it (or *below* it if the z-coordinate is a negative value). Figure 15.3 illustrates this concept.

FIGURE 15.3:

Two identical objects at different z-coordinates

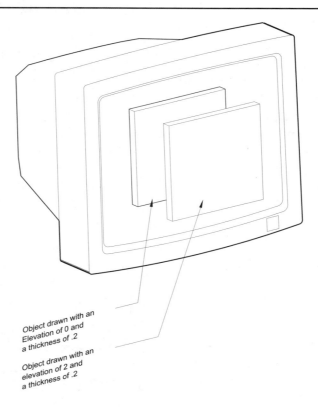

Object drawn with an Elevation of 0 and a thickness of .2

Object drawn with an elevation of 2 and a thickness of .2

Changing a 2D Plan into a 3D Model

In this exercise, you will turn the 2D Unit drawing into a 3D drawing by changing the properties of the wall lines. You will also learn how to view the 3D image.

1. Start AutoCAD and open the Unit file or use `15a-unit.dwg` from the companion CD-ROM.   *Save as   cmkunit3d*

2. Set the current layer to Wall, and freeze all the other layers except Jamb. Remember that Freeze is the option just to the right of the lightbulb in the Layer Properties Manager dialog box.

3. Turn on the grid (if it isn't on already). Your screen should look like Figure 15.4.

4. Click View ➤ 3D Views ➤ SW Isometric. Your view now looks as if you are standing above and to the left of your drawing, rather than directly above it (see Figure 15.5). The UCS icon helps you get a sense of your new orientation. The grid also shows you the angle of the drawing surface.

FIGURE 15.4:

The Plan view of the walls and door jambs

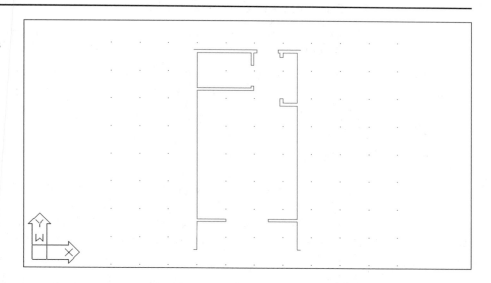

NOTE   The interior walls of the bathroom are not visible because the layer on which the bathroom block was inserted was frozen. For the purpose of this exercise, you can ignore the bathroom wall. Since the bathroom is a block, you cannot change the thickness property of the wall without using the In-place Xref and Block Edit tool.

FIGURE 15.5:

A 3D view of the floor plan

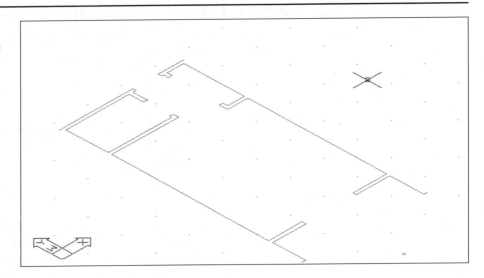

5. Select all the objects in the drawing.

6. Click the Properties tool on the Standard toolbar, or right-click and select Properties from the popup menu.

7. In the Properties dialog box, locate the Thickness option, then double-click the 0 value in the right-hand column.

8. Enter **8'**↵ (metric users should enter **244**↵). The walls and jambs now appear to be 8' (244cm) high.

9. Close the Properties dialog box.

Figure 15.6 shows the extruded wall lines. You can see through the walls because this is a *Wireframe view*. A Wireframe view shows the volumes of a 3D object by showing the lines representing the intersections of surfaces. Later, this chapter will discuss how to make an object's surfaces opaque in order to facilitate a particular point of view for a drawing.

In step 4, you were able to quickly obtain a 3D view from a set of 3D View options. You'll learn more about these options as you progress through this chapter.

NOTE	Notice that when you extruded the walls, the interior bathroom walls did not change with the others. This is because those walls are part of a block. You must redefine the block to change the thickness of the objects it contains.

FIGURE 15.6:

The wall lines, extruded (Wireframe view)

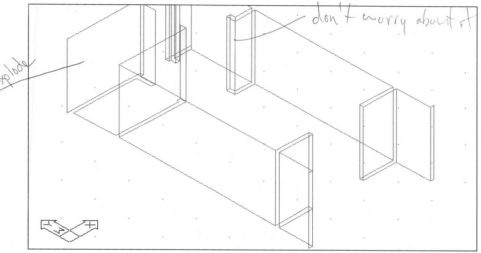

Next you will change the elevation of the door headers by moving them in the z-axis using grips.

1. First, zoom out a bit to get all of the drawing in view, as shown in Figure 15.7. You can use the Pan and Zoom tools in this 3D view as you would in a 2D view.

2. Turn on the Ceiling layer. The door headers appear as lines on the floor where the door openings are located.

3. Click the two magenta lines representing the header over the balcony door. As you do so, notice that your cursor's shape conforms to the 3D view.

4. Shift+click the midpoint grips of these two lines.

5. Click again one of the hot grips.

6. At the ** STRETCH ** prompt, enter @0,0,7'↵ (metric users should enter @0,0,214↵). Don't forget to indicate feet for the 7. The lines move to a new position 7' (214cm) above the floor (see Figure 15.7).

FIGURE 15.7:

The header lines at the new elevation

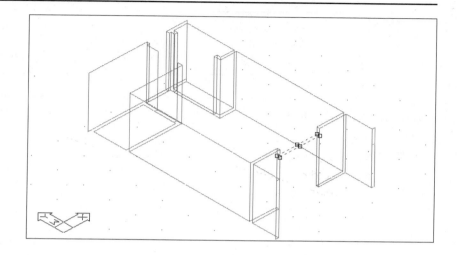

7. Click the Properties button on the Object Properties toolbar and change the thickness of the header to 1' (30cm) using the Thickness input box. Click OK.

8. Click the four lines representing the door header for the closet and entry.

9. Repeat steps 3 through 7. Your drawing will look like Figure 15.8.

10. Use the View Control dialog box (choose View ➤ Named Views) to create a new view under the name of 3D. See *Saving Views* in Chapter 6 if you need help saving views.

FIGURE 15.8:

The headers with the new thickness

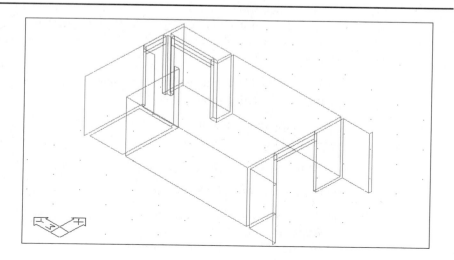

You could have used the Move command to move the lines to their new eleva-tion, entering the same **@0,0,7'** at the Specify second point of displacement or <use first point as displacement>: prompt for Move. Because you must select objects to edit them using grips, with the Move command, you save a step by not having to select the lines a second time for the Properties tool.

Creating a 3D Object

Though you may visualize a design in 3D, you will often start sketching it in 2D and later generate the 3D views. When you know from the start what the thickness and height of an object will be, you can set these values so that you don't have to extrude the object later. The following exercise shows you how to set elevation and thickness before you start drawing.

1. Choose Format ➤ Thickness.

2. Enter **12"**⏎ at the Enter new value for THICKNESS <0.0000>: prompt. Metric users should enter **30**⏎. Now as you draw objects, they will appear 12" (30cm).

3. Draw a circle representing a planter at one side of the balcony (see Figure 15.9). Make it 18" (45cm for metric users) in diameter. The planter appears as a 3D object with the current thickness and elevation settings.

FIGURE 15.9:

The planter

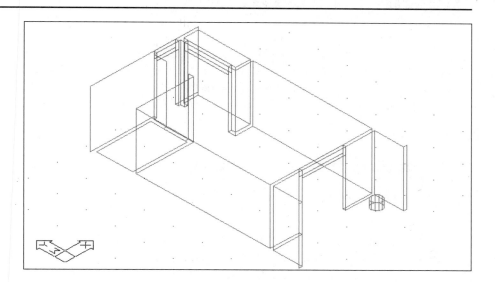

If you use the same thickness and elevation often, you can even create a template file with these settings so they are readily available when you start your drawings. The command for setting thickness and elevation is Elev. You can also use the Elevation and Thickness system variables to set the default elevation and thickness of new objects.

Having set the thickness setting to 12" (30cm), everything you draw will have a thickness of 12 inches (30cm) until you change it back to 0 or some other setting.

You can also change the default elevation from 0 to some other positive or negative value. To do this, you type **Elev⏎** and then enter the elevation you want. You are then prompted for a thickness as well.

Giving objects thickness and modifying their elevation is a very simple process, as you have seen. With these two properties, you can create nearly any three-dimensional form you need. Next, you will discover how to control your view of your drawing.

Viewing a 3D Drawing

Your first 3D view of a drawing is a Wireframe view. It appears as if it were an open model made of wire; none of the sides appear solid. This section describes how to manipulate the Wireframe view so you can see your drawing from any angle. This section will also describe how, once you have selected your view, you can view the 3D drawing as a solid object with the hidden lines removed. You will also learn methods for saving views for later recall.

Finding Isometric and Orthogonal Views

First, let's start by looking at some of the viewing options available. You used one option already to get the current 3D view. That option, View ➢ 3D Views ➢ SW Isometric, brings up an Isometric view from a southwest direction, where north is the same direction as the y-axis. Figure 15.10 illustrates the three other Isometric View options: SE Isometric, NE Isometric, and NW Isometric. In Figure 15.10, the cameras represent the different viewpoint locations. You can get an idea of their location in reference to the grid and UCS icon shown in Figure 15.10.

FIGURE 15.10:

This diagram shows the isometric viewpoints for the four Isometric views available from the View ➤ 3D Views cascading menu.

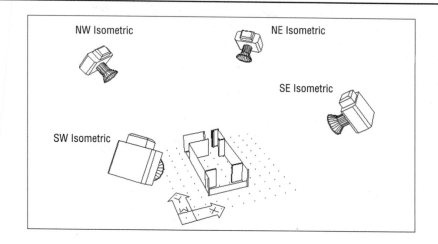

Another set of options available on the View ➤ 3D Views cascading menu are Top, Bottom, Left, Right, Front, and Back. These are Orthogonal views that show the sides, top, and bottom of the model, as shown in Figure 15.11. In this figure, the cameras once again show the points of view.

To give you a better idea of what an Orthogonal view looks like, Figure 15.12 shows the view that you see when you choose View ➤ 3D Views ➤ Right. It is a side view of the unit.

FIGURE 15.11:

This diagram shows the six viewpoints of the Orthogonal view options on the View ➤ 3D Views cascading menu.

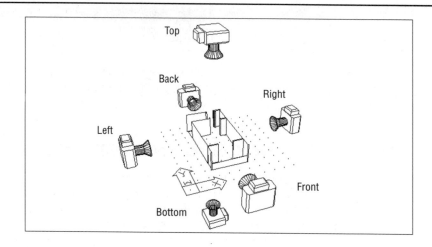

FIGURE 15.12:

The view of the unit model you see when you choose View ➤ 3D Views ➤ Right

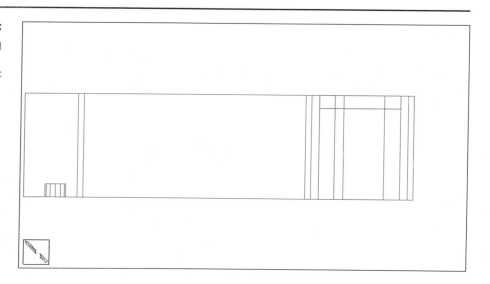

When you use any of the View options described here, AutoCAD attempts to display the extents of the drawing. You can then use the Pan and Zoom tools to adjust your view.

If you find you use these View options frequently, you may want to open the View toolbar.

This toolbar offers quick, single-click access to all the options discussed in this section. To open it, right-click any toolbar, and then click Viewpoint on the Toolbars dialog box.

Using a Dialog Box to Select 3D Views

You now know that you can select from a variety of "canned" viewpoints to view your 3D model. You can also fine-tune your view by indicating an angle from the drawing's x-axis and from the floor plane using the Viewpoint Presets dialog box. The following steps show you how it works.

1.   Click View ➤ 3D Views ➤ Viewpoint Presets, or type **Vp↵**. The Viewpoint Presets dialog box appears (see Figure 15.13). The square dial to the left lets

you select a viewpoint location in degrees relative to the x-axis. The semicircle to the right lets you select an elevation for your viewpoint.

2. Click the area labeled 135 in the upper-left of the square dial. Then click the area labeled 60 in the right-hand semicircle. Notice that the pointer moves to the angle you've selected and the input boxes below the graphic change to reflect the new settings.

3. Click OK. Your view changes according to the new settings you just made.

Other settings in this dialog box let you determine whether the selected view angles are relative to the World Coordinate System or to the current User Coordinate System (UCS is discussed in Chapter 16). You can also go directly to a Plan view by clicking the Set to Plan View button.

There are a couple of features of the Viewpoint Presets dialog box that are not readily apparent. First of all, you can select the exact angle indicated by the label of either graphic by clicking anywhere inside the outlined regions around the pointer (see Figure 15.13). For example, in the graphic to the left, click anywhere in the region labeled 90 to set the pointer to 90 exactly.

You can set the pointers to smaller degree increments by clicking within the pointer area. For example, if you click in the area just below the 90 region in the left graphic, the pointer moves to that location. The angle will be slightly greater or less than 90°.

FIGURE 15.13:

The Viewpoint Presets dialog box

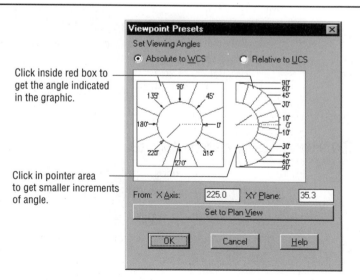

Click inside red box to get the angle indicated in the graphic.

Click in pointer area to get smaller increments of angle.

If you want to enter an exact value from the x-axis or x-y plane, you can do so by entering an angle value in the input boxes provided. You can obtain virtually any view you want using the options offered in the Viewpoint Presets dialog box.

NOTE   Another tool called 3D Orbit can help you visualize your model. 3D Orbit is similar to 3D orbit tools found in other 3D programs. You'll get a detailed look at 3D Orbit in Chapter 16.

Visualizing Your 3D Model

As you work with your 3D model, you will want to get an idea of how it looks with hidden lines removed. Frequently, object intersections and shapes are not readily apparent until you can see what object lies in front of others.

AutoCAD provides two helpful viewing commands for this situation. First, the Hide command allows you to quickly view your drawing with the hidden lines removed. You can then assess where surfaces are and get a better feel for the model. Hide is also an option at plot time, allowing you to create printed line drawings of a 3D model. You can then render the hard copy using manual techniques if you want.

The second command, Shademode, lets you work with your 3D model as if it is composed of opaque surfaces instead of lines. Shademode also has a variety of options for controlling how colors are applied. You can't plot views as they appear when Shademode is turned on. It is intended only as a visualization aid for constructing 3D models.

Let's begin by looking at the Hide command and then discuss the Shademode command.

Removing Hidden Lines

Hide is perhaps the easiest of all the AutoCAD 3D viewing commands to use. Try the following to see a hidden-line view of your model.

1. Restore the view you saved earlier with the name 3D using the View dialog box. This shows you that you can store and recall 3D views as well as 2D views.

2. Choose View ➤ Hide, or enter **Hi**↵ at the command prompt. AutoCAD displays this message:

    Regenerating drawing

    If the drawing is a complex one, a graphic bar appears in the status bar showing the progress of the hidden-line removal. When AutoCAD is done, the image appears with the hidden lines removed (see Figure 15.14).

3. After you've reviewed the results of the View ➤ Hide, choose View ➤ Regen or type **Re**↵ to return to your Wireframe view.

FIGURE 15.14:

A unit in the apartment building drawing with hidden lines removed

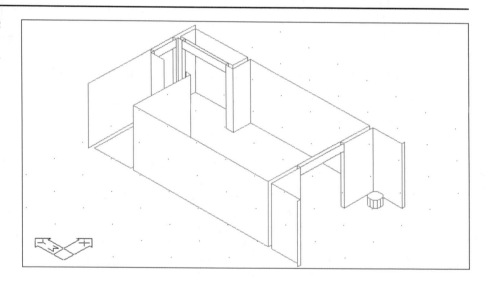

TIP

You can also plot a view with hidden lines removed by checking the Hide Objects check box in the Plot Configuration dialog box before you start your plot. Using the Hide Objects option generally adds only a few minutes to your plot time. If you're plotting a Layout tab, you need to turn on the Hideplot property of the viewport containing the 3D view.

This hidden-line view remains until your drawing is regenerated. Note that you cannot use the View command to save a hidden-line view. You can, however, save this view as a Slide.

NOTE

The Hide command does not hide text objects, unless the text objects have a thickness.

Although it did not take much time to perform a hidden-line removal on this drawing, the more complex the 3D drawing, the longer the Hide command takes. But even the most complex model you create does not take much more than several minutes.

WARNING

If you want to use the Zoom Realtime tool after you use the Hide command, you must choose View ➤ Regen.

Using a Shaded Mode with Your 3D Model

If you're used to working with Wireframe 3D images, the Hide command is usually good enough to give you an idea of how your model looks from time to time as you work on it. But when you want to get an even better visualization of the form your model is taking on, it's time for the Shademode command. To see how Shademode works, try the following exercise.

NOTE

The Shademode command is set up as a toolbar with several tools. Each tool issues the Shademode command and applies a different option. If you prefer, you can enter the Shademode command at the command prompt and enter the appropriate options to get the same results as the toolbar tools.

1. First, open the Shade toolbar by right-clicking any toolbar, then selecting Shade from the popup menu. The Shade toolbar appears.

2. Click the Flat Shaded tool on the Shade toolbar. You can also select View ➤ Shade ➤ Flat Shaded. Notice that a ground plane appears. This is an aid to help you better visualize the model and it isn't actually part of your drawing.

3. Click the GRID button in the status bar. Notice that the 3D grid turns off. Click the GRID button again to turn it back on. The grid you see with the shaded view does not reflect the grid spacing you set in the Drafting Settings dialog box. It's only there to help you visualize the plane represented by the x-y axes at 0 elevation. It also shows you the limits of your drawing, just like the standard grid.

4. Click the Flat Shaded, Edges On tool from the Shade toolbar, or choose View ➢ Shade ➢ Flat Shaded, Edges On from the menu bar. Notice that this time, the edge of the surfaces is highlighted to help you see the surfaces (see Figure 15.15).

5. Now click the Hidden tool or choose View ➢ Shade ➢ Hidden. Your drawing changes to look similarly to the way it looked when you used the View ➢ Hide option. But there is a difference in this option.

6. Choose View ➢ Regen. The view doesn't change. AutoCAD remains in a Shaded view mode until you click 2D Wireframe on the Shade toolbar or View ➢ Shade ➢ 2D Wireframe.

7. Click the 2D Wireframe tool in the Shade toolbar. Your drawing returns to the Wireframe view you started with. Remember this tool when you want to return to the standard 2D Wireframe view of your drawing.

FIGURE 15.15:

The Unit plan shaded using the Flat Shaded, Edges On option

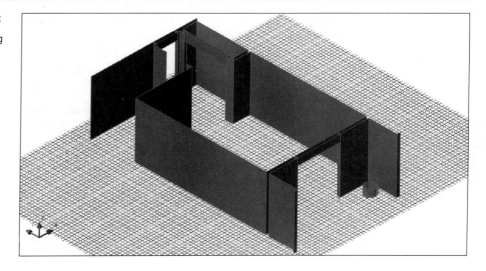

The Hidden Shade mode allows you to better visualize your 3D drawing. Depending on the type of model and its complexity, you can even work on it with the Hidden Shade mode turned on. You can always go back to the Wireframe view using the 2D Wireframe option. In fact, there may be times when you will want to "see through" a wall or other object while you're editing your 3D model. That's when the 2D Wireframe view will be more helpful.

Before you continue editing the Unit plan, you may want to know the functions of the other options on the Shade toolbar. The 3D Wireframe option displays a view similar to the 2D Wireframe view, with the addition of the ground plane you first saw in step 2. The other two options, Gouraud Shade and Gouraud Shade, Edges On are both used to get a smooth shade effect on curved surfaces as shown in Figure 15.16. These Gouraud options don't have an effect on flat surface models like the Unit plan.

FIGURE 15.16:

A sphere shaded using different Shade modes

2D Wireframe   Hidden   Flat Shaded   Gouraud Shaded   Flat Shaded Edges On   Gouraud Shaded Edges On

The Edges On options display the edge of flat surfaces. The spheres in Figure 15.16 are made up of flat surfaces, which can be seen in the Hidden example. The Gouraud Shade options smooth out the facets of the sphere. The Gouraud Shade, Edge On option shows the edges of the facets even though the smoothing effect is on.

There is a third method for visualizing your model that allows you to place varying light sources in your drawing. The AutoCAD rendering functions on the Render toolbar let you adjust light reflectance of surfaces, smooth out faceted surfaces such as spheres and cylinders, and place light sources accurately. You'll get a chance to work with the rendering functions in Chapter 17. For now, let's look at some other factors that affect how a 3D model will look when it is shaded or when hidden lines are removed.

Getting the 3D Results You Want

You've seen how you can make an opaque vertical surface just by changing the thickness property of an object. To make a horizontal surface appear opaque, you must draw it with a wide polyline, a solid hatch, or a 3D Face. For example, consider a table: You might represent the tabletop with a rectangle and give it the appropriate thickness, but the top appears to be transparent when the lines are hidden. Only the sides of the tabletop become opaque. To make the entire tabletop opaque if the tabletop is an irregular shape, you can use a solid hatch or an object called a *region*. Chapter 18 discusses regions. When the lines are hidden, the tabletop appears to be opaque (see Figure 15.17).

FIGURE 15.17:

One table using lines for the top, and another using a solid fill

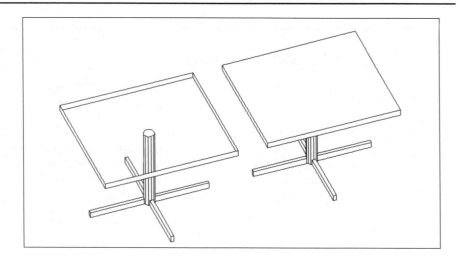

When a circle is used as an extruded form, the top surface appears opaque when you use the Hide command. Where you want to show an opening at the top of a circular volume, as in a circular chimney, you can use two 180° arcs (see Figure 15.18).

FIGURE 15.18:

A circle and two joined arcs

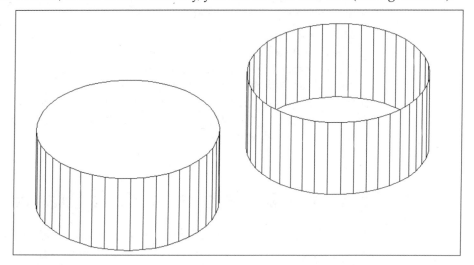

For complex horizontal surfaces, you can use a combination of wide polylines, solids, and 3D Faces to create them. For example, a sidewalk on a street corner would use a donut for the rounder corner, and solids or 3D Faces at either side for the straight portion of the sidewalk. It's okay to overlap surfaces to achieve the effect you want. Polylines are useful for creating window mullions or other shapes that might be formed by a straight extrusion in the real world. (You'll learn how to create a curved extruded shape in Chapter 18).

Setting Layers Carefully

Bear in mind that the Hide command that you used first to hide the Wireframe view hides objects that are obscured by other objects on layers that are turned off. For example, if a couch in the corner of the studio unit is on a layer that is off when you use Hide, the lines behind the couch are hidden even though the couch does not appear in the view (see Figure 15.19). You can, however, freeze any layer containing objects that you do not want affected by the hidden-line removal process. This is important to be aware of since the Hide command reproduces what you see when you plot your drawing. In fact, you can use the Hide command to test your 3D model before you print.

FIGURE 15.19:

A couch hiding a line, when the layer is turned on (top) and turned off (bottom)

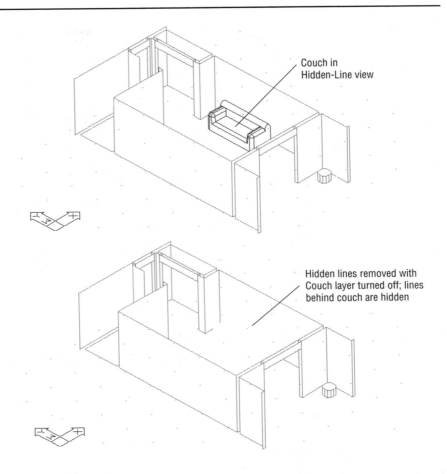

Couch in
Hidden-Line view

Hidden lines removed with
Couch layer turned off; lines
behind couch are hidden

Drawing 3D Surfaces

In your work with 3D so far in this chapter, you have simply extruded existing forms, or you have set AutoCAD to draw extruded objects. But extruded forms have their limitations. Using just extruded forms, it's hard to draw diagonal surfaces in the z-axis. AutoCAD provides the 3D Face object to give you more flexibility in drawing surfaces in three-dimensional space. The 3D Face produces a 3D surface where each corner can be given an x, y, and z value. By using 3D Faces in conjunction with extruded objects, you can create a 3D model of just about anything. When you view these 3D objects in a 2D Plan view, you will see them as 2D objects showing only the x and y positions of their corners or endpoints.

Using Point Filters

Before you start working with 3D surfaces, you should have a good idea of what the z-coordinate values are for your model. The simplest way to construct surfaces in 3D space is to first create some layout lines to help you place the endpoints of 3D Faces.

AutoCAD offers a method for 3D point selection, called *filtering*, that simplifies the selection of z-coordinates. Filtering allows you to enter an *x*, *y*, or *z* value by picking a point on the screen and telling AutoCAD to use only the *x*, *y*, or *z* value of that point, or any combination of those values. If you don't specify a z-coordinate, the current elevation setting is assumed.

In the following exercises, let's imagine you decide to add a new two-story unit to your apartment design. You will add a stair rail to the studio apartment to access that second floor. In doing this, you will practice using 3D Faces and filters. You'll start by doing some setup, so you can work on a copy of the Unit file and keep the old Unit plan for future reference.

1. Save the Unit file, and then use File ➤ Save As to create a drawing called Unitloft from the current file. (You can also use the Unitloft.dwg file supplied on the companion CD-ROM.)

2. Choose Format ➤ Thickness and set the Thickness to 0.   *unit3d*

3. Set the current layer to Wall.

Now you are ready to lay out your stair rail.

1. Click the Line tool on the Draw toolbar.

2. At the Specify first Point: prompt, Shift+click the right mouse button to bring up the Osnap menu; then pick Point Filters ➤ .xy. As an alternative, you may enter **.xy**↵ instead of using the Osnap menu. By doing this, you are telling AutoCAD that you are going to first specify the x-coordinate and y-coordinate for this beginning point, and then later indicate the z-coordinate.

NOTE   Notice the .X, .Y, and .Z options on the Object Snap menu (Shift+right-click). These are the 3D filters. By choosing one of these options as you select points in a 3D command, you can filter an *x*, *y*, or *z* value, or any combination of values, from that selected point. You can also enter filters through the keyboard.

---

3. At the `Specify first Point: .xy of:` prompt, pick a point that is 2'-7" (79cm for metric users) from the corner of the bathroom near coordinate 25'-6",25'-5". (Metric users use the coordinate 777,775.) This will be the first line at the bottom of the stair rail. (You don't need to be too exact because we are just practicing.)

4. At the `(need Z):` prompt, enter **9'**↵ (the z-coordinate). Metric users enter **274**↵.

5. At the `Specify next point or [Undo]:` prompt, pick .xy again from the Osnap menu, or enter **.xy**↵.

6. Enter **@12' <270**↵. Metric users enter **@365<270**↵. This locates the x-coordinate and y-coordinate for the other end of the stair rail.

7. At the `(need Z):` prompt, enter **0**↵.

8. Press ↵ to end the Line command. Your drawing should look like Figure 15.20.

FIGURE 15.20:

3D view of the stair rail

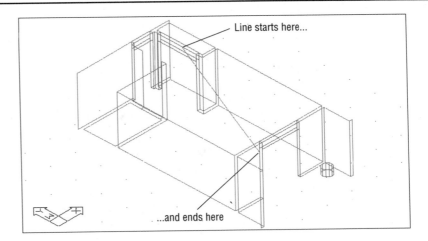

Line starts here...

...and ends here

Now you will copy the line vertically to draw the top of the stair rail.

1. Click the Copy Object button on the Modify toolbar.

2. Select the 3D line you just drew, and press ↵.

3. At the `Specify base point or displacement, or [Multiple]:` prompt, pick any point on the screen.

4. At the prompt

   `Specify second point of displacement or <use first point as displacement>:`

   enter **.xy⏎**, and then enter **@⏎**. This tells AutoCAD that your second point will maintain the x-coordinate and y-coordinate of the first point.

5. At the `(need Z)` prompt, enter **3'6"⏎** to place the copy 3'-6" on the z-axis. Metric users should enter **106⏎** to place the copy 106cm on the z-axis. A copy of the 3D line appears 3'-6" (106cm) above the original.

In step 4 you specified that the second point used the same x-coordinate and y-coordinate of the base point, so you only needed to enter the z value for the second point. In the earlier exercise, you used a relative coordinate to move door headers to a position 7' higher than their original location. You could have used the same method here to copy the line vertically, but in this exercise you got a chance to see how the point filter works.

Creating Irregular 3D Surfaces

Sometimes you will want to draw a solid surface so that when you remove hidden lines, objects will appear as surfaces rather than wireframes. If you were to continue drawing the side of the stair rail using lines, the side of the stair rail would appear transparent. So the next step is to fill in the side using 3D Faces.

TIP   It generally makes life easier to first draw a wireframe of your object using lines, and then use their endpoints to fill in the surfaces.

Loading the Surfaces Toolbar

The 3DFace command and AutoCAD's 3D shapes are located in the Surfaces toolbar. Right-click any toolbar, then click Surfaces in the popup menu.

Adding a 3D Face

Now that you've opened the Surfaces toolbar, you can begin to draw 3D Faces.

1. Zoom in to the two lines you just created, so you have a view similar to Figure 15.21.

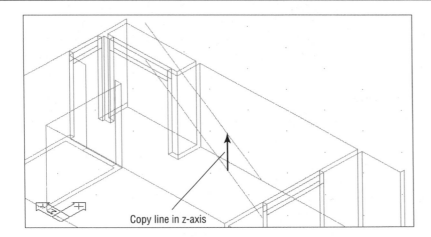

Copy line in z-axis

2. Click the 3D Face button on the Surfaces toolbar, or type **3f↵**. You can also choose Draw ➤ Surfaces ➤ 3D Face.

3. At the Specify first point or [Invisible]: prompt, use the Osnap overrides to pick the first of the four endpoints of the 3D lines you drew. Be sure the Ortho mode is off.

> **TIP**
>
> The Running Osnap mode can help you select endpoints quickly in this exercise. See Chapter 3 if you need help remembering how to set up the Running Osnap mode.

4. As you continue to pick the endpoints, you are prompted for the second, third, and fourth points.

NOTE

With the 3DFace command, you pick four points in a circular fashion, as shown in Figure 15.22. Once you've drawn one 3D Face, you can continue to add more by selecting more points.

---

5. When the `Specify third point or [Invisible] <exit>:` prompt appears again, press ↵ to end the 3DFace command. A 3D Face appears between the two 3D lines. It is difficult to tell if they are actually there until you use the Hide command, but you should see vertical lines connecting the endpoints of the 3D lines. These vertical lines are the edges of the 3D Face (see Figure 15.22).

FIGURE 15.22:

The 3D Face

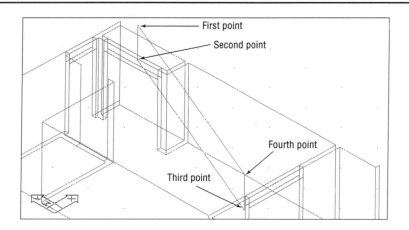

NOTE

When the `Specify third point or [Invisible] <exit>:` prompt reappears, you can draw more 3D Faces if you like. The next 3D Face will use the last two points selected as the first two of its four corners—hence the prompt for a third point.

---

6. Copy the 3D Face you just drew 5" horizontally in the 0-angle direction.

7. Use the 3DFace command to put a surface on the top and front side of the rail, as demonstrated in the top and middle images of Figure 15.23.

8. Use the Intersection Osnap override to snap to the corners of the 3D Faces.

9. Use the Hide command to get a view that looks like the bottom image of Figure 15.23.

10. Copy the three 3D Faces you just created 3' horizontally in the 0-angle direction.

11. Now you can save the `Unitloft.dwg` file.

The top and front faces of the stair rail, and the stair rail with the hidden lines removed

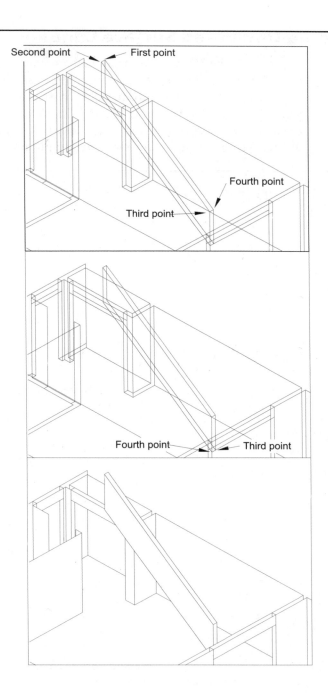

Hiding Unwanted Surface Edges

When using the 3DFace command, you are limited to drawing surfaces with four sides. You can, however, create more complex shapes by simply joining several 3D Faces. Figure 15.24 shows an odd shape constructed of three joined 3D Faces. Unfortunately, you are left with extra lines that cross the surface as shown in the top image of Figure 15.24; but you can hide those lines by using the Invisible option under the 3DFace command, in conjunction with the Splframe variable.

FIGURE 15.24:

Hiding the joined edge of multiple 3D Faces

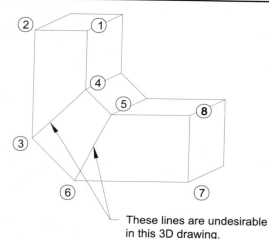

These lines are undesirable in this 3D drawing.

Drawing an odd-shaped surface using 3DFace generates extra lines. The numbers in the drawing to the left indicate the sequence of points selected to create the surface.

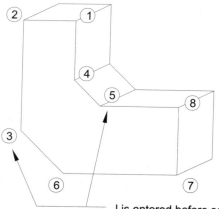

I is entered before selecting points 3 and 5.

By drawing the same surface using the I option before selecting the appropriate points, the unwanted lines will be hidden. This drawing indicates where the I option is issued in the point-selection sequence.

To make an edge of a 3D Face invisible, start the 3DFace command as usual. While selecting points, just before you pick the first point of the edge to be hidden, enter **I**⏎ as shown in the bottom image of Figure 15.24. When you are drawing two 3D Faces sequentially, only one edge needs to be invisible to hide their joining edge.

You can make invisible edges visible for editing by setting the Splframe system variable to 1. Setting Splframe to 0 causes AutoCAD to hide the invisible edges. Bear in mind that the Splframe system variable can be useful in both 3D and 2D drawings.

TIP   The Edge option on the Surfaces toolbar lets you change an existing visible 3D Face edge to an invisible one. Click the Edge button and then select the 3D Face edge to be hidden.

Using Predefined 3D Surface Shapes

You may have noticed that the Surfaces toolbar offers several 3D surface objects, such as cones, spheres, and torus (donut-shaped). All are made up of 3D Faces. To use them, click the appropriate button on the Surfaces toolbar. When you select an object, AutoCAD prompts you for the points and dimensions that define that 3D object; then AutoCAD draws the object. This provides quick access to shapes that would otherwise take substantial time to create.

Things to Watch Out for When Editing 3D Objects

You have seen how you can use the Copy command on 3D lines and 3D Faces. You can also use the Move and Stretch commands on 3D lines, 3D Faces, and 3D shapes to modify their z-coordinate values—but you have to be careful with these commands when editing in 3D. Here are a few tips to keep in mind:

- The Scale command will scale an object's z-coordinate value, as well as the standard x-coordinate and y-coordinate. Suppose you have an object with an elevation of two units. If you use the Scale command to enlarge that object by a factor of 4, the object will have a new elevation of 2 units times 4, or 8 units. If, on the other hand, that object has an elevation of 0, its elevation will not change, because 0 times 4 is still 0.

Continued on next page

- Array, Mirror, and Rotate (on the Modify toolbar) can also be used on 3D lines, 3D Faces, and 3D shapes, but these commands won't affect their z-coordinate values. Z-coordinates can be specified for base and insertion points, so take care when using these commands with 3D models.

- Using the Move, Stretch, and Copy commands (on the Modify toolbar) with object snaps can produce some unpredictable and unwanted results. As a rule, it is best to use point filters when selecting points with Osnap overrides. For example, to move an object from the endpoint of one object to the endpoint of another on the same z-coordinate, invoke the .XY point filter at the `Specify base Point...` and `Specify second Point...` prompts before issuing the endpoint override. Proceed to pick the endpoint of the object you want; then enter the z-coordinate, or just pick any point to use the current default z-coordinate.

- When you create a block, the block will use the UCS that is active at the time the block is created to determine its own local coordinate system. When that block is later inserted, it will orient its own coordinate system with the current UCS. (UCS is discussed in more detail in Chapter 16.)

Turning a 3D View into a 2D AutoCAD Drawing

There are many architectural firms that use AutoCAD 3D models to study their designs. Once a specific part of a design is modeled and approved, they convert the model into 2D elevations, ready to plug into their elevation drawing.

At the end of Chapter 11, you learned about a method you can use to convert a 3D model into a 2D AutoCAD drawing. If you need more accuracy in the conversion, configure the AutoCAD Plotter for an ADI Plotter. Set it up to plot a .dxb file. Your plots then generate .dxb files, which you can import using the Insert ➤ Drawing Exchange Binary option in the menu bar. This opens the Select DXB File dialog box from which you can select the appropriate .dxb file.

Creating and Using Slides

Three-dimensional graphics are often handy for presentations, and 3D AutoCAD images are frequently used for that purpose, as well as for producing drafted 2D drawings. You may want to show off some of your 3D work directly from the computer screen. However, if your drawings are complicated, your audience may get impatient waiting for the hidden lines to be removed. Fortunately, AutoCAD provides two commands that let you save a view from your screen in a form that will display quickly.

The Mslide and Vslide commands both save a view as a file on disk. Such a view is called a *slide*. You can display a slide any time you are in the AutoCAD drawing editor. Slides display at redraw speed, no matter how complex they may be. This means you can save a slide of a hidden-line view of your 3D drawing and recall that view quickly at any time.

Slides can also be used for reference during editing sessions, instead of panning, zooming, or viewing. A slide cannot be edited, however, nor will it be updated when you edit the drawing.

Creating Slides

In the following exercise, you will make a few slides of the Unit file.

1. Open the Unit file and click the Hide button on the Render toolbar to get a hidden-line view of the unit.

2. Type **Mslide.⏎** at the command prompt.

3. In the File dialog box, click Save to accept the default filename, Unit.sld. (The default slide name is the same name as the current drawing, with the extension .sld.) The actual drawing file is not affected.

4. Zoom in to the bathroom, and use Mslide to save another view called Unit-bath, this time without the hidden lines removed.

5. When the File dialog box appears, highlight the File input box at the bottom of the dialog box, enter **Unitbath.⏎**, and click OK.

Viewing Slides

Now that you've saved two views, let's see how to view them.

1. Zoom back to the previous view and then type **Vslide.⏎**.

2. In the File dialog box, locate and select Unitbath.dwg and click Open. The slide of the bathroom appears. You can move the cursor around the view and start commands in the normal way, but you cannot edit or obtain information from this slide.

3. Start Vslide again.

4. This time, click Open in the dialog box to accept the default slide filename, Unit. The 3D view of the unit appears with its hidden lines removed. Because slides display at redraw speed, you don't have to wait to view the unit without its hidden lines.

NOTE   Any command that performs a redraw also returns you to the current drawing.

5. Choose View ➤ Redraw to return to the drawing being edited.

6. Open the Plan file and use the Vslide command to view the Unitbath slide again. As you can see, you are able to call up the slide from any file, not just the one you were in when you created the slide.

7. Now create a Slide of the Plan file and call it Plan1.

Next, you'll get to see how you might automate a slide presentation using the slides you just created.

Automating a Slide Presentation

As mentioned in Chapter 7, Script (Tools ➤ Run Script) can be used to run a sequence of commands automatically. Let's create a script file to automatically show the slides you made in the last exercise.

A script file is really nothing more than a list of "canned" AutoCAD commands and responses. In this example, you'll add the Delay command, whose sole function is to pause a script for a specific length of time.

1. Create a new file called Show.

2. Use a text editor like the Windows Notepad to create a file called Show.scr, and enter the following lines into this file, pressing ↵ at the end of each line:

```
vslide
unit
```

```
delay 3000
vslide
unitbath
delay 3000
vslide
Plan1
```

These lines are a sequence of predetermined instructions to AutoCAD that can be played back later. Save this file in the same place where your slide files are located. When you play this script file, each line is entered at the AutoCAD command prompt, just as you would enter it through the keyboard. Notice that the Vslide command is executed before each slide, which is then followed by the line delay 3000, which tells AutoCAD to pause roughly 3,000 milliseconds after each Vslide command is issued (you can substitute another value if you like). If no delay is specified, the next slide comes up as soon as the previous slide is completed.

You can also have the slides repeat themselves continuously by adding the Rscript command at the very end of the Show.scr file. You may want to do this in a presentation intended for casual viewing, such as an exhibit in a display area with people passing through. To stop a repeating script, press the Backspace key.

Now try playing the script.

1. Return to AutoCAD, and then choose Tools ➤ Run Script, or enter **Script**↵.

2. In the Select Script File dialog box, highlight and pick the file you just created (Show.scr) from the file list, and then click OK.

The slides you saved will appear on the screen in the sequence in which you entered them in the Show.scr file.

Creating a Slide Library

You can group slide files together into one file to help keep your slides organized—for example, by project or by drawing type. Slide libraries also save disk space, since they often require less space than the total consumed by the individual slide files.

Slide files are also used to create custom dialog boxes that show sample views of objects. An example of such a dialog box is the 3D Objects dialog box, which is displayed when you select Draw ➤ Surfaces ➤ 3D Surfaces.

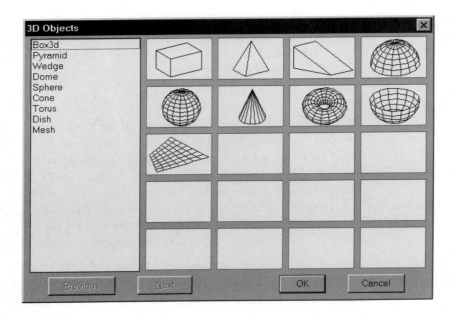

The tool you use to create a slide library is the Slidelib.exe utility that comes with AutoCAD. This utility can be found in the \Support\ subdirectory of AutoCAD 2000. To create a slide library, follow these steps.

1. Use a word processor and make a list of the slides you want to include in the library. For the slides you created earlier, it would look like the following:

   ```
   unit
   unitbath
   plan1
   ```

   Notice that you do not have to include the .sld extension in the filenames in your list.

2. Save this list as a plain text file, with an appropriate name. For this example, call it Slide1.lst. Be sure it is saved in the same directory as your slide files.

3. Locate the Slidelib.exe program; you should find it in \Support\ subdirectory. Be sure your Slidelib.exe file is in the same directory as your slide list file and slide files.

   Do not include the filename extension; the Slidelib utility program automatically adds the file extension .slb. For example, if you use Plans as the library name in step 4, a slide library file called Plans.slb is created.

4. Open a DOS window and go to your AutoCAD \Support\ subdirectory.

5. At the DOS prompt, enter **slidelib Myslides < slide1.lst**↵. A file named Myslides.slb is created. The library name can be any legal DOS filename, but don't use filenames over eight characters long, such as those allowed by Windows 95/98.

Now let's test your slide library. To view a slide from a slide library, you use the Vslide command. This time, however, you will specify the filename differently. Instead of picking a slide name from the dialog box, you must enter the name at the prompt line in a special format. The name must be entered with the library name first, followed by the individual slide name in parentheses.

1. Open a new temporary file called Temp, and at the AutoCAD command prompt, enter **Vslide**↵.

2. In the File dialog box, click the Type It button. This causes the dialog box to close and lets you complete the command from the command line.

3. At the Slide file< current file name>: prompt, enter **Myslides(plan1)**↵. The slide appears in the drawing area.

WARNING   If you placed the slide library file in a directory other than the current one, be sure to enter the directory name before the slide library name in step 3.

To use slide libraries from a script, you use the slide library and slide name following the Vslide command, as in the following example:

```
vslide
myslides(unit)
delay 3000
vlside
myslides(unitbath)
delay 3000
vslide
myslides(plan1)
delay 3000
rscript
```

You've seen how you can save and display 3D views quickly and how you can automate a presentation of slides using scripts. With these tools, you can create an impressive, fast-paced presentation.

If You Want to Experiment...

Architects traditionally use 3D models made from cardboard or *chipboard* to help others visualize their ideas. And if you've ever taken a class in architectural design, chances are you've had to make such a model yourself. 3D modeling on a computer is faster and a lot more fun than creating a physical chipboard model, and in some cases it can show you things that a physical model cannot.

The following exercise is really just for fun. It shows you how to do a limited form of animation, using View ➤ 3D Viewpoint, the Mslide command, and scripts.

1. Open the Unit plan.

2. Do a hidden-line removal; then use Mslide to create a slide called V1.

3. Click and drag the Inquiry button on the Object Properties toolbar, and then select Locate Point on the flyout. Pick a point in the center of the floor plan. This marks the view center for the next step.

4. Enter **Vpoint.⏎ R.⏎** at the command prompt.

5. At the Enter angle at XY plane: prompt, enter **235⏎**; at the next prompt, press ⏎.

6. Do another hidden-line removal, and use Mslide again to create a slide called **V2**.

7. Repeat steps 4 through 6, but this time increase by 10 the angle value you entered at step 5 (to **245**). At step 6, increase the slide name by 1 (to **V3**).

8. Keep repeating steps 4 through 6, increasing the angle value by 10 each time and increasing the slide filename by 1. Repeat these steps at least five more times.

9. Use a text editor to create a script file called `Animate.scr`, containing the following lines, pressing ⏎ at the end of each line:

```
Vslide v1
Vslide v2
Vslide v3
Vslide v4
Vslide v5
Vslide v6
```

```
Vslide v7
Vslide v8
Rscript
```

10.   Return to AutoCAD. At the command prompt, enter **Script** and click Animate in the File dialog box. Then click OK and watch the show.

11.   Press the Esc key or Backspace to end the show.

You might also want to try creating an animation that moves you completely around the Unit plan.

Here's another suggestion for experimenting: To practice drawing in 3D, turn the kitchen of your 3D Unit drawing into a 3D object. Make the cooking top 30" high and add some cabinet doors.

Have fun!

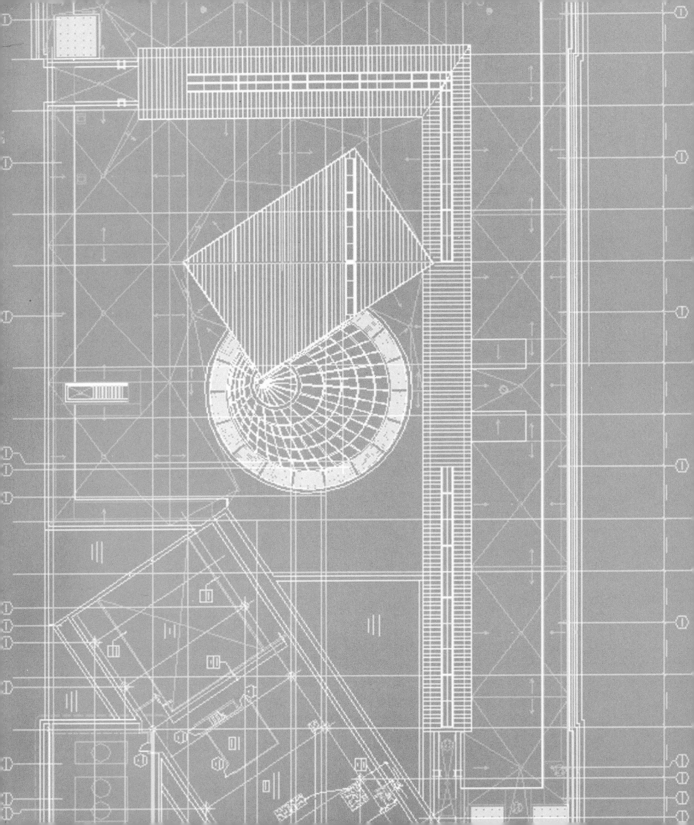

Using Advanced 3D Features

AutoCAD's extended set of tools for working with 3D drawings lets you create 3D objects with few limitations on shape and orientation. This chapter focuses on the use of these tools, which help you easily generate 3D forms and view them in both the Perspective and Orthogonal modes.

Mastering the User Coordinate System

The User Coordinate System (UCS) allows you to define a custom coordinate system in 2D and 3D space. In fact, you've been using a special UCS called the World Coordinate System (WCS) all along.

By now you are familiar with the L-shaped icon in the lower-left corner of the AutoCAD screen, containing the letters W, X, and Y. The W indicates that you are currently in the WCS; the X and Y indicate the positive directions of the x- and y-axes. WCS is a global system of reference from which you can define other User Coordinate Systems.

It may help to think of these AutoCAD User Coordinate Systems as different drawing surfaces, or two-dimensional planes. You can have several User Coordinate Systems at any given time. By setting up these different UCSs, you are able to draw as you would in the WCS in 2D, yet draw a 3D image. Suppose you want to draw a house in 3D with doors and windows on each of its sides. You can set up a UCS for each of the sides; then you can move from UCS to UCS to add your doors and windows (see Figure 16.1). Within each of these UCSs, you draw your doors and windows as you would in a typical 2D drawing. You can even insert elevation views of doors and windows that you have created in other drawings.

FIGURE 16.1:

Different User Coordinate Systems in a 3D drawing

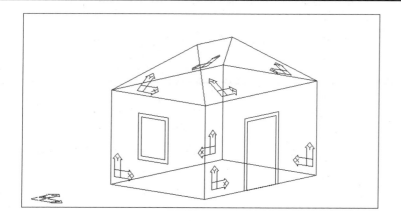

In this chapter you will be experimenting with a number of different views and UCSs. All of the commands you will use are available both at the command line and via the menu bar. In addition, a number of the UCS commands can be accessed from the UCS toolbar.

Defining a UCS   In the first set of exercises, you will draw a chair that you can later add to your 3D Unit drawing. In drawing this chair, you will be exposed to the use of the UCS, as well as to some of the other 3D capabilities available in AutoCAD.

Begin the chair by drawing the seat and seat back.

1. Start AutoCAD and create a new file called `Barcelon`.

2. Set up your drawing as an architectural drawing with a scale of 1"=1'-0" on an 8 1/2" × 11" sheet. You will want to set the upper-right corner of the limits to 132 × 102. If you're a metric user, you'll be drawing the chair at a scale of 1 to 10 on an A4 sheet. Your work area should be 297 × 210, which is the equivalent of a 297cm by 210cm area.

TIP

If you are a metric user and you prefer to work in millimeters, then you can set the upper-right corner of the limits to 2970,2100. Then, when the book specifies a length or coordinate, multiply the specified value by 10. For example, 50cm becomes 500mm. Coordinate 50,50 becomes 500,500. Your scale factor would also change to 100.

---

3. Choose View ➢ Zoom ➢ All or type **Z↵ A↵**.

4. To draw the seat of the chair, click the Rectangle tool on the Draw toolbar. Draw a rectangle measuring 20" in the x-axis and 30" in the y-axis. Position the rectangle so the lower-left corner is at the coordinate 2'-0",2'-0" (see the top image of Figure 16.2). Metric users should draw a rectangle that is 50cm by 76cm with its lower-left corner at coordinate 50,50.

5. To draw the back of the chair, draw another rectangle 17" in the x-axis and 30" in the y-axis, just to the right of the previous rectangle (see the top image of Figure 16.2). Metric users should make this rectangle 43cm by 76cm.

6. Choose View ➢ 3D Views ➢ SW Isometric. This gives you a 3D view from the lower-left of the rectangles, as shown in the bottom image of Figure 16.2.

7. Select the two rectangles, then click the Properties tool on the Standard toolbar.

8. At the Properties dialog box, enter **3** in the Thickness setting and click OK. This gives the seat and back a thickness of 3". Metric users should make the thickness 7.6cm.

9. Close the Properties dialog box.

10. Zoom out a bit and give yourself some room to work.

FIGURE 16.2:

The chair seat (top) and back (bottom) in the Plan and Isometric views

Notice that the UCS icon appears in the same plane as the current coordinate system. The icon will help you keep track of which coordinate system you are in. Now you can see the chair components as 3D objects.

Next, you will define a UCS that is aligned with one side of the seat.

1. Right-click any toolbar, and at the popup menu, select UCS. The UCS toolbar appears.

2. Click the Display UCS Dialog tool in the UCS toolbar.

The UCS dialog box appears.

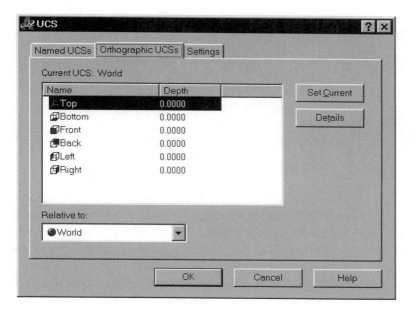

3. Select the Orthographic UCSs tab to view a set of predefined UCSs.

4. Select Front in the list box. Figure 16.3 shows the orientation of the Front UCS.

5. Click the Set Current button to make the Front UCS the current one.

6. Click OK to close the dialog box.

The Orthographic UCSs tab offers a set of predefined UCSs for each of the six standard orthographic projection planes. Figure 16.3 shows these UCSs in relation to the World Coordinate System. You can also access these orthographic UCSs from the Tools ➤ Orthographic UCS cascading menu, or from the UCS dialog box.

FIGURE 16.3:

The six predefined UCS orientations

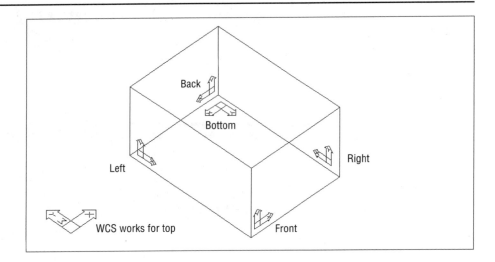

Since a good part of 3D work involves drawing in these orthographic planes, AutoCAD supplies these ready-made UCS orientations for quick access. But you aren't limited to these six orientations by any means. If you're familiar with mechanical drafting, you'll see that the orthographic UCSs correspond to the typical orthographic projection used in mechanical drafting. If you're an architect, the Front, Left, Back, and Right UCSs correspond to the south, west, north, and east elevations of a building. Before you continue building the chair model, you'll want to move the UCS to the surface on which you will be working. Right now, the UCS has its origin located in the same place as the WCS origin. You can move a UCS so that its origin is anywhere in the drawing where it's needed.

1. Click the Origin UCS tool in the UCS toolbar.

2. Use the Endpoint Osnap and click the bottom-front corner of the chair seat, as shown in Figure 16.4. The UCS icon moves to indicate its new origin's location.

FIGURE 16.4:

Setting up a UCS

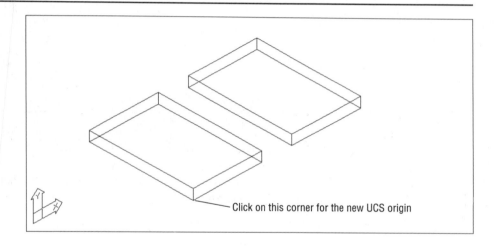

Click on this corner for the new UCS origin

The operation you just performed created a new UCS based on the Front UCS you selected from the UCS dialog box. Now as you move your cursor, you'll see that the origin of the UCS icon corresponds to a 0,0 coordinate. Though you've got a new UCS, the World Coordinate still exists, and you can always return to it when you need to.

Saving a UCS

Once you've gone through the work of creating a UCS, you may want to save it, especially if you think you'll want to come back to it later on. Here's how to save a UCS.

1. Click Display UCS Dialog on the UCS toolbar. You can also choose Tools ➢ Named UCS. The UCS dialog box appears.

2. Make sure the Named UCS tab is selected, and then highlight the Unnamed option in the Current UCS list box.

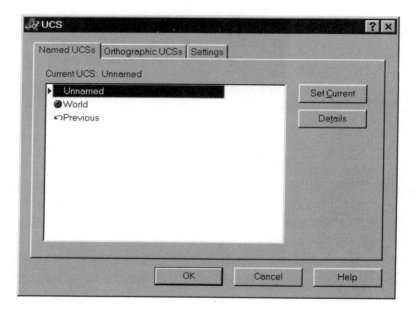

3. Right-click Unnamed, and then select Rename from the list box. The item changes to allow editing.

4. Type **3DSW**↵ for the name of your new UCS.

5. Click OK to exit the dialog box.

   Your UCS is now saved under the name of 3DSW. You'll be able to recall it from the UCS dialog box, or from other methods that you'll learn about later in this chapter.

Working in a UCS

Next, you will want to arrange the seat and back and draw the legs of the chair. Your UCS is oriented so that you can easily adjust the orientation of the chair components to their proper orientation. As you work through the next exercise, notice that while you are manipulating 3D objects, you are really using the same tools you've used to edit 2D objects.

1. Click the seat back to expose its grips.

2. Click the bottom grip, as shown in the first image of Figure 16.5.

3. Right-click the mouse to open the Grip Edit popup menu.

4. Select Rotate from the menu. Notice how the seat back now rotates with the movement of the cursor. Take a moment to play with this rotation, as it may take a while to grow accustomed to it. Since this is an Isometric view, you can get an optical illusion effect.

5. Type **80.**⌐ to rotate the seat back 80°. Your view will look like the second image of Figure 16.5.

6. Click the bottom grip shown in the second image of Figure 16.5.

7. Right-click the mouse again and select Move.

8. Using the Endpoint Osnap, click the top corner of the chair seat, as shown in the second image of Figure 16.5, to join the chair back to the seat.

9. Click both the chair seat and back; then click the bottom-corner grip of the seat, as shown in the third image of Figure 16.5.

10. Right-click the mouse; then at the Grip Edit popup menu, click Rotate.

11. Enter **–10.**⌐ to rotate both the seat and back a minus 10 degrees. Press the Esc key twice to clear the grips. Your chair will look like Figure 16.6.

The new UCS orientation enabled you to use the grips to adjust the chair seat and back. All of the grip rotation in the previous exercise was confined to the plane of the new UCS. Mirroring and scaling will also occur in relation to the current UCS.

FIGURE 16.5:

Moving the components of the chair into place

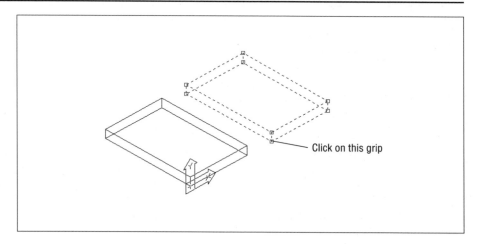

Click on this grip

FIGURE 16.5
CONTINUED:

FIGURE 16.5
CONTINUED:

Moving the components of
the chair into place

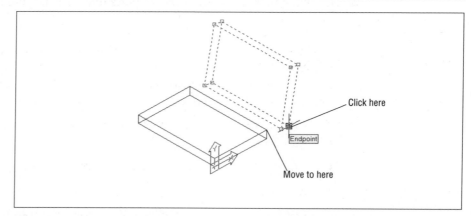

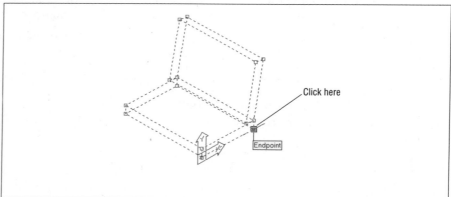

FIGURE 16.6:

The chair, after rotating and
moving the components
into place

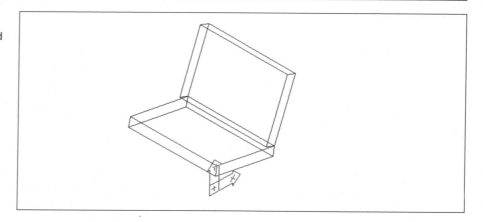

Now to finish the chair seat and back, add a 3D Face to their top and bottom surfaces.

1. To help you visualize what's going on as you add the 3D Face, turn on the Hidden Shade mode by choosing View ➤ Shade ➤ Hidden. Or, if you have the Shade toolbar open, you can click the Hidden tool.

2. Click the 3D Face button on the Surfaces toolbar, or choose Draw ➤ Surfaces ➤ 3D Face, to draw a surface over the top sides of the chair seat and back. Start the 3D Face in the leftmost corner of the seat and work in a counterclockwise fashion.

NOTE   To display the Surfaces toolbar, right-click any toolbar, then choose Surfaces from the Toolbars dialog box. If you need help with the 3DFace command, see Chapter 15.

3. Add the 3D Faces to the bottom of the chair seat and to the chair back, as shown in Figure 16.7.

4. When you've finished adding the 3D Faces, turn off the Hidden Shade mode. Choose View ➤ Shade ➤ 2D Wireframe.

FIGURE 16.7:

The 3D view of your drawing so far, showing where to pick points for the 3D Face

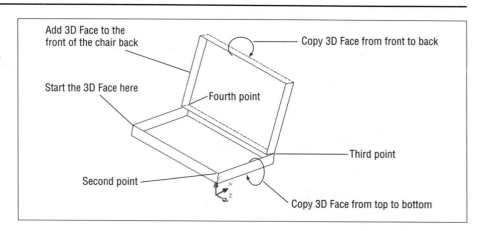

Normally, when picking points for 3D Faces, it doesn't matter where you start selecting points. But for the purpose of this tutorial, you selected points for the seat's 3D Face starting at the leftmost corner and working in a counterclockwise fashion. The way you create the chair seat will influence the action of some UCS command options which you'll use later in this chapter.

Controlling the UCS Icon

If the UCS icon is not behaving as described in the exercises of this chapter, then chances are that its settings have been altered. You can control the behavior of the UCS icon through the UCS dialog box. To access the UCS dialog box, choose Tools ➤ Named UCS. You can also click the Display UCS Dialog tool on the UCS II or UCS toolbar. Once you've opened the dialog box, click the Settings tab.

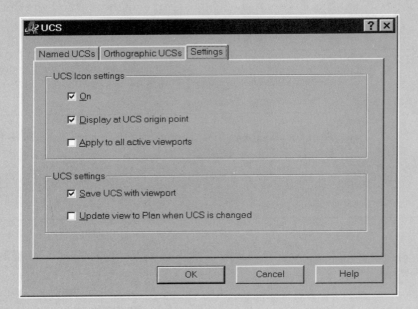

The settings in the UCS Icon Settings group affect the way the UCS icon behaves. Normally, the On and Display at UCS Origin Point check boxes are checked. If On is not checked, you won't see the UCS Icon at all. If Display at UCS Origin Point is not checked, the UCS icon will remain in the lower-left corner of the drawing window, no matter where its origin is placed in the drawing.

If you have multiple viewports set up in a drawing, you can set these two options independently for each viewport. The third option, Apply to All Active Viewports, forces the first two settings to apply in all viewports.

Continued on next page

Two more options appear in the UCS settings group. If you have multiple viewports open, the Save UCS with Viewport option allows AutoCAD to maintain a separate UCS for each viewport. The Update View to Plan When UCS is Changed option forces the display to show a plan view of the current UCS. This means that if you change a UCS orientation, AutoCAD will automatically show a plan view of the new UCS orientation.

Using Viewports to Aid in 3D Drawing

In Chapters 7 and 12, you were introduced to AutoCAD's floating viewports in Paper Space. In this section, you will use *tiled* viewports to see your 3D model from several sides at the same time. This is helpful in both creating and editing 3D drawings because it allows you to refer to different portions of the drawing without having to change views. Tiled viewports are created directly in Model Space.

1. Select View ➤ Viewports ➤ Named Viewports. The Named Viewports dialog box appears.

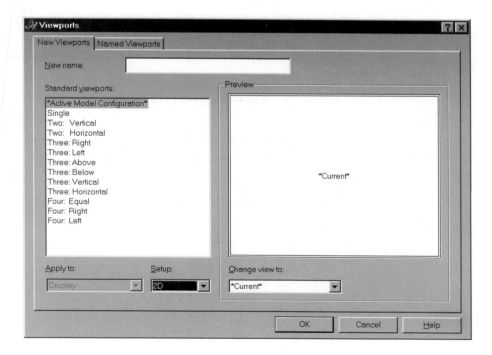

2. Make sure the New Viewports tab is selected, then click Three: Right from the Standard Viewports list on the left. The window on the right changes to display a sample of the viewport configuration. It shows three rectangles, which represent the viewports, arranged with two on the left and one larger one to the right. Notice that each rectangle is labeled as Current. This tells you that the current view will be placed in each viewport.

3. Open the Setup drop-down list at the bottom of the dialog box and select 3D. Now notice that the labels in the viewport sample change to indicate Top, Front, and SE Isometric. This is close to the arrangement that you'll want, but you need to make one more adjustment. The viewport to the right, SE Isometric, shows the backside of the chair. You want an SW Isometric view in this window.

4. Click the SE Isometric viewport sample. Notice that the sample viewport border thickens to indicate that it is selected.

5. Open the Change View To drop-down list just below the sample viewports and select SW Isometric. The label in the selected viewport changes to let you know that the view will now contain the SW Isometric view. Notice that the list contains the standard four isometric views and the six orthogonal views. By clicking a sample viewport and selecting an option from the Change View To drop-down list, you can arrange your viewport views in nearly any way you want.

6. To keep this viewport arrangement, enter **My Viewport Setup** in the New Name input box.

7. Now click OK. Your display changes to show three viewports arranged as they were indicated in the Viewports dialog box (see Figure 16.8).

8. To check to see that your viewport was saved, Choose View ➢ Viewports ➢ Named Viewports to open the Viewports dialog box again.

9. Click the Named Viewports tab. My Viewport Setup is listed in the Named Viewports list box. If you click it, a sample view of your viewport arrangement appears on the right.

10. After you've reviewed the addition to the Named Viewports list, close the dialog box.

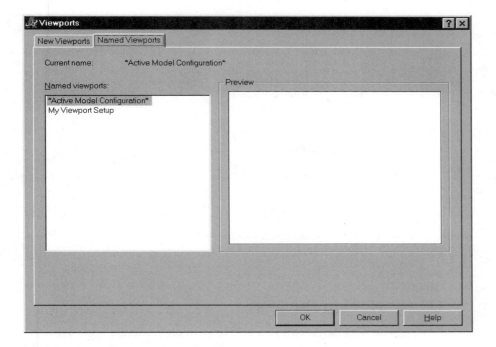

Now take a close look at your viewport setup. Notice that the UCS icon in each of the two orthogonal views in the two left viewports are oriented to the plane of the view. AutoCAD allows you to set up a different UCS for each viewport. The top view uses the WCS since it is in the same plane as the WCS. The side view has its own UCS, which is parallel to its view. The isometric view to the right retains the UCS you saved—namely the 3DSW UCS.

Another Viewports dialog box option you didn't try is the Apply To drop-down list in the New Viewports tab of the Viewports dialog box.

This list shows two options: Display and Current Viewport. When Display is selected, the option you choose from the Standard Viewports list applies to the overall display. When Current Viewport is selected, the option you select applies to the selected viewport in the sample view in the right side of the dialog box. You can use the Current Viewport option to build multiple viewports in custom arrangements.

FIGURE 16.8:

Three viewports, each displaying a different view

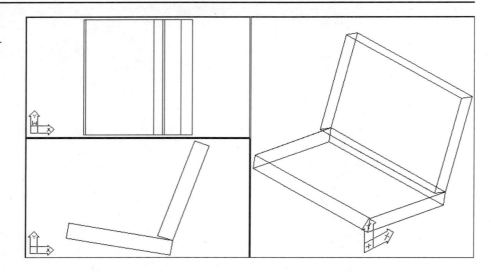

FIGURE 16.8:

Three viewports, each displaying a different view

Adding the Legs

The next items you will add to your chair are the legs. Before you do that, you'll want to set up the 3DSW UCS in the side view of your chair.

1. Click the lower-left viewport to make it active.

2. Click the Display UCS Dialog tool on the UCS toolbar.

3. Select the Named UCSs tab, then select 3DSW from the list of UCSs.

4. Click the Set Current button. The triangular marker to the left of the UCS names moves to 3DSW.

5. Click OK.

Now you're ready to draw the legs using the coordinate information shown in Figure 16.9.

Now let's finish off the chair by adding legs.

1. Go to the side view of the chair and move the chair seat and back vertically in the y-axis 8.5" or 21.6cm for metric users. Make sure you select all the lines and 3D Faces for the move. You may have to pan the view down so that the entire chair is displayed.

TIP If you anticipate moving a group of 3D objects frequently, use the Group command to group objects together. The Group command is especially useful in 3D work, since you can group sets of objects together for easy manipulation, yet you can still edit the individual objects within a group.

2. Next, draw two curved polylines, as shown in Figure 16.9. You may have to adjust your view so that you can draw the legs more easily. You don't have to be absolutely perfect about placing or shaping these lines.

3. Use the grips of the polylines to adjust their curve, if necessary.

4. Use Modify ➣ Polyline to give the polylines a width of 0.5" (1.27cm for metric users).

5. Use the Properties dialog box to give the polylines a thickness of –2" (minus 2 inches). Metric users should make the thickness –5cm. Notice that as you draw and edit a polyline, it appears in both the Plan and 3D views.

6. Close the Properties dialog box when you are done changing the thickness property.

NOTE Polylines are the best objects to use for 3D, because you can generate complex shapes easily by giving the polylines thickness and width.

FIGURE 16.9:

Drawing the legs of the chair. Metric coordinates are shown in brackets.

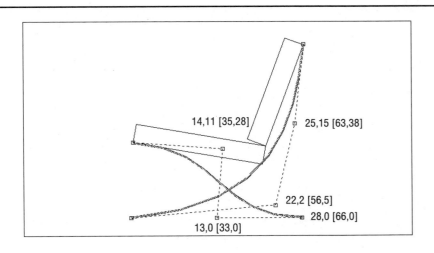

14,11 [35,28]   25,15 [63,38]

22,2 [56,5]

28,0 [66,0]

13,0 [33,0]

7. Click the top view of the chair in the upper-left viewport.

8. Turn the Ortho mode on, and then click the Mirror tool on the Modify toolbar.

9. In the upper-left viewport, click the two polylines representing the chair legs, then press ↵.

10. At the First point of mirror line: prompt, use the Midpoint Osnap and select the midpoint of the chair seat, as shown in Figure 16.10.

11. At the second point, pick any location to the right of the point you selected, so that the rubber-banding line is exactly horizontal.

12. Press ↵ at the Delete old object: prompt. The legs are mirrored to the opposite side of the chair. Your screen should look similar to Figure 16.10.

NOTE   Notice that the broken-pencil UCS icon has shifted to the viewport in the lower-left corner. This icon tells you that the current UCS is perpendicular to the plane of that view.

FIGURE 16.10:

Mirroring the legs from one side to another

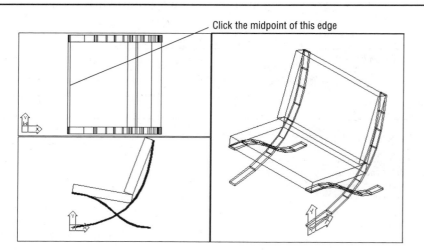

Click the midpoint of this edge

Your chair is now complete. Let's finish up by getting a better look at it.

1. Click the viewport to the right showing the isometric view.

2. Open the Viewport dialog box and select the New Viewport tab.

3. Select Single from the Standard Viewports list, and then click OK.

4. Choose View ➤ Hide to get a view of your chair with the lines hidden, as shown in Figure 16.11.

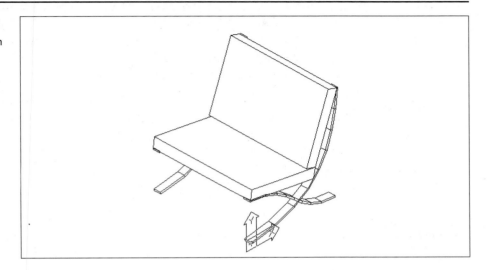

Controlling the UCS   You've seen how you can select a UCS from a set of pre-defined UCSs. You can frequently use these preset UCSs and make minor adjustments to them to get the exact UCS you want.

There are also a number of other ways to define a UCS. You can, for example, use the 3D Face of your chair seat as the definition for a UCS. In the following set of exercises, you will get some practice moving your UCS around. Learning how to move effortlessly between UCSs is crucial to your mastering the creation of 3D models, so you'll want to pay special attention to the command options shown in these procedures. These options are accessible from either the Tools ➤ UCS cascading menu or the UCS toolbar.

UCS Based on Object Orientation

You can define a UCS based on the orientation of an object. This is helpful when you want to work on a predefined object to fill in detail on its surface plane.

1. Click the Object UCS tool on the UCS toolbar, or choose Tools ➤ New UCS ➤ Object. You can also type **UCS↵ OB↵**.

2. At the Select object to align UCS: prompt, pick the 3D Face used to define the top surface of the chair seat. Because the 3D Face and the polyline outline of the seat share a common edge, you may need to use the Selection Cycling feature to pick the 3D Face. The UCS icon shifts to reflect the new coordinate system's orientation (see Figure 16.12).

TIP If you have a Hidden-Line view, selection cycling will not work for picking 3D Faces. Issue a Regen to return to a wireframe view.

FIGURE 16.12:

Using the Object option of the UCS command to locate a UCS

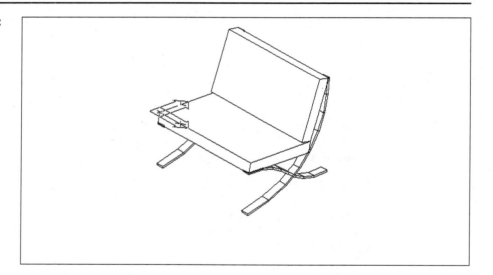

Orientation of the UCS Origin Remember earlier in the chapter when you drew the 3D Face for the seat in a specific way? Well, the location of the UCS origin and its orientation depend on how that 3D Face was created. If you had drawn it other than as instructed, the UCS you defined using the Object option in the above exercise would not have been generated as described.

Table 16.1 describes how an object can determine the orientation of a UCS.

TABLE 16.1:   Effects of Objects on the Orientation of an UCS

Object Type	UCS Orientation
Arc	The center of the arc establishes the UCS origin. The x-axis of the UCS passes through the pick point on the arc.
Circle	The center of the circle establishes the UCS origin. The x-axis of the UCS passes through the pick point on the circle.
Dimension	The midpoint of the dimension text establishes the origin of the UCS origin. The x-axis of the UCS is parallel to the x-axis that was active when the dimension was drawn.
Line	The endpoint nearest the pick point establishes the origin of the UCS, and the x-z plane of the UCS contains the line.
Point	The point location establishes the UCS origin. The UCS orientation is arbitrary.
2D Polyline	The starting point of the polyline establishes the UCS origin. The x-axis is determined by the direction from the first point to the next vertex.
Solid	The first point of the solid establishes the origin of the UCS. The second point of the solid establishes the x-axis.
Trace	The direction of the trace establishes the x-axis of the UCS with the beginning point setting the origin.
3D Face	The first point of the 3D Face establishes the origin. The first and second points establish the x-axis. The plane defined by the 3D Face determines the orientation of the UCS.
Shapes, Text, Blocks, Attributes, and Attribute Definitions	The insertion point establishes the origin of the UCS. The object's rotation angle establishes the x-axis.

UCS Based on Offset Orientation

There may be times when you want to work in a UCS that has the same orientation as the current UCS but is offset. For example, you may be making a drawing of a building that has several parallel walls offset with a sawtooth effect (see Figure 16.13). You can easily hop from one UCS to another parallel UCS by using the Origin option.

1. Click the Origin UCS tool on the UCS toolbar, or choose Tools ➤ New UCS ➤ Origin. You can also type **UCS↵ O↵**.

2. At the `Origin point <0,0,0>:` prompt, pick the bottom end of the chair leg, just below the current UCS origin. The UCS icon shifts to the end of the leg, with its origin at the point you picked (see Figure 16.14).

FIGURE 16.13:

Using the Origin option to shift the UCS

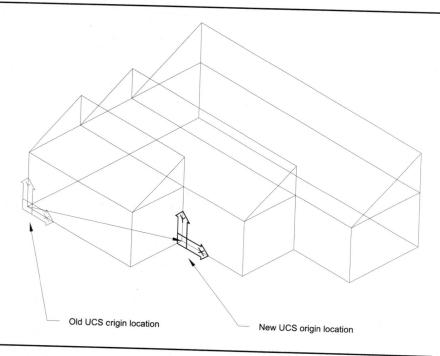

Old UCS crigin location   New UCS origin location

FIGURE 16.14:

Moving the origin of the UCS

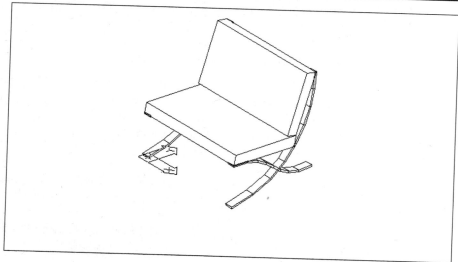

Moving vs. Creating a UCS Origin

The Origin UCS tool creates a new UCS that you can save under its own name. Another option that is very similar to the Origin UCS tool is the Move UCS option on the Tools pull-down menu. At first glance, they seem to do the same thing, that is, create a new UCS by moving an existing UCS's origin. There is a subtle difference between the two, however. The Tools ➤ Move UCS option is intended to move an existing named UCS to a new location. It doesn't actually create a new one. For example, if you use Move UCS to move the 3DSW UCS you created earlier in this chapter, then when you recall 3DSW, it will appear in its new location. On the other hand, if you use the Origin UCS tool to change the origin of the 3DSW UCS, Auto-CAD creates an entirely different UCS and maintains the original location of 3DSW.

The Tools ➤ Move UCS option can also be found on the UCS II toolbar. You'll get a chance to work with the UCS II toolbar in the next section.

UCS Rotated Around an Axis

Now suppose you want to change the orientation of the x-, y-, or z-axis of a UCS. You can accomplish this by using the X, Y, or X Axis Rotate UCS options on the UCS toolbar. Let's try rotating the UCS about the z-axis to see how this works.

1. Click the Z Axis Rotate UCS tool on the UCS toolbar, or choose Tools ➤ New UCS ➤ Z Axis Rotate. You can also type **UCS⏎ Z⏎**. This will allow you to rotate the current UCS around the z-axis.

2. At the Rotation angle about Z axis <0>: prompt, enter **90** for 90°. The UCS icon rotates to reflect the new orientation of the current UCS (see Figure 16.15).

Similarly, the X and Y Axis Rotate UCS options allow you to rotate the UCS about the current x- and y-axis, respectively, just as you did for the z-axis above. The X and Y Axis Rotate UCS tools are very helpful in orienting a UCS to an inclined plane. For example, if you want to work on a plane of a sloped roof of a building, you can first use the Origin UCS tool to align the UCS to the edge of a roof and then use the X Axis Rotate UCS tool to rotate the UCS to the angle of the roof slope, as shown in Figure 16.16.

FIGURE 16.15:

Rotating the UCS about the
z-axis

FIGURE 16.15:

Rotating the UCS about the
z-axis

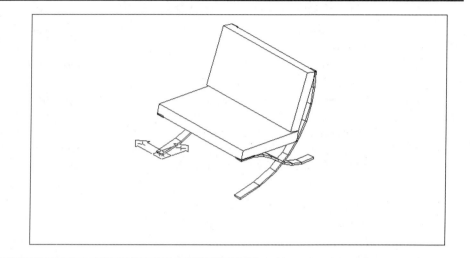

FIGURE 16.16:

Moving a UCS to the plane
of a sloping roof

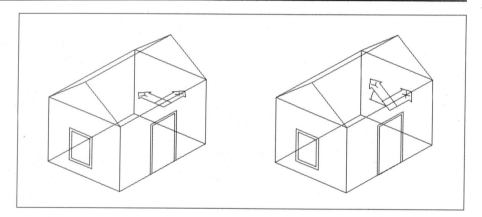

Finally, you can skew the UCS using the Z Axis Vector option. This is useful
when you need to define a UCS based on a z-axis determined by two objects.

1. Click the Z Axis Vector UCS tool on the UCS toolbar, or choose Tools ➤ UCS ➤
    Z Axis Vector. You can also type **UCS⏎ ZA⏎**.

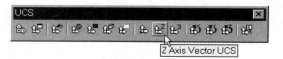

2. At the `Origin point <0,0,0>:` prompt, press ↵ to accept the default, which is the current UCS origin. You can shift the origin point at this prompt if you like.

3. At the next prompt:

   `Point on positive portion of Z-axis <0'-0", 0'- 0", 0'-1">:`

   use the Endpoint Osnap override and pick the other chair leg end, as shown in Figure 16.17. The UCS twists to reflect the new z-axis of the UCS.

WARNING   Because your cursor location is in the plane of the current UCS, it is best to pick a point on an object using either the Osnap overrides or the coordinate filters.

FIGURE 16.17:

Picking points for the Z Axis Vector option

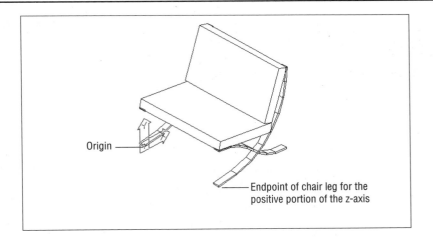

Origin

Endpoint of chair leg for the positive portion of the z-axis

Orienting a UCS in the View Plan

Finally, you can define a UCS in the current view plane. This is useful if you want to switch quickly to the current view plane for editing or for adding text to a 3D view.

Click the View UCS tool on the UCS toolbar, or choose View ➤ Set UCS ➤ View. You can also type **UCS**↵ **V**↵. The UCS icon changes to show that the UCS is aligned with the current view.

AutoCAD uses the current UCS origin point for the origin of the new UCS. By defining a view as a UCS, you can enter text to label your drawing, just as you would in a technical illustration. Text entered in a plane created in this way appears normal (see Figure 16.18).

FIGURE 16.18:

Adding text to a 3D view using the View option of the UCS command

The Barcelona Chair

Now you've finished your tour of the UCS command. Set the UCS back to the World Coordinate System and save the `Barcelon.dwg` file.

You've explored nearly every option in creating a UCS, except for one. In the next section, you'll learn about the 3 Point option for creating a UCS. The 3 Point option is the most versatile method for creating a UCS, but it is a bit more involved than some of the other UCS options.

TIP   A new feature in AutoCAD 2000 is the ability to save a UCS with a view. Choose View ➤ Named Views, then select the Named Views tab of the Views dialog box. Click the New button. At the New View dialog box, enter a name for your new view, then make sure the Save UCS with View option is checked. By default, Auto-CAD saves the current UCS with the view. You can also choose a UCS to save with a new view using the UCS Name drop-down list.

Creating Complex 3D Surfaces

In the previous example, you drew a chair composed of objects that were mostly straight lines or curves with a thickness. All the forms in that chair were defined in planes perpendicular to each other. For a 3D model such as this, you can get by using the Orthographic UCSs. At times, however, you will want to draw objects that do not fit so easily into perpendicular or parallel planes. The following exercise demonstrates how you can create more complex forms using some of Auto-CAD's other 3D commands.

Laying Out a 3D Form

In this next group of exercises, you will draw a butterfly chair. This chair has no perpendicular or parallel planes to work with, so you will start by setting up some points that you will use for reference only. This is similar in concept to laying out a 2D drawing. You will construct some temporary 3D lines to use for reference. These temporary lines will be your layout. These points will define the major UCSs needed to construct the drawing. As you progress through the drawing construction, notice how the reference points are established to help create the chair.

1. If it isn't open already, open the Barcelon drawing, and then use File ➢ Save As to save the file under the name Btrfly.

2. Choose View ➢ 3D Views ➢ Plan View ➢ World UCS. Then choose View ➢ Zoom ➢ All to display the overall area of the drawing.

> **NOTE** You will draw the butterfly chair almost entirely while viewing it in 3D. This approach is useful when you are creating complex shapes.

3. Erase the entire contents of the drawing, and then make sure you are in the WCS by choosing Tools ➢ UCS ➢ World.

4. Click Rectangle on the Draw toolbar. Draw a rectangle 20" square with its first corner at coordinate 36,36. Metric users should draw a rectangle 51cm square, with its first corner at coordinate 81,81.

5. Use the Offset tool to offset the square 4" out, so you have two concentric squares with the outer square measuring 28". Metric users should offset 10cm for an outer square measuring 71cm.

6. Move the larger of the two squares, the 28" square, to the left 2". Metric users should move the larger square 5cm to the left. Your screen should look similar to Figure 16.19.

7. Choose View ➤ 3D Viewpoint ➤ SW Isometric. This will give you a view from the lower-left side of the rectangles.

8. Zoom out so the rectangles occupy about a third of the drawing area window.

FIGURE 16.19:

Setting up a layout for a butterfly chair

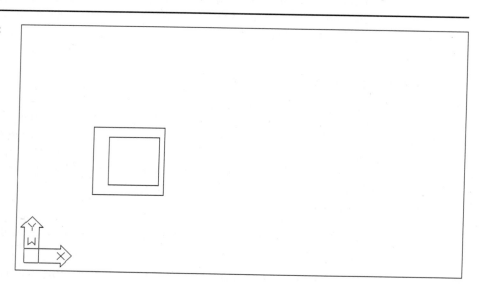

Now you need to move the outer rectangle in the z-axis so that its elevation is 30" (76cm for metric users).

1. Click the outer rectangle, and then click one of its grips.

2. Right-click to open the Grip Edit popup menu.

3. Select Move, and then enter @0,0,30⏎. Metric users should enter @0,0,76⏎. This tells AutoCAD to move the rectangle a 0 distance in both the x- and y-axis, and 30" (or 76cm) in the z-axis.

4. Pan your view downward so it looks similar to Figure 16.20.

5. Use the Line tool and draw lines from the corners of the outer square to the corners of the inner square, as shown in Figure 16.18. Use the Endpoint Osnap to select the exact corners of the squares. This is the layout for your chair—not yet the finished product.

FIGURE 16.20:

The finished chair layout

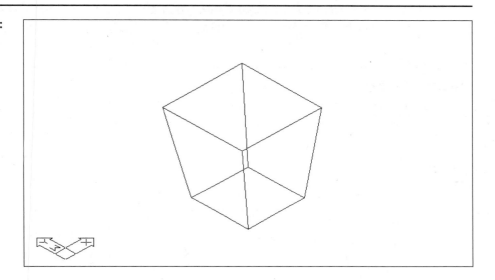

Spherical and Cylindrical Coordinate Formats

In the foregoing exercise, you used relative Cartesian coordinates to locate the second point for the Move command. For commands that accept 3D input, you can also specify displacements by using the *Spherical* and *Cylindrical Coordinate* formats.

The Spherical Coordinate format lets you specify a distance in 3D space while specifying the angle in terms of degrees from the x-axis of the current UCS and degrees from the x-y plane of the current UCS (see the top image of Figure 16.19). For example, to specify a distance of 4.5" (11.43cm) at a 30° angle from the x-axis and 45° from the x-y plane, enter **@4.5<30<45**. (**@11.43<30<45** for metric users). This refers to the direct distance, followed by a < symbol; then the angle from the x-axis of the current UCS followed by another < symbol; then the angle from the x-y plane of the current UCS. To use the spherical coordinate format to move the rectangle in the exercise, enter **@30<0<90** at the Second point: prompt or **@76<0<90** for metric users.

The Cylindrical Coordinate format, on the other hand, lets you specify a location in terms of a distance in the plane of the current UCS and a distance in the z-axis. You also specify an angle from the x-axis of the current UCS (see the bottom image of Figure 16.21). For example, to locate a point that is a distance of 4.5" (11.43cm) in the plane of the current UCS, at an angle of 30° from the x-axis, and a distance of 3.3" (8.38cm) in the z-axis, enter **@4.5<30,3.3** (**@11.43<30,8.38** for metric users). This refers to the distance of the displacement as it relates to the plane of the current

UCS, followed by the < symbol; then the angle from the x-axis, followed by a comma; then the distance in the z-axis. Using the cylindrical format to move the rectangle, you enter **@0<0,30** at the Second point: prompt or **@0<0,76** for metric users.

FIGURE 16.21:

The Spherical and Cylindrical Coordinate formats

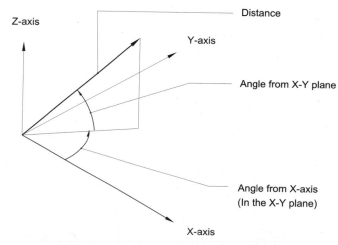

[Distance] < [Angle from X-axis] < [Angle from X-Y plane]

The Spherical Coordinate Format

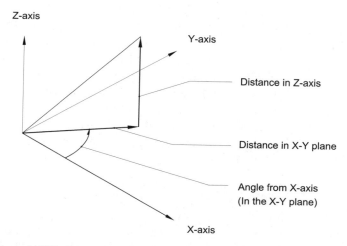

[Distance in X-Y plane] < [Angle from X-axis] , [Distance in Z-axis]

The Cylindrical Coordinate Format

Using a 3D Polyline

Now you will draw the legs for the butterfly chair using a 3D polyline. This is a polyline that can be drawn in 3D space.

1. Choose Draw ➤ 3D Polyline, or type **3p**↵.

2. At the First point: prompt, pick a series of points, as shown in Figure 16.22, using the Endpoint and Midpoint Osnap.

TIP　　This would be a good place to use the Running Osnaps feature.

---

3. Draw another 3D polyline in the mirror image of the first (see Figure 16.22).

4. Erase the rectangles and connecting lines that make up the frame.

FIGURE 16.22:

Using 3D polylines to draw the legs of the butterfly chair

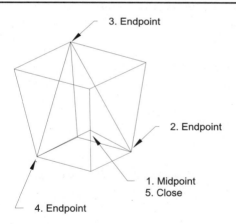

3. Endpoint

2. Endpoint

1. Midpoint
5. Close

4. Endpoint

Draw a polyline in the sequence shown to the left. Use the Osnap overrides indicated in the figure.

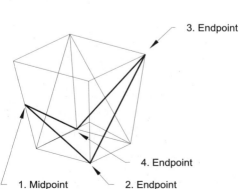

3. Endpoint

4. Endpoint

1. Midpoint
5. Close

2. Endpoint

Repeat the process for the other part of the chair legs.

All objects, with the exception of lines, 3D Faces, 3D Meshes, and 3D polylines, are restricted to the plane of your current UCS. The Pline command can only be used to draw polylines in one plane, but the 3DPoly command allows you to create a polyline in three dimensions. Three-dimensional polylines cannot, however, be given thickness or width.

Creating a Curved 3D Surface

Next, you will draw the seat of the chair. The seat of a butterfly chair is usually made of canvas and drapes from the four corners of the chair legs. You will first define the perimeter of the seat using arcs, and then use the Edge Surface tool on the Surfaces toolbar to form the shape of the draped canvas. The Edge Surface tool creates a surface based on four objects defining the edges of that surface. In this example, you will use arcs to define the edges of the seat.

To draw the arcs defining the seat edge, you must first establish the UCSs in the planes of those edges. Remember, in the last example you created a UCS for the side of the chair before you could draw the legs. In the same way, you must create a UCS defining the planes that contain the edges of the seat.

Since the UCS you want to define is not orthogonal, you will need to use the three-point method. This lets you define the plane of the UCS based on three points.

1. Click the 3 Point UCS tool on the UCS toolbar. You may also choose Tools ➢ UCS ➢ 3 Point, or type **UCS**↵ **3**↵. This option allows you to define a UCS based on three points that you select.

> **NOTE**   Remember, it helps to think of a UCS as a drawing surface situated on the surface of the object you wish to draw or edit.

2. At the Specify new origin point <0,0,0>: prompt, use the Endpoint Osnap to pick the bottom of the chair leg to the far left, as shown in the top panel of Figure 16.23. This is the origin point of your new UCS.

3. At the `Point on positive portion of the X axis:` prompt, use the End-point Osnap to pick the bottom of the next leg to the right of the first one, as shown in the top panel of Figure 16.23.

FIGURE 16.23:

Defining and saving three UCSs

Set up the Front UCS

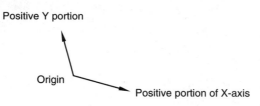

Set up the Side UCS

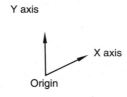

Set up the Back UCS

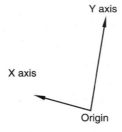

4. At the `Point on positive - Y portion of the UCS X-Y plane:` prompt, pick the top corner of the butterfly chair seat, as shown in the top panel of Figure 16.23. The UCS icon changes to indicate your new UCS.

5. Now that you have defined a UCS, you need to save it so that you can return to it later. Click Display UCS Dialog from the UCS toolbar, or choose Tools ➢ UCS ➢ Named UCS. You can also type **UC**↵. The UCS dialog box appears.

6. With the Named UCSs tab selected, right-click the Unnamed item in the list box, then select Rename.

7. Enter **Front Side**↵.

8. Click OK to exit the UCS dialog box.

WARNING   Don't skip step 4. If you do, you will not get the results you want when you start picking the arc's endpoints in step 5. AutoCAD only draws arcs in the current UCS. Remember: Only lines, 3D polylines, and other 3D objects can be drawn in three-dimensional space. All other objects can be drawn only in the current UCS.

You've defined and saved a UCS for the front side of the chair. As you can see from the UCS icon, this UCS is at a non-orthogonal angle to the WCS. Continue by creating UCSs for the other four sides of the butterfly chair.

1. Define a UCS for the side of the chair as shown in the middle image of Figure 16.23. Use the UCS Control dialog box to rename this UCS Left Side, just as you did for Front Side in steps 5 through 8. Remember that you renamed the Unnamed UCS.

2. Repeat these steps again for a UCS for the back of the chair, named Back. Use the bottom image of Figure 16.23 for reference.

3. Open the UCS dialog box again, and in the Named UCSs tab, highlight Front Side.

4. Click the Current button, and then click OK. This activates Front Side as the current UCS.

5. Choose Draw ➤ Arc ➤ Start, End, Direction.

6. Draw the arc defining the front edge of the chair (see Figure 16.24). Use the Endpoint Osnap override to pick the top endpoints of the chair legs as the endpoints of the arc. (If you need help with the Arc command, refer to Chapter 3.)

7. Repeat steps 3 through 7 for the UCS named Side, and then again for the UCS named Back—each time using the top endpoints of the legs for the endpoints of the arc.

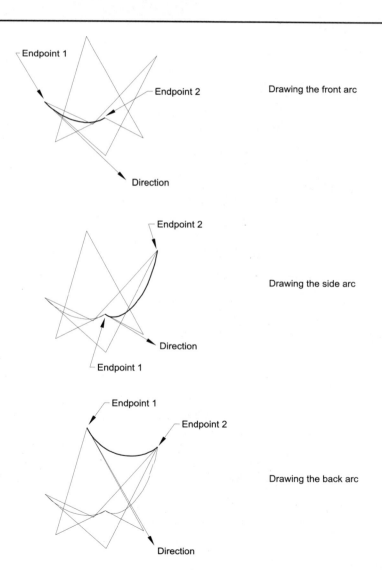

Endpoint 1

Endpoint 2

Direction

Drawing the front arc

Endpoint 2

Direction

Endpoint 1

Drawing the side arc

Endpoint 1

Endpoint 2

Direction

Drawing the back arc

Next, you will mirror the side-edge arc to the opposite side. This will save you from having to define a UCS for that side.

1. Click World UCS on the UCS toolbar. This restores the WCS. The reason for doing this is that you want to mirror the arc along an axis that is parallel to the plane of the WCS. Remember that you must go to the coordinate system that defines the plane you wish to work in.

2. Click the arc you drew for the side of the chair (the one drawn on the Side UCS).

3. Click the midpoint grip of the arc in the Side UCS; then right-click the mouse and select Mirror.

4. Enter **C**↵ to select the Copy option.

5. Enter **B**↵ to select a new base point for the mirror axis.

6. At the `Base point:` prompt, use the Intersect Osnap to pick the intersection of the two lines in the Front plane.

7. Next, use the Intersection override to pick the intersection of the two legs in the Back plane. Refer to Figure 16.25 for help. The arc should mirror to the opposite side, and your chair should look like Figure 16.26.

8. Press the Esc key twice to clear the grips.

FIGURE 16.25:

Mirroring the arc that defines the side of the chair seat

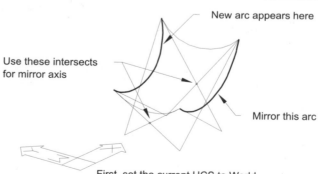

FIGURE 16.26:

Your butterfly chair so far

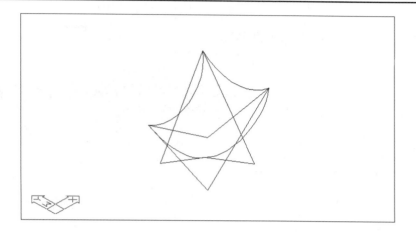

Quick Hops to Your UCSs

If you find you're jumping from one saved UCS to another, you'll want to know about the UCS II toolbar. The UCS II toolbar offers a drop-down list that contains all of the saved UCSs in a drawing. You can use this list as a quick way to move between UCSs that you've set up, or even between the predefined orthogonal UCSs.

Two other tools on the UCS II give you access to the UCS dialog box and the Move UCS origin tool, which moves an existing UCS to another location. As with all toolbars, you can open the UCS II toolbar by right-clicking any toolbar and then selecting UCS II from the popup menu.

Finally, let's finish off this chair by adding the mesh representing the chair seat.

1. Click the Edge Surface tool on the Surfaces toolbar, or enter **Edgesurf.**⏎ at the command prompt.

NOTE   To display the Surfaces toolbar, choose Tools ➤ Toolbars ➤ Surfaces.

2. At the Select edge 1: prompt, pick the arc on the Front UCS.

3. At the Select edge 2: prompt, pick the next arc on the Side UCS.

WARNING   For the command to work properly, the arcs (or any set of objects), used with the Edge Surface option to define the boundary of a mesh, must be connected exactly end-to-end.

4. Continue to pick the other two arcs in succession. (The arcs must be picked in a circular fashion, not crosswise.) A mesh appears, filling the space between the four arcs. Your chair is now complete.

5. Use View ➤ Hide to get a better view of the butterfly chair. You should have a view similar to Figure 16.27.

6. Save this file.

At this point, you've been introduced to a few of the options on the Surfaces toolbar. You'll get a chance to use these later in this chapter. Next, you'll learn how to edit mesh objects like the Butterfly chair's seat.

FIGURE 16.27:

The completed butterfly chair

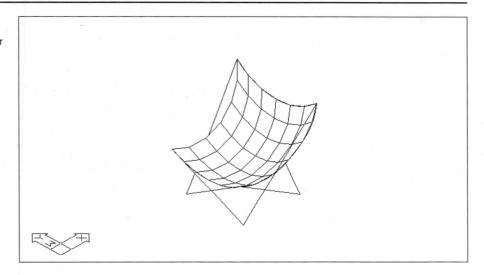

Adjusting the Settings That Control Meshes

As you can see, the seat in our butterfly chair is made up of rectangular segments. If you want to increase the number of segments in the mesh (to get a look like that in Figure 16.28), you can change the Surftab1 and Surftab2 system variables. Surftab1 controls the number of segments along edge 1, the first edge you pick in the sequence; and Surftab2 controls the number of segments along edge 2. AutoCAD refers to the direction of edge 1 as m and the direction of edge 2 as n. These two directions can be loosely described as the x- and y-axes of the mesh, with m being the x-axis and n being the y-axis.

NOTE   See Chapters 13 and 14 and Appendix D for more information on system variables.

In Figure 16.28, the setting for Surftab1 is 24, and for Surftab2 the setting is 12. The default value for both settings is 6. If you would like to try different Surftab settings on the chair mesh, you must erase the existing mesh, change the Surftab settings, and then use the Edge Surface tool again to define the mesh.

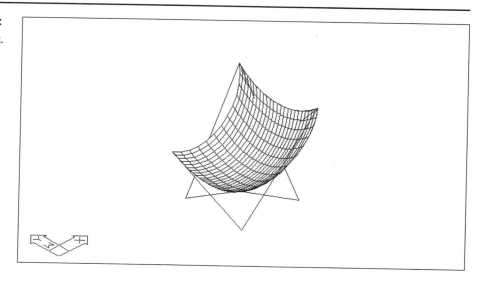

Creating a 3D Mesh by Specifying Coordinates

If you need to draw a mesh like the one in the previous example, but you want to give exact coordinates for each vertex in the mesh grid, you can use the 3DMesh command. Suppose you have data from a survey of a piece of land; you can use 3DMesh to convert your data into a graphic representation of its topography. Another use of the 3DMesh command is to plot mathematical data to get a graphic representation of a formula.

Because you must enter the coordinate for each vertex in the mesh, 3DMesh is better suited in scripts or AutoLISP programs, where a list of coordinates can be applied automatically to the 3DMesh command in a sequential order. See Chapter 19 and the *ABCs of AutoLISP*, which is on the companion CD-ROM for more information on AutoLISP.

Other Surface-Drawing Tools

In the last example, you used the Edge Surface tool to create a 3D surface. There are several other 3D surface commands available that allow you to generate complex surface shapes easily.

TIP   All the objects described in this section, along with the meshes described earlier, are actually composites of 3D Faces. This means that these 3D objects can be exploded into their component 3D Faces, which in turn can be edited individually.

Using Two Objects to Define a Surface

The Ruled Surface tool on the Surfaces toolbar draws a surface between two 2D objects, such as a line and an arc or a polyline and an arc. This command is useful for creating extruded forms that transform from one shape to another along a straight path. Let's see firsthand how the Ruled Surface tool works.

1. Open the file called `Rulesurf.dwg` from the companion CD-ROM. It looks like the top image of Figure 16.29. This drawing is of a simple half-circle, drawn using a line and an arc. Ignore the diagonal blue line for now.

2. Move the line between the arc endpoints 10 units in the z-axis.

3. Now you are ready to connect the two objects with a 3D surface. Click the Ruled Surface tool on the Surfaces toolbar, or choose Draw ➤ Surfaces ➤ Ruled Surface.

4. At the `Select first defining curve:` prompt, place the cursor toward the right end of the arc and click it.

5. At the `Select second defining curve:` prompt, move the cursor toward the right end of the line and click it, as shown in the bottom image of Figure 16.29. The surface will appear as shown in Figure 16.30.

WARNING   The position you use to pick the second object will determine how the surface is generated.

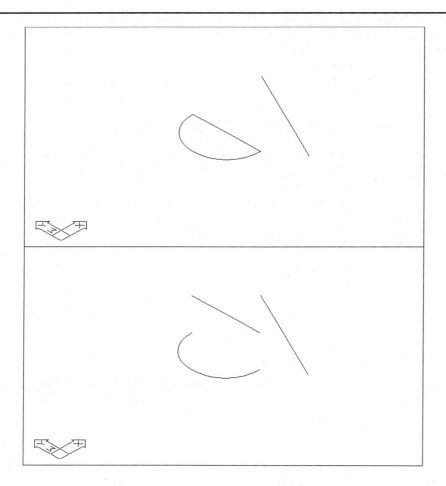

The location you use to select the two objects for the ruled surface is important. You selected specific locations on the arc and line so that the ruled surface is
generated properly. Had you selected the opposite end of the line, for example,
your result would look more like Figure 16.31. Notice that the segments defining
the surface cross each other. This crossing effect is caused by picking the defining
objects near opposite endpoints. The arc was picked near its lower end, and the
line was picked toward the top end. At times, you may actually want this effect.

FIGURE 16.30:

The Rulesurf surface

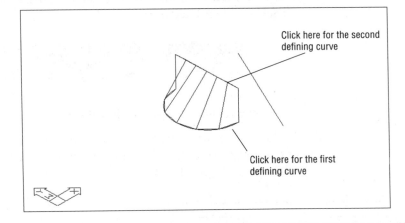

Click here for the second
defining curve

Click here for the first
defining curve

FIGURE 16.31:

The ruled surface redrawn
by using different points to
select the objects

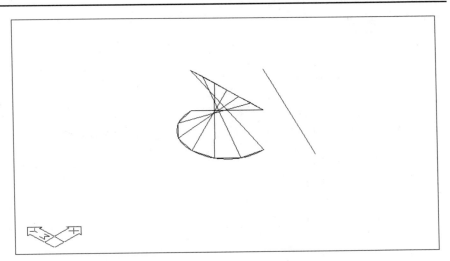

Extruding an Object along a Straight Line

The Tabulated Surface tool also uses two objects to draw a 3D surface, but instead of drawing the surface between the objects, the Tabulated Surface tool extrudes one object in a direction defined by a direction vector. The net result is an extruded shape that is the length and direction of the direction vector. To see what this means firsthand, try the following exercise.

1. While still in the Rulesurf drawing, click the Undo button in the Standard toolbar to undo the ruled surface from the previous exercise.

2. Click the Tabulated Surface tool from the Surface toolbar, or choose Draw ➤ Surfaces ➤ Tabulated Surfaces.

3. At the `Path curve:` prompt, click the arc.

4. At the `Select Direction Vector:` prompt, click the lower end of the blue line farthest to the right. The arc is extruded in the direction of the blue line, as shown in Figure 16.32.

FIGURE 16.32:

Extruding an arc using a line to indicate the extrusion direction

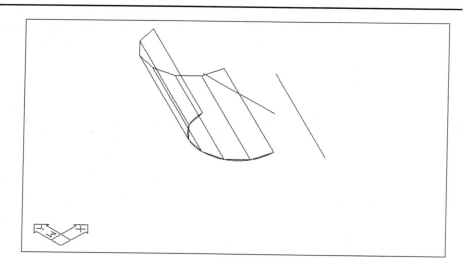

The direction vector can be any object, but AutoCAD will only consider the object's two endpoints when extruding the path curve. Just as with the Ruled Surface tool, the point at which you select the direction vector object affects the outcome of the extrusion. If you had selected a location near the top of the blue line, the extrusion would have gone in the opposite direction from the exercise.

Since the direction vector can point in any direction, the Tabulated Surface tool allows you to create an extruded shape that is not restricted to a direction perpendicular to the object being extruded.

The path curve defining the shape of the extrusion can be an arc, circle, line, or polyline. You can use a curve-fitted polyline or a spline polyline to create more complex shapes, as shown in Figure 16.33.

FIGURE 16.33:

Some samples of other shapes created using the Ruled Surface and Tabulated Surface tools

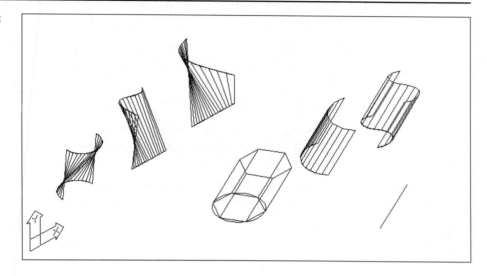

If you want to increase the number of facets in either the Ruled Surface or Tabulated Surface tools, set the Surftab1 system variable to the number of facets you desire.

Extruding a Circular Surface

The Revolved Surface tool allows you to quickly generate circular extrusions. Typical examples are vases or teacups. The following exercise illustrates how the Revolved Surface tool is used to draw a pitcher. You'll use an existing drawing that has a profile of the pitcher already drawn.

1. Open the `Pitcher.dwg` file from the companion CD-ROM. This file contains a polyline profile of a pitcher as well as a single line representing the center of the pitcher (see the top image of Figure 16.34). The profile and line have already been rotated to a position that is perpendicular to the WCS. The grid is turned on so you can better visualize the plane of the WCS.

2. Click the Revolved Surface tool on the Surfaces Toolbar.

3. At the Select Path Curve: prompt, click the polyline profile, as shown in the top image of Figure 16.34.

4. At the Select Axis of Revolution: prompt, click near the bottom of the vertical line representing the center of the vase, as shown in the top image of Figure 16.34.

5. At the Start angle <0>: prompt, press ↵ to accept the 0 start angle.

6. At the Included angle (+=ccw, -=cw) <Full circle>: prompt, press ↵ to accept the Full Circle default. The pitcher appears, as shown in the bottom image of Figure 16.34.

FIGURE 16.34:

Drawing a pitcher using the Revolved Surface tool

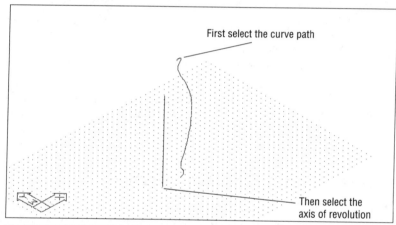

First select the curve path

Then select the axis of revolution

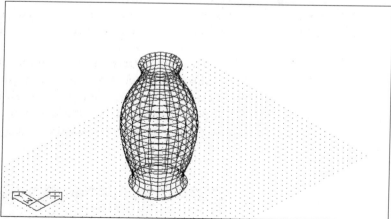

Notice that the pitcher is made up of a faceted mesh, like the mesh that is created by the Edge Surface tool. Just as with the Edge Surface tool, you can set the number of facets in each direction using the Surftab1 and Surftab2 system variable settings. Both Surftab1 and Surftab2 were already set to 24 in the Pitcher.dwg file, so the pitcher shape would appear fairly smooth.

You may have noticed that in steps 5 and 6 of the previous exercise, you have a few options. In step 5, you can specify a start angle. In this case, you accepted the 0 default. Had you entered a different value, 90 for example, then the extrusion would have started in the 90° position relative to the current WCS. In step 6, you have the option of specifying the angle of the extrusion. Had you entered 180, for example, your result would have been half the pitcher. You can also specify the direction of the extrusion by specifying a negative or positive angle.

Editing a Mesh

Once you've created a mesh surface with either the Edge Surface or Revolved Surface tool, you can make modifications to it. For example, suppose you want to add a spout to the pitcher you created in the previous exercise. You can use grips to adjust the individual points on the mesh to reshape the object. Here, you must take care how you select points. The UCS will become useful for editing meshes, as shown in the following exercise.

1. Zoom into the area shown in the first image of Figure 16.35.

2. Click the pitcher mesh to expose its grips.

3. Shift+click the grips shown in the second image of Figure 16.35.

4. Click the grip shown in the third image of Figure 16.35 and slowly drag the cursor to the left. As you move the cursor, notice how the lip of the pitcher deforms.

5. When you have the shape of a spout similar to the second image of Figure 16.35, select that point. The spout is fixed in the new position.

You can refine the shape of the spout by carefully adjusting the position of other grip points around the edge of the pitcher. Later, when you render the pitcher, you can apply a smooth shading value so that the sharp edges of the spout are smoothed out.

Adding a spout to the
pitcher mesh

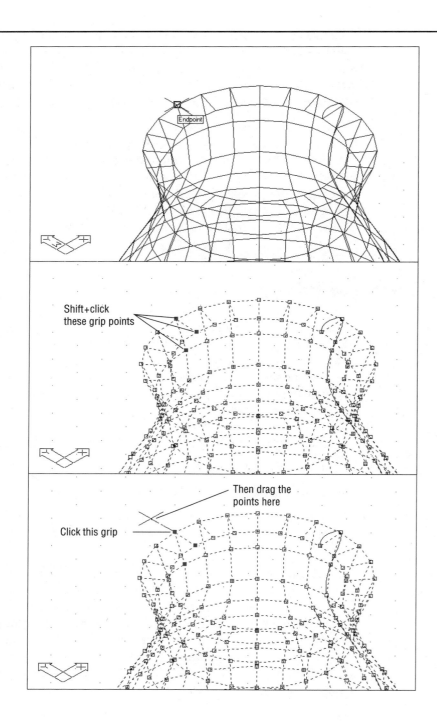

This exercise shows how easy it is to make changes to a mesh by moving individual grip locations. You may want to know, however, that when you move mesh grips manually (as opposed to entering coordinates), their motion is restricted to a plane that is perpendicular to the current UCS. You can use this restriction to your advantage. For example, if you want to move the spout downward at a 30° angle, rotate the UCS so it is tipped at a 30° angle in relation to the top of the pitcher. Then edit the mesh grips as you did in the previous exercise.

Another option would be to specify a *relative* coordinate as opposed to selecting a point. By specifying a coordinate, such as **@.5<50**, you do not have to move the UCS. Using this method, however, removes you from the spontaneity of being able to select a point visually.

Other Mesh-Editing Options

You can use Modify ➤ Object ➤ Polyline to edit meshes in a way similar to editing polylines. When you choose this option and pick a mesh, you get the following prompt:

```
Edit vertex/Smooth surface/Desmooth/Mclose/Nclose/Undo/eXit <X>:
```

Here are the descriptions of these options:

Edit Vertex   Allows you to relocate individual vertices in the mesh.

Smooth Surface   This option is similar to the Spline option for polylines. Rather than having the mesh's shape determined by the vertex points, the Smooth Surface option adjusts the mesh, so that mesh vertices act as control points that pull the mesh—much as a spline frame pulls a spline curve.

TIP   You can adjust the amount of pull the vertex points exert on a mesh by using the Smooth Surface option in conjunction with the Surftype system variable.

Desmooth   Reverses the effects of the Smooth Surface option.

Mclose and **Nclose**   Allow you to close the mesh in either the *m* or *n* direction. When either of these options is used, the prompt line changes, replacing Mclose or Nclose with Mopen or Nopen and allows you to open a closed mesh.

The Edit Polyline tool on the Modify II toolbar performs the same function as Modify ➤ Object ➤Polyline.

Moving Objects in 3D Space

AutoCAD provides two tools for moving objects in 3D space: Align and 3D Rotate. Both of these commands are found on the Rotate flyout of the Modify toolbar. They help you perform some of the more common moves associated with 3D editing.

Aligning Objects in 3D Space

In mechanical drawing, you often create the parts in 3D and then show an assembly of the parts. The Align command can greatly simplify the assembly process. The following exercise describes how Align works.

1. Choose Modify ➤ 3D Operation ➤ Align, or type **Al**↵.

2. At the `Select objects:` prompt, select the 3D source object you want to align to another part. (The *source object* is the object you want to move.)

3. At the `1st source point:` prompt, pick a point on the source object that is the first point of an alignment axis, such as the center of a hole or the corner of a surface.

4. At the `1st destination point:` prompt, pick a point on the destination object to which you want the first source point to move. (The *destination object* is the object with which you want the source object to align.)

5. At the `2nd source point:` prompt, pick a point on the source object that is the second point of an alignment axis, such as another center point or other corner of a surface.

6. At the `2nd destination point:` prompt, pick a point on the destination object indicating how the first and second source points are to align in relation to the destination object.

7. At the `3rd source point:` prompt, you can press ↵ if two points are adequate to describe the alignment. Otherwise, pick a third point on the source object that, along with the first two points, best describes the surface plane you want aligned with the destination object.

8. At the `3rd destination point:` prompt, pick a point on the destination object that, along with the previous two destination points, describes the plane with which you want the source object to be aligned. The source object will move into alignment with the destination object.

Figure 16.36 gives some examples of how the Align tool works.

FIGURE 16.36:

Aligning two 3D objects

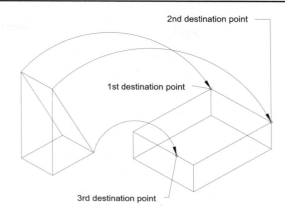

2nd destination point

1st destination point

3rd destination point

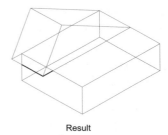

Result

Rotating an Object in 3D

If you just want to rotate an object in 3D space, the Modify ➤ 3D Operation ➤ Rotate 3D option on the menu bar can simplify the operation. Once you've selected this option and selected the objects you want to rotate, you get the following prompt:

```
Axis by Entity/Last/View/Xaxis/YAxis/Zaxis/<2points>:
```

This prompt is asking you to describe the axis of rotation. Here are descriptions of the options presented in the prompt:

> **Entity**   Allows you to indicate an axis by clicking an object. When you select this option, you are prompted to pick a line, circle, arc, or 2D polyline

segment. If you click a line or polyline segment, the line is used as the axis of rotation. If you click a circle, arc, or polyline arc segment, AutoCAD uses the line passing through the center of the circle or arc and perpendicular to its plane as the axis.

Last Uses the last axis that was used for a 3D rotation. If no previous axis exists, you are returned to the `Axis by Entity/Last/View/Xaxis/YAxis/ Zaxis/<2points>:` prompt.

View Uses the current view direction as the direction of the rotation axis. You are then prompted to select a point on the view direction axis to specify the exact location of the rotation axis.

Xaxis/Yaxis/Zaxis Uses the standard x-, y-, or z-axis as the direction for the rotation axis. You are then prompted to select points on the x-, y-, or z-axis to locate the rotation axis.

<2points> Uses two points you provide as the endpoints of the rotation axis.

This completes the lesson on creating and editing 3D objects. You have had a chance to practice using nearly every type of object available in AutoCAD. You might want to experiment on your own with the predefined 3D shapes offered on the Surfaces toolbar. In the next section, you'll discover how you can generate perspective views.

Viewing Your Model in Perspective

So far, your views of 3D drawings have been in *parallel projection*. This means that parallel lines appear parallel on your screen. Although this type of view is helpful while constructing your drawing, you will want to view your drawing in true perspective from time to time, to get a better feel for what your 3D model actually looks like.

AutoCAD provides the 3D Orbit tool to help you get the 3D view you want. You can use the 3D Orbit tool to refine your parallel projection views, but it is also the gateway to perspective views of your model. 3D Orbit has a lot of features and settings. With this in mind, you may want to begin these exercises when you know you have an hour or so to complete them all at one sitting.

If you are ready now, let's begin!

1. Open the Setting.dwg file from the sample files off of the CD-ROM. You'll use this file to practice using the 3D Orbit tool. This file contains a simple 3D model of some chairs, a table, and a lamp.

2. Right-click any toolbar and then select 3D Orbit from the popup list. Open the View toolbar as well.

To set up your view, use the Camera tool on the View toolbar.

1. Choose the Camera tool on the View menu.

2. At the Specify new camera point: prompt, click the lower-left corner of the drawing, as shown in Figure 16.37.

3. At the Specify new camera target: prompt, click the center of the circle that appears in the middle of the drawing, as shown in Figure 16.37. Your view changes to a side view of the chairs, as shown in Figure 16.38.

FIGURE 16.37:

Selecting the camera and target points

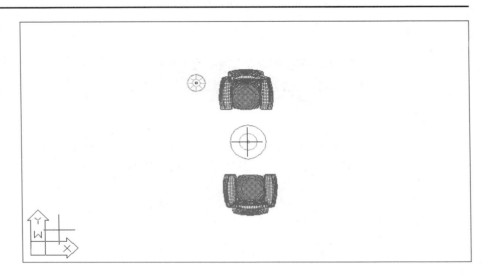

FIGURE 16.38:

The side view of the chairs

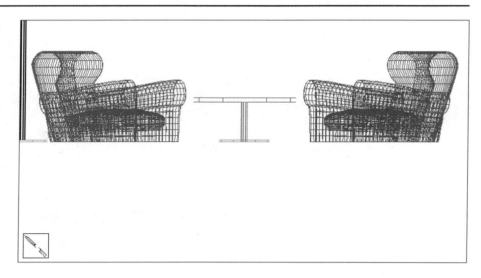

This new view is from the camera point that you specified in step 2. The view's center is the target point you selected in step 3. Now you're ready to use the 3D Orbit tool. The camera and target points you selected are at the 0 coordinate on the z-axis, so your view is aimed at the bottom of the chairs. That's why the view is oriented toward the top of the screen.

1. Click the 3D Orbit tool on the 3D Orbit toolbar. You can also select 3D Orbit from the Standard toolbar.

You see a circle with four smaller circles at its cardinal points. This circle is called an *arcball*. It helps you control your view, along with the cursor.

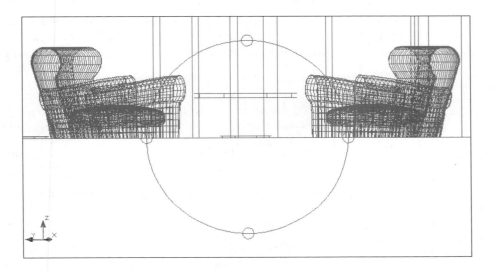

2. Place the cursor on the small circle at the top of the arcball. The cursor changes its appearance to a vertically elongated ellipse.

3. Click and drag the cursor downward from the top circle of the arcball but don't let go yet. The view follows your cursor and the motion is restrained in to a vertical one. When you've got a view similar to Figure 16.39. Release the mouse button.

FIGURE 16.39:

The view after clicking and dragging the top arcball circle

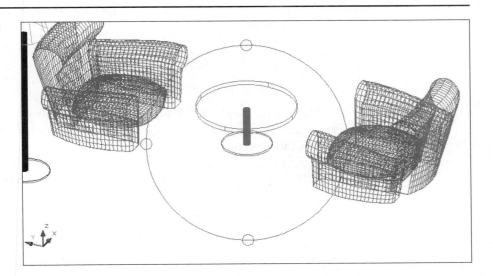

When you click and drag the circle at the top or bottom of the arcball, your view rotates about the target point you selected in step 3 of the first exercise. You can relocate the rotation point by using the Camera tool to select a new target point.

Now let's continue by rotating the view sideways.

1. Place the cursor on the circle on the left side of the arcball. Notice that this time, the cursor changes to look like a ellipse that is elongated horizontally.

2. Click and drag the cursor to the left from this circle on the arcball, but don't let go. The view now rotates about the target point from left to right.

3. Position your view so it looks like Figure 16.40, then release the mouse.

FIGURE 16.40:

The view after clicking and dragging the left arcball circle

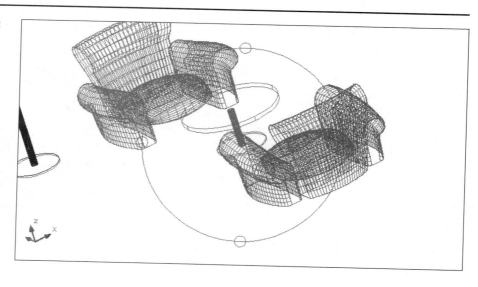

By now, you should have a feel for the way the arcball works. You click and drag until you get the view you want. But right now, the view is not exactly right. You'll want to rotate the view to straighten it out.

1. Move the cursor to the outside of the arcball. Notice that it now looks like a circle.

2. With the cursor outside of the arcball, click and drag downward. The view rotates in the direction that you move the cursor.

3. Adjust the view until it looks similar to the one in Figure 16.41.

When the cursor appears as a circle, you can rotate the view in the view plane. This allows you to "straighten" your view once you've moved your viewpoint or camera location.

You've tried nearly all of the arcball options. There's one more option that is a combination of the top and side circles.

1. Place the cursor inside the arcball. The cursor now looks like two superimposed ellipses.

2. Click and drag the cursor and move it in a slight circular motion. Notice how the view pivots in all directions about the target point.

3. Return the view to the one shown in Figure 16.41.

FIGURE 16.41:

The view straightened out

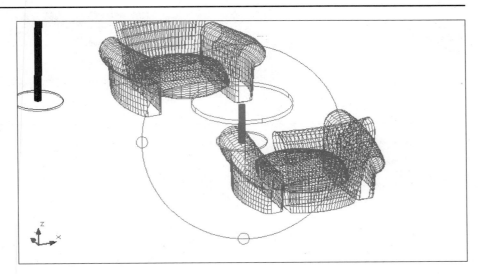

This last option gives you a bit more freedom to move the view, though it can be a bit unwieldy.

TIP	You can change the target point, and therefore the point around which your 3D Orbit view rotates, by using the Camera tool on the View toolbar. Click the Camera tool, then press ↵ when you are prompted for a camera location. Then select the new target location. You can use an object in your drawing as a selection point.

Turning on a Perspective View

The view is still a bit high in the AutoCAD window. You will want to move it downward to include more of the lamp and the chair at the top. You're also still viewing your drawing in a parallel projection mode. In the next exercise, you'll switch to a perspective view, then use the Pan tool to center your view.

1. Right-click and select Projection ➤ Perspective from the popup menu. Your view changes to a perspective one. The view is a bit high so you'll want to use the 3D Orbit Pan tool to center your view.

2. Right-click and select 3D Pan from the popup menu. You can also select Pan from the 3D Orbit toolbar. The arcball disappears and the cursor turns into the familiar Pan cursor.

3. Click and drag the view downward to center the table top in the view. Your view should look like Figure 16.42.

FIGURE 16.42:

The perspective view after panned downward

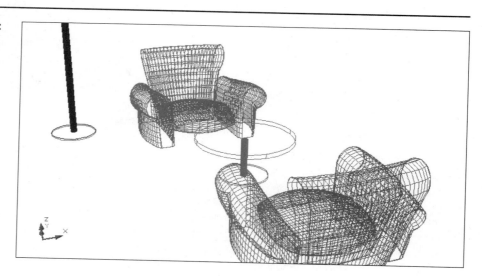

You saw several things happen in this brief exercise. First, you saw how easy it is to obtain a perspective view. You were also introduced to the 3D Orbit popup menu. This menu offers a few options that don't appear on the 3D Orbit toolbar. You also used the 3D Pan tool on the 3D Orbit toolbar.

The 3D Pan tool on the 3D Orbit toolbar works just like the standard Pan tool you've been using all along, but there is a difference. You may have noticed that when you panned your view, the perspective changed as you panned. The effect is similar to that of looking out of a car's side window as you move down the highway. When you pan your view using the 3D Pan tool on the 3D Orbit toolbar, you are moving both the camera viewpoint and the target point together. This maintains your camera and target orientation while moving the overall scene.

Using Some Visual Aids

You're still in 3D Orbit mode, even though you don't see the arcball anymore. This can be a bit confusing. You can use a visual aid to remind yourself that 3D Orbit is still active.

1. Right-click and then select Visual Aids ➢ Compass from the popup menu. The 3D Orbit Compass appears.

2. Right-click again and select Visual Aids ➢ Grid. A grid appears at the 0 z-coordinate.

3. To help visualize the forms of the objects in this scene, turn on the shade mode. Right-click and then select Shading Modes ➢ Hidden. You've already seen both the Grid and the Hidden Shade mode in Chapter 15. Figure 16.43 shows how your view will look after turning on the Compass, Grid, and Hidden Shade mode.

FIGURE 16.43:

The view with the Compass, Grid, and Hidden shade modes turned on

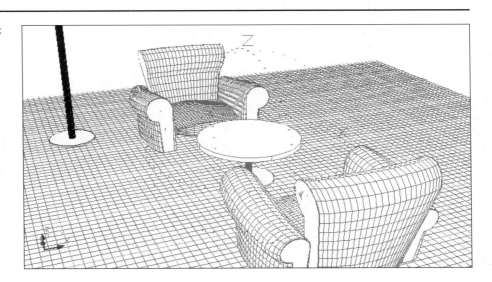

You may have noticed that the options under the Shading Modes cascading menu were the same options available from the Shade Mode toolbar. They're offered in the 3D Orbit popup menu for easy access, in case you want to view your model with hidden lines removed.

Adjusting the Camera

The 3D Orbit arcball lets you rotate your camera location about the target. You've also seen how the Pan option moves both the target and the camera to view a different part of your 3D model. All of these tools maintain the distance between the target and the camera. In the following set of exercises, you learn how to use the tools available that allow you to fine-tune your camera location and characteristics.

Start by changing the distance between the camera and target.

1. Right-click and then choose More ➤ Adjust distance from the popup menu. You can also choose the 3D Adjust Distance tool from the 3D Orbit toolbar.

The cursor turns into a double-headed arrow in a perspective view.

2. Click and drag the mouse downward. As you do, the view recedes as if you were backing away from the scene. You are moving the camera away from the target location.

3. Adjust your view so that it looks like Figure 16.44.

FIGURE 16.44:

The view after using the 3D Adjust Distance tool

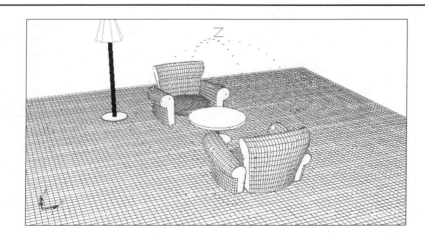

You can adjust the camera distance from the target by clicking and dragging up or down. An upward motion brings the camera closer to the target. A downward motion moves the camera away.

At first glance, the Zoom option on the 3D Orbit toolbar appears to do the same thing as the 3D Adjust Distance option. However, the Zoom option actually has a very different effect on the display. The Zoom option has the effect of enlarging or reducing the size of the image, but it does so by changing the field of view of the camera. This is like using a telephoto lens on a camera. You can zoom in on a scene without actually changing your position relative to the scene.

A telephoto lens does its work by changing its focal length. By increasing its focal length, you get a closer view. By decreasing the focal length, you see more of the scene. If you shorten the focal length a lot, the image begins to distort, like the image in a fish-eye lens. The Zoom option of the 3D Orbit tool works in the same way. Try the following exercise to see firsthand.

1. Right-click and select Orbit from the popup menu. The arcball returns.

2. Click the circle on the right side of the arcball and drag the view to the right so you get a side view of both the chairs.

3. Use the Arcball to adjust your view so it looks like Figure 16.45.

FIGURE 16.45:

The side view of the chairs after rotating the view horizontally

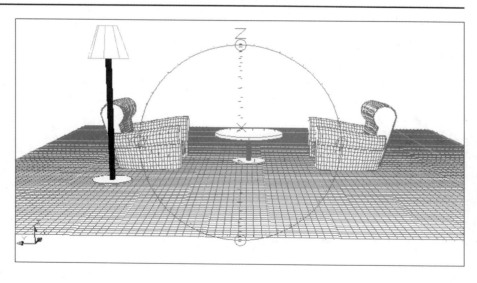

Next, you'll temporarily leave the 3D Orbit tool to turn on a layer.

1. Right-click and then select Exit from the popup menu to exit the 3D Orbit tool.

2. Use the Layer drop-down list to locate and turn on the Wall layer. You'll see some walls appear in the foreground.

3. Click the 3D Orbit tool in the Standard toolbar and then right-click and select Zoom. You can also select the Zoom tool from the 3D Orbit toolbar.

4. Click and drag the mouse slowly downward. As your view moves slowly away, it also begins to distort. The vertical walls start to splay outward more and more as you zoom out, as shown in the top image in Figure 16.46. You also see the 3D Orbit compass distort.

5. Bring your view back to normal by clicking and dragging the mouse upward until you have a view similar to the lower image of Figure 16.46.

FIGURE 16.46:

A view of the walls begins to distort when zooming out.

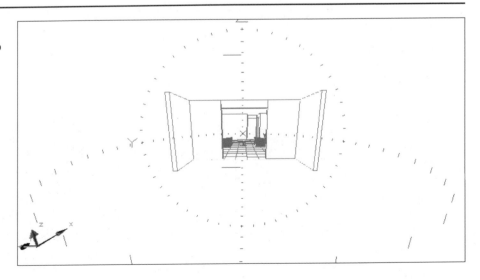

FIGURE 16.46
CONTINUED:

A view of the walls begins to distort when zooming out.

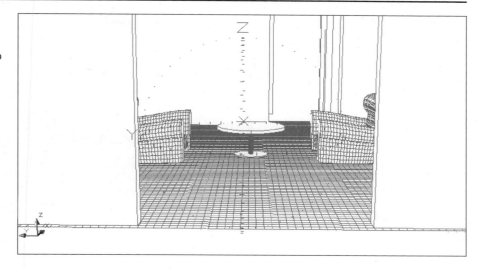

In this exercise, you turned on the walls of the room and then used the Zoom option to see its affects. As you zoomed back, you were actually changing the field of view, or focal length of the camera, to that of a wide-angle lens. You can control the focal length in a more precise way by using another command outside of the 3D Orbit tool—the Dview command. The following exercise will show you how you can precisely set the focal length of the camera.

1. Right-click and then choose Exit from the popup menu.

2. Enter **Dv**⌐⌐ **Z**⌐. Your display changes to show a crude house. This is a visual aid for the Dview command; your drawing hasn't changed.

3. You see the `Specify lens length:` prompt, with the current lens focal length shown in brackets as a default.

4. Type **35**⌐ for a 35-mm lens focal length. Your view changes to offer a wider view of the room as shown in Figure 16.47.

5. Press ⌐ again to exit the Dview command.

The Dview command offers the same functions as the 3D Orbit tool, but it is much more difficult to use. However, it does offer the ability to precisely set the camera focal length. This one feature can be of great use when setting up views of interior spaces in an architectural model.

FIGURE 16.47:

The view of the room after setting the camera focal length to 35mm

Now, suppose you want to move the target of your view upward slightly to encompass more of the back of the room. You can accomplish this by rotating the camera. Here's how it's done.

1. Click the 3D Orbit tool from the Standard toolbar. Then right-click and select More ➢ Swivel Camera. You can also click the 3D Swivel tool in the 3D Orbit toolbar. The cursor changes to a camera icon with a curved arrow.

2. Click and drag the mouse upward to view more of the back wall of the room so that it looks similar to Figure 16.48.

FIGURE 16.48:

The room after swiveling
the camera upward

Using Clipping Planes to Hide Parts of Your View

The walls in the foreground obscure the current view of the interior of the room. While this may be an accurate view of your model, you may want to remove parts of your model that obstruct your view in the foreground. To do this, you can use clipping planes.

1. While in the 3D Orbit mode, right-click, and then select More ≻ Adjust Clipping Planes. The Adjust Clipping Planes dialog box appears. It shows your model as though you were looking at it from above.

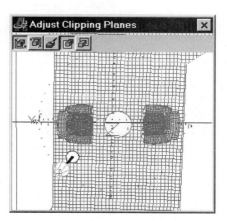

Also notice that the view of the room in the AutoCAD window changes. You see more of the room and the chairs appear to be sliced in half.

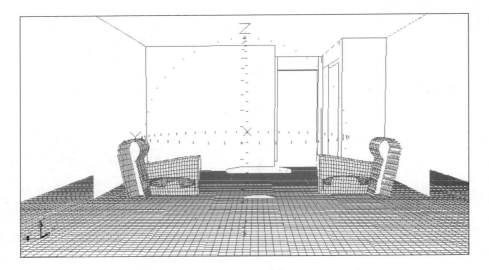

2. Right-click in the Adjust Clipping Planes dialog box. The popup menu that appears offers several options.

3. Make sure the Adjust Front Clipping option shows a checkmark next to it; then click the screen to close the popup menu. This allows you to adjust the front clipping plane. You can also press the Adjust Front Clipping button on the dialog box toolbar.

4. Place the cursor over the horizontal line in the middle of the dialog box, then click and drag downward. The line moves downward. This line represents the location of the front clipping plane in relation to the objects in the drawing. Notice what happens to your view in the main part of the Auto-CAD window as you move the clipping plane. The chairs become whole again, and the lamp appears. Move the cursor up and down to see the effect.

5. Move the clipping plane downward until it is just past the lamp toward the bottom of the dialog box.

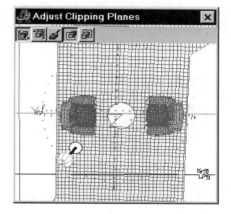

6. Close the Adjust Clipping Planes dialog box. Your view should now show more of the room, as shown in Figure 16.49.

FIGURE 16.49:

The interior view of the room with the front clipping plane turned on

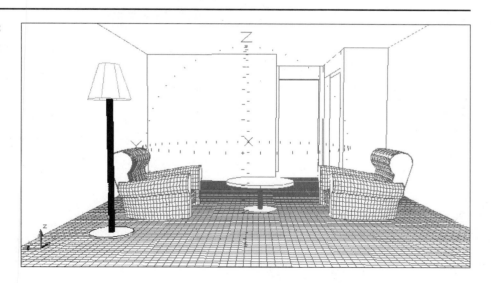

The front clipping plane is turned on as soon as you open the Adjust Clipping Planes dialog box. You can then adjust the clipping plane by moving in the dialog

box. In addition, you can turn on and adjust a back clipping plane to hide objects in the back of your scene, as shown in Figure 16.50. To do this, you turn on the back clipping plane; then adjust it just as you did the front clipping plane. Two buttons control these functions in the Adjust Clipping Planes dialog box: The Adjust Back Clipping lets you adjust the location of the back clipping plane, and the Back Clipping On/Off turns the back clipping plane on or off.

A third option, the Create Slice button, lets you move both the back and front clipping planes in unison. All of these options are also on the Adjust Clipping Planes popup menu.

FIGURE 16.50:

Effects of the clipping planes

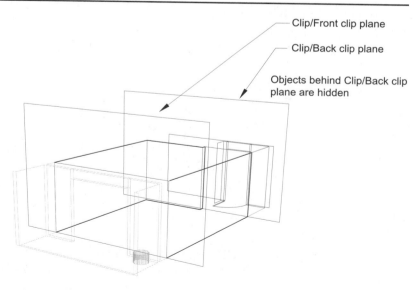

Clip/Front clip plane

Clip/Back clip plane

Objects behind Clip/Back clip plane are hidden

Objects in Clip/Front of front clip plane are hidden

Getting a Simple Animation of Your View

The last 3D Orbit option you'll learn about is one that is perhaps more fun than practical. You can get a simple animated view of your model that rotates your view about the target point. Try this exercise to see how it works.

1. To make this animation a bit more interesting, turn on the Gouraud shading mode. While in 3D Orbit mode, right-click and then select Shading Modes ➤ Gouraud Shaded.

2. Right-click again; then select More Continuous Orbit. You can also select 3D Continuous Orbit from the 3D Orbit toolbar.

3. Click and drag to the left just a short distance. Your view begins to spin in a clockwise direction. The distance you click and drag controls the speed of the spin.

4. Click anywhere to stop the rotation; then click and drag to the right. This time the model spins in a counter-clockwise direction.

5. Click again to stop the spinning.

6. After you've reviewed the results of this exercise, close the `Setting.dwg` file without saving it.

The 3D Continuous Orbit option is better suited to viewing single objects rather than the interior of a room, but this exercise shows what can be done with this option.

This concludes your tour of the 3D Orbit tool. You've used nearly every option available in this tool. With this knowledge, you should be able to set up practically any view you want. You covered a lot of ground here, so you may want to review this section before you work in 3D again.

If You Want to Experiment...

You've covered a lot of territory in this chapter, so it may be a good idea to play with these commands to help you remember what you've learned. Try the exercise shown in Figure 16.51.

FIGURE 16.51:

Drawing a 3D overstuffed couch

Draw the shape shown to the right using a spline curve polyline.

Use Modify > 3D Operation > Rotate 3D to rotate the curve 90 degrees.

Use View > 3D Views > SW Isometric to get a 3D view of the shape.

Copy the shape in the Y axis so it looks similar to this view. Add arcs connecting the bottom endpoints of the shapes.

Make two more copies of the shape and rotate them so they are oriented as shown to the right.

Add more arcs to the endpoints of these new shapes.

Set the Surftab1 system variable to 12, and the Surftab2 system variable to 24.

Use the Edgesurf command to create the mesh forming the couch back and arms.

Mirror the meshes to create the arms for the other side.

Draw some cushions and add them to your couch.

Steps for Rotate 3D:
Select curve
2nd point
1st point
Rotation angle = 90°

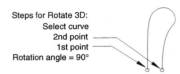

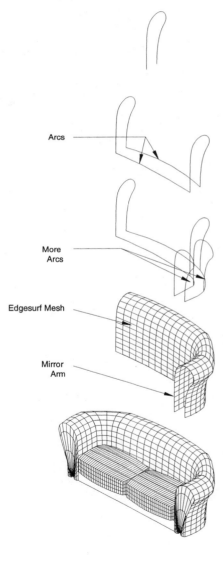

Arcs

More Arcs

Edgesurf Mesh

Mirror Arm

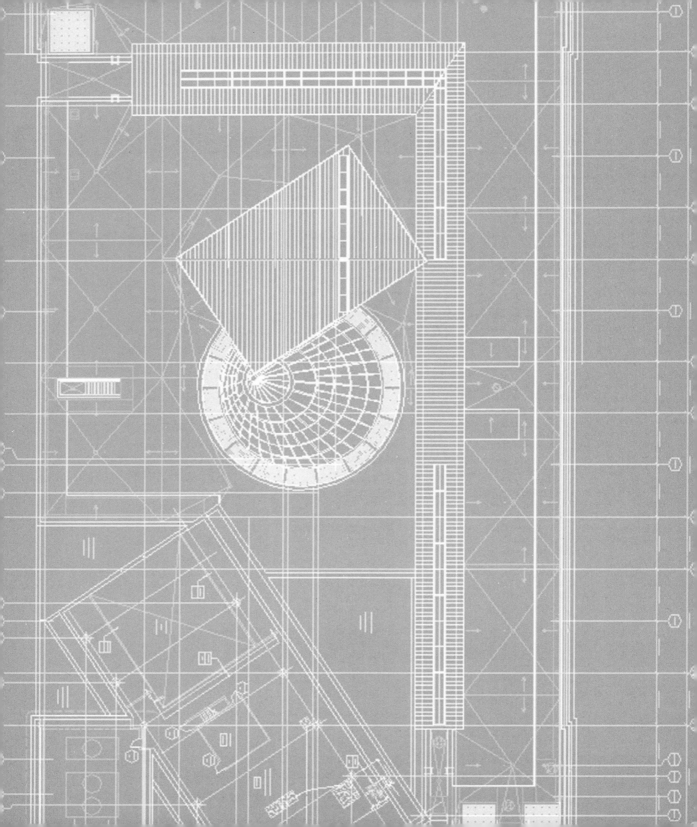

CHAPTER

SEVENTEEN

17

3D Rendering in AutoCAD

Just a few years ago, it took the power of a workstation to create the kind of images you will create in this chapter. Today, you can render not just a single image, but several hundred images to build computer animations. And with the explosion of game software, the Internet, and virtual reality, real-time walk-through sessions of 3D computer models are nearly as commonplace as word processors.

In this chapter, you'll learn how you can use rendering tools in AutoCAD to produce rendered still images of your 3D models. With these tools, you can add materials, control lighting, and even add landscaping and people to your models. You also have control over the reflectance and transparency of objects, and you can add bitmap backgrounds to help set the mood.

Things to Do Before You Start

You will want to take certain steps before you start working with the rendering tools so you won't run into problems later. First, make sure you have a lot of free disk space on the drive where Windows is installed. Having 100 megabytes of free disk space will ensure that you won't exceed your RAM capacity while rendering. This may sound like a lot, but remember, you are attempting to do with your desktop computer what only workstations were capable of a few years ago. Also, make sure there is plenty of free disk space on the drive where your Auto-CAD files are kept.

Creating a Quick Study Rendering

Throughout this chapter, you will work with a 3D model that was created using AutoCAD's solid modeling tools (you'll learn more about solid modeling in Chapter 18). The model is of two buildings on a street corner. You'll start by creating a basic rendering using the default settings in the Render dialog box.

1. Open the Facade.dwg file from the companion CD-ROM.

2. Open the Render toolbar from the Toolbar dialog box.

3. Choose View ➤ Render ➤ Render, or click the Render tool in the Render toolbar.

The Render dialog box appears. In time, you will become intimately familiar with this dialog box.

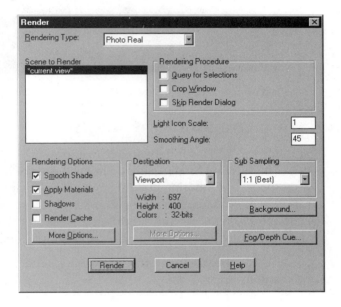

4. Click the Render button. AutoCAD takes a minute or two to render the current view. While it's working, you will see messages in the Command window showing you the progress of the rendering. When AutoCAD is done, the model appears as a surface-shaded model (see Figure 17.1).

When you render a model without any special settings, you get what is called a *Z buffer shaded model*. The surfaces are shaded in their color and the light source is, by default, from the camera location. This view is much like a Hidden-Line view with color added to help distinguish surface orientation. You can actually get a similar view using the Flat Shade tool on the Shade toolbar.

FIGURE 17.1:

The Facade model rendered using all the default settings

Simulating the Sunlight Angle

The ability to add a sunlight source to a drawing is one of AutoCAD's key features. This is a tool used frequently in the design of buildings in urban and suburban settings. Neighboring building owners will want to know if your project will cast darkening shadows over their homes or workplaces. The Sun option lets you accurately simulate the sun's location in relation to a model and its surrounding buildings. AutoCAD also lets you set up multiple light sources other than the sun.

So let's add the sun to our model to give a better sense of the buildings form and relationship to its site.

1.   Choose View ➤ Render ➤ Lights, or click Lights on the Render toolbar.

TIP   Whenever you are creating a new light or other object with the Rendering tool, you usually have to give it a name first, before you can do anything else.

2. In the Lights dialog box, choose Distant Light from the drop-down list next to the New button toward the bottom left.

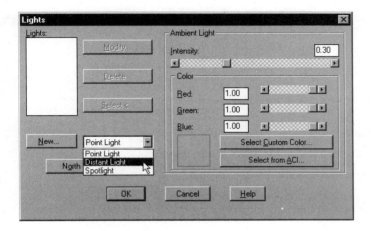

3. Click the New button. The New Distant Light dialog box appears.

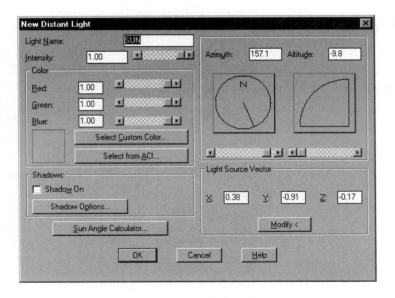

4. Type **SUN** in the Light Name input box toward the top of the dialog box. This dialog box lets you control various aspects of the light source, such as color and location.

5. Because you want to simulate the sun in this example, click the button labeled Sun Angle Calculator. The Sun Angle Calculator dialog box appears.

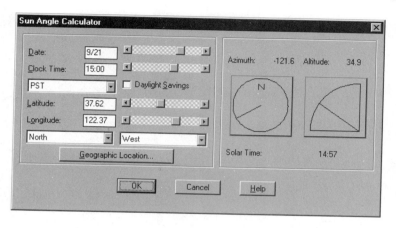

Notice that you have options for setting the date and time to determine the exact location of the sun. In addition, you have the option to indicate where true polar north is in relation to your model. AutoCAD assumes polar north is at the 90° position in the WCS.

6. One important factor for calculating the sun angle is finding your location on the earth. Click the Geographic Location button. The Geographic Location dialog box appears.

Here you can tell AutoCAD where your building is located in the world.

7. For the sake of this tutorial, suppose the Facade model is a building in San Francisco, California, USA. Select North America from the drop-down list above the map.

8. Locate and select San Francisco, CA in the scrolling list to the left of the map. Notice that the Latitude and Longitude input boxes below the list change to reflect the location of San Francisco. For locations not listed, you can enter values manually in those input boxes.

9. Now click OK to return to the Sun Angle Calculator dialog box. Set the Date for 9/21 and the time for 14:00 hours. Notice that the graphic to the right of the dialog box adjusts to show the altitude and azimuth angle of the sun for the time you enter.

10. Click OK in the Sun Angle Calculator dialog box and the New Distant Light dialog box, and then click OK again in the Lights dialog box.

11. Choose View ➤ Render ➤ Render, or click Render on the Render toolbar. Then click the Render button in the Render dialog box. Your model will be shaded to reflect the sun's location (see Figure 17.2).

FIGURE 17.2:

The Facade model with the sun light source added

Notice that the building itself looks darker than before, and that the ground plane is lighter. Remember that in the first rendering, the light source was the same as the camera location, so the wall facing you received more direct light. In this last rendering, the light source is at a glancing angle, so the surface appears darker.

This section mentioned that you can set the direction of polar north. This is accomplished by clicking the North Location button in the Lights dialog box. When selected, this button opens the North Location dialog box, shown in Figure 17.3. With this dialog box, you can set true north in any of the following three ways:

- Click the graphic to point to the direction.

- Use the slide bar at the bottom to move the arrow of the graphic and adjust the value in the input box.

- Enter a value directly into the input box.

You also have the option to indicate which UCS is used to set the north direction. For example, you may have already set a UCS to point to the true north direction. You only need to select the UCS from the list and leave the angle at 0.

FIGURE 17.3:

The North Location dialog box

Improving the Smoothness of Circles and Arcs

You might notice that at times when using the Render, Hide, or Shade tool, solid or region arcs appear segmented rather than curved. This may be fine for producing layouts or backgrounds for hand-rendered drawings, but for final plots, you will want arcs and circles to appear as smooth curves. You can adjust the accuracy of arcs in your hidden, rendered, or shaded views through a setting in the Options dialog box.

Continued on next page

The Rendered Object Smoothness setting in the Display tab of the Options dialog box can be modified to improve the smoothness of arcs. Its default setting is .5, but you can increase this to as high as 10 to smooth out faceted curves. In the `Facade.dwg` model, you can set Rendered Object Smoothness to 1.5 to render the arch in the entry as a smooth arc instead of a series of flat segments. This setting can also be adjusted using the Facetres system variable.

Adding Shadows

There is nothing like adding shadows to a 3D rendering to give the model a sense of realism. AutoCAD offers three methods for casting shadows. The default method is called Volumetric Shadows. This method takes a considerable amount of time to render more complex scenes. When using AutoCAD's Ray Trace option (described later in this chapter), shadows will be generated using the Ray Trace method. The third method, called Shadow Map, offers the best speed but requires some adjustment to get good results. Shadow Map offers a soft-edge shadow. While shadow maps are generally less accurate than the other two methods, the soft-edge option offers a level of realism not available in the other two methods.

In the following exercise, you will use the Shadow Map method. It requires the most amount of adjustments and yields a faster rendering.

1. Choose View ➤ Render ➤ Lights, or click Lights on the Render toolbar.

2. In the Lights dialog box, make sure SUN is highlighted, and then click Modify. The Modify Distant Light dialog box appears.

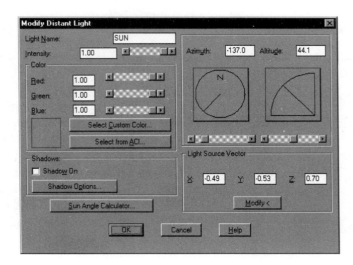

> **TIP**
> When adding shadows, remember that you must turn on the Shadow option for both the Render dialog box *and* for each light that is to cast a shadow.

3. Click the Shadow On check box, and then click the Shadow Options button. The Shadow Options dialog box appears.

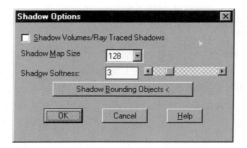

4. In the Shadow Map Size input box, select 512 from the drop-down list. This is the actual number of pixels used to create the shadow map.

5. Click the Shadow Bounding Objects button. The dialog box temporarily disappears to allow you to select objects from the screen. This option allows you to select the objects you want to cast shadows.

6. Select the entire Facade building. Don't select any of the building next to it. When you are done, press ↵. The Shadow Options dialog box reappears.

7. Click OK to close the Shadow Options dialog box, and then click OK in the Modify Distant Light dialog box. It may take several seconds before the dialog box closes.

8. When you get to the Lights dialog box, click OK to close it.

9. Click the Render button on the Render toolbar.

10. In the Render dialog box, click the Shadows check box, and then click the Render button. After a minute or two, the model appears rendered with shadows (see Figure 17.4).

Don't panic if the shadows don't appear correct. The Shadow Map method needs some adjustment before it will give the proper shadows. The default settings are appropriate for views of objects from a greater distance than our current view. The following exercise will show you what to do for close-up views.

1. Open the Render dialog box again, and then click the button labeled More Options. The Photo Real Render Options dialog box appears.

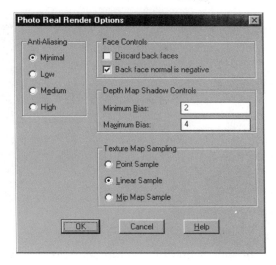

2. In the Depth Map Shadow Controls group, change the Minimum Bias value from 2 to .1.

3. In the same group, change the Maximum Bias value from 4 to .2.

4. Click OK to close the Photo Real Render Options dialog box, and then click Render. Your next rendering will show more accurately drawn shadows (see Figure 17.5).

FIGURE 17.4:

The Facade model rendered with shadows using the Shadow Map method

The shadow still looks a bit rough. You can further refine the shadow's appearance by increasing the Shadow Map Size to greater than 512. This setting can be found in the Shadow Options dialog box in step 4 of the exercise just before the last one. Figure 17.6 shows the same rendering with the Shadow Map Size set to 1024. As you increase the map size, you also increase render time and the amount of RAM required to render the view. If you don't have enough free disk space, you may find that AutoCAD will refuse to render the model. You will then either have to free up some disk space or decrease the map size.

Notice that the shadow has a soft edge. You can control the softness of the shadow edge using the Shadow Options dialog box you saw in the exercise before the last one. The Shadow Softness input box and slide bar let you sharpen the shadow edge by decreasing the value or soften it by increasing the value. The soft shadow is especially effective for renderings of building interiors or scenes where you are simulating artificial light.

Adding Materials

The rendering methods you've learned so far can be of enormous help in your design effort. Simply being able to see how the sun affects your design can be of enormous help in selling your ideas or helping get plans through a tough planning board review. But the look of the building is still somewhat cartoonish. You can further enhance the rendering by adding materials to the objects in your model.

Let's suppose you want a granite-like finish to appear on the Facade model. You will also want the building next to the Facade model to appear as a glass tower. The first step to adding materials is to acquire the materials from AutoCAD's materials library.

1. Choose View ➤ Render ➤ Materials or click Materials on the Render toolbar.

The Materials dialog box appears.

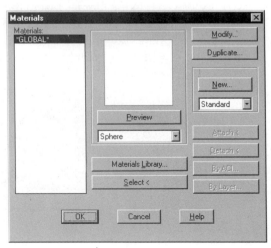

2. Click the Materials Library button in the middle of the dialog box. The Materials Library dialog box appears.

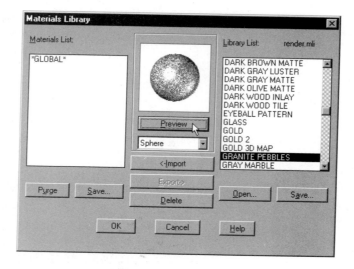

3. In the Library List box, find and select Granite Pebbles so it is highlighted. This is the material you will assign to the facade.

4. Click the Preview button in the middle of the dialog box. A view of the material appears on a sphere, giving you an idea of what the material looks like.

5. Click the Import button. Notice that Granite Pebbles now appears in the Materials List box to the left. This list box shows the materials you've transferred to your drawing.

6. Now locate Glass in the Library List to the right and select it. Click the Preview button again to see what it looks like. Notice that the preview shows a transparent sphere showing some reflected light. You may notice a textured effect caused by the low color resolution of the AutoCAD display.

7. Click the Import button again to make Glass available in the drawing; then click OK to exit the Materials Library dialog box.

Once you've acquired the materials, you will have to assign them to objects in your drawing.

1. In the Materials dialog box, highlight the Granite Pebbles item shown in the list to the left, and then click the Attach< button in the right half of the dialog box. The dialog box temporarily disappears, allowing you to select the objects you want to appear as Granite Pebbles.

2. Click the Facade model, including the steps, columns, and arched entrance, and then press ↵. After a moment, the Materials dialog box appears again.

3. Click Glass on the Materials list box.

4. This time you'll assign a material based on its layer. Click the By Layer button to the right of the dialog box. The Attach by Layer dialog box appears.

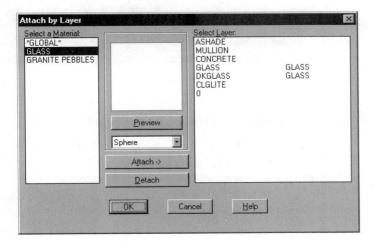

5. Shift+click Glass and Dkglass from the Select Layer list to the right, and then click the Attach button. Notice that the word Glass now appears next to the layer names you selected, indicating that the Glass material is now associated with those layers.

6. Click OK to exit the Attach by Layer dialog box; then click OK again to exit the Materials dialog box.

7. Now render your model. You may want to take a break at this point, as the rendering will take a few minutes. When AutoCAD is done, your rendering will look like Figure 17.7.

FIGURE 17.7:

The Facade model with the glass and granite pebbles materials added

Adjusting the Materials' Appearance

The Facade model looks more like it has an Army camouflage paint job instead of a granite finish. Also, the glass of the office tower is a bit too transparent. Fortunately, you can make several adjustments to the materials. You will want to reduce the scale of the granite pebbles material so it is in line with the scale of the model. You will also want to darken the glass material so it looks more like the tinted glass used in modern office buildings. You'll start with the granite pebbles.

1. Choose View ➤ Render ➤ Materials.

2. In the Materials dialog box, select Granite Pebbles from the Materials list, and then click the Modify button. The Modify Granite Material dialog box appears.

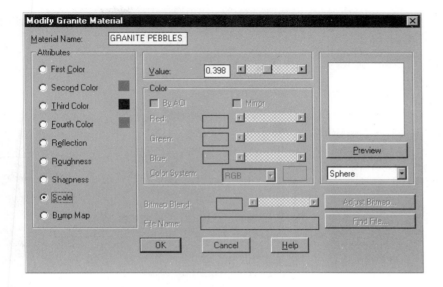

3. Click the Scale radio button in the Attributes button group in the left-hand side of the dialog box.

4. Change the Value input box near the top of the dialog box from .398 to .010. This reduces the scale of the material.

5. Click OK to return to the Materials dialog box.

The Modify Granite Material dialog box offers a variety of options that let you control reflectivity, roughness, color, transparency, and, of course, scale. The Help button in the Modify Granite Material dialog box provides a brief description of these options. As you'll see when you continue with the next exercise, not all materials have the same options.

1. Select Glass from the Materials list, and then click the Modify button again. The Modify Standard Material dialog box appears.

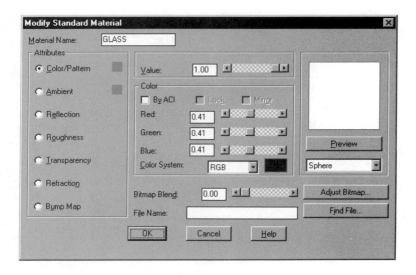

Notice that this dialog box offers a slightly different set of Attributes options than those offered in the Modify Granite Material dialog box you edited in the previous exercise.

2. Select the Transparency radio button in the Attributes button group, and then adjust the Value option downward to .55. This has the effect of darkening the glass.

3. Select the Color/Pattern radio button; then, in the Color button group, adjust the Red value to 69, the Green value to 60, and the Blue to .58. This gives the glass a bronze tint.

4. Select Cube from the drop-down list just below the Preview button, and then click the Preview button to get a preview of the color settings.

5. Click OK in both the Modify Standard Material and Materials dialog boxes to exit them.

6. Render the view with the new material settings. After a few minutes, your view will look something like Figure 17.8.

There are four basic types of materials: Standard, Marble, Granite, and Wood. Each type has its own set of characteristics that you can adjust. You can even create new materials based on one of the four primary types of materials. Now let's continue by making another adjustment to the material settings.

FIGURE 17.8:

The Facade model after modifying the material settings

The granite surface of the Facade is a bit too strong. You can reduce the graininess of the granite by further editing in the Modify Granite Material dialog box.

1. Click the Materials tool on the Render toolbar, and then select Granite Pebbles from the Materials list, and then choose Modify.

2. In the Modify Granite Material dialog box, click the Sharpness Attribute radio button. Then set the Value input box to .20.

3. Click OK, and then click OK again in the Materials dialog box.

4. Choose View ➣ Render ➣ Render, and then click the Render button of the Render dialog box. Your rendering appears after a few minutes with a softer granite surface (see Figure 17.9).

FIGURE 17.9:

The rendered image with a softer granite surface

Adding a Background Scene

You could continue by adding and adjusting materials to the other parts of the model, but try dressing up your view by including a sky. To do so, you need to set up the background.

1. Open the Render dialog box, and then click the button labeled Background. The Background dialog box appears.

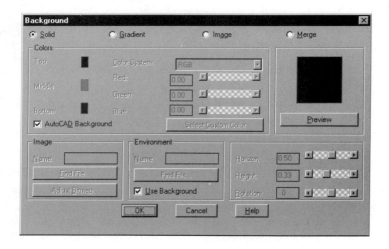

2. In the row of radio buttons across the top, find and click Image. Notice that several of the options near the bottom of the dialog box are now available.

3. Click the Find File button at the bottom left of the dialog box. The Background Image dialog box appears. This is a typical AutoCAD file dialog box.

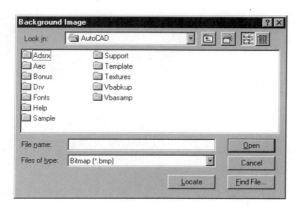

4. Use the Background Image dialog box to locate the Sky.tga file. It can be found in the \Textures\ subdirectory of the \AutoCAD2000\ directory.

5. Once back in the Background dialog box, click Preview to see what the file looks like. Sky.tga is a bitmap image of a blue sky with clouds.

6. Click OK. Then, once back in the Render dialog box, click Render. The background appears behind the model, as shown in Figure 17.10.

This example added a bitmap image for a background, but you can use other methods to generate a background. For example, you might prefer to use a gradient shade or color for the background. This can help give a sense of depth to the image (see Figure 17.11). You can, of course, add a single color to the background if you prefer.

To create a gradient background, select the Gradient radio button at the top of the Background dialog box. You can then adjust the color for the top, middle, and bottom third of the background. AutoCAD automatically blends the three colors from top to bottom to create the gradient colors.

FIGURE 17.10:

The Facade model rendered with a sky bitmap image for a background

Effects with Lighting

Up to now, you've only used one light source, called a Distant Light, to create a sun. You have two other light sources available to help simulate light: point-light sources and spotlights. This section will show you some examples of how you can use these types of light sources, along with some imagination, to perform any number of visual tricks with them.

Simulating the Interior Lighting of an Office Building

Our current rendering shows a lifeless-looking office building. It's missing a sense of activity. You might notice that when you look at glass office buildings, you can frequently see the ceiling lights from the exterior of the building—provided the glass isn't too dark. In a subtle way, those lights lend a sense of life to a building.

To help improve the image, you'll add some ceiling lights to the office building. You've already supplied the lights in the form of square 3D Faces arrayed just at the ceiling level of each floor, as shown in Figure 17.12.

In this section, you will learn how to make the ceiling lights appear illuminated.

1. Start by assigning a reflective material to the squares. Choose View ➤ Render ➤ Materials and then click the Materials Library button.

2. In the Materials Library dialog box, locate and select White Plastic from the Library List at the right, and then click Import.

3. Click OK to exit the Materials Library dialog box. Then in the Materials dialog box, highlight White Plastic in the list to the left and click the By Layer button.

4. In the Attach by Layer dialog box, make sure White Plastic is highlighted in the Select a Material list to the left; then click the Clglite layer in the Select Layer list to the right.

5. Click the Attach-> button. The word White Plastic appears next to the Clglite layer name in the Select Layer list.

6. Click OK to exit the Attach by Layer dialog box, and then click OK to exit the Materials dialog box.

FIGURE 17.12:

The 3D Face squares representing ceiling light fixtures

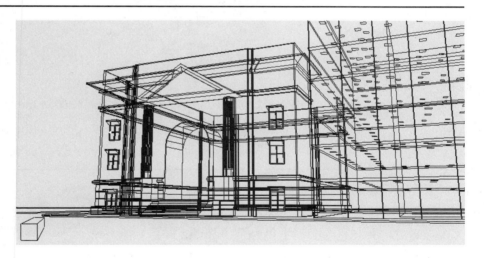

You now have a reflective, white material assigned to the ceiling fixtures. But the reflective material alone will not give the effect of illuminated lights. You need a light source that can be reflected by the fixtures, giving the impression of illumination. For this, you'll use a point-light source.

1. Choose View ➤ 3D Viewpoint ➤ SE Isometric to get an Isometric view of the model.

2. Zoom into the base of the office building so your view is similar to Figure 17.13.

3. Choose View ➤ Render ➤ Lights. Then in the Lights dialog box, select Point Light from the New drop-down list; then click the New button. The New Point Light dialog box appears.

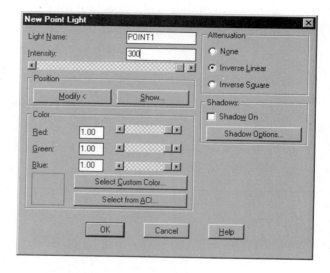

4. Enter **Point1** for the light name. Then enter **300** in the Intensity input box.

5. Click the Modify button, and then select a point at the very center of the office building base, as shown in Figure 17.13.

FIGURE 17.13:

Selecting the point-light source location in the SW Isometric view

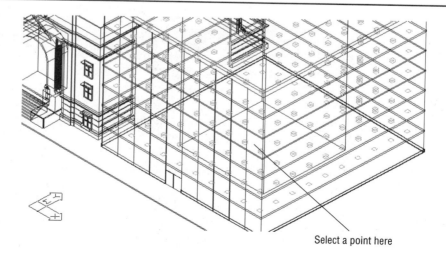

Select a point here

6. Click OK to exit the New Point Light dialog box, and then click OK in the Lights dialog box.

7. Choose View ➤ Named Views. Then at the Named Views dialog box, select 3DFront and click the Restore button.

8. Click OK to exit the Named Views dialog box.

9. Go ahead and render the view. After a minute, you will have a rendered view similar to Figure 17.14.

FIGURE 17.14:

The rendered view with ceiling lights

The new point light in conjunction with the 3D Face light fixture adds a sense of life and depth to the office building. Notice that despite the fact that the light is located inside the box representing the office core, the light manages to strike all the lights of all the floors as if the floors and core were transparent. Since you didn't turn on the Shadow feature for the point-light source, its light passes through all the objects in the model.

There is even light falling on the granite facade building illuminating the inside of the arched entrance. This shows that with careful use of lighting, you can bring out some of the detail in the Facade model that might otherwise get lost with the distant light source.

Of course, you can use point-light sources in a more traditional way, representing lightbulbs or other nondirectional light sources. But by playing with light source location and shadow, you can create effects to help enhance your rendering.

Simulating a Night Scene with Spotlights

Spotlights are lights that are directed. They are frequently used to provide emphasis and are usually used for interior views or product presentations. In this exercise, you'll set up a night view of the facade model using spotlights to illuminate the facade.

You'll start by setting up a view to help place the spotlights. Once they are placed, you'll make some adjustments to them to get a view you want.

1. Choose View ➤ 3D Viewpoint Presets ➤ SE Isometric; then zoom into the facade so your view looks similar to Figure 17.15.

2. Choose View ➤ Render ➤ Lights. Then in the Lights dialog box, select Spotlight from the New drop-down list.

3. Click New. Then in the New Spotlight dialog box, enter **Spot-L**. This designates a spotlight you will place on the left side of the facade.

4. Enter **400** in the Intensity input box. Then click the Modify< button.

5. At the `Enter Target Location:` prompt, use the Nearest Osnap and select the point on the window, as indicated in Figure 17.15.

6. At the `Enter Light Location:` prompt, select the point indicated in Figure 17.15. Once you've selected the light location, you return to the New Spotlight dialog box. You can, in the future, adjust the light location if you choose.

7. Click OK. Then in the Lights dialog box, click New again to create another spotlight.

8. This time, enter **Spot-R** for the name. Enter **400** for the intensity as before.

9. Click the Modify< button and select the target and light locations indicated in Figure 17.16.

10. Click OK to exit the New Spotlight dialog box, and then click OK again in the Lights dialog box. You now have two spotlights on your building.

11. Choose View ➤ Named Views and restore the 3DFront view.

12. Render the model (you should know how this is done by now). Your view will look similar to Figure 17.17.

The rendered view has a number of problems. First, the sunlight source needs to be turned off. Second, the spotlights are too harsh. You can also see that the spotlights don't illuminate the center of the building, so you'll need to add some lighting at the entrance. These problems will be solved in the next section.

FIGURE 17.15:

Selecting the points for the first spotlight

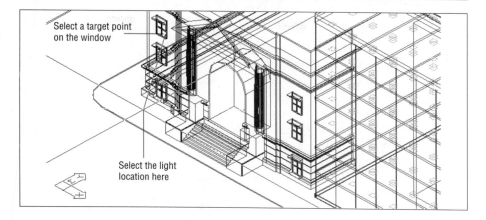

Select a target point on the window

Select the light location here

FIGURE 17.16:

Selecting the points for the second spotlight

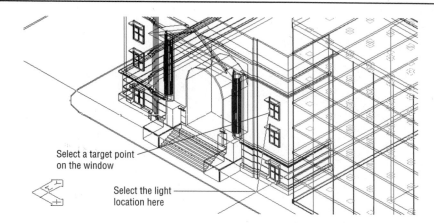

Select a target point on the window

Select the light location here

FIGURE 17.17:

The rendered view of the model with the spotlights

Controlling Lights with Scenes

The first problem is how to turn off the sun. You can set the sunlight intensity value to 0 using the Modify Distant Light dialog box. Another way is to set up a scene. AutoCAD lets you combine different lights and views into named scenes. These scenes can then be quickly selected at render time so you don't have to adjust lighting or views every time you want a specific setup. Here's how it works.

1. Choose View ➤ Render ➤ Scenes, or click the Scenes tool on the Render toolbar.

The Scenes dialog box appears.

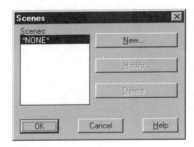

2. Click New. The New Scene dialog box appears.

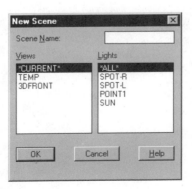

3. Enter **NIGHT** for the scene name. The name appears in the Scene Name input box.

4. Select 3DFRONT from the Views list and then Shift+click SPOT-L, SPOT-R, and POINT1 in the Lights list.

5. Click OK. Notice that now you have NIGHT listed in the Scenes list in the Scenes dialog box.

6. Click New again, and then type **DAY**.

7. Select 3DFRONT from the Views list, and SUN and POINT1 from the Lights list. Then click OK. You now have two scenes set up.

8. Click OK, and then open the Render dialog box. Notice that you have DAY and NIGHT listed in the Scene to Render list box in the upper left of the Render dialog box.

9. Select NIGHT, and then click the Render button. Your view will look like Figure 17.18.

FIGURE 17.18:

Rendering the night scene

Notice that without the sunlight source, your view is considerably darker. You will now add a few more light sources and adjust some existing ones.

1. Choose View ➢ 3D Viewpoint Presets ➢ SE Isometric, and then zoom into the office building so your view looks similar to Figure 17.19.

2. Open the Lights dialog box, select Point Light from the New drop-down list, and click New.

3. Enter the name **Point2**, and then give this new point light an intensity value of **500**.

4. Click the Modify< button, and place the Point2 light in the center of the office building in the same location as Point1.

5. Click OK; then create another point-light source and enter the name **Point3**. Enter an intensity of **150**.

6. Click the Modify< button, adjust your view so it looks similar to Figure 17.20, and then place the light in the facade entrance, as shown in Figure 17.20. Use the .X, .Y, and .Z point filters to select the location of the light.

7. Click OK. Then in the Lights dialog box, select Spot-L from the list and click Modify<.

8. In the Modify Spotlight dialog box, change the Falloff value in the upper right to **80**.

9. Click OK, and then repeat steps 7 and 8 for the Spot-R spotlight.

10. Click OK in the Modify Spotlight dialog box.

11. In the Lights dialog box, increase the ambient light intensity to **50**, and then click OK.

FIGURE 17.19:

Adding another point-light source to the office building

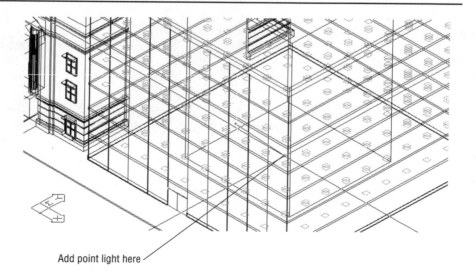

Add point light here

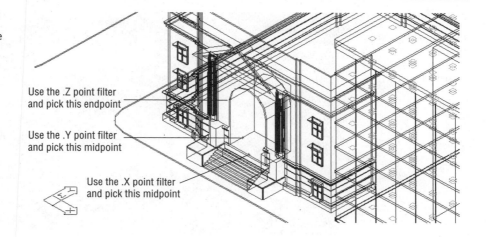

FIGURE 17.20:

Adding a point-light source for the entrance to the facade

Use the .Z point filter and pick this endpoint

Use the .Y point filter and pick this midpoint

Use the .X point filter and pick this midpoint

You've got the new lights installed and the spotlights adjusted. Before you render your scene, you need to include the new lights in the scene you set up for the night rendering.

1. Choose View ➤ Render ➤ Scene.

2. Highlight Night in the Scenes list, and then click the Modify button.

3. Shift+click Point2 and Point3 in the Lights list, and then Alt+click Point1 to deselect it.

4. Click OK in both the Modify Scene and Scenes dialog boxes.

5. Choose Render and make sure Night is selected in the Scene to Render list.

6. Click the Render button. Your view will look similar to Figure 17.21.

The new rendering is brighter. You can also see the effects of an increased falloff for the spotlights. They don't have the sharp edge they had in the first night rendering, and the light is spread in a wider radius, illuminating more of the lower portion of the facade.

You also see another by-product of using the Scenes tool. You didn't have to return to the 3DFront view to render the model. Since the 3DFront view is included in the scene information, AutoCAD automatically rendered the model from that view when the Night scene was selected. If you were to issue the Regen command now, you would see that AutoCAD still maintains the SE Isometric view.

FIGURE 17.21:

The night rendering with added lights and an increased falloff area for the spotlights

Adding Reflections and Detail with Ray Tracing

You've been gradually building up the detail and realism in your renderings by adding light and materials. In this section, you'll learn how using a different rendering method can further enhance your 3D models. Up until now, you've been using the standard AutoCAD rendering method. Ray Tracing can add interest to a rendering, especially where reflective surfaces are prominent in a model. In this section, you'll use the Ray Tracing method to render your model after making a few adjustments to the glass material.

What Is Ray Tracing?

To make a long, complicated story short, Ray Tracing simulates the way light works. And it does it in somewhat of a reverse way. Ray Tracing analyzes the light path to each pixel of your display, tracing the light or "ray" from the pixel to the light origin as it bounces off objects in your model. Ray Tracing takes into account the reflectivity and, in the case of glass, the refraction of light as it is affected by objects in the model. Because more objects in a model offer more surfaces to reflect light, Ray Tracing becomes more time-consuming as the

Continued on next page

number of objects increases. Also, since each pixel is analyzed, a greater image size increases the render time geometrically. For example, by doubling the width and height of the view size, you are essentially increasing the number of pixels by four times.

AutoCAD offers Ray Tracing as an option for rendering both shadows and the entire scene. The Ray Trace options offer greater accuracy in exchange for slow rendering time. If you choose to select ray-traced shadows, for example, you can expect at least a fourfold increase in rendering time. Rendering an entire scene can increase rendering time by an order of magnitude.

Needless to say, if you are in a time crunch, you will want to save Ray Tracing just for the essential final renderings. Use the Photo Real or other rendering type options in the Render dialog box for study rendering or for situations that don't require the accuracy of Ray Tracing.

Assigning a Mirror Attribute to Glass

Glass is a complex material to model in computer renderings. The AutoCAD standard rendering method simply gives glass a transparency with some "highlight" reflection. But glass has both refractive and reflective attributes that make it difficult to model. Because Ray Tracing models the way light works, it is especially well suited to rendering views that contain large areas of glass.

To demonstrate what Ray Tracing can do, you'll use it to render the Facade model that happens to contain an office building with a typical glass exterior. You'll start by making an adjustment to the glass material to make it appear more reflective.

1. Choose View ➤ Render ➤ Materials, and then in the Materials dialog box, highlight Glass in the list box and click the Modify button.

2. Click the Reflection radio button in the Attributes button group.

3. Click the Mirror check box in the Color button group, and then click OK to close the Modify Standard Material dialog box.

4. Click OK again in the Materials dialog box, and then open the Render dialog box.

5. Choose Photo Raytrace from the Rendering Type list box at the top of the dialog box.

6. Click the More Options button. The Photo Raytrace Render Options dialog box appears.

7. Set the Minimum Bias setting to **.1** and the Maximum Bias setting to **.2**. Whenever you change the rendering type, you must reset these settings. AutoCAD does not automatically transfer these settings to different rendering types.

8. Click OK, and then select Day from the Scene to Render list. Next, click the Background button.

9. In the Background dialog box, make sure the Use Background check box is checked in the Environment button group; then click the OK button. This tells AutoCAD to reflect the background image in the glass.

10. Click the Render button. Your view will look similar to Figure 17.22.

FIGURE 17.22:

The Facade model rendered with the Ray Tracing method

The sky bitmap used as a background is faintly reflected in the glass of the office building. The office building has also become brighter from the reflection. Also notice the secondary reflection of the interior ceiling on the west interior wall of the office.

The brightness of the office building is a bit overwhelming, so you will want to adjust the glass material to tone it down.

1. Choose View ➤ Render ➤ Materials. Then with the Glass material highlighted, select Modify.

2. In the Modify Standard Material dialog box, make sure the Color/Pattern radio button is selected. Then set the Value setting above the Color button group to **.20**. This helps darken the office building.

3. Click OK to close the Modify Standard Material dialog box, and then click OK in the Materials dialog box.

4. Render the scene again. Your view will look something like Figure 17.23.

FIGURE 17.23:

The rendering with a lower Color/Pattern setting for the Glass material

You can further reduce the brightness of the office building by reducing the intensity value of the point-light source you added early in this chapter.

Getting a Sharp, Accurate Shadow with Ray Tracing

In the beginning of this chapter, you learned how to use the Shadow Map method for casting shadows. Shadow maps offer the feature of allowing a soft-edge shadow in exchange for accuracy. For exterior views, you may prefer a sharper shadow. The Facade example loses some detail using the Shadow Map method; in particular, the grooves in the base of the building disappear. By switching to the Ray Tracing method for casting shadows, you can recover some of this detail.

1. Choose View ➢ Render ➢ Lights. Then from the Lights list, select Sun and click Modify.

2. In the Modify Distant Light dialog box, click the Shadow Options button.

3. In the Shadow Options dialog box, click the Shadow Volumes/Ray Traced Shadows check box to place a checkmark there.

4. Click OK in all the dialog boxes to exit them and return to the AutoCAD view.

5. Render the view using the Photo Ray Trace rendering type. Your view will look like Figure 17.24.

Notice that you can now see the rusticated base clearly. The shadows also appear sharper, especially around the surface detail of the Facade model.

Creating and Adjusting Texture Maps

You've already seen how you can assign a material to an object by adding the granite pebbles and glass materials to the buildings in the Facade3.dwg file. Many of these materials make use of bitmap image files to simulate textures. You can create your own surface textures or use bitmaps in other ways to help enhance your rendering. For example, you can include a photograph of existing buildings that may exist within the scene you are rendering.

Figure 17.25 shows a bitmap image that was scanned into the computer and edited using a popular paint program. Now imagine that this building is across the street from the Facade model, and you want to include it in the scene to show its relationship to your building.

FIGURE 17.25:

A photographic image of a building that was scanned into a computer and saved as a bitmap file

The following exercise will show you how it's done.

1. Click Redraw on the Standard toolbar, and then adjust your view so it looks like the top image of Figure 17.26.

2. Draw a line 133 feet long, as shown in the top image of Figure 17.26.

3. Change the thickness of the line to 80' using the Properties tool.

4. Choose View ➢ Render ➢ Materials. Then in the Materials dialog box, click New. Notice that the New Standard Material dialog box is the same as the dialog box for the Glass material. The settings are not the same, however.

5. Enter **Build1** for the material name.

6. Make sure the Color/Pattern radio button is selected, and then click the Find File button in the lower-right corner of the dialog box.

7. Click the List Files of Type drop-down list. Notice that you have several file types from which to choose.

8. Choose GIF from the list, and then locate the Market2.gif file. This file comes with the other sample files on the companion CD-ROM.

9. Choose Open to exit this dialog box. Then click OK in the New Standard Material dialog box.

10. In the Materials dialog box, make sure Build1 is selected in the Materials list, and then click the Attach< button.

11. Select the line you added in step 2, and then press ↵.

12. Click OK to exit the Materials dialog box, and then render the scene. Your view will look like the bottom image of Figure 17.26.

FIGURE 17.26:

Adding a bitmap image of a building to your rendering

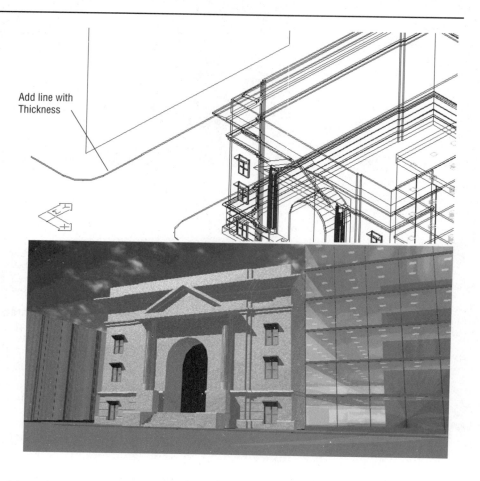

Add line with Thickness

The bitmap image does not appear properly in the rendered view. Instead, it looks like a vertical streak of colors. When you see this streaking, you know your bitmap image or material is not properly aligned with the object to which it is attached. The following exercise introduces you to the tools you need to properly align a bitmap image to an object.

1. Redraw the screen. Then choose View ➤ Render ➤ Mapping, or click Mapping on the Render toolbar.

2. At the `Select objects:` prompt, select the extruded line you created in the last exercise. The Mapping dialog box appears.

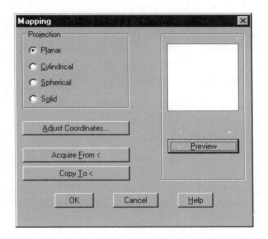

3. Click the Adjust Coordinates button. The Adjust Planar Coordinates dialog box appears.

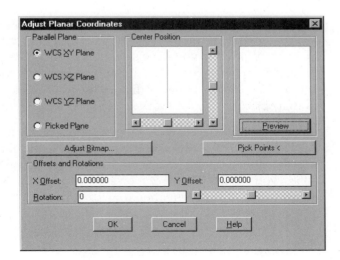

Notice the rectangle in the area labeled Center Position. This shows the relationship of the bitmap image to the object to which it has been assigned. All you can see is a vertical line.

4. Click the WCS YZ Plane radio button. The plane defined by the y- and z-axes is parallel to the surface on which you want the bitmap to appear.

5. Click the Preview button. Now you can see how the bitmap will appear on the vertical surface. You now need to adjust the positioning of the bitmap.

6. First, you want to increase the size of the bitmap in relation to the surface so the image of the building completely covers the surface. To do this, you need one other dialog box. Click the Adjust Bitmap button. The Adjust Object Bitmap Placement dialog box appears (see the top image of Figure 17.27).

7. Enter .95 in the Scale input box to the left of the U, and then enter .76 in the Scale input box to the left of the V. The U is the horizontal direction scale and the V is the vertical direction scale.

8. Click the Preview button to view the effect of the scaling. Notice that the image is larger but still not centered vertically.

9. Use the vertical Offset sliders to move the outer rectangle in the graphic upward so it looks like the bottom image of Figure 17.27, and then click the Preview button again. Now the image fits within the rectangle.

10. Click OK in each of the dialog boxes to close them, and then render the model. Your view will look like Figure 17.28.

Notice that the image of the building across the street now appears correctly and no longer looks like vertical streaks. Neither are there any odd blank spaces on the building. As you have seen in the previous exercise, the Adjust Object Bitmap Placement dialog box allows you to stretch the image vertically or horizontally in case the image is distorted and needs to be fitted to an accurately drawn object.

Another option is to use a paint program to refine the bitmap image before it is used in AutoCAD. AutoCAD attempts to place the bitmap accurately on a surface, so if the bitmap is fairly clean and doesn't have any extra blank space around the edges, you can usually place it on an object without having to make any adjustments other than its orientation.

FIGURE 17.27:

The Adjust Object Bitmap
Placement dialog box

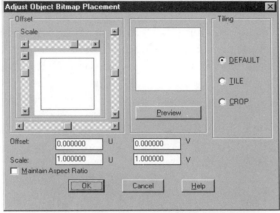

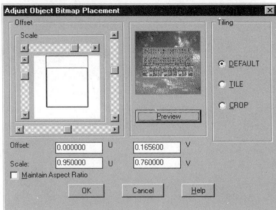

FIGURE 17.28:

The rendered view with the
bitmap image adjusted

Adding Landscape and People

There's nothing like adding landscaping and people to a rendering to add a sense of life and scale. Computer images, in particular, need landscape props because they tend to appear cold and somewhat lifeless. AutoCAD offers a set of pre-built landscape objects to help soften the appearance of your rendering. Let's see how you can add a few trees and people to the Facade model.

1. Choose View ≻ Redraw, and then choose View ≻ Render ≻ Landscape New. You can also click the Landscape New tool on the Render toolbar.

The Landscape New dialog box appears.

2. Click Quaking Aspen in the Library list, and then click Preview to view the item.

3. Use the slider just below the Preview button and change the Height value from 20 to 100, the highest setting.

4. Click the Position< button, and then click the point indicated in the top image of Figure 17.29 to place the tree in front of the buildings. You may have to adjust your view.

5. Click the View Aligned check box to deselect this option. This option is explained later in this section.

6. Click OK. The tree appears as a rectangle with a text label telling you what it is, as shown in the bottom image of Figure 17.29.

7. Copy the tree to the positions indicated in the bottom image of Figure 17.29.

8. Now render the view. You will see a view similar to Figure 17.30.

The trees you added are actually two-dimensional bitmap images. If you view the model from a glancing angle, the trees will begin to look thinner and you will see that they are indeed two-dimensional. Two of the options in the Landscape New dialog box offer some options to reduce the 2D effect. The View Aligned option you turned off in step 5 forces the tree to be aligned to your point of view, so you never see the object edge-on. Another option, Crossing Faces, creates two images of the object to appear. Each image is crossed over the other, as shown in Figure 17.31, creating an almost 3D look.

FIGURE 17.29:

Placing the trees in the Facade model

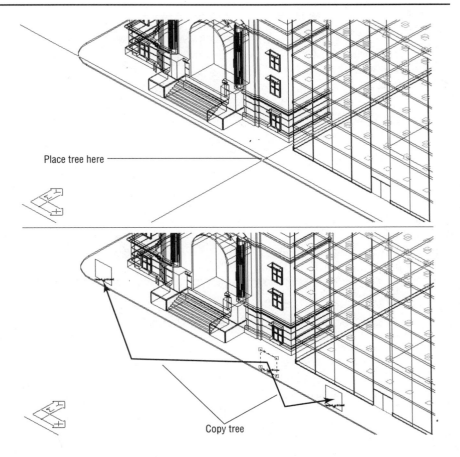

Place tree here

Copy tree

FIGURE 17.30:

The rendered view of the model with the trees

FIGURE 17.31:

The Crossing Faces option used with a landscape object

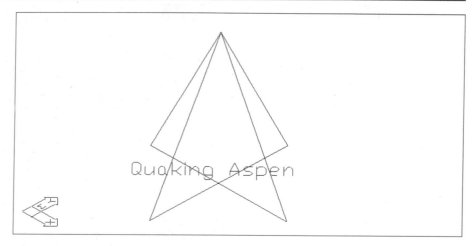

New Object Types in AutoCAD

If you were to use the List tool to find out what the landscape objects were, you would find that that they are called Plant or People. Does AutoCAD 2000 have some new object types you don't know about? The answer is maybe.

Continued on next page

AutoCAD 2000 allows third-party developers to add new object types that aren't native to the program itself. This is a fairly revolutionary idea. AutoCAD uses this capability by adding Plant and People objects. However, there is a problem with adding new object types: You need the third-party application to view and edit the objects you create. When the application is not present, the new objects become what Autodesk calls *proxies*. Proxies allow themselves to be edited with a limited set of editing tools. The level of "editability" of proxies is determined by the application that created them.

Where AutoCAD's rendering tools are concerned, the application is always present, so you are always able to edit the trees and people.

The ability to add new object types to an AutoCAD drawing has some far-reaching implications. The possibilities for third-party developers are enormous, and you, the end user, will benefit in many ways. The Landscape tool in AutoCAD is an example of what can be done.

There are a few things wrong with this rendering. The trees are too small, and they appear to be shaded on the wrong side. The shadows on the trees don't reflect the location of the Distant Light setting in the model. The street is also unusually empty for a daytime scene. The trees are easily fixed using standard AutoCAD editing tools. You can also add some people using the Landscape New tool in the Render toolbar.

1. Redraw the screen, and then click one of the trees to expose its grips.

2. Click the grip at the base of the tree, right-click the mouse, and select Rotate from the popup menu.

3. Type **180↵** to rotate the tree 180 degrees.

4. Click the grip again, right-click the mouse, and this time select Scale.

5. Enter **2.4↵** to increase the size of the tree by 2.4 times.

6. Repeat steps 1–5 for each of the other trees.

7. Open the Landscape New dialog box again and select People #1 from the list.

8. Enter a Height value of **66**, and then use the Position button to place the people at the entrance of the Facade building (see Figure 17.32). The people will appear as triangles in the Wireframe view. (Make sure you use the Nearest Osnap override to place the people.)

9. Click OK. Then repeat steps 7 and 8 to place People #2 in front of the office building between the trees (see Figure 17.32).

10. Render the view. Your view will look similar to Figure 17.33.

FIGURE 17.32:

Placing people in the scene

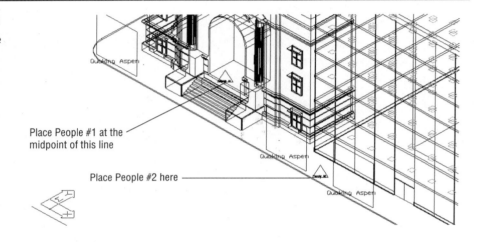

Place People #1 at the midpoint of this line

Place People #2 here

FIGURE 17.33:

The view after rendering, with the trees adjusted and people added

The shadows of the trees now match the sun's location, and they are a size better suited to the model. However, notice that the people are not lit very well. This is because when you placed them, you did not turn off the View Align option. Therefore, they are facing your view tilted slightly away from the sun. This has the effect of darkening their image.

You can use View ➤ Render Landscape Edit to change the settings for landscape objects. You will be prompted to select an object. Once you do, the Landscape Edit dialog box appears, which is identical to the Landscape New dialog box. From there, you can make changes to the settings for the selected landscape object.

Other Rendering Output Options

Throughout this chapter, you have been rendering to the AutoCAD drawing area. You can also render to a file, which enables you to recall the image at any time in any application, or render to the Render window. From there, you have a number of options in dealing with the rendered image.

Rendering to the Render Window

The Render window lets you control the resolution and color depth of your image. It also lets you save the images that you render in the Windows .bmp format. Another advantage of the Render window is that you can render several views and then compare them before you decide which ones to save.

1. Open the Render dialog box, and then select Render Window from the Destination drop-down list near the bottom of the dialog box.

2. Click Render. After a moment the Render window appears. It then takes a minute or two before the image finishes rendering and appears in the window.

Notice that the image is within its own window. If you render another view, that view will also appear in its own window, leaving the previous renderings undisturbed. You can use File ➤ Save in the Render window to save the file as a .bmp file for later editing or printing, or you can print directly from the Render window. You can also use the Render window to cut and paste the image to another application or to view other files in the .bmp format.

To set the size of renderings, you use the File ➤ Option tool in the Render window. This option opens the Windows Render Options dialog box (see Figure 17.34). Here, you can choose from two standard sizes or enter a custom size for your rendering. You can also choose between 8-bit (256 colors) and 24-bit (16 million colors) color depth. Changes to these settings don't take effect until you render another view.

FIGURE 17.34:

The Windows Render Options dialog box

Rendering Directly to a File

Rendering to the Render window allows you to view and compare your views before you save them. However, you can only save your views in the .bmp format. If you plan to further edit the image in an image-processing program, this may not be a problem. But if you want to use your image file with a program that requires a specific file format, you may want to render directly to a file. Here's how it's done.

1. Open the Render dialog box, and then select File in the Destination button group in the lower middle of the dialog box.

2. Choose More Options at the bottom of the Destination button group. The File Output Configuration dialog box appears.

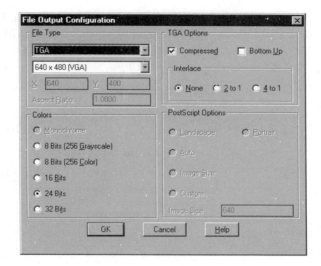

3. Click the File Type drop-down list to see the options. You can save your image in .gif, .tga, .tif, .pcx, or even PostScript format. There are also several other formats available. You might also notice the other options available in the dialog box, such as color depth, resolution, and compression. Not all these options are available for all the file types. For example, .gif is limited to 256 colors, so the other color options will not apply to .gif files.

4. Click OK to return to the Render dialog box, and then click the Render button. The Rendering File dialog box appears, prompting you for a filename for your image.

5. Enter **Facade1**. AutoCAD adds the filename extension for you.

6. Click OK and AutoCAD proceeds to render to the file.

As AutoCAD renders to the file, it tells you how much of the image has been rendered in the command line.

Improving Your Image and Editing

There will be times when you will be rushing to get a rendering done and won't want to wait for each trial rendering to become visible. AutoCAD offers several tools that can save you time by limiting the resolution or area being rendered.

Suppose you just want to render the area where you've added a tree to make sure it is in the right location. The following exercise will show you how this is done.

1. Choose View ➤ Named Views, and then restore the 3DFront view.

2. Open the Render dialog box and set the Destination option to Viewport.

3. Click the Crop Window check box to activate this option, and then click the Render button.

4. The prompt `Pick Crop Window to Render:` appears. Select the area shown in Figure 17.35, indicated by the rubber-banding square. Once you select the window, AutoCAD renders only the area you selected.

FIGURE 17.35:

Selecting the crop window

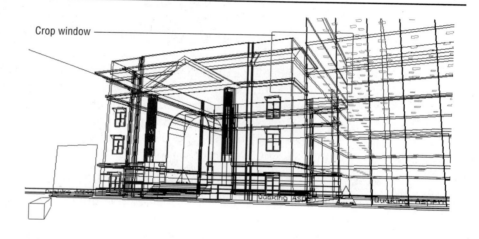

Crop window

The Crop Window option is a working tool and is not available when File or Render Window are selected as destinations.

You can also select specific objects to be included in the rendering by checking the Query for Selections check box in the Render dialog box. This option asks you to select a set of objects before it proceeds to render. You can render to all three destination options with Query for Selections turned on.

If you want to get a quick rendering with a reduced resolution to check composition, you can use the Sub Sampling drop-down list. Try the following exercise to see how it works.

1. Open the Render dialog box, and then open the Sub Sampling drop-down list.

2. Choose 3:1 from the list, make sure the Crop Window option is unchecked, and then click the Render button. Your view will render faster, but will look a bit crude (see Figure 17.36).

FIGURE 17.36:

A rendered view with the Sub Sampling option set to 3:1

The different ratios in the Sub Sampling option tell you how many pixels are being combined to reduce the resolution of the image. For example, 3:1 combines three pixels into one to reduce the resolution to a third of the original.

Smoothing Out the Rough Edges

The Sub Sampling option increases the jagged appearance of your rendering because of the reduced resolution. For your final rendering, you can actually improve the smoothness of edges and thereby increase the apparent resolution by using the Anti-Aliasing option in the Render dialog box. This option performs a kind of computer trick that reduces the jagged appearance of object edges. Anti-Aliasing blends the color of two adjacent contrasting colors. This gives the effect of smoothing out the "stairstep" appearance of a computer-generated image. The improvement to your rendering can be striking. Try the following exercise to see firsthand what Anti-Aliasing can do.

1. Open the Render dialog box, and then click the More Options button.

2. In the Raytrace Rendering Options dialog box, click the Medium radio button in the Anti-Aliasing button group, and then click OK.

3. Select 1:1 from the Sub Sampling drop-down list, and then click the Render button. The rendering takes several minutes, so you may want to take a break at this point. When the rendering is done, it will look similar to Figure 17.37.

FIGURE 17.37:

A rendering with the Anti-Aliasing setting set to Medium

Notice that the edges of the buildings are much smoother. You can also see that the vertical mullions of the office building are more clearly defined. One negative point is that the texture effect of the Facade model has been reduced. You may have to increase the scale value for the Granite Pebbles material setting to bring the texture back.

As you can see from this exercise, you trade off rendering speed for a cleaner image. You will want to save the higher Anti-Aliasing settings for your final output.

If You Want to Experiment...

In this chapter, you've participated in a guided tour of AutoCAD's rendering tools and have seen the main features of this product. Because of space considerations, this chapter didn't go into the finer details of many of its features, but you now have the basic knowledge from which to build your rendering skills. Without too much effort, you can adapt much of what you've learned here to your own projects. If you need more detailed information, use the Help button found in all the Render dialog boxes.

Computer rendering of 3D models is a craft that takes some time to master. Experiment with these rendering tools to see firsthand the types of results you can expect. You might want to try different types of views like an Isometric or Elevation view, the latter of which is shown in Figure 17.38. With a bit more detail added, this rendered elevation could fit nicely into a set of renderings for a presentation.

FIGURE 17.38:

An Elevation view of the Facade model

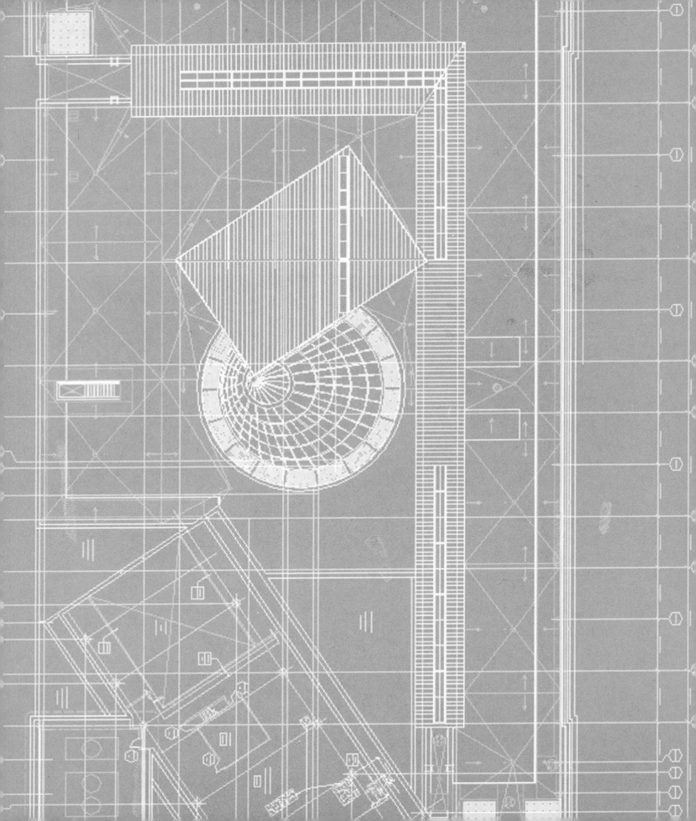

18

Mastering 3D Solids

- Understanding Solid Modeling

- Creating Solid Forms

- Creating Complex Primitives

- Editing Solids

- Enhancing the 2D Drawing Process

- Finding the Properties of a Solid

- Taking Advantage of Stereolithography

- If You Want to Experiment...

So far, you have been creating 3D models according to a method called *surface modeling*: As you drew, you used 3D Faces to give your models form and the appearance of solidity. But there is another method that you can use to create 3D computer models: *solid modeling*.

With surface models, drawing a simple cube requires several steps; with solids, you can create a cube with one command. Having created a solid model, you can assign materials to it and have the computer find physical properties of the model, such as weight and center of mass. It is easier to create models by using solid modeling, and there are many advantages to the technique, especially in mechanical design and engineering.

Solid modeling was once thought to require more computational power than most personal computers could offer, but with today's powerful microcomputer hardware, solid modeling is well within the reach of most PC users. AutoCAD offers built-in solid modeling functions, which you will explore in this chapter.

Understanding Solid Modeling

Solid modeling is a way of defining 3D objects as solid forms rather than as wireframes with surfaces attached. When you create a 3D model using solid modeling, you start with the basic forms of your model—cubes, cones, and cylinders, for instance. These basic solids are called *primitives*. Then, using more of these primitives, you begin to add to or subtract from your basic forms. For example, to create a model of a tube, you first create two solid cylinders, one smaller in diameter than the other. Then you align the two cylinders so they are concentric and tell AutoCAD to subtract the smaller cylinder from the larger one. The larger of the two cylinders then becomes a tube whose inside diameter is that of the smaller cylinder, as shown in Figure 18.1.

Several primitives are available for modeling solids in AutoCAD (see Figure 18.2).

FIGURE 18.1:

Creating a tube using solid modeling

Create two cylinder primitives, one for the outside diameter and one for the inside diameter.

Cylinder for inside diameter

Cylinder for outside diameter

Superimpose the cylinder for the inside diameter onto the cylinder for the outside diameter.

Use the Subtract command to subtract the inside diameter cylinder from the outside diameter cylinder.

FIGURE 18.2:

The solids primitives

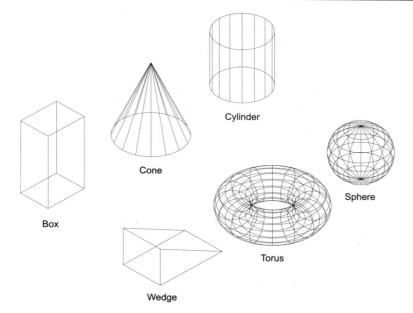

Cylinder

Cone

Sphere

Box

Torus

Wedge

These shapes—box, wedge, cone, cylinder, sphere, and donut (or *torus*)—can be joined in one of four ways to produce secondary shapes. The first three, demonstrated in Figure 18.3 using a cube and a cylinder as examples, are called *Boolean operations*. (The name comes from the nineteenth-century mathematician George Boole.) There are three joining methods, as follows:

Intersection   Uses only the intersecting region of two objects to define a solid shape.

Subtraction   Uses one object to cut out a shape in another.

Union   Joins two primitives so they act as one object.

FIGURE 18.3:

The intersection, subtraction, and union of a cube and a cylinder

A solid box and a solid cylinder are superimposed.

The intersection of the primitives creates a solid cylinder with the ends skewed.

The cylinder subtracted from the box creates a hole in the box.

The union of the two primitives creates a box with two round pegs.

A fourth option, *interference*, lets you find exactly where two or more solids coincide in space—similar to the results of a union. The main difference between interference and union is that interference allows you to keep the original solid shapes, while union discards the original solids, leaving the form represented by their intersection. With interference, you can have AutoCAD either show you the shape of the coincident space or create a solid based on the coincident space's shape.

Joined primitives are called *composite solids*. You can join primitives to primitives, composite solids to primitives, and composite solids to other composite solids.

Now let's take a look at how these concepts let us create models in AutoCAD.

NOTE   To simplify the exercises in this chapter, all of the instructions in the exercises are unitless; that is, the book doesn't specify inches or centimeters. This way, users of both the metric and English measurement systems will be able to use the exercises without having to deal with duplicate information.

Creating Solid Forms

In this section, you will begin to draw the object shown in Figure 18.4. In the process, you will explore the creation of solid models by creating primitives and then setting up special relationships between them.

FIGURE 18.4:

This steel bracket was created in and rendered in AutoCAD.

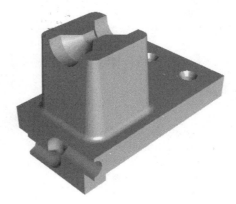

Displaying the Solids Toolbar

All of the commands you will use to create the solids primitives, and many of the commands you can use for editing solids, are accessible on the Solids toolbar.

Right-click any toolbar and select Solids from the popup menu. The Solids tool-bar appears.

Open the Solids Editing toolbar as well. Now you're ready to begin creating basic solids.

Creating Primitives

Primitives are the basic building blocks of solid modeling. At first, it may seem limiting to have only six primitives to work with, but consider the varied forms you can create with just a few two-dimensional objects. Let's begin by creating the basic mass of our steel bracket. First, prepare your drawing for the exercise.

1. Create a new file called `Bracket`.

2. Right-click the SNAP button on the status bar, then in the Drafting Settings dialog box, set the Snap spacing to **0.5** and turn on the Grid and Snap modes.

3. Turn on the dynamic coordinate readout by pressing F6. You'll use the read-out to help guide you in selecting points in the exercises that follow.

Now start building the solid model.

1. Click the Box tool on the Solids toolbar, or enter **BOX**↵. You may also choose Draw ➢ Solids ➢ Box.

2. At the `Specify corner of box or [CEnter] <0,0,0>:` prompt, pick a point at coordinate 3,2.5.

3. At the `Specify corner or [Cube/Length]:` prompt, enter **@7,4**↵ to create a box with a length of 7 and a width of 4.

4. The `Specify height:` prompt that appears next is asking for the height of the box in the z-axis. Enter **1**↵.

You've now drawn your first primitive, a box that is 7 units long by 4 units wide by 1 unit deep. Now, let's change the view so you can see the box more clearly. Use the Vpoint command to shift your view so you are looking at the WCS from the lower left.

5. Open the Viewpoint Presets dialog box (choose View ➤ 3D Views ➤ Select), and then enter **225** in the From X Axis input box and **19.5** in the XY Plane input box.

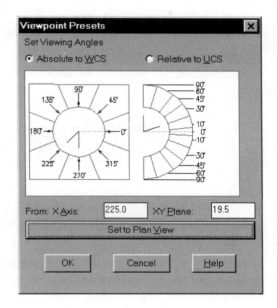

6. Click OK, and then adjust your view so it looks similar to Figure 18.5.

FIGURE 18.5:

The first stage of the bracket

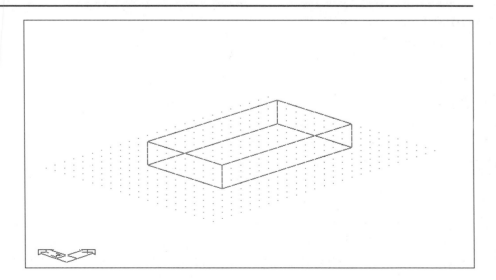

Turning a 2D Polyline into a 3D Solid

Now let's add another box to form the lower lip of the bracket. This time, you'll create a box primitive from a polyline.

1. Click the Polyline tool on the Draw toolbar.

2. At the From point: prompt, start the polyline from the coordinate .5,2.5.

3. Continue the polyline around to create a rectangle that is 1 unit in the x-axis and 3 units in the y-axis. Your drawing will look like Figure 18.6.

4. Click the Extrude tool on the Solids toolbar, or type **EXT**↵.

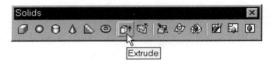

5. At the Select objects: prompt, pick the polyline and press ↵.

6. At the Specify height of extrusion or [Path]: prompt, type **1**↵.

7. At the Specify angle of taper for extrusion <0>: prompt, press ↵ to accept the default taper of 0°. (You'll see what the Taper option does in a later exercise.) The polyline now extrudes in the z-axis to form a bar, as shown in Figure 18.7.

8. Type **R**↵ to redraw the screen.

FIGURE 18.6:

The polyline drawn in place

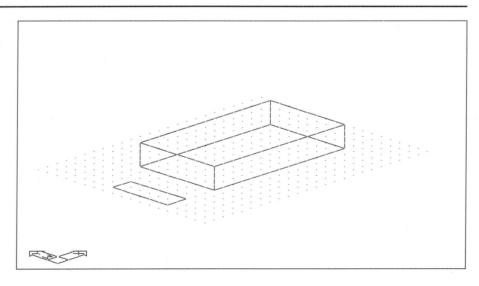

FIGURE 18.7:

The converted polyline box

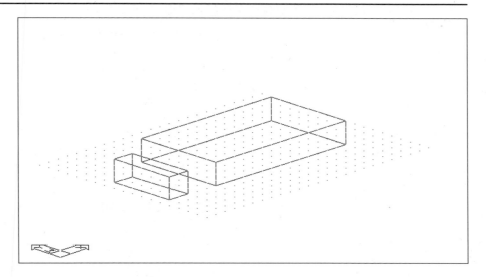

You've now drawn two box primitives using the Box and the Extrude options on the Solids toolbar. Just for variety's sake, this exercise had you create the smaller box by converting a polyline into a solid, but you could just as easily have used the Box option for that as well. The Extrude option converts polylines, circles, and traces into solids. (Regular lines, 3D lines, 3D Faces, and 3D polylines cannot be extruded.)

Other Solids Options

Before you continue, let's examine the commands for primitives that you haven't had a chance to use yet. Refer to Figures 18.8 through 18.11 to understand the terms used with these other primitives.

> **Cone↵ (Cone icon on the Solids toolbar)**   Draws a circular cone or a cone with an elliptical base. Drawing a circular cone is much like drawing a circle, with an added prompt asking for a height. The Ellipse option acts like the Ellipse command (on the Draw toolbar), with an additional prompt for height.

FIGURE 18.8:

Drawing a solid cone

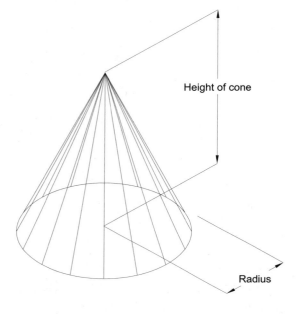

Height of cone

Radius

Sphere.↵ (Sphere icon on the Solids toolbar) Acts like the Circle command, but instead of drawing a circle, it draws a sphere.

FIGURE 18.9:

Drawing a solid sphere

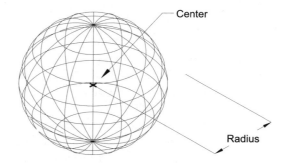

Center

Radius

Torus.↵ (Torus icon on the Solids toolbar) Creates a torus (a donut-shaped solid). You are prompted for two diameters or radii, one for the diameter or radius of the torus and another for the diameter or radius of the tube portion of the torus.

FIGURE 18.10:

Drawing a solid torus

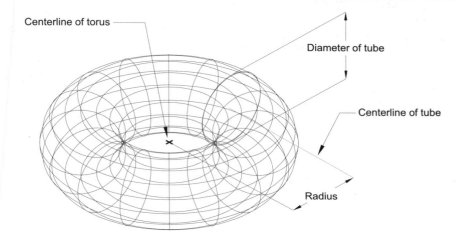

Centerline of torus

Diameter of tube

Centerline of tube

Radius

Wedge↵ (Wedge icon on the Solids toolbar)   Creates a wedge-shaped solid. This command acts much like the Box command you used to draw the bracket. You have the choice of defining the wedge by two corners or by its center and a corner.

FIGURE 18.11:

Drawing a solid wedge

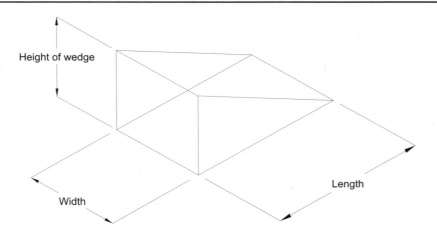

Height of wedge

Width

Length

In the following exercises you will be creating and combining solid primitives. The commands required to create complex solids are available on the Solids Editing toolbar.

Joining Primitives

Now let's see how the two box objects you created are joined. First, you'll move the new box into place, and then join the two boxes to form a single solid.

1. Start the Move command, pick the smaller of the two boxes, and then press ↵.

2. At the `Base point:` prompt, use the Midpoint Osnap override and pick the middle of the back edge of the smaller box, as shown in the top image of Figure 18.12.

3. At the `Second point:` prompt, pick the middle of the bottom edge of the larger box, as shown in the bottom image of Figure 18.12.

FIGURE 18.12:

Moving the smaller box

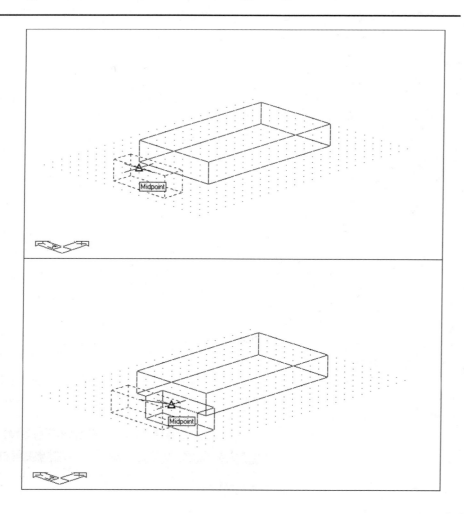

4. Choose Modify ➤ Solids Editing ➤ Union, or type **Uni**↵. You may also click Union on the Solids Editing toolbar.

5. At the Select objects: prompt, pick both boxes and press ↵. Your drawing now looks like Figure 18.13.

FIGURE 18.13:

The two boxes joined

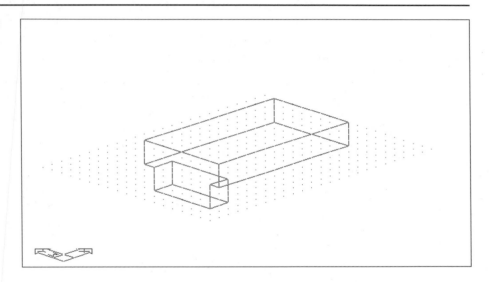

As you can see in Figure 18.13, the form has joined to appear as one object. It also acts like one object when you select it. You now have a composite solid made up of two box primitives.

Now let's place some holes in the bracket. In this next exercise, you will discover how to create negative forms to cut portions out of a solid.

1. Click the Cylinder tool on the Solids toolbar, or type **Cylinder**↵. You may also choose Draw ➤ Solids ➤ Cylinder.

2. At the `Specify center point for base of cylinder or [Elliptical]` `<0,0,0>:` prompt, pick a point at the coordinate 9,5.5.

3. At the `Specify radius for base of cylinder or [Diameter]:` prompt, enter **.25**.

NOTE   As with the Circle command, you can enter **D** to specify a diameter or enter a radius value directly.

---

4. At the `Specify height of cylinder or [Center of other end]:` prompt, enter **1.5**↵. The cylinder is drawn.

5. Copy the cylinder two inches in the negative direction of the y-axis, so your drawing looks like Figure 18.14.

FIGURE 18.14:

The cylinders added to the drawing

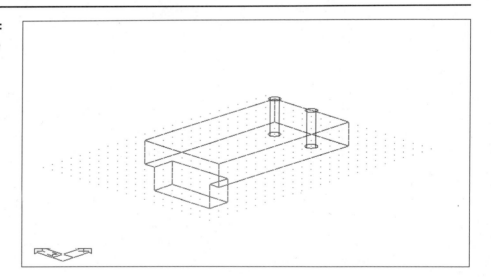

You now have the cylinder primitive, but you still need to define its relationship to the composite solid you created from the two boxes.

1. Choose Modify ➤ Solids Editing ➤ Subtract, or type **Su**↵. You may also click the Subtract tool on the Solids Editing toolbar.

2. At the Select solids and regions to subtract from... Select objects: prompt, pick the composite solid of the two boxes and press ↵.

3. At the Solids and regions to subtract... Select objects: prompt, pick two of the cylinders and press ↵. The cylinder has now been subtracted from the bracket.

4. To view the solid, choose View ➤ Hide. You'll see a Hidden-Line view of the solid, as shown in Figure 18.15.

FIGURE 18.15:

The bracket so far, with hidden lines removed

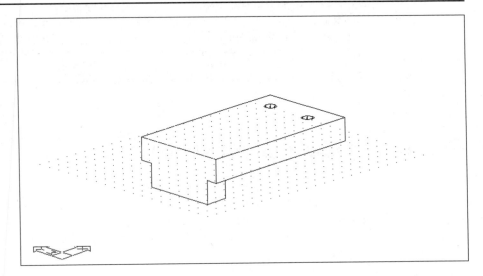

As you've learned in the earlier chapters in Part IV, Wireframe views, such as the one in step 3, are somewhat difficult to decipher. Until you use the Hide command (step 4), you cannot tell for sure that the subtracted cylinder is in fact a hole. Using the Hide command frequently will help you keep track of what's going on with your solid model.

In step 3 of the previous exercise, you may have noticed that the cylinders changed shape to conform to the depth of the bracket. You'll also recall that you drew the cylinder at a height of 1.5 units, not 1 unit, which is the thickness of the bracket. Having drawn the cylinder taller than needed, you can see that when AutoCAD performed the subtraction, it ignored the portion of the cylinder that doesn't affect the bracket. AutoCAD always discards the portion of a primitive that isn't used in a Subtract operation.

What Are Isolines?

You may have noticed the message that reads:

```
Current wire frame density:  ISOLINES=4
```

This message tells you the current setting for the Isolines system variable. The Isolines system variable controls the way curved objects, such as cylinders and holes, are displayed. A setting of 4 causes cylinders to be represented by four lines with circles at each end. You can see this in the holes that you've created for the Bracket model in the previous exercise. You can change the Isolines setting by entering **Isoline.⏎** at the command prompt. You then enter a value for the number of lines to use to represent surfaces. This setting is also controlled by the Contour Lines Per Surface option in the Display tab of the Options dialog box.

Creating Complex Primitives

As you learned earlier, you can convert a polyline into a solid using the Extrude option on the Solids toolbar. This process lets you create more complex primitives. In addition to the simple straight extrusion you've already tried, you can also extrude shapes into curved paths, or you can taper an extrusion.

Tapering an Extrusion

Next, you'll take a look at how you can taper an extrusion to create a fairly complex solid with little effort.

1. Draw a 3×3 closed polyline at the top of the current solid. Start at the back-left corner of the bracket at coordinate 3.5,3,1, and then draw the 3×3 closed polyline to fit in the top of the composite solid, as shown in Figure 18.16.

WARNING Remember to use the Close option to create the last side of the box.

2. Click the Fillet tool on the Modify toolbar. At the `Select first object or [Polyline/Radius/Trim]:` prompt, type **R⏎** to set the radius of the fillet.

3. At the prompt for the fillet radius, type **.5**↵.

4. At the command prompt, press ↵ to again issue the Fillet command, and then type **P**↵ to tell the Fillet command that you want to chamfer a polyline.

5. Click the polyline. The corners become rounded.

6. Click the Extrude button on the Solids toolbar, or enter **Ext**↵ at the command prompt.

7. At the `Select objects:` prompt, pick the polyline you just drew and press ↵. (As the prompt indicates, you can pick polylines or circles.)

8. At the `Specify height of extrusion or [Path]:` prompt, enter **3**↵.

9. At the `Specify angle of taper for extrusion <0>:` prompt, enter **4** for 4° of taper. The extruded polyline looks like Figure 18.17.

10. Now join the part you just created with the original solid. Choose Modify ➤ Boolean ➤ Union, and then select the extruded part and the rectangular solid just below it.

NOTE   In step 9, you can indicate a taper for the extrusion. Specify a taper in terms of degrees from the z-axis, or enter a negative value to taper the extrusion outward. Or press ↵ to accept the default, 0°, to extrude the polyline without a taper.

FIGURE 18.16:

Drawing the 3 × 3 polyline box

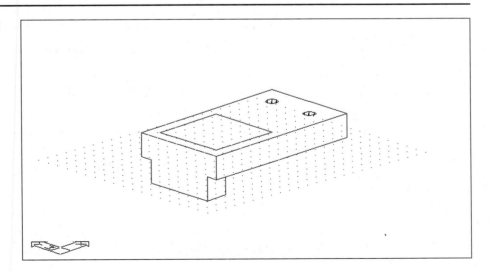

FIGURE 18.17:

The extruded polyline

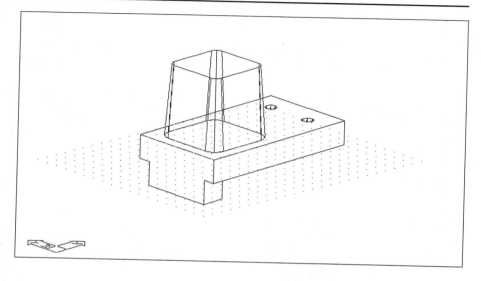

Extruding on a Curved Path

As demonstrated in the following exercise, the Extrude command lets you extrude virtually any polyline shape along a path that is defined by a polyline, arc, or 3D polyline.

1. Choose View ➤ Zoom ➤ Extents and turn off the grid.

2. Choose View ➤ Hide. This helps you view and select parts of your model in the following steps.

3. Start by placing the UCS on a vertical plane perpendicular to the back of the bracket. Choose Tools ➤ Orthographic UCS ➤ Left.

4. Start a polyline at the point shown in the top image of Figure 18.18. Use the Midpoint Osnap to make sure you select the midpoint of the vertical corner edge. After you locate the first point, enter the following coordinates:

   ```
   @2<180
   @1<270
   @2<180
   ```

   When you are done, your drawing should look like the bottom image of Figure 18.18.

5. Click the Fillet tool on the Modify toolbar, and then type **R↵** to set the fillet radius.

6. Enter **.4↵** for the fillet radius.

7. Press ↵ to reissue the Fillet command, and then type **P↵** to select the Polyline option.

8. Click the polyline you drew on the backside of the solid.

9. Choose Tools ➤ New UCS ➤ Y, and then enter **90↵**. This rotates the UCS 90 degrees around the y-axis so the UCS is perpendicular to the front face of the solid.

10. Draw a circle with a 0.35-unit radius at the location shown in the second image of Figure 18.18.

TIP The Hidden-Line view of the solid in Figure 18.18 shows a lot of extra facets on the curved portion of the model. You can set up AutoCAD so these extra facets don't appear. Open the Options dialog box and place a check by the Show Silhouettes in Wireframe option on the Display tab.

At this point, you've created the components needed to do the extrusion. Next, you'll finish the extruded shape.

1. Click the Extrude button on the Solids toolbar, click the circle, and then press ↵.

2. At the Specify height of extrusion or [Path]: prompt, type **P↵** to enter the Path option.

3. At the Select extrusion path: prompt, click the polyline curve. AutoCAD pauses a moment and then generate a solid "tube" that follows the path. The tube may not look like a tube because AutoCAD draws extruded solids such as this with a single line showing its profile.

4. Click the Subtract tool on the Solids Editing toolbar or choose Modify ➤ Solid Editing ➤ Subtract, and then select the rectangular solid.

5. Press ↵. At the Select objects: prompt, click the curved solid and press ↵. The curved solid is subtracted from the square solid. Your drawing will look like Figure 18.19.

FIGURE 18.18:

Setting up your drawing to create a curved extrusion

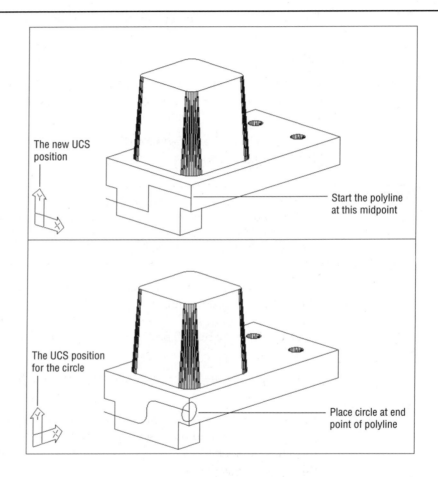

In this exercise, you used a curved polyline for the extrusion path, but you can use any type of 2D or 3D polyline, as well as lines and arcs, for an extrusion path.

FIGURE 18.19:

The solid after subtracting
the curve

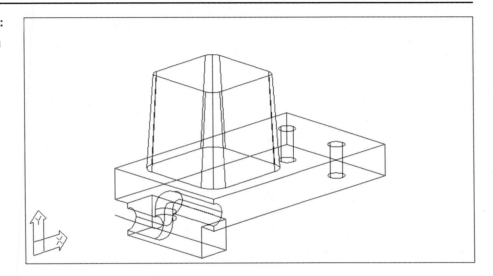

Revolving a Polyline

When your goal is to draw an object that is circular, the Revolve command on the
Solids toolbar is designed to let you create a solid that is revolved, or swept in a
circular path. Think of Revolve's action as similar to a lathe that lets you carve a
shape from a spinning shaft. In this case, the spinning shaft is a polyline, and rather
than carving it, you define the profile and then revolve the profile around an axis.

In the following exercise, you will draw a solid that will form a slot in the tapered
solid.

1. Zoom in to the top of the tapered box, so you have a view similar to Fig-
    ure 18.20.

2. Turn the Snap mode off.

3. Return to the WCS by choosing Tools ➤ New UCS ➤ World.

4. Next, choose Tools ➤ New UCS ➤ Origin.

5. At the Origin: prompt, use the Midpoint Osnap override and pick the mid-
    point of the top surface, as shown in Figure 18.20.

FIGURE 18.20:

An enlarged view of the top of the tapered box and the new UCS location

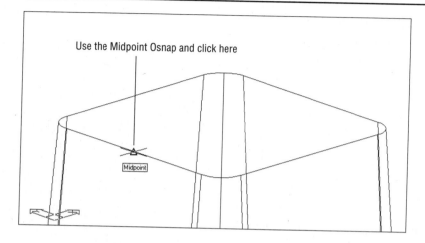

6. Set the Snap distance to **0.25** and turn on Polar Tracking.

7. Draw a polyline using Polar Tracking with the following polar coordinates:

   ```
   Start at -0.25,0
   0.75<90
   0.75<0
   0.7071<315
   0.5<0
   0.7071<45
   0.75<0
   0.75<270
   ```

8. When you've finished, type **C**↵ to close the polyline. AutoCAD will not revolve an open polyline. Your drawing should look like Figure 18.21.

9. Click the Revolve tool on the Solids toolbar, or type **Rev**↵ at the command prompt.

FIGURE 18.21:

Drawing the polyline

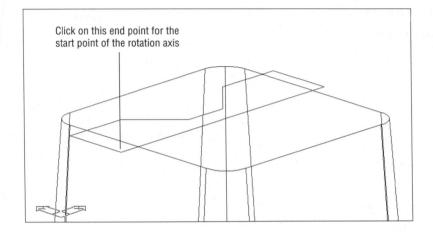

Click on this end point for the
start point of the rotation axis

10. At the `Select objects:` prompt, pick the polyline you just drew and press ↵.

11. When you see the next prompt:

    `Axis of revolution - Object/X/t/<Start point of axis>:`

    use the Endpoint Osnap override and pick the beginning endpoint of the polyline you just drew.

12. Turn on the Ortho mode (press F8) and turn off the Snap mode (press F9). Then pick a point to the far left of the screen so that the rubber-banding line is parallel with the x-axis of the current UCS.

13. At the `Angle of revolution <full circle>:` prompt, press ↵ to sweep the polyline a full 360°. The revolved form appears, as shown in Figure 18.22.

You have just created a revolved solid that will be subtracted from the tapered box to form a slot in the bracket. But before you subtract it, you need to make a slight change in the orientation of the revolved solid.

1. Choose Modify ➤ 3D Operation ➤ Rotate 3D.

2. At the `Select objects:` prompt, select the revolved solid and press ↵.

3. At the prompt

    `Axis by Entity/Last/View/Xaxis/Yaxis/Zaxis/<2point>`

    use the Midpoint Osnap and click the right-side edge of the top surface, as shown in Figure 18.23.

FIGURE 18.22:

The revolved polyline

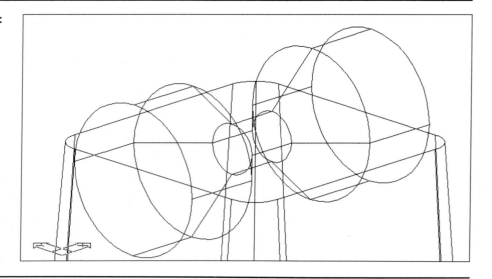

FIGURE 18.23:

Selecting the points to rotate the revolved solid in 3D space

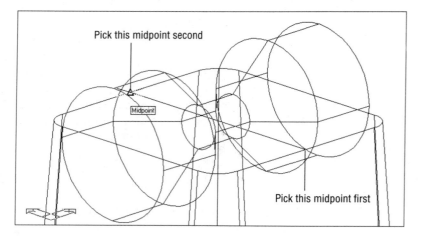

Pick this midpoint second

Midpoint

Pick this midpoint first

4. At the 2nd point on axis: prompt, use the Midpoint Osnap again and click the opposite side of the top surface, as shown in Figure 18.23.

5. At the <Rotation angle>/Reference: prompt, type **5**↵. The solid rotates 5°.

6. Click the Subtract tool on the Solids Editing toolbar or choose Modify ➤ Solids Editing ➤ Subtract, click the tapered box, and then press ↵.

7. At the Select objects: prompt, click the revolved solid and press ↵. Your drawing looks like Figure 18.24.

FIGURE 18.24:

The composite solid

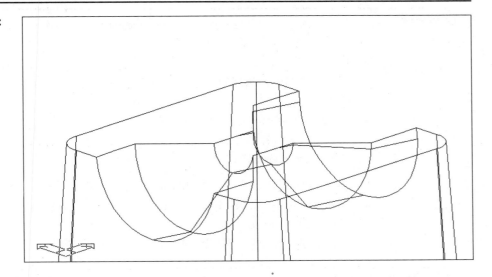

Editing Solids

Basic solid forms are fairly easy to create. The refinement of those forms requires some special tools. In this section, you'll learn how to use some familiar 2D editing tools to edit a solid as well as some new tools. You'll also be introduced to the Slice tool that lets you cut a solid into two pieces.

Splitting a Solid into Two Pieces

Perhaps one of the more common solid editing tools you'll use is the Slice tool. As you might guess from its name, Slice allows you to cut a solid into two pieces. The following exercise demonstrates how it works.

1. Zoom to the previous view and return to the World Coordinate System.

2. Click the Slice tool on the Solids toolbar, or type **Slice**↵.

NOTE   In step 3, you could select more than one solid. The Slice command would then slice all the solids through the plane indicated in steps 4 and 5.

3. At the `Select object:` prompt, click the part you've been working on and press ⏎.

4. At the prompt

   ```
   Specify first point on slicing plane by [Object/
   Zaxis/View/XY/YZ/ZX/3points] <3points>:
   ```

   type **XY**⏎. This lets you indicate a slice plane parallel to the x-y plane.

5. At the `Point on XY plane <0,0,0>:` prompt, type **0,0,.5**⏎. This places the slice plane at the z-coordinate of .5 units. You can use the Midpoint Osnap and pick any vertical edge of the rectangular solid.

NOTE   If you want to delete one side of the sliced solid, you can indicate the side you want to keep by clicking it in step 6, instead of entering **B**⏎.

6. At the `Specify a point on desired side of the plane or [keep Both sides]:` prompt, type **B**⏎ to keep both sides of the solid. AutoCAD will divide the solid horizontally, one-half inch above the base of the part, as shown in Figure 18.25.

FIGURE 18.25:

The solid sliced through the base

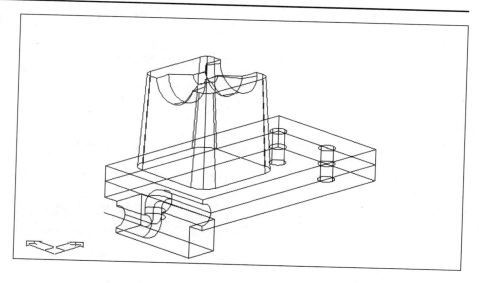

The Slice Options

There were several options in step 4 of the previous exercise that are worth discussing here. Here are descriptions of those options:

Object   Lets you select an object to define the slice plane.

Zaxis   Lets you select two points defining the z-axis of the slice plane. The two points you pick will be perpendicular to the slice plane.

View   Generates a slice plane that is perpendicular to your current view. You are prompted for the coordinate through which the slice plane must pass—usually a point on the object.

3point   Is the default, and lets you select three points defining the slice plane. Normally, you would pick points on the solid.

XY/YZ/ZX   Pick one of these to determine the slice plane based on the x-, y-, or z-axis. You are prompted to pick a point through which the slice plane must pass.

Rounding Corners with the Fillet Tool

Your bracket has a few sharp corners that you may want to round in order to give the bracket a more realistic appearance. You can use the Construct menu's Fillet and Chamfer commands to add these rounded corners to your solid model.

1. Adjust your view of the model so it looks similar to the top image of Figure 18.26.

2. Click the Fillet tool on the Modify toolbar.

3. At the `Select first object or [Polyline/Radius/Trim]:` prompt, pick the edge indicated in the top image of Figure 18.26.

4. At the `Enter fillet radius:` prompt, type .2↵.

5. At the `Select an edge or [Chain/Radius]:` prompt, type C↵ for the Chain option. Chain lets you select a series of solid edges to be filleted.

6. Select one of the other three edges at the base of the tapered form, and press ↵ when you are done.

7. Choose Hide on the Render toolbar, or type **Hide**↵, to get a better look at your model, as shown in the bottom image of Figure 18.26.

As you saw in step 5, Fillet acts a bit differently when you use it on solids. The Chain option lets you select a set of edges, instead of just two adjoining objects.

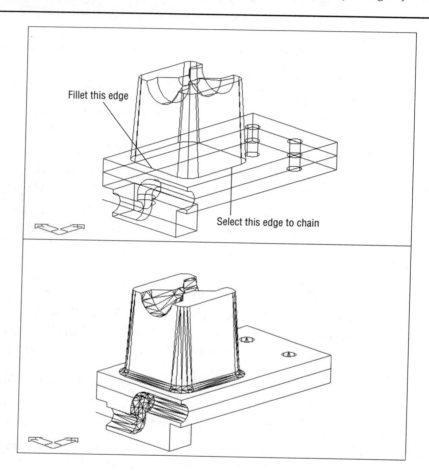

Chamfering Corners with the Chamfer Tool

Now let's try chamfering a corner. To practice using Chamfer, you'll add a countersink to the cylindrical hole you created in the first solid.

1.   Type **Regen.** to return to a Wireframe view of your model.

2. Click the Chamfer tool on the Modify toolbar, or type **Cha**.

Chamfer

3. At this prompt

    `Select first line or [Polyline/Distance/Angle/Trim/Method]:`

    pick the edge of the hole, as shown in Figure 18.27. Notice that the top surface of the solid is highlighted, and the prompt changes to `Enter surface selection option [Next/OK (current)] <OK>:`. The highlighting indicates the base surface, which will be used as a reference in step 5. (You could also type **N.⏎** to choose the other adjoining surface, the inside of the hole, as the base surface.)

FIGURE 18.27:

Picking the edge to chamfer

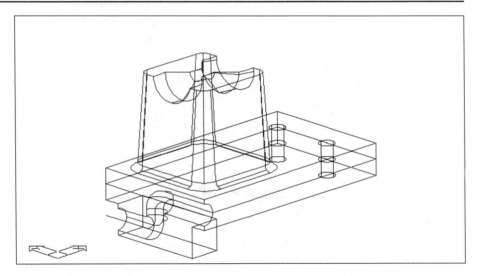

4. Press ⏎ to accept the current highlighted face.

5. At the `Specify base surface chamfer distance <0.5000>:` prompt, type **.125⏎**. This indicates that you want the chamfer to have a width of .125 across the highlighted surface.

6. At the `Specify other surface chamfer distance <0.5000>:` prompt, type **.2**⏎.

7. At the `Select an edge or [Loop]:` prompt, click the edges of both holes and then press ⏎. When it is done, your drawing will look like Figure 18.28.

8. After reviewing the work you've done here, save the `Bracket.dwg` file.

NOTE   The Loop option in step 7 lets you chamfer the entire circumference of an object. You don't need to use it here because the edge forms a circle. The Loop option is used when you have a rectangular or other polygonal edge you want to chamfer.

FIGURE 18.28:

The chamfered edges

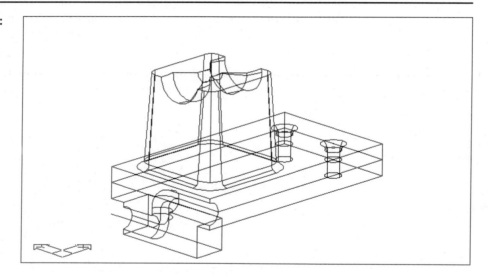

Using the Solid Editing Tools

You've added some refinements to the Bracket model by using some standard AutoCAD editing tools. There is a set of tools that is specifically geared toward editing solids. You already used the Union and Subtract tools found on the Solids Editing toolbar. In this section, you'll explore some of the other tools available on that toolbar.

To help keep the exercises simple and easy to understand, you'll be using an existing 3D model called `Solidedit.dwg`. This file will help to demonstrate the Solids Editing tools.

Moving a Surface

The first tool you'll try is the Move tool. The Move tool moves the surface of a solid.

1. Open the `Solidedit.dwg` file. This file is set up with the Hidden Shade mode turned on so you can see the form more easily.

2. Click the Move Faces tool in the Solids Editing toolbar, then click the back edge of the model, as shown in Figure 18.29. Notice that two surfaces are highlighted. These are the faces that will be moved unless you indicate otherwise. To isolate the back surface, you will remove the top surface from the selection set.

3. At the `Select faces or [Undo/Remove/ALL]:` prompt, type **R.**⏎. The prompt changes to read `Remove faces or [Undo/Add/ALL]:`. Now any highlighted object you select will be removed from the selection set.

4. Click the edge of the top surface, as indicated in Figure 18.29. The top surface is removed from the selection set.

5. Press ⏎ to finish your selection.

6. At the `Specify a base point or displacement:` prompt, click any point near the back face.

7. At the `Specify a second point of displacement:` prompt, enter **@.6<0.**⏎ to move the surface 0.6 units to the right.

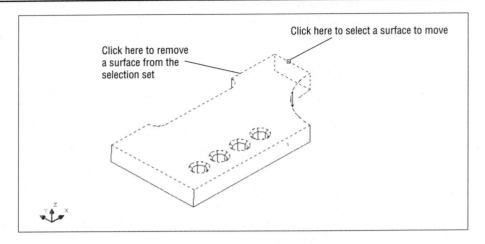

Once you've selected the surface you want to move, the Move Faces tool acts just like the Move command. Notice how the curved side of the model extends its curve to meet the new location of the surface. This shows you that AutoCAD attempts to maintain the geometry of the model when you make changes to the faces.

Try Move Faces again, but this time, move a set of faces on the interior of the model.

1. Click the Move Faces tool again.

2. Click the countersink hole closest to the foreground, as shown in Figure 18.30. Then click the straight shaft of the hole, as shown in Figure 18.30.

3. Press ↵ to finish your selection, then click any point on the screen.

4. Enter @1<90↵. The hole moves 1 unit in the y-axis.

In some instances, AutoCAD will not be able to move surfaces. This usually occurs when an adjoining surface is too complex.

FIGURE 18.30:

Moving the countersink
hole in the model

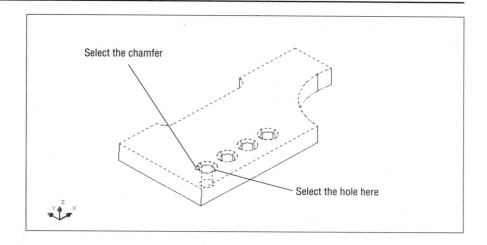

Select the chamfer

Select the hole here

Offsetting a Surface

Now suppose you want to decrease the radius of the arc in the right corner of the
model, and you also want to thicken the model by the same amount as the decrease
in the arc radius. To do this, you can use the Offset Faces tool.

1. Click the Offset Faces tool on the Solids Editing toolbar.

2. Click the lower edge of the curved surface, as shown in Figure 18.31. Notice
   that both the curved surface and the bottom of the model are highlighted.
   You can add or remove surfaces from the selection set as you did in the previous two exercises. Here, you'll just stick with the selection set you have.

3. Press ↵ to finish your selection, then at the Specify the offset distance:
   prompt, enter .5↵. The surfaces move to their new location.

FIGURE 18.31:

Selecting a surface to offset

FIGURE 18.31:

Selecting a surface to offset

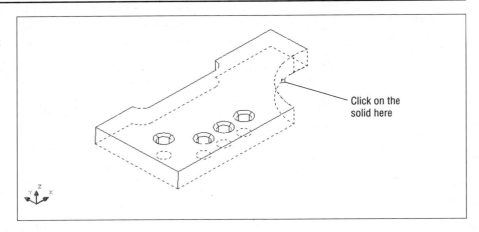

Click on the
solid here

FIGURE 18.32:

The model after offsetting
the curved and bottom
surface

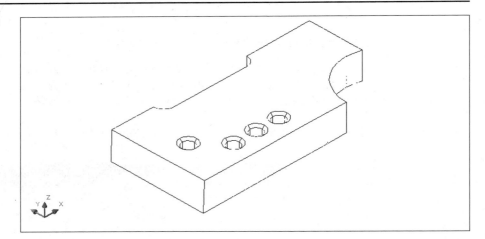

Deleting a Surface

Now suppose you've decided to eliminate the curved part of the model altogether.
You can delete a surface using the Delete Faces tool.

1. Click the Delete Faces tool on the Solids Editing toolbar.

2. At the `Select faces or [Undo/Remove]:` prompt, click the bottom edge of the curve as you did in the last exercise. You'll need to remove the bottom surface from the selection set, otherwise this operation won't work.

3. Type **R↵** and then select the back edge of the bottom surface to remove it from the selection set. The curved surface remains highlighted.

4. Type ↵ to finish your selection. The curve disappears and a corner forms in its place, as shown in Figure 18.33.

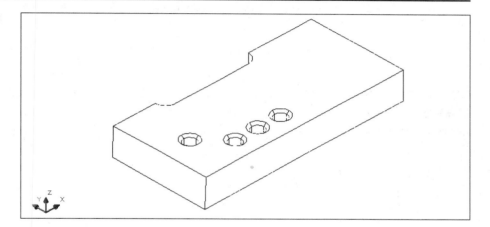

When you attempt to delete surfaces, keep in mind that the surface you delete must be recoverable by other surfaces in the model. For example, you cannot remove the top surface of a cube expecting it to turn into a pyramid. That would require the sides to change their orientation, which is not allowed in this operation. You can, on the other hand, remove the top of a box with tapered sides. Then, when you remove the top, the sides converge to form a pyramid.

Rotating a Surface

All of the surfaces of the model are parallel or perpendicular to each other. Imagine that your design requires two sides to be at an angle. You can change the angle of a surface using the Rotate Faces tool.

1. Click the Rotate Faces tool on the Solids Editing toolbar.

2. At the `Select faces or [Undo/Remove]:` prompt, select the corner edge in the foreground, as shown in Figure 18.34, then press ↵. The two surfaces facing you are highlighted.

3. At the `Specify an axis point or [Axis by object/View/Xaxis/Yaxis/Zaxis] <2points>:` prompt, use the Endpoint Osnap to select the bottom of the corner, as shown in Figure 18.34.

4. At the `Specify the second point on the rotation axis:` prompt, use the Endpoint Osnap to select the top of the corner as shown in Figure 18.34. The two points you just selected specify the axis of rotation for the surface rotation.

5. At the `Specify a rotation angle or [Reference]:` prompt, enter 4↵. The two surfaces change their orientation, as shown in Figure 18.35.

FIGURE 18.34:

Defining the axis of rotation

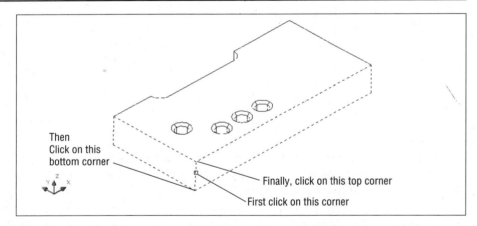

Then
Click on this
bottom corner

Finally, click on this top corner

First click on this corner

FIGURE 18.35:

The model after rotating two surfaces

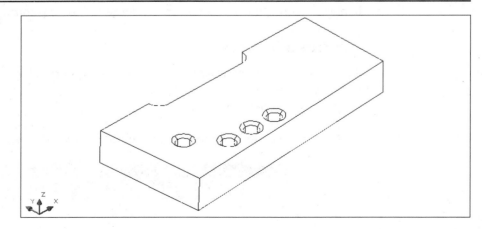

Tapering Surfaces

In an earlier exercise, you saw how to create a new tapered solid using the Extrude command. But what if you want to taper an existing solid? Here's what you can do to taper an existing 3D solid.

1. Choose the Taper Faces tool from the Solids Editing toolbar.

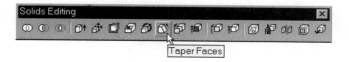

2. Click the three corners of the model, as indicated in Figure 18.36. You may have to approximate the location of the back corner to select it.

3. Press ↵ to finish your selection.

4. At the `Specify the base point:` prompt, use the Endpoint Osnap to click the bottom corner in the foreground of the model, as shown in Figure 18.36.

5. At the `Specify another point along the axis of tapering:` prompt, use the Endpoint Osnap to click the top corner, as shown in Figure 18.36.

6. At the `Specify the taper angle:` prompt, enter **4**↵. The sides of the model are now tapered 4 degrees inward at the top, as shown in Figure 18.37.

FIGURE 18.36:

Selecting the surfaces to taper and indicating the direction of the taper

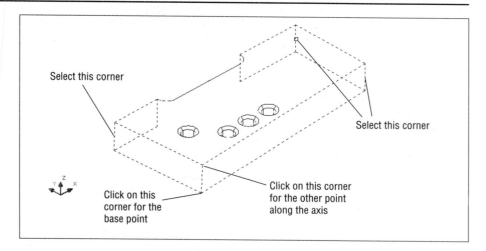

Select this corner

Select this corner

Click on this corner for the base point

Click on this corner for the other point along the axis

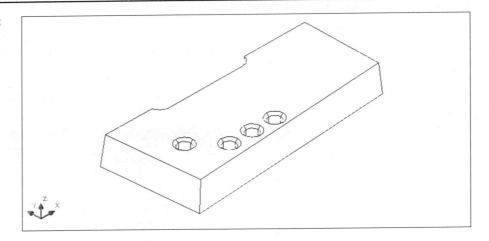

Extruding a Surface

You used the Extrude Faces command to create two of the solids in the Bracket
model. The Extrude command requires a closed polygon as a basis for the extrusion. The Solids Editing toolbar offers the Extrude Faces tool that will extrude a
surface of an existing solid. The following exercise demonstrates how it works.

1.   Click the Extrude Faces tool on the Solids Editing toolbar.

2.   Click the bottom edge of the front surface of the model, as shown in Fig-
     ure 18.38.

3.   You don't want to extrude the bottom surface of the model so type **R**↵ then
     click the back edge of the highlighted bottom surface, as shown in Figure 18.38.

4.   Press ↵. The `Specify height of extrusion or [Path]:` prompt appears.
     Notice that this is the same prompt you saw when you used the Extrude com-
     mand earlier in this chapter.

5.   Enter .5↵ for an extrusion height of 0.5 units.

6. At the Specify angle of taper for extrusion <0>: prompt, enter **45**↵ to taper the extrusion at a 45° angle. Your model now adds the extrusion, as shown in Figure 18.39.

FIGURE 18.38:

Selecting the surfaces for extrusion

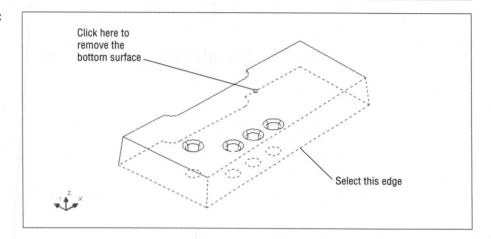

Click here to remove the bottom surface

Select this edge

FIGURE 18.39:

The model with a surface extruded and tapered

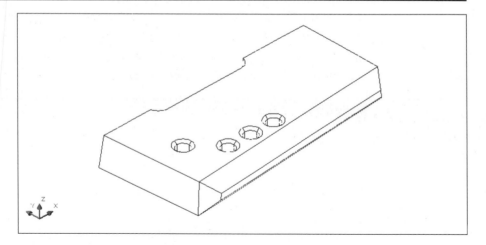

You can extrude multiple surfaces at one time if you need to by selecting more surfaces after step 2. In this exercise, you removed a selected surface in step 3 so that only one surface is extruded.

Other than those features, the Extrude Faces tool works just like the Extrude command.

Turning a Solid into a Shell

In many situations, you'll want your 3D model to be a hollow, rather than solid mass. The Shell tool lets you convert a solid into a shell. Here's an example of how it might be used.

1. Choose the Shell tool from the Solids Editing toolbar.

2. Click the model. The entire model is highlighted. AutoCAD assumes you want to shell the entire object with a few faces completely removed. The `Remove faces or [Undo/Add/ALL]:` prompt appears and you see the object selection cursor indicating that you can select objects for removal.

3. Click the top-front corner of the solid, as shown in Figure 18.40, to remove the two surfaces that adjoin that edge.

4. Press ⏎ to finish your selection.

5. At the `Enter the shell offset distance:` prompt, enter **.1**⏎. The solid becomes a shell with a 0.1 wall thickness, as shown in Figure 18.41.

6. After studying the results of the Shell tool, type **U**⏎ to undo the shell operation in preparation for the next exercise.

FIGURE 18.40:

Selecting the edge to be removed

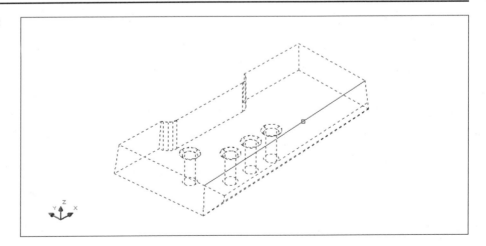

FIGURE 18.41:

The solid model after using the Shell tool

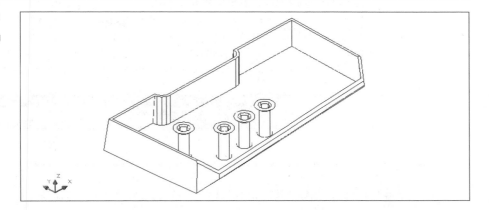

The shell thickness is added to the outside surface of the solid, so when you're constructing your solid with the intention of creating a shell, you need to take this into account.

Copying Faces and Edges

There may be times when you want to create a copy of a surface of a solid to analyze its area or to produce another part that mates to that surface. The Copy Faces tool creates a copy of any surface on your model. The copy it produces is a type of object called a *region*. You'll learn more about regions later in this chapter. Right now, let's see how the Copy Faces tool works.

1. Click the Copy Faces tool on the Solids Editing toolbar.

2. Click the front-top edge of the model, the same one shown in Figure 18.40 in the Shell exercise. Two surfaces are highlighted.

3. Press ↵ to finish your selection.

4. Click a base point for the copy, then enter **@10<315**.

5. Choose View ➢ Zoom ➢ Extents or type **Z↵ E↵** to view the entire drawing. The copied surfaces appear to the right of the solid.

The copies of the surfaces are opaque and can hide objects behind them when you perform a hidden-line removal (View ➢ Hide).

Another tool that is similar to Copy Faces is Copy Edges. It works in a similar way, but instead of selecting surfaces as in step 2, you select all the edges you want to make copies of. The result is a series of simple lines representing the edges of your model. This tool can be useful if you want to convert a solid into a set of 3D Faces. The Copy Edges tool will create a framework onto which you can add 3D Faces.

Using the Command Line for Solids Editing

The Solids Editing tools are actually options of a single AutoCAD command called Solidedit. If you prefer to use the keyboard, here are some tips on using the Solidedit command. When you first enter **Solidedit** at the command prompt, you see the following prompt:

```
Enter a solids editing option [Face/Edge/Body/Undo/eXit] <eXit>:
```

You can select the Face, Edge, or Body option to edit the various parts of a solid. The Face option offers the following prompt:

```
[Extrude/Move/Rotate/Offset/Taper/Delete/Copy/coLor/Undo/eXit]
<eXit>:
```

The options from this prompt produce the same results as their counterparts in the Solid Editing toolbar. The Edge option from the first prompt offers the following prompt:

```
Enter an edge editing option [Copy/coLor/Undo/eXit] <eXit>:
```

The Copy option lets you copy a surface and the coLor option lets you add color to a surface. The Body option from the first prompt offers following prompt:

```
[Imprint/seParate solids/Shell/cLean/Check/Undo/eXit] <eXit>:
```

These options also perform the same functions as their counterparts on the Solid Editing toolbar. As you work with this command, you can use the Undo option to undo the last Solidedit option you used without exiting the command.

Adding Surface Features

You'll start by inserting an object that will be the source of the imprint. Then you will imprint the main solid model with the object's profile.

1. Choose Insert ➤ Block.

2. In the Insert dialog box, click Browse, then locate the `Imprint.dwg` file in the `\Figures\` directory and select it.

3. In the Insert dialog box, make sure that the Explode option is checked and remove the checkmark for the Specify On-Screen check box in the Insertion Point group.

4. Click OK. The block appears in the middle of the solid.

5. Click the Imprint tool.

6. Click the main solid model.

7. Click the imported solid.

8. At the `Delete the source object <N>:` prompt, enter **Y**↵.

You now have an outline of the intersection between the two solids imprinted on the top surface of your model. To help the imprint stand out, try the following steps to change its color.

1. Click the Color Faces tool on the Solid Editing toolbar.

2. Click the imprint from the last exercise. The imprint and the entire top surface is highlighted.

3. At the `Select faces or [Undo/Remove/ALL]:` prompt, type **R**↵, then click the outer edge of the top surface to remove it from the selection set.

4. Press ↵. The Select Color dialog box appears.

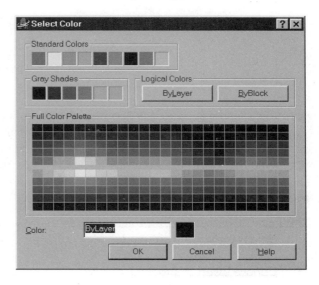

5. Click the red color sample at the top of the dialog box, then click OK. The imprint is now red.

6. Press ↵ three times to exit the command.

7. To see the full effect of the Color Faces tool, choose View ➤ Shade ➤ Flat Shade. The imprint appears as a solid red area.

If you want to remove an imprint from a surface, use the Clean tool on the Solids Editing toolbar. Click the Clean tool, then click the imprint you want to remove. If the imprint has a color, then the color will "bleed" out to the surface where the imprint was placed.

Separating a Divided Solid

While in the process of editing solids, you may end up with two separate solid forms that were created from one solid, as shown in Figure 18.42. Even though the two solids appear separated, they act like a single object. In these situations, Auto-CAD offers the Separate tool in the Solids Editing toolbar. To use it, just click the Separate tool, then select the solid that has become separated into two forms.

FIGURE 18.42:

When the tall, thin solid is subtracted from the larger solid, the result is two separate forms, yet they still behave as a single object.

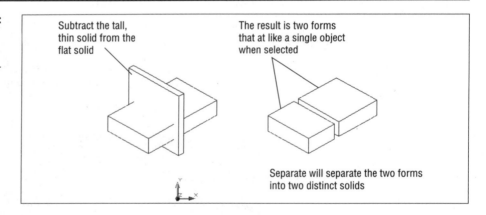

Subtract the tall, thin solid from the flat solid

The result is two forms that at like a single object when selected

Separate will separate the two forms into two distinct solids

You've seen how each of the Solids Editing tools works through some simple examples. You aren't limited to using these tools in the way shown in this section and this book cannot anticipate every situation you may encounter as you create your solid models. These examples are intended as an introduction to these tools, so feel free to experiment with them. You can always use the Undo option to backtrack in case you don't get the results you expect.

TIP   Figure 18.42 is included in the sample figures under the name of `Separate.dwg` on the companion CD-ROM. You can try the Separate tool on this file on your own.

This concludes your tour of the Solids Editing toolbar. Next, you'll learn how to use your 3D solid models to quickly generate 2D working drawings.

Enhancing the 2D Drawing Process

Using solids to model a part—such as the Bracket and the Solidedit examples used in this chapter—may seem a bit exotic, but there are definite advantages to modeling in 3D, even if you want to draw the part in only 2D as a page in a set of manufacturing specs.

The exercises in this section show you how to quickly generate a typical mechanical drawing from your 3D model using Paper Space and the Solids toolbar. You will also examine techniques for dimensioning and including hidden lines.

TIP   If your application is architecture, and you've created a 3D model of a building using solids, you can use the tools described in this section to generate 2D elevation drawings from your 3D solid model.

Drawing a Standard Top, Front, and Right-Side View

One of the more common types of mechanical drawings is the *orthogonal projection*. This style of drawing shows the top, front, and right-side view of an object. Sometimes a 3D image is also added for clarity. You can derive such a drawing within a few minutes, once you have created your 3D solid model. The first step is to select a sheet title block. The title block consists of a border and an area in the lower-right corner for notes and other drawing information.

NOTE   If you need to refresh your memory about using Paper Space, refer to Chapter 12.

Setting Up a File with a Title Block

The first step is to create a file using one of AutoCAD's template files designed for mechanical applications.

1. If you haven't done so already, save the Bracket.dwg file from the earlier exercise, and then Choose File ➢ New.

2. In the Create New Drawing dialog box, click the Use a Template button.

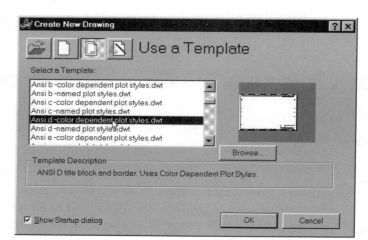

3. From the Select a Template list box, select Ansi d-color dependant plot styles.dwt, and then click OK. A title block appears, along with a viewport to Model Space.

4. Use File ➤ Save As to save this file as Bracket_title.dwg.

You are now in Floating Model Space. Though it may not be obvious at first glance, the title block is in Paper Space and an active Model Space viewport is inside the title block.

WARNING If for some reason you do not see a listing of template files in the Create New Drawing dialog box, you will need to set up AutoCAD to look for these files in the right place. Normally, AutoCAD looks in the \Program Files\AutoCAD2000\ Template directory for template files. Check the Template Drawing File Location listing in the Files tab of the Options dialog box. See *Configuring AutoCAD* in Appendix B for details.

Importing the 3D Model

The next step is to insert the Bracket solid model into this drawing. Remember that while you are in a floating Model Space viewport, anything you do affects Model Space. So in the next exercise, you will use the Insert tool to import the Bracket drawing into the Model Space of this new drawing.

1. Choose Insert ➤ Block.

2. In the Insert dialog box, click the File button.

3. At the Select Drawing File dialog box, locate and select the `Bracket.dwg` file and click Open.

4. Back in the Insert dialog box, make sure that the Explode check box in the lower-left corner of the dialog box is checked. Click the Specify On Screen check box in the Insertion Point group to deselect this option.

5. Click OK. The drawing appears in the viewport.

There's one more step to take before you actually set up the orthogonal views. You want to make the current viewport display a front view of the bracket. This is easily done with a single menu bar option.

1. Choose View ➤ 3D Views ➤ Front. The Viewport view changes to show the front view of the model.

2. Choose View ➤ Zoom ➤ Scale, and then type **1xp**↵ to give the view a 1-to-1 scale. This has the same effect as setting the Standard Scale property of the viewport to a value of 1:1. The view is now in proper scale to the title block.

3. Choose View ➤ Paper Space, and then using its grips, resize the viewport so it is just large enough to display the model, as shown in Figure 18.43. To expose the viewport grip, click the inner border of the title block, as shown in Figure 18.43.

4. Move the viewport to a location similar to the one shown in Figure 18.43.

FIGURE 18.43:

Resizing the viewport so it is just large enough to contain the view of the bracket

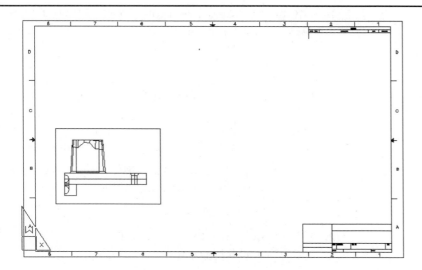

Creating the Orthogonal Views

Now you are ready to create the orthogonal views. The next part will seem simple compared with the steps you had to take to set up the title block and viewport.

1. Click the Setup View tool on the Solids toolbar, or choose Draw ➤ Solids ➤ Setup ➤ View.

2. At the `Ucs/Ortho/Auxiliary/Section/<Exit>:` prompt, type **O**↵.

3. At the `Pick Side of Viewport to Project:` prompt, place the cursor on the right side of the viewport so that a Midpoint Osnap marker appears, as shown in the top image of Figure 18.44. A rubber-banding line appears.

4. At the `View Center:` prompt, click a point to the right of the viewport, at about half the width of the viewport. The right-side view of the bracket appears, as shown in the bottom image of Figure 18.44. Click again to adjust the horizontal position of the right-side view.

5. Once you're satisfied with the location of the view, press ↵. You don't have to be too precise at this point because you will be able to adjust the view's location later.

6. At the `Clip First Corner:` prompt, click a location below and to the left of the right-side view, as shown in the continued image of Figure 18.44.

7. At the `Clip Other Corner:` prompt, click above and to the right of the view, as shown in the continued image of Figure 18.44.

8. At the `View Name:` prompt, enter **rightside**↵. Notice that the `Ucs/Ortho/Auxiliary/Section/<Exit>:` prompt appears again. This allows you to set up another view.

At this point, you can exit the Setup View tool by pressing ↵, but you need another view. Continue with the following steps to create the top view.

9. Type **O**↵ again, but this time, at the `Pick side of Viewport to Project:` prompt, click the top edge of the front-view viewport.

10. Follow steps 4 through 8 to create a top view. In step 4, click a point above the viewport instead of to the right.

11. Name this third viewport **Top**.

12. When you return to the `Ucs/Ortho/Auxiliary/Section/<Exit>:` prompt, press ↵ to exit the command.

Each new view you create using the Setup View tool is scaled to match the original view from which it is derived. As you saw from step 3, the view that is generated depends on the side of the viewport you select. If you had picked the bottom of the viewport, a bottom view would be generated, which would look the same as the top view until you use the View ➤ Hide option to see it as a Hidden-Line view.

FIGURE 18.44:

Adding the Orthogonal views in Paper Space

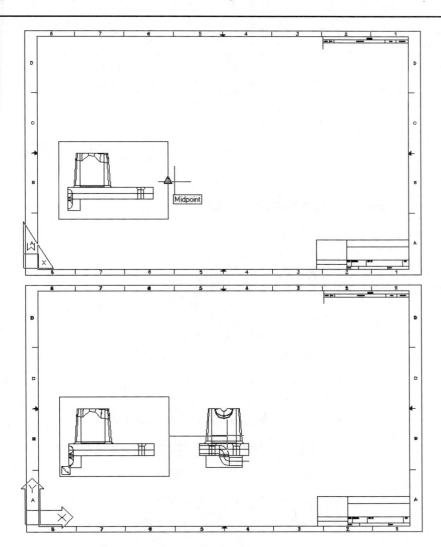

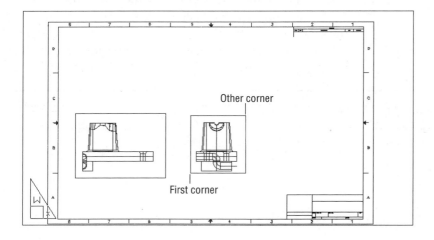

Creating an Isometric View

In this section, you will add an Isometric view to your Paper Space layout at a 1-to-1 scale. You can use the Setup View tool to accomplish this, but you'll need to set up a UCS to which the Setup View tool can refer. The following explains how to set up such a UCS for an Isometric view.

1. Click the Model tab to go to Model Space.

2. Choose View ➤ 3D Views ➤ SE Isometric to get an Isometric view of the model.

3. Choose Tools ➤ New UCS ➤ View to set the UCS to be parallel to the current view plane.

4. Choose Tools ➤ UCS ➤ Named UCS to open the UCS Control dialog box.

5. Rename the current Unnamed UCS to SEIsometric.

6. Choose View ➤ Paper Space to return to the Paper Space view of your model.

Notice that even though you changed your view in Model Space, the Paper Space viewports maintain the views as you last left them.

Now you're ready to create a viewport showing the same Isometric view you set up in Model Space.

1. Click the Setup View tool on the Solids toolbar.

2. At the `Ucs/Ortho/Auxiliary/Section/<Exit>:` prompt, type **U**↵.

3. At the `Named/World/?/<Current>:` prompt, press ↵ to accept the current UCS.

4. At the `Enter view scale<1.0000>:` prompt, press ↵ to accept the scale of 1.

5. At the `View center:` prompt, click a point above and to the right of the original viewport. The Isometric view of the model appears, as shown in Figure 18.45. If you don't like the view's location, you can continue to click points until the view's location is just where you want it.

6. Press ↵ when you are satisfied with the view's location.

7. At the `Clip First corner:` prompt, window the Isometric view to define the viewport border.

8. Name the view `SEIsometric`.

9. Press ↵ to exit the Setup View tool.

FIGURE 18.45:

Adding a viewport for the Isometric view

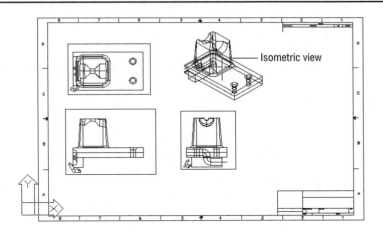

Isometric view

There were a lot of steps involved in creating these views. However, imagine the work involved if you had to create these views manually, and you'll appreciate the power of these few simple tools.

Creating Hidden-Line Views

You aren't quite finished yet. Typically, orthographic projections, such as the top, front, and right-side view, will show the hidden portions of the model with dashed lines. For example, the holes toward the right end of the bracket would be shown dashed in the front view. You could set up the viewports to do a hidden-line removal at plot time, but this would not create the effect you want.

Fortunately, AutoCAD offers the Setup Profile tool to quickly generate a proper Orthographic Projection view of your solid model. Take the following steps to create your first hidden-line view.

1. First, go to Floating Model Space by double-clicking the lower-left viewport.

3. Choose Setup Profile from the Solids toolbar, or choose Draw ➤ Solids ➤ Setup ➤ Profile.

4. Click both halves of the solid model, and then press ↵.

5. At the `Display hidden profile lines on separate layer?` `<Y>`: prompt, press ↵.

6. At the `Project profile lines onto a plane?` `<Y>`: prompt, press ↵.

7. At the `Delete tangential edges?` `<Y>`: prompt, press ↵. AutoCAD will work for a moment, and then the command prompt will appear with no apparent change to the drawing.

You don't see the effects of the Setup Profile tool yet. You'll need to make the solid model invisible to display the work that was done by the Setup Profile tool. You'll also have to make a few layer changes to get the profile views just right.

1. Double-click an area outside the viewport or click the MODEL button on the status bar to return to Paper Space.

2. Zoom into the front view so it fills most of the display area.

3. Turn off Layer 0 (zero). If it is the current layer, you will get a message telling you that you are about to turn off the current layer. Go ahead and click OK. You've just turned off the layer of the solid model, leaving the profile created by the Setup Profile tool. Notice that you only see an image of the front view.

4. Open the Layer Properties Manager (click the Layers tool in the Object Properties toolbar or choose Format ➤ Layer from the menu bar).

5. Select the layer whose name begins with the "PH" prefix.

6. Change its line type to Hidden. You may need to load the hidden-line type.

7. Once you've changed the line type, click OK to exit the Layer Properties Manager dialog box. The front view now displays hidden lines properly with dashed lines, as shown in Figure 18.46.

FIGURE 18.46:

The front view after using the Setup Profile tool

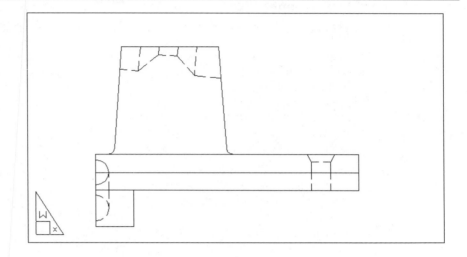

The Setup Profile tool creates a 2D drawing of your 3D model. This 2D drawing is projected onto an imaginary plane that is parallel to the view from which you selected the model while using the Setup Profile tool. To see this clearly, take a look at your model in Model Space.

1. Click the Model tab to go to Model Space.

2. Turn Layer 0 back on. You see the projected 2D view next to the 3D model, as shown in Figure 18.47.

FIGURE 18.47:

The projected view next to the 3D solid model

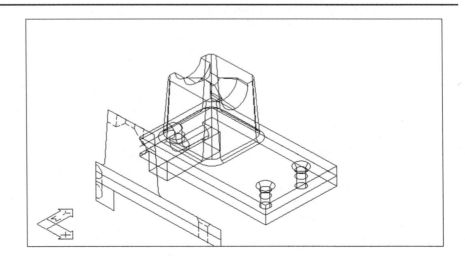

Creating a 2D Projection from Your 3D Model

Another tool on the Solids toolbar creates 2D drawings of 3D solid models. The Setup Drawing tool does nearly the same thing as the Setup Profile tool, with some differences. First of all, the Setup Drawing tool only works with viewports that are created by the Setup View tool. It automatically turns off the layer on which the solid model resides. So once it has created a 2D view, you can see the results without having to adjust layer settings. Also, unlike the Setup Profile tool, Setup Drawing leaves the 2D drawing objects as individual objects ready to be edited, instead of turning them into blocks.

Finally, the Setup Drawing tool creates layers whose names offer a better description of their purpose. For example, if you use Setup Drawing to create a 2D drawing of the right-side view, you will get layers entitled Rightside-dim, Rightside-hid, and Rightside-vis. These layer names are derived from the View name from which the 2D drawing is derived. Setup Drawing adds the -dim, -hid, and -vis suffixes to the view name to create the layer name. These suffixes are abbreviations for dimension, hidden, and visible.

Adding Dimensions and Notes in Paper Space

Although I don't recommend adding dimensions in Paper Space for architectural drawings, it may be a good idea for mechanical drawings like the one in this chapter. By maintaining the dimensions and notes separate from the actual model, you keep these elements from getting in the way of your work on the solid model. You also avoid the confusion of having to scale the text and dimension features properly to ensure that they will plot at the correct size.

NOTE   See Chapters 8 and 9 for a more detailed discussion of notes and dimensions.

As long as you set up your Paper Space work area to be equivalent to the final plot size, you can set dimension and text to the sizes you want at plot time. If you want text 1/4" high, you set your text styles to be 1/4" high.

To dimension, just make sure you are in Paper Space (View ➣ Paper Space), and then use the dimension commands in the normal way. However, there is one thing you do have to be careful of: If your Paper Space viewports are set to a scale other than 1 to 1, you must set the Annotation Units option in the Dimension Style dialog box to a proper value. The following steps show you how.

1. Choose Dimension ➣ Style.

2. In the Dimension Style Manager dialog box, make sure you have selected the style you want to use, and click Modify.

3. In the Modify Dimension Style dialog box, click the Primary Units tab.

4. In the Scale factor input box under the Measurement Scale group, enter the value by which you want your Paper Space dimensions multiplied. For example, if your Paper Space views are scaled at one-half the actual size of your model, you enter **2** in this box to multiply your dimensions' values by 2.

TIP To make sure the value you need in step 4 is correct, just determine what scale factor you need for your Paper Space drawing to get its actual size; that's the value you need to enter.

---

5. Click the Apply to Layout Dimensions Only check box. This ensures that your dimension is scaled only while you are adding dimensions in Paper Space. Dimensions added in Model Space are not affected.

6. Click OK to close the Modify Dimension Style dialog box, then OK again in the Dimension Style Manager dialog box.

You've had to complete a lot of steps to get the final drawing you have now, but, compared to having to draw these views by hand, you have undoubtedly saved a great deal of time. In addition, as you will see later in this chapter, what you have is more than just a 2D drafted image. With what you have created, further refinements are now quite easy.

Drawing a Cross-Section

One element of your drawing that is missing is a cross-section. AutoCAD will draw a cross-section through any part of the solid model. In the following exercise, you will draw such a cross-section.

1. First, save your drawing so you can return to this stage (in case you don't want to save the results of the following steps).

2. Choose Tools ➤ New UCS ➤ World.

3. Click the Section tool on the Solids toolbar.

4. At the Select objects: prompt, click both halves of the solid model and press ↵.

5. At the prompt

    Section plane by Object/Last/Zaxis/View/XY/YZ/ZX/<3points>

    enter **ZX**↵. This tells AutoCAD you want to cut the solid in the plane defined by the x- and z-axes.

6. At the Point on ZX plane: prompt, pick the midpoint of the top-right surface of the solid (see the top image of Figure 18.48). The section cut appears, as shown in the bottom image of Figure 18.48.

FIGURE 18.48:

Selecting the point on the z-x plane to define the section-cut outline

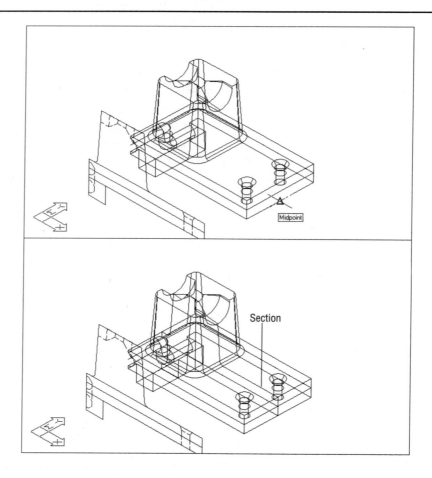

The section shown in the bottom image of Figure 18.48 is a type of object called a *region*. In the next section, you'll learn how regions share some characteristics with 3D Solids.

Using 3D Solid Operations on 2D Drawings

You can apply of some of the features described in this chapter to 2D drafting by taking advantage of AutoCAD's *region* object. Regions are two-dimensional objects to which you can apply Boolean operations.

Try the following optional exercise, which demonstrates how two Boolean operations, Union and Subtract, work on 2D objects.

1. If you have been working through the tutorial on 3D solids, save the Bracket drawing now.

2. Open the `Region.dwg` drawing supplied on the companion CD-ROM. You will see the drawing shown in the top image of Figure 18.49. The objects in this drawing are circles and closed polylines.

3. Click the Region tool on the Draw toolbar, or type **Reg**↵.

4. At the `Select objects:` prompt, click all the objects in the drawing and press ↵. AutoCAD converts the objects into regions.

5. Move the two circles and the hexagons into the positions illustrated in the bottom image of Figure 18.49. (For this demonstration exercise, you don't have to worry about matching the positions exactly.)

6. Choose Modify ➢ Boolean ➢ Union.

7. At the `Select objects:` prompt, click the rectangle and the two circles. The circles merge with the rectangle to form one object.

8. Choose Modify ➢ Boolean ➢ Subtract, and then click the newly created region and press ↵.

9. At the next `Select objects:` prompt, click the two hexagons. Now you have a single, 2D solid object in the shape of a wrench, as shown in the continued image of Figure 18.49.

You can use regions to generate complex surfaces that might include holes or unusual bends (see Figure 18.50). There are two things you should keep in mind:

- Regions act like surfaces; when you remove hidden lines, objects behind the regions are hidden.

- You can explode regions to edit them. (You can't do this with solids.) However, exploding a region causes the region to lose its surface-like quality, and objects will no longer hide behind its surface(s).

FIGURE 18.49:

Working with regions in the Region.dwg file

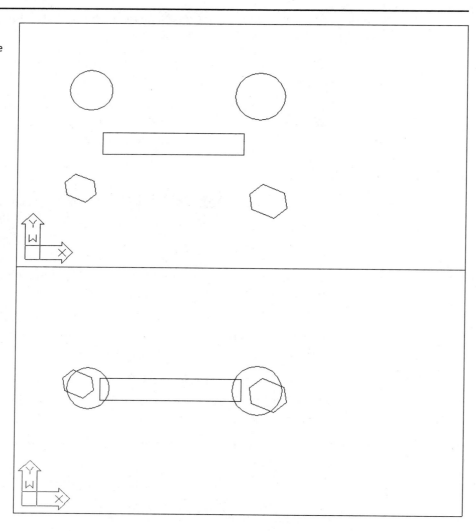

FIGURE 18.49 CONTINUED:

Working with regions in the Region.dwg file

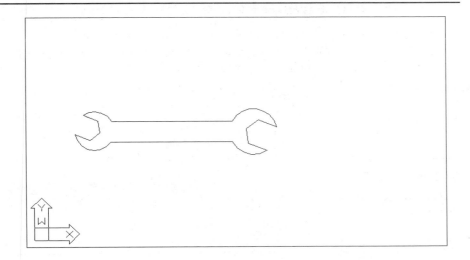

FIGURE 18.50:

You can use the regional model to create complex 2D surfaces for use in 3D surface modeling.

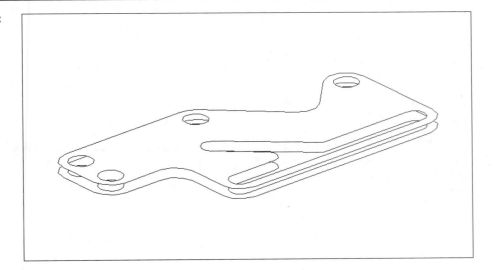

Finding the Properties of a Solid

All of this effort to create a solid model isn't just to create a pretty picture. Once your model is drawn and built, you can obtain information about its physical properties. In this section, you will look at a few of the commands that let you gather such information.

Finding a Model's Mass Properties

You can find the volume, the moment of inertia, and other physical properties of your model by using the Massprop command. These properties can also be recorded as a file on disk so you can modify your model without worrying about losing track of its original properties.

1. Open the Bracket drawing you worked on through most of this chapter.

2. Click and drag the Distance tool on the Standard toolbar. Select Mass Properties on the flyout, or enter **Massprop↵**.

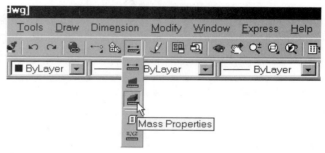

3. At the `Select objects:` prompt, select the two halves of the solid model. AutoCAD will calculate for a moment, and then it displays a list of the object's properties, as shown in Figure 18.51.

```
AutoCAD Text Window                                              _ □ X
Edit
Command:  MASSPROP
Select objects: 1 found

 elect objects:  |
 ----------------      SOLIDS      ----------------

Mass:                   35.1657
Volume:                 35.1657
Bounding box:      X: 2.9990   --  10.0000
                   Y: 2.5000   --  6.5000
                   Z: 0.4990   --  4.0000
Centroid:          X: 5.5725
                   Y: 4.5055
                   Z: 1.7242
Moments of inertia: X: 886.9826
                    Y: 1318.5188
                    Z: 1924.6475
Products of inertia: XY: 882.4382
                     YZ: 272.9676
                     ZX: 317.4906
Radii of gyration:  X: 5.0222
                    Y: 6.1233
                    Z: 7.3980
Press ENTER to continue:
Principal moments and X-Y-Z directions about centroid:
                    I: 61.3669 along [0.9424 -0.0061 -0.3344]
                    J: 121.9476 along [-0.0229 0.9963 -0.0826]
                    K: 126.0628 along [0.3337 0.0855 0.9388]

Write to a file ? <N>:
Command: |
```

Taking Advantage of Stereolithography

A discussion of solid modeling wouldn't be complete without mentioning *stereolithography*. This is one of the more interesting technological wonders that has appeared as a by-product of 3D computer modeling. Stereolithography is a process that generates resin reproductions of 3D computer solid models. It offers the mechanical designer a method of rapidly prototyping designs directly from AutoCAD drawings. The process requires special equipment that will read computer files in a particular format.

AutoCAD supports stereolithography through the Stlout command. This command generates an .stl file, which can be used with *Stereolithograph Apparatus* (*STA*) to generate a model. You must first create a 3D solid model in AutoCAD; then you can proceed with the following steps to create the .stl file.

1. Choose File ➢ Export.

2. In the Export Data dialog box, open the Save as Type drop-down list and select Lithography (*.stl). Click the Save button.

TIP   You can also type **Stlout**↵ at the command prompt to bypass steps 1 and 2.

---

3. At the Select a single solid for STL output: prompt, select a solid or a set of solids, and press ↵. All solids must reside in the positive x-, y-, and z-coordinates of the World Coordinate System.

The AutoCAD 3D solids are translated into a set of triangular-faceted meshes in the .stl file. You can use the Facetres system variable to control the fineness of these meshes. See Chapter 17 for more information on Facetres.

If You Want to Experiment...

This chapter has focused on a mechanical project, but you can, of course, use solids to help simplify the construction of 3D architectural forms. If your interest lies in architecture, try drawing the window in Figure 18.52. (Imagine trying to create this window without the solid-modeling capabilities of AutoCAD!)

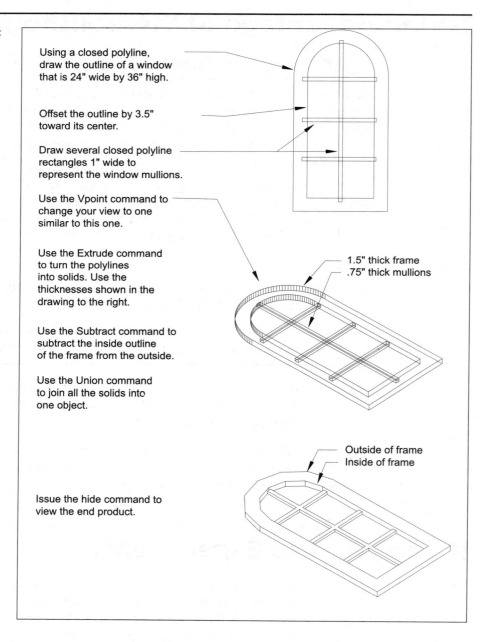

Using a closed polyline, draw the outline of a window that is 24" wide by 36" high.

Offset the outline by 3.5" toward its center.

Draw several closed polyline rectangles 1" wide to represent the window mullions.

Use the Vpoint command to change your view to one similar to this one.

Use the Extrude command to turn the polylines into solids. Use the thicknesses shown in the drawing to the right.

1.5" thick frame
.75" thick mullions

Use the Subtract command to subtract the inside outline of the frame from the outside.

Use the Union command to join all the solids into one object.

Outside of frame
Inside of frame

Issue the hide command to view the end product.

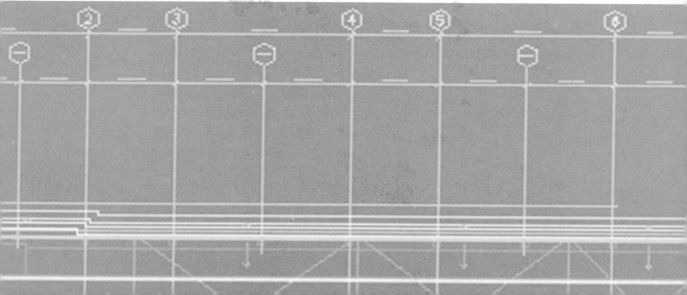

PART V

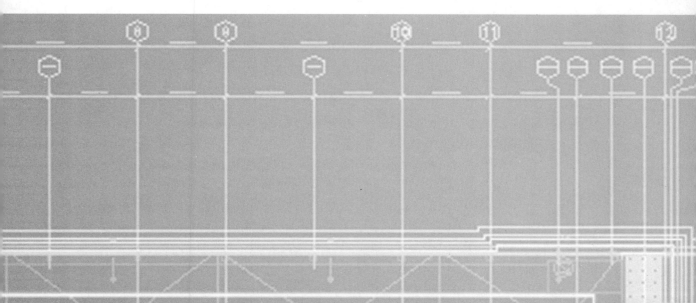

Customization: Taking AutoCad to the Limit

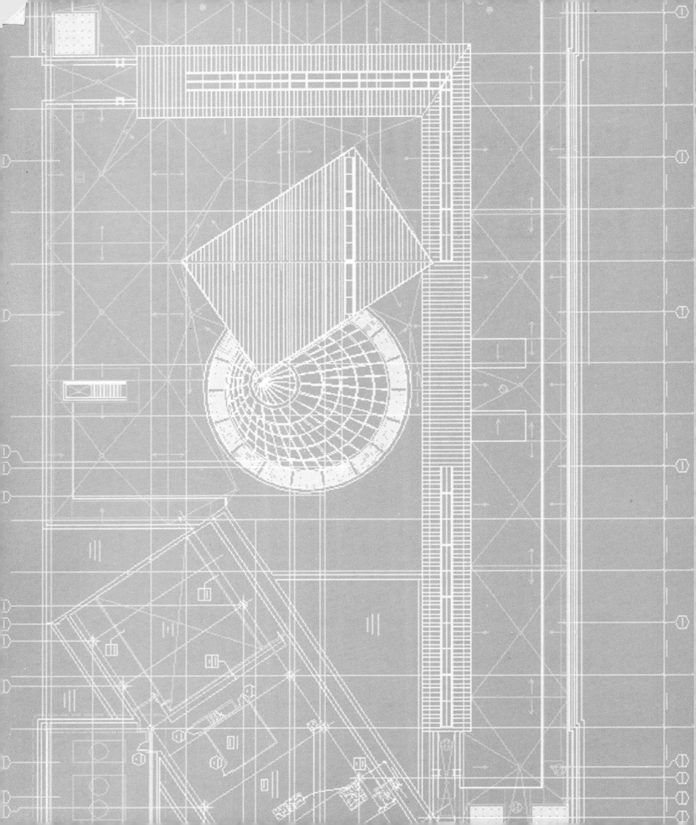

CHAPTER

NINETEEN

19

Introduction to Customization

- Enhancements Straight from the Source

- Utilities Available from Other Sources

- Putting AutoLISP to Work

- Managing Your AutoLISP and VBA Library

- Creating Keyboard Macros with AutoLISP

- Using Third-Party Software

- Getting the Latest Information from Online Services

- If You Want to Experiment...

AutoCAD offers a wealth of features that you can use to improve your productivity. But even with these aids to efficiency, there are always situations that can use further automation. In this chapter, you'll be introduced to the different ways AutoCAD can be customized and enhanced with add-on utilities.

First, you'll discover how the AutoCAD Express Tools can help boost your productivity. Many of these utilities were created using the programming tools that are available to anyone, namely AutoLISP and VBA. Next, you'll learn how to load and run AutoLISP utilities that are supplied on this book's companion CD-ROM. By doing so, you'll be prepared to take advantage of the many utilities available from user groups and online services. Finally, you'll finish the chapter by taking a look at how third-party applications and the Internet can enhance AutoCAD's role in your workplace.

Enhancements Straight from the Source

If you've followed the tutorial in this book, you've already used a few add-on programs that come with AutoCAD, perhaps without even being aware that they were not part of the core AutoCAD program. This section will introduce you to the AutoCAD Express tools: a set of AutoLISP, ARX, and VBA tools that showcase these powerful customization environments. The best part about the Express Tools is that you don't have to know a thing about programming to take advantage of them.

There are so many of these Express tools that this chapter can't provide step-by-step instructions on all of them. Instead, you will get a detailed look at some of the more complicated tools and read shorter descriptions for other tools. Let's start with the Express Layer tools.

Opening the Express Toolbars

If you don't have the Express toolbars on your screen, here's how to open them.

1. Right-click any toolbar, then select Customize at the bottom of the popup menu. The Toolbars dialog box appears.

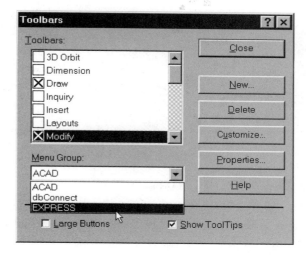

2. Open the Menu Group drop-down list at the bottom of the dialog box, then select Express. The Toolbars list box changes to show a listing of toolbars available from the Express menu group.

3. Click the check box to the left of each item in the list.

4. Click Close to close the Toolbars dialog box.

NOTE   You'll get a chance to learn more about the Toolbars dialog box in Chapter 20.

You now have all of the Express toolbars on your screen. If you don't want to have them all on your screen, just keep one of them open; when you want to open any of the other Express toolbars, right-click the remaining Express toolbar and select the other toolbars you want to open from the popup menu.

Now let's take a look at the Express Layer toolbar.

Loading the Express Tools

If you installed AutoCAD using the Typical Installation option, you may not have installed the AutoCAD Express tools yet. Fortunately, you can install these utilities separately without having to reinstall the entire program.

Continued on next page

Proceed as if you are installing AutoCAD for the first time. When you see the Setup Choices dialog box, choose the Add button to add new components to the current system. You will see an item called Express in the Custom Components dialog box that appears next. Place a check in the Bonus check box, and then proceed with the installation. When Setup is finished, open AutoCAD and load the Express menu. See Chapter 20 for more detailed information on loading menus.

Tools for Managing Layers

In a survey of AutoCAD users, Autodesk discovered that one of the most frequently used features in AutoCAD was the Layer command. As a result, the layer controls in AutoCAD have been greatly improved. Still, there is room for some improvement. The Express Layer tools include some shortcuts to controlling layer settings as well as one major layer enhancement called the Layer Manager.

TIP   All of the bonus tools discussed in this section have keyboard command equivalents. Check the status bar when selecting these tools from the toolbar or pulldown menu for the keyboard command name.

Saving and Recalling Layer Settings

The Layer Manager lets you save layer settings. This can be crucial when you are editing a file that serves multiple uses, such as a floor plan and reflected ceiling plan. You can, for example, turn layers on and off to set up the drawing for a reflected ceiling Plan view, and then save the layer settings. Later, when you need to modify the ceiling information, you can recall the layer setting to view the ceiling data. The following steps show you how the Layer Manager works.

1. In AutoCAD, open the 14a-unit.dwg file. Open the Layer Properties Manager dialog box and turn on all the layers except the Notes and Flr-pat layers. Your drawing should look similar to the top image of Figure 19.1.

2. Click the Layer Manager tool in the Express Layer Tools toolbar.

The Layer Manager dialog box appears.

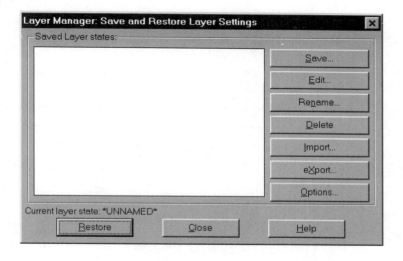

3. Click the Save button. The Layer State Name dialog box appears.

4. Enter **blank floor plan**, and then click OK. The Layer Manager dialog box reappears. Notice that the name you entered for the layer state appears in the list box.

5. Click the Close button.

6. Now open the Layer Properties Manager dialog box again and turn on the Flr-pat and Notes layers and turn off the Ceiling layer. Your drawing will look like the bottom image of Figure 19.1.

7. Click the Layer Manager tool again.

8. Click BLANK FLOOR PLAN in the list, and then click Restore.

9. Click Close. Your drawing reverts to the previous view with the Notes and

Flr-pat layers turned off and the Ceiling layer on.

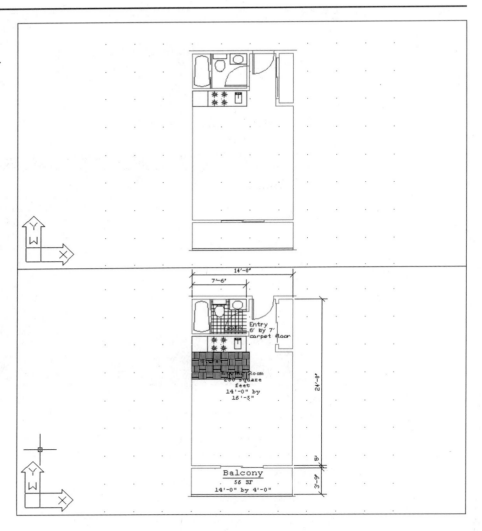

The layer states are saved with the file so you can retrieve them at a later date. As you can see from the Layer Manager dialog box, you have a few other options. Here is a listing of those options and what they do:

Edit   Opens the Layer Properties Manager dialog box to let you edit the settings for a layer state. Highlight the layer state in the list, and then choose Edit.

Rename   Lets you rename an existing layer setting.

Delete   Deletes a layer state from the list.

Import   Imports a set of layer states that have been exported using the Export option of this dialog box.

Export   Saves a set of layer states as a file. By default, the file is given the name of the current file with the .lay filename extension. You can import the layer state file into other files.

Options   Lets you control which layer options are saved as part of the layer state. When you click Options, you see the Layer Manager: Restore Options dialog box. This dialog box consists of a set of check boxes. You check the options you want to have saved by the Layer Manager. By default, all of the layer options are saved. The options offered in the Layer Manager: Restore Options dialog box are: ON/OFF status, Thaw/Freeze status, Thaw/Freeze in Current Viewport status, Lock/Unlocked status, Color status, Linetype status, Lineweight status, Plot status, and Plot Style status.

Changing the Layer Assignment of Objects

In addition to the Layer Manager, the Express Layer toolbar offers two tools that change the layer assignments of objects. The Match Objects Layer tool is similar to the Match Properties tool, but is streamlined to just operate on layer assignments. After choosing this tool, you first select the object or objects you wish to change, and then you select an object whose layer you wish to match.

The Change to Current Layer tool changes an object's layer assignment to the current layer. This tool has long existed as an AutoLISP utility and you'll find that you'll get a lot of use from it.

Controlling Layer Settings through Objects

The remaining set of Express Layer tools lets you make layer settings by selecting objects in the drawing. The tools in this set are simple to use: Just click the tool, and then select an object. These tools are so helpful, you may want to consider docking them permanently in your AutoCAD window. The following list describes what each tool does.

Isolate Objects Layer   Turns off all the layers except for the layer of the selected object.

Freeze Object Layer   Freezes the layer of the selected objects.

Turn Objects Layer Off   Turns off the layer of the selected object.

Lock Objects Layer   Locks the layer of the selected object. A locked layer is one that is visible but cannot be edited.

Unlock Object Layer   Unlocks the layer of the selected object.

Deleting a Layer While Preserving Its Contents

Every now and then, you will inherit an AutoCAD file from some other office or individual and you'll want to convert its layering system to one more suited to the way you work. This usually involves renaming and deleting layers. The Layer Merge Express tool is a great aid in this effort.

Layer Merge can be found by choosing Express ➤ Layers ➤ Layer Merge. It works by first moving all the objects from one layer to another existing layer. You can either select objects to indicate the layer you want, or you can type in the layer names. Once the objects are moved, Layer Merge deletes the empty layer. Another related tool is Layer Delete (Express ➤ Layers ➤ Layer Delete). This tool will completely delete a layer and its contents.

Tools for Editing Text

It seems that you can never have enough text-editing features. Even in the realm of word processors, there are innumerable tools for setting fonts, paragraphs, tabs, and tables. Some programs even check your grammar. While you're not trying to write the great American novel in AutoCAD, you are interested in getting your text in the right location, at the right size, with some degree of style. This often means using a mixture of text and graphics editing tools. Here are some additional tools that will help ease your way through some otherwise difficult editing tasks.

Masking Text Backgrounds

One problem AutoCAD users frequently face is how to get text to read clearly when it is placed over a hatch pattern or other graphic. The Hatch command will hatch around existing text leaving a clear space behind it. But what about those situations where you must add text *after* a hatch pattern has been created? Or what about those instances where you need to mask behind text that is placed over non-hatch objects, such as dimension leaders or raster images?

The Text Mask tool addresses this problem by masking the area behind text with a special masking object called a Wipeout. Try the following exercise on the 14a-unit.dwg file to see firsthand how it works.

1. In the Unit file, make sure the Flr-pat and Notes layers are turned on.

2. Adjust your view so you see the kitchen area as it appears in the top image of Figure 19.2. Notice that the Kitchen label is obscured by the floor's hatch pattern.

3. Choose the Text Mask tool from the Express Text Tools toolbar.

You'll see the following message:

```
Current settings: Offset factor = 0.3500, Mask type = Wipeout
Select text objects to mask or [Masktype/Offset]:
```

4. Here you can enter the amount of space you want around the text as a percentage of the text height or you can select a different type of object for the mask.

5. Select the Kitchen text and click the Living Room text. When you're done selecting text, press ↵. You'll see the message

```
Masking text with a Wipeout
Wipeout created.
1 text items have been masked with a Wipeout.
```

The text appears on a clear background, as shown in the bottom image of Figure 19.2.

Text Mask creates an object called a Wipeout that masks other objects behind the text. Wipeout is not a standard AutoCAD object; it is a new object created through AutoCAD's programming interface.

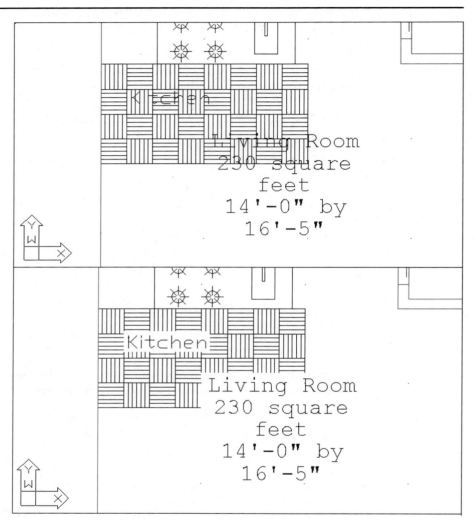

If you prefer to use a 3D Face or Solid to hide the background of text, you can do so by entering **M⏎** at the prompt in step 3. You see the following prompt asking you to select a Mask type:

```
Specify entity type to use for mask [Wipeout/3dface/Solid] <Wipeout>:
```

Enter the mask type at this prompt, and you'll return to the previous prompt.

If you want more room around the text, you can enter **O**⏎ at the prompt in step 3. You can then enter a value for the margin around the text.

The Wipeout object has its own little quirks that you will want to know about. To get a bit more familiar with Wipeout objects, try the following exercise.

1. Click the Kitchen text. Notice that both the text and the Wipeout object are selected.

2. Click Move on the Modify toolbar.

3. Move the text and Wipeout object to the right about 12 inches or 30cm for metric users. The text seems to disappear.

4. Type **Re**⏎ to issue a Regen. The text appears once again.

The text and Wipeout objects are linked so that if you select the text, you automatically select the Wipeout object. Also, the display order of the two objects gets mixed up when you move them so you need to issue a Regen command to restore the text's visibility. You can also edit or erase the Wipeout object. There is a description on how to edit Wipeout objects in the *Express Standard Tools* section later in this chapter.

If you want to delete the Wipeout background, use the Express ➤ Text ➤ Unmask Text option. This option prompts you to select an object. You then select the masked text and the Wipeout background disappears.

Next, you'll look at ways to globally change text objects.

Finding and Replacing Text

While the Find and Replace tool isn't really an Express tool, it is an example of a former Express tool that has been moved into the main part of the program. This is one tool that users had been asking for a long time.

Find and Replace works like any other find and replace tool in a word-processing program. There are a few options that work specifically with AutoCAD. Here's how it works.

1. Click the Find and Replace tool on the Standard toolbar.

The Find and Replace dialog box appears.

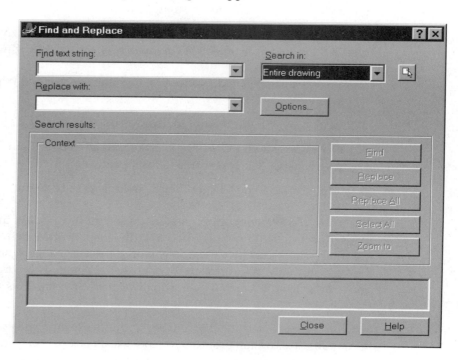

2. Enter the text you want to locate in the Find Text String input box.

3. Enter the replacement text in the Replace With input box.

4. Click Find. When AutoCAD finds the word, it appears in the Context window, along with any other text next to the word.

5. If you have any doubts, click the Zoom to button to display the text in the AutoCAD drawing area.

6. Finally, when you've made certain that this is the text you want to change, click Replace.

If you want to replace all of the occurrences of a word in the drawing, click Replace All. You can also limit your find and replace operation to a specific area of your drawing by clicking the Select Object button in the upper-right corner of the Find and Replace dialog box.

When you click the Select Objects button, the Find and Replace dialog box disappears temporarily to allow you to select a set of objects or a region of your drawing. Find and Replace will then limit its search to those objects or the region you select.

You can further control the types of objects that Find and Replace looks for by clicking the Options button. This opens the Find and Replace Options dialog box.

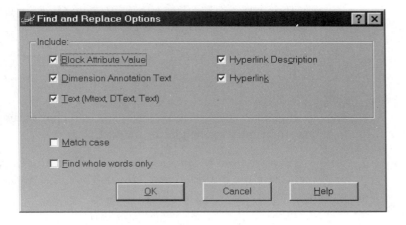

With this dialog box, you can refine your search by limiting it to blocks, dimension text, standard text, or hyperlink text. You can also determine whether to match case or find whole words only.

Adding Linked Text Documents

One of the more frustrating and time-consuming aspects to drafting is editing lengthy notes. General notes and specifications change frequently in the life of a project so editing notes can be a large part of what you do in AutoCAD. Frequently, notes are written by someone else, perhaps a specification writer, who doesn't work directly with the drawings.

You can improve the efficiency of note editing by using OLE to cut and paste notes into your drawing (see Chapter 14 for more on OLE). That way, you or the specification writer can edit the note and it will be automatically updated in drawings that contain pasted copies of the note. There are some drawbacks to OLE-linked text documents. However, the biggest problem is that you have little control over the text size and font.

To make note editing easier, AutoCAD supplies the Remote Text object. This is a special object that is linked to an external text document. Like an OLE object, a Remote Text object will automatically update its contents whenever its source document changes. To use Remote Text objects, take the following steps.

1. Choose Express ➤ Text ➤ Remote Text or type **Rtext.⏎** at the command prompt.

2. At the `Enter an option [Style/Height/Rotation/File/Diesel] <File>:` prompt, press ⏎. The Select Text File dialog box appears. This is a typical file dialog box that lets you locate and select a file for import.

3. Select a file and click Open.

4. At the `Specify start point of RText:` prompt, position the text in the drawing.

5. At the `Enter an option [Style/Height/Rotation/Edit]:` prompt, enter **H.⏎**, then enter the height for the text.

As you can see from the prompt in step 5, you can specify the text style, height, and rotation for the imported text. You also have the option to edit the text from within AutoCAD.

Since the Remote Text object is linked to the original document you selected in step 3, whenever that original document is edited, the Remote Text object in your drawing will be updated automatically, in a way similar to Xrefs.

Automatically Update Drawing Information Labels

Another way to use Remote Text is to use it to add labels of the drawing's general information, such as the name of the file, the date it was last edited, and the person who did the editing. This information is usually placed in the corner of the drawing for reference so that a print of a drawing can be easily associated with a drawing file.

Remote Text can be used to keep track of this information. Even if the name of the file or its location on the hard drive changes, Remote Text will automatically update labels displaying this information. Here's an example of how to set up Remote Text to do this.

1. Choose Express ➢ Text ➢ Remote Text or type **Rtext**↵ at the command prompt.

2. At the `Enter an option [Style/Height/Rotation/File/Diesel] <File>:` prompt, enter **D**↵ to select the Diesel option. The Edit Rtext dialog box appears.

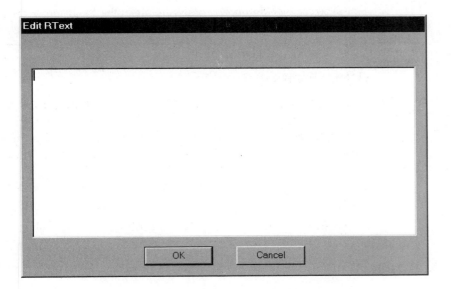

3. Enter the following text: **Drawing name and location: $(getvar, "dwg-prefix")$(getvar, "dwgname")**.

4. Click OK. The text string appears as a rectangle in the drawing next to your cursor.

5. Click a location for the text, which is usually placed in the lower-left corner of a drawing title block. The text displays the drawing location and name.

6. At the `Enter an option [Style/Height/Rotation/Edit]:` prompt, type **R**↵ then enter **90** to rotate the text 90 degrees.

This example uses the Diesel option of the Remote Text tool. Diesel is one of many macro programming languages AutoCAD supports. The text `$(getvar, "dwgprefix")$(getvar, "dwgname")` is the diesel code that extracts the current drawing location and name from the file. This code is translated into the actual directory listing and filename of the current drawing. This is how Remote Text reads the Dwgprefix and Dwgname system variables of the file. If the file is moved to another location or if it is renamed, Remote Text reads the dwgprefix and dwgname system variables and updates the label containing this code. You'll learn more about the Diesel option in Chapter 20.

TIP   You can type **dwgprefix** or **dwgname** at the command prompt to see the information that Remote Text is reading.

Other Express Text Tools

You've learned about several of the main text-editing tools in the Express Text Tools toolbar and Express pull-down menu. There are several more text-editing tools that you may find useful. By now, you should feel comfortable in exploring these tools on your own. The following is a brief description to get you started:

Text Fit   Lets you visually stretch or compress text to fit within a given width.

ArcAlignedText   Creates text that follows the curve of an arc. If the arc is stretched or changed, the text follows the arc's shape. This is one of the more interesting bonus text-editing tools offering a wide range of settings presented in a neat little dialog box.

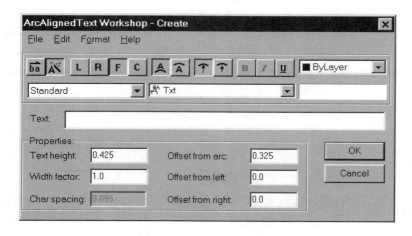

Explode Text   Converts the individual characters in a text object into polylines. Beware! This tool can take some time while it works.

If you want text to follow a curved path, take a look at the `Txtpath.lsp` utility on the companion CD-ROM. It draws text on a spline curve to follow virtually any contour you want. (See Appendix C for more information about this utility.)

Express Block Tools

Every now and then, you run into a situation where you want to use objects within a block to trim or extend to, or perhaps you may want to copy a part of a block to another part of your drawing. Here are six tools that will let you do these things. They're fairly simple to use, so the following descriptions should be enough to get you started.

Copy Nested Entities   Lets you copy single objects within a block. You are only allowed to select objects individually—one click at a time. The copied objects will be placed on the current layer.

Trim to Block Entities   Lets you trim to objects in a block. It works just like the standard Trim command with the exception that you must select the objects to trim to individually.

Extend to Block Entities   Lets you extend to objects in a block. It also works like its standard counterpart with the exception that you must select the objects you wish to extend to individually.

List Xref/Block Entities   Displays basic information about an Xref or block.

Global Attribute Edit   On the Express Block Tools toolbar simplifies the global editing of attribute text.

Explode Attributes to Text   On the Express Block Tools toolbar explodes blocks containing attributes so that the attribute values are converted into plain single-line text.

The Extended Clip tool, described later in this chapter allows you to hide portions of a block that you do not want to display.

Express Standard Tools

The Express Standard toolbar seems to be the answer to most AutoCAD users' wish lists. As with many of the Express tools discussed so far, these tools have been floating around in the AutoCAD user community as AutoLISP utilities. However, some are completely new. This section starts with a look at one tool that has been on my wish list for quite some time.

Multiple Entity Stretch

The Stretch command has always been limited by the fact that you can only select one set of vertices. The Multiple Entity Stretch tool removes that limitation and makes stretching multiple objects a simpler task. Here's how it works.

1. Click the Multiple Entity Stretch tool on the Express Standard toolbar.

    You'll see the following message:

    ```
    Define crossing windows or crossing polygons...
    CP(crossing polygon)/<Crossing First point>:
    ```

2. Start to place crossing windows around the vertices you want to stretch. You may also enter **Cp**↵ and proceed to place crossing polygons around the vertices.

3. When you are done selecting vertices, press ↵.

4. Go ahead and select a base point and second point to move the vertices.

Streamlined Move Copy and Rotate

The Move Copy Rotate tool combines these three functions into one tool. It's like a streamlined Grip Edit tool without the grips. Here's how it works.

1. Click the Move Copy Rotate tool or select Express ➤ Modify ➤ Move Copy Rotate.

2. Select the objects you want to edit, then press ↵.

3. Click a base point.

4. At the [Move/Copy/Rotate/Scale/Base/Undo]<eXit>: prompt, enter the option you want to use; for example, type C. You can also right-click and select Copy from the popup menu. The object or objects you selected in step 2 now follow your cursor.

5. Click a location for your copy. You can continue to select more points to create multiple copies.

6. When you are finished making copies, press ↵. The [Move/Copy/Rotate/Scale/Base/Undo]<eXit>: prompt returns, allowing you to make further edits.

7. Press ↵ to exit the Move Copy Rotate tool.

The Move Copy Rotate tool acts like the Move or Copy command up until step 4. From step 4 on, you can do any number of operations on the selected objects as listed in the prompt.

Quick Multiple Trims with Extended Trim

The Extended Trim tool is actually best described by its title in the Express pull-down menu: Cookie Cutter Trim. It is capable of trimming a set of objects to a closed shape, such as a circle or closed polyline. You can, for example, use it to cut out a star shape in a crosshatch pattern. You can also trim multiple objects to a line or arc as well. To use it, do the following.

1. Choose Extended Trim on the Express Standard toolbar, or select Express ➤ Modify ➤ Cookie Cutter Trim.

2. Select an object that is to be the trim boundary; that is, the object to which you want to trim.

3. Click the side of the selected object that you want trimmed.

Extended Trim only allows you to select a single object to trim to, but it trims multiple objects quickly and with fewer clicks of the mouse.

Editing Multiple Polylines with Multiple Pedit

If you only want to change the properties of polylines, you may want to use the
Multiple Pedit tool.

The Multiple Pedit tool works exactly like the standard Pedit command (found
by choosing Modify ➤ Object ➤ Polyline) with two exceptions: It does not offer the
Edit Vertex option and you are not limited to a single polyline. This means that you
can select multiple polylines to change their width, curvature, or open/close status.
Multiple Pedit also lets you easily convert multiple lines and arcs into polylines.

Perhaps one of the most common uses for the Multiple Pedit tool is to change the
width of a set of lines, arcs, and polylines. If you include lines and arcs in a selection
set with this tool, they are converted into polylines and the specified width is applied.

Masking Areas with Wipeout

Chapter 6 described two methods for masking hatch patterns behind graphics in a
space-planning example. A third method is to use the Wipeout tool. Wipeout creates an object called a Wipeout, which acts like a mask. If you read the previous section on the Text Mask tool, you've gotten a glimpse at how Wipeout works because
the Text Mask tool uses the Wipeout object. The following exercise demonstrates
how to use the Wipeout tool in another application.

Imagine that you've set up a Paper Space layout showing an enlarged view of
one of the units of the studio apartment building from this book. You want to
show dimensions and notes around the unit, but there are too many other objects
in the way. The Wipeout tool can be of great help in this situation. Here's how.

1. Open the 19wipe.dwg file. This is one of the sample files on the companion
    CD-ROM. When you open this file, you will be in Paper Space.

2. While still in Paper Space, zoom in to the typical Unit plan so your view looks
    similar to Figure 19.3.

3. Create a layer called Wipeout and make it current.

4. Switch to Floating Model Space by double-clicking inside the Model Space viewport or by clicking the PAPER button in the status bar.

5. Draw the closed polyline shown in Figure 19.3. You don't have to be exact about the shape; you can adjust it later.

6. Click Wipeout on the Express Standard toolbar.

7. At the `Wipeout Frame/New <New>:` prompt, press ↵ to accept the default New option.

8. At the `Select a polyline:` prompt, select the polyline you just drew.

9. At the `Erase polyline? Yes/No <No>:` prompt, enter **Y**↵ to erase the polyline. The area enclosed by the polyline is masked out.

FIGURE 19.3:

Adding a polyline to the enlarged Unit plan

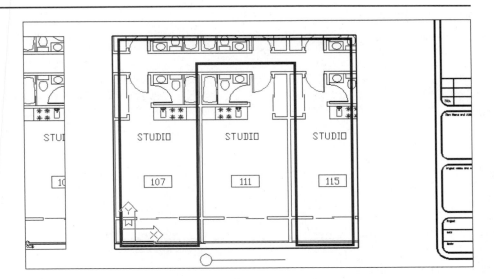

The Wipeout object has a border that can be turned on and off. When visible, you can click the Wipeout border and use its corner grips to reshape the area that it covers. You can also erase, move, or copy the Wipeout object using its border. In the example of the Unit plan, you will want to hide the Wipeout border. Take the following steps to turn off the Wipeout border's visibility.

1. Click the Wipeout button in the Express Standard toolbar.

2. At the Frame/New <New>: prompt, type **F**↵.

3. At the OFF/ON <ON>: prompt, type **OFF**↵. The frame disappears.

When the frame is off, you cannot edit the Wipeout object. Of course, you can turn it back on using the Frame option you used in step 2 of the previous exercise. By the way, if you need to edit the Text Mask tool described earlier in this chapter, you use the Frame option described in the previous exercise to turn on the Text Mask border.

With the Wipeout object in place and its border turned off, you can add dimensions and notes around the image without having the adjoining graphics interfere with the visibility of your notes. Figure 19.4 shows the Unit plan with the dimensions inserted from the individual Unit plan file.

FIGURE 19.4:

The Unit plan with dimensions added and the viewport border adjusted to hide the graphics beyond the Wipeout object

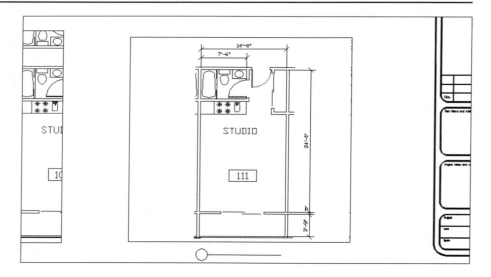

There is one more point to address here. If you switch to Paper Space and zoom out to view the entire Paper Space drawing, you'll notice that the Wipeout object appears in the overall plan at the top of the screen (see Figure 19.5). Fortunately, you can freeze the Wipeout layer in the viewport with the Overall view to hide the Wipeout object.

FIGURE 19.5:

The Wipeout object as it appears in the overall Plan view

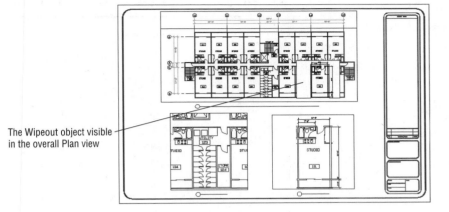

The Wipeout object visible in the overall Plan view

Drawing Revision Clouds

A *revision cloud* is a cloud-like outline drawn around parts of a drawing that have been revised. They are used to alert the viewer to any changes that have occurred in the design of a project since the drawings were last issued. Revision clouds are fairly common in most types of technical drawings, including architectural, civil, and mechanical drawings.

As simple as they might appear, revision clouds are difficult to draw using the standard tools offered by AutoCAD. But now there is a single tool that makes them easy to draw. Try using the Revision Cloud tool on the 19wipe.dwg file by following these steps.

1. If you haven't already done so, switch your drawing to Paper Space.

2. Click the Revision Cloud tool. Then click a point near the right side of the viewport that shows a view of the Unit plan, as shown in Figure 19.6.

3. Move the cursor in a counterclockwise direction to encircle the Unit plan view. As you move the cursor, the cloud is drawn.

4. Bring the cursor full circle back to the point from which you started. When you approach the beginning of the cloud, the revision cloud closes and you exit the Revision Cloud tool.

FIGURE 19.6:

Drawing a revision cloud

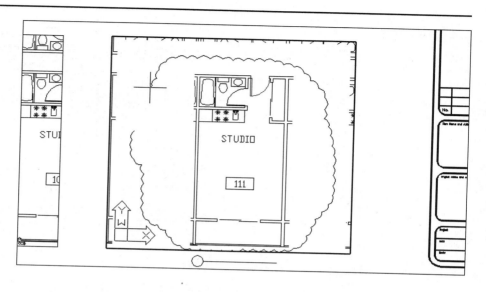

If you need to change the size of the arcs in the revision cloud, you can do so in step 2 by entering **A⏎**. You can then enter an arc length. Also note that you must draw the cloud in a counterclockwise direction; otherwise, the arcs of the cloud will point in the wrong direction.

Keeping Your Xref Files Together with Pack 'n Go

The Xref feature of AutoCAD has helped streamline the production of large architectural projects. The San Francisco Main Library project, in particular, benefited from Xrefs. But Xrefs also introduce one major problem. When it comes time to send the AutoCAD files to other consultants, you have to figure out which files are external references for other files. In a large project, management of Xrefs can become a major headache.

The Pack 'n Go utility is designed to help you manage Xrefs, as well as most other external resources that an AutoCAD drawing may depend on, such as line-type definitions and text fonts. Here's how it works.

1. Click the Pack 'n Go tool in the Express Standard toolbar.

The Pack & Go dialog box appears.

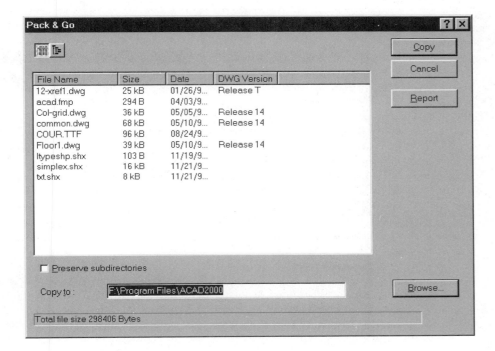

This dialog box shows all external references and resources the current file is using. It also allows you to move all of these resources into one location, such as a directory you've set up to collect a set of files to send to a client or consultant.

2. To choose a location for the copies of your files, click the Browse button in the lower-right corner of the dialog box. A Browse for Folder dialog box lets you locate and select a folder in which to place your copies.

3. Click Copy to copy all the drawing files and resources to the selected directory.

In addition to the files and resources, Pack 'n Go generates three script files designed to convert the drawing files into any format from Release 12 to Release 14. (See Chapter 15 for more on script files.)

Another helpful feature of the Pack 'n Go tool is the report generator. If you click the Report button in the Pack & Go dialog box, a Report dialog box opens, providing a written description of the current file and it resources.

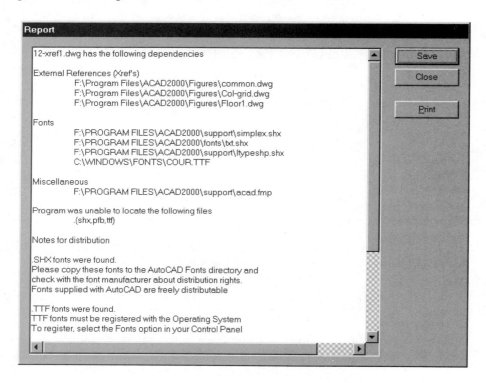

You can save this report as a text file by clicking the Save button. Such a report can be used as a Readme file when sending drawings to clients or consultants.

Creating Custom Hatch Patterns with Super Hatch

AutoCAD offers a large variety of hatch patterns from its Boundary Hatch dialog box. But there are times when none of those patterns will fulfill your needs. This is where the Super Hatch tool comes in. With Super Hatch, you can create virtually any hatch pattern you want. You can use objects in your drawing as a basis for a hatch pattern, or you can import bitmap images and use them to form a hatch pattern, like tiled wallpaper in the Windows background. The following exercise shows you how to use Super Hatch.

1. Open the sample file from the Figures folder called Superhatch.dwg. You'll see a block of the Sybex logo on the left side of the screen and a

rectangular area to the right. In this exercise, you'll turn that logo into a hatch pattern.

2. Click the Super Hatch tool.

The SuperHatch dialog box appears.

3. Click the Select Existing button. The SuperHatch dialog box disappears.

4. Click the arrow. It becomes highlighted and a magenta rectangle appears encircling the arrow.

5. At this point, you can indicate the area you want repeated in your pattern. The default is the extents of the image as indicated by the magenta rectangle.

6. Click the two points shown in Figure 19.7 to indicate the area that you want repeated. The rectangle changes to reflect the new area. You can repeat the area selection until you get exactly the area you want.

7. Press ⏎ to move on to the next step.

8. Click the interior of the rectangle to indicate the area you want to hatch. If you have multiple hatch areas, you can continue to select them at this step.

9. Press ⏎ to finish your selection of hatch areas. The logo appears repeated as a pattern within the rectangle as shown in Figure 19.8.

FIGURE 19.7:

Selecting the area to be repeated

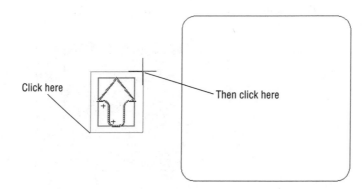

FIGURE 19.8:

The hatch pattern

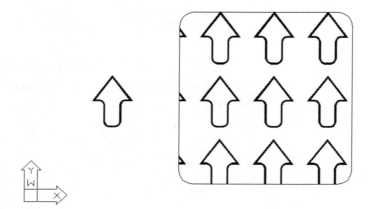

The object you select using the Select Existing option of the SuperHatch dialog box must be a block. You can modify that block using the techniques described in Chapter 6 and the changes will appear in the hatch pattern, as shown in Figure 19.9.

As you can see from the SuperHatch dialog box, you can incorporate Xrefs, blocks, and even image files. Each of these options prompts you to insert the object before you convert it into a hatch pattern. You use the usual insertion method for the type of object you select. For example, if you choose the Block option, you are prompted for an insertion point, the X and Y scale factors, and a rotation angle. For image files, you see the same Image dialog box that you see when you insert an image file, offering the options for insertion point, scale, and rotation. Figure 19.10 shows a sample hatch pattern with an image file used instead of an AutoCAD block.

FIGURE 19.9:

The hatch pattern after the block is modified

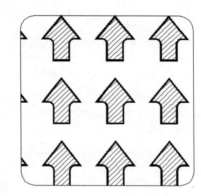

FIGURE 19.10:

A hatch pattern using a bitmap image

Using Add-On Utilities on the San Francisco Main Library Project

While the San Francisco Main Library project was a successful use of AutoCAD, it had its ups and downs. Perhaps one of the biggest problems occurred when a large number of AutoCAD drawings had to be transferred between the architects, SMWM, and the CAD specialists who were producing the drawings, Technical Publications.

As mentioned in previous chapters, the San Francisco Main Library project made extensive use of the Xref feature in AutoCAD. Xrefs were a great time-saver overall, but frequently, the links between the Xref source files and their receiving files were lost when they were transferred from the architect to the CAD specialist. This was the result of the architect and CAD specialist having their own, separate directory structures for the CAD drawings, which tended to confuse AutoCAD. Extra time was spent reestablishing links between drawings and their Xrefs.

Had there been a tool like the Pack 'n Go utility, the Xref problems would not have occurred and the project would have gone much more smoothly. Pack 'n Go would have also helped in managing the many different text fonts used on the project.

But despite the minor glitches, the application of AutoCAD in the San Francisco Main Library project was quite successful, due in part to Technical Publications' extensive use of other add-on utilities available at the time. Many of those same utilities can be found in the On-Screen AEC add-on available on the companion CD-ROM, some of which are even duplicated in the Express tools described in this chapter.

Tools in the Express Pull-Down Menu

Most of the Express tools discussed so far are available as options in the Express pull-down menu. There are some additional options in the pull-down menu you won't see in any of the toolbars. You won't want to miss these additional tools. They can greatly enhance your productivity on any type of project.

Controlling Shortcuts with the Command Alias Editor

Throughout this book, you've been learning about the keyboard shortcuts to the commands of AutoCAD. All of these shortcuts are stored in a file called Acad.pgp in the \Program Files\AutoCAD 2000\Support\ directory. In the past, you had to edit this file with a text editor to modify these command shortcuts (otherwise know as *command aliases*). But to make your lives simpler, Autodesk supplies the Command Alias Editor, which automates the process of editing, adding, or removing command aliases from AutoCAD.

NOTE   At the time of this writing, the Alias Editor was included as part of the Express tools. However, subsequent releases of AutoCAD may not include the Alias Editor or other express tools. Check the Autodesk Web site for more information.

In addition, the Command Alias Editor lets you store your own alias definitions in a separate file. You can then recall your file to load your own command aliases. Here's how the Command Alias Editor works.

1. Choose Express ➤ Tools ➤ Command Alias Editor. The AutoCAD Alias Editor dialog box appears.

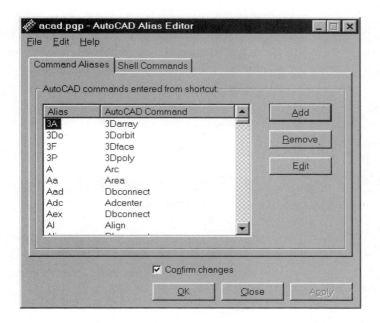

2. As you can see from the button options, you can add a new alias or delete or edit an existing alias. If you click the Add button, you see the New Command Alias dialog box.

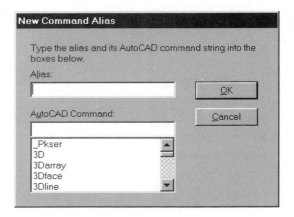

In this dialog box, you enter the desired alias in the Alias input box, and then select the command from the list box below. You can also enter a command or macro name, such as Wipeout, in the input box. When you click the Edit option in the AutoCAD Alias Editor dialog box, you see a dialog box identical to this one with the input boxes already filled in.

3. When you are done creating or editing an alias, click OK. The AutoCAD Alias Editor dialog box reappears.

4. Click OK to exit the dialog box. You see a warning message.

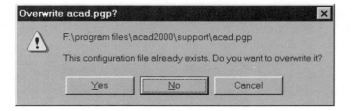

This message is telling you that you are about to overwrite the Acad.pgp file.

5. Click No to leave the Acad.pgp file untouched. The Save As dialog box then appears. In the Save As dialog box, enter an alternate filename, such as Myalias.pgp, to store your personal set of command aliases.

6. Once you've entered a name and saved your settings, a message appears telling you that your new settings have taken effect. Click OK to return to AutoCAD.

If you're a veteran AutoCAD user, you may have become accustomed to your own set of command aliases. If so, you may want to leave the original Acad.pgp file alone and create your own .pgp file as suggested in step 5. Then, whenever you use AutoCAD, you can open the AutoCAD Alias Editor, and choose File ➤ Open and load your personal .pgp file. From then on, the aliases in your file will supersede those of the standard Acad.pgp file.

Full Screen AutoCAD

AutoCAD users can't seem to get enough drawing space. The Full Screen Auto-CAD tool is for those AutoCAD users who are never satisfied with the amount of drawing area their screen may provide.

When you choose Express ➤ Tools ➤ Full Screen AutoCAD, the AutoCAD drawing area is pushed to the maximum area available. The AutoCAD title bar is hidden, as is the menu bar. You can access the menu bar by pushing the cursor to the top of the screen until you see a diskette icon, then click and drag. The menu bar momentarily appears, allowing you to select an option.

To return to the normal AutoCAD window, point to the top edge of the screen until you see the diskette icon, then click and hold to display the menu bar. Choose Express ➤ Tools ➤ Full Screen AutoCAD and you return to the standard AutoCAD view.

Clipping a Raster Image, Xref, or Block to a Curved Shape with Extended Clip

In Chapters 12 and 14, you saw how you can clip portions of an Xref or raster image so that only a portion of these objects is visible. One limitation to the Raster Clip option is that you can only clip areas defined by straight lines. You cannot, for example, clip an area defined by a circle or ellipse.

The Extended Clip tool is designed for those instances where you absolutely need to clip a raster image or block to a curved area. The following steps show you how it works.

1. Create a clip boundary using a curved polyline or circle.

2. Choose Express ➤ Modify ➤ Extended Clip.

3. Click the boundary.

4. Click the Xref, block, or image you wish to clip.

5. At the `Enter max error distance for resolution of arcs <7/16">:` prompt, press ⏎. The Xref, block, or image clips to the selected boundary.

6. You may erase the boundary you created in step 1 or keep it for future reference.

Extended Clip really doesn't clip to the boundary you created, but instead, approximates that boundary by creating a true clip boundary with a series of very short line segments. In fact, the prompt in step 5 lets you specify the maximum allowable distance between the straight-line segments it generates and the curve of the boundary you create (see Figure 19.11).

Once you've created a boundary using Extended Clip, you can edit the properties of the boundary using Modify ➢ Clip➢ Xref for Xrefs and blocks, or Modify ➢ Clip ➢ Image for raster images.

FIGURE 19.11:

Extended Clip allows you to set the maximum distance from the your clip boundary and the one it generates.

Creating a Custom Line Type with Make Linetype

Most of the time, the line types provided by AutoCAD are adequate. But if you're looking for that perfect line type, you can use the Make Linetype tool to make your own. Here's how it works.

1. Open the `Custom1type.dwg` sample file from the `Figures` directory. The sample drawing is made up of simple lines with no polylines, arcs, or circles. When you create your own line-type prototype, make sure the lines

are all aligned. Draw a single line and break it to form the segments of the line type (see Figure 19.12). Also make sure it is drawn to the actual plotted size.

2. Choose Express ➤ Tools ➤ Make Linetype. The MKLTYPE dialog box appears.

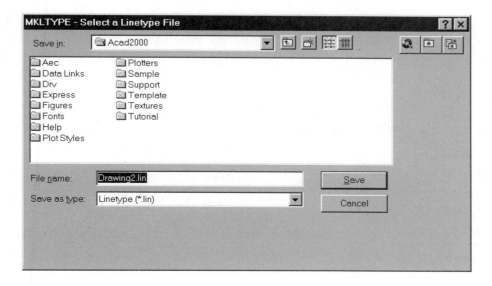

3. Enter **myltype** in the File Name input box and select a location for the file, then click OK.

4. At the Enter a linetype name: prompt, enter **MyLinetype**, or any name you want to use to describe the line type. The name must be a single word.

5. At the Enter linetype description: prompt, enter a description for your line type. This can be a sentence that best describes your line type.

6. At the Specify starting point for line definition: prompt, pick one endpoint of the sample line type.

7. At the Specify ending point for line definition: prompt, pick a point just past the opposite end of the sample line type. Pick a point past the endpoint of the sample to indicate the gap between the end of the first segment of the line type and the beginning of the repeating portion as shown in Figure 19.12.

8. At the Select objects: prompt, select the sample line type lines. When you're done, press ↵. You now have a custom line type.

To load your custom line type, use the Linetype Manager dialog box (Format ➤ Linetype) to locate your line-type file and load the line type. You can also get to the Linetype Manager by clicking the Linetype drop-down list in the Properties toolbar and selecting Other.

If you send your file to someone else, make sure you include your custom line-type files with the drawing file. Otherwise, anything drawn using your custom line type will appear as a continuous line and your recipient will get an error message saying that AutoCAD cannot find your line-type file.

The Make Linetype tool creates a single line-type file for each line type you create. The line-type file is a simple ASCII text file. If you end up making several line types, you can combine your line-type files into one file using a simple text editor like Windows Notepad. Don't use Windows WordPad or Microsoft Word because those programs will introduce special codes to the line-type file.

If you want to understand more about line-type creation and customization, see *Creating Custom Line Types and Hatch Patterns* in Chapter 20.

FIGURE 19.12:

Creating a custom line type using the Make Linetype tool

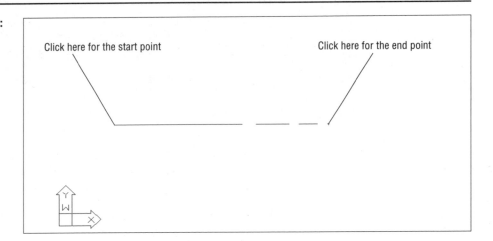

Creating Custom Shapes as an Alternative to Blocks

Shapes are a special type of AutoCAD object that are similar to blocks. They are usually simple symbols made up of lines and arcs. Shapes take up less memory and can be displayed faster, but they are much less flexible than blocks, and they are not very accurate. You cannot use Object Snaps to snap to specific parts of a shape, nor can you explode them. They are best suited for symbols or as components in complex line types.

Shapes have always been difficult to create. In the past, you could not create a shape by drawing it. You had to create something called a *shape definition* using a special code. A shape definition is just an ASCII file containing a description of the geometry of the shape. Creating such a file was a tedious, arcane process that few users bothered with.

With the introduction of complex line types in recent versions of AutoCAD, interest in shapes has revived. To make it easier for users to create shapes, Auto-CAD 2000 offers a tool that will create a shape definition file for you based on a line drawing. Try this simple exercise to learn how you can create and use a shape.

1. Open the `Makeshape.dwg` sample file. This file contains a simple drawing of an upward pointing arrow. It contains lines and arcs.

2. Select Express ➤ Tools ➤ Make Shape. The MKSHAPE dialog box appears. This is a typical file dialog box allowing you to specify a name and location for your shape definition file.

3. Enter **Arrow** in the File Name input box, then locate the `Figures` directory to place your new file there.

4. Click OK to create your file.

5. At the `Enter the name of the shape:` prompt, enter **Arrow⏎**.

6. At the `Enter resolution <128>:` prompt, enter **512⏎**. Shapes are defined with a square matrix of points. All of the endpoints of lines and arcs must be on a point within that matrix. At this prompt, you can define the density of that matrix. A higher density will give you a better-looking shape, but you don't want to get carried away with this setting.

7. At the `Specify insertion base point:` prompt, select the tip of the arrow, as shown in Figure 19.13. This will be the insertion point of your shape, which is similar to the insertion point of a block.

8. At the `Select objects:` prompt, select the entire arrow. Press ⏎ when you've selected the arrow.

You'll see a series of messages telling you what AutoCAD is doing. The last message will tell you whether AutoCAD was successful in creating the shape file and it will tell you the location and name of the new shape file.

```
Compilation successful. Output file F:\Program
Files\ACAD2000\Figures\arrow.shx contains 309 bytes.
```

FIGURE 19.13:

Creating a shape from an existing drawing

Click here for the insertion base point

To see how your shape came out, try the following steps. In this exercise, you'll learn how to load and insert a shape.

1. Type **Load**↵ at the command prompt. The Select Shape File dialog box appears. This is a typical file dialog box.

2. Go to the Figures folder, locate the file Arrows.shx, and click Open to load it.

3. Now type **Shape**↵.

4. At the Enter shape name or [?]: prompt, type **Arrow**↵. Now you'll see the arrow follow the cursor as you move it across the drawing area.

> **NOTE** If you've forgotten the name of a shape you are loading, you can enter a **?** to get a listing of available shapes.

5. At the Specify insertion point: prompt, click to the right of the original arrow.

6. At the Specify height: prompt, press ↵ to accept the default of 1.

7. At the Specify rotation angle: prompt, enter **45**↵. The arrow appears at a 45° angle.

In many ways, a shape acts like a block, but you cannot snap to any of its points. It is also less accurate in its representation than a block, though for some applications, this may not be a great concern. Finally, you cannot use complex shapes such as splines or 3D objects for your shape. You can only use lines and arcs.

Still, you may find shapes useful in your application. As mentioned earlier, you can include shapes in line-type definitions. See Chapter 20 for a description on how to create a line type that includes shapes as part of the line.

NOTE   If you plan to send a file containing shapes to someone else, make sure to include the shape file with the drawing file. See the Pack 'n Go Express tool to learn how you can quickly put a "package" of drawings and their support files together.

Filleting Polylines

One of the more frequently used tools is the Fillet tool. It is great for joining endpoints of lines together. You can also use the Fillet tool to join the endpoint of a polyline and a line. Unfortunately, Fillet won't join two polyline endpoints. This can be frustrating, especially if you are trying to join a set of polylines to form a single polyline. As you learned in Chapter 13, polylines must meet exactly end to end before you can join them.

The Express tools come to the rescue with the Polyline Join tool. Polyline Join lets you connect the endpoints of two polylines in a way similar to the Fillet command. You also have the option to connect the endpoints with a line segment. The following exercise demonstrates how Polyline Join works.

1. Open the Pljoin.dwg file from the Figures directory.

2. Choose Express ➤ Modify ➤ Polyline Join, or type **Pljoin**↵.

3. At the Select objects: prompt, select the two lines, then press ↵.

4. At the Enter fuzz distance or [Jointype]: prompt, click two points to define a distance that is roughly the same as the distance between the two endpoints of the polyline as shown in Figure 19.14. The endpoints of the polylines join.

If you didn't get the results as indicated in step 4, the Polyline Join settings may be set to something other than Fillet. You can change the way Polyline Join works by entering **J**↵ at the prompt in step 4. You then see the following prompt:

```
Enter join type [Fillet/Add/Both]:
```

Enter **F**↵ to make Polyline Join fillet two polylines or enter **A**↵ to make Polyline Join add a line segment between the two polylines. The Both option adds a line segment and fillets the endpoints of polylines.

FIGURE 19.14:

Filleting a polyline

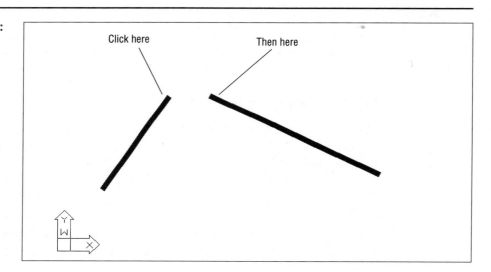

Using the Anti-Selection Tools

Sometimes it seems that there aren't enough selection tools available in Auto-CAD. Chapter 2 described the various methods you can use to select groups of objects to build a selection set, a set of objects selected for an operation such as a Move or Copy. The Express Selection tools offer a set of tools that let you create a selection set by subtraction. These tools work by first asking you to select all the objects on a layer, or even the entire drawing. You then select the object you do not want in the selection set. Once you've removed objects from the selection set, you can proceed with whatever command you want to use to edit the selection set. You can use the Previous Selection option at the Select objects: prompt to use the selection set you build with the Express Selection tools.

The Express Selection tools work like the standard selection options, only in reverse. Instead of adding objects to the selection set, objects are subtracted from the selection set. Here's a view of the Express Selection tools menu showing the options available.

A tool called Get Selection Set at the top of the menu sets up your selection set based on layers. When you choose Get Selection Set, you are prompted to select an object whose layer contains all the objects you want to select. You can press ↵ to create a selection set of all the objects in the drawing. From there, you can use the Exclude Selection option to exclude objects from the selection set. You don't really need to use this option if you want to select all the objects in a drawing except the ones you specify.

If you prefer to type in your selection options at the `Select objects:` prompt, you can do so by entering the standard selection option, preceded by '**EX**. For example, to exclude a set of objects using a window, enter '**EXW**, then proceed to place a window around the object you want to exclude from the selection set. To exclude objects with a crossing window, enter '**EXC**, and so on. If you're selecting objects before you issue a command, to use grip editing for example, you can enter the selection option without the apostrophe. AutoCAD then selects everything except the selected object.

Dimstyle Export and Dimstyle Import

Most AutoCAD users really only need to set up their dimension styles once, then make minor alterations for drawing scale. You can set up your dimension styles in a template file, then use that template whenever you create new drawings. That way, your dimension styles will already be set up the way you want them.

But frequently, you will receive files that were created by someone else who may not have the same ideas about dimension styles as you do. Normally, this would mean that you would have to recreate your favorite settings in a new dimension style. Now with the Express tools, you can export and import dimension styles at any time, saving you the effort of recreating them. Here's how it works.

1. Open a file from which you wish to export a dimension style.

2. Choose Express ➤ Tools ➤ Dimstyle Export, or enter **Dimex**.⅃. The Dimension Style Export dialog box appears.

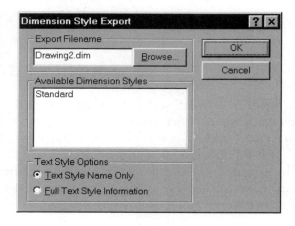

3. Click the Browse button at the top of the dialog box to locate and name a file for storing your dimension style. AutoCAD appends the .dim filename extension.

4. Click Open in the Open dialog box. If the file you specified does not exist, AutoCAD asks you if you want to create it. Click OK to create a new .dim file.

5. Select the name of the dimension style you want to export from the Available Dimension Styles list box.

6. Click the Full Text Style Information radio button to include all the information regarding the associated text style.

7. Click OK. A message appears in the Command window telling you that your dimension style was successfully exported.

To import a style you've exported, take the following steps.

1. Open a file into which you want to import a dimension style.

2. Choose Express ➢ Tools ➢ Dimstyle Import, or type **Dimim**⏎. The Dimension Style Import dialog box appears.

3. Click the Browse button to open the Open dialog box.

4. Locate and select the dimension style file you saved earlier, and then click Open.

5. Click either the Keep Existing Style or Overwrite Existing Style radio button to choose which action to take.

6. Click OK.

Options for Selecting Objects, Attaching Data to Objects, and Updating Polylines

This last set of options is less likely to get as much use as the others discussed so far, so this section includes a brief description of them without going into too much detail. They're actually fairly easy to use, and you shouldn't have any trouble trying them out.

Selection Tools ➢ Get Selection Set   Lets you create a selection set based on layer and type of object. You can either enter a layer or object type when prompted to do so, or select a representative object from the screen.

Tools ➢ Xdata Attachment   Lets you attach extended data to objects. Extended data is usually only used by AutoLISP, ADS, or ARX applications. You are asked to select the object that will receive the data, and then for an application name that serves as a tag to tell others who the data belongs to. You can then select a data type. Once this is done, you can enter your data.

Tools ➢ List Entity Xdata   Displays extended data that has been attached to an object.

Utilities Available from Other Sources

The utilities listed in the previous section are just a few samples of the many utilities available for AutoCAD. Other sources for AutoLISP utilities are the AutoCAD journals *Cadence* and *Cadalyst*. Both offer sections that list utilities written by readers and editorial staff. If you don't already have a subscription to one of these publications and want to know more about them, their contact information follows:

> *Cadence* Magazine published by Miller Freeman Inc., 525 Market Street, Suite 500, San Francisco, CA 94105
>
> URL: `http://www.cadence-mag.com`
>
> *Cadalyst* published by Advanstar Inc., 131W. First St., Duluth, MN 55802-2065
>
> URL: `http://www.cadonline.com`

Finally, the companion CD-ROM included with this book contains some freeware and shareware utilities.

Also on the CD-ROM, I have included my own AEC (architecture, engineering, civil) software offering basic architectural utilities, such as a symbols library, automatic door and window insertion program, and reference symbols. If you're using AutoCAD's 3D features, you'll also want to check out the Eye2eye 3D viewer. Eye2eye lets you easily create perspective views using a camera and target object. For more information on what is included on the companion CD-ROM, see Appendix C.

Putting AutoLISP to Work

Most high-end CAD packages offer a macro or programming language to help users customize their systems. AutoCAD has *AutoLISP*, which is a pared-down version of the popular LISP artificial intelligence language.

Don't let AutoLISP scare you. In many ways, an AutoLISP program is just a set of AutoCAD commands that help you build your own features. The only difference is that you have to follow a different set of rules when using AutoLISP. But this isn't so unusual. After all, you had to learn some basic rules about using

AutoCAD commands, too—how to start commands, for instance, and how to use command options.

If the thought of using AutoLISP is a little intimidating to you, bear in mind that you don't really need substantial computer knowledge to use this tool. In this section, you will see how you can get AutoLISP to help out in your everyday editing tasks, without having to learn the entire programming language.

Other Customization Options

If you are serious about customization, you'll want to know about Autodesk's ObjectARX programming environment that allows Microsoft Visual C++ programmers to develop full applications that work within AutoCAD. ObjectARX allows programmers to create new objects within AutoCAD as well as add functionality to existing objects. ObjectARX is beyond the scope of this book so to find out more, contact your AutoCAD dealer or visit Autodesk's Web site at www.autodesk.com.

If you are familiar with Visual Basic, AutoCAD offers Visual Basic ActiveX Automation as part of its set of customization tools. ActiveX Automation offers the ability to create macros that operate across different applications. It also gives you access to AutoCAD objects through an object-oriented programming environment. Automation is a broad subject, so Chapter 98 is devoted to this topic.

Loading and Running an AutoLISP Program

Many AutoCAD users have discovered the usefulness of AutoLISP through the thousands of free AutoLISP utilities that are available from bulletin board and online services. In fact, it's quite common for users to maintain a "toolbox" of their favorite utilities on a diskette. But before you can use these utilities, you need to know how to load them into AutoCAD. In the following exercise, you'll load and use a sample AutoLISP utility found on the companion CD-ROM.

1. Start AutoCAD and open the 14a-unit.dwg file again.

2. Choose Tools ➤ Load Application. The Load/Unload Applications dialog box appears.

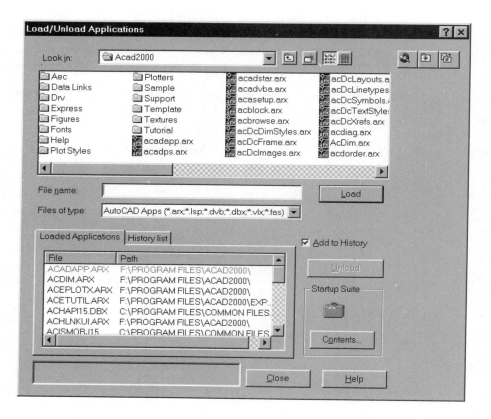

3. In the file list box, locate and select the Getarea.lsp file from the companion CD-ROM. It is included among the sample drawing files in the \Figures\ directory.

4. Highlight Getarea.lsp and click the Load button. The message Getarea.lsp successfully loaded appears in the message box at the very bottom of the dialog box. If you scroll down the list in the Loaded Applications tab, you also see Getarea.lsp listed there, which tells you that it is loaded.

5. Click Close to close the Load/Unload Applications dialog box.

6. Now enter **getarea**↵.

7. At the `Pick point inside area to be calculated:` prompt, click inside the Unit plan.

8. At the `Select location for area note:` prompt, pick a point just above the door to the balcony. A label appears displaying the area of the room in square feet.

You have just loaded and used an AutoLISP utility. As you saw in the Load/Unload Applications dialog box, there are several other utilities you can load and try out. You'll be introduced to a few more of these utilities later on in Appendix C, but for now, let's look more closely at the Load/Unload Applications dialog box.

NOTE   The functions of some of the more popular AutoLISP utilities have become part of the core AutoCAD Program. Tools like Match Properties and Make Objects Layer Current have been around as AutoLISP utilities since the earliest releases of AutoCAD.

Managing Your AutoLISP and VBA Library

The Load/Unload Applications dialog box gives you plenty of flexibility in managing your favorite AutoLISP utilities, You can also manage your VBA and ADS applications. As you saw from the previous exercise, you can easily find and select utilities using this dialog box. If you find that you use a custom application often, you can include it in the History list of the Load/Unload Applications dialog box.

1. Choose Tools ➤ Load Applications again to open the Load/Unload Applications dialog box.

2. Click the Add to History check box.

3. Click the History List tab.

4. Select `Getarea.lsp` again from the list of applications at the top of the dialog box.

5. Click Load. `Getarea.lsp` appears in the History List.

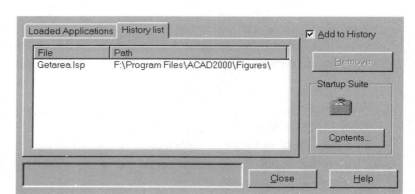

6. Click Close to close the Load/Unload Applications dialog box.

Now when you exit AutoCAD, the dialog box retains the name of the `Getarea.lsp` utility in the History List tab. When you want to load `Getarea.lsp` in a future session, you won't have to hunt it down. You can highlight it in the History List tab, then load it from there. You can add as many items as you want to your History list, or remove items by highlighting them and clicking the Remove button. The History list works with all types of applications that AutoCAD supports.

Loading AutoLISP Programs Automatically

As you start to build a library of AutoLISP and VBA applications, you may find that you use some of them all the time. You can set up AutoCAD to automatically load your favorite applications. To do this, you use the Startup Suite in the Load/Unload Applications dialog box.

1. Choose Tools ➤ Load Applications to open the Load/Unload Applications dialog box.

2. Click the Contents button or the suitcase icon of the Startup Suite group. The Startup Suite dialog box appears.

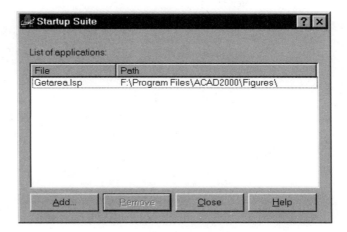

TIP You can also drag and drop files into the Startup Suite list from the Windows Explorer or other drag-and-drop compatible applications.

3. Click the Add button. The Add File to Startup Suite dialog box opens. This is a typical file dialog box that allows you to search for and select a file.

4. Locate and select the Getarea.lsp file in the \Figures\ directory, then click Add. The Startup Suite dialog box reappears and Getarea.lsp is listed.

5. Click Close, then click Close again in the Load/Unload Applications dialog box.

   From now on, Getarea.lsp will be loaded automatically whenever you start AutoCAD. You can add several files to the Startup Suite list, or remove them by selecting them in the list, then clicking the Remove button.

Creating Keyboard Macros with AutoLISP

You can write some simple AutoLISP programs of your own that create what are called *keyboard macros*. Macros—like script files—are strings of predefined keyboard entries. They are invaluable for shortcuts to commands and options you use frequently. For example, you might find that, while editing a particular drawing, you often use the Break command to break an object at a single point. Here's a way you should turn this operation into a macro.

1. Open the Unit file and, at the command prompt, enter the following text. Be sure you enter the line exactly as shown here. If you make a mistake while entering this line, you can use the I-beam cursor or arrow keys to go to the location of your error to fix it.

```
(defun C:breakat () (command "break" pause "f" pause "@"))↵
```

2. Next, enter **breakat**↵ at the command prompt. The Break command starts and you are prompted to select an object.

3. Click the wall on the right side of the unit.

4. At the `Enter First Point:` prompt, click a point on the wall where you want to create a break.

5. To see the result of the break, click the wall again. You will see that it has been split into two lines, as shown in Figure 19.15.

FIGURE 19.15:

With the grips exposed, you can see that the wall is split into two lines.

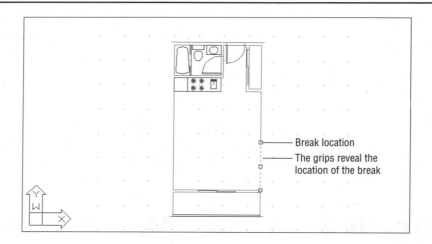

— Break location

— The grips reveal the location of the break

You've just written and run your first AutoLISP macro! Let's take a closer look at this very simple program (see Figure 19.16). It starts out with an opening parenthesis, as do all AutoLISP programs, followed by the word defun. Defun is an AutoLISP function that lets you create commands; it is followed by the name you want to give the command (Breakat, in this case). The command name is preceded by C:, telling defun to make this command accessible from the command prompt. If the C: were omitted, you would have to start Breakat using parentheses, as in (Breakat).

FIGURE 19.16:

Breakdown of the Breakat macro

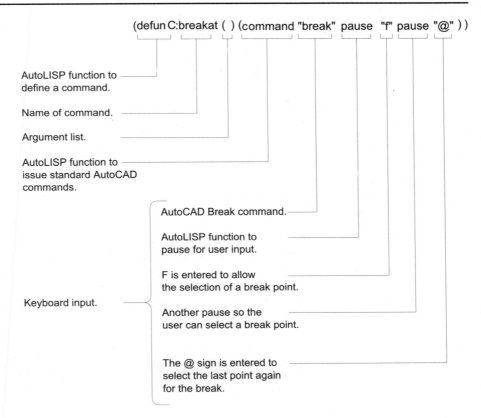

(defun C:breakat ( ) (command "break" pause "f" pause "@"))

AutoLISP function to define a command.

Name of command.

Argument list.

AutoLISP function to issue standard AutoCAD commands.

AutoCAD Break command.

AutoLISP function to pause for user input.

F is entered to allow the selection of a break point.

Keyboard input.

Another pause so the user can select a break point.

The @ sign is entered to select the last point again for the break.

After the command name is a set of open and closing parentheses. This encloses what is called the *argument list*. The details aren't important; just be aware that these parentheses must follow the command name.

Finally, a list of words follows, enclosed by another set of parentheses. This list starts with the word command. Command is an AutoLISP function that tells AutoLISP that whatever follows should be entered just like regular keyboard input. Only one item in the Breakat macro—the word pause—is not part of the keyboard input series. Pause is an AutoLISP function that tells AutoLISP to pause for input. In this particular macro, AutoLISP pauses to let you pick an object to break.

Notice that most of the items in the macro are enclosed in quotation marks. Literal keyboard input must be enclosed in quotation marks in this way. The `pause` function, on the other hand, does not require quotation marks because it is a proper function, one that AutoLISP can recognize.

Finally, the program closes with two closing parentheses. All parentheses in an AutoLISP program must be in balanced pairs, so these two parentheses close the opening parenthesis at the start of the `command` function as well as the opening parenthesis back at the beginning of the `defun` function.

Storing AutoLISP Macros as Files

When you create a program at the command prompt, such as you did with the `Breakat` macro, AutoCAD remembers it only until you exit the current file. Unless you want to recreate this macro the next time you use AutoCAD, you can save it by copying it into an ASCII text file with a .lsp extension, as shown in the following example, where the `Breakat` macro is saved, along with some other macros I use often.

Figure 19.17 shows the contents of a file named `Keycad.lsp`. This file contains the macro you used previously, along with several others. The other macros are commands that include optional responses. For example, the third item, `defun c:corner`, would cause AutoCAD to start the Fillet command, enter an **R↵** to issue the Radius option, and finally enter a **0** for the fillet radius. Table 19.1 shows the command abbreviations and what they do.

FIGURE 19.17:

The contents of Keycad.lsp

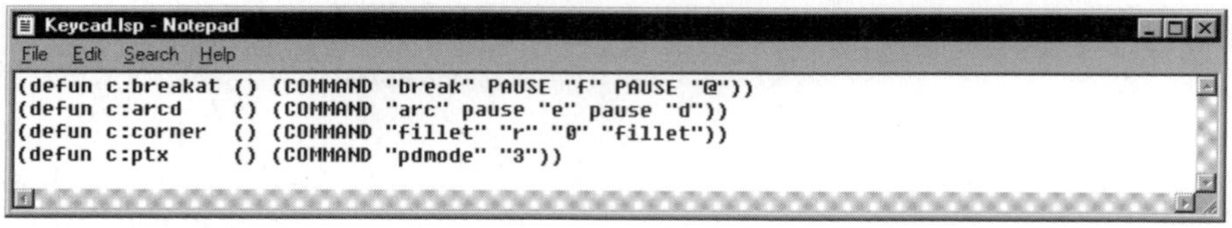

```
Keycad.lsp - Notepad
File  Edit  Search  Help
(defun c:breakat () (COMMAND "break" PAUSE "F" PAUSE "@"))
(defun c:arcd    () (COMMAND "arc" pause "e" pause "d"))
(defun c:corner  () (COMMAND "fillet" "r" "0" "fillet"))
(defun c:ptx     () (COMMAND "pdmode" "3"))
```

TABLE 19.1: The Shortcut Key (Command Abbreviations) Macros Provided by the Keycad.lsp File

Abbreviation	Command or Action Taken
breakat	Breaks an object at a single point
arcd	Draws an arc using the Start, End, Direction sequence
corner	Sets the fillet radius to 0; then starts the Fillet command
ptx	Sets the point style to be in the shape of an X

Use the Windows Notepad application and copy the listing in Figure 19.17. Give this file the name Keycad.lsp, and be sure you save it as an ASCII file. Then, whenever you want to use these macros, you don't have to load each one individually. Instead, you load the Keycad.lsp file the first time you want to use one of the macros, and they're all available for the rest of the session.

Once it is loaded, you can use any of the macros contained within it just by entering the macro name. For example, entering **pts**↵ will set the point style to the shape of an X.

Macros loaded in this manner will be available to you until you exit AutoCAD. Of course, you can have these macros loaded automatically every time you start Auto-CAD by including the Keycad.lsp file in the Startup Suite of the Load/Unload Applications dialog box. That way, you don't have to remember to load it in order to use the macros.

Now that you have some firsthand experience with AutoLISP, I hope these examples will encourage you to try learning more about this powerful tool. If you would like to learn more about AutoLISP, the book *The ABCs of AutoLISP* is included on the companion CD-ROM. This 400-page book, converted into an electronic document, is a complete resource for AutoLISP, including tutorials and example programs.

Using Third-Party Software

One of the most significant reasons for AutoCAD's popularity is its strong support for third-party software. AutoCAD is like a chameleon; it can change to suit its environment. Out of the box, AutoCAD may not fulfill the needs of some users. But by incorporating one of the over 300 third-party add-ons, you can tailor AutoCAD to suit your specific needs.

This section discusses a few of the third-party add-ons that are popular today, so you'll know about some of the possibilities open to you while using AutoCAD. This section will give you an idea of the scope of third-party software. For more information on the myriad of third-party tools out there, check out the Autodesk Web site at http://www.autodesk.com.

Custom-Tailoring AutoCAD

The needs of an architect are far different from those of a mechanical designer or a civil engineer. Third-party developers have created some specialized tools that help users of specific types of AutoCAD applications.

Many of these tools come complete with libraries of parts or symbols, AutoLISP, ADS, or ARX programs, and menus—all integrated into a single package. These packages offer added functions to AutoCAD that simplify and speed up the Auto-CAD user's work. For example, most AEC (architectural or engineering construction) add-ons offer utilities for drawing walls, inserting doors and windows, and creating schedules. These functions can be performed with the stock AutoCAD package but usually require a certain amount of effort. Certainly, if you have the time, you can create your own system of symbols, AutoLISP programs, and menus, and often this is the best way of molding AutoCAD to your needs. However, when users want a ready-made solution, these add-ons are invaluable.

TIP   The companion CD-ROM includes a basic AEC add-on called On-Screen AEC. This add-on provides the basic tools for creating architectural CAD drawings, as well as some great utilities for your everyday use.

Specialized third-party add-ons are available for AEC, mechanical, civil engineering, piping, mapping, finite element analysis, numeric control, GIS, and many other applications. They can save you a good deal of frustration and time, especially if you find just the right one for your environment. Like so many things, however, third-party add-ons can't be all things to all people. It is likely that no matter which add-on you purchase, you will find something lacking. When you're considering custom add-ons, make sure that there is some degree of flexibility in the package, so if you don't like something, you can change it or add to it later.

Check with your AutoCAD dealer for information on third-party add-ons. Most AutoCAD dealers carry the more popular offerings. You might also want to get involved with a user group in your area.

Third-Party Product Information on the World Wide Web

The World Wide Web is another good place to start looking for the third-party add-ons. In particular, you will want to take a look at the Autodesk Resource Guide Web site at www.autodesk.com/products/autocad/index.htm. You can get there by selecting Help ➢ Autodesk on the Web ➢ Autodesk Developers Resource Guide Homepage. While you're at it, you may want to check out the other options on the Autodesk on the Web cascading menu. It offers links to support, technical bulletins, upgrades, and other valuable information.

Autodesk's Own Offerings

Autodesk also offers a wide variety of add-ons to AutoCAD from simple symbols libraries to full-blown, industry-specific applications. There are offerings for architecture, civil, mechanical, mapping, data management, and 3D Visualization. Check out the Autodesk Web site for full details.

Getting the Latest Information from Online Services

There are many resources available for the AutoCAD user. Perhaps the most useful resources are today's popular online services and in AutoCAD-related newsgroups. If you don't already subscribe to one, you would do well to get a modem and explore the AutoCAD newsgroups, departments, or forums on online services.

To start with, check out the two Internet newsgroups that are devoted to AutoCAD users:

- `Alt.cad.autocad`
- `comp.cad.autocad`

Both of these newsgroups offer a forum for you to discuss your AutoCAD questions and problems with other users. Most Internet browsers let you access newsgroups. For example, you can open a News window from Netscape Communicator by choosing Window ➢ Netscape News. From the Netscape News window, choose File ➢ Add Newsgroup, and then enter the name of the newsgroup into the input box that pops up. From then on, you can read messages, reply to posted messages, or post your questions.

Another online service that offers help to AutoCAD users is America Online (AOL). Although it doesn't offer a direct line to Autodesk, there is a forum for AutoCAD users to exchange ideas and troubleshooting tips. AOL also offers a library of AutoCAD-related utilities. To get to the AutoCAD folder in AOL, choose Go To ➢ Keyword. Then in the Keyword dialog box, enter **CAD** and click GO.

Cadalyst and *Cadence*, the two North American magazines devoted to AutoCAD mentioned earlier, both have their own Web sites. *Cadalyst* is at `http:\\www.cadonline.com`; *Cadence* is at `http:\\www.cadence.com`. Also, check out the

Sybex Web site at `http:\\www.sybex.com` for the latest information on more great books on AutoCAD. Finally, check out my own site—`http:\\www.omura.com`—for information concerning this and other books, files, and links to other AutoCAD resources.

If You Want to Experiment...

Try to think of some other keyboard macros that you would like to create. For example, you might try to create a macro that copies and rotates an object at the same time. This operation is a fairly common one that can be performed using the grip edit options, but you can reduce the number of steps needed to copy and rotate by creating a macro. Review the section entitled *Creating Keyboard Macros with AutoLISP* for help.

Here are some hints to get you started:

- Use the Copy command to copy an object in place.

- Use the same coordinate, like 0,0, for the base point and the second point.

- Use the Last Selection option to rotate the last object selected, which happens to be the original object that was copied.

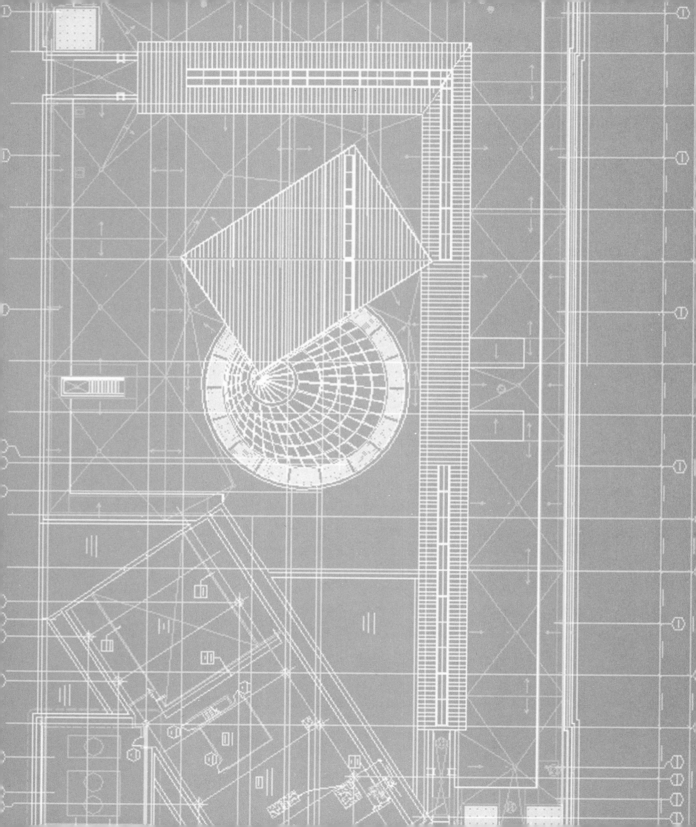

Integrating AutoCAD into Your Projects and Organization

- Customizing Toolbars

- Customizing Toolbar Tools

- Adding Your Own Pull-Down Menu

- Understanding the Diesel Macro Language

- Creating Custom Line Types

- Creating Hatch Patterns

- If You Want to Experiment…

AutoCAD offers a high degree of flexibility and customization, allowing you to tailor the software's look and feel to your requirements. This chapter shows how you can adapt AutoCAD to fit your particular needs. You will learn how to customize AutoCAD by modifying its menus. You will learn how to create custom macros for commands that your work group uses frequently. You'll look into the inner working of menu files, line-type and hatch-pattern definitions, and you'll learn to create new custom toolbars and tools.

Customizing Toolbars

The most direct way to adapt AutoCAD to your way of working is to customize the toolbars. AutoCAD offers new users an easy route to customization. You can create new toolbars, customize tools, and even create new icons. In this section, you'll discover how easy it is to add features to AutoCAD.

Taking a Closer Look at the Toolbars Dialog Box

Throughout this book, you've used the Toolbars dialog box to open toolbars that are specialized for a particular purpose. The Toolbars dialog box is one of the many entry points to customizing AutoCAD. Let's take a closer look at this dialog box to see what other options it offers besides just opening other toolbars.

1. Right-click the Draw toolbar, and then select Customize. The Toolbars dialog box opens.

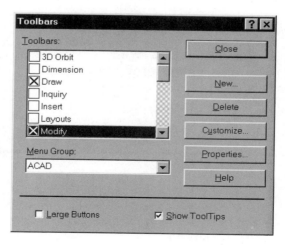

The Toolbars list box shows a listing of all the toolbars available in AutoCAD.

2. Scroll the list box up until you see Inquiry. Highlight it and then click the Properties button. The Toolbar Properties dialog box appears.

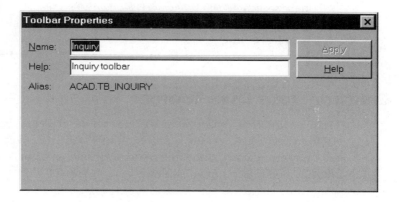

The Name input box controls the title that appears in the toolbar's title bar. The Help input box contains the help message that appears in the status line.

3. Click Close in the Toolbars dialog box to close both dialog boxes.

As you can see from the Toolbar Properties dialog box, you can rename a toolbar and alter its help message, if you choose. Here are brief descriptions of some of the other options in the Toolbars dialog box:

Close   Closes the dialog box.

New   Lets you create a new toolbar.

Delete   Deletes a toolbar from the list.

Customize   Opens the Customize Toolbars dialog box from which you can click and drag predefined buttons.

Properties   Opens the Toolbar Properties dialog box.

Help   Displays helpful information about the Toolbars dialog box.

Large Buttons   Changes all the tools to a larger format.

Show ToolTips   Controls the display for the tool tips.

You'll get to use most of these other options in the following sections.

NOTE   Typically, AutoCAD stores new toolbars and buttons in the `Acad.mns` file (see *The Windows Menu Files* sidebar later in this chapter). You can also store them in your custom menu files. Once you've created and loaded your menu file, as described in the section *Adding Your Own Pull-Down Menu* later in this chapter, choose your menu from the Menu Group pull-down list in the New Toolbar dialog box described below.

Creating Your Own Toolbar

You may find that instead of using one toolbar or flyout, you are moving from flyout to flyout from a variety of different toolbars. If you keep track of the tools you use most frequently, you can create your own custom toolbar containing your favorite tools. Here's how it's done.

1. Right-click any icon in any toolbar, then select Customize in the popup menu. The Toolbars dialog box opens.

2. Click the New button. The New Toolbar dialog box appears.

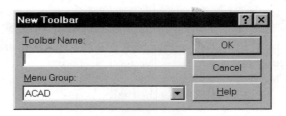

3. Enter **My Toolbar** in the Toolbar Name input box, and then click OK. A small, blank toolbar appears in the AutoCAD window.

Notice that ACAD appears in the Menu Group list box and My Toolbar now appears in the Toolbars list box. You can now begin to add buttons to your toolbar.

4. Click Customize in the Toolbars dialog box. The Customize Toolbars dialog box appears.

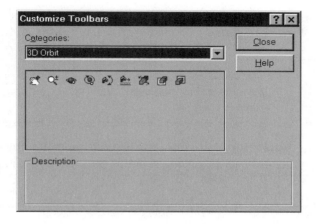

5.   Open the Categories pull-down list. Notice that the list contains the main categories of commands.

6.   Choose Draw from the list. The list box displays all the tools available for the Draw category. Notice that the dialog box offers several additional arc and circle tools not found in the Draw toolbar.

7.   Click the first tool in the top row: the Line tool. You'll see a description of the tool in the Description box at the bottom of the dialog box.

8.   Click and drag the Line tool from the Customize Toolbars dialog box into the new toolbar you just created. The Line tool now appears in your toolbar.

9.   Click and drag the Arc Start End Direction tool to your new toolbar.

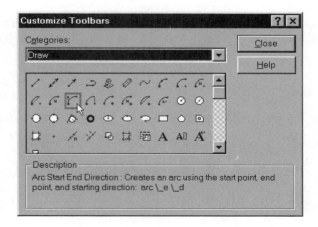

10.   Exit the Customize Toolbars dialog box and the Toolbars dialog box.

You now have a custom toolbar with two buttons. You can add buttons from different categories if you like. You are not restricted to buttons from one category.

NOTE　　If you need to remove a tool from your toolbar, click and drag it out of your toolbar into the blank area of the drawing. Do this while the Customize Toolbars dialog box is open.

AutoCAD treats your custom toolbar just like any other toolbar. It appears when you start AutoCAD and remains until you close it. You can recall it by the same method described in the first exercise.

Opening Toolbars from the Command Line

You may want to know how to open toolbars using the command line. This can be especially helpful if you want to create toolbar buttons that open other toolbars.

1. Type **–Toolbar**↵ at the command prompt (don't forget to include the minus sign at the beginning of the Toolbar command).

2. At the `Toolbar Name <All>:` prompt, enter the name of the toolbar you want to open.

3. At the `Show/Hide/Left/Right/Top/Bottom/Float <Show>:` prompt, press ↵. The toolbar appears on the screen.

A typical button macro for opening a toolbar might look like this:

```
^c^cToolbar[space]ACAD.Arc[space][space]
```

Here, the `[space]` is added for clarity. You would press the spacebar in its place. This example shows a macro that opens the Arc toolbar (`ACAD.Arc`).

As the prompt in step 3 indicates, you can specify the location of the toolbar by left, right, top, or bottom. Float lets you specify the location and number of rows for the toolbar.

The following list shows the toolbar names available in the standard AutoCAD system. Use the following names with the Toolbar command:

ACAD.TB_OBJECT_PROPERTIES

ACAD.TB_STANDARD

Continued on next page

ACAD.TB_DIMENSION

ACAD.TB_DRAW

ACAD.TB_EXTERNAL_DATABASE

ACAD.TB_INQUIRY

ACAD.TB_INSERT

ACAD.TB_LAYOUTS

ACAD.TB_MODIFY

ACAD.TB_MODIFY_II

ACAD.TB_OBJECT_SNAP

ACAD.TB_3D_ORBIT

ACAD.TB_REFEDIT

ACAD.TB_REFERENCE

ACAD.TB_RENDER

ACAD.TB_SOLIDS

ACAD.TB_SOLIDS2

ACAD.TB_SURFACES

ACAD.TB_UCS

ACAD.TB_UCS2

ACAD.TB_VIEWPOINT

ACAD.TB_VIEWPORTS

ACAD.TB_ZOOM

ACAD.TB_WEB

Notice that the toolbar names in the Toolbars dialog box do not match those shown in this list. You can find the "true" name of a toolbar by highlighting it in the Toolbars dialog box, and then clicking Properties. The toolbar's true name is displayed under Alias.

Customizing Toolbar Tools

Now let's move on to more serious customization. Suppose you want to create an entirely new button with its own functions. For example, you may want to create a set of buttons that will insert your favorite symbols. Or you might want to create a toolbar containing a set of tools that open some the other toolbars that are normally "put away."

Creating a Custom Button

In the following set of exercises, you'll create a button that inserts a door symbol. You'll add your custom button to the toolbar you just created.

1. Open the Toolbars dialog box again, and then click Customize.

2. Select Custom from the drop-down list. The list box now shows two blank buttons, one for a single command and another for flyouts. (The one for flyouts has a small triangle in the lower-right corner.)

3. Click and drag the single command blank button to your new toolbar.

4. Right-click the blank button in your new toolbar. The Button Properties dialog box appears. This dialog box lets you define the purpose of your custom button.

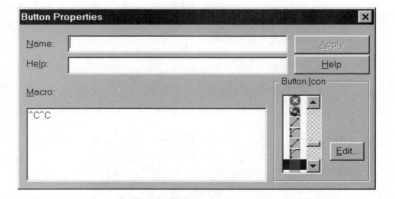

Let's pause for a moment to look at this dialog box. The Name input box lets you enter a name for your button. This name will appear as a tool tip. You must enter a name before AutoCAD will create the new button definition.

The Help input box just below the name lets you add a help message. This message will appear in the lower-left corner of the AutoCAD window when you point to your button.

The Macro area is the focus of this dialog box. Here, you can enter the keystrokes you want to "play back" when you click on this button.

Finally, to the right, you see a scroll bar that lets you scroll through a set of icons. You'll also see a button labeled Edit. When you highlight an icon in the scroll box, and then click Edit, an Icon Editor tool appears allowing you to edit an existing icon or create a new icon.

Now let's go ahead and add a macro and new icon to this button.

1. In the Name input box, enter **Door**. This will be your tool tip for this button.

2. In the Help input box, enter **Inserts a single door**. This will be the help message for this button.

3. In the Macro input box, enter the following: **^C^C–insert door**.

    Make sure you include the minus sign before the word **insert**. This indicates that you want to use the command-line version of the Insert command.

TIP

You can put any valid string of keystrokes in the Macro input box, including AutoLISP functions. See Chapter 21 or the *ABCs of AutoLISP* on the companion CD-ROM for more on AutoLISP. You can also include pauses for user input using the backslash (\) character. See the *Pausing for User Input* section later in this chapter.

Note that the two ^Cs already appear in the Macro input box. These represent two Cancels being issued. This is the same as pressing the Esc key twice. It ensures that when the macro starts, it cancels any unfinished commands.

You follow the two Cancels with the Insert command as it is issued from the keyboard. If you need help finding the keyboard equivalent of a command, consult the *AutoCAD 2000 Instant Reference* on the companion CD-ROM, which contains a listing of all the command names.

WARNING   It is important that you enter the exact sequence of keystrokes that follow the command, otherwise your macro may get out of step with the command prompts. This will take a little practice and some going back and forth between testing your button and editing the macro.

After the Insert command, there is a space, and then the name Door appears. This is the same sequence of keystrokes you would enter at the command line to insert the door drawing you created in Chapters 2 and 3. You could go on to include an insertion point, scale factor, and rotation angle in this macro, but these options are better left for the time when the door is actually inserted.

Creating a Custom Icon

You have all the essential parts of the button defined. Now you just need to create a custom icon to go with your door button.

1. In the Icon scroll box, scroll down the list until you see a blank icon.

2. Click the blank icon, and then click Edit. The Button Editor appears.

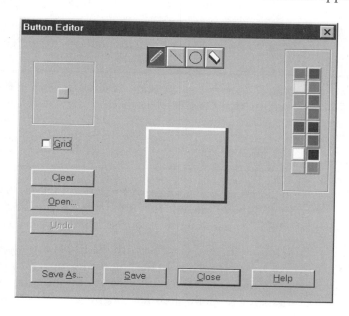

NOTE If you prefer, you can use any of the predefined icons in the scroll box. Just click the icon you want to use, and then click Apply.

The Button Editor is like a very simple drawing program. Across the top are the tools to draw lines, circles, and points as well as an eraser. Along the right side, you see a color toolbar from which you can choose colors for your icon button. In the upper left, you see a preview of your button. The following describes the rest of the options:

Grid Turns a grid on and off in the drawing area. This grid can be an aid in drawing your icon.

Clear Erases the entire contents of the drawing area.

Open Opens a .bmp file to import an icon. The .bmp file must be small enough to fit in the 16 × 16 pixel matrix provided for icons (24 × 24 for large-format icons).

Save As Saves your icon as a .bmp file under a name you enter.

Save Saves your icon under a name that AutoCAD provides, usually a series of numbers and letters.

Close Exits the Button Editor.

Help Displays helpful information about the features of the Button Editor.

Undo Undoes the last operation you performed.

Now let's continue by creating a new icon.

3. Draw the door icon shown here. Don't worry if it's not perfect; you can always go back and fix it.

4. Click Save, and then click Close.

5. In the Button Properties dialog box, click Apply. You'll see the icon appear in the button in your toolbar.

6. Now click the Close button of the Toolbars dialog box.

WARNING   The Door drawing must be in the default directory, or in the **Acad** search path before the door button will be inserted.

---

7. Click the Door icon on your new toolbar. The door appears in your drawing ready to be placed.

You can continue to add more buttons to your toolbar to build a toolbar of symbols. Of course, you're not limited to a symbols library. You can also incorporate your favorite macros or even AutoLISP routines that you may accumulate as you work with AutoCAD. The possibilities are endless.

Setting the Properties of Flyouts

Just as you added a new button to your toolbar, you can also add flyouts. Remember that flyouts are really just another form of a toolbar. This next example shows how you can add a copy of the Zoom toolbar to your custom toolbar, and then make adjustments to the properties of the flyout.

1. Right-click the Door icon in the toolbar you just finished. The Toolbars dialog box opens with My Toolbar already highlighted.

2. Click Customize, and then in the Customize Toolbars dialog box, open the pull-down list and select Custom.

3. Click and drag the flyout button from the list box into the My Toolbar toolbar.

TIP   To delete a button from a toolbar, open the Toolbars dialog box, and then click Customize. When the Customize Toolbars dialog box appears, click and drag the button you want to delete out of the toolbar and into the drawing area.

You now have a blank flyout to which you can add your own icon. Let's see what options are available for flyout buttons.

4. Close the Customize Toolbars dialog box, and then right-click the new, blank flyout button you just added to your toolbar. The Flyout Properties dialog box appears.

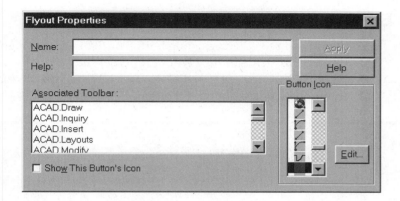

Notice how this dialog box resembles the Button Properties dialog box you used in the previous exercise. But instead of the Macro input box, you see a list of associated toolbars.

5. Scroll down the list of toolbar names until you find ACAD.Zoom. This is a pre-defined toolbar, although it can be a toolbar you define yourself.

6. Highlight ACAD.Zoom, and then enter **My Zoom Flyout** in the Name input box. Enter **My very own flyout** in the Help input box.

7. Locate an icon in the icon scroll box that looks like a magnifying glass, and click it.

8. Click the check box labeled Show This Button's Icon so that a checkmark appears in the box.

9. Click Apply. The flyout button in the My Toolbar toolbar shows the icon you selected.

10. Close the Toolbars dialog box, and then place the arrow cursor on the flyout to display its tool tip. Notice that your new tool tip and help message appear.

11. Click and drag the Zoom icon, and then select Zoom In from the flyout. Notice that even though you selected Zoom In, the original Zoom icon remains as the icon for the flyout.

Step 11 demonstrates that you can disable the feature that causes the last flyout to appear as the default on the toolbar. You disabled this feature in step 8 by checking the Show This Button's Icon check box.

Editing Existing Buttons

If you want to edit an existing button or flyout, you can go directly to either the Button Properties or the Flyout Properties dialog box by double-right-clicking a button. Once one of these dialog boxes is open, you can make changes to any component of the button definition.

The Windows Menu Files

As you create and modify buttons and toolbars, you see messages momentarily appear in the status line at the bottom of the AutoCAD window. These messages are telling you that AutoCAD is creating new menu files. AutoCAD creates several menu files it uses in the course of an editing session.

Here's a brief rundown of what those different menu files are

Acad.mnu   This file is the source text file that contains the information required to build the AutoCAD menu. If you are a programmer, you would use this file to do detailed customization of the AutoCAD menu. Here, you can edit the pull-down menus, image tiles, buttons, etc. Most users won't have a need to edit this file.

Acad.mnc   This file is AutoCAD's translation of the **Acad.mnu** file. AutoCAD translates, or "compiles," the **Acad.mnu** file so that it can read the menu faster.

Acad.mns   This file is a text file created by AutoCAD containing the source information from the .mnu file plus additional comments. This file is rewritten whenever an .mnu file is loaded. If you make changes or additions to toolbars, you'll want to keep a backup copy of this file to preserve those changes. The **Acad.mns** file can be used like an **Acad.mnu** file as a source text file to build the AutoCAD menu.

Acad.mnr   This file is the menu resource file. It is a binary file that contains the bitmap images used for buttons and other graphics.

As you create or edit icon buttons and toolbars, AutoCAD first adds your custom items to the **Acad.mns** file. It then compiles this file into the **Acad.mnc** and **Acad.mnr** files for quicker access to the menus. If you reload the MNU version of your menu, AutoCAD recreates the MNS file, thereby removing any toolbar customization you may have done.

Note that the **Acad.mns** file is the file you need to copy to other computers to transfer your custom buttons and toolbars. Also, if you create your own pull-down menu files, as in the **Mymenu.mnu** example in this chapter, AutoCAD creates the source, compiled, and creates the resource files for your custom menu file. You have the option to store new toolbars in your custom menu through the Menu Group pull-down list of the New Toolbar dialog box.

Adding Your Own Pull-Down Menu

In addition to adding buttons and toolbars, AutoCAD lets you add pull-down menu options. This sections looks at how you might add a custom pull-down menu to your AutoCAD environment.

Creating Your First Pull-Down Menu

Let's start by trying the following exercise to create a simple pull-down menu file called My Menu.

1. Using a text editor, like the Windows Notepad, create a file called Mymenu.mnu, containing the following lines:

```
***POP1
[My 1st Menu]
[Line]^c^c_line
[-]
[->More]
[Arc-SED]^c^c_arc \_e \_d
[<-Break At]^c^c(defun c:breakat ()+
(command "break" pause "f" pause "@")+
);breakat
[Fillet 0]^c^c_fillet r 0;;
[Point Style X]'pdmode 3
***POP2
[My 2nd Menu]
[door]^c^cInsert door
[Continue Line]^C^CLINE;;
```

2. Save this file, and be sure you place it in your \AutoCAD2000\Support\ directory.

WARNING   Pay special attention to the spaces between letters in the commands described in this chapter. (You need not worry much about whether to type uppercase or lowercase letters.)

Once you've stored the file, you've got your first custom pull-down menu. You may have noticed some familiar items among the lines you entered. The menu contains the Line and Arc commands. It also contains the Breakat macro you worked on in Chapter 19; this time, that macro is broken into shorter lines.

Now let's see how My Menu works in AutoCAD.

Loading a Menu

In the following exercise, you will load the menu you have just created and test it out. The procedure described here for loading menus is the same for all menus, regardless of their source.

1. Choose Tools ➤ Customize Menus. The Menu Customization dialog box appears.

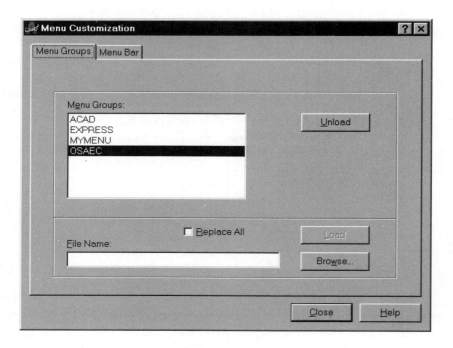

2. Click the Menu Groups tab. Then click Browse at the bottom of the dialog box. The Select Menu file dialog box appears.

3. Click the Files of Type drop-down list, and then select Menu Template (*.mnu).

4. Locate the Mymenu.mnu file, highlight it, and then click Open. You return to the Menu Customization dialog box.

5. Click Load. You see a warning message telling you that you will lose any toolbar customization you have made. This only refers to the specific menu you are loading. Since you haven't made any toolbar customization changes to your menu, you won't lose anything.

6. Click Yes. The warning dialog box closes and you see the name of your menu group listed in the Menu Group list box.

7. Click the Menu Bar tab at the top of the dialog box. The dialog box changes to show two lists.

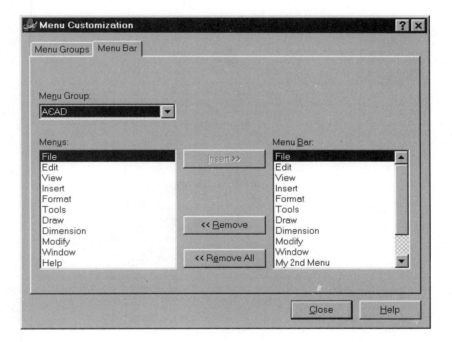

On the left is the name of the current menu group. The list on the right shows the currently available pull-down menus.

8. Click the Menu Group drop-down list, then select MYMENU. The names of the pull-down menus in your menu file appear.

9. Highlight Help in the right-hand column. This tells AutoCAD you want to add your pull-down menu in front of the Help pull-down menu.

10. Highlight My 1st Menu from the list on the left, then click the Insert >> button. My 1st Menu moves into the right-hand column and it appears in the AutoCAD menu bar.

11. Highlight My 2nd Menu from the list on the left, and then click Insert >> again. My 2nd Menu is copied to the right-hand column and it also appears in the menu bar.

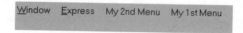

12. Close the Menu Customization dialog box.

13. Draw a line on the screen, and then try the option My 1st Menu ➤ More ➤ Break At.

With just an 11-line menu file, you created a menu that contains virtually every tool used to build menus. Now let's take a more detailed look at how menu files work.

How the Pull-Down Menu Works

Let's take a closer look at the Mymenu.mns file. The first item in the file, ***POP1, identifies the beginning of a pull-down menu. The text just below the first line is My 1st Menu enclosed in square brackets. This is the title of the pull-down menu; this text appears in the toolbar. Every pull-down menu must have this title element.

Following the title, each item in the list starts with a word enclosed in brackets; these words are the options that actually appear when you open the pull-down menu. If you were to remove everything else, you would have the menu as it appears on the screen. The text that follows the item in brackets conveys instructions to Auto-CAD about the option.

Finally, in the My 1st Menu sample, you see ***POP2. This is the beginning of a second pull-down menu. Again, you must follow this with a pull-down menu title in square brackets. Below the title, you can add other menu options.

Calling Commands

Now look at the Line option in the Mymenu.mnu listing. The two Ctrl+C (^C) elements that follow the square brackets will cancel any command that is currently operative. The Line command follows, written just as it would be entered through the keyboard. Two Cancels are issued in case you are in a command that has two levels, such as the Edit Vertex option of the Pedit command (Modify ➤ Object ➤ Polyline).

The underscore character (_) that precedes the Line command tells AutoCAD that you are using the English-language version of this command. This feature lets you program non-English versions of AutoCAD using the English-language command names.

You may also notice that there is no space between the second ^C and the Line command. A space in the line would be the same as a ↵. If there were a space between these two elements, a ↵ would be entered between the last ^C and the Line command, causing the command sequence to misstep. Another way to indicate a ↵ is by using the semicolon, as in the following example:

```
[Continue Line]^C^CLINE;;
```

TIP When you have many ↵s in a menu macro, using semicolons instead of spaces can help make your macro more readable.

In this sample menu option, the Line command is issued, and then an additional ↵ is added. The effect of choosing this option is a line that continues from the last line entered into your drawing. The two semicolons following the word Line tell AutoCAD to start the Line command, and then issue ↵ twice to begin a line from the endpoint of the last line entered. (AutoCAD automatically issues a single ↵ at the end of a menu line. In this case, however, you want two ↵s, so they must be represented as semicolons.)

Pausing for User Input

Another symbol used in the menu file is the backslash (\); it is used when a pause is required for user input. For example, when you select the Arc-SED option in My 1st Menu, it starts the Arc command and then pauses for your input.

```
[Arc-SED]^c^c_arc \_e \_d
```

NOTE   The underscore character (_) that precedes the command name and option input tells AutoCAD that you are entering the English-language versions of these commands.

The space between ^c^c_arc and the backslash (\) represents the pressing of the spacebar. The backslash indicates a pause to allow you to select the starting endpoint for the arc. Once you have picked a point, the _e represents the selection of the Endpoint option under the Arc command. A second backslash allows another point selection. Finally, the _d represents the selection of the Direction option. Figure 20.1 illustrates this.

FIGURE 20.1:

The execution of the Arc menu item

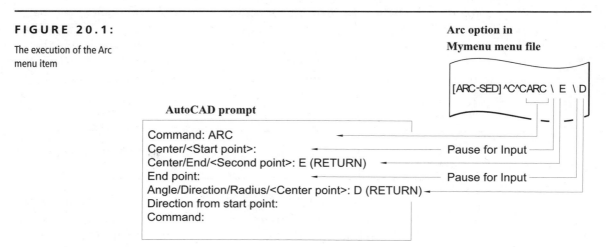

If you want the last character in a menu item to be a backslash, you must follow the backslash with a semicolon.

Using the Plus Sign for Long Lines

As you browse through the Acad.mnu file, notice that many of the lines end with a plus sign (+). The length of each line in the menu file is limited to about 80 characters, but you can break a line into two or more lines by adding a plus sign at the end of the line that continues, like this:

```
[<-Break At]^c^c(defun c:breakat ()+
(command "break" pause "f" pause "@")+
);breakat
```

It's okay to break an AutoLISP program into smaller lines. In fact, it can help you read and understand the program more easily.

This example showed how to include the Breakat AutoLISP macro in a menu. Everything in this segment is entered just as it would be with the keyboard. The plus sign is used to indicate the continuation of this long item to the subsequent lines, and the semicolon is used in place of ⏎.

Creating a Cascading Menu

Look at the More option in the File pull-down menu group; it starts with these characters: ->. This is the way you indicate a menu item that opens a cascading menu. Everything that follows the [->More] menu item will appear in the cascading menu. To indicate the end of the cascading menu, you use the characters <-, as in the [<-Rotate90] menu item farther down. Anything beyond this <- item appears in the main part of the menu. If the last item in a cascading menu is also the last item in the menu group, you must use <-<-, as in [<-<-.XZ].

Placing Division Lines and Dimmed Text in Pull-Down Menus

Two symbols are used to place dividing lines in your pull-down menus. One is the *double-hyphen* symbol (--). This is used to divide groups of items in a menu; it will expand to fill the entire width of the pull-down menu with a line of hyphens. The other option is the *tilde* symbol (~). If the tilde precedes a bracketed option name, that option will be dimmed when displayed; when clicked on, it will have no effect. You have probably encountered these dimmed options on various pull-down menus in the programs you use. When you see a dimmed menu item, it usually means that the option is not valid under the current command.

Loading AutoLISP Macros with Your Submenu

As you become a more advanced AutoCAD user, you may find that you want to have many of your own AutoLISP macros load with your menus. This can be accomplished by combining all of your AutoLISP macros into a single file. Give this file the same name as your menu file with the .mnl filename extension. Such a file will be automatically loaded with its menu counterpart. For example, say you have a file called `Mymenu.mnl` containing the Breakat AutoLISP macro. Whenever you load `Mymenu.mns`, `Mymenu.mnl` is automatically loaded along with it, giving you access to the Breakat macro. This is a good way to manage and organize any AutoLISP program code you want to include with a menu.

Adding Help Messages to Pull-Down Menu Items

Earlier in this chapter, you learned how to include a help message with a button. The help message appears in the status bar of AutoCAD window when you highlight an option. You can also include a help message with a pull-down menu item.

First, you must give your pull-down menu file a menu group name. This helps AutoCAD isolate your file and its help messages from other menus that might be loaded along with yours. To give your menu file a group name, add the following line at the top of the file:

```
***MENUGROUP=MYMENU
```

where *MYMENU* is the name you want for your menu group name.

Next, you have to add an ID name to each menu item that requires a help message. The following example shows how this might be done for the My 1st Menu example you used earlier:

```
***MENUGROUP=MYMENU
***POP1
[My 1st Menu]
ID_1line      [Line]^c^c_line
[-]
[->More]
ID_1arc-sed  [Arc-SED]^c^c_arc \_e \_d
ID_1breakat  [<-Break At]^c^c(defun c:breakat ()+
(command "break" pause "f" pause "@")+
```

```
);breakat
ID_1fillet0    [Fillet 0]^c^c_fillet r 0;;
ID_1pointx     [Point Style X]'pdmode 3
***POP2
[My 2nd Menu]
[door]^c^cInsert door
[Continue Line]^C^CLINE;;
```

The ID name starts with the characters ID followed by an underscore character (_), and then the name for the menu item. Several spaces are added so the menu items align for clarity. Each menu item must have a unique ID name.

Finally, you add a section at the end of your file called ***HELPSTRINGS. For this example, it would look like the following code.

```
***HELPSTRINGS
ID_1line      [Draws a line]
ID_1arc-sed   [Draws an arc with start, end, direction]
ID_1breakat   [Breaks an object at a single point]
ID_1fillet0   [Sets the Fillet radius to zero]
ID_1pointx    [Sets the Point style to an X]
```

The menu item ID names are duplicated exactly, followed by several spaces, and then the actual text you want to have appear in the status line, enclosed in brackets. The spaces between the ID and the text are for clarity.

WARNING The ID names are case sensitive, so make sure they match up in both the HELPSTRINGS section and in the menu section.

Once you've done this, and then loaded the menu file, you will see these same messages appear in the status bar when these menu options are highlighted. In fact, if you browse your Acad.mnu file, you will see similar ID names. If you prefer, you can use numbers in place of names.

Creating Accelerator Keys

Perhaps one of the more popular methods for customizing AutoCAD has been the keyboard accelerator keys. Accelerator keys are Ctrl or Shift key combinations that invoke commonly used commands or tools in AutoCAD. The Osnaps are a popular candidate for accelerator keys, as are the display commands.

To add accelerator key definitions to AutoCAD, you need to add some additional code to your menu file. The following is an example of what you can add to the Mymenu.mnu file to define a set of accelerator keys.

```
***ACCELERATORS
[CONTROL+SHIFT+"E"]endp
[CONTROL+SHIFT+"X"]int
ID_1breakat    [CONTROL+SHIFT+"B"]
```

The ***ACCELERATORS line at the top is the group heading, similar to the ***HELP-STRINGS heading in that it defines the beginning of the section. This is followed by the accelerator descriptions.

There are two methods shown in the previous example for defining an accelerator key. The first two bracketed text items follow the format you've already seen for the pull-down menu. But instead of the menu text in square brackets, you see the keys required to invoke the action that follows the brackets. So in the first line:

```
[CONTROL+SHIFT+"E"]endp
```

the CONTROL+SHIFT+"E" tells AutoCAD to enter the Endpoint Osnap (**endp**) whenever the Ctrl+Shift+E key combination is pressed. Notice that the E is in quotation marks and that all the characters are uppercase. Follow this format for quotation marks and capitalization when you create your own accelerator keys.

A second method is shown in the third line:

```
ID_1breakat    [CONTROL+SHIFT+"B"]
```

Here, the ID_1breakat is used to associate a keystroke combination with a menu option, not unlike the way it is used to associate a menu item with a help string. This line tells AutoCAD to issue the Breakat macro listed earlier in the menu whenever the Ctrl+Shift+B key combination is pressed.

You can use either Ctrl or Shift individually or together in combination with most keys on your keyboard, including the function keys. You can also assign keys without the Ctrl or Shift options. Note that the function keys and the Esc key are already defined, so take care that you don't redefine them unless you really want to. Table 20.1 contains a brief listing of some of the special keys you can define and how you need to specify them in the menu file.

TABLE 20.1:   Key Names to Use in Your Accelerator Key Definitions

Key	Format Used in AutoCAD Menu
Numeric keypad	"NUMPAD0" through "NUMPAD9"
Ins	"INSERT"
Del	"DELETE"
Function keys	"F2" through "F12"
Up arrow	"UP"
Down arrow	"DOWN"
Left arrow	"LEFT"
Right arrow	"RIGHT"

WARNING   Although you can use the F1 and Esc keys for accelerator keys, their use is discouraged because they serve other functions for both Windows and AutoCAD.

Understanding the Diesel Macro Language

If you browse through the Acad.mnu file, you'll see many menu options that contain odd-looking text beginning with a dollar sign ($). In some instances, the dollar sign is used to tell AutoCAD to open a popup menu. But in many cases, it is used as part of the Diesel macro language. Diesel is one of many macro languages AutoCAD supports, and it can be used to perform some simple operations. Like AutoLISP, it makes use of parentheses to enclose program code.

You can actually use Diesel at the AutoCAD command line using a command called Modemacro. The Modemacro command sends information to the status line. Diesel can be used with Modemacro to perform some simple tasks. Try the following exercise to try Diesel for yourself.

1.   Type **Modemacro.⏎** at the command prompt.

2. At the `Enter new value for MODEMACRO, or . for none:` prompt, enter **$(/,25,2)**↵. You'll see the answer to the equation in the far-left side of the status line.

```
Command: modemacro
Enter new value for MODEMACRO, or . for none <"">: $(/,25,2)
Command:
```
```
12.5  16.9132, 7.2424, 0.0000        SNAP GRID ORTHO POLAR OSNAP OTRACK LWT MODEL
```

3. To clear the status line, enter **Modemacro**↵.↵.

The equation you entered in step 2 is referred to as an *expression*. The structure of Diesel expressions is similar to that of AutoLISP. The dollar sign tells AutoCAD that the information that follows is a Diesel expression.

A Diesel expression must include an operator of some sort, followed by the items to be operated on. An *operator* is an instruction to take some specific action such as adding two numbers together or dividing one number by another. Examples of mathematical operators include the plus sign (+) for addition and forward slash (/) for division.

The operator is often referred to as a *function* and the items to be operated on as the *arguments* to the function or simply, the arguments. So, in the expression (/,25,2), the / is the function and the 25 and 2 are the arguments. All Diesel expressions, no matter what size, follow this structure and are enclosed by parentheses.

Parentheses are important elements of an expression. All parentheses must be balanced; for each left parenthesis, there must be a right parenthesis.

You can do other things with Diesel besides performing calculations. In Chapter 19, you used Diesel to place text in the drawing using the Remote Text tool. There, the Getvar function was used to obtain the drawing prefix and name, which Remote Text converted into text in the drawing. Try the following to see how Diesel uses Getvar.

1. Type **Modemacro**↵ again.

2. Type **$(getvar,dwgprefix)**↵. The location of the current drawing appears in the status bar.

3. Press ↵ to reissue the Modemacro command, then type **$(getvar,dwgname)**↵. Now the name of the drawing appears in the status bar.

In this example, the Getvar function extracts the drawing prefix and name and displays it in the status line. Getvar can be used to extract any system variable you want. If you've been working through the tutorials in this book, you've seen that virtually all AutoCAD settings are also controlled through system variables. (Appendix D contains a list all the system variables.) This can be a great tool when you are creating custom menus because with Getvar, you can "poll" AutoCAD to determine its state. For example, you can find out what command is currently being used. Try the following exercise to see how this works.

1. Click the Line tool in the Drawing toolbar.

2. Type **'Modemacro**⤶. The apostrophe at the beginning of Modemacro lets you use the command while in another command.

3. Type **$(getvar,cmdnames)**⤶. The word `line` appears in the status bar indicating that the current command is the Line command.

Diesel can be useful in a menu when you want your menu option to perform a specific task depending on which command is currently active.

Using Diesel in a Menu

So far, you've been experimenting with Diesel through the Modemacro command. To use Diesel in a menu requires a slightly different format. You still use the same Diesel format of a dollar sign followed by the expression, but you don't use the Modemacro command to access Diesel. Instead, you use $M=. You can think of $M= as an abbreviation for Modemacro.

Here's a Diesel expression that you can use in a menu:

```
[Blipmode on/off]'Blipmode $M=$(-,1,$(getvar,Blipmode))
```

This menu option turns Blipmode on or off. Blipmode is a feature that displays point selections in the drawing area as tiny crosses. These tiny crosses, or *blips* as they are called, do not print and can be cleared from the screen with a redraw. They can be helpful when you need to track your point selections.

In this example, the Blipmode command is invoked, then the $M= tells AutoCAD that a Diesel expression follows. The expression

```
$(-,1,$(getvar,Blipmode))
```

returns either a 1 or a 0, which is applied to the Blipmode command to either turn it on or off. This expression shows that you can nest expressions within each other. The most deeply nested expression is evaluated first, so AutoCAD evaluates

```
$(getvar,blipmode)
```

to begin with. This returns either a 1 or 0, depending on whether Blipmode is on or off. Next, AutoCAD evaluates the next level in the expression:

```
$(-,1,getvar_result)
```

where *getvar_result* is either a 1 or 0. If *getvar_result* is 1, then the expression looks like

```
$(-,1,1)
```

which returns a 0. If *getvar_result* is 0 then the expression looks like

```
$(-,1,0)
```

which returns a 1. In either case, the end result is that the Blipmode command is assigned a value that is opposite to the current Blipmode setting.

Using Diesel as a Menu Option Label

In the previous example, you saw how Diesel can be used in a menu to read the status of a command, then return a numeric value to alter that status. You can also use Diesel as part of the menu option label. The following expression shows the same menu listing you've already seen, with a twist. It includes Diesel code as the menu option label, as follows:

```
[$(eval,"Blipmode =" $(getvar,blipmode))]'BLIPMODE $M=$(-,1,$(getvar,
blipmode))
```

NOTE   When Diesel is used as the menu name, you don't need the $M= code.

Normally, you see the menu name within the square brackets at the beginning of this menu listing, but here you see some Diesel instructions. These instructions tell AutoCAD to display the message Blipmode = 1 or Blipmode = 0 in the menu, depending on the current Blipmode setting.

Here's how it works. You see the familiar $(getvar,blipmode) expression, this time embedded within a different expression. You know that $(getvar,blipmode) returns either a 1 or 0 depending on whether Blipmode is on or off. The outer expression

```
$(eval,"Blipmode =" getvar_result)
```

displays the word Blipmode = then combines this word with *getvar_result*, which as you've learned, will be either 1 or 0. The eval function evaluates any text that follows it and returns its contents. The end result is the appearance of Blipmode = 1 or Blipmode = 0 in the menu, depending on the status of Blipmode. Here's what the option looks as it appears in a menu.

You can get even fancier by setting up the Menu option label to read Blipmode On or Blipmode Off by using the If Diesel function. Here's that same menu listing with additional Diesel code to accomplish this:

```
[$(eval,"Blipmode " $(if,$(getvar,blipmode),"Off","On"))]'BLIPMODE
$M=$(-,1,$(getvar,blipmode))
```

In this example, the simple $(getvar,blipmode) expression is expanded to include the If function. The If function reads the result of $(getvar,blipmode) then returns the Off or On values depending on whether $(getvar,blipmode) returns a 0 or 1. Here's a simpler look at the expression:

```
$(if, getvar_result, "Off", "On")
```

If *getvar_result* returns a 1, then the If function returns the first of the two options listed after *getvar_result*, which is Off. If *getvar_result* returns a 0, then the If functions returns On. The second of the two options is optional. Here's how the fancier Blipmode option appears in a menu.

You've really just skimmed the surface of what Diesel can do. To get a more detailed description of how Diesel works, look at the AutoCAD Help Topics dialog box. Choose Help ➤ AutoCAD Help, then in the Help Topics dialog box, click the Index tab. Enter **Diesel** in the input box at the top and you'll see a listing of topics that deal with Diesel.

For fun, try adding this Blipmode menu listing to your `Mymenu.mnu` file under the [`Continue Line`] option, then reload the menu file and check the results.

```
[$(eval,"Blipmode " $(if,$(getvar,blipmode),"Off","On"))]'BLIPMODE
$M=$(-,1,$(getvar,blipmode))
```

Make sure the last line in your menu file is followed by a ⏎.

If you feel you've learned enough to do some work with Diesel, Table 20.2 shows some of the commonly used Diesel functions. Check the AutoCAD Help Topics dialog box for a more detailed list.

TABLE 20.2: A Sample of Diesel Functions. Note That to Indicate True or False, Diesel Uses 1 or 0.

Code	Function	Example	Result	Comments
+	Add	$(+,202,144)	346	
−	Subtract	$(-,202,144)	58	
*	Multiply	$(*,202,144)	29088	
/	Divide	$(/,202,144)	1.4028	
=	Equal to	$(=,202,144)	0	If numbers are equal, then 1 is returned.
<	Less than	$(<,202,144)	0	If first number is less than second, then 1 is returned.
>	Greater than	$(>,202,144)	1	If first number is less than second, then 0 is returned.
!	Not equal to	$(!,202,144)	1	If numbers are equal, then 0 is returned.
<=	Less than or equal to	$(+,202,144)	0	If first number is less than or equal to second, then 1 is returned.
>=	Greater than or equal to	$(+,202,144)	1	If first number is less than or equal to second, then 0 is returned.
eq	Equal string	$(eq,"Yes", "No")	0	If both text strings are the same, then 1 is returned.
eval	Evaluate text	$(eval,"Here I Am")	Here I Am	Returns text in quotes.

Continued on next page

TABLE 20.2 CONTINUED: A Sample of Diesel Functions. Note That to Indicate True or False, Diesel Uses 1 or 0.

Code	Function	Example	Result	Comments
getvar	Get system variable value	`$(getvar,ltscale)`	Current line-type scale	
if	If/Then	`$(if,1,"Yes","No")`	Yes	The second argument is returned if the first argument evaluates to 1. Otherwise, the third argument is returned. The third argument is optional.

Creating Custom Line Types

As your drawing needs expand, you may find that the standard line types are not adequate for your application. Fortunately, you can create your own. This section explains how to go about creating your own custom line types.

Chapter 19 shows you a simplified way to create line types using the Express Make Linetype tool. In this section, you'll get an in-depth view of the process of creating line types. You'll also learn how to create complex line types that cannot be created using the Express Make Linetype tool.

Viewing Available Line Types

Although AutoCAD provides the line types most commonly used in drafting (see Figure 20.2), the dashes and dots may not be spaced the way you would like, or you may want an entirely new line type.

NOTE   AutoCAD stores the line types in a file called **Acad.lin**, which is in ASCII format. When you create a new line type, you are actually adding information to this file. Or, if you create a new file containing your own line-type definitions, it, too, will have the extension .lin. You can edit line types as described here, or you can edit them directly in these files.

To create a custom line type, use the Linetype command. Let's see how this handy command works, by first listing the available line types.

1. Open a new AutoCAD file.

2. Enter **–Linetype**↵ at the command prompt. (Don't forget the minus sign at the beginning of the word Linetype.)

3. At the ?/Create/Load/Set prompt, enter ?↵.

4. In the File dialog box that appears, locate and double-click ACAD in the listing of available line-type files. You get the listing shown in Figure 20.3, which shows the line types available in the Acad.lin file along with a simple description of each line. Figure 20.3 shows a few of the standard line types and the ISO and complex line types. (See Figure 4.8 for a complete listing of standard line types.)

FIGURE 20.2:

The standard AutoCAD line types

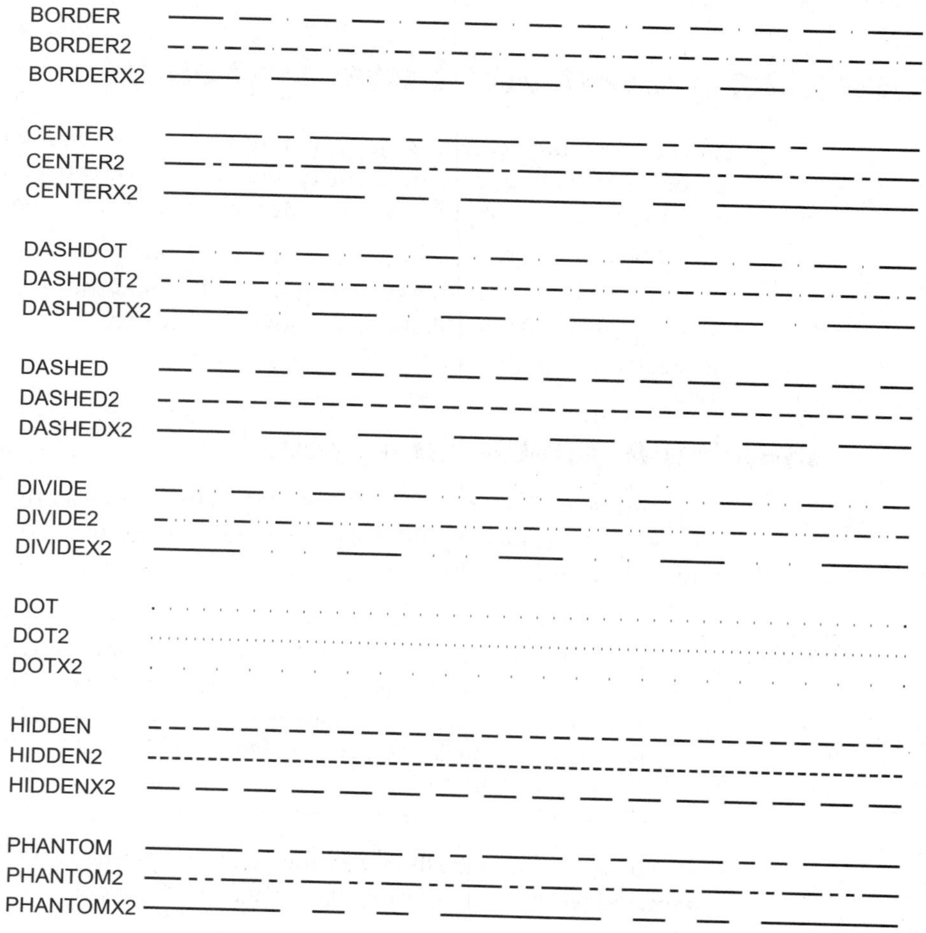

BORDER	
BORDER2	
BORDERX2	
CENTER	
CENTER2	
CENTERX2	
DASHDOT	
DASHDOT2	
DASHDOTX2	
DASHED	
DASHED2	
DASHEDX2	
DIVIDE	
DIVIDE2	
DIVIDEX2	
DOT	
DOT2	
DOTX2	
HIDDEN	
HIDDEN2	
HIDDENX2	
PHANTOM	
PHANTOM2	
PHANTOMX2	

FIGURE 20.3:

The lines in this listing of standard line types were generated with the underscore key (_) and the period (.), and are only rough representations of the actual lines.

```
BORDER          Border    __ __ . __ __ . __ __ . __ __ .
BORDER2         Border (.5x)  _._._._._._._._._._._._._.
BORDERX2        Border (2x) ___ ___ ___   .   ___ ___ .
CENTER          Center   ___ _ ___ ___ _ ___ ___ _ ___
CENTER2         Center (.5x) __ _ __ __ _ __ __ _ __ __

CENTERX2        Center (2x) _____ __ _____ __ _____
DASHDOT         Dash dot  __ . __ . __ . __ . __ . __ .
DASHDOT2        Dash dot (.5x) _._._._._._._._._._._._._._.
DASHDOTX2       Dash dot (2x) ___ . ___ . ___ . ___ .
DASHED          Dashed   __ __ __ __ __ __ __ __ __ __

DASHED2         Dashed (.5x) _ _ _ _ _ _ _ _ _ _ _ _ _ _ _ _
DASHEDX2        Dashed (2x) ___ ___ ___ ___ ___ ___ ___
DIVIDE          Divide   __ . . __ . . __ . . __ . . __
DIVIDE2         Divide (.5x) _ .. _ .. _ .. _ .. _ .. _ .._
DIVIDEX2        Divide (2x) _____   . .   _____   . .  _

DOT             Dot . . . . . . . . . . . . . . . . . .
DOT2            Dot (.5x) ....................................
DOTX2           Dot (2x) .   .   .   .   .   .   .   .   .
HIDDEN          Hidden   __ __ __ __ __ __ __ __ __ __ __
HIDDEN2         Hidden (.5x) _ _ _ _ _ _ _ _ _ _ _ _ _ _ _

HIDDENX2        Hidden (2x) ____ ____ ____ ____ ____ ____
PHANTOM         Phantom  _____ __ __ _____ __ __ _____
PHANTOM2        Phantom (.5x) ___ _ _ ___ _ _ ___ _ _ ___
PHANTOMX2       Phantom (2x) _____     ____     ____

ACAD_ISO02W100  ISO dash  __ __ __ __ __ __ __ __ __ __
ACAD_ISO03W100  ISO dash space  __   __   __   __   __
ACAD_ISO04W100  ISO long-dash dot ____ . ____ . ____ . _
ACAD_ISO05W100  ISO long-dash double-dot ____ .. ____ .. ____ .
ACAD_ISO06W100  ISO long-dash triple-dot ____ ... ____ ... ____
ACAD_ISO07W100  ISO dot . . . . . . . . . . . . . .

ACAD_ISO08W100  ISO long-dash short-dash ____ _ ____ _ ____ _
ACAD_ISO09W100  ISO long-dash double-short-dash ____ _ _ ____ _
ACAD_ISO10W100  ISO dash dot  _ . _ . _ . _ . _ . _ . _ .
ACAD_ISO11W100  ISO double-dash dot __ __ . __ __ . __ __ . __
ACAD_ISO12W100  ISO dash double-dot __ .. __ .. __ .. __ ..

ACAD_ISO13W100  ISO double-dash double-dot __ __ . . __ __ . .
ACAD_ISO14W100  ISO dash triple-dot __ . . . __ . . . __ . .
ACAD_ISO15W100  ISO double-dash triple-dot __ __ . . . __ __ . . . _
FENCELINE1      Fenceline circle ----O-----O----O-----O----O---
FENCELINE2      Fenceline square ----[]-----[]----[]-----[]----

TRACKS          Tracks -|-|-|-|-|-|-|-|-|-|-|-|-|-|-|-|-|-|-|-|
BATTING         Batting SSSSSSSSSSSSSSSSSSSSSSSSSSSSSSSSSSSSSSSS
HOT_WATER_SUPPLY  Hot water supply ---- HW ---- HW ---- HW ----
GAS_LINE        Gas line ----GAS----GAS----GAS----GAS----GAS---
ZIGZAG          Zig zag /\/\/\/\/\/\/\/\/\/\/\/\/\/\/\/\/\/\/\/
```

Creating a New Line Type

Next, try creating a new line type.

1.   At the ?/Create/Load/Set: prompt, enter **C↵**.

2. At the `Name of linetype to create:` prompt, enter **Custom.↵** as the name of your new line type.

3. Notice that the file dialog box you see next is named Create or Append Line-type File. You need to enter the name of the line-type file you want to create or add to. If you pick the default line-type file, ACAD, your new line type is added to the `Acad.lin` file. If you choose to create a new line-type file, Auto-CAD opens a file containing the line type you create and adds .lin to the file-name you supply.

4. Let's assume you want to start a new line-type file. Enter **Newline.↵** in the File Name input box.

> **NOTE** If you had accepted the default line-type file, ACAD, the prompt in step 5 would say `Wait, checking if linetype already defined`.... This protects you from inadvertently overwriting an existing line type you may want to keep.

5. At the `Descriptive text:` prompt, enter a text description of your line type. You can use any keyboard character as part of your description, but the actual line type can be composed only of a series of lines, points, and blank spaces. For this exercise, enter:

   Custom - My own center line _____ _ _____ ↵

   using the underscore key (_) to simulate the appearance of your line.

6. At the `Enter pattern (on next line):` prompt, enter the following numbers, known as the line-type code (after the a that appears automatically):

   1.0,-.125,.25,-.125 ↵

> **WARNING** If you use the Set option of the –Linetype command to set a new default line type, you will get that line type no matter what layer you are on.

7. At the `New definition written to file. ?/Create/Load/Set:` prompt, press ↵ to exit the –Linetype command.

Remember, once you've created a line type, you must load it in order to use it, as discussed in the *Assigning Line Types to Layers* section of Chapter 4.

TIP You may also open the **Acad.lin** or other .lin file with Windows Notepad and add the descriptive text and line-type code directly to the end of the file.

The Line-Type Code

In step 6 of the previous exercise you entered a series of numbers separated by commas. This is the line-type code, representing the different lengths of the components that make up the line type. The separate elements of the line-type code are explained as follows:

- The **1.0** following the **a** is the length of the first part of the line. (The **a** that begins the line-type definition is a code that is applied to all line types.)

- The first **−.125** is the blank or broken part of the line. The minus sign tells AutoCAD that the line is *not* to be drawn for the specified length, which is 0.125 units in this example.

- Next comes the positive value of **0.25**. This tells AutoCAD to draw a line segment 0.25 units long after the blank part of the line.

- Finally, the last negative value, **−.125**, again tells AutoCAD to skip drawing the line for the distance of 0.125 units.

This series of numbers represents the one segment that is repeated to form the line (see Figure 20.4). You could also create a very complex line type that looks like a random broken line, as in Figure 20.5.

FIGURE 20.4:

Line-type description with plotted line

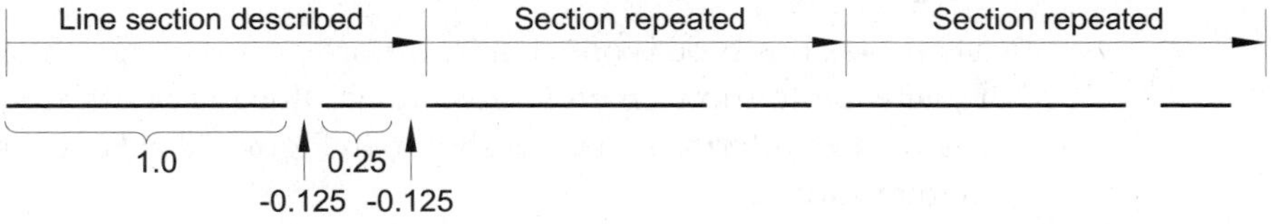

Line section described | Section repeated | Section repeated

1.0   0.25
-0.125 -0.125

FIGURE 20.5:

Random broken line

You may be wondering what purpose the a serves at the beginning of the line-type code. A line type is composed of a series of line segments and points. The a, which is supplied by AutoCAD automatically, is a code that forces the line type to start and end on a line segment rather than a blank space in the series of lines. At times, AutoCAD stretches the last line segment to force this condition, as shown in Figure 20.6.

FIGURE 20.6:

AutoCAD stretches the beginning and the end of the line as necessary.

| Stretched | | Stretched |

NOTE The values you enter for the line-segment lengths are multiplied by the Ltscale factor, so be sure to enter values for the *plotted* lengths.

As mentioned in the beginning of this section, you can also create line types outside AutoCAD by using a word processor or text editor such as Windows Notepad. The standard Acad.lin file looks like Figure 20.3 with the addition of the code used by AutoCAD to determine the line-segment lengths.

Normally, to use a line type you have created, you have to load it, through either the Layer or the Linetype dialog box (Format ➢ Layers, or Format ➢ Linetype). If you use one of your own line types frequently, you may want to create a button macro, so it will be available as an option on a menu.

Creating Complex Line Types

A complex line type is one that incorporates text or special graphics. For example, if you want to show an underground gas line in a site plan, you normally show a line with an intermittent G, as shown in Figure 20.7. Fences are often shown with an intermittent X.

For the graphics needed to compose complex line types, use any of the symbols found in the AutoCAD font files discussed in Chapter 8. Just create a text style using these symbol fonts, and then specify the appropriate symbol by using its corresponding letter in the line-type description.

To create a line type that includes text, use the same line-type code described earlier, with the addition of the necessary font file information in brackets. For example, say you want to create the line type for the underground gas line mentioned above. You add the following to your Acad.lin file:

```
*Gas line -- G -- G --
a,1.0,-0.25, ["G", standard, S=.2, R=0, X=-.1, Y=-.1], -0.25
```

The information in the square brackets describes the characteristics of the text. The actual text that you want to appear in the line is surrounded by quotation marks. Next are the text style, scale, rotation angle, X displacement, and Y displacement.

FIGURE 20.7:

Samples of complex line types

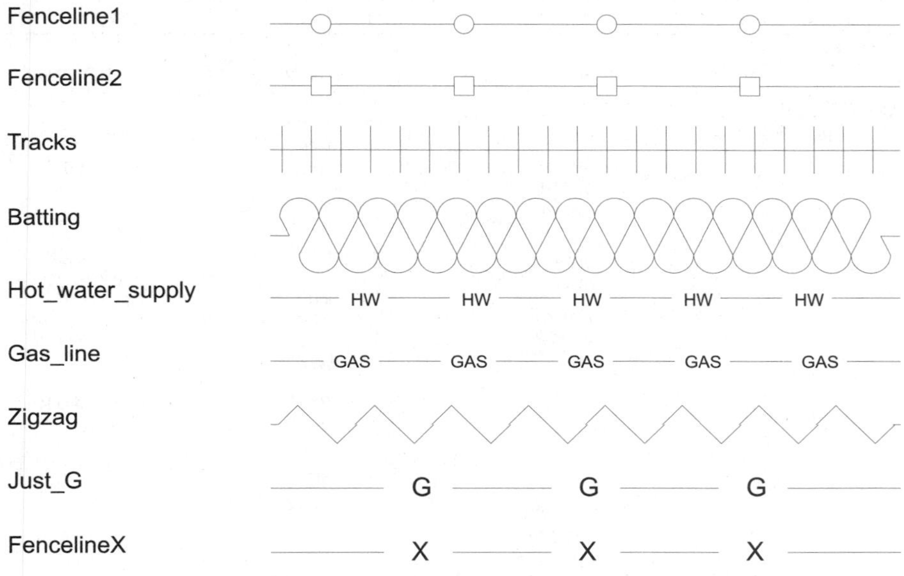

Fenceline1	
Fenceline2	
Tracks	
Batting	
Hot_water_supply	HW HW HW HW HW
Gas_line	GAS GAS GAS GAS GAS
Zigzag	
Just_G	G G G
FencelineX	X X X

WARNING   You cannot use the –Linetype command to define complex line types. Instead, you must open the **Acad.lin** file using a text editor, such as Windows Notepad, and add the line-type information to the end of the file. Make sure you don't duplicate the name of an existing line type.

You can substitute the rotation angle (the R value) with an A, as in the following example:

```
a,1.0,-0.25, ["G", standard, S=.2 A=0, X=-.1, Y=-.1], -0.25
```

This has the effect of keeping the text at the same angle, regardless of the line's direction. Notice that in this sample, the X and Y values are a   -.1; this will center the Gs on the line. The scale value of .2 will cause the text to be .2 units high, so the -.1 is half the height.

In addition to fonts, you can also specify shapes for line-type definitions. Instead of letters, shapes display symbols. Shapes are stored not as drawings, but as definition files, similar to text-font files. In fact, shape files have the same .shx filename extension as text files and are also defined similarly. Figure 20.8 shows some symbols from shape files supplied with the companion CD-ROM.

FIGURE 20.8:

Samples of shapes available on the companion CD-ROM

ST.SHX	ES.SHX	PC.SHX	LTYPESHP.SHX
opt-x	con1	dip14	track1
obl-x	cap		
pro-x	pnp	dip18	
opt-m	mark		box
bol-m	jump	dip24	bat
pro-m	zener		zig
opt-c	nor	dip8	circ1
obl-c	and	dip16	
pro-c	buffer		
opt-r	box	dip20	
obl-r			
pro-r	res	dip40	
opt-p	diode		
obl-p	npn		
pro-p	arrow		
opt-perp	con2		
obl-perp	or		
pro-perp	xor		
opt-parallel	nand		
obl-parallel	inverter		
pro-parallel	neg		
	feedthru		

To use a shape in a line-type code, you use the same format as shown previously for text. However, instead of using a letter and style name, you use the shape name and the shape filename, as in the following example:

```
*Capline, ====
a,1.0,-0.25,[CAP,ES.SHX,S=.5,R=0,X=-.1,Y=-.1],-0.25
```

This example uses the CAP symbol from the Es.shx shape file. The symbol is scaled to .5 units with 0 rotation and an X and Y displacement of −.1.

Here is another example that uses the arrow shape you created in Chapter 19.

```
*Arrowline, --|---|---|
a,1.0,-0.25,[ARROW,ARROW.SHX,S=.5,R=0,X=-.1,Y=-.1],-0.25
```

Just as with the Capline example, the ARROW symbol in this example is scaled to .5 units with 0 rotation and an X and Y displacement of –.1. Here's what it the Arrowline line type looks like when used with a spline.

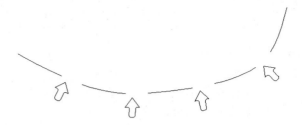

Creating Hatch Patterns

AutoCAD provides several predefined hatch patterns you can choose from (see Figure 20.9), but you can also create your own. This section demonstrates the basic elements of pattern definition.

Unlike line types, hatch patterns cannot be created while you are in an AutoCAD file. The pattern definitions are contained in an external file named Acad.pat. This file can be opened and edited with a text editor that can handle ASCII files, such as the Windows Notepad. Here is one hatch pattern definition from that file:

```
*square,Small aligned squares
0, 0,0, 0,.125, .125,-.125
90, 0,0, 0,.125, .125,-.125
```

You can see some similarities between pattern descriptions and line-type descriptions. They both start with a line of descriptive text, and then give numeric values defining the pattern. However, the numbers in pattern descriptions have a different meaning. This example shows two lines of information. Each line represents a line in the pattern. The first line determines the horizontal line component of the pattern and the second line represents the vertical component. Figure 20.10 shows the hatch pattern defined in the example.

FIGURE 20.9:

The standard hatch patterns

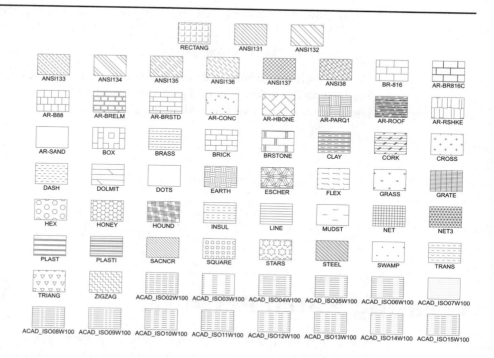

FIGURE 20.10:

Square pattern

A pattern is made up of *line groups*. A line group is like a line type that is arrayed a specified distance to fill the area to be hatched. A line group is defined by a line of code, much as a line type is defined. In the square pattern, for instance, two lines—one horizontal and one vertical—are used. Each of these lines is duplicated in a fashion that makes the lines appear as boxes when they are combined. Figure 20.11 illustrates this point.

FIGURE 20.11:

The individual and combined line groups

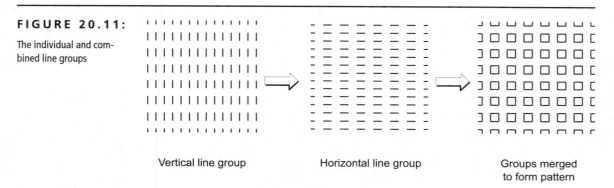

Vertical line group   Horizontal line group   Groups merged to form pattern

Look at the first line in the definition:

```
0, 0,0, 0,.125, .125,-.125
```

This example shows a series of numbers separated by commas; it represents one line group. It actually contains four sets of information, separated by blank spaces:

- The first component is the 0 at the beginning. This value indicates the angle of the line group, as determined by the line's orientation. In this case, it is 0 for a horizontal line that runs from left to right.

- The next component is the origin of the line group, 0,0. This does not mean that the line actually begins at the drawing origin (see Figure 20.12). It gives you a reference point to determine the location of other line groups involved in generating the pattern.

NOTE If you have forgotten the numeric values for the various directions, refer back to Figure 2.4 in Chapter 2, which shows AutoCAD's system for specifying angles.

FIGURE 20.12:

The origin of the patterns

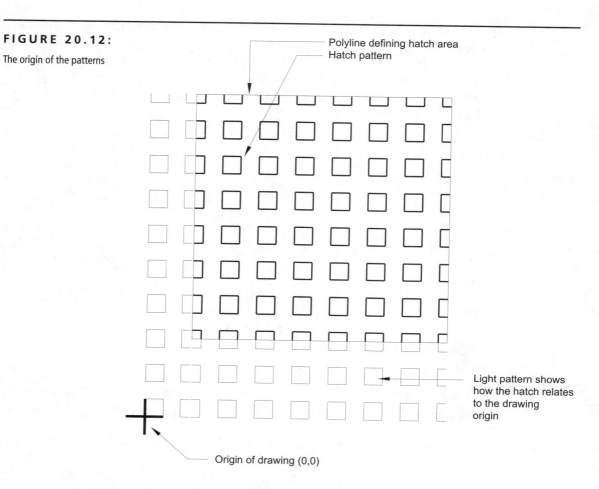

Polyline defining hatch area

Hatch pattern

Light pattern shows how the hatch relates to the drawing origin

Origin of drawing (0,0)

- The next component is 0, .125. This determines the distance for arraying the line and in what direction, as illustrated in Figure 20.13. This value is like a relative coordinate indicating x and y distances for a rectangular array. It is not based on the drawing coordinates, but on a coordinate system relative to the orientation of the line. For a line oriented at a 0° angle, the code 0, .125 indicates a precisely vertical direction. For a line oriented at a 45° angle, the code 0, .125 represents a 135° direction. In this example, the duplication occurs 90° in relation to the line group, because the x value is 0. Figure 20.14 illustrates this point.

FIGURE 20.13:

The distance and direction of duplication

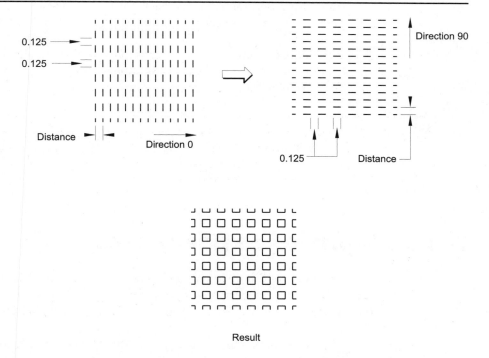

Result

FIGURE 20.14:

How the direction of the line group copy is determined

The X and Y coordinate values given for the array distance are based on the orientation of the line group.

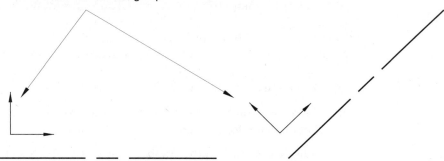

- The last component is the actual description of the line pattern. This value is equivalent to the value given when you create a line type. Positive values are line segments and negative values are blank segments. This part of the line-group definition works exactly as in the line-type definitions you studied in the previous section.

This system of defining hatch patterns may seem somewhat limiting, but you can actually do a lot with it. Autodesk managed to come up with 53 patterns—and that was really only scratching the surface.

TIP If you want to include thick lines in your hatch patterns, you have to "build up" line widths with multiple line-type definitions. You may also use the SuperHatch Express tool discussed in Chapter 19.

If You Want to Experiment...

In the first part of this chapter, you learned that you can create your own toolbars, then you went on to learn how to create your own menu. Try adding custom toolbars to the menu you created in the *Adding Your Own Pull-Down Menu* section.

1. If you haven't done so already, load the Mymenu.mnu file into the AutoCAD menu bar.

2. Right-click a button in any toolbar, then select Customize in the popup menu. The Toolbars dialog box opens.

3. Select Mymenu from the Menu Group drop-down list.

Since you don't have toolbars coded into your menu file, the Toolbars list box is empty. The next step is to add a toolbar to your custom menu.

1. Click the New button. The New Toolbar dialog box appears.

2. Enter **My Toolbar** in the Toolbar Name input box, and then click OK. A small, blank toolbar appears in the AutoCAD window.

3. Click Customize in the Toolbars dialog box. The Customize Toolbars dialog box appears.

4. Open the Categories pull-down list. Notice that the list contains the main categories of commands.

5. Choose Draw from the list. The list box displays all the tools available for the Draw category. Notice that the dialog box offers several additional arc and circle tools not found in the Draw toolbar.

6. Click the first tool in the top row: the Line tool. You'll see a description of the tool in the Description box at the bottom of the dialog box.

7. Click and drag the Line tool from the Customize Toolbars dialog box into the new toolbar you just created. The Line tool now appears in your toolbar.

8. Click and drag the Arc Start End Direction tool to your new toolbar.

9. Exit the Customize Toolbars dialog box and the Toolbars dialog box.

AutoCAD saves your addition in a file called Mymenu.mns. The contents of Mymenu.mns contains all of the code you wrote when you created the Mymenu.mnu file, plus the code needed for the toolbar you added in this last exercise. You can preserve your toolbar additions to your menu file by making a copy of Mymenu.mns and renaming it to Mymenu.mnu.

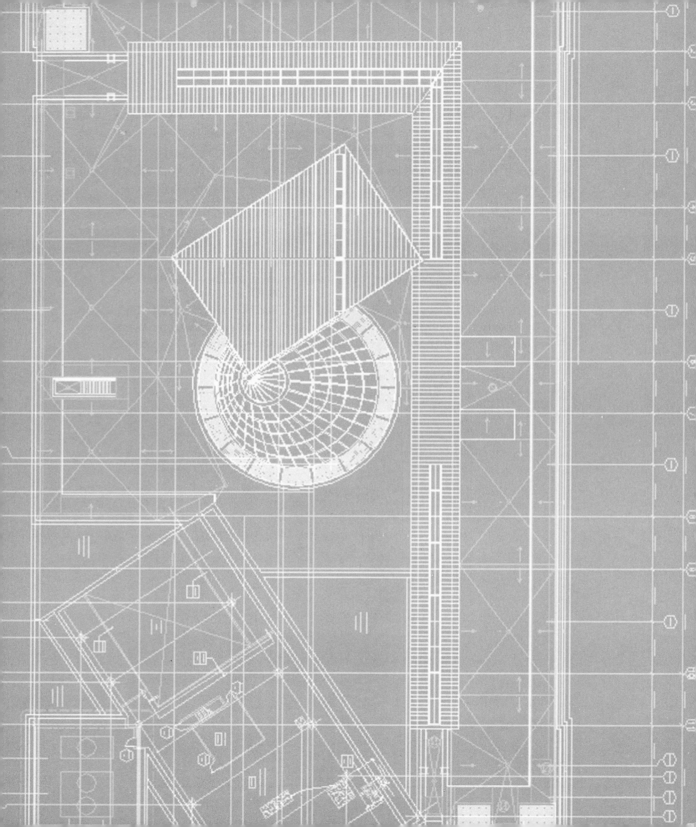

CHAPTER
TWENTY-ONE

Introduction to VBA in AutoCAD

- Understanding ActiveX Automation

- Writing VBA Code

- Using Procedures

- Variables and Constants

- Control Structures

- Built-In Functions

- Error Handling

- Converting from AutoLISP to VBA

- If You Want to Experiment...

Visual Basic for Applications (VBA) is integrated as a standard part of Auto-CAD 2000. This means that you can use VBA for all of your AutoCAD development tasks, instead of (or in addition to) ObjectARX and AutoLISP. If you're already familiar with some dialect of BASIC, you'll find that VBA is easy to learn. If you're a seasoned AutoLISP developer, you may find the VBA way of doing things to be odd, but after a while it will make sense. There's a table at the end of this chapter that will help you translate AutoLISP concepts to their VBA equivalents.

Shortcuts

To Launch the Visual Basic Editor

Select Tools ➢ Macro ➢ Visual Basic Editor.

To Load a VBA Project

Select Tools ➢ Macro ➢ Load Project.

To Create a New Procedure

Type **Sub** or **Function** and the name of the procedure in a module.

To Test a Procedure

In the Immediate window, type the name of a sub, or a question mark, and type in the name of the function, plus any required arguments in parentheses.

To Define a Variable

Use Dim plus the variable name and type.

To Define a Constant

Use Const plus the constant name and data.

To Prevent Spelling Mistakes from Creating Unwanted Variables

Place Option Explicit at the top of every module.

To Store Multiple Items of Information

Declare and use an array for a fixed number of items, or a collection for a variable number of items.

To Branch within Your Code

Use If...Then...Else or Select Case.

Continued on next page

To Loop within Your Code

Use a For loop for a fixed number of iterations, or a Do loop for a variable number of iterations.

To Display a Message to the User

Use the MsgBox function.

To Request Input from the User

Use the InputBox function.

To Handle Errors

Use On Error GoTo to direct all errors to an error trap in your code.

Getting Started with VBA

Microsoft's VBA package supplies two things to AutoCAD. First, there's the VBA language engine itself, which does the job of interpreting any VBA code you write when your application is executed. Second, there's the VBA Integrated Development Environment (IDE), which provides you with the tools for editing and debugging your VBA code. In this chapter, you'll learn the basics of the VBA language itself. The next chapter describes the IDE and how to integrate VBA code with the AutoCAD user interface. However, you need to know just enough about the IDE to type in and execute procedures to follow along with this chapter, so here's a quick introduction.

Launching the VBA IDE

To open the VBA editor, select Tools ➤ Macro ➤ Visual Basic Editor from an Auto-CAD drop-down menu. This opens the VBA editor in a separate window. You can use the Windows taskbar to move back and forth between the editor and the main AutoCAD window. You can also move from the editor to the AutoCAD window by clicking the View AutoCAD button at the left end of the Editor toolbar, or by selecting View ➤ AutoCAD from an editor menu. The Alt+F11 key combination also moves you from the editor back to AutoCAD. Pressing Alt+F11 again takes you from the main AutoCAD window back to the VBA editor.

TIP You can also open the editor automatically when you load a VBA project. To do so, choose Tools ➤ Macro ➤ Load Project and make sure the Open Visual Basic Editor check box is selected.

Creating a New Module

At any given time, you can have more than one VBA project open in AutoCAD. (You do not need to have any project open, however.) All of the components in a project are loaded at the time the project is opened. A project can consist of any of these components:

- Modules
- Class modules
- UserForms

A module is a container for VBA code. A class module is the VBA component used to define a new type of object. A UserForm is a customizable user interface component. Class modules are an advanced topic, and you'll learn about User-Forms in Chapter 99 (which is on the CD), but for now, let's just create a standard module. This will be a place where you can execute code samples.

If you have AutoCAD open with a default blank drawing loaded, you'll find that this drawing includes a default VBA project named ACADProject. To insert a new module, select Insert ➤ Module from the IDE menus, or click the Insert Module button on the Standard toolbar. This creates a new module and opens that module in the editor. The editor can display many modules at once, since it's a Multiple Document Interface (MDI) application. While you're learning VBA, you'll probably find it useful to maximize the module you're working with.

Creating and Running a New Procedure

Modules hold VBA code, but one module can contain a lot of code. In VBA, code is broken up into procedures. You'll learn about the different types of procedures in a moment, but for now, let's just create one. In the Module1 window, type **Sub HelloWorld** and press the Enter key. VBA will insert parentheses at the end of the procedure definition, and automatically create an End Sub line to mark the end of

the procedure. Now type **MsgBox "Hello World"** in between the Sub and End
Sub lines. Notice that VBA provides you with Quick Info about the arguments for
the MsgBox function. For now, you can just ignore these. Click the mouse anywhere off the line you've just typed to accept it and clear the Quick Info.

Now that you've created a procedure, let's run it. You can run procedures interac-
tively in the VBA environment by using the Immediate window (sometimes called
the Debug window). This window may already be displayed at the bottom of the
IDE. If not, you can open it using View ➤ Immediate Window or the Ctrl+G keystroke combination.

Type **HelloWorld** into the Immediate window to tell VBA to execute the HelloWorld procedure that you just created. The MsgBox statement creates a popup
message in your AutoCAD window (and, incidentally, makes the AutoCAD window the active window, as shown in Figure 21.1).

Click OK in this dialog box to return to the VBA IDE. If you've followed along
with the instructions in this section, your screen will look like Figure 21.2.

FIGURE 21.1:

Results of the HelloWorld
procedure

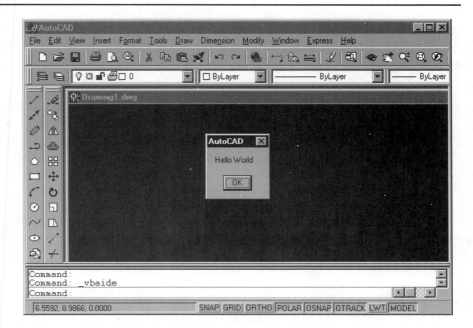

FIGURE 21.2:

The HelloWorld procedure in the VBA IDE

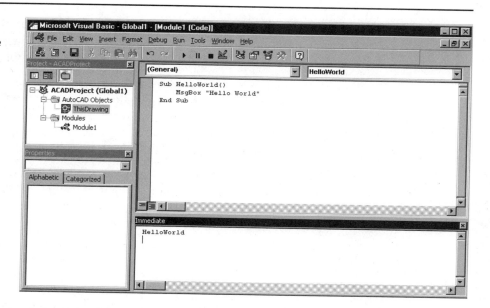

Procedures

Your VBA code is stored in procedures, which themselves are grouped into modules. Procedures come in two flavors: Function procedures, and Sub procedures, usually just called *Functions* and *Subs*. In this section, you'll learn how to create and call both types of procedures and how to pass information back and forth between procedures.

Subs and Functions

The difference between Subs and Functions is that Functions return a value to the caller, while Subs do not.

NOTE   Actually, it's more correct to say that Functions *can* return a value, since you can actually execute a Function with a syntax that tells VBA to throw the return value away. This chapter, though, will concentrate on learning enough VBA to do useful work as quickly as possible, without digging into every corner of the language. For a more advanced discussion of VBA, see *VBA Developer's Handbook*, by Ken Getz and Mike Gilbert (Sybex, 1997; ISBN# 0-7821-1951-4).

While there is an Insert ➤ Procedure item on the VBA menu, it's really unnecessary. That's because, as you saw previously for a Sub, it's simpler just to type in the Sub or Function keyword, name the procedure, and let VBA do the rest. As illustrated in the following example, you can create one of each type of procedure by typing only four words into a module (the **boldface** statements are the parts you need to type; VBA will supply the rest):

```
Sub ShowSquare()

End Sub
Function ReturnSquare()

End Function
```

Arguments

The ShowSquare and ReturnSquare procedures both square a number provided by the user. To do this, you need to equip each procedure with an argument. An argument is a placeholder for information that will be supplied at runtime. Let's also add the code to these two procedures to make them deliver the square. Here's the modified version:

```
Sub ShowSquare(x)
    Debug.Print x * x
End Sub
Function ReturnSquare(x)
    ReturnSquare = x * x
End Function
```

In each of these procedures, x is an argument. At runtime (that is, when you actually execute the procedure) you must supply a value for the argument. Figure 21.3 shows the Immediate window after executing each of these procedures.

FIGURE 21.3:

Executing the ShowSquare and ReturnSquare procedures

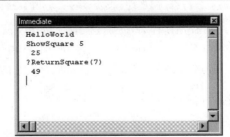

Note that the calling syntax differs between Functions and Subs. For a Sub, you simply supply the name of the procedure, followed by any arguments the Sub takes, without parentheses. To call a Function from the Immediate window, you use the ? operator (think of this operator as meaning "What is the value of?") followed by any arguments the Function takes, surrounded by parentheses.

Although both procedures provide the same output in the sample, they use different methods to provide that output. The Sub calls Debug.Print, which is a special bit of VBA syntax that takes whatever follows it on the line and prints it to the Immediate window. The Function assigns the result to its own name. This has the effect of making that the return value of the Function.

Of course, one procedure can call other procedures. In the following example, the CallBoth procedure executes both of the other two procedures:

```
Sub CallBoth(x)
    Dim y
    ShowSquare x
    y = ReturnSquare(x)
End Sub
```

Here, y is a local variable: a place to store a bit of information (you'll learn more about variables in the next section). To call a Function procedure from within another procedure, you assign the value of the Function procedure to a local variable.

> **TIP** You can also execute a Sub procedure by using the special Call keyword, in which case the procedure's arguments must be enclosed in parentheses. That is, the statements `ShowSquare 4` and `Call ShowSquare(4)` are equivalent. Most developers use the former syntax because it requires less typing.

Optional and Named Arguments

VBA supports two types of argument: optional and named (actually, every argument in VBA is a named argument). Here's a Function definition that uses both:

```
Function Increment(Original, Optional Amount = 1)
    Increment = Original + Amount
End Function
```

In this example, both Original and Amount are named arguments. In addition, Amount is an optional argument, with a default value of 1. You can execute the Increment procedure from the Immediate window in a variety of ways:

```
?Increment(5,2)
?Increment(5)
?Increment(Original:=5)
?Increment(Original:=5, Amount:=2)
?Increment(Amount:=2, Original:=5)
```

The first example treats the arguments positionally, supplying a value for each one in order. The second example does the same, but does not supply a value for the Amount argument. In this case, the Amount argument defaults to 1, and the result of the Function is 6 (try it yourself!). The third example also omits the optional argument, but uses the named argument syntax of `Name:=Value` to make it clear what information is being supplied. The fourth and fifth examples show that you can supply arguments in whatever order you like if you're using named arguments.

TIP

Don't try to mix named and positional arguments. If you supply a named argument for any argument to a procedure, use named arguments for all the information you pass.

Variables and Constants

Until now, you haven't learned about one big part of most actual procedure declarations: data types. Technically, all of the arguments and return values up to this point have been *variants*. You can think of a variant as a multipurpose data type that can hold anything. In this section, you'll see that there are also special-purpose data types, as well as some other ways to store data than in simple variables.

Data Types

VBA supports ten specific types of data. Table 21.1 shows these data types and the range of data that each one can hold.

TABLE 21.1: VBA Data Types

Data Type	Holds
Boolean	True or False (VBA considers −1 to be the native True value, but will interpret any non-zero value as True.)
Byte	0 to 255, without rounding
Integer	−32,768 to 32,767, without rounding
Long	−2,147,483,648 to 2,147,483,647, without rounding
Currency	−922,337,203,685,477.5808 to 922,337,203,685,477.5807, without rounding
Single	−3.402823E38 to −1.401298E−45 and 1.401298E−45 to 3.402823E38, possibly with rounding
Double	−1.79769313486232E308 to −4.94065645841247E−324 and 4.94065645841247E−324 to 1.79769313486232E308, possibly with rounding
Date	Any date or time value
String	Text data from 0 to 2E31 characters
Variant	Can hold any of the other types as well as Null (a special value for uninitialized variants and database fields)

You can declare the type of a procedure argument, a variable, or a function return type with the As keyword. For example, you might rewrite the ShowSquare, Return-Square, and CallBoth procedures this way:

```
Sub ShowSquare(x As Integer)
    Debug.Print x * x
End Sub
Function ReturnSquare(x As Integer) As Long
    ReturnSquare = x * x
End Function
Sub CallBoth(x As Integer)
    Dim y As Long
    ShowSquare x
    y = ReturnSquare(x)
End Sub
```

NOTE   Many developers and authors working with VBA use a naming convention that specifies prefix characters for variable names to indicate their type. For example, an integer might be named intX and a string variable strName. The earlier examples in this chapter didn't use a naming convention. From here on, though, this chapter will use the Reddick VBA Naming Convention, which is probably the most widely used naming convention in the industry.

You can explicitly declare a variable As Variant, and use it to hold any type of data that VBA is capable of handling. You can also leave the As clause off a variable declaration entirely, in which case VBA implicitly provides a variant. While this technique does free you from having to worry about data types, it also means that VBA won't do any checking at runtime to see whether data is reasonable. If you declare a variable As Integer and try to put a character string in it, VBA will give you an error; if you declare the same variable As Variant, VBA has no idea that you didn't want it to accept strings.

Scope and Lifetime

Variables declared within procedures are *local variables*. They're of use only to that procedure, and indeed, only when the procedure is running. But VBA provides several other ways to declare variables. This code fragment shows all the ones you'll commonly need:

```
Option Explicit

Public gstrSharedWithEveryone As String
Private mstrSharedRightHere As String

Public Sub Procedure1(varArg1 As Variant)
    Dim intI As Integer
End Sub

Private Sub Helper(varArg2 As Variant)
    Static intJ As Integer
End Sub
```

You can break down these declarations as follows:

- gstrSharedWithEveryone is a *public variable* (called a *global variable* in earlier versions of VBA). This variable can be used by any procedure in any module in the project.

- mstrSharedRightHere is a *module-level variable*. This variable can be used by any procedure in the module where it's defined.

- varArg1 and varArg2 are *local arguments*. They can only be used by the procedures in whose argument list they appear.

- intI is a *local variable*. It can only be used by the procedure in which it is defined.

- intJ is also a local variable. It can only be used by the procedure in which it is defined.

This distinction—between public, module-level, and local variables—is commonly referred to as the *scope* of the variable. Using the previous example, gstrSharedWithEveryone has global scope, mstrSharedRightHere has module scope, and intI has local scope.

There's also a second factor to consider in declaring variables, that of *lifetime*. Global and module scope variables have *project lifetime:* They are created when the project is loaded, and if you set a value into one of these variables, they keep that value until the project is unloaded (or you deliberately set another value into them). Local variables have *procedure lifetime:* They're created when you execute the procedure, and discarded when the procedure is finished. However, you can use the Static keyword (as shown for intJ above) to declare a local variable with project lifetime. What this means is that the value of the variable persists across calls to the procedure. If you run Helper more than once (and it contains additional code, not shown here, to assign a value to the variable), you'll find that intJ contains the last value you set into it, rather than being reinitialized each time.

The *Option Explicit* Statement

You may have noticed the line Option Explicit in the code example in the previous section. This is a VBA statement that you can insert into any of your code modules (once per module, and by convention at the top). The effect of this statement is to tell VBA that you intend to explicitly declare all of your variables before using them. If you omit Option Explicit, VBA will automatically create a variant-type variable for any variable you use without declaration.

This option can protect you against an annoying and hard-to-find error. For example, if you *don't* have Option Explicit set, this is legal VBA:

```
Function Oops() As Long
    Dim LongVariableName As Integer
    LongVariableName = 4
```

```
    Oops = LongVariableName * LongVarriableName
End Function
```

Even though it's legal, the Function as written will return 0, not 16, because one of the variable names is spelled differently than the other two, causing VBA to assign it separate storage. If you try to run this procedure in a module with `Option Explicit` set, though, you'll get an immediate compilation error: Variable Not Defined from VBA.

TIP   You can check for compilation errors at any time in VBA by selecting Debug ➢ Compile ACADproject.

Setting `Option Explicit` is so important that there's a way to tell VBA to do this for you in every new module. Select Tools ➢ Options ➢ Editor from the VBA drop-down menus and you'll get the Editor Options dialog box, shown in Figure 21.4. Check the Require Variable Declaration check box (by default it's unchecked) and you'll never have to worry about including `Option Explicit` again yourself. Make this the first thing you do after installing AutoCAD, before you write any code at all.

FIGURE 21.4:

The Editor Options dialog box

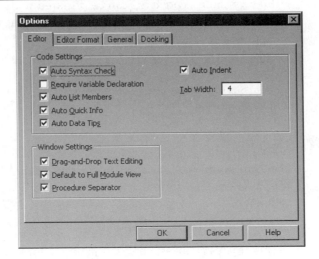

Constants

VBA supports *constants*—names for values that won't change during the course of your application. You can use constants to make your code more readable. For example, even though VBA doesn't provide an automatic function to convert degrees into radians, it's easy enough to write one:

```
Function DegreesToRadians1(dblDegrees As Double) _
 As Double
     DegreesToRadians1 = (dblDegrees / 180) * 3.14159
 End Function
```

TIP   The underscore (_) followed by the Enter key (⏎) combination serves as a line-continuation character in VBA, so the first two lines of this example are one line as far as the VBA interpreter is concerned.

Although it's easy enough to see what this example does, you can make it a bit clearer by using a constant to represent the magic number:

```
Function DegreesToRadians2(dblDegrees As Double) _
 As Double
     Const Pi = 3.14159
     DegreesToRadians2 = (dblDegrees / 180) * Pi
 End Function
```

Like variables, constants can be declared with local, module, or global scope. If you needed Pi in many places, you might define it as a global constant instead:

```
Public Const Pi = 3.14159
Function DegreesToRadians3(dblDegrees As Double) _
 As Double
DegreesToRadians3 = (dblDegrees / 180) * Pi
End Function
```

Arrays

You can group VBA variables into *arrays*—numbered collections of variables of the same type. To declare an array, you simply tell VBA how many elements it will have:

```
Dim strK(1 To 5) As String
```

This creates an array, strK, with storage for five strings, numbered 1 through 5. You can assign values to members of an array, or read them out again:

```
Sub ArrayDemo()
    Dim strK(1 To 5) As String
    strK(1) = "H"
```

```
        strK(2) = "e"
        strK(3) = "l"
        strK(4) = "l"
        strK(5) = "o"
        Debug.Print strK(1), strK(2), strK(3), _
          strK(4), strK(5)
    End Sub
```

Arrays tend to be of limited use in VBA, since in many instances, collections (see below) prove more useful. However, they're critical for one thing in AutoCAD: the VBA representation of a point in AutoCAD's Model Space is as an array of doubles. Here's what the code for drawing a line in AutoCAD might look like:

```
Sub DrawLine()
    Dim ptStart(1 To 3) As Double
    Dim ptEnd(1 To 3) As Double
    ptStart(1) = 1
    ptStart(2) = 1
    ptStart(3) = 1
    ptEnd(1) = 2
    ptEnd(2) = 2
    ptEnd(3) = 2
    ThisDrawing.ModelSpace.AddLine ptStart, ptEnd
End Sub
```

Each of the arrays holds the information necessary to locate one point. The first, second, and third elements of the array hold, respectively, the x-, y-, and z-coordinates of the point in AutoCAD's model space.

Collections

VBA collections provide an alternative to arrays for keeping track of multiple items. Unlike arrays, which are designed to hold things that can be identified by number, collections are designed for random access. You can think of a collection as a place to stash anything you like and to retrieve it later by name.

The CollectionDemo procedure demonstrates the syntax that you use working with collections:

```
Sub CollectionDemo()
    Dim col As Collection
    Set col = New Collection
```

```
' Add three items to the collection
col.Add 5, "First"
col.Add 9, "Second"
col.Add 12, "Third"

' Retrieve items by name
Debug.Print col.Item("First")
Debug.Print col("Second")
Debug.Print col("Third")

' Retrieve items by index
Debug.Print col.Item(1)
Debug.Print col(2)
Debug.Print col(3)

' Remove an item from the collection
col.Remove 2

' And show how many items are left
Debug.Print col.Count
End Sub
```

Although you declare a collection with the same Dim keyword that you use for other variables, you must also *initialize* the collection. That's because a collection is a type of *object variable*—one that has more complex properties than just a storage location for data. Initializing the variable is the purpose of this line:

```
Set col = New Collection
```

The New keyword tells VBA to create an object of the type Collection, and the Set keyword tells VBA to make the col variable a way to refer to this new object.

Add is a *method* of the Collection object. This method takes two arguments, the first being the item to add, and the second being a key value that can be used later to refer to the item. You can add anything to a collection. In this case, you're adding the three numbers 9, 5, and 12.

The next two sections of the sample show that you can retrieve items either by key or by index (position) within the collection. Note that the keyword Item can be specified or omitted when using either syntax. That's because Item is the *default method* of the collection object.

Finally, you can use the Remove method to remove an item from a collection, and the Count *property* to show the current number of items in a collection.

Objects, Methods, and Properties

You'll run into objects, methods, and properties throughout VBA. If you've looked at the AutoCAD object model, you've already run across all three of these:

- An object is any type of variable that has complex behavior. For example, the Document object in AutoCAD represents an entire drawing file.

- A method is anything that an object knows how to do. The methods of the Document object include the Open and Regen methods. You can think of methods as the verbs for an object.

- A property is anything that describes an object. The properties of the Document object include the Name and ActiveLinetype properties. You can think of properties as the adjectives describing an object.

In addition to the objects provided by AutoCAD, VBA has a number of built-in objects, including the collection object you've just seen. Later in this chapter you'll learn how to use class modules to create your own objects.

Control Structures

Although the original BASIC language lacked many features, most of those deficiencies have been remedied in modern versions of BASIC, such as VBA. VBA is now a full-fledged structured programming language, with a full set of control structures for looping, branching, and flow of control. This section will describe the control structures that are most often useful in applications.

The *If...Then...Else* Structure

To handle branching, VBA uses an If...Then...Else structure, as shown in the following example:

```
Function IfDemo(intNum As Integer) As String
    If intNum = 1 Then
        IfDemo = "One"
    ElseIf intNum = 2 Then
        IfDemo = "Two"
```

```
        ElseIf intNum = 3 Then
            IfDemo = "Three"
        Else
            IfDemo = "I dunno"
        End If
    End Function
```

In this structure, each `If` or `ElseIf` keyword is followed by a *Boolean condition*—something that can be evaluated as either True or False. When VBA comes to a condition that evaluates as True, it executes the statements that follow that condition. If you include an `Else` clause, that set of statements is executed if none of the conditions is True. Note the `End If` statement that is required to terminate the conditional. Figure 21.5 shows the result of executing IfDemo with a variety of inputs.

FIGURE 21.5:

Testing the IfDemo procedure

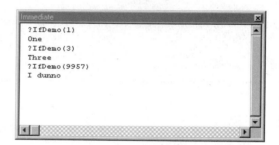

```
? IfDemo(1)
One
? IfDemo(3)
Three
? IfDemo(9957)
I dunno
```

The *Select Case* Statement

Deeply nested `If...Then...Else` loops can be very difficult to decipher. Always beware of difficult code, because it's a potential maintainability nightmare: If you need to modify such code, the chance of introducing a new error is all too large. Fortunately, VBA provides an alternative branching structure for such situations, the `Select Case` statement. Here's an example of the `Select Case` statement syntax:

```
Function CaseDemo(intNum As Integer) As String
    Select Case intNum
        Case 1
            CaseDemo = "One"
        Case 2
            CaseDemo = "Two"
        Case 3 To 5
            CaseDemo = "Between Three and Five"
        Case 7, 9
```

```
            CaseDemo = "7 or 9"
        Case Else
            CaseDemo = "I dunno"
    End Select
End Function
```

The Select Case statement works by comparing the specified expression (in this example, intNum) to each case in turn, until it finds one that matches. At that point, the code in that particular case is executed. Here, the return value of the procedure is determined by the matching case. As you can see, the case can be a particular value, a range of values (3 to 5) or a collection of values (7, 9). You can use the Select Case statement with any type of variable. The values of the individual cases must be the same data type as the variable.

For Loops

VBA provides several looping structures for repetitively executing code. The For loop is perhaps the simplest of these, providing a way to execute a set of statements a predetermined number of times. The For loop works by incrementing or decrementing a counter:

```
Sub ForDemo()
    Dim intI As Integer

    ' Simple For loop: intI is incremented by
    ' one each time the loop is executed
    For intI = 1 To 5
        Debug.Print intI
    Next intI

    ' For loop with increment: in this case,
    ' 2 is added to intI with each loop
    For intI = 1 To 5 Step 2
        Debug.Print intI
    Next intI

    ' Reverse For loop: here, intI is
    ' decremented each time through the loop
    For intI = 5 To 1 Step -1
        Debug.Print intI
    Next intI
End Sub
```

For loops are most useful when you know exactly how many times you need to execute the loop. Often, you'll use a For loop to process the elements in an array. If you're dealing with a collection, you may be better off using a Do loop, as shown in the next section.

Do Loops

Do loops provide an alternative to For loops when you don't know how many times you need to execute the loop but know when you need to stop. The simplest Do loop executes a statement as long as some condition is True and stops as soon as it is False:

```
Sub DoDemo1(intInput As Integer)
    Do While intInput > 0
        Debug.Print intInput;
        intInput = intInput - 1
    Loop
End Sub
```

Figure 21.6 shows the output from this loop.

FIGURE 21.6:

Output of a simple Do loop

NOTE The semicolon at the end of the **Debug.Print** statement tells VBA to put additional results on the same line of output.

You can also cause a Do loop to be executed as long as a particular condition is False by using Until instead of While:

```
Sub DoDemo2(intInput As Integer)
    Do Until intInput = 0
        Debug.Print intInput;
```

```
        intInput = intInput - 1
    Loop
End Sub
```

Do loops also allow you to test the condition at the end of the loop rather than at the top, as shown in the next two examples:

```
Sub DoDemo3(intInput As Integer)
    Do
        Debug.Print intInput;
        intInput = intInput - 1
    Loop While intInput > 0
End Sub
Sub DoDemo4(intInput As Integer)
    Do
        Debug.Print intInput;
        intInput = intInput - 1
    Loop Until intInput = 0
End Sub
```

TIP   A **Do** loop with the test at the end will always execute at least once, even if it would have been skipped entirely if the test were at the start of the loop.

The *GoTo* Operator

In addition to branching and looping, VBA includes an operator to transfer flow of control to another place in the program. This is the infamous GoTo, which causes execution to resume at a different spot (a *label*) in the procedure:

```
Sub GoToDemo()
    Debug.Print "In the demo"
    GoTo GoHere
    Debug.Print "This won't print"
GoHere:
    Debug.Print "This will print"
End Sub
```

In this example, GoHere is a label, a nonexecutable statement that serves only to mark a place in the procedure. Although using a GoTo statement is often associated with sloppy, hard-to-decipher programming, this statement is essential in error handling in VBA, as you'll see later in this chapter. Otherwise, you can almost always avoid GoTo statements in your code.

VBA Functions

VBA includes a wide variety of built-in functions. While this section can't cover all of them, you will learn about the most useful ones here. You may want to review the Functions section of the VBA online help for a more comprehensive list. You can also use the Object Browser (see Chapter 99, which is on the accompanying CD) to view all of the VBA functions.

Operators

VBA includes support for a variety of operators. Table 21.2 summarizes these operators. Although VBA includes fairly complex operator precedence rules governing the order in which operators are evaluated, you can always use parentheses to force a particular order of operations.

TABLE 21.2:   VBA Operators

Operator	Meaning
^	Exponentiation (2^3 = 8)
-	Negation
*	Multiplication (2*3 = 6)
/	Division (6/3 = 2)
\	Integer division (8\3 = 2)
Mod	Modulus
+	Addition
-	Subtraction
&	String concatenation ("A" & "B" = "AB")
=	Logical equality (If A = 5)
<>	Logical inequality (If A <> 5)
<	Less Than
>	Greater Than
<=	Less Than or Equal To

Continued on next page

TABLE 21.2 CONTINUED: VBA Operators

Operator	Meaning
>=	Greater Than or Equal To
Like	Wildcard string comparison
Is	Object equivalence
Not	Logical Not
And	Logical And
Or	Logical Or
Xor	Logical Exclusive Or
Imp	Logical Implication
Eqv	Logical Equivalence

Quick Info

With the variety of built-in functions that VBA provides, you might find it difficult to remember the arguments that you have to supply to make each function work. That's why VBA provides *Quick Info*, a way of prompting you on screen for the arguments to a function. Figure 21.7 shows Quick Info in action.

FIGURE 21.7:

VBA Quick Info

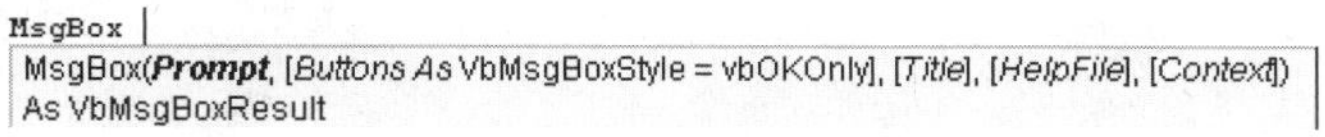

```
MsgBox |
MsgBox(Prompt, [Buttons As VbMsgBoxStyle = vbOKOnly], [Title], [HelpFile], [Context])
As VbMsgBoxResult
```

In this example, the Prompt argument is required. The other arguments are optional, as shown by the square brackets surrounding each argument. The Buttons As argument must be one of the values in the built-in enumeration VbMsgBoxStyle, which you can view using the Object Browser or by starting to enter the argument. Finally, the return value of the function will be one of the values allowed by the VbMsgBoxResult enumeration.

As you work with VBA, you'll probably find Quick Info very helpful. If you reach the point where you have learned the arguments for every function and Quick Info is becoming intrusive, you can disable it by selecting the Tools ➢ Options ➢ Editor.

User Interface Functions

VBA provides two functions that are extremely useful for creating a user interface to your procedures. The MsgBox function displays a dialog box on screen, and returns information about which button the user clicked to dismiss the dialog box. The InputBox function prompts the user for information.

The MsgBox function takes five arguments:

```
Msgbox(Prompt[, Buttons][, Title][, HelpFile, Context]
```

TIP Square brackets in VBA syntax examples indicate optional arguments.

The Prompt and Title arguments supply the text and caption for the dialog box. The Buttons argument controls the appearance of the dialog box; it accepts a series of constants that you can see by checking the IntelliSense help for the function. The last two arguments allow you to specify a help file and help topic to be used if the user presses F1 while the dialog box is displayed.

Figure 21.8 shows the dialog box produced by the following statement:

```
MsgBox "Unable to Save File", _
    vbAbortRetryIgnore + vbCritical, "File Error"
```

FIGURE 21.8:

Sample dialog box from MsgBox

The return value from a call to the MsgBox function is a constant that indicates which button the user clicked. Although these constants are numeric, you should always use the built-in VBA constants to evaluate this return value. That will make your code more readable, and protects you against potential future changes to the literal values of the various constants. The MsgBoxDemo procedure shows this technique.

```
Sub MsgBoxDemo()
    Dim intRet As Integer
    intRet = MsgBox("Unable to Save File", _
     vbAbortRetryIgnore + vbCritical, "File Error")
```

```
    Select Case intRet
        Case vbAbort
            Debug.Print "You chose Abort"
        Case vbRetry
            Debug.Print "You chose Retry"
        Case vbIgnore
            Debug.Print "You chose Ignore"
    End Select
End Sub
```

The InputBox function uses seven arguments, although most of the arguments are optional:

```
InputBox( Prompt[, Title][, Default][, XPos][, YPos] _
[, HelpFile, Context]
```

Again, the Prompt and Title arguments control the text and caption of the dialog box. The Default argument provides a default return value, and the next two arguments allow you to specify where the dialog box will appear on screen. As an example, Figure 21.9 shows the dialog box generated by the following call:

```
InputBox "Enter a Number", "Numeric Prompt", 27
```

The return value from the InputBox function is a variant containing the value that the user typed into the edit control in the dialog box.

FIGURE 21.9:

Sample InputBox

String Functions

VBA supports a wide variety of text-string manipulation functions. Historically, BASIC dialects have been very strong in string handling, and VBA is no exception. Table 21.3 shows the most important of these functions.

TABLE 21.3:   Some VBA String Functions

Function	Results
Asc(strX)	Returns the ASCII value of the first character in strX.
Chr(n)	Returns a string whose ASCII value is n.
InStr(Start, str1, str2)	Returns the position in str1 where str2 occurs as a substring. Starts looking at position Start.
LCase(strU)	Returns the lowercase translation of strU.
Len(strX)	Returns the number of characters in strX.
LTrim(strX)	Removes leading spaces from strX.
Mid(strX, Start, Length)	Returns a string of Length characters starting at position Start in strX.
Right(strX, n)	Returns n characters from the right end of strX.
RTrim(strX)	Removes trailing spaces from strX.
Space(n)	Returns a string consisting of n spaces.
Trim(strX)	Removes both leading and trailing spaces from strX.
UCase(strL)	Returns the uppercase translation of strL.

Mathematical Functions

VBA includes most of the common mathematical functions (in addition to the mathematical operators that you've already seen). Table 21.4 lists the more important of these functions.

TABLE 21.4:   Some VBA Mathematical Functions

Function	Results
Abs(x)	Returns the absolute value of x.
Atn(x)	Returns the arctangent of x.
Cos(x)	Returns the cosine of x.
Int(x)	Returns the largest integer less than or equal to x.

Continued on next page

TABLE 21.4 CONTINUED: Some VBA Mathematical Functions

Function	Results
Log(x)	Returns the natural logarithm of x.
Rnd(x)	Returns a random number if x is positive.
Sgn(x)	Returns 1 if **x** is positive and −1 if x is negative.
Sin(x)	Returns the sine of x.
Sqr(x)	Returns the square root of x.
Tan(x)	Returns the tangent of x.

NOTE   Like AutoCAD, VBA requires that arguments to trigonometric functions be expressed in radians.

Date/Time Functions

VBA has a selection of functions to help you work with dates and times. It's also possible to do your own date and time arithmetic, once you understand how dates and times are stored. All date and time variables are double-precision floating points, and contain a number of days and partial days since an arbitrary zero date. That means that you can add seven, for example, to a date variable, and get the same date in the following week.

Table 21.5 shows some of the built-in functions that will help you work with dates and times in your code. Two of these functions, DateAdd and DateDiff, work with intervals. The allowable interval codes are shown in Table 21.6.

TABLE 21.5: Some of VBA's Date and Time Functions

Function	Results
Time()	Returns the current time.
Date()	Returns the current date.

Continued on next page

TABLE 21.5 CONTINUED: Some of VBA's Date and Time Functions

Function	Results
Now()	Returns the current date and time.
DateAdd(Interval, number, date)	Adds the specified number of intervals to the specified date.
DateDiff(Interval, Date1, Date2)	Returns the number of intervals between Date1 and Date2.
Weekday(Date)	Returns the day of the week that the specified date falls on.

TABLE 21.6: Interval Codes

Code	Interval
yyyy	Year
q	Quarter
m	Month
y	Day of year (1 to 366)
d	Day
w	Weekday
ww	Week
h	Hour
n	Minute
s	Second

Error Handling

It's important to make sure that your VBA code handles any errors that occur in the course of your application. Errors don't necessarily mean that you've written "bad" code. In VBA, it's often necessary to provoke errors in the normal course of an application. For example, to determine whether there's a diskette in a drive, it's simplest to just try to write a file to that drive and intercept the error that occurs if the drive is empty.

In this section, you'll learn how to develop code with error handling and see how to use the Err and Debug objects to derive information about errors.

Using *On Error GoTo*

VBA's default behavior in response to errors is quite simple: It's designed to halt operations and notify the user. For example, suppose you run this function from the Immediate window with an input of 0:

```
Function ErrorDemo1(intX As Integer) As Integer
    ErrorDemo1 = 10 / intX
End Function
```

Of course, you can't divide ten by 0, so this call will cause a runtime error. Figure 21.10 shows the result.

FIGURE 21.10:

Untrapped runtime error

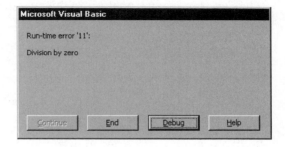

In the dialog box that reports the runtime error, clicking the End button will simply end execution of all code, while clicking the Debug button will suspend execution of the code and highlight the line that caused the error.

In most applications, this default behavior is unacceptable. You'll generally use the VBA On Error GoTo statement to send all errors to a particular spot (label) in your code, and deal with the errors there, to prevent VBA's default error handling from taking over. The ErrorDemo2 function shows how this might be accomplished for our sample function.

```
Function ErrorDemo2(intX As Integer) As Integer
    On Error GoTo HandleErr
    ErrorDemo2 = 10 / intX
```

```
ExitHere:
    Exit Function
HandleErr:
    Select Case Err.Number
        Case 11 ' Division by zero
            MsgBox "Zero is not a legal input"
        Case Else
            MsgBox Err.Number & " " & Err.Description, _
                vbCritical, "Error in ErrorDemo2"
    End Select
    Resume ExitHere
End Function
```

Here's a step-by-step analysis of this function.

1. The `On Error GoTo` statement tells VBA that in case of any error, it should resume execution at the label HandleErr.

2. The function then continues with its normal operation.

3. If nothing goes wrong, the `Exit Function` statement will be the last statement to be executed.

4. If any error occurs, execution continues at HandleErr.

5. The `Select Case` statement makes a decision based on the error number (see the next section for a discussion of the Err object).

6. The function includes a special message for one particular error, division by 0, that the function designer was anticipating.

7. For any other error, the function posts an information message to the user. This doesn't provide any additional information over that which VBA supplies by default, but by handling the error, the function prevents execution from being halted.

8. The `Resume ExitHere` statement clears the error condition and allows execution to continue at the ExitHere label. By always exiting the function at the same point, you can avoid some future maintenance problems.

The error-handling skeleton used in this function is typical of VBA error handling. If you're building an application for distribution to others, you'll want to include an error handler similar to this in every procedure.

The Err Object

In the sample error-handling code, you may have noticed the references to Err.Number and Err.Description. These are two *properties* of the Err *object*, a self-contained piece of functionality built into VBA. Just as AutoCAD has an object model (discussed extensively in Chapter 98, which is on the accompanying CD), VBA itself supplies a few objects. If an error occurs in your code, you can determine what the error is by checking the properties of the Err object, which will reflect the most recent error (if no error has occurred, Err.Number will be 0).

Table 21.7 shows the most important properties of the Err object.

TABLE 21.7:   Properties of the Err Object

Property	Meaning
Number	Number of the most recent error
Description	Text of the most recent error
Source	Source of the most recent error. For example, if an error occurs when working with controls on a form, the Source will be MSForms.
LastDllError	Error number from a call to the Windows API

The Debug Object

Another VBA object that can be useful when dealing with code is the Debug object. The Debug object supports a single method, Print, that allows your code to send a message to the Immediate window. If you can't figure out quite what's going wrong when code is misbehaving, you can use the Debug object to help sort things out. For example, if there's a variable lngCount that is getting set to an unexpected value, you can cause your code to print the current value of the variable to the Immediate window by inserting the following line:

```
Debug.Print lngCount
```

The Debug object only has an effect when you're running your code in the editor. When users interact with your application, they won't see these messages.

Converting from AutoLISP to VBA

VBA is not a replacement for AutoLISP. There are still many things that are easy to do in AutoLISP that are difficult or impossible from VBA. You shouldn't assume that VBA is the preferable technology just because it's the newer one.

On the other hand, the ease of designing dialog boxes with UserForms (covered in Chapter 99, which is on the CD that accompanies this book) and the accessibility of VBA make it a compelling language for simple applications that require a user interface. You may find yourself porting existing AutoLISP code partially or entirely to new VBA utilities to make use of VBA features.

While there's no automated tool for converting from AutoLISP to VBA, nor exact equivalents for every AutoLISP command, there are similarities between any pair of programming languages. If you're familiar with AutoLISP, you'll find the equivalences in Table 21.8 useful as you come up to speed on VBA.

TABLE 21.8: AutoLISP to VBA Conversions

AutoLISP Command	VBA Equivalent
+	+
-	-
*	*
/	/
=	=
/=	<>
<	<
<=	<=
>	>
>=	>=
~	Not
1+	+ 1
1-	- 1

Continued on next page

TABLE 21.8 CONTINUED: AutoLISP to VBA Conversions

AutoLISP Command	VBA Equivalent
abs	Abs
ads	Application.ListADS
alert	MsgBox
and	And
angle	Utility.AngleFromXAxis
angtof	Utility.AngleToReal
angtos	Utility.AngleToString
arx	Application.ListARX
arxload	Application.LoadARX
arxunload	Application.UnloadARX
ascii	Asc
atan	Atn
atof	CDbl
atoi	Cint
chr	Chr
close	Close
cond	Select Case
cos	Cos
dictadd	Dictionaries.Add
dictnext	Dictionaries.Item
dictremove	Dictionary.Delete
dictrename	Dictionary.Rename
dictsearch	Dictionary.GetName, Dictionary.GetObject
entmake	ActiveDocument.Add*XXXX*

Continued on next page

TABLE 21.8 CONTINUED: AutoLISP to VBA Conversions

AutoLISP Command	VBA Equivalent
entupd	Entity.Update
equal	Eqv
error*	Err
exp	Exp
expt	^
findfile	Dir
fix	Fix, Int, or Cint
float	CDbl
foreach	For Each/Next
getangle	Utility.GetAngle
getcfg, getenv	Preferences object
getcorner	Utility.GetCorner
getdist	Utility.GetDistance
getint	Utility.GetInteger
getkword	Utility.GetKeyword
getorient	Utility.GetOrientation
getpoint	Utility.GetPoint
getreal	Utility.GetReal
getstring	Utility.GetString
getvar	Application.GetVariable
graphscr	Application.Caption
handent	Handle property
if	If/Then/Else
itoa	Str

Continued on next page

TABLE 21.8 CONTINUED: AutoLISP to VBA Conversions

AutoLISP Command	VBA Equivalent
last	Ubound
list	ReDim
listp	IsArray
log	Log
logand	And
logior	Or
lsh	Imp
max	Max
min	Min
minusp	< 0
nentsel	SelectionSet.SelectAtPoint
nitget	Utility.InitializeUserInput
null	IsNull
numberp	TypeName
open	Open
polar	Utility.PolarPoint
read-char	Input
read-line	Line Input
regapp	RegisteredApplications.Add
rem	Mod
repeat	Do/While
rtos	Utility.RealToString
set	Set
setvar	Application.SetVariable

Continued on next page

TABLE 21.8 CONTINUED: AutoLISP to VBA Conversions

AutoLISP Command	VBA Equivalent
sin	Sin
sqrt	Sqr
ssadd	SelectionSets.Add
ssdel	SelectionSet.Delete
ssget	SelectionSet.SelectOnScreen
sslength	SelectionSet.Count
ssname	SelectionSet.Name
startapp	Shell
strcase	StrConv
strcat	&
strlen	Len
substr	Mid
trans	Utility.TranslateCoordinates
ver	Application.Version
vports	Viewports
wcmatch	Like
while	Do/While
write-char, write-line	Print
xload	Application.LoadADS
xunload	Application.UnloadADS
zerop	= 0

If You Want to Experiment...

The easiest way to experiment with VBA is to just start using it. The sample file supplied with this chapter, `ch21.dvb`, contains all of the examples from this chapter. You should open this file, located in the "code" folder on this book's CD, and try the sample procedures. Then try adding some of your own procedures to the same modules, or create a module of your own to hold your own test procedures.

In Chapter 99 (on the CD that accompanies this book), you'll see how to integrate your VBA code with AutoCAD and AutoCAD objects. In the meantime, you should just become familiar with VBA syntax. Some tasks you might try to do with VBA include:

- Extract the portion of a full path's filename following the last slash to return just the filename.

- Write a procedure that returns the average of a set of numbers stored in an array.

- Write a procedure that uses the Pythagorean theorem to return the distance between two points in a 2D or 3D drawing.

You'll also find a number of sample VBA projects in the AutoCAD Samples/VBA folder on your hard drive if you've done a full install of AutoCAD.

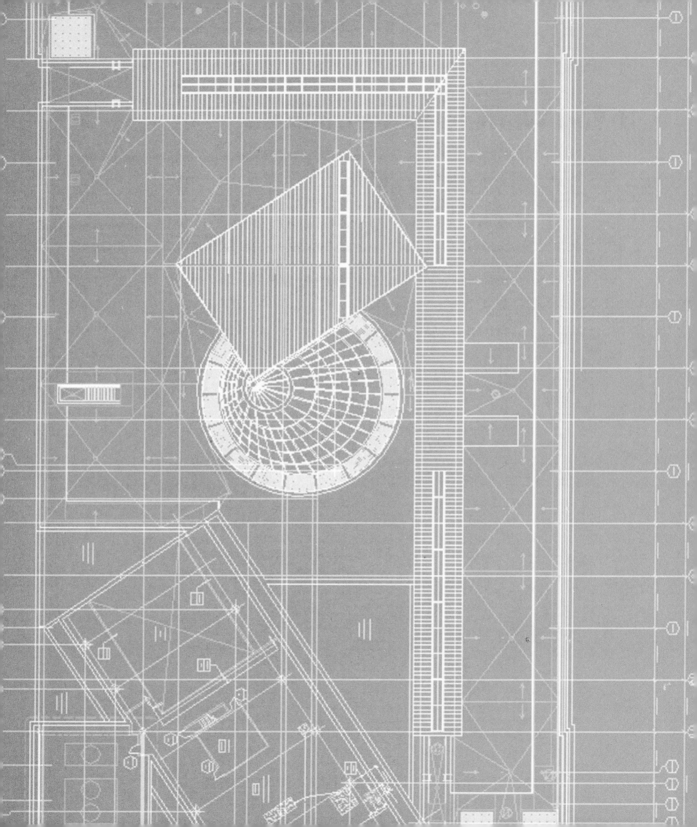

Integrating AutoCAD into Your Work Environment

- Managing Your Drawings with the DesignCenter

- Sharing Drawings on the World Wide Web

- Adding Hyperlinks to Connect to Other Drawings or Web Pages

- Supporting Your System and Working in Groups

- Establishing Office Standards

- Maintaining Files

- Using Networks with AutoCAD

- Keeping Records

- Understanding What AutoCAD Can Do for You

Whether you're a one-person operation working out of your home or one of several hundred AutoCAD users in a large company, file sharing and file maintenance becomes the focus of much of your time. In a more interconnected world, the volume of messages and files crossing our path seems to be constantly on the rise. In addition, the Internet has allowed us to be more mobile, adding more complexity to our file management tasks.

In this chapter, you'll learn about some of the tools that AutoCAD offers to help you manage your files and the files you share with others. You'll also examine some general issues that arise while using AutoCAD in a workgroup environment. In this discussion, you may find help with some problems you have encountered when using AutoCAD in your particular work environment. This chapter also discusses the management of AutoCAD projects.

Managing Your Drawings with the DesignCenter

As you start to build a library of drawings, you'll find that you're reusing many of the components of existing drawing files. Most of the time, you will probably be producing similar types of drawings with some variation, so you'll reuse drawing components like layer settings, dimension styles, and layouts. It can be a major task just to keep track of all the projects you've worked on. It's especially frustrating when you remember setting up a past drawing in a way that you know would be useful in a current project, but you can't remember that file's name or location.

AutoCAD 2000 offers the DesignCenter to help you keep track of the documents you use in your projects. You can think of the DesignCenter as a kind of super Windows Explorer that is focused on AutoCAD files. The DesignCenter lets you keep track of your favorite files and it helps you locate files, blocks, and other drawing components. In addition, you can import blocks and other drawing components from one drawing to another by using a simple click and drag. If you've been diligent about setting the unit format of your drawings, then you can use the DesignCenter to import symbols and drawings of different unit formats into a drawing and the symbols will maintain their proper size. For example, a 90-cm door symbol from a metric drawing can be imported into an English unit drawing and the DesignCenter will translate the 90-cm metric door size to a 35.43-inch door.

Getting Familiar with the DesignCenter

At first glance, the DesignCenter looks a bit mysterious. But it only takes a few mouse clicks to reveal a tool that looks very much like the Windows Explorer. Try the following steps to get familiar with the DesignCenter.

1. Open AutoCAD to a new file, and then click the DesignCenter tool in the Standard toolbar.

The DesignCenter appears docked in the left side of the AutoCAD window.

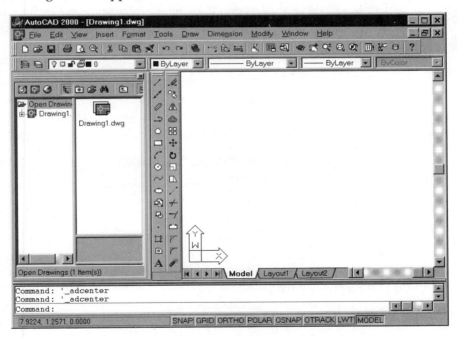

NOTE   If your DesignCenter view doesn't look like this, with the DesignCenter window divided into two parts, click the Tree View Toggle tool in the DesignCenter toolbar. The tree view opens on the left side of the DesignCenter window.

---

2. Click the Desktop tool in the DesignCenter toolbar.

The DesignCenter displays a listing of the Favorites directory. What you are actually looking at is a view into the C:\Windows\Favorites\Autodesk\ directory. You see the single DesignCenter shortcut icon. You can add more shortcuts to this directory as you work with the DesignCenter. You may also see a view showing the tree structure of the files you have open in AutoCAD.

3. Double-click the grab bars at the top of the DesignCenter window. The Design-Center window moves away from its docked position to a floating one.

4. Place your cursor on the lower-left corner of the DesignCenter window so a double-headed diagonal arrow shows, then click and drag the corner out so that you have an enlarged DesignCenter window that looks similar to Figure 22.1. By the way, the view on the right containing the DesignCenter folder is called the Palette view and the view on the left is called the Tree view (see Figure 22.1).

FIGURE 22.1:

The DesignCenter window

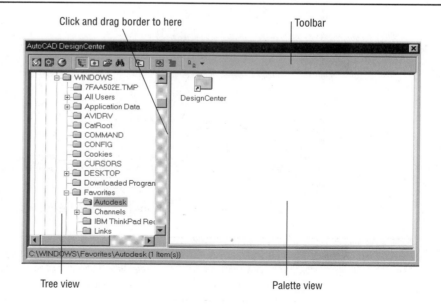

5. Place your cursor on the border between the Tree view and the Palette view until you see a double-headed cursor. Then click and drag the border to the right to enlarge the Tree view until it covers about one-third of the window.

6. Finally, use the scroll bar at the bottom to adjust your view of the Tree view so you can easily read its contents.

Once set up like this, you can see the similarities between the DesignCenter and the Windows Explorer. You can navigate your computer or network using the Tree view, just as you would in Windows Explorer. There are a few differences however. Try the following exercise to see what those differences are.

1. Double-click the DesignCenter shortcut in the Palette view. The view changes to display the contents of the DesignCenter Directory under the \AutoCAD2000\ Samples\ directory.

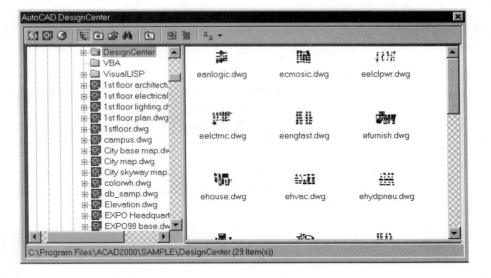

2. Instead of the usual listing of files, you see sample images of each file. These are called *preview icons*.

3. Click the Views tool in the toolbar. The Palette view changes to show the files in another format.

4. Click the Views tool again and the view changes again. The Views tool is similar to the Large Icon, Small Icon, List and Detail options in Windows Explorer.

5. Click the file named `Eanlogic.dwg` to select it.

You can see an enlarged version of the preview icon of a selected file by clicking the Preview tool in the DesignCenter toolbar.

The view appears at the bottom of the Palette view. The preview can be helpful if you prefer viewing files and drawing components as a list in the main part of the Palette view.

Another option on the toolbar that offers more information on your drawings is the Description tool.

When you click the Description tool, the DesignCenter displays any text information that has been included with the drawing or block. To see an example of how this works, do the following.

1. Use the Tree view of the DesignCenter to locate and select the directory containing the file called `14a-unit.dwg`. This should be in a directory called `Figures` if you used the default installation for the figures from the companion CD-ROM.

2. Click the `14a-unit.dwg` file, then click the Description tool in the DesignCenter toolbar. You'll see a description of the file at the bottom of the Palette window.

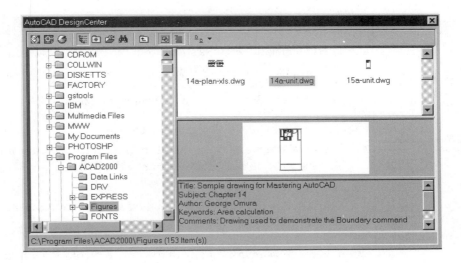

The information you see was added using the Properties dialog box (File ➤ Drawing Properties) described in Chapter 14.

Both the preview icon and the Description tool can offer help in identifying files that you may be looking for. Once you find a file, you can click and drag it into the Tree view to organize your files into separate directories, or you can click and drag them into Windows Explorer.

You can also add files to the Favorites folder under the Windows directory by right-clicking, then selecting Add to Favorites. The file itself won't be moved to the Favorites folder but instead, a shortcut to the file will be created in the Favorites folder. If you want to work on organizing your Favorites folder, you can open a window to the Favorites folder by right-clicking on a file in the Palette view and selecting Organize Favorites. A window to the Favorites folder appears.

Since you'll be working with the sample drawings from the companion CD-ROM, go ahead and add the Figures directory to the Favorites folder.

1. Locate the Figures directory in the Tree view then right-click it.

2. Select Add to Favorites from the popup menu.

3. To go directly to the Favorites folder, click the Favorites tool in the DesignCenter toolbar.

The Favorites folder appears in the Palette view.

4. Double-click the Figures shortcut in the Palette view. You return to the contents of the Figures directory.

You can go beyond just looking at file listings. You can look inside files to view their components.

1. In the Palette view, locate the file named 16a-unit.dwg and double-click it. You see a listing of its components in the Palette view. The Tree view also shows the file highlighted.

2. Double-click the Block listing in the Palette view. Now you see a listing of all of the blocks in 16a-unit.dwg.

From here, you can import any of the drawing components from the Design-Center palette into an open drawing in AutoCAD. But before you try that, try a few other features of the DesignCenter.

Using the Favorites Tool in the AutoCAD File Dialog Boxes

As you use AutoCAD, you may notice a set of tools in the upper-right corner of nearly all of the file dialog boxes.

The Add to Favorites tool creates a shortcut to a file and places it in the Favorites folder. You can then easily retrieve that file by clicking the Look in Favorites tool and selecting the shortcut to the file. You can use the Favorites folder like a collection of bookmarks to those files that you use frequently. Instead of searching your hard disk or your network for a file, use the Look in Favorites tool to go directly to your favorite file. Be aware, however, that if the file is moved from its location at the time the shortcut was made, the shortcut won't work. You'll have to delete the old shortcut and establish a new one using the Add to Favorites tool.

Opening and Inserting Files with the DesignCenter

With the DesignCenter, you can locate the files you are looking for more easily because you can view thumbnail preview icons. But often, that isn't enough. For example, you may want to locate all of the files that contain the name of a particular manufacturer in an attribute of a drawing.

Once you've found the file you're looking for, you can load it into AutoCAD by right-clicking the filename in the Palette view, then selecting Open in Window. Try it with the following exercise.

1. Click the Up tool in the DesignCenter toolbar twice. This takes you up two levels in the Palette view from the view of the drawing blocks to the list of filenames.

2. In the Palette view of the DesignCenter, locate the 12c-unit2.dwg sample.

3. Right-click 12c-unit2.dwg, then select Open in Window. The drawing appears in the AutoCAD window.

Another way to open files from the DesignCenter is to click and drag the filename from the Palette view of the DesignCenter into a blank AutoCAD window, but not into an open file. If you already have a few files open, minimize them by clicking the Minimize button in the drawing window.

Once this is done, you can click and drag a file into AutoCAD's gray window background.

If you want to insert a file into another drawing as a block, you can do so by clicking and dragging the file from the DesignCenter Palette view into an open drawing window. You will then be prompted for insertion point, scale, and rotation angle. If you prefer to use the Insert dialog box to insert a drawing from the DesignCenter, right-click the filename in the Palette view, and then select Insert As Block. The Insert dialog box opens, offering you the full set of insert options, as described in Chapter 3.

Finally, you can attach a drawing as an Xref by right-clicking a file in the Palette view of the DesignCenter, then selecting Attach as Xref. The External Reference dialog box appears, offering the insertion point, scale, and rotation options similar to the Insert dialog box. This is the same dialog box described in Chapter 6 in the section *Using External References*.

Finding and Extracting the Contents of a Drawing

Aside from the convenience of being able to see thumbnail views of your drawing, the DesignCenter may not seem like much of an improvement over Windows Explorer. But the DesignCenter goes beyond Windows Explorer in many ways. One of the main features of the DesignCenter is that it allows you to locate and extract components of a drawing.

Imagine that you want to find a specific block in a drawing. You remember the name of the block, but you don't remember the drawing you put it in. You can search the contents of drawings using the DesignCenter's Find dialog box. In the following exercise, you will search for a block named s-door1 among a set of files.

1. In the DesignCenter toolbar, click the Find tool.

The Find dialog box appears. It looks similar to the Find tool that comes with Windows.

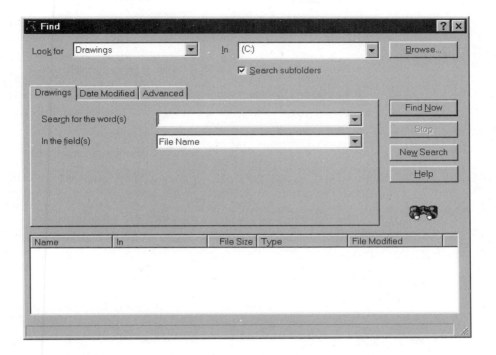

2. Select the drive that contains the sample drawings from the companion CD-ROM from the In drop-down list.

3. Select Blocks from the Look for drop-down list. As you can see from the list, you can look for a variety of drawing component types.

4. Enter **kitchen2-metric.↵** in the Search for the name input box. The binocular icon in the lower-right corner will move back and forth telling you that it is working. After a minute or two, you'll see the name of the block in the window at the bottom of the dialog box.

5. Right-click the block name, then select Load into Palette. The DesignCenter displays the block in the Palette view and the file that contains the block appears in the Tree view.

As you can see from this example, the Find dialog box can be helpful in finding items that are buried in a set of drawings. In the exercise, you searched for a block, but you can search for any named drawing component, including attribute data and text. For example, if you want to find all attributes that contain the name ABC

Manufacturing Company in your drawings, you can do so with the DesignCenter Find dialog box. Here is a summary of its features.

In Lets you select the drive you want to search.

Look for Options Lets you select the type of item to search for. The options are: Drawings, Drawings and Blocks, Layers, Layouts, Linetypes, Textstyles, and Xrefs.

Browse Lets you locate a specific directory to search.

Search Subfolders Lets you determine whether Find searches subfolders in the drive and directory you specify.

Find Now Starts the search process.

Stop Cancels the current search.

New Search Clears all of the settings for the current search so you can start fresh on a new search.

Help Opens the AutoCAD help system to the Find topic.

When you select Drawings from the Look for drop-down list, you see a set of additional tabs in the Find dialog box. Here is a description of the options you'll find in those additional tabs.

Drawings tab Contains two options.

> **Search for the Word(s)** Lets you specify the text to search for in the drawing properties fields.

> **In the Field(s)** Lets you specify the field of the Drawing Properties dialog box to search through, including filename, title, subject, author, and keyword. These are the fields you see when you choose File ➤ Drawing Properties.

Date Modified tab Lets you limit search criteria based on dates.

Advanced tab Offers three options to further limit your search to specific types of drawing data or to a range of dates:

> **Containing** Lets you select from a list of data to search for, including block name, block and drawing description, attribute tag, and attribute value.

> **Containing text** Lets you specify the text to search for in the types of data you select from the Containing option.

Size is Lets you restrict the search to files greater than or less than the size you specify.

Once you've found the block using the DesignCenter, you can click and drag the block into your open drawing. In the following exercise, you'll do just that, but with a slight twist. The block you've found is drawn in centimeters, but you'll be inserting the Kitchen2-metric block into a drawing named 12c-unit2.dwg, which was created in the English measurement system. If you were to insert the Kitchen2-metric block into 12c-unit2.dwg, the kitchen would be exactly 2.54 times larger than it should be for 12c-unit2.dwg. But as you'll see, the DesignCenter takes care of scaling for you.

1. In AutoCAD, make sure the 12c-unit2.dwg sample drawing is loaded.

2. In the DesignCenter, click and drag the Kitchen2-metric block from the Palette view into the 12c-unit2.dwg window in AutoCAD. The kitchen appears at the appropriate scale.

3. To see that the DesignCenter did indeed adjust the scale of the Kitchen2-metric block, click it, then right-click and select Properties.

4. Check the Scale X, Scale Y, and Scale Z settings in the Geometry category. Notice that they show .3937 as the scale factor instead of 1.

5. After reviewing the Properties dialog box, close it.

You may recall from Chapter 3 that you have the opportunity to specify the type of units the drawing is set up for in the Units dialog box under the Drawing Units for DesignCenter Blocks button group. The DesignCenter uses this information when you drag and drop blocks from the DesignCenter into an open drawing. This is how the DesignCenter is able to correctly scale a block drawn in metric to a drawing that is drawn in the English format.

Blocks aren't the only type of drawing component you can click and drag from the Palette view. Line types, layouts, dimension styles, and text styles can all be imported from files on your computer or network through the DesignCenter's Palette view.

TIP Since you can easily drag and drop blocks from the DesignCenter into an open drawing, you can use files as a place to store symbols. Set up a few files that just contain the blocks you use as symbols. When you start to build a drawing, use the DesignCenter to open the file containing the symbols you need, then click and drag the symbols from the Palette view into your drawing.

Exchanging Data between Open Files

You've seen how you can extract a block from a file stored on your hard drive and place it into an open drawing, but what if you want to copy a block from one open drawing to another open drawing? You change the way the Tree view displays data so that it shows only the files that are loaded in AutoCAD. The following exercise demonstrates how this works.

1. In AutoCAD, make sure that 12c-unit2.dwg is open, then open the 12c-unit2-metric.dwg file.

2. In the DesignCenter, click the Open Drawings tool in the toolbar. The Tree view changes to display only the drawings that are open.

3. Click the plus sign (+) to the left of the 12c-unit2.dwg filename in the Tree view. The list expands to show the listing of components in 12c-unit2.dwg.

4. Click Blocks in the Tree view. The Palette view changes to show a list of blocks available in 12c-unit2.dwg.

5. Locate the Kitchen block in the Palette view.

6. Click and drag Kitchen from the Palette view into the open 12c-unit2-metric.dwg drawing in AutoCAD. You see the block move with the cursor. Once again, the DesignCenter has automatically scaled the block to the appropriate size, this time from English to metric.

7. Click anywhere in the drawing to place the Kitchen block.

In this example, you inserted a block from one open drawing into another drawing. If you prefer to use the Insert dialog box, you can right-click the block name in step 6 and select Insert Block. The Insert dialog box appears, allowing you to set the insertion point, scale, and rotation options.

Viewing Data in Different Ways

You can alter the way the Palette view displays its data. For example, you can view the data as a list or as a set of icons. If a block is created with a preview icon, you can view that icon from the Palette view.

1. If it isn't selected already, click the Kitchen block in the Palette view.

2.   Click the Preview tool in the DesignCenter toolbar. You see a preview image at the bottom of the Palette view.

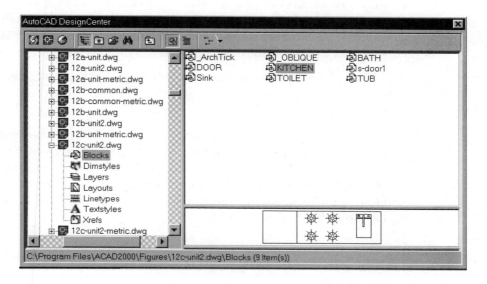

3.   Click the Description tool in the DesignCenter toolbar. A text description of the Kitchen block appears at the bottom of the Palette view.

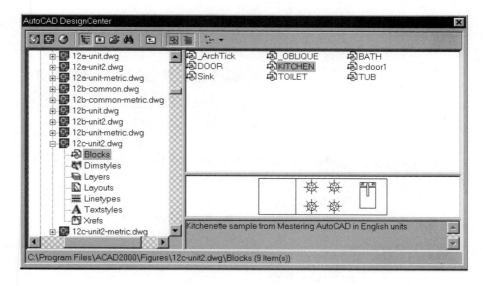

Just as with drawings, you can see a preview icon and descriptive text for blocks. In Chapter 3, when you first created a block, you had the option to save a preview icon with the block. This is where that preview icon can be really helpful. The preview icon gives you a chance to see what the block looks like when you use the DesignCenter to browse through your drawing files. If you don't save a preview icon, you'll see the same block icon that was displayed in the previous Palette view.

The text description can also be added at the time that you create the block. Before saving the block, enter a description in the Description input box of the Block Definition dialog box.

If you're updating older drawing files to be used with the DesignCenter, you can add text descriptions to blocks using the Make Block tool in the Draw toolbar. Click the Make Block tool, then in the Block Definition dialog box, select the name of a block from the Name drop-down list. Enter the description you want for this block in the Description input box toward the bottom of the Block Definition dialog box. When you're finished, click OK.

Loading Specific Files into DesignCenter

You've seen how you can locate files through the Tree view and Palette view. If you already know the name and location of the file you want to work with, you can use the traditional method of using a file dialog box to open files in the DesignCenter.

1. Click the Load tool in the DesignCenter toolbar. The Load the DesignCenter Palette dialog box appears.

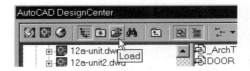

2. Locate and select the sample `Nozzle3D.dwg` that was installed from the companion CD-ROM, then click Open.

3. The Palette view shows the contents of `Nozzle3D.dwg` and the Tree view shows its location in the hierarchical list.

TIP   You can also load, view, and import the contents of a file that is posted on the World Wide Web. To do this, use the Search the Web tool in the Load the DesignCenter Palette dialog box. See *Opening and Inserting .dwg Files from the Web* later in this chapter.

If you want to open a file in the DesignCenter that you've recently opened, you can use the History tool in the toolbar.

1. Click the History tool. The Tree view closes and you see a list of the most recent files you've worked on.

2. Locate 12c-unit2.dwg and double-click it. The Tree view returns, displaying the file you selected and the Palette view displays the contents of the selected file.

3. After reviewing the results of step 2, close the DesignCenter and all of the drawings you've opened so far in this chapter. You don't have to save them.

The DesignCenter offers some great features that will prove invaluable to AutoCAD users in a workgroup environment. While these examples show you how to use the DesignCenter on a stand-alone computer, you can just as easily perform the same functions across a network, or even across the Internet, provided you have password access to remote sites.

In the next part of this chapter, you'll look at ways that you can use the Internet to share your drawings with others.

Sharing Drawings on the World Wide Web

The World Wide Web has become a major part of the computer industry and is quickly becoming a part of everyday life. If you're in business, any business, a Web presence is seen as a necessity, even if you don't think anyone will ever use it. But the Web offers AutoCAD users some real, practical benefits through its ability to publish drawings and other documents online. AutoCAD gives you tools that allow you to post drawings on the Web that others can view and download. In the architectural or engineering construction (AEC) industry in particular, this can

mean easier access to documents needed by contractors, engineers, cost estima-
tors, and others involved in the design, bidding, and construction of architectural
projects. Suppliers of products can post symbols libraries of their products or even
3D solid models.

In this section, you'll learn about the tools AutoCAD provides for publishing
and accessing drawings on the Web. This section assumes some knowledge on
your part of the HTML format used to create Web pages, and a basic familiarity
with browsing the Web and using FTP sites. First, you'll learn how to create a
Web-viewable drawing.

Using Your Web Space

Nearly all Internet service providers (ISPs) offer *Web space* as part of their basic package.
Web space is an area on your Internet provider's computer reserved for you alone. You can
place your Web page documents there for others to view. Of course, along with the Web
space you get your own Web address. If you are using the Internet now, but aren't sure
whether you can use your Internet account to post Web pages, check with your ISP. You
may already have the Web space and not even know it.

Once you've established your Web space, you'll need to know how to post your Web
pages. If you need help in this area, Sybex offers *Mastering Web Design* (Sybex, 1997).

Creating a Web-Compatible Drawing

AutoCAD users have been looking for ways to publish their drawings on the Web for
some time. The earlier efforts involved capturing bitmap images of drawings and
adding them to Web pages. While this is fairly simple to do, this method allowed for
only the crudest of images to be displayed. Drawings had to be limited in size and resolution to make them easily accessible. If you wanted to add URL links (clickable areas
on an image that open other documents), you had to delve into the inner workings of
Web page design.

NOTE   URL stands for Uniform Resource Locator and is a standard system for addressing
Internet locations on the World Wide Web.

Fortunately, Autodesk has come up with the DWF drawing file format. DWF allows you to easily add vector format images to your Web pages. These images can be viewed using the same pan and zoom tools available in AutoCAD, thereby allowing greater detail to be presented. In addition, you can embed URL links that can open other documents with a single mouse click. These links can be attached to objects or areas in the drawing.

Creating a DWF File

In most cases, you will want to create a Web-viewable drawing file that looks similar to your printed output. You can think of your DWF files as plot that you can post on the Web. So to create a DWF file, you go through the AutoCAD plot system. The following exercise shows you exactly what to do.

1. Open the `Plan.dwg` file in AutoCAD. You can use the `12a-plan.dwg` file from the companion CD-ROM if you didn't create the `Plan.dwg` file on your own.

2. Choose File ➤ Plot to open the Plot Settings dialog box.

3. Click the Plot Device tab, then select DWF ePlot PC3 from the Name drop-down list. You may also select DWF Classic PC3 to produce an earlier version of a DWF file.

4. In the Plot to File group of the Plot Device tab, enter the filename and select a location for the DWF file.

5. Click the Plot Settings tab and select the area you want to plot from the Plot area group.

6. Click OK in the Plot dialog box to proceed with the creation of the DWF file.

You can control the DWF plot as you would any plot, although the sheet size is meaningless in this situation since your DWF file is not dependant on a fixed media size.

Configuring the DWF Output

In addition to the settings available in the Plot dialog box, you can make some special configuration adjustments to the DWF plotter configuration file. Here is where to find those configuration settings.

1. Choose File ➢ Page Setup, then in the Page Setup dialog box, select the Plot Device tab.

2. Make sure the DWF ePlot PC3 or the DWF Classic PC3 configuration file is listed in the Name list box.

3. Click the Properties button to the right of the Plotter Configuration Name drop-down list. The Plotter Configuration Editor appears.

4. Make sure the Device and Document Settings tab is selected, then click the Custom Properties listing in the dialog box.

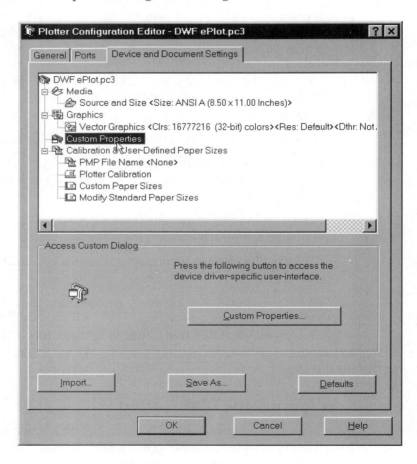

5. Click the Custom Properties button that appears in the lower half of the dialog box. The DWF Properties dialog box appears.

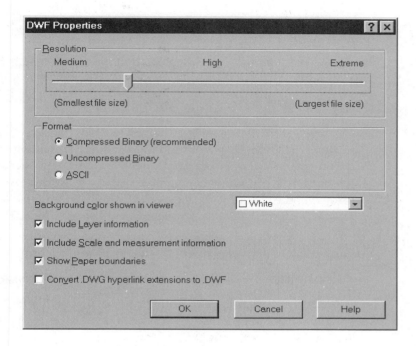

In this dialog box, you can set the resolution, format, and background color and paper boundary for your DWF file. You can also specify whether to include layer and scale information or whether you want to include any hyperlinks from the source drawing.

6. Click OK after making your settings. The Plotter Configuration Editor dialog box reappears. Once you make the custom properties settings, you can save any new settings under the DWF ePlot.PC3 file, or create a new DWF PC3 plot configuration file. To save any setting changes you have made, click the Save As button in the Plotter Configuration Editor dialog box, then select the PC3 file you want to save the settings to.

7. Click OK in the Plotter Configuration Editor to return to the Page Setup dialog box.

8. Click OK to exit the Page Setup dialog box.

NOTE   For more information on PC3 plot configuration files, see Chapter 7.

Once you've made your custom configuration settings in step 5, you needn't open the Plotter Configuration Editor dialog box again the next time you plot a DWF file. If you save your new settings as a new PC3 file, you can select it from the File drop-down list of the Plotter Configuration group. You needn't re-enter the custom settings again.

Now let's continue by adding the .dwf file to a Web page file.

Adding a DWF File to a Web Page

Creating a DWF file is simple. Adding it to a Web page can be a bit more work. This section will assume that you are familiar with the creation and editing of HTML documents. HTML stands for Hypertext Markup Language, but don't let the fancy title scare you. The fundamentals of HTML are really quite easy to learn. If you need to know more about HTML, check out *HTML: No Experience Required* (Sybex, 1997). Now let's proceed with the instructions.

If you want to just embed a DWF file in your HTML file, you can add the following line to your HTML file and the DWF file will appear in the browser.

```
<EMBED SRC="drawingname.dwf" WIDTH="640" HEIGHT="480" ALIGN="BOTTOM">
```

Replace *drawingname.dwf* with the name of your drawing. The width and height specifications can be whatever you want them to be. If you want to add all of the bells and whistles to your DWF document, you can do the following.

1. Open your HTML document, either in a word processor or in a Web page creation program.

2. Insert the following code in the location where you want the DWF file to appear.

```
<object
 classid ="clsid:B2BE75F3-9197-11CF-ABF4-08000996E931"
 codebase = "ftp://ftp.autodesk.com/pub/autocad/plugin/ _
whip.cab#version=2,0,0,0"
 width=400
 height=300 >
<param name="Filename"  value="drawingname.dwf">
<param name="View"      value="10000,20000 30000,40000">
<param name="Namedview" value="viewname">
<embed name= drawingname src="drawingname.dwf"
 pluginspage=http://www.autodesk.com/products/autocad/
 whip/whip.htm
```

```
width=400
height=300
view="10000,20000 30000,40000"
namedview="INITIAL">
</object>
```

This code includes all the data required for both Netscape Communicator and Microsoft Internet Explorer. You'll want to keep the code for both browsers in your HTML file so that users of both browsers can view your drawings.

This example contains some generic code. You'll want to make a few changes to it to make it applicable to your specific DWF file. The items in *italics* are the ones you will want to change. Let's look at them one by one so you know exactly how to replace them in your file.

Determining Files and Opening Views

As you scan down the code, you'll see two lines labeled width and height:

```
width=400
height=300 >
```

These two lines are for the benefit of Microsoft Internet Explorer. The numeric values in this bit of code determine the size of your drawing in the Internet Explorer window. They describe the width and height in pixels. You can replace the numbers here to whatever value you want, but keep them in a range that will fit neatly in a typical Web page format.

The next set of lines determines the actual filename and opening view for the DWF file.

```
<param name="Filename"  value="drawingname.dwf">
<param name="View"      value="10000,20000 30000,40000">
<param name="Namedview" value="viewname">
<embed name= drawingname src=" drawingname.dwf"
```

The first three lines shown here are for Microsoft Internet Explorer. In the first line, replace the italicized letters with your own .dwf filename. You can also specify a URL to a .dwf file at another location, such as http://www.omura.com/sample.dwf.

The next two lines describe the view name to which Internet Explorer is to open the .dwf file, or the actual coordinates for the opening view. Use one or the other, but don't use both view parameters.

NOTE   With regard to the view name in the HTML code, AutoCAD will create a view called *Initial* when you create the .dwf file. This view will be of the drawing at the time that the .dwf file is created. You may want to use the Initial view name just to simplify your page creation efforts.

The fourth line is for the benefit of Netscape Communicator. Again, you enter the name of the .dwf file here in place of the *drawingname.dwf* letters. You'll also see name = *drawingname*. This lets you identify the drawing with Java and JavaScript applications. You can replace the italicized name with your own name. Also, it doesn't have to be the drawing name.

Further down the listing you will see the width, height, and view parameters repeated:

```
width=400
 height=300
 view="10000,20000 30000,40000"
 namedview="viewname">
```

This set of parameters is intended for Netscape Communicator users and should match the data you provide for Microsoft Internet Explorer in the previous set of lines.

Your Internet Provider Needs to Know...

Finally, whether you are using an Internet provider or an in-house Web server, your server will need to be able to recognize the .dwf file type. You will need to inform your Webmaster that you intend to use the .dwf file in your Web page. The Webmaster then needs to add the MIME type of "drawing/x-dwf" to the Internet server. This registers the .dwf file type with the Internet server software enabling others to view your drawings online.

Viewing Your Web Page

Once you have your HTML file completed, you are ready to view it with a browser. You will need Version 3.0 or higher of either Microsoft Internet Explorer or Netscape Communicator *and* the Autodesk Whip 3.1 driver. This driver can be obtained from the Autodesk Web page. The Whip driver comes in the form of installation files that are fairly large. Set aside at least half an hour of download time.

Once the installation file is downloaded, double-click it and follow the instructions. Your browser is located automatically, then prompts you for a location for the Whip driver software. Once this is done, you're ready to view your page!

NOTE   You may have noticed that the sample HTML code you saw in the previous section included some Web addresses. These addresses allow a viewer without the Whip driver to automatically locate and download the driver when they attempt to view your page.

The companion CD-ROM contains a sample page in case you are in a hurry to see how .dwf files look on a Web page. The following exercise steps you through the opening and viewing of that sample page. This will give you a chance to see just how useful a .dwf file can be.

1. Using Windows Explorer, locate the `houseplan.html` file from the companion CD-ROM and double-click it. Your Internet browser opens with a view of a simple floor plan.

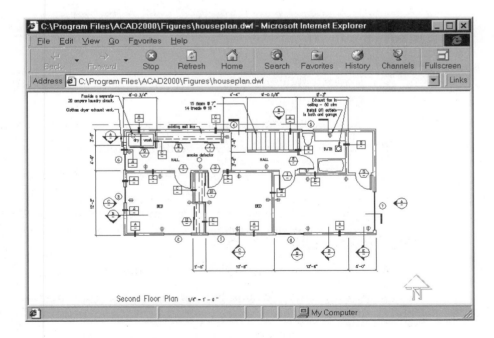

As you move the mouse over the image, you'll see the Pan Realtime hand cursor.

2. Click and drag the Pan Realtime cursor over the image. Notice that it works just like the Pan Realtime tool in AutoCAD.

3. Right-click the mouse. A popup menu appears.

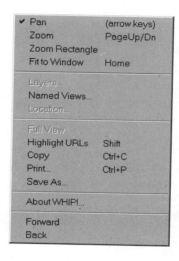

Notice that this menu is also similar to the one you see in AutoCAD, with some additions.

4. Select Zoom from the menu. The cursor changes to the Zoom Realtime cursor.

5. Zoom in on the view as you would in AutoCAD.

6. Adjust your view so you see the lower-left corner of the plan, similar to Figure 22.2.

7. Double-click the wall reference symbol shown in Figure 22.2. A new page appears showing a wall type detail drawing associated with the symbol that you clicked.

8. Click the button labeled Back on the button bar to return to the previous page.

9. Click the door symbol shown in Figure 22.2. This time you see a page showing the door schedule.

In this example, you saw how you can click an area of the drawing to get to another drawing. These clickable objects are called *URL links* or *hyperlinks*. It is possible to set up these URL links to open the actual wall detail associated with the symbol. In the next section, you'll learn how these links were created.

FIGURE 22.2:

Exploring a Web page containing a DWF file

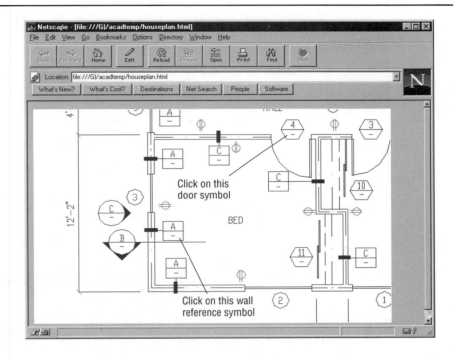

Adding Hyperlinks to Connect to Other Drawings or Web Pages

The file you opened in your browser in the previous exercise contains the HTML code you looked at in the previous section entitled *Adding a DWF File to a Web Page*. Only the names of the embedded DWF files were modified to include the floor plan. The ability to have a clickable object in the browser's view of the plan comes from the DWF file itself. You add links to connect objects in your drawing to other HTML files before you save your drawing in the DWF format.

To add such links, you use the Hyperlink tool in AutoCAD. You aren't limited to creating links to DWF files. You can create links to text documents, other drawing files, or any type of file you want.

Once you add links to objects, you can use those links to open the linked file just by selecting the object and right-clicking on a blank area in the drawing. You don't have to turn your drawing into a .dwf file to take advantage of hyperlinks.

Creating Hyperlinks

The following shows you how links were added to the plan you saw in the previous exercise.

1. In AutoCAD, open the file called houseplan.dwg.

2. Choose Insert ➤ Hyperlink.

3. At the Select objects: prompt, click the hexagonal door symbols, as shown in Figure 22.3.

4. When you're done, press ↵. (In the sample file you looked at previously, you added a link to all of the hexagonal symbols.) The Insert Hyperlink dialog box appears.

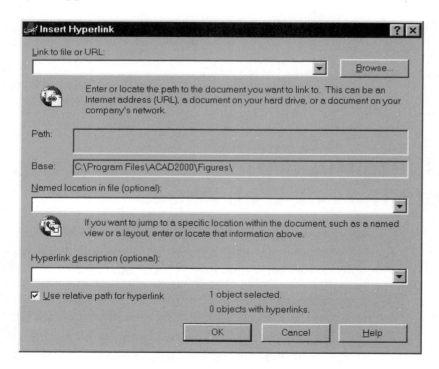

5. Click the Browse button in the upper-right corner of the dialog box. The Browse the Web–Select Hyperlink dialog box appears.

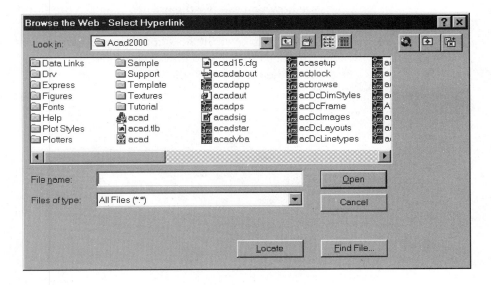

6. Locate the `Doorsch.html` file in the `\Figures\` subdirectory and select it.

7. Click Open. The Insert Hyperlink dialog box reappears. Notice that `Doorsch.html` appears in the list box at the top of the dialog box.

8. Make sure that the Use Relative Path for Hyperlink option is not checked, then click OK.

FIGURE 22.3:

The door symbol in the Houseplan.dwg file

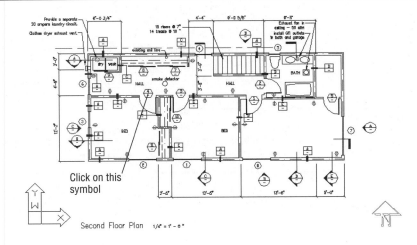

The link you just created is stored with the drawing file. You can then create a DWF file from this drawing and the link will be preserved in the DWF file.

Now let's see how you can use the link from within the AutoCAD file.

1. Move your cursor over the hexagonal door symbol. Notice that the cursor changes to the Hyperlink icon when it is placed on the symbol. It also shows the name of the file to which the object is linked.

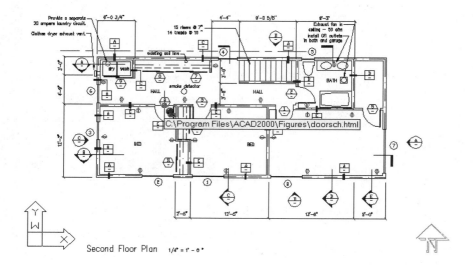

Second Floor Plan   1/4" = 1'-0"

This tells you that the object is linked to another document somewhere on your system, network, or the World Wide Web.

2. Click the hexagonal door symbol to select it.

3. Right-click a blank area of the drawing. In the popup menu, select Hyperlink ➤ `C:\Program Files\ACAD2000\Figures\doorsch.html`.

Your default Web browser opens and displays the file `doorsch.html`.

WARNING   If you have installed the sample figures from the companion CD-ROM on another drive or directory location, the Hyperlink menu option will reflect this new location and will be different from the one shown in step 3.

You used the `doorsch.html` file as an example in these exercises, but this could have been a text file, a spreadsheet, a database, or even another AutoCAD file. AutoCAD will start the application associated with the linked file and open the file.

Editing and Deleting Hyperlinks

You can edit or delete the hyperlink by doing the following.

1. Choose Insert ➤ Hyperlink.

2. Click the object whose link you wish to edit, then press ↵. The Insert Hyperlink dialog box appears.

3. You can now change the link, or click the Remove Link button in the lower-left corner of the dialog box to delete the link altogether.

When you create a hyperlink that connects to an AutoCAD drawing file, you can set up the link to open a specific view in the drawing. You do this by entering the name of the view in the Named Location in File input box of the Edit Hyperlink dialog box. This also works with word-processed documents by entering the name of a bookmark in the Named Location in File input box. If you're linking to an HTML document, you can put an anchor name in this input box to go to a specific anchor.

The inclusion of hyperlinks in drawing files and DWF files opens a world of new possibilities in the way that you work with drawings. You can link product specifications directly to the objects in the drawing that represent that product. You can also link to extended data beyond the simple symbol or graphic in a drawing, such as a database table or spreadsheet.

You don't have to limit your links to HTML files containing AutoCAD drawings. You can link to all sorts of Web documents, to drawings on your computer or your companies network, and even to documents on other sites. For example, you can enter `http://www.autodesk.com` in the Link to File or URL input box of the Edit Hyperlink dialog box to link the hexagonal door symbols to the Autodesk Web site.

Viewing and Removing Links

A couple of other tools on the Internet Utilities toolbar allow you to view or remove the URLs associated with objects and areas. The List URL tool will display the URL attached to an object or area. The Detach URL tool will clear the URL that is attached to an area or object. If you have difficulty remembering which objects have URLs assigned to them, you can use the Select URL tool to highlight all the objects and areas that have URLs attached to them.

Opening and Inserting .dwg Files from the Web

If you find you need to share your AutoCAD drawings with a lot of people, you can post your files on your Web site and allow others to download them. This is typically done through a Web page by assigning a graphic or a string of text to a file. A person viewing your page can then click the graphic or text to start the download process.

AutoCAD also offers a way to open files directly from a Web page. You'll need to know the name of the file you are downloading, but beyond that, the process is quite simple. Try downloading a sample drawing from my Web page at www .omura.com to see how this process works.

1. First, make the connection to your ISP.

2. With AutoCAD open, choose File ➤ Open. The Select File dialog box appears.

3. Click the Search the Web tool.

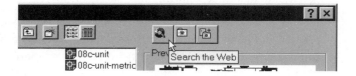

The Browse the Web dialog box appears.

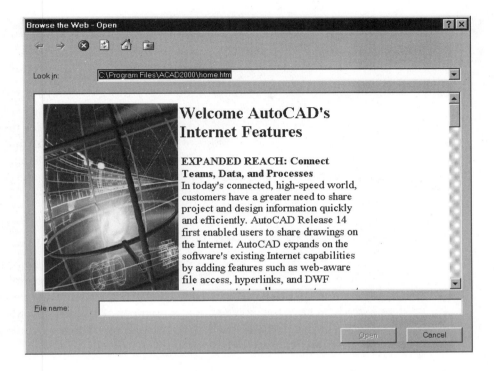

4. Enter **www.omura.com**↵ in the Look in drop-down list. The www.omura.com opening Web page appears. As you can see, the AutoCAD Browse the Web dialog box acts as a Web browser.

5. Enter **sample.dwg**↵ in the File Name input box. The sample drawing is downloaded and appears in the drawing editor.

The Search the Web button you saw in step 3 is present in all of the File dialog boxes that you encounter in AutoCAD. This means that you can import blocks, Xrefs, and even raster image files from Web sites, as long as you know the names of the files you want to import.

TIP   You can also click and drag a DWF file from a Web page into AutoCAD to download and open a .dwg file, provided that a .dwg file with the same name as the DWF file exists on the Web site.

Supporting Your System and Working in Groups

So far in this book you have worked with AutoCAD as an individual learning a program. However, chances are you are usually not alone when you use AutoCAD on a project. Your success with AutoCAD may depend as much on the people you work with as on your knowledge of the program. The last half of this chapter will look at some of the issues you may face as a member of an interactive group: selecting a system and obtaining support for it; what happens once that system arrives in the office; and some ways you can manage your system.

Getting Outside Support

It helps to have knowledgeable people to consult when questions arise. Most often, the vendor who sells the CAD system is also the source for technical support. Another source is an independent CAD consultant. And don't overlook colleagues who have had some solid experience with AutoCAD. Most likely, you will tap all three of these sources at one point or another as you start to implement an AutoCAD system in your work.

> **TIP**
>
> It is well worth searching for a knowledgeable vendor. Your vendor can save you several times their sales commission in work hours that your office might otherwise spend trying to solve hardware and software problems. Your vendor can also help you set up a system of file organization and management—something that can become a nightmare if left unattended.

It can be difficult to find a vendor who understands your special needs. This is because the vendor must have specialized knowledge of computers as well as knowledge of design or production. A good vendor should offer training and phone support, both of which are crucial to productive use of a program with as much complexity as AutoCAD. Some vendors even offer user groups as a means of maintaining an active and open communication with their clients. Here are some further suggestions:

- In addition to your vendor, you may want to find an independent consultant who is familiar with AutoCAD. Although it may be harder to find a good CAD consultant than to find a good vendor, the consultant's view of your needs is unbiased by the motivation to make a sale. The consultant's main goal is to help you gain productivity from your CAD system, so he or she will be more helpful in these areas than your average vendor.

- Get references before you use anyone's services. Your own colleagues may be the best source of information on vendors, consultants, and even hardware. You can learn from their good fortune or mistakes.

- Don't rely on magazine reviews and product demonstrations at shows. These can often be misleading or offer incomplete information. If you see something you like, test it before you buy it. For some products this may be difficult, but because of the complex nature of computer-aided design and drafting, it is important to know exactly what you are getting.

Choosing In-House Experts

Perhaps even more important than a good vendor is an individual within your office who knows your CAD system thoroughly. Ideally, everyone closely involved in your drafting and design projects should be a proficient AutoCAD user, but it is impractical to expect everyone to give time to system management. Usually one individual is chosen for this task. It can often be a thankless one, but when the going gets rough, an in-house expert is indispensable.

NOTE If you find that a task can be automated, a knowledgeable in-house person can create custom macros and commands on the spot, saving your design or production staff hundreds of work hours—especially if several people are performing that task. Your in-house authority can also train new personnel and answer users' questions.

In a smaller office, the in-house authority may need to be an expert on design, production, and computers—all rolled into one. The point is that to really take advantage of AutoCAD or any CAD system, you should have access to some in-house expertise. AutoCAD is a powerful tool, but that power is wasted if you don't take advantage of it.

However, you must be aware that the role of the in-house expert will require significant time spent away from other tasks. Dealing with questions about the program's use can be disruptive to the expert's own work, and writing custom applications is often at least a part-time job in itself. Keep this under consideration when scheduling work or managing costs on a project. It also pays to keep the following in mind:

- The in-house expert should be a professional trained in your firm's field of specialization, rather than someone with a computer background. Every architect or engineer on your staff represents years of training, while learning AutoCAD can take a matter of weeks or months. The expert-to-be, however, should be willing to develop some computer expertise.

- Running a CAD system is not a simple clerical task. It takes not only clear thinking and good organizational skills, but good communication skills as well. The in-house authority should have some interest in teaching, and the ability to be patient when dealing with interruptions and "stupid" questions. He or she may well be a manager and will need access to the same information as any key player on your design team.

- If you have several computers, you may also want to obtain some general technical support. Especially if your company is implementing its first computer environment, many questions will arise that are not directly related to AutoCAD. The technical support person will be able to answer highly technical questions for which a computer background is required, more so than familiarity with your professional specialty.

- Consider contracting with an outside consultant to occasionally provide additional support. This will allow development of custom applications without waiting for your staff to develop the necessary skills. A consultant can also help train your staff and even fill in from time to time when production schedules become too tight.

Acclimatizing the Staff

Once an AutoCAD system is installed and operational, the next step is to get the staff acquainted with that system. This can be the most difficult task of all. In nearly every office, there is at least one key person who resists the use of computers. This can be a tremendous obstacle, especially if that individual is at management level—although nearly anyone who is resisting the project goals can do damage. The human capacity to undermine the most sincere efforts is astounding, and when coupled with a complex computer system, the results can be disastrous. Unfortunately, there is no easy solution to this problem aside from fostering a positive attitude toward the CAD system's capabilities and its implementation.

AutoCAD has a way of adding force to everything you do, both good and bad. Because AutoCAD is capable of reproducing work rapidly, it is very easy to unintentionally multiply errors until they are actually out of hand. This also holds true for project management. Poor management tends to be magnified when AutoCAD comes into the picture. You are managing yet another dimension of information— blocks, symbols, layers, and so on. If the users cannot manage and communicate this information, problems are sure to arise.

On the other hand, a smooth-running, well-organized project is reflective of the way AutoCAD enhances your productivity. In fact, good management is essential for realizing productivity gains with AutoCAD. A project on AutoCAD is only as good as the information you provide and the manner in which the system is administered. Open communication and good record-keeping are essential to the development and integrity of a design or a set of drawings. The better managed a project is, the fewer problems arise, and the less time is required to get results.

Discussing CAD management procedures in your project kickoff meetings will help get people accustomed to the idea of using the system. Exchanging information with your consultants concerning your CAD system standards is also an important step in keeping a job running smoothly from the start, especially if they are also using AutoCAD.

Learning the System

Learning AutoCAD can be time consuming. If you are the one who is to operate the AutoCAD system, at first you won't be as productive as you were when you were doing everything manually, and don't expect to perform miracles overnight. Once you have a good working knowledge of the program, you still have to integrate it into your day-to-day work. It will take you a month or two, depending on how much time you spend studying AutoCAD, to get to a point where you are entering drawings with any proficiency. It also helps to have a real project you can work on while you are in training. Choose a project that doesn't have a tight schedule, so that if anything goes wrong, you have enough time to make corrections.

Remember that it is important to communicate to others what they can expect from you. Otherwise, you may find yourself in an awkward position because you haven't produced the results that someone anticipated.

Making AutoCAD Use Easier

Not everyone in your organization needs to be an AutoCAD expert, but in order for your firm to obtain maximum productivity from AutoCAD, almost everyone involved in design or production should be able to use the system. Designers especially should be involved, since AutoCAD can produce significant time-savings in the design phase of a project.

You may want to consider an add-on software package to aid those who need to use AutoCAD but who are not likely to spend a lot of time learning it. These add-ons automate some of the typical functions of a particular application. They can also provide ready-made office standards for symbols and layers. Add-ons are available for architects, circuit board designers, electrical engineers, civil engineers, and mechanical designers, to name a few.

TIP
If you are serious about being productive with AutoCAD, you will want to develop custom applications. See Chapter 19 to find out more about customization and third-party software.

Add-ons shouldn't be viewed as the only means of using AutoCAD within your office, but rather as aids to casual users, and partners to your own custom applications. No two offices work alike and no two projects are exactly the same, so add-ons cannot be all things to all people. Remember that AutoCAD is really a graphics tool whose commands and interface can be manipulated to suit any project or office. And that is the way it should be.

Managing an AutoCAD Project

If you are managing a project that is to be put on AutoCAD, be sure you understand what it can and can't do. If your expectations are unreasonable, or if you don't communicate your requirements to the design or production team, friction and problems may occur. Open and clear communication is of the utmost importance, especially when using AutoCAD or any CAD program in a workgroup environment. Here are some further points to consider:

- If your office is just beginning to use AutoCAD, be sure to allow time for staff training. Generally, an individual can become independent on the program after 24 to 36 hours of training. ("Independent" means able to produce drawings without having to constantly refer to a manual or call in the trainer.) This book should provide enough guidance to accomplish this level of skill.

- Once at the point of independence, most individuals will take another month or so to reach a work rate comparable to hand drafting. After that, the individual's productivity will depend on his or her creativity and problem-solving ability. These are very rough estimates, but they should give you an idea of what to expect.

- If you are using a software add-on product, the training period may be shorter, but the user won't have the same depth of knowledge as someone who isn't using the enhancements. As mentioned earlier, this kind of education may be fine for casual users, but you will reach an artificial upper limit on productivity if you rely too heavily on add-ons.

As you or your staff members are learning AutoCAD, you will need to learn how to best utilize this new tool in the context of your office's operations. This may mean rethinking how you go about running a project. It may also mean training coworkers to operate differently.

For example, one of the most common production challenges is scheduling work so that check plots can be produced on a timely basis. Normally, project members have grown accustomed to looking at drawings at convenient times as they progress, even when there are scheduled review dates. With AutoCAD, you won't have that luxury. You will have to consider plotting time when scheduling drawing review dates. This means that the person doing the drawings must get accurate information in time to enter last-minute changes and to plot the drawings.

Establishing Office Standards

Communication is especially important when you are one of many people working on the same project on separate computers. A well-developed set of standards and procedures helps to minimize problems that might be caused by miscommunication. In this section, you'll find some suggestions on how to set up these standards.

Establishing Layering Conventions

You have seen how layers can be a useful tool. But they can easily get out of hand when you have free reign over their creation and naming. This can be especially troublesome when more than one person is working on the same set of drawings. The following scenario illustrates this point.

One day, the drawing you are working on has twenty layers. Then the next day, you find that someone has added six more layers, with names that have no meaning to you whatsoever. You don't dare delete those layers or modify the objects on them, for fear of retaliation from the individual who put them there. You ask around, but no one seems to know anything about these new layers. Finally, after spending an hour or two tracking down the culprit, you discover that the layers are not important at all.

With an appropriate layer-naming convention, you can minimize this type of problem (though you may not eliminate it entirely). A too-rigid naming convention can cause as many problems as no convention at all, so it is best to give general guidelines rather than force everyone to stay within narrow limits. As mentioned in Chapter 6, you can create layer names in a way that allows you to group them using wildcards. AutoCAD allows up to 31 characters in a layer name, so you can use descriptive names.

Line weights should be standardized in conjunction with colors. If you intend to use a service bureau for your plotting, check with them first; they may require that you conform to their color and line-weight standards.

TIP If you are an architect, engineer, or in the construction business, check out some of the CAD layering standards set forth by the American Institute of Architects (AIA) and the Construction Standards Institute (CSI).

Maintaining Files

As you use your computer system, you will generate files rapidly. Some files will be garbage, some will be necessary but infrequently used, and others will be current job files or system files that are constantly used. In addition, AutoCAD automatically creates backup files (they have the filename extension .bak). If something is wrong with the most recent version, you can restore the .bak file to a drawing file by simply changing the .bak extension to .dwg. You may or may not want to keep these backup files.

NOTE An AutoCAD backup file is a copy of the most recent version of the file before you issued the last Save or End command. If you save the .bak files, you will always have the next-to-most recent version of a file.

All these files take up valuable space, and you may end up with insufficient room for your working files. Because of this, you will want to regularly clear the unused files from the hard disk by erasing unwanted files and archiving those that are used infrequently. You may even want to erase current files from your hard disk once they have been backed up on floppy disks. It's wise to do this at every editing session, so you don't confuse meaningful files with garbage. You may want to erase all your .bak files, as well, if you don't care to keep them.

TIP You can set up AutoCAD so that it does not create the .bak files. Open the Options dialog box, click the Open and Save tab, and then remove the checkmark from the Create Backup Copy with Each Save option.

Backing Up Files

Besides keeping your hard disk clear of unused and inactive files, consider backing it up daily or at least once a week. This might be done by the in-house expert, network manager, or the technical support staff. You needn't back up the entire hard disk, just those crucial drawing files you've been slaving over for the past several months. When you do back up your entire hard disk, you save the configuration of all your programs and the directory structure. In the event of a hard disk failure, you won't have to reinstall and reconfigure all your software. You just restore the backups once the problem with the hard disk is remedied.

If you're in a network environment, chances are that you are storing your files on a server that is backed up daily. Individual computer configurations can also be backed up through the server.

> **NOTE** In the event that you do have a system failure and some files become corrupted, AutoCAD has a built-in file-recovery routine. Whenever it attempts to load a corrupted file, it will tell you the file is corrupted and proceed to fix the problem as best it can. See Appendix A for more on this feature.

A good policy to follow is to back up your entire hard disk every week, and your data files every day, as a compromise to backing up everything daily.

Tape backup systems are the preferred backup method for a hard disk. These systems transfer the contents of your hard disk onto a tape cartridge or cassette. The software to operate the tape system is usually provided as part of the system. A tape backup system allows you to start the backup process and then walk away to do something else. Some systems offer timed backup so you don't even have to think about starting them—it simply happens at a predetermined time, usually in the evening.

Besides tape backup systems, you may want to obtain a system that will let you archive drawing files on a project-by-project basis. Recordable or rewritable CD-ROMs have become a popular medium for project archiving. They can also double as a means to distribute drawings or other project files to clients and consultants.

There are also other, faster, more flexible options, such as rewritable optical drives that can store 500MB to 1GB of data. Such a system usually costs twice as much as a recordable CD-ROM drive. Rewritable optical drives can be invaluable, however, in situations where large amounts of data must be archived and readily retrieved.

Labeling Hard Copies

A problem you will run into once you start to generate files is keeping track of which AutoCAD file goes with which hard copy drawing. It's a good idea to place an identifying tag on the drawing (that will plot with the drawing) in some inconspicuous place. As well as the filename, the tag should include such information as the date and time the drawing was last edited, who edited it, and what submission the plot was done for. All these bits of information can prove helpful in the progress of a design or production project (see Figure 22.4).

FIGURE 22.4:

You can promote good drawing management by using a small note identifying the file used to generate the drawing.

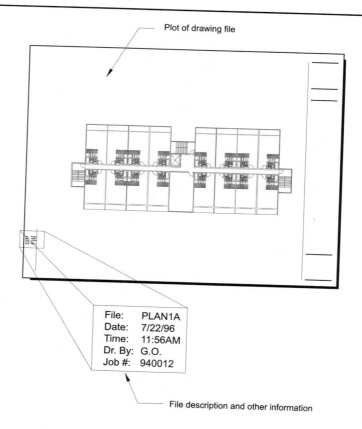

Plot of drawing file

File:	PLAN1A
Date:	7/22/96
Time:	11:56AM
Dr. By:	G.O.
Job #:	940012

File description and other information

TIP

The Batch Plot utility described in Chapter 7 allows you to add a descriptive label to your drawings. Also, many of the modern inkjet plotters feature a plot-stamping function.

Using Networks with AutoCAD

In an effort to simplify your file maintenance, you will want to consider installing a network to connect your computers. Networks offer a way to share files and peripherals among computers in different locations.

Two basic types of networks can be used with AutoCAD: *dedicated file server/client* systems and *peer-to-peer* systems. The dedicated file server offers you a way to maintain files on a single computer. The computers connected to the server are referred to as *clients* or *nodes*. You can store all of your common symbols, AutoLISP programs, custom menus, and working files on the server, thus reducing the risk of having duplicate files. The client computers are simpler and less powerful. They use the server as their main storage device, accessing the programs and data stored on the server through the network. Networks with servers also have all the peripheral output devices connected to the server. This centralized type of system offers the user an easier way of managing files.

NOTE   In simplified terms, a *dedicated file server* is a storage device, often a computer with a large-capacity hard disk, that acts as a repository of data. A server will often have a tape backup device to facilitate regular system backup.

A peer-to-peer network does not use a server. Instead, each computer has equal status and can access files and peripherals on other computers on the network. Generally, this type of network is less expensive because you don't need to dedicate a computer to the single task of being a server. Peripherals such as plotters and printers are shared among computers. Even hard disks are shared, although access to directories can be controlled at each computer.

Networks can be useful tools in managing your work, but they can also introduce new difficulties. For some network users, file-version control becomes a major concern. Speed of file access can be another problem. No matter what form of network you have or install, you will need a network manager whose duties include backing up files in the server and making sure that the network's output devices are operating as they should. Used properly, a network can save time by easing the flow of information between computer users; it must, however, be managed carefully.

Here are some tips on using AutoCAD on a network:

- Use a star topology for your network, with an active hub and a dedicated server.

- Configure AutoCAD to store temporary files on the client or node computer.

- Configure your network version of AutoCAD for multiple swap files and local code pages, and set the AutoCAD preferences to use the client or node computer for swap files. (See Appendix A for more on these tasks.)

Keeping Records

Computers are said to create "the paperless office." As you work more and more with them, however, you may find that quite the opposite is true. Although you can store more information on magnetic media, you will spend a good deal of time reviewing that information on hard copy because it is very difficult to spot errors on a computer monitor. When you use AutoCAD on large projects, another level of documentation must also exist: a way of keeping track of the many elements that go into the creation of drawings.

TIP   Your companion CD-ROM has AutoLISP utilities that will generate log files for you automatically. See the section on the AEC utilities in Appendix C for details.

Because job requirements vary, you may want to provide a layer log to keep track of layers and their intended uses for specific jobs, or better yet, use the Layer Manager Express tool described in Chapter 19. In addition, to manage blocks within files, a log of block names and their insertion values can help. Finally, plan to keep a log of symbols. You will probably have a library of symbols used in your work group, and this library will grow as your projects become more varied. Documenting these symbols will help to keep track of them.

Another activity that you may want to keep records for is plotting—especially if you bill your clients separately for computer time or for analyzing job costs. A plot log might contain such information as the time spent on plotting, the type of plot done, the purpose of the plot, and even a list of plotting errors and problems that arise with each drawing.

Although records may be the last issue on your mind when you are working to meet a deadline, in the long run they can save time and aggravation for you and the people you work with.

Understanding What AutoCAD Can Do for You

Some of you may have only a vague idea of what AutoCAD can contribute to your work. You think it will make your drafting tasks go faster, but you're not sure exactly how. Or you may believe it will help you produce better-quality drawings. Some people expect AutoCAD will make them better designers or allow them to produce professional-quality drawings without having much drawing talent. All these things are true to an extent, and AutoCAD can help you in some ways that are less tangible than speed and quality.

Seeing the Hidden Advantages

You have learned how AutoCAD can help you meet your drafting and design challenges by allowing you to visualize your ideas more clearly and by reducing the time it takes to do repetitive tasks. AutoCAD also forces you to organize your drawing process more efficiently. It changes your perception of problems and, though it may introduce new ones, the additional accuracy and information AutoCAD provides will minimize errors.

AutoCAD also provides drawing consistency. A set of drawings done on Auto-CAD is more legible and consistent, reducing the possibility of errors caused by illegible handwriting or poor drafting. In our litigious culture, this is a significant feature.

Finally, because AutoCAD systems are becoming more prevalent, it is easier to find people who can use it proficiently. As this group of experts grows, training will become less of a burden to your company.

As you have seen, AutoCAD is a powerful software tool, and like any powerful program, it is difficult to master. I hope this last chapter has given you the incentive to take advantage of AutoCAD's full potential. Remember: Even after you've learned how to use AutoCAD, there are many other issues that you must confront while using AutoCAD in an office environment.

Unlike words, drawings have few restrictions. The process of writing requires adherence to the structures of our language. The process of drawing, on the other hand, has no fixed structure. For example, there are a million ways to draw a face or a building. For this reason, your use of AutoCAD is much less restricted, and there are certainly potential uses for it that are yet to be discovered. I encourage you to experiment with AutoCAD and explore the infinite possibilities it offers for solving your design problems and communicating your ideas.

I hope *Mastering AutoCAD 2000* has been of benefit to you and that you will continue to use it as a reference. If you have comments, criticisms, or ideas about how to improve the next edition of this book, write to me at the address below. And thanks for choosing *Mastering AutoCAD 2000*.

George Omura

Omura Illustration

P.O. Box 357

Albany, CA 94706-0357

E-Mail: gomura@sirius.com

PART VI

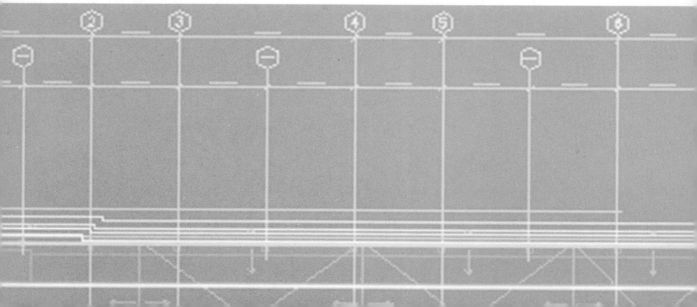

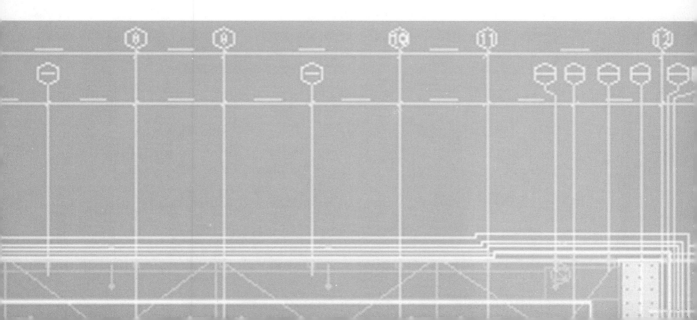

Appendices

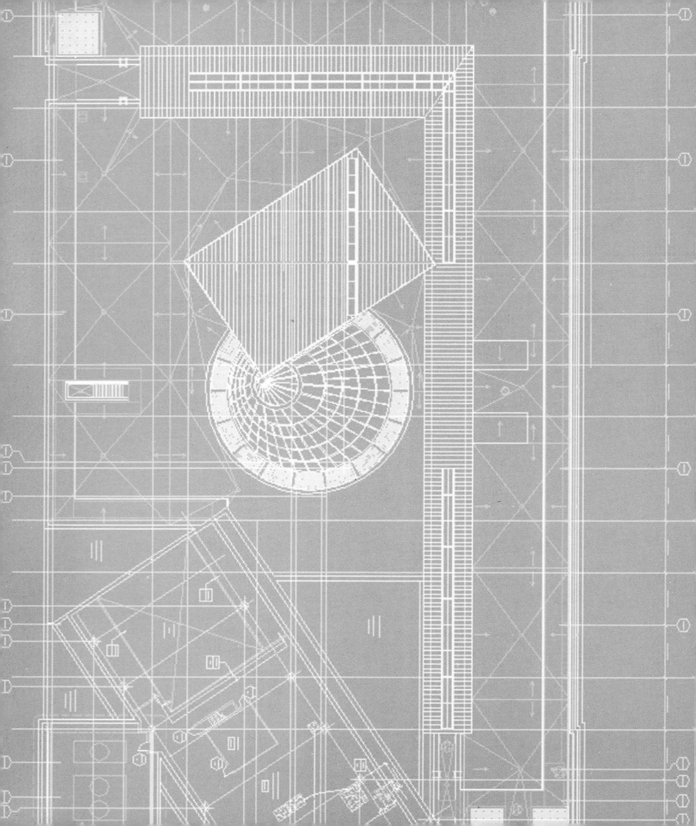

APPENDIX
A

Hardware and Software Tips

Because some of the items that make up an AutoCAD system are not found on the typical desktop system, I have provided this appendix to help you understand some of the less common items you may need. This appendix also discusses ways you can improve AutoCAD's performance through software and hardware.

The Graphics Display

There are two issues to consider concerning the graphics display: *resolution* and *performance*.

If you are running Windows 95/98 or Windows NT, then in all probability you already have a high-resolution display card for your monitor. If you haven't set up your system yet, then a high-resolution display card and monitor is a must. SVGA or XVGA display cards are inexpensive and offer high-quality display.

Graphics performance comes down to speed. To enhance graphics performance you need to consider the following resources:

AGP Bus   Contemporary motherboards use high-speed AGP expansion slots that offer the fastest video throughput available. Check that yours is a system of this type. There are also options for using multiple monitors in Windows 98 that have been popular among AutoCAD users in the past. Multiple monitors offer AutoCAD users the option to view multiple documents more easily.

Video RAM   If you are shopping for a display system, you should also make sure that it has 4–8 megabytes of *video RAM*. Standard video cards typically have at least 4 megabytes of video RAM. Greater amounts of up to 32 megabytes will give you noticeably better performance with AutoCAD.

Pointing Devices

Our most basic means of communicating with computers is the keyboard and pointing device. Most likely, you will use a mouse, but if you are still in the market for a pointing device, choose an input device that generates smooth cursor movement.

Some of the lesser-quality input devices cause erratic movement. When looking for an input device other than a mouse, choose one that provides positive feedback, such as a definitive button click when you pick an object on the screen. Many low-cost digitizers have a very poor button feel that can cause errors when you are selecting points or menu options.

In general, use a high-resolution mouse if you do not plan to do any tracing. If you must have the use of a tablet menu, or if you know you are going to trace drawings, then get a digitizer, but be sure it is of good quality.

The Digitizing Tablet

If you need to trace large drawings, you may want to consider a digitizing tablet. It is usually a rectangular object with a pen-like *stylus* or a device called a *puck*, which resembles a mouse. It has a smooth surface on which to draw. The most common size is 4" × 5", but digitizing tablets are available in sizes up to 60" × 70". The tablet gives a natural feel to drawing with the computer because the movement of the stylus or puck is directly translated into cursor movement. While many digitizers come with a stylus, you will want a multi-button puck to work with AutoCAD.

A digitizing tablet's puck often has *function buttons*. These buttons can be programmed through the AutoCAD menu file system to start your most frequently used commands, which is much faster than searching through an on-screen menu. You can also select commands from the tablet's surface if you install the *menu template* supplied with AutoCAD. A menu template is a flat sheet of plastic with the AutoCAD commands printed on it. You can select commands simply by pointing at them on the template. If you have a digitizing tablet, refer to Appendix B, which tells you how to install a template.

AutoCAD supports Wintab-compatible digitizers. If your digitizer has a Wintab driver, you can use your digitizer as both a tracing device (to trace drawings on a tablet) and as a general pointing device for Windows to choose program menu items.

Your Wintab digitizer must be installed and configured under Windows. Check that it is working in Windows before enabling it in AutoCAD, otherwise you will not be able to use the digitizer as a pointing device (mouse). To enable the digitizer in AutoCAD, choose Tools ➤ Options, then select the System tab. In the System tab, open the Current Pointing Device drop-down list and select Wintab-compatible digitizer ADI 4.2–by Autodesk, Inc.

Output Devices

Output options vary greatly in quality and price. Quality and paper size are the major considerations for both printers and plotters. Nearly all printers give accurate drawings, but some produce better line quality than others. Some plotters give merely acceptable results, while others are quite impressive in their speed, color and accuracy.

AutoCAD 2000 can use the Windows 95/98 or Windows NT *system printer*, so any device that Windows supports is also supported by AutoCAD. AutoCAD also gives you the option of plotting directly to an output device, although Autodesk recommends that you set up your plotter or printer through Windows and then select the device from the Plot Configuration group in the Plot Device tab of the Plot or Page Setup dialog box.

Printers

There are so many types of printers available these days that it has become more difficult to choose the right printer for your application. This section describes the broad categories of printers available and how they relate to AutoCAD. You will also want to consider the other uses for your printer, such as word-processing or color graphics. Here are a few printing options:

Laser Printers   Produce high-quality line work output. The standard office laser printer is usually limited to 8 1/2" × 11" paper; however, 11" × 17" laser printers for graphics and CAD work are now becoming affordable, and are commonly used for proof plots. Resolution and speed are the major considerations if you are buying a laser printer. An output of 300 DPI (dots per inch) produces very acceptable plots, but 600 DPI is fast becoming the standard. You should look also for a laser printer with sufficient built-in memory to improve spooling and plotting speeds.

Inkjet or Bubble Jet Printers   Offer speed and quality output. Some inkjet printers even accept 17" × 22" paper and offer PostScript emulation at up to 720 DPI. Since inkjet printers are competitively priced, they can offer the best solution for low-cost check plots. And the 17" × 22" paper size is quite acceptable for half-size plots, a format that more architects and engineers are using.

PostScript Printers   If you want to use a PostScript device to output your drawings, the best method is to use File ➤ Export or the Psout command. These options convert your drawing into a true PostScript file. You can then send your file to a PostScript printer or typesetting machine. This can be especially useful for PCB layout where you require photo negatives for output. If you are an architect who needs presentation-quality drawings, you may want to consider using the Encapsulated PS (*.eps) option in the Export Data dialog box. Often service bureaus who offer a raster plotter service can produce E-size PostScript output from a PostScript file. The uses of this option are really quite open-ended.

Another option is to export your drawing to an illustration program such as Adobe Illustrator 8 and make any refinements to your drawing there. You can save files in the AutoCAD 2000 DXF file format or use the File ➤ Export option to export files to the Windows Metafile format. Most illustration programs accept either of these formats.

Plotters

Printer technology has changed significantly over the past 10 years since the early versions of AutoCAD. This is especially true in the area of large format plotters. Output devices intended for CAD were once dominated by pen plotters, but now color inkjet plotters and printers are commonplace. Inkjet technology offers far greater flexibility and speed, giving you many more options in the look of your output. Autodesk has completely retooled the plotter section of AutoCAD to reflect these new options. Most of these new features can be found in the Plot Device tab of the Plot dialog box.

You can also find laser or electrostatic plotters at a much higher price. Black-and-white inkjet plotters offer the best value; they are fast and fairly inexpensive compared to the older pen plotters they supersede. For a bit more expense, you can step up to a color plotter. Black-and-white plotters are capable of printing raster images in larger formats, and they can print patterns and screens for highlight effects.

If you need large plots but feel you can't afford a large plotter, many blueprint companies and even some copy centers offer plotting as a service. This can be a very good alternative to purchasing your own plotter. Check with your local blueprinter or CAD service bureau.

Fine-Tuning the Appearance of Output

If you open the Plot or Page Setup dialog box and click the Plot Device tab, you'll see the options that offer control over how your plotter or printer works.

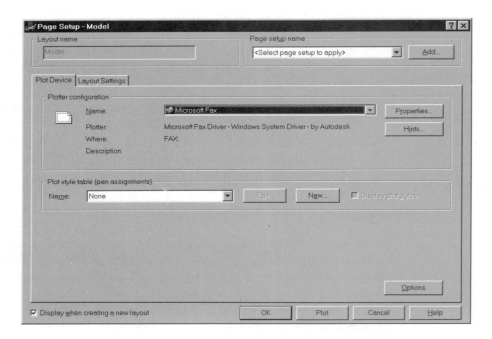

There are four button groups in this tab:

- Plotter Configuration
- Plot Style Table (Pen Assignments)
- What to Plot
- Plot to File

These button groups seem innocent enough, but behind two of these groups lies a vast set of options that can be quite intimidating. You've already seen how the Plot Style Table options work in Chapter 7. This section covers the options available when you click the Properties button in the Plotter Configuration group.

Making Detailed Adjustments with the Plotter Configuration Options

The Plotter Configuration options allow you to adjust those printer or plotter settings that you may not need to access all the time, but may want to adjust on occasion. These settings are fairly technical in nature and include things like the port your printer is connected to, the quality of bitmap image printing, custom paper sizes, and printer calibration, which lets you adjust your plotter for any size discrepancies in output. You won't be using most of these settings often, but you will want to know that they exist just in case you find yourself in a situation where you need to make some subtle change to your printer's configuration. You can also use these options to create multiple configurations of the same plotter for quick access to custom settings.

You'll want to know that all of the settings in this group are stored in a file with the .PC3 filename extension. You can store and recall any number of configuration files for situations that call for different plotter settings. PC3 files are normally stored in the Plotters folder under the main AutoCAD2000 folder.

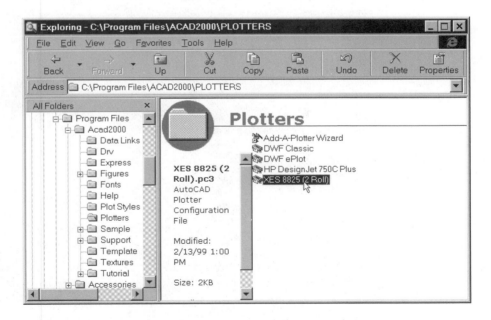

The Plotter Configuration button group offers a drop-down list from which you can select a printer or file output configuration. If a PC3 file exists for a plotter configuration, the drop-down list will display it, and it will display any Windows system printer. Once you've selected an output device from the list, you can click the Properties button to access the Plotter Configuration Editor dialog box.

TIP
You can configure AutoCAD to create bitmap files in the most common file formats such as TIFF, Targa, and PCX, or create Autodesk's DWF file format for the Internet. Once you've configured AutoCAD for these types of output, this is where you select the file output type.

The Plotter Configuration Editor dialog box offers three tabs. The General tab displays a list of Windows drivers that this configuration uses, if any, and there is a space for your own comments.

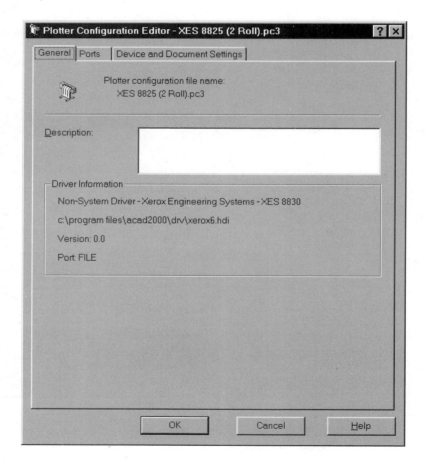

TIP

You can access and edit the plotter configuration settings without opening Auto-CAD. To do this, locate the PC3 file in the **Plotters** subdirectory under the **Auto-CAD2000** directory, then double-click it.

The Ports tab lets you determine where your plotter data is sent. This is where you want to look if you are sending your plots to a network plotter, or if you decide you want to create plot files. You can also select the Autospool feature, which allows you to direct your plot to an intermediate location for distribution to the appropriate output device.

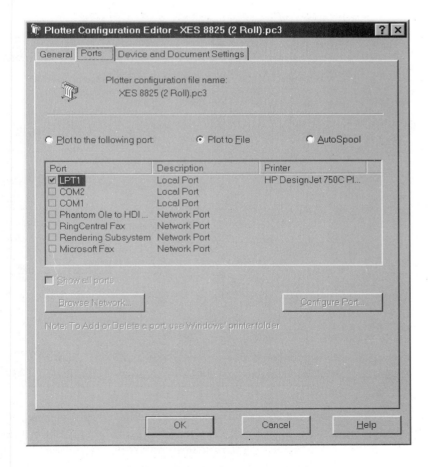

The Device and Document Settings tab is the main part of this dialog box. It offers a set of options ranging from OLE output control to custom paper sizes. The main list box offers options in a hierarchical list, similar to a directory listing in Windows Explorer. Toward the bottom of the dialog box are three buttons labeled Import, Save As, and Defaults. These buttons let you import configuration settings from earlier versions of AutoCAD, save the current settings as a file, or return the settings to their default values.

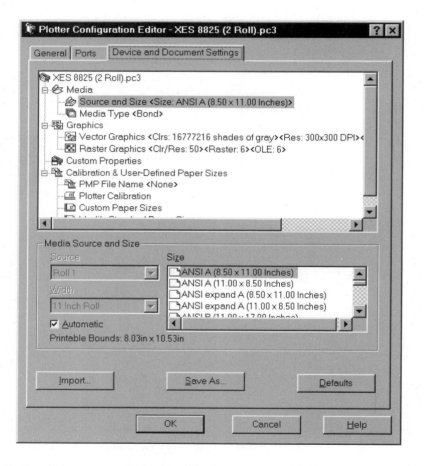

The list has four main categories: Media, Graphics, Custom Properties, and Calibration and User-Defined Paper Sizes. Not all of the options under these categories are available in all plotters. When you select an item from this list, the area just below the list displays the options associated with that item. The following describes each category and its options.

The images you see in the following descriptions are those offered for the Xerox
Engineering Systems XES8825.

Media

Some plotters, like the Xerox Engineering Systems 8800 series, offer options for the
source and size of printer media and for the media type. If the Source and Size option
is available, the dialog box offers a listing of the source, such as sheet feed or roll, and
the sheet size. The Media Type option lets you choose from bond, vellum, glossy, or
any other type of media that is specifically controlled by the plotter. Duplex Printing,
when available, controls options for double-sided printing in printers that support
this feature. Media Destination, when available, lets you select a destination for output such as collating or stapling in printers that support such features.

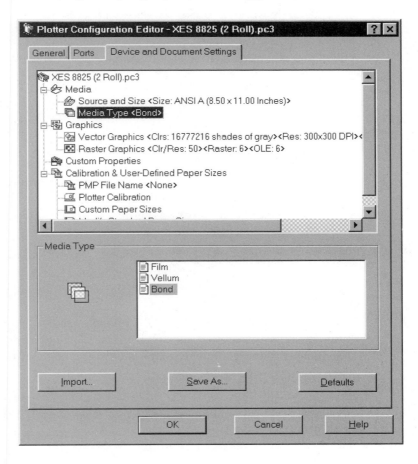

Physical Pen Configuration (Shown Only for Pen Plotters)

Pen plotters have features that diverge from the typical laser or inkjet printer or plotter. When these options are present, they let you control some of the ways that AutoCAD generates data for pen plotters. Here is a listing of those pen plotter feature settings:

Prompt for Pen Swapping   Stops the plotter to allow you to switch pens. This feature is designed primarily for single-pen plotters.

Area Fill Correction   Tells AutoCAD to compensate for pen width around the edges of a solid-filled area in order to maintain dimensional accuracy of the plot.

Pen Optimization Level   Sets how AutoCAD sorts pen movement for optimum speed. AutoCAD does a lot of preparation before sending your drawing to the plotter. If you are using a pen plotter, one of the things it does is optimize the way it sends vectors to your plotter, so your plotter doesn't waste time making frequent pen changes and moving from one end of the plot to another just to draw a single line.

Physical Pen Characteristics   Lets you set assign plotter pen numbers to AutoCAD colors, adjust the speed of individual pens, and assign pen widths.

Graphics

These settings give you control over both vector and raster output from your plotter. The Vector Graphics settings let you control resolution and color depth, as well as control the method for creating shading. If you want to configure your printer for virtual pens, select 255 Virtual Pens under the Color Depth option.

The Raster Graphics settings slider gives you control over the quality of any bitmap images. If this setting is placed all the way to the left, then raster images will not be plotted. As you move the slider farther to the right, the raster image quality increases, the speed of printing decreases, and memory requirements increase. The OLE Settings slider controls the quality of OLE linked or embedded files. If this setting is placed all the way to the left, then OLE objects will not be printed. As you move the slider farther to the right, OLE image quality and memory requirements increase while speed is reduced.

The Tradeoff slider lets you choose how the Raster and OLE sliders improve speed. You can choose between lower resolution or lower colors.

For printers and plotters that support TrueType fonts, the TrueType Text options allow you to select between plotting text as graphics or as TrueType text.

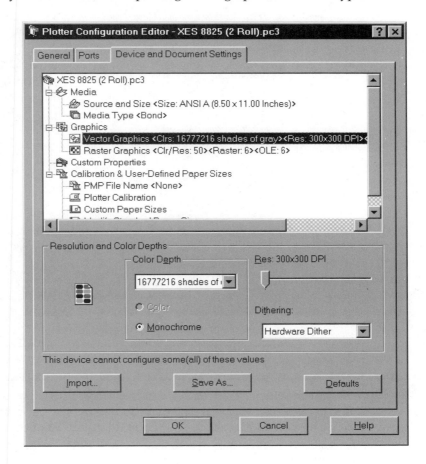

Custom Properties

This is a single option that displays the Custom Properties button in the lower part of the dialog box. By clicking the Custom Properties button, you are given access to the same printer or plotter settings that are available from the Windows system printer settings. These settings can also be accessed by choosing Start ➣ Settings ➣ Printers, then right-clicking the desired printer and selecting Properties.

The options offered through the Custom Properties button often duplicate many of the items listed in the Device and Documents list. If an option is not accessible from the Device and Documents list, check the options offered under the Custom Properties button.

Initialization String

Some plotters require pre-initialization and post-initialization codes, in the form of ASCII text strings, to "get the plotter's attention." If you have such a plotter, this option lets you enter such strings.

Calibration and User-Defined Paper Sizes

The options in the Calibration and User-Defined Paper Sizes listing offer some of the more valuable options in this dialog box. In particular, the Calibration option can be useful in ensuring the accuracy of your plots.

Plotter Calibration   If you find that your printer or plotter is not producing an accurate plot, you should focus on the calibration option. If your plotter stretches or shrinks your image in one direction or another, the calibration option lets you adjust the width and height of your plotter's output. To use it, click the Plotter Calibration listing under Calibration and User-Defined Paper Sizes.

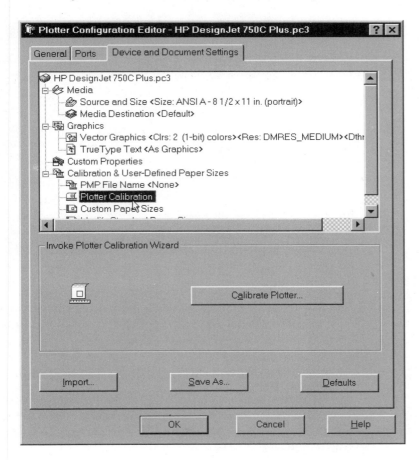

A button appears labeled Calibrate Plotter. Click this button to open the Calibrate Plotter wizard as shown in Figure A.1.

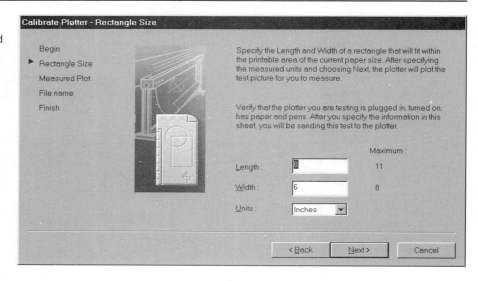

You can use the Calibrate Plotter wizard to plot a sample rectangle of a specific size. You then measure the rectangle and check its dimensions against the dimensions that it is supposed to be. If there are any discrepancies between the plotted dimensions and the dimensions you select in the wizard, you can then enter the actual plotted size, then print out another test rectangle. You can repeat this process until your plotted rectangle exactly matches the dimensions entered into the wizard.

Toward the end of the Calibrate Plotter wizard's steps, you'll be asked to give a name for a Plot Model Parameter (PMP) file that will store your calibration data. The PMP file also stores any custom paper size information that you may input from other parts of the Calibration and User-Defined Paper Sizes options. This file is then associated with the PC3 file that stores your plotter configuration data.

If you have more than one PC3 file for your plotter, you can associate the PMP file to other PC3 files using the PMP File Name option in the Device and Document Settings list box. This option is the first item under the Calibration and User-Defined Paper Sizes category.

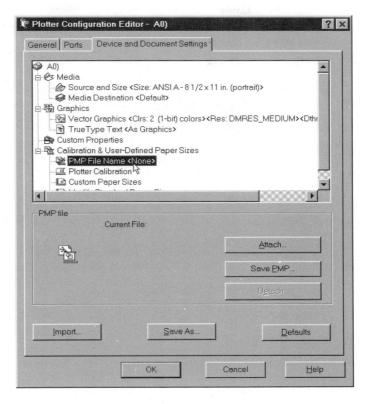

To associate a PMP file to a PC3 plotter configuration file, select the PC3 file from the Name drop-down list of the Plot Device tab in the Plot dialog box. Click the Properties button, then in the Device and Document Settings tab, click the PMP File Name listing. The PMP options appear in the bottom of the dialog box. Click the Open File button, then select the PMP file from the Open dialog box. Click OK. You'll see that the PMP file has been added to the PMP file name listing.

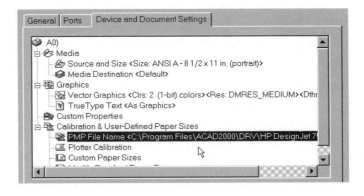

Custom Paper Sizes   Some plotters will offer custom paper sizes. This is usually offered for printers and plotters that you've set up to use the AutoCAD drivers instead of the Windows system drivers. If your plotter offers this option, you'll see a list box and a set of buttons when you select Custom Paper Sizes.

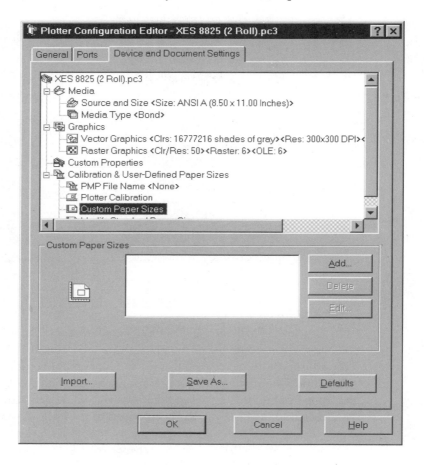

If you click the Add button, you'll see the Custom Paper Size wizard.

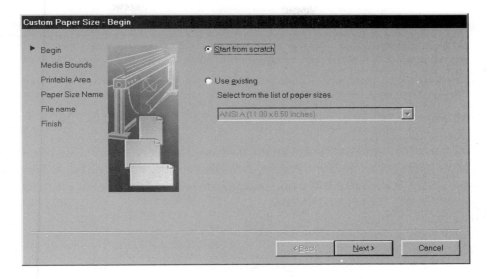

The Custom Paper Size wizard lets you set the sheet size and margin, as well as the paper source. This information is then saved in a PMP file. You are asked to provide a specific name for the custom paper size, which will be listed in the Custom Paper Size list box.

Once you've created a custom paper size, you can edit or delete it using the Edit or Delete buttons in the Custom Paper Size options

Modify Standard Paper Size   The last item in the Device and Document Settings list is the Modify Standard Paper Size option. If this option is available, it allows you to adjust the margins of a standard paper size.

NOTE   If you are using an older pen plotter, you will see the Physical Pen Configuration options in the Device and Document Settings list box. These additional options give you control over pen speed, pen optimization, and area fill correction.

Import, Save As, and Defaults

The Import, Save As, and Defaults buttons at the bottom of the Plot Configuration Editor let you import or save your plotter settings as PC3 files, which you will recall from the Plot Device tab of the Plot and Page Setup dialog box, as described earlier in this appendix. The Import button lets you import PCP and PC2 files from earlier versions of AutoCAD. Save As lets you save your current settings under an existing or new PC3 file name. The Defaults button restores the default settings, if any, for the current plotter configuration.

Fine-Tuning PostScript File Export

AutoCAD provides the PostScript user with a great deal of control over the formatting of the PostScript file that is output with the File ➤ Export and the Psout command. The options range from font-substitution mapping to custom PostScript Prologue data.

However, AutoCAD does require you to master the PostScript programming language to take full advantage of AutoCAD PostScript output. Most of this control is offered through a file named Acad.psf. This is the master support file for the Psin and Psout commands. You can customize the PostScript file created by Psout by making changes in the Acad.psf file. Acad.psf is divided into sections that affect various parts of the PostScript output. Each section begins with a title preceded by an asterisk. The following briefly describes these sections:

*fonts   Lets you control font substitution. You can assign a PostScript font to an AutoCAD font file or PostScript .PFB file used in the drawing.

*figureprologue   Defines the procedures used for embedding figures included with Psin PostScript images.

*isofontprologue   Defines the procedures used to re-encode fonts in order to be compatible with the ISO 8859 Latin/1 character set.

*fillprologue   Defines the code used in the Psout file to describe area fills.

*fill   Is a section where you can include your own custom fill patterns.

Most of these sections, with the exception of the *fonts section, will be of little use to the average user; but if you are a PostScript programmer, you can take advantage of these sections to customize your PostScript output.

You will also want to know about the Psprolog system variable. This system variable instructs Psout to include your custom prolog statement in its PostScript output. (See Chapter 14 for details on using Psout.) You add your custom prolog to the Acad.psf file using a text editor. The prolog should begin with a section heading that you devise. The heading can say anything, but it must begin with an asterisk like all the other section headings. Everything following the heading, up to the next heading or the end of the file, and excluding comments, will be included in the Psout output file. The following shows a sample prolog that converts color assignments to line widths in a way similar to pen plotters:

```
*widthprolog
/ACADLayer { pop } def
/ACADColor { pop pop pop dup 0.5 mul setlinewidth pop} def
/ACADLtype { pop
userdict /Linedict known not { /Linedict 100 dict def } if
1 index cvn Linedict exch known not {
mark 1 index { dup 0 eq { pop 1 72.0 div } if abs } forall
counttomark 2 add ~-1 roll astore exch pop
1 index cvn exch Linedict begin def end }
{ pop } ifelse
Linedict begin cvx exec 0 setdash end } bind def
/bd{bind def}bind def /m{moveto}bd /l{lineto}bd /s{stroke}bd
/a{arc}bd /an{arcn}bd /gs{gsave}bd /gr{grestore}bd
/cp{closepath}bd /tr{translate}bd /sc{scale}bd /co{concat}bd
/ff{findfont}bd /sf{setfont}bd /sh{show}bd /np{newpath}bd
/sw{setlinewidth}bd /sj{setlinejoin}bd /sm{setmiterlimit}bd /cl{clip}bd
/fi{fill}bd
%%EndProlog
```

A complete discussion of Psout and Psin's PostScript support is beyond the scope of this book. If you are interested in learning more, consult the PostScript section of the *AutoCAD Customization* manual. You can also learn a lot by looking at the Post-Script files produced by Psout, browsing the Acad.psf file, and consulting the following publications:

- *Understanding PostScript* by David Holzgang (Sybex, 1992)

- *PostScript Language Program Design* by Adobe Systems Incorporated (Addison-Wesley Publishing Company, Inc., 1990)

- *PostScript Language Reference Manual* by Adobe Systems Incorporated (Addison-Wesley Publishing Company, Inc., 1991)

- *PostScript Language Tutorial and Cookbook* by Adobe Systems Incorporated (Addison-Wesley Publishing Company, Inc., 1989)

You can also add a PostScript plotter to the plotter configuration. When you do this, AutoCAD plots the drawing as a series of vectors, just like any other plotter. If you have any filled areas in your drawing and you are plotting to a PostScript file, the vectors that are used to plot those filled areas can greatly increase plot-file size and the time it takes to plot your PostScript file.

Memory and AutoCAD Performance

Next to your computer's CPU, memory has the greatest impact on AutoCAD's speed. How much you have, and how you use it, can make a big difference in whether you finish that rush job on schedule or work late nights trying. This section will clarify some basic points about memory and how AutoCAD uses it.

AutoCAD 2000 is a virtual memory system. This means that when your RAM memory resources reach their limit, part of the data stored in RAM is temporarily moved to your hard disk to make more room in RAM. This temporary storage of RAM to your hard disk is called *memory paging*. Through memory paging, Auto-CAD will continue to run, even though your work might exceed the capacity of your RAM.

AutoCAD uses memory in two ways. First, it stores its program code in RAM. The more programs you have open under Windows, the more RAM will be used. Windows controls the use of memory for program code, so if you start to reach the RAM limit, Windows will take care of memory paging. The second way Auto-CAD uses memory is for storing drawing data. AutoCAD always attempts to store as much of your drawing in RAM as possible. Again, when the amount of RAM required for a drawing exceeds the actual RAM available, AutoCAD will page parts of the drawing data to the hard disk. The paging of drawing data is controlled strictly by AutoCAD. Since RAM is shared with both program code and drawing data, your drawing size, the number of files you have open in Auto-CAD, and the number of programs you have open under Windows will affect how much RAM you have available. For this reason, if you find your AutoCAD editing session is slowing down, try closing other applications you might have open or close files that you are no longer using. This will free up more memory for AutoCAD and the drawing file.

AutoCAD and Your Hard Disk

You will notice that AutoCAD will slow down when paging occurs. If this happens frequently, the best thing you can do is add more RAM. But you can also improve the performance of AutoCAD under these conditions by ensuring that you have adequate hard-disk space and that any free hard-disk space has been *defragmented* or *optimized*. A defragmented disk will offer faster access, thereby improving paging speed.

With previous versions of Windows, you were recommended to set up a permanent swap file. With Windows 95/98 or Windows NT, this is not necessary. Windows dynamically allocates swap-file space. However, you should make sure that there is enough free space on your hard disk to allow Windows to set up the space. A good guideline is to allow enough space for a swap file that is four times the size of your RAM capacity. If you have 32MB of RAM you need to allow space for a 128MB swap file (at a minimum). This will give your system 128MB of virtual memory.

What to Do for "Out of RAM" and "Out of Page Space" Errors

After you have used AutoCAD for some time, you may find some odd-looking files with an .ac$ extension in the \Windows\Temp\ directory. These files are the temporary files for storing unused portions of a drawing. They often appear if AutoCAD has been terminated abnormally. You can usually erase these files without any adverse effect.

If you've discarded all the old swap files and your disk is still unusually full, there may be some lost file clusters filling up your hard disk. Lost clusters are pieces of files that are not actually assigned to a specific file. Often they crop up when a program has terminated abnormally. To eliminate them and free up the disk space they're using, exit AutoCAD and run ScanDisk, which is a standard Windows accessory.

Finally, if you are not in the habit of emptying your Recycle bin, you should do so now. Every file that you "delete" using the Windows Explorer is actually passed to the Recycle bin. You need to clear this out regularly. If you are regular Internet user, check your Internet cache directory for unnecessary files.

AutoCAD Tools to Improve Memory Use

AutoCAD 2000 offers some tools to help make your use of system memory more efficient. Partial Open and the Spacial and Layer indexes let you manage the memory use of large drawings and multiple open files by reducing the amount of a file that is loaded into memory. Using these tools, you can have AutoCAD open only those portions of a file that you want to work on.

Using Partial Open to Conserve Memory and Improve Speed

Use the Partial Open option in the File dialog box when you know you are only going to work on a small portion or particular set of layers of a large drawing. Choose File ➢ Open, locate and select the file you want to open, then click the Partial Open button.

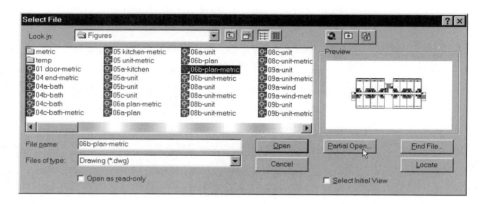

When you click this button, you see the Partial Open dialog box.

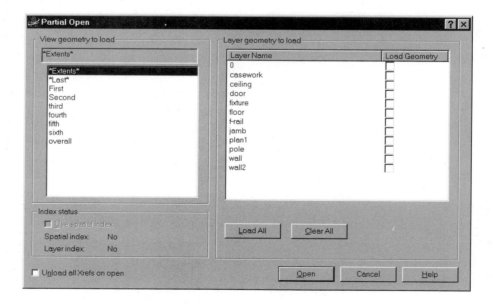

You can use this dialog box to open specific views of your drawing by selecting the view name from the View Geometry to Load list box. Only the geometry displayed in the selected view will be loaded into memory. This does not limit you to only that view as you edit the drawing. Subsequent views will cause AutoCAD to load the geometry of those views as needed.

You can further limit the amount of a drawing that is loaded into memory by selecting only those layers you want to work. Place a check next to the layers you want in the Layer Geometry to Load list box.

Once a file is opened using the Partial Open option, you can always make further adjustments by choosing File ➢ Partial Load. This opens the Partial Load dialog box, which offers the same options as the Partial Open dialog box. The Partial Load dialog box is not available for files that are opened normally without using the Partial Open option.

Using Spatial and Layer Indexes to Conserve Memory

The Spatial and Layer indexes are lists that keep a record of geometry in a drawing. A Spatial index lists a drawing's geometry according to the geometry's location in space. A Layer index lists the drawing's geometry according to layer assignments. These indexes offer more efficient memory use and faster loading times for drawings that are being used as Xrefs. These indexes take effect only when Demand Load is turned on (see *Controlling Xref Settings in the Options Dialog Box* in Chapter 6 for more on Demand Load). The Layer index allows AutoCAD to load only those layers of an Xref that are not frozen. AutoCAD uses the Spatial index to load only objects in an Xref that are within the boundary of a clipped Xref.

You can turn on the Spatial and Layer indexes for a file through the Indexctl system variable. Indexctl has four settings:

- A 0 setting is the default. This turns off Spatial and Layer indexing.

- A setting of 1 turns on Layer indexing

- A setting of 2 turns on Spatial indexing.

- A setting of 3 turns on both Layer and Spatial indexing.

To use the Indexctl system variable, type **Indexctl**↵ then at the `Enter new value for INDEXCTL <0>:` prompt, enter the number of the setting option you want to use.

> **NOTE**
>
> The Partial Open option in the File dialog box includes the Index Status button group, which offers information on the index status of a drawing. If the drawing you're opening has the Spatial or Layer indexing turned on, you can use it by checking the Spatial Index check box.

Using the Incremental Save Percentage to Conserve Disk Space

If your disk is getting crowded and you need to squeeze as many files as you can onto it, you can reduce the amount of wasted space in a file by adjusting the Incremental Save value in the Open and Save tab of the Options dialog box. By setting the Incremental Save value to a lower value, you can reduce the size of files to some degree. The tradeoff is slower performance when saving files. See *Open and Save Tab* in Appendix B for more information on this setting.

Another related option is to turn off the .bak file option, also located in the Open and Save tab of the Options dialog box. Each time you use File ➤ Save or File ➤ Save As, AutoCAD creates a backup copy of your file with the .bak file extension. By turning the Create Backup Copy with Each Save option, .bak files are not created, thereby saving disk space. This option is also found in the Open and Save tab of the Options dialog box.

When Things Go Wrong

AutoCAD is a complex program, and at times things don't go exactly right. If you run into problems, chances are they won't be insurmountable. Here are a few tips on what to do when things don't work.

Difficulty Starting Up or Opening a File

The most common reason why you'll have difficulty opening a file is a lack of free disk space. If you encounter errors attempting to open files, check to see if you have adequate free disk space on all your drives.

If you've recently installed AutoCAD but you cannot get it started, you may have a configuration problem. Before you panic, try reinstalling AutoCAD from scratch. Particularly if you are installing the CD-ROM version, this does not take long (see Appendix B for installation instructions). Before you reinstall AutoCAD, use the Uninstall program to remove the current version of AutoCAD first. Also make sure you have your authorization code, serial number, and CD-Key handy. Make sure that you've closed all other programs when you run the AutoCAD installation. As a final measure, restart your computer when you've completed the installation.

Restoring Corrupted Files

Hardware failures can result in data files becoming corrupted. When this happens, AutoCAD is unable to open the drawing file. Fortunately, there is hope for damaged files. In most cases, AutoCAD will run through a file-recovery routine automatically when it attempts to load a corrupted file. If you have a file you know is corrupted, you can start the file-recovery utility by choosing File ➢ Drawing Utilities ➢ Recover. This opens the Select File dialog box, allowing you to select the file you want to recover. Once you enter the name, AutoCAD goes to work. You get a series of messages, most of which have little meaning to the average user. Then the recovered file is opened. You may lose some data, but a partial file is better than no file at all, especially when the file represents several days of work.

Another possibility is to attempt to recover your drawing from the .bak file—the last saved version before your drawing was corrupted. Rename the drawing .bak file to a .dwg file with a different name, and then open it up. The drawing will contain only what was in your drawing when it was previously saved.

If you want to restore a file that you've just been working on, you can check the file named `Auto.sv$`. This is the file AutoCAD uses to store your drawing during automatic saves. Change the .sv$ filename extension to .dwg, and then open the file.

There may be situations when a file is so badly corrupted it cannot be restored. By backing up frequently, the inconvenience of such an occurrence can be minimized. You may also want to consider the Microsoft Office Plus package, which allows you to schedule backups and scan and defragment your drives during off hours. Programs such as ScanDisk can spot problem areas on your hard disk before they cause trouble.

Troubleshooting

AutoCAD is a large, complex program, so you are bound to encounter some difficulties from time to time. This section covers a few of the more common problems experienced while using AutoCAD.

You can see but cannot select objects in a drawing someone else has worked on.

This may be happening because you have a Paper Space view instead of a Model Space view. To make sure you're in Model Space, type **Tilemode**↵, and then type **1**↵. Or you can turn on the UCS icon (by typing **Ucsicon**↵ **On**↵. If you see the triangular UCS icon in the lower-left corner, then you are in Paper Space. You must go to Model Space before you can edit the drawing.

Another item to check is the layer lock setting. If a layer is locked, you won't be able to edit objects on that layer.

Grips do not appear when objects are selected.

Make sure the Grips feature is enabled (Tools ➤ Grips). See Appendix B for details.

When you select objects, it doesn't work the way it appears in this book.

Check the Selection settings to make sure they are set the same way as the exercise specifies (Tools ➤ Selection). See Chapter 2 for details.

Text appears in the wrong font style, or an error message says AutoCAD cannot find font files.

When you are working on files from another company, it's not uncommon that you will encounter a file that uses special third-party fonts that you do not have. You can usually substitute standard AutoCAD fonts for any fonts you don't have without adverse effects. AutoCAD automatically presents a dialog box that lets you select font files for the substitution. You can either choose a font file or press the Esc key to ignore the message. (See Chapter 8 for more on font files.) If you choose to ignore the error message, you may not see some of the text that would normally appear in the drawing.

You can't import DXF files.

Various problems can occur during the DXF import, the most common of which is that you are trying to import a DXF file into an existing drawing rather than a new drawing. Under some conditions, you can import a DXF file into an existing drawing using the Dxfin command, but AutoCAD may not import the entire file.

To ensure that your entire DXF file is safely imported, choose File ➤ Open and select *.DXF from the File Type pull-down list. Then import your DXF file.

If you know the .DXF file you are trying to import is in the ASCII format and not a Binary .DXF, take a look at the file with a text editor. If it contains odd-looking lines of characters, chances are the file is damaged or contains extra data that AutoCAD cannot understand. Try deleting the odd-looking lines of characters, and then import the file again (make a backup copy of the file before you attempt this).

A file cannot be saved to disk.

Frequently, a hard drive will fill up quickly during an edit session. AutoCAD can generate temporary and swap files many times larger than the file you are editing. This might leave you with no room left to save your file. If this happens, you can empty the Recycle Bin to clear some space on your hard drive, or delete old Auto-CAD .bak files you don't need. *Do not delete temporary AutoCAD files.*

AutoCAD does not display all the Paper Space viewports.

AutoCAD uses substantial memory to display Paper Space viewports. For this reason, it limits the number of viewports it will display at one time. Even though viewports don't display, they will still plot. Also, if you zoom in on a blank viewport while in Paper Space, you will be able to see its contents. The viewport regains visibility because you are reducing the number of viewports shown on the screen at one time.

You can increase the number of viewports AutoCAD will display at one time by resetting the Maxactvp system variable. (This is usually set to 48.) Be forewarned, however, that increasing the Maxactvp setting will cause AutoCAD to use more memory. If you have limited memory on your system, this will slow down Auto-CAD considerably.

AutoCAD becomes impossibly slow when adding more Paper Space viewports.

As mentioned for the preceding problem, AutoCAD consumes memory quickly when adding viewports. If your system resources are limited, you can reduce the Maxactvp system variable setting so that AutoCAD displays fewer viewports at one time. This will let you work on a file that has numerous viewports without causing a decrease in your computer's performance. Try reducing Maxactvp to 8, and then reduce or increase the setting until you find the optimum value for your situation. Alternatively, you can use the Mview OFF option to turn off viewports when you are not working in them.

AutoCAD won't open a large file and displays a "Page File Full" message.

AutoCAD will open drawing files larger than can fit into your system's RAM. In order to do this, however, AutoCAD attempts to store part of the drawing in a temporary file on your hard drive. If there isn't room on the hard drive, AutoCAD will give up. To remedy this problem, clear some space on your hard drive. It is not uncommon for AutoCAD to require as much as 10MB of hard-disk space for every 1MB of a drawing file.

The keyboard shortcuts for commands are not working.

If you are working on an unfamiliar computer, chances are the keyboard shortcuts (or command aliases) have been altered. The command aliases are stored in the Acad.pgp file. If you have installed the AutoCAD 2000 Express Menu (see Appendix B for installation instructions), you can modify the keyboard shortcuts by using the Command Alias Editor option on the Express menu. Choose Express ➤ Tools ➤ Command Alias Editor, or type **aliasedit** at the command prompt. Then you may add, remove, or edit the keyboard shortcut codes. See Chapter 19 for more information on the Alias Editor.

Plots come out blank.

Check the scale factor you are using for your plot. Often, a blank plot means your scale factor is making the plot too large to fit on the sheet. Try plotting with the Scale to Fit option. If you get a plot, then you know your scale factor is incorrect. See Chapter 7 for more on plotting options. Check your output before you plot by using the Full Preview option in the Plot Configuration dialog box.

You cannot get your drawing to be properly oriented on the sheet.

If you want to change the orientation of your drawing on a plotted sheet, and the Plot Configuration orientation options don't seem to work, try rotating the UCS to align with your desired plot view, and then type **Plan.⌡**. Adjust the view to display what you want to have plotted, and then use the View command (View ➤ Named Views) to save this view. When you are ready to plot, use the View option in the Plot Configuration dialog box and plot the saved view, instead of rotating the plot.

Dimensions appear as lines and text and do not act the way the are described in this book.

The Dimaso system variable is off, or was turned off when the dimension was created. Another possibility is that the dimension was reduced to its component objects using the Explode command. Make sure Dimaso is on by typing **Dimaso**↵ **on**↵. Unfortunately, an exploded dimension or one that was created with Dimaso turned off cannot be converted to a true dimension object. You must redraw the dimension.

A file containing Xref appears to be blank or parts are missing.

AutoCAD cannot find the Xref file. Use the External Reference dialog box (Insert ➣ External Reference) to reestablish connection with the Xref file. Once the External Reference dialog box is open, select the missing Xref from the list, and then click the Browse button and locate and select the file using the Browse dialog box.

As you draw, little marks appear on your screen where you have selected points.

The Blipmode system variable is on. Turn it off by typing **Blipmode**↵ **off**↵.

When you attempt to open a text file to extract attributes, you see an error message.

There are two possible sources of this problem. The first is that you did not save your attribute template file as a plain ASCII text file. You can do so in most word processors, including WordPad, by choosing File ➣ Save As, and then selecting the Text Document option from the Save as Type drop-down list. To ensure that you are creating a plain ASCII text file, you can use the Windows Notepad application to create your attribute templates.

The second possible problem is that you did not place a ↵ at the end of the last line of text in your attribute template file.

A file you want to open is read-only, even though you know no one else on the network is using the file.

Every now and then, you may receive a file that you cannot edit because it is read-only. This frequently happens with files that have been archived to a CD-ROM. If you have a file that is read-only, try the following:

1. Locate the read-only file with Windows Explorer, then right-click the filename.

2. Select Properties from the popup menu.

3. At the Properties dialog box, select the General tab.

4. At the bottom of the Properties dialog box, click the Read-Only check box to remove the check for that option.

Tracking vectors do not appear in the drawing as described in this book.

Make sure that the AutoTrack features are turned on. See the discussion of the Drafting tab of the Options dialog box in Appendix B in the section *Configuring AutoCAD*.

The Hyperlink icon does not appear as described in Chapter 24.

Make sure the Hyperlink options are turned on in the User Preferences tab of the Options dialog box.

When you open new files, the drawing area is not the same as described in this book.

Make sure you're using the correct default unit style for new drawings. At the Create New Drawing dialog box, click the Start from Scratch button, then select the appropriate unit style from the Default Settings button group. If you are using feet and inches, select English (feet and inches). If you are using metric measurements, select Metric. AutoCAD will use the `Acad.dwt` file template for new English measurement drawings and the `Acadiso.dwt` template for metric measurement drawings. You can also use the Measureinit system variable to set the default unit style.

When you offset polylines, such as rectangles or polygons, the offset object has extra line segments or rounded corners.

Set the Offsetgap system variable to 0. Offsetgap controls the behavior of the line segments of offset polylines. When set to 0, the individual line segments of a polyline are extended to join end to end. If it is set to 1, the line segments remain their original length and are joined with an arc. If set to 2, the line segments remain their original length and are joined by a straight-line segment.

The `Slidelib.exe` DOS tool doesn't seem to work.

`Slidelib.exe` is a DOS application, so it needs all of its files and resources in the same directory where it resides; or you can set a DOS path to those resources. Setting a DOS path is a bit too involved to explain here. To simplify things, make sure your slide files and your text file containing the list of slides are in the same directory as `Slidelib.exe`. If you prefer, you may move `Slidelib.exe` to the location of your slides and slide list.

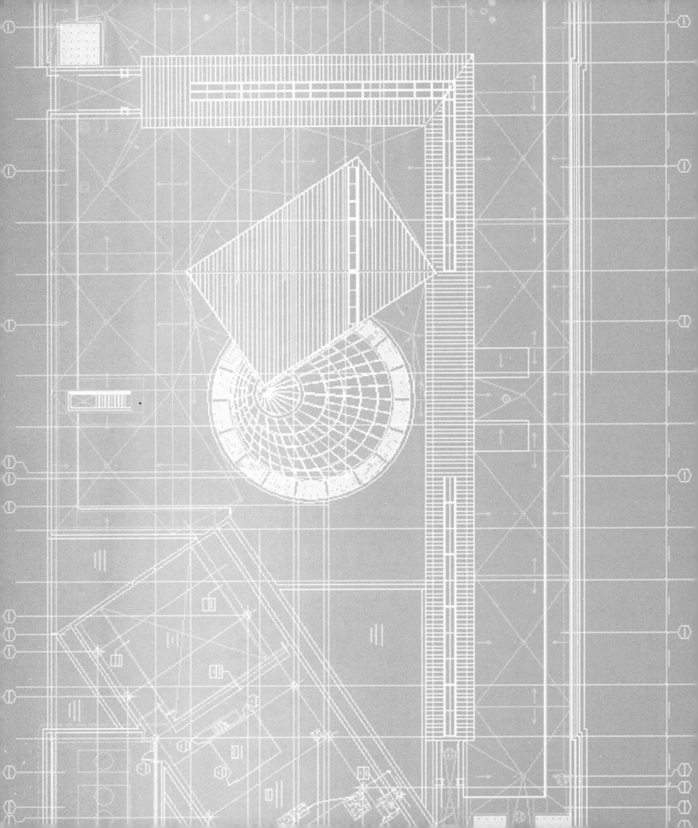

Installing and Setting Up AutoCAD

This appendix gives you information on installing AutoCAD 2000 on your system and describes the system parameters that you will want to set to configure AutoCAD to meet the needs of your operating environment. Throughout this appendix, the system variable associated with a setting, when available, is included at the end of an option description, enclosed in brackets. System variables are settings that allow you to control the AutoCAD's behavior when using commands and features. You'll find a detailed description of the AutoCAD system variables in Appendix D.

Before Installing AutoCAD

Before you begin the installation process, be sure you have a drive with at least 100MB of free disk space. In addition, you should know your AutoCAD vendor's name and phone number.

You will also want to have at least an additional 50MB of free disk space for Auto-CAD *temporary files* and *swap files*, plus another 20MB for the tutorial files you will create. (Temporary and swap files are system files AutoCAD creates as it works. You don't have to deal with these files directly, but you do have to allow room for them. If you want to know more about these files, see Appendix A.) If you are installing AutoCAD on a drive other than the one on which Windows is installed, make sure you have about 50MB free on the Windows drive. AutoCAD also stores temporary files there.

Finally, have your AutoCAD vendor's name and phone number ready. You will be asked to enter this information during the installation. You will also want to have your network and single-user authorization code ready. These can be obtained by calling the toll-free number listed in your AutoCAD package. Single-user systems have a 30-day grace period, so you can install and use AutoCAD without having to enter your authorization code right away.

Installing the AutoCAD Software

After you've made sure you have enough disk space and you've closed all other programs, proceed with the following steps to install AutoCAD:

1. To begin your installation, be sure the AutoCAD CD-ROM is in your CD-ROM drive.

2. If the AutoCAD 2000 Master Setup does not automatically start, click the Windows Start button and choose Run.

3. At the Run dialog box, enter **D:setup** in the input box. Enter the drive letter of your CD-ROM in place of the **D** in this example. Click OK when you are ready. You see the AutoCAD 2000 Master Setup dialog box warning you to make sure all other programs are closed. Click OK to continue.

4. The Welcome dialog box appears, asking you to be sure you have closed all other applications. Do so, then click Next.

5. The next dialog box is the Software License Agreement. Read it. If you accept the terms, select your home country from the Select Your Country of Residence drop-down list, then click I Accept. The Next> button becomes available. Go ahead and click Next.

6. In the Serial Number dialog box, enter the serial number and CD Key, and then click Next.

7. Next, you see the Personal Information dialog box. To personalize AutoCAD, you are asked for your name, company, and AutoCAD vendor's name and telephone number. This information will be displayed on the opening Auto-CAD screen, so don't enter anything you'll regret later.

8. You are then asked to confirm the information you entered. If you changed your mind, you can go back and change the information in the previous dialog box. Otherwise, click Next.

9. Select the location for your AutoCAD files. The tutorial assumes you have AutoCAD on drive C and in a folder called \Program Files\AutoCAD2000\— these are the defaults during the installation. When you're done, click Next. If the installation location does not exist, you will see a message to this effect and asking if it is OK for the Installer to create it. Click OK.

10. In the next dialog box, choose the type of setup you want. You have the choice of Typical, Full, Compact, or Custom. I encourage you to choose the Full installation, as this will enable you to take advantage of the Express utilities discussed in Chapter 19. When you are done, click Next.

11. The installation will create a program folder with a set of AutoCAD-related programs and documents. Enter a name for this folder in the next dialog box or choose to accept the default folder name, AutoCAD 2000. Once you've selected a program folder name, click Next.

12. At the Assign an Editor for Textbased Files dialog box, you can determine the text editor AutoCAD will use whenever you attempt to edit any of AutoCAD's customizable files. The default is the Windows Notepad application, which is usually adequate for most applications. Click Next after you've selected a text editor.

13. You finally get a Setup Confirmation dialog box showing you a listing of program components the Installation will install. Click Next to begin the actual file installation. This can take several minutes.

14. Once the installation is done, you will see the AutoCAD 2000 Setup dialog box asking you if you want to restart your computer. Go ahead and click OK to do that now. It's usually better to restart your computer immediately after installing AutoCAD, if it requests that you do so. Remove your AutoCAD CD-ROM from your computer; otherwise, you may see the AutoCAD installation dialog box again when you restart your system.

Once you've installed AutoCAD, you'll have to obtain an authorization code.

1. Start AutoCAD by double-clicking the AutoCAD 2000 shortcut on the Windows Desktop.

2. You will then see a message telling you that you have 30 days to authorize your copy of AutoCAD. You will also have a choice to authorize AutoCAD 2000 now or defer authorization and open AutoCAD.

3. If you choose to authorize AutoCAD and click Next, you'll see the Authorization wizard begin page. Here you can select the method of authorization. You can also tell AutoCAD if you are an individual user or a member of a company that has purchased AutoCAD. If you are connected to the Internet, choose World Wide Web for the authorization method. The World Wide Web option offers the quickest way to obtain the authorization code.

4. Click Next. You'll see the Codes page of the Authorization wizard. If you are upgrading to AutoCAD 2000, enter your previous serial number in the space provided. Select your country, then click Next.

5. For the next several pages of the Authorization wizard, you will be asked questions about your use of AutoCAD. Once you are done, you will be connected to the AutoCAD Web site and then given an authorization code. Once you have the code, the next time you start AutoCAD choose Authorize again, select Already Have an Authorization Code in the Authorization wizard begin page, and then enter the number in the space provided.

Installing Other AutoCAD Components

If you didn't install some of the AutoCAD components, like the Express tools or the database tools, and you would like to install them, take the following steps:

1. Place your AutoCAD 2000 CD-ROM in your computer's CD-ROM drive.

2. Click Start ➤ Run.

3. At the Run dialog box, enter **D:setup**, where **D** is the drive letter of your CD-ROM drive.

4. Click OK.

5. Click Next at the Welcome dialog box.

6. At the Setup Choices dialog box, click Add.

7. At the Custom Components dialog box, select the items you want to install from the list of components. When you have completed your selection, click Next.

8. You may be asked if you want to select an editor for text-based files. Select one, then click Next.

9. You see the Setup Confirmation dialog box just as you did when you initially installed AutoCAD. Click Next. AutoCAD will begin the installation.

10. Click OK if you are asked to restart your computer.

After AutoCad 2000 is installed, you have the option to install the AutoCad 2000 Migration Assistance. For more information, read the following section.

The AutoCAD 2000 Migration Assistance

AutoCAD 2000 offers many new features to make your work easier and more efficient. But upgrading to a new version of AutoCAD can cause a number of problems from file version conflicts to customization retooling. The AutoCAD 2000 Migration Assistance is a suite of utilities designed to help make your upgrade to AutoCAD 2000 as painless as possible. The following list describes the utilities available from the Migration Assistance:

Batch Drawing Converter   Lets you convert a set of drawings from one version to another. For example, you can convert a whole directory of drawing files from Release 14 to AutoCAD 2000, including plotter line width settings, using this tool. Or you can convert a set of files back to Release 12 to send to clients or associates who need files in that format.

AutoLISP Compatibility Analyzer   Lets you examine your custom AutoLISP applications for compatibility with AutoCAD 2000. This utility scans your AutoLISP code and locates specific items that need to be updated. It even offers suggestions for those updates. You can then make the changes on the spot.

Menu and Toolbar Porter   Gives you an easy way to move your custom menus and toolbars from previous versions of AutoCAD to AutoCAD 2000. This tool can save you hours of re-editing AutoCAD menu files to preserve your custom applications.

Command Alias (PGP) Porter   Gives you an easy way to move your custom keyboard shortcuts from earlier versions of AutoCAD to AutoCAD 2000. Just as with the Menu and Toolbar Porter, the Command Alias Porter makes quick work of what would otherwise be a tedious, time-consuming process.

Color to Name Tool   Solves the problem of having to choose between color plot styles and named plot styles. If you imported an earlier version of a drawing to AutoCAD 2000 using a color plot style, but you decide later to change the plot style of the file to a named plot style, this tool lets you perform the conversion. See Chapter 7 for a detailed description of plot styles.

Network Deployment Tool   This tool is a 30-day trial edition of Lanovation's PictureTaker. This program allows you to automatically install and configure multiple AutoCAD configurations over a network.

Serial Number Harvester   Lets you keep track of multiple AutoCAD serial numbers over a network. It helps you with installation and authorization of multiple seats of AutoCAD.

ScriptPro   This is a handy utility that lets you apply a script to a set of files. You only need to write the script once, then load it into ScriptPro. ScriptPro takes care of opening and closing the drawing files and applying the script to the files you select. This is one tool you'll find useful, regardless of whether you are migrating up to AutoCAD 2000 or just starting out with AutoCAD. See Chapter 15 for more on scripts.

Compatibility Information   This is a Web document designed to help CAD managers with migration issues.

Installing the AutoCAD Migration Assistance

At the end of the AutoCAD 2000 installation, you have the option to install the Migration Assistance. You can go ahead and install it, or you can exit the Installer and install the Migration Assistance at a later time. To install the Migration Assistance separate from the main AutoCAD installation, take the following steps:

1. Click Start ➤ Run.

2. At the Run dialog box, enter **D:msetup,** where **D** is the drive letter of your CD-ROM drive.

3. Click OK.

4. At the AutoCAD 2000 Master Setup dialog box, select Install the AutoCAD 2000 Migration Assistance, then click OK.

5. At the Welcome screen, click Next.

6. At the Choose Destination Location dialog box, select a location for the Migration Assistance, then click Next.

7. At the Select Program Folder dialog box, select a program folder, then click Next.

8. You are asked to confirm the location for the Migration Assistance. Click Yes. AutoCAD will proceed to install the Migration Assistance.

9. The AutoCAD Migration Assistance installation will begin to install a program called ScriptPro. Click Next.

10. Click Yes at the Software License Agreement dialog box.

11. At the Check Setup Information dialog box, check the information, then click Next. ScriptPro will be installed.

12. When the installation is complete, you'll see a message informing you that you can run ScriptPro batch projects by typing **ScriptPro** at the AutoCAD command prompt. Click OK to finish.

The utilities offered by the AutoCAD 2000 Migration Assistance are for intermediate to advanced users and are aimed primarily at those responsible for managing a large number of AutoCAD seats. Some of the tools are useful to individual users as well. The utilities are fairly easy to use so this book doesn't go into the details of how to use each one. You'll want to explore the Batch Drawing Converter and the ScriptPro utility regardless of the size of your office. If you do a lot of customization, you'll also want to check out the AutoLISP Compatibility Analyzer, the Menu and Toolbar Porter, and the Command Alias Porter.

The Program Files

The \Program Files\AutoCAD2000\ folder contains a number of other folders.

This book's tutorial assumes you are working from the directory where the program files are stored. However, if you prefer to work from a different directory, be sure you have set a path for the AutoCAD directory; otherwise, AutoCAD will not start properly. Consult your DOS manual for more information on Path statements.

Here are brief descriptions of each subdirectory's contents:

Express   Contains the Express tools and samples described in Chapter 19. You won't see this directory unless you've installed the Express tools or performed the Full AutoCAD installation.

Data Links   Contains the Data Link files for AutoCAD's dbConnect feature.

Fonts   Contains AutoCAD fonts.

Help   Contains AutoCAD help documents.

Plot Styles   Contains the plot styles.

Plotters   Contains the plotter configuration files.

Sample   Contains sample drawing files, as well as sample ActiveX, DesignCenter, VBA, and VisualLISP files.

Support   Contains the files that define a variety of AutoCAD's functions for use with the DOS version of AutoCAD.

Template   Contains AutoCAD template files.

Textures   Contains texture files for AutoCAD's rendering feature.

Tutorial   Contains Autodesk's own sample tutorial files.

Configuring AutoCAD

In this section, you will learn how to *configure* AutoCAD. By configure, I mean to set up AutoCAD to work the way you want it to work. You can configure AutoCAD at any time during an AutoCAD session through the Options dialog box.

The tutorials in this book assume that you are using the default Options settings. As you become more familiar with the workings of AutoCAD, you may want to make adjustments to the way AutoCAD works using the Options dialog box. Many of the options in the Options dialog box can also be set through system variables.

This dialog box can be accessed by clicking on Tools ➤ Options. It is further divided into sections shown as tabs across the top of the dialog box. The following subsections describe the settings available on each of the tabs.

TIP   Many of the options you see in the Options dialog box show an AutoCAD file icon. This icon indicates that the option's setting is saved with the file, as opposed to being saved as part of AutoCAD's default settings.

Files

The Files tab is where you tell AutoCAD where to place or find files it needs to operate. It uses a hierarchical list, similar to the one presented by Windows Explorer. You first see the general topics listed in the Search Path, File Names, and File Location list boxes. You can expand individual items in the list by clicking the plus sign shown to the left of the item.

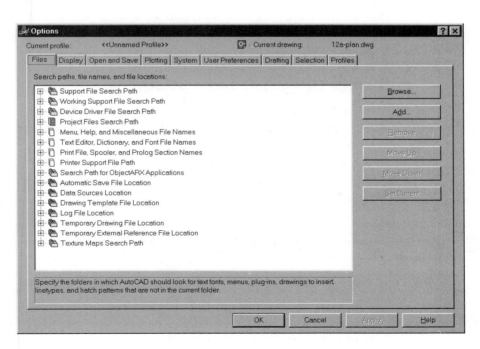

The following explanations describe what each item in the list box is for. Chances are you won't have to use most of them, while others you may change occasionally.

NOTE	The related system variable is shown in brackets at the end of the description of each item.

Support File Search Path

AutoCAD relies on external files for many of its functions. Menus, text fonts, line types, and hatch patterns are a few examples of features that rely on external files. The Support File Search Path item tells AutoCAD where to look for these files. You can add directory paths to this listing by clicking the Add button and entering a new path or using the Browse button. It's probably not a good idea to delete any of the existing items under this heading unless you really know what you are doing.

If you are familiar with using environment variables, you can include them in the search paths.

Working Support File Search Path

The Working Support File Search Path item contains a read-only list of the support file search path for the current session, including any special settings that may be included with command switches and environment settings.

Device Driver File Search Path

The Device Driver File Search Path item locates the device drivers for AutoCAD. Device drivers are applications that allow AutoCAD to communicate directly with the printers, plotters, and input devices. In most cases, you do not have to do anything with this setting.

Project Files Search Path

Eventually, you will receive files from a consultant or other AutoCAD user that are dependent on Xref or raster images. Often, such files will expect the Xref or raster image to be in a particular directory. When such files are moved to another location with a different directory system, Xref-dependent files will not be able to find their Xrefs. The Support File Search Path item allows you to specify a directory where Xrefs or other dependent files are stored. If AutoCAD is unable to find an Xref or other file, it will look in the directory you specify in this listing [Projectname].

To specify this directory, highlight Project File Search Path, and then click the Add button. AutoCAD suggests Project1 as the directory name. You can change the name if you prefer. Click the plus sign next to Project1, and then click Browse to select a location for your project file search path. The project file search path is stored in a system variable called Projectname.

Menu, Help, Log, and Miscellaneous File Names

This item lets you set the location of a variety of support files including menu, help, automatic save, log, and configuration files. It also lets you set the default Internet address for the Launch Browser button on the AutoCAD Standard toolbar. If you have a network installation, you can also set the License Manager location on your network.

Text Editor, Dictionary, and Font File Names

Use this item to set the location of the text editor [Mtexted], the Custom and Standard dictionaries [Dctmain, Dctust], and the alternate font and font mapping files [Fontalt]. Chapter 8 describes this item in more detail.

Print File, Spooler, and Prolog Section Names

You can specify a print filename other than the default that is supplied by AutoCAD whenever you plot to a file. The Spooler option lets you specify an application intended to read and plot a plot file. The Prolog option is intended for PostScript export. It lets you specify the Prolog section from the Acad.psf file that you want AutoCAD to include with exported Encapsulate PostScript files. See Appendix A and Chapter 14 for more information on exporting PostScript files and the Acad.psf file [Psprolog].

Print Support File Path

There are several support files associated with the AutoCAD printing and plotting system. This item allows you to indicate where you want AutoCAD to look for these files.

Search Path for ObjectARX Applications

If you have custom ObjectARX applications, you can tell AutoCAD where they are stored using this item. You can include multiple listings.

Automatic Save File Location

You can indicate the location for AutoCAD's Automatic Save file using this item [Savefilepath].

Data Source Location

This item lets you specify the location for ODBC Data Link files for linking Auto-CAD drawings to database files.

Drawing Template File Location

When you select the Use a Template option in the Create New Drawing dialog box, AutoCAD looks at this setting for the location of template files. You can modify this setting, but chances are you won't need to.

Log File Location

With this item you can indicate where log files are to be placed [Logfilepath].

Temporary Drawing File Location

AutoCAD creates temporary files to store portions of your drawings as you work on them. You usually don't have to think about these temporary files until they start crowding your hard disk, or if you are working on a particularly large file on a system with little memory. This item lets you set the location for temporary files. The default location is the \Windows\Temp\ directory. If you have a hard drive that has lots of room and is very fast, you may want to change this setting to a location on that drive to improve performance [Tempprefix, read-only].

Temporary External Reference File Location

If you are on a network and you foresee a situation where another user will want to open an Xref of a file you are working on, you can set the Demand Load setting in the Performance tab to Enable with Copy. This causes AutoCAD to make and use a copy of any Xref that is currently loaded. This way, the original file can be opened by others. The Temporary External Reference File Location lets you specify the directory where AutoCAD will store this copy of an Xref [Xloadpath].

Texture Maps Search Path

This item specifies the location for AutoCAD Render texture maps. In most cases, you won't have to change this setting. You can, however, add a directory name to this item for your own texture maps as you acquire or create them.

Display

The settings on this tab let you control the appearance of AutoCAD. You can make AutoCAD look completely different with these settings if you choose. Scroll bars, fonts, and colors are all up for grabs.

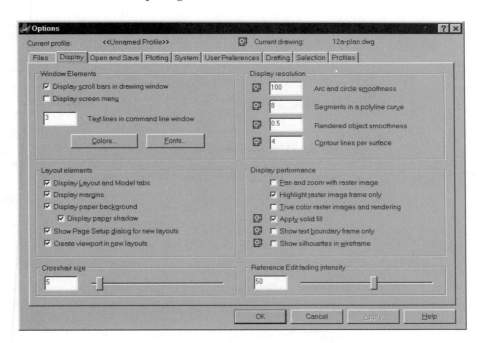

Window Elements

These options control the general settings for the AutoCAD windows:

Display Screen Menu Turns on the old AutoCAD format screen menu that once appeared on the right side of the screen. If you really must have it displayed, this is where you can turn it back on.

Display Scroll Bars in Drawing Window   Lets you turn the scroll bars on and off. If you've got a small monitor with low resolution, you may want to turn the scroll bars off for a larger drawing area.

Text Lines in Command Line Window   Lets you increase or decrease the number of text lines displayed. If you feel comfortable with AutoCAD and don't need to refer to the prompt too often, you may want to decrease this value to get a larger drawing area.

Colors   Opens a dialog box that lets you set the color for the various components of the AutoCAD window. This is where you can change the background color of the drawing area if you find that black doesn't work for you.

Fonts   Opens a dialog box that lets you set the fonts of the AutoCAD window. You can select from the standard set of Windows fonts available in your system.

Display Resolution

These options control the way different types of objects are displayed in AutoCAD. You can choose between display accuracy or speed.

Arc and Circle Smoothness   Controls the appearance of arcs and circles, particularly when you zoom in on them. In some instances, arc and circles will appear to be octagons, even though they will plot as smooth arcs and circles. If you want arcs and circles to appear smoother, you can increase this setting. An increase will also increase memory use. This setting is also controlled by the Viewres system variable [Viewres].

Segments in a Polyline Curve   Controls the smoothness of polyline curves. Increase the value to make curved polylines appear smoother and less segmented. Decrease the value for improved display performance. This option is also set by the Splinesegs system variable [Splinesegs].

Rendering Object Smoothness   Controls the smoothness of curved solids when they are rendered or shaded. Values can range from 0.01 to 10 [Facetres].

Contour Lines Per Surface   Lets you set the number of contour lines used to represent solid, curved surfaces. Values can range from 0 to 2047 [Isolines].

Layout Elements

These options control the display of elements in the Paper Space layout tabs. See Chapters 7 and 12 for more information.

Display Performance

You can adjust a variety of display-related settings from this group.

Pan and Zoom with Raster Image　Controls the way raster images react to realtime pans and zooms. If this option is checked, raster images move with the cursor. Turn this option off for better performance [Rtdisplay].

Highlight Raster Image Frame Only　Determines how raster images appear when selected. Turn this option on for better performance [Imagehlt].

True Color Raster Images and Rendering　Determines whether raster images and rendered images are displayed in true color. Turn this option off for better performance.

Apply Solid Fill　Controls the display of filled objects such as wide polylines and areas filled with the solid hatch pattern. This option is also controlled by the Fillmode system variable. See Chapter 14 for more information on filled polylines and the solid hatch pattern. Turn this option off for better performance [Fillmode].

Show Text Boundary Frame Only　Controls the way text is displayed. Turn this option on to display text as rectangular boundaries [Qtextmode].

Show Silhouettes in Wireframe　Controls whether surface meshes for solid models are displayed. Turn this option off for better performance [Dispsilh].

Crosshair Size

This slider controls the size of the crosshair cursor. You can set this to 100 percent to simulate the full-screen crosshair cursor of earlier versions of AutoCAD [Cursorsize].

Reference Fading Intensity

This slider controls the display of non-selected objects during in-place reference editing. See Chapter 6 for more information on in-place reference editing [Xfadectl].

Open and Save

The Open and Save tab offers general file-related options such as automatic save and the default file version for the Save and Save As options.

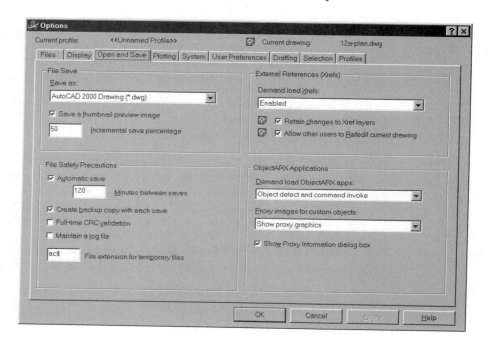

File Save

You can control how AutoCAD saves files by using the options in this group.

Save As   This drop-down list lets you set the default file type for the File ➤ Save and File ➤ Save As options. If you are working in an environment that requires Release 14 files as the standard file type, you can use this option to select Release 14 as the default file type. You can also set up AutoCAD to save DXF files by default.

Save a Thumbnail Preview Image   Lets you determine whether a preview image is saved with a drawing. Preview images are used in the AutoCAD

File dialog box and the DesignCenter to let you preview a file before opening it [Rasterpreview].

Incremental Save Percentage   Controls the degree to which the incremental save feature is used whenever you use the File ➢ Save or File ➢ Save As options. An incremental save improves the time it takes to save a file to disk, but it also makes the file size larger. If you have limited disk space, you can set this value to 25. A value of 0 turns off incremental save altogether, but will reduce AutoCAD performance. This option is also controlled through the Isavepercent system variable [Isavepercent].

External Reference

These options let you control memory and layer features of Xrefs.

Demand Load Xrefs   Lets you turn on the Demand Load feature of Xrefs. Demand Load helps to improve the performance of files that use Xrefs by loading only those portions of an Xref drawing that are required for the current open drawing. This option is a drop-down list with three options: Disabled turns off demand loading, Enable turns demand loading on, and Enabled with Copy turns on demand loading using a copy of the Xref source file. This last option allows others on a network to edit the Xref source file while you're working on a file that also uses the file [Xloadctl].

Retain Changes to Xref Layers   Lets you save layer settings of Xref files in the current drawing. This does not affect the source Xref file. With this setting turned off, the current file will import the layer settings of the Xref file when it loads the Xref file. This setting is also set by the Visretain system variable [Visretain].

Allow Other Users to Refedit Current Drawings   Lets you determine whether others can simultaneously edit a file that you are editing. This option is intended to allow others use the Modify ➢ In-Place Xref and Block Editing option (the Refedit command) on files that you currently have loaded in AutoCAD [Xedit].

File Safety Precautions

These options control the automatic backup features of AutoCAD.

Automatic Save   Offers control over the Automatic Save features. You can turn it on or off using the check box or set the frequency at which files are saved using the Minutes Between Saves input box. You can set the location for the automatic save files using the Automatic Save File Location listing in the Files tab of the Options dialog box. You can also set the frequency of automatic save through the Savetime system variable [Savefilepath, Savefile].

Create Backup Copy with Each Save   Lets you determine whether a .bak file is saved along with every save you perform. You may turn this option off to conserve disk space. You can also use the Isavebak system variable to turn this option on or off [Isavebak, Tempprefix].

Full-Time CRC Validation   Controls the cyclic redundancy check feature which checks for file errors whenever a file is read by AutoCAD. This feature is helpful in troubleshooting hardware problems in your system.

Maintain a Log File   Lets you record the data in the AutoCAD text window. See Chapter 14 for more on this feature. You can set the location for log files in the Files tab of the Options dialog box [Logfilemode, Logfilename].

File Extension for Temporary Files   Lets you set the filename extension for AutoCAD temporary files. These are files AutoCAD uses to temporarily store drawing data as you work on a file. If you are working on a network where temporary files from multiple users may be stored in the same directory, you may want to change this setting to identify your temporary files.

Object ARX Applications

AutoCAD allows users and third-party developers to create custom objects that usually require the presence of a custom ObjectARX application to support the object. These options control the way AutoCAD treats custom objects and their related ObjectARX applications.

Demand Load ObjectARX Apps   Controls when a supporting third-party application is loaded if a custom object is present in a file. This option offers several settings that are selectable from a drop-down list. The available settings are Disable Load on Demand, Custom Object Detect, Command

Invoke, and Object Detect and Command Invoke. Disable Load on Demand prevents AutoCAD from loading third-party applications when a custom object is present. Custom Object Detect causes AutoCAD to automatically load an ARX application if a custom object is present. Command Invoke loads a custom application when you invoke a command from that application. The Object Detect and Command Invoke option loads an ARX application when either a custom object is present or when you invoke a command from that application [Demandload].

Proxy Images for Custom Objects   Offers a drop-down list with three settings that control the display of custom objects when the objects supporting ARX applications are not present on your system. Do Not Show Proxy Graphics turns off the display of custom objects. Show Proxy Graphics displays the custom object. Show Proxy Bounding Box shows a bounding box in place of the custom object.

Show Proxy Information Dialog Box   Lets you determine whether the Show Proxy Information warning dialog box is used. When this option is checked, the Show Proxy Information warning appears when a drawing with custom objects is opened but the objects, associated ARX application cannot be found by AutoCAD [Proxynotice].

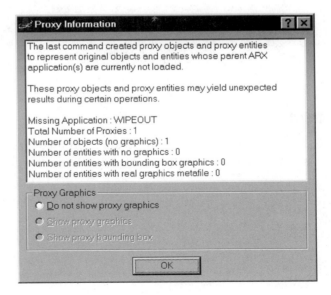

Plotting

The Plotting tab of the Options dialog box offers settings related to printing and plotting. See *Understanding the Plotting Tab on the Options Dialog Box* in Chapter 7 for a description of these options.

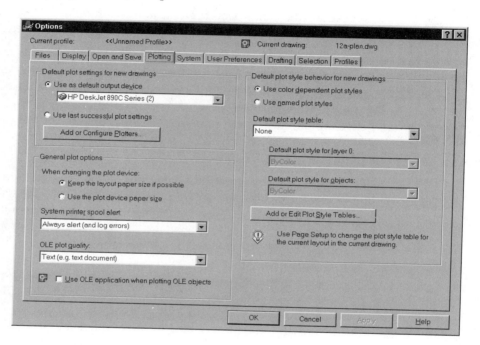

System

These options in the System tab offer control over some of AutoCAD's general interface settings such as the display drivers and pointing devices.

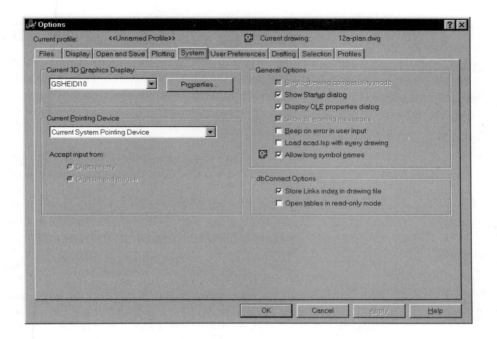

Current 3D Graphic Display

This group offers a drop-down list and a Properties button. The drop-down list offers any available 3D graphics display systems. The GSHEIDI10 default option is Autodesk's own Heidi 3D Graphics display system. Other options may be provided by third-party vendors.

The Properties button opens the 3D Graphics System Configuration dialog box that offers further options controlling the 3D Orbit and Shade Mode tools. The options presented with the Properties button will differ depending on the option selected in the drop-down list. If you are using the default GSHEIDI10 display system, see *Adjusting AutoCAD's 3D Graphics System* later in this appendix.

Current Pointing Device

You can choose the type of pointing device you want to use with AutoCAD through the options in this group. The drop-down list offers Current System Pointing Device and Wintab Compatible Digitizer. If you want to just use the default Windows pointing device, choose Current System Pointing Device. If you have a digitizer that uses the Wintab driver, you can select Wintab Compatible Digitizer.

You can further limit AutoCAD's use to the Wintab compatible digitizer by selecting the Digitizer Only radio button. If you select the Digitizer and Mouse radio button, AutoCAD will accept input from both devices.

General Options

This set of check boxes allows you to set options related to the general operation of AutoCAD such as the Startup dialog box and a few interface options.

Single-Drawing Compatibility Mode   Lets you control whether Auto-CAD allows you to open multiple documents or whether it limits you to a single document, as in earlier versions of AutoCAD [Sdi].

Show Startup Dialog   Lets you control the display of the Startup dialog box. If you turn the Startup dialog box off by removing the check from the Show Startup Dialog option in the Startup Dialog box, you can restore the Startup dialog box here.

Display OLE Properties Dialog   Lets you control the display of the OLE Properties dialog box. The OLE Properties dialog box normally appears when you insert OLE objects into an AutoCAD drawing. You can turn this feature off by removing the check by the Display OLE Properties Dialog when pasting new OLE objects option in the OLE Properties dialog box. You can restore the OLE Properties dialog box using this option.

Show All Warning Messages   Lets you control the display of all warning dialog boxes that show the Don't Display This Warning Again option. When you turn this option on, all warning dialog boxes are restored.

Beep on Error in User Input   Turns on an alarm beep that sounds whenever there is an input error.

Load Acad.lsp with Every Drawing   Lets you determine whether an Acad .lsp file is loaded with every drawing. If you are used to using an Acad.lsp file with your AutoCAD system, you can check this option; otherwise, Auto-CAD will only load the Acaddoc.lsp file [Acadlspasdoc].

Allow Long Symbol Names   Allows you to use long names for items such as layer, block, line-type and text-style names. With this option turned on, you can enter names of up to 255 characters [Extnames].

dbConnect Options

These check boxes offer controls over the dbConnect feature.

Store Links Index in Drawing File   Lets you determine where database link data is stored. If this option is checked, link data is stored in the drawing that is linked to a database. This increases file size and file-loading time.

Open Tables in Read-Only Mode   Lets you limit access to database files.

User Preferences

The options in the User Preferences tab allow you to adjust the way AutoCAD reacts to user input.

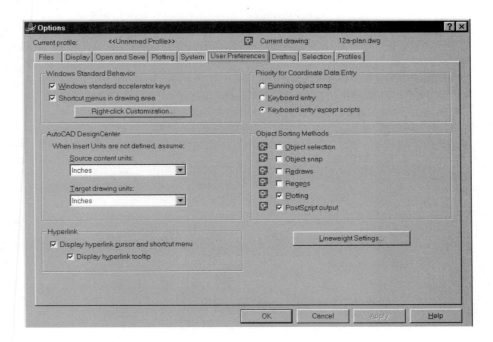

Windows Standard Behavior

These settings allow you to control how AutoCAD reacts to keyboard accelerators and mouse right-clicks.

Standard Accelerator Keys Causes AutoCAD to use the standard Windows behavior for Ctrl+C (Copy to Clipboard) and Ctrl+V (Paste from Clipboard) keystrokes. When this is not checked, AutoCAD interprets Ctrl+C as a Cancel and Ctrl+V as a Viewport Toggle.

Shortcut Menus in Drawing Areas Lets you see the shortcut popup menu when you right-click. When this option is not checked, AutoCAD responds to a right-click with a ↵ [Shortcutmenu].

Right-Click Customization Opens the Right-Click Customization dialog box which offers further options for the behavior of the right-click on AutoCAD.

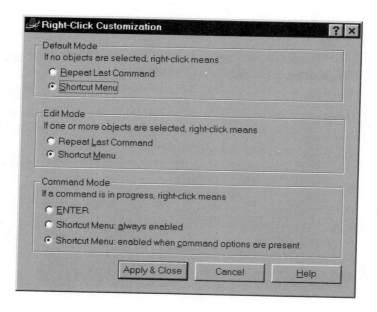

AutoCAD DesignCenter

These settings control how the DesignCenter determines the scale of blocks when blocks are given a unitless setting for their DesignCenter unit type. Each drop-down list offers the standard set of unit types that are available in the Block Definition dialog box under the Insert Units drop-down list. See Chapter 6 for more information on Blocks and Chapter 22 for information on the DesignCenter [Insunits].

Hyperlink

These options control the display of the Hyperlink icon and the shortcut popup menu.

Priority for Coordinate Data Entry

These options control the way AutoCAD responds to coordinate input.

> **Running Object Snap**   Forces AutoCAD to use Running Osnaps at all times [Osnapcoord].
>
> **Keyboard Entry**   Allows you to use keyboard entry for coordinate input. The Keyboard Entry Except Scripts option allows you to use keyboard entry for coordinate input, except in scripts [Osnapcoord].

Object Sorting Method

These options let you determine how objects are sorted during the specified operations. If an item is checked, the sort method is based on the order in which objects are drawn. If the item is not checked, the sort method is based on how AutoCAD optimizes the order of objects for display and file performance. For example, if you place a check in the Object Selection check box, AutoCAD offers the most recently drawn object of two overlapping objects when you attempt to select the object with a selection cursor. If you place a check in the Redraws and Regens options, AutoCAD restores the view of the drawing in the order that objects were created [Sortents].

Lineweight Settings

This option opens the Lineweight Settings dialog box. See Chapters 7 and 12 for more information about the Lineweight Settings dialog box.

Drafting

The Drafting tab offers settings that relate to the drawing cursor, including the AutoSnap and AutoTracking features.

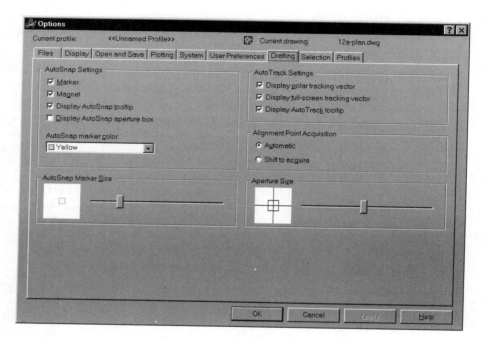

AutoSnap Settings

The options in this group control the AutoSnap features that are engaged when you use Osnaps.

Marker Turns on the small, square graphic that appears on the Osnap location. If you prefer not to see this marker, remove the check next to the Marker option [Autosnap].

Magnet Causes the Osnap cursor to "jump to" an Osnap location as the cursor moves close to that location [Autosnap].

Display AutoSnap Tooltip   Controls the display of the Osnap tool tip [Autosnap].

Display AutoSnap Aperture Box   Displays a square over the cursor whenever Osnaps are active. If you are familiar with earlier versions of AutoCAD, you'll recognize the Aperture Box as the graphic used to indicate Osnaps in earlier versions of AutoCAD before the AutoSnap feature was introduced [Apbox].

AutoSnap Marker Color   Lets you determine the color for the AutoSnap marker.

AutoSnap Marker Size

This option lets you control the size of the AutoSnap marker.

AutoTracking Settings

These options offer control over the tracking vector used for Polar Tracking and Osnap Tracking.

Display Polar Tracking Vector   Turns the Polar Tracking vector on or off [Trackpath].

Display Full-Screen Tracking Vector   Lets you control whether the tracking vector appears across the full width of the drawing window or stops at the cursor location or the intersection of two tracking vectors [Trackpath].

Display AutoTracking Tooltip   Turns the Osnap Tracking tool tip on or off [Autosnap].

Alignment Point Acquisition.

This option lets you determine the method for acquiring Osnap Tracking alignment points.

Aperture Size

This option lets you set the size of the Osnap aperture pickbox [Aperture].

Selection

The options in the Selection tab of the Options dialog box control the way you select objects in AutoCAD. You can also make adjustments to the Grips feature.

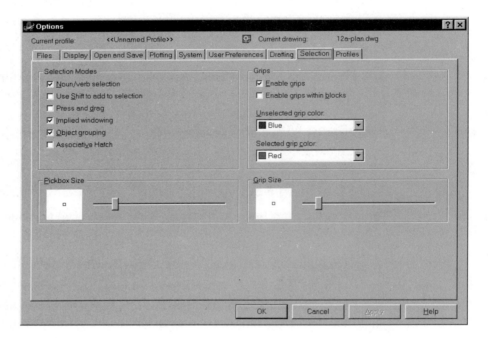

Selection Modes

The Selection Modes group lets you control the degree to which AutoCAD conforms to standard graphical user interface (GUI) methods of operation. It also lets you adjust the size of the Object Selection pickbox.

Noun/Verb Selection   Makes AutoCAD work more like other Windows programs. If you are used to working with other graphical environments, you may want to turn on some of the other options in the Selection Settings dialog box. [Pickfirst].

Use Shift to Add   Lets you use the standard GUI method of holding down the Shift key to pick multiple objects. When the Shift key is not held down, only the single object picked or the group of objects windowed will be selected. Previously selected objects are deselected, unless the Shift key is held down during selection. To turn this feature on using system variables, set Pickadd to 0 [Pickadd].

Press and Drag   Lets you use the standard GUI method for placing windows: First, click and hold down the Pick button on the first corner of the window; then, while holding down the Pick button, drag the other corner of the window into position. When the other corner is in place, you let go of the Pick button to finish the window. This setting applies to both Verb/Noun and Noun/Verb operations. In the system variables, set Pickadd to 1 for this option [Pickdrag].

Implied Windowing   Causes a window or crossing window to automatically start if no object is picked at the `Select objects:` prompt. This setting has no effect on the Noun/Verb setting. In the system variables, set Pickadd to 1 for this option [Pickauto].

Object Grouping   Allows you to select groups as single objects [Pickstyle].

Associative Hatch   Allows you to select both a hatch pattern and its associated boundary with a single pick [Pickstyle].

Pickbox Size

This slider lets you adjust the size of the pickbox [Pickbox].

Grips

These options control the grips feature.

Enable Grips   Turns on the Grips feature.

Enable Grips within Blocks   Turns on the display of grips within blocks. While you cannot edit grips within blocks, you can use grips within blocks as selection points [Gripblock].

Unselected Grip Color   Lets you select a color for grips that are exposed but not selected [Gripcolor].

Selected Grip Color   Lets you set the color for grips that are exposed and selected [Griphot].

Grip Size

This slider lets you adjust the size of grips [Gripsize].

Profiles

If you are using Windows NT, you know that a user profile is saved for each login name. Depending on the login name you use, you will have a different Windows setup. The Profiles tab offers a similar function for AutoCAD users. You can store different settings from the Options dialog box in a profile and recall them at any time. You can also save them to a file with the .arg extension, then take that file to another system. It's a bit like being able to take your Options settings with you wherever you go.

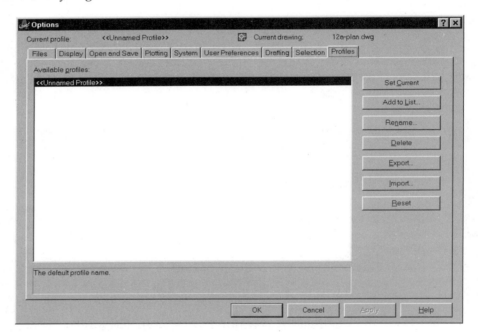

The main part of the Profiles tab displays a listing of available profiles. The default <<Unnamed Profile>> is the default profile. As you add more profiles, they will appear in the list.

To create a new profile, you highlight a profile name from the list, and then click Add to List. A Copy Profile dialog box appears, allowing you to enter a profile name and a description of the profile. The description appears in the box below the list on the Profiles tab whenever that profile is selected.

Once you've created a new profile, you can modify the settings on the other tabs of the Options dialog box and the new settings will be associated with the new profile. Profiles will store the way menus are set up so they can be used as an aid to managing both your own customization schemes and other third-party software.

Profiles can also be a way to manage multiple users on the same computer. Each user can maintain his or her own profile so they don't have to fight over how AutoCAD is set up. Here is a brief listing of the options on the Profiles tab:

Set Current   Installs the settings from the selected profile.

Add to List   Creates a new profile from an existing one.

Rename   Allows you to rename a profile and change its description.

Delete   Removes the selected profile from the list.

Export   Lets you save a profile to a file.

Import   Imports a profile that has been saved to a file.

Reset   Resets the values for a selected profile to its default settings.

Configuring the Tablet Menu Area

If you own a digitizing tablet and you would like to use it with the AutoCAD tablet menu template, you must configure your tablet menu.

1. First, securely fasten your tablet menu template to the tablet. Be sure the area covered by the template is completely within the tablet's active drawing area.

2. Choose Options ➤ Tablet ➤ Configure. The following prompt appears:

    ```
    Digitize upper left corner of menu area 1:
    ```

    For the next series of prompts, you will be locating the four tablet menu areas, starting with menu area 1 (see Figure B.1).

3. Locate the position indicated in Figure B.1 as the upper-left corner of menu area 1. Place your puck or stylus to pick that point. The prompt changes to

    ```
    Digitize lower left corner of menu area 1:
    ```

4. Again, locate the position indicated in Figure B.1 as the lower-left corner of menu area 1.

5. Continue this process until you have selected three corners for four menu areas.

6. When you are done selecting the menu areas, you get the following prompt:

    ```
    Do you want to respecify the Fixed Screen Pointing Area?
    ```

    Type **Y**↵ and then choose the position indicated in Figure B.1.

7. Finally, you get this prompt:

```
Digitize upper right corner of screen pointing area:
```

Pick the position indicated in Figure B.1.

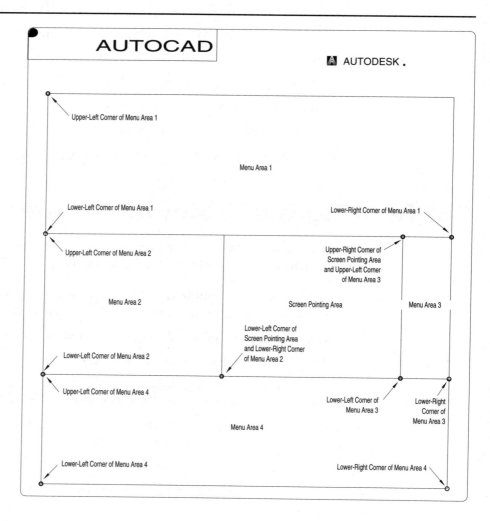

The three prompts that remain refer to a *floating screen pointing area*. This is an area on your tablet that allows you to select menu options and other areas on your screen outside the drawing area. This option is necessary because when you set up a digitizer for tracing, access to areas outside the drawing area is temporarily disabled.

The floating screen pointing area lets you access pull-down menus and the status bar during tracing sessions (see Chapter 11).

8. If you never intend to trace drawings with your tablet, then answer **N**⏎ to all three prompts. Otherwise, do the following three steps.

9. At the following prompt:

    ```
    Do you want to specify the Floating Screen Pointing Area? <N>:
    ```

    type **Y**⏎.

10. At the prompt

    ```
    Do you want the Floating Screen Pointing Area to be the same size
    as the Fixed Screen Pointing Area? <Y>:
    ```

    type **Y**⏎ if you want the floating screen pointing area to be the same as the fixed screen pointing area, the area you specified in steps 6 and 7. Type **N**⏎ if you want to use a separate area on your tablet for the floating screen pointing area.

11. The last prompt asks if you want to use the F12 function key to toggle the floating screen pointing area on and off. (This is similar to the F10 key function of earlier releases of AutoCAD). Enter **Y**⏎ or **N**⏎, depending on whether you want to specify a different function key for the floating screen pointing area or not.

AutoCAD will remember this configuration until you change it again. Quit this file by selecting File ➤ Exit.

Turning on the Noun/Verb Selection Method

If, for some reason, the Noun/Verb Selection method is not available, here are instructions on how to turn it back on.

1. Choose Tools ➤ Options. Then at the Options dialog box, select the Selection tab.

2. In the Selection Modes button group, find the Noun/Verb Selection setting. Click the check box to turn this option on.

3. Click OK.

If it wasn't there before, you should now see a small square at the intersection of the crosshair cursor. This square is actually a pickbox superimposed on the cursor. It tells you that you can select objects, even while the command prompt appears at the bottom of the screen and no command is currently active. As you have seen earlier, the square will momentarily disappear when you are in a command that asks you to select points.

You can also turn on Noun/Verb Selection by entering **'Pickfirst⏎** at the command prompt. When you are asked for New value for PICKFIRST <0>:, enter **1⏎** (entering **0** turns the Pickfirst function off). The Pickfirst system variable is stored in the AutoCAD configuration file. See Appendix D for more on system variables.

Turning on the Grips Feature

If, for some reason, the Grips feature is not available, here are instructions for turning it back on:

1. Choose Tools ➤ Options. Then at the Options dialog box, select the Selection tab.

2. At the left of the dialog box are the Select Settings check boxes. Click the Enable Grips check box in the upper-right side of the dialog box.

3. Click OK and you are ready to proceed.

The Selection tab of the Options dialog box also lets you determine whether grips appear on objects that compose a block (see Chapter 4 for more on blocks), as well as set the grip color and size. These options can also be set using the system variables described in Appendix D.

You can also turn the Grips feature on and off by entering **'Grips⏎**. At the New value for GRIPS <0>: prompt, enter a **1** to turn grips on, or **0** to turn grips off. Grips is a system variable that is stored in the AutoCAD configuration file.

Setting Up the Tracking Vector Feature

If you find that AutoCAD does not display a tracking vector as described in the early chapters in this book or that the tracking vector does not behave as described, chances are this feature has been turned off or altered. Take the following steps to restore the Tracking Vector so that it behaves as described in this book.

1. Open the Options dialog box by selecting Tools ➤ Options.

2. Click the Drafting tab.

3. Click all three of the AutoTracking Settings options so that a checkmark shows for each option.

4. Make sure there is a checkmark by the Marker, Magnet, and Display AutoSnap tool tip options in the AutoSnap Settings group.

5. Make sure the Automatic radio button in the Alignment Point Acquisition group is selected.

6. Click OK to exit the dialog box.

Adjusting AutoCAD's 3D Graphics System

You can adjust the performance of AutoCAD's 3D graphic system through the 3D Graphic System Configuration dialog box. You can open this dialog box by selecting the System tab of the Options dialog box and clicking the Properties button in the Current 3D Graphics Display group.

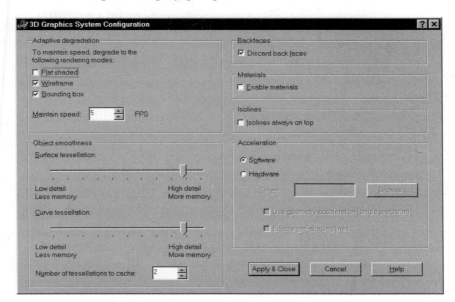

This dialog box offers control over the way AutoCAD displays 3D models when you use the 3D Orbit tool or when you are using a Shade mode. Here is a listing of the options for the GSHEIDI10 3D Graphics System Configuration dialog box.

Adaptive Degradation

The 3D Orbit tool allows you to adjust your view in real time, which places high demands on your display system. To maintain the smoothness of the real-time update of your 3D views, AutoCAD will degrade the display while performing the view transformation. The options under Adaptive Degradation let you set the level to which the view is degraded while using the 3D Orbit tool.

Flat Shaded   Causes AutoCAD to degrade the 3D view to flat shaded mode.

Wireframe   Causes AutoCAD to degrade the 3D view to wireframe mode.

Bounding Box   Causes AutoCAD to degrade the 3D view to show bounding boxes to indicate objects.

Maintain Speed FPS   Lets you set the frame rate in frames per second for the realtime display of 3D objects. Higher values require greater performance from your display system.

Object Smoothness

The options in this group determine the smoothness of 3D objects when they are shaded. To simulate smoothness, the AutoCAD Heidi 3D Graphics system divides curved surfaces into triangles called *tessellations*.

Surface Tessellation   Controls the amount of detail shown for surfaces. Greater detail requires more surface tessellation, which in turn requires more system memory.

Curve Tessellation   Controls the amount of detail shown for curved surfaces. Greater detail requires more surface tessellation, which in turn requires more system memory.

Number of Tessellations to Cache   Controls the number of tessellations that are cached. A cache is a part of memory reserved to store frequently used data. AutoCAD will always cache one tessellation. Caching two tessellations will improve the appearance and performance of 3D objects when you use multiple viewports.

Backfaces

In most 3D rendering systems, surfaces have just one visible side. The backsides of surfaces are invisible. This doesn't matter for objects such as cubes and spheres, where you only see one side of a surface at any given time; but in some situations, you may see both sides of a surface, such as a single surface used as a wall.

If your drawing is composed of mostly closed objects like cubes and spheres, where you will only see one surface, you can place a check by the Discard Backfaces check box to improve system performance. If you have lots of single surfaces that will be viewed from both sides, you will want to leave this option turned off.

Materials

This option determines whether material assignments to surfaces are displayed. If this feature is turned on, performance is degraded.

Isolines

If you use either the Flat Shaded/Edges On or Gouraud Shaded/Edges On options, you'll see the outlines of surfaces and surface tessellations displayed. With the Isolines Always on Top option turned on, these outlines and tessellations appear on both the front and back faces of surfaces.

Acceleration

This option lets you determine whether you use software or hardware acceleration to perform 3D drawing tasks.

Software   Causes AutoCAD to use software to draw 3D objects.

Hardware   Causes AutoCAD to use hardware to draw 3D objects, when hardware acceleration is available.

Use Geometry Acceleration (Single Precision)   Causes AutoCAD to use hardware acceleration for object geometry. This option is only available when the Hardware option is selected and your graphics hardware supports geometry acceleration.

Enable Anti-aliasing Lines   Causes AutoCAD to smooth out lines and remove the jagged appearance of lines and arcs. This option is only available when the Hardware option is selected and your graphics hardware supports anti-aliasing.

Enable Stereo Viewing   Allows AutoCAD to make use of stereo viewing for graphic systems that support it.

Setting Up ODBC for AutoCAD

In Chapter 10, you learned how to set up AutoCAD to link to database files. You also learned how to set up a file-based data source name (DSN) through a Data Link file in the \AutoCAD2000\Data Link\ directory. You then used the DSN to link AutoCAD to your database. You can also set up a DSN through the ODBC Data Source Administrator in the Windows Control Panel. Take the following steps:

1. Choose Start ➤ Settings ➤ Control Panel from the Windows Desktop to open the Windows Control Panel.

2. Locate the ODBC (32-bit) utility and double-click it. The ODBC Data Source Administrator dialog box appears.

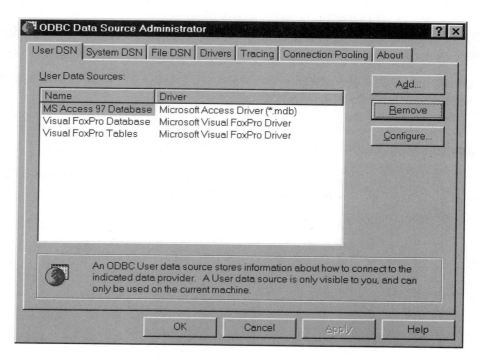

3. Select the User DSN tab or the System DSN tab, then click the Add button.

4. At the Create New Data Source dialog box, select a driver for your database, then click Finish.

NOTE
The dbConnect tutorial in Chapter 10 showed you how to create a file DSN through a Data Link file. The process is the same for the File DSN tab in the ODBC Data Source Administrator dialog box.

The options from this point will vary, depending on the database driver you select in step 4. In general, you will add a data source name and select a database file. Once you've done that, you will return to the User DSN tab or System DNS tab. You then click OK to exit the Data Source Administrator.

Once you've created a DSN, you can connect to the data source described by your DSN by editing the properties of the Data Link file you create in the `Data Link` directory under the `AutoCAD2000` directory.

1. Using Windows Explorer, open the `Data Link` directory under the `AutoCAD2000` directory.

2. Right-click an existing Data Link file or create a new Data Link file as described in *Creating a Data Link File* in Chapter 10 and right-click your new Data Link file.

3. In the Data Link Properties dialog box, select the Connection tab.

4. Click the Use Data Source Name radio button.

5. Open the Use Data Source Name drop-down list and select the DSN you created with the ODBC Data Source Administrator.

6. Click OK to exit the Data Link Properties dialog box.

The next time you open the dbConnect dialog box in AutoCAD, you'll be able to link to your database through your new DSN.

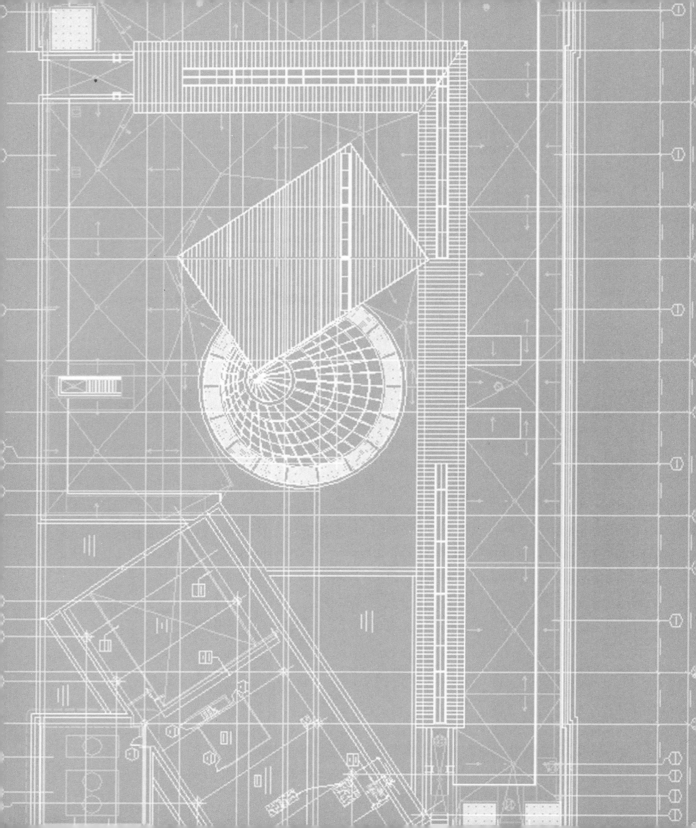

APPENDIX

C

What's on the Companion CD-ROM

This appendix describes the materials supplied on the companion CD-ROM that comes with this book. The CD-ROM contains a number of useful utilities and resources that you can load and run at any time. Before you use them, however, it's best to get familiar with AutoCAD 2000. Many of these utilities work within Auto-CAD from the command line or as options on the pull-down menus, and they offer prompts in a way similar to most other AutoCAD commands. Other utilities are stand-alone applications.

The Mastering AutoCAD Bonus Software

To help you get the most from AutoCAD and this book, I've included a set of programs and files. Once you load the CD-ROM, the Sybex interface will guide you to the following utilities:

Figures   Is a directory of the drawings used in this book. If you follow the tutorial chapter by chapter, you'll create these figures yourself. If you want to do the exercises out of sequence, use these files as needed.

AEC   Is a directory of the set of utilities described later in this appendix. These utilities are mostly aimed at the AEC environment but any AutoCAD user will find them helpful. I've included two versions of AEC, one for user in the US and another for metric users.

Eye2eye   Is a directory of the Eye2eye add-on to AutoCAD, described later in this appendix. Eye2eye makes perspective viewing of your 3D models a snap.

AutoCAD 2000 Instant Reference   Is on the companion CD-ROM in PDF format. This is the definitive companion to *Mastering AutoCAD 2000* that is full of detailed descriptions of AutoCAD's commands and tools.

ABCs of AutoLISP   Is a complete tutorial and reference book for AutoLISP, the AutoCAD macro-programming language. This book has been a favorite of end users and developers alike, and it's now in an easy-to-use Web browser format.

ActiveX samples   Help you get started with ActiveX Automation in Auto-CAD. You can use these examples along with Chapter 21 to explore the newest customization feature of AutoCAD.

Whip!   Allows you to view AutoCAD drawings over the Internet. It gives you full Pan and Zoom capabilities as well as access to Web links embedded in AutoCAD files.

TutoHelp Fundamentals   Is an interactive software program to help you learn and review AutoCAD.

JASC's PaintShop Pro   Is an image-editing program that makes a great partner with AutoCAD. It allows you to edit bitmap image files with advanced editing tools and supports pressure-sensitive drawing tablets.

JASC's QuickView   Is a powerful image file manager. You can quickly view a wide variety of bitmap and vector image files directly from Windows Explorer without having to open them in image-editing programs. You can even view HPGL files to check your AutoCAD plots before sending them to your plotter. (HPGL files need a filename extension of .HPG or .HPGL before they can be viewed by QuickView).

Opening the Installation Program

The software discussed in this appendix can be easily installed using the interface and installation program on the CD-ROM. Take the following steps to open the installation program:

1. Insert the *Mastering AutoCAD 2000* CD-ROM in your CD-ROM drive.

2. The Sybex interface will launch automatically. You will first see the License Agreement screen.

3. After you've read the agreement and accepted the terms, click Accept. You then see the *Mastering AutoCAD 2000* software installation interface.

From here, you can select the software you wish to install. For details on each of these options, read the following related sections.

Installing and Using the Sample Drawing Files

The `Figures` directory contains sample drawing files for the exercises in this book. These drawings are provided for you in the event that you decide to skip some of the book's tutorial material. With these files, you can open the book to any chapter and start working, without having to construct the drawings from earlier.

1. Start the *Mastering AutoCAD 2000* software installation program, as described earlier in this appendix.

2. Click the Figures button.

3. Click Continue. You see the WinZip Self-Extractor dialog box. You have the option to accept the default directory shown in the input box, or enter a different location for the files.

4. When you've entered the location for the sample files, click Unzip. The sample files will be installed on your computer.

5. Click Close to return to the main installation program screen.

6. Proceed with another installation or click Exit.

Once you've installed the sample files, you have access to them during the exercises.

Installing the Bonus Add-On Packages

The companion CD-ROM also includes two add-on packages called On-Screen AEC and Eye2eye. On-Screen AEC is a set of AutoLISP macros and architectural symbols, all integrated with a standard AutoCAD menu. This package provides the basic tools you'll need to start creating architectural drawings. In addition, it contains many time-saving tools to aid all users, not just architects, in editing their drawings.

Eye2eye is a utility that replaces the AutoCAD Dview command with an easy-to-use method for creating perspective views. Eye2eye uses a camera-target metaphor to let you place viewpoints and view directions in a drawing.

Installing On-Screen AEC

Follow these steps to install On-Screen AEC:

1. Start the *Mastering AutoCAD 2000* software installation program, as described earlier in this appendix.

2. Click the AEC button.

3. Click Continue. You see the WinZip Self-Extractor dialog box. You have the option to accept the default directory shown in the input box, or you may enter a different location for the files. I recommend that you install the AEC files in a subdirectory called AEC under the `\Program Files\AutoCAD2000\` directory where AutoCAD is installed.

4. When you've entered the location for the AEC files, click Unzip. The files will be installed on your computer.

5. Click Close to return to the main installation program screen.

6. Click Exit, and then start AutoCAD.

7. Start AutoCAD and choose Tools ➤ Options.

8. Click the Files tab at the top of the Options dialog box.

9. Click Support Files Search Path.

10. Click the Add button, and then click Browse.

11. Locate and select the `\Program Files\AutoCAD2000\AEC\` directory, and then click OK.

12. Click OK in the Options dialog box.

On-Screen AEC is now installed and ready for use. The next section describes how to load the On-Screen AEC menu.

Loading the On-Screen AEC Menu

Now you are ready to load the On-Screen AEC menu to give you access to the symbols and utilities offered there. You will load a partial menu that will give you full access to all the AEC tools. Here's how it's done.

1. Once back in AutoCAD, choose Tools ➤ Customize Menu, or type **Menuload**↵. The Menu Customization dialog box appears. Click the Menu Group tab.

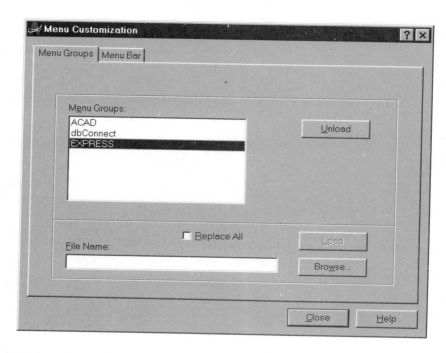

2. Click the Browse button at the bottom of the dialog box. The Select Menu File dialog box appears.

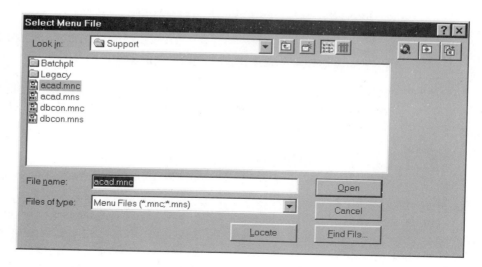

3. Locate the file name Osaec.mnu, and then double-click it. You return to the Menu Customization dialog box and the Osaec.mnu file name appears in the File Name input box.

4. Click the Load button just above the Browse button. A warning message appears. Press ↵. AutoCAD takes a moment to load the menu. The AEC toolbar appears on the screen.

5. Click the Menu Bar tab at the top of the dialog box. The dialog box changes to reveal the Menu Bar tab options.

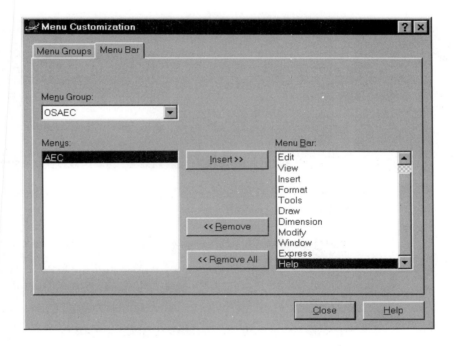

6. Open the Menu Group drop-down list, then select OSAEC.

7. In the Menu Bar list box to the right, click Help to highlight it. This determines where the AEC pull-down menu will appear in the menu bar.

8. Click the button labeled Insert >>. AEC appears just above Help in the Menu Bar list box, and you will see AEC appear in the AutoCAD menu bar at the top of the AutoCAD Window.

You are now ready to use On-Screen AEC. Follow the instructions presented in the following section.

Using the AEC Utilities

On-Screen AEC is a basic architectural symbols library package. This package supplies utilities for creating doors, plumbing and electrical fixtures, wall patterns, and wall intersection cleanup. It also includes many time-saving utilities to help you work faster and more efficiently. Even if your application doesn't involve architecture, you may want to install On-Screen AEC just to take advantage of these utilities.

Getting Started with On-Screen AEC

Once you've installed the AEC software, you can begin to use On-Screen AEC. You may want to start by clicking the Setup Drawing option in the AEC menu to bring up a dialog box you can use to set up your drawing. Once the setup is done, you will have a drawing area equivalent to your sheet size, with a grid representing 1-inch intervals on the final plot area.

Using AEC to Add Walls, Doors, Symbols, and Stairs

Let's begin by taking a look at some of the basic architectural features available with AEC.

Adding Walls

To draw walls, you could use AutoCAD's Multiline feature, but Multilines are a bit difficult to edit. Another alternative is to use the Walls option on the AEC menu. Here's how it works.

1. Choose AEC ➤ Walls, or click Wall from the AEC palette. The Wall Setup dialog box appears.

2. Select the options you want to apply to the wall, and then proceed to select points to draw the walls.

3. To stop picking points, press ↵.

4. At the Close last corner: prompt, you can enter Y↵ to close your wall, or N↵ to exit the Walls utility without closing the wall.

Here is a description of the options in the Wall Setup dialog box:

Offset direction   Lets you control the position of the wall in relation to the points you select. The Center option centers the wall along the points you pick. The Up and Down options place one side of the wall on the points you pick, while the other side appears above (Up) or below (Down) the points you pick as you select points from left to right.

Relative to Location   Lets you start a wall relative to a point in your drawing instead of from the first point you pick.

Wall Width   Lets you enter a width for your wall.

If you've installed the metric version of the AEC utilities, you'll see the following additional options:

Draw Cavity Wall   Lets you add additional lines to indicate a cavity wall.

Cavity Wall Thickness for one side   Lets you determine the width of the cavity wall on one side.

Cavity Width   Lets you specify the width of the cavity. Subtract the cavity wall thickness and cavity width from the overall wall width to get the cavity wall thickness on the opposite side.

Adding a Door

The door utility can be used only in the World Coordinate System (WCS). If you are in another UCS, switch back to the WCS temporarily to insert a door using this utility. Also, you must have drawn walls using the Wall utility to place doors.

1. Choose AEC ➤ Doors, and then select a door from the cascading menu. (To see what the door styles look like, select the Open Toolbar option at the bottom of the menu to open the Door palette. You can then select a door type from the palette.)

2. Once you select a door, pick a reference point along the wall (see Figure C.1). This should be a known point, such as an interior corner or the midpoint of a wall. You will later enter a value to determine the distance from this point to the door hinge.

3. Pick a point on the opposite side of the wall, as shown in Figure C.1.

4. Again using Figure C.1 as your guide, pick a point along the wall indicating where the door opening will appear in relation to the last point selected.

5. When the command prompt asks you for a door width, enter a width or press ↵ to accept the default door width shown in the < > brackets.

6. Enter the distance from the reference point you picked earlier (step 3) that you want to place the door hinge. For example, if you picked the inside corner of a room for the reference point and you want the door to be 4 inches from that corner, enter 4↵.

FIGURE C.1:

Select this sequence of points when adding a door.

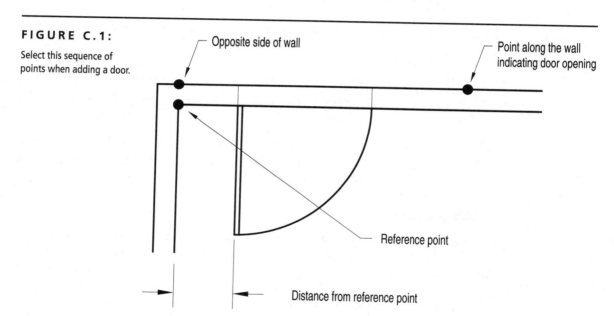

Notice the Settings option near the bottom of the menu. This lets you set the layers on which to place the door, the door header, and the door jamb. Once these layers are set, AutoCAD will remember them until you change them again. These layer settings affect newly inserted doors only, not previously inserted doors.

Adding a Wall Pattern

The following steps show you how to select and pick points for a wall pattern.

1. Choose AEC ➤ Wall Patterns.

2. From the cascading menu, select the wall pattern you want, or click Open Toolbar to open the Wall Pattern palette.

3. At the `Pick wall at beginning of pattern:` prompt, use the Osnap modes to select a point along the wall where the pattern is to start. For example, you can pick the intersection of two walls using the Intersect Osnap mode.

> **NOTE**   You must use an Osnap mode to select the beginning point of the pattern, or the pattern may not align properly with the wall.

4. At the `Pick the opposite side of the wall:` prompt, pick any point on the opposite side of the wall from the last point you picked.

5. At the `Pick end of the wall pattern:` prompt, pick a point indicating the end of the wall pattern. This point should be on the same side of the wall as the last point you picked.

The wall pattern appears between the first and last points you selected.

Adding Symbols

Take the following steps to add symbols to a drawing. If you would like to modify the AEC-supplied symbols to fit your own work environment, you can find them in the AEC subdirectory.

1. Pull down the AEC menu, and choose one of the three categories of symbols. A cascading menu appears which displays a list of symbols.

2. Choose the name of the symbol you want to use, or you can choose Open Toolbar from the menu to have better access to them (see Figure C.2).

3. Answer the insertion point and rotation angle prompts on the command line. The symbol appears in the location you select.

FIGURE C.2:

The toolbars available on the AEC menu

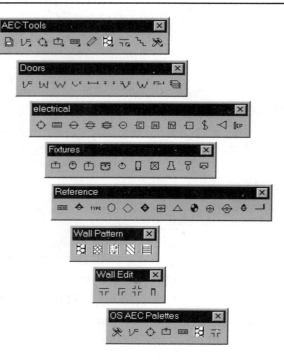

Adding Stairs

The AEC menu also includes a stair-drawing option; the following steps show you how it works.

1. Choose AEC ➤ Draw Stairs.

2. At the Pick first corner of stair: prompt, pick a point locating one corner of the first stair-tread nosing (see Figure C.3).

3. At the Pick second corner of stair: prompt, pick the other corner of the nosing.

4. At the Pick third corner of stair: prompt, pick the other end of the stair run.

5. Answer the following four prompts:

```
Enter minimum run of stair <10.00>:
Enter maximum rise of stair <7.50>:
Enter hand rail extension at top of stair <12.00>:
Enter hand rail extension at bottom of stair <12.00>:
```

The stairs appear within the three points you select, complete with handrails.

FIGURE C.3:

Adding stairs

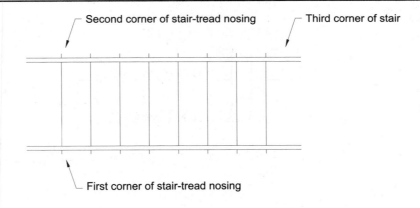

Second corner of stair-tread nosing

Third corner of stair

First corner of stair-tread nosing

Using the Wall Cleanup Utilities

The cleanup utilities will join double lines into tee, corner, and cross formations. The lines joined must be simple lines, not polylines or multilines. (To join multilines, use the Mledit command. To join polylines, use the Join option of the Pedit command.)

Cleaning Up Tee Wall Intersections

To clean up tee wall intersection, do the following:

1. Choose AEC ➣ Wall Cleanup.

2. Select Tee from the cascading menu.

3. At the `Pick intersection with window:` prompt, use a selection window to enclose the intersection of the walls forming the tee.

4. At the `Indicate leg of tee using axis:` prompt, pick a point to one side of the leg of the tee. A rubber-banding line appears from the point you select.

5. Pick a second point so that the rubber-banding line crosses over the two lines of the leg of the tee. Take care not to cross over any lines other than those of the tee leg.

The tee intersection joins into a smooth tee intersection, as shown in Figure C.4.

FIGURE C.4:

Joining a tee intersection

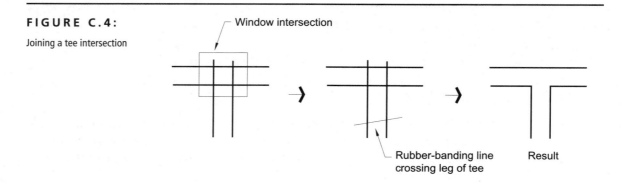

Cleaning Up Corner Wall Intersections

To clean up corner wall intersections, do the following:

1. Choose AEC ➤ Wall Cleanup and select Corner.

2. At the `Select intersection with window:` prompt, window the intersection of the walls forming the corner.

3. At the `Pick inside of corner:` prompt, a rubber-banding line appears. Pick a point on the inside of the corner. Try to pick this point so that the rubber-banding line divides the angle formed by the two walls exactly in half.

The walls first disappear and then reappear with the corner cleaned up, as shown in Figure C.5.

FIGURE C.5:

Joining a corner

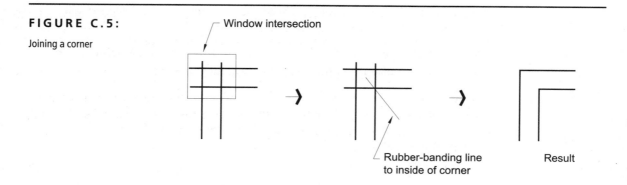

Cleaning Up Crossing Wall Intersections

This function only works if all the lines forming the walls are continuous through the intersection. If this is the case, take the following steps:

1. Choose AEC ➤ Wall Cleanup and choose Intersect.

2. At the `Select Intersection with Window:` prompt, window the intersection of the walls.

3. At the `Pick Narrow Bisecting Angle of Intersection:` prompt, pick a point between the intersecting walls, as close to midway between the two walls as possible. If the walls are not perpendicular, pick a point between the narrower angle between the walls.

The walls first disappear, and then reappear with the intersection cleaned up, as shown in Figure C.6.

FIGURE C.6:

Joining two intersecting walls

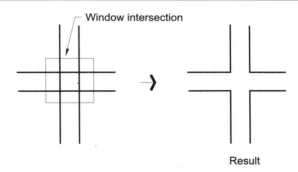

Closing the End of a Wall

This function can be used on any two lines that need to be closed.

1. Click AEC ➤ Wall Cleanup and choose Close End.

2. At the `Select end of wall with crossing line:` prompt, indicate the end of the wall that you want to close by picking two points that cross the end of the wall. The end of the wall closes.

Using the General Utilities

Along with the AEC utilities, the companion CD-ROM has several other general-purpose utilities to help you edit your drawings. These utilities are helpful no matter what your field of interest. Take a moment to read through the following descriptions and see if you haven't had a need for at least one or two of these tools.

If you want to use these utilities from a menu, you can find them on the AEC menu. They are located in the lower half of the AEC pull-down menu.

Text-Related Utilities

AutoCAD has improved its text-handling capabilities over the years, but you may still want some help in this area. This section describes some utilities that will fill many of the voids still remaining in AutoCAD's text-handling functions.

Drawing Text on a Curve

If you work on maps in which text has to follow some geographic feature, this utility will be helpful. The Text on a Path option on the AEC ➤ Text menu draws text on a curved polyline or arc. You must first draw the polyline or arc.

1. Choose AEC ➤ Text and select Text on a Path.

2. At the Pick path for text: prompt, click the polyline you have created to define the path.

3. At the Enter text: prompt, enter the text you want to follow the path, and press ↵.

4. At the Reverse Text? prompt, enter Y↵ if you want the text to appear in a reverse direction. The text will appear momentarily.

Editing Several Single-Line Text Objects at Once

The Edit Dtext Block (Edsp) option on the AEC ➤ Text menu allows you to use DOS Edit to make changes to a group of single-line text objects created using Dtext.

1. Click AEC ➤ Text and choose Edit Dtext Block.

2. At the Save to file/<Edit>? prompt, enter S↵ to save text in a file for later retrieval. Enter E↵ to edit the text in DOS Edit, and proceed to step 4.

3. If you entered **S.**↵, you are prompted with `Enter name of file to be saved <Filename.doc>:`. You can enter a different filename, if you want, or press ↵ to accept the default.

4. The next prompt you see is:

    `Sort text by vertical location (this takes some time) ? <N>:`

    Here you have the option to have Edit Dtext Block sort text so it appears in the text file in the same order it appears in the drawing. This only applies to columns of text, so don't use this option unless you plan to select a column of text for editing.

5. At the `Select text:… Select objects:` prompt, select the set of single-line text you want to edit.

NOTE   At this point, you also have the choice to exit AutoCAD entirely and make changes to your text file at a later time. If you choose to do this, be sure you save your file before exiting AutoCAD; otherwise, Edsp won't be able to update your text later. The next time you open the file, load Edsp, enter **(Sp_update).**↵, and the text in your drawing will be updated.

---

6. Next, using a word processor, open the file you just created, make your changes, and then return to the drawing.

7. Enter **(Sp_update).**↵. The changes you made to your saved file are applied to your drawing.

8. If you chose to enter ↵ in step 2, AutoCAD loads a text editor and your selected text appears on the screen for you to edit. Once you've made your changes, choose File ➤ Exit. Be sure you answer Yes to save your changes. You will return to your drawing, and your text will be updated to reflect the changes you have made.

Quickly Changing Single Lines

You probably often run across the situation where you need to change several lines of text to make them all say the same thing. Instead of changing each line individually, use the Quick Text Edit utility on the AEC ➤ Text menu. It's an easy-to-use utility that lets you select a set of text objects and change them all at once.

1. Click AEC ➤ Text and choose Quick Text Edit.

2. At the `Pick text to be changed… Select objects:` prompt, select the lines of text you want to change.

3. At the `Enter new string:` prompt, enter the text you want to appear in place of the selected lines.

Changing Numeric Sequences

If one of your frequent chores is having to change the sequence of numbers—the numbering in parking stalls, for example, or sequential numbers in a table—the Sequential Numbers option (on the AEC ➤ Text menu) helps you do this quickly and easily. This utility lets you control the unit style of the numbers, as well as the increment of increase for each number in the sequence.

1. Choose AEC ➤ Text and select Sequential Numbers.

2. At the `ETS Pick numbers to be changed in order of increment:` prompt, select the text objects that are to be converted into a new sequence of numbers. Select the objects in the order the numbers are to appear.

3. At the `Enter unit type Scientific/Decimal/Engin/Arch <D>:` prompt, enter the unit style you want.

4. At the `Enter precision value:` prompt, enter the decimal accuracy you want for the numbers.

5. At the `Enter increment value:` prompt, enter the amount of increase for each number in the sequence.

6. At the `Enter new beginning value:` prompt, enter the first number of the sequence. AutoCAD then proceeds to change the selected objects into sequential numbers.

Changing the Height of Text Objects

One of the more frequently requested utilities is one that will change text height. The Change Text Style utility on the AEC ➤ Text menu does this—and it also alters nearly any other property of a group of text objects. Unfortunately, it doesn't operate on multiline text.

1. First, create a text style with the height you want.

2. Choose AEC ➤ Text and select Change Text Style.

3. At the `Select objects:` prompt, select the text whose height you want to change.

Housekeeping Utilities

When you're working with a group of people, it is often helpful to keep a record of your layers and blocks. Your coworkers can then refer to these records to find out the assigned contents and purpose of existing layers and blocks. The two utilities described in this section create ASCII log files of your work.

Keeping a Log of Your Blocks

The Block Log utility on the AEC ➤ Blocks menu is a simple macro that creates a log file of blocks. You can specify a name for the file or use the default name, which is usually the drawing name with the .blk extension. The log file will contain the date and a space for remarks. You can edit the file using a text editor to add comments or view and print the file. Here's how it works.

1. Choose AEC ➤ Blocks ➤ Block Log.

2. At the `Enter name of block file <filename>:` prompt, enter a block name or press ↵ to accept the default. If no file exists with the name you enter, a new file will be created; otherwise, the current block information will be appended to an existing file.

Keeping a Log of Your Layers

The Layer Log utility does essentially the same thing as the Block Log utility described previously, except that it creates an ASCII file log of your layers. This utility creates or appends to a file with the .LAY extension. The following steps show you how to use it.

1. Choose AEC ➤ Layers ➤ Layer Log.

2. At the `Enter name of layer file <filename>:` prompt, enter a name or press ↵ to accept the default.

General Productivity Tools

The utilities in this section offer general help in drawing and editing.

Changing the Thickness of Lines

The Thicken utility on the AEC ➤ Drawing Aids menu changes the width of a set of lines, polylines, or arcs by converting objects to wide polylines. This is useful if you like to control line thickness directly in your drawing, rather than relying on plotter pen settings.

1. Choose AEC ➤ Drawing Aids ➤ Thicken.

2. At the prompt, enter the thickness you want for your lines.

3. At the `Select objects:` prompt, select the lines, arcs, or polylines you want to change, and then press ↵.

NOTE If you want to change the width of circles, you must break them with a very small break.

Joining Broken Lines

It is considered bad form to leave disjointed lines in a CAD drawing. By the term "disjointed," I mean lines that appear to be continuous but are actually made up of several line segments. The Join Lines utility on the AEC ➤ Drawing Aids menu will help you clean up such lines, or just close a gap in any broken line except a polyline.

1. Choose AEC ➤ Drawing Aids ➤ Join Lines.

2. At the `Select Two Lines to Be Joined:` prompt, pick the lines that are broken.

NOTE The Join Lines utility does not work on polylines. You can, however, use grips to first move a polyline endpoint to join the endpoint of the second polyline, and then use the Pedit command's Join option to connect them.

Attribute Template Files, Simplified

Creating and using attributes can be trying for the beginner and even the intermediate user. Extracting attribute data is even more difficult. The Create Attrib .Templt. option on the AEC ➤ Drawing Aids menu eases these chores by letting you easily create an attribute template file that tells AutoCAD what data to extract.

1. Choose AEC ➤ Drawing Aids ➤ Create Attrib.Templt.

2. At the `Name of attribute template file:` prompt, enter the name you want for your template. Don't bother adding an extension; the utility will do that for you.

3. At the `?/Enter name of attribute tag:` prompt, enter the name of the tag you wish to extract. You can also enter **?⏎** to get a listing of existing tags.

4. At the `Is the attribute a Number or Character <C/N>?` prompt, enter **C⏎** or **N⏎** to specify the attribute as a character or number.

5. At the `Enter number of digits or characters:` prompt, enter the number of characters or digits you want reserved for the attribute.

6. If you entered **N⏎** in step 4, you'll see the `Enter number of decimal places wanted:` prompt next. Enter the number of decimal places you want to reserve for your number.

7. Repeat steps 3 through 5 for each attribute. These prompts will continue until you press ⏎ at the `?/Enter name of attribute tag:` prompt in step 3.

Cookie Cutter for Objects

There may be times when you want to export a portion of a drawing that is enmeshed in a larger set of objects. The Cut Out option on the AEC ➤ Drawing Aids menu offers a "cookie-cutter" tool for breaking out objects that are bound into a larger system of objects. The following steps show you how to use the Cut Out option.

1. Choose AEC ➤ Drawing Aids ➤ Cut Out.

2. At the `Pick first point of Fence/Select:` prompt, pick a point to start a fence. This fence defines that area to be cut out.

3. At the `Next point:` prompt, pick the next point of the fence.

4. At the Next point/Close: prompt, continue to pick points defining the area you want to cut out.

5. At the last point of your fence, enter **C↵** to close the fence. The program will break each line, polyline, and circle that it encounters.

You can also predefine a fence by drawing a polyline in the shape of the area you want to cut out. Then, in step 2 you enter **S↵**. At the prompt Pick line or Pline defining cut location: prompt, select an object, and the fence will cut objects along the line or polyline.

There are a few restrictions when using the Cut Out option:

•   You cannot use polyline arcs or splines for fence paths. If you want to cut an arc path, approximate the arc using a spline curve.

•   The fence cannot cut blocks, text, arcs, or splines. In addition, it will not reliably cut fitted polylines.

Counting Blocks

Is there a simple way to count the occurrences of blocks in a drawing? Yes. Perhaps the easiest method is to use the Selection Filters option on the Assist menu to select the blocks you want. Then choose Assist ➤ Select Objects ➤ Previous to display the number of selected items. This is fine for counting individual block occurrences, but what if you want a quick count of several block definitions? The Count Blocks utility on the AEC ➤ Blocks menu gives you a listing of blocks and the number of times they occur in your drawing. It also saves the list as a file with the same name as your drawing and the .blk extension. Here's how it works.

1. Choose AEC ➤ Blocks ➤ Count Blocks.

2. At the Enter name(s) of blocks to count or RETURN for all: prompt, enter the names of the blocks you want to count, separated by commas. Or you can press ↵ to count all the blocks in the drawing.

AutoCAD lists the blocks and their count. When the counting is done, an ASCII file is created to store the information displayed on the screen.

Creating Keyboard Macros

In Chapter 19, you learned how you can use AutoLISP to create a keyboard macro. I've included an AutoLISP program utility with On-Screen AEC that will do the work for you. This utility, Macro on the AEC ➤ Drawing Aids menu, allows you to record specific points in your drawing and also lets you insert pauses in your macro where you need them. To create a macro, follow these steps.

1. Choose AEC ➤ Drawing Aids ➤ Macro.

2. At the Enter keys to define: prompt, enter the name of the macro. This is what you will enter at the command prompt to start your macro.

3. At the Will this macro require open ended object selection? prompt, enter Y↵ if you want to be able to select objects without restrictions. This means you can use all the standard selection options whenever you run your macro. If you do enable this option, however, you must use the Previous setting (described at the end of this procedure) in the main part of your macro to indicate where you want the selected objects to be applied.

4. At the Previous/?=Pause/*=Point/#=done/<Keystroke>: prompt, enter the keystrokes of your macro or enter one of the options, as described in the following list.

Here are descriptions of the options in the Previous/?=Pause/*=Point/ #=done/<Keystroke>: prompt:

> **Previous**   Is used to indicate when the selected objects should be applied in your macro. Use this option where you anticipate the Select objects: prompt. If you have enabled open-ended object selection (step 3 above), you must include this option.
>
> **?**   Places a pause for input in the macro. Use this option when you want the macro to stop and wait for point or text input.
>
> *****   Lets you pick a point on the screen or enter a coordinate. This value becomes a fixed value in the macro.
>
> **#**   Ends the macro keystroke input and stores the macro in memory (or, optionally, on disk).

Eye2eye

Eye2eye is a set of AutoLISP utilities that aid the viewing of 3D models in Auto-CAD. If you find you are struggling with the AutoCAD Dview command, these utilities will be of benefit to you.

Installing Eye2eye

Here's how to install Eye2eye:

1. Start the *Mastering AutoCAD 2000* software installation program as described earlier in this appendix.

2. Click the Eye2eye button.

3. Click Continue. You see the WinZip Self-Extractor dialog box. You have the option to accept the default directory shown in the input box, or you may enter a different location for the files. I recommend that you install the Eye2eye files in a subdirectory called `Eye2eye` under the `\Program Files\AutoCAD2000\` directory where AutoCAD is installed.

4. When you've entered the location for the Eye2eye files, click Unzip. The files will be installed on your computer.

5. Click Close to return to the main installation program screen.

6. Click Exit.

7. Start AutoCAD and choose Tools ➢ Options.

8. Click the Files tab at the top of the dialog box.

9. Click Support Files Search Path.

10. Click the Add button, and then click Browse.

11. Locate and select the `\Program Files\AutoCAD2000\Eye2eye\` directory, and then click OK.

12. Click OK in the Options dialog box.

Eye2eye is now available for loading and use. The next section describes how to access the Eye2eye features.

Using Eye2eye

Eye2eye is based on the idea of using a camera and target object to control your perspective views. I call the camera and target objects *eyes*, hence the name Eye2eye. To set up a view, you simply place the camera, or Eyeto block (see Figure C.7), where you want your point of view. You then place the target, or Eyefrom block, where you want your center of attention. You then use Eye2eye's Showeye command to display the perspective.

FIGURE C.7:

The Eyeto block used with Eye2eye

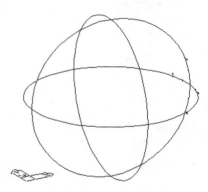

The following list gives a brief description of all of the Eye2eye commands:

Showeye   Displays the current eye-target perspective view in the current viewport. Be sure to have the desired viewport active before using this command.

Findeye   Draws a temporary vector between the camera and target points to help locate these points.

Crosseye   Displays a view that reverses the camera and target locations.

Mtarg   Moves the target location. You must be in an Orthogonal view for this command.

Meye   Moves the camera location. You must be in an Orthogonal view for this command.

Seteye   Allows you to turn the Perspective mode on or off, set camera focal length, turn the camera and target objects on or off, pan the Perspective view, or set up multiple viewports for Eye2eye.

Paneye   Lets you pan the Perspective view. This is useful for fine-tuning your Perspective view.

Matcheye   Sets the camera and target objects to the current Perspective view. You must be in a Perspective viewport to use this command. This is useful when you've changed your view using methods outside of the Eye2eye command set, such as the Dview command.

Eye2eye assumes that you have a fairly good grasp of AutoCAD's 3D functions and the use of Paper Space viewports. It is best suited as a tool for viewing your model after you've created the basic massing.

Once you have a 3D model built, load the Eye2eye utilities by entering the following at the command prompt:

```
(load "eye2eye")
```

You can also use Tools ➤ Load Applications. At the dialog box, click the File button and locate and load the Eye2eye.lsp file in the \Program Files\Auto-CAD2000\Eye2eye\ directory.

After you've loaded Eye2eye, set up multiple viewports with the following steps.

1. Open a file containing a 3D model. Set up your display so that you can see all of the model and leave some room for the camera location. Make sure this is a plan or top-down view.

2. Go to the World Coordinate System and enter **Eye2eye**⏎ at the command prompt.

3. Since this is the first time you are using Eye2eye, you are prompted to pick a camera point. Do so. Don't worry about the exact placement of your camera just yet, you will get a chance to adjust its location later. The camera object, a block called Eyeto, appears.

4. Next, you are prompted to select a target location. Do so. As with the camera location, it isn't important to place the target in an exact location at this time. You can easily adjust it later. Eye2eye will create a new Layout tab called Eye2eye and set up four viewports: one large viewport (to the right) for your Perspective view and three smaller viewports (to the left) for your top, front, and left-side Orthogonal views. You will use the Orthogonal views to manipulate the camera and target points (see Figure C.8). You are now ready to use the Eye2eye utilities.

5. You'll also see the prompt:

```
Perspctv Off/ON/Focal lngth/Pan/cLose eyes/Show eyes/ fInd eyes/
move Camera/move Target/Hide/Match prspctv/eXit:
```

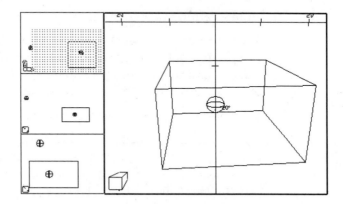

Because your views are in Paper Space, you can easily enlarge or resize a view
for easy editing. Just remember that while using the Eye2eye utilities, you must
be in tiled Model Space.

You are now ready to use the Eye2eye utilities. The options shown in the Eye2eye
prompt perform some of the same functions that are described in the beginning of
this section:

Perspctv Off/ON   Turns the Perspective mode off or on in the Perspective
viewport.

Focal length   Changes the focal length of the "camera."

Pan (Paneye)   Lets you pan the Perspective view. This is useful for fine-
tuning your Perspective view.

Close eyes   Turns off the layer on which the camera and target "eyes" reside.
This turns off the visibility of the eyes.

Show eyes   Turns on the layer on which the camera and target eyes reside.
This turns on the visibility of the eyes.

Find eyes   Helps you locate the camera and target eyes by zooming into
an area that just includes the eyes. You must be in a non-Perspective viewport before this option will take effect.

Move Camera (Meye)   Moves the camera location. You must be in an Orthogonal view for this command.

Move Target (Mtarg)   Moves the target location. You must be in an Orthogonal view for this command.

Hide   Performs a hidden-line removal on the Perspective view.

Match prspctv (Matcheye)   Sets the camera and target objects to the current Perspective view. You must be in a Perspective viewport to use this command. This is useful when you've changed your view using methods outside of the Eye2eye command set, such as the Dview command.

Exit   Terminates the Eye2eye command.

NOTE To simplify your use of Eye2eye, you may also want to install the Eye2eye menu. Use the instructions for installing .MNU files in Chapter 20 to install the `Eye2eye.mnu` file that is located in the `Eye2eye` directory. Once installed, the Eye2eye options will be available from a pull-down menu or from a handy toolbar.

Using Eye2eye for Model Construction

If you want to use Eye2eye as a tool to help you construct your 3D model, be sure you set up your Model Space work area *before* you proceed with the above steps. You can use the Ddsetup utility provided with Eye2eye to accomplish this. To use Ddsetup, enter **(load "ddsetup")**⏎ at the command prompt, and then enter **Ddsetup**⏎. A dialog box appears, from which you can choose a unit style, sheet size, and scale. Once you've selected the appropriate options, click OK. The drawing is then set up according to your selections. You will also see the grid dots. They are set to represent one-inch intervals at your final plot size.

You can now setup Eye2eye as described previously.

Setting the Eyes

Try moving the camera and target objects in the Orthogonal views. You can use the Meye and Mtarg commands to help you locate the camera and target objects. When you use these commands, a temporary red-and-green vector is drawn to show you the location of the camera and target. The red portion of the vector shows the direction of the camera while the green portion shows the direction of the target. Use the Redraw command to remove the vectors. They are not true AutoCAD objects and will not plot.

Mtarg and Meye work just like the Move command but you don't have to select an object; the camera (Meye) or target (Mtarg) is automatically selected. You only need to select the base point and second point for the move. You can also use the standard AutoCAD Move command to move the camera and target.

As you move the eye and target location with Mtarg and Meye, the Perspective viewport will automatically update to display the new eye-to-target orientation. If you happen to move the eye or target blocks using the Move command, you can update the Perspective viewport by clicking the Perspective viewport and entering **Showeye.**⌐. A Perspective view based on the camera-target locations is displayed. You can then use the AutoCAD View command to save your view or go on to make minor adjustments. For example, you can use the Paneye command to adjust your perspective view before saving it.

Controlling the Eyes

You will notice some lines and numbers on the Perspective view. These are parts of the camera object showing you the angle below or above horizontal in 10-degree increments. You can turn off the display of camera and target objects by using the Hide Eyes option of the Seteye command. To turn them back on again, use the Show Eyes option. Alternately, you can simply turn the Eyes layer on or off. The Eyes layer is the layer on which the Eyeto and Eyefrom blocks were constructed.

The ActiveX Automation Samples

With AutoCAD 2000, you now have a new way to create custom applications in AutoCAD. ActiveX Automation is a new feature that allows AutoCAD users to take control of AutoCAD, either by creating Visual Basic applications or through other applications that support ActiveX Automation.

Chapter 98 provides an introduction to ActiveX Automation as it relates to Auto-CAD. There are some sample applications included on the CD-ROM that you can experiment with when you're reading Chapter 98. The following steps show you how to access those examples.

1. Start the *Mastering AutoCAD 2000* software installation program, as described earlier in this appendix.

2. Click the ActiveX Samples button. You'll see a list of samples you can install.

3. Click the name of the sample set of files you want to install, then follow the instructions that appear on the screen.

4. Proceed with another installation or click Exit.

AutoCAD Instant Reference

Mastering AutoCAD 2000 was designed to help AutoCAD users by demonstrating commands in the context of everyday activities that you might encounter in your work. It shows you what commands to use in a given situation. As a result, this book doesn't always show every option or permutation of a command. This is where the *AutoCAD 2000 Instant Reference* comes in.

The *AutoCAD 2000 Instant Reference* is the perfect companion to *Mastering AutoCAD 2000*. You can think of it as a dictionary of AutoCAD commands that describes each command in detail, including all of the command options.

The CD-ROM contains a Modern Age version of the *AutoCAD 2000 Instant Reference*. You will need to install the Modern Age book viewer (also on this CD-ROM) to use this online book.

1. Start the *Mastering AutoCAD 2000* software installation program, as described earlier in this appendix.

2. Click the *AutoCAD 2000 Instant Reference* button.

3. Follow the directions provided.

ABCs of AutoLISP

Previous editions of this book included an introduction to AutoLISP. In this edition of the book, the AutoLISP information has been replaced with a chapter on ActiveX Automation. In place of the introduction to AutoLISP, a complete AutoLISP tutorial and source book is included on the companion CD-ROM. The *ABCs of AutoLISP* offers a more detailed look at AutoCAD's macro-programming language.

The *ABCs of AutoLISP* is in a format that can be viewed using any Internet Web browser, such as Netscape Communicator or Microsoft Internet Explorer. To use it, simply install it on to your hard drive and double-click the Contents.HTM or

`ABC's_of_AutoLISP.htm` file. The following steps show you how to install the *ABCs of AutoLISP*.

1. Start the *Mastering AutoCAD 2000* software installation program, as described earlier in this appendix.

2. Click the AutoLISP button. You see a brief description of the *ABCs of AutoLISP* and the default location where it will be installed.

3. Click Continue. You see the WinZip Self-Extractor dialog box. You have the option to accept the default directory shown in the input box, or you may enter a different location for the files.

4. When you've entered the location for the sample files, click Unzip. The files will be installed on your computer.

5. Click Close to return to the main installation program screen.

6. Proceed with another installation or click Exit.

If you want to uninstall the *ABCs of AutoLISP*, simply delete the folder containing the files for the *ABCs of AutoLISP*. The *ABCs of AutoLISP* is an HTML document and does not directly affect your system registry or add any programs to your system.

The Whip! Plug-In

Chapter 19 discusses how you can add drawings to a Web page. Before you can view such drawings, you need to install the Whip4 plug-in for your Web browser. You can obtain this plug-in from the Autodesk Web site, but as a convenience, Whip! 4 is included on the CD-ROM.

To install Whip! 4, make sure that you have Netscape Navigator/Communicator 3.0 or later installed. Next, perform the following steps.

1. Make sure all other programs are closed.

2. Start the *Mastering AutoCAD 2000* software installation program, as described earlier in this appendix.

3. Click the Whip! 4 button. The Whip! 4 installation program starts.

4. Follow the instructions to complete the Whip! 4 installation.

If you are using Microsoft Internet Explorer, perform the following steps:

1. If your system requires that you log on to your Internet Service Provider (ISP) before opening your Web browser, do so now.

2. Go to `http://www.autodesk.com/products/whip/install.htm`.

3. Choose "Installing Whip! as an ActiveX control for Microsoft Internet Explorer."

The Whip4 ActiveX Control software takes about 20 minutes to download if you're using a 28.8 modem. When it is done, you will be asked if you want to restart your computer. Once the installation is complete, your Internet Explorer will be able to view AutoCAD .dwf files online.

PaintShop Pro, TutoHelp, QuickView, and Visual Stitcher

The *Mastering AutoCAD 2000* CD-ROM contains trial versions of PaintShop Pro, TutoHelp, QuickView, and Visual Stitcher. These programs help round out your needs as an AutoCAD user.

Each program provides its own installation utility. You can select these programs from the *Mastering AutoCAD 2000* CD-ROM installation menu, then follow the instructions that appear. You may also use Windows Explorer to locate the installation utility for the program you want to install, then double-click it to begin installation.

If you decide to remove an installed program, use the Add/Remove programs utility in the Windows Control Panel to completely remove the program.

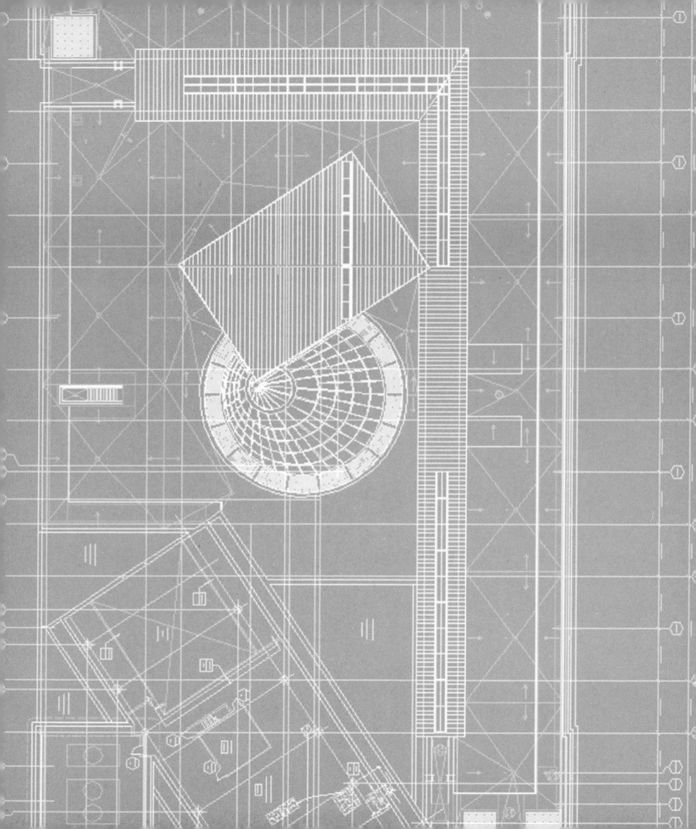

System and Dimension Variables

System variables let you fine-tune your AutoCAD environment. Dimension variables govern the specific dimensioning functions of AutoCAD.

System variables are accessible directly from the command prompt, and transparently (while in another command), by entering the variable name preceded by an apostrophe. These variables are also accessible through the AutoLISP interpreter by using the Getvar and Setvar functions as well as through ActiveX Automation.

This appendix is divided into two sections, *Setting System Variables* and *Setting Dimension Variables.* This division is somewhat artificial, because as far as AutoCAD is concerned, there is no difference between system variables and dimension variables—you use both types of variables the same way. But because the set of dimension variables is quite extensive, they are separated here for clarity.

At the end of this appendix, you will also find a detailed description of the Dimension Style dialog boxes. They are presented here to maintain clarity in Chapter 9 where the main discussion of dimensions is presented.

Setting System Variables

Table D.1 lists the variables, and notes whether they are read-only or adjustable. Most of these variables have counterparts in other commands, as listed in the table. For example, Angdir and Angbase can be adjusted using the Ddunits command (Format ➤ Units). Many, such as Highlight and Expert, do not have equivalent commands. These must be adjusted at the command line (or through AutoLISP).

TABLE D.1: System Variables. Items Marked with an Asterisk Are New in AutoCAD 2000.

Variable Name	Associated Command	Where Saved	Use
Acadlspasdoc*	Options	Registry	Controls the loading of the **Acad.1sp** file when present. 0 = load only into first drawing (initial value); 1 = into every opened drawing.
Acadprefix	Options	*NA*	The AutoCAD environment setting.

Continued on next page

TABLE D.1 CONTINUED: System Variables. Items Marked with an Asterisk Are New in AutoCAD 2000.

Variable Name	Associated Command	Where Saved	Use
Acadver	*NA*	*NA*	The AutoCAD version number.
Acisoutver	Acisout	With drawing	Controls ACIS version of SAT files.
Adcstate* (read-only)	*NA*	Registry	Indicates the current display state of the AutoCAD DesignCenter: 0 = closed; 1 = opened.
Aflags	Units	*NA*	Controls attribute mode settings: 1 = invisible; 2 = constant; 4= verify; 8=preset.
Angbase	Units	With drawing	Controls direction of 0° angle, relative to the current UCS.
Angdir	Units	With drawing	Controls positive direction of angles: 0 = counterclockwise; 1 = clockwise.
Apbox	Draw and Edit commands	Registry	Displays Autosnap aperture box when Autosnap is activated: 0 = off, 1 = on.
Aperture	Draw and Edit commands	Registry	Sets size of Osnap cursor in pixels.
Area (read-only)	Area	*NA*	Displays last area calculation; use with Setvar or AutoLISP's Getvar function.
Attdia	Insert/Attribute	With drawing	Controls the Attribute dialog box: 0 = no dialog box; 1 = dialog box.
Attmode	Attdisp	With drawing	Controls attribute display mode: 0 = off; 1 = normal; 2 = on.
Attreq	Insert	With drawing	Controls the prompt for attributes: 0 = no prompt or dialog box for attributes (attributes use default values); 1 = normal prompt or dialog box upon attribute insertion.
Auditctl	Config	Registry	Controls whether an audit file is created: 0 = disable; 1 = enable creation of .ADT file.
Aunits	Units	With drawing	Controls angular units: 0 = decimal degrees; 1 = degrees-minutes-seconds; 2 = grads; 3 = radians; 4 = surveyor's units.

Continued on next page

TABLE D.1 CONTINUED: System Variables. Items Marked with an Asterisk Are New in AutoCAD 2000.

Variable Name	Associated Command	Where Saved	Use
Auprec	Units	With drawing	Controls the precision of angular units determined by decimal place.
Autosnap	Draw/Edit	Registry	Controls Autosnap display and features: 0 = everything off; 1 = marker on; 2 = Snaptip on; 4 = magnet on.
Backz (read-only)	Dview	With drawing	Displays distance from Dview target to back clipping plane.
Bindtype*	Xref	NA	Controls the way Xref names are handled when bound to a file: 0 = maintain Xref filename prefix (initial value); 1 = remove Xref filename prefix.
Blipmode	NA	With drawing	Controls appearance of blips: 0 = off; 1 = on.
Cdate (read-only)	Time	NA	Displays calendar date/time read from system date (*YYYY MMDD .HHMMSSMSEC*).
Cecolor	Color	With drawing	Controls current default color assigned to new objects.
Celtscale	NA	With drawing	Controls current line-type scale for individual objects.
Celtype	Linetype	With drawing	Controls current default line type assigned to new objects.
Celweight*	Lineweight	With drawing	Controls the default line weight for new objects: −1 = Bylayer; -2 = Byblock; -3 = Default as set by Lwdefault. Specific line-weight values may also be entered in millimeters.
Chamfera	Chamfer	With drawing	Controls first chamfer distance.
Chamferb	Chamfer	With drawing	Controls second chamfer distance.
Chamferc	Chamfer	With drawing	Controls chamfer distance for Angle option.

Continued on next page

TABLE D.1 CONTINUED: System Variables. Items Marked with an Asterisk Are New in AutoCAD 2000.

Variable Name	Associated Command	Where Saved	Use
Chamferd	Chamfer	With drawing	Controls chamfer angle for Angle option.
Chammode	Chamfer	NA	Controls method of chamfer: 0 = use two distances; 1 = use distance and angle.
Circlerad	Circle	NA	Controls the default circle radius: 0 = no default.
Clayer	Layer	With drawing	Sets the current layer.
Cmdactive (read-only)	NA	NA	Displays whether a command, script, or dialog box is active: 1 = command active; 2 = transparent command active; 4 = script active; 8 = dialog box active (values are cumulative, so 3 = command and transparent command are active).
Cmddia	NA	Registry	Controls use of dialog boxes for some commands: 0 = don't use dialog box; 1 = use dialog box.
Cmdecho	AutoLISP	NA	With AutoLISP, controls display of prompts from embedded AutoCAD commands: 0 = no display of prompt; 1 = display prompts.
Cmdnames (read-only)	NA	NA	Displays the English name of the currently active command.
Cmljust	Mline	With drawing	Sets method of justification for multi-lines: 0 = top; 1 = middle; 2 = bottom.
Cmlscale	Mline	With drawing	Sets scale factor for Multiline widths: a 0 value collapses the multiline to a single line; a negative value reverses the justification.
Cmlstyle (read-only)	Mline	With drawing	Displays current multiline style by name.
Compass*	3DOrbit	NA	Controls the display of the 3D compass: 0 = off (initial value); 1 = on.

Continued on next page

TABLE D.1 CONTINUED: System Variables. Items Marked with an Asterisk Are New in AutoCAD 2000.

Variable Name	Associated Command	Where Saved	Use
Coords	F6, Ctrl+D	With drawing	Controls coordinate readout: 0 = co-ordinates displayed only when points are picked; 1 = absolute coordinates dynamically displayed as cursor moves; 2 = distance and angle displayed during commands that accept relative distance input.
Cplotstyle*	Plot/Pagesetup	With drawing	Controls the default plot style for new objects. Startup values are ByLayer, ByBlock, Normal, and User Defined.
Cprofile* (read-only)	Options	Registry	Displays the current profile name.
Ctab* (read-only)	(tabs)	With drawing	Displays the name of the current tab.
Cursorsize	NA	Registry	Determines size of crosshairs as a percentage of the screen size (1–100).
Cvport (read-only)	Vports	With drawing	Displays ID number of current viewport.
Date (read-only)	Time	NA	Displays date and time in Julian format.
Dbmod (read-only)	NA	NA	Displays drawing modification status: 1 = object database modified; 2 = symbol table modified; 4 = database variable modified; 8 = window modified; 16 = view modified.
Dctcust	Spell	Registry	Sets default custom spelling dictionary filename, including path.
Dctmain	Spell	Registry	Sets default main spelling dictionary filename; requires specific keywords for each language. See AutoCAD Help for complete list of keywords.
Deflplstyle*	Plotstyle	With drawing	Sets the default plot style for new layers.
Defplstyle*	Plotstyle	Registry	Sets the default plot style for new objects.

Continued on next page

TABLE D.1 CONTINUED: System Variables. Items Marked with an Asterisk Are New in AutoCAD 2000.

Variable Name	Associated Command	Where Saved	Use
Delobj	*NA*	With drawing	Controls whether source objects used to create new objects are retained: 0 = delete objects; 1 = retain objects.
Demandload	*NA*	Registry	Controls loading of third-party applications required for custom objects in drawing (0–3).
Diastat (read-only)	*NA*	*NA*	Displays how last dialog box was exited: 0 = Cancel; 1 = OK.
Dispsilh	All curved solids	With drawing	Controls silhouette display of curved 3D solids: 0 = no silhouette; 1 = silhouette curved solids.
Distance (read-only)	Dist	*NA*	Displays last distance calculated by Dist command.
Donutid	Donut	*NA*	Controls default inside diameter of a donut.
Donutod	Donut	*NA*	Controls default outside diameter of a donut.
Dragmode	*NA*	With drawing	Controls dragging: 0 = no dragging; 1 = if requested; 2 = automatic drag.
Dragp1	*NA*	Registry	Controls regeneration-drag input sampling rate.
Dragp2	*NA*	Registry	Controls fast-drag input sampling rate.
Dwgcheck*	*NA*	Registry	Controls the display of a warning dialog box indicating that a drawing was last edited in a program other than AutoCAD. 0 = suppress dialog box; 1 = display dialog box when needed.
Dwgcodepage (read-only)	*NA*	With drawing	Displays code page of drawing (see Syscodepage).
Dwgname (read-only)	Open	*NA*	Displays drawing name and drive/directory, if specified by user.

Continued on next page

TABLE D.1 CONTINUED: System Variables. Items Marked with an Asterisk Are New in AutoCAD 2000.

Variable Name	Associated Command	Where Saved	Use
Dwgprefix (read-only)	*NA*	*NA*	Displays drive and directory of current file.
Dwgtitled (read-only)	*NA*	*NA*	Displays whether a drawing has been named: 0 = untitled; 1 = named by user.
Edgemode	Trim, Extend	Registry	Controls how trim and extend boundaries are determined: 0 = boundaries defined by object only; 1 = boundaries defined by objects and their extension.
Elevation	Elev	With drawing	Controls current 3D elevation relative to current UCS.
Expert	*NA*	*NA*	Controls prompts, depending on level of user's expertise: 0 = normal prompts; 1 = suppresses **About to regen** and **Really want to turn the current layer off** prompts; 2 = suppresses **Block already defined** and **A drawing with this name already exists** prompt for Block command; 3 = suppresses **An item with this name already exists** prompt for the Linetype command; 4 = suppresses **An item with this name already exists** prompt for the UCS/Save and Vports/Save options; 5 = suppresses **An item with this name already exists** prompt for Dim/Save and Dim/Override commands.
Explmode	Explode	With drawing	Controls whether blocks inserted with different *x*, *y*, and *z* values are exploded: 0 = blocks are not exploded; 1 = blocks are exploded.
Extmax (read-only)	Zoom	With drawing	Displays upper-right corner coordinate of extents view.
Extmin (read-only)	Zoom	With drawing	Displays lower-left corner coordinate of extents view.

Continued on next page

TABLE D.1 CONTINUED: System Variables. Items Marked with an Asterisk Are New in AutoCAD 2000.

Variable Name	Associated Command	Where Saved	Use
Extnames*	Options	With drawing	Controls the length of names for named objects in AutoCAD: 0 = limits names to 31 characters; 1 = allow up to 255 characters.
Facetratio*	Shade, Hide	*NA*	Controls aspect ratio of faceting of curved 3D surfaces. Value is zero or 1, where 1 increases the density of the mesh.
Facetres	Shade, Hide	With drawing	Controls appearance of smooth curved 3D surfaces when shaded or hidden. Value can be between 0.01 and 10. The higher the number, the more faceted (and smoother) the curved surface, and the longer the time needed for shade and hidden-line removal.
Filedia	Dialog box	Registry	Sets whether a file dialog box is used by default: 0 = don't use unless requested with a ~ (a tilde); 1 = use whenever possible.
Filletrad	Fillet	With drawing	Controls fillet radius.
Fillmode	Fill	With drawing	Controls fill status: 0 = off; 1 = on.
Fontalt	Open, Dxfin, other File ➤ Import options	Registry	Lets you specify an alternate font when AutoCAD cannot find the font associated with a file. If no font is specified for Fontalt, AutoCAD displays a warning message and a dialog box where you manually select a font.
Fontmap	Open, Dxfin, other import functions	Registry	Similar to Fontalt, but lets you designate a set of font substitutions through a font mapping file. Example line from mapping file: `romans:c:\Program Files\AutoCAD2000\fonts\times.ttf`. This substitutes Romans font with Times TrueType font. Font-mapping file can be any name, with extension .FMP.

Continued on next page

TABLE D.1 CONTINUED: System Variables. Items Marked with an Asterisk Are New in AutoCAD 2000.

Variable Name	Associated Command	Where Saved	Use
Frontz (read-only)	Dview	With drawing	Controls front clipping plane for current viewport; use with View mode system variable.
Fullopen* (read-only)	Open	NA	Displays whether the current drawing is fully or partially opened.
Gridmode	Grid	With drawing	Controls grid: 0 = off; 1 = on.
Gridunit	Grid	With drawing	Controls grid spacing.
Grips	Grips	Registry	Controls use of grips: 0 = grips disabled; 1 = grips enabled (default).
Gripblock	Grips	Registry	Controls display of grips in blocks: 0 = show insertion point grip only; 1 = show grips of all objects in block.
Gripcolor	Grips	Registry	Controls color of unselected grips. Choices are integers from 1 to 255; default is 5.
Griphot	Grips	Registry	Controls color of hot grips. Choices are integers from 1 to 255; default is 1.
Gripsize	Grips	Registry	Controls grip size (in pixels), from 1 to 255 (default is 3).
Handles (read-only)	NA	With drawing	Displays status of object handles: 0 = off; 1 = on.
Hideprecision	Hide, Shade	NA	Controls the Hide/Shade precision accuracy: 0 = single precision; 1 = double precision.
Highlight	Select	NA	Controls whether objects are highlighted when selected: 0 = none; 1 = highlighting.
Hpang	Hatch	NA	Sets default hatch pattern angle.
Hpbound	Hatch	Registry	Controls type of object created by Hatch and Boundary commands: 0 = region; 1 = Polyline.

Continued on next page

TABLE D.1 CONTINUED: System Variables. Items Marked with an Asterisk Are New in AutoCAD 2000.

Variable Name	Associated Command	Where Saved	Use
Hpdouble	Hatch	*NA*	Sets default hatch doubling for user-defined hatch pattern: 0 = no doubling; 1 = doubling at 90°.
Hpname	Hatch	*NA*	Sets default hatch pattern name; use a period (.) to set to no default.
Hpscale	Hatch	*NA*	Sets default hatch pattern scale factor.
Hpspace	Hatch	*NA*	Sets default line spacing for user-defined hatch pattern; cannot be 0.
Hyperlinkbase*	Hyperlink	With drawing	Sets the base location for hyperlink addresses. If left blank, the drawing path is used.
Imagehlt*	Options	Registry	Controls highlighting of raster images: 0 = frame only; 1 = entire image.
Indexctl	NA	With drawing	Controls whether layer and spatial indexes are created and saved in drawings: 0 = no index; 1 = Layer index; 2 = Spatial index; 3 = both.
Inetlocation	Browser	Registry	Stores the Internet location used by the BROWSER command.
Insbase	Base	With drawing	Controls insertion base point of current drawing.
Insname	Insert	*NA*	Sets default block or filename for Insert command; enter a period (.) to set to no default.
Insunits*	Units	With drawing	Sets the units value for the Design-Center insert: 0 = unitless; 1 = inches; 2 = feet; 3 = miles; 4 = millimeters; 5 = centimeters; 6 = meters; 7 = kilometers; 8 = microinches; 9 = mils; 10 = yards; 11 = angstroms; 12 = nanometers; 13 = microns; 14 = decimeters; 15 = decameters; 16 = hectometers; 17 = gigameters; 18 = astronomical units; 19 = light years; 20 = parsecs.

Continued on next page

TABLE D.1 CONTINUED: System Variables. Items Marked with an Asterisk Are New in AutoCAD 2000.

Variable Name	Associated Command	Where Saved	Use
Insunitsdef-source*	Units	Registry	Sets the default source units. Values are the same as Insunits.
Insunitsdeftarget*	Units	Registry	Sets the default target units. Values are the same as Insunits.
Isavebak	Save	Registry	Controls the creation of BAK files: 0 = no BAK file created; 1 = BAK file created.
Isavepercent	Save	Registry	Determines whether to do a full or an incremental save based on the amount of wasted space tolerated in a drawing file: (0–100).
Isolines	Curved solids	With drawing	Specifies the number of lines on a Solid's surface to help visualize its shape.
Lastangle (read-only)	Arc	NA	Displays ending angle for last arc drawn.
Lastpoint	NA	NA	Sets or displays coordinate normally referenced by the @.
Lastprompt	NA	NA	Saves last string echoed to the command line.
Lenslength (read-only)	Dview	With drawing	Displays focal length of lens used for perspective display.
Limcheck	Limits	With drawing	Controls limit checking: 0 = no checking; 1 = checking.
Limmax	Limits	With drawing	Controls coordinate of drawing's upper-right limit.
Limmin	Limits	With drawing	Controls coordinate of drawing's lower-left limit.
Lispinit	Load	Registry	Preserves AutoLISP-defined functions and variables beyond current drawing session: 0 = AutoLISP variables preserved; 1 = AutoLISP functions valid for current session only.

Continued on next page

TABLE D.1 CONTINUED: System Variables. Items Marked with an Asterisk Are New in AutoCAD 2000.

Variable Name	Associated Command	Where Saved	Use
Locale (read-only)	NA	NA	Displays ISO language code used by your version of AutoCAD.
Logfilemode	NA	Registry	Determines whether log file is recorded or not: 0 = log file off; 1 = log file on.
Logfilename	NA	Registry	Specifies name/path of log file.
Logfilepath*	Options	Registry	Sets the path for the log file.
Loginname (read-only)	NA	NA	Displays user's login name.
Ltscale	Ltscale	With drawing	Controls the global line-type scale factor.
Lunits	Units	With drawing	Controls unit styles: 1 = scientific; 2 = decimal; 3 = engineering, 4 = architectural, 5 = fractional.
Luprec	Units	With drawing	Controls unit accuracy by decimal place or size of denominator.
Lwdefault*	Lineweight	Registry	Sets the default line weight. Values are specified in millimeters x 100 (25 = 0.25mm).
Lwdisplay*	Lineweight	With drawing	Determines whether line weights are displayed: 0 = not displayed; 1 = displayed.
Lwscale*	Lineweight	With drawing	Determines whether line weights are scaled with plotter scale settings or are absolute values: 0 = scaled with plot; 1 = absolute value.
Lwunits*	Lineweight	Registry	Sets the display of line weight units: 0 = inches; 1 = millimeters.
Maxactvp	Viewports/ Vports	With drawing	Controls maximum number of viewports to regenerate at one time.
Maxobjmem	NA	NA	Specifies the amount of virtual memory that can be used before AutoCAD starts paging a drawing out to disk.

Continued on next page

TABLE D.1 CONTINUED: System Variables. Items Marked with an Asterisk Are New in AutoCAD 2000.

Variable Name	Associated Command	Where Saved	Use
Maxsort	NA	Registry	Controls maximum number of items to be sorted when a command displays a list.
Mbuttonpan*	Options	Registry	Determines the behavior of the pointing devices wheel or third button: 0 = behavior determined by menu file; 1 = click-and-drag panning.
Measureinit	Open	Registry	Sets the unit style for new drawings. Determines whether metric or English template file should be used. Determines which default line type and hatch pattern files should be used: 0 = English; 1 = metric.
Measurement	Bhatch, Linetype	With drawing	Sets drawing units as English or metric: 0 = English; 1 = metric.
Menuctl	NA	Registry	Controls whether side menu changes in response to a command name entered from the keyboard: 0 = no response; 1 = menu response.
Menuecho	NA	NA	Controls messages and command prompt display from commands embedded in menu: 0 = display all messages; 1 = suppress menu item name; 2 = suppress command prompts; 4 = Disable ^P toggle of menu echo; 8 = debugging aid for DIESEL expressions.
Menuname (read-only)	Menu	With drawing	Displays name of current menu file.
Mirrtext	Mirror	With drawing	Controls mirroring of text: 0 = disabled; 1 = enabled.
Modemacro	NA	NA	Controls display of user-defined text in status line.
Mtexted	Mtext	Registry	Controls name of program used for editing Mtext objects.

Continued on next page

TABLE D.1 CONTINUED: System Variables. Items Marked with an Asterisk Are New in AutoCAD 2000.

Variable Name	Associated Command	Where Saved	Use
Nomutt*	NA	NA	Suppresses message display (muttering): 0 = normal display; 1 = suppress messages.
Offsetdist	Offset	NA	Controls default offset distance.
Offsetgaptype*	Offset	Registry	Controls how polyline line segments are joined when offset: 0 = extend line segments to join ends; 1 = keep line segments the same length and join endpoints with arcs; 2 = keep line segments the same length and join endpoints with lines.
Olehide	NA	Registry	Controls display of OLE objects.
Olequality*	Options	Registry	Controls the quality of OLE objects: 0 = line art; 1 = text; 2 = graphics; 3 = photograph; 4 = high quality photograph.
Olestartup*	Options	With drawing	Determines whether the source application of an OLE object is loaded when the OLE object is plotted: 0 = No load; 1 = load.
Opmstate* (read-only)	Properties	Registry	Displays the current state of the Properties dialog box: 0 = not open; 1 = open.
Orthomode	F8, Ortho	With drawing	Controls Ortho mode: 0 = off; 1 = on.
Osmode	Osnap	With drawing	Sets current default Osnap mode: 0 = none; 1 = endpoint; 2 = midpoint; 4 = center; 8 = node; 16 = quadrant; 32 = intersection; 64 = insert; 128 = perpendicular; 256 = nearest; 512 = quick. If more than one mode is required, enter the sum of those modes.
Osnapcoord	Osnap	Registry	Controls whether coordinates entered at the command line use running object snaps: 0 = Running Osnaps settings override; 1 = keyboard entry overrides; 2 = keyboard entry overrides, except in scripts.

Continued on next page

TABLE D.1 CONTINUED: System Variables. Items Marked with an Asterisk Are New in AutoCAD 2000.

Variable Name	Associated Command	Where Saved	Use
Paperupdate*	Plot	Registry	Controls the display of paper size warning message: 0 = display warning if the paper size in a paper space layout is not supported by the specified plotter. 1 = adjust paper size to conform with plotter configuration.
Pdmode	Ddptype	With drawing	Controls type of symbol used as a point during Point command.
Pdsize	Point	With drawing	Controls size of symbol set by Pdmode.
Pellipse	Ellipse	With drawing	Controls type of object created with Ellipse command: 0 = true NURBS ellipse; 1 = polyline representation of ellipse.
Perimeter (read-only)	Area, List	NA	Displays last perimeter value derived from Area and List commands.
Pfacevmax (read-only)	Pface	NA	Displays maximum number of vertices per face. (*PFaces* are 3D surfaces designed for use by third-party software producers and are not designed for end users.)
Pickadd	Select	Registry	Determines how items are added to a selection set: 0 = only most recently selected item(s) become selection set (to accumulate objects in a selection set, hold down Shift while selecting); 1 = selected objects accumulate in a selection set as you select them (hold down Shift while selecting items to remove those items from the selection set).
Pickauto	Select	Registry	Controls automatic window at `Select objects:` prompt: 0 = window is enabled; 1 = window is disabled.
Pickbox	Select	Registry	Controls size of object-selection pickbox (in pixels).

Continued on next page

TABLE D.1 CONTINUED: System Variables. Items Marked with an Asterisk Are New in AutoCAD 2000.

Variable Name	Associated Command	Where Saved	Use
Pickdrag	Select	Registry	Controls how selection windows are used: 0 = click each corner of the window; 1 = Shift+click and hold on first corner, then drag and release for the second corner.
Pickfirst	Select	Registry	Controls whether you can pick object(s) before you select a command: 0 = disabled; 1 = enabled.
Pickstyle	Group, Hatch	With drawing	Controls whether groups and/or associative hatches are selectable: 0 = neither are selectable; 1 = groups only; 2 = associative hatches only; 3 = both groups and associative hatches.
Platform (read-only)	*NA*	*NA*	Identifies the version of AutoCAD being used.
Plinegen	Pline/Pedit	With drawing	Controls how polylines generate line types around vertices: 0 = line-type pattern begins and ends at vertices; 1 = line-type patterns ignore vertices and begin and end at polyline beginning and ending.
Plinetype	Pline	Registry	Controls whether AutoCAD creates optimized 2D polylines and/or converts existing polylines to optimized polylines: 0 = polylines in existing drawings are not converted, *and* new polylines are not optimized; 1 = polylines in existing drawings are not converted, *but* new polylines are optimized; 2 = polylines in existing drawings are not converted, *and* new polylines are optimized.
Plinewid	Pline	With drawing	Controls default polyline width.
Plotid	Plot	Registry	Sets default plotter based on its description.
Plotlegacy*	Options	Registry	Allows the use of scripts for plotting: 0 = scripts not allowed; 1 = allows the use of scripts.

Continued on next page

TABLE D.1 CONTINUED: System Variables. Items Marked with an Asterisk Are New in AutoCAD 2000.

Variable Name	Associated Command	Where Saved	Use
Plotrotmode	Plot	Registry	Controls orientation of your plotter output.
Plotter	Plot	Registry	Sets default plotter, based on its integer ID.
Plquiet*	NA	Registry	Controls the display of dialog boxes for batch plotting and scripts: 0 = display dialog boxes; 1 = do not display dialog boxes.
Polaraddang*	Dsettings	Registry	Sets the value of the Additional angle setting of the Polar Snap tab of the Drafting Settings dialog box. You may enter up to 10 angles of 25 characters each separated with semicolons.
Polarang*	Dsettings	Registry	Sets the Increment Angle setting of the Polar Snap tab of the Drafting Settings dialog box.
Polardist*	Dsettings	Registry	Sets the Polar Snap distance.
Polarmode*	Dsettings/Options	With drawing	Sets Polar and Object Snap Tracking settings. The value is the sum of four pairs of codes as follows. Polar angle measurement: 0 = absolute; 1 = relative. Object Snap tracking: 0 = orthogonal only; 2 = use Polar Tracking settings. Use additional Polar Tracking angles: 0 = no; 4 = yes. Acquire Object Snap Tracking points (Options dialog box): 0 = automatically; 8 = Shift to acquire.
Polysides	Polygon	NA	Controls default number of sides for a polygon.
Popups (read-only)	NA	NA	Displays whether the current system supports pull-down menus: 0 = no; 1 = yes.
Projectname	Options	Registry	Assigns a project name to a drawing. The project name can be associated with one or more folders.

Continued on next page

TABLE D.1 CONTINUED: System Variables. Items Marked with an Asterisk Are New in
AutoCAD 2000.

Variable Name	Associated Command	Where Saved	Use
Projmode	Trim, Extend	Registry	Controls how the Trim and Extend commands affect objects in 3D: 0 = objects must be coplanar; 1 = trims/extends based on a plane parallel to the current UCS; 2 = trims/extends based on a plane parallel to the current view plane.
Proxygraphics	NA	With drawing	Controls whether images of proxy objects are stored in a drawing: 0 = images not stored; 1 = images saved.
Proxynotice	NA	Registry	Issues a warning to the user when a proxy object is created, i.e., when user opens a drawing containing custom objects created using an application which is not loaded: 0 = no warning; 1 = warning displayed.
Proxyshow	NA	Registry	Specifies if and how proxy objects are displayed: 0 = No display; 1 = graphic display of all proxy objects; 2 = only bounding box shown.
Psltscale	Pspace	With drawing	Controls Paper Space line-type scaling.
Psprolog	Psout	Registry	Controls what portion of the **ACAD.PSF** file is used for the prologue section of a PSOUT output file. Set this to the name of the section you want to use.
Psquality	Psin	Registry	Controls how images are generated in AutoCAD with the Psin command. Value is an integer: 0 = only bounding box is drawn; >0 = number of pixels per AutoCAD drawing unit; <0 = outline with no fills, and absolute value of setting determines pixels per drawing units.
Pstylemode*	Options	Drawing	Determines the type of plot styles used in new or imported drawings: 0 = color plot styles; 1 = named plot styles.

Continued on next page

TABLE D.1 CONTINUED: System Variables. Items Marked with an Asterisk Are New in AutoCAD 2000.

Variable Name	Associated Command	Where Saved	Use
Pstylepolicy*	NA	Registry	Determines whether object colors are associated with its plot style: 0 = no association; 1 = association.
Psvpscale*	Vports	NA	Sets the default view scale factor for new viewports. Values must be positive real: 0 = scale to fit.
Pucsbase*	Ucsman	With drawing	Stores the name of a UCS that you want to use as the base for orthographic UCS settings. Paper Space only.
Qtextmode	Qtext	With drawing	Controls the quick text mode: 0 = off; 1 = on.
Rasterpreview	Save	Registry	Controls whether raster preview images are saved with the drawing and sets the format type: 0 = No preview image created; 1 = BMP preview image.
Refeditname* (read only)	Refedit	NA	Displays the current reference-editing state of a drawing.
Regenmode	Regenauto	With drawing	Controls Regenauto mode: 0 = off; 1 = on.
Re-init	Reinit	NA	Reinitializes I/O ports, digitizers, display, plotter, and **ACAD.PGP**: 1 = digitizer port; 2 = Plotter port; 4 = digitizer; 8 = display; 16 = PGP file reload.
Rtdisplay	Rtpan, Rtzoom	Registry	Controls display of raster images during realtime Pan and Zoom.
Savefile (read-only)	Autosave	Registry	Displays filename that is autosaved.
Savename (read-only)	Save	NA	Displays user filename under which file is saved.
Savetime	Autosave	Registry	Controls time interval between automatic saves, in minutes: 0 = disable automatic save.

Continued on next page

TABLE D.1 CONTINUED: System Variables. Items Marked with an Asterisk Are New in AutoCAD 2000.

Variable Name	Associated Command	Where Saved	Use
Screenboxes (read-only)	Menu	Registry	Displays number of slots or boxes available in side menu.
Screenmode (read-only)	NA	Registry	Displays current display mode: 0 = text; 1 = graphics; 2 = dual screen.
Screensize (read-only)	NA	NA	Displays current viewport size in pixels.
SDI	NA	Registry	Determines whether AutoCAD allows multiple documents or limits user to single document editing: 0 = multiple documents; 1 = single document; 2 = indicates single documents because loaded third-party application does not support multiple documents (read only); 3 = same as 2 with SDI set to 1 by user.
Shadedge	Shade	With drawing	Controls how drawing is shaded: 0 = faces shaded, no edge highlighting; 1 = faces shaded, edge highlighting; 2 = faces not filled, edges in object color; 3 = faces in object color, edges in background color.
Shadedif	Shade	With drawing	Sets difference between diffuse reflective and ambient light. Value represents percentage of diffuse reflective light.
Shortcutmenu*	Right-click	Registry	Controls the Default, Edit, and Command mode shortcut menus. For multiple options, use the sum of option values: 0 = restore R14 behavior; 1 = Default mode shortcut enabled; 2 = Edit mode shortcut enabled; 4 = Command mode shortcut enabled; 8 = Command mode shortcut enabled only when options are shown in command line.
Shpname	Shape	NA	Controls default shape name.
Sketchinc	Sketch	With drawing	Controls sketch record increment.

Continued on next page

TABLE D.1 CONTINUED: System Variables. Items Marked with an Asterisk Are New in AutoCAD 2000.

Variable Name	Associated Command	Where Saved	Use
Skpoly	Sketch	With drawing	Controls whether the Sketch command uses regular lines or polylines: 0 = line; 1 = polyline.
Snapang	Snap	With drawing	Controls snap and grid angle.
Snapbase	Snap	With drawing	Controls snap, grid, and hatch pattern origin.
Snapisopair	Snap	With drawing	Controls isometric plane: 0 = left; 1 = top; 2 = right.
Snapmode	F9, Snap	With drawing	Controls snap toggle: 0 = off; 1 = on.
Snapstyl	Snap	With drawing	Controls snap style: 0 = standard; 1 = isometric.
Snaptype*	Snap	Registry	Controls whether polar or grid snap is current: 0 = grid snap; 1 = polar snap.
Snapunit	Snap	With drawing	Controls snap spacing given in x and y values.
Solidcheck*	Solidedit	NA	Controls solid validation for 3D solids in current session: 0 = off; 1 = on.
Sortents	NA	Registry	Controls whether objects are sorted based on their order in database: 0 = disabled; 1 = sort for object selection; 2 = sort for object snap; 4 = sort for redraws; 8 = sort for Mslide; 16 = sort for regen; 32 = sort for plot; 64 = sort for Psout.
Splframe	Pline, Pedit, 3DFace	With drawing	Controls display of spline vertices, defining mesh of a surface-fit mesh, and display of "invisible" edges of 3D Faces: 0 = no display of spline vertices, display only fit surface of a smoothed 3D Mesh, and no display of "invisible" edges of 3D Face; 1 = spline vertices are displayed, only defining mesh of a smoothed 3D Mesh is displayed, "invisible" edges of 3D Face are displayed.

Continued on next page

TABLE D.1 CONTINUED: System Variables. Items Marked with an Asterisk Are New in AutoCAD 2000.

Variable Name	Associated Command	Where Saved	Use
Splinesegs	Pline, Pedit	With drawing	Controls number of line segments used for each spline patch.
Splinetype	Pline, Pedit	With drawing	Controls type of spline curve generated by Pedit spline: 5 = quadratic B-spline; 6 = cubic B-spline.
Surftab1	Rulesurf, Tabsurf, Revsurf, Edgesurf	With drawing	Controls number of facets in the *m* direction of meshes.
Surftab2	Revsurf, Edgesurf	With drawing	Controls number of facets in the *n* direction of meshes.
Surftype	Pedit	With drawing	Controls type of surface fitting used by the Pedit command's Smooth option: 5 = quadratic B-spline surface; 6 = cubic B- spline surface; 8 = Bezier surface.
Surfu	3Dmesh	With drawing	Controls surface density in the *m* direction.
Surfv	3Dmesh	With drawing	Controls surface density in the *n* direction.
Syscodepage (read-only)	*NA*	*NA*	Displays system code page specified in ACAD.XMX.
Tabmode	Tablet	*NA*	Controls tablet mode: 0 = off; 1 = on.
Target (read-only)	Dview	With drawing	Displays coordinate of perspective target point.
Tdcreate (read-only)	Time	With drawing	Displays time and date of file creation in Julian format.
Tdindwg (read-only)	Time	With drawing	Displays total editing time in days and decimal days.
Tducreate* (read-only)	Time	With drawing	Displays the time and date that a drawing was created.
Tdupdate (read-only)	Time	With drawing	Displays time and date of last file update in Julian format.

Continued on next page

TABLE D.1 CONTINUED: System Variables. Items Marked with an Asterisk Are New in AutoCAD 2000.

Variable Name	Associated Command	Where Saved	Use
Tdusrtimer (read-only)	Time	With drawing	Displays user-controlled elapsed time in days and decimal days.
Tdupdate* (read-only)	Time	With drawing	Displays the time and date of last update or save.
Tempprefix (read-only)	NA	NA	Displays location for temporary files.
Texteval	NA	NA	Controls interpretation of text input: 0 = AutoCAD takes all text input literally; 1 = AutoCAD interprets "(" and "!" as part of an AutoLISP expression, unless either the Text or Dtext command is active.
Textfill	Text	Registry	Controls display of Bitstream, TrueType, and PostScript Type 1 fonts: 0 = outlines; 1 = filled.
Textqlty	Text	With drawing	Controls resolution of Bitstream, True-Type, and PostScript Type 1 fonts: values from 1.0 to 100.0. The lower the value, the lower the output resolution. Higher resolutions improve font quality but decrease display and plot speeds.
Textsize	Text Dtext	With drawing	Controls default text height.
Textstyle	Text, Dtext	With drawing	Controls default text style.
Thickness	Elev	With drawing	Controls default 3D thickness of object being drawn.
Tilemode	Mspace/ Pspace	With drawing	Controls Paper Space and viewport access: 0 = Paper Space and viewport objects enabled; 1 = strictly Model Space.
Tooltips	Icon tool palettes	Registry	Controls display of tool tips: 0 = off; 1 = on.
Tracewid	Trace	With drawing	Controls trace width.

Continued on next page

TABLE D.1 CONTINUED: System Variables. Items Marked with an Asterisk Are New in AutoCAD 2000.

Variable Name	Associated Command	Where Saved	Use
Trackpath*	Options	Registry	Controls the display of the tracking vector: 0 = full screen; 1 = only between alignment points; 2 = no Polar Tracking vector; 3 = no Polar or Object Snap Tracking vector.
Treedepth	Treestat	With drawing	Controls depth of tree-structured spatial index affecting speed of AutoCAD database search. First two digits are for Model Space nodes; second two digits are for Paper Space nodes. Use positive integers for 3D drawings and negative integers for 2D drawings. Negative values can improve speed of 2D operation.
Treemax	Regen, Treedepth	Registry	Limits memory use during regens by limiting maximum number of nodes in spatial index created with the Treedepth command.
Trimmode	Chamfer, Fillet	Registry	Controls whether lines are trimmed during the Chamfer and Fillet commands: 0 = no trim; 1 = trim (as with pre-Release 13 versions of AutoCAD).
Tspacefac*	Mtext	NA	Sets multiline text line spacing as a percentage of text height. Valid range is between 0.25 and 4.0.
Tspacetype*	Mtext	NA	Controls multiline text line spacing quality: 1 = use tallest letter for basis of line spacing; 2 = use text height specification a basis of line spacing.
Tstackalign*	Mtext	With drawing	Controls text alignment for stacked text: 0 = bottom; 1 = center; 2 = top.
Tstacksize*	Mtext	With drawing	Sets stacked fraction text height as percent of normal text height. Valid range is 1 to 127.
Ucsaxisang*	UCS	Registry	Sets the default rotation angle for x-, y-, or z-axis option of UCS command.

Continued on next page

TABLE D.1 CONTINUED: System Variables. Items Marked with an Asterisk Are New in AutoCAD 2000.

Variable Name	Associated Command	Where Saved	Use
Ucsbase*	UCS	With drawing	Sets the name of the UCS used as a basis for orthographic UCS options.
Ucsfollow	UCS	With drawing	Controls whether AutoCAD automatically changes to Plan view of UCS while in Model Space: 0 = UCS change does not affect view; 1 = UCS change causes view to change with UCS.
Ucsicon	Ucsicon	With drawing	Controls UCS icon: 1 = on; 2 = UCS icon appears at origin.
Ucsname (read-only)	Ucs	With drawing	Displays name of current UCS.
Ucsorg (read-only)	Ucs	With drawing	Displays origin coordinate for current UCS relative to World Coordinate System.
Ucsortho*	Ucs	With drawing	Controls whether the UCS follows orthographic views: 0 = does not follow; 1 = follow orthographic view.
Ucsview*	View	With drawing	Controls whether a UCS is saved with a named view: 0 = not saved; 1 = saved.
Ucsvp*	Vport	With drawing	Controls whether the UCS follows the orientation of a new viewport: 0 = current UCS; 1 = follow orientation of viewport view.
Ucsxdir (read-only)	Ucs	With drawing	Displays x direction of current UCS relative to World Coordinate System.
Ucsydir (read-only)	Ucs	With drawing	Displays y direction of current UCS relative to World Coordinate System.
Undoctl (read-only)	Undo	NA	Displays current state of Undo feature: 1 = Undo enabled; 2 = only one command can be undone; 4 = Autogroup mode enabled; 8 = group is currently active.
Undomarks (read-only)	Undo	NA	Displays number of marks placed by Undo command.

Continued on next page

TABLE D.1 CONTINUED: System Variables. Items Marked with an Asterisk Are New in AutoCAD 2000.

Variable Name	Associated Command	Where Saved	Use
Unitmode	Units	With drawing	Controls how AutoCAD displays fractional, foot-and-inch, and surveyor's angles: 0 = industry standard; 1 = Auto-CAD input format.
Useri1–Useri5	AutoLISP/Diesel	With drawing	Five user variables capable of storing integer values.
Userr1–Userr5	AutoLISP/Diesel	With drawing	Five user variables capable of storing real values.
Users1–Users5	AutoLISP/Diesel	With drawing	Five user variables capable of storing string values.
Viewctr (read-only)	*NA*	With drawing	Displays center of current view in coordinates.
Viewdir (read-only)	Dview	With drawing	Displays camera-viewing direction in coordinates.
Viewmode (read-only)	Dview	With drawing	Displays view-related settings for current viewport: 1 = perspective on; 2 = front clipping on; 4 = back clipping on; 8 = UCS follow on; 16 = front clip not at a point directly in front of the viewer's eye.
Viewsize (read-only)	*NA*	With drawing	Displays height of current view in drawing units.
Viewtwist (read-only)	Dview	With drawing	Displays twist angle for current viewport.
Visretain	Layer	With drawing	Controls whether layer setting for Xrefs is retained: 0 = current layer color; linetype and visibility settings retained when drawing is closed; 1 = layer settings of Xref drawing always renewed when file is opened.
Vsmax (read-only)	*NA*	With drawing	Displays coordinates of upper-right corner of virtual screen.
Vsmin (read-only)	*NA*	With drawing	Displays coordinates for lower-left corner of virtual screen.

Continued on next page

TABLE D.1 CONTINUED: System Variables. Items Marked with an Asterisk Are New in AutoCAD 2000.

Variable Name	Associated Command	Where Saved	Use
Whiparc*	*NA*	Registry	Controls the tessellation of circles and arcs: 0 = tessellated; 1 = not tessellated.
Wmfbkgnd*	Export	*NA*	Sets the way backgrounds and borders are generated in exported Windows metafiles: 0 = transparent backgrounds, no borders; 1 = background same as AutoCAD background, border is reverse color of background.
Worlducs (read-only)	UCS	*NA*	Displays status of WCS: 0 = current UCS is not WCS; 1 = current UCS is WCS.
Worldview	Dview, Vpoint	With drawing	Controls whether the Dview and Vpoint commands operate relative to UCS or WCS: 0 = current UCS is used; 1 = WCS is used.
Writestat* (read-only)	*NA*	*NA*	Displays the current drawings read/write status: 0 = read-only; 1 = drawing can be written to.
Xclipframe	Xref	With drawing	Controls visibility of Xref clipping boundaries: 0 = clipping boundary is not visible; 1 = boundary is visible.
Xedit*	Options	With drawing	Controls Refedit availability of current drawing: 0 = not available for in-place Xref editing; 1 = available for in place Xref editing.
Xfadectl*	Options	*NA*	Controls fading intensity in percent value for objects not selected while using Refedit (in-place Xref editing). Valid range is 0 to 90.
Xloadctl	Xref, Xclip	Registry	Controls Xref demand loading, and creation of copies of original Xref: 0 = no demand loading allowed, entire Xref drawing is loaded; 1 = demand loading allowed, and original Xref file is kept open; 2 = demand loading allowed, using a copy of Xref file stored in AutoCAD temp files folder.

Continued on next page

TABLE D.1 CONTINUED: System Variables. Items Marked with an Asterisk Are New in AutoCAD 2000.

Variable Name	Associated Command	Where Saved	Use
Xloadpath	Xref	Registry	Creates a path for storing temporary copies of demand-loaded Xref files.
Xrefctl	Xref	Registry	Controls whether Xref log files are written: 0 = no log files; 1 = log files written.
Zoomfactor*	Mouse Wheel	Registry	Controls the amount of zoom applied to a drawing when the mouse wheel is turned. Valid range is between 3 and 100. Default is 10.

Setting Dimension Variables

In Chapter 9, nearly all of the system variables related to dimensioning are shown with their associated options in the Dimension Styles dialog box. Later in the appendix you'll find a complete discussion of all elements of the Dimension Styles dialog box and how to use it.

This section provides further information about the dimension variables. For starters, Table D.2 lists the variables, their default status, and a brief description of what they do. You can get a similar listing by entering **–Dimstyle.⌐** at the command prompt, then typing **ST** to select the Status option. Alternatively, you can use the AutoCAD Help system. This section also discusses a few system variables that do not show up in the Dimension Styles dialog box.

TABLE D.2: The Dimension Variables

Dimension Variable	Default Setting	Description
		General Dimension Controls
Dimaso	On	Turns associative dimension on and off.
Dimsho	On	Updates dimensions dynamically while dragging.

Continued on next page

TABLE D.2 CONTINUED: The Dimension Variables

Dimension Variable	Default Setting	Description
		General Dimension Controls
Dimstyle	Standard	Name of current dimension style.
Dimtmove	0	Sets the way dimension text behaves when moved: 0 = move dimension line with text; 1 = add leader and move text freely; 2 = no leader and move text freely.
Dimupt	Off	Controls user positioning of text during dimension input: 0 = automatic text positioning; 1 = user defined text positioning allowed.
		Scale
Dimscale	1.0000	Overall scale factor of dimensions.
Dimtxt	.18 (approx. 3/16")	Text height.
Dimasz	.18 (approx. 3/16")	Arrow size.
Dimtsz	0"	Tick size.
Dimcen	.09 (approx. 3/32")	Center mark size.
Dimlfac	1.0000	Multiplies measured distance by a specified scale factor.
		Offsets
Dimexo	.0625 or 1/16"	Extension line origin offset.
Dimexe	.18 (approx. 3/16")	Amount extension line extends beyond dimension line.
Dimdli	.38 (approx. 3/8")	Dimension line offset for continuation or base.
Dimdle	0"	Amount dimension line extends beyond extension line.
		Tolerances
Dimalttz	0	Controls zero suppression of tolerance values: 0 = leaves out zero feet and inches; 1 = includes zero feet and inches; 2 = includes zero feet; 3 = includes zero inches; 4 = suppresses leading zeroes in decimal dimensions; 8 = suppresses leading zeroes in decimal dimensions.
Dimdec	4	Sets decimal place for primary tolerance values.
Dimtdec	4	Sets decimal place for tolerance values.

Continued on next page

TABLE D.2 CONTINUED: The Dimension Variables

Dimension Variable	Default Setting	Description
		Tolerances
Dimtp	0"	Plus tolerance.
Dimtm	0"	Minus tolerance.
Dimtol	Off	When on, shows dimension tolerances.
Dimtolj	1	Controls vertical location of tolerance values relative to nominal dimension: 0 = bottom; 1 = middle; 2 = top.
Dimtzin	0	Controls zero suppression in tolerance values: 0 = leaves out zero feet and inches; 1 = includes zero feet and inches; 2 = includes zero feet; 3 = includes zero inches; 4 = suppresses leading zeroes in decimal dimensions; 8 = suppresses leading zeroes in decimal dimensions; 12 = suppresses leading and trailing zeroes in decimal dimensions.
Dimlim	Off	When on, shows dimension limits.
		Rounding
Dimazin*	0	Controls zero suppression for angular dimensions: 0 = display all zeros; 1 = suppress leading zeros; 2 suppress trailing zeros; 3 = suppress all zeros.
Dimrnd	0"	Rounding value.
Dimzin	0	Controls zero suppression dimension text: 0 = leaves out zero feet and inches; 1 = includes zero feet and inches; 2 = includes zero feet; 3 = includes zero inches; 4 = suppresses leading zeroes in decimal dimensions; 8 = suppresses leading zeroes in decimal dimensions; 12 = suppresses leading and trailing zeroes in decimal dimensions.
		Dimension Arrow & Text Control
Dimadec	-1	Controls the number of decimal places shown for angular dimension text: 1 = uses the value set by Dimdec dimension variable; 0–8 = Specifies the actual number of decimal places to be shown.
Dimatfit*	3	Controls the way text and arrows are placed when there is not enough room to fit both within extension lines: 0 = place both outside extension lines; 1 = move arrows first; 2 = move text fires; 3 = move either text or arrows, whichever is best fit.

Continued on next page

TABLE D.2 CONTINUED: The Dimension Variables

Dimension Variable	Default Setting	Description
		Dimension Arrow & Text Control
Dimaunit	0	Controls angle format for angular dimensions; settings are the same as for Aunits system variable.
Dimblk	" "	Predefined or user-defined arrow block name. You can enter a user-defined block name or one of the following: _DOT, _DOTSMALL, _DOTBLANK, _ORIGIN, _ORIGIN2, _OPEN, _OPEN90, _OPEN30, _CLOSED, _SMALL, _OBLIQUE, _BOXFILLED, _BOXBLANK, _CLOSEDBLANK, _DATUMFILLED, _DATUMBLANK, _INTEGRAL, ARCHTICK.
Dimblk1	" "	Predefined or user-defined arrow block name for first end of dimension line used with Dimsah. See Dimblk for valid options.
Dimblk2	" "	Predefined or user-defined arrow block name for second end of dimension line used with Dimsah. See Dimblk for valid options.
Dimdsep*	. (period)	User-defined separator for decimals when dimension units are set to decimal.
Dimfit	3	Controls location of text and arrows for extension lines, if space is not available for both: 0 = text and arrows placed outside; 1 = text has priority, arrows are placed outside extension lines; 2 = arrows have priority; 3 = AutoCAD chooses between text and arrows, based on best fit; 4 = a leader is drawn from dimension line to dimension text when space for text not available; 5 = no leader.
Dimfrac*	0	Sets the fraction format for architectural and fractional formats: 0 = vertical; 1 = diagonal; 2 = not stacked.
Dimgap	1/16" or 0.09"	Controls distance between dimension text and dimension line.
Dimjust	0	Controls horizontal dimension text position: 0 = centered between extension lines; 1 = next to first extension line; 2 = next to second extension line; 3 = above and aligned with the first extension line; 4 = above and aligned with second extension line.
Dimldrblk*	0	Sets the arrow type for leaders: 0 = standard closed filled arrow; (period) = no arrow. See Dimblk for valid options.
Dimlunit*	Off	Sets unit style for all dimension types except angular: 1 = scientific; 2 = decimal; 3 = engineering; 4 = architectural; 5 = fractional; 6 = Windows Desktop.
Dimsah	Off	Allows use of two different arrowheads on a dimension line. See Dimblk1 and Dimblk2.

Continued on next page

TABLE D.2 CONTINUED: The Dimension Variables

Dimension Variable	Default Setting	Description
		Dimension Arrow & Text Control
Dimtfac	1.0"	Controls scale factor for dimension tolerance text.
Dimtih	On	When on, text inside extensions is horizontal.
Dimtoh	On	When on, text outside extensions is horizontal.
Dimtad	0	When on, places text above the dimension line.
Dimtix	Off	Forces text between extensions.
Dimtvp	0	Controls text's vertical position based on numeric value.
Dimtxsty	Standard	Controls text style for dimension text.
Dimunit	2	Controls unit style for all dimension style groups except angular. Settings are same as for Lunit system variable.
		Dimension & Extension Line Control
Dimsdl	Off	Suppresses the first dimension line.
Dimsd2	Off	Suppresses the second dimension line.
Dimse1	Off	When on, suppresses the first extension line.
Dimse2	Off	When on, suppresses the second extension line.
Dimtofl	Off	Forces a dimension line between extension lines.
Dimsoxd	Off	Suppresses dimension lines outside extension lines.
		Alternate Dimension Options
Dimalt	Off	When on, alternate units selected are shown.
Dimaltf	25.4000	Alternate unit scale factor.
Dimaltd	2	Alternate unit decimal places.
Dimalttd	2	Alternate unit tolerance decimal places.
Dimaltu	2	Alternate unit style. See Lunits system variable for values.
Dimaltz	0	Controls the suppression zeroes for alternate dimension values.

Continued on next page

TABLE D.2 CONTINUED: The Dimension Variables

Dimension Variable	Default Setting	Description
		Alternate Dimension Options
Dimpost	" "	Adds suffix to dimension text.
Dimapost	" "	Adds suffix to alternate dimension text.
		Colors and Lineweights
Dimclrd	0 or *ByBlock*	Controls color of dimension lines and arrows.
Dimclre	0 or *ByBlock*	Controls color of dimension extension lines.
Dimclrt	0 or *ByBlock*	Controls color of dimension text.
Dimlwd	*ByBlock*	Controls the line weight of dimension lines. Valid values are Bylayer, Byblock, or integer representing 100th millimeter.
Dimlwe	*Byblock*	Controls the line weight of extension lines. Valid values are Bylayer, Byblock, or integer representing 100th millimeter.

Finally, for those of you who might want to write macros, scripts, or AutoLISP programs to control dimension styles, you'll learn about using two options of the DIMSTYLE command to set and recall dimension styles from the command line: **–Dimstyle↵ S↵** and **–Dimstyle↵ R↵**.

If you want to change a setting through the command line instead of through the Dimension Styles dialog box, you can enter the system variable name at the command prompt.

Controlling Associative Dimensioning

You can turn off AutoCAD's *associative dimensioning* by changing the Dimaso setting. The default for Dimaso is On.

The Dimsho setting controls whether the dimension value is dynamically updated while a dimension line is being dragged. The default for this setting is On.

Storing Dimension Styles through the Command Line

Once you have set the dimension variables as you like, you can save the settings by using the Dimstyle command. The Dimstyle/Save command records all of the current dimension variable settings (except Dimaso) with a name you specify.

1. At the command prompt, enter **–Dimstyle**↵.

2. At the [Save/Restore/Status/Variables/Apply/?] <Save>: prompt, type ↵.

3. When the Enter name for new dimension style or [?]: prompt appears, you can enter a question mark (**?**) to get a listing of any dimension styles currently saved, or you can enter a name under which you want the current settings saved.

For example, suppose you change some of your dimension settings through dimension variables instead of through the Dimension Styles dialog box, as shown in the following list:

Dimtsz   0.044

Dimtad   On

Dimtih   Off

Dimtoh   Off

These settings are typical for an architectural style of dimensioning; you might save them under the name Architect, as you did in an exercise in Chapter 9. Then suppose you change other dimension settings for dimensions in another format—surveyor's dimensions on a site plan, for example. You might save them with the name Survey, again using the Save option of the Dimstyle command. When you want to return to the settings you used for your architectural drawing, use the Restore option of the Dimstyle command, described in the next section.

Restoring a Dimension Style from the Command Line

To restore a dimension style you've saved using the Dimstyle Save option:

1. At the command prompt, enter **–Dimstyle**↵.

2. At the [Save/Restore/STatus/Variable/Apply/?] <Restore>: prompt, type ↵.

3. At the following prompt:

   Enter dimension style name or [?] or <select dimension>:

   you have three options: Enter a question mark (**?**) to get a listing of saved dimension styles; enter the name of a style, such as Arch, if you know the name of the style you want; or use the cursor to select a dimension on the screen whose style you want to match.

Notes on Metric Dimensioning

The AutoCAD user community is worldwide and many of you may be using the metric system in your work. As long as you are not mixing U.S. (feet and inches) and metric measurements, using the English version of AutoCAD is fairly easy. With the Units command, set your measurement system to decimal, then draw distances in millimeters or centimeters. At plot time, select the mm radio button (millimeters) under Paper Size and Paper Units in the Plot dialog box. Also, be sure you specify a scale that compensates for differences between millimeters and centimeters.

If your drawings are to be in both foot-and-inch and metric measurements, you will be concerned with several settings, as follows:

Dimlfac Sets the scale factor for dimension values. The dimension value will be the measured distance in AutoCAD units times this scale factor. Set Dimlfac to 25.4 if you have drawn in inches but want to dimension in millimeters. The default is 1.00. If you want to scale dimension values from millimeters to inches, use a value of 0.03937.

Dimalt Turns the display of alternate dimensions on or off. Alternate dimensions are dimension text added to your drawing, in addition to the standard dimension text.

Dimaltf Sets the scale factor for alternate dimensions (i.e., to metric from English). The default is 25.4, which is the millimeter equivalent of 1". If you are using metric ISO units, the default will be 0.03937 which is the inch equivalent of 1mm.

Dimaltd Sets the number of decimal places displayed in the alternate dimensions.

Dimapost Adds suffix to alternate dimensions, as in 4.5mm.

If you prefer, you can use the metric template drawing supplied by AutoCAD.

1. Create a new drawing.

2. In the Create New Drawing dialog box, select the Use A Template option.

3. Click the filename ACADISO.DWT, and click OK to open the template.

This drawing is set up for metric/ISO standard drawings.

You can also use the Metric radio button in the Start From Scratch option of the Create New Drawing dialog box. This is the dialog box you see when you choose File ➤ New, or when you start AutoCAD. When you choose Metric from the Create New Drawing dialog box, subsequent new files will be set to metric by default.

If the Create New Drawing dialog box does not appear when you open Auto-CAD or choose File ➤ New, you can restore it by using the Show Startup Dialog option in the System tab of the Options dialog box.

A Closer Look at the Dimension Style Dialog Boxes

As you saw in Chapter 9, you can control the appearance and format of dimensions through dimension styles. You can create new dimension styles or edit existing ones. This section describes all the components of the dialog boxes you use to create and maintain dimension styles.

The Dimension Style Manager Dialog Box

The Dimension Style Manager dialog box is the gateway to dimension styles. With this dialog box, you can create new dimension style, edit existing ones, or make an existing dimension style current.

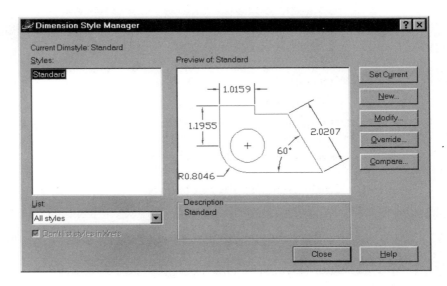

The following sections describe the options available in the Dimension Style Manager dialog box.

Preview of <Standard>

The image you see in the right half of the Dimension Style Manager dialog box gives you a preview of your dimension style. It shows a sample of most of the types of dimensions you'll use, formatted the way you specified when you created or modified your dimension style.

Styles

The Styles list box displays the available dimension styles. You can highlight the dimension style names in the Styles list box to indicate a style to be used with the Set Current, New, Modify, and Override options. You can also right-click a style name, then rename or delete the selected style.

List

The List drop-down list lets you control what is listed in the Styles list box. You can display either all the styles available or only the styles in use in the drawing.

Don't List Styles in Xrefs

The Don't List Styles in Xrefs check box lets you determine whether dimension styles in Xrefs are listed in the Styles list box.

Set Current

The Set Current button lets you set the dimension style highlighted in the Styles list box to be current.

New

The New button lets you create a new dimension style or modify the dimension type of an existing dimension style. The New button will use the dimension style that is highlighted in the Styles list box as the basis for the new style. This option opens the Create New Dimension Style dialog box.

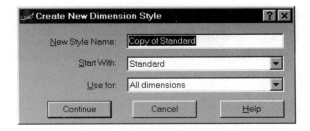

At the New Dimension dialog box, you can enter the name for your new dimension style. You can also select the source dimension style on which you new dimension style will be based.

New Style Name   Lets you specify the name for your new dimension style.

Start With   Lets you select an existing style on which to base your new dimension style.

User For   Lets you choose a dimension type for your new dimension style. For a completely new dimension style, use the All Dimensions option in the Use For drop-down list. If you want to modify the specifications for a particular dimension type of an existing dimension style, select a dimension type from this list. Your modified dimension type will appear in the Styles list box under the main style you specify in the Start With drop-down list. Once you've modified a dimension type, the new type will be applied to any new dimensions.

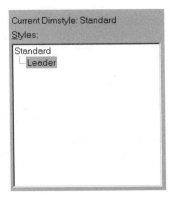

Once you've entered your options in the Create New Dimension Style dialog box, click Continue. You see the New Dimension Style dialog box described in the next section. When you are finished setting up your new style, you will see it listed in the Styles list box.

Modify

The Modify button lets you modify the dimension style that is selected in the Styles list box. This option opens the Modify Dimension Style dialog box described in the next section.

Override

The Override button lets you create a temporary dimension style based on an existing style. You may want to use this option if you need to create a dimension that differs only slightly from an existing style.

To use the Override option, select a style from the Styles list box, then select Override. You'll see the Override Current Style dialog box described in the next section. Once you create an override, you'll see it listed as <style overrides> in the Styles list box right under the style you used to create the override.

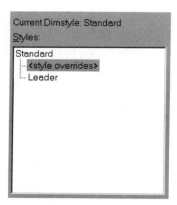

The override then becomes the default dimension style until you select another one from the Styles list. When you select a different style to be current, you will see a message telling you that the unsaved style will be discarded. To save an override style, select the override from the Styles list box, then click New. Click Continue at the Create New Dimension Style dialog box, then click OK at the New Dimension Style dialog box. You can also merge the Override style with its source style by right-clicking the <style overrides> listing and selecting Save to current style.

Compare

The Compare button lets you compare the differences between two dimension styles. When you click the Compare button, the Compare Dimension Styles dialog box appears.

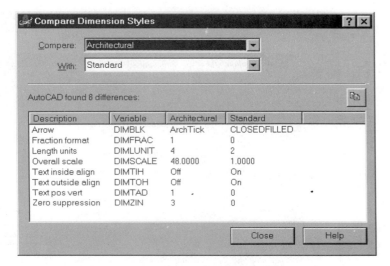

You can select the two styles you want to compare from the Compare and With drop-down lists. The differences will appear in the list box. The button just above the upper-right corner of the list box copies the contents of the list box to the Windows clipboard allowing you to save the comparison to a word-processed document.

The New/Modify/Override Dimension Style Dialog Box

When you select the New option in the Dimension Style Manager dialog box, then select Continue at the Create New Dimension Style dialog box, the New Dimension Style dialog box appears.

You will also see this same dialog box under a different name when you select the Modify or Override buttons in the Dimension Style Manager dialog box. The options in this dialog box let you determine all the characteristics of your dimension style. The following sections offer detailed descriptions of each available option.

NOTE
The equivalent dimension style variables are shown in brackets at the end of the description of each option.

Lines and Arrows Tab

The options in the Lines and Arrows tab give you control over the appearance of dimension and extension lines, arrowheads, and center marks. Figure D.1 shows an example of some of the dimension components that are affected by these options. The value you enter here for distances should be in final plot sizes and will be multiplied by the dimension scale value in the Fit tab to derive the actual extension distance in the drawing.

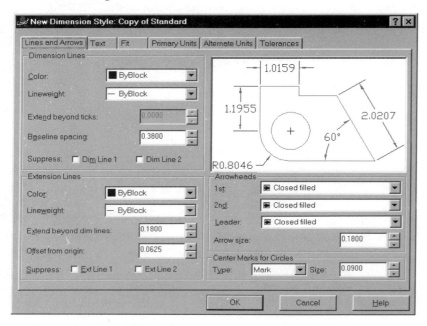

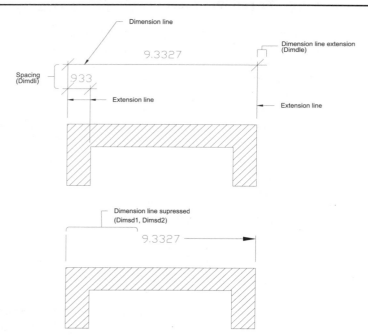

Examples of how some of the Lines and Arrows tab options affect dimensions

**FIGURE D.1
CONTINUED:**

Examples of how some of
the Lines and Arrows tab
options affect dimensions

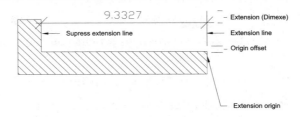

Dimension Lines Group   The following options let you control the general behavior characteristics of the dimension lines:

Color   Lets you set the color of the dimension line [Dimclrd].

Lineweight   Lets you set the line weight for dimension lines [Dimlwd].

Extend Beyond Ticks   Lets you set the distance that the dimension line extends beyond the extension lines. The value you enter here should be in final plot sizes and will be multiplied by the dimension scale value in the Fit tab to derive the actual extension distance in the drawing [Dimdle].

Baseline Spacing   Lets you specify the distance between stacked dimensions [Dimdli, Dimbaseline].

Suppress   Check boxes lets you suppress the dimension line on either side of the dimension text [DimLine1, DimLine2].

Extension Lines Group   The following options let you control the general behavior and characteristics of the extension lines:

Color   Lets you set the color for extension lines [Dimclre].

Lineweight   Lets you set the line weight for extension lines [Dimlwe].

Extend beyond dim lines   Lets you set the distance that extension lines extend beyond dimension lines [Dimexe].

Offset from origin   Lets you set the distance from the extension line to the object being dimensioned [Dimexo].

Suppress   Check boxes lets you suppress one or both extension lines [Ext Line1, Ext Line2].

Arrowheads Group   The following options let you select the type and sizes of arrowheads for dimensions and leaders:

1st   Drop-down list lets you select the type of arrowhead to use on dimension lines. By default, the 2nd arrowhead automatically changes to match the arrowhead you specify for this setting [Dimblk1].

2nd Drop-down list lets you select a different arrowhead from the one you select for 1st [Dimblk2].

Leader Drop-down list lets you specify an arrowhead for leader notes [Dimldrblk].

Arrow size Lets you specify the size for the arrowheads [Dimasz].

Center Marks for Circles Group The following options let you set the center mark for radius and diameter dimensions:

Type Drop-down list lets you select the type of center mark used in radius and diameter dimensions. Mark draws a small cross mark, Line draws a cross mark and centerlines, None doesn't draw anything [Dimcen].

Size Lets you specify the size of the center mark [Dimcen].

Text Tab

The options in the Text tab offer control over the appearance of the dimension text. You can set the text style and default location of text in relation to the dimension line. If the text style you select for your dimension text has a height value of 0, you can set the text height from this tab.

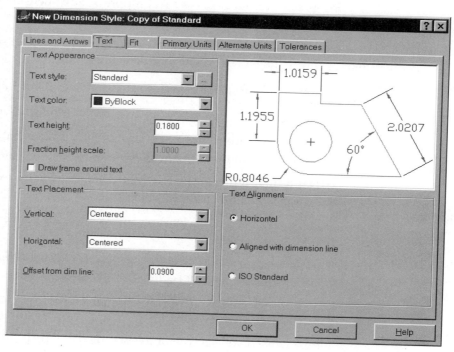

Text Appearance   The following options give you control over the appearance of text:

> **Text style**   Drop-down list lets you select an existing text style for your dimension text. You can also create a new style for your dimension text by clicking the Ellipses button [Dimtxsty].
>
> **Text color**   Drop-down list lets you select a color for your dimension text [Dimclrt].
>
> **Text height**   Lets you specify a text height for dimension text. This option is only valid for text styles with 0 height [Dimtxt].
>
> **Fraction height scale**   Lets you specify a scale factor for the height of fractional text. This option is only available when Architectural or Fractional is selected in the Primary Units tab [Dimtfac].
>
> **Draw frame around text**   Check box draws a rectangle around the dimension text when selected [Dimgap].

Text Placement   The following options give you control over the placement of text, including the ability to specify the distance of text from the dimension line:

> **Vertical**   Drop-down list lets you set the vertical position of the text in relation to the dimension line. The options are Centered, Above, Outside, and JIS. Centered places the text in line with the dimension line. The dimension line is broken to accommodate the text. Above places the text above the dimension line leaving the dimension line unbroken. Outside places the text away from the dimension line at a location farthest away from the object being dimensioned. JIS places the text in conformance to the Japanese Industrial Standards [Dimtad].
>
> **Horizontal**   Drop-down list lets you set the location of the text in relation to the extension lines. The options are Centered, 1st Extension Line, 2nd Extension Line, Over 1st Extension Line, and Over 2nd Extension Line. Centered places the text between the two extension lines. 1st Extension Line [extension lines. 2nd Extension Line places the text next to the second extension line but still between the two extension lines. Over 1st Extension Line places the text above the first extension line and aligned with the first extension line. Over 2nd Extension Line places the text above the second extension line and aligned with the second extension line [Dimjust].
>
> **Offset from dim line**   Lets you determine the distance from the baseline of text to the dimension line when text is placed above the dimension line. It also lets you set the size of the gap between the dimension text and the

endpoint of the dimension line when the text is in line with the dimension line. You can use this option to set the margin around the text when the dimension text is in a centered position that breaks the dimension line into two segments [Dimgap].

Text Alignment   The following options give you control over the alignment of text in relation to the dimension line:

Horizontal   Keeps the text in a horizontal orientation, regardless of the dimension line orientation.

Aligned with dimension line   Aligns the text with the dimension line.

ISO standard   Aligns the text with the dimension line when it is between the extension lines; otherwise the text is oriented horizontally [Dimtih, Dimtoh].

Fit Tab

The options in the Fit tab let you fine-tune the behavior of the dimension text and arrows under special conditions. For example, you can select an optional placement for text and arrows when there isn't enough room for them between the extension lines.

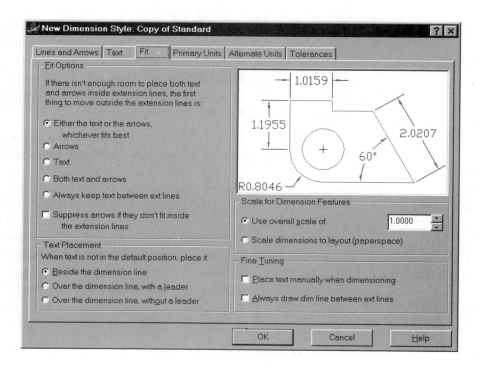

Fit Options   The Fit Options radio buttons let you determine which dimension component is moved when there isn't enough room between the extension lines for either or both the text or the arrows.

> **Either the Text or the Arrows, Whichever Fits Best**   Automatically determines whether text, arrows, or both text and arrows will fit between the extension lines, then places them accordingly. For example, if there isn't enough room for both text and arrows, and the text is wider than the two arrows combined, then the text will be placed outside the extension lines. If the width of the arrows is greater than the width of the text, then the arrows will be moved outside the extension lines. If the gap between the extension lines is too narrow for either the text or arrows, then both the arrows and the text will be moved outside of the extension lines [Dimatfit].
>
> **Arrows**   Moves the arrows outside the extension line when there isn't enough room for both arrows and text between the extension lines. If the gap between the extension lines is too narrow for either the text or the arrows, both the arrows and the text will be moved outside of the extension lines [Dimatfit].
>
> **Text**   Moves the text outside the extension line when there isn't enough room for both arrows and text between the extension lines. If the gap between the extension lines is too narrow for either the text or the arrows, both the arrows and the text will be move outside of the extension lines [Dimatfit].
>
> **Both Text and Arrows**   Moves both the text and the arrows outside the extension line when there isn't enough room for both arrows and text between the extension lines [Dimatfit].
>
> **Always Keep Text between Ext Lines**   Places the text between the extension lines, regardless of whether the text will fit between the extension lines [Dimtix].
>
> **Suppress Arrows If They Don't Fit Inside Extension Lines**   Removes the arrows entirely if they don't fit between the extension lines [Dimsoxd].

Text Placement   The Text Placement radio buttons determine how the dimension text will behave when it is moved from its default location.

> **Beside the Dimension Line**   Keeps the text in its normal location relative to the dimension line [Dimtmove].

Over the Dimension Line, with a Leader Lets you move the dimension text, independent of the dimension line. A leader is added between the dimension line and the text [Dimtmove].

Over the Dimension Line, without a Leader Lets you move the dimension text, independent of the dimension line. No leader is added [Dimtmove].

Scale for Dimension Features These options offer control over the scale of the dimension components. You can set a fixed scale or you can allow the dimension components to be scaled depending on the Paper Space viewport in which they are displayed.

Use Overall Scale Of Radio button and input box let you determine the scale of the dimension components. All of the settings in the Dimension Style dialog box will be scaled to the value you set in the input box if this radio button is selected [Dimscale].

Scale Dimension to Layout (Paper Space) Will scale all of the dimension components to the scale factor assigned to the Paper Space viewport in which the drawing appears [Dimscale].

Fine Tuning The following two check boxes offer miscellaneous settings for dimension text and dimension lines:

Place Text Manually When Dimensioning Allows you to manually place the dimension text horizontally along the dimension line when you are inserting dimensions in your drawing [Dimupt].

Always Draw Dim Line between Ext Lines Forces AutoCAD to draw a dimension line between the extension lines no matter how narrow the distance is between the extension lines [Dimtofl].

Primary Units Tab

The options in the Primary Units tab let you set the format and content of the dimension text, including the unit style for linear and angular dimensions.

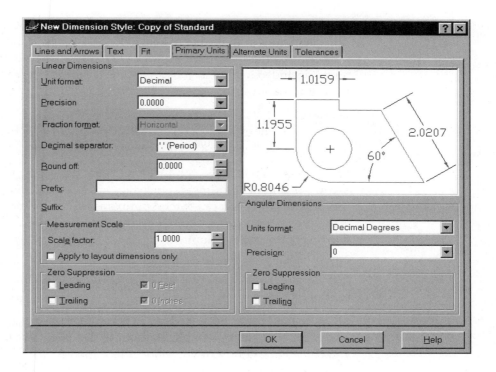

Linear Dimensions   The following options offer control over the unit style and the formatting of dimension text for linear dimensions:

> **Unit Format**   Drop-down list lets you determine the unit style of the dimension text. The options are: scientific, decimal, engineering, architectural, fractional, and Windows Desktop. You must set this option independent of the overall drawing units setting (Format ➤ Units) if you want the dimension text to appear in the appropriate style [Dimunit].
>
> **Precision**   Drop-down list lets you set the precision of the dimension text. This option will round off the dimension text to the nearest precision value you set. It does not affect the actual precision of the drawing [Dimdec].
>
> **Fraction Format**   Drop-down list is only available for architectural and fractional unit formats. This option lets you select between vertically stacked, diagonally stacked, and horizontal fractions [Dimfrac].

Decimal Separator Drop-down list lets you select a decimal separator for dimension unit formats that display decimals. You can choose between a period, a comma, or a space. If you want to use another dimension separator not included in the list, you can use the Dimsep system variable to specify a custom dimension separator [Dimsep].

Round Off Lets you determine the degree of round-off applied to dimensions. For example, you can set this option to 0.25 to round off dimensions to the nearest .25 or 1/4 of a unit [Dimrnd].

Prefix Lets you include a prefix for all linear dimension text. For example, if you want all of your linear dimension text to be preceded by the word "Approximately," you can enter **Approximately** in this input box. Control codes may be used for special characters. See Chapter 8 for more information on control codes [Dimpost].

Suffix Lets you include a suffix for all linear dimension text. Control codes may be used for special characters. See Chapter 8 for more information on control codes [Dimpost].

Measurement Scale: Scale Factor Lets you set a scale factor for the dimension text. This option will scale the value of the dimension text to the value you enter. For example, if you want your dimensions to display distances in centimeters, even though the drawing was created in inches, you can enter **2.54** for this option. Your dimension text will then display dimensions in centimeters. Conversely, if you want to have your dimension text show dimensions in inches, even though you've created your drawing using centimeters, you would enter **0.3937** (the inverse of 2.54) for this option [Dimlfac].

Measurement Scale: Apply to Layout Dimensions Only Causes AutoCAD to apply the measurement scale factor to Paper Space layouts only. With this option checked, the Dimlfac dimension variable gives a negative value [Dimlfac].

Zero Suppression Lets you suppress zeros so they do not appear in the dimension text. For dimensions other than architectural, you can suppress leading and trailing zeros. For example, 0.500 becomes .500 if you suppress leading zeros. It becomes 0.5 if you suppress trailing zeros. For architectural dimensions, you can suppress zero feet or zero inches, although typically, you would not suppress zero inches [Dimzin].

Angular Dimensions   The following options allow you to format angle dimensions:

> **Units Format**   Drop-down list lets you select a format for angular dimensions. The options are decimal degrees, degrees/minutes/seconds, grads, radians, and surveyor [Dimaunit].
>
> **Precision**   Lets you set the precision for the angular dimension text [Dimadec].
>
> **Zero Suppression**   Lets you suppress leading or trailing zeros in angular dimensions [Dimazin].

Alternate Units Tab

The Alternate Units tab lets you apply a second set of dimension text for linear dimensions. This second set of text can be used for alternate dimension styles or units. Typically, alternate units are used to display dimensions in metric if your main dimensions are in feet and inches.

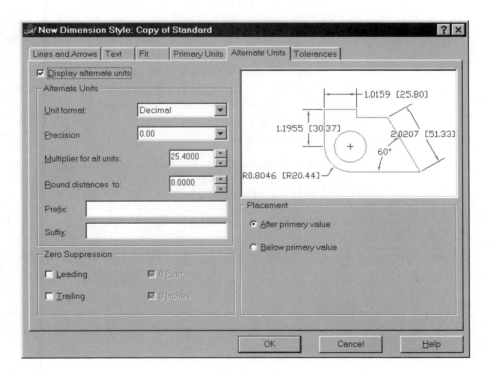

Linear Dimensions   The following options offer control over the unit style and the formatting of dimension text for linear dimensions:

> **Display Alternate Units**   Check box turns on alternate units. This causes AutoCAD to include an additional dimension text in the format you specify in the Alternate Units tab [Dimalt].
>
> **Unit Format**   Drop-down list lets you determine the unit style of the dimension text. The options are scientific, decimal, engineering, architectural stacked, fractional stacked, architectural, fractional, and Windows Desktop. You must set this option independent of the overall drawing units setting (Format ➤ Units) if you want the dimension text to appear in the appropriate style [Dimaltu]. You can adjust the size of fractions relative to the main dimension text by using the Dimfac dimension variable.
>
> **Precision**   Drop-down list lets you set the precision of the dimension text. This option will round off the dimension text to the nearest precision value you set. It does not affect the actual precision of the drawing [Dimaltd].
>
> **Multiplier for Alt Units**   Lets you set a multiplier value for the dimension text. This option will multiply the value of the dimension text to the value you enter. For example, if you want your alternate dimensions to display distances in centimeters even though the drawing was created in inches, you can enter **2.54** for this option. Your alternate dimension text will then display dimensions in centimeters. Conversely, if you want to have your alternate dimension text show dimensions in inches, even though you've created your drawing using centimeters, you would enter **0.3937** (the inverse of 2.54) for this option [Dimaltf].
>
> **Round Distances To**   Lets you determine the degree of round-off applied to dimensions. For example, you can set this option to 0.25 to round off dimensions to the nearest .25 or 1/4 of a unit [DImaltrnd].
>
> **Prefix**   Lets you include a prefix for all linear dimension text. For example, If you want all of your linear dimension text to be preceded by the word "Approximately," you can enter **Approximately** in the Prefix input box. Control codes may be used for special characters. See Chapter 8 for more information on control codes [Dimpost].
>
> **Suffix**   Lets you include a suffix for all linear dimension text. Control codes may be used for special characters. See Chapter 8 for more information on control codes [Dimapost].

Zero Suppression Lets you suppress zeros so they do not appear in the dimension text. For dimensions other than architectural, you can suppress leading and trailing zeros. For example, 0.500 becomes .500 if you suppress leading zeros. It becomes 0.5 if you suppress trailing zeros. For architectural dimensions, you can suppress zero feet or zero inches, though typically, you would not suppress zero inches [Dimaltz].

Placement The following options let you determine the location for the alternate units:

After Primary Value Places the alternate dimension text behind and aligned with the primary dimension text [Dimapost].

Below Primary Value Places the alternate dimension text below the primary dimension text and below the dimension line [Dimapost].

Tolerances Tab

The options in the Tolerance tab offer the inclusion and formatting of tolerance dimensions text.

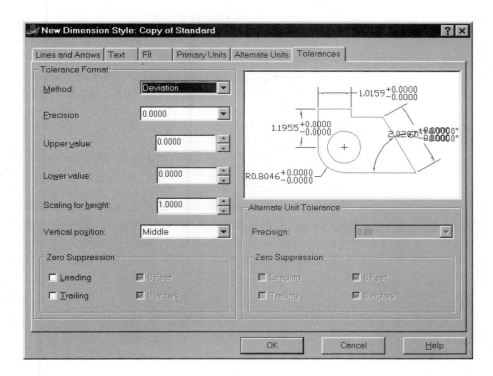

Tolerance Format   The following options offer control over the format of tolerance dimension text:

Method   Lets you turn on and set the format for the tolerance dimension text. The options are None, Symmetrical, Deviation, Limits, and Basic. None turns off the tolerance dimension text. Symmetrical adds a plus/minus tolerance dimension. This is a single dimension preceded by a plus/minus sign. Deviation adds a stacked tolerance dimension showing separate upper and lower tolerance values. The Limits option replaces the primary dimension with a stacked dimension showing maximum and minimum dimension values. The Basic option draws a box around the primary dimension value. If an alternate dimension is used, the box encloses both primary and alternate dimension text [Dimtol, Dimlim, (minus) Dimgap].

Precision   Drop-down list lets you set the precision of the tolerance dimension text. This option will round off the dimension text to the nearest precision value you set. It does not affect the actual precision of the drawing [Dimtdec].

Upper Value   Lets you set the upper tolerance value for the Symmetrical, Deviation, and Limits tolerance methods [Dimtp].

Lower Value   Lets you set the lower tolerance value for the Deviation and Limits tolerance methods [Dimtm].

Scaling for Height   Lets you adjust the size for the tolerance dimension text as a proportion of the primary dimension text height [Dimtfac].

Vertical Position   Lets you determine the vertical position of the tolerance text. The options are Top, Middle, and Bottom. Top aligns the top tolerance value of a stacked pair of values with the primary dimension text. The Middle option aligns the gap between stacked tolerance values with the primary dimension text. The Bottom option aligns the bottom value of two stacked tolerance values with the primary dimension text [Dimtolj].

Zero Suppression   Lets you suppress zeros so they do not appear in the dimension text. For dimensions other than architectural, you can suppress leading and trailing zeros. For example, 0.500 becomes .500 if you suppress leading zeros. It becomes 0.5 if you suppress trailing zeros. For architectural dimensions you can suppress zero feet or zero inches, though typically, you would not suppress zero inches [Dimtzin].

Alternate Unit Tolerance　　The following options offer control over the precision and zero suppression of alternate tolerance dimensions:

Precision　　Drop-down list lets you set the precision of the alternate tolerance dimension text. This option will round off the dimension text to the nearest precision value you set. It does not affect the actual precision of the drawing [Dimalttd].

Zero Suppression　　Lets you suppress zeros so they do not appear in the dimension text. For dimensions other than architectural, you can suppress leading and trailing zeros. For example, 0.500 becomes .500 if you suppress leading zeros. It becomes 0.5 if you suppress trailing zeros. For architectural dimensions you can suppress zero feet or zero inches, though typically, you would not suppress zero inches [Dimalttz].

Importing Dimension Styles from Other Drawings

Dimension styles are saved within the current drawing file only. You don't have to recreate the dimension style for each new drawing, however. If you have loaded the Express menu (see Appendix B for installation instructions), you can import a dimension style that was created in another drawing.

First, save the dimension style using the Express ➤ Dimension ➤ Dimstyle Export option. The dimension style is saved to a user-specified .dim file. For example, you might call it `Architect.dim` or `Survey.dim`.

To restore an exported dimension style, choose Express ➤ Dimension ➤ Dimstyle Import. The selected .dim file is loaded into your current drawing.

Drawing Blocks for Your Own Dimension Arrows and Tick Marks

If you don't want to use the arrowheads supplied by AutoCAD for your dimension lines, you can create a block of the arrowheads or tick marks you want, to be used in the Arrowheads group of the Dimension Styles/Geometry dialog box.

TIP　　To get to the Arrowhead options, go to the Lines and Arrows tab of the New, Modify, or Override Dimension Style dialog box.

For example, suppose you want to have a tick mark that is thicker than the dimension lines and extensions. You can create a block of the tick mark on a layer you assign to a thick pen weight, and then assign that block to the Arrowhead setting. This is done by first opening the Geometry dialog box from the Dimension Styles dialog box (click the Dimension Styles button on the Dimensioning toolbar to open the Dimension Styles dialog box.) Next, choose User Arrow from the first pull-down list in the Arrowheads group. At the User Arrow dialog box, enter the name of your arrow block.

When you draw the arrow block, make it one unit long. The block's insertion point will be used to determine the point of the arrow that meets the extension line, so make sure you place the insertion point at the tip of the arrow. Because the arrow on the right side of the dimension line will be inserted with a zero rotation value, create the arrow block so that it is pointing to the right (see Figure D.2). The arrow block is rotated 180° for the left side of the dimension line.

FIGURE D.2:

The orientation and size of a block used in place of the default arrow

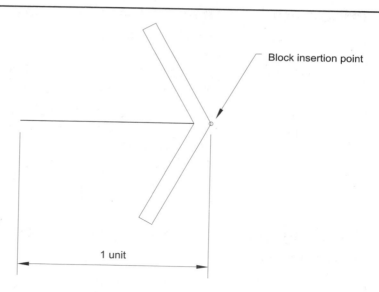

Block insertion point

1 unit

To have a different type of arrow at both ends of the dimension line, create a block for each arrow. Then, in the Dimension Styles/Geometry dialog box, choose User in the drop-down list for the first arrowhead, and enter the name of one block. Then choose User in the drop-down list for the second arrowhead, and enter the name of the other block.

INDEX

Note to the Reader: Throughout this index **boldfaced** page numbers indicate primary discussions of a topic. *Italicized* page numbers indicate illustrations.

NUMBERS

B

D

E

G

#

I

J

K

L

M

N

O

T

What's on the CD

This CD-ROM is packed with valuable resources, including two electronic versions of Sybex books, add-ons, utilities, references, and drawing files from the exercises in this book. More specifically, the CD-ROM includes:

- *Auto CAD 2000 Instant Reference,* a Sybex best-seller, now an electronic book. This is the definitive companion to *Mastering AutoCAD 2000,* providing detailed descriptions of AutoCAD's commands and tools.

- *ABCs of AutoLISP* is a complete tutorial and reference book for AutoLISP, the AutoCAD macro-programming language. This book has been a favorite of end users and developers alike, and it's now in an easy-to-use Web-browser format.

- **AEC On-Screen** is an architectural add-on that gives you the basic symbols library for drawing floor plans. It also provides utilities to simplify floor plan layout and drawing setup. It also includes general utilities to help make any drawing task easier. You can choose from either the US version or the metric version.

- **TutoHelp Fundamentals** is an interactive software program to help you learn and review AutoCAD.

- **Visual Stitcher** is a powerful but easy-to-use image-stitching application.

- **Eye2eye** is an add-on utility that greatly simplifies the process for obtaining 3D perspective views of your 3D models. No more lost views and unwieldy commands. Set your views using an easy-to-use camera and target metaphor.

- **ActiveX samples** help you get started with Automation in AutoCAD. You can use these examples along with Chapter 21 to explore the newest customization feature of AutoCAD.

- **Whip! 4** allows you to view AutoCAD .dwf drawings over the Internet. It gives you full Pan and Zoom capabilities as well as access to Web links embedded in AutoCAD files.

- **JASC's PaintShop Pro** is an image-editing program that makes a great partner with AutoCAD. It allows you to edit bitmap image files with advanced editing tools and supports pressure-sensitive drawing tablets.

- **JASC's QuickView** is a powerful image file manager. You can quickly view a wide variety of bitmap and vector image files directly from Windows Explorer without having to open them in image-editing programs. You can even view HPGL files to check your AutoCAD plots before sending them to your plotter.

- **All the drawing files** from the exercises in the book are included so you can easily study any topic at any time. You can experiment with the files on your own without worrying about losing or corrupting them.

- **Additional VBA and ActiveX chapters** discuss using applications such as Microsoft Visual Basic or Microsoft Excel and how they interact with AutoCAD. These chapters also show you how you can use the VBA programming language and user interface tools to build user-friendly front-ends for your AutoCAD applications. The AutoCAD object model is also introduced.